Government by the people

National edition

Government by the people
9th edition

James MacGregor Burns
Williams College

and J. W. Peltason
University of Illinois

with Thomas E. Cronin
University of California, Santa Barbara
Aspen Institute for Humanistic Studies

Prentice-Hall, Inc., Englewood Cliffs, New Jersey

JK
274
B853
1975

Library of Congress Cataloging in Publication Data

BURNS, JAMES MACGREGOR.
Government by the people: national edition

Bibliography:
1. United States—Politics and government—Handbooks, manuals, etc. I. Peltason, Jack Walter, joint author. II. Cronin, Thomas E., joint author. III. Title.

JK274.B853 1975 320.4'73 74-32101
ISBN 0-13-361089-6

Parts 1-7 © 1975, 1972, 1969, 1966, 1963, 1960, 1957, 1954, 1952 by Raymond H. Young. All rights reserved. No part of this book may be reproduced in any form without permission in writing from the publisher. Printed in the United States of America.

10 9 8 7 6 5 4 3 2

Prentice-Hall International, Inc., London
Prentice-Hall of Australia, Pty. Ltd., Sydney
Prentice-Hall of Canada, Ltd., Toronto
Prentice-Hall of India Private Ltd., New Delhi
Prentice-Hall of Japan, Inc., Tokyo

Design by Ben Kann
Photo research by Mira Schachne
Illustrations by Eric G. Hieber Associates

PHOTO CREDITS:

ABC Photo Release. Page 504

California Historical Society, San Francisco. Page 68

CBS Photo Division. Page 504

Culver Pictures. Pages 21, 24, 27, 31, 50, 62, 70, 228, 637

Lawrence Frank, Rapho Guillumette. Pages 278, 284, 336

Magnum Photos. Page 8

NBC Photo. Page 272

United Press International. Pages 8, 87, 201, 213, 262, 279, 321

United States Department of Agriculture. Page 644

Wide World. Pages 3, 76, 95, 101, 125, 142, 152, 165, 172, 174, 217, 253, 257, 260, 279, 303, 304, 312, 320, 344, 351, 353, 356, 358, 362, 367, 370, 371, 372, 378, 388, 393, 395, 406, 410, 422, 429, 434, 443, 447, 454, 460, 464, 465, 469, 490, 493, 494, 499, 504, 508, 520, 525, 528, 540, 547, 550, 551, 558, 562, 570, 571, 575, 577, 584, 586, 590, 594, 596, 612, 622, 627, 633, 655, 674, 681, 692, 701

Contents

MAR 7 1979
131335

Part Seven
Government in action *545*

Preface
about a new era and old problems

In early 1975, as a heavily Democratic Congress confronted a strongly Republican president, the United States seemed to be passing into a new political era. The agony of Watergate was over—though not the scarring memories, nor some of the trials. Politicians' thoughts were more attuned to the future than the past—especially to the approaching election year of 1976, which would also be the nation's bicentennial. For almost a decade Americans had been transfixed by the moral and strategic issue of Vietnam and by the moral and legal issue of Watergate. Now they were facing new and baffling economic crises at home and abroad.

If the nation was indeed entering a new political phase, however, it was doing so with a political system plagued by familiar divisions and inadequacies.

"Government by the people" was a divided government. The midterm elections of 1974 not only bolstered Democratic strength in Congress; they sent to Capitol Hill a host of Democratic senators and representatives hostile to President Ford's economic policies. Checks and balances were alive and well in Washington.

President Ford was trying to shape his own executive structure and presidential style. Watergate had put the presidency under a cloud; some Americans reacted by proposing to weaken if not emasculate the whole institution. Yet the people were still looking to the White House for political, legislative, and executive leadership.

The standing of Congress—especially of the lower chamber—had risen as a result of the judicious handling of the impeachment proceedings against President Nixon. But Congress seemed unable still to reform or modernize itself—even to bring its committee structure up to date.

The reputation of the judiciary had also soared as the Supreme Court and lower federal courts met the challenge of Watergate. But the very success of federal judges in dealing with thorny problems sharpened the old questions: To what degree should the political branches shove problems onto judicial institutions? To what degree should judges make essentially political decisions?

The political environment was still cloudy and even polluted. Voting turnout dropped in the 1974 election, as it had done in the preceding ones. Party support continued to decline at the grass roots. Both parties sought to revitalize themselves; the Democrats even held an unprecedented "mini-convention" in December 1974 for this purpose—but the results were ambiguous. Cynics doubted that the passage of a new campaign finance law would curb the power of Big Money.

There were signs of revitalization. Voters in 1974 elected the first woman governor to be chosen on her own right, the first woman chief justice of a state

Supreme Court, and a host of women legislators at the national and state levels. California and Colorado elected blacks as lieutenant governors. New Mexico chose its first governor with a Spanish surname in over half a century. A thrity-three-year-old political scientist won the governorship of Oklahoma.

But the problems confronting such new officials continued to swell and fester—inflation, unemployment, poverty, faltering environmental controls, badly distributed medical care, rising taxes, archaic public transportation, along with world crises of population growth, hunger, disease, despair.

Ever since its inception, *Government By the People* has endeavored to acknowledge the problems inside government and confronting government—especially the supreme paradox of a government framed in the eighteenth century trying to deal with the stupendous problems of the twentieth. The original authors have sought to keep the book "up to date" by massive revisions that over the years have produced virtually new volumes. We felt that this new edition presented a special opportunity for new emphases and orientations in the light of deepening public distrust in their leadership.

Hence we are pleased that Thomas E. Cronin has joined us as a contributing author to this volume. We had been impressed by his critique of the "textbook view of the presidency" and we concluded that we wanted this kind of freshness and revisionism to be part of this new edition. He has contributed measureably to all parts of the book, but especially to the chapters on the presidency, on Congress, and on the policy and political linkages between White House and Capitol Hill.

We wish to call attention of readers to James A. Burkhart and Raymond L. Lee, *Guide to "Government by the People"* designed to give students an opportunity to participate more directly in the learning process. These two authors have also produced a new edition of *A Systems Approach to Teaching Government with "Government by the People,* and a new test booklet is available as another supplementary aid to instructors.

This edition, like the previous, is dedicated to "those students committed to the most difficult and revolutionary of activities—thinking."

New editions of this book have always been heavily dependent on a heavy infusion of fresh ideas, hard criticism, and scholarly research findings from some of the ablest people in the discipline of political science. Because of the change and tumult attending recent political developments—especially Watergate—we especially value the contributions made to this edition by Benjamin R. Barber, Michael Couzens, Roger H. Davidson, Richard E. Dawson, Martha Derthick, Delmer D. Dunn, Robert L. Lineberry, and John E. Moore.

We have had the benefit also of more specific suggestions and criticism from: David Ahola, Berndt G. Angman, John S. Chambers, Kenneth N. Ciboski, Scott Cole, Wayne G. Delevan, Eric Elliott, John George, John H. Gilbert, Thomas Hindson, Earl Kohler, Eugene L. Lazare, Lawrence Lorensen, John Lovelace, Thomas M. Mongar, Casimo Naspinsky, Sydney A. Reid, G. Ellis Sandoz, Donald Scott, Roy W. Shin, Gerald Stollman, Joellen Thurber, Hendrik Van Dalen, William Winters, and Ivan Youngberg.

Trienah Meyers, Stewart Burns, and Michael Clough made substantive and editorial contributions to the work. For editorial and production assistance we wish also to thank Frances Buckley, Carolyn Higgs, Mrs. Irish Langton, Janice Parrill, and Ina Patterson. Amy Midgley, Ann Torbert, and their associates at Prentice-Hall, Ben Kann, Mira Schachne, and Kitty Woringer, made important contributions to a most demanding publishing enterprise. For encouragement and suggestions we also thank our wives.

J.M.B.
J.W.P.
T.E.C.

Government by the people

Part One Democratic government in america

Chapter 1 Government by the people?

"When in the course of human events . . . we hold these truths to be self-evident. . . . All men are created equal . . . they are endowed by their Creator with certain unalienable rights . . . among these are Life, Liberty and the pursuit of Happiness. . . ."

As Americans prepared to celebrate the bicentennial of the Declaration of Independence from Great Britain, orators were polishing the marvellous old phrases. Historians were reminding us that the American Revolution had been pitched on a high moral plane, that it marked the birth of far-reaching democratic reforms, that the Declaration led directly to the state and national bills of rights. Political scientists were noting that our Declaration had served as a model for other peoples shaking off colonial rule—that Vietnamese revolutionaries at the end of World War II, for example, had borrowed for their proclamation of independence almost the very words of that celebrated earlier revolutionary, Thomas Jefferson.

Independence should be forever commemorated with shows, games, sports, guns, balls, bonfires, and illuminations, John Adams wrote his wife Abigail, and the 1976 celebrants of the 1776-style revolution were not idle. Philadelphia was readying its "Historic Square Mile" with its cluster of historic shrines—Carpenter's Hall, where the first Continental Congress met; Independence Hall, where the Declaration of Independence had been signed in 1776 and the Constitution drawn up eleven years later; Congress Hall, where the first Congress of the United States met. New York City was restoring five square blocks of a section of its old seaport where clipper ships, the fastest vessels afloat, had brought in goods from four continents. Boston was reminding us that this was where it all started—with a "massacre" near the old State House; in Lexington, with a clash on a village green; and in Concord, with a struggle around a little bridge. Washington, D.C., was planning a festival of American folklife on the Mall; Southern cities would open up homes that had been built before the Revolution; Virginia offered Williamsburg and Charlottesville.

The whole nation would be one great celebration. President Ford and Vice-President Rockefeller would preside at major occasions. Leonard

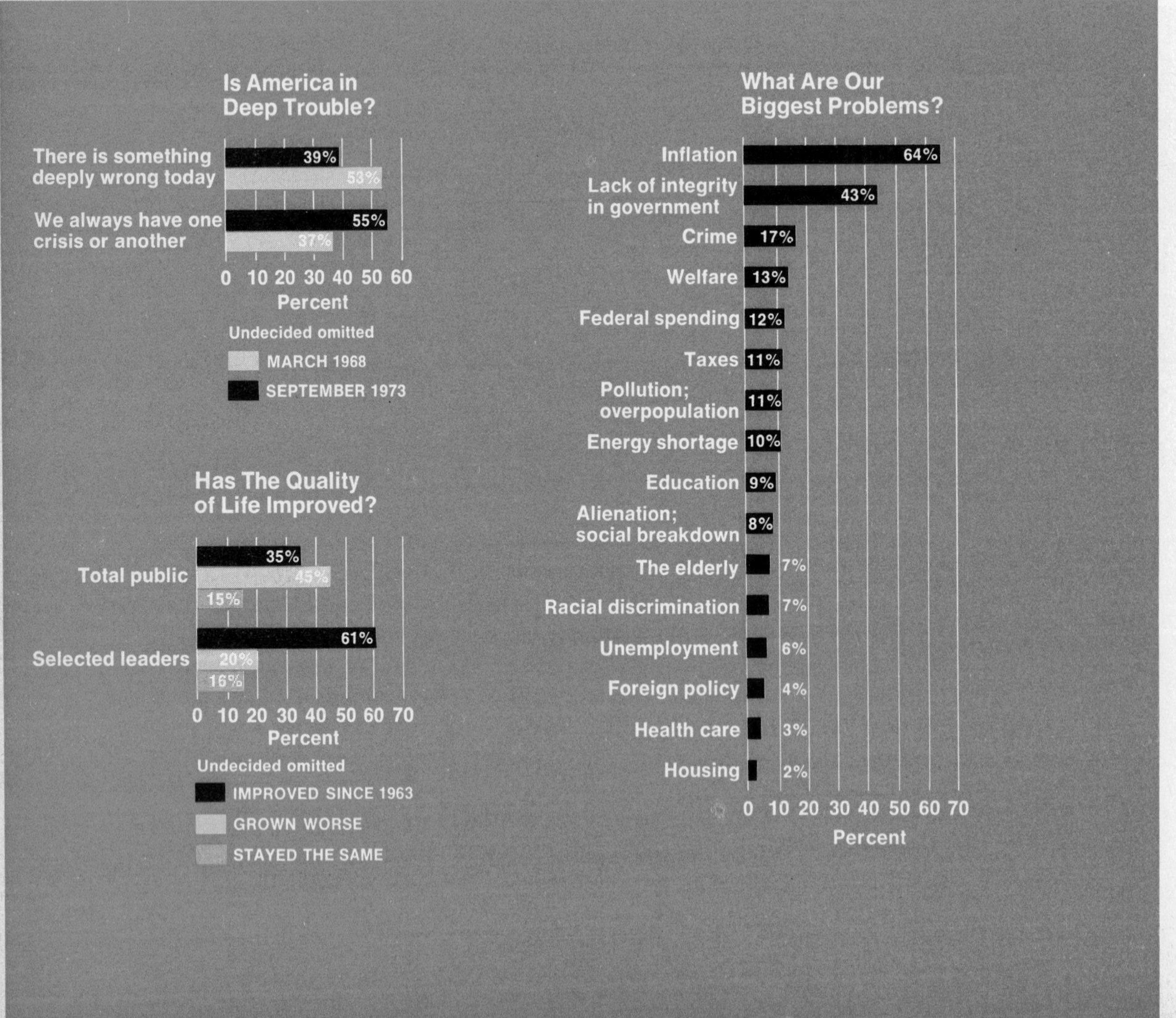

Bernstein was commissioned to write a symphony. Nevada planned to restore the old railroad between Virginia Center, heart of the fabled Comstock Lode, and Reno, center of gambling, divorce, and fun. Colorado undertook to resurrect the buildings of Central City, the gleaming hub of the gold and silver rush. . . .

Somewhat lost in the feverish activity was the question: just what were we celebrating?

Do we have anything to celebrate?

The melancholy fact was that, at the start of the mid-seventies, Americans were in anything but a celebratory mood about the state of the nation. Rather, they were caught in a crisis of confidence. Something, they

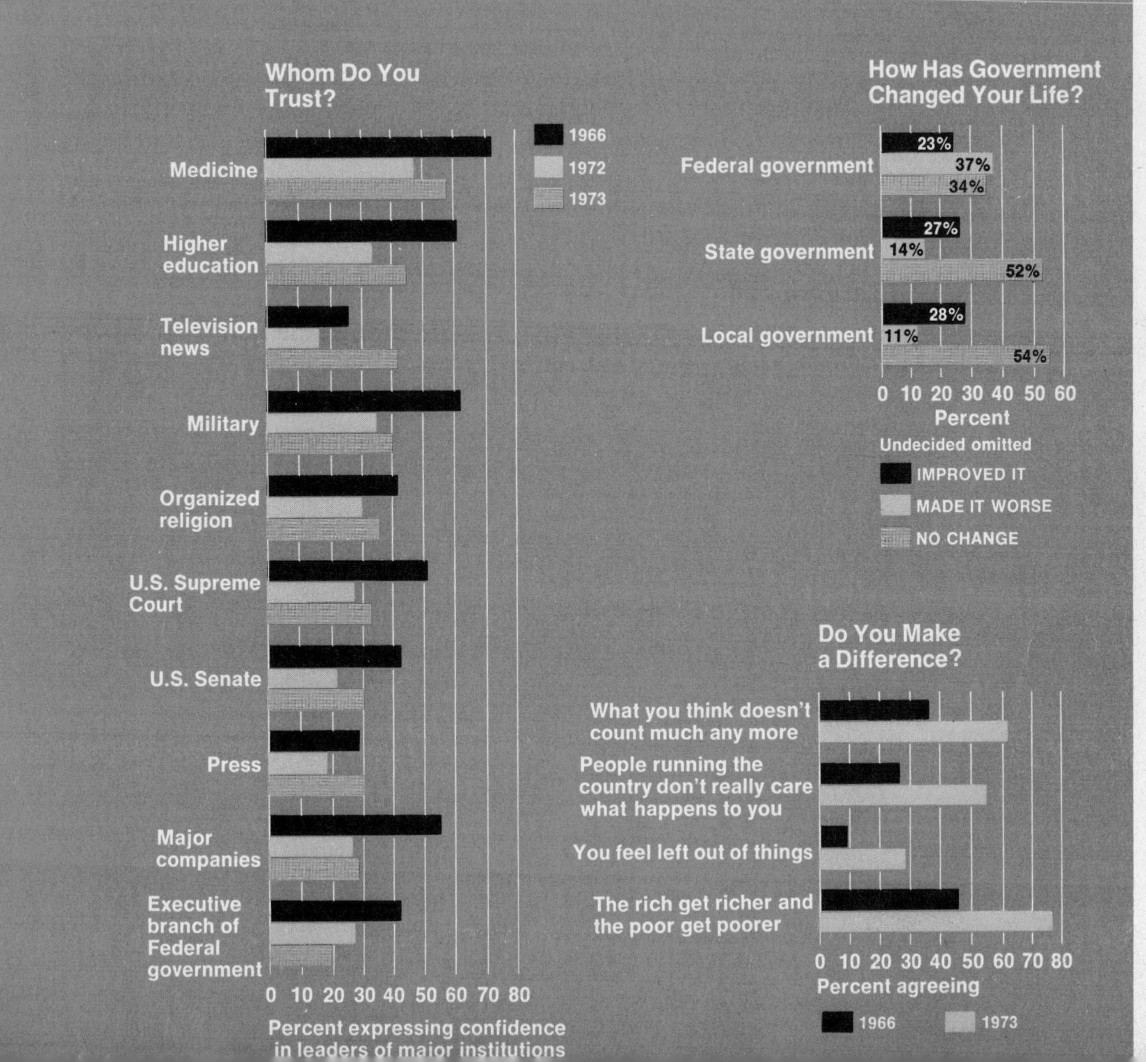

felt, had gone deeply wrong with their country. They had lost much of their respect for most of the nation's important institutions. In particular they felt angry with government—they felt alienated from it, cynical toward it. These were the findings not of confirmed pessimists but of a comprehensive public opinion survey conducted by a respected polling organization and commissioned by a subcommittee of the United States Senate.[1]

"SOMETHING IS DEEPLY WRONG"

Not since the 1968 assassinations of Martin Luther King and Robert F. Kennedy had a majority of Americans felt "there is something deeply wrong in America" today. These are no ordinary times of crisis. A North Carolina tobacco farmer said: "The whole moral character of the country is going downhill or we wouldn't have had a Watergate crisis. People in the top of government are power hungry and they will do almost anything to get and keep their power. They want nothing but raw power. And that's just downright corrupting."

A feeling of alienation and powerlessness had sharply increased in the past decade, as the charts on pages 4 and 5 suggest.

Trust and respect for the leaders of the nation's key institutions had plummeted. Those expressing a "great deal of confidence" in medicine had dropped from 72 to 57 percent since 1966; in colleges and universities, 61 to 44 percent; in the military, 62 to 40 percent; in organized religion, 41 to 36 percent; in major corporations, 55 to 28 percent; in organized labor, 22 to 18 percent. Television news had risen in public respect, but not very far. The only persons commanding a "great deal" of confidence from a majority of Americans in the poll were doctors and local trash collectors!

The people directed much of their disrespect toward their political leaders. Since Watergate was coming to a climax when the poll was taken, it was not surprising that the presidency had fallen from a "great confidence" rating in seven years from 41 to 19 percent. But the Senate, the House, and even the Supreme Court had also been sharply diminished in public attitudes. All levels of government had lost credibility, but especially the national government. An hourly rate worker in Detroit said: "To me the federal government is taxes, period." People seemed to have little contact with government except through taxes or law enforcement. Only 11 percent looked to the federal government for help, though more turned to local and state governments.

[1] "Confidence and Concern: Citizens View American Government," a survey of public attitudes by the Subcommittee on Intergovernmental Relations of the Committee on Government Relations, United States Senate (Government Printing Office, December 1973). Louis Harris and Associates conducted the poll in the fall of 1973. See also Louis Harris, *The Anguish of Change* (Norton, 1973).

HOW MIXED A PICTURE?

The picture was not one of utter gloom. The vast majority felt that government *could* work effectively. Both the public and its leaders shared a faith "in the ability of government, especially the unpopular federal establishment, to subordinate special influence to the general welfare and to bring in first-rate people whose first priorities will be 'helping the country' and 'caring about the people.'" Both officials and the public viewed organized citizens' groups as a more and more respected means of channeling people's energies into effective collective action.

Some contended, moreover, that the last ten years—despite the "poor mouthing" of the doom theorists and nay-sayers—had been a period of unprecedented progress—in health, housing, income, jobs, satisfaction with one's work, and general happiness. John Kennedy's New Frontier and Lyndon Johnson's Great Society, they said, had really paid off in substantial social and economic progress, despite some mistakes and false starts. They noted that when Americans were asked by Gallup pollsters, "In general, how happy would you say you are—very happy, fairly happy, or not happy?" 38 percent answered "very happy" in 1947, 43 percent in 1970, and 52 percent in 1973. And young people turned out to be the happiest of all, and expected their futures to be better.[2] If the Declaration had called for the "pursuit of happiness," we seemed to have a right to celebrate our progress on this score at least.

But the optimists still had to concede that even those who talked cheerfully felt themselves to be beset by many problems. And critics of "America 1976" contended that the trouble lay much deeper than such obvious failings as poverty, racial discrimination, perverse combinations of inflation and recession, costly misadventures abroad, inadequate health and housing, and much else. These critics believe that these are but *symptoms* of far more basic ills in the society and polity. They see environmental decay as resulting from uncontrolled technology. They see crime and lawlessness stemming from a general disintegration of the social fabric. They see poverty as caused by inequality entrenched in our economic and political structures. Above all, they see the decline in individual liberty and popular control of government as resulting from the power of huge corporate institutions and impersonal government bureaucracies.

Popular pessimism seemed to reflect these concerns. And the feeling of malaise was not confined to young Eastern liberals or radicals. That feeling was stronger in the Midwest, South, and West than in the East. People in their fifties were more concerned than those in their forties and thirties, and young adults less than either. Blacks were more concerned than whites, the poor more than the rich. But majorities in almost all categories felt that something was deeply wrong in America.

[2]Ben J. Wattenberg, *The Real America* (Doubleday, 1974), based largely on U.S. Census data.

People were quite specific about the problems facing the nation. Plagued by soaring prices, they named the economy in general and inflation in particular as the issue they were most concerned about. Next was "integrity in government"—named by 43 percent in 1973 and by only 5 percent the year before! Next came crime, drugs, welfare reform, pollution and ecology, taxes, the energy shortage, education, alienation and social breakdown. Two great issues of earlier years—racial discrimination and war in Indochina—were near the bottom of the list.

"If you could sit down and talk with the president," people were asked, "what two or three things would you like to tell him?" The vast majority wanted him to "listen to the people more," get better advisers, stop being so secretive, and cooperate more with Congress. Others were more concerned about foreign policy and the state of the economy. But few if any of those who thought about being "leaders for a day" indicated that they would tell the president how wonderful the system was. They were not in a mood to celebrate.

On the eve of the bicentennial year, there was no evidence that the concerns of Americans had diminished. Some Americans were of a mood to celebrate the bicentennial less with games and bonfires than with some hard thought about what 1776 had meant and what 1976 could mean. They were remembering that after all it was a *revolution* that was being celebrated, and while they were in no mood to stage another one, the times might call for some revolutions in *thinking*. Some felt that 1976 could best be marked by a deep probing into what America had aspired to be, what it had become, what it could be.

A few remembered that Thoreau had advised: "Probe the earth and see where your main roots are." It seemed like good advice for a bicentennial year—and for any year.

Pessimism and feelings of malaise about American society in the early 1970s were not confined to young Eastern liberals and radicals. People of all ages and from all walks of life felt that something was deeply wrong in America.

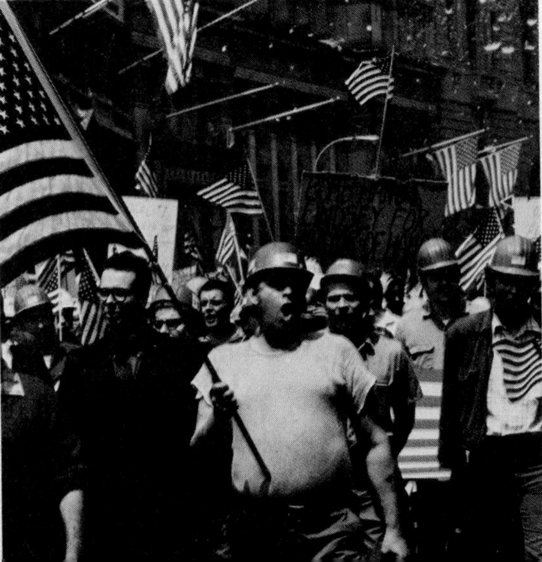

Democracy as an ultimate end

The main roots of the American version of "government by the people" lie in the Enlightenment—in the eruption of new ideas that spread through Western Europe during the eighteenth century. This new "light" was first of all *critical;* it put under piercing illumination the accepted faith and wisdom of the day, and it attacked and ridiculed most of the doctrines of the established and authoritarian church and state. But ultimately it was enormously positive. From the fresh and passionate thinking of the radicals of the day stemmed most of our democratic notions of individual liberty, political rights, equality, even participation.

Leading these radicals was a remarkable group of philosophers and publicists who punctured the old myths less with artillery salvos than with wit and satire. Thus Voltaire on Equality: "What does one dog owe to another or one horse to some other horse? Nothing. No animal depends on his fellow. But man, having received from God the light we call reason, has with it made himself—what? A slave nearly everywhere. . . ."

Terms must be defined if we are not ourselves to become slaves to the "tyranny of words." Consider the key word, *democracy.* Like most value-laden words, democracy has been defined in hundreds of ways. It is also used indiscriminately to denote highly different political systems; the communist regime in East Germany, for example, is officially called the German Democratic Republic. The word comes from two Greek roots—*demos,* the people, and *kratis,* authority—and was used by the Athenians to mean government by the many, as contrasted with government by the few (oligarchy) or by one (autocracy). Here we define democracy both as ultimate ends and instrumental means, both as *goals* basic to humankind and as a *method*—for example, free and fair elections—best calculated to realize those human goals. The means and the ends, the goals and the method, are closely interrelated.

BASIC ENDS OF DEMOCRATS

First, democrats recognize the fundamental dignity and importance of the *individual.* This emphasis on the supreme worth of the individual runs unbroken through democratic thought. It is woven into the writings of Thomas Jefferson, especially in the Declaration of Independence—*all* men are endowed by their Creator with certain *unalienable* rights. The doctrine of individualism insists that we must, in the words of the philosopher Immanuel Kant, "So act as to treat humanity, whether in thine own person or in that of any other, in every case as an end withal, never as a means only." Individualism makes the person, rich or poor, black or white, male or female, the *central* measure of value. The state, the union, the corporation are measured in terms of their usefulness to individuals.

Does the primacy of the individual seem so obvious a goal that all must believe in it? Many do not. The doctrine of *statism* has powerfully influenced many societies; this doctrine makes the state the measure of value. Democrats refuse to glorify the state, even when it is pictured as simply the collective will of all the people. To a democrat the state has no meaning except in terms of each of the individuals that compose it.

Second, democrats recognize the right of each individual to be treated as a unique and inviolable human being. They do not insist that all persons are equal in talents or virtues; they do insist that one person's claim to life, liberty, and property must be recognized as much as any other's. This right raises difficult questions of how equal rights can be secured, but the principle of equality of right is clear.

Third, democrats are convinced that liberty is desirable in itself, that freedom is good in itself. *Liberty* or *freedom* (used interchangeably here) means that every individual must have full opportunity to choose his own goals in life and the means to reach those goals. The core of liberty is *self-determination*. Liberty is not simply the *absence* of external restraint on a person; it means the individual's power to act positively to reach his goals.

Democracy claims to be centered in the individual person. The freedom to make real, meaningful choices is essential to the things that make one a human being. It is only by acting as free and responsible persons that we are able to exploit our full capacity for individual growth. Moreover, both history and reason suggest that individual liberty is the key to *social progress*. The greater people's freedom, the greater the chance of discovering better ways of life. Progress is stifled wherever an authoritarian group—or even rigid social custom—imposes an orthodoxy that none may question. Further, to deny a person freedom causes personal frustration, which in turn may erupt into aggressive, antisocial behavior.

These basic values of democracy do not necessarily coexist with one another happily in a particular society. The concept of the economically

Thomas Jefferson's rough draft of the Declaration of Independence.

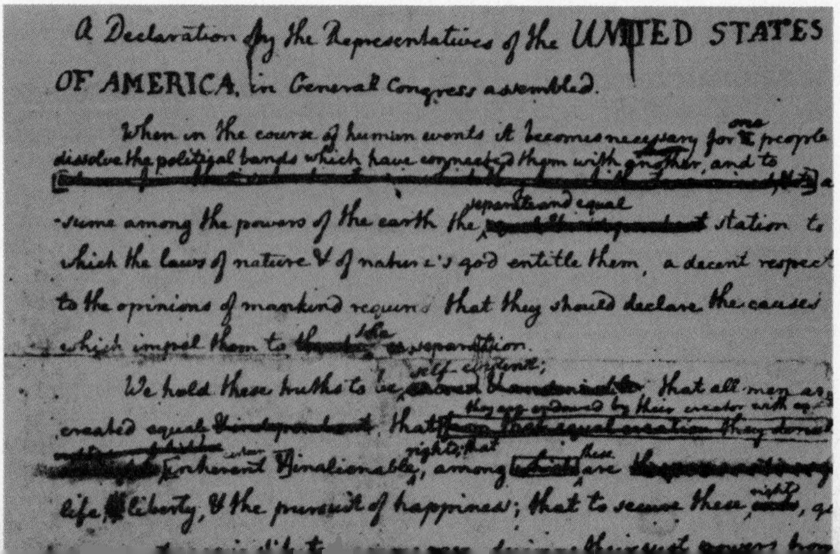
A Declaration by the Representatives of the UNITED STATES OF AMERICA, in General Congress assembled.

When in the course of human events it becomes necessary for one people to dissolve the political bands which have connected them with another, and to
-sume among the powers of the earth the separate and equal station to which the laws of nature & of nature's god entitle them, a decent respect to the opinions of mankind requires that they should declare the causes which impel them to the separation.

We hold these truths to be self-evident; that all men are created equal; that they are endowed by their creator with
inherent & inalienable rights; that among these are life, liberty, & the pursuit of happiness; that to secure these rights,

motivated, private, even "selfish" kind of *individualism* may conflict with the older tradition of public virtue and collective welfare—of the citizen as a participant in the *general welfare*. Freedom as the *liberation* of the individual may conflict with freedom as the *alienation* of man from his fellow men or from his communities. The concept of *individual self-determination* may conflict with that of *collective decision-making* for the national welfare or the public good. More concretely, the right of a mill owner to run his factory as he pleases, as compared to the right of a millhand in that factory to join a union, or even to share in the running of the plant, illustrates this type of conflict in everyday life.

GOALS OF AMERICAN DEMOCRACY

Democracy, said Maury Maverick, is "liberty plus groceries." Probably the single most powerful idea in American history has been that of individual liberty. It was for life, liberty, and the pursuit of happiness that independence was declared; it was to secure the blessings of liberty that the Constitution was drawn up and adopted. There is no way to prove, of course, that liberty has been this powerful a concept for Americans; we had no scientific polling for the first century and a half of our national existence (even if that would have proved anything). But consider our patriotic anthems—it is to the "sweet land of liberty" that we sing. Or take a coin out of your pocket. Unless something has happened since these words were written, that penny, nickel, dime, quarter, or half dollar proclaims not authority, security, brotherhood, individualism, but *liberty*.

Liberty is a fuzzy as well as a compelling concept, of course, and much depended on how Americans would define it as they measured their practical decisions by the yardstick of freedom. During the early decades of the republic, the American concept of liberty was essentially negative. The main impetus of Jeffersonian democracy was to throw off the burdens of established governments, churches, and other institutions. These negative liberties were made explicit in the Bill of Rights of the Constitution. Free speech, free press, freedom of religion, freedom of assembly, and the rest—the main role of government was to *remove* constraints on persons' liberties.

During most of the nineteenth century liberty as "freedom *from*" interlocked with the dominant economic and social doctrine of laissez faire. Under this doctrine "economic man" must be freed of governmental impediments that might thwart him in reaching maximum efficiency and productivity. The state, it was argued, must intervene no more then was absolutely necessary to protect life and property; further intervention, such as minimum wages, health protection, or even compulsory vaccination, was both immoral in theory and improper in fact. The idea was simple—the less governmental power, the more individual liberty.

But what was the meaning of liberty when, not governments but other *individuals*—employers, lynch mobs, plantation owners, labor bosses, police officers—deprived persons of their liberties? Slavery forced Americans to rethink their ideas of liberty. "The world has never had a good definition of the word liberty," Abraham Lincoln declared in an 1864 speech, "and the American people, just now, are in want of one. We all declare for liberty; but in using the same word we do not all mean the same thing. With some the word liberty may mean for each man to do as he pleases with himself, and the product of his labor; while with others the same word may mean for some men to do as they please with other men. . . ."[3] He used the homely example of the shepherd who drives the wolf from the sheep's throat, for which the sheep thanks the shepherd as his liberator, while the wolf denounces him for the same act as the *destroyer* of liberty.

With the advent of intensive industrialization, urbanization, agrarian and labor discontent, of unions, depressions, social protest, and of leaders like William Jennings Bryan, Theodore Roosevelt, Robert La Follette, Eugene Debs, and Woodrow Wilson, liberty became invested with far more positive meanings. Americans slowly came to understand a crucial fact—men and women, crowded more and more together, lived amid growing webs of all kinds, personal and private, institutional and psychological. To abolish one type of restraint such as Negro slavery might mean increasing another type of restraint such as wage slavery. To cut down on governmental restraint of liberty might simply mean increasing *private* economic and social power. The question was not simply of liberating people from *government;* it was how to use government to free people from *non*governmental curbs on liberty as well.

Such a concept meant that liberty might be converging with another concept, *equality*, which some had seen as opposed to liberty. Next to liberty, equality is probably the most vital concept in American thought. "All men are created equal and from that equal creation they derive rights inherent and unalienable, among which are the preservation of liberty and the pursuit of happiness." Those were the words of Jefferson's first draft of the Declaration and they indicate the primacy of the concept. Tocqueville, Bryce, Laski, and other foreigners who investigated American democracy—especially the Jacksonian, abolitionist, populist, and progressive movements—were struck by the thrust of egalitarian thought and practice, both in our political and social lives.

But what did equality mean? Hard questions emerged from the press of events. What *kind of* equality? Economic, political, legal, social, something else? Equality for *whom?* Blacks, as well as whites? Children and teenagers as well as adults? Equality merely of *opportunity?*—almost all Americans said they wanted that—but also of *condition?* This last question was the toughest. Did equality of opportunity simply mean that everyone should have *the same place at the starting line*—and after that the devil take the hindmost, as in a horse race? Or did it mean that there would be an effort to equalize most or all of the factors *that*

[3]Speech at Sanitary Fair, 1864.

during the course of a person's lifetime might determine how well he or she made out socially or economically?

Herbert Hoover effectively posed the issue when he said: "We, through free and universal education, provide the training of the runners; we give to them an equal start; we provide in government the umpire of fairness in the race. . . ."[4] Franklin D. Roosevelt sought to answer the question when he proclaimed first the Four Freedoms—significantly freedom from *want* and *fear* as well as freedom of speech and religion—and later a "second Bill of Rights." Under this second bill of rights, he said, Americans had accepted the idea that a new basis of security and prosperity can be established for all, regardless of station, race, or creed. This meant good housing, health, jobs, social security for all. The New Deal and its successor programs—Truman's Fair Deal, Kennedy's New Frontier, Johnson's Great Society—in both their achievements and failures have carried out the egalitarian implications of the second bill of rights.

What has happened is that two concepts once seen as opposites have found a meeting point in a philosophy that calls for government both to help broaden people's *social* and *economic* liberties, and to prevent other institutions (corporations or unions or landlords) from constricting persons' liberties—at the same time that government must restrict *itself* from interfering with liberty. This is no small task, and it is not always performed well. But the idea is an exciting one. It means that Americans, perhaps without being wholly conscious of it, have brought about a convergence between the values of liberty and equality that were once considered antithetical. No longer could one say flatly, "the more government, the less liberty." But neither could one say the opposite. Everything depended on the impact of government and other restraining and liberating forces on a person's sum total of liberties.

Maury Maverick was only half right, some Americans would contend. The values of American democracy are not only liberty *plus* groceries but the *interrelation* between the two. The values of liberty and equality interlock and stimulate each other at some points; they are in a state of opposition or at least tension at other points; and at still other points they do not relate to each other at all. Pushed too far, liberty becomes license and unbridled individualism; pushed too far, equality could mean leveling, a dull mediocrity, and even the erosion of liberty. Just how to strike a fruitful balance is a question around which much of our political combat revolves.

Democracy as political means

Some favor democracy not only because they believe it stands for human goals such as liberty and equality, but also because they see de-

[4]Herbert Hoover, *American Individualism* (Doubleday, Page, 1922), p. 9.

mocracy as the best *process* available for governing a complex society. If those who admire democracy for the human ends it represents can be called "principle democrats," those who see democracy essentially as a *technique* of self-government can be called "process democrats." Process democrats grant that the procedures of democracy do not guarantee that "justice will be done," but they contend that the chances are better under "government by the people" than any other procedures they know of.

FUNDAMENTAL DEMOCRATIC PROCESSES

The crucial democratic mechanism in all genuinely popular governments is a system of free, fair, and open elections. Democratic governments take many different forms, but democratic elections have at least four essential elements:

"Gad, when I think of the power the people have . . . It just isn't fair."

© 1965 Los Angeles Times; reprinted by permission.

1. All citizens should have *equal voting power.* This does not mean that all must or will have *equal political influence.* Some persons, because of wealth, talent, or position, have much more power than others. How much extra influence key figures should be allowed to exercise in a democracy is one of the exacting questions that face democrats. But as a bedrock matter, no matter whether one is president or pick-and-shovel laborer, newspaper publisher or lettuce picker, middle-aged political scientist or nineteen-year-old student of politics—each casts only one vote at the polls.

2. Voters should have the right of access to facts, to criticism, to competing ideas, to the views of all candidates, including "extremists." If government monopolizes or edits all sources of information, the election is obviously a sham. Here again, the extent to which different ideas actually receive equal attention is a troubling problem because of the nature of the mass media, the special access of the president to television and the press, the inability of many lower-income people to make their ideas known. But the principle of free competition of ideas during an election is essential.

3. Citizens must be free to organize for political purposes. Obviously individuals can be more effective in most situations when they join with others in a party, a pressure group, a protest movement, a demonstration—in whatever activity does not abridge the constitutional rights of others.

4. Elections are decided by majorities (or at least pluralities). Those who get the most votes win, even if the winning side seems to be made up of idiots, nonentities, and scoundrels and the minority of the wise and "right-minded." The persons chosen by the majority take office. How much power the winners may then wield over the losing minority is another perplexing problem of democratic government, but there is no question that the winners take office and assume formal authority. It is important to note what is *not* included in the concept of democracy as a means. "Process democrats" do not judge a democracy by its policy output. Their concern is with the *procedures* for making policy and not with the rightness of the policy that is made.

Their central point is this. Government *by* the people usually will produce government *for* the people. But the very reason they are committed to democratic government is that they reject the notion that it is possible to define "scientifically" what the public interest is. If one believes, as did Plato, that decisions about public policy are of the same nature as, say, a decision as to how to build a boat, then it would follow that the best way to make policy is to turn everything over to a group of specialists or experts. Then like Plato one would favor a system that placed authority in the hands of philosopher-kings or perhaps, in today's terms, in the hands of the "best and the brightest" or other so-called experts. Process democrats, on the other hand, take their stand with Aristotle, who argued that although an expert cook knows better than the nonexpert how to bake a cake, the person who eats it is the better judge of whether it tastes good. As A. D. Lindsay put it, the average voter may not know how government can stop his shoe from pinching, but he does know whether it pinches or not.

Most Americans do not trust experts that much. As President Eisenhower stated in his farewell address: "Yet in holding scientific research and discovery in respect, as we should, we must also be alert to the equal and opposite danger that public policy could itself become the captive of a scientific-technological elite." Few democrats—especially process democrats—wish to shift the control of our destinies from voters and their elected leaders to some new priesthood of technocratic systems analysts.

THE AMERICAN SYSTEM: DEMOCRATIC AND CONSTITUTIONAL

The Founding Fathers were both principle democrats and process democrats. Their genius lay in their relating the *goals* of democracy to the *methods* of democracy. If the Declaration of Independence was more concerned with the goals of free men such as liberty and equality, the Constitution focussed more on the processes that could help realize these goals without sacrificing other values such as controlled power, stability, continuity, due process, balanced decision-making. For two centuries American politicians, jurists, and other leaders have been enormously influenced by the resounding success of the revolutionaries of 1776 and 1787 in working out effective and durable political processes. The Watergate scandals were a dramatic warning, process democrats remind us, that to flout and abuse democratic processes is to threaten both the means and ends of a free people.

Almost all governments, of course, have a constitution—that is, certain agreed on ways by which government proceeds. In this sense both the Soviet Union and Communist China have constitutions. But for process democrats the term constitutional government has come to have a more specific and restricted meaning—namely a government where there are clearly recognized and regularly applied limits on the power of those who govern. Officials have only the power delegated to them by the constitution, and any official who exceeds the scope of his authority surrenders his claim to obedience. By this definition Great Britain, India, France, Canada, and the United States are constitutional governments, but the Soviet Union is not, for the people of that country have—short of revolution—limited checks on the power of their rulers.

The American system of government, then, is both democratic and constitutional. There are recognized limits as to what government may do—even a government elected by vote of the people. The individual has rights that the government lacks the constitutional authority to deny. Not everyone agrees on the concrete content of these rights, but it is agreed there are certain things that government may not do and other things it may do only according to proper and fair procedure. At a minimum, the government may not deprive any person of his life, liberty, or property except by just and fair procedures of the law. Beyond this minimum there are countless abuses of process that could hardly be catalogued but have come to our attention dramatically such as governmental spying on private citizens, burglarizing the opposition party's headquarters, using the Internal Revenue Service to report on opponents' federal income tax returns, and many other unsavory episodes.

Into the third century

As the bicentennial of the Declaration of Independence neared, some Americans were so disturbed by the failures of the American system, especially by the Watergate scandals and the forced resignation of a president, that they had a novel concept as to how to celebrate the founding of the nation. The spirit of 1776 had been the spirit of revolution against existing institutions, they reminded us, or at the very least had marked a time of fundamental reassessment of the governmental system the early Americans lived under. Why not approach the bicentennial in the same spirit—of celebration of achievements to be sure, but also of probing our main roots, reexamining our government, perhaps reforming our institutions? If we could pursue this task effectively enough in the next decade, they suggested, then we could look forward to a truly joyful observance in 1987, when we would celebrate the bicentennial of the writing of the Constitution.

One did not have to take this gloomy a view of the 1976 bicentennial to agree that profoundly important questions about the American political system had come to the fore in recent years and had to be faced by

The drafting of the Declaration of Independence.

students of American government. Three questions—really sets of questions—will underlie the exposition in the coming chapters:

1. *Is the American governmental system today participatory, representative, responsible?* By participatory, we mean a governmental decision-making process in which most persons, if they choose to do so, are able to participate. By representative we mean a governmental leadership that, while it may not be a mirror of people's attitudes or of their division into classes, races, interests, regions, and the like, is sensitive to the needs and opinions of these different groups. By responsible we mean a leadership that must report fully to the people on what it is doing, can be held accountable by the voters in elections, and keeps in mind the long-term needs of the whole people and not merely the short-term interests of organized groups.

In considering this question we must remember that the framers did not favor a government that would be directly participated in, be representative of, or responsive to the mass of people. They sought to subdue both the spirit of faction and the thrust of majorities. Their prime concern was how to fashion a viable but limited government. The framers had not seen a political party in the modern sense and would have spurned it if they had. They believed not in an arousing, mobilizing kind of leadership but in a stabilizing, balancing, magisterial leadership—the kind George Washington was expected to supply and did supply. Today we have *high-pressure politics*—strongly organized groups, potent and volatile public opinion dominated by opinion-making agencies, parties vying to mobilize nationwide majorities, celebrity-leaders intimately covered by the media. How responsive are our political agencies to fast-moving changes in public attitudes and moods?

2. *Could a constitution written in the eighteenth century still be serviceable in the twentieth?* Our basic charter had been shaped to meet the needs of a small country composed mainly of agrarian interests, on a new continent separated by three months of sailing time from Europe. How can it serve the needs of a huge, urbanized, industrialized nation that can be reached from abroad by electronic communication in split seconds and by nuclear missiles in minutes? The Constitution, we will note over and again in the coming pages, fragments power and divides it among different officials; today we seem to need concerted governmental effort to meet the massive problems facing us. The Founding Fathers had worked out democratic processes that would, they believed, help realize the principles implicit in the American revolution. Yet the system so devised seems unable to make policy intelligently or enforce programs effectively—or so it appears to many critics. What new processes might be required in the wake of the fundamental economic, social, intellectual, organizational, and military events that have reshaped the nation in two centuries of unceasing change?

3. *Is our constitutional and political system a "government by the people," or is it but a facade behind which elite groups really run America?* This is the gravest charge raised against the American system because it strikes at the heart of our claims that we have a democratic system. Elites, it is charged, dominate the mass media, organized interest groups, the courts, legislatures, and bureaucracies; elites wrote the Constitution originally and control the interpretation of it; elites are powerful enough to keep the prime "popular" instrumentalities such as elections, candidates, political parties, and even elected officials—notably congressmen—from having much control over government.

These three appraisals of our government do not by any means exhaust the possible critiques of the system. There is a *conservative* critique that stresses a different type of failing—the tendency of big government to get too big and powerful, take on tasks that should be left to private industry, regulate the individual unduly, tax him to death, and then waste his money on "boondoggles" and other make-work activities. *Reactionaries* believe all this and much more; they would like to turn the clock back and return to an earlier, happier day when life was simpler and cheaper, and government was harmless. Such views are serious and important, and they will receive attention in the chapters to follow. But by the mid-1970s the major attacks on the American system aim at its alleged lack of democracy and responsiveness to the people, and it is these attacks that will mainly occupy us.

Part Two The rules and how they grew

A PROBLEM GUIDE

Felix Frankfurter once observed that "talking constitutionality" was a disease that afflicted many Americans. One may wonder why we should care about what went on in Philadelphia during the summer of 1787 or how the Constitution later developed. Our concern with constitutional history is not that of an antiquarian. We are interested in the "rules of the game" and their origins and evolvement because of their *present* effect on who wins and loses in American politics and government. By identifying the values and interests that the framers intended to advance, we set the stage for a basic question of this book: What values and interests does the American system favor today?

Forty men gathered in Philadelphia in 1787 to write the Constitution. They faced the problem of building a national government strong enough to perform its tasks but not so strong as to antagonize the people. They also faced the problem of compromising among many different ideas of government and many different interests and sections. Chapter 2 describes how the framers met these problems.

The Constitution posed further problems, however, that have challenged Americans ever since 1787. Basically, a constitution both grants and controls power. Ideally, it gives the leaders enough power to meet the nation's needs, but it also prevents them from abusing this power. It sets up the rules that determine how leaders must win office (for example, through fair elections) and how they must exercise power once they are in office.

Now the framers—and most other Americans in 1787—feared government, especially a *national government,* even though they knew that some government was necessary. So they designed a government that could handle the tasks facing the nation but that would not be able to seize or wield too much power. To check national power the framers depended on two devices: (1) *free and fair elections,* so nobody could take elective office unless he was acceptable to most of the voters; and (2) an elaborate system of *balancing power.*

This system of balancing power is the heart of our constitutional system and rests, in turn, on two devices: (1) a *distribution of governmental power* among the several branches of the national government (for example, between president and Congress); and (2) a *system of checks and balances* that makes the branches of government responsible to different sources of popular support (for example, senators are elected by state electorates; representatives by numerous small districts based on *population*).

Although this system has stood the test of time, it created a set of difficult problems: is a system of checks and balances that was adequate for the horse-and-buggy age good enough for the space age? Does it allow the people direct and strong control over their leaders? By dividing up national power among many officials, each responding to different groups of voters, does it make coordinated policies too difficult? Does it allow leaders to "pass the buck" so that the voters have trouble finding out who does what, when, and how well? Does the Constitution incorporate a systematic bias in favor of the elites at the expense of the masses? Chapter 3 takes up this set of problems.

Closely related is the question of how flexible and adaptable our Constitution should be. After all, it was drawn up almost two centuries ago, and the demands on government are much greater now. Is the Constitution a timeless charter whose principles and methods are as sound today as ever? Or should we adopt a new one more attuned to the needs of today? Chapter 3 discusses these questions too.

Finally, there are the problems created by *federalism*—the division of power between the national and state governments. Our country has undergone vast economic, social, and military changes, and the national government has taken on heavier and heavier burdens. Relatively, the states have lost ground. Is federalism obsolete? Does it deprive the national government of the power it needs to handle its huge tasks? Or is federalism as valid as ever? Chapters 4 and 5 deal with these and related problems.

Examining these questions will help us organize our thinking about the basic problem of Part Two. Can we and should we maintain a constitutional system largely shaped in 1787 in the face of the urgent demands of the 1970s? Part Two sets forth these problems, but they, and others, will reappear throughout the book.

Chapter 2 The birth of a nation

On a bright Sunday afternoon in May 1787, General George Washington, escorted by three other generals and a troop of light horses, arrived in Philadelphia to the sound of chiming bells and cheering citizens. After depositing his baggage, Washington went to call on an old friend, Benjamin Franklin. They had many important matters to discuss and much to work out. For Washington, as a delegate from Virginia, and Franklin, as a delegate from Pennsylvania, were in the vanguard of a group of illustrious men who were to spend the hot summer of 1787 writing a new constitution for the thirteen American states.

A constitution that is to endure must reflect the hard experience and high hopes of the people for whom it is written. Those who framed our Constitution did not, of course, complete the job of constitution-making, for it is a process that began long before the Constitutional Convention met and that still continues today. Constitutions – even written ones – are growing and evolving organisms rather than documents that are merely "struck off, at a given time, by the brain and purpose of man" (as Gladstone once described our Constitution).

Toward independence and self-government

The first immigrants to this continent brought with them English political concepts and institutions. For the next 150 years these English ideas were adapted to fit the conditions of the New World. (Sometimes we forget that this nation was part of the British Empire for almost as long as it has been independent.) By July 4, 1776, the colonists had shaped basic governmental arrangements, some of which still serve us.

THE KINDLING OF NATIONALISM

But despite their experience with government within the colonies, the colonists had little training in *inter*colonial problems, for under a divide-and-rule policy, London tried to keep the colonies separate and dependent on England. The colonists themselves developed little sense of unity until the events leading to the Revolutionary War stirred latent American patriotism. Until a few years before the Revolution, most colonists considered themselves Englishmen, and their national loyalty was to the British Crown. The local loyalty of each was to his colony, not to America, although there was some sectional feeling based on familiarity and identity of interests; thus New England, the South, and, to a lesser extent, the Middle Colonies became identifiable communities. Among the people themselves, there were no common American loyalties, no consciously shared experiences, no universally held ideas.

But the groundwork for the development of American nationalism was being laid. During the French and Indian War, known in Europe as the Seven Years' War, American war heroes began to emerge. Gradually the colonists became aware of American, as distinct from English or purely regional, interests. "By the early 1770s, the colonists were sufficiently different from their English contemporaries that they comprised a political community—embryonic in some respects, perhaps, but nonetheless a distinct American political community."[1] Persistent trouble with the mother country intensified this sense of American identity.

Prior to the end of the French and Indian War, the imperial authorities had allowed the colonists to handle their own affairs with relatively little interference from London. But, at considerable expense, the British had driven the French from the North American continent and had made new territories available for settlement. The ministers therefore decided it would be only fair to ask the colonists to pay some of the cost of defending their own frontiers. Steps were taken to raise revenue among the Americans, to enforce trade regulations more rigorously, and generally to tighten English control over colonial affairs. But what seemed just to the English authorities was viewed differently on this side of the Atlantic. Colonial businessmen wanting to develop their own industries, merchants and shippers wishing to trade with nations other than England, planters believing they could get better prices from the Dutch and French than from the English, speculators wishing to buy western land—these and others chafed under the heavier taxes and harsher restrictions.

[1]Richard L. Merritt, *Symbols of American Community, 1735–1775* (Yale University Press, 1966), p. 182.

"You know, the idea of taxation *with* representation doesn't appeal to me very much either."

Drawing by Handelsman; © 1970 The New Yorker Magazine, Inc.

But these restless colonists hardly thought of independence; they merely wanted Parliament to repeal the onerous laws and to leave the colonists alone. However, to make more effective their protests, which were couched in legal and constitutional phraseology, these essentially conservative men stirred up the feelings of other elements in the colonies. Many of the small artisans, lesser merchants, and farmers were not directly affected by the tax and trade laws, and many of them did not have the right to vote; nevertheless, the actions of the English government affronted their developing national feeling. Leadership of the protest movement began to pass from the hands of the more restrained group to those who were asking for more radical action—men like Sam and John Adams in Massachusetts and Patrick Henry and Thomas Jefferson in Virginia. These leaders gave more stress to the concepts of the natural rights of men and of government resting on the consent of the governed and less stress to constitutional and legal arguments. They started to talk about individual liberty and human rights.[2]

These arguments had a double edge. They could be used against the dominant groups *within* the colonies as well as against the British.

[2] J. F. Jameson, *The American Revolution Considered as a Social Movement* (Princeton University Press, 1926; reprinted Peter Smith, 1950). For a detailed analysis of American political thought from 1765 to 1776, see Clinton Rossiter, *Seedtime of the Republic* (Harcourt, 1953); for political thought from 1776 to 1787, see Gordon S. Wood, *The Creation of the American Republic: 1776–1787* (University of North Carolina Press, 1969).

Gradually some of the conservatives began to lose their enthusiasm for protest, fearing that revolution might lead not merely to changes in Empire relations but also to domestic reform. Popular feeling against England, however, became sharper. The colonists were forced, first for political and then for military purposes, to join together in defense of their common cause. Colonial leaders began to keep in closer touch with one another. The Committees of Correspondence, the Stamp Act Congress, and the First Continental Congress stimulated awareness of the common bond and gave the colonists experience in intercolonial cooperation. Finally, in 1775, the Second Continental Congress spoke for *Americans.*

THE SURGE TOWARD INDEPENDENCE

Even after minutemen began fighting with redcoats in 1775, many Americans found the idea of independence quite unacceptable and hoped for reconciliation with England. But the fighting continued through the months, and the English government refused to make concessions to American demands. In August 1775 the King issued a proclamation declaring the colonies to be in a state of rebellion, and in December 1775 Parliament forbade all trade with the colonies. These actions played into the hands of the radicals and strengthened their cause. Then, in January 1776, Thomas Paine issued his pamphlet *Common Sense*, calling on Americans to proclaim their independence. Seldom in

The burden of the Stamp Act (expressed here by a Pennsylvania colonist) helped unite Americans in the surge toward independence.

The TIMES are Dreadful, Dismal Doleful Dolorous, and DOLLAR-LESS

An Emblem of the Effects of the STAMP

O! the fatal Stamp

Thursday, *October* 31, 1765. THE NUMB. 1195.

PENNSYLVANIA JOURNAL; AND WEEKLY ADVERTISER.

EXPIRING: In Hopes of a Resurrection to LIFE again.

I AM sorry to be obliged to acquaint my Readers, that as The STAMP-ACT, is fear'd to be obligatory upon us after the *First of November* ensuing, (the *fatal To morrow*) the Publisher of this Paper unable to bear the Burthen, has thought it expedient TO STOP awhile, in order to deliberate, whether any Methods can be found to elude the Chains forged for us, and escape the insupportable Slavery, which it is hoped, from the last Representations now made against that Act, may be effected. Mean while, I must earnestly Request every Individual of my Subscribers, many of whom have been long behind Hand, that they would immediately Discharge their respective Arrears that I may be able, not only to support myself during the Interval, but be better prepared to proceed again with this Paper, whenever an opening for that Purpose appears, which I hope will be soon WILLIAM BRADFORD history has a single pamphlet had so much influence. "It rallied the undecided and the wavering, and proved a trumpet call to the radicals."[3]

The clamor for independence intensified. On May 10, 1776, Congress advised the colonies to adopt new governments and five days later declared "that the exercise of every kind of authority under the . . . Crown should be totally suppressed." This May 15 resolution "was the real declaration of independence, . . . the most important act of the Continental Congress in its history."[4] On June 7, Richard Henry Lee, following instructions from the Virginia Assembly, moved in the Second Continental Congress "that these United Colonies are, and of right ought to be, Free and Independent States." After bitter debate, Lee's motion was adopted on July 2. The Congress had already appointed a committee, consisting of Thomas Jefferson, John Adams, Benjamin Franklin, Roger Sherman, and Robert Livingston, to prepare a formal declaration of "the causes which impelled us to this mighty resolution." This Declaration of Independence was adopted on July 4, 1776.

The Declaration is more than a justification of rebellion. It is also a statement of the American democratic creed, "designed to justify the past and chart the future."[5] and set forth in succinct and eloquent language. Let us look again at the first sentences:

> We hold these truths to be self-evident, that all men are created equal, that they are endowed by their Creator with certain unalienable Rights, that among these are Life, Liberty and the pursuit of Happiness.—That to secure these rights, Governments are instituted among Men, deriving their just powers from the consent of the governed,—that whenever any Form of Government becomes destructive of these ends, it is the Right of the People to alter or to abolish it, and to institute new Government, laying its foundation on such principles, and organizing its powers in such form, as to them shall seem most likely to effect their Safety and Happiness.

Here we find the democratic beliefs in natural rights, in popular consent as the just basis for political obligations, in limited government, and in the right of the people to revolt against tyrannical government.

SOME INTELLECTUAL LUGGAGE

To most American patriots in 1776, these doctrines were just plain common sense. Jefferson, who wrote the Declaration, stated in a letter to Henry Lee that he did not feel it his duty to set out "new principles . . . never before thought of," but to "place before mankind the common sense of the subject, in terms so plain and firm as to command their assent, and to justify ourselves in the independent stand we are compelled to take." These ideas had become fully synthesized in America.

[3]S. E. Morison, H. S. Commager, and W. E. Leuchtenburg, *The Growth of the American Republic*, 6th ed. (Oxford University Press, 1969), I, 171.

[4]Wood, *American Republic: 1776–1787*, p. 132.

[5]Ralph Barton Perry, *Puritanism and Democracy* (Vanguard, 1944), pp. 124–25.

But in essence they were part of the intellectual luggage that the colonists had brought with them, or later imported, from the Old World.

The man most responsible for popularizing these doctrines was John Locke, whose famous *Second Treatise of Civil Government*, written a century before, had been used to justify the English Revolution of 1688. Locke's arguments were tailormade for the defense of the American cause. He profoundly influenced the patriot leaders, and his ideas, along with some of his phraseology, found their way into the Declaration.

Prior to the establishment of organized society and government, Locke had written, people lived in a state of nature. This was not a lawless condition, however, because the natural law was known to all through the use of reason and was binding on all. (The meaning of "natural law" has been argued by philosophers for centuries; for our purposes it is enough to think of the laws of nature as inherent, inescapable rules of proper human behavior—laws, in Cicero's words, that are in accordance with nature, apply to all, and are unchangeable and eternal.) According to the natural law, each individual has a basic, inalienable right to life, liberty, and that property with which he has mixed his own labor. Whoever deprives another of the natural rights violates the natural law and can justly be punished.

Most people obeyed the natural law, but living in a state of nature was inconvenient. There were always a few lawless souls; and whenever a person's natural rights were violated, he had no recourse but to enforce the law himself. Furthermore, when people had differences, there was no impartial judge to whom they could turn for a decision. Therefore, people decided to end this inconvenience by contracting among themselves to form a society and to establish a government for the purpose of protecting each person's natural rights. By the terms of this social contract, each individual promised to abide by the decisions of the majority and to surrender to society the private right to enforce the law.

Government was thus limited by the purpose for which it was established. It had only the authority to enforce the natural law. When government becomes destructive of the people's inalienable rights, it ceases to have a claim on their allegiance. The people then have the duty to revolt and to create a government better designed to promote their natural rights.

Does this sound like a radical doctrine? It must be remembered that while Locke's ideas would give power to the people, they also put checks on that power. Depending on one's interpretation of natural rights, these theories could be used either to strengthen or to weaken the right of the people to control their relations with one another through the agency of government.[6]

[6]Willmoore Kendall, *John Locke and the Doctrine of Majority Rule* (University of Illinois Press, 1941). See also Peter Laslett, ed., *Locke's Two Treatises of Government* (Cambridge University Press, 1960). For a view of Locke as a defender of natural rights to restrain the political majority (the view accepted by most of the framers), see Carl L. Becker, *The Declaration of Independence: A Study of the History of Political Ideas* (Knopf, 1951).

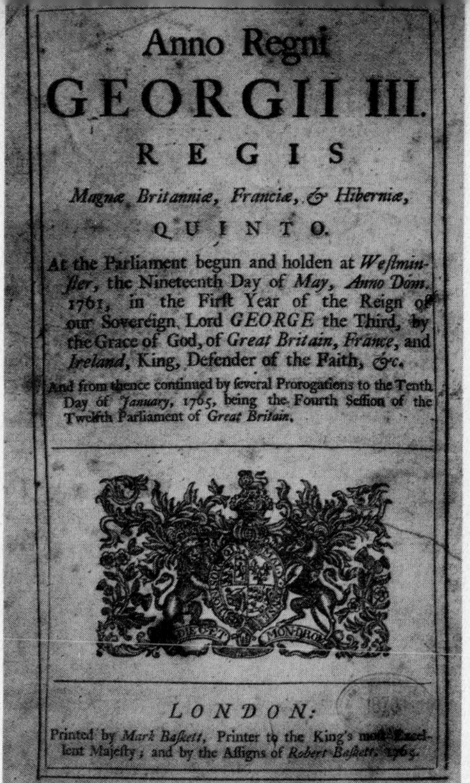

Anno Regni

GEORGII III.

REGIS

Magnæ Britanniæ, Franciæ, & Hiberniæ,

QUINTO.

At the Parliament begun and holden at *Weſtminſter*, the Nineteenth Day of *May*, *Anno Dom.* 1761, in the Firſt Year of the Reign of our Sovereign Lord *GEORGE* the Third, by the Grace of God, of *Great Britain*, *France*, and *Ireland*, King, Defender of the Faith, *&c.*

And from thence continued by ſeveral Prorogations to the Tenth Day of *January*, 1765, being the Fourth Seſſion of the Twelfth Parliament of *Great Britain*.

LONDON:

Printed by *Mark Baſkett*, Printer to the King's moſt Excellent Majeſty; and by the Aſſigns of *Robert Baſkett*. 1765.

Colonists protest the Stamp Act by burning the stamps (left). Right, the document that started all the trouble—the first page of the unpopular Stamp Act.

Early Americans were also influenced by other Old World philosophers. One of the most prominent of these was Montesquieu, who, in the time of Louis XIV and Louis XV, believed that liberty must be secured *against* government. Montesquieu's importance lies in the fact that he had a very practical scheme—*the separation of powers*—to keep government from violating man's natural right to liberty. The way to prevent the abuse of power is to check power with power, said Montesquieu, by giving some authority to the legislative branch, some to the executive, and some to the judicial. This kind of organization safeguards liberty against government.

These were the ideas that set the intellectual tone during the period when Americans were replacing English authority with their own government. Broadly speaking, the forefathers leaned more heavily on Locke in setting up government under the Articles of Confederation, more heavily on Montesquieu in framing the Constitution of 1787.

Experiment in confederation

Alexis de Tocqueville, the perceptive nineteenth-century French visitor to the New World, asserted, "The great advantage of the Americans is that they have arrived at a state of democracy without having to endure a democratic revolution. . . ."[7] Tocqueville had not forgotten the war of 1776. He meant that the American Revolution was primarily a rebellion of colonies against an empire. But even in this respect, "The Americans [other than blacks] were not an oppressed people; they had no crushing imperial shackles to throw off. In fact, the Americans knew they were probably freer and less burdened with cumbersome feudal and hierarchical restraints than any part of mankind in the eighteenth century."[8] In the modern sense, it was hardly a revolution; there were no sharp breaks with the past and no great social, economic, or political upheavals. Contrast the colonists' demand for the "rights of Englishmen" with the Frenchmen's demand for the "rights of man" in 1789.

Americans experienced a conservative revolution that sought a return to a previous condition of utopian simplicity rather than an advance to a utopian future. "Indeed, what is truly extraordinary about the Revolution is that few Americans ever felt the need to repudiate their English heritage for the sake of . . . what ought to be. . . . Even the fact that Americans jettisoned a monarch and suddenly and without much internal debate adopted a republican government marked no great upheaval."[9] Thomas Jefferson observed in the summer of 1777 that Americans "seem to have deposited the monarchical and taken up the republican government with as much ease as would have attended their throwing off an old and putting on a new suit of clothes."[10] As a result the American Revolution did not open class wounds. Neither a radical tradition nor one of reaction developed. The political system based on such a revolution centered on consensus rather than conflict.

And yet in significant ways the new governments were different from those existing before the Revolution. There were no kings. There were no imperial representatives. The English had tried to regulate the colonists from London; now power was to be held firmly in the hands of state governments. But this was not all, for just to be free from London was not the most important aim of the Revolution; it was to protect liberty, to insure that neither imperial authorities nor local ones would be able to trample on people's freedoms. Americans therefore wrote new state constitutions that incorporated bills of rights, abolished most religious qualifications, and liberalized property and taxpaying requirements for voting.[11] Although outside the South free black males had

[7]*Democracy in America*, ed. F. Bowen (Sever and Francis, 1872), II, 13. For other statements of the same view, see Daniel J. Boorstin, *The Genius of American Politics* (University of Chicago Press, 1953), p. 68; and Louis Hartz, *The Liberal Tradition in America* (Harcourt, 1955).

[8]Wood, *American Republic, 1776–1787*, p. 3.

[9]*Ibid.* p. 10.

[10]Quoted by Wood, p. 92, Jefferson to Benjamin Franklin, August 2, 1777. In Boyd, ed., *Jefferson Papers*, II, 26.

[11]Elisha P. Douglass, *Rebels and Democrats* (University of North Carolina Press, 1955). See also R. R. Palmer, *The Age of the Democratic Revolution* (Princeton University Press,

about the same political privileges as white men, little was done about slavery. The abolition of that evil was to take another half century and a Civil War. Nor was there any concern shown for the political, civil, or legal rights of women, although in New Jersey women could vote if they could meet the property qualifications. The expansion of liberty was limited to white males.

The most glaring difference between the old colonial charters and the new state constitutions was the concentration of power in the legislatures. The legislative branches had enhanced their prestige as champions of popular causes. The emphasis on the consent of the governed, borrowed from Locke and others, also stressed the legislature as the repository of that consent. The office of governor, on the other hand, smacked of royalty and stirred unpleasant memories. In most of the states governors were made dependent on the legislature for election, their term of office was shortened, their veto power reduced, their power to appoint officials curbed. Judges, too, smacked of royalty, and the new state legislatures overrode judicial decisions and scolded judges whose rulings were unpopular. The legislative branch, complained *Federalist No. 48* later, was "drawing all power into its impetuous vortex."

THE ARTICLES OF CONFEDERATION

What about the central government? The Continental Congress, like the colonial legislatures, had assumed governmental powers at the outbreak of hostilities. Although the Congress appointed General Washington commander in chief of the Continental Army, carried on negotiations with foreign countries, raised and supported troops, and borrowed and printed money, its powers were based only on a revolutionary act. A more permanent constitutional arrangement was needed. Accordingly, in June 1776, the Congress created a committee to draft a constitution. A few days after the Declaration of Independence was adopted, this committee submitted a plan for a "league of friendship and perpetual Union," but not until a year later, after months of debate, did Congress submit the Articles of Confederation to the states for their approval. Within two years all the states except Maryland had ratified the Articles; but unanimous consent was required, and the Articles did not go into effect until 1781, when Maryland finally ratified.

The Articles more or less constitutionalized existing arrangements. They frankly established only a league of friendship and cooperation—not a national government. Each state retained its "sovereignty, free-

---

1959), pp. 217–35; Chilton Williamson, *American Suffrage: From Property to Democracy, 1760–1860* (Princeton University Press, 1960), p. 92; Robert A. Rutland, *The Birth of the Bill of Rights, 1776–1791* (University of North Carolina Press, 1955); Richard Ashcraft, "Locke's State of Nature: Historical Fact or Moral Fiction?" *American Political Science Review* (September 1968) pp. 898–915; Samuel Eliot Morison, *The Oxford History of the American People* (Oxford University Press, 1965), p. 276; Hannah Arendt, *On Revolution* (Viking 1963), p. 139.

dom, and independence, and every power, jurisdiction, and right" that was not *expressly* delegated to "the United States, in Congress assembled." The states had jointly declared their independence of the King and had jointly fought against him, but they considered themselves free and independent sovereignties and were loath to part with any of their newly won powers. After fighting a war against centralized authority, they did not want to create another central government, even though it would be American rather than English. Most of the patriots shared the belief that republican governments could exist only in small states and feared that a strong central government would fall into the hands of those who would nullify the work of the Revolution.

There was, nevertheless, a universal recognition of the need for "the more convenient management of the general interests of the United States," and for this purpose a congress was established in which each state was to be represented by not fewer than two nor more than seven delegates. The voting in Congress was by state, each state having one vote regardless of size or contributions to the general treasury. Delegates were chosen by the state legislatures, and their salaries were paid from their respective state treasuries. Because the delegates were state representatives rather than national legislators, they were subject to recall by their state legislatures.

Under the Articles, Congress was given the power to determine peace and war, to make treaties and alliances, to coin money, to regulate trade with the Indians, to borrow money, to issue bills of credit, to build and equip a navy, to establish a postal system, and to appoint senior officers of the United States Army (composed of state militias). In short, Congress was given substantially the same powers that the Continental Congress had already been exercising.

The two most important powers *denied* to Congress were the power to levy taxes and the power to regulate commerce, for it was the British government's abuse of these two powers that had precipitated the Revolutionary War. All that Congress could do was to ask the states for funds and hope that the state governments would collect taxes and turn the money over to the central treasury. And though the states promised to refrain from discriminating against one another's trade, Congress had no power to prevent such discrimination or to pass positive measures to promote national commerce. Only through treaties could Congress regulate foreign commerce, but here, too, it had no enforcement powers.

Clearly Congress under the Confederation was a feeble body. Furthermore, neither a federal executive nor a federal judiciary existed to enforce what decisions the Congress did make. There was simply the promise of each state to observe the Articles and abide by the decisions of Congress. The Articles—more like a treaty than a constitution—were ratified by the several state legislatures, not by the voters. The Articles could be amended, but—again more like a treaty than a constitution—the approval of all thirteen state legislatures was needed. In some re-

Attack on Fort St. Philip, French and Indian War.

spects the national government was like the United Nations today, although the similarity has often been exaggerated.

Nevertheless, the government created by the Articles of Confederation was what most people wanted. They believed that the goals of the Revolution could be achieved only through strong local governments and that centralized authority was dangerous. A truly national government at this time could have been established only by the sword and probably would have been destroyed by the sword. The Articles reflected public sentiment and rested on political reality. A unified national government cannot be created by documents; it must either be based on the support of interests and individuals within the community or be held together by force.

POSTWAR PROBLEMS

The war was over and independence won. Could the new nation—a nation just becoming conscious of its own nationality—survive? The practical difficulties confronting it would have tested the strongest and best-entrenched government. Within the limits of its powers, the government of the Confederation did an excellent job: it adopted a program for governing and developing western lands; it established diplomatic relations with other nations; it laid the foundations of a central bureaucracy; and it met the financial problems growing out of the war. By the time the Constitutional Convention assembled, the postwar depression was giving way to a period of business and commercial expansion.

Yet the problems were great and the central government was unable to provide strong leadership. Newly won independence deprived Americans of some of the special commercial privileges they had enjoyed as members of the British Empire. The profitable trade with the

English West Indies was prohibited. Congress found it difficult to negotiate favorable trade treaties with other nations because of a general belief in Europe that the states would not comply with the treaties. The Spanish closed the mouth of the Mississippi at New Orleans to all American goods, and Barbary pirates freely looted American shipping in the Mediterranean. There was no uniform medium of exchange, because each state provided its own money, which fluctuated greatly in value. Paper money issued by Congress to finance the war was circulating at about one thousandth of its face value. Lacking confidence in the ability of Congress to redeem its pledges, creditors were reluctant to lend money to the central government except at high interest rates. Public securities sold at a fraction of their face value. The states themselves began to default in their payments to the federal treasury. Each state regulated its own commerce, some discriminating against their neighbors; and the lack of uniformity of trade regulations made it difficult to develop interstate commerce. The end of the war reduced the sense of urgency that had helped to unite the several states, and conflicts among the states were frequent.

Within the states, affairs went badly too. Delinquent debtors—primarily farmers, who faced the loss of their property and the prospect of debtors' prison—began to exert pressure on the state legislatures for relief. In several of the states they were successful, and the legislatures extended the period for the payment of mortgages, issued legal-tender paper money for the payment of debts, and scaled down the taxes. Creditors resented these interferences. Throughout the nation the conflicts grew bitter between debtor and creditor, between poor and rich, between manufacturer and shipper.

To add to the difficulties, neither the English nor the states would live up to the terms of the treaty of peace. The English refused to withdraw their troops from the western frontier until American debtors had paid their English creditors and until the states had repaid the Loyalists for confiscated property. Congress lacked the power to force either the English or the states to comply. To the English on the west and the Spanish and French in the south, the new nation, internally divided and lacking a strong central government, made a tempting prize.

MOVEMENT FOR REVISION

Was it surprising that in the face of postwar problems, foreign threats, and conflicts among the various sectional and economic interests, some became disillusioned about the republican ideals of 1776? In the states people came to be disturbed by the inadequacies of their state governments in which unrestrained power had been vested in the legislative assemblies. The radicals, who had engineered the Revolution, either began to change their views or to lose power. In many states the constitutions were revised to strengthen the role of the governor and to provide for more independence for the judges.

What of the national government—if it could be called a government? The elite had never been satisfied with the Articles of Confederation, considering them too democratic and too feeble. The inability of the Confederation to provide a strong union against foreign dangers, to prevent the states from interfering with business, and to pay its creditors added to the conviction of the conservatives that the central government must be strengthened and that checks must be placed on the state governments. They undoubtedly did, for partisan purposes, "paint dark the picture of the times and blame the supposed woes of the country on the Articles of Confederation,"[12] but they were genuinely alarmed. It was, after all, their contracts that the state legislatures were interfering with, their bonds that the central government was unable to pay, their businesses that needed uniform commercial regulations and national protective tariffs, their manufacturing for which they wanted bounties. But beyond this, they were concerned about the dangers of foreign attack, disunion, anarchy, and tyranny.

These fears were sharpened by the growth of a small but powerful group, composed chiefly of men who had never believed in government by the people. These men began to argue publicly that republican government was a failure—that a strong monarchical government was needed to protect persons and property. Washington, who, fortunately for the nation, would have nothing to do with the persistent attempts to make him a king or dictator of the United States, wrote in alarm in August 1786 to John Jay, Secretary of Foreign Affairs:

> What astonishing changes a few years are capable of producing! I am told that even respectable characters speak of a monarchical form of Government without horror. . . . But how irrevocable and tremendous! What a triumph for our enemies to verify their predictions! What a triumph for the advocates of despotism to find that we are incapable of governing ourselves, and that systems founded on the basis of equal liberty are merely ideal and fallacious! Would to God that wise measures be taken in time to avert the consequences we have but too much reason to apprehend.[13]

Those who believed that measures should be taken felt the situation was so critical that it would not be enough merely to revise the Articles of Confederation. To save republicanism they wanted to alter the basic nature of the Union and to create a strong central government with coercive powers. The proponents of a new national government therefore set about—and this may be their greatest contribution—to create a republican government that did not require "a virtuous people for its sustenance," but which could be made to work by and for ordinary people. They hoped to create a central government that would succeed

[12]Merrill Jensen, *The Articles of Confederation* (University of Wisconsin Press, 1940), p. 245.

[13]John C. Fitzpatrick, ed., *The Writings of George Washington* (U.S. Government Printing Office, 1938), XXVIII, 503.

where the states had failed, in John Dickinson's words, "to protect the worthy against the licentious."[14] Clearly the movement for revision "was both a progressive attempt to salvage the Revolution in the face of its imminent failure and a reactionary effort to restrain its excesses."[15]

The desire to control internal dissensions and to stabilize republicanism was not the only reason why the nationalists felt that drastic changes were required. Pressures toward unity also stemmed from fear of outside military and diplomatic threats. A weak, internally divided nation invited outside intervention.[16]

How to proceed? How could closer union be achieved and a strong national government established? Although there was growing recognition of the need to amend the Articles in order to give Congress the power to collect taxes and to regulate commerce among the states, many Americans were still suspicious of a central government with coerceive powers over them. Many of the people did not think the times were so bad, certainly not bad enough to call for any basic alterations in the governmental structure. Nevertheless, practical problems of boundaries, navigation, and tariffs continued to arise, and often these problems were common to most or all of the states. In January of 1786, the Virginia legislature, guided by James Madison, invited the other states to send delegates to a meeting in Annapolis to discuss the possibility of establishing uniform trade regulations. At least this was the ostensible purpose of the convention. But, as Madison wrote Jefferson, "Many gentlemen both within and without Congress wish to make this meeting subservient to a plenipotentiary Convention for amending the Confederation."[17]

When the Convention met in Annapolis in the late summer of 1786, only five states sent delegates, and many who wanted action lost hope. But not Alexander Hamilton, who seized the opportunity to push through the Convention a discreetly worded resolution requesting the five legislatures of the states represented at the Convention to appoint commissioners to meet at Philadelphia on the second Monday of May 1787 "to devise such further provisions as shall appear to them necessary to render the Constitution of the Federal Government adequate to the exigencies of the Union." Although the resolution did not require action by Congress, a copy was sent to it and to the governors of the other states, both "from motives of respect" and with the hope that Congress and the other states might also endorse the proposed convention.[18] Congress, apathetic and perhaps suspicious that Hamilton had

[14]Wood, *American Republic*, 1776–1787.

[15]*Ibid.*

[16]William H. Riker, *Federalism: Origin, Operation, Significance* (Little, Brown, 1964), pp. 19–20.

[17]Quoted in Charles Warren, *The Making of the Constitution* (Little, Brown, 1937), p. 22.

[18]Julius Goebel, Jr., *Antecedents and Beginnings to 1801* (Macmillan, 1971), p. 199.

more in mind than amending the Articles, was loath to act. Some state legislatures appointed delegates, but throughout the nation not much more than polite interest was shown.

INCIDENT IN MASSACHUSETTS

Western Massachusetts had long been the home of "unhappy Tumults and Disorders," and the towns west of the Connecticut River had been in a "state of virtual rebellion from the governing authorities of the East," throughout the Revolutionary period.[19] But in the fall and winter of 1786–87, events in western Massachusetts seemed to justify the dire predictions that the country was on the verge of anarchy. Many farmers who faced imprisonment through inability to pay their mortgages or their taxes rallied around Daniel Shays, a Revolutionary War captain. The angry farmers—many called them a mob—marched into Northampton where they blocked the entrance to the courthouse and forcibly restrained the judges from foreclosing mortgages on farms.

The militia put down the uprising, but the revolt sent a shudder down the spines of the more substantial citizens. "Indeed, it was as if all the imaginings of political philosophers for centuries were being lived out in a matter of years in the hills of New England."[20] The outraged General Knox, Secretary of War, wrote to Washington: "This dreadful situation has alarmed every man of principle and property in New England. . . . Our government must be braced, changed or altered to secure our lives and property. . . ."[21] As the story of this open rebellion spread through the nation, it took on lurid overtones and, in the minds of many, became a personal threat to life and fortune. Some reacted by abandoning any pretense of support for republican principles. Madison warned that the "turbulent scenes" in Massachusetts had done inexpressible injury to the republican cause and had caused a "propensity toward Monarchy" in the minds of some leaders.[22]

The more respectable leaders were not ready to plunge into either monarchy or disunion. Fortunately, an instrument was at hand that promised a better way to deal with the crisis—the proposed Philadelphia Convention. Shays' Rebellion served as a catalyst, and throughout the states there was a quickening of interest in the recommendation of the Annapolis Convention. Seven states appointed delegates without waiting for Congress to act. Finally Congress jumped on the Convention bandwagon with a cautiously worded request to the states to appoint delegates for the "sole and express purpose of revising the Articles of Confederation . . . to render the Federal Constitution adequate

[19]Wood, *American Republic, 1776–1787*, pp. 284–85.

[20]*Ibid.*

[21]Women, *Making of the Constitution*, p. 31.

[22]Madison to Edmund Pendleton, February 28, 1787. Cited in Warren, p. 45.

to the exigencies of Government, and the preservation of the Union." The careful congressmen specified that no recommendation would be effective unless approved by Congress and confirmed by all the state legislatures as provided by the Articles.

Eventually every state except Rhode Island appointed delegates. (The debtors and farmers who controlled the Rhode Island legislature suspected that the very purpose of the Convention would be to place limits on their power.) Some of the delegations were bound by instructions only to consider amendments to the Articles of Confederation. Delaware went so far as to forbid her representatives to consider any proposal that would deny any state equal representation in Congress.

The Philadelphia story

The first step in the birth of the new nation had been the destruction of English governmental authority; the second step was the creation of new state governments to replace the colonial governments. The Constitutional Convention, which began in Philadelphia in the summer of 1787, was the third step. The delegates to the Convention were presented with a condition, not a theory. They had to establish a national government with enough power to provide for the common defense and to prevent the nation from degenerating into anarchy or despotism.

Although seventy-four delegates were appointed by the various states, only fifty-five put in an appearance in Philadelphia, and, of these, approximately forty took a real part in the work of the Convention. But it was a distinguished gathering. Many of the most important men of the nation were there—successful merchants, planters, bankers, and lawyers, former and present governors and congressional representatives (thirty-nine of the delegates had served in Congress). As theorists, they had read Locke, Montesquieu, and other philosophers. As men of affairs, they were interested in the intensely practical job of constructing a national government. Theory played its part, but experience was to be their main guide.

THE CAST

Although most of the Revolutionary leaders eventually supported the Constitution in the ratification debate, only eight of the fifty-six signers of the Declaration of Independence were present at the Constitutional Convention. Among the Revolutionary leaders absent were Jefferson, Paine, Henry, Richard Henry Lee, Sam and John Adams, and John Hancock. The Convention was as representative as most meetings of the time. Of course, there were no women or blacks. Although the delegates to the Convention were mainly aristocrats, in the 1780s the common man was not expected to participate in politics (even today small farmers and working people are seldom found in the ranks of Congress). Of the active participants at the Constitutional Convention, several men stand out as the prime movers.

Alexander Hamilton was, as already noted, one of the most impassioned proponents of a strong national government. He had been the engineer of the Annapolis Convention and as early as 1778 had been urging the necessity for invigorating the national government. Born in the West Indies, he lacked strong local attachments and was dedicated to the vision of a unified and powerful United States. Hamilton had come to the United States when only sixteen and while still a student at Kings College (now Columbia University) had won national attention by his brilliant pamphlets in defense of the colonial cause. During the war he served as General Washington's aide, and his war experiences confirmed his distaste for a Congress so weak that it could not even supply its troops with enough food or arms.

From Virginia came two of the leading delegates—General George Washington and James Madison. Even at that time Washington was "first in war, first in peace, and first in the hearts of his countrymen." Although active in the movement to revise the Articles of Confederation, he had been extremely reluctant to attend the Convention and accepted only when persuaded that his prestige was needed for its success. When the Virginia legislature placed his name at the top of its list of delegates, the importance of the Convention was made manifest. Washington was unanimously selected to preside over the meetings. According to the records, he spoke only twice during the deliberations, but his influence was felt in the informal gatherings as well as during the sessions. The universal assumption that Washington would become the first President under the new Constitution inspired confidence in it.

James Madison, slight of build and small in voice, was only thirty-six years old at the time of the Convention, but he was one of the most learned members present. Despite his youth, he had helped frame Virginia's first constitution and had served in both the Virginia Assembly and in the Congress. Realizing the importance of the Convention, Madison had spent months preparing for it by studying the history of Greek confederacies and Italian republics. During the deliberations, he sat in the front of the room and kept full notes on what was said and done. These notes are our major source of information about the Convention. Madison was also a leader of the group who favored the establishment of a strong national government.

The Pennsylvania delegation rivaled that of Virginia, its membership including Benjamin Franklin and Gouverneur Morris. Franklin, at 81, was the Convention's oldest member, and, as one of his fellow delegates said, "He is well known to be the greatest philosopher of the present age." Second only to Washington in the esteem of his countrymen, Franklin enjoyed a world reputation unrivaled by that of any other American. He was one of the first to hold a vision of a strong and united America.

Gouverneur Morris, " a very handsome, bold, and—the ladies say—a very impudent man," was more eloquent than brilliant. He addressed the Convention more often than any other person. His views were those of an aristocrat with disdain for both the rabble and the uncouth moneymakers. The elegance of the language of the Constitution is proof of his facility with the pen, for he was responsible for the final draft.

Luther Martin of Maryland, John Dickinson of Delaware, and William Paterson of New Jersey were not in agreement with a majority of the delegates, but they ably defended the position of those who insisted on equal representation for all states.

Clearly, the Convention was made up of the political elite of the colonies. That men of the stature of Washington and Madison undertook the difficult journey to Philadelphia reflects their deep concern over the state of the Union, and their expectation that major changes were in the wind.

The proceedings of the Convention were kept secret, and delegates were forbidden to discuss any of the debates with outsiders in order to encourage the delegates to speak freely. It was feared that if a member publicly took a firm stand on an issue, it would be harder for him to change his mind after debate and discussion. Also, looking ahead to the ratification struggle, the members knew that if word of the inevitable disagreements got out it would provide ammunition for the many enemies of the Convention. There were critics of this secrecy rule, but without it, agreement might have been impossible.

CONSENSUS

The Constitutional Convention is usually discussed in terms of three famous compromises: the compromise between large and small states over representation in Congress, the compromise between North and South over the counting of slaves for taxation and representation, and the compromise between North and South over the regulation and taxation of foreign commerce. But this emphasis obscures the fact that there were many other important compromises and that on many of the more significant issues most of the delegates were in substantial agreement.

A few delegates might have personally favored a limited monarchy, but all supported *republican* government, and this was the only form of government seriously considered at the Convention. It was the only form that would be acceptable to the nation. Most important, all the delegates were *constitutionalists,* who opposed arbitrary and unrestrained government, whether monarchical, aristocratic, or democratic.

The common philosophy accepted by most of the delegates was that of *balanced government.* They wanted to construct a national government in which no single interest would dominate the others. Because the men in Philadelphia represented groups alarmed by the tendencies of the agrarian interests to interfere with property, they were primarily concerned with balancing the government in the direction of protection for property and business. There was an almost universal concurrence in the remark of Elbridge Gerry (delegate from Massachusetts): "The evils we experience flow from the excess of democracy. The people do not want virtue, but are dupes of pretended patriots." Likewise there was substantial agreement with Gouverneur Morris' statement that property was the "principal object of government."

Benjamin Franklin favored extending the right to vote to male non-property owners, but most of the delegates agreed in general that freeholders (owners of land) were the best guardians of liberty and that only they could be counted on to resist the "dangerous influence of those multitudes without property and without principle." James Madison voiced the fear that those without property, if given the right to vote, would either combine to deprive the property owners of their rights or would become the "tools of opulence and ambition." The delegates agreed in principle on restricted suffrage, but they differed over the kind and amount of property that one must own in order to vote. Moreover, as the several states were in the process of relaxing freehold qualifications for the vote, the framers recognized that they would jeopardize approval of the Constitution if they should make the federal franchise more restricted than the franchises within the states.[23] As a result, each state was left to determine the qualifications for electing members to the House of Representatives, the only branch of the national government in which the electorate was given a direct voice.

Within five days of its opening, the Convention, with only Connecticut dissenting, voted to approve the Fourth Virginia Resolve that "a national government ought to be established consisting of a supreme legislative, executive, and judiciary." This decision to establish a *national government resting on and exercising power over individuals* proposed to alter the nature of the central government profoundly, changing it from a league of states to a national government.

There was little dissent from proposals to give the new Congress all the powers of the old Congress plus all other powers in which the separate states were negligent or in which the harmony of the United States might be disrupted by the exercise of individual legislation. The framers agreed that a strong executive, which had been lacking under the Articles, was necessary to provide the energy and direction for the general government. And an independent judiciary was also accepted without much debate. Franklin favored a single-house national legislature, but almost all the states had had two-chamber legislatures since colonial times and the delegates were used to the system. Bicameralism also conformed to their belief in the need for balanced government, the upper house representing the aristocracy and offsetting the more democratic lower house. So the delegates established two chambers in the national government too.

[23]John P. Roche, "The Founding Fathers: A Reform Caucus in Action," *American Political Science Review* (December 1961), pp. 799–816, emphasizes the importance of such political considerations in the framers' deliberations.

CONFLICT

There were serious differences among the various groups, especially between the representatives of the large states, who favored a strong national government, which they expected to be able to dominate, and the delegates from the small states, who were anxious to avoid being dominated.

The Virginia delegation took the initiative; it had caucused during the delay before the Convention and, as soon as the Convention was organized, was ready with fifteen resolutions. These resolutions, the Virginia Plan, called for a strong central government. The legislature was to be composed of two chambers. The members of the lower house were to be elected by the voters, those of the upper house to be chosen by the lower chamber from nominees submitted by the state legislatures. Representation in both branches was to be on the basis of either wealth or numbers, thus giving the more populous and wealthy states—Virginia, Massachusetts, and Pennsylvania—a majority in the legislature.

The Congress thus created was to be given all the legislative power of its predecessor under the Articles of Confederation and the right "to legislate in all cases in which the separate States are incompetent." Furthermore, it was to have the authority to veto state legislation in conflict with the proposed constitution. The Virginia Plan also called for a national executive, to be chosen by the legislature, and a national judiciary with rather extensive jurisdiction. The national Supreme Court, along with the executive, was to have a qualified veto over acts of Congress.

For the first few weeks the Virginia Plan dominated the discussion at the Convention. But by June 15, additional delegates from the small states had arrived, and they began to counterattack. They rallied around William Paterson of New Jersey, who presented a series of resolutions known as the New Jersey Plan. Paterson did not question the need for a greatly strengthened central government, but he was concerned about how this strength would be used. The New Jersey Plan would give Congress the right to tax and regulate commerce and to coerce recalcitrant states but would retain a single-house legislature in which all states would have the *same vote, regardless of their size*. It provided for a plural national executive and for a national Supreme Court with considerable authority. The New Jersey Plan contained the germ of what eventually came to be a key provision of our Constitution—the supremacy clause. The national Supreme Court was to hear appeals from state judges, and the supremacy clause would require all the judges—state and national—to treat laws of the national government and the treaties of the United States as part of the supreme law of each of the states.[24]

Paterson was maneuvering to force concessions from the larger states. He favored a strong central government but not one that the big states

[24]Robert H. Birkby, "Politics of Accommodation: The Origin of the Supremacy Clause," *Western Political Quarterly* (March 1966), p. 27.

could control. And he raised the issue of practical politics: to adopt the Virginia Plan, which created a powerful national government dominated by Massachusetts, Virginia, and Pennsylvania and eliminated the states as important units of government, would be to court defeat for the Convention's proposals in the ratification struggle to come.

But the large states resisted, and for a time the Convention was deadlocked. The small states argued that states should be represented equally in Congress, at least in the upper house. The large states were adamant, insisting that representation in both houses be based on population or wealth and that national legislators be elected by the electorate rather than by the state legislatures. Finally, a Committee of Eleven was elected to devise a compromise and on July 5 it presented its proposals. Because of the prominent role of the Connecticut delegation, this plan has since been known as the Connecticut Compromise. It called for an upper house in which each state would have an equal vote, but for a lower house in which representation would be based on population and in which all bills for raising or appropriating money would originate. This was a setback to the large states, who agreed only when the smaller states made it clear that this was their price for union. After equality of representation in the Senate was accepted, most objections to the establishment of a strong national government dissolved.

The Southern states wanted slaves to be counted in determining representation in the House of Representatives. It was finally agreed that a slave should count as three-fifths of a free person, both in determining representation in the House and in apportionment of direct taxes. Southerners were also fearful that a Northern majority in Congress might discriminate against Southern trade. They had some basis for this concern. John Jay, Secretary of Foreign Affairs for the Confederation, had proposed a treaty with Great Britain that would have given advantages to Northern merchants at the expense of Southern exporters. To protect themselves, the Southern delegates insisted on requiring a two-thirds majority in the Senate for the ratification of treaties.

The delegates, of course, found other issues to argue about. Should the national government have lower courts or would one federal Supreme Court be enough? This issue was resolved by postponing the decision; the Constitution states that there *shall* be one Supreme Court and that Congress *may* establish inferior courts. How should the President be selected? For a long time the Convention accepted the idea that the President should be elected by the Congress. But it was feared that either the Congress would dominate the President or vice versa. Election by the state legislatures was rejected because of distrust of these bodies. Finally, the electoral college system was decided upon. This was perhaps the most original contribution of the delegates, and is one of the most criticized provisions in the Constitution.

After three months, the delegates ceased debating. On September 17, 1787, they assembled for the impressive ceremony of signing the document they were recommending to the nation. All but three of those still present signed; others, who opposed the general drift of the Convention, had already left. Their work over, the delegates adjourned to the City Tavern to relax and to celebrate a job well done.

WHAT MANNER OF MEN?

Were the delegates an inspired group of men who cast aside all thoughts of self-interest? Were they motivated by the desire to save the Union or by the desire to save themselves? Was the Convention the inevitable result of the weaknesses of the Articles? Was it a carefully maneuvered coup d'état on the part of certain elites? Was the difference between those who favored and those who opposed the Constitution mainly economic? Or was the difference mainly regional?

Students of history and government have held various opinions concerning these and other questions. During the early part of our history, the members of the Convention were the object of uncritical adulation; the Constitution was the object of universal reverence. Early in the twentieth century, a more critical attitude was inspired by J. Allen Smith and Charles A. Beard. Smith, in his *The Spirit of American Government* (1911), painted the Constitution as the outgrowth of an antidemocratic reaction, almost a conspiracy, against the rule of majorities. Beard's thesis was that the Constitution represented the platform of the propertied groups who wanted to limit state legislatures and strengthen the national government as a means of protecting property. In his influential book *An Economic Interpretation of the Constitution* (1913), Beard described the economic holdings of the delegates and argued that their support or opposition to the Constitution could best be explained in terms of their financial interests. He explicitly denied that he was charging the Founding Fathers with writing the Constitution for their personal benefit; rather, he contended that men's political behavior reflects their broad economic interests.

Some more recent historians have questioned the soundness of Beard's scholarship and challenged his interpretation of the data. Robert E. Brown points out that there was no great propertyless mass in the United States and that "practically everybody was interested in the protection of property." "We would be doing a grave injustice to the political sagacity of the Founding Fathers," Brown has noted, "if we assumed that property or personal gain was their only motive."[25] Forrest McDonald, after looking into Beard's data, has concluded that the "economic interpretation of the Constitution does not work," although he concedes an "economic interpretation renders intelligible many of the forces at work in the making of the Constitution."[26] David G. Smith concludes, "The delegates . . . protected property, but especially in

[25]*Charles Beard and the Constitution* (Princeton University Press, 1956), pp. 197–98.

[26]*We the People: The Economic Origins of the Constitution* (University of Chicago Press, 1958), pp. vii, 415.

order to remove sources of discord, foster economic growth, and develop interest in the government. They destroyed the dependence of the government upon the states, but more in the interests of a national citizenship than fear of democracy. . . ."[27] Gordon S. Wood sees the conflict over the Constitution as one between differing political ideologies, based on social lines. He writes, "There were many diverse reasons in each state why men supported or opposed the Constitution that cut through any sort of class division. . . . Nevertheless, despite all of the confusion and complexity, the struggle over the Constitution . . . can best be understood as a social one. . . . The quarrel was fundamentally one between aristocracy and democracy."[28]

Analysis of the votes in the Convention shows that the voting patterns cannot be explained by large versus small states, or by the economic interests of the delegates, or by the class interests represented by the state delegations, or the distribution of real property in the states.[29] On the other hand, states that were geographically contiguous did tend to vote together.

The various interpretations of the American Revolution, of which the writing of the Constitution was part, reflect the changing styles of contemporary affairs as current political debates are read backwards into our past. But the various interpretations also reflect the fact that "The American Revolution . . . was so complex and contained so many diverse and seemingly contradictory currents that it can support a wide variety of interpretations and may never be comprehended in full."[30]

Beard himself recognized that men are motivated by a complex of factors, both conscious and unconscious. Self-interest, economic or otherwise, and principles are inextricably mixed in human behavior, and the framers were not much different from today's political leaders. The Founding Fathers were neither gods for whom self-interest or economic considerations were of no importance nor selfish elitists who thought only in terms of their own pocketbooks. They were, by and large, aristocrats fearful of the masses, but they were committed to an aristocracy of merit, of education, of accomplishment and not of birth or wealth. The framers were concerned with the Union and they wanted to protect the nation from aggression abroad and dissension at home. Stability and strength were needed to protect their own interests—but also to secure the unity and order indispensable for the operation of a democracy.

[27] *The Convention and the Constitution* (St. Martin's Press, 1965), p. 31.

[28] Wood, *American Republic, 1776–1787* pp. 484–85.

[29] S. Sidney Ulmer, "Subgroup Formation in the Constitutional Convention," *Midwest Journal of Political Science* (August 1966), p. 302.

[30] Jack P. Greene, "The Reappraisal of the American Revolution in Recent Historical Literature," in Jack P. Greene, ed., *The Reinterpretation of the American Revolution, 1763–1789* (Harper & Row, 1968), p. 2.

To adopt or not to adopt

The delegates had gone far. They had not hesitated to contravene Congress's instructions about ratification or to ignore Article XIII of the Articles of Confederation. This article declared the Union to be perpetual and prohibited any alteration in the Articles unless agreed to by the Congress and *by every one of the state legislatures*—a provision that had made it impossible to amend the Articles. But the Convention delegates boldly declared that the Constitution should go into effect when ratified by *popularly elected conventions* in *nine states*. They had substituted this method of ratification for both practical considerations and reasons of principle. Not only were the delegates aware that there was little chance of securing approval of the new Constitution in all of the state legislatures, but many felt that the Constitution should be ratified by an authority higher than any governmental body. A constitution based on popular approval would have a higher legal and moral status. The Articles of Confederation had been a compact of state governments, but the Constitution was to be a "union of people."[31]

But even this method of ratification was not going to be easy. The nation was not ready to adopt the Constitution without a thorough debate, and soon two camps sprang up. The supporters of the new government, by cleverly appropriating the name of Federalists, took some of the sting out of the charges that they were trying to destroy the states and establish an all-powerful central government. By dubbing their opponents Antifederalists, they pointed up the negative character of the arguments of those who opposed ratification.

The split was in part geographical. The seaboard and city regions tended to be Federalist strongholds. The vast back-country regions from Maine through Georgia, inhabited by farmers and other relatively poor people, were areas in which the Antifederalists were most strongly entrenched. But, as in all political contests, no single factor—geographical or economic or ideological—completely accounted for the division between Federalist and Antifederalist. For example, in Virginia the leaders of both sides came from the same general social and economic class. New York City and Philadelphia strongly supported the Constitution, but so did predominantly rural New Jersey.

From our vantage point of hindsight, many of the criticisms raised by the Antifederalists obviously were unfounded and many of their fears unjustified. It used to be the fashion among historians and political scientists to picture these opponents of our Constitution as small-minded, selfish men who could not see beyond their own local interests. With the introduction of a more critical attitude toward the Founding Fathers, there was a swing to the other extreme; the Antifederalists were then described as the true defenders of liberty and democracy, fighting the economically motivated aristocratic Federalists. Both these generali-

[31]Max Farrand, ed., *The Records of the Federal Convention of 1787* (Yale University Press, 1911), II, 93, 476.

zations are exaggerated. Each side included able and enlightened men as well as those with less admirable motives, and, judged within the context of the eighteenth century, both Federalists and Antifederalists were confirmed defenders of republican government.

The great debate was conducted with pamphlets, papers, letters to editors, and speeches. The issue was important and the interest of those concerned intense, but the argument, in the main, was carried on in a temperate manner. This great debate stands even today as an outstanding example of a free people using open discussion to determine the nature of their fundamental laws.

THE GREAT DEBATE

In general, the Antifederalist argument developed along these lines: There is much merit in the proposed Constitution, but it contains many provisions that show the aristocratic bias of its authors. It calls for the creation of a "consolidated system" that would in the end destroy republican government and individual liberty as well as the independence of the states.[32] It lacks adequate guarantees of the people's fundamental rights. Present conditions are not so bad as the Federalists make out; we are at peace, and there is no danger of internal dissension. We do need a correction of the Articles of Confederation but a correction that preserves, as the Constitution does not, the power of the states and the freedom of the people. We should not ratify the proposed Constitution; but after it has been fully discussed and its defects made apparent, a second convention should be called to revise the Articles in the light of these discussions.

The Antifederalists were suspicious of the intentions of the delegates to the Convention; the delegates had exceeded their instructions, deliberated in secret, and presented a constitution that established a powerful national government. Said Amos Singletary, delegate from a western town in the Massachusetts ratifying convention, member of the Massachusetts legislature, and a veteran of the Revolutionary army:

> Mr. President, if any body had proposed such a constitution as this in that day [the Revolutionary period], it would have been thrown away at once. . . . These lawyers, and men of learning, and moneyed men, that talk so finely, and gloss over matters so smoothly, to make us poor illiterate people swallow down the pill, expect to get into Congress themselves; they expect to be the managers of this Constitution, and get all the power and all the money into their own hands, and then they will swallow up all of us little folks, like the great *Leviathan*, Mr. President; yes, just as the whale swallowed up *Jonah*.

The Federalists, on the other side, argued that there were just two al-

[32]John D. Lewis, ed., *Anti-Federalists versus Federalists* (Chandler, 1967), p. 2; Robert Allen Rutland, *The Ordeal of the Constitution: The Antifederalists and the Ratification Struggle of 1787–1788* (University of Oklahoma Press, 1966).

ternatives—adoption of the Constitution or disunion. They insisted that the Confederation was hopelessly defective and that, unless it was quickly altered, the Union would be lost. Arguing that union was indispensable to liberty and security, they defended the Constitution as conforming to the true principles of republican government. They admitted that it was not perfect but held that it was the best that could be obtained and that the way was open to correct such deficiencies as were uncovered through time and experience.

One of the best attacks produced by the Antifederalists was a series of articles written by Richard Henry Lee, the man who had introduced the resolution in the Second Continental Congress calling for independence. Lee's *Letters of the Federal Farmer*, published in the fall of 1787, were widely circulated throughout the nation. On the other hand, *The Federalist*, a series of essays, is without doubt the best defense of the Constitution. Charles and Mary Beard have written, "From that day to this *The Federalist* has been widely regarded as the most profound single treatise on the Constitution ever written and as among the few masterly works on political science produced in all the centuries of history."[33] These essays were written by Alexander Hamilton, James Madison, and John Jay. Over the name of Publius, they were published serially in the New York papers during the winter of 1787.

Perhaps the most telling criticism of the proposed Constitution made by Lee and others was its failure to include a bill of rights.[34] The Federalists argued that a bill of rights would be superfluous. The general government had only delegated powers, and there was no need to specify that Congress could not, for example, abridge freedom of the press. It had no power to regulate the press. Moreover, the Federalists argued, to guarantee *some* rights might be dangerous because it would then be thought that rights *not* listed could be denied. Contradictorily, they pointed out that the Constitution protected some of the most important rights—trial by jury in federal criminal cases, for example. Hamilton and others also insisted that paper guarantees were weak reeds on which to depend for protection against governmental tyranny.

The Antifederalists were unconvinced. If some rights were protected, what could be the objection to providing constitutional protection for others? Without a bill of rights, what was to prevent Congress from using one of its delegated powers in such a manner that free speech would be abridged? If bills of rights were needed in state constitutions to limit

[33]Charles A. Beard and Mary R. Beard, *A Basic History of the United States* (New Home Library, 1944), p. 136. Gottfried Dietze's *The Federalist: A Classic on Federalism and Free Government* (Johns Hopkins Press, 1960) is one of the few monographic analyses of these important state papers. There are also two other editions of *The Federalist* available, that of Benjamin F. Wright (Harvard University Press, 1961), which contains an excellent introductory essay, and that of Jacob E. Cooke (Wesleyan University Press, 1961), which provides exhaustive annotations.

[34]Rutland, *Birth of the Bill of Rights.* See also Alpheus T. Mason, *The States Rights Debates: Antifederalism and the Constitution* (Prentice-Hall, 1964), pp. 4, 66–97.

state governments, why was one not needed in the national constitution to limit the national government—a government farther from the people and with a greater tendency, it was argued, to subvert natural rights? The Federalists, forced to concede, agreed to add a bill of rights if and when the new Constitution was approved.

THE POLITICS OF RATIFICATION

Despite the great debate, many people remained apathetic. The only direct voice the electorate had in the writing and adopting of our Constitution was in choosing delegates to the state ratifying conventions. In Connecticut and in New York all adult males were allowed to vote for representatives to the ratifying conventions, and in most of the other states suffrage requirements were liberalized. From 80 to 85 percent of the adult white males[35] were eligible to vote for delegates, yet only a fraction of those qualified to vote actually did so. "The Constitution was adopted with a great show of indifference."[36]

The political strategy of the Federalists was to secure ratification in as many states as possible before the opposition had time to organize. The Antifederalists were handicapped. They lacked access to the newspapers, most of which supported ratification. Their main strength was in the rural areas, under-represented in some state legislatures and difficult to arouse to political action. They needed time to perfect their organization and collect their strength. The Federalists, composed of a more closely knit group of leaders throughout the colonies, moved in a hurry. "Unless the Federalists had been shrewd in manipulation as they were sound in theory, their arguments could not have prevailed."[37]

In most of the small states, now propitiated by equal Senate representation, ratification was gained without difficulty; Delaware was the first state to ratify. The first large state to take action was Pennsylvania. The Federalists presented the Constitution to the state legislature immediately after the Philadelphia Convention adjourned in September 1787, urging the legislators to call for the ratifying convention to adopt the new Constitution. But the legislature was about to adjourn, and the Antifederalist minority felt that this was moving with unseemly haste (Congress had not even formally transmitted the document to the legislature for its consideration!). They wanted to postpone action until after the coming state elections, when they hoped to win a legislative majority and so forestall calling a ratifying convention. When it became clear that the Federalists were going to move ahead, the Antifederalists left the legislative chamber. With two short of a quorum, business was brought to a standstill. But Philadelphia, the seat of the legislature, was

[35]Williamson, *American Suffrage*, pp. 111–12.

[36]Brown, *Charles Beard and the Constitution*, pp. 69, 197. See also A. C. McLaughlin, *A Constitutional History of the United States* (Appleton, 1935), pp. 220–21.

[37]Morison and Commager, *Growth of the American Republic*, 5th ed., I., 296.

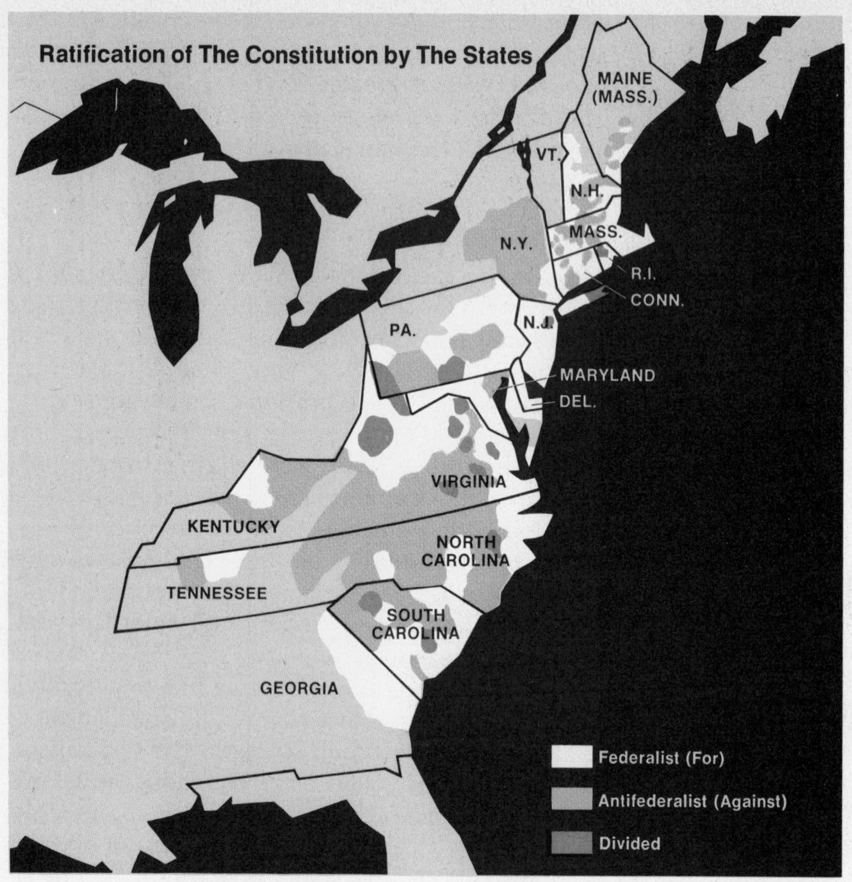

a Federalist stronghold. The next morning two Antifederalists were roused from their quarters, carried into the legislative chamber, and forced to remain. With a quorum thus obtained, the resolution calling for election of delegates to a ratifying convention was adopted.[38] Under the astute generalship of James Wilson, the Pennsylvania convention ratified by a vote of 46 to 23 in December 1787, the opposition coming from the western districts.

By early 1788 New Jersey, Connecticut, and Georgia had also ratified. The scene of battle then shifted to Massachusetts, a key state and a doubtful one. John Hancock and Samuel Adams had not declared themselves, and these men of '76, with their great popular following, held the balance of power. The Federalists cleverly pointed out to Hancock that Washington would be the first president and that therefore the vice-president would undoubtedly be a New Englander. What citizen of New England was more distinguished than John Hancock? Whether or not this hint was the cause, Hancock eventually came out for ratifica-

[38]Goebel, *Antecedents and Beginnings*, p. 267.

tion, and Adams was persuaded to vote for approval after securing a promise that a bill of rights would be forthcoming after adoption. Even so, Massachusetts ratified by the narrow margin of 187 to 168.

By June 1788, Maryland, South Carolina, and New Hampshire had ratified, so the nine states required to bring the Constitution into effect had been obtained. But neither Virginia nor New York had taken action, and without them the new Union would have little chance of success. Virginia was the most populous state and the home of many of the nation's outstanding leaders, and New York was important geographically.

The Virginia ratifying convention rivaled the Constitutional Convention in the caliber of its delegates. James Madison was the captain of the Federalist forces, and he had able lieutenants in Governor Randolph and young John Marshall. Patrick Henry, George Mason, and James Monroe within the convention and Richard Henry Lee outside led the opposition. Henry attacked the proposed government, point by point, with great eloquence; Madison turned back each attack quietly but cogently. At the critical juncture, Washington sent a letter to the convention urging unqualified ratification. This tipped the scale, and Virginia ratified. News was rushed to New York.

The great landowners along the Hudson, unlike their Southern planter friends, were opposed to the Constitution. They feared federal taxation of their holdings, and they did not want to abolish the profitable tax that New York had been levying on the trade and commerce of other states. When the convention assembled, the Federalists were greatly outnumbered, but they were aided by the strategy and skill of Hamilton and by word of Virginia's ratification. New York approved by a margin of three votes.

Although North Carolina and Rhode Island still remained outside the Union (the former ratified in November 1789 and the latter six months later), the new nation was created. In New York, a few members of the old Congress assembled to issue the call for elections under the new Constitution, and then Congress adjourned *sine die,* that is without setting a day for reconvening.

Chapter 3 The living Constitution

For a time, some people remained skeptical of the new Constitution. After watching merchants and mechanics march side by side in a parade celebrating ratification, a Bostonian remarked sourly that "it may serve to please children, but freemen will not be so easily gulled out of their liberties." On the other hand, a Philadelphian said that the procession in his city had "made such an impression on the minds of our young people that 'federal' and 'union' have now become part of the household words of every family in the city." This effect on the youth was significant, for it was on the younger generation that hopes for the new government depended.

The adoption of the Constitution coincided with the return of prosperity. Markets for American goods were opening in Europe, and business was pulling out of its postwar slump. Such events seemed to justify Federalist claims that adoption of the Constitution would correct the nation's ills. Within a surprisingly short time the Constitution lost its partisan character; Antifederalists vied with Federalists in honoring it. Politicians differed less and less over whether the Constitution was good. More and more they began to argue over what it meant.

As the Constitution won the support of Americans, it began to take on the aura of natural law itself.

Here was the document into which the Founding Fathers had poured their wisdom as into a vessel; the Fathers themselves grew ever larger in stature as they receded from view; the era in which they lived and fought became a Golden Age; in that age there had been a fresh dawn for the world, and its men were giants aginst the sky; what they had fought for was abstracted from its living context and became a set of "principles," eternally true and universally applicable.[1]

This adoration of the Constitution was important as a means of bringing unity into the diversity of the new nation. Like the Crown in Britain, the Constitution became a symbol of national loyalty, a unifying symbol that evoked both emotional and rational support from all Americans regardless of their differences. The framers' work became part of the American creed; it stood for liberty, equality before the law, limited government—indeed, for whatever anyone wanted to build into it.

But the Constitution is also a supreme and binding law that both *grants* and *limits* powers. "In framing a government which is to be administered by men over men," wrote Madison in *The Federalist*, "the great difficulty lies in this: you must first enable the government to control the governed; and in the next place oblige it to control itself." The Constitution is both a *positive* instrument of government, enabling the governors to control the governed, and it is a *restraint* on government, enabling the ruled to check the rulers.

In what ways does the Constitution limit the power of the national government? In what ways does it create national power? How has it managed to serve both as a great symbol of national unity and at the same time as a somewhat adaptable and changing instrument of government?

Checking power with power

It is strange, perhaps, to begin by stressing the ways in which the Constitution *limits* national power. Yet we must keep in mind the dilemma that the framers faced. They wanted a more effective national government but at the same time were keenly aware that the people would not accept too strong a central control. Accordingly, they allotted certain powers to the national government and reserved the rest for the states. In short, they established a system of *federalism* (the nature and problems of which will be taken up in Chapters 4 and 5). But this distribution of powers, they felt, was not enough. Other ways of limiting the national government were needed.

The most important device to make public officials observe the constitutional limits on their powers is for voters to go to the polls and throw out of office those who abuse power. But the framers were not

[1]Max Lerner, *Ideas for the Ice Age* (Viking, 1941), pp. 241–42.

willing to depend solely on such *political* controls, because they did not fully trust the people's judgment. The people might be misled and vote a demagogue into office. Thomas Jefferson, a firm democrat, put it this way: "Free government is founded on jealousy, and not in confidence. . . . In questions of power, then, let no more be heard of confidence in man, but bind him down from mischief by the chains of the Constitution."[2] Even more important, the framers feared that a majority faction might use the new central government to deprive minorities of their rights. "A dependence on the people is, no doubt, the primary control on the government," Madison admitted, "but experience has taught mankind the necessity of auxiliary precautions." Thus the framers made part of the Constitution two arrangements—*separation of powers,* and *checks and balances*—that they hoped would prevent public officials from abusing their power, or any one group of people, even a majority, from capturing control of the government and tyrannizing the rest of the people.

DIVIDING NATIONAL POWER

The first step was the *separation of powers,* that is, dividing constitutional authority among the three branches of the national government. In *Federalist No. 47* James Madison wrote, "No political truth is certainly of greater intrinsic value, or is stamped with the authority of more enlightened patrons of liberty, than that . . . the accumulation of all powers, legislative, executive, and judiciary, in the same hands . . . may justly be pronounced the very definition of tyranny."

But the force of this logic alone does not account for the incorporation of the doctine of separation of powers in our Constitution. This doctrine had been, as we have seen, the operating practice in the colonies for over a hundred years. Only during the Revolutionary period was the doctrine compromised and authority concentrated in the hands of the legislature, and the experience confirmed the belief in the merits of separation of powers. Many of the framers attributed the evils of state government and the want of energy of the central government to the lack of a strong executive who could both check legislative abuses and give energy and direction to administration.

But dividing power was not enough. For there was always the danger—from the framers' point of view—that different officials with different powers might pool their authority and act together. Separation of powers by itself would not prevent government branches and officials from responding to the same pressures—for example, an overwhelming majority of the voters. If dividing power was not enough, what else could be done?

[2]Quoted in Alpheus T. Mason, *The Supreme Court: Palladium of Freedom* (University of Michigan Press, 1962), p. 10.

CHECKS AND BALANCES: AMBITION TO COUNTERACT AMBITION

The framers' answer was a system of *checks and balances,* which provides that the president, legislators, and judges, although mutually dependent in performing their constitutional functions, are given *political* as well as legal independence. The framers made these officials politically independent of one another by making them responsive to different constituencies. The president was to be chosen by a group of *electors*, so that he would have different loyalties and represent different interests from senators, chosen by *state legislators;* from representatives, directly elected by *local constituencies;* and from judges, holding office for life and appointed by the president with the consent of the Senate.

The framers were also careful to arrange matters so that a majority could win control over only part of the government at one time. A popular majority might take control of the House of Representatives in an off-year election, but the president, representing previous sentiment, would still have two years to go. The majority might win the presidency, but other forces might still control the Senate.

Moreover, each branch of the national government is given some responsibilities toward performing the functions of the others, and each is given some authority to control the operations of the others. The doctrine of separation of powers, when combined with checks and balances, is one of *interdependence* rather than independence. "The great security against a gradual concentration of the several powers in the same department," wrote Madison, "consists in giving to those who administer each department the necessary constitutional means and personal motives to resist encroachment on the others. . . . Ambition must be made to counteract ambition." Thus, Congress enacts law, the president can veto them, and Congress can repass them over his veto. The Supreme Court can invalidate laws passed by Congress and signed by the president, but the chief executive appoints the judges with the Senate's concurrence. The president administers the laws, but Congress provides the money for him and his agencies. The Senate and the House of Representatives have an absolute veto on each other. The framers created not a government of separated powers but a "government of separated institutions *sharing* powers."[3]

The framers felt it was the legislative branch that was most likely to take over the whole government. "In republican government," Madison wrote, "the legislative authority necessarily predominates." It was in part to meet this problem that the framers decided on two houses and made them responsible to different constituencies. Said Madison, the two houses were rendered "by different modes of election and different principles of action, as little connected with each other as the nature of their common functions and their common dependence on the society will admit."

Finally, if this did not work, there were the judges. It was not until

[3]Richard E. Neustadt, *Presidential Power* (John Wiley, 1960), p. 33.

some years after the Constitution was in operation that the judges asserted the power of *judicial review*—the right to refuse to enforce those laws of Congress that in the judges' opinion are unconstitutional (see Chapter 14). But from the beginning the judges were expected to check the legislature and the groups that the congressional majority might represent. "Independent judges," wrote Alexander Hamilton in *Federalist No. 78*, would be "an essential safeguard against the effects of occasional ill humors in society."

Could such a system really work? What if a majority of the people should get control of all branches of government and force through radical and impulsive measures? The framers knew that if, over a period of years, the great majority of the voters wanted to take a certain step, nothing could stop them. Nothing, that is, except despotic government, and they did not want that. The men of 1787 reasoned that all they could do—and this was quite a lot—was to stave off, temporarily, full control of the popular majority.

It may seem surprising that the people—or at least the large number of them who were suspicious of the new Constitution—did not object to these "auxiliary precautions," which often are barriers to action by a popular majority. But the Antifederalists were deeply suspicious of officeholders and were even more anxious than the Federalists to see the power of national authorities defined and restrained.[4]

Early Americans (and perhaps their descendents two centuries later) did not look on government as an instrument they could seize with their votes and use for their own purposes; they viewed it as something to be handcuffed, hemmed in, and rendered harmless. The separation of powers and the system of checks and balances were intended to make it difficult for a majority to gain control of the government. Equally important, they were intended to keep those who govern from exceeding their constitutional authority.

The framers, distrustful both of elites and the masses, deliberately built inefficiency into our political system. These constitutional limitations on the exercise of governmental power have profound contemporary significance. Almost two hundred years after the ratification of the Constitution, Americans continue to debate whether it is desirable to maintain these limits under the vastly different conditions of the 1970s. Crucial questions remain: are these checks necessary or sufficient to prevent abuses of political power? Is the greater danger that governments will not do the right things or that they will do the *wrong* things? Do these limitations work to prevent abuses, or do they make coherent governmental action in public interest difficult if not impossible?

A STUDY IN CONTRASTS

Although many Americans are raising questions about the efficacy of

[4]Cecelia M. Kenyon, "Men of Little Faith: The Anti-Federalists on the Nature of Representative Government," *William and Mary Quarterly* (January 1955), pp. 3–43.

our governmental institutions, we tend to take the system of checks and balances for granted. The separating and dispersing of power seem to be the very essence of constitutional government. Like Madison, and especially since the revelations of Watergate, we view the amassing of power by any one branch of government as the essence of tyranny. Yet it is quite possible for a government to be constitutional without such an apparatus. In the British system, the voters elect members of Parliament from districts throughout the nation (much as we elect members of the House of Representatives). The members of the House of Commons have almost complete constitutional power. The leaders of the majority party serve as executive ministers, who collectively form the Cabinet, with the prime minister as its head. Any time the executive officers lose support of the majority in the Commons, they must resign or call for new elections. The House of Lords once could check the Commons, but now is almost powerless. There is no high court with the power to void acts of Parliament; the prime minister cannot veto them (though he may ask the Crown to dissolve Parliament and call for elections for members of the House of Commons). And, of course, Englishmen take their system as much for granted as we do our own.

The British system is based on majority rule—that is, a majority of the voters elect a majority of the legislators, who can put through (virtually without hindrance) the majority's program as long as the parliamentary majority stays together, at least until the next election. Ours usually depends for action on the agreement of many elements of the society, comprising more than a majority. The British system *concentrates* control and responsibility in the legislature; ours *diffuses* control and responsibility among the several organs of government.

We have a written document called the Constitution; Britain does not. Yet both systems are constitutional in the sense that the rulers are subject to regular restraints. Clearly constitutionalism requires something much more basic than the existence of a document—witness the military dictatorships whose "constitutions" bear no relation to the exercise of political power. The limitations that our written Constitution and the conventions of the unwritten British constitution impose on all those who exercise governmental power rest on underlying values, attitudes, and norms that exist in both societies. One of the major concerns of political scientists today is to identify the social prerequisites of constitutional democracy. Although research in this area is far from conclusive, it seems certain that constitutional government requires more than any one particular set of formal legal rules.[5]

[5]See Seymour Martin Lipset, *Political Man* (Doubleday, 1959), Chaps. 2, 3; Seymour Martin Lipset, Martin Trow, and James Coleman, *Union Democracy* (Free Press, 1956); Harry Eckstein, *A Theory of Stable Democracy* (Princeton University Center of International Studies, 1961); Charles F. Cnudde and Deane E. Neubauer, eds., *Empirical Democratic Theory* (Markham, 1969); Robert W. Jackman, "On the Relation of Economic Development to Democratic Performance," *American Journal of Political Science* (August 1973), pp. 611ff; Paul H. Conn, "Social Pluralism and Democracy," *American Journal of Political Science* (May 1973), pp. 237ff.

CHECKS AND BALANCES: MODIFICATIONS

Fragmentation of political power remains basic, but several developments have modified the way the checks and balances that the Founding Fathers so carefully placed in our constitutional system actually work.

1. *Rise of national political parties.* Parties have served to some extent as unifying factors, drawing together the president, senators, representatives, and even judges behind common programs. But the parties, in turn, have been splintered and weakened by the necessity of working through a system of fragmented governmental power.

2. *Changes in electoral methods.* The framers wanted the president to be chosen by wise, independent men free from popular passions and hero worship. Almost from the beginning, however, presidential electors have acted as automata, and have pledged prior to elections to cast their electoral vote for their party's presidential candidate. And senators, who were originally elected by state legislatures, are today chosen directly by the people.

3. *Establishment of agencies deliberately designed to exercise all three functions—legislative, executive, and judicial.* When the government began to regulate the economy and detailed rules had to be made and judgments rendered on highly complex matters such as policing compe-

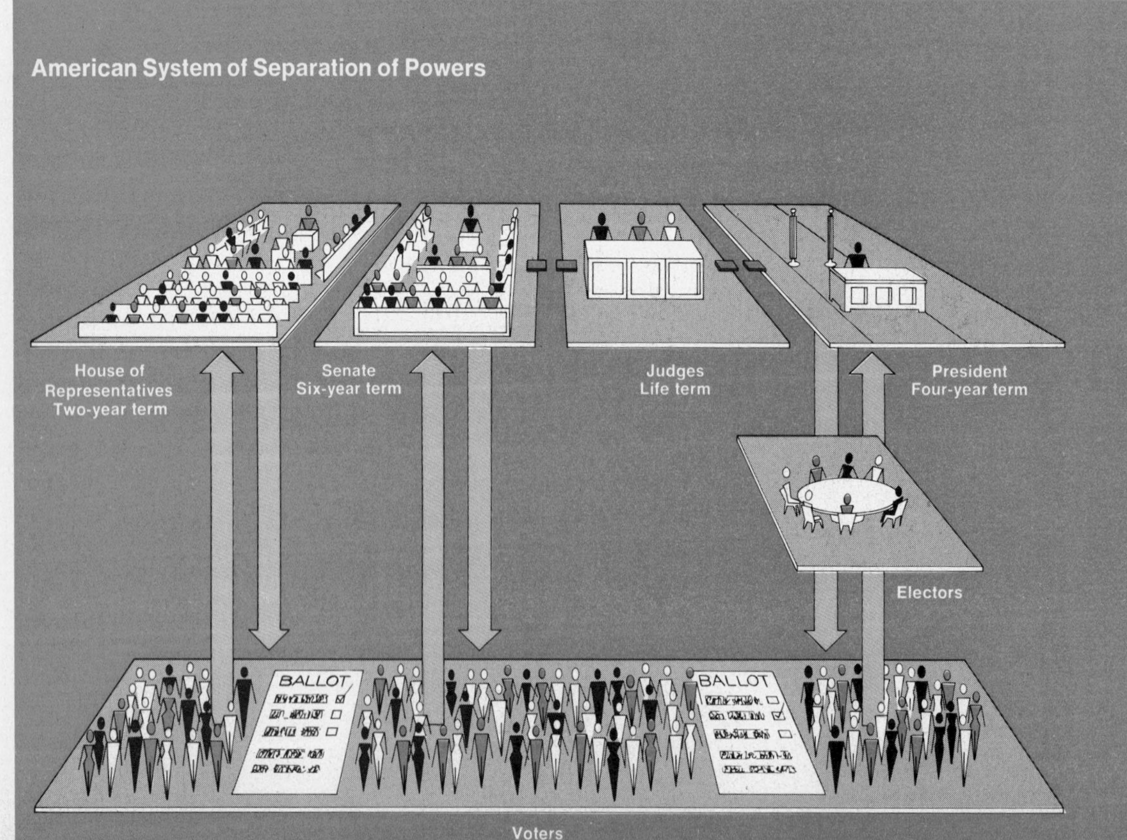

tition or preventing energy shortages, it was difficult to assign responsibility to an agency without blending the powers to make and apply rules and to decide disputes.

4. *Changes in technology.* Atomic bombs, television, computers, instant communications—these and other alterations in our environment create conditions for the operation of governmental agencies that are qualitatively different from those that existed two centuries ago. In some ways these new technologies have enhanced the powers of the president, in others they have given additional leverage to organized interests working through Congress, in others they have given greater independence and influence to nongovernmental agencies such as the press. Governmental power remains fragmented, but the system of checks and balances operates differently from the way it did in 1789 when there were no televised congressional investigating committee hearings, no FBI using electronic listening devices, no *New York Times* with a national constituency, no presidential press conferences, no live coverage of presidential visits to foreign nations.

5. *The emergence of the United States as a world power and the existence of recurrent crises.* Today crises and problems anywhere in the world become crises and problems for the United States, and vice versa. The need to deal with perpetual emergency has concentrated power in the hands of the chief executive and his immediate staff.

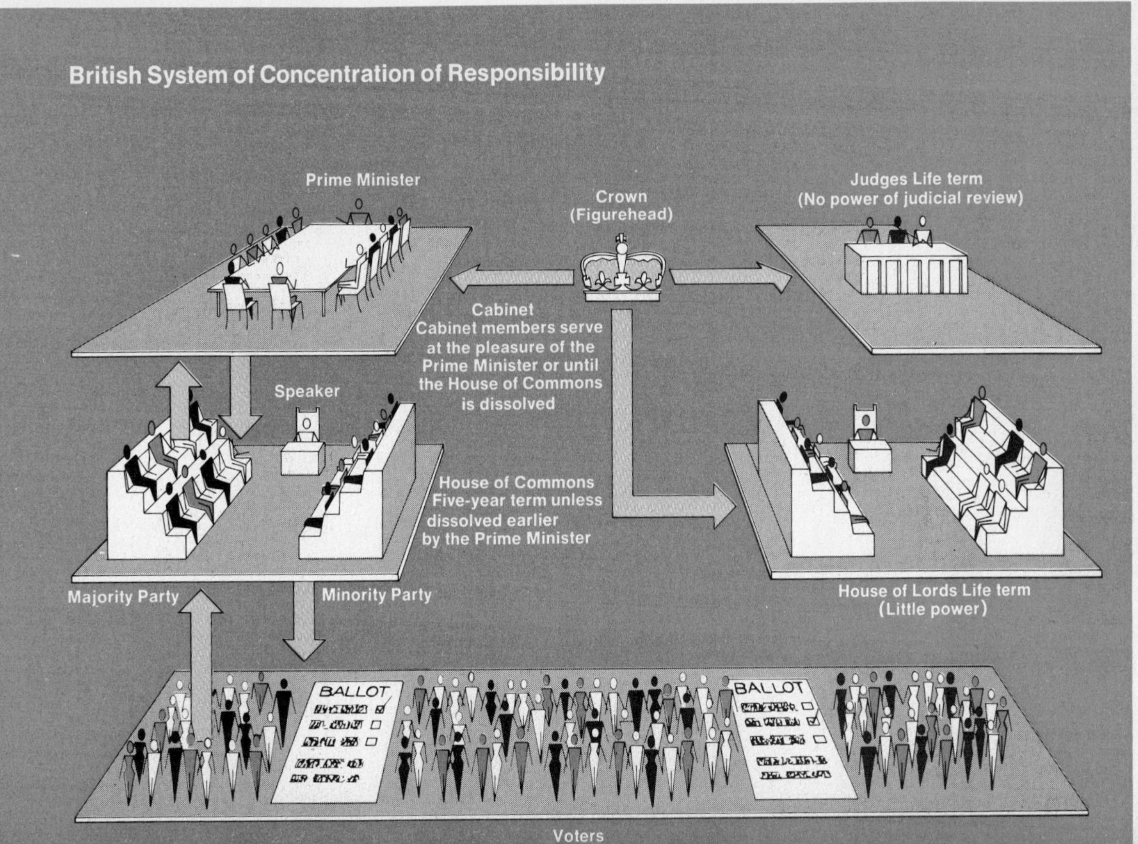

6. *The office of the president has become a unifying, sometimes a divisive, but always a dominating agency of the national government.* Drawing on its constitutional, political, and emergency powers, the presidency has been able to overcome some of the restraints imposed by the Constitution on the exercise of cohesive governmental power—to the applause of some, to the alarm of others.

The Constitution as instrument of government

As careful as the Founding Fathers were to limit the powers they conferred on the national government, the main reason they had assembled in Philadelphia was to create a *strong* national government. They had learned that weak central government, incapable of governing, is a greater danger to liberty than a powerful government. They wished to establish a national government within the framework of a federal system and to endow it with enough authority to meet the exigencies of all times. They knew that, to endure, the government must be capable of meeting the needs of future generations whose problems could not be anticipated. They did not try to put down all the rules in black and white; they made their grants of power general, leaving the way open for succeeding generations to fill in the details and organize the structure of government in accordance with experience.

Consequently, our formal, written Constitution is only the skeleton of our system and is supplemented by a number of fundamental rules that must be considered part of our constitutional system in its larger sense. Without an understanding of the rules of the "informal" Constitution, we would have an incomplete and even misleading picture of our government, because it is primarily through changes in our *informal* Constitution that our constitutional system is kept up to date. These changes are to be found in certain basic statutes and historical practices of Congress, decisions of the Supreme Court, actions of the president, and customs and usages of the nation.

CONGRESSIONAL ELABORATION

Because the framers gave Congress the authority to prescribe the structural details of the national government, it is unnecessary to amend the Constitution every time a change is needed. Examples of congressional elaboration appear in such fundamental legislation as the Judiciary Act of 1789, which laid the foundations of our national judicial system; in the laws establishing the organization and functions of all federal executive officials subordinate to the president; and in the rules of procedure, internal organization, and practices of the Congress itself.

The Watergate revelations of 1973 and the urgent question of 1974 about applying the impeachment process to President Nixon provide a dramatic example of the role of Congress in constitutional elaboration. The constitutional language is sparse: It is primarily up to Congress to give meaning to that language. Article I—the Legislative Article—stipulates that the House of Representatives shall have the sole power of impeachment and the Senate the sole power to try all impeachments, and that the Senators when sitting for that purpose "shall be on oath or affirmation," with the chief justice of the United States presiding in the event the president is being tried. The Article provides that conviction on impeachment charges requires the concurrence of two-thirds of the senators present, and that judgments shall extend no further than removal from office and disqualification to hold any office under the United States, but that a person convicted shall also be liable to indictment, trial, judgment, and punishment according to the law. In Article II—the Executive Article—the Constitution stipulates that the "President, Vice-President, and all civil officers of the United States, shall be removed from Office on Impeachment for, and Conviction of, Treason, Bribery, or other high Crimes and Misdemeanors." The Article also excepts cases of impeachment from the president's pardoning power. Article III—the Judicial Article—exempts cases of impeachment from the jury trial requirement.

We have relatively little congressional elaboration to go on with respect to impeachment. As James Bryce wrote in his celebrated *American Commonwealth* (1888), "Impeachment . . . is the heaviest piece of artillery in the congressional arsenal, but because it is so heavy it is unfit for ordinary use. It is like a hundred-ton gun which needs complex machinery to bring it into position, an enormous charge of powder to fire it, and a large mark to aim at."[6]

Prior to 1974, the House of Representatives had investigated for possible impeachment about sixty-five persons, had voted charges against twelve, and the Senate had convicted four (all federal judges). One judge resigned after being impeached and the charges against him were dropped, although resignation does not give immunity from being tried on impeachment charges for acts committed while in office.

The first person impeached by the House was Senator Blount. The Senate expelled him but decided that members of Congress are not liable to removal by the impeachment process. When Jefferson became president and found the federal courts manned by partisan Federalists, he argued that impeachment procedures should be used to remove from office incompetent or politically objectionable officers, especially judicial ones appointed in effect for life, even if they had not committed a legal wrong. The House did impeach Associate Justice Samuel Chase, an especially fierce Federalist, and many thought that if the Senate convicted Chase, the next to be impeached would be Chief Justice Marshall. But the Senate failed to convict Chase, and its action was construed to mean that political objections, or even misconduct in office that fell

[6]James Bryce, *The American Commonwealth*, 3rd ed. (Macmillan, 1911), I, 212.

short of "high crimes or misdemeanors," were not impeachable offenses. Again, when the House impeached President Andrew Johnson in 1868 but the Senate failed to convict, even though by a margin of only one vote, it tended to confirm the narrow construction of the Constitution that the only grounds for impeachment is criminal conduct or something close to it.

However, two successful impeachments of lower federal judges, one in 1913 and the other in 1936, restored a somewhat broad construction, at least as applied to judges. In both instances the Senate voted to convict and remove from office judges charged with serious misconduct in office, but in neither case was the charge on which the judge was removed related to a criminal offense.

By the time of Watergate and the impeachment case against President Nixon, past congressional practices had rejected either the *broadest* view that officers may be removed because of political objections or unpopularity—a view that if it had been adopted might have given us a parliamentary type of government—or on the other hand the *narrowest* construction that the only impeachable offenses are those that involve violations of the criminal laws. Rather, the established position of the Congress is that an impeachable offense, especially for a president elected by a vote of the people for a fixed term, although not necessarily criminal in nature, must relate to seriously improper conduct reflecting substantial violation of constitutional responsibilities and a clear dereliction of duty.

Other questions about the impeachment process remain for Congress and the courts to answer. Are persons subject to impeachment also subject to criminal prosecution while they are in office, or must they be removed from office before standing trial? The answer is not likely to be the same for the president, the vice-president, or a federal judge. Judge Otto Kerner was convicted of a criminal offense while still holding office as a federal appeals court judge, but this would not necessarily serve as a precedent as applied to the president. Vice-President Agnew's resignation after deciding not to contest a charge of a criminal offense made it unnecessary to face the question as far as the vice-presidency is concerned. May conduct occurring before occupancy of the office in question be grounds for removal through the impeachment procedures? Again, Vice-President Agnew's resignation made it unnecessary for Congress to face that issue with respect to charges of misconduct stemming from his prior service as governor of Maryland. If an officer is first tried for a criminal offense, are the House and Senate bound by a judicial determination of guilt or innocence as it applies to impeachment? May the president withhold information the House and Senate believe relevant to the pursuit of their responsibilities under the impeachment clauses? In the *United States v. Nixon* (1974) the Supreme Court pointedly ignored the question when it ruled that the president's executive privilege did not extend to withholding information from a federal judge needed for a criminal trial (see p. 147).

The House Judiciary Committee deliberately chose not to seek judicial enforcement for its subpoenas directed to President Nixon but it did vote to recommend to the House as one of the articles of impeachment his refusal to supply the Committee with requested information. President Nixon's resignation avoided a resolution of this clash between the House Judiciary Committee and the president. But most scholars feel that the president has a constitutional obligation to furnish the House and Senate with the information they request in order to carry out their respective obligations under the impeachment clauses.

The Nixon affair well illustrates the role of congressional elaboration of our constitutional system. It shows that the system is still growing: Congress applied to contemporary conditions the impeachment procedures placed in the Constitution by the framers in the eighteenth century, who in turn were drawing on the experiences of four hundred years of English history.[7]

PRESIDENTIAL PRACTICES

Presidential practices also have had much to do with the development of our constitutional system. Although there has been no change in the formal constitutional powers of the president, his position is dramatically different today from what it was in 1789. The presidency has become the pivotal office of our national government; the president has become a key *legislator* as well as the chief executive.

Presidential practices also explain—in part—the growing significance of the office of vice-president, as presidents have given their running mates more important roles to perform. At the same time the public has become more aware of the importance of the vice-presidency as dramatically demonstrated by the death in office of President Roosevelt, the assassination of President Kennedy, and the resignation of President Nixon. Television has played its part in making the people aware of the personality of the vice-president. Whereas it used to be a politically dead-end office, today it has become a major stepping-stone to the White House. Within weeks after his appointment as vice-president, Gerald Ford, who prior to that time was not even mentioned as a presidential candidate, was leading the Republican list in the opinion polls for the 1976 presidential elections.

CUSTOMS AND USAGES

Customs and usages of the nation have rounded out our governmental system. Presidential nominating conventions and other party activities are examples of constitutional usages. Although no specific mention of

[7]For historical background, see Raoul Berger, *Impeachment: The Constitutional Problems* (Harvard University Press, 1973); Irving Brant, *Impeachment: Trial and Errors* (Knopf, 1972).

The Child Labor Amendment to the Constitution has still not been ratified more than fifty years after its submission. However, the Supreme Court has since changed the construction of the Constitution and the amendment is no longer needed to outlaw child labor.

these practices is in the written Constitution, they are fundamental to an understanding of our constitutional system. In fact, it has been primarily through the extraconstitutional development of national political parties and the extension of the suffrage within the states that our Constitution has become democratized. A broader electorate began to exercise control over the national government; the presidential office was made more responsive to the people; the relationship between Congress and the president was altered; and, through the growth of political parties, some of the Constitution's blocks to majority rule were overcome.

JUDICIAL INTERPRETATION

Judicial interpretation of the Constitution, especially by the Supreme Court, has played an important part in the continuous process of modernizing the constitutional system. American judges have the power of judicial review—that is, the authority to refuse to enforce those laws that the judges think are in conflict with the Constitution. As a result, the Supreme Court has become the authoritative interpreter of the Constitution.

Judicial review introduces an element of rigidity into our system. Nevertheless, the words of the Constitution are broad and ambiguous enough to allow divergent interpretations. As conditions have changed and new national demands have developed, the Supreme Court's interpretation of the Constitution has changed to accommodate these new conditions and to reflect these new demands. In the words of Woodrow Wilson, "The Supreme Court is a constitutional convention in continuous session." The establishment of judicial review itself is a classic example of the importance of judicial interpretation in the development of our constitutional system.

Because the Constitution is so flexible and because it allows for easy adaptation to changing times, it does not require frequent formal amendment. The advantages of this flexibility may be appreciated when the national Constitution is compared with the rigid and overly specific state constitutions. Many state constitutions, more like legal codes than basic charters, are so detailed that the hands of public officials are often tied. State constitutions leave so little discretion to those who govern that in order to adapt state governments to changing conditions, the constitutions must be amended frequently or replaced every generation or so.

A RIGID OR FLEXIBLE CONSTITUTION?

This picture of a constantly changing national constitutional system disturbs many people. How, they argue, can you have a constitutional government when the Constitution is constantly being twisted by interpretation and changed by informal methods? This view fails to distinguish between two aspects of the Constitution. As an expression of basic and timeless personal liberties, the Constitution does not and should not change. For example, no government can destroy the right to free speech and remain a constitutional government. In this sense the Constitution *is* timeless and essentially unchanging.

But when we consider the Constitution as an instrument of government and a positive grant of power, we realize that if it does not grow with the nation it serves, it will soon be pushed aside. The framers could not have conceived of the problems that the government of more than two hundred million citizens in an industrial state would have to face in the 1970s. The general purposes of government remain the same—to establish liberty, promote justice, ensure domestic tranquillity, and provide for the common defense. But the powers of government adequate to accomplish these purposes in 1787 are simply inadequate in the 1970s.

"We the people"—the people of today and tomorrow, not just the people of 1787—ordain and establish the Constitution. "The Constitution," wrote Jefferson, "belongs to the living and not to the dead." So firmly did he believe this that he advocated a new constitution for every generation. But new constitutions have not been necessary, because in a less formal way each generation has taken part in the never-ending process of developing the original Constitution.

Because of its remarkable adaptability, the Constitution has survived the rigors of democratic and industrial revolutions, the turmoil of civil war, the tensions of major depressions, and the dislocations of world wars. The problem is, then, to preserve the Constitution in its role as a protector of fundamental liberties, as a preserver of the essentials of justice and democracy upon which our system is based, and at the same time to permit government to operate in accordance with the wishes of the people and to adapt itself to new conditions.

Changing the letter of the Constitution

The framers knew that future experience would call for changes in the text of the Constitution itself and that some means of formal amendment was necessary. Accordingly, they set forth two ways to propose amendments to the Constitution and two ways to ratify them, and they saw to it that amendments could not be made by simple majorities.

PROPOSING AND RATIFYING

Pandora Project.

©1967 Herblock in *The Washington Post.*

The first method of proposing amendments — the only one that has been used — is by a two-thirds vote of both houses of Congress. The second method is by a national convention called by Congress at the request of the legislatures of two-thirds of the states. During the first hundred years of its existence, Congress received only ten such petitions from state legislatures, but since 1893 over 300 such petitions have been filed.

The second method is full of imponderables. Who determines whether the necessary number of state legislatures have petitioned for a convention? If Congress called a convention into being, how would delegates be chosen and how many votes would each state have? Could the convention propose amendments on a variety of subjects, perhaps even an entirely new constitution? Who determines the method of ratification, Congress or the convention? Where would the convention assemble? Because we have not had a constitutional convention since the adoption of the present Constitution, we have no precedents. But there never appeared to be much urgency about these questions, so scholars were the only ones who had much interest in them. The general assumption was that these were political questions to be answered by Congress, either by a general law covering all such conventions or by Congress at the time it called a convention into being.

At the end of the last decade, these questions ceased, at least for the moment, to be of only academic interest; for only one short of the required number of state legislatures had petitioned Congress to call a national constitutional convention. The purpose was to propose an amendment that would reverse the impact of Supreme Court rulings requiring both chambers of state legislatures to be apportioned on the basis of population. In 1971 the Senate Judiciary Committee proposed a law that, if it had been adopted, would have established procedures relating to constitutional conventions. It called for giving to each state in such a convention as many delegates as it has members in the House and Senate, provided for delegates to be elected, imposed a limitation on such conventions against considering any except the amendments referred to it, and allowed Congress to determine the method of ratification. The flurry of excitement died down when no more petitions for a convention were forthcoming and Congress failed to act on the proposal.

Since state legislatures have now been reapportioned to reflect population, additional proposals for a constitutional convention to deal with this issue seem unlikely. Such a convention could well be called, however, on other topics—for example, abortion, capital punishment, and school busing. And the national concern about the constitutional crisis surrounding the Watergate affair has added some political interest to proposals by a few academics for a basic reformation of our constitutional system. But Congress shows little disposition to call a convention: there is no legal way to force Congress to do so, even if the necessary two-thirds of the state legislatures should petition for it. It seems probable that in the future, as in the past, whenever pressures develop for a constitutional change, Congress will propose the amendments to bring it about rather than call a convention to do so. (Perhaps Congress remembers the fate of its predecessor at the hands of the convention it called into being in 1787!)

After an amendment has been proposed, it must be ratified by the states. Again, two methods are provided—by approval of the legislatures in three-fourths of the states or by approval of specially called ratifying conventions in three-fourths of the states. Congress determines which method of ratification shall be used.

A state may change its mind and ratify an amendment after it has voted against ratification, but the weight of opinion is that once a state has approved a proposed amendment it cannot subsequently change its mind and "unratify." (This question could come to the fore in the ratification battles over the Equal Rights Amendment, see p. 70.)

A state must ratify proposed amendments within a reasonable time. Congress determines what a reasonable time is, and the modern practice is for Congress to stipulate that an amendment is not to become part of the Constitution unless approved by the necessary number of states within seven years from the date of its submission. In 1924 when it proposed the Child Labor Amendment, Congress failed to set any time limit for its ratification. To date twenty-eight states have done so. Even if ten more states were to ratify (the three-fourths applies to the number of states presently in the Union, not the number at the time the amendment was proposed), it seems unlikely that Congress would consider that the amendment had been ratified within a reasonable time—more than fifty years after its submission.

The procedure of submitting amendments to *legislatures* instead of to ratifying conventions has been criticized, because it permits the Constitution to be changed without any clear expression of the electorate's

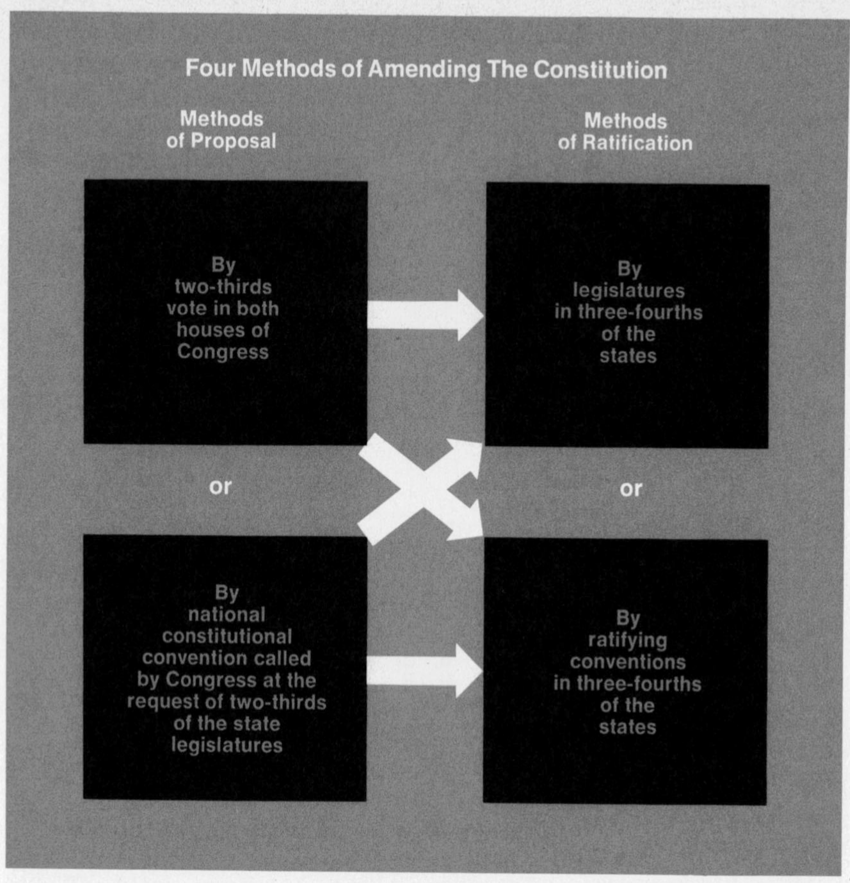

desires. State legislators who do the ratifying may even have been elected before the proposed amendment was submitted to the states. In any event, state legislators are chosen because of their views on schools, taxation, bond issues, and other matters, or because of their personal popularity—they are almost never elected because of their stand on a proposed constitutional amendment.

Despite these objections to ratification by legislatures, the only amendment that has been submitted to ratifying *conventions* is the Twenty-first (to repeal the Eighteenth, or Prohibition Amendment). The "wets" rightly believed that repeal had a better chance of success with conventions than with the rural-dominated state legislatures. This strategy, rather than any desire to submit the question to the electorate, was the important factor.[8]

The major obstacle to the adoption of constitutional amendments has not been ratification but getting Congress to propose amendments in the first place. Although dozens of resolutions proposing amendments

[8]Philip J. Martin, "Convention Ratification of Federal Constitutional Amendments," *Political Science Quarterly* (March 1967), p. 61.

are introduced in every session—over 6,000 since 1789—few make any headway. But what Congress proposes is usually ratified. Of thirty-two amendments proposed, twenty-six have been ratified. The proposed Equal Rights Amendment, the possible Twenty-seventh Amendment, is presently before the state legislatures. Four of the unratified amendments were proposed before the Civil War; since then, only the Child Labor Amendment has failed to win the necessary state approvals. (Because the Supreme Court changed its construction of the Constitution after the amendment had been proposed, the amendment is no longer needed to permit Congress to outlaw child labor.)

The president has no formal authority over constitutional amendments. His veto power does not extend to them, although his political influence in getting amendments through Congress is often crucial. Nor may governors veto approval of amendments by their respective legislatures, because the Constitution vests ratification in the legislatures alone.

The entire amending procedure has been criticized because neither a majority of the voters at large nor even a majority of the voters in a majority of the states can formally alter the Constitution. But when a majority of the people are serious in their desire to bring about changes in our constitutional system, their wishes are usually implemented either by formal amendment or by the more subtle methods of interpretation and adaptation.

As we have mentioned, the flexibility of our federal Constitution has reduced the need for formal amendments. If we disregard the Bill of Rights, which for all practical purposes may be considered part of the original document, the Constitution has been amended only sixteen times, and two of these amendments, the Eighteenth and Twenty-first, involving prohibition, cancel each other. The sixteen amendments adopted since the Bill of Rights are difficult to classify, but they may be grouped somewhat arbitrarily into the following categories: (1) those whose chief importance is to add to or subtract from the power of the national government; (2) those whose main effect is to limit the power of the state governments; (3) those whose chief impact has been to add to or subtract from the role of the electorate; and (4) those making structural changes in governmental machinery.

CHANGES IN NATIONAL POWER

The eleventh amendment When the Constitution was adopted, it was generally assumed that no private individual could sue a state in federal court without the consent of the state. But in 1793, when the Supreme Court ruled otherwise in the case of *Chisholm v. Georgia,* there was immediate alarm lest citizens flood the federal courts with suits against states defaulting on their debts. The Eleventh Amendment, which became part of the Constitution in 1798, took from federal courts the jurisdiction to hear suits commenced by individuals against a state, except with the consent of the state. The amendment, however, should not be read too literally. The state's consent can be implied if it engages in certain activities.[9] Nor does the amendment prevent an individual from appealing from a state to the federal courts, even if a state is the other party to the case. Chief Justice Marshall wrote many years ago that such an appeal is not a new proceeding commenced by the individual against a state, but a continuation of the proceeding started by the state.[10]

But by far the most significant exception to the Eleventh Amendment is the series of decisions that have held that if a public official acts in a manner that violates the Constitution or federal laws, he or she is not protected from a suit in federal courts initiated by individuals, even if the official is carrying out duties imposed on him by a state law. As Chief Justice Burger wrote for the Court in upholding the right of the parents of students who died at Kent State to sue state officials in federal courts, "it has been settled that the Eleventh Amendment provides no shield for a state official confronted by a claim that he had deprived another of a federal right under the color of state law."[11]

The thirteenth amendment The Thirteenth Amendment abolished slavery; in addition, it authorized Congress to legislate against any attempt to hold a human being in slavery or involuntary servitude. In 1968, the amendment took on additional importance when the Supreme Court ruled *(Jones v. Mayer)* that the amendment authorizes Congress to legislate against racial discrimination whether imposed by public officials or by private individuals, for such discrimination is to impose on human beings a badge of slavery (see Chapter 7).

The sixteenth amendment In 1895 the Supreme Court, overruling a long line of precedents, for all practical purposes denied to the federal government the power to levy a graduated income tax.[12] The Sixteenth Amendment, which was adopted in 1913, empowered the national government to collect such a tax.

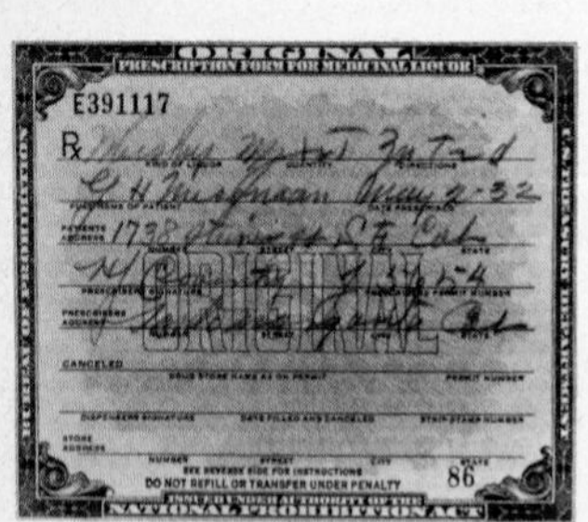

"Medicinal" liquor was widely prescribed during prohibition.

The eighteenth amendment Adopted in 1919, the Eighteenth Amendment was the culmination of a long struggle of the prohibitionists against the use of alcoholic beverages. The amendment gave Congress the power to prevent the manufacture, sale, or transportation of liquors. Although the amendment was ratified by all but two state legislatures, prohibition did not have the support of large groups of people, especially in urban areas. A bootlegging industry thrived, and prohibition,

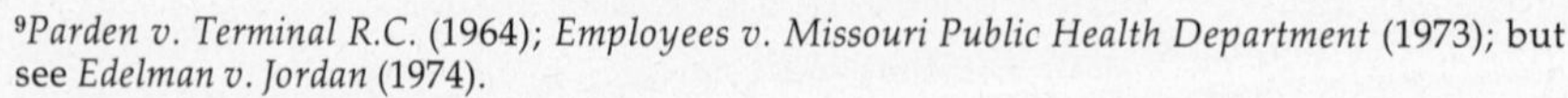

[9]*Parden v. Terminal R.C.* (1964); *Employees v. Missouri Public Health Department* (1973); but see *Edelman v. Jordan* (1974).

[10]*Cohens v. Virginia* (1821).

[11]*Ex parte Young* (1908); *Scheuer v. Rhodes* (1974).

[12]*Pollock v. Farmers' Loan and Trust Co.* (1895).

instead of cutting down the consumption of alcohol, served mainly to enrich criminals and to foster a callous attitude toward the law.

The twenty-first amendment After thirteen years of disappointment and the outbreak of the Great Depression (which made new taxes desirable), the Twenty-first Amendment was adopted in 1933, repealing the Eighteenth. It did more than restore the status quo, for it gave states greater authority to regulate intoxicating beverages than other items of interstate commerce.

Formal amendments, it is clear, have not been very important in adding to or detracting from the power of the federal government. One amendment (the Eleventh) took away power that the national government was not thought to have had; one (the Sixteenth) added power that it was believed to have had; one grant of power (the Eighteenth) was subsequently repealed; and one amendment (the Thirteenth) gave the national government power that for a hundred years had little significance because of narrow judicial interpretation.

LIMITING STATE POWER

The fourteenth and fifteenth amendments Along with the Thirteenth, the Fourteenth and Fifteenth Amendments were adopted following and as a result of the Civil War. Whereas the major purpose of the Thirteenth was to free the slaves, the major purpose of the Fourteenth was to make them citizens and to protect their civil rights and of the Fifteenth to protect their right to vote. Although only the objectives of freedom and citizenship were immediately accomplished, the amendments have had other consequences not generally anticipated; for example, the Supreme Court for a time used the Fourteenth Amendment to give constitutional sanction to the economic doctrine of laissez faire (see Chapter 8).

Two crucial clauses of the Fourteenth Amendment require states to guarantee *equal protection of the laws* to all persons and prohibit them from depriving any person of life, liberty, or property without *due process of law.* The equal protection and due process clauses of the Fourteenth Amendment are the Constitution's means of protecting our civil rights from infringement by state governments and have been the basis of many of the Supreme Court's decisions defending individual freedom.

These amendments substantially increased the power of the Supreme Court to review actions of the state governments and might well be placed among those that added to the power of the national government—or at least to the judicial branch of that government.

The nineteenth amendment Adopted in 1920, the Nineteenth Amendment deprives the states (and the national government) of the right to deny any citizen the right to vote because of sex. Although women were

Suffragettes campaigning for the vote shortly before ratification of the nineteenth amendment.

voting in many states prior to its adoption, the amendment was the final step in providing the constitutional framework for universal suffrage.

The proposed twenty-seventh amendment The Nineteenth Amendment did not affect laws dealing with the ownership of property, jury service, marriage and divorce, labor regulations, or other matters; and its ratification did not end discrimination based on sex. Not until November of 1971 in *Reed v. Reed* did the Supreme Court invalidate a law because it discriminated against women or hint that the equal-protection clause of the Fourteenth Amendment might render classifications based on sex constitutionally suspect (see p. 184).

On March 22, 1972, a half century after the first introduction in Congress of a proposal for an equal-rights amendment, ERA, as it is called, was submitted to the state legislatures for ratification. (They have until March 22, 1979, to approve.) Prior to its submission, unsuccessful attempts were made to amend it to guarantee that women would be exempt from combat military duty and to authorize Congress and the states to enact laws to promote and protect the health and safety of women. Proponents of ERA feared that such alterations in its simple language—"Equality of rights under the law shall not be denied or abridged by the United States or by any State on account of sex"—would permit the reintroduction of sexually discriminatory legislation under the guise of protection.

In order to give Congress and the state legislatures time to make the necessary changes in the laws, the amendment is not to become effective until two years after its ratification. When effective, the amendment by its own force will render unconstitutional all *laws* and *governmental* action that discriminate against any person because of her or *his* sex.

The twenty-fourth amendment Ever since 1939 Congress has had under consideration proposals to eliminate poll taxes either by amendment or by statute. The Twenty-fourth Amendment, proposed in 1962 and adopted in 1964, forbids any state to require either the payment of a poll tax or any other action in lieu of payment of such a tax as a condition for voting in any election for a president or for members of Congress.[13] However, the amendment allows states to impose a poll tax as a condition for voting for state or local officials. At the time of the amendment's adoption, four states still had poll taxes. But in 1966 the Supreme Court held[14] that the equal-protection clause of the Fourteenth Amendment precludes a state from imposing a poll tax as a requirement for voting in *any* election. This decision, in effect, rendered the Twenty-fourth Amendment superfluous—an intriguing example of the interplay of constitutional change by formal amendment and judicial interpretation.

The twenty-sixth amendment In 1971, after the Supreme Court held a federal law lowering the voting age to eighteen to be valid for federal but not for state or local elections (see p. 191), Congress proposed an amendment to permit otherwise qualified persons eighteen years of age or older to vote in all elections. Ratification was swift, partly because without it many states would have been faced with the cost and administrative difficulty of keeping separate registration books, ballots, and voting apparatus for federal and for state and local elections.

CHANGING THE POWER OF THE VOTERS

The seventeenth amendment Adopted in 1913, the Seventeenth Amendment provides that United States senators be chosen directly by the electorate instead of being selected by the state legislatures. According to the original Constitution, the House of Representatives was the only branch of the national government that the electorate chose directly. But the rise of political parties and the extension of suffrage within the states brought the presidential office under the control of the voters by the 1830s. From then on it was only a matter of time before the people would demand the right to choose their senators as well.

As the twentieth century opened, the people in many of the states were, in effect, choosing their senators, because the legislatures were simply ratifying the results of popular referenda. But in other states it was charged that great sums of money were being used to bribe state legislators into choosing as senators men of wealth and conservative outlook. The Senate came to be dubbed the Millionaires' Club, and individual senators were tagged as representatives, not of the people but of the steel trust, the sugar trust, the railroad trust, and so on. The de-

[13] *Harman v. Forssenius et al.* (1965).

[14] *Harper v. Virginia Board of Elections* (1966).

mand for constitutional change became insistent. Several times the House of Representatives approved an amendment that would require direct election, but the Senate resisted. Finally, in 1912, the Senate capitulated. The Seventeenth Amendment, passed that year, rounded out the process by which the political branches of the national government were made more directly responsive to the voters.

The twenty-second amendment Adopted in 1951, the Twenty-second Amendment prevents one from being elected to the office of president more than twice and stipulates that a person succeeding to the presidency and serving more than two years may be elected president in his own right only once. The chief significance of the amendment, however, is that it limits the electorate. Prior to the third-term election of Franklin D. Roosevelt in 1940, one of the unwritten usages of the American Constitution was that a person should not run for and the voters should not elect a person to this high office more than twice. In 1940 and again in 1944, a majority of the voters, aided by Roosevelt, "amended" this unwritten rule. But with the adoption of the Twenty-second Amendment, the restriction on the political majority was made formal.

The twenty-third amendment Ratified in March 1961, the Twenty-third Amendment grants the citizens of the District of Columbia the right to vote in presidential elections for the first time since the district was founded in 1802. The amendment provides that the district shall have the number of electoral votes it would be entitled to if it were a state but in no event more than the least populous state. This means that the District of Columbia will have only three votes in the electoral college, the minimum allowed to the least populous state, and fewer votes than the District would have if it were a state.

In 1970 Congress by law gave to the District the right to send a nonvoting delegate to the House of Representatives, but it would take another amendment to give the District residents *voting* representatives in both chambers of Congress.

CHANGING THE CONSTITUTIONAL STRUCTURE

The twelfth amendment The Twelfth Amendment was adopted in 1804 to correct a deficiency in the original Constitution. The original provisions for the selection of president and vice-president provided that electors be chosen in each state according to the method prescribed by the state legislature and that each elector, without consultation with others, was to vote for the two men he deemed best qualified to serve as president. The person with the most votes, provided the number of votes represented a majority of the electors, was to be president, and the person with the next highest number of votes was to be vice-president. It was generally expected that the electors in the several states would cast their votes for such a multitude of local and national candidates that no one would receive a majority. In such cases the House of Representatives, voting by state, was to choose the president from among the five men with the most votes. In the event that two men received the same number of votes, each representing a majority of the number of electors (remember, each elector cast two electoral votes), the House was to choose between them.

The rise of national politicial parties made this system unworkable. By the time the presidential election of 1800 took place, the electors had become party functionaries pledged to vote for the candidates of their own parties. In that year the Republicans, whose candidates were Jefferson for president and Aaron Burr for vice-president, elected a majority of the electors. Each Republican elector, as pledged, cast one of his ballots for Jefferson and one for Burr, so that each man had the same number of electoral votes. As a result, the election was thrown into the House of Representatives, still controlled by the Federalists. For a while, the Federalists toyed with the idea of electing Burr to the presidency; to some Federalist leaders this would have been the lesser of two evils. It was only with the greatest difficulty that Jefferson was finally installed in the White House. Soon thereafter, the Twelfth Amendment was adopted. Each elector now votes separately for president and for vice-president, and the candidate with the majority of the votes in each case is elected. In the event no candidate receives a majority of the votes for president, the House, voting by states, chooses from among the three persons with the most electoral votes. If no person receives a majority of the votes cast for vice-president, the Senate chooses between the two with the most votes.

The twentieth amendment Popularly known as the "lame-duck" amendment, this measure was inspired largely by Senator George Norris of Nebraska. Before it was adopted, a president elected in November did not take office until the following March, and congressmen chosen at the same time did not legislate until thirteen months after their election. Meanwhile, congressmen who had been defeated in the elections continued to represent—or misrepresent—their constituents in the short and ineffective December-to-March session. The Twentieth Amendment rearranged the schedule of congressional and presidential terms so that congressmen elected in November now begin their duties on January 3, and the president takes office on January 20.

The twenty-fifth amendment Ratified in 1967, the Twenty-fifth Amendment confirms prior practice that on the death of the president, the vice-president becomes not acting president but president. It also provides that in the event the president should resign, the vice-president becomes president, not just acting president. But of greater significance, it provides a procedure to determine whether an incumbent president is unable to discharge the powers and duties of his office, and it establishes procedures to fill a vacancy in the vice-presidency.

Eighteen times the office of vice-president has been vacant, creating the unsatisfactory situation of leaving the line of presidential succession open to the secretary of state or (after 1947) the speaker of the House, men not chosen for their suitability to serve as acting president of the United States. The Twenty-fifth Amendment provides that in the event there is a vacancy in the office of the vice-president, the president shall nominate a vice-president who shall take office upon confirmation by a majority vote of both houses of Congress. This procedure ensures the appointment of a vice-president in whom the president has confidence. If the vice-president has to take over the presidency, he can be expected to reflect the policies of the person the people had originally elected to the office.

The procedures for filling a vacancy in the vice-presidency were put to their toughest tests in 1973 and again in 1974 when they were used in circumstances not anticipated by their framers—first to fill a vacancy created by the forced resignation of Vice-President Agnew, and then in 1974 to fill a vacancy created by the accession to the presidency of Gerald Ford after the forced resignation of President Nixon. After Agnew's resignation, there was briefly some confusion about what might happen if President Nixon were forced out of office after he sent his nomination to Congress but before Congress had acted on it—a dangerous hiatus, for the most dangerous moment in the life of a constitutional government comes when there is any doubt or confusion about who has the legitimate right to exercise power. But in a relatively short time Congress, controlled by the opposition party, confirmed Gerald Ford as vice-president. Ford was then the minority leader of the House and the nominee of a president who himself was subject to an impeachment inquiry. Congress carefully checked into Ford's background but limited its inquiry to questions of honesty and integrity, and, in keeping with the spirit of the amendment, avoided matters of policy so that the vice-president might be a person reflecting the policy positions of the man elected to the White House. Then, after Nixon's resignation, President Ford used the amendment to nominate as vice-president Nelson Rockefeller who, although twice removed from the electorate, assumed the vice-presidency when confirmed by Congress.

The amendment also provides procedures to deal with the situation when questions are raised about the ability of the president to carry out his duties because of serious and sustained illness. Such a situation has occurred several times. In the future the responsibility to act is vested in the vice-president "and a majority of either the principal officers of the executive department"—that is, the cabinet or "of such other body as Congress may by law provide." Whenever the vice-president and a majority of the cabinet (Congress has left the responsibility there) are of the opinion that the president is unable to discharge the powers and duties of his office, they are so to state in writing to the president pro tempore of the Senate and to the speaker of the House. Upon such a written declaration, the vice-president is to serve immediately as acting president and continue to do so until the president transmits in writing to the president pro tempore of the Senate and the speaker of the House his declaration that he is prepared to resume his responsibilities. If the vice-president and a majority of the cabinet do not think the president is ready to resume his duties, they have four days to notify the Congress. The Congress must then assemble within forty-eight hours and come to a decision within twenty-one days. The presumption, however, favors the president. It requires a two-thirds vote of both houses to keep the president from taking over his responsibilities in the face of his declaration that he is able to do so.

The one principal feature of our constitutional system that remains to be examined is *federalism,* one of the most important "auxiliary precautions" against the abuse of power. The United States is not the only or even the oldest federal union, but it was the first to operate successfully a federal system on a continental scale. This has been one of America's major contributions to the science and art of government.

Chapter 4
American federalism: constitutional dynamics

American federalism 1787-style and 1970s-style are as different as a stage-coach and a spaceship. Since 1787 our federal system has been molded by a dynamic society and altered by the thoughts and actions of millions of men and women. This chapter will explore the nature of American federalism and its constitutional structure.

A *federal system of government* is one in which a constitution divides governmental powers between the central, or national, government and the constituent governments (called states in the United States), giving substantial functions to each. Neither the central nor the constituent government receives its powers from the other; both derive them from a common source, a constitution. This constitutional distribution of powers cannot be altered by the ordinary process of legislation—for example, by an act of the national legislature or by acts of the several constituent governments. Finally, both levels of government operate through their own agents and exercise power directly over individuals. Among the countries that have a federal system of government are the United States, Canada, Switzerland, India, Mexico, and Australia.[1]

[1] "Constitutional Law: Distribution of Powers," *International Encyclopedia of the Social Sciences* (Macmillan, 1968), III, 301. The description of federalism is based on Arthur W. MacMahon, *Administering Federalism in a Democracy* (Oxford University Press, 1972), pp. 3–5.

A *unitary,* as opposed to a federal, *system of government* is one in which a constitution vests all governmental power in the central government. The central government, if it so chooses, may delegate authority to constituent units but what it delegates it may also take away. Britain, France, Israel, and the Philippines are examples of this unitary form of government, and, in the United States, the relation between states and their subdivisional governments, such as counties and cities, is ordinarily of this sort.

Some students distinguish a *confederation* from a federation by defining the former as a government in which the constituent governments by constitutional compact create a central government but do not give it power to regulate the conduct of individuals. The central government makes regulations for the constituent governments but it exists and operates only through their sufferance. The thirteen states operating under the Articles of Confederation fit this definition.

Unfortunately for our understanding of federalism, the founders of our Constitution used the term *federal* to describe what we now would call a confederate form of government.[2] Moreover, today *federal* is frequently used as a synonym for *national;* that is, people often refer to the government in Washington as "the federal government." In an exact sense, of course, the states *and* the national government make up our federal system.

Governments range along a continuum from highly centralized unitary governments (in form and fact) through centralized federations to leagues of sovereign nations. And every nation is in a constant but gradual process of changing this "mix." To determine where decisions are made and functions are performed, one must look not only at constitutional documents and political institutions but also at a nation's political behavior and practices. Constitutional forms "may or may not accurately express the social, cultural, and political realities of the society being studied."[3] The Soviet Union, for example, has a federal constitution, but because of the centralized and disciplined nature of the Communist party, constituent unions of the U.S.S.R. have less independent authority than do the local governments under the British unitary constitution.[4]

As a way of distributing power, federalism raises key questions of representation and responsibility. What groups gain, what groups lose under the division of authority between national and state governments? To what extent does federalism advance or retard the welfare of the whole nation? Federalism also sharpens the elitist-pluralist debate.

[2]Martin Diamond, "What the Framers Meant by Federalism," in Robert A. Goldwin, ed., *A Nation of States* (Rand McNally, 1963), pp. 24–41.

[3]Charles D. Tarlton, "Symmetry and Asymmetry as Elements of Federalism: A Theoretical Speculation," *Journal of Politics* (November 1965), p. 866.

[4]See Rufus Davis, "The 'Federal Principle' Reconsidered," in Aaron Wildavsky, ed., *American Federalism in Perspective* (Little, Brown, 1967), p. 31.

To what extent does dispersing power among one national, fifty state, and thousands of local governments fulfill the pluralist ideal of a wide distribution of power? To what extent, paradoxically, does it tend to support the elite-theorist charge of an actual *concentration* of power behind the facade of dispersion?

Why federalism?

Why do we have a federal form of government? In part, because in 1787 there was no other practical choice. After confederation had been tried and found wanting, the only choice open to those who wanted a more closely knit union was federation. A unitary system was ruled out, because the leaders knew that the overwhelming majority of the people were too deeply attached to the state governments to permit the states to be subordinated to central rule. Total amalgamation of the states into a single unitary government was impossible short of military conquest by the more populous states.

Today, it would be feasible to operate democratically a unitary system even in a large country. But in the United States of 1787, distances were too great, methods of transportation and communication too slow, and the techniques of democracy too new to have made possible the operation of a large unitary state by democratic methods. In the absence of widespread cohesion and nationally shared sentiments, such a union could have been held together only by force. Federalism 1787-style went as far in the direction of union as public opinion and the technology of the time permitted.

Federalism has also been the ideal system for "the great enterprise of appropriating the North American Continent to western civilization."[5] It has enabled the Union to expand from thirteen states to fifty without any disruption or revision of the governmental structure. As people moved into a new territory, they drew up a state constitution, which was then approved by the Congress and the president. Each new state became a member of the Union with the same powers and responsibilities as the original thirteen; the only changes required were the addition of new desks in the Senate and House of Representatives in Washington and new stars on the flag.

The factors that led to the creation of our federal system in 1787 and that sustain it in the 1970s should not be confused with the arguments for and against federalism. (In large measure we retain federalism because our political and electoral structure is sufficiently decentralized to preserve the independence of the states in the face of the strong pressures that incline us to central controls.) But the arguments in behalf of federalism, whatever their merits, provide an ideological tone for debate that political leaders affront at their own peril. Public debate takes place within the context of all groups' insisting that their actions will "strengthen the federal system."

[5]Edward S. Corwin, "American Federalism—Past, Present, and Future," Princeton University Bicentennial Address, October 7, 1946.

Confederation

The People

The People

Central Government

State

State

State

State

The People

The People

The Confederation was a union of states. The central government received power from the states and had no direct authority over the people.

—and Federation

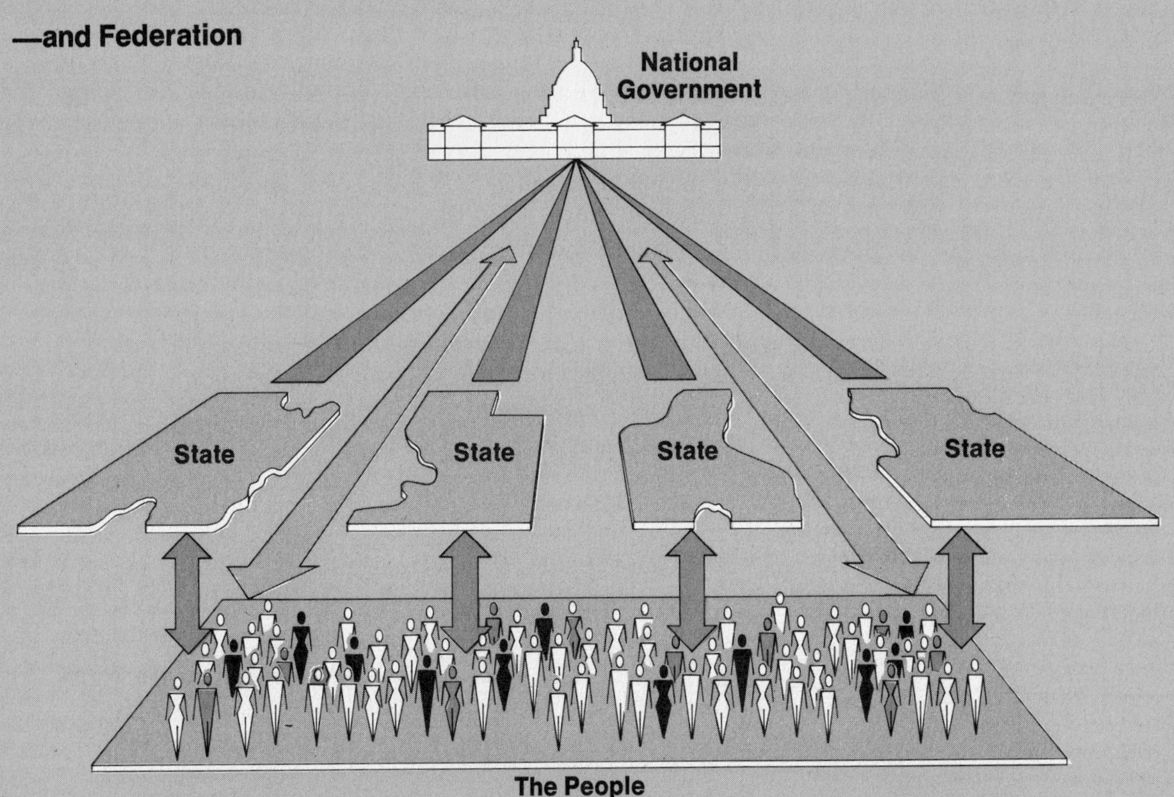

The Federal Union is a union of people. The national government and state governments receive power from the people and exercise authority directly over them.

UNITY WITHOUT UNIFORMITY

Even if a unitary state had been politically possible in 1787, it probably would not have been chosen, for federalism was and still is regarded as the appropriate form of government for the people of the United States. It is thought to be ideally suited to the needs of a relatively heterogeneous people who are spread over a large continent, who are suspicious of concentrated power, and who desire unity but not uniformity.

Federalism institutionalizes the American suspicion of concentrated power, for Americans tend to equate freedom and federalism. We often forget that in the rest of the world federal forms have not been notably successful in preventing the rise of tyrannies, and that many unitary governments are democratic. The assumption that federalism is a major factor in preserving democracy is questionable, but federalism "lessens the risk of a monopoly of political power by providing a number of independent points where the party that is nationally in the minority at the time can maintain itself while it formulates and partly demonstrates its policies and capabilities and develops new leadership."[6] Conversely, if, as Madison pointed out in *Federalist No. 10*, "factious leaders . . . kindle a flame within their particular states," national leaders can check the spread of the "conflagration into other states."

This diffusion of power, of course, has the defects of its virtues—it makes it difficult for a national majority to carry into effect a program of action, and it permits a majority in control of a state government to frustrate the consensus as expressed by national agencies of government. Whether this is an advantage or a disadvantage depends on one's political outlook. To the Founding Fathers it was an advantage; they feared that the mass of people "without property or principle" would seize control of the government. Federalism, they hoped, would make such a seizure less probable, because national majorities could be checked by local majorities. Of course—and this is a point often overlooked—the size of the nation and the multiplicity of interests within it are the greatest obstacles to the formation of an arbitrary, single-interest majority. But if such a majority should be formed, the fact that it would have to work through a federal system would restrain its powers.

Under a federal system, local issues do not have to be thrust into the national arena, thereby making it easier to develop a consensus on national problems. National politicians and parties do not have to iron out every difference on every issue in every state, because issues that might prove irreconcilable in Congress are disposed of in the state legislatures.

The size of the United States, with its many diverse cultures, makes it difficult to set national norms for local issues. Suppose for example, that Congress had to establish a single uniform national policy on divorce, gun control, abortion, or dress codes for schools. Or take the issue of the

[6]Arthur W. MacMahon, "The Problems of Federalism," *Federalism, Mature and Emergent* (Doubleday, 1955), p. 11.

regulation of alcoholic beverages. Many persons consider the moderate use of hard drink as one of the amenities of life and the prohibition of its sale as an infringement on personal liberty. Others are convinced that the unlimited sale of alcohol harms health and morals, causes social problems, and that its sale should be prohibited or closely regulated. Our federal system permits these battles to be fought in the state legislatures. There is no need to enforce a single standard on the divergent areas of the nation. As Martha Derthick has pointed out, "The opportunities that the federal system provides for distributing the burden of political decision-making may contribute to the stability of the system as a whole. . . . The fact that, for all its problems, the U.S. Congress is still the most vigorous of the legislatures of the major nations may be attributed partly to the opportunities the federal system provides for responding to pressures for action while limiting the risks of the response."[7]

FEDERALISM AND INNOVATION

According to both the old and the new conventional wisdoms, federalism encourages experimentation. The old wisdom has it that the states serve as proving grounds, trying out new procedures that, if they fail, are limited to a few states but that if successful, can be adopted by other states and the national government. The Federal Rehabilitation Act of 1965 reflects the innovative practices of some of the states in the field of corrections. The Federal Highway Safety Act of 1967 was built on state experiences. Georgia was the first to permit eighteen-year-olds to vote. New York has shown the way in its assault on water pollution; California has pioneered air pollution control programs; New York, Massachusetts, Oregon, and Wisconsin established fair employment practice commissions before Congress got around to doing so. (By executive order, however, President Franklin D. Roosevelt created such a commission before any state did.) Many states altered their abortion laws before the Supreme Court acted (whether this is progress or regression, like so many questions of politics, depends upon one's values).[8] About a fourth of the states abolished the death penalty before the Supreme Court imposed constitutional reasons for doing so (see p. 245).

The *new* wisdom puts more emphasis on the ability of the national government to encourage experimentation and is skeptical of the states' ability to do so. As Judge Wright asserts, "Mr. Justice Brandeis' wonderful laboratory theory for state government experimentation has

[7]Martha Derthick, *The Influence of Federal Grants: Public Assistance in Massachusetts* (Harvard University Press, 1970), p. 196.

[8]Ira Sharkansky, *The Maligned States: Policy Accomplishments, Problems and Opportunities* (McGraw-Hill, 1972), p. 13; see also Jack L. Walker, "The Diffusion of Innovations Among the American States," *American Political Science Review* (September 1969), pp. 880–99.

shipwrecked on the contemporary fact of industrial mobility. No state dare impose sweeping new regulations on industry, for their imposition would drive away business concerns whose presence in the state opens up employment opportunities and accounts for vital tax resources."[9] The national government with its greater tax resources can sponsor research, provide demonstrations, encourage national distribution of the results, and national action gives industry no incentive to move from one state to another to avoid controls.

But whether the new or the old wisdom is correct, at least we do have fifty-one semi-autonomous governments, and this permits action at one level and at one place where it may not be possible to secure it at the other level and at another place. This action, this experimentation, provides experience that may be used, if we wish to use it, to assess the consequences of various practices and programs for adoption or rejection elsewhere within the federal system.

Federalism is also defended on the grounds that it keeps governed and governors in close and continuing contact and gives the electorate a greater voice in governmental affairs. Few of us can serve the national government as president, congressman, cabinet member, or even high level administrator, but many thousands can participate in the operations of state and local government.

We have to be cautious, however, about the conventional generalization that the state and local governments are "closer to the people" than is the national government.[10] Closer in what sense? Some people are more involved in local and state politics than with national affairs, but most people identify more often with national officials than with those of their own state. Voter participation in state elections is below that in national elections. Among school children the evidence suggests "the state level is the last about which learning takes place."[11] Polling results show that the public believes that the federal government gives taxpayers more for their tax dollars than do state and local governments.[12] Nevertheless, states and their local units remain very much a part of the political life of those involved in public matters. In recent years, probably as a result of Watergate, confidence in state and local governments has increased while that in national officials has declined.[13] Whatever the current ups and downs of public attitudes, as Jennings and Zeigler

[9]J. Skelly Wright, "The Federal Courts and the Nature and Quality of State Law," in S. I. Shuman, ed., *The Future of Federalism* (Wayne State University Press, 1968), pp. 75–76.

[10]Morton Grodzins, "Centralization and Decentralization in the American Federal System," in Robert A. Goldwin, ed., *A Nation of States* (Rand McNally, 1963), pp. 9–15.

[11]Fred I. Greenstein, *Children and Politics* (Yale University Press, 1965), p. 155.

[12]Advisory Commission on Intergovernmental Relations, 15th Annual Report, *The Year in Review* (January 1974), pp. 5–6.

[13]Report by Louis Harris and Associates, Inc., of a survey conducted for a subcommittee of the Senate Government Operations Committee in the *New York Times*, December 3, 1973.

conclude, "The states still loom large in the perspectives of the American public. Any attempted juggling of political units involving the states would probably confront a reservoir of mass attachments to the states as political entities."[14] Whatever the merits or demerits of federalism, it is a fact of our political life—and will remain so.

Constitutional structure of American federalism

The formal constitutional framework of our federal system may be stated simply: The national government has only those powers, with one important exception, delegated to it by the Constitution; the states have all the powers not delegated to the central government except those denied to them by the Constitution; but within the scope of its operations, the national government is supreme. Furthermore, some powers are specifically denied to *both* the *national* and *state* governments; others are specifically denied *only* to the *states;* still others are denied *only* to the *national* government. Here is an outline of the constitutional structure of our federal system.

POWERS OF THE NATIONAL GOVERNMENT

The Constitution, chiefly in the first three Articles, delegates legislative, executive, and judicial powers to the national government. In addition to these *express* powers, the Constitution delegates to Congress those *implied* powers that may be reasonably inferred from the express powers. The constitutional basis for the implied powers of Congress is the "necessary and proper clause" (Article I, Section 8), which gives Congress the right "to make all Laws which shall be necessary and proper for carrying into Execution the forgoing powers, and all other powers vested . . . in the Government of the United States."

In the field of foreign affairs the national government has *inherent* powers that do not depend on specific constitutional grants but grow out of the very existence of a nation-state. The national government has the same authority in dealing with other nations as it would if it were a unitary government. For example, the government of the United States may acquire territory by discovery and occupation even though there is no specific constitutional basis for such acquisition. Even if the Constitution were silent about foreign affairs—which it is not—the national government would have as "necessary concomitants of its nationality" the right to declare war, make treaties, and appoint and receive ambassadors.[15]

[14]M. Kent Jennings and Harmon Zeigler, "The Salience of American State Politics," *American Political Science Review* (June 1970), p. 535.

[15]*United States v. Curtiss-Wright Export Corporation* (1936).

POWERS OF THE STATES

The Constitution reserves to the states all powers not granted to the national government subject only to the limitations of the Constitution. Powers that are not by express provision of the Constitution or by judicial interpretation exclusively conferred on the national government may be *concurrently* exercised by the states as long as there is no conflict with national law. For example, the states have concurrent powers with the national government to levy taxes and to regulate commerce internal to each state.

These rather simple statements about the concurrent powers of the states and the national government conceal difficult constitutional questions which we can but note and highlight. Take the power to tax: a state may levy a tax even on the same item as does the national government—gasoline taxes are an example. But a state cannot by a tax "unduly burden" a function of the national government or interfere with the operation of a national law or abridge the terms of a treaty of the United States. Who decides whether a state tax is an "undue burden" on a national function? Ultimately, the Supreme Court.

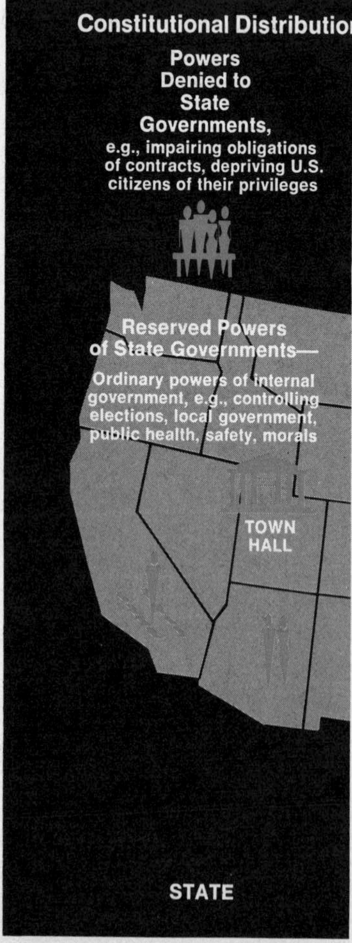

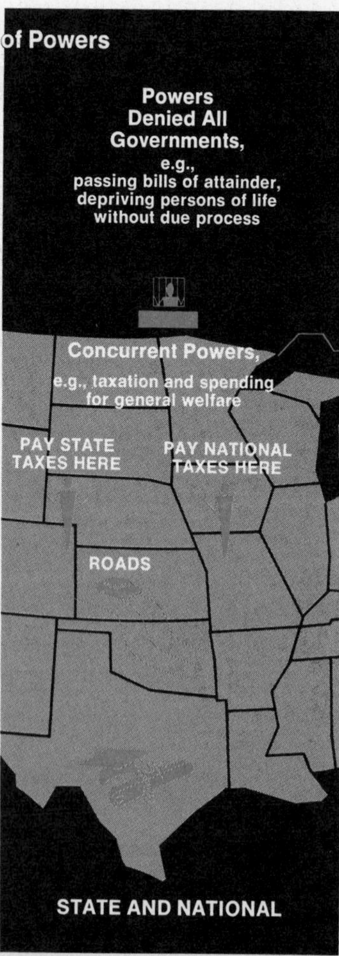

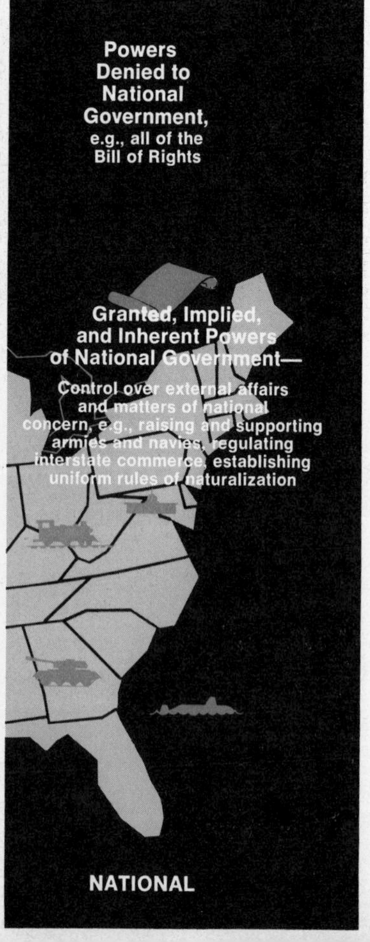

What about regulations of commerce? Here the issues are even more complicated. The Supreme Court has ruled that when Congress has not acted the states may regulate those local aspects of interstate commerce that do not require uniform national treatment, and they may apply their laws designed to protect the public to interstate commercial activities, provided those laws do not unduly burden, obstruct, or discriminate against such commerce. Who decides? Again, in the silence of Congress, ultimately the Supreme Court. For example, the Court has upheld state laws imposing speed limits on trains within city limits and requiring the elimination of grade crossings, but it has invalidated laws requiring trains to stop at every crossing.[16]

What of state regulations designed to protect consumers from fraud, guard the public health, or collect a fair share of taxes from those who use state roads or other public facilities? Again, if there is no clear congressional direction, the Supreme Court must decide whether such regulations are within the reserved powers of the state or if they are preempted by, or come into conflict with, superior federal regulation, or if they unduly burden interstate commerce. For example, the Supreme Court has ruled that states and cities may not impose a curfew on jet take-offs and landings at airports, but they could impose boarding charges on airline passengers to help defray the costs of airport construction and security (subsequently Congress outlawed such charges).[17] A few other examples out of the scores of cases that the Court has had to decide: Illinois could collect a use tax on the privilege of taking gasoline from storage and putting it into United Airlines planes in Chicago even though the fuel was being used for interstate flights; Florida could impose more stringent antipollution regulations than those imposed by federal law on ships in its coastal waters.[18]

In deciding these many disputes stemming from the concurrent powers of the states and the national government, the Supreme Court has a trying responsibility. Clearly the grant of power to Congress to regulate commerce among the states was designed to protect such commerce from discriminatory treatment and to prevent the "balkanization" of our national economy. Our economic wealth is in large measure due to the fact that our economy has not been subjected to trade barriers and diverse regulation by fifty state legislatures. On the other hand the commerce clause was not designed to permit business firms to hide behind it in order to avoid paying their share of taxes or to escape compliance with regulations deemed by state legislatures necessary to protect public health, welfare, safety, and morals. The Supreme Court remains the most important arbiter of these competing claims.

[16]*Erb v. Morasch* (1900); *Erie Railroad Co. v. Board of Public Utility Commissioners* (1921); *Seaboard Air Line Ry. Co. v. Blackwell* (1917); see also *Southern Pacific v. Arizona* (1945) and cases mentioned therein.

[17]*City of Burbank v. Lockheed Air Terminal* (1973); *United Airlines v. Mahin* (1973); *Evansville-Vanderburg Airport Authority District v. Delta Airlines* (1972).

[18]*United Airlines v. Mahin* (1973); *Askew v. American Waterways Operations Inc.* (1973).

NATIONAL SUPREMACY

Article VI states: "This Constitution, and the Laws of the United States which shall be made in Pursuance thereof; and all Treaties made . . . under the Authority of the United States, shall be the supreme Law of the Land; and the Judges in every state shall be bound thereby; any Thing in the Constitution or Laws of any State to the Contrary notwithstanding." Moreover, all officials, state as well as national, are bound by constitutional oath to support the Constitution of the United States.

States may not use their reserved powers to frustrate national policies. (It should be recognized that local units of governments are agents of the states. What states cannot constitutionally do, local units cannot do. In our discussion of the constitutional structure of federalism, local units are subsumed in all references to the states.)

For a time the application of the familiar principle of national supremacy created some controversy as applied to treaties. But it is now well established that so long as a treaty does not abridge a specific provision of the Constitution, it is constitutional even if it regulates matters, or gives Congress the power to regulate them, that may not be within the direct scope of the law-making power specifically granted by the Constitution to the national government.[19]

CONSTITUTIONAL LIMITS ON THE POWERS OF THE NATIONAL AND STATE GOVERNMENTS

The Constitution imposes certain restraints on the national or state governments or both. For example, states are prohibited from making treaties, impairing the obligations of contracts, coining money, or, except with the consent of Congress, collecting duties on exports or imports or making compacts with other states. And most important, the Constitution imposes restraints on both national and state governments in order to protect individual liberties. These restraints designed to protect individual freedoms are set forth in large measure in Article I, the Bill of Rights, and the Thirteenth, Fourteenth, Fifteenth, and Nineteenth Amendments.

CONSTITUTIONAL OBLIGATIONS OF THE NATIONAL GOVERNMENT TO THE STATES

The Constitution obligates the national government to guarantee to each state a republican form of government. The Constitution does not define what is meant by a republican form—the framers undoubtedly used the term to distinguish it from a monarchy on the one hand and a pure, direct democracy on the other—and the Supreme Court has held that the enforcement of this guarantee is a congressional responsibility.[20] Congress determines that a state has a republican form of govern-

[19] *Missouri v. Holland* (1920).

[20] *Pacific States Telephone and Telegraph Co. v. Oregon* (1912).

ment if it permits the congressional representatives of the state to take their seats in Congress.

In addition to guaranteeing to each state a republican form of government, the national government is obliged by the Constitution to protect the states against domestic insurrection. Congress has delegated authority to the president to send troops to quell insurrections on the request of the proper state authorities. This gives the president the power to determine which of contending factions is the proper authority in a state. President Tyler's decision was binding on the courts when he threatened to send federal troops to protect the Rhode Island government against the "domestic insurrection" of a rival government contending for the right to speak for the state.[21]

HORIZONTAL FEDERALISM: INTERSTATE CONSTITUTIONAL RELATIONS

What obligations does the Constitution impose on the states in their dealings with one another? Three clauses of the Constitution, taken from the Articles of Confederation, require the states to give full faith and credit to one another's public acts, records, and judicial proceedings; to extend to one another's citizens the privileges and immunities of their own citizens; and to return persons who are fleeing from justice in sister states.

Full faith and credit The full-faith-and-credit clause is one of the most technical provisions of the Constitution. In general, it requires each state to enforce civil judgments of sister states and to accept their public rec-

[21]*Luther v. Borden* (1849).

There has been much controversy over whether the governor of New York abused his power when he called out state troopers to quell the disturbance at Attica prison, but an equally valid question is whether prisoners were justified in claiming constitutional rights following the rebellion.

ords and acts as valid documents. (It does not require states to enforce the criminal laws of sister states; in fact, in most cases for one state to enforce the criminal laws of another would be unconstitutional.) The clause applies especially to noncriminal judicial proceedings. Suppose Smith obtains a $5,000 judgment against Jones from the Pennsylvania courts, but then Jones moves to California and refuses to pay up. Although California will not automatically enforce the judgment of the Pennsylvania courts, under the full-faith-and-credit clause Smith does not have to convince a California judge or jury that he is entitled to damages from Jones. In appropriate proceedings the California courts will give full faith and credit to the Pennsylvania judgment without any inquiries into the merits of the legal dispute.[22]

Some idea of the complexity of the problems growing out of the full-faith-and-credit clause is suggested by the question of how much faith and credit a state must give to a divorce decree, a civil judgment granted by another state. Clearly, a divorce granted by a state to two bona fide residents must be given full faith and credit by all the other states, even though they might not themselves have granted the divorce for the grounds alleged. On the other hand, what if Mrs. A, a citizen of North Carolina, goes to Reno, Nevada, in order to avoid the divorce laws of her own state, stays just the six weeks necessary to establish residence in Nevada, obtains a divorce in a proceeding in which Mr. A is not represented, and returns to North Carolina? Must North Carolina give full faith and credit to the divorce? Not necessarily, for the Supreme Court has held that under certain circumstances it is permissible for the courts of other states to rule that the divorce-granting state lacked jurisdiction over the parties; hence, there would be no validly obtained divorce decree to which full faith and credit must be given. In our example, North Carolina would not be required by the Constitution to recognize Mrs. A's divorce, though in Nevada it would, of course, be unquestioned.

Interstate privileges and immunities States may not deny to citizens of other states the full protection of the law, the right to engage in peaceful occupations, or access to the courts. States may not tax citizens of other states at a disciminatory rate or otherwise arbitrarily interfere with the use of their property within the state. In short, states must extend to citizens of other states the privileges and immunities of their own citizens. However, this does not extend to political rights, such as voting and serving on juries, or admission to institutions, such as schools or hospitals, that are publicly supported.

Extradition The Constitution asserts that a state shall deliver to the proper officials a criminal who has fled from another state, when requested to do so by the governor of the state from which the criminal has fled. Congress has supplemented this provision by making the governor of the state to which the fugitive has fled responsible for return-

[22]Harold W. Chase, "The Lawyers Need Help with 'the Lawyer's Clause,'" in Gottfried Dietze, ed., *Essays on the American Constitution* (Prentice-Hall, 1964), pp. 104–10.

ing him. However, despite the use of the word *shall*, the federal courts will not order governors to surrender (extradite) persons wanted in other states. Recently a governor of Michigan, horrified at the conditions under which men lived in a prison farm, refused to hand over a fugitive to Arkansas officials. There was nothing that Arkansas could do about it. Normally, however, extradition is handled in a routine fashion. Furthermore, Congress has partially closed this "gap" by making it a federal crime to flee from one state to another for the purpose of avoiding prosecution for a felony.

In addition to these three obligations, the Constitution also requires the states to settle their disputes with one another without the use of force. States may carry their legal arguments to the Supreme Court or may negotiate *interstate compacts*, which may also be used to establish interstate agencies and to solve joint problems. Before interstate compacts become effective, the approval of Congress is required, an approval that is sometimes given in advance. After a compact has been signed and approved by Congress, it becomes binding on all signatory states, and its terms are enforceable by the Supreme Court. Not all agreements among states, however, require congressional approval—only those, the Supreme Court held in 1893, "tending to increase the political power of the States, which may encroach upon or interfere with the just supremacy of the United States."[23]

THE CONSTITUTIONAL STRUCTURE OF FEDERALISM: THE REALITIES TODAY

This brief outline of the constitutional structure of federalism oversimplifies, and especially as related to the division of powers between the national government and the states, even misleads. For as Michael D. Reagan has written, "form can remain constant while the content changes radically. This is, in fact, what has happened to federalism."[24]

As recently as the Great Depression of the 1930s, constitutional scholars and Supreme Court justices debated whether Congress had the authority to enact legislation dealing with agriculture, labor, education, housing, and welfare. Only a decade or so ago, there were constitutional questions about the authority of Congress to legislate against racial discrimination. And it remains technically correct to state that Congress lacks any *general* grant of authority to do whatever it thinks necessary and proper in order to promote the general welfare or to preserve domestic tranquillity. But as a result of the rise of a national economy, the growth of national demands on Washington, the emergence of a world in which war could destroy us in a matter of minutes, our constitutional system has evolved to the point where the national government has ample constitutional authority to deal with any national or international program. As an eminent jurist has written: "Bluntly stated, in major respects the federal government is no longer a government of limited

[23]*Virginia v. Tennessee* (1893).

[24]Michael D. Reagan, *The New Federalism* (Oxford University Press, 1972), p. 4.

powers. Changes in social reality and in judicial interpretation of several key rubrics of Article I constitutional authority make it possible for the federal government to legislate pervasively in almost any area. State law, in many of the eddies where it does still govern, is no more secure than a tenancy at will, terminable at Washington's pleasure."[25]

There may be a few subjects—for example, regulation of marriage and divorce—about which the Supreme Court might interpose objections to national legislation because of the principles of federalism, but it is now fairly accurate (even if technically incorrect) to say that Congress has power to do whatever it believes is necessary and proper to promote the general welfare.

Federalism, in short, no longer imposes serious constitutional restraints on the power of Congress, or the president, or the federal courts. Today constitutional restraints on national power stem from provisions that protect the liberties of the people rather than from those relating to the powers of the individual state governments. Still, the distribution of governmental authority between the national and state governments is of great significance. For despite the growth of national constitutional authority, states are vital and active governments backed by significant political forces. Federalism as a process remains a vital aspect of our political life.

Triumph of the nationalist interpretation

This summary of contemporary constitutional construction of our federal system jumps over two hundred years of conflict and proclaims victory, at least for the moment, for the nationalists' interpretation of that system. (The debate between those who favor national action as against those in favor of state and local levels continues, but it does so generally outside the framework of *constitutional* principles.) But this victory for the nationalist construction of the Constitution is a recent one. Throughout most of our history it has had to contend with a states' rights interpretation.

The constitutional arguments revolving around federalism grew out of specific issues: whether the national government had the authority to outlaw slavery in the territories; whether states had the authority to operate racially segregated schools; whether Congress could regulate labor relations. The debates were frequently couched in lofty constitutional language and appeals were made to the great principles of federalism, but the struggles were very practical ones to determine who was to get what, where, and how, and who was to do what to whom.

Among those who championed the states' rights interpretation, albeit with varying emphasis and differing concerns, were Thomas Jefferson,

[25]Wright, "The Federal Courts and the Nature and Quality of State Law from the Point of View of a Federal Judge," p. 73.

John C. Calhoun, the Supreme Court from the 1920s to 1937, and today George Wallace.

The basic premise of the states' righters is that the Constitution is an intergovermental treaty among sovereign states which thereby created the central government and gave it carefully limited authority. Because the national government is thus nothing more than an agent of the states, every one of its powers should be narrowly construed. In case of doubt whether the states had given a particular function to the general government or reserved it for themselves, the doubt should be resolved in favor of the states.

The states' righters hold that the national government should not be permitted to exercise its delegated powers in such a way as to interfere with activities reserved to the states. The Tenth Amendment, it is claimed, makes this emphatic: "The powers not delegated to the United States by the Constitution, nor prohibited by it to the States, are reserved to the States respectively, or to the people."

Underlying the states' righters' fundamental position is their insistence that the state governments are closer to the people and therefore that they more accurately reflect the people's wishes than does the national government, which they view as a distant and essentially external authority. They maintain further that the national government is inherently heavy-handed and bureaucratic and that in order to preserve our federal system and our liberties the central authority must be carefully circumscribed.

The *nationalist* position, supported, again with varying emphasis, by Chief Justice John Marshall, Abraham Lincoln, Theodore Roosevelt, Franklin Roosevelt, and, throughout most of our of history, the Supreme Court, rejects the whole concept of the Constitution as an interstate compact. Rather, the Constitution is a supreme law ordained and established by the people. The national government, it is held, is an agent of the people, not of the states, for it was the people who drew up the Constitution and created the national government. The sovereign people gave the national government sufficient power to accomplish the great objectives listed in the Preamble. They intended that the central government's powers should be liberally construed and that it not be denied authority unless there is a clear absence of constitutional sanction.

The nationalists contend that the national government is not a foreign entity but a government of all the people; each state speaks for only some of the people. Of course the Tenth Amendment reserves powers to the states, but as Chief Justice Stone said, "The Tenth Amendment states but a truism that all is retained which has not been surrendered" (*United States v. Darby*, 1941). The amendment does not deny the national government the right to exercise to the fullest extent all the powers given to it by the Constitution. The supremacy of the national government does however restrict the states, for a government representing part of the people cannot be allowed to interfere with a government representing all of them.

McCULLOCH V. MARYLAND: A NATIONALIST VICTORY

In 1819, in the famous case of *McCulloch v. Maryland,* the Supreme Court had the first of many chances to choose between these two interpretations of our federal system. Maryland had levied a tax against the Baltimore branch of the Bank of the United States, a semi-public agency which had been established in accordance with a law of Congress. McCulloch, the cashier of the bank, refused to pay on the ground that a state could not tax an instrument of the national government. Maryland's attorneys responded that in the first place that the national government did not have the power to incorporate a bank, but even if it did, the state had the power to tax it.

Maryland was represented before the Court by some of the most distinguished men of the bar, including Luther Martin, a delegate to the Constitutional Convention who had left early in the deliberations when it became apparent that a strong national government was in the making. Martin, basing his argument against the constitutionality of the bank on the states' rights view of federalism, pointed out that the power to incorporate a bank is not one of the powers expressly delegated to the national government. He contended that Article I, Section 8, Clause 18, which gives Congress the right to choose whatever means are necessary and proper to carry out its delegated powers, should, like all grants of national power, be narrowly construed. So interpreted, the clause gives Congress only the power to choose those means and to pass those laws absolutely essential to the execution of its expressly granted powers. Because a bank is not absolutely necessary to the exercise of any of its delegated powers, Congress has no authority to establish it.

What about Maryland's right to tax the bank? Martin's position was simply stated: The power to tax is one of the powers reserved to the states, which they may use as they see fit.

The national government was represented by equally distinguished counsel, chief of whom was Daniel Webster. Webster conceded that the power to create a bank is not one of the express powers of the national government. But the power to pass laws necessary and proper to carry out enumerated powers is expressly delegated to Congress, and this power should be interpreted generously to mean that Congress has authority to enact any legislation convenient and useful in carrying out delegated national powers. Therefore, Congress may incorporate a bank as an appropriate, convenient, and useful means of exercising the granted powers of collecting taxes, borrowing money, and caring for the property of the United States.

As to Maryland's attempt to tax the bank, Webster contended that though the power to tax is reserved to the states, states cannot use their reserved powers to interfere with the operations of the national government. The Constitution leaves no room for doubt: In case of conflict between the national and state governments, the former is supreme.

In 1819 the Supreme Court was presided over by Chief Justice John Marshall, a nationalist and an advocate of a broad interpretation of the central government's constitutional authority. Speaking for a unanimous Court, Marshall rejected every one of Maryland's contentions. In his usual forceful style, he wrote: "We must never forget that it is a *constitution* we are expounding. . . . [A] constitution intended to endure for ages to come, and consequently, to be adapted to the various crises of human affairs." "The government of the Union," he continued, "is emphatically and truly a government of the people. In form and substance it emanates from them, its powers are granted to them, and are to be exercised directly on them. . . . It can never be to their interest and cannot be presumed to have been their intention, to clog and embarrass its execution, by withholding the most appropriate means." Marshall summarized his views on how the powers of the national government should be broadly construed in these now-famous words: "Let the end be legitimate, let it be within the scope of the Constitution, and all means which are appropriate, which are plainly adapted to that end, which are not prohibited, but consist with the letter and spirit of the Constitution, are constitutional."

Having thus established the doctrine of implied national powers, Marshall set forth the doctrine of national supremacy. No state, he said, can use its reserved taxing powers to tax a national instrument. "The power to tax involves the power to destroy. . . . If the right of the states to tax the means employed by the general government be conceded, the declaration that the Constitution, and the laws made in pursuance thereof, shall be the supreme law of the land, is empty and unmeaning declamation."

The long-range significance of *McCulloch v. Maryland* in providing an ideological support for the developing forces of nationalism can hardly be overstated. The arguments of the states' righters, if accepted, would have strapped the national government in a constitutional straitjacket and denied it the powers needed to handle the problems of an expanding nation. In all probability, the Constitution would have been replaced many years ago as succeeding generations were forced, once again, to render the central government adequate to the needs of each new age. Marshall's vision accounts in part for the longevity of our Constitution, the oldest written constitution in the world today.

Growth of the national government

The structure of American federalism is little changed since 1787, but the way we actually operate this system is drastically different. The words of the Constitution, wrote Justice Holmes in *Missouri v. Holland* (1920), called into life a being whose development "could not have been foreseen completely by the most gifted of its begetters. It was enough for them to realize or to hope that they had created an organism; it has taken a century and has cost their successors much sweat and blood to prove that they created a nation." The Constitution established a framework in which a national government could develop, but it was some time before a viable national community to support this national government actually existed.

The nationalists' interpretation of government finally triumphed at Appomattox Courthouse after the Civil War, but, from the beginning of our political history, events have vindicated their position. It has made no difference whether the party in power has been Federalist, Jeffersonian, Whig, Republican, or Democratic—the national government's sphere has constantly expanded.

CONSTITUTIONAL BASIS OF THE GROWTH

How has the expansion occurred? Not by amendment. The formal constitutional powers of the national government are essentially the same today as they were in 1789. But the Supreme Court (building on Marshall's work in *McCulloch v. Maryland*), the Congress, the president, and—ultimately—the people have taken advantage of the Constitution's flexibility to permit the national government to exercise the powers needed to fight wars and depressions and to serve the needs of a modern industrial nation. The full scope of the central government's consitutional powers has been used to support this expansion of functions, but there are three major constitutional pillars on which the expansion has developed.

The war power The national government is responsible for protecting the nation from external aggression and, when necessary, for waging war. In a world community that has known total war and that lives under the threat of total destruction, the power needed to provide for the common defense is of a scope never dreamed of in 1789. No longer does military strength depend solely on troops in the field; it also depends on the ability to mobilize the nation's industrial might and to apply its scientific knowledge to the tasks of defense. Everything from the physics courses taught in the schools to the conservation of natural resources and the maintenance of a prosperous economy affects the nation's military strength.

In brief, the national government has the power to wage war and to do what is necessary and proper to wage it successfully. In these times this almost means the power to do anything that is not in direct conflict with constitutional guarantees.

The power to regulate interstate and foreign commerce Congressional authority extends to all commerce that affects more than one state and to all those activities, wherever they exist or whatever their nature, whose control is necessary and proper to regulate interstate and foreign commerce. The term *commerce* includes all commercial intercourse—the production, buying, selling, and transporting of goods. The power to regulate is the power to prescribe the rules by which this commerce is governed, that is, the right to foster, prohibit, promote, protect, or defend all commerce that affects more states than one.

The commerce clause packs a tremendous constitutional punch. It has been construed to cover more than commercial or business transactions. In these few words the national government has been able to find constitutional justification for regulating a wide range of human activity and property. Today there are few aspects of our economy that do not affect commerce in more states than one. When farmer Filburn plants wheat on his own farm to feed his own children and chickens, his actions affect the price of wheat in the interstate market, and therefore his activities are within the scope of congressional authority. When a steel company fires men because they belong to a labor union, it enhances the danger of industrial strife and threatens the flow of goods in interstate commerce. Thus, national laws regulating employer-employee relations in industries that affect interstate commerce have been upheld as necessary and proper means to protect the free flow of commerce.

The commerce clause can also be used to sustain legislation that goes beyond commercial matters. When the Supreme Court upheld the 1964 Civil Rights Act forbidding discrimination because of race, religion, or national origin in places of public accommodation, it said, "Congress' action in removing the disruptive effect which it found racial discrimination has on interstate travel is not invalidated because Congress was also legislating against what it considers to be moral wrongs." Discrimination restricts the flow of interstate commerce; interstate commerce was being used to support discrimination; therefore, Congress could legislate against the discrimination. Moreover, the law could be applied even to local places of public accommodation since these local incidents of discrimination have a substantial and harmful impact on interstate commerce. "If it is interstate commerce that feels the pinch, it does not matter how local the operation that applies the squeeze."[26]

Some have accused the Supreme Court of making strained interpretations of the commerce clause in order to justify national regulation. Al-

[26]*Heart of Atlanta Motel v. United States* (1964); see also *Perez v. United States* (1971).

These senators didn't mind posing in the old Supreme Court chamber where cots were set up for them during the marathon civil rights session in the senate in 1960.

though Justice Black did not question that Congress could bar racial discrimination under its powers stemming from the Fourteenth Amendment, he felt the commerce clause should not be stretched "so as to give the federal government complete control over every little remote country place of recreation in every nook and cranny of every precinct and county in every one of the fifty states."[27] But Justice Black dissented alone. Most observers feel that the Supreme Court has simply recognized the obvious integration of our economic and social life. Wheat planted in people's backyards does, as a matter of economic fact, affect the interstate price of wheat. A strike in Pittsburgh or Detroit does affect commerce in California and New York. Discrimination by innkeepers and restaurant owners does make it burdensome to travel in interstate commerce.

The power to tax and spend for the general welfare Congress lacks constitutional authority to pass laws solely on the ground that the laws will promote the general welfare, but it may raise taxes and spend money to promote the general welfare. This distinction between legislating and appropriating frequently makes little difference. For example, Congress lacks constitutional power to regulate education or agriculture directly, but Congress has the power to appropriate money to support education or to pay farmers subsidies, and by attaching conditions to its grants of money Congress may regulate what it could not constitutionally control by legal fiat.

Because Congress puts up the money, it has a strong voice in determining how it shall be spent. By withholding or threatening to withhold funds, the national government can influence state operations or regulate individual conduct. For example, the 1964 Civil Rights Act provides that "No person in the United States shall, on the ground of race, color, or national origin, be excluded from participation in, be denied the benefits of, or be subjected to discrimination under any program or activity receiving Federal financial assistance." (Subsequent legislation extends these restraints on the use of most federal funds to cover discrimination because of sex.) Federal authorities are directed by the act to develop regulations that will ensure that federal funds, whether loans or grants, are not being used to support programs from which persons are excluded because of race, sex, or national origin.

Until recently, Congress' authority to appropriate money was almost beyond constitutional challenge. In 1923 the Supreme Court had ruled in *Frothingham v. Mellon* that a taxpayer's contribution to the treasury was not sufficient to give him the right to challenge before a federal court the constitutionality of a federal appropriation. Then in 1968 in *Flast v. Cohen* the Supreme Court severely modified the *Frothingham* doctrine. It held that taxpayers could challenge, as a violation of the establishment-of-religion and free-exercise clauses, grants to the states under the 1965 Elementary and Secondary Education Act for the

[27]Dissent in *Daniel v. Paul* (1969).

purchase of instructional materials for public and private, including church-operated, schools. The Supreme Court did set conditions to such taxpayer suits: A taxpayer not only must establish a logical link between himself and the particular spending challenged but must point to a specific constitutional limitation on the congressional power to tax and to spend; a taxpayer may not invoke the power of federal courts merely to question an appropriation because he thinks it unwise.

In addition to using its appropriating authority for regulatory purposes, Congress may levy taxes that have a regulatory impact; for example, Congress has so heavily taxed white-phosphorus matches that it is no longer profitable to manufacture and sell these dangerous items. However, Congress may not use its taxing powers to deprive persons of specific rights secured by the Constitution, as it was reminded in 1968 (*Marchetti v. United States* and *Haynes v. United States*) when the Supreme Court declared unconstitutional two tax laws that forced persons to incriminate themselves, contrary to the guarantee of the Fifth Amendment (see pp. 232–33). One of these laws required owners of sawed-off shotguns and other such weapons to file registration papers showing possession of weapons illegal under most state laws. The other law required professional gamblers to declare that they were engaging in activities that are illegal in forty-nine states by filing a federal tax statement and securing a federal license, both the statement and the license being available to law enforcement officials.

Congress may also use its taxing powers "to induce" states to adopt certain kinds of programs. For example, Congress has levied a tax on employers but allows them to deduct from it the state taxes they pay to support state unemployment compensation. Because the employer has to pay this money anyhow, all the states have been induced to establish unemployment compensation programs.

These three constitutional powers—the war power, the power over interstate commerce, and the power to tax and spend for the general welfare—have made possible a tremendous expansion of federal functions. If all the laws Congress has passed in pursuance of these powers were wiped off the statute books, the size of the federal government and the scope of its functions would shrink drastically.

Umpiring the federal system

Although today there are few doubts about the national government's constitutional authority to deal with issues impacting on the nation, whether they be civil rights, the speed limits on highways, or the kinds of Christmas lights we may display, there are still constant conflicts between those who wish national action and those who believe that particular matters are better left to the states. Judges, and most especially those on the Supreme Court, continue to play a vital role as one of the umpires of the federal system.

THE ROLE OF THE SUPREME COURT

In many instances Congress has not acted and the judges must decide, when appropriate lawsuits are brought before them, whether state or local regulations will be permitted. Even when Congress acts, often there are questions about whether or not Congress intends to preempt state regulations. For example, do federal regulations on controlling pollution of the air and water *preempt* or *supplement* state regulations? And there are even still a few occasions in which the Supreme Court has to face the issue of whether Congress has exceeded its constitutional authority and invaded the reserved powers of the state. In fact as recent as 1970 the Supreme Court declared unconstitutional a provision of a federal law, the Voting Rights Act of 1970, on the grounds that Congress lacked the authority to supersede state power to set the age requirements for voting for state officials.[28] (The Twenty-sixth Amendment resulted from that decision.)

The Supreme Court's role as the principal umpire of the federal system is not merely an exercise in legal interpretation. For as Robert H. Jackson wrote before he became a Supreme Court justice: "This political role of the Court has been obscure to laymen—even to most lawyers. It speaks only through the technical form of the lawsuit, which is not identified with politics in the popularly accepted sense. Yet these lawsuits are the chief instrument of power in our system. Struggles over power that in Europe call for regiments of troops, in America call out battalions of lawyers."[29]

The constitutional struggle that concerned Justice Jackson is more or less over, with the victory going to the national government. But the Supreme Court continues to play a role in legitimizing the exercise of national power. To quote Richard Leach: "As the country becomes more national in its orientation, federalism is inefficient, slow, and cumbersome, and to overcome these difficulties, the combined efforts of public opinion, economic and social pressure, and political and legislative action find ways to bypass its limitations. The Supreme Court, by legitimizing these shortcuts, in a sense enables the nation to have its cake and eat it too, in that it provides the mechanism by which the major national needs and aspirations can be satisfied with at least some dispatch and efficiency and without forcing the issue and arousing the ancient forces of disunion once again."[30]

The Supreme Court, itself a branch of the national government, has often been accused of bias. The states, it has been charged, have had to play against the umpire as well as against the national government itself. Over the years the Court's decisions have favored national powers,

[28]*Oregon v. Mitchell* (1970).

[29]*The Struggle for Judicial Supremacy* (Knopf, 1941), p. xi.

[30]Richard H. Leach, *American Federalism* (Norton, 1970), p. 81; see also Loren P. Beth, "The Supreme Court and American Federalism," *Saint Louis University Law Journal* 10 (Spring 1966), 376 ff.; Paul A. Freund, "The Supreme Court and the Future of Federalism," in Shuman, ed., *Future of Federalism*, p. 37ff.

including its own powers vis à vis state courts. Especially in recent years, the Supreme Court has shown less of a tendency to favor local regulations than has Congress.

Those who control the state governments have often been severe in their criticism of the Court for its decisions curtailing their authority. But despite the frequent criticism of the Supreme Court, few would deny it the power to review *state* actions. As Justice Holmes once remarked, "I do not think the United States would come to an end if we lost our power to declare an Act of Congress void. I do think the Union would be imperiled if we could not make that declaration as to the laws of the several states."[31] Or, as Justice Story wrote many years earlier, a review by the Supreme Court of the constitutional decisions of state courts is necessary to maintain "uniformity of decisions throughout the whole United States, upon all subjects within the purview of the constitution. . . . Judges of equal learning and integrity, in different states might differently interpret a statute, or a treaty of the United States, or even the Constitution itself."[32]

OTHER UMPIRES (AND CONTESTANTS) OF THE FEDERAL SYSTEM

The Supreme Court is not the only umpire of the federal system; Congress has much to say about the distribution of functions and the extent to which federal or state standards will prevail. Through Congress are heard powerful local and state political interests. Congress adopts laws imposing federal standards or supplementing state programs. After Congress acts, the president and federal administrators take over. They approve the guidelines for enforcing federal laws, decide which projects to approve, and have a considerable role in determining how rigorously federal standards shall be applied.

However, we should not be misled into thinking that it is a simple matter for federal authorities to impose their views on state and local communities. On a single issue the dominant political power is not always on the side of those favoring national standards. A coalition of political forces may secure an act of Congress, but countervailing pressures may be applied when it comes to enforcing that act.

The complexities of the political process are well illustrated by the Elementary and Secondary Education Act of 1965 in which Congress provided funds so that state and local school officials could develop special programs for the poor. Federal authorities had great difficulty in influencing how the funds were used at the state and local levels. In the first place, federal educational authorities had no particular desire to engage in political battles with their counterparts in local school systems. But it was not simply "the lack of will . . . but lack of political muscle" that kept federal educational administrators from having an impact at the local level. They knew that in case of a crunch congress-

[31]*Collected Legal Papers* (Harcourt, 1920), pp. 295–96.

[32]*Martin v. Hunter's Lesee* (1816).

men would be "sure to be more responsive to the wishes of state and local school officials than to the desires of bureaucrats in the executive branch."[33] In short, "The federal system—with its disperson of power and control—not only permits but encourages the evasion and dilution of federal reform, making it nearly impossible for the federal administrator to impose program priorities; those not diluted by Congressional intervention, can be ignored during state and local implementation."[34]

The constitutional structure of federalism—a summary

Over the last two hundred years, our federal constitutional system has evolved into something that is only slightly different in form but significantly different in fact from the one we began with. Whether or not we ever had a system in which it was possible to talk about neat constitutional divisions between the powers of the national and the state governments, it is certainly no longer accurate to do so today. Today the national government's constitutional authority is seldom restrained by constitutional principles flowing from the federal system.

But to recognize that the national government has the constitutional authority to do whatever Congress thinks may be necessary and proper to do is not the same as saying that federalism is dead. The patterns of American politics are not simple and they make generalizations dangerous. The political tides do not all move in the same direction. Although during the last two centuries constitutional power has moved toward the center, political power remains dispersed. Our federal system remains very much alive. "If there is anything sure in the world of politics, it would appear to be the certainty that the American federal system will continue to be used as the basic container for American government."[35] States remain active and significant political communities. Conflicts between national and state majorities continue to be active on our political agenda as do the issues of centralization versus decentralization. The spirit and rhetoric of federalism are heard in our electoral contests.

What has happened is that we no longer spend so much time debating the *law* of federalism. We have now moved to the *politics* of federalism. As now construed, the Constitution gives us the option to decide through the political process what we want to do, who is going to pay, and how we are going to get it done.

[33]Jerome T. Murphy, "Title I of ESEA: The Politics of Implementing Federal Educational Reform." *Harvard Educational Review*, 41 (February 1971), p. 45.

[34]*Ibid.* p. 60.

[35]Leach, *American Federalism*, p. x.

Chapter 5 American federalism: politics and problems

The state and national governments are not hard, solid objects that collide with sharp impact. They *mesh* with one another, for they are made up of people who govern, and are governed by, other people. To talk of states' rights is but a shorthand way of referring to the rights of people who live in states and to the authority of officials elected by them. Texans, not Texas, have rights.

National and state governments are arenas in which differing groups engage in political combat over public policies. Congressmen and state legislators often respond to the same groups and express the same ideas, and we have "national-state cooperation." At other times, congressmen and state legislators represent sharply different combinations of interests, and we have "national-state conflict." This conflict between the national and state officials is just one facet of the continuing struggle among groups that makes up our politics. "Federalism does not involve a struggle between the nation and the states, but rather a struggle among interests who have favorable access to one of the two levels of government."[1]

[1]Harmon Zeigler, *Interest Groups in American Society* (Prentice-Hall, 1964), p. 48.

The politics of federalism

From the day the colonists first set foot on the soil of the New World, Americans have been arguing about the "proper" division of powers between central and local governments. From time to time various governmental commissions and private study groups have attempted to determine the proper distribution of power, but the experts discovered, as did the Founding Fathers in 1787, that there are no objective, scientific standards to distinguish the respective functions.

The questions are political in nature. At one time or another Northerners, Southerners, businessmen, farmers, workers, Federalists, Democrats, Whigs, and Republicans have thought it improper to vest a particular function in the national government. They have opposed "control by Washington" in the name of maintaining the federal system. But underlying the debates have been such issues as slavery, labor-management relations, government regulation of business, civil rights, and welfare.

With the advent of the New Deal and the growth of organized labor's influence at the national level, most business groups became devotees of the rights of states. The national government came to be controlled by persons in whom many businessmen had little confidence and over whom they had less influence. They discovered that state legislatures and state courts were more likely than their national counterparts to make decisions favored by businessmen. As Carl B. Swisher observed, "It behooves us . . . to take thought before drenching our handkerchiefs when the National Association of Manufacturers and the American Bar Association bewail the prostrate position of the states before the federal colossus. These mourners are not shedding tears over the lamentable conditions of New Hampshire and North Carolina and Montana and Texas but over the enterprise caught in the grip of the federal regulatory hand. . . ."[2] On the other hand, labor leaders found national agencies more responsive to their claims. It is not surprising that while business groups have been quick to defend the states against what they call the "federal octopus," labor leaders have emphasized the need for national action and have charged the states with being dominated by "special interests."

Until recently, those who favor segregation dominated most governments in the South. They feared that national officials, responding to different political majorities, would support integration. Naturally, segregationists sang the virtues of local governments "close to the people;" they were quick to emphasize the dangers of overcentralization, and argued at great length that the regulation of civil rights was not a proper function of the national government. This appeal to states' rights in what was an attempt, ultimately unsuccessful, to secure the support of a national majority typifies the political technique of trying to give an

[2] *The Growth of Constitutional Power in the United States* (University of Chicago Press, 1946), p. 33.

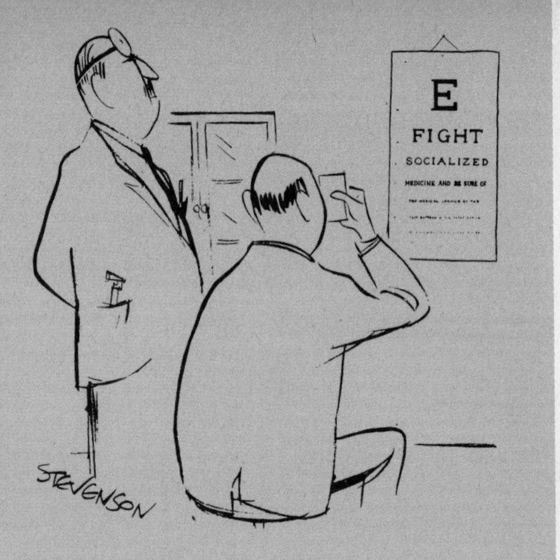

Drawing by Stevenson; © 1958 The New Yorker Magazine, Inc.

ideological wrapping to a political position in order to maximize support for it.

The debate continues. Those confident that the decisions made by Congress and federal administrators are more apt to reflect values they approve are likely to be skeptical about revenue-sharing (see pp. 113–17) or other procedures that give more discretion to state and local officials. Those who expect to have maximum influence at the state and local level tend to support arrangements that enhance the role of state and local authorities.

Today, however, the politics of federalism have become more complicated than in the past. As a leading student of federalism has pointed out: "Perhaps there was a time when it was possible to generalize casually about specific interests being satisfied by different planes of government. . . . Today it is simply no longer true about significant interests."[3] Take, for example, the business interests. By the 1960s, they were no longer so singlemindedly in favor of state as against national action. They discovered that "Federal regulation meant one set of rules or standards rather than fifty, and even more important federal rules would represent a compromise between those calling for stringent regulation and those disposed to keep regulation minimal while at least some states would establish more stringent rules or set higher standards."[4] In 1966 the automobile industry changed its position against federal regulation of safety standards to favor preemptive federal regulation when it realized that by doing so it could avoid the more stringent regulations being imposed by California and New York, which control some 20 percent of the market.

Even in the area of civil rights, the issue of national versus state action has become more complicated. Although the ability of Southern

[3]Daniel J. Elazer, *American Federalism: A View from the States*, 2nd ed. (Crowell, 1972), p. 213.

[4]*Ibid.*, p. 215–16.

Left, the jobless demonstrate in the Pennsylvania senate gallery in 1936 over the failure of the state to accede to their relief demands. Right, the midwest leg of the 1968 Poor People's March on Washington demanding federal aid.

states to obstruct civil rights legislation naturally made most blacks look to Washington for protective legislation, again, as Elazar points out, in 1968 by the time Congress passed open-housing legislation "over 115 million Americans, including the overwhelming majority of blacks living outside of the South, were living under state open-housing laws, some of many years standing."[5]

Conservative ideology continues to favor state and local action; liberal ideology tends to support national action. But changes of recent years have begun to erode the consistency of these positions. The virtues of participation by urban groups in the affairs of their schools and their local communities; the increasing black control over the inner cities; Republican conservatives winning the presidency—these events have led some liberal spokesmen to rethink the values of local action, and some conservatives have been appreciating the advantages of national standards.

Of course, national conflicts with states seldom involve two ideologically distinct interest groups lining up against each other on the issue of which level of government should prevail. Nor do these conflicts involve all the states on one side and the national government on the other. States have a formal, legal equality, but "the federal relationship (and the politics of federalism) means something very much different to nearly every participant unit in the system."[6] As Fesler has warned,

[5]*Ibid.*, p. 212.

[6]Charles D. Tarlton, "Symmetry and Asymmetry as Elements of Federalism: A Theoretical Speculation," *Journal of Politics* (November 1965), p. 861.

"generalizations about national-state relations must be read (and preferably advanced) with caution. . . . Eight of the fifty states contain about half of the national population; in four states the federal government owns between sixty-four and ninety-four percent of the land; the states of Alaska and Wyoming each receive federal grants-in-aid that per capita are about six times what New Jersey or Florida receives. . . ."[7] And the politics of national-state relations are much affected by differences among the states. The more a state differs in its political, economic, and social make-up from the rest of the nation, the more likely will that state's policies conflict with the policies being espoused by national spokesmen. Witness the difference in the nature of relations between Alabama and the national government and New York and the national government.[8]

The politics of national growth

In Chapter 4 we discussed the constitutional bases for the expansion of the role of the national government. But why has this expansion of national functions occurred? Certainly not because of any superior logic of one side over the other. Rather, "big government" has come about because of deep-seated changes in our society and as the result of the pushing and hauling of conflicting interest groups.

Since 1789 we have grown from a poor, sparsely populated agricultural society to a rich, densely populated industrial nation. The United States has grown from a weak, isolated debtor nation to a powerful creditor that plays a central role in the world community. Clearly, such profound alterations in any society would have a powerful impact on the government of that society. People's attitudes toward the national government have changed, too. Whereas the government of the Confederation was viewed in the 1780s as a distant, even foreign government, today most people identify their fortunes more closely with Washington than they do with their state governments. The railroad, telegraph, telephone, radio, airplane, and television have made the activities of federal officials familiar to all. Most people do not even know when their state legislature is in session, but what happens in Washington is known throughout the land in a matter of minutes. Likewise, citizens of other states are no longer considered foreign. The automobile made us a nation on the move. Two hundred years of common experiences, especially the fighting of two world wars, have cemented the Union and made Washington the focus of attention. Moreover, an urban industrial society requires much closer regulation than a rural agri-

[7]James W. Fesler, "Approaches to the Understanding of Decentralization," *Journal of Politics* (August 1965), p. 537, n. 1.

[8]Tarlton, "Symmetry and Asymmetry," p. 871.

cultural one. A thousand people in the country might need only one police officer, because informal pressures can be counted on to maintain order. The same number of people living in the city, with its impersonal and diversified make-up, might require five police to enforce social sanctions.

The states have had to expand their functions, but, because many of our problems have become national in scope, even greater responsibilities have devolved on the national government. In recent decades the national government has gradually taken over a greater role in business regulation, law enforcement, consumer protection, education, housing, civil rights, and welfare. Much that was local in 1789, or even in 1860, is now national. A state could supervise the relations between a small merchant, who bought and sold his products within the local market, and his few employees. But only the national government can supervise the relations between a nationally organized industry that buys and sells its materials all over the world and its thousands of employees organized into national unions. With the industrialization of the United States there came about a concentration of economic power, first in the form of businesses and later in the form of labor unions. These units, which, along with professional organizations, are private governments exercising political as well as economic power, necessitated the coalescing of national governmental power. If the unit of public government is not as powerful as the unit of private government it is to supervise, the regulated often regulates the regulator. The activities of the UAW or AT&T are too far-flung and their power is too formidable to enable the states to provide the needed social control. General Motors has twice the total revenue of the state of California and four times as many employees. Big business, big agriculture, big labor, all must add up to big government.

As industrialization progressed, various powerful interests began to make demands on the national government. First the business groups, who were largely responsible for building industrial America, called on the government for aid in the form of tariffs, a national banking system, a uniform and stable currency, and subsidies to railroads, airlines, and the merchant marine. Once the business groups obtained what they wanted and felt strong enough to take care of themselves, they began generally to oppose governmental aid to other groups. But then farmers learned that the national government could give them more aid in solving their economic problems than could their states, and they too began to demand help. The farm groups used their powers to secure such laws as regulation of the railroads, antitrust legislation, paper currency, parcel post, and, finally, government support for farm prices. By the beginning of the present century, urban groups in general, and organized labor in particular, began to press their demands. Workers found that they could not organize unions with a hostile government issuing injunctions and calling out troops. They began to work for restrictions on injunctions and for friendly administrations. With increased industrialization and urbanization, city dwellers, including blacks who have migrated from the South to the northern central cities, began to make claims on the federal treasury for funds to provide housing, welfare, educational benefits, mass transportation, and all the other things they consider necessary to make our big cities habitable.

INADEQUACIES OF THE STATES

Why could not the states provide these services? Why have they not done so? In part because of geographical inadequacies. Many of our states' boundaries were blocked out on the map with little reference to underlying geographic, social, or historical realities; with the passage of time, growing discrepancies have developed between state boundaries and human problems. Many natural regions, such as river valleys, are cut in half by the surveyor's line. Many large cities have grown up along state boundaries, which means that cohesive metropolitan areas—New York City, Kansas City, and Washington, D.C., for example—are fragmented between two or three states. When the people of a river valley or a metropolitan region want their governments to act to conserve human or natural resources, they often find that no one state has jurisdiction to deal with the problems of the entire area.

Many of the problems affecting citizens most directly—housing, race relations, air pollution, energy, economic security—require resources available only to the national government. In the 1930s, states had neither the tax resources nor a wide enough area jurisdiction to achieve recovery from the Great Depression; the national government was forced to act. In the 1970s, faced wth disorder and an urgent need to improve life for the millions of Americans living in the core of our large cities, the national government had to move on a massive scale, a scale beyond the fiscal or governmental capacity of our states.

Federalism and the urban crisis

"There has in fact never been a time when federal, state, and local functions were separate and distinct."[9] The national government has long been involved in what was often thought to be the primary preserve of the state and local governments. But today the national government is involved deeply and comprehensively in every aspect of American society. This involvement of the national government in the lives and af-

[9]Morton Grodzins, "Centralization and Decentralization in the American Federal System," in Robert A. Goldwin, ed., *A Nation of States* (Rand McNally, 1963), pp. 6–7. See also Martha Derthick, *Between State and Nation: Regional Organizations of the United States* (Brookings Institution, 1974); and Daniel J. Elazar, *The American Partnership: Intergovernmental Cooperation in the Nineteenth Century United States* (University of Chicago Press, 1962).

fairs of our states and cities has come about through the use and modification of an old technique—the grant-in-aid. And the scope of national involvement has added complications and confusions to intergovernmental relations; it is bringing new dimensions to old political conflicts.

THE TRADITIONAL GRANT SYSTEM

Prior to the Great Depression of the 1930s, Congress provided some funds to the states for such clearly national functions as the building of post roads. Then during the Depression fourteen programs were added to cover such new services as welfare, employment assistance, public and child health care, public housing, and school lunches. From the end of World War II to the 1960s more programs were established: for example, airports, hospitals, urban renewal, and library services.

By the beginning of the Kennedy Administration there were forty-four federal grant programs. In most instances the national government provided funds to the states by a formula, so much going to each state. Grants of this kind were conditional: each state that wanted to participate in a program had to put up some of its own funds to match the fed-

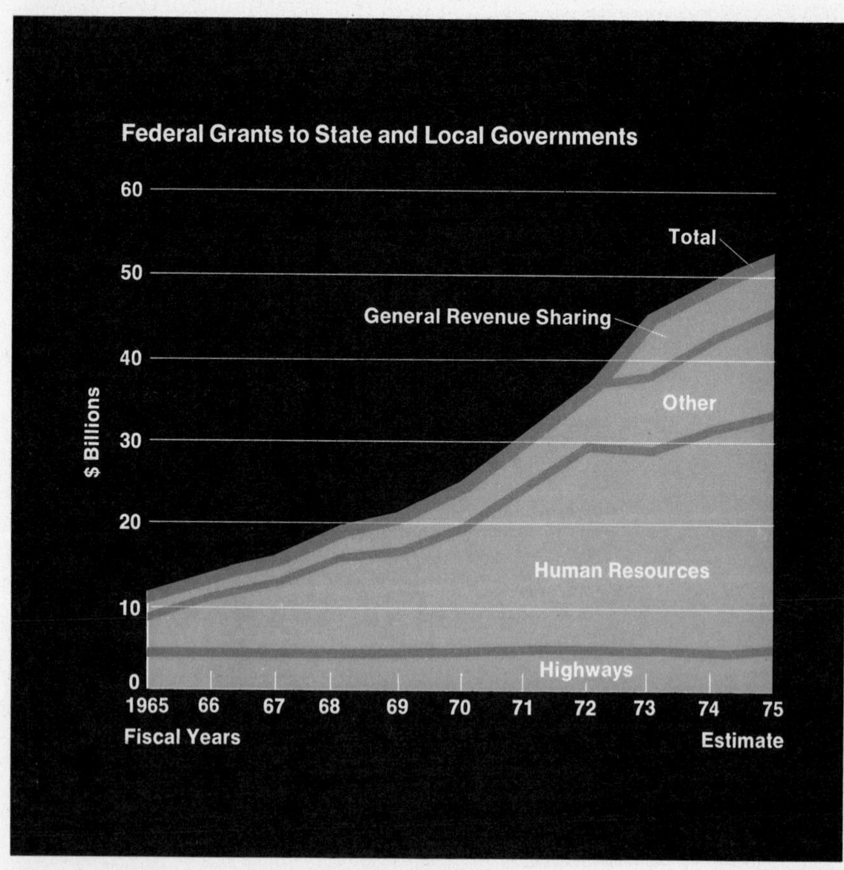

eral grant, agree to establish agencies to expend the funds, submit plans for advance approval, permit inspection by national officials of the completed work, and place the employees who administered the grant under a merit system. Although Congress determined for what purposes states received federal funds, governors and state legislators had an active role in determining how the programs were implemented. Except for highways and welfare services, federal dollars were not then a sizable proportion of state and local spending.

THE PROJECT GRANT SYSTEM

The 1960s brought an explosion of federal programs. Faced with demands from local communities, especially from our big cities, Congress responded with billions to build houses, provide urban transportation, get rid of slums, fight crime, clean up air and water, provide health insurance for the aged. Rural areas such as Appalachia were also provided federal dollars. In the ten-year period of the 1960s, federal grants in dollar terms increased by 189 percent.

Today the state and local governments are receiving from the national government about 23 percent of the money they are spending. The national government is turning back to the states and local communities about 17 percent of the federal tax revenues. Twenty-one national departments and agencies are administering over 400 separate grant programs for the benefit of fifty states, 78,000 local units of government, and millions of individuals. There are so many federal grant programs that some local governments have specialized personnel with computers just to keep track of them. The Advisory Commission on Intergovernmental Relations found that the number of grant catalogs being issued about federal programs was "proliferating to the point" that it published a catalog of catalogs. It covers nine single-spaced pages.[10]

Most of the programs launched since 1960 do not distribute funds to states automatically according to a set formula. Rather they establish project grants—an approach under which state or local agencies applying for federal assistance prepare applications, submit them to the nearest federal regional office—"and hope for the best."[11] Eligibility to receive a federal grant in some programs is extended to nongovernmental agencies, including individuals. And for many of the programs the federal government supplies all the funds. The project grant approach permits Congress and the national administration to decide where the money is most needed. They can bypass state governments and place the money directly "on the target."

[10]Advisory Commission on Intergovernmental Relations, *Eleventh Annual Report* (U.S. Government Printing Office, 1970), p. 3.

[11]*Ibid.*, p. 2.

DIRECT FEDERALISM

Federal officials have dealt directly with city and country officials since the early nineteenth century. But not until the Great Depression, not really until the urban crisis of the sixties and seventies, did federal-city relations become significant in terms of either dollars or politics. As the urban crisis came to the forefront of domestic politics, the president and the Congress became increasingly responsive to urban values and demands. Today there are at least seventy programs that directly relate to big-city issues.

Most of the newer federal programs bypass the state governments, and because of the belief that "the poor and the black—especially the latter—would never get a fair shake from State governments, especially in the South,"[12] some have been framed to minimize state participation. Some have even attempted to circumvent City Hall and deal directly with agencies created to represent the poor.

"The expansion of direct federalism has given local governments unmistakable status as a third component of the system. The national government has become the champion of the cities in attacking the tough urban problems produced by density and poverty. The states remain vital partners in the system, but their future is in question."[13]

Governors and state legislators, of course, do not like to see federal funds go directly to city officials. On the other hand, city officials favor such assistance—provided they have control over it. When Congress authorized federal grants to community action groups outside the structure of local governments in order to involve poor people in the administration of antipoverty programs, city officials complained about being bypassed just as loudly as had state officials. Congress responded by returning antipoverty programs to local authorities.

Many large cities—actually city-states in many respects—have more influence within the circles of the national government than they do in their own state legislatures, which are dominated by rural and suburban representatives. President Eisenhower told the Conference of State Governors, "Today, for help in urban problems, committees of Mayors are far more likely to journey to Washington than to their own state capitals."[14] Mayor Richard Daley of Chicago told a congressional committee, "I think a city the size of Chicago should be able to go directly to its Federal Government with its programs, because we find in many instances the greater responsiveness and greater understanding."[15] And

[12]Advisory Commission on Intergovernmental Relations, *Metropolitan America: Challenge to Federalism* (U.S. Government Printing Office, 1966), p. 3.

[13]John M. DeGrove, "Help or Hindrance to State Action? The National Government," in Alan K. Campbell, ed., *The States and the Urban Crisis* (Prentice-Hall, 1970), p. 151.

[14]Address by the President at the 1957 Governors' Conference, *Report of the Joint Federal–State Action Committee* (U.S. Government Printing Office, 1957), p. 20.

[15]*Hearings on Federal–State–Local Relations before a Subcommittee of the House Committee on Government Operations*, 85th Cong., 1st sess., 1957, p. 391.

former Mayor Stokes of Cleveland stated simply, "Why run to the federal government? Because that's where the money is."[16]

THE GRANT SYSTEM IN TRANSITION

The vast proliferation of grants during the 1960s brought increasing confusion and uncertainty. Faced with what they called a "management mess," angry that they had been granted no voice in so many programs, governors began to insist that Washington accord them a more direct role in the grant system. Mayors, although not eager to see governors given any greater involvement, nonetheless pressed for a more coherent and adequately funded program of federal assistance.

The Nixon Administration responded with a variety of moves to simplify and unify federal grant programs. The Office of Management and Budget issued orders giving state, and in some instances city, authorities a chance to comment before federal grants were made within their respective jurisdictions. And to secure greater coherence in the field, the president ordered most federal agencies to decentralize into ten regional headquarters. In each region there is a Federal Regional Council, and each council is chaired by a presidential designee. These Federal Regional Councils are to work with governors and local executives in developing coordinated federal programs as they apply to each respective region.

But of a more fundamental nature, President Nixon proposed to drastically shift the federal grant system. He recommended that we move away from detailed categorical grants—in which Congress and federal administrative authorities stipulate in considerable detail how the funds shall be used—to programs that give more discretion to state and local officials.

The most unconditional type of grants are called *general* revenue-sharing grants. Here Congress merely turns over tax dollars to state and local governments with few or even no strings. *Special* revenue-sharing grants would consolidate existing programs into broad areas; for example, subventions would be given to the states and local governments for urban community development, education, manpower training, law enforcement, transportation, and so on. *Block* grants are somewhat narrower in focus but still bring together detailed categorical grants into larger units that give state and local units more discretion in their use.

For more than a decade, Congress considered revenue-sharing proposals of various kinds, block grants, and a variety of other ways to give money to the states with fewer strings attached. But action was slow. Congressmen who control federal appropriations and federal administrators who administer them are reluctant to see any changes made in the federal grant system, and in this they have had the powerful support of the groups who benefit from the existing arrangements. But

[16]*Chicago Tribune*, March 4, 1968.

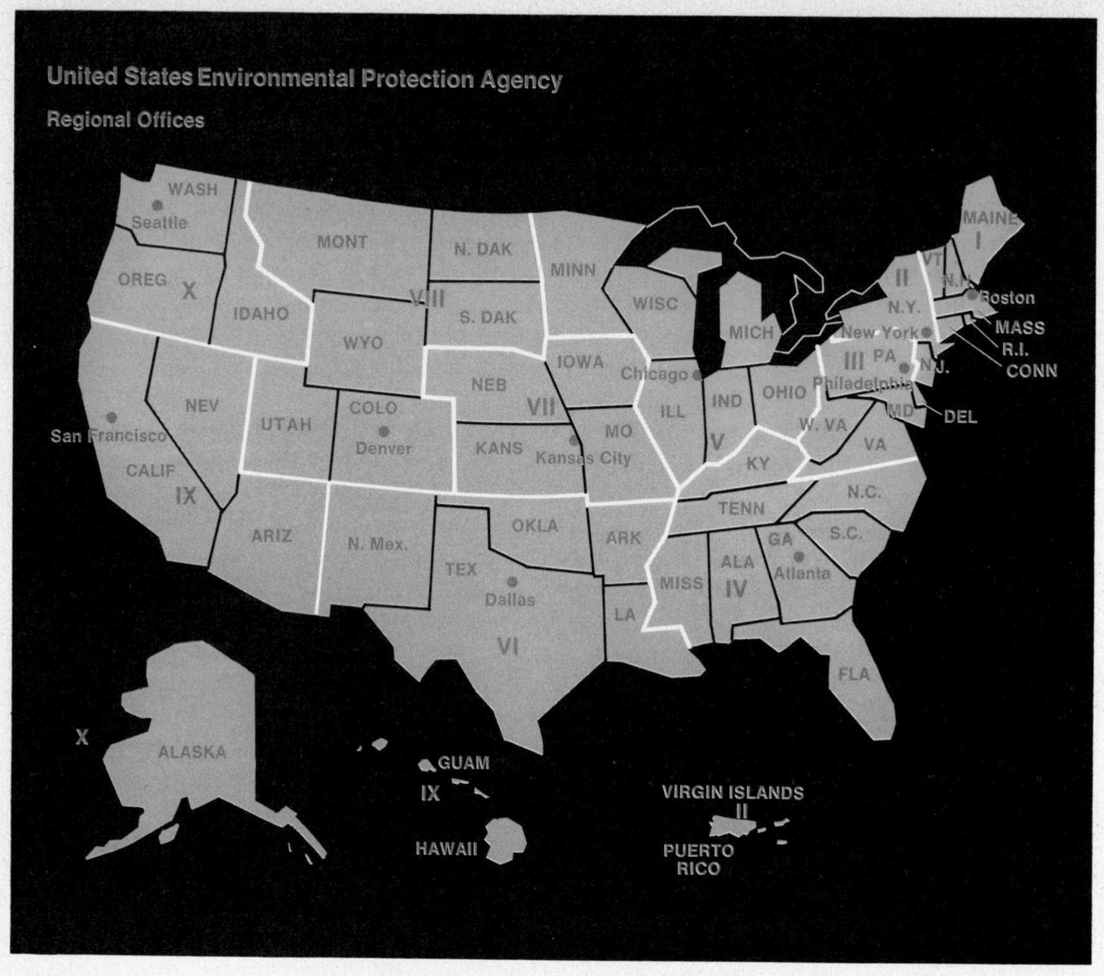

some progress was made. In 1966 Congress consolidated a dozen separate public health programs into the Partnership in Health Act that gives funds to each state subject only to the approval of a state plan by the United States Surgeon General. The Crime Control and Safe Streets Act of 1968 provides block grants to the states with the stipulation that a certain percentage of the money be passed on to local governments. By the middle of the 1970s, Congress had also consolidated some categorical grant programs in education and manpower training into larger and more comprehensive blocks.

However, President Nixon wanted to move faster. He asked Congress to give him the authority to consolidate existing categorical programs subject only to veto by Congress. This technique, which has been used during the last several decades to reorganize executive agencies, would have put the initiative for altering the form of federal grants in the hands of an office somewhat less accessible than the Congress to those who favor the status quo. But Congress refused to delegate such authority to the president. The most it would do in this area was to adopt the 1968 Intergovernmental Cooperation Act that provides more flexibility in the administration of federal grants.

REVENUE-SHARING

In view of congressional reluctance to approve block grants and its refusal, so far, to approve special revenue-sharing, many were surprised when in the fall of 1972 Congress did approve *general* revenue-sharing. Undoubtedly it did so because the State and Local Fiscal Assistance Act of 1972, while providing state and local governments with more dollars, by itself did not threaten any existing program. (After the adoption of the act, the Nixon Administration tried to impound federal funds authorized and appropriated by other federal programs, in part on the grounds that revenue-sharing provides a substitute for them. In most instances federal courts upheld those who challenged the president's authority to withold funds appropriated by Congress.)

The 1972 Fiscal Assistance Act provides funds to be drawn from a five-year authorization and appropriation beginning with over $5 billion in 1972 and scheduled to increase to almost $6.5 billion in 1976. Two-thirds of the funds are going to nearly 38,000 general-purpose units of local governments; the other third to the states. Other than the general constitutional and legal restriction that none of these federal funds can be used to support any programs that discriminate against any person because of race, national origin, or sex, the only limit on the federal dollars is that the funds cannot be used to match other federal grant programs. Local governments also face a very general limitation that the money must be spent on "priority expenditures." Priority expenditures are very broadly defined to cover public safety, environmental protection, public transportation, health, recreation, libraries, social services for the poor or aged, and financial administration.

Many argued that the money should not be given to state and local governments unless they first adopted certain procedural and structural reforms—for example, merit systems, modern accounting practices, consolidation of small units. But the act contains no such conditions and provides that all general-purpose governmental units are eligible to participate. "The unwanted effect will be, at least to some extent, to freeze the existing governmental structure and to prop it up, without regard to its viability."[17]

NEW FEDERALISM, PROS AND CONS

As is true of most debates over governmental structure, the arguments

[17]Advisory Commission on Intergovernmental Regulations, *14th Annual Report. Striking a Better Balance: Federalism in 1972* (U.S. Government Printing Office, 1973), p. 6.

about revenue-sharing and about the Nixon–Ford New Federalism, involve more than just considerations of efficiency and economy. There are also basic differences about what is desirable public policy and most importantly, differing anticipations of who will gain or lose by the various procedures. Michael D. Reagan, a scholar of federalism and an opponent of revenue-sharing, argues that Congress and federal administrators are more likely to put the money where it is most needed—that is, largely in the cities. He does not trust state and local officials. He put it very directly: "State governments are structurally inadequate and politically weak even when they are not actually corrupt."[18] Vernon E. Jordan, Jr., executive director of the National Urban League, contends that revenue-sharing will hurt the blacks and other disadvantaged groups. Revenue-sharing, he writes, "would take present programs out of the purview of competent and relatively sympathetic federal agencies and turn their funds over to state and local government for uses that may not be as relevant to the needs of the minority community. . . . I have little faith in the competence and record of fifty state governments and thousands of local governments to make humane judgments and institute responsible programs. And I fear that many agencies, most of them small community groups, will be left out in the cold, with the result that the black and minority communities will suffer tragically."[19]

Proponents of revenue-sharing argue to the contrary. They insist that for the first time in decades states and cities will have the funds to permit them to govern. Their weaknesses, they argue, have stemmed from inflexible financial resources. They contend that the record hardly establishes that federal categorical programs are always effective in putting the dollars where the need is greatest. "Under the present project grant system, distributions appear to have been heavily influenced by skillful local administrators, powerful Congressmen, and the desire of federal administrators to spread funds broadly to build a base of political support for their program."[20] These things, rather than the amount of poverty in a city or some objective determination of need, seem to affect how the present system operates.

Elazar argues, "I do not doubt that, in some places, greater local responsibility for making and administering public policy will engender results that liberals . . . will find disagreeable. In other places, the result will be just as disturbing to conservatives. . . . " But he concludes, "Today there is simply no justification for thinking that the states and localities, either in principle or in practice, are less able to do the job than the federal government."[21]

[18]Michael D. Reagan, *The New Federalism* (Oxford University Press, 1972), p. 111.

[19]Vernon E. Jordan, Jr., "Local Control Hurts Blacks," *Wall Street Journal* (September 19, 1973), p. 13.

[20]Richard P. Nathan and Martha Derthick, "Local Control Helps Everyone," *Wall Street Journal* (September 10, 1973), p. 12.

[21]Daniel J. Elazar, "The New Federalism: Can the States Be Trusted?" *Public Interest* (Spring 1974), p. 102.

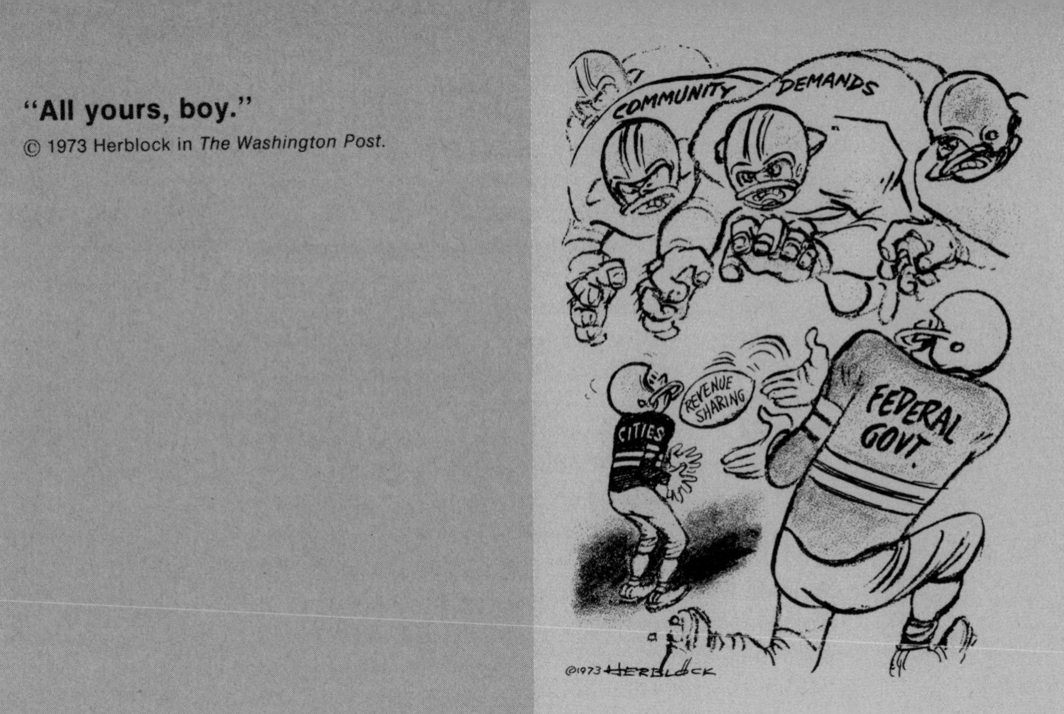

"All yours, boy."

© 1973 Herblock in *The Washington Post.*

Aaron Wildavsky, who appears to be more or less neutral about revenue-sharing, predicts that a consequence of revenue-sharing will be to blur further the responsibility "for not solving our latest set of insoluble problems." He writes "Cities are now beginning to understand that they are getting a little money and a lot of trouble. Increasingly they become the center of demand and lack the capacity to respond. . . . The consequence, of course, need not be all bad: people with demands to make will find it more worthwhile to approach the cities and states because these will have more to give."[22]

Closely related to the debate over whether or not state and local governments can be trusted to spend federal dollars at their own discretion is the concern over which state and local authorities are to be given the responsibility for deciding how the funds are to be spent. Most proponents of revenue-sharing have promoted the idea that the funds should be given to the *elected state* and *local officials*, especially the governors and the mayors, and the generalists who report to them, rather than to *functional specialists* such as health administrators, education officials, welfare agents, and so on. For the arguments about the forms of grants involve much more than mere differences between national officials on one side and state and local officials on the other. More often the battles are between elected state and local officials who favor no-strings-attached federal grants to themselves, and on the other side national, state, and local administrative specialists who favor federal grants only to programs controlled by professional specialists like themselves.

[22]Aaron Wildavsky, "Government and the People," *Commentary*, 56 (August 1973), 28.

Specialists, such as highway officials, welfare authorities, educators, are likely to have more in common with each other, whether they work for the national government or a state or local agency, than with the elected officials of their respective governments. These specialists get together at professional meetings, read common journals, and jointly defend the "independence" of their programs from the attempts by elected officials to regulate them. They have politically powerful allies on citizen advisory committees and in other client groups who work to keep their particular special programs "out of politics"—that is, not subject to control by governors or mayors or state legislators or city councils. Their "independence" is well secured if there is a federal grant program providing funds directly to the specialists and subject to being spent only in their area.

These alliances among specialists, or "guilds," as Harold Seidman calls them, are a kind of fourth branch of government. It is a branch, Senator Muskie has charged, that "has no direct electorate, operates from no set perspective, is under no special control, and moves in no particular direction."[23] We condemn governors and mayors, writes Seidman, "for their failure to prescribe cures for urban blight, substandard housing, pollution, poverty, and crime; but in too many cases we deny them the means to take remedial action" by directing federal funds to agencies not subject to their jurisdiction. "In contrast to governors and mayors," Seidman continues, "the guilds are supported by strong powerful bases within the federal establishment and have developed a close rapport with functionally oriented congressional committees. They have a capacity to block or delay reform measures which they suspect contain hidden traps."[24]

How have block grants and revenue-sharing worked? The results so far from the block grant programs have not been particularly encouraging even to those who advocate them. In public health Congress has already started to recategorize them and it has provided for special programs in the areas of kidney diseases, cancer, and communicable disease control for migrant agricultural workers. Nor did the block grant system in public health work, as hoped, to strengthen the role of governors. In many states, authority to administer the state health program was granted to an agency removed from the direct administrative supervision of the governor. The 1968 Crime Control Act block grant feature has also not been lacking for critics. The Law Enforcement Assistance Administration (LEAA), the federal agency created within the Department of Justice to administer the program, has been accused by congressional and other critics of failing to monitor properly state programs, and the states have been accused by some of spending an

[23]Senate Committee on Government Operations, Subcommittee on Intergovernmental Relations, *The Federal System as Seen by State and Local Officials* (U.S. Government Printing Office, 1963), p. 2.

[24]Harold Seidman, *Politics, Position, and Power: The Dynamics of Federal Organization* (Oxford University Press, 1970), pp. 158, 162.

inordinate amount of money on hardware. Other block grant programs in education and manpower are too recently established to permit evaluation of their consequences.

General revenue-sharing has just started, but its opponents contend that the states and cities are wasting the funds. Proponents, however, contend that revenue-sharing is already beginning to revitalize state and local units by giving them the funds they need to meet their responsibilities. The Advisory Commission on Intergovernmental Relations has the responsibility to monitor the impact of revenue-sharing. ACIR's first report suggests that states are using some of the moneys for tax relief and that local governments, especially the smaller ones, because of uncertainty that the funds will continue to be available, prefer to use them for buildings and other kinds of capital projects rather than for new operating programs that would have to be supported with fresh dollars year after year. However, as ACIR concludes, "Any definitive evaluation of the program would have to await the experience of at least a few more years. . . ."[25]

It would be misleading to give too much emphasis to the form of federal financing. Those who look to revenue-sharing to revitalize state and local units and to provide for more coordinated and coherent programming are likely to be disappointed, as will those who fear it will dismantle the federally managed welfare state. The form of federal funding is simply not that important. Organizational behavior, political climate, and bargaining among groups and political units are more likely to determine policy than are the source and flexibility of funding, although the latter factor obviously does make some difference.[26]

FEDERAL GRANT PROGRAMS: SOME QUESTIONS

It is important to understand the contemporary debates within the nation, the Congress, and the political science fraternity about modernizing, or at least changing, the federal grant system. It is also important to keep in mind some of the bigger questions scholars are just beginning to ask but are not yet able to answer. Among these are the following:

What is the *flow* of *influence?* From the national government to state and local governments or vice versa? Murphy, for example, found that the fear of federal dominance of state educational programs has been caused by a misperception of power relationships in education. "If anything, research suggests that the states' problem is not federal control, but rather local autonomy."[27]

Does the fact that states and local governments can get federal funds

[25]Advisory Commission on Intergovernmental Relations, *15th Annual Report, The Year in Review* (U.S. Government Printing Office, 1974), p. 4.

[26]Jerome T. Murphy, "Title V of ESEA: The Impact of Discretionary Funds on State Educational Bureaucracies," *Harvard Educational Review*, 43 (August 1973), 384–85.

[27]*Ibid.*, p. 367.

make them more or less responsive to *particular constituents?* Does the amount and kind of federal funding available alter the kinds of constituents to which state and local units will respond?

Does the federal grant system help to maintain and reinforce *regional pluralism* by enabling local majorities who control state and local governments to pursue their goals independently of the wishes of the national majorities? Or does it work the other way—that is, are federal grants used by the national majorities to bring state and local governments, and the groups to which they respond, under the control of national majorities? Certainly federal funds have been important levers in forcing states and cities and local school districts to adopt desegregation programs, in compelling universities and other federal contracting agencies to take affirmative action to hire and upgrade employment opportunities for women, blacks, and other victims of discrimination. On the other hand, the greater the number of dollars and the fewer the federal controls, the more states, cities, school districts, housing authorities, and other local units can do what the *local majority* wants done rather than what Congress, the federal agencies, and those to whom they respond want done.

These are important questions of political science and of politics. The answers involve analysis of evidence of what has happened and is likely to happen. Even more, they involve choices as to the kind of society we want and knowledge of the kinds of procedures that are most likely to produce it.

STATES AND THE URBAN CRISIS

One close student of the subject, after a hard look at the states, came to the conclusion that we might as well give up on them as instruments to solve urban problems. In many states he found a distrust of big-city government, a rural orientation, a provincial outlook, a spirit of nostalgia. He believes that the only hope is to work to strengthen the link between the federal government and the cities.[28] And the Advisory Commission on Intergovernmental Relations, a federal agency with an important involvement by state officials, has warned, "The States are on verge of losing control over the metropolitan problem: if they lose this control they lose the major responsibility for domestic government in the United States and in turn surrender a vital role in the American Federal System."[29]

The prediction that the states are doomed is not new: In 1933, Luther Gulick, seeing state governments helpless before the onslaught of the Great Depression, stated, "I do not predict that the States will go, but

[28]Roscoe C. Martin, *The Cities and the Federal System* (Atherton Press, 1965), p. 77.

[29]*Eighth Annual Report of the Advisory Commission on Intergovernmental Relations* (U.S. Government Printing Office, 1967), p. 9.

affirm that they have gone."[30] Thirty years later, Senator Dirksen intoned that before too long, "The only people interested in state boundaries will be Rand-McNally."[31]

In many states reapportionment, which had been expected to increase the voice of the big cities, led rather to an alliance of the suburbs, rural areas, and small towns against those who live in the inner cities. As former Mayor Stokes of Cleveland complained, "One man-one vote hasn't changed a thing so far as the central city is concerned. Instead of the farmer with his conservatism and detachment, you now have the man from suburbia, who is as conservative and detached, and sometimes as hostile to the city, as the rural member."[32] Suspicion and conflict are characteristic of the relations between many governors and the mayors of the big cities. Many states lack governmental structures to permit mobilization of resources to attack social issues; many lack the political will to do so.

On the other hand, there are signs that hard political realities are beginning to result in a revitalization of the state role in the handling of urban problems. As the problems of pollution, crime, poverty, lack of jobs, and underfinanced schools—which have long plagued the urban poor—are also being felt in the suburbs, governors and state legislators are becoming more and more involved with these issues. More than half of the states, including all those with large cities, now have special agencies to deal with urban problems. Many states are now helping local governments construct sewage-treatment plants, improve mass transportation, and provide more adequate housing.

Our metropolitan areas are also discovering that even with federal funding they need help from their own state houses. The 228 metropolitan areas in the United States are governed on the average by ninety-one different governments, some by as many as a thousand. With authority so scattered among the central city and its suburbs and special purpose districts, they are looking to the states to help reorganize their governmental systems.

As Daniel R. Grant observes, "The best political guess . . . is a highly mixed bag with contents varying all the way from states which continue the present tradition of grudging involvement and passive indifference, to a small and select group of states which take the bull by the horns and restructure metropolitan government. . . ."[33] It is likely that we shall see a "differential approach to federal-state relations." At present, when federal programs are being designed, for example, to deal

[30] "Reorganization of the States," *Civil Engineering* (August 1933), p. 421; quoted by Terry Sanford in *Storm Over the States* (McGraw-Hill, 1967), p. 21.

[31] *New York Times* (August 8, 1965), section IV, p. 2; quoted by Sanford, *ibid.*, p. 37.

[32] Quoted by A. James Reichley, "The Political Containment of the Cities," in Campbell, *The States and the Urban Crisis*, p. 173.

[33] Daniel R. Grant, "Urban Needs and State Response," in Campbell, *ibid.*, p. 83.

with problems of poverty, any suggestion that states be given a role in their administration is likely to be met with the question, "Do you want to give that kind of power to George Wallace?"[34] In the future it may be that a state that establishes a strong program to assist the cities will be given a greater voice in the administration of federal programs than one where the administrative capacity is lacking or where leadership is hostile to the objectives to be accomplished.

Although Americans have strong attachments to their states, their concerns are with more immediate problems—clean air, equal rights, jobs, safety in the streets. They are willing to use whatever agencies or combinations thereof they feel can best serve their needs and represent their interests. Federal-state-local relations now as always are undergoing change. As Tocqueville noticed over a hundred years ago, "I have never been more struck by the good sense and the practical judgment of the Americans than in the manner in which they elude the numberless difficulties resulting from their Federal Constitution."[35]

The future of federalism

There are some who consider federalism a midway station between a confederation and a unitary state. These critics argue that modern techniques of transportation and communication have destroyed the barriers of time and distance that originally gave rise to federalism. In short, they insist that federalism has become obsolete.

Harold J. Laski, the late British political scientist, socialist writer, and critic of American federalism, argued that federalism

> is insufficiently positive in character; it does not provide for sufficient rapidity of action; it inhibits the emergence of necessary standards of uniformity; it relies upon compacts and compromises which take insufficient account of the urgent category of time; it leaves the backward areas a restraint, at once parasitic and poisonous, on those which seek to move forward. . . .[36]

Laski charged that our national government lacks the constitutional authority to control vested business interests and that the state governments are reluctant to regulate them lest these business interests withdraw their patronage and go elsewhere. He predicted that public pressures would force positive national action, eventually leading to the abandonment of federalism. But Laski was not so much predicting the end of our federal system as he was arguing for its abolition. Favoring

[34]Sundquist and Davis, *Making Federalism Work*, p. 271.

[35]*Democracy in America*, ed. Phillips Bradley (Knopf, 1944), I, 167.

[36]"The Obsolescence of Federalism," *The New Republic*, (May 3, 1939), pp. 367–69.

more vigorous national regulation of business and more positive government management of the economy, he believed that the federal system stood in the way of achieving these goals.

William H. Riker agrees with Laski that federalism benefits economic interests, but he concludes that these benefits "pale beside the significance of the benefits to Southern segregationist whites . . . who have been given the freedom to oppress Negroes, first as slaves and later as a depressed caste. . . . The judgment to be passed on federalism in the United States is therefore a judgment on the values of segregation and racial oppression."[37]

Daniel J. Elazar comes to a different conclusion. He finds that all the traditional arguments in favor of federalism are demonstrated by American experience and that federalism as it operates in the United States is stronger than ever. He concludes, "In sum, the virtue of the federal system lies in its ability to develop and maintain mechanisms vital to the perpetuation of the unique combination of governmental strength, political flexibility, and individual liberty, which has been the central concern of American politics."[38] And rather than finding federalism to be obsolete, a transitional stage in governmental development, Carl J. Friedrich, a renowned student of the subject, asserts: "Whenever democratization and industrialization reach an advanced stage, the demand for effective decentralization and/or federalization becomes insistent, as new groups discover their distinctive identity. Short of general anarchy, federalizing such communities appears to be the only solution; sometimes in the interest of greater unity, at other times in the interest of greater diversity."[39]

Perhaps we attribute to federalism difficulties for which it is only partly responsible. We are a nation of continental proportions with a rich variety of sections and groups. Even if the federal form of government were abolished tomorrow, there would still be a South and a New England. Giant capitalists and trade unionists would remain strong, and white supremacists would still oppose the passage and enforcement of civil rights laws. Even without federalism there would be local units of government, and local majorities would use these units to resist national majorities. True, the ideology of states' rights and the general support for federalism have permitted segregationists and others who dominate state governments to work for their goals in the name of local self-government, but such appeals are not unknown in governments that operate under the unitary forms. And as far as the constitutional structure of federalism is concerned, today the national government has all the constitutional power it needs to deal with virtually every problem of national scope.

[37]*Federalism: Origin, Operation, Significance* (Little, Brown, 1964), pp. 152–53.

[38]*American Federalism*, p. 227.

[39]*Trends of Federalism in Theory and Practice* (Praeger, 1968), p. viii.

Federalism today: a summary

Federalism is a political system influencing which groups achieve which goals through which levels of government. Over time the national government has expanded in response to nationwide unification, social trends, and economic problems, and also to the inadequacies of the states. Today the national government grants many billions annually to state and local governments; just how this money is distributed, to which lower governments, and with what federal "strings" is a hot political issue. The cities in particular are demanding easier access to federal money, and more of it. Federalism, despite all its complexities and failings, is still a vital and dynamic system.

Federalism is also a continuing controversial issue in American politics. Those pluralists who believe representative democracy should divide power widely among many independent governments believe in the system and would like to reform and strengthen it. Some elite-theorists see federalism as a device that so divides power as to *atomize* it; behind the facade of federalism, they contend, financial, military, and other powerful elites gain their ends because they can employ private *concentrated* power against public *dispersed* power. They cannot do this, some pluralists reply, because the elites themselves are divided by the pervasive force of American social pluralism and governmental federalism.

Part Three Civil liberties and citizenship

A PROBLEM GUIDE

How can we maintain the proper balance between liberty and order, between diversity and uniformity, between individual rights and collective needs? This is the main problem taken up in Part Three. To many Americans the safeguarding and broadening of individual freedom—of civil liberties and civil rights—is the most important task of a democratic society. These are the lofty and historic rights of the Western tradition—freedom of religion, freedom of speech, freedom of assembly, freedom of the press, equality under the law.

When we think of protecting these freedoms of the individual, we usually think of protecting them *against* government. But in a democracy the protection of the rights of the individual against the government is only part of the problem (though probably the major part). A person's freedom from governmental oppression is of little use, after all, except in a peaceful, orderly society. Hence citizens seek to achieve both peace and order, both liberty and equality, through government.

The problem, then, is how to balance individual rights against collective needs, remembering always that individual freedom and social order are necessary to each other. Chapter 6 describes how Americans have tried to achieve this balance in several important areas—freedom of religion and of speech and of the press, for example. Which goals—individual liberties or collective needs—should be the main goals if they come into conflict with each other? When and under what conditions should one or the other receive priority? Who should decide—judges, legislators, or someone else?

We have been talking about individual liberties, such as freedom of speech; there is also the matter of civil rights, such as the right to equal opportunity in education, jobs, housing, and the right to vote. Chapter 7 takes up the constitutional guarantees and political battles behind the idea that no person should suffer because of race, religion, national origin, sex, or other qualities irrelevant to individual merit. In Chapter 8 we describe a different but equally important type of right—the right not to be arbitrarily deprived of life, liberty, and property. Both sets of rights—civil rights and (mainly) procedural rights—pose the problem of the balance of individual rights against collective needs.

Implicit in this discussion is the fact that individual freedom may be threatened directly by other individuals as well as by government. A person trying to speak from a soapbox may be knocked down by a mob and arrested by a police officer. Or the officer may protect him from the mob—a case of government guarding the liberty of one individual against other individuals. It is always advisable, when considering a problem of individual freedom, to ask the question *Whose* civil liberties are to be protected, against *what*, by *whom*, and *how*?

Chapter 8 also deals with the rights of immigrants, aliens, and citizens. The Constitution does not guarantee the right of admission to the United States; aliens do not enjoy all the privileges of American citizens. But important issues of liberty are involved in our treatment of noncitizens.

Chapter 6 The first amendment and the first freedoms

"Congress shall make no law," declares the First Amendment, "respecting an establishment of religion, or prohibiting the free exercise thereof; or abridging the freedom of speech, or of the press; or the right of the people peaceably to assemble, and to petition the Government for a redress of grievances." Here in bold and imposing terms are the fundamental supports of a free society—freedom of *conscience* and freedom of *expression.*

Although the framers drafted the Constitution, in a sense it was the people who drafted our basic charter of liberties. The Constitution drawn up at Philadelphia included no specific guarantee of the basic freedoms—an omission that aroused suspicion and distrust among the people at large. In order to win ratification, the Federalists promised to correct this oversight, and in the very first session of the new Congress they lived up to their promise. Congress proposed amendments that were ratified by the end of 1791 and became part of the Constitution. These ten amendments are known as the Bill of Rights.

Note that the Bill of Rights is addressed to the *national* government. As John Marshall held in *Barron v. Baltimore* (1833), the Bill of Rights limits the national but not the state governments. Why not the states? In the 1790s the people were confident they could control their own state officials, and most of the state constitutions already had bills of rights. It was the new and distant central government that the people feared.

But as it turned out, those popular apprehensions of 1790 were largely misplaced. The national government, responsive to tens of millions of voters from a variety of races, creeds, religions, and economic groups, has shown less tendency to curtail civil liberties than have state and local governments. It was not long after the Bill of Rights was adopted that some people began to recognize the mistake of exempting state governments from the prohibitions of the national Bill of Rights. True, each state constitution also includes a bill of rights, but for the most part state judges have not been inclined to apply these bills of rights vigorously to protect civil liberties.

With the adoption of the Fourteenth Amendment in 1868, which *does* apply to the states, litigants tried to persuade the Supreme Court to construe the due-process clause of this amendment to mean that the states are limited in the same way that the Bill of Rights limits the national government. At a minimum, they contended, freedom of speech should be brought within the confines of the Fourteenth Amendment. For decades the Supreme Court refused to interpret the Fourteenth Amendment in this way. Then in 1925, in *Gitlow v. New York,* the Supreme Court announced: "For present purposes we may and do assume that freedom of speech and of press—which are protected and liberties protected by the due process clause of the Fourteenth Amendment from impairment by the states." *Gitlow v. New York* was a decision of major, almost revolutionary significance. Since that date, beginning in the 1940s and at a rapid rate in the 1960s, the Supreme Court has brought within the protection of the Fourteenth Amendment almost every applicable provision of the Bill of Rights (see pp. 245–48).

Today virtually all Americans agree that governmental power should not be used to interfere with the freedoms of speech and conscience. Yet the country seems to be almost constantly involved in quarrels about specific applications of these restraints. It is all very well to venerate our liberties in general. The trouble arises when we move from generalities to *specifics.* "All declare for liberty," wrote Justice Reed, "and proceed to disagree among themselves as to its true meaning."[1] In few areas are the problems more difficult to resolve and the differences more intense than in that of religious freedoms.

A wall of separation

The very first words of the First Amendment are emphatic, "Congress shall make no law respecting an establishment of religion." The Fourteenth Amendment has been construed to impose the same restrictions on state and local governments.

[1] *Breard v. Alexandria* (1951).

Some have argued that this Establishment Clause does not forbid governmental support for religion but simply prohibits *favoritism* toward a particular religion. But the Supreme Court has consistently and unequivocally rejected this construction of the law. As Justice Powell said for the Court, "It is now firmly established that a law may be one 'respecting the establishment of religion' even though its consequence is not to be promote a 'state religion,' and even though it does not aid one religion more than another but merely benefits all religions alike."[2] Or as Justice Black said, "In the words of Jefferson, the clause against establishment of religion by law was intended to erect 'a wall of separation between Church and State.' "[3] On the other hand, "It is equally well established . . . that not every law that confers an 'indirect,' 'remote,' or 'incidential' benefit upon religious institutions is, for that reason alone, constitutionally invalid."[4]

Sometimes the line between the permissible and the forbidden governmental involvement with religion can only be "dimly perceived," and Jefferson's metaphoric "wall of separation" has become "as winding as the famous serpentine wall" he designed for the University of Virginia.[5] But recently the Supreme Court has put forward a three-part test to determine whether a statute violates the Establishment Clause: first, it must reflect a clear secular legislative purpose; second, its primary effect must neither advance nor inhibit religion; third, it must avoid "excessive government entanglement with religion." In other words, the Establishment Clause is designed to prevent three main evils: "sponsorship, financial support, and active involvement of the sovereign in religious activity."[6]

Because of the Establishment Clause, states may not introduce nondenominational devotional exercise into the public school curriculum or the devotional reading of the Bible or the recitation of the Lord's Prayer.[7] A state may not, as Arkansas tried to do, prohibit the teaching of evolution or the use of books discussing the Darwinian theory because it is deemed to conflict with the interpretation of the Book of Genesis.[8] School authorities may not permit religious instructors to come into the public school buildings during the school day to provide religious instruction, even on a voluntary basis.[9] On the other hand, the Constitution does not prevent the study of the Bible or religion in public schools when presented as part of a *secular* program of education.

[2]*Committee for Public Education and Religious Liberty v. Nyquist* (1973).

[3]*Everson v. Board of Education* (1947).

[4]*Committee for Public Education and Religious Liberty v. Nyquist* (1973).

[5]Justice Jackson concurring in *Illinois ex rel McCollum v. Board of Education* (1948).

[6]*Waltz v. Tax Commission* (1970); *Lemon v. Kurtzman* (1971).

[7]*Engel v. Vitale* (1962); *Abington School District v. Schempp* (1963).

[8]*Epperson v. Arkansas* (1968).

[9]*Illinois ex rel McCollum v. Board of Education* (1948).

And a 1952 decision permitting schools to release students from part of the compulsory school day in order to secure religious instruction, provided it takes place outside the school building, has not been reversed, despite what appears to be a conflict between the reasoning in support of this ruling and the since-proclaimed construction of the Establishment Clause.[10]

The Supreme Court has also approved Sunday closing laws. The Court majority, conceding that these laws originally had a religious purpose and effect, reasoned that they have now taken on a secular purpose and effect of providing a day of rest, recreation, and family togetherness.[11]

Not until 1970 did the Supreme Court finally consider the long-established practice of exempting church property from taxation. Chief Justice Burger, speaking for seven members of the Court *(Waltz v. Tax Commission)*, after noting that the exemption applies to other kinds of nonprofit institutions, concluded that it neither advances nor inhibits religions, is neither sponsorship nor hostility, and unlike a direct subsidy does not involve excessive entanglement between church and state—in fact involved *less* entanglement of government with religion than there would be if churches were subject to taxation. In dissent Justice Douglas said that he could not see any constitutional difference between a direct money grant to a church and a tax exemption for it. In his view, both are actually subsidies to religion, and hence unconstitutional.

One of the more troublesome and controversial areas involves the attempt by more than three-fourths of the states to provide some kind of financial assistance to parochial schools. (There are *state* as well as national constitutional restrictions. "More rigid prohibitions against grants of public funds to sectarian schools may be found in thirty-eight state constitutions" than that contained in the national Constitution.)[12] Obviously a state may not grant tax funds to religious schools to teach religion. But proponents have argued that the aid they have given is to the *school children*, not to the religion. And the Supreme Court, using the child-benefit justification, by a five-to-four vote did sustain the payments out of tax funds to reimburse parents for bus fares to send children to church (as well as to public) schools,[13] a decision that has since been characterized by Justice Powell as "approaching the verge of impermissible state aid."[14] The Supreme Court has also approved the use of tax funds to furnish secular textbooks for pupils in private as well

[10]*Zorach v. Clausen.*

[11]*McGawn v. Maryland* (1961).

[12]Carnegie Commission on Higher Education, *The Capitol and the Campus* (McGraw-Hill, 1971), p. 93.

[13]*Everson v. Board of Education* (1947).

[14]*Committee for Public Education v. Nyquist* (1973).

as in public schools,[15] except those private schools that exclude pupils because of race or religion.[16] And the Court found no violation of the Establishment Clause in tax grants and the use of state bonds to permit church-related colleges and universities to build buildings not used for religious purposes or religious exercises.[17] (It is not always clear which colleges are sectarian and which are not.)

In each of these cases the justices recognized that the actions of the state and federal governments might indirectly provide some benefit to religion, but in each instance a majority were persuaded that the programs had a secular purpose and effect, involved no excessive entanglement of government in religion, and chiefly provided benefits for students rather than for religions.

On the other side of the ledger, the Court has ruled that tax funds may not be used to reimburse church-operated elementary and secondary schools or otherwise supplement their financial resources in order to pay for the salaries of teachers even of secular subjects; nor can a state make payments to reimburse such schools for the maintenance and repair of school facilities and equipment designed to enhance the health, welfare, and safety of pupils, nor reimburse these schools for the cost of testing pupils in secular subjects.[18] The Supreme Court has also declared unconstitutional payments to reimburse parents for the tuition they paid to send their children to private schools, the great majority of such schools being sectarian.[19] The Court has also ruled constitutionally impermissible a state rule that allows parents to deduct from their state income taxes payments made to send children to sectarian schools.[20]

How did the Court justify these distinctions? If state funds can be used to pay for secular textbooks used in church schools, why cannot such funds be used to pay for teachers of secular subjects, or for the preparation of school tests? Because, said the justices, "A textbook's content is ascertainable, but a teacher's handling of a subject is not."[21] And, "Routine teacher-prepared texts . . . are 'an integral part of the teaching process' " and there is substantial potential inherent in the situation that the texts will be used "to inculcate students in the religious precepts of the sponsoring church."[22] Although a state may have the appropriate purpose of aiding education and assisting pupils in secular

[15] *Board of Education v. Allen* (1968).

[16] *Norwood v. Harrison* (1973)

[17] *Tilton v. Richardson* (1971).

[18] *Lemon v. Kurtzman* (1971); *Committee for Public Education v. Nyquist* (1973); *Levitt v. Committee for Public Education* (1973).

[19] *Committee for Public Education v. Nyquist* (1973).

[20] *Sloan v. Lemon* (1973).

[21] *Lemon v. Kurtzman* (1971).

[22] *Levitt v. Committee for Public Education* (1973).

learning, when it pays for teachers or gives religious schools funds to prepare texts, there is a substantial risk of the constitutionally fatal effect of tax funds being used to provide religious instruction.

But if it is constitutionally permissible to make grants of public funds to church colleges for buildings, why cannot a state make grants to elementary and secondary schools to maintain and repair facilities? Because, argues the Supreme Court, grants to colleges can readily be limited to buildings that are not to be used to teach religion or for religious exercises, but grants to maintain school facilities are likely to result in the funds being used for facilities to teach religious precepts. Yet, if a state tries to establish procedures to guarantee that maintenance grants only go to facilities that are used for secular teaching, it is likely to run afoul of the "excessive entanglement with religion" doctrine. Furthermore, at the university level, so it is contended, religious indoctrination is less likely to permeate the entire program than it is in elementary and secondary schools. And college students are less impressionable and susceptible to indoctrination, so said four members of the Supreme Court, than are those in high school and grade school.[23] Therefore, capital grants to church-operated colleges for secular buildings run little risk of involving state funds in programs relating to religious instruction. Such grants do not require the state to establish elaborate procedures or to become excessively entangled with religion in order to isolate public funds for secular purposes.

As for the state reimbursing tuition or providing tax exemptions for those who pay tuition for their children to attend church-operated schools, these practices directly provide state aid for religion in contrast to the "indirect and incidential benefits that flowed to sectarian schools for programs aiding all parents by supplying bus transportation and secular textbooks for their children."[24]

In view of the political pressures for aid to parochial schools, the Supreme Court has not said its last word about the constitutionality of the many attempts by states to find constitutional ways to provide assistance, directly or indirectly, to sectarian schools. Indeed, the Supreme Court in 1974 *(Wheeler v. Barrera)* pointed out that Congress in Title I of the Elementary and Secondary Education Act of 1965 left it up to each state to find constitutional ways for children from educationally deprived areas to receive assistance administered by public officials but not to exclude those attending private schools. The Court hinted, without deciding, that if a public school teacher, solely under public control, were sent into a parochial school to teach a special remedial course a few hours a week it might not violate the Establishment Clause.

States will find it difficult, however, to get around the constitutional prohibitions. As Justice Powell has pointed out, "We are not unaware that . . . those who have endeavored to formulate systems of state aid

[23]*Tilton v. Richardson* (1971); *Hunt v. McNair* (1973).

[24]*Sloan v. Lemon* (1973).

to nonpublic education may feel that the decisions of this Court have, indeed, presented them with the 'insoluable paradox.' " If the program makes no attempt to isolate the funds so that they are used only for secular purposes, it runs the risk of failing the effect test; but if the state adopts regulations designed to keep the funds from spilling over into religious activities, it runs the risk of failing the excessive-governmental-entanglement-with-religion part of the test. "But," said Justice Powell, "if novel forms of aid have not readily been sustained by this Court, the 'fault' lies not with the doctrines which are said to have created a paradox, but rather with the Establishment Clause itself. . . ."[25]

Each may worship in his or her own way

The Constitution not only forbids the establishment of religion, but it also enjoins Congress and the states from passing any law "prohibiting the free exercise thereof." "Tensions inevitably exists between the Free Exercise and the Establishment Clause . . . and it may not be possible to promote the former without offending the latter."[26] For example, a law that requires a person to do something that offends his religion might interfere with the free exercise of religion, but to exempt him from the law because of his religious convictions might be to favor religion and offend the Establishment Clause. "The Court has struggled to find a neutral course between the two Religion Clauses, both of which are cast in absolute terms, and either of which, if expanded to a logical extreme, would tend to clash with the other."[27]

The right to hold any or no religious *belief* is absolute, one of the few absolute rights that exists in organized society. One's religious beliefs are inviolable, and no government in the United States has any authority whatsoever to compel the acceptance of or to censor any creed. A state may not compel a religious belief nor deny any person any right or privilege because of his or her beliefs or lack of them. Religious oaths as a condition of public employment or to run for public office are unconstitutional.[28] In fact the only time the Constitution mentions the word "religion" is to state, "no religious test shall ever be required as a Qualification to any Office or public Trust under the United States" (Article VI).

The right to *advocate* one's religion, like the right to advocate anything else, may be curbed only when there is danger that the advocacy will result in immediate and substantial injury to the rights of others.

Although carefully protected, the right to *practice* one's religion has

[25] *Sloan v. Lemon* (1973).

[26] *Committee for Public Education v. Nyquist* (1973).

[27] *Waltz v. Tax Commission* (1970).

[28] *Torcaso v. Watkins* (1961).

less protection than its advocacy or the right to hold particular beliefs. As the Supreme Court has said, "It was never intended that the First Amendment . . . could be invoked as protection against legislation for the punishment of acts inimical to the peace, good order, and morals of society."[29] Religious convictions do not ordinarily exempt one from complying with otherwise valid and nondiscriminatory laws designed to protect the public peace, health, safety, and morals. However, the Supreme Court will scrutinize closely laws that infringe on religious practices and insist upon some compelling public purpose. "Only those interests of the highest order and those not otherwise served can overbalance legitimate claims to the free exercise of religion."[30]

The Supreme Court has upheld laws forbidding the practice of polygamy as applied to Mormons; laws requiring vaccination of school children as applied to Christian Scientists; laws forbidding business activities on Sunday in order to promote health and rest as applied to Orthodox Jews.[31]

On the other hand, the Supreme Court has ruled that a state may not require Jehovah's Witnesses (or for that matter anyone else) to participate in a public school flag salute ceremony.[32] Similarly, parents have a constitutionally protected right to send their children to sectarian schools if they so wish.[33] Moreover, in the face of three centuries of established Amish religious practices, the Supreme Court ruled that Wisconsin could not compel the Amish to send their children to any kind of school beyond the eighth grade (through the eighth grade is within the constitutional power of the state).[34] Nor would the Supreme Court permit a state to deny unemployment compensation to Sabbatarians who refuse to accept positions that require them to work on Saturday.[35] (Here is another example of the tension between the two Religion Clauses: to require those who have religious scruples to work on Saturday or forfeit unemployment compensation interferes with the free exercise of their religion, while to exempt them from the requirement of accepting work on Saturday but not exempt those who have no such religious scruples comes close to giving governmental support to religion.)

What of those who have religious scruples against bearing arms? The Supreme Court has held that such scruples do not give one a constitutional exemption from the draft laws (or from paying taxes), but Congress has chosen to exempt from the military draft persons who by rea-

[29]*Reynolds v. United States* (1879).

[30]*Wisconsin v. Yoder* (1973).

[31]*McGowan v. Maryland* (1961) and cases cited therein.

[32]*Board of Education v. Barnette* (1943).

[33]*Pierce v. Society of Sisters* (1925).

[34]*Wisconsin v. Yoder* (1972)

[35]*Sherbert v. Verner* (1963).

son of religious belief are conscientiously opposed to participating in war. Congress has not exempted, however, those who are against participation on "political, sociological, or philosophical grounds." The Supreme Court, in part to avoid a clash between the Free Exercise and the Establishment Clause, has construed the word religious so broadly that any deeply held humanistic opposition to participate in *any* and *all* wars is included within the congressionally granted exemption. Those who object just to a particular war, however, are not exempt. In World War II, as a result, many Jehovah's Witnesses spent years in prison because they could not meet the test of opposition to all wars. They said they planned to fight in only one, on the day of the final clash between Grace and Reprobation at Armageddon. And in the Vietnam War many failed to win conscientious objector status because their opposition was not to fighting in all wars, but in that particular war.[36]

The Supreme Court's rulings as it tries to accommodate the clashing views about the proper construction of the Religion Clauses always stir up sharp criticism. The cases arouse intense emotions. The problem of drawing the constitutional line is difficult. But in a world where many nations are sharply divided into religious factions, "the amicable accommodation of religious difference in America has been a significant achievement of our political experience.[37]

Free speech and free people

Most democrats assume that government by the people is based on the individual's right to speak freely, to organize in groups, to question the decisions of the government, and to campaign openly against it. Only through free and uncensored expression of opinion can the government be kept responsive to the electorate and can governmental power be transferred peacefully. Elections, separation of powers, and constitutional guarantees are meaningless unless each person has the right to speak frankly and to hear and judge for himself the worth of what others have to say.

Despite the fundamental importance of free speech in a democracy, some people seem to believe that speech should be free only for those who agree with them. Once we leave the level of abstractions and move to the level of specific questions or conflicts, there is a discouragingly low level of support for free speech among the public.[38] If one asks someone whether he believes in freedom of speech or the Bill of Rights,

[36]*Welsh v. United States* (1970); *Gillette v. United States* (1971).

[37] Alan P. Grimes, *Equality in America: Religion, Race, and the Urban Majority* (Oxford University Press, 1964), p. 41.

[38]Samuel Krislov, *The Supreme Court and Political Freedom* (Free Press, 1968), pp. 39 ff., summarizes and cites much of the relevant literature.

the answer wll probably be Yes, but if one asks whether a Communist or a spokesman from General Electric or an advocate of the view that race conditions intelligence should be allowed to speak on a college campus in order to recruit persons to join the Communist party or work for General Electric or be converted to their views, the answer is often No. One study, for example, reported that one out of two persons thought that newspapers should not be permitted, even in peacetime, to criticize the government.[39] Such people ask why evil or ignorant persons should be permitted to spread falsehoods and confuse the minds of others. Why should they be allowed to utter dangerous ideas that stir up trouble among the people or subvert our democratic society?

THE BEST TEST OF TRUTH

Believers in democracy insist on free debate and the unlimited exchange of ideas because they feel that no group has a monopoly on truth, that no group has the right to establish in the field of politics absolute standards of what is true and what is false. A person may be convinced that he is right, that truth is on his side, but in the midst of debate he appeals, not to a philosopher-king, commissar, or oracle of wisdom, but to the power of his reason. As Justice Holmes wrote: "The best test of truth is the power of the thought to get itself accepted in the competition of the market." The insistence on free speech for others stems from the recognition that people are not infallible, that perhaps the other person is right or, at least, that "I might be wrong."

Free speech is not simply the personal right of individuals to have his or her say; it is also the right of the rest of us to hear them. John Stuart Mill, whose *Essay on Liberty* is the classic defense of free speech, put it this way: "The peculiar evil of silencing the expression of opinion, is that it is robbing the human race. . . . If the opinion is right, they are deprived of the opportunity of exchanging error for truth; if wrong, they lose, what is almost as great a benefit, the clearer perception and livelier impression of truth, produced by its collision with error."[40]

Freedom of speech is not merely freedom to express ideas that differ slightly from ours; it is, as the late Justice Jackson said, "freedom to differ on things that go to the heart of the matter." Some people profess to believe in free speech, but they draw the line at ideas they consider abhorrent or dangerous. But what is a dangerous idea? Who decides? The heresies of yesterday are often the orthodoxies of today. In the realm of political ideas, who can find an objective, eternally valid standard of right? The search for truth is an endless one. It involves the possibility—even the inevitability—of error. The search cannot go on un-

[39]CBS Poll, "60 Minutes," April 14, 1970.

[40]John Stuart Mill, "Essay on Liberty," in Edwin A. Burtt, ed., *The English Philosophers from Bacon to Mill* (Modern Library, 1939), p. 961.

less it proceeds unfettered in the minds and speech of men. This means, in the words of Justice Holmes, not only free thought for those who agree with us, "but freedom for the thought we hate."

In short, to forbid the expression of ideas an the ground that they are dangerous is to set oneself up as an infallible judge of what speech should be permitted. Such presumptuousness stifles the fearless exchange of opinions and short-circuits the procedures of democratic government that are protected by the First Amendment. This, at least, is the assumption of democrats.

CONSTITUTIONAL GUARANTEES

Despite the fact that the First Amendment emphatically denies the national government the power to pass any law abridging freedom of speech, the amendment has never been interpreted in such sweeping terms. Liberty of expression is important, but it is not absolute. Like almost all rights, the right to freedom of speech and press is limited by the fact that its free exercise "implies the existence of an organized society maintaining public order without which liberty itself would be lost in the excess of unrestrained abuses."[41] How is the line to be drawn between permissible and unconstitutional restraint on freedom of expression?

In discussing the constitutional power of government to regulate speech, it is useful to distinguish among belief, speech, and action. At one extreme is the right to *believe* as one wishes, a right about as absolute as any can be for people living in organized societies. Despite occasional deviations in practice, the traditional American view is that *thoughts* are inviolable and that no government has the right to punish a person for beliefs or to interfere in any way with freedom of conscience.

At the other extreme from belief is *action,* which is constantly constrained. We may believe it perfectly all right to go sixty miles an hour through an intersection, but if we do so we may be punished. Because one man's action directly affects the liberty and property of others, "his right to swing his arm ends where the other fellow's nose begins."

Speech stands somewhere between belief and action. It is not an absolute, or almost absolute, right as is belief, but it is not so exposed to governmental restraint as is action. There are certain categories of expression—the obscene, the seditious, the libelous, commercial speech, fighting words—where the problem is one of defintion in order to distinguish between what is protected by the First Amendment and what is not. We shall turn shortly to these problems. But what about speech outside of these categories?

[41]*Cox v. New Hampshire* (1941).

THE HOLMES-BRANDEIS CLEAR-AND-PRESENT DANGER TEST

The first test used by the Supreme Court to distinguish between protected and unprotected speech was announced by Justice Holmes in *Schenck v. United States* (1919): "The question in every case is whether the words are used in circumstances and are of such a nature as to create a clear and present danger that they will bring about substantive evils" that Congress had a right to prevent. "Furthermore, no danger flowing from speech can be deemed clear and present," wrote Justice Brandeis (concurring in *Whitney v. California*, 1927), "unless the incidence of the evil is so imminent that it may befall before there is opportunity for full discussion."

Holmes and Brandeis, although conceding that speech is not an absolute right, felt it to be so fundamental that under our Constitution no government has authority to suppress speech or punish a person for what he has said unless the connection between the speech and illegal action is so close that the speech itself takes on the character of the action. The Holmes-Brandeis clear-and-present-danger formula is primarily a rule to determine the sufficiency of the evidence. It requires that before being allowed to punish a person for speaking or writing, a government must prove clearly that the speech presents an imminent danger of a major substantive evil. Note that it is not *any* clear and present danger but only danger of a substantive evil that the government has a right to prevent—for example, rioting, destruction of property, or forceful overthrow of the government.

Let us see how the clear-and-present-danger test might be applied. Suppose a legislature has made it illegal to utter in public scurrilous and abusive remarks about members of another race. Under the clear-and-present-danger doctrine, a person could be punished for making such remarks only if at the trial the government has convincing evidence that the particular remarks clearly and presently might have led to a riot or some other serious substantive evil that the government rightfully may prevent.

THE DANGEROUS-TENDENCY DOCTRINE

Although the clear-and-present-danger doctrine was the first to receive formal Supreme Court support, the dangerous- or bad-tendency doctrine, stemming from the common law, is older, and it too at various times has been the official doctrine of the Court, most notably in *Gitlow v. New York* (1925). According to adherents of the dangerous-tendency doctrine, the Constitution, rather than requiring government to stay its hand until there is a clear and present danger flowing from a particular speech, implies that government may outlaw speech that has a *tendency* to lead to a substantive evil. Furthermore, those who espouse this view contend that it is primarily a legislative and not a judicial responsibility to determine what kinds of speech have a dangerous tendency. Once the legislature has made it a crime to say or write certain things that have a dangerous tendency, persons may be punished for using the forbidden words even if no immediate danger flows from their speech. For the legislature has already decided that such words are dangerous.

Now let us take the example used above and see how those who believe in the dangerous-tendency doctrine would apply it. Since the legislature has already determined that scurrilous and abusive racial remarks are dangerous, and because it is not unreasonable to conclude that such comments have a tendency to stir up riot, they would argue, all that is necessary to convict a person is to show that he in fact made such comments.

THE PREFERRED-POSITION DOCTRINE

Another test, the preferred-position doctrine, was the official view of the Supreme Court during the 1940s and is presently supported by several of the justices. This doctrine is an extension of the clear-and-present-danger formula—indeed, some of its supporters come close to the position that freedom of expression is an absolute right. Those who espouse the preferred-position interpretation believe that the First Amendment freedoms hold the highest priority in our constitutional hierarchy and that courts have a special responsibility to scrutinize with extra care laws trespassing on these freedoms. Whereas legislative majorities are free to experiment and adopt various schemes regulating our economic lives, when they tamper with freedom of speech they close the channels of the political process by which error can be corrected. Any law that on its face limits the First Amendment freedoms is presumed to be unconstitutional. Only if the government can show that limitations on speech are absolutely necessary to avoid extremely imminent and extremely serious substantive evils are such limitations to be tolerated.

If the preferred-position doctrine were applied to our example of a law against abusive racial remarks, the law would be declared unconstitutional. Restraints on such abusive speech are not absolutely necessary to prevent riots, according to this doctrine, and whatever danger may flow from such abusive remarks does not justify a restriction on free comment. Moreover, supporters of the preferred-position doctrine contend that it is not merely the application of this law to a particular speaker that is unconstitutional but that the law itself violates the Constitution.

These three doctrines are subject to a variety of interpretations and applications. And they are not the only formulas that the Supreme Court uses to measure the constitutionality of laws regulating speech. Among the other tests or doctrines or rules of thumb, perhaps the most important are the following:

Prior restraint Of all forms of governmental interference with expression, judges are most suspicious of those that impose restraints prior to publication, including licensing requirements before a speech can be made, a motion picture shown, a newspaper published. The Supreme Court has not gone so far as to declare all forms of prior censorship unconstitutional, but "a prior restraint on expression comes to this Court with a 'heavy presumption' against its constitutionality. . . . The Government thus carries a heavy burden of showing justification for the enforcement of such a restraint."[42]

In the celebrated case *New York Times Company v. United States* (1971) the Supreme Court, by six-to-three vote, held that the government had not met this burden when the attorney general secured a court injunction against the publication by the *Times*, the *Washington Post*, and other newspapers of parts of the Pentagon Papers, a classified study of the "History of U.S. Decision-Making Process on Viet Nam Policy." Although three justices, Black, Douglas, and Brennan, made it clear that in their view the First Amendment forbids a court to impose, however briefly and for whatever reason, any prior restraint on a newspaper, the prevailing view was that in this particular instance the government had failed to show that the publication of these particular documents would cause immediate and specific damage to the nation's security.

In fact the Supreme Court has never approved of any general practice of prior restraint on any medium except motion pictures, and these only to prevent the showing of obscenity. Even in this area there is great suspicion of the censor. As Justice Brennan has pointed out, "Because the censor's business is to censor, there inheres the danger that he may well be less responsive than a court . . . to the constitutionally protected interests in free expression."[43] In practice the censor's views of what the public should be allowed to see may be conclusive. States or cities that wish to subject motion pictures to prior censorship must establish carefully defined standards and provide procedures that ensure swift and easy judicial review of the censor's decisions.[44]

Vagueness Any law is unconstitutional if it "either forbids or requires the doing of an act in terms so vague that men of common intelligence must necessarily guess at its meaning and differ as to its application. . . ."[45] Laws touching First Amendment freedoms are required to meet an even more rigid standard. These laws must not allow those who administer them so much discretion that the administrators could discriminate against those whose views they disapprove. Also the laws must not be so vague that persons are afraid to exercise protected freedoms for fear of running afoul of the law. The Supreme Court has struck down laws that condemn sacrilegious movies or publications of "crimi-

[42]*Organization for a Better Austin v. Keefe* (1971); *Bantam Books Inc. v. Sullivan* (1963).

[43]*Freedman v. Maryland* (1965).

[44]*Teitel Film Corp. v. Cusak* (1968).

[45]*Lanzetta v. New Jersey* (1939)

nal deeds of bloodshed or lust . . . so massed as to become vehicles for inciting violent and depraved crimes" because no one would know for sure what is or is not allowed.[46]

Overbreadth Closely related to the vagueness doctrine and often merging with it is the requirement that a statute relating to First Amendment freedoms cannot be so broad in scope that it sweeps within its prohibitions protected as well as nonprotected activities. For example, a loyalty oath that would endanger protected forms of association as well as illegal activities would be unconstitutional. A legislature must deal more directly and precisely with the kinds of activities it has a right to prohibit. The Court opined in one decision, "The overly broad statute . . . creates a danger zone within which protected expression may be inhibited. . . . Even the prospect of ultimate failure of . . . prosecutions by no means dispels its chilling effect on protected expression." In another, "Because First Amendment freedoms need breathing space to survive, government may regulate in the area only with narrow specificity."[47] Since the very presence on the statute books of an overbroad statute can be used to repress freedom of speech and association, such a statute, rather than just a specific application of it, may be declared unconstitutional on its face.

Least means Related to both vagueness and overbreadth and often merged with these tests is the requirement that the legislative choice be narrowly restricted to the evil to be curbed. Outside the area of First Amendment freedoms, judges ordinarily will not invalidate a law just because the legislature might have chosen some other means to deal with a particular problem. But if the law impinges on the First Amendment, "even though the governmental purpose be legitimate and substantial, that purpose cannot be achieved by means that broadly stifle fundamental personal liberties when that end can be more narrowly achieved."[48] For example, a state may protect the public from the improper practice of the law, but it may not do so by a law forbidding organizations to make legal services available to their members.[49] There are other means to protect the public that do not impinge on the rights of free association.

The balancing doctrine All judges, whatever language they use to express their opinions, weigh a variety of factors in making their decisions. But for some time the balancing doctrine took on a more restrict-

[46]*Burstyn v. Wilson* (1952) and *Winters v. New York* (1948).

[47]Respectively, *Dombrowski v. Pfister* (1965) and *NAACP v. Button* (1963); see also *Gooding v. Wilson* (1972).

[48]*Shelton v. Tucker* (1960).

[49]*NAACP v. Button* (1963) and *Brotherhood of Railroad Trainmen v. Virginia* (1964).

ed meaning and referred to a particular doctrine, especially as espoused by Justices Frankfurter and Harlan.

Essentially the Frankfurter–Harlan position was a protest by those who think the First Amendment should not be read in absolute terms, who reject the notion that First Amendment freedoms are any more sacred than any other constitutional freedoms, who believe that judges should not apply standards to measure the constitutionality of laws impinging on First Amendment freedoms that differ from those that are used to measure any other kinds of laws, and who think that judges have no mandate to protect these freedoms that is any different from their responsibilities in any other area. Laws regulating First Amendment freedoms, like all laws, must be judged by balancing the interests to be secured by the regulation against the amount of freedom that is lost or impaired. Thus Justice Harlan, ruled that Congress' concern to preserve the nation against Communist subversion overbalances a witness' right before a congressional investigating committee to refuse to answer questions about his possible involvement with the Communist party.[50]

In more recent years, the Supreme Court's decision indicate that

> balancing of the Frankfurter variety has not turned out to be the dominant general formula for free speech cases that it once appeared to be becoming. [The] Court's emphasis on the need for overriding and compelling state interests before the balance will fall in its favor suggests something like a return to the old balancing-cum-preferred-position technique that coexisted with the clear-and-present-danger rule in the early forties. . . . For how much difference is there between saying that speech interests will be given special weight and saying that unless the state's interests are especially weighty they cannot overbalance speech.[51]

Whatever the doctrines, doctrines do not decide cases—judges do. And judges are constantly searching and seeking and explaining; hence the Supreme Court may undergo doctrinal changes especially when it deals with issues that lack a national consensus. Doctrines are judges' starting points, not their conclusions; each case requires them to weigh a variety of factors. *What* was said? *Where* was it said? *How* was it said? What was the *intent* of the person who said it? What were the *circumstances* in which it was said? *Which* government is attempting to regulate the speech? The city council that speaks for a few people or the Congress that speaks for a wide variety of people? (Only a very few *congressional* enactments have ever been struck down because of conflict with the First Amendment.) *How* is the goverment attempting to regulate the speech? By prior censorship? by punishment after the speech? *Why* is the government attempting to regulate the speech? To protect

[50]*Barenblatt v. United States* (1959).

[51]Martin Shapiro, *Freedom of Speech: The Supreme Court and Judicial Review* (Prentice-Hall, 1966), p. 83.

the national security? to keep the streets clean? to protect the rights of unpopular religious minorities? to prevent criticism of those in power? These and scores of other considerations are involved. And there is the future question of how much deference judges should show to the legislature's attempt to adjust these conflicting claims. In short, no test has been devised that will automatically weigh all the factors.

Freedom of the press

Today, information is seldom spread through streetcorner meetings or public assemblies, the historic centers of debate. Rather, it is broadcast wholesale by the press, television, radio, movies, and other media of communication. The Supreme Court has been zealous in guarding freedom of the press from governmental restriction. But how broad is this freedom?

Sometimes freedom of the press comes into conflict with another basic right—trial by an impartial judge and jury in a calm and judicial atmosphere. When newspapers and other mass media report in vivid detail the facts of a lurid crime and secure press releases from the prosecutor, it may be impossible to hold a trial in an atmosphere free from hysteria or to secure a jury that can decide in an impartial manner. In England the emphasis is on the side of fair trial. British courts do not hesitate to hold in contempt newspapers that comment on pending criminal proceedings. In the United States the emphasis is on the side of free comment. The Court has sustained the right of the press to criticize judges, even to the point of allowing editors to threaten judges with political reprisals unless they deal with defendants in a certain fashion. As Justice Douglas put it, "Judges are supposed to be men of fortitude, able to thrive in a hardy climate" (*Craig v. Harney*, 1947).

Juries, on the other hand, are more susceptible to prejudicial comments and events. Thus a defendant was given a new trial because, after his indictment, a congressional investigating committee had conducted open hearings that, the judges believed, so inflamed public opinion that a fair trial was impossible. Similarly, the Supreme Court had reversed convictions when prejudical newspaper publicity and prosecutors' statements to the press or the televising of the accused reading a confession have so aroused a community that a jury selected from the community could not be impartial.[52]

Is a defendant deprived of due process if, over his objection, the judge allows television cameras into the courtroom? Four justices of the Supreme Court were of the view that the mere fact that the trial is being televised is so likely to influence the behavior of judge, jury, witnesses,

[52]*Delaney v. United States*, U.S.S.C.A. (1952); *Irvin v. Dowd* (1961); *Rideau v. Louisiana* (1963), and cases cited therein. See also Justice William O. Douglas, "The Public Trial and the Free Press," *American Bar Association Journal*, XLVI (1960), 840.

and defendants and is so inherently contrary to the idea of quiet and calm deliberation that televising trials is a violation of due process. The other justices would ban television from a courtoom only if there is evidence that its impact on a particular judge, jury, or witness interferes with a fair trial.[53]

The American Bar Association, concerned about sensational newspaper coverage, has adopted a series of rules designed, not to curb what newspapers may print, but to restrain what prosecutors, defense attorneys, judges, court employees, police, and other law enforcement officers should release. Although the ABA rules are not the law (though some judges have begun enforcing them), they do conform to the spirit of recent Supreme Court decisions instructing trial judges to use their authority to prevent the release before and during trials of prejudicial information that makes it difficult for the accused to be tried in an atmosphere that promotes calm and fair deliberations. Many newspapers have criticized the new ABA rules as infringing on the guarantee of a free press and have been urging judges not to follow them.[54]

THE PRESS AND THE CAMPUS

Although lower federal courts have ruled that administrators of public

[53]*Estes v. Texas* (1965) and *Shepperd v. Maxwell* (1966).

[54]For commentary and copy of ABA rules, see *American Bar Association Journal* (April 1968), pp. 343–51.

Clarence Darrow, left, at the trial of Leopold and Loeb, which was described as the country's most sensational murder trial.

universities, even if they function as the publishers, are restrained by the First Amendment in dealing with student newspapers, the Supreme Court has not as yet ruled on this matter. The Court has held, however (*Papish v. University of Missouri Curators*, 1972), that a publicly supported university may not expel a student for distributing what authorities considered to be an indecent newspaper. The university may regulate the time, place, and manner of the distribution of printed matter on campus, but "the mere dissemination of ideas—no matter how offensive to good taste—on a state university campus may not be shut off in the name alone of 'conventional decency.'" The three dissenting justices felt that the materials were legally obscene, but that even if they were not of the nature that would justify a criminal conviction, the Constitution does not forbid a university from disciplining a student for distributing on campus publications "which are at the same time obscene and infantile." The dissenters also chided their colleagues for being unwilling to use in their own opinion the four-letter words—(the familiar "code abbreviations" were used)—the majority felt were not of a nature to sustain disciplinary action against a student.

A RIGHT TO REPLY?

Some critics have charged that the "press lords" enjoy ample opportunity to have their say, but that ordinary citizens, including most officeholders, find difficulty in getting their side of the issues presented. Especially when a newspaper levels an attack against a person, they argue, the editor should be required to give space for a reply to those he criticizes.

Whatever might be the merits to such arguments, the Supreme Court has shown little sympathy toward legislative attempts to force a right to reply. A unanimous court (*Miami Herald Publishing Co. v. Tornillo*, 1974) ruled unconstitutional a Florida law requiring newspapers to provide free space for verbatim replies by candidates for public office criticized by a paper. Speaking for the Court, Chief Justice Burger said that a newspaper involves a "crucial process" of editorial judgment that the state may not regulate. "A responsible press," he wrote, "is an undoubtedly desirable goal, but press responsibility is not mandated by the Constitution and like many other virtues, it cannot be legislated." A year before the Court had given a somewhat similar negative response to those who had argued that groups should be given a right of access to television (see p. 154). In fact, the only intrusion into the editorial judgments of newspapers and broadcasters that the Court has so far sustained involved classified advertisements (see p. 153).

CENSORSHIP AT THE SOURCE

Is there freedom of the press to *obtain* news as well as to print it? Recently newsmen and others have charged that censorship at the source

"This is awful—It's not one of ours."

© 1971 Herblock in *The Washington Post.*

is undermining their ability to keep the people informed. Governments have always withheld information, especially during time of war, and it is generally agreed that some public business is best done in secret. But during the Cold War years, public officials began to classify more and more information as confidential, secret, or top secret, and made it a crime to divulge it.

Does the government have the authority to punish a newsman for publishing classified documents? We have had as yet no Supreme Court test of the issue. The Nixon Administration brought Daniel Ellsberg to trial for releasing the Pentagon Papers, but the case was dismissed after the Department of Justice's violations of his civil rights were brought to the trial judge's attention. In the *New York Times* case, some members of the Court hinted that although the government in that instance lacked authority to restrain the publication of the Pentagon Papers, they were not so sure that it could not punish the newspaper for publishing the classified documents. Despite rumors that some newspapers were going to be prosecuted for doing so, no such action was taken against them.

The Pentagon Papers incident did revive interest in the abusive use by the executive branch of its authority to classify documents and thereby keep them from the public. Justice Stewart in his opinion in the *New York Times* case pointed out, "[W]hen everything is classified, then nothing is classified, and the system becomes one to be disregarded by the cynical and careless and to be manipulated by those intent on self-protection or self-promotion." A good security system, he said, should provide "maximum possible disclosure, recognizing that secrecy can best be preserved when credibility is truly maintained." Justice Douglas, dissenting in another case, pointed out, ". . . [A]nyone who has ever been in the executive branch knows how convenient the 'Top Secret' or 'Secret' stamp is, how easy it is to use, and how it covers perhaps for decades the footprints of a nervous bureaucrat or a wary executive."[55]

Congress has liberalized access to public records. The Freedom of Information Act of 1966 makes all such records public, but it excepts those specifically required by the president to be kept secret in the interest of national defense or foreign policy, private financial transactions, personnel records, criminal investigation files, interoffice memoranda and letters used in the decision-making process of the executive branch, and a few other categories. Persons denied access to records are entitled to a speedy hearing before a federal district judge who is to determine if the agency has acted properly, and the burden is on the agency to sustain the action in refusing to grant the materials. The Supreme Court (*EPV v. Mink*, 1973) interpreted the Act to mean that if the president or his agents classified a document as one that should not be made public in the interest of national security, the courts lacked authority to look into the validity of that classification.

Following the Mink decision in 1974 Congress amended over President Ford's veto the Freedom of Information Act by permitting courts to exercise an independent judgment on whether information has properly been classified, by requiring the government to pay legal fees incurred in taking a freedom-of-information case to court, by requiring the federal agencies to act more quickly on requests for information, by more precise definitions of national security, by more specific guidelines for those authorized to classify documents, by faster declassification, and by more effective protection for those documents that should be kept secret.

In the spring of 1972, President Nixon issued a new executive order designed to correct some of the abuses in the overclassification of documents. The order stipulates that classification shall be solely on the basis of national security considerations, defined as those that bear directly on the effectiveness of our national defense or the conduct of foreign relations. It states that an entire document should not be classified merely because parts of it contain secret information. It stipulates that in no case shall information be classified to conceal inefficiency or administrative error, or to prevent embarrassment to persons or a department. It reduced the number of agencies given authority to use secret stamps and required each official with stamping power to be so designated by the head of the agency in writing. And the order establishes a watchdog committee to oversee its enforcement and to handle appeals. This Interagency Classifications Review Committee operates under the National Security Council.[56]

Skeptics remain unconvinced that the new executive order will result in more effective enforcement against misuse of the classification system. Said Congressman William Moorhead, "This is a step forward, but

[55]*EPA v. Mink* (1973).

[56]Executive Order 11652, March 8, 1972, effective July 1, 1972, thirty-seven *Federal Register* 5209.

only a small step when the fact is that earlier directives prohibiting overclassification never were enforced."[57]

A NEWSPERSON'S RIGHT TO WITHHOLD INFORMATION

What of the right of reporters to withhold information from grand juries, legislative committees, and other agencies of government? Most newspersons contend that unless they can assure confidentiality to their source, they will not get the information they need to keep the public informed. But the Supreme Court has ruled (*Branzburg v. Hayes*, 1972) that reporters, and presumably scholars, have no First Amendment right to withhold information from grand or other kinds of juries. In this particular set of cases the newspersons did not claim an absolute privilege, but they did assert that they should not be forced either to appear or to testify unless sufficient grounds are shown for believing that the reporter possesses information relevant to a crime that is being investigated, that the information is not available from other sources, and that the need for the information is sufficiently compelling. But Justice Stewart, speaking for the Court, quoted approvingly from Jeremy Bentham, "Were the Prince of Wales, the Archbishop of Canterbury, and the Lord High Chancellor, to be passing by in the same coach, while a chimney-sweeper and a barrow-woman were in dispute about a halfpennyworth of apples, and the chimney-sweeper or the barrow-woman were to think proper to call upon them for their evidence, could they refuse it? No, most certainly." The majority concluded: " 'The public has a right to every man's evidence,' except those persons protected by a constitutional, common-law, or statutory privilege," and that if any privilege were to be given to newspersons, it should be done by act of Congress and of the states.

The dissenting justices argued that the "Court's crabbed view of the First Amendment . . . would invite state and federal authorities to undermine the historic independence of the press by attempting to annex the journalistic profession as an investigative arm of the government. . . . When neither the reporter nor his source can rely on the shield of confidentiality against unrestrained use of the grand jury's subpoena power, valuable information will not be published and the public dialogue will inevitably be impoverished."

Congress has responded to the Supreme Court's suggestion in the Branzburg decision (that Congress is in the better position to weigh the conflicting claims) by considering a federal shield law. But so far it has not acted. In the meantime the attorney general has issued guidelines limiting federal prosecutors' discretion in the issuance of subpoenas to

[57]Quoted in Samuel J. Archibald, "Access to Government Information—the Right before First Amendment," *The First Amendment and the News Media,* Annual Chief Justice Earl Warren Conference on Advocacy in the United States (Roscoe Pound-American Trial Lawyers Foundation, 1973), p. 71.

newspersons. Twenty states have shield laws already, and others are considering their adoption.

EXECUTIVE PRIVILEGE AND UNITED STATES V. RICHARD M. NIXON

Although not directly related to the conflicts over the claim by newspersons of the right to withhold information from grand juries, one is reminded of the claim of President Nixon, and his predecessors, that he had a constitutional right to withhold information even from Congress and the courts if he considered its release would jeopardize national security or interfere with confidentiality of advice given to the president. In the celebrated case of *United States v. Nixon* (1974), the Supreme Court ruled that a president does not have an absolute executive privilege to withhold information. He is subject to a subpoena for materials relevant to a criminal prosecution.

This historic decision – historic in more than one sense, for it was the first time the Supreme Court has decided a matter directly involving the president as a party to a case, in contrast to his agents – rightly focused attention on the Supreme Court's rejection of the president's claim that he has an absolute executive privilege, and that he, rather than the courts, has the final say about what information to release and what to withhold. But perhaps overlooked was the fact that the Court fully recognized that a president does have a *limited* executive privilege.

In the first place if a president claims the privilege because disclosure would reveal military or diplomatic secrets, the courts should show "utmost deference" to his decision. And even outside of these areas, his "singularly unique" role requires that great efforts be made to insure that his communications are kept confidential. To this end the trial judge was instructed to look at the subpoenaed materials *in camera* (in secret), release to the prosecutor and thus eventually to the public only the information the judge thought related to the trial, and return the other material to the president "restored to its privileged" status. He is also to be protected against "vexations and unnecessary subpoenas."

LIBEL

Libel prosecutions have often been a favorite weapon to suppress criticism of government officials and to prevent discussion of public issues. But through a progressive raising of the constitutional standards, the danger of civil damages or criminal prosecution for libel no longer constitutes a serious threat to free communication. As far as public officials and public figures are concerned, no person may be made to pay damages or be punished for any comments he or she makes about such a person unless it can be proved that the comments were maliciously made with a knowledge of their falsity or with reckless disregard for whether they are true or false.[58] The mere fact that a statement is wrong or even defamatory is not sufficient to sustain a charge of libel.

The constitutional standards for libel actions brought by private individuals is not so rigid. By a bare majority *(Gertz v. Robert Welch Inc.)*, indicating that the decision is not likely to be the last word, the Court ruled that states could allow damage awards to *private citizens* for defamatory falsehoods if there is evidence of negligence or fault. However, if this less rigid standard is used, damages must be limited to compensation for actual injury to the plaintiff and his or her reputation.

OBSCENITY

What of smut? Obscene publications are not entitled to constitutional protection, but the members of the Supreme Court, like everybody else, have had great difficulty in determining how obscenity is to be constitutionally defined. As Justice Harlan pointed out, "The subject of obscenity has produced a variety of views among the members of the Court unmatched in any course of constitutional adjudication."[59] And as Justice Brennan has written, "No other aspect of the First Amendment has, in recent years, commanded so substantial a commitment of our time, generated such disharmony of views, and remained so resistant to the formulation of stable and manageable standards."[60] Since the Supreme Court entered the field in 1957, there have been over seventy-five separate opinions written by the justices.

In *Miller v. California* (1973) Chief Justice Burger, speaking for only five members of the Court, once again tried to clarify and redefine the constitutional standards: A work may be considered legally obscene provided: (1) the average person, applying contemporary standards of the forum community would find that the work, taken as a whole, appeals to a prurient interest in sex; (2) it depicts or describes in a patently offensive way sexual conduct specifically defined by the applicable law; and (3) the work, taken as a whole, lacks serious literary, artistic, political, or scientific value. The Chief Justice specifically rejected part of the previous test—the so-called *Memoirs v. Massachusetts* (1966) formula—that had been applied by the Supreme Court, namely, no work should be judged obscene unless it was "utterly without redeeming social value." The Chief Justice argued such a test made it impossible for a state to outlaw hard-core pornography. He also said the standard of offensiveness could be of the forum community—rather than the nation at large—opening the possibility that a book or movie might be legally obscene in one state or city but not in another.

[58]*New York Times v. Sullivan* (1964); *Curtis Publishing Co. v. Butts* (1967); *Rosenbloom v. Metromedia, Inc.* (1971) and cases cited therein.

[59]*Interstate Circuit, Inc. v. City of Dallas* (1968).

[60]*Paris Adult Theatre I v. Slaton* (1973).

Did the *Miller* decision mean that henceforth the local communities could ban whatever a prosecutor could persuade a jury was obscene? There were many who hoped so; there were many who feared so. They read *Miller* to mean that the Supreme Court would no longer review each book or movie in order to second-guess the decision of local authorities. But how far could the local community go? What if it decided to ban "Little Red Riding Hood"? After all, who really knows what went on in that bedroom?

A year after the *Miller* decision, the Supreme Court in *Jenkins v. Georgia* (1974), although reaffirming that the standard of offensiveness was to be that of the forum community, warned that "It would be a serious misreading of *Miller* to conclude that juries have unbridled discretion in determining what is patently offensive." Appellate courts, said Justice Rehnquist speaking for the majority, should closely review jury determinations to insure compliance with constitutional standards. And the Supreme Court itself, after such a review, ruled that the movie *Carnal Knowledge* was not patently offensive, contrary to the conclusion of a jury in Albany, Georgia.

Four members of the Supreme Court would go even farther than the majority. They include Justice Stewart who once said that although he could not define hard-core pornography, "I know it when I see it."[61] But after struggling to develop a constitutional definition, he joined two of his brethren, Justices Brennan and Marshall, in finally coming to the conclusion that it is impossible to do so without endangering protected speech and miring the court in a "case-by-case determination of obscenity." These justices would let adults see or read whatever they wished. Justice Douglas would go even farther. He argues that obscenity, no matter how defined, is like other forms of speech and that sexually oriented expression is constitutionally protected no matter to whom it is sold or directed.

The Supreme Court majority of five, although holding obscenity is not entitled to constitutional protection, have insisted upon the government's proceeding under statutes narrowly drawn to define specifically the kinds of sexual conduct persons are forbidden to portray in word or picture. Moreover, a government cannot make it a crime for a bookseller merely to offer an obscene book for sale; it must be shown that he or she did so *knowingly*. Otherwise booksellers would avoid placing on their shelves materials that some policeman or prosecutor might consider objectionable, and thus the public would be deprived of an opportunity to purchase and read anything except the "safe and sanitary."[62]

The mere private possession of obscene materials cannot be made a crime. But a person may be convicted for transporting such literature in interstate commerce or importing it from abroad even if it is for his or

[61]*Jacobellis v. Ohio* (1964).

[62]*Smith v. California* (1959).

her own use.[63] These limitations on the right to read privately lead Justice Douglas to observe in dissent that "a person can read whatever he desires . . . only if one wrote or designed a tract in his attic, printed or processed it in his basement, so as to be able to read it in his study."[64]

Except for Justice Douglas, all the justices, including those who dissented in *Miller* and in *Jenkins*, would permit regulation of what minors can see or read. And, again except for Justice Douglas, the justices have concluded that what is not considered legally obscene for adults may be so for minors. The Supreme Court, recognizing the state's special interest in protecting young people, has approved regulations that prohibit the knowing sale to minors of "girlie magazines" that would not be considered obscene if sold to adults.[65] But even under this "variable-obscenity" doctrine, governments are not free to move at will. For example, a Dallas ordinance was declared unconstitutional that forbade motion picture exhibitors to allow minors to see pictures that a motion picture classification board had determined unsuitable for minors. The board's standards were too vague; it classified as "not suitable for minors" films that a majority of its members thought "likely to incite or encourage crime, delinquency, or sexual promiscuity."[66]

States are primarily responsible for regulating obscene literature, but ever since Anthony Comstock started a national crusade against dirty literature in the 1880s, Congress has had a concern with the subject. Congress has outlawed the importation into the United States of pornographic materials. It has made it a crime to send such materials through the mails or interstate commerce, even to willing adults, even as transported by a person in his brief case on an airline for his own private use.[67]

The Supreme Court has treated somewhat differently, however, those laws that authorized postal authorities to exclude from the mails publications they concluded to be obscene and to cut off all incoming mail to the alleged pornographers. These laws rested on the assumption that the use of the mails is a privilege that the government may terminate at its discretion. But in 1965 in *Lamont v. Postmaster General* the Court—on a different issue—rejected this assumption and adopted the view of Justice Holmes: "The United States may give up the Post Office when it sees fit, but while it carries it on, the use of the mails is almost as much a part of free speech as the right to use our tongues." Congress, said the Court, cannot condition the right of an addressee to receive foreign Communist political propaganda on his returning an official notice say-

[63]*Stanley v. Georgia* (1969); *United States v. Reidel* (1971); *United States v. Thirty-seven Photographs* (1971); *United States v. Orito* (1973); *Hamling v. United States* (1974).

[64]*United States v. 12,200-ft. Reels of Super 8 MM Film* (1973).

[65]*Ginsberg v. New York* (1968).

[66]*Interstate Circuit, Inc. v. City of Dallas* (1968).

[67]*United States v. Orito* (1973).

ing that he wanted to receive it. "The regime of this Act," said the Court, "is at war with the 'uninhibited, robust, and wide-open debate and discussion that are contemplated by the First Amendment.' " This was the first time the Court had ever ruled that an act of Congress violated the First Amendment. Six years later the Court unanimously extended the *Lamont* decision to void laws authorizing postal authorities to make administrative determinations of obscenity, exclude it from the mails, and cut off all mail to persons sending it.[68]

On the other hand, the Supreme Court has sustained a law giving any householder unlimited power to ask the postmaster to order a mailer to delete his name from all mailing lists and refrain from sending any advertising material that the householder in his sole discretion believes to be "erotically arousing or sexually provocative." It does not make any difference if the householder includes in such a category a "dry-goods catalogue." This is not governmental censorship. The "mailer's right to communicate must stop at the mailbox of an unreceptive addressee."[69] The Supreme Court's decision would seem to support the 1970 Postal Reorganization Act provision that authorizes the Postal Service to maintain current lists of persons who have stated that they do not wish to receive "sexually oriented advertisements." Mailers of unsolicited advertisements are prohibited from sending such advertisements to persons whose names appear on the list.

Until 1952 motion pictures were considered entertainment rather than communication and therefore were not protected by the free speech and press guarantees of the Constitution. Seven states and numerous cities require all exhibitors to submit all films to censors, who determined, without any legal restraints, what could and could not be shown. Then in 1952 *(Joseph Burstyn, Inc. v. Wilson),* the Supreme Court brought the movies under the protection of the Constitution when it held that New York authorities lacked constitutional power to prevent the showing of a film because the authorities thought it to be "sacrilegious." Not only does *sacrilegious* lack precise meaning, the Court held, but government has no right to censor movies solely because they may offend some people's religious sensibilities. Since the *Burstyn* decision, the Supreme Court, in case after case, has upset attempts to ban motion pictures that various censors have alleged "tended to corrupt morals," or were "harmful," or presented "acts of sexual immorality as desirable." The only grounds on which a government may prevent the showing of a film is proof that it is obscene.

The Supreme Court has allowed films to be treated differently from books or newspapers. It has refused to hold that prior censorship of films is necessarily unconstitutional under all circumstances.[70] However, laws calling for prior submission of all films to a review board are

[68]*Blount v. Rizzi* (1971).

[69]*Rowan v. Post Office Department* (1970).

[70]*Times Film Company v. City of Chicago* (1961).

constitutional only if the review board is required promptly to grant a license or promptly to go to court for a prompt judicial hearing and determination that the film in question is obscene, and the burden is on the board to prove to the court that the film is in fact obscene.[71]

Censorship of films and books may be imposed by a variety of means other than formal action. In some cities a local group, such as the Legion of Decency may put pressure on the authorities, and local police have been known to threaten an exhibitor or a bookseller with criminal prosecution if he persists in showing films or selling books of which some local people disapprove. Such a threat is often enough to compel exhibitors to stop showing the films or selling the books. Of course any group is free to stay away from pictures or books that it dislikes, even to try to persuade others to stay away. What the Constitution forbids is the use of the coercive powers of government.

Today, fears about obscenity appear to have replaced the seventeenth-century fears about heresy and the 1950s fears about sedition. After the Supreme Court entered the field to protect reading and other materials from the too-heavy hand of the censor, Congress in 1967 responded to public concerns by creating an eighteen-member Commission on Obscenity and Pornography to study the traffic in obscene literature, to determine if there is a causal relationship between this matter and antisocial behavior, and to make recommendations to Congress on what kind of legislation it should adopt. The commission—all of whose members except one were appointed by President Johnson—reported in 1970 that there is no evidence that exposure to obscene materials adversely affects moral attitudes or causes criminal behavior. It recommended that all legislation prohibiting the sale of such materials to adults be repealed.[72] President Nixon repudiated the commission's report. The Senate went to the unusual length, by a sixty-to-five vote, of rejecting the recommendations.

In view of these negative responses, and in view of the fact that the commission itself favored legislation to prevent the unwarranted intrusion of sexually explicit materials upon individuals and to keep such materials from young persons, regulation of obscene books, motion pictures, and other materials is likely to continue. Conflicts over how it should or should not be regulated are going to remain lively parts of our political debates, especially at the community level.

FIGHTING WORDS

There are certain well-defined and narrowly limited classes of speech "which by their very utterance inflict injury or tend to incite an immediate breach of peace" (*Chaplinsky v. New Hampshire*, 1942) which governments may justifiably punish. The state must treat these "fighting words" by carefully and narrowly drawn statutes not susceptible of

[71]*Freedman v. Maryland* (1965) and *Teitel Film Corp. v. Cusak* (1968).

[72]*Report of the Commission on Obscenity and Pornography* (Bantam Books, 1970), pp. 62–67.

application to protected expression.[73] And the category of what will be considered fighting words is very narrow—for example, a four-letter word used in relation to the draft and worn on a sweater is not a fighting word, at least when not directed to any specific person.[74]

COMMERCIAL SPEECH

The Supreme Court has not ruled unequivocally that commercial speech is without protection of the First Amendment, but it has certainly permitted it to be regulated in a manner that would not be allowed for other kinds of communication. The Federal Communications Commission and the Federal Trade Commission, for example, have been allowed to ban completely certain kinds of advertisements without constitutional objection. Cities have been permitted to regulate the distribution of commercial handbills in ways not allowed for political handouts.[75]

May a newspaper be forbidden to list help wanted advertisements classifed by sex? Justice Powell, speaking for a five-man majority, ruled that advertisements of such a nature are commercial speech unprotected by the First Amendment. They do not communicate information or express opinions, but merely are proposals for possible employment. Since hiring on the basis of sex is illegal, advertisements on this basis, like those proposing sale of narcotics or soliciting prostitution, Powell argued, could also be banned. He warned, however, that governments could not interfere with the publication by a newspaper, whether through news columns or advertisements, of communications indicating sex preferences or advocating sexism. Justice Stewart in dissent contended that no government has the power to tell any newspaper in advance what it can and cannot print or to interfere with its editorial judgments about what to put in its pages, including its classified advertisements. "The camel's nose is in the tent," he warned. "If governments can order a newspaper to print classified ads in a certain way, nothing will prevent government from dictating the layout of the news pages."[76]

OTHER MEANS OF COMMUNICATION

Radio and Television Radio and especially television have increasingly become the most important means for the distribution of news to the mass public as well as the primary forum used by state and national candidates to appeal for votes. The Supreme Court has had to deal with

[73]*Gooding v. Wilson* (1972); *Lewis v. New Orleans* (1974).

[74]*Cohen v. California* (1971).

[75]*Valentine v. Christensen* (1942); *Lehman v. City of Shaker Heights* (1974).

[76]*Pittsburgh Press Company v. Pittsburgh Commission on Human Relations* (1973).

the difficult problem of applying the First Amendment whose principles were first developed when the town meeting, the handbill, and the street speaker served as the chief marketplace for ideas.

Congress has established a system of private broadcasting, recently supplemented by the Public Broadcasting System, subject to general regulation by the Federal Communications Commission. Broadcasters use publicly owned airwaves, and no one has a constitutional right to use these facilities without a license.[77] The FCC grants these licenses for limited periods and makes regulations consistent with the "public convenience, interest, or necessity." Congress has specifically denied the commission the authority to censor what is transmitted or to interfere with the right of free speech, and the First Amendment would prevent such censorship if the FCC tried to impose it. But the First Amendment does not prevent the FCC from refusing to renew a license if in its opinion a broadcaster has not served the public interest or from imposing regulations designed to insure fair coverage of events.

Congress and the FCC have adopted the Fairness Doctrine, which imposes on licensees the obligation to see that issues of public significance are covered adequately and to reflect differing viewpoints. If a paid sponsor is unavailable to present an opposing view, the broadcaster must provide free time. He must initiate programming on public issues if no one seeks to do so. In case a person is subject to personal attack, the licensee has an obligation to notify the person attacked and give him or her an opportunity to respond. If the licensee makes editorial statements or endorses candidates, he must give opponents an opportunity to respond. And in the case of candidates for public office Congress has imposed an equal-time requirement.

Regulations imposed on the broadcaster or telecaster are greater than those on newspaper publishers. As Justice White said for the Court in upholding the Fairness Doctrine, "This is not to say that the First Amendment is irrelevant to public broadcasting. . . . But it is the rights of viewers and listeners, not the right of the broadcasters, which is paramount. . . . Congress need not stand idly by and permit those with licenses to ignore the problems which beset the people or to exclude from the airways anything but their own views of fundamental questions."[78]

Does a group, like a political party, a candidate, or those who organize to promote particular political views, have a consitutional or legal right to access to radio or television time if it is willing to pay for it? Or does a licensee have a constitutional and legal right to refuse to accept paid political announcements if in its journalistic judgment it would be wise to do so? As we have noted, a unanimous Supreme Court concluded that so far as newspapers are concerned there is no constitutional right to reply, and a state may not interfere with a journalist's

[77]*National Broadcasting Co. v. United States* (1943).

[78]*Red Lion Broadcasting Co. v. Federal Communications Commission* (1969).

decision about what to print. But so far as broadcasters are concerned, the Supreme Court had a more difficult time answering these questions. It could not muster a majority who could agree on the reasons, but seven justices concluded that neither the Federal Communications Act nor the First Amendment requires broadcasters to accept paid editorial advertisements. The opinion of Chief Justice Burger, for the plurality, after observing that if broadcasters had to accept all paid editorials there would be a substantial risk that those with the most money could monopolize the airwaves, concluded that the First Amendment did not require broadcasters to accept such paid announcements, but neither does it forbid the FCC and Congress to impose some kinds of access requirements if they wished. Justice Douglas was with the majority in this case, but he is of the view that the First Amendment forbids Congress or the FCC from imposing any such restraints on the journalistic judgments of the licensees. On the other side, Justices Brennan and Marshall argued that a ban by broadcasters, acquiesced in by the FCC, violates the First Amendment rights of those who wish to buy time.[79]

The coming of cable television is likely to ease somewhat the access problems since it will provide more channels for more groups. It is undoubtedly going to raise new problems of applying the principles of free speech to new technologies. Not the least will be the interrelations between federal licensing and local regulations. To this point the Supreme Court has not had to face the issue squarely, although the courts of appeals have ruled that state laws requiring a license to show a motion picture to the public may not be applied to films shown over television. Will the courts so hold for films shown over closed-circuit cable television?

Handbills The distribution of religious and political pamphlets, leaflets, and handbills to the public—a historic weapon in the defense of liberty—is constitutionally protected. The Supreme Court has been quick to strike down ordinances interfering with this right. Of course, cities may prosecute those who engage in fraud or libel or who deliberately litter the streets, but keeping the streets clean does not justify interference with the right to pass out political or religious literature. When Los Angeles tried to outlaw the distribution of anonymous handbills, the Supreme Court ruled that the city's interest in identifying those who might be responsible for fraud, false advertising, or libel was not substantial enough to justify a ban on all anonymous handbills.[80]

Picketing Picketing is protected by the First and Fourteenth Amendments; therefore, a state law forbidding all peaceful picketing carried on for any purpose would be an unconstitutional invasion of freedom of

[79] *Columbia Broadcasting System, Inc. v. Democratic National Committee* (1973).

[80] *Talley v. California* (1960).

speech.[81] However, "picketing involves elements of both speech and conduct, i.e., patrolling," and "because of this intermingling of protected and unprotected elements, picketing can be subjected to controls that would not be constitutionally permissible in the case of pure speech."[82] Even peaceful picketing can be restricted by a state if it is conducted for an illegal purpose.[83] As far as trade-union picketing is concerned federal regulations are so comprehensive and preempt so many areas from state regulation that the power of states to interfere with such picketing is much narrower than it might appear if one looked only at decisions relating to freedom of speech.[84]

Symbolic speech When engaged in to communicate an idea, conduct is even less protected by the First and Fourteenth Amendments than is picketing, as David Paul O'Brien and his three companions discovered when they burned their draft cards in violation of a specific congressional regulation that makes it a crime to do so knowingly and deliberately. O'Brien argued that the First Amendment protects "all modes of communication of ideas by conduct." But Chief Justice Warren, speaking for eight members of the Supreme Court, stated, "We cannot accept the view that an apparently limitless variety of conduct can be labelled speech whenever the person engaging in the conduct intends thereby to express an idea."[85] Congress had chosen a necessary and proper means of enforcing its power to call men to the military services.

The line, of course, between speech and conduct is not easy to draw. A majority of the justices, after carefully distinguishing between questions such as length of skirts, type of clothing, hair style, deportment, and group demonstrations, held that school authorities had violated the Constitution when they suspended two students who defied their principal by quietly and passively wearing black armbands to school to protest the war in Vietnam. Justice Black, long a vigorous champion of free speech, wrote a vigorous dissent: "I think . . . that the armbands did exactly what the elected school officials and principal foresaw they would, that is, took the students' mind off their class work.[86]

Freedom of assembly and petition

The right to assemble peaceably applies, not only to meetings in private homes and meeting halls, but to meetings held in public streets and

[81] *Thornhill v. Alabama* (1940).

[82] *Amalgamated Food Employees Local 590 v. Logan Valley Plaza, Inc.* (1968).

[83] *International Brotherhood of Teamsters v. Vogt* (1957).

[84] Martin Shapiro, *Law and Politics in the Supreme Court* (Free Press, 1964), pp. 75–142.

[85] *United States v. O'Brien* (1968).

[86] *Tinker v. Des Moines School District* (1969).

parks, which, the Supreme Court has said, since ". . . time out of mind have been used for purposes of assembly . . . and discussing public questions" (*Hague v. C.I.O.*, 1939). But, under the guise of exercising freedom of peaceful assembly and petition, people are not free to incite riots, to block traffic, to take over a school, to seize and hold the office of a mayor (or a university chancellor), to hold parades, or to make speeches in the public streets during rush hours—and the government may make reasonable regulations over time, place, and manner in order to preserve order.

The courts will look carefully at regulations and police actions that obstruct the right of public assembly, especially in circumstances that raise a suspicion that a law is not being applied evenhandedly. The Supreme Court is unwilling to approve regulations that let public authorities determine, at their own discretion, which groups will be allowed to hold public meetings, or laws that are so vague that they give the police broad discretion to determine whom to arrest and courts latitude to decide whom to convict.

Governments may regulate the use of the streets, but they must do so by precisely drawn and fairly administered statutes which are neutral concerning differing points of view. The Supreme Court, for example, sustained a Louisiana law that made it an offense to picket or parade in or near a courthouse with the intent to influence a judge, juror, witness, or to impede the administration of justice.[87] It also upheld an ordinance of the city of Rockford, Illinois, which prohibits persons while on the grounds adjacent to a building in which school is in session from making a noise or diversion that disturbs or tends to disturb the peace or good order of the school session.[88] On the other hand, the Court struck down a Louisiana statute that defined disturbing the peace so broadly that it would permit arrest merely for holding a meeting on a public street.[89] It also struck down a Chicago ordinance that prohibited all picketing within 150 feet of school except one that was involved with a labor dispute. Such a regulation, by allowing some kinds of picketing while forbidding other kinds, slipped from the neutrality of a time-and-place regulation into a concern about content.[90]

What of unpopular groups whose peaceful public meetings and nonviolent demonstrations in the public streets and parks arouse others to violence? May police arrest them and judges convict the demonstrators? If the answer were yes, then the right of unpopular minorities to hold meetings would be seriously curtailed. It is almost always easier for the police to maintain order by curbing the peaceful meetings of the unpopular minority than to move against those threatening the violence. On the other hand, if police never have the right to order a group to dis-

[87]*Cox v. Louisiana* (1965).

[88]*Grayned v. City of Rockford* (1972).

[89]*Cox v. Louisiana* (1965).

[90]*Police Department of Chicago v. Mosley* (1972).

perse, public order is at the mercy of those who may resort to street demonstrations just to create public tensions and provoke street battles.

The Supreme Court has refused to give a categorical answer; it depends on the circumstances. Several years ago (*Feiner v. New York,* 1951) the Court upheld the conviction for "unlawful assembly" of a sidewalk speaker who continued to talk after being ordered to stop by the only two policemen present. There was no evidence that the police interfered because of objection to what was being said. But in view of the hostile response of the audience, the police were fearful that a fight might ensue that they could not prevent or contain. Judges have also approved of the police breaking up demonstrations in front of public school buildings by segregationists who by taunts and threats have tried to intimidate school authorities, parents, and children attempting to carry out a court-ordered desegregation program.

The *Feiner* case has never been overruled, but since then the Supreme Court has tended to emphasize the need for governments to move under more precisely drawn statutes; it has refused to approve police interference with public meetings where there is a strong suspicion that local authorities failed to make a good-faith attempt to protect peaceful demonstrators who were not interfering with the substantial rights of others. For example, in *Edwards v. South Carolina* (1963) the Supreme Court reversed the conviction of 187 black high school and college students who were arrested for holding a mass meeting in front of the South Carolina State House to protest denial of their civil rights. A crowd of about 300 onlookers watched the demonstration. The police protected the demonstrators for about forty-five minutes and then gave the students fifteen minutes in which to disperse. When they refused to do so, they were arrested and convicted for breach of the peace. The Supreme Court stressed that this was not a prosecution for violation of a precise and narrowly drawn statute limiting or prescribing specific conduct, such as interfering with traffic. All that had happened was that the opinions being expressed had been sufficiently opposed by a majority of the community to attract a crowd and necessitate police protection. "The Fourteenth Amendment," said the Court, "does not permit a State to make criminal the peaceful expression of unpopular views." Justice Clark, the lone dissenter, argued that the right to express views does not include the right to do so under circumstances where law-enforcement officers conclude in good faith that a dangerous disturbance is imminent.

In 1969 the Supreme Court followed the *Edwards* rather than the *Feiner* precedent when it reversed the conviction under a disorderly conduct statute of Dick Gregory and other demonstrators who had marched in a peaceful and orderly procession, under police protection, from city hall to the mayor of Chicago's residence to press their claims for desegregation of the schools. As they marched in front of the mayor's home a large and growing number of onlookers became unruly toward the demonstrators. For some time the police tried to maintain order, but when they concluded that there was an imminent threat of violence they demanded that the demonstrators disperse. The command was not obeyed, and Gregory and his followers were arrested and subsequently convicted of disorderly conduct. Although the Supreme Court reversed the decision, the Court made it clear that the situation would have been different if Chicago had acted under ordinances specifically forbidding demonstrations after certain hours in residential areas or under ordinances making it an offense to disobey a police officer when there is an imminent threat of violence and the police have made all reasonable efforts to protect the demonstrators from hostile bystanders. The Supreme Court's objection was to the fact that Gregory and his followers had been charged with and convicted of disorderly conduct when there was no evidence that they had been disorderly. Justices Douglas and Black concurred, but they went out of their way to emphasize: "Speech and press are, of course, to be free. . . . But picketing and demonstrating can be regulated like other conduct of men. We believe that the homes of men, sometimes the last citadel of the tired, the weary and the sick, can be protected by government from noisy, marching, trampling, threatening picketers and demonstrators bent on filling the minds of men, women, and children with fears of the unknown."[91]

Again in *Coates v. Cincinnati* (1971) the Court struck down on its face an ordinance which forbade three or more persons to assemble on sidewalks and there conduct themselves in a manner annoying to persons passing by. Justice Stewart, speaking for the Court, ruled that the ordinance was void for vagueness and overbreadth. He said, "The city is free to prevent people from blocking sidewalks, obstructing traffic, littering streets, committing assaults, or engaging in countless other forms of antisocial conduct. It can do so through the enactment and enforcement of ordinances directed with reasonable specificity toward the conduct to be prohibited. . . . It cannot constitutionally do so through the enactment and enforcement of an ordinance whose violations may entirely depend upon whether or not a policeman is annoyed."

What of public facilities, such as libraries, courthouses, schools, and swimming pools, that are designed to serve purposes other than demonstrations? As long as persons assemble to use such facilities within the normal bounds of conduct, they may not be constitutionally restrained from doing so. However, if they attempt by demonstrations such as sit-ins to interfere with programs or try to appropriate facilities for their own use, a state has the constitutional authority to punish such activities, provided the discretion accorded to those enforcing the law is properly limited and discriminatory application of the laws does not take place. In *Brown v. Louisiana* (1965), for example, the Supreme Court, by a five-to-four vote, ruled that five blacks could not be punished for breach of the peace for merely remaining quietly in a library for ten to fifteen minutes in order to protest racial discrimination. There was no

[91]*Gregory et al. v. Chicago* (1969). See also *Bachellor v. Maryland* (1970); *Shuttlesworth v. Birmingham* (1969).

disorder and no intent to provoke a breach of the peace, and the protestors had a right "by silent and reproachful presence to protest the unconstitutional segregation of public facilities." But Justice Black, speaking for the four dissenting justices, wrote, "Though the First Amendment guarantees the right of assembly and the right of petition. . . . it does not guarantee to any person the right to use someone else's property, even that owned by government and dedicated to other purposes, as a stage to express dissident ideas."

A year later, a different five-to-four division of the Court, this time with Justice Black speaking for the majority, sustained a conviction for "trespass with a malicious and mischievous intent" of students from Florida A & M University. The students had marched to the jailhouse to protest the arrest and jailing of some of their fellow students the day before and, more generally, to protest against segregation within the jail. They refused to leave when ordered to do so by the sheriff. Justice Black emphasized that jails are built for security purposes and are not open to the general public and that the Constitution does not preclude a state from "evenhanded enforcement of its general trespass statute . . . to preserve the property under its control for the use to which it is lawfully dedicated."[92] People who wish to protest do not have a constitutional right to do so "whenever and however and wherever they please." Justice Douglas, speaking for the four dissenting justices, argued that the jailhouse—just as an executive mansion, legislative chamber, or statehouse—is one of the seats of government and that when it "houses political prisoners or those who may think they are unjustly held, it is an obvious center for protest." Douglas chided the majority for treating this "petition for redress of grievances" as an ordinary trespass action.

What of private property and the right to protest? The right to assemble and to petition does not include the right to trespass on privately owned property. The state may protect owners against those who attempt to convert property to their own use even if they are doing so to express ideas.

Under certain conditions, however, owners of private property are subject to the same restraints that the First (and Fourteenth) Amendment imposes on governments. A company-owned town open to the public has long been held to be governed by the First Amendment. Shopping centers are also limited by the Constitution to some extent: The management of such centers are free, so far as the Constitution is concerned, to prohibit the distribution of handbills on the premises of the center if they relate to non-center matters (such as opposition to the draft), but they cannot prohibit the distribution of handbills expressing employee grievances against employers located in the center.[93]

[92] *Adderly v. Florida* (1966).

[93] *Marsh v. Alabama* (1946); *Amalgamated Food Employee's Local 590 v. Logan Valley Plaza* (1968); *Lloyd Corp. v. Tanner* (1972).

Does the right of peaceful assembly and petition include the right nonviolently but deliberately to violate a law? Again we have no unequivocal answer. The Supreme Court has sustained the right of persons to refuse peacefully to comply with segregation ordinances that are clearly unconstitutional. But speaking in general terms, civil disobedience, even if peacefully engaged in, is not a protected right. When Dr. Martin Luther King and his followers refused to comply with a state court's injunction that forbade them to parade in Birmingham without first securing a permit, the Supreme Court sustained their conviction even though there was a serious doubt about the constitutionality of the injunction and the ordinance upon which it was based. Justice Stewart, speaking for the five-man majority, said, "No man can be judge in his own case, however exalted his station, however righteous his motives, and irrespective of his race, color, politics, or religion." Persons are not "constitutionally free to ignore all the procedures of the law and carry their battles to the streets."[94] The four dissenting justices emphasized that one does have a right to defy peacefully an obviously unconstitutional statute or injunction.

The many five-to-four votes of the Supreme Court in drawing a line that will preserve the rights of persons to assemble and peacefully to petition and demonstrate—but that will not deprive state and local authorities of the right to maintain order and preserve the rights of all—reflect the complexity of the problem. An explanation of the Supreme Court's attempt to distinguish between legitimate use of public authority to preserve order and the unconstitutional use of public authority to suppress the right to assemble only begins to state the problem. The Court cannot police the nation. In thousands of local communities, those who really determine the extent to which people are free to exercise their constitutional right to assemble peacefully and to express unpopular views are the local law enforcement authorities, and these officials, in turn, usually reflect the views and values of the communities they serve. Despite Supreme Court opinions, some peaceful demonstrators still are arrested and some demonstrations still are stopped. Thousands of dollars and months later, convictions may be reversed. In the meantime the peaceful protestors may be silenced. Again, we have an example of the fact that the Supreme Court can *outline* but cannot *secure* constitutional rights unless its decisions are backed by the dominant political views and values and forces of the nation.

Freedom of association

The right to organize for the peaceful promotion of political causes is not precisely mentioned in the Constitution, but as the Supreme Court

[94] *Walker v. Birmingham* (1967).

has said, "It is beyond debate that freedom to engage in association for the advancement of beliefs and ideas is an inseparable aspect of the 'liberty' protected by the Constitution."[95]

Of course this right, like other rights, under certain conditions may be regulated. Some years back the Supreme Court ruled that the mere registration with the attorney general of the names of members of certain Communist organizations would not in itself violate the Constitution (but individual Communists could not be forced to register, for this would violate their rights against self-incrimination—see p. 232.[96] Although the publicity resulting from the disclosure that a person is a member of a Communist organization would impair the ability of the Communist party to recruit members, and it would subject individual Communists to social ostracism and economic reprisal, the Court majority was influenced by evidence that Communist organizations were not seeking to promote their goals by peaceful means. And even earlier, the Supreme Court sustained a state law aimed at breaking up the Ku Klux Klan by making it a crime for persons to parade on the public streets with their faces masked.[97]

The Supreme Court treated quite differently the attempts by some southern states only a few years ago to prevent persons from joining the National Association for the Advancement of Colored People. This organization, which proceeds in large measure by pressing lawsuits, had aroused considerable hostility among white citizens in areas where segregationist traditions were strong. Southern states and cities tried by a variety of means to discourage persons from joining the NAACP, even to the extent of trying to outlaw the organization. One of the most frequently attempted anti-NAACP tactics was to force the NAACP to reveal the names of its members. In many areas, if it had become known that a person belonged to the NAACP, he or she risked loss of employment, economic reprisal, even physical coercion. Under such circumstances, disclosure of membership lists would have interfered with the right to join a lawful organization. Unless the state could show some compelling public purpose, it could not force the NAACP to hand over membership lists.[98]

Along these same lines, the Supreme Court ruled that Arkansas could not demand a list of all organizations to which its teachers belonged (the list ostensibly being required to determine their fitness to teach). Arkansas could get the information it was entitled to without having to impose a requirement which would discourage membership in lawful but unpopular organizations.[99]

The Supreme Court even declared that Illinois had unconstitutionally

[95]*NAACP v. Alabama* (1958); *United States v. Robel* (1967); *Kusper v. Pontikes* (1973).

[96]*Communist Party v. Subversive Activities Control Board* (1961).

[97]*Bryant v. Zimmerman* (1928).

[98]*Bates v. Little Rock* (1960); *NAACP v. Alabama* (1958); *NAACP v. Button* (1963).

[99]*Shelton v. Tucker* (1960).

infringed on the right of political association when the state prohibited a person from voting in the primary of one political party if he or she had voted in the primary of another party within the preceding twenty-three months. The dissenting justices pointed out that those denied the right to vote in one primary election were free to associate with the party and vote for its candidates in the general election; they argued that this relatively limited interference with the right to associate was justified by a state's legitimate concern in reserving the right to participate in the selection of a party's candidates to adherents of that party.[100]

Freedom of association, like other First Amendment rights, is also constitutionally protected on the campuses of state-supported universities. To illustrate: the president of a state college, after a hearing concluded that the local chapter of the Students for a Democratic Society was not independent of the national SDS, which he found to have a philosophy of disruption and violence. Therefore, he ruled the local chapter could not use the facilities of the college for its meetings. Although the Supreme Court emphasized that a state college could refuse a student organization access to its facilities unless it would affirm in advance its willingness to adhere to reasonable campus rules, a unanimous Court declared the college could not, as in this instance, deny such privileges to an organization because of its disapproval of its aims or a generalized apprehension that its activities could lead to disruptions.[101]

What of the freedom *not* to associate? May a state compel lawyers to join a bar association or allow unions to make membership in a union a condition for securing or retaining employment? To oversimplify a complex problem, the Supreme Court has been willing to sustain such laws provided arrangements are made to insure that no individual is required to give his money to support the political activity of the association.[102] These precedents are likely to be cited if there are legal challenges to the use for political purposes of some of the fee money that some public instutions collect from students and then turn over to student organizations.

There are also difficult constitutional issues presented by the conflict between an individual's rights to choose his associates and the civil rights of others. We shall return to this problem when we discuss the powers of the national and state governments to protect the civil rights of those being discriminated against.

Subversive conduct and seditious speech

"If there is any fixed star in our constitutional constellation," Justice Jackson said, "it is that no official, high or petty, can prescribe what

[100]*Kusper v. Pontikes* (1973).

[101]*Healy v. James* (1972).

[102]*International Association of Machinists v. Street* (1961); *Lathrop v. Donohue* (1961).

shall be orthodox in politics, nationalism, religion, or other matters of opinion. . . ."[103] Any group can champion whatever position it wishes, whether vegetarianism, feminism, sexism, communism, fascism, black nationalism, white supremacy, Zionism, anti-Semitism, Americanism, Republicism, or Democraticism. But what of those who are unwilling to abide by democratic methods and go beyond mere advocacy and attempt through force or violence to impose their views upon others? Here is a perplexing problem for a democratic government: How to protect itself against antidemocrats who are working to destroy the democratic system, but at the same time to preserve our constitutional freedoms and democratic procedures.

TRAITORS, SPIES, SABOTEURS, REVOLUTIONARIES

Laws aimed at acts of violence, espionage, sabotage, or treason in themselves raise no constitutional questions, nor do they infringe on protected constitutional liberties. However, they can be used to intimidate if they are loosely drawn or indiscriminately administered. The framers of the Constitution—themselves considered traitors by the English government—knew the dangers of loose definitions of treason. Accordingly, they carefully inserted a constitutional definition by stating that treason consists only of the overt acts of giving aid and comfort to the enemies of the United States or levying war against it. Furthermore, in order to convict a person of treason, the Constitution requires the testimony of two witnesses to the overt treasonable acts or the defendant's confession in open court.

But treason does not exhaust the limits of the constitutional power of the national government to move against conduct designed to subvert the democratic system. Congress, for example, has made it a crime to engage in espionage or sabotage; to cross interstate boundaries or use the mails or interstate facilities to bomb buildings and schools (passed in 1960 and aimed at the white segregationists who were alleged to have blown up black churches and used force to intimidate black leaders and their white allies); or to cross state lines or use interstate facilities with the intent to incite a riot (the so-called Rap Brown law passed in 1968 aimed at black militants who were alleged to foment riots); or to conspire to do any of the above.

More often than not, when the government prosecutes under such laws the charge is conspiracy rather than the charge that somebody has actually committed a violent act. It is easier to prove conspiracy than to get evidence to sustain a charge against a named defendant that he or she has thrown a brick, planted a bomb, engaged in a riot, or committed an act of violence. But conspiracy charges, although long known to Anglo-American jurisprudence, are especially dangerous to civil liberties for they can be abused by prosecutors to intimidate the politically unpopular.

[103] *West Virginia State Board of Education v. Barnette* (1943).

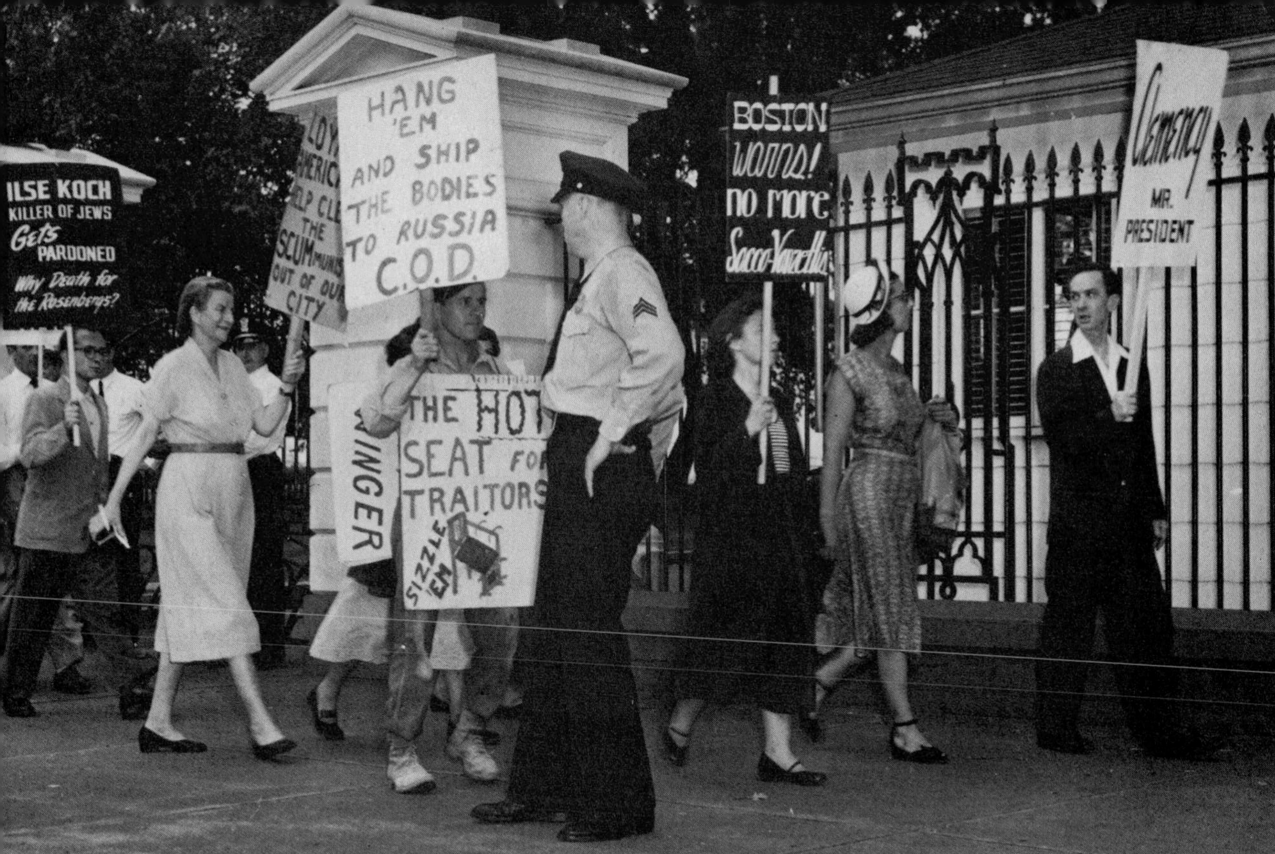
ILSE KOCH
KILLER OF JEWS
Gets
PARDONED
Why Death for the Rosenbergs?
HANG 'EM AND SHIP THE BODIES TO RUSSIA C.O.D.
OUT OF OUR CITY
BOSTON
warns!
no more
Clemency
MR. PRESIDENT
THE HOT SEAT FOR TRAITORS
SIZZLE 'EM

Demonstrators picket in front of the White House while awaiting the Supreme Court decision in the case of convicted atom spies Julius and Ethel Rosenberg. Persons at left and right carry signs on behalf of the Rosenbergs; to the left of the policeman are people carrying slogans with opposite sentiments.

Often the application of these laws against various kinds of "seditious" conduct leads to charges of "political trials." To call a trial a "political trial" is a conclusion rather than a description, for one person's political trial is another's act of justice. This is well illustrated by the famous Chicago Eight trial that grew out of demonstrations at the Democratic Convention of 1968. The charges were conspiracy to cross state lines with intent to incite a riot as well as making certain speeches for the purpose of inciting a riot after having traveled in interstate commerce. Although five defendants were convicted of the substantive charge (they all were acquitted on the conspiracy count), the court of appeals reversed the decision on the grounds that the jury had been improperly selected and that the judge and prosecutor had improperly demonstrated a deprecatory manner toward the defendants and their counsel.

For the most part the highly charged prosecutions of the late 1960s and the early 1970s against political radicals and black militants for allegedly engaging in, or conspiring to engage in, violent acts led either to verdicts of not guilty or reversals on appeal. To some, this is evidence that our court system is strong and can be counted on to protect the innocent. To others it is evidence of the inability of the government to bring to justice those who should have been punished for their deeds. And to still others it is evidence of how governments can use legal procedures to intimidate adherents of unpopular causes. For even if defendants are finally acquitted, the effort and expense of defending themselves in court has an intimidating impact on political dissenters. Historians, journalists, political scientists, and others will be debating the lessons of these trials for many years.

There is little dispute, however, that Congress probably violated the Constitution when as part of the Internal Security Act of 1950 it outlawed any conspiratorial action, peaceful or violent, designed to contribute substantially to the establishment of a foreign-controlled dictatorship in the United States. The Department of Justice has never made an attempt to prosecute anybody under this provision, which is not aimed at specific acts or at the use of violence or unlawful means but attempts to make certain political goals illegal.

SEDITIOUS SPEECH

It is one thing to punish persons for what they do; it is quite another to punish them for what they *say*. The story of the development of free government is in large measure the story of making clear this distinction between speech and other kinds of activity and of restricting the power of government to define and punish seditious speech. Until recent centuries, seditious speech was so broadly defined that all criticism of those in power was considered criminal. As late as the eighteenth century in England, seditious speech was defined as covering any publication intended to incite disaffection against the king or the government or to raise discontent among the people or to promote feelings of ill will between different classes.[104] And it did not make any difference if what was said was true. On the contrary, "the greater the truth the greater the libel." For if one charged the king's ministers with being corrupt and in fact they were corrupt, such a charge would more likely cause discontent among the people than if it were false.

The adoption of the Constitution and the Bill of Rights did not result in a quick, easy victory for those who wished to establish free speech in the United States.[105] In 1798, only seven years after the First Amendment had been ratified, Congress passed the first national sedition law. These were perilous times for the young republic, for war with France seemed imminent. The Federalists, in control of both Congress and the presidency, were so stung by the criticisms of the Jeffersonian Republicans that they persuaded themselves that national safety required a little suppression of speech. The Sedition Act made it a crime to utter false, scandalous, or malicious statements intended to bring the govern-

[104]Zechariah Chafee, Jr., "The Great Liberty: Freedom of Speech and Press," in Alfred H. Kelly, ed., *Foundations of Freedom in the American Constitution* (Harper & Row, 1958), p. 79.

[105]Leonard Levy, *Legacy of Suppression* (Harvard University Press, 1960), and *Freedom of the Press from Zenger to Jefferson* (Bobbs-Merrill, 1966).

ment or any of its officers into disrepute or "to incite against them the hatred of the good people of the United States."[106]

The popular reaction to the Sedition Act helped defeat the Federalists in the elections of 1800. They had failed to grasp the core of the democratic idea that a person may criticize the government of the day, may work for its downfall, may oppose its policies, and still be loyal to the nation.

THE SEDITION ACT OF 1918

Not until World War I did such a severe measure again become the law of the land. In 1918 Congress made it a crime to print, write, or publish any "disloyal, profane, scurrilous, or abusive language about the form of government of the United States or the Constitution . . . or any language intended to bring the form of government of the United States, or the Constitution of the United States, or the military forces . . . or the flag . . . or the uniform of the Army and Navy . . . into contempt, scorn, contumely, or disrepute."

This drastic measure was not aimed at talk that might lead to specific kinds of illegal activity. Rather, it made the speech itself illegal. Like the Sedition Act of 1798, this law made it a crime not only to advocate illegal activities but even to criticize the government. Loosely drawn and poorly administered, it was applied at a time when many people, emotionally aroused by the war, were willing to restrict the liberties of their fellow citizens. As a result of the combined effort of state laws against anarchy and sedition and federal laws against interfering with drafting men for the army, it became a crime "to advocate heavier taxation instead of bond issues, to state that conscription was unconstitutional. . . , to say that the sinking of merchant vessels was legal, to urge that a referendum should have preceded our declaration of war, to say that war was contrary to the teachings of Christ."[107] A twenty-one-year-old girl was sentenced to fifteen years in jail for taking part in the scattering of pamphlets attacking President Wilson and opposing American intervention in Russia.[108] During the "red scare" that followed the war, judges and juries punished hundreds of people who expressed ideas to which their neighbors objected.

THE SMITH ACT OF 1940

The next sedition law, the first to apply in peacetime since the Sedition Act of 1798, was the Smith Act of 1940. It forbids persons with the intent

[106]See James Morton Smith *Freedom's Fetters: The Alien and Sedition Laws and American Civil Liberties* (Cornell University Press, 1956).

[107]Zechariah Chafee, Jr., *Free Speech in the United States* (Harvard University Press, 1941), p. 51; John P. Roche, *The Quest for the Dream* (Macmillan, 1963), pp. 26–76.

[108]*Abrams v. United States* (1919).

to bring it about to advocate forceful overthrow; to distribute, with disloyal intent, matter teaching or advising the overthrow of government by violence; and to organize knowingly or to help organize any group having such purposes.

In *Dennis v. United States* (1951) a majority of the justices agreed that the Smith Act could be constitutionally applied to the leaders of the Communist party who had been charged with conspiring to advocate the violent overthrow of the government, but when the Department of Justice and, in many states, local prosecutors began to go after second-string Communist leaders, the Supreme Court modified its earlier decision. First (*Pennsylvania v. Nelson*, 1956) it ruled that the Smith Act precluded state prosecutions for seditious advocacy against the national government. Then (in *Yates v. United States*, 1957) it held that the *Dennis* decision had been misunderstood. The Smith Act did not outlaw the advocacy of the abstract doctrine of violent overthrow. Justice Harlan explained: "The essential distinction is that those to whom the advocacy is addressed must be urged *to do* something now or in the future, rather than merely *to believe* in something." And more recently the Supreme Court narrowed the *Dennis* holding even further: a state may not proscribe advocacy of the use of force or of law violation "except where such advocacy is directed to inciting or producing *imminent* lawless action and is likely to incite or produce such action."[109]

From this brief survey it seems clear that seditious speech, if narrowly defined to cover only the advocacy of immediate concrete acts of violence, is not constitutionally protected. Such narrowly construed antisedition laws leave totalitarians free to work to achieve their political objectives so long as they abandon the use of force as a means of bringing it about or its specific and immediate advocacy.

THE INTERNAL SECURITY ACT OF 1950

When the Cold War turned into a hot one in Korea, Congress responded with the Internal Security Act of 1950. In addition to the previously mentioned ineffective provision that outlaws conspiratorial action designed to establish a totalitarian dictatorship in the United States, the act strengthens the laws against espionage and sedition, adds to alien registration requirements, makes it more difficult for Communist aliens to enter or remain in the United States, and established procedures to be used in the event of a national emergency to detain any person who could "reasonably" be expected to engage in acts of sabotage or espionage. The detention provisions were never used and on the recommendation of President Nixon were repealed by Congress in 1971.

The most significant part of the act was the creation of the five-person Subversive Activities Control Board that was to determine, on the request of the attorney general, if a particular organization was commu-

[109]*Brandenburg v. Ohio* (1969); *Hess v. Indiana* (1973).

nist or if particular individuals were members of such organizations. After final review of the determinations, including judicial appeals, certain disabilities were to be imposed on these organizations.

The act was almost totally ineffective. Although eleven years after the adoption of the act, the Supreme Court upheld the findings of the Board that the Communist party was indeed a communist organization, as defined by the act, the decision had little consequence.[110] The Supreme Court declared unconstitutional every attempt to impose the sanctions of the act.[111] In the late 1960s by a variety of devices Congress tried to salvage the act and reinvigorate the Board but to no avail. Finally Congress failed to appropriate funds for the Board and it ceased to operate in 1973.

THE COMMUNIST CONTROL ACT OF 1954

In the Communist Control Act of 1954, Congress tried to deprive the Communist party and its successors of "any of the rights, privileges, and immunities attendant upon legal bodies created under the laws of the United States" or any of the states. For the first time in our history, the national government tried to outlaw a political party and to deny some citizens of the opportunity to use the traditional instruments of democracy to achieve their political goals. The act presents a variety of substantial constitutional issues, but so far they have not been raised before the Supreme Court because there has been little attempt to enforce it. The Communist party still operates and its candidates are on the ballot in many states.[112]

Disloyalty: loyalty-security programs

Since 1939 Communists, Nazis, and Fascists have been disqualified from federal employment. During World War II, all applicants for government jobs were carefully investigated and access to classified and secret information was denied to all except those who had been cleared. Then in 1947 President Truman, responding to public concern over disclosures of Communist espionage, created by executive order the first comprehensive and systematic federal loyalty-security program.

This program, as modified by acts of Congress, presidential executive orders, and Supreme Court decisions, now requires an investigation of each applicant for a position in the federal executive branch, the extent of the investigation varying with the nature of the job for which he or

[110] *Albertson v. Subversive Activities Control Board* (1965).

[111] *Aptheker v. Secretary of State* (1964); *United States v. Robel* (1967).

[112] See *Communist Party v. Catherwood* (1961); *Communist Party of Indiana v. Whitcomb* (1974).

she is being considered. The applicant will be denied employment if evidence is uncovered that he or she would not be a good security risk because of untrustworthiness, liability to blackmail, drunkenness, and so on.

Federal employees holding sensitive positions—those directly involving national security—may be summarily dismissed if at any time evidence is uncovered that brings their security status into question. The employee is entitled to a hearing, but the government is under no legal obligation to disclose the name of his accusers or the precise nature and source of the information against him.

For the most part, the Supreme Court has avoided a direct ruling on the constitutionality of the federal security program, but it has narrowly construed the security laws and the applicable executive orders. It has been especially suspicious of those aspects of the security regulations that attempt to extend their coverage to nongovernmental employees such as defense plant workers.[113] The Court has rejected the old notion that working for the government is a privilege which the government can condition at its discretion, but at the same time it has stated (*Cole v. Richardson*, 1972) "there is no constitutionally protected right to overthrow a government by force, violence, or illegal or unconstitutional means." The federal government (and the states) may make reasonable efforts to ensure that those who work for it are not actively involved in attempting to promote its illegal overthrow.

What of the state and local governments? Although few positions occupied by state and local officials directly affect our national security, they too have been concerned about the loyalty of their employees. During the 1950s some states got so carried away that they even tried to impose loyalty oaths on students in public universities, public accountants, occupants of public housing projects, and persons applying for unemployment compensation. One state even included wrestlers and fighters on the list of those who were subject to loyalty oaths, on the grounds—according to the executive secretary of the state athletic commission—that "we didn't want to license a professional boxer or wrestler who might become a hero in the eyes of youthful fans and then discover he was a communist."[114]

Positive oaths that require one to swear or affirm loyalty to the United States or a state as a condition of employment have not presented substantial constitutional objection. But oaths that reverse the normal presumption of innocence and proceed on the assumption that one is disloyal unless he swears to the contrary have run into constitutional obstacles. The Court has struck down oaths that one does not *believe* in force, violence, or communism. It has struck down all except the most narrowly drawn oaths that advocate immediate violent overthrow. It has been unwilling to permit oaths that bring within their net persons

[113]*Vitarelli v. Seaton* (1959); *Greene v. McElroy* (1959).

[114]*Whitehill v. Elkins* (1967).

who are members of an organization that may have unlawful purposes, but who themselves do not participate in the organization's unlawful activities or share in its unlawful purposes.[115] Although by a four-to-three vote the Supreme Court recently did uphold the right of Massachusetts to require from its employees, in addition to the traditional oath of positive support, an oath "to oppose the overthrow of the government by force, violence, or by an illegal or unconstitutional method," it did so only after the majority had construed the oath as requiring nothing more than a promise to abide by the constitutional system in the future.[116]

DISLOYALTY AND DEMOCRACY

Those who support governmental limitations on persons who are organized to destroy democracy argue that these antidemocrats are not entitled to any rights because they are at war with our whole democratic system. They insist that antidemocratic groups, unless carefully controlled, will take advantage of their status as political parties or as organized assocations to camouflage underground activities. Only by denying such groups their veil of secrecy, they argue, can innocent persons be protected. Democratic government, it is contended, must curtail the freedom of those who would destroy freedom.

Most agree that it is appropriate to protect our system against those who are conspiring to destroy it by force. But we should not do so by means that jeopardize the democratic system we are acting to preserve. Times of national peril or internal tension call not for repression of constitutional freedoms but steadfast defense of them.

[115]*Communist Party of Indiana v. Whitcomb* (1947) and cases cited therein.

[116]*Cole v. Richardson* (1972).

Chapter 7 Equality under the law

Consider again the ringing words of the Declaration of Independence: "We hold these truths to be self-evident, that all men are created equal, that they are endowed by their Creator with certain unalienable Rights, that among these are Life, Liberty, and the pursuit of Happiness. . . ." The Declaration does not talk about the equality of white, Christian, or Anglo-Saxon men but of *all* men. This creed of individual dignity and equality is older than our Declaration of Independence; its roots go back at least as far as the teachings of Judaism and Christianity. To act by this creed, to bring practice into conformity with principles, has long been a central preoccupation of Americans.

No doubt it might make some sense to consider the safeguarding of civil rights as a function of government, one of the areas of public policy. Yet unlike other government functions, establishing civil rights policy has the fundamental character of implementing part of the Constitution. For what we are really talking about when we talk about civil rights is the question of whether black Americans or Mexican Americans or American Indians or women are to be given the constitutional rights and the educational and social opportunities to take full part in the political system created by the American Constitution.

Certain liberties are essential to the operation of democratic government. But these liberties are not merely means of attaining self-government; they are ends in themselves. They exist not to protect the government; the government exists to protect them. Our forefathers called them natural rights—today we speak of *human* rights—but the belief is still the same, the belief in the moral primacy of people over government and in the dignity and worth of each individual.

"Our inability to achieve [an] . . . accommodation of racial differences has been our most conspicuous political failure."[1] Today no problem is more compelling than that of ensuring to every American his or her basic civil rights—rights to enjoy life and liberty and to pursue happiness—without discrimination because of race, religion, national origin, sex, or any other attribute not relevant to the right to enjoy life and the pursuit of happiness. American democracy, despite its many triumphs, has not extended civil rights to all people, especially not to blacks, Latinos, American Indians, or to women. From the time they are born until they die these minorities and many women suffer handicaps that other Americans do not face; they are victims of history. These injustices are injuries that Americans live with daily.

What should we do to protect civil rights and to extend opportunities for those who have been discriminated against? These questions have been of significance in our presidential elections; they give rise each year to battles in Congress and to debates in the state legislatures and city councils. And what we do, or fail to do, has significance beyond our national borders. Peoples everywhere follow the treatment of our minorities, especially those of a racial character, with more than casual interest. But it is not only the black, brown, and yellow people of the world who are concerned, for all who hear us talk of democracy—including Americans themselves—may lose faith in a society that denies in fact the very rights that it promises in theory.

Denial of equal rights not only negates the equality that the Declaration of Independence asserts—it is also contrary to the guarantees of the Constitution. For under the Constitution each person has the right to live and work and participate in public affairs, free of discrimination because of his race, religion, sex, or national origin. The Constitution provides two ways of protecting these civil rights: first, by seeing to it that *government itself* imposes no discriminatory barriers; second, by granting the national and state governments authority to act positively to protect civil rights against interference by *private* individuals. In this chapter we shall be concerned with both these aspects, government as a *threat* to civil rights and government as the *protector* of civil rights.

To secure racial justice—an overview

In order to put into context the court decisions, laws, and other kinds of governmental action relating to civil rights, it may be useful to review

[1]Alan P. Grimes, *Equality in America: Religion, Race, and the Urban Majority* (Oxford University Press, 1964), p. 41. See also John P. Roche, *The Quest for the Dream* (Macmillan, 1963).

briefly the accelerating drive to make real the promises of the Declaration of Independence and the Constitution of the United States. For the civil rights crusade is not just a series of legal decisions and statutes, as important as they may be, but an involvement of the entire social, economic, and political system of the United States. Governmental action and reaction is as much the result as the cause of the civil rights movement.

The difficulty of resolving racial tensions and providing justice is not unique to this nation. Racial tensions are probably the most divisive internal issues faced by any society, but they are not the only causes of internal division—witness the white-against-white religious battles in Northern Ireland, the black-against-black conflicts in Nigeria. As Matthew Holden has pointed out, "nowhere in this world has ethnic diversity been easily reconciled with political order and equality. . . . These problems are more difficult when they are combined with the criteria of democracy, constitutionalism, and welfare statism," than for polities like those of the Soviet Union "which neither pretend to nor desire the terms of democratic constitutionalism."[2] Yet it is unclear whether states like the Soviet Union have done any better with these problems than have the democracies.

Ku Klux Klan members marched in silent protest against passage of the Civil Rights Act of 1964.

Americans have had a special confrontation with the problem of race—before, during, and after the Civil War. Because the North won that war, the Thirteenth, Fourteenth, and Fifteenth Amendments—to abolish slavery and all badges of servitude, and grant to blacks all rights enjoyed by every other American—became part of the Constitution. Congress enacted a series of civil rights laws to enforce these promises and established special programs, such as the Freedman's Bureau, to provide educational and social services to the recently freed slaves.

But before these programs had a significant impact, the political community of white Americans became reunited. By 1877, Northern political leaders abandoned blacks to their fate at the hands of their former white masters. The president no longer concerned himself with the enforcement of civil rights laws, Congress ceased to enact new ones, and the Supreme Court either declared civil rights acts unconstitutional or so narrowly construed them that they were ineffective. The Court also gave such limited construction to the Thirteenth, Fourteenth, and Fifteenth Amendments as protections against racial discrimination that there ceased to be any effective limitation on the authority of the dominant white groups to drive blacks from the political arena.

By the end of the century, white supremacy reigned unchallenged in the South, where most blacks lived at the time. Despite the Constitution, blacks were kept from the polls, forced to accept menial jobs, and denied educational opportunities. In 1896 the Supreme Court, by an eight-to-one vote, gave constitutional sanction to governmentally im-

[2]Matthew Holden, Jr., *The Divisible Republic: Part II, The White Man's Burden* (Abelard-Schuman, 1973), p. 257.

posed racial segregation (see p. 187). Even if the Court had declared segregation unconstitutional at that time, a decision so contrary to popular feeling and political realities would have had little immediate impact. Blacks were considered by many whites, North and South, to be childlike. Southern political leaders openly and unapologetically espoused white supremacy. In 1896 blacks were lynched at an average of one every ninety to one hundred hours, and few citizens, black or white, raised a voice in protest.

During World War I blacks began to migrate to Northern cities, and by then there were small beginnings toward educational opportunities and jobs. These trends were accelerated by the New Deal and World War II. And the South, through urbanization and industrialization, became more like the rest of the nation. As the migration of blacks out of the rural South into Southern and Northern cities shifted the racial composition of cities, the votes of blacks became important in national elections. There were more jobs, more social gains. And above all, these changes created a black middle class to which segregation as a symbol of servitude and a cause of inequality became a primary target. By the middle of the twentieth century urban blacks were no longer passive recipients of white men's favors but active and politically powerful citizens. There was a growing, persistent, and insistent demand for the abolition of color barriers.

GOVERNMENT BEGINS TO RESPOND

The first branch of the national government to become sensitized to these growing pressures from black Americans was the presidency. Because of the special nature of the electoral college and the pattern of our political system, by the 1930s no person in the White House, or hoping to live there, could afford to ignore the aspirations of blacks. The commitment of our presidents to the cause of equal protection under the laws became translated into the appointment of federal judges more sympathetic to a construction of the Thirteenth, Fourteenth, and Fifteenth Amendments in the manner originally intended by those who proposed them.

In the 1930s blacks started to resort to litigation to secure their rights, especially to challenge the doctrine of segregation as a sham and a device to impose discrimination. They emphasized litigation because at the time they had no alternative; they lacked the political power to make their demands effective before either the state legislatures or the Congress.

By the 1950s civil rights litigation began to have its impact. Under the leadership of the Supreme Court, federal judges started to construe the Fourteenth Amendment to reverse earlier decisions that rendered it and federal legislation ineffective. The Supreme Court outlawed all forms of governmentally imposed racial segregation and struck down most of the devices that had been used so long by state and local authorities to keep blacks from voting.[3] Presidents, too, were using their executive authority to end, or to attempt to end, segregation in the armed services and federal employment and were directing more of the resources of the Department of Justice to enforce whatever civil rights laws were available.

Finally, as the 1950s came to a close, the emerging national consensus in favor of positive governmental action to protect civil rights and the growing political voice of blacks began to have their impact on Congress. Until then, the House of Representatives had frequently adopted civil rights bills, but the intense opposition of Southern Democrats and the indifference of many conservative Republicans, combined with Senate rules that gave an advantage to a determined minority, made it impossible to secure positive Senate action. In the 1956 elections, for the first time since the New Deal there was a substantial movement of black voters into the Republican column, especially in the cities. Neither party could consider the black vote "safe"; neither could ignore the demands of those urging civil rights legislation; neither wanted to be tagged as opposed to civil rights. Southern Democrats, though still powerful enough to force concessions, were no longer able to block all civil rights legislation. Finally, in 1957, Congress overrode a Southern filibuster in the Senate and enacted the first civil rights law since Reconstruction. Repeatedly during the 1960s came additional and significant civil rights legislation. By the 1970s all branches of the national government, reflecting a widespread and politically strong national consensus, had placed their weight behind those fighting racism.

During the 1960s the issues and the battles changed. During the 1950s, the conflict had been seen primarily as an attempt to use the weight of national authority to compel white Southerners to cease using state governments to segregate blacks into inferior schools, parks, libraries, houses, and jobs. The major effort was to put down determined and sustained Southern resistance to the Supreme Court's frontal attack on segregation in the schools. Representatives of the Deep South were trying to curb the Court. Southern state legislatures, dominated by members from small towns and rural areas where segregationist sentiments were most deep-seated, reached back to pre-Civil War precedents and asserted the right to "interpose" and resist the Supreme Court's mandates; some even claimed the right to declare the Court's decisions null and void. A host of organizations sprang up to fight for segregation. The more ardent segregationists insisted not only that school boards had no duty to obey the Supreme Court but that authorities should resist judicial decrees by every possible means. Although decrying force, they urged parents to barricade and boycott schools in order to keep black children from attending schools previously reserved for whites. When violence flared, attempts to use police and military

[3]For a general history of Supreme Court decisions affecting the constitutional rights of blacks, see Loren Miller, *The Petitioners* (Meridian Books, 1967).

forces to contain it were met with cries of "federal tyranny" and "police brutality."

At first, blacks had to stand up to such resistance without much help from federal authorities. Only when law and order collapsed completely or when there was open defiance of the orders of federal judges did the president intervene. By the end of the 1960s this had changed. The Department of Justice, the president, and the Congress moved to compel compliance with desegregation. Resistance to it still persists, but now the whole nature of the struggle to secure racial justice has altered.

1963 A TURNING POINT

A decade after the Supreme Court declared public school segregation to be unconstitutional, most black children in the South still attended segregated schools. Furthermore, in the North, segregation in housing and education remained the established pattern in the cities. Congress had enacted laws, judges had issued injunctions, presidents had proclaimed executive orders and appointed commissions—so most legal barriers in the path of equal rights had fallen. But black Americans still could not buy a house where they wanted, secure the job they needed, find educational opportunities for their children, or walk secure in the knowledge that they would not be subjected to insults. And what had once been thought of as a Southern problem was recognized as a national problem.

By 1963 the struggles in the courtrooms were being supplemented by a massive social, economic, and political movement. What had been largely a conflict arousing the emotions and commitments of the more highly educated and economically secure blacks gripped the feelings of thousands of men and women, from the domestic servant to the Nobel Prize winner.

The black revolt of 1963 did not come unannounced, and its immediate background did not stem directly from the struggle to desegregate the public schools. In one sense it began when the first Negro slave was educated 300 years ago, but its more immediate origin was in 1955 in Montgomery, Alabama, when the black community engaged in a boycott of the city buses to protest segregation on them. The boycott worked. And from the Montgomery incident the civil rights movement produced its first charismatic leader—the Reverend Martin Luther King, who, through his Southern Christian Leadership Conference and his doctrine of nonviolent resistance, provided a new dimension to the struggle for civil rights. By the early 1960s, new organizational resources to support and sponsor sit-ins, freedom rides, live-ins, and mass demonstrations came into existence in almost every city.

In the summer of 1963 the forces of social discontent created a national crisis. It started with a demonstration in Birmingham, Alabama, which was countered by the use of fire hoses, police dogs, and mass arrests, and culminated in a march in Washington, D.C., where over

200,000 people heard King speak of his dream of the day when children "will live in a nation where they will not be judged by the color of their skin, but by the content of their character." By the time the summer was over there was hardly a city that had not had a demonstration, protest, or sit-in; in many, there were riots. This direct action had some effect: civil rights ordinances were enacted in many cities and existing legislation broadened; more schools were desegregated that fall than in any year since 1956; and at the national level, President Kennedy urged Congress to enact a comprehensive civil rights bill. But Congress did not act.

Late in 1963, the nation's grief over the assassination of John Kennedy, who had become identified with civil rights goals, added political fuel to the drive for federal action. President Johnson gave the adoption of civil rights legislation the highest priority of his program. On July 2, 1964, after months of debate, President Johnson signed the Civil Rights Act of 1964 into law.

BLACK MILITANCY, BLACK AWARENESS, AND BLACK POWER[4]

At the close of the 1960s, the legal phases of the civil rights movement had about come to a close. Restraints previously imposed on black Americans through the use of the instruments of government by white Americans had been more or less removed. But as "things got better," discontent became more intense. Once the chains of slavery began to be withdrawn, the stings that remained hurt more. When blacks had been completely subjugated, they had lacked resources to defend themselves. But, as is true of almost all social revolutions, as conditions began to improve, demands became more and more insistent. And the millions of impoverished black Americans, like the white Americans who came before them, have demonstrated growing impatience with the discrimination that remains—the same frustrations that are now heard by the dispossessed around the world.

Many black Americans feel that changes are not coming large enough or soon enough. But many white Americans disagree. Some, though believing in equal rights, think that until blacks secure education and social resources, they will be unable to profit from the opportunities presently available; others view direct action as confirmation of their long-held view that the black must be "kept in his place." Black Americans have persisted in their pursuit of equal rights, and the attitudes between and within white and black America have hardened.

It is not surprising that this highly volatile situation should give way to racial violence and disorders. By 1965, the year of the Watts riots in Los Angeles, it was all too clear that disorders were becoming a part of the American scene. In 1966 and 1967 these disorders increased in scope

[4]See Joel D. Aberbach and Jack L. Walker, "The Meanings of Black Power," *American Political Science Review* (June 1970), pp. 367–88.

House divided.

From *The Herblock Gallery* (Simon & Schuster, 1968).

and intensity, with the Detroit riot in July 1967 being the worst race riot in modern American history.

In July 1967 President Johnson appointed a special Advisory Commission on Civil Disorders to investigate the origins of the disorders and to recommend measures to prevent or contain such disasters in the future. "Not even the sternest police action," said the president, "nor the most effective federal troops can ever create lasting peace in our cities." The president concluded:

> The only genuine, long-range solution for what has happened lies in an attack—mounted at every level—upon the conditions that breed despair and violence. All of us know what those conditions are: ignorance, discrimination, slums, poverty, disease, not enough jobs. We should attack these conditions—not because we are frightened by conflict, but because we are fired by conscience. We should attack them because there is simply no other way to achieve a decent and orderly society in America.

The single most characteristic feature of the eleven-person Commission, which came to be known as the Kerner Commission after its chairman, then Governor Otto Kerner of Illinois, was that both its black and white members were drawn from the "moderate and responsible establishment." Once the commission issued its report, however, personalities faded into relative insignificance. In stark, clear language, a unanimous commission said, "What white Americans have never fully understood—but what the Negro can never forget—is that white society is deeply implicated in the ghetto. *White institutions created it, white institutions maintain it, and white society condones it.*"

TWO SOCIETIES?

The basic conclusions of the commission was that "our nation is moving toward two societies, one black, one white—separate and unequal" and that "only a commitment to national action on an unprecedented scale" could stem this trend. National action, said the commission, should be based on these objectives:

> Opening up opportunities to those who are restricted by racial segregation and discrimination, and eliminating all barriers to their choice of jobs, education and housing.
>
> Removing the frustration of powerlessness among the disadvantaged by explicitly helping them to deal with the problems that affect their own lives and by increasing the capacity of our public and private institutions to respond to these problems.
>
> Increasing communication across racial lines to destroy stereotypes, halt polarization, end distrust and hostility, and create common grounds for efforts toward public order and social justice.[5]

[5] *Report of the National Advisory Commission on Civil Disorders* (U.S. Government Printing Office, 1968).

To fulfill these objectives, the commission made sweeping recommendations concerning employment, education, housing, and the welfare system.[6] Although the Vietnam War, the Nixon resignation, and the partial calming down of racial tensions have diverted attention momentarily away from questions about how the two nations—black and white—can live together in peace and with justice, this remains our most important internal issue.

Where do we stand? As legal barriers have been progressively lowered by civil rights legislation and judicial decisions, the remaining restraints appear to be primarily economic and social. Not that there is complete compliance with the legislation; ways are still found to thwart, circumvent, or obstruct the force of these laws, especially those that apply to housing and employment. But what now appears to stand in the way of faster and more effective advancement by the impoverished blacks of our cities and rural countryside is lack of modern job skills, poor education, inadequate housing and income; and future legislation is more likely to be aimed at creating programs to overcome these handicaps than was the civil rights legislation of the 1960s.

There will be continuing friction among black Americans (and white Americans), not only over the means of achieving the goals of equality but over ends as well. A few black Americans see violent action as the only way to get "the system" to respond; more believe that changes can be brought about through peaceful direct action, but most apparently still favor the traditional electoral and political methods of bargaining, negotiation, and building coalitions with other political interests.[7] Black Americans also differ over where such strategy should lead. Some see complete integration of the races as the end; others—such as the black nationalists—see complete separation of the races as the only realistic solution. Still others see cultural pluralism as the answer: a society in which there will remain identifiable black and white communities, but communities that individuals are free to move into and out of, just as in many large cities there are Irish and Polish and Greek neighborhoods, neighborhoods of choice rather than of compulsion.

THREE SOCIETIES OR MORE?

The rise of black militancy and the struggle for racial justice has stimulated other minorities, most especially Latinos and American Indians, to organize and to insist that they too be accorded the rights promised by the Declaration of Independence and secured by the Constitution. To black power has been added brown power, sometimes as an ally, sometimes as an opponent, but all part of the rising political activity of what has come to be called euphemistically "disadvantaged groups."

[6]*Ibid.*, Chap. 17.

[7]See Matthew Holden, Jr., *The Divisible Republic: Part I, The Politics of the Black 'Nation'* (Abelard-Schuman, 1973), especially pp. 42–131.

And as the 1960s came to a close, these forces of discontent with the status quo were dramatically augmented by a revival of the long-smoldering feminist movement now called Women's Liberation. Although the Nineteenth Amendment had ended discrimination against women as voters, it had not brought to an end the discrimination they suffered in employment, schooling, freedom to manage property, and a host of other disabilities imposed on them either by law or social custom.

Finally as the 1970s opened, there was also a revival of concern about the "ethnics" – that is, white Americans not of Anglo-Saxon heritage. In the past the American model was supposedly to become the melting pot in which all persons regardless of background would become more and more alike. But in part as a reaction to the rise of the blacks and browns, in part as a statement in defense of ethnic neighborhoods, but also in part as a recognition of the values of cultural pluralism, we are now also beginning to hear about Polish power and Irish power. We are also hearing an insistence that it is as wrong to stereotype all blue-collar ethnics as Archie Bunkers as it is to stereotype all blacks as "Yassuh boss."

More than two hundred and fifteen million Americans of all colors and ethnic backgrounds have managed, not always wisely or fairly, to operate within the framework of a single society and government. The challenge is to move from survival as a nation to give reality to the promise of equal justice for all.

These are the social and political realities of the struggle for justice. But what have been the governmental response and initiatives in the areas of segregation, voting, criminal justice, housing, employment, and public accommodations? Before we examine them, it is valuable first to review the constitutional standards that relate most directly to the questions of equal justice under the law.

Equal protection under the laws – what does it mean?

The Fourteenth Amendment declares, "No state [including any subdivision thereof] shall . . . deny to any person within its jurisdiction the equal protection of the laws." Although there is no equal-protection clause limiting the national government, the Fifth Amendment's due process clause has been construed to impose the same restraints on the national government.

The Constitution does not forbid the government from making distinctions among people, for it could not legislate without doing so. What the Constitution forbids is *unreasonable* classifications. In general, a classification is unreasonable when there is no relation between the classes it creates and permissible governmental goals. For example, a law prohibiting redheads from voting would be unreasonable, because there is no relation between having red hair and the ability to vote. On the other hand, laws denying to persons under eighteen the right to vote, to marry without the permission of their parents, or a license to drive a car are reasonable because there seems to be (at least to most persons over eighteen) a relationship between chronological age and the ability to vote sensibly, marry wisely, and drive safely. Similarly, the Supreme Court has held that it is reasonable to treat the rich different from the poor for the purpose of levying taxes (but not for voting), and to classify property according to its use for zoning purposes.

The traditional test to determine whether a law complies with the equal protection requirement places the burden of proof upon those attacking the law. If any facts can be pointed out that would justify a classification, it will be sustained. "It's enough that the State action be rationally based and free from invidious discrimination. . . . It does not offend the Constitution because the classification is not made with mathematical nicety or because in practice it results in some inequality."[8] To illustrate, the Supreme Court upheld Illinois's exemption of individuals from paying personal property taxes while at the same time imposing such taxes on corporations. Said Justice Douglas for the Court, "Where taxation is concerned, and no specific federal right, apart from equal protection, is imperiled, the states have large leeway in making classifications and drawing lines which in their judgment produce reasonable systems of taxation."[9]

SUSPECT CLASSIFICATIONS

But the Supreme Court's deference to the judgment of the legislatures and its use of the less exacting "rational basis" test does not hold in two situations. The first is when a suspect classification is involved; the second is when a fundamental right is involved. First consider the situation when a suspect classification is involved.

There are certain classifications that are "odious to our system," "constitutionally suspect," "subject to the most rigid scrutiny," and in most instances irrelevant. Race, alienage, national origin, and illegitimacy are clearly such classifications.[10] So is religion, although there is no specific Supreme Court decision to this effect, probably because states have seldom tried to classify persons on the basis of their particular religion. The Court has left us somewhat confused about wealth, but it would appear that laws that have an adverse effect on the totally indigent are to be considered as dealing with a constitutionally suspect classification. Sex may be added to the suspect list, although only four justices have specifically stated that they so consider it.[11]

[8] *Dandridge v. Williams* (1970); *Jefferson v. Hackney* (1972); *Kahn v. Shevin* (1974).

[9] *Lehnhausen v. Lake Shore Auto Parts Co.* (1973).

[10] *San Antonio School District v. Rodriguez* (1973); *Frontiero v. Richardson* (1973); *Gomez v. Perez* (1973) and cases cited therein.

[11] *Frontiero v. Richardson* (1973); *Kahn v. Shevin* (1974).

Constitutionally suspect classifications, explained Justice Powell, are of persons "saddled with such disabilities, or subject to such a history of purposeful unequal treatment, or relegated to such positions of political powerlessness as to command extraordinary protection from the majoritarian political process."

When a law comes before the Court involving a suspect classification, the normal presumption of constitutionality is reversed. It is not sufficient that the law merely be a reasonable and rational means for handling a particular problem. Rather, the Supreme Court must be persuaded that there is some "compelling public interest" to justify the law, and the state must demonstrate that there is no alternative way less restrictive in its impact on the suspect classification to accomplish the compelling public purpose.

Of all the suspect classifications perhaps the most suspect are those based on *race*. The Supreme Court has come very close to ruling that any classification based on race is necessarily unreasonable. However, despite its deep suspicion of such classifications the Court has not made a blanket prohibition of all racial classifications. Indeed during the Second World War, the Supreme Court sustained the right of the government to force American citizens of Japanese ancestry to leave their homes and their jobs on the West Coast and to go to what were euphemistically called "relocation camps."

Since World War II, the Supreme Court appears to agree with the first Justice Harlan, who, dissenting in *Plessy v. Ferguson*, stated, "The Constitution is color blind." With one clear and one possible exception, the Court has refused to sustain any law based on a racial classification for whatever purpose: marriage, schools, parks, prison. The one clear exception is that the Court has *upheld* judicial decrees that order the assignment of pupils and teachers to schools on a racial basis as a means of dismantling racially segregated school systems. The Court noted, "Just as the race of students must be considered in determining whether a constitutional violation has occurred, so also must race be considered in formulating a remedy. To forbid, at this stage, all assignments made on the basis of race, would deprive school authorities of the one tool absolutely essential to fulfillment of their constitutional obligation to eliminate existing dual school systems."[12]

The other possible exception is that the Court (*Morton v. Mancari*, 1974) ruled that the preference the Bureau of Indian Affairs gives to Indians in original hiring and promotions over non-Indians does not constitute invidious racial discrimination. A unanimous court was obviously much influenced by the long historical and constitutionally prescribed special relationship between the national government and the Indian tribes, and described the employment preference as "an employment criterion reasonably designed to further the cause of Indian self-government."

[12]*North Carolina State Board v. Swann* (1971).

More difficult constitutional questions are presented by the various affirmative action programs that deliberately weigh the scales in favor of blacks, women, and other groups who have been subjected to discrimination. (India amended its Constitution to overcome the equivalent of our equal-protection clause in order to allow special treatment for persons of low caste.) In 1974 the Supreme Court dodged the issue when it dismissed as moot the challenge of a white law student to his university's affirmative action program designed to provide special opportunities for blacks *(DeFunis v. Odegaard).* The issue is of such national importance that the Supreme Court is likely to confront it again in the near future.

CLASSIFICATION BY SEX

What of classifications based on sex? It was as late as 1971 before any classification based on sex was declared to violate the equal-protection clause. Prior to that time state laws excluding or restricting women's participation on juries had been sustained, as well as many laws purporting to provide special protection for women, such as one in Ohio forbidding any woman other than the wife or daughters of an owner of a tavern to serve as barmaids.[13]

The 1964 Civil Rights Act makes illegal laws or company regulations of firms affecting interstate commerce imposing job discrimination on women. Then in the fall of 1971, a unanimous Court in *Reed v. Reed* stated that the preference Idaho gave to fathers over mothers in the administration of their children's estates "cannot stand in the face of the Fourteenth Amendment's command that no State deny the equal protection to any person within its jurisdiction. A criterion based on sex for the purpose of administering estates," said the justices, "is arbitrary and wholly unrelated to the objective of the statute."

Two years later, the Supreme Court by a vote of eight to one (*Frontiero v. Richardson,* 1973) struck down as unconstitutional a federal law providing for dependency benefits for the wives of all male military officers but only for such husbands of female officers who were dependent on their wives for over one half of their support. Justice Brennan, speaking for three other justices, ruled that sex, like race, was a suspect classification. He conceded that this has not always been the construction of the Constitution. "Indeed," he wrote, "there can be no doubt that our Nation has had a long and unfortunate history of sex discrimination. Traditionally, such discrimination was rationalized by an attitude of 'romantic paternalism' which, in practical effect put women, not on a pedestal, but in a cage." Four other justices concurred in the judgment, but refrained from holding that sex is a suspect classification. Justice Powell pointed out that the proposed Equal Rights Amendment is currently before the nation so that it might make this choice, if it so wishes, through the amendatory process.

[13]*Goesaert v. Cleary* (1948).

Then to add to the confusion, in 1974 *(Kahn v. Shevin)* six members of the Court speaking through Justice Douglas (who in the *Frontiero* case had joined in the view that sex classifications are suspect and to be considered presumptively unconstitutional) sustained a Florida statute granting widows, but not widowers, an annual $500 property exemption on their taxes. Justice Douglas treated this as a routine tax law, subject only to the rational means test, and ruled that Florida could reasonably conclude that a lone woman is more likely to face financial difficulties than a lone man. The dissenting justices contended that if the state was anxious to help the poor it should have limited its exemption to those who are poor, whether male or female.

The Supreme Court further complicated the issue of sex as a suspect classification when it ruled (*Geduldig v. Aiello*, 1974) that a California disability insurance program for private employees that excludes from coverage disabilities resulting from normal pregnancy does not violate the equal-protection clause. The Court applied the traditional test and said that California could decide what risks would be covered and what excluded so long as it did not discriminate against any specific groups. Here women as a group received as much from the program as did men. The three dissenting justices argued that the Court was retreating from its *Frontiero* decision that required a more severe constitutional test for laws that created gender-based classifications.

In short, until the Equal Rights Amendment is adopted, which will make sex classifications unacceptable, the Supreme Court seems to be making sex a suspect classification but not as clearly so as is race. But, the adoption of ERA will not end all constitutional questions; questions would still arise over sex-related classifications. For example, may a state for some purposes treat mothers differently from other people?

FUNDAMENTAL RIGHTS

The Supreme Court also subjects state regulations to especially stringent scrutiny when the laws impinge on "fundamental rights." The justices are not too clear what makes a right fundamental, but Justice Powell, speaking for a five-man majority in *San Antonio School District v. Rodriguez* (1973), explained that it is not the social importance of the right nor the justices' conclusions about the significance of the right that determines whether or not it is fundamental, but whether *it is explictly or implictly guaranteed by the Constitution.* Under this test the right to travel has been held to be fundamental in this constitutional sense, along with the right to vote and First Amendment rights, but not the right to an education or to housing or to welfare benefits. Important as are these latter rights, there is nothing in the Constitution guaranteeing to any person that the government will provide them with an education, a house, welfare benefits, or are there any specific constitutional provisions protecting these rights from governmental regulation.[14]

[14] *San Antonio School District v. Rodriguez* (1973) and cases cited therein.

Once the Court decides that a right is fundamental, laws impinging on it, like those impacting suspect classifications, must meet the more stringent constitutional test: the state must demonstrate a compelling public need and persuade the Court that it has acted by procedures that impose the least possible restraint on the fundamental right in question.

SUBSTANTIVE EQUAL PROTECTION

This new construction of the equal-protection clause as applied to fundamental rights or suspect classifications is called *substantive* equal protection. It would be tedious to list all the cases in which it has been applied in recent years, but here are a few examples: a state may not make persons who have resided within the state for less than a year ineligible to vote (fifty days is permissible);[15] a state may not make ownership of property a requirement to serve on a school board;[16] a state may not make it a crime for a doctor to prescribe a contraceptive device to an unmarried person;[17] a state may not by filing fees keep indigents from getting on ballots;[18] a state may not deprive illegitimate children from suing their biological fathers for support or from recovering damages for the wrongful death of their parents;[19] a state may not require indigents to pay a fee before being allowed to sue for divorce (but such requirements have been upheld as applied to bankruptcy proceedings).[20]

The life and death of Jim Crow

This review of the Supreme Court's interpretation of the equal-protection clause gets us considerably ahead of our story. We must return to the last century.

Laws requiring the segregation of blacks and whites date only from the end of the nineteenth century.[21] Prior to that time it was social custom and economic status, rather than law, that kept the two races apart. But segregationists began to insist that laws were needed to maintain racial segregation, and before long, Southern states and cities had made it a crime for whites and blacks to ride in the same car on a train, attend

[15] *Dunn v. Blumstein* (1972).

[16] *Turner v. Fourche* (1970).

[17] *Eisenstadt v. Baird* (1972).

[18] *Lubin v. Panish* (1974).

[19] *Weber v. Aetna Casualty and Surety Co.* (1972).

[20] *Boddie v. Connecticut* (1971).

[21] C. Vann Woodward, *The Strange Career of Jim Crow*, rev. ed. (Oxford University Press, 1968).

the same theater, or go to the same school. "Jim Crow" laws, as they came to be called, soon blanketed Southern life. How could these laws be adopted and enforced in the face of the equal-protection clause?

IS SEGREGATION DISCRIMINATION?: PLESSY V. FERGUSON

In 1896 the Supreme Court, in *Plessy v. Ferguson*, endorsed the view that racial segregation did not constitute discrimination and that states by law could require the separation of races in public places as long as equal accommodations were provided for all. Even equal accommodations were not required except for services provided by public funds or for a limited category of public utilities, such as trains and buses. Under this *separate-but-equal* formula, several states, most of which were in the South, enforced segregation in transportation, places of public accommodation, and education.

The *Plessy* decision was forward-looking for its time, because it did require equality as the price for a state to adopt a program of compulsory segregation. But for many years the "equal" part of the formula was meaningless. States segregated blacks into unequal facilities and blacks lacked a political voice to protest. The Supreme Court did not help. In 1899, for example, the Court found no denial of equal protection in the fact that a county provided a high school for white citizens but none for the sixty black children in the district.[22] The passage of time did not lessen the inequality. In 1950, in all the segregated states, there were fourteen medical schools for whites, none for blacks; sixteen law schools for whites, five for blacks; fifteen engineering schools for whites, none for blacks; five dentistry schools for whites, none for blacks.

Beginning in the late 1930s blacks started to file lawsuits challenging the separate-but-equal doctrine. They cited facts to show that in practice separate-but-equal always resulted in discrimination against blacks. However, the Supreme Court was not yet willing to upset the doctrine directly. Rather, it began to undermine it. The Court scrutinized each situation and in case after case ordered facilities to be equalized.

THE END OF SEPARATE-BUT-EQUAL: *BROWN V. BOARD OF EDUCATION*

Finally, in the spring of 1954 in *Brown v. Board of Education*, the Supreme Court reversed its 1896 holding as applied to public schools and ruled that "separate but equal" is a contradiction in terms and that segregation is itself discrimination. A year later, the Court ordered school boards to proceed with all deliberate speed to desegregate public schools at the earliest practicable date.[23]

[22]*Cumming v. County Board of Education* (1899). See also J. W. Peltason, *Fifty-eight Lonely Men: Southern Federal Judges and School Desegregation* (University of Illinois Press, 1971), p. 248.

[23]*Brown v. Board of Education* (1955).

It was one thing for the Supreme Court to declare unconstitutional racial segregation in the public schools. It has been another to abolish such segregation. In the South, some school officials tried to circumvent desegregation orders by assigning pupils to segregated schools for reasons other than race, closing schools to which blacks had been assigned, using the pretext of violence as justification for delaying action. In the North, racial segregation in housing resulted in de facto segregation, with black children often being crowded into the worst schools with the least resources.

In the years since the *Brown* decisions, federal judges have struck down a whole battery of evasive schemes. In the Little Rock, Arkansas, case (*Cooper v. Aaron*, 1958), in an opinion signed by all members of the Court individually—an unprecedented move to indicate their unanimity and strength of conviction—the Court stated, "The constitutional rights of children not to be discriminated against in school admission on grounds of race or color . . . can neither be nullified openly and directly by state legislators or state executives or judicial officers, nor nullified indirectly by them through evasive schemes for segregation whether attempted ingeniously or ingenuously." Community opposition, even violent protests, said the Court, could not justify and delay: "Law and order are not . . . to be preserved by depriving the Negro children of their constitutional rights."

Beginning in 1963, the Supreme Court gradually reversed its second *Brown* decision granting school districts time to prepare for desegregation. In 1969 the Court stated unequivocally: "Continued operation of racially segregated schools under the standard of 'all deliberate speed' is no longer constitutionally permissible. School districts must immediately terminate dual school systems based on race and operate only unitary school systems."[24]

Congress and the presidency have gradually increased their involvement in bringing about desegregation. The 1964 Civil Rights Act authorized the attorney general to initiate desegregation suits. But of even greater significance, the act stipulates that federal dollars—of major importance since the adoption of the Elementary and Secondary Education Act of 1965—must be withdrawn from any school district or public institution of higher education that discriminates "on the ground of race, color, or national origin"—the Education Act of 1972 adds sex to the list—in "any program or activity receiving federal financial assistance."[25] (It was under the 1964 Civil Rights Act and the HEW regulations designed to implement it that the Supreme Court ruled that San Francisco school system had an obligation to provide English language instruction for the more than 1,800 students of Chinese ancestry who do

[24]*Alexander v. Board of Education* (1969).

[25]Gary Orfield, *The Reconstruction of Southern Education: The Schools and the 1964 Civil Rights Act* (John Wiley, 1969), p. 355.

The Reverend Martin Luther King, Jr. was an early leader in the struggle for black integration. His peaceful protests often led to further demonstrations, marches, and police arrest.

not speak English.)[26] The act, in addition, makes federal funds available to help school districts desegregate.

One of the burning issues of the times is whether the Constitution demands merely that school districts not require racial separation or whether authorities have a positive duty to achieve racially balanced schools by such means as pupil assignment or busing of children from one neighborhood to another. By and large Congress has been hostile to busing. The Civil Rights Act of 1964, for example, defined desegregation as *not* meaning "the assignment of students to public schools in order to overcome racial imbalance," and stipulated that nothing in the act shall "expand any official or court of the United States" authority to require busing. The Nixon Administration refused to withhold funds from or bring suit against districts which adopted desegregation programs that contained "neutral assignment plans" and that had no provision for busing, with the result that a large measure of de facto segregation remained.

In 1971 the Supreme Court in *Swann v. Charlotte-Meckleburg Board of Education* and companion cases, in a unanimous decision, held that a district judge could, among other things, order a school district as a

[26]*Lau v. Nichols* (1974).

means of eliminating all vestiges of state-imposed segregation to bus students a reasonable distance beyond their own neighborhoods. "All things being equal," said Chief Justice Burger, "with no history of discrimination, it might well be desirable to assign pupils to schools nearest their homes." But in districts that previously operated segregated systems "desegregation plans cannot be limited to walk-in schools." In short, a school district which previously operated a segregated system has an obligation to act positively to achieve desegregation, and a federal judge has authority to order them to do so. In areas where there has not been a history of governmentally imposed school segregation, however, authorities if they wish may bus children from one neighborhood to another in order to achieve some kind of racial balance but have no constitutional responsibility to do so.

What about de facto school segregation that results from the concentration of blacks in the central city and of whites in the suburbs?[27] A federal judge in Detroit (who was upheld by the court of appeals) concluded that the Detroit schools could not be properly desegregated if considered in isolation. Since, he ruled, school districts are "no more than arbitrary lines on a paper drawn for political convenience," he ordered the assignment and busing of pupils throughout the entire Detroit metropolitan area—that is, the city and fifty-four adjacent school districts.

But the Supreme Court (*Milliken v.* Bradley, 1974) by a five-to-four vote reversed this decision. The majority, speaking through Chief Justice Burger, ruled that at least in metropolitan areas where it was not shown that the school district lines had been drawn for the purpose of maintaining segregation, and where there was no evidence that the suburban districts were being operated in a racially discriminatory fashion, a judge should not order cross-district busing. To do so, the Chief Justice commented, would make the judge in effect the superintendent of schools for the entire metropolitan area, a task "which few, if any, judges are qualified to perform and one which would deprive the people of control of schools through their elected representatives."

The dissenting justices were especially biting in their comments. Justice Douglas called the decision a dramatic retreat from *Plessy v. Ferguson* because the black children of Detroit were not only to be kept in separate schools, but they are not even to be equal to those of the white children in the suburbs. Justice White said the majority had ignored the role of the state and had left the people of Detroit with no effective remedy to overcome school segregation. Justice Marshall commented that "unless our children begin to learn together, there is little hope that our people will ever learn to live together."

Obviously the Court's decision in this and the other busing cases does not end the matter. The highly charged nature of busing is such that like other emotionally packed issues, Congress, president, and the

[27]Robert L. Green, *Northern School Desegregation: Educational, Legal, and Political Issues* (National Society for the Study of Education, 1974).

electorate—and not merely the judges—are participating in its resolution. Proposals for constitutional amendments and laws to forbid court-ordered school busing are before Congress. Busing was a hotly debated issue in the 1972 elections, and it is likely to be a heated subject throughout the 1970s.

WHERE DO WE STAND?

By the fall of 1970, *de jure* (required by law) segregation had all but disappeared, even in the Deep South. Nonetheless, many black children still attend schools in which there are no or very few white students. More children attend de facto segregated schools in the North than in the South.

Some blacks have become disillusioned about securing integrated schools or even the desirability of integration. The general counsel of the New York City Commission on Human Rights told a Senate committee: "You are simply not going to integrate most of the children now trapped inside the sprawling ghettos of Chicago, Detroit, Philadelphia, St. Louis, New Orleans, Houston, and many other cities. . . . And to pretend that it might be done is to play a cruel hoax on those black communities searching desperately for better education."[28]

De jure segregation is gone, or at least almost gone. De facto segregation remains. Many black children are still denied an adequate education. Nonetheless, "Even though the reordering of race relations in Southern (and Northern) schools was halting and incomplete . . . no nation has accomplished without war or revolution, a social transformation as profound and as rapid as that implied by the partial integration of the schools of the South."[29]

Color and other bars at the polls

The Constitution leaves to the states the power to determine suffrage qualifications for all elections, but states are subject to a variety of constitutional restraints in exercising this power. The main thrust of the constitutional restraints on state power is to prevent interference with the right to vote because of race or sex. But this is not the only limitation.

In the Voting Rights Act of 1970 Congress stipulated that eighteen should be the age qualification for voting in all elections, thus superseding the regulations of almost all of the states. In the same year, however, the Supreme Court came to the somewhat surprising conclusion *(Oregon v. Mitchel)* that the act of Congress was unconstitutional as

[28]As reported in *Congressional Quarterly Weekly Report* (September 1970), p. 2177.

[29]Orfield, *Reconstruction of Southern Education*, p. 355.

applied to elections for *state* or *local* officials, but constitutional as applied to elections for *president* and for *Congress.*

This strange result came about because four justices felt that the states have authority under the Constitution to set reasonable suffrage requirements and that an age qualification of twenty-one, adopted by most of the states, was not unreasonable. On the other hand, four other justices felt that Congress has authority to implement the Fourteenth Amendment and if Congress believes that twenty-one is unreasonable its regulation should supersede state regulation for all elections. (A similar reasoning had been used when the Court earlier upheld a provision of the Voting Rights Act of 1965 setting aside a New York English literacy requirement even though conceding the requirement to be constitutional.)[30] Justice Black was the "swing man." He argued that Article I, Section 4, giving Congress authority to supersede state regulations as to "times, places, and manner" of elections for federal offices, includes the power to set an age qualification, but that that power does not extend to state and local elections, and, he argued, unless the state sets an unreasonable qualification neither Congress nor the Supreme Court can set it aside. As we have noted, following the Supreme Court's decision in *Oregon v. Mitchell,* Congress proposed a constitutional amendment to make eighteen-year-olds eligible to vote in all elections. The Twenty-sixth Amendment was quickly ratified, and the issue was resolved.

The Supreme Court has ruled that the Constitution also forbids a state from excluding nonparents or nontaxpayers from voting for members of school boards or for bond issues.[31] (However, it ruled otherwise with respect to requirements that one be a landowner in order to vote for the board of directors of water control and irrigation districts.)[32] The Court has also held that Texas could not prohibit "any member of the Armed Forces of the United States who moved to Texas from voting in any election." "The uniform of our country . . . must not be the badge of disfranchisement for the man or woman who wears it," the Court declared, and "a state may not fence out from the Franchise a sector of the population for fear of how it will vote."[33] Similarly Maryland was told that it could not bar residents of federal reservations from voting.[34]

But the major thrust of the Fourteenth Amendment has been to prevent states from making racial qualifications for voting. And what the Fourteenth Amendment does implicitly, the Fifteenth does explicitly: "The right of citizens of the United States to vote shall not be denied or abridged by the United States or by any State on account of race, color, or previous condition of servitude." The Fifteenth Amendment also empowers Congress to enact any law necessary and proper to enforce the prohibitions of the amendment.

[30]*Katzenbach v. Morgan* (1966).

[31]*Phoenix v. Kolodziejski* (1970); *Kramer v. Union Free School District* (1969)

[32]*Sayler Land Company v. Tulare Basin Water Storage District* (1973).

[33]*Carrington v. Rash* (1965).

[34]*Evans v. Cornman* (1970).

For over a decade after the Civil War, the provisions of the Fourteenth and Fifteenth Amendments were backed up by federal troops. Blacks, in alliance with Northern radical Republicans (carpetbaggers) and certain white Southerners (scalawags), assumed full control of some state governments. The new regimes passed good laws as well as bad, but they were loathed by "patriotic" white Southerners. Then came the counterrevolution. Even before federal troops were withdrawn from the South in 1877, white Democrats had begun to regain power. Organizing secret societies such as the Knights of the White Camellia and the Ku Klux Klan, the aroused Southerners set out to restore Southern government to white rule. Often they resorted to threats, force, and fraud, to midnight shootings, burnings, and whippings. Many blacks concluded that it would be healthier to stay away from the polls than to insist on their vote, and the carpetbaggers began to retreat north.

CIRCUMVENTING THE FOURTEENTH AND FIFTEENTH AMENDMENTS "LEGALLY"

Once they had regained control of Southern state governments, Southern Democrats resolved to continue to keep the black from voting. At first they continued to rely on social pressures and threats of violence. But toward the end of the nineteenth century, for the first time since the Civil War, there were two strong political parties—the Democrats and the Populists—in many parts of the South. White supremacists were fearful that the parties might compete for the black's vote and that the blacks might come to have a balance-of-power role. To continue to rely on extralegal and illegal means to disfranchise the blacks had disadvantages: It undermined the moral fabric of the society, and a too flagrant use of force and fraud might cause the president and Congress to intervene. So white supremacists searched for "legal" means.

Southern leaders reasoned that if they could pass laws that, while ostensibly not denying blacks the right to vote because of their race, deprived them of it on other grounds, the blacks would find it difficult to challenge the laws in the courts. Some whites protested, saying that such laws could be used against whites as well as blacks. But the likelihood that the laws would keep poor whites from voting did not disturb the conservative leaders of the Democratic party who were in control of some Southern states, for they were often just as anxious to undermine white support for the Populist party as they were to disfranchise blacks. Leaders in the states where blacks constituted a large minority and sometimes even a majority skillfully played on memories of black rule and Northern intervention. "The disfranchisement movement of the 'nineties,'" said V. O. Key, "gave the Southern states the most impressive systems of obstacles between the voter and the ballot box known to the democratic world."[35]

In the 1940s the Supreme Court began to strike down one after anoth-

[35]V. O. Key, Jr., *Southern Politics* (Knopf, 1949), p. 555.

er of the devices used to keep blacks from voting. In 1944 *(Smith v. Allwright)* the Court declared the "white primary" unconstitutional. In 1957 it held that racial gerrymandering was contrary to the Fifteenth Amendment.[36] The Twenty-fourth Amendment got rid of the poll tax in federal elections, and in 1966 the Court held that the Fourteenth Amendment forbade the tax as a condition in any election.[37]

As the white primary, poll taxes, racial gerrymandering, and other laws were struck down, those wishing to deny blacks the right to vote placed primary reliance on registration requirements. On the surface, these requirements appeared to be perfectly proper. It was the manner in which they were administered that kept blacks from the polls, for they were often applied by white election officers while white policemen stood guard, with white judges hearing appeals—if any—from decisions of registration officials.

Registration officials often seized on the smallest error in an application blank as an excuse to disquality a voter. In one parish in the state of Louisiana, after four white voters filed affidavits in which they challenged the legality of the registration of black voters on the grounds that these voters had made an "error in spilling" *(sic)* in their applications, registration officials struck 1,300 out of approximately 1,500 black voters from the voting rolls.[38] In other instances, blacks were denied the right to register because when they stated their ages, they did not stipulate precisely to the day: "I am twenty-one years, six months, and five days old."

In many Southern areas literacy tests were administered by registration officials to discriminate against blacks. Some Southern states, either as an additional requirement or as a substitute for literacy tests, required an applicant to demonstrate to the satisfaction of election officials that he understood the national and state constitutions and, further, that he was a person of good character. Whites were often asked simple questions; blacks were asked questions that would baffle a Supreme Court justice. In Louisiana, 49,603 illiterate white voters were able to persuade election officials they could understand the Constitution, but only two black voters were able to do so.

ACTION BY THE NATIONAL GOVERNMENT

For over twenty years federal courts, under the leadership of the Supreme Court, carefully scrutinized voting laws and procedures in cases brought before them. But this case-by-case approach did not open the voting booth to millions of blacks, especially those living in rural areas of the Deep South. As the United States Civil Rights Commission re-

[36]*Gomillion v. Lightfoot* (1960).

[37]*Harper v. Virginia* (1966).

[38]*Report of the United States Commission on Civil Rights* (U.S. Government Printing Office, 1959), pp. 103–4.

ported, "Suits must proceed in a single court at a time, and they are time consuming, expensive, and difficult. After one law or procedure is enjoined, the state or country would adopt another."[39]

Finally Congress began to act. At first, as in the Civil Rights Acts of 1957 and 1960, the major responsibility was left with the courts. Civil rights statutes protecting the right to vote were strengthened, and the Department of Justice was authorized to seek injunctions. Then in the 1964 act, strengthened by the Voting Rights Act of 1965, Congress, without going outside the courtroom framework, set aside, for federal elections, literacy tests for persons who had completed the equivalent of the sixth grade in an accredited school under the American flag and prohibited the denial of the right to vote because of minor errors on application forms. (The American-flag requirement was stipulated by the 1965 Voting Rights Act in order to protect the right to vote of Puerto Ricans who had moved to the mainland, many of whom are not able to pass literacy tests given in English.)

The 1964 Civil Rights Act had hardly been enacted when events in Selma, Alabama, dramatically showed the inadequacy of dependence on the courts as the major federal instrument to prevent racial barriers in polling places. The voter registration drive in that city by Martin Luther King and his associates produced police arrests, further demonstrations, marches on the state capitol, and the murdering of two civil rights workers, but there was no major dent in the color bar at the polls. Martin Luther King's Selma protests culminated in President Johnson's making a dramatic address to the nation and to the Congress in which he called for federal action which would ensure that no person would be deprived of his right to vote in any election for any office because of the color of his skin. Congress responded with an even stronger measure.

THE VOTING RIGHTS ACT OF 1965

The Voting Rights Acts of 1965 was a major departure from the approach of the prior civil rights acts, which depended first on legal action and then, after the lawsuit was over, on state and local officials to carry the court order into effect. Together with its 1970 amendments, the act authorized direct action by federal executives to register voters and to see to it that they are allowed to vote and that their ballots are honestly counted.[40]

By 1965, discrimination against black voters was concentrated in about one hundred rural counties in Alabama, Georgia, Louisiana, Mis-

[39]*Ibid.*, and United States Commission on Civil Rights, *Civil Rights: Excerpts* (U.S. Government Printing Office, 1961), p. 18.

[40]The constitutionality of the Voting Rights Act was upheld in *South Carolina v. Katzenbach* (1966).

sissippi, North Carolina, and South Carolina.[41] The Voting Rights Act of 1965 concentrated on these areas. In states or political subdivisions in which less than 50 percent of the voting-age population was registered to vote on November 1, 1965 (now amended to November 1, 1968), or actually voted in the 1964 presidential elections (now amended to the 1968 presidential elections), and which required on that data a literacy, understanding, or good-character test, the attorney general was given authority, *without intervening court action*, to order the suspension of the test until 1975 and to call upon the Civil Service Commission to appoint federal examiners. Outside the covered areas (and unless Congress extends the act after 1975), the attorney general must secure approval for the appointment of federal examiners by carrying his complaint of voter discrimination to a federal court. (The 1970 amendments extended coverage to some districts in Alaska, Arizona, California, Idaho, Oregon, and New York City.)

The workings of the law are of interest: Federal examiners (and state and local officials) are to ignore literacy and other tests that have been used to discriminate against blacks and make their own examination to see which voters are qualified under the laws of the state. And to keep states from constantly changing voter requirements in order to prevent blacks from registering, in the areas covered new voting laws, including legislative reapportionment,[42] are not to be effective until 1975 unless approved by the attorney general or a three-judge district court for the District of Columbia. The burden of proof is on the state to show that the proposed changes are free of a racially discriminatory effect. Each month, federal examiners transmit to the appropriate election officials a list of voters they have determined are qualified to vote.

If election officials turn away from the polls any voter that the federal examiners have determined is entitled to vote, the examiners may go into a federal district court and secure an order impounding all the ballots until persons entitled to vote are allowed to do so. In addition, the attorney general may appoint poll watchers to enter voting places to ensure that the votes of all qualified persons are properly counted. And it is a federal offense, punishable by five years in prison and a $5,000 fine, for anybody, private citizen or public official, to intimidate or otherwise interfere with any person attempting to exercise his right to vote.

States or political subdivisions subject to the Voting Rights Act of 1965 may seek exemption from it only by proving to a three-judge district court for the District of Columbia that during the last ten years they have not kept blacks from voting because of their race. Significantly

[41]United States Commission on Civil Rights, *Civil Rights*, p. 15. See also H. D. Price, *The Negro and Southern Politics* (New York University Press, 1957), and Margaret Price, *The Negro and the Ballot in the South* (Southern Regional Council, 1959). See also Richard Claude, *The Supreme Court and the Electoral Process* (Johns Hopkins Press, 1970), pp. 108–43.

[42]*Georgia v. United States* (1973).

Congress placed this matter outside the jurisdiction of federal district judges sitting in the states and subdivisions subject to the act. Some of the latter judges had shown an unwillingness in past legal proceedings to scrutinize carefully state and local regulations discriminating against black voters or to apply civil rights statues with vigor.

The 1970 amendments, in addition to extending the act to 1975, suspend the use of literacy tests in all states, provide that any otherwise qualified person can vote in a presidential election in the place in which he has lived for thirty days immediately prior to that election, and lower from twenty-one to eighteen the voting age for all elections. The Supreme Court has sustained the constitutionality of the basic act, the suspension of literacy tests, and the congressional standard for residency for voting in presidential elections, and the eighteen-year-old voting requirement to vote for congressmen and presidential electors. The Twenty-sixth Amendment governs the age requirement for voting in all elections.

With the Voting Rights Act of 1965 and its 1970 amendments, federal authority has displaced that of the states over voting requirements and the supervision of elections, especially in those areas that have a past history of discrimination against blacks. Federal officials are now mandated to enroll and protect the right to vote of all those who are qualified. States still determine the basic qualifications for voting, but Congress has determined that it is necessary and proper for the national government to enforce the requirements of the Fourteenth and Fifteenth Amendments.

THE RESULTS

A decade after the Voting Rights Act was enacted, more than 4,000,000 blacks had registered to vote in the eleven Southern states. More than 1,000 blacks are holding state, local, or party office in the South.

For the moment, restraints on black voting and registration in most areas appear to be more economic and social than legal. Although the Civil Rights Act of 1968 makes harassment of voters a serious federal crime, persons urging blacks to register and vote and work in behalf of black candidates in some places still report that they are subject to some harassment.[43] But today threats are more likely to be subtle than overt.

Clearly blacks have become an important factor in Southern political life. The black vote can no longer be ignored by those running for public office. It is especially important where the political situation does not become polarized around race—that is, where voters do not find race such a salient issue that all whites vote for only white candidates and all blacks vote for only black candidates. Except in local areas where blacks outnumber whites, the black minority is most likely

[43]United States Commission on Civil Rights, *Political Participation* (U.S. Government Printing Office, 1968), p. 20.

to have the largest political impact where its votes can provide the margin of victory. In a growing number of areas and election contests, public officials no longer find that it is politically profitable to be identified with the more extreme white supremacists.

In the North, black voting power is beginning to assert itself in practical politics. Northern urban centers have long had large concentrations of Negro voters, and with their numbers increasing—some to majority status—they are beginning to flex their political muscles. The election of black mayors in cities such as Cleveland, Los Angeles, Gary, Atlanta, and Washington, D. C., and the increase of blacks in elective and appointive positions at the state and local levels generally—are evidence of the growing influence of black Americans in the American political process.

The struggle for color-blind justice

Of all the sectors of the civil rights front, perhaps the most difficult to deal with by means of legislation, and the one in which the role of the national government was until recently the most limited, is the administration of justice. The Constitution reserves to the states the primary responsibility for finding, prosecuting, and convicting persons who violate the laws, with the national government's functions being chiefly restricted to enforcing federal laws and supervising action by the states to secure compliance with constitutional standards.

In the 1930s the Supreme Court started to use the Fourteenth Amendment to reverse convictions by state and local courts where there was evidence that blacks failed to receive fair treatment. The Court could free blacks who had been jailed unfairly, but this left untouched the police and prosecutors who had deprived blacks of their rights. Although urged to pass protective federal legislation, Congress failed to do so. Nevertheless, President Roosevelt created a Civil Rights Section in the Department of Justice to do what it could to enforce the remnants of the civil rights laws still remaining from Reconstruction days.

The Civil Rights Section, now a Division, found it difficult to enforce these laws. Even if convictions were obtained, the punishment was seldom more than a year's imprisonment. Federal trials had to be held in front of juries selected in accord with the local state practice. (The Jury Selection and Service Act of 1968 has taken care of this particular problem.) The archaic laws made proof difficult—for example, the Department of Justice was unable to sustain a conviction against Sheriff Claude M. Screws of Georgia who, along with a deputy, was alleged to have beaten for fifteen to thirty minutes a handcuffed black prisoner with their fists and a "solid-bar blackjack about eight inches long and weighing two pounds." (The prisoner died.) The department was unable to prove that Screws had acted with the specific intent in mind to prive his prisoner of his constitutionally secured rights.[44] Nor was the Department of Justice able to persuade a jury to convict some South Carolina state troopers who it alleged had fired into a crowd, killing three students and wounding twenty-seven others. The students were at the time demonstrating against a segregated bowling alley near the campus of their college.[45]

But even using these Reconstruction statutes, the department did have some success: three Mississippi officers and four who conspired with them were convicted for their part in the murders of three civil rights workers; in another case two persons were given a ten-year sentence for their part in the killing of a black educator.[46]

Other than these criminal statutes, about the only other federal law that offered much help to blacks in securing their rights was the Civil Rights Act of 1871, which opened federal courts to suits for damages and injunctions against officials alleged to have deprived persons of rights secured by the Constitution. Because this act provided for civil rather than criminal remedies, damages could be won and injunctions obtained without having to prove that the officers had a specific intent to deprive a person of his federally protected rights. Blacks, working mainly through the NAACP, had some notable successes with the act of 1871, but private litigants often found it difficult to gather evidence and to challenge state and local authorities, and it could even be dangerous for them and for the lawyers who represented them. One white lawyer, for example, told the United States Commission on Civil Rights:

> I was born in North Carolina and raised in the hills of Eastern Tennessee, and I am in favor of the Civil Rights Statutes but must live with this as silent as the grave. I see my clients beat, abused and run over all of the time and there is nothing much I can do, because when I try in Federal Court I wind up with the hell beat out of me.[47]

The failure of state and local governments to apply justice evenhandedly, the murdering within a few years of dozens of civil rights leaders, the bombing of scores of homes, and the punishment of only a few persons for these acts caused Congress gradually to enlarge the role of the Department of Justice. The Supreme Court has more broadly construed existing legislation[48] and, most importantly, has removed any doubts about Congress' constitutional authority to do whatever is necessary and proper to protect persons against racial discrimination—whether

[44]*Screws v. United States* (1945).

[45]Richard Harris, *Justice, the Crisis of Law, Order, and Freedom in America* (Dutton, 1970), pp. 189–95.

[46]*United States v. Price* (1966); *United States v. Guest* (1966).

[47]United States Commission on Civil Rights, *Report on Justice* (U.S. Government Printing Office, 1961), p. 69. Also see generally the Commission's *Report on Law Enforcement*, 1965.

[48]*United States v. Price* (1966); *United States v. Guest* (1966); *Griffin V. Breckenridge* (1971).

imposed by state officials, local authorities, or private individuals. Congress has responded with new and more adequate legislation.

In 1964 Congress authorized the attorney general to intervene, whenever he thinks the case is of public importance, in any civil suit in which there is an allegation of the denial of equal protection of the laws. Using this authority, the Department of Justice intervened in several major suits against school districts, both in the North and the South, and in a few instances, against authorities of an entire state. Then, as part of the Civil Rights Act of 1968, Congress adopted specific federal criminal legislation to protect persons in the exercise of their civil rights against injury, intimidation, or interference either by private individuals or public officials. Under this act, it became a federal crime to interfere with or attempt to interfere with or injure any person because he is voting or campaigning in any election, serving on a federal or state jury, working for a federal agency, attending a public school, or using a common carrier or public accommodation. Also protected under the law are persons who are trying to encourage or help persons secure these civil rights. Commission of any of the acts interdicted by the federal law is also a violation of state law, so Congress limited federal prosecutions to those instances when the attorney general certifies in writing that federal prosecution is in the public interest and necessary to secure substantial justice—thus the federal authorities will not act if the state does. Also, Congress provided for uniform provisions that should avoid any discrimination in the selection of federal juries.

The Civil Rights Act of 1968 further strengthened the Justice Department's authority to protect constitutional rights and to act against racially motivated crimes. The Department's more active role has already had an impact; it has alerted state and local officers to the fact that they violate at their own peril the rights and privileges protected by the Constitution. But as the Civil Rights Commission has reported, "Little can be done directly to prevent police brutality itself until the police are more carefully selected, trained and controlled."[49]

Racial and sexual barriers to homes, jobs, and public accomodations

Until recently those who wanted to keep blacks or Jews or Latinos or Indians or any other kind of person from buying homes in their neighborhood or eating lunches at the same counters or working in the same plants could have used the power of government to enforce these discriminatory practices, especially those relating to race. Not so today. Laws and government regulations that interfere with equal access to homes, jobs, or public accommodations are now unconstitutional.

What of discriminatory action by *private individuals?* Although it is

[49]United States Commission on Civil Rights, *Report on Justice*, p. 9.

likely to be a violation of federal and state laws, such action does not violate the Constitution unless it is aided, supported, or encouraged by governmental action. "Where the impetus for the discrimination is private, the State must have 'significantly involved itself with invidious discriminations' in order for the discriminatory action to fall within the ambit of constitutional prohibition."[50]

Persons who wish to do so may place covenants in deeds restricting the use of their property to persons of particular races or religious or nationalities, but no court or other public official may enforce such covenants because this would be state-aided discrimination.[51] In like manner, private schools may exclude blacks or whites or adopt religious qualifications, but if the schools receive any financial or other public support their conduct becomes subject to the limitations of the equal-protection clause.[52] The Supreme Court has also held that trade unions whose right to engage in collective bargaining is protected by federal laws may not discriminate.[53] And the Court has come very close to the proposition that holding and conducting elections in which public officials are nominated or elected is a governmental function. Whoever discharges these functions is restrained by the Constitution.[54]

The Supreme Court inspects closely whenever there is a suspicion of state involvement in discriminatory conduct. It found that when a state

[50]*Moose Lodge No. 107 v. Irvis* (1972).

[51]*Shelly v. Kraemer* (1948); *Barrows v. Jackson* (1953).

[52]*Norwood v. Harrison* (1973).

[53]*Conley v. Gibson* (1957).

[54]*Terry v. Adams* (1953).

Using several pens, President Lyndon Johnson signs into law the "War on Poverty" bill (1964). He said that the bill would stimulate a "new era of progress for those who have not shared in America's prosperity."

leased space to a restaurant in a public parking garage, the action of the restaurant could no longer be considered purely private under the equal-protection clause.[55] On the other side, the mere receiving of a liquor license from a state does not by itself make the discriminatory conduct of a private club the action of the state.[56]

The Supreme Court did find state involvement sufficient to bring the equal-protection clause into play when it declared unconstitutional an amendment to the California Constitution that in effect rendered unenforceable previously enacted legislation forbidding racial discrimination in the sale of real estate. The people of California in amending their Constitution were making it more difficult for blacks than for whites to buy houses.[57] Similarly, a charter amendment of Akron, Ohio, requiring open housing—but no other—ordinances to be submitted to popular referendum came into conflict with the equal-protection clause: Here again the power of government was being used to make it more difficult for those who favor open housing legislation to secure its enactment than for those who favor other kinds of legislation.[58]

The Supreme Court refused, however, to extend the Akron precedent when it upheld a California constitutional provision requiring approval by a majority of the local voters before any city or county public housing authority could develop or acquire a low-rent housing project. Justice Black, speaking for a five-man majority (in *James v. Valtierra*, 1971) pointed out that California was not imposing any requirement that would make it more difficult for blacks than for whites to find a place to live, but was merely using a long-established procedure "to give citizens a voice on questions of public policy." Justice Marshall, speaking for three dissenting justices, argued that even though California's action was on its face racially neutral, the Fourteenth Amendment protects not merely against racial discrimination but also against economic discrimination. And in many communities the racial question in fact is involved in disputes over the location of low-income housing, especially when an attempt is made to place such projects in suburbs.

What if blacks or others are arrested for trespass or other offenses as a result of their sitting-in at lunch counters and other facilities that are privately owned but open to the public? Some argue that if owners of privately owned businesses wish to refuse service to blacks, the state may protect their right to do so. But the Supreme Court had no difficulty in deciding that it is an unconstitutional state action if state-enforced custom or state laws force operators of places of public accommodation to refuse nonsegregated service or if private owners work with state officials to keep people from being served because of their race.[59] A state

[55]*Burton v. Wilmington Parking Authority* (1966).

[56]*Moose Lodge No. 107 v. Irvis* (1972).

[57]*Reitman v. Mulkey* (1967).

[58]*Hunter v. Erickson* (1968).

[59]*Adickes v. S. H. Kress & Co.* (1970) and cases cited therein.

cannot constitutionally prosecute or arrest persons for peacefully attempting to secure their rights, and those who act under force of state law to deprive persons of their civil rights are liable for civil damages as well as criminal prosecution. The question of discrimination by a place of public accommodation when there is no governmental pressure to do so is not likely to come up, for with the passage of the Civil Rights Act of 1964 (see p. 206) few businesses any longer have a legal right to discriminate against their customers because of race even if they would like to do so.

Furthermore, in *Jones v. Mayer* (see p. 209), the Supreme Court has robbed the doctrine of state action of some of its significance. The Thirteenth Amendment, which covers private as well as state action, is now being construed to authorize Congress to legislate against various kinds of racial discrimination whether or not it is state supported. There is no longer the need to show state involvement in the discriminatory conduct to provide constitutional justification for the enactment and application of federal civil rights legislation.

STATE CIVIL RIGHTS PROGRAMS

As Justice Douglas has pointed out, the Constitution creates "a zone of privacy which precludes government from interfering with private clubs or groups. The associational rights which our system honors permit all white, all black, all brown and all yellow clubs to be established. They also permit all Catholic, all Jewish, or all agnostic clubs to be established. Government may not tell a man or a woman who his or her associates must be. The individual can be as selective as he desires."[60] But as Chief Justice Burger said for the Court, "although the Constitution does not proscribe private bias, it places no value on discrimination. . . . Invidious private discrimination may be characterized as a form of exercising freedom of association protected by the First Amendment, but it has never been accorded affirmative constitutional protection."[61]

Although private acts of discrimination do not violate the Constitution, and some such acts are even entitled to constitutional protection, no one has a constitutionally protected right to injure others. And just as a state may protect a person's property rights, so may it protect a person's civil rights.

Should governments use their powers to make it illegal for landlords and landladies, employers, trade unions, private schools, managers of businesses, and others to discriminate against persons because of their race or color or nationality or sex? No, say some people; prejudice cannot be eradicated by laws. But if laws cannot eradicate prejudice, they can help to eliminate discriminatory *conduct* that deprives people of their right to be treated as human beings.

[60]*Moose Lodge No. 107 v. Irvis* (1972).

[61]*Moose Lodge No. 107 v. Irvis* (1972).

Most states *outlaw* segregation and other kinds of racial, religious, or national origin discrimination. Some states (and the federal government) are beginning to outlaw discrimination based on sex. Discrimination by owners and operators of public places of recreation and accommodation has long been a tort (civil wrong) under the common law; most states have special statutes making it a criminal or civil offense to refuse service to patrons because of race, religion, or national origin, with clauses forbidding discrimination because of sex being added in some states. In addition, many states have adopted fair employment laws which are increasingly being amended to protect against sex-based as well as racial, religious, and national origin discrimination. Some states have made it illegal for school and university authorities to discriminate racially or religiously, except with respect to religion in the case of church-operated schools. But most states allow private institutions to admit on the basis of sex if they so wish. (The federal government is beginning to forbid discrimination by educational institutions—including private institutions—on sex lines as well as racial ones if the institution receives federal funds. However, exceptions include undergraduate institutions, military schools, and religious schools which still may operate single-sex institutions.) More than half the states and many cities forbid landlords and landladies to deny tenants a place to live because of their race, religion, or national origin, and, in recent years, sex is being added as an unacceptable reason for denial of housing. Almost all states forbid discrimination (including sex-based discrimination) in public employment.

The weakness of some of these civil rights statutes is that they make no special provision for enforcement other than by regular court action instituted by public prosecutors or through the initiation of lawsuits by the person being discriminated against. Frequently, the person denied a job or a room or service has neither the knowledge to bring the matter to the attention of a prosecutor nor the money to undertake a civil suit. Moreover, many prosecutors have been somewhat less than eager to take action.

The ineffectiveness of criminal laws against discrimination and of dependence on damage suits brought by the aggrieved person has led many states and cities to establish special agencies with a responsibility to hear and determine charges of civil rights violations and with authority to issue judicially enforceable complaints against offenders. These human relations commissions, as they are often called, frequently also engage in educational programs and have been successful in providing substantial protection against discrimination in employment, places of public accommodation, housing, and educational institutions.

THE NATIONAL SHIELD AND SWORD

What of the national government? It was the hope of some of the congressmen who proposed the Fourteenth Amendment over 100 years ago that its ratification would authorize federal action against nongovernmental discrimination. And Section 5 of that amendment does state, "The Congress shall have power to enforce, by appropriate legislation, the provisions of this article." So in 1875 Congress made it a federal offense for any owner or operator of a public conveyance, hotel, or theater to deny accommodations to any person because of his race or color. But in the *Civil Rights Cases* (1883), the Supreme Court invalidated this law on the ground that the Fourteenth Amendment applies only to state action and does not give Congress authority to forbid discrimination by private individuals.

What of the Thirteenth Amendment? Unlike the Fourteenth this amendment applies to all persons and not just to those acting under the color of law. By its own force it outlaws all forms of involuntary servitude. It also empowers Congress to pass whatever laws are necessary and proper to prevent slavery or involuntary servitude. For a hundred years some people, including the first Justice Harlan, argued that the Thirteenth Amendment gives Congress authority to legislate against all the badges of slavery—that is, against racial discrimination in all its forms, regardless of its source. But the Supreme Court construed the Thirteenth Amendment so narrowly that slavery meant only physical compulsion or peonage (a condition of compulsory servitude based on indebtedness of the worker to the employer). Thus it was held that Congress received no power from the Thirteenth Amendment to legislate against racial discrimination.

Then, in *Jones v. Mayer Co.* (1968), Justice Stewart, speaking for a seven-man majority, adopted the view of the first Justice Harlan (his grandson, the second Justice Harlan, dissented). The immediate question before the Court was the meaning and constitutionality of an 1866 act relating to the purchase of property. Justice Stewart stated that the Thirteenth Amendment became part of the Constitution so that Congress could have the power to remove the "badges of slavery" from the nation. "When racial discrimination," he wrote, "herds men into ghettos and makes their ability to buy property turn on the color of their skin, then it too is a relic of slavery. . . . At the very least, the freedom that Congress is empowered to secure under the Thirteenth Amendment includes the freedom to buy whatever a white man can buy, the right to live wherever a white man can live. If Congress cannot say that being a free man means at least this much, then the Thirteenth Amendment made a promise that the Nation cannot keep."

The Supreme Court has reaffirmed *Jones v. Mayer* several times (*Tillman v. Wheat-Haven Recreation Assn.*, 1973): There can no longer be any doubt about the constitutional authority of Congress to enact whatever legislation it thinks necessary in order to protect persons against suffering any disabilities because of their race, whether the disabilities are imposed by private or state action.

Prior to these wider constructions of its constitutional powers, Congress had to rely on its power to regulate commerce among the states in order to extend federal protection against discriminatory acts, as it did in 1964 when it adopted a sweeping Civil Rights Act to protect persons against discrimination in places of public accommodation and employment.

PLACES OF PUBLIC ACCOMMODATION

For the first time since Reconstruction, Congress, through the Civil Rights Act of 1964, authorized the massive use of federal authority to combat privately imposed racial discrimination. Title II forbids discrimination in places of accommodation and makes it a federal offense to discriminate against any customer or patron because of his race, color, religion, or national origin. It applies to any inn, hotel, motel, or lodging establishment (except establishments with fewer than five rooms and occupied by the proprietor—in other words, small boarding houses); to any restaurant or gasoline station that offers to serve interstate travelers or serves food or products of which a substantial portion have moved in interstate commerce; and to any motion picture house, theater, concert hall, sports arena, or other place of entertainment that customarily presents films, performances, athletic teams, or other sources of entertainment that are moved in interstate commerce. Title II also applies to any establishment that attempts to discriminate or segregate in response to state law or order of any public official.

The attorney general may initiate proceedings as well as intervene in cases initiated by aggrieved individuals. States with laws against discrimination in places of public accommodation are given thirty days to see if they can bring about compliance. Federal judges may refer complaints to the Community Relations Service (see p. 209) in order to seek voluntary compliance. But if these procedures fail, judges are to provide prompt hearings with direct appeals to the Supreme Court whenever the attorney general believes the case is of general public importance.

Within a few months of the enactment of Title II, the Supreme Court unanimously sustained its constitutionality (*Heart of Atlanta Motel v. United States*, 1964). Faced with the adoption of Title II, the determination of the Department of Justice to enforce it, and an organized program of testing by blacks to publicize lack of compliance, most larger establishments in most cities, including those in the South, have opened their doors to all customers.

EMPLOYMENT

Title VII of the Civil Rights Act of 1964, as amended, makes it an unfair employment practice for any employer, including state and local agencies such as universities, or trade union in any industry affecting interstate commerce, to discriminate in any fashion or to segregate any person because of race, color, religion, sex, national origin, or age for those between forty and sixty-five. Religious institutions such as schools may use religious standards, and exceptions to the ban against discrimination may be made when there are bona fide occupational qualifications reasonably necessary to the normal operations of a particular business or enterprise. The law covers firms or unions affecting interstate commerce and having fifteen or more employees or members.

Employers and trade unions subject to the act are required to keep records and make them available to federal authorities and to take affirmative action to bring about nondiscriminatory hirings. In addition Title VII has been supplemented by the Equal Pay Act of 1963 with its amendments, the Equal Employment Opportunities Act of 1972 covering federal employment, and Title IX, Prohibition of Sex Discrimination, added in 1972 to the Higher Education Act of 1965.

The Equal Employment Opportunity Commission, consisting of five members appointed by the president with the consent of the Senate, has primary responsibility for bringing about compliance with Title VII. EEOC works with state authorities and uses conciliation wherever possible. If this fails, however, the EEOC, since the 1972 amendments, can through its own general counsel secure a court order directing the employer or trade union to cease its discriminatory conduct. EEOC is entitled to an expeditious court hearing on its complaints. If the Commission believes that a firm or trade union is engaged in a willful and persistent pattern of resistance, it may request a prompt hearing before a three-judge federal court from which direct appeals to the Supreme Court are possible.

Title VII has been construed to prohibit employment practices which operate to exclude minorities or women when the practice cannot be shown to be related to on-the-job performance. For example, a company may not require prospective employees to take tests that may be neutral on their face if the tests cannot be shown to be job related and if they exclude persons who are capable of performing effectively in the desired position.[62]

Until 1972, EEOC did not have much enforcement clout. It is too early to tell what the impact of its new legal powers will be. In addition to Title VII, presidential executive orders require all contractors and subcontractors (including universities) of the federal government to adopt and implement affirmative action programs to insure a properly balanced labor force. Failure to do so can lead to loss of federal funds.[63]

HOUSING: THE CIVIL RIGHTS ACT OF 1968 AND THE DISCOVERY OF THE ACT OF 1866

Discrimination in housing has remained one of the most intractable of

[62] *Griggs v. Duke Power Co.* (1971); *McDonnell Douglas Corp. v. Green* (1973).

[63] Richard P. Nathan, *Jobs and Civil Rights: The Role of the Federal Government in Promoting Equal Opportunity and Employment and Training* (prepared for the United States Commission on Civil Rights by the Brookings Institution, 1969).

"Well, I'll be darned! It was already unlocked."

Copyright © 1968 The Chicago Sun-Times; reproduced by courtesy of Wil-Jo Associates, Inc., and Bill Mauldin.

our social problems and, in turn, has had an impact on school desegregation and the isolation of black Americans from the suburbs. Residential segregation results not from the use of governmental power to force segregated housing but from the refusal of lending agencies, brokerage agencies, and owners and operators of houses and apartments to allow blacks to rent or buy homes for their families except within certain restricted areas.

In 1948, the Supreme Court *(Shelly v. Kraemer)* held that the judges of the land would no longer enforce racially restrictive covenants. And in 1962 President Kennedy ordered the Federal Housing Administration, the Veterans Administration, and other federal housing authorities to cease making federal funds or help available to any project that was operated on a segregated basis. Yet most of the nation's housing was still denied to black Americans, and they had to pay more for what was available. Then in 1968 Congress enacted the Civil Rights Act of 1968. The act covers 80 percent of all housing for rent or sale, exempting from its coverage only private individuals owning not more than three houses who sell or rent their houses without the services of a real estate agent and who do not indicate any preference or discrimination in their advertising; dwellings that have no more than four separate living units in which the owner maintains a residence (the so-called Mrs. Murphy boarding houses); and religious organizations and private clubs housing their own members on a noncommercial basis. For all other housing, the Civil Rights Act proscribes the refusal to sell or rent to any person because of his race, color, religion, or national origin. No discriminatory advertising is to be permitted, and so-called blockbusting techniques—that is, attempts to persuade persons to sell or rent a dwelling by representing that blacks or any other racial or religious group, are about to come into the neighborhood—are outlawed. Real estate brokers and lending institutions are also prohibited from discriminatory practices.

Although the attorney general may initiate action under the Civil Rights Act of 1968 whenever he finds a pattern of discrimination, the act primarily depends for its enforcement upon "private attorneys general"—that is, on the persons injured by the discriminatory conduct. The injured party does not necessarily have to be black, for a white person denied the opportunity to live in an integrated community also has been injured and has standing to sue.[64] The aggrieved person first must file a complaint with the Secretary of the Department of Housing and Urban Development. If this fails to bring relief, he or she may file a suit in any court for injunctive relief and for damages. (In a suit for damages, the defendant has a constitutional right to demand a jury trial.[65]

The only criminal provisions of the act cover those who interfere with any person's attempting to comply with the act or secure his rights under it.

[64]*Trafficante v. Metropolitan Life Insurance Co.* (1972).

[65]*Curtis v. Loether* (1974).

The Civil Rights Act of 1968 had not even had time to become effective when, as we have noted, the Supreme Court announced its decision in *Jones v. Mayer Co.* (1968). Mr. and Mrs. Jones had filed a complaint three years before against a housing development in St. Louis that had refused to sell them a home because Mr. Jones was black. At that time few people thought they had much chance to win their case. Congress had enacted no civil rights laws to cover housing since the moribund act of 1866, and even if it did, there was some doubt about its power to make discrimination by private persons a federal offense. Even if the Joneses won, it was assumed the Supreme Court would base its decision on state involvement in the discrimination because of the financial support the state had given to the developer.

The Joneses cited the Civil Rights Act of 1866, which reads, "All citizens of the United States shall have the same right, in every state and territory, as is enjoyed by white citizens thereof to inherit, purchase, lease, sell, hold, and convey real and personal property." Because of the Supreme Court's long-standing requirement of state action to bring the Fourteenth Amendment into play and its narrow construction of the Thirteenth, the 1866 act had been more or less forgotten. But the Supreme Court sustained the Joneses' petition and ruled that the Congress of 1866 meant what it had said and that the Thirteenth Amendment gave Congress ample authority to enact the law. How did the Court reconcile the fact that only a few months before, in the Civil Rights Act of 1968, Congress adopted legislation to cover discrimination in housing with more limited coverage than the act of 1866? The Supreme Court argued that the two acts reinforce each other—the 1968 act provides remedies to enforce the 1866 act.

THE FEDERAL PRESENCE AND CIVIL RIGHTS

The recently expanded involvement of the national government in the field of civil rights has imposed on the established federal agencies a variety of new enforcement responsibilities as well as producing many new agencies. The Equal Employment Opportunity Commission has already been mentioned. The Community Relations Service, now located in the Department of Justice, was created by the Civil Rights Act of 1964. It serves as a conciliation service working with community leaders when conflict between the races has shown the lack of any local machinery to bring leaders from both races together. Federal judges may refer to the service complaints relating to public accommodations to see if it can obtain voluntary compliance.

The six-member United States Commission on Civil Rights, created by the Civil Rights Act of 1957, serves as a national clearing house on civil rights matters. Its public hearings and reports to the Congress have focused national and congressional attention on the more flagrant violations of civil rights, and its recommendations have had a major impact on congressional legislation and executive actions.

The Civil Rights Commission was especially critical of the Nixon Administration. "Federal civil rights enforcement proceeds at a snail's pace," the Commission charged. "It lacks creativity, resources, a sense of urgency, a firmness in dealing with violators—and most important—a sense of commitment." The commission reported: "The enforcement failure [of the early 1970s] was the result, to a large extent, of placing the responsibility for ensuring racial and ethnic justice upon a massive Federal bureaucracy which for years had been an integral part of a discriminatory system." The problem was not only the inherent conservatism of the bureaucracy, the commission argued, but the fact that agency heads were fearful that if they actively attended to civil rights concerns they would lose favor with the constituents they serve and with the Congress. "Moreover, since nonenforcement was an accepted mode of behavior, any official who sought to enforce civil rights laws with the same zeal applied to other statutes ran the risk of being branded as an activist, a visionary, or a troublemaker. Regrettably, there were few countervailing pressures. Minorities still lacked the economic and political power to influence or motivate a reticent officialdom."[66]

Although not all agree with the accuracy of the commission's negative report on the effectiveness of the federal enforcement efforts, its emphasis on the need for civil rights forces to maintain countervailing pressures on federal agencies reflects the findings of political scientists in many policy areas: those who wish to alter behavior cannot assume that they will accomplish their purpose merely by persuading Congress to enact a law or a court to issue an order. The policy-making process never stops.

Though sometimes overlooked in discussions of federal civil rights activities, the various poverty, educational, manpower training, and similar programs are very much part of the federal civil rights efforts. These programs are designed to provide federal dollars and technical assistance to states, local communities, and private agencies in order to develop programs to provide individuals with job skills. For blacks and Latinos, more than other groups, have felt the impact of technological change that has made large numbers of unskilled jobs obsolete. Discriminated against, forced into urban ghettos, and burdened by the social ills of all groups that have been subjected to these conditions, blacks and Latinos suffer especially high unemployment rates. Whether programs can be designed, funded, and implemented that will effectively provide persons with the skills to permit them to break out of the vicious cycle of discrimination and poverty may be of more significance than any specific civil rights act.

[66]United States Commission on Civil Rights, *Federal Civil Rights Enforcement Effort—A Reassessment* (U.S. Government Printing Office, 1973), pp. 3, 11.

Equality today: a summary

It is easy to get lost in the maze of federal and state civil rights laws, to become confused by the refined distinctions made in courts of law, and to perceive the struggle to secure civil rights as one involving only constitutional and legal questions. But we are what we are, and the laws and constitutional provisions are what they are, because of a complicated interaction among social, economic, legal, and political developments.[67]

The federal presence in civil rights was a long time in coming. As we have seen, after the Civil War the federal government tried briefly to secure for the recently freed slaves some measure of protection. But blacks were largely uneducated, illiterate, and completely dependent on the white community. Moreover, they were an insignificant political force. In 1877 the federal government withdrew from the field and left the blacks to their own resources. For decades, blacks did not count politically or economically or socially, and, as a result, they were segregated and discriminated against.

At the end of World War II, there began a national debate over civil rights. Black leaders and others urged Congress to adopt federal laws to protect civil rights. But white Southerners and many others contended that federal civil rights laws would upset the federal system and lead to a dangerous centralization of power. They insisted that national legislation would create more problems than it solved. A national program could not be enforced if it overrode local public opinion, they contended. Let the states do the job, for they could protect civil rights by laws adapted to the attitudes of the local citizenry. Anyway, they added, "you can't legislate morality."

Champions of national action argued that states had failed to protect civil rights and that, in fact, in many areas the state governments themselves were the major instruments of discrimination. Furthermore, the denial of civil rights is not merely a local matter, for it has national and international implications. The Constitution promises to every person who lives in the United States equal treatment before the law without respect to his or her race, religion, or national origin, and it is up to the national government to see that this promise is kept. Whatever the speculative merits of local rather than national action, as a matter of practical political fact, civil rights could be extended only by the national majority using the power of the national government. For, as one white Southerner noted, "not one concrete step toward full rights for the southern Negro—whether in voting or education—has been achieved without the intervention of the national government."[68] By

[67]Grimes, *Equality in America*, pp. 41–85.

[68]James W. Prothro, "A Southerner's View of a Southerner's Book," *The Reporter* (September 20, 1956), p. 46.

the end of the 1950s, the debate over whether the national government had a responsibility to protect civil rights was over. The question became, What should it do?

By the mid-1970s, discrimination had become a tougher challenge to American liberals than to conservatives. Black, brown, red, and white militants were challenging not just the defense of the *status quo* but the liberal pluralist value structure of individual liberty and equality. Some of them demanded recognition less for their individual rights than for their rights as a group—as blacks, as Indians, as Latinos. Some were contending that equality was not enough—what they wanted was *reverse* discrimination. They wanted laws to be passed and enforced deliberately for their benefit; they wanted a social and economic "handicap" much like the handicap that favors the weaker golfer. Still others were protesting that American democratic pluralism could not do the job at all: the pluralist system was too slow, too cumbersome, too respectful of the rights of those standing in the way of progress, whereas the problem—the tangle of knotted social factors that maintain the ghetto in a city, the century-old sense of inferiority and repression in the country, and the "culture of poverty" everywhere—was simply beyond the capacity of pluralist democracy to solve.

Each year more and more blacks, Latinos, and Indians exercise their voting power. Increasingly, they are comprehending more clearly the connection between voting and better schools, houses, and jobs. And with these advances, more and more blacks and Latinos and Indians are coming to insist on full participation in the political, economic, and social life of the country. The impact of their political power when combined with the increasingly militant voice of women is being felt long before every member of each discriminated-against group has become politically self-conscious. What is happening in the United States is part of the worldwide "revolution of rising expectations." Colonialism is dead. White supremacy is dying. There is no stopping place between the granting of a few rights and full citizenship. Blacks, Latinos, American Indians, and women are demanding the same rights as other citizens. No Americans have asked for more than this—or settled long for less.

Chapter 8 Rights to citizenship, life, liberty, and property

Public officials have great power. Under certain conditions they can seize our property, throw us into jail, and, in extreme circumstances, even take our lives. Under some conditions they can take away our citizenship. It is necessary to vest great power in those who govern—it is also dangerous. It is so dangerous that to keep officials from becoming tyrants we are unwilling to depend on the ballot box alone. For we know that political controls have little impact when a majority uses governmental power to deprive unpopular minorities of their rights.

Because public power can be dangerous, we parcel it out in small chunks and surround it with elaborate restraints. No single official can, by himself, decide to take our life, liberty, or property. And officials must proceed according to established forms. If they act outside the scope of their authority or contrary to the law, be they the president or a policeman, they have no claim to obedience.

The Constitution also protects our right to become and to remain a citizen, a right basic to the concept of self-government. True, all nations have rules that determine nationality—the condition of membership in, owing allegiance to, and being the subject of a nation-state—but in democratic theory citizenship is something more than nationality, something more than merely being a subject. *Citizenship* in a democracy is an *office* and, like other offices, carries with it certain powers and responsibilities.

The Constitution protects citizenship

It was not until 1868, with the adoption of the Fourteenth Amendment, that this basic right of membership in the body politic was given constitutional protection. This amendment makes "all persons *born or naturalized* in the United States and subject to the jurisdiction thereof . . . citizens of the United States and of the State wherein they reside." All persons born in the United States, with the minor exception of children born to foreign ambassadors and ministers (but not consuls), are citizens of this country regardless of the citizenship of their parents. (Congress has defined the United States to include Puerto Rico, Guam, and the Virgin Islands.)

The Fourteenth Amendment does not of its own force make members of Indian tribes citizens of the United States or of the state in which they reside. But by act of Congress Indians are American citizens, they have the right to vote, to use state courts, and when they leave Indian reservations to exercise all the rights and obligations of any other citizen. Indians living on reservations are subject to preemptive regulation by the national government and are wards of the nation. The relations of Indian tribes with the United States are complex: they are regarded not as states, not as nations possessed of the full attributes of sovereignty, but as a separate people, with the power of regulating their own internal relations.[1]

The Fourteenth Amendment confers citizenship according to the principle of *jus soli*—by place of birth. In addition, Congress has granted, under certain conditions, citizenship at birth according to the principle of *jus sanguinis*—by blood. A child born of an American parent living abroad becomes an American citizen at birth provided one of his citizen parents had been physically present in the United States prior to the child's birth. In order to retain citizenship derived through only one citizen parent, a person must come to the United States and live here for at least five years between his fourteenth and twenty-eighth birthdays.

Citizenship may also be acquired by naturalization, collective or individual. The granting of citizenship to Puerto Ricans in 1917 by an act of Congress is an example of collective naturalization. Individual naturalization requirements are determined by Congress.

Today, with a few minor exceptions any nonenemy alien over eight-

[1]*McClanahan v. Arizona State Tax Commission* (1973).

een years of age who has been lawfully admitted for permanent residence and who has resided in the United States for at least five years and in a state for at least six months is eligible for naturalization. An eligible alien who wishes to become a citizen files a petition of naturalization, verified by two witnesses, with the clerk of a court of record, federal or state. Then an official of the Immigration and Naturalization Service examines the petitioner to ensure that he has met the residence requirements, can read, write, and speak English, and is of good moral character. The official must also determine that the petitioner understands and is attached to the fundamentals of the history, principles, and form of government of the United States; that he is well disposed toward the good order and happiness of this country; and that he does not now, nor did within the last ten years, believe in, advocate, or belong to an organization that supports opposition to organized government, overthrow of government by violence, or the doctrines of world communism or any other form of totalitarianism.

The examiner makes his report to the judge. The final step is a hearing in open court. If the judge is satisfied that the petitioner is qualified, the applicant renounces all allegiance to his or her former country and swears to support and defend the Constitution and laws of the United States against all enemies and to bear arms in behalf of the United States when required by law. (Those with religious beliefs against the bearing of arms are allowed to take an oath to serve in the armed forces as noncombatants or to perform work of national importance under civilian direction.) Then the court grants a certificate of naturalization.

LOSS OF CITIZENSHIP

Naturalized citizenship may be revoked by court order if the government can prove that it was procured by concealment of a material fact or by willful misrepresentation. In addition, citizenship, however acquired, may be voluntarily renounced. Under existing statutes, an American citizen living outside the United States may formally renounce his citizenship before an American diplomatic or consular official. A person living in the United States may formally renounce his citizenship only during time of war and only with the approval of the attorney general.

Congress seems to believe that it has the power to strip a person of citizenship as a penalty for the commission of certain kinds of crimes and for certain kinds of conduct that it has determined to be incompatible with undivided allegiance to the United States. The Supreme Court thinks otherwise. The justices have had difficulty in articulating their arguments and in developing a coherent and consistent majority position, but in essence the Court has ruled that what the Constitution gives, Congress may not take away. Justice Black (*Afroyim v. Rusk*, 1967), speaking for a five-man majority, unequivocally stated, "Congress has no power under the Constitution to divest a person of his United States citizenship absent his voluntary renunciation thereof."

Of the several types of conduct that Congress has stipulated are to be construed as expatriating acts, five have been challenged in the courts. By a closely divided vote the Court has declared four unconstitutional: voting in a foreign election; conviction by a court-martial of desertion during time of war; departing from or remaining outside the United States in time of war or national emergency to avoid military service; and residence by a naturalized citizen in the country of his national origin for more than three years.[2] In 1971, *(Rogers v. Bellei)*, again by five to four, the Court upheld the power of Congress to deny citizenship to a person born outside the United States to one citizen parent if that person does not return to the United States for five years between the ages of fourteen and twenty-eight. The Fourteenth Amendment, said the Court majority (consisting in part of President Nixon's appointees), does not apply except to persons born or naturalized in the United States. Justice Black in sharp dissent wrote, "This precious Fourteenth Amendment American citizenship should not be blown around by every passing political wind that changes the composition of this Court."

Among the stipulated acts of expatriation that have still not been challenged, the following appear to conflict with Supreme Court doctrine, for they can hardly be considered voluntary renunciation of citizenship and do apply to persons born or naturalized in the United States: conviction of treason, of attempting to overthrow the government by force, or of conspiring to advocate forceful overthrow; serving in the armed forces of another state without the approval of the secretary of state and secretary of defense; and accepting a job in a foreign state that is open only to the citizens of that state.

RIGHTS OF AMERICAN CITIZENSHIP

American citizenship confers some very special rights. First of all, an American citizen obtains state citizenship merely by residing in a state. (*Residence*, as used in the Fourteenth Amendment, means domicile, the place one calls home. The legal status of *domicile* should not be confused with the fact of physical presence. A person may be living in Washington, D.C., but be a citizen of California—that is, he may consider California home. Domicile, or residence, is a question primarily of intent.) And it is from state citizenship that many of our most important rights flow. For example, states determine—subject to constitutional limitations—who shall vote. Although states could confer the right to vote on aliens, no state today does so and citizenship is an essential (but not sufficient) requirement to vote and to hold office.

[2]*Afroyim v. Rusk* (1967); *Trop v. Dulles* (1958); *Kennedy v. Mendoza-Martinez* (1963); and *Schneider v. Rusk* (1964). Also see John P. Roche, "The Expatriation Decisions: A Study in Constitutional Improvisation and the Uses of History," *American Political Science Review* (March 1964), pp. 72–80.

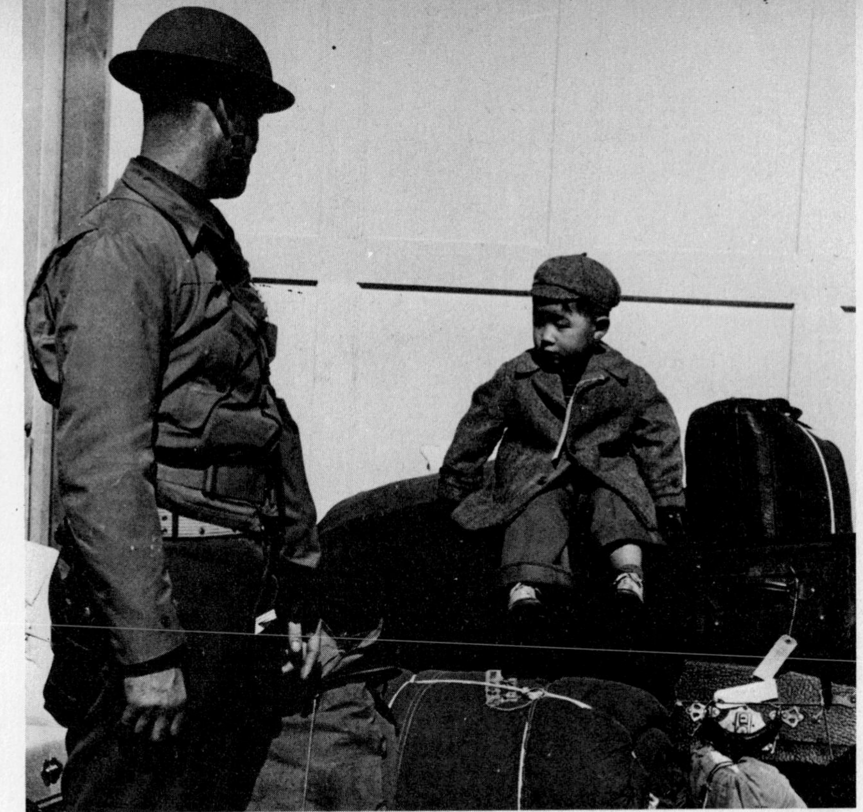

During World War II thousands of persons, both Japanese aliens and Americans of Japanese descent, were taken from their homes on the West Coast and sent to relocation centers. This small evacuee was one of them.

Do American citizens have rights other than the right to become a citizen of the state in which they reside? The Supreme Court in the *Slaughter House Cases* (1873) carefully distinguished between privileges of United States citizens and of state citizens, holding that the only privileges attaching to national citizenship are those that "owe their existence to the Federal Government, its National Character, its Constitution, or its laws." These privileges of United States citizenship have never been completely enumerated, but they include the right to use the navigable waters of the United States; to assemble peacefully; to petition the national government for redress of grievances; to be protected by the national government on the high seas; to vote, if qualified to do so under state laws, and to have one's vote counted properly; and to travel throughout the United States.

The right to travel This right has in recent years become the subject of considerable litigation. Except for persons under legal restraint—committed to jail, subject to the draft, out on bail, and so forth—all American citizens may travel throughout the nation, and no state may impose any barriers to this freedom of movement. During World War II, however, the national government forced American citizens of Japanese ancestry to move from their homes to relocation centers. The Supreme Court reluctantly approved this denial of their liberty, accepting as reasonable the decision of military commanders that such measures were necessary to prevent sabotage and espionage. But the Supreme Court insisted that after the loyalty of these people was established, restrictions could not be placed on their freedom to travel that were not legally imposed on all other persons.[3]

Do American citizens have the right to travel abroad, or is that a privilege that the government may limit at its discretion? Until World War I, no passports were required, though one could be obtained as a convenience if wanted. Then, other nations began to demand passports before they would grant visas to our citizens. Under present law and presidential directives, when the United States is at war or in a state of national emergency proclaimed by the president, it is unlawful, except as otherwise provided by the president, for any citizen to leave or enter the United States unless he bears a valid passport. Presidential proclamations have brought these provisions into effect since 1941, and, except for travel to a few nations—Mexico and Canada, for example—no citizen can lawfully leave the United States without a passport.

For many years the Department of State contended that Congress had given it wide authority to determine who could have a passport and under what conditions. The Department continues to contend that it may deny passports to persons whose travel abroad may, in the judgment of the Secretary of State, "be prejudicial to the orderly conduct of foreign relations of the United States or otherwise be prejudicial to the interests of the United States." But in recent years the Supreme Court has concluded that the right to travel is part of the liberty protected by the Fifth Amendment.[4] So far the Court has declared unconstitutional only one congressional provision, that making it a crime for any member of a registered communist organization to apply for a passport,[5] but it has narrowly construed the authority of the Department of State. The Court held that the department is authorized to impose area restrictions whenever and wherever it feels that travel by an American citizen is not in the best interest of the United States,[6] but the Court in another case ruled that Congress had not made it a crime to travel into a restricted area.[7] Invalidation of a passport for travel to certain countries merely announces to the bearer that if he or she goes to such a country, the citizen cannot be assured of the protection of the United States. It does not mean that the citizen is committing a crime. If Congress specifically makes such travel a federal offense, the Supreme Court will have to face the constitutional issue.

The right to live in the United States The right of a citizen to come to the

[3]*Korematsu v. United States* (1944); *Ex parte Endo* (1944).

[4]*Kent v. Dulles* (1958).

[5]*Aptheker v. Secretary of State* (1964).

[6]*Zemel v. Rusk* (1965).

[7]*United States v. Laub* (1967).

United States and to live here is not subject to any congressional limitation. Aliens have no such right.

Congress has complete constitutional power to decide which aliens shall be admitted to the United States and under what conditions they shall remain. Despite the fact, as President Franklin D. Roosevelt reminded the Daughters of the American Revolution, that "all of us are descended from immigrants and revolutionists," Congress has made it difficult for aliens to enter the United States (though compared to many other nations, admission to the United States is relatively easy).

Beginning in 1875 Congress imposed the first of the so-called qualitative limitations, to exclude certain types of "undesirables." During World War I and with the 1924 Immigration Act, Congress set a limit on the number of immigrants who could be admitted to the United States and created a national-origin system which discriminated against those immigrants from southern and southeastern Europe and Asia. Then in 1965 Congress, after years of political pressures, adopted a new immigration policy. Under present law there is a ceiling of 170,000 immigrants a year for all countries outside of the Western Hemisphere, and no more than 20,000 a year from any one country. For nationals within this hemisphere the ceiling is 120,000 a year. Within these overall ceilings, preferences are given to members of the arts and professions, refugees driven from their homes by political or racial persecution, and for relatives of American citizens. Minor unmarried children, spouses, or parents of American citizens may enter without regard to quota limitations.

Once here, aliens remain in this country at the sufferance of the national government; aliens who enter illegally may be expelled without much ado. Because the Supreme Court has ruled that deportation, despite its drastic consequences, is a civil rather than a criminal proceeding, the constitutional safeguards that protect persons accused of crimes do not come into play. Aliens may be deported for acts that were not grounds for banishment when they were performed and for a variety of reasons, such as two convictions for crimes involving moral turpitude, joining an organization that advocates revolutionary doctrines, or engaging in activities that the attorney general believes are "subversive to the national security."

Although the Supreme Court has recently tended to construe narrowly congressional statutes dealing with deportation and exclusion of aliens, it has reaffirmed Congress's full and complete power to exclude aliens and to prescribe the conditions of their entry. The Court has gone so far as to permit Congress to delegate to the attorney general the discretion to exclude aliens merely because they have advocated or published communist doctrines. "Over no conceivable subject is the legislative power of Congress more complete than it is over the admission of aliens."[8]

[8]*Kleindienst v. Mandel* (1972).

RIGHTS OF ALIENS

Aliens have no constitutional right to come to or to remain in the United States, but while here they are protected by the Constitution. And most of the protective provisions of the Constitution are not limited to citizens. More often it speaks of the rights of *persons.* Congress and the states, for example, have no more authority to interfere with an alien's freedom of religion than with that of a citizen.

Since, as we have noted, alienage is a suspect classification, laws relating to aliens are subject to close judicial scrutiny. To illustrate: the Supreme Court has ruled that a state may not deny aliens the right to be admitted to the bar.[9] Present federal laws excluding aliens from federal employment have not been challenged, but the Court has held that a state may not impose a flat ban on the employment of aliens to all state jobs.[10] It hinted strongly that if a state were to exclude aliens from policy-making positions such action would be considered constitutional. The Supreme Court has also held that although the Civil Rights Act of 1964 protects aliens along with citizens from being discriminated against because of their race, sex, religion, age, or national origin, the act does not make it illegal for private employers to refuse to hire aliens.[11]

Constitutional protection of property

By *property rights* we mean the rights of an individual to own, use, rent, invest, or contract for property. From Aristotle, through the English philosopher Harrington, to the Founding Fathers, there has run a persistent emphasis on the close connection between liberty and ownership of property, between property and power. This emphasis has been reflected in American political thinking and American political institutions. A major purpose of the framers of our Constitution was to establish a government strong enough to protect each person's right to use and enjoy his property and, at the same time, a government so limited that it could not encroach upon that right. The framers were disturbed by the efforts of some state legislatures in behalf of debtors at the expense of creditors (see Chapter 2). So in the Constitution they forbade states to make anything except gold or silver legal tender for the payment of debts or to pass any law "impairing the obligation of contracts."

THE CONTRACT CLAUSE

The obligation-of-contracts clause of the Constitution was designed to

[9] *Sugarman v. Dougall* (1973).

[10] *In Re Griffiths* (1973).

[11] *Espinoza v. Farah Mfg. Co.* (1973).

prevent states from enacting legislation to extend the period during which debtors could meet their payments or otherwise relieve them of their contractual obligations. The framers had in mind an ordinary contract between private persons. But beginning with Chief Justice John Marshall, the Supreme Court expanded the coverage of the clause to prevent states from altering in any way privileges previously conferred on a corporation.[12]

In effect the contract clause was being used to protect vested property at the expenses of the power of the states to guard the public welfare. Gradually, however, the Court began in the 1880s to restrict the coverage of the contract clause and to subject contracts, like other forms of property, to the states' power to protect the public health, safety, welfare, or morals. In 1934 the Supreme Court went so far as to hold that even contracts between individuals—the very ones the contract clause was intended to protect—could be modified by state law in order to avert social and economic catastrophe.[13]

But in the 1880s, just as the contract clause ceased to be an important block to state regulation of property, the due process clause took over.

DUE PROCESS OF LAW

Perhaps the most difficult parts of the Constitution to understand are the clauses in the Fifth and Fourteenth Amendments that forbid national and state governments, respectively, to deny any person his life, liberty, or property without due process of law. These due process clauses have resulted in more Supreme Court decisions than has any other in the Constitution, although the equal-protection clause is about to catch up. Even so, it is impossible to give due process any exact and completely satisfactory explanation. Indeed, the Supreme Court itself has refused to give it a precise definition.

There are two kinds of due process—*procedural* and *substantive. Procedural* due process refers to the methods by which a law is enforced, but there are several ways in which a law itself, on its face, as enacted by a legislative body may violate the procedural due process requirement.

First, the statute may be vague. "A statute which either forbids or requires the doing of an act in terms so vague that men of common intelligence must necessarily guess at its meaning and differ as to its application, violates the first essential of due process of law."[14] A vague statute fails to provide adequate warning, contains insufficient guidelines for law enforcement officials, and sets juries and courts at large. Here are some examples of laws struck down for vagueness: a statute making it a crime "to treat contemptuously the flag,"[15] a "suspicious

[12]*Fletcher v. Peck* (1810).

[13]*Home Building and Loan Association v. Blaisdell* (1934).

[14]*Connally v. General Constr. Co.* (1926); *Smith v. Goguen* (1974).

[15]*Ibid.*

"What's so great about due process? Due process got me ten years."

Drawing by Handelsman; © 1970 The New Yorker Magazine, Inc.

persons ordinance" that made it illegal for any person to be found on a street at late or unusual hours without any visible or lawful business and who could not give a satisfactory account for himself;[16] a vagrancy ordinance that declared to be vagrants a wide variety of ill-defined classes such as "rogues and vagabonds," "dissolute persons who go about begging," "common night walkers," and so on.[17]

A second way in which a law itself may deny a person procedural due process is by creating a statutory presumption of guilt "where there is no rational connection between the facts proved and the facts presumed." For example, the Court has declared unconstitutional laws that created a presumption that a firearm in the possession of a person convicted of a crime of violence has been transported or received in violation of a law,"[18] and that possession of marijuana or cocaine creates the presumption that the drugs were obtained through an illegal importation.[19] (The constitutionality of such a presumption in the case of heroin has been sustained, since little if any heroin is made in this country and virtually all of it is illegally imported.)[20]

Traditionally, however, procedural due process refers to the *procedures* by which a law is applied. It requires, to paraphrase Daniel Webster's famous definition, a procedure that "hears before it condemns, proceeds upon inquiry, and renders judgment only after a trial" in which the essentials of justice have been preserved. Originally procedural due process was limited to criminal prosecutions. It now applies to many different kinds of governmental proceedings, not just to courtroom hearings. Among the other forums where procedural due process is required are juvenile hearings, disbarment proceedings, determinations of eligiblity for welfare payments, parole revocations, legislative contempt proceedings, congressional committees and administrative tribunals, disciplinary proceedings in state universities and colleges.[21]

In determining if procedural due process is required, it makes no difference whether the activity that is involved is called a "privilege" or a "right." Moreover, the liberty that is protected is more than freedom from being thrown into jail, and the property that is secured goes beyond mere ownership of real estate, things, or money. However, "the range of interests protected by procedural due process is not infinite." For example, a state does not have to give a nontenured faculty member a hearing before it decides not to renew his appointment. True, a faculty member is entitled to freedom of speech, along with everybody else,

[16]*Palmer v. City of Euclid, Ohio* (1971).

[17]*Paparchristou v. City of Jacksonville* (1972).

[18]*Tot v. United States* (1943).

[19]*Leary v. United States* (1969).

[20]*Turner v. United States* (1970).

[21]*Groppi v. Leslie* (1973); *Goldberg v. Kelly* (1970); *In re Gault* (1967); *Thorpe v. Housing Authority* (1969); *UGSA v. Peltason* (1974).

and he cannot be denied that freedom without due process, but "the interest in holding a teaching job at a state university, simpliciter, is not itself a free speech interest" nor one that cannot be denied without procedural due process.[22]

"Once it is determined that due process applies, the question remains what process is due."[23] What is due varies with the kind of interest involved and the nature of the proceedings. As applied in a federal courtroom, due process requires as a minimum the careful observance of the provisions of the Bill of Rights as outlined in amendments four through eight. For other kinds of proceedings, courtroom procedures are not necessarily essential for there to be due process. The question in each instance is what must be done to insure *fundamental fairness.* It is hard to generalize because of the wide variety of governmental proceedings involved. But at a minimum there must be adequate notice and an opportunity to be heard. The hearing required must be appropriate to the interest involved and the kind of procedure concerned—it does not necessarily have to be formal or adversary in nature. To illustrate, a nonprobationary federal employee may be dismissed for cause without a preremoval hearing, although before it can be made final such a hearing must be held.[24] An old-age aid recipient is entitled to a hearing with the right to present oral evidence before his aid may be terminated, but he is not entitled to have the state furnish him with legal counsel.[25] A juvenile cannot be declared delinquent without a hearing in which he is given the right to confront hostile witnesses and to cross-examine them, to present oral evidence, and to be represented by counsel. The level of proof must demonstrate his delinquency beyond any reasonable doubt, but he is not entitled to have the decision made by a jury.[26] A prisoner facing disciplinary proceedings should be provided written notice of the alleged violation and reasons for the action, but he is not entitled to confront his accusers or to cross-examine adverse witnesses, or to have legal counsel.[27]

SUBSTANTIVE DUE PROCESS

Whereas procedural due process places limits on the manner in which governmental power may be exercised, substantive due process has to do not with the procedures but with the *content* of the law, which it requires to be reasonable and fair. Whereas procedural due process

[22]*Board of Regents v. Roth* (1972).

[23]*Morrissey v. Brewer* (1972).

[24]*Arnett v. Kennedy* (1974)

[25]*Goldberg v. Kelly* (1970).

[26]*In re Gault* (1967); *McKeiver v. Pennsylvania* (1971).

[27]*Wolff v. McDonnell* (1974).

primarily restrains the executive and judicial branches, substantive due process mainly limits the law-making branch. Substantive due process means that even if a law has been legally passed and is being properly applied, if the law itself is unreasonable, it is unconstitutional. Or to put it another way, procedural due process limits the way in which governmental power may be exercised, substantive due process places limits on what the government may regulate, regardless of the procedures it uses.

For an example of a substantive due process claim, suppose that a state legislature should adopt a law requiring employers to pay all employees precisely the same salary paid to the president of the firm. An employer being prosecuted for violating this law might object that the law is unreasonable and that even if he is given a fair trial, to make him comply with the law would be to deprive him of his property without due process of the law—that is, the law itself is unreasonable. Or take some real examples: pregnant women denied by state laws the right to have abortions and physicians denied the right to provide such for their patients have argued with some success that such laws are unreasonable and therefore unconstitutional (*Roe v. Wade,* 1973). Similarly, the Supreme Court held that school board regulations requiring a teacher to cease teaching past the fourth month of pregnancy and barring her from returning to the classroom until three months after the birth of her child are a denial of due process—that is, the regulations were thought by a majority of the judges to be unnecessarily stringent and to interfere unreasonably with the liberty of a female teacher to bear a child.[28]

Along with the adoption of substantive due process, the Supreme Court expanded the meaning of "property" and "liberty," especially the latter. It has been expanded to denote "not merely freedom from bodily restraint but also the right of the individual to contract, to engage in any of the common occupations of life, to acquire useful knowledge, to marry, establish a home and bring up children, to worship God according to the dictates of his own conscience, and generally to enjoy those common law privileges long recognized as essential to the orderly pursuit of happiness by free men."[29]

Prior to 1937, the most important phase of this new liberty protected by the Supreme Court was "liberty of contract"—that is, business liberty. Indeed, the adoption of the doctrine of substantive due process and the simultaneous expansion of the meaning of liberty rendered the Supreme Court, for a time, the final arbiter of our economic and industrial life. During this period, the Supreme Court was dominated by conservative gentlemen who considered almost all social welfare legislation unreasonable. They used the due process clause to strike down laws regulating hours of labor, establishing minimum wages, regulating prices, and forbidding employers to discharge workers for union mem-

[28]*Cleveland Board of Education v. LaFleur* (1974).

[29]*Meyer v. Nebraska* (1923).

bership. The Supreme Court, for a time elevating the doctrine of laissez faire into a constitutional principle, vetoed laws adversely affecting property rights unless the judges could be persuaded that such laws were necessary to protect the public health or safety.

But what is "unreasonable"? What is "necessary"? The trouble with the substantive interpretation of due process is that the view of the reasonableness of a law depends on one's economic, social, and political views. In democracies, elected officials are supposed to accommodate the clashing notions of reasonableness and to decide what regulations of liberty and property are needed to promote the public welfare. When the Supreme Court substitutes its own ideas of reasonableness for the legislature's, it acts like a superlegislature. But how competent are judges to say what the nation's economic policies should be? Or other kinds of policies?

Under the impact of this criticism, the Supreme Court since 1937 has largely abandoned the doctrine of "liberty of contract" and in general has refused to apply the doctrine of substantive due process to laws regulating the economy.[30] The Court now consists of justices who believe that deciding which are reasonable regulations of the uses of property is a *legislative* and not a judicial responsibility. As long as the justices see some connection between such a law and the promotion of the public welfare, the Supreme Court will not interfere, even if the justices personally believe the law to be unwise.

The abandonment of the doctrine of substantive due process as a limit on the government's power to regulate property rights has not presaged a return to the old narrow conception of liberty or to the abandonment of substantive due process. Quite the contrary, since 1937 the word "liberty" of the Fifth and Fourteenth Amendments has been expanded to include the *basic civil liberties*, and substantive due process has been given new life as a limitation on governmental power in the field of these liberties.

Furthermore, as we have noted, since the 1960s the Supreme Court has developed a substantive interpretation of the equal-protection clause to supplement the substantive interpretation of due process. And just as prior to 1937, liberal justices in dissents, and liberal commentators, used to chide conservative justices in the majority for using substantive due process to impose their own ideas of what was a reasonable regulation of the economy upon the nation, so today conservative judges, still in the minority, and commentators, are contending that once again the Supreme Court justices in the majority are going beyond the bounds of their responsibilities to substitute their own ideas of what is desirable public policy on the people's elected representatives. Justice Rehnquist, for example, the Court's most outspoken conservative, has accused his colleagues of imposing their own preferences when they ruled that the legislatures could not forbid abortions

[30]See for example, *North Dakota Pharmacy Bd. v. Snyder's Store* (1973).

during the first three months of pregnancy, could do so to protect the health of the mother and fetus during the second three months, and could forbid them altogether during the last three months of pregnancy.[31] In another case he chided the majority for what he thought was going beyond the language of the Constitution when they declared a state lacked authority to restrict residency status for those attending its public universities to those who were residents at the time of admission.[32]

The justices who support the majority position, of course, deny that they are reviving the discredited doctrine of substantive due process or substituting their own values for those of the legislature. They insist they are merely applying the commands of the Constitution. They argue that there is a fundamental difference between what they are doing in protecting *civil liberties* and what the conservative pre-1937 justices did to protect *property rights.* They argue that the conservative justices were writing into the Constitution the principles of laissez-faire economics whereas the present justices are extracting from the Constitution the principles of civil liberties.

The fact is that the notion that laws must be reasonable has deep roots in natural-law concepts and a long history in the American constitutional tradition. For most Americans most of the time, it is not sufficient merely to say that a law reflects the wishes of the popular or legislative majority. We also want our laws to be just. And we continue to rely heavily on judges to decide what is just. These tensions between democratic procedures and judicial guardians are ones to which we shall return when we discuss the role of the judges in Chapter 14.

EMINENT DOMAIN

Many government regulations affect the value of the property we own, sometimes making it worth more, sometimes less. For example, a zoning law restricting a particular area to residential uses may decrease the immediate value of a particular individual's property. (Maybe he was planning to use his land for a gas station.) The government does not have to remunerate the owner for such losses, so he loses money—but the rest of the community may gain.

What if the government goes beyond reasonable regulation and takes property? Both the national and state governments have a constitutional right to do so, to exercise what is known as the power of eminent domain. But the Constitution requires that property be seized only for public purposes—for example, to build a highway or school or military installation—and that the owner must be paid a fair price. If there is any

[31] *Roe v. Wade* (1973).

[32] *Vlandis v. Kline* (1973). For a review of the intellectual issues, see Jacob W. Landynski, "Due Process and the Concept of Ordered Liberty," *Hofstra Law Review* (Winter 1974), pp. 1 ff.

dispute about what price is fair, the final decision is made by the courts.

To sum up, where do we stand today in terms of constitutional protection of property? The obligation-of-contracts clause is no longer a major barrier to state regulation of property, and substantive due process has been abandoned as a judicially enforced limit on legislative regulation of our economy. The constitutional limits on the power of eminent domain remain as important as ever. But our right to use our property is not above regulation in the public interest. What regulations are needed is determined by the legislatures; the national courts will intervene only if the laws are outrageously arbitrary and unreasonable or are being applied without procedural due process.

Freedom from arbitrary arrest, questioning, and imprisonment

James Otis's address in 1761 protesting arbitrary searches and seizures by English customs officials was the opening salvo of the American Revolution; as John Adams later said, "American independence was then and there born." The Fourth Amendment states: "The right of the people to be secure in their persons, houses, papers, and effects, against unreasonable searches and seizures, shall not be violated, and no Warrants shall issue, but upon probable cause, supported by Oath or affirmation, and particularly describing the place to be searched, and the persons or things to be seized."

WHAT IS AN UNREASONABLE SEARCH AND SEIZURE?

Despite what we see in television police dramas and sometimes read about in the news, lawmen—federal, state, or local—have no general right to invade homes and break down doors. They are not supposed to search people except under certain narrowly defined conditions; and they have no right to arrest except under prescribed circumstances. This is a highly technical area in which the Supreme Court itself has difficulty in determining what the Constitution means. As Justice Powell has written, "Searches and seizures are an opaque area of the law; flagrant Fourth Amendment abuses will rarely escape detection but there is a vast twilight zone with respect to which our own 'decisions . . . are hardly noted for their predictability.' "[33] And the law in this area is constantly changing. It is on the reasonableness of searches and seizures that the Burger Court has been especially likely to move away from the more restrictive decisions of the Warren Court

In general, any search by the police made without a warrant issued by a magistrate is unreasonable. The *exceptions* to the warrant requirement, and the list grows under the Burger Court, are as follows:

[33]Concurring in *Schneckloth v. Bustamonte* (1973) and quoting from Justice Harlan in *Ker v. California* (1963).

1. Searches of automobiles that the police have probable cause to believe contain evidence of crimes or are being used to commit crimes.[34]

2. A police officer may stop and frisk a suspect if he has reason to believe that he is dealing with an armed and dangerous person, regardless of whether or not he has probable cause to arrest the individual for a crime. The search must be confined to find weapons that could be used to assault the officer.[35]

3. When making a lawful arrest, police may make a warrantless full search of the arrestee's person and the area under his immediate custody and control.[36] The Burger Court has extended such searches to cover the effects in possession of the arrestee at the place where he is detained.[37]

4. The Burger Court has combined exceptions two and three to create what the minority thinks to be a new exception. If the initial frisk, even if undertaken when the officer lacked probable cause to make an arrest, uncovers evidence that justifies an arrest, then the arrest can be used to justify a further search. In *Adams v. Williams* (1972), an officer, acting on an informer's tip, approached a person sitting in a car. The policeman ordered the suspect to get out of the car, but the suspect merely rolled down the window. The officer saw a weapon on the suspect's waistband. He arrested him—although the mere possession of the weapon was not a crime—and made a search and found heroin. Justice Rehnquist, speaking for the Court, said, "The Fourth Amendment does not require a policeman who lacks the precise level of information necessary for probable cause to arrest to simply shrug his shoulders and allow a crime to occur or a criminal to escape." The dissenting justices argued that the majority had ignored the fact that the stop-and-frisk exception to the warrant requirement of the Fourth Amendment had been "begrudgingly" granted only to protect the safety of officers of the law.

[34]*Carroll v. United States* (1925); *Cardwell v. Lewis* (1974).

[35]*Terry v. Ohio* (1968).

[36]*Chimel v. California* (1969); *United States v. Robinson* (1974); *Gustafson v. Florida* (1974).

[37]*United States v. Edwards* (1974).

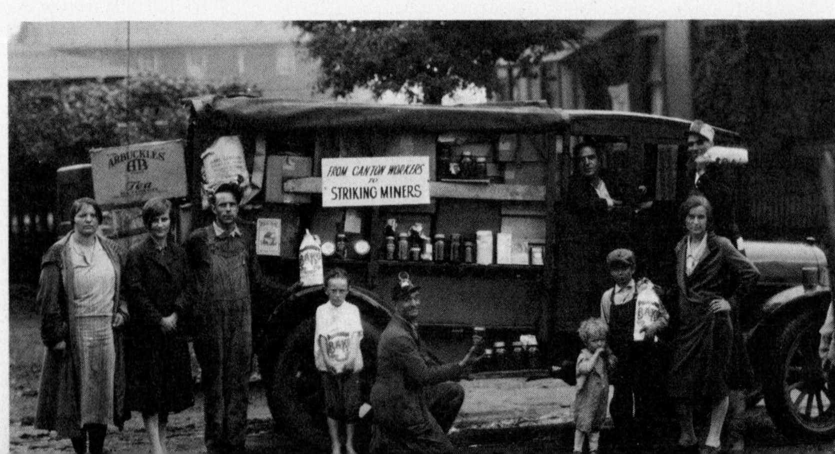

Early efforts of miners to unionize were sometimes thwarted by unconstitutional means. Union organizers were sometimes subject to police harassment.

5. When there is probable cause to make an arrest, even if one is not made, limited search necessary to preserve highly evanesent evidence such as scrapings under fingernails is permitted.[38]

6. A search based on consent voluntarily given, even if the person who gives it is not first notified that he or she has a right to refuse to grant permission, is allowed even if the police officer has no probable cause either to seek a warrant or to make a lawful arrest.[39]

With the above exceptions, prior to engaging in a search, police are supposed to appear before a neutral and detached magistrate for a warrant. (The magistrate need not be a legally trained judge, but a prosecutor or a state attorney general will not do.)[40] The officer under oath must present some evidence to demonstrate that he has probable cause to believe that the search will produce evidence of a crime. The magistrate must "perform his 'neutral and detached' function and not serve merely as a rubber stamp for the police." The warrant he issues must describe what places are to be searched and what things are to be seized. A mere blanket authorization to search indiscriminately violates the Constitution. The premises protected against unreasonable searches and seizures include any place a person has a legitimate right to be, including hotel rooms, rented homes, apartments of friends, or even telephone booths.

The Fourth Amendment also protects persons against unreasonable arrests or police detentions. However, since people, like automobiles, are movable, the courts are more lenient in permitting warrantless arrests of individuals than warrantless searches of homes. The police may make arrests without warrants whenever they have probable cause to believe that a person has committed or is about to commit a crime.

The Fourth Amendment covers searches by governmental agencies other than the police—i.e., health inspectors, social workers—and premises other than homes—i.e., businesses of various kinds. But the Courts are less likely to insist on warrants prior to searches and to impose less restrictive conditions on such searches than for those made by the police. No warrant is required, for example, for home visits by case workers to insure that recipients of welfare are complying with the law.[41] If permission to make such a visit is refused, aid can be cut off, although no criminal penalty can be imposed. Warrantless inspections are also permitted to insure compliance with regulations by federally licensed dealers in liquor and firearms.[42] A field inspector for an enviromental protection agency does not need a warrant to go on to property

[38]*Cuppy v. Murphy* (1973).

[39]*Schneckloth v. Bustamonte* (1973); *United States v. Matlock* (1974).

[40]*Shadwick v. City of Tampa* (1972); *Collidge v. New Hampshire* (1971).

[41]*Wyman v. James* (1971).

[42]*Colonnade Catering Corp. v. United States* (1970); *United States v. Biswell* (1972).

and make a test of smoke coming from a stack which he had sighted as a possible violation of regulations from "the open fields."[43] But health inspectors may not make entree without a warrant if a householder refuses permission. The inspector, however, can readily get a warrant from a magistrate: he does not have to demonstrate probable cause that the law is being violated, merely that he is performing his lawful duties.[44]

The inventions of science have confronted judges with new problems in applying the prohibition against unreasonable searches and seizures. Obviously, the framers of the Fourth Amendment had in mind physical objects such as books, papers, letters, and other kinds of documents that they felt should not be seized by police officers except on the basis of limited search warrants issued by magistrates. But what of tapping phone wires or using electronic devices to eavesdrop?[45] In *Olmstead v. United States,* decided in 1928, a bare majority of the Supreme Court held that there was no unconstitutional search unless there was seizure of physical objects or an actual physical entry into a premise. Justices Holmes and Brandeis wrote vigorous dissents in which they argued that the Constitution should be kept abreast of modern times and that the "dirty business" of wiretapping produced the same evil invasions of privacy that the framers had in mind when they wrote the Fourteenth Amendment.

Forty years later, in *Katz v. United States* (1967), the Supreme Court adopted the Holmes-Brandeis position: "The Fourth Amendment protects people—and not simply 'areas'—against unreasonable searches and seizures," and the use by police officers of electronic devices to overhear a conversation inside a public telephone booth is a search and seizure within the meaning of the Constitution. "Wherever a man may be, he is entitled to know that he will remain free from unreasonable searches, and seizures."

Since conversations are now constitutionally protected against unreasonable searches and seizures, several states have adopted statutes authorizing the police to obtain warrants to intercept conversations. (The Supreme Court declared New York's statute unconstitutional for its failure to establish sufficiently precise standards.)[46] And despite President Johnson's objection that the statute would lead to a "nation of snoopers bending through the keyholes of the homes and offices of America, spying on our neighbors," Congress in the Omnibus Crime Control and Safe Streets Act of 1968 authorized procedures for intercepting conversations by federal, state, and local police.

[43] *Air Pollution Variance Board of Colorado v. Western Alfalfa Corp.* (1974).

[44] *See v. City of Seattle* (1967); *Camara v. Municipal Court* (1967).

[45] See Walter F. Murphy, *Wiretapping on Trial: A Case Study in the Judicial Process* (Random House, 1965).

[46] *Berger v. New York* (1967).

The 1968 act, although making it a federal crime for any unauthorized person to tap telephone wires or use or sell in interstate commerce electronic bugging devices, authorizes the attorney general to secure permission for federal agents to engage in bugging by applying for a warrant from a federal judge for a whole range of specified federal offenses. The attorney general must authorize the wiretapping personally or through an assistant attorney general specifically designated by him for that purpose. This authority may not be further delegated.[47]

At the state level the act authorizes the principal prosecuting attorney of any state or political subdivision to apply to a state judge for a warrant approving of wiretapping or oral intercepts for felonies. Judges are to issue warrants only if they decide that probable cause exists that a crime is being, has been, or is about to be committed and that information relating to that crime may only be obtained by the intercept.

In addition to these intercepts under warrant, the act permits police officers to act without a warrant for forty-eight hours in "an emergency situation relating to conspiratorial activities threatening the national security" or involving organized crime. The president is even empowered by the act to authorize intercepts by "nonpolice" in national security cases and evidence obtained by such methods is to be admissible in federal courts.

In the few cases that have come before it under the act, the Supreme Court has construed it as narrowly as possible. A unanimous Court held that the president's authority to protect the nation against foreign attack and violent overthrow does not include the right, without judicial warrant, to authorize electronic surveillance of persons suspect of domestic subversion. Justice Powell, speaking for the Court (*United States v. United States District Court*, 1972), said, "The danger to political dissent is acute where the Government attempts to act under so vague a concept as the power to protect 'domestic security.' " The Court pointedly did not rule on the scope of the constitutionality of the practice of presidents to authorize surveillance over the activities of agents of foreign powers, within and without the country. However, the Court in no way has ever hinted that a president has any constitutional authority to authorize a breaking in and entry for surveillance purposes.

THE EXCLUSIONARY RULE

Combining the Fourth Amendment prohibition against unreasonable searches and seizures with the Fifth Amendment injunction that no person shall be compelled to be a witness against himself—and using the Fourteenth Amendment (*Mapp v. Ohio*, 1961) to make its ruling applicable to the state and local courts—the Supreme Court has ruled that evidence unconstitutionally obtained cannot be used in a criminal trial against persons from whom it was seized. The exclusionary rule,

[47] *United States v. Giordano* (1974).

however, does not extend to grand jury proceedings. Grand juries may consider all evidence even if it has been obtained improperly.[48]

The exclusionary rule was adopted in large part to deter police misconduct; the police are seldom prosecuted for making illegal searches and seizures nor are they made to pay civil damages. The exclusionary rule is about the only sanction available to the judges to enforce the requirements of the Fourth Amendment, and it is ineffective if the police are not particularly interested in using the evidence to prosecute.

There are critics of the rule, including some justices of the Supreme Court. They ask, Why should the government be denied the use of the best available evidence merely because the police have misbehaved? They argue that the solution is to punish the police for their misconduct rather than letting other law violators go free. So far, however, these arguments have not prevailed.

Shadowed.

© 1971 Herblock in *The Washington Post.*

THE RIGHT TO REMAIN SILENT

During the seventeenth century, certain special courts in England forced confessions of heresy and sedition from religious dissenters. It was in response to these practices that the British privilege against self-incrimination developed, and it was because the framers of our Bill of Rights were familiar with the history of these odious confessions that they included within the Fifth Amendment the provision that no person shall be compelled to testify against himself in criminal prosecutions. The protection against self-incrimination is designed to strengthen a fundamental principle of Anglo-American justice—that no person has an obligation to prove innocence. Rather, the burden is on the government to prove guilt.

Literally read, the privilege against self-incrimination applies only in criminal prosecutions, but it has always been interpreted to protect any person subject to questioning by any agency of government. Hence, a witness before a congressional committee, for example, may refuse to answer incriminating questions. But to invoke the privilege, it is not enough that the witness's answers might be embarrassing, lead to public disapproval or loss of job, or might incriminate others; there must be a reasonable fear that the answers might support a national or state criminal prosecution or "furnish a link in the chain of evidence needed to prosecute" him for a crime.[49] If a defendant refuses to take the stand in his own defense, the judge must warn the jury not to draw any adverse inferences from his silence. However, if a defendant elects to take the stand, he cannot claim the privilege against self-incrimination to prevent cross-examination by the prosecution.

The self-incrimination clause may not be denied to a person because he or she is a public employee or government contractor. Governments may not dismiss employees or deny contracts to persons who invoke

[48]*United States v. Calandra* (1974).

[49]*Blau v. United States* (1950).

their right to remain silent when subject to official interrogation by grand juries and other governmental agencies (although they may be dismissed if they refuse to answer to their superiors about matters closely related to their official duties.)[50]

Until the Supreme Court brought the privilege against self-incrimination within the scope of the Fourteenth Amendment and until it permitted the privilege to be invoked to prevent incrimination by either national or state governments, a person could find himself "whipsawed" between national and state authorities. He could not refuse to answer questions put to him by national authorities for fear of state prosecution, and vice versa. Thus federal and state authorities working together could use the machinery of one government to compel evidence to be used in the courts of the other government. Recent rulings of the Supreme Court have put a stop to these practices.[51]

Sometimes authorities would rather have answers from a witness than prosecute. If the immunity granted is as broad as the protection provided by the self-incrimination clause, then a witness may be compelled to respond under pain of fine or jail. Congress has established procedures whereby prosecutors and congressional committees may secure from a federal judge a grant of immunity for a witness.

For many decades the immunity granted was "transactional immunity"—that is, a person compelled to answer questions could not be prosecuted for any crimes uncovered as the result of the compelled testimony. Then in 1970, Congress restricted the scope of the immunity that could be given to a witness. No longer is he guaranteed he will not be prosecuted for any crimes uncovered, but merely that the government will not use any of the information directly or indirectly derived from the compelled testimony. By a close vote, the Supreme Court (*Kastigar v. United States*, 1972), ruled that this "use and derivate use immunity" is coextensive with the constitutional privilege, and therefore is sufficient to compel testimony over a claim of the privilege against self-incrimination. However, if a person granted immunity is subsequently prosecuted, the government has an affirmative duty to prove to the court that the evidence it proposes to use is wholly independent of the compelled testimony.

Congress may confer immunity from federal or state prosecution, but a state may not completely immunize a witness from prosecution by federal authorities. However, if a state grants a witness immunity, federal officials may not use the evidence disclosed by the state proceedings, although they are free to make their own investigations.

THE THIRD DEGREE

The questioning of suspects by the police is a key procedure for solving crimes—and also one that can easily be abused. Police officers some-

[50]*Garrity v. New Jersey* (1967); *Lefkowitz v. Turley* (1973).

[51]*Malloy v. Hogan* (1964); *Murphy v. Waterfront Commission* (1964).

times forget or ignore the constitutional rights of suspects, especially of those who are frightened and ignorant. Torture, detention incommunicado, and sustained interrogation to wring confessions from suspects are common practices in police states, and such tactics are not completely unknown in the United States. What is the good of constitutional protections at the time of a trial, or the guarantee of the right to assistance of counsel at the trial, or the presumption of innocence if, long before an accused is brought before the court, he is detained and, without the help of an attorney, forced to prove his innocence to the police? What happens in the police station can reduce the courtroom proceedings to a mere formality.

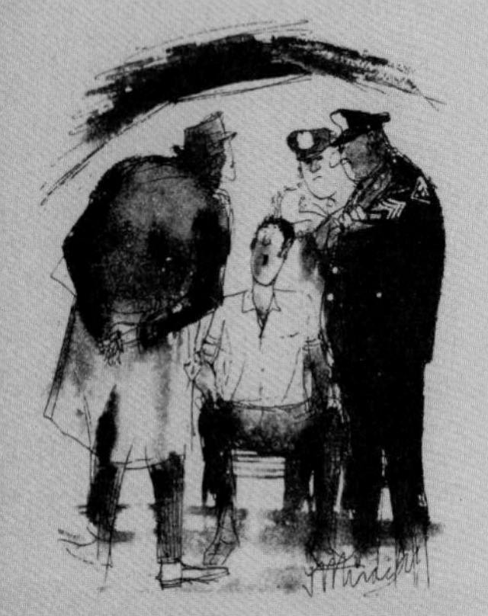

"Why, this is a revelation! I never dreamed I had so many rights."

Drawing by J. Mirachi; © 1970 The New Yorker Magazine, Inc.

Judges, especially those on the Supreme Court, have tried to stamp out police brutality. The Supreme Court has ruled that even though there may be sufficient evidence to support a conviction apart from a confession, the admission into evidence of a coerced confession violates the self-incrimination clause, deprives a person of the assistance of counsel guaranteed by the Sixth and Fourteenth Amendments, deprives a person of due process, and vitiates the entire proceeding.[52]

The federal rules of criminal procedure and the laws of all our states require officers to take those whom they have arrested before a magistrate promptly; the magistrate is to inform the person in custody of his or her constitutional rights and to allow him to get in touch with friends and to seek legal advice. The police have no lawful right to hold a person for questioning prior to a hearing before the magistrate, but they are often tempted to question first. Sometimes they lack the evidence to make an arrest stick but feel that if they can interrogate the suspect before he knows of his constitutional right to remain silent, they can get him to confess.

At first the Supreme Court merely adopted a rule that no confession, whether voluntary or involuntary, obtained while a person was being illegally detained by federal officers could be used in federal courts. Beginning in 1957, despite mounting criticism from many police officers and congressmen, the Supreme Court handed down a series of decisions, sometimes based on the self-incrimination clause of the Fifth Amendment, sometimes on the right-to-counsel clause of the Sixth, sometimes on the due process clause of the Fifth and Fourteenth, that began to cast doubt on the constitutional validity of any *in camera* interrogation of persons suspected of crime by federal or state police.

Then in 1966 *(Miranda v. Arizona)*, by a five-to-four vote the Supreme Court announced that henceforth no conviction—federal or state—could stand if evidence introduced at the trial had been obtained by the police as the result of "custodial interrogation," unless the suspect had been (1) notified that he is free to remain silent, (2) warned that what he says may be used against him in court, (3) told that he has a right to have his attorney present during the questioning, (4) informed that if

[52] *Payne v. Arkansas* (1958).

he cannot afford to hire his own lawyer, an attorney would be provided for him, and (5) permitted at any stage of the police interrogation to terminate it. If the suspect answers questions in the absence of his attorney, the prosecution must be prepared to demonstrate that the suspect knowingly and intelligently waived his rights to remain silent and to have his own lawyer present. Failure to comply with these requirements will lead to reversal of a conviction even if other independent evidence would be sufficient to establish guilt.

As might be expected, there are many critics of the Supreme Court's decision; they argue that the Court has unnecessarily and severely limited the ability of the police to bring criminals to justice. (The importance of pretrial interrogation and investigation procedures to the administration of justice is underscored by the fact that roughly 90 percent of all criminal convictions result from pleas of guilty and never reach the trial stage.)[53] Persuaded by these critics, Congress in 1968, in Title II of the Crime Control Bill, adopted rules for federal trials that may be in conflict with some aspects of the decision *Miranda*.[54] And the Supreme Court itself, under the leadership of President Nixon's post-*Miranda* appointees, has started to back away from that decision. In *Harris v. New York* (1971) Chief Justice Burger, speaking for a five-man majority, stated that the right to take the stand in one's own defense does not include the right to commit perjury. Although the prosecution may not introduce as evidence of guilt statements of the defendant that were obtained by police absent the *Miranda* warning and without counsel present, still such statements can be used to attack a defendant's credibility if he takes the stand and makes statements inconsistent with what he previously told the police. Justice Douglas, speaking for the dissenters, argued that the impact of the *Harris* ruling will be to force a defendant to refrain from testifying if he wishes to deprive the prosecution of the opportunity to use evidence obtained in violation of the *Miranda* ruling, and that *Harris* will undermine the impact of *Miranda* as a deterrent of police practices in disregard of the Constitution. "It is monstrous," he wrote, "that the courts should aid or abet the lawbreaking police officers."

Three years later, Douglas was the only dissenter when the Supreme Court ruled (*Michigan v. Tucker*, 1974) that the testimony of a witness could be used even though police had learned the identity of the witness by questioning the defendant without giving him the full *Miranda* warning. The police had advised the defendant that statements he made would be used against him, and asked him if he wanted an attorney but failed to advise him that he would be furnished counsel free of charge if he could not pay for such services himself. Although the questioning

[53]Donald J. Newman, *Conviction: The Determination of Guilt or Innocence Without Trial* (Little, Brown, 1966), p. 3.

[54]Adam Caryle Breckenridge, *Congress Against the Court* (University of Nebraska Press, 1970), p. 95.

took place before the *Miranda* decision was handed down, the Court majority suggested that this was not the controlling factor in its decision to allow to be used testimony not of the defendant, but of a witness uncovered by this interrogation of the defendant. Said Justice Rehnquist, "Just as the law does not require that a defendant receive a perfect trial, only a fair one, it cannot realistically require that policemen investigating serious crimes make no errors whatsoever."

THE RIGHT OF PRIVACY

There is no mention of the right of privacy in the Constitution, but in the last decade the Supreme Court has come to recognize personal privacy as one of the rights protected by the Constitution. The Court has done this by putting together some elements of the Fourth and Fifth Amendments, the First Amendment's protection for one's intellect, interests, tastes, and beliefs; the liberty protected by the due process clause of the Fifth and Fourteenth Amendments, and the rights reserved to the people by the Ninth Amendment.

The Supreme Court has used the developing doctrine of the right to privacy to rule that states cannot intrude into marital privacy in order to outlaw the sale or use of contraceptives.[55] But perhaps the most dramatic illustration of how the right of privacy has been used by the Court is its decision in *Roe v. Wade* (1973), previously noted, restricting the power of a state legislature to regulate the conditions of abortions (see p. 224).

THE WRIT OF HABEAS CORPUS

Even though the framers did not think a Bill of Rights necessary, they considered certain rights important enough to be included in the original Constitution. Foremost is the guarantee that the writ of habeas corpus will be available unless suspended in time of rebellion or invasion. Permission to suspend the writ is found in the article setting forth the powers of Congress, so presumably only Congress has the right to suspend it.

As originally used, the writ was merely an inquiry by a court to determine whether or not a person was being held in custody as the result of an act of a court with proper jurisdiction. But over the years it has developed into a remedy "available to effect discharge from any confinement contrary to the Constitution or fundamental law."[56] Simply stated, the writ is a court order to any person having another in his custody directing the official to produce the prisoner in court and explain to the judge why he is being held. A person held in custody or subject to restraint applies under oath, usually through his attorney, and states why

[55] *Griswold v. Connecticut* (1965).

[56] *Preiser v. Rodriguez* (1973).

he believes he is being unlawfully held. The judge then orders the jailer to show cause why the writ should not be issued. Testimony can be taken if there is a dispute over the facts. If the judge finds that the petitioner is being unlawfully detained, he may order the prisoner's immediate release.

The case of Messrs. Duncan and White is a good example of one use of the writ. Duncan and White were civilians who had been convicted by military tribunals and were being held by military authorities in Hawaii during World War II. They filed petitions for writs of habeas corpus in the district court of Hawaii, citing both statutory and constitutional reasons to prove that the military had no right to keep them in prison. The court then asked the military officers to show cause why the petition should not be granted. The military replied that Hawaii had become part of an active theater of war, that the writ of habeas corpus had been suspended, that martial law had been established, and that consequently the district court had no jurisdiction to issue the writs. Moreover, the military answered, even if the writ of habeas corpus had not been suspended, it should not be issued in this case because the military trials of Duncan and White were valid. After hearing both sides, the district court, in an action eventually approved by the Supreme Court, agreed with Duncan and White and issued writs ordering their release.[57]

Under our federal system, state courts may not issue writs to inquire why a person is being held by national authorities, but federal judges may intervene to inquire about those restrained by state authorities, provided the petitioner has first sought and been denied relief in the state courts. The expansion in recent decades of the federal court's habeas corpus jurisdiction to permit more extensive postconviction review by federal district judges of the judgments of state courts in criminal cases is a major point of contention between many state and federal judges. As a state judge wrote, "The . . . assumption . . . that federal court protection is needed in addition to state court protection which cannot be trusted with the task . . . has raised the hackles or blood pressure of many of my state court colleagues."[58]

EX POST FACTO LAWS AND BILLS OF ATTAINDER

The Constitution forbids both the national and state governments to pass ex post facto laws or enact bills of attainder (Article I, Sections 9 and 10).

An *ex post facto law* is a retroactive criminal law that works to the detriment of an individual—for example, a law making a particular act a crime that was not a crime when committed or a law increasing the

[57]*Duncan v. Kahanamoku* (1946).

[58]Charles S. Desmond, "The Federal Courts and the Nature and Quality of State Law," in S. I. Shuman, ed., *The Future of Federalism* (Wayne State University Press, 1968), p. 97.

punishment for a crime after it was committed. The prohibition of ex post facto laws does not prevent the passage of retroactive civil laws—for example, increasing income tax rates as applied to income already earned—nor does it prevent the passage of retroactive penal laws that work to the benefit of an accused—for example, a law decreasing a punishment or changing the rules of evidence to make conviction more difficult.

A *bill of attainder* is a legislative act inflicting punishment on specified individuals without judicial trial. Bills of attainder have been rare in American history, but Congress has enacted two in the last three decades. In 1943 Representative Martin Dies, then chairman of the House Committee on Un-American Activities, denounced from the floor of Congress thirty-nine officials as "crackpot, radical bureaucrats." He singled out three of these men for special abuse. Shortly afterward, Congress attached a rider to an appropriation bill naming these three employees and ordering that they receive no salary from the federal government until the president had reappointed them and the Senate had confirmed their nominations. The Supreme Court eventually ruled (in *United States v. Lovett*, 1946) that by accusing the men of disloyalty and denying them their pay, Congress had punished them without a trial and thus had violated the constitutional prohibition against bills of attainder.

In 1959 Congress made it a crime for a member of the Communist party to serve as an officer or an employee of a labor union. Chief Justice Warren, speaking for a five-man majority pointed out that Congress possesses power under the commerce clause to enact legislation designed to protect that commerce from political strikes. However, the 1959 enactment did not set forth a general rule, but designated by name members of a particular political group and imposed a punishment on them. This was a bill of attainder. The Chief Justice wrote, "Congress possesses full legislative authority, but the task of adjudication must be left to other tribunals."[59]

Rights of persons accused of crime

That the innocent will go free and that the guilty will be punished; that rich and poor, educated and ignorant will secure justice under law—these are among the most ancient and honorable goals of free nations. Some feel that the rights of persons accused of crime are less important than other civil liberties, but, as Justice Frankfurter observed, "The history of liberty has largely been the history of observance of procedural safeguards." These safeguards, moreover, have frequently "been forged in controversies involving not very nice people." Their purpose is not "to convenience the guilty but to protect the innocent."

[59]*United States v. Archie Brown* (1965).

The rights of persons accused of crime by the national government can be found in the Fourth, Fifth, Sixth, and Eighth Amendments. In order to gain some idea of the application of these constitutional safeguards, we shall follow the fortunes and misfortunes of John T. Crook (a fictitious name).

Crook sent circulars through the mails soliciting purchases of stock in a nonexistent gold mine, an action contrary to at least three federal laws. When postal officers uncovered these activities, they went to the district court and secured from a United States magistrate—a court-appointed official who assists the judges—warrants for the arrest of Crook and to search his home for copies of the circulars. They found Crook at home, read the *Miranda* warning to him, emphasizing especially his right to remain silent and to have the assistance of counsel, showed him the warrants, arrested him for using the mails to defraud, and found and seized some of the circulars mentioned in the search warrant.

Crook was promptly brought before a federal district judge who again emphasized to Crook that he had the constitutional *right to the assistance of counsel.* What was once merely a right to be represented by an attorney during a trial if a defendant wanted and could afford such help, is now a positive obligation in federal trials (*Johnson v. Zerbst*, 1938) and since 1963 also in state trials (*Gideon v. Wainwright*, 1963), to see to it that all persons subject to any kind of custodial interrogation are represented by a lawyer. Unless the record clearly shows that the accused was fully aware of what he or she was doing and waived the right to counsel, absence of such counsel will render criminal proceedings unconstitutional. The right extends to all trials, including juvenile delinquency proceedings,[60] for all offenses for which an accused may be deprived of his liberty, whether considered felonies or misdemeanors (*Argesinger v. Hamilton*, 1972), whether or not a jury trial is required. Only trials in which fines are the sole penalty are exempt from the assistance of counsel requirement. And this assistance is required at every stage of a criminal proceeding where substantial rights may be affected—preliminary hearings, bail hearings, trial, sentencing, and appeal. (Assistance of counsel is not automatically required at parole and probation revocation hearings, but under certain circumstances in order for there to be due process such assistance may be necessary.)[61] In this particular proceeding, after the judge outlined to Crook his right to the assistance of counsel, upon learning of his indigency, the judge appointed an attorney to represent him. (See p. 251 for procedures used in federal courts to pay for attorneys for the indigent.)

Bail was set at $1,500 and Crook was held over until the convening of the next federal grand jury. After posting bond, Crook was permitted his freedom as long as he remained within the limits of the judicial district.

[60]*In re Gault* (1967).

[61]*Gagnon v. Scarpelli* (1973).

The Eighth Amendment forbids imposition of *excessive bail*, for it is a basic principle of American justice that no person is guilty until pronounced so after a fair trial. To set bail higher than necessary to assure the presence of a defendant at his trial is "excessive." The Bail Reform Act of 1966 allows federal judges to release persons without bail if, after taking into account such factors as past record or family and community ties, bail seems unnecessary. For capital crimes, judges may refuse to release a person on bail, for no amount of money may be sufficient to ensure that one who stands in jeopardy of losing his life will be around for his trial. And in 1970 Congress authorized judges in the District of Columbia to detain prior to trial persons accused of dangerous crimes or crimes of violence if after a hearing the judge concludes that release could endanger the safety of the community. Although this authorization of preventive detention has rarely been used, it raises serious constitutional questions.

When the next grand jury was convened, the United States district attorney brought before the twenty-three jurors evidence to indicate that Crook had committed a federal crime. Grand jurors are concerned not with a person's guilt or innocence, but merely with whether there is enough evidence to warrant bringing him to trial. No person has a right to appear before a grand jury, but may be invited or ordered to do so. If a majority of the grand jurors agree that a trial is justified, they return what is known as a *true bill*, or indictment. Except in cases arising in the military forces involving service-connected crimes,[62] the national government cannot force any person to stand trial for any serious crime except on *grand jury indictment*. In our particular case, the grand jury was in agreement with the United States district attorney and returned a true bill against Crook.

After a copy of the indictment was served on Crook, he was again ordered to appear before a federal district judge. The Constitution guarantees the accused *the right to be informed of the nature and cause of the accusation* so that he can prepare his defense; consequently, the federal prosecutor had seen to it that the indictment clearly stated the nature of the offense and that copies had been properly served on Crook and his lawyer.

Actually, Crook's attorney, prior to his hearing, had discussed with the United States Attorney's Office the possibility of Crook pleading guilty to a lesser offense. This kind of "plea bargaining"—so familiar since Watergate—is often used. Prosecutors, faced with more charges than they can handle, often prefer to accept a guilty plea to a reduced charge rather than to prosecute for the more serious offense. And defendants are often willing to "cop a plea" to a lesser offense to avoid the risk of more serious punishment.

But when a defendant pleads guilty to a lesser offense, he waives his constitutional rights and under most circumstances is forever precluded

[62]*O'Callahan v. Parker* (1969); *Relford v. Commandant* (1971).

from raising objections to his conviction—for example, that the grand jury that indicted him had been improperly empaneled.[63] This is why a judge before accepting a guilty plea ordinarily will interrogate the defendant to insure that his attorney has explained the alternatives to him and that he knows what he is doing when he enters a plea of guilty. It never came to this in Crook's case, however, since after discussing the matter with his attorney, he elected to stand trial on the charge and entered a plea of not guilty.

After indictment, Crook's bail was raised to $3,000. Now the federal government was obliged to give him *a speedy and a public trial*, the word speedy, however, should not be taken too literally. Crook had to be given time to prepare his defense. And defendants often ask for delays since these work to their advantage. The crowded nature of many court dockets often leads to delay, although federal courts have recently adopted a rule of procedure that requires them to state in advance the time limits in which the case must be brought to a hearing. For if the government denies the accused a speedy trial in a constitutional sense, the remedy is drastic. It is not merely that the conviction may be reversed, but the case must be dismissed outright.[64]

Crook's lawyer pointed out that under the Sixth Amendment, he had a right to trial before an impartial jury selected from the state and district where the alleged crime was committed, for he was being tried for a serious crime—that is, one defined by the court as being punishable by more than six months in prison or a $500 fine.[65] Federal law provides for juries of twelve in federal courts; but if Congress wished, it could provide for juries of other sizes, the Supreme Court recently held (*Williams v. Florida*, 1970). The Sixth Amendment apparently still requires federal juries to convict by a unanimous vote, but this holding is tenuous; the Supreme Court gave its approval to nonunanimous verdicts in state courts, with four justices explictly stating that in their view such verdicts do not violate the Sixth Amendment (*Apodaca v. Oregon*, 1972).

An impartial jury, and one that meets the requirements of due process and equal protection, consists of persons who represent an unbiased cross-section of the community. Although blacks, for example, are not entitled to a jury on which there are blacks, they are entitled to a jury from which persons have not been excluded because of their race.[66] So, by the way, are whites—that is, a white or a black is deprived of his or her constitutional rights if tried by a jury from which whites or blacks have been excluded because of race.[67] Such actions would also

[63] *Tollet v. Henderson* (1973); but see *Blackledge v. Perry* (1974).

[64] *Strunk v. United States* (1973).

[65] *Dyke v. Taylor Implement Manufacturing Co.* (1968).

[66] *Coleman v. Alabama* (1967).

[67] *Peters v. Kiff* (1972).

A General View of The Criminal Justice System

This chart seeks to present a simple yet comprehensive view of the movement of cases through the criminal justice system. Procedures in individual jurisdictions may vary from the pattern shown here. The differing weights of line indicate the relative volumes of cases disposed of at various points in the system, but this is only suggestive since no nationwide data of this sort exist.

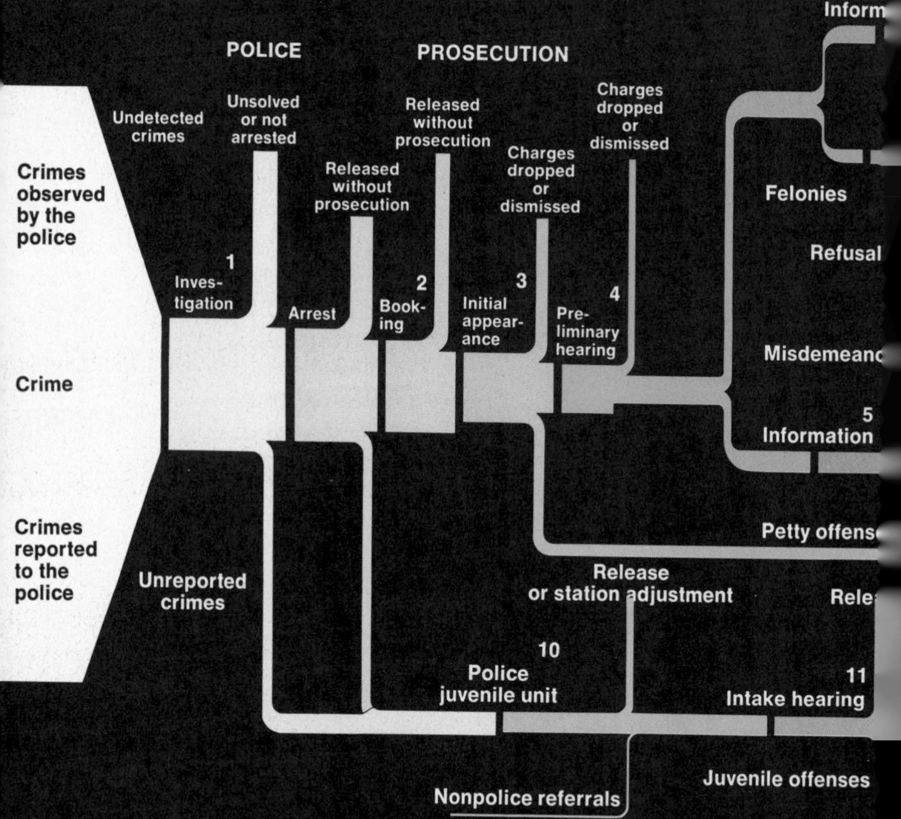

1 May continue until trial.
2 Administrative record of arrest. First step at which temporary release on bail may be available.
3 Before magistrate, commissioner, or justice of peace. Formal notice of charge, advice of rights. Bail set. Summary trials for petty offenses usually conducted here without further processing.
4 Preliminary testing of evidence against defendant. Charge may be reduced. No separate preliminary hearing for misdemeanors in some systems.
5 Charge filed by prosec information submitted Alternative to grand ju used in felonies, almos misdemeanors.
6 Reviews whether gove sufficient to justify tria grand jury system; oth

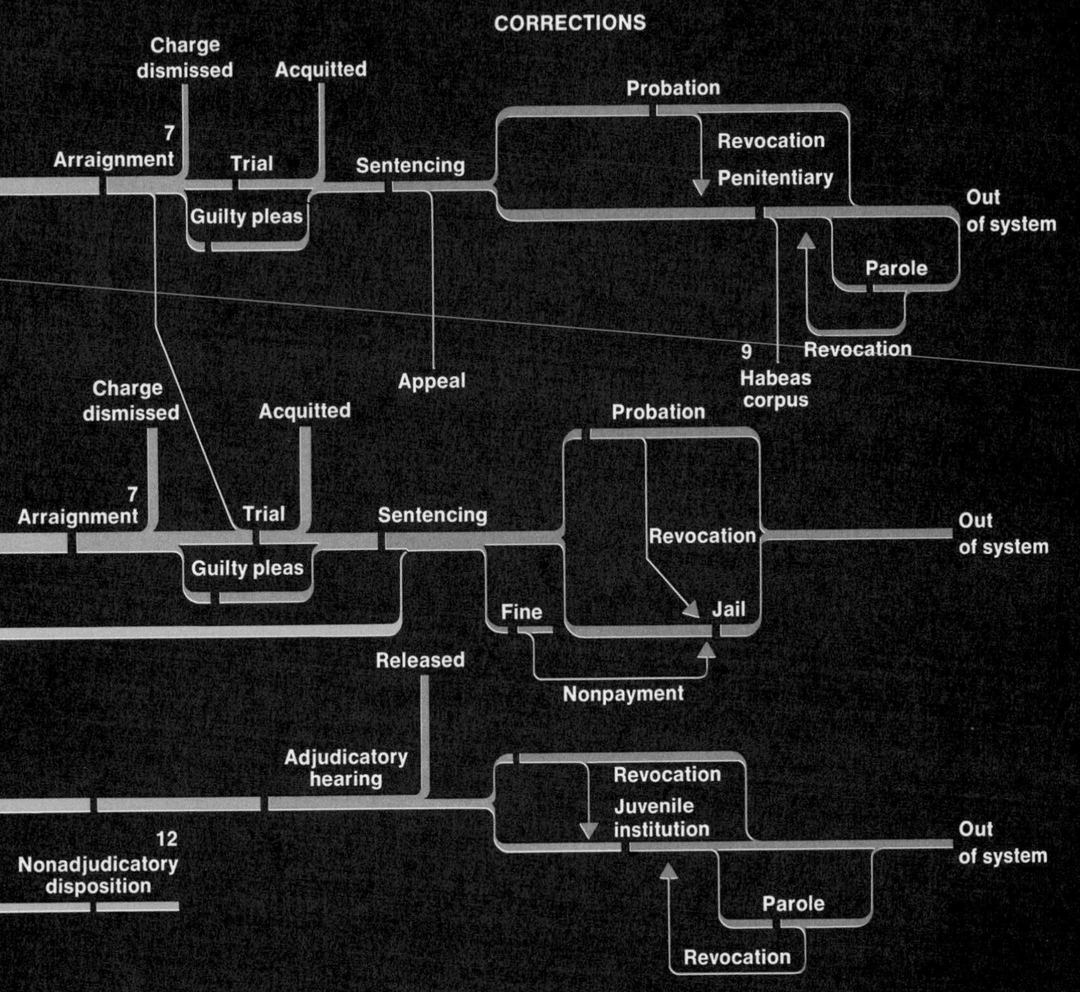

7 Appearance for plea; defendant elects trial by judge or jury (if available); counsel for indigent usually appointed here in felonies. Often not at all in other cases.

8 Charge may be reduced at any time prior to trial in return for plea of guilty or for other reasons.

9 Challenge on constitutional grounds to legality of detention. May be sought at any point in process.

10 Police often hold informal hearings, dismiss or adjust many cases without further processing.

11 Probation officer decides desirability of further court action.

12 Welfare agency, social services, counselling, medical care, etc., for cases where adjudicatory handling not neded.

violate the civil rights of the persons denied the opportunity to serve on juries.[68] And with respect to those categories to which the Constitution gives especial protection—race, religion, national origin, alienage, and probably sex—a defendant's attorney has a right to question potential jurors about their attitudes toward persons of the defendant's particular category. The Supreme Court, however, refused to make it a matter of constitutional right for bearded defendants to interrogate jurors about their possible prejudice against persons with beards; the Court left this to the discretion of the trial judge.[69]

In preparation of his defense, Crook told his lawyer that he had dinner with George Witness on the night on which he was charged with sending the damaging circulars. The attorney took advantage of Crook's constitutional right to obtain *witnesses in his favor* and had the judge subpoena Witness to appear at the trial and testify. Witness could have refused to testify on the grounds that his testimony would tend to incriminate him, but he agreed to do so. Crook himself, however, chose to use his constitutional right not to be a witness against himself and refused to take the witness stand. He knew that if he did so, the prosecution would have a right to cross-examination, and he was fearful of what might be uncovered. The federal judge conducting the trial cautioned the jury against drawing any conclusions from Crook's reluctance to testify—although nothing could prevent the jurors from being affected. All prosecution witnesses appeared in court and were available to defense cross-examination, because the Constitution insists that the accused has the *right to be confronted with the witnesses against him.*

At the conclusion of the trial, the jury rendered a verdict of guilty. The judge then raised Crook's bail to $5,000 and announced that he would hand down a sentence on the following Monday. The Eighth Amendment forbids the *levying of excessive fines* and the inflicting of *cruel and unusual punishments.* When the judge, in accord with the law, gave Crook the maximum punishment of $5,000 and five years in the penitentiary, the punishment could not be considered cruel and unusual.

The ban against cruel and unusual punishment forbids, for example, making drug addiction a crime because this would inflict punishment simply for being ill.[70] On the same grounds the mere act of being a chronic alcholic cannot be made a crime, but a closely divided Court held that such a person could be punished for appearing drunk in a public place.[71]

What of capital punishment? There are many who believe that for a nation that considers itself civilized, any form of capital punishment should be declared cruel and unusual. Eleven states have banned capital punishment. Since June 1967, no one has been executed by any state or

[68]*Carter v. Jury Commissioners* (1970).

[69]*Ham v. South Carolina* (1973).

[70]*Robinson v. California* (1962).

[71]*Powell v. Texas* (1968).

by the national government. And in *Furman v. Georgia* (1972), the Supreme Court by a five-to-four vote held that as the legal system presently operates, the imposition of capital punishment is cruel and unusual.

Only Justices Brennan and Marshall stated that they consider capital punishment to be per se unconstitutional. Justice Douglas voted against it because as it is presently imposed, it falls more heavily on the poor and the despised. Justices White and Stewart limited their holding to present conditions under which judges and juries have such wide discretion in determining whether or not the death sentence should be imposed. The four dissenting justices, expressing their own distaste for the death penalty, accused the majority of usurping the role of the legislature, ignoring 191 years of historical precedent, and imposing their own values on the country. As a result of the *Furman* decision, in many states death penalty statutes have been revised to restrict the discretion of judges and juries as to when the penalty shall be imposed. The issue will be back before the Supreme Court in the near future.

But back to Crook. The court of appeals rejected his contention that the judge had improperly instructed the jury, the Supreme Court refused to review the case, and Crook was sent to a federal prison.

The nationalization of the Bill of Rights

While still in the federal penitentiary, Crook was taken by federal authorities before the state courts to answer charges that he had also committed a state crime. Since Crook was entitled to a speedy trial on these state charges, the state could not wait until he had been permanently released by federal authorities before bringing him to justice.[72]

Crook, through his state-appointed attorney, protested that he had already been tried by the federal government for using the mails to defraud, and he pointed to the Fifth Amendment provision that no person shall be "subject for the same offense to be twice put in jeopardy of life or limb." This double jeopardy limitation, Crook's attorney pointed out, has been construed by the Supreme Court (*Benton v. Maryland* 1969) to be part of the Fourteenth Amendment and therefore a limit on the power of a state.

The judge answered, "The Supreme Court has said that double jeopardy prevents two criminal trials by the *same* government for the same offense."[73] (Trial by a state and one of its municipalities is trial by the same government.)[74] It does not prevent punishment by the state and the national governments for the same offense. He pointed to a 1959 Supreme Court decision (somewhat undermined by more recent deci-

[72]*Dickey v. Florida* (1970).

[73]*United States v. Lanza* (1922); *One Lot Emerald Cut Stones v. United States* (1972).

[74]*Waller v. Florida* (1970).

sions, but still not reversed) that sustained a state conviction of a man for robbing a bank after he had previously been acquitted of the same offense by a federal court.[75]

What constitutional rights can Crook claim in the state courts? In the first place, every state constitution contains a bill of rights listing practically the same guarantees against state abridgment that the Bill of Rights in the national Constitution contains against national abridgment. By and large, however, state judges have been less inclined than federal judges to construe constitutional guarantees of their own state constitutions liberally in favor of those accused of crime.

To what extent does the national Constitution protect courtroom procedures from state abridgment? The Bill of Rights does not apply to the states, but the Fourteenth Amendment does, and it contains two clauses of great importance—the due process and the equal-protection clauses. As we have noted the equal-protection clause forbids discriminatory conduct in courtroom procedures, and for some time a persistent minority of the Supreme Court justices has argued that the due process clause of the Fourteenth Amendment should be construed to impose on the states exactly the same limitations that the Bill of Rights imposes on the national government. The Supreme Court still has not gone so far as to make the due process clause of the Fourteenth Amendment a mirror image of the Bill of Rights and it still has not adopted the doctrine of "total incorporation," or as it is sometimes called, "absoption," but it has come very close to this position.

Until recently the official doctrine of the Court was that only those rights "implicit in the concept of ordered liberty" that are so important that neither "liberty nor justice would exist if they were sacrificed" are, so to speak, automatically included within the Fourteenth Amendment. Outside the scope of these rights, the test in each case was whether the procedures adopted by a state were fundamentally fair—not whether the procedures were those required of the national government by the Bill of Rights.

This formula, known as the *Palko* test or the doctrine of selective incorporation, was formulated by Justice Cardozo.[76] Using it, the Court distinguished between such rights as First Amendment freedoms, which are so fundamental that there can be no liberty or justice if they are lost, and indictment by grand jury or trial before a jury in civil cases. Replacement of these latter rights by other procedures would not necessarily be a denial of justice or liberty.

Beginning in the 1930s and accelerating after 1964, the Supreme Court has selectively incorporated provision after provision of the Bill of Rights into the requirements of the due process clause of the Fourteenth Amendment. Moreover, it has revised the *Palko* test. Instead of asking if a particular safeguard is necessary for a civilized society, the Court now

[75]*Bartkus v. Illinois* (1959).

[76]*Palko v. Connecticut* (1937).

asks if such a safeguard is fundamental to an Anglo-American regime of ordered liberty.

Today, the Fourteenth Amendment imposes on the states all the requirements of the Bill of Rights except those of the Second, Third, Seventh and Tenth Amendments. The Supreme Court, however, may refrain from accepting the doctrine of total incorporation in order to allow the states to use such procedures as indictment by information. Twenty-eight states, for example, allow the prosecuting attorney to dispense with grand jury indictments for all but the most serious crimes. The prosecutor simply files an information affidavit that he has evidence in his possession to justify a trial.

Dissenting justices and other critics argue that the "onward march of the . . . discredited incorporation doctrine" undermines our federal system. The Constitution, they contend, leaves each state free to adopt whatever procedures for administering justice that its own legislature and courts desire, provided these procedures result in fundamental fairness, and Supreme Court justices should refrain from subjecting "state legal processes to enveloping federal judicial authority."[77]

The Court majority and their defenders respond that the vague, subjective test of fundamental fairness requires the Supreme Court "to intervene in the state judicial process with considerable lack of predictability and with a consequent likelihood of considerable friction." The failure of state courts either to apply the provisions of their state constitutions or properly to construe Supreme Court rulings on due process led to such shocking examples of injustice that the Supreme Court had to set forth clear and imperative constitutional standards. With the elaboration for state courts of the same rules that have long been followed by national courts, the state judges will know in advance how to proceed. "And, to deny to the states the power to impair a fundamental constitutional right is not to increase federal power, but, rather, to limit the power of *both* federal and state governments in favor of safeguarding the fundamental rights and liberties of the individual."[78]

Now that for practically all purposes the Bill of Rights has been incorporated into the Fourteenth Amendment, future constitutional battles are likely to develop between those who argue, like the late Justice Black, that "the first section of the Fourteenth Amendment not only incorporates the specifics of the first eight amendments, but it is *confined to them*,"[79] and those who believe, like Justice Douglas, that in addition to incorporating all the specific provisions of the Bill of Rights, the due process clause protects other fundamental rights too – for example, the right to privacy. Justice Douglas sees the Supreme Court as the

[77]*Benton v. Maryland* (1969). See also Francis William O'Brien, "Juries and Incorporation in 1971," *Washington University Law Quarterly*, (Winter 1971), pp. 1–43.

[78]Justice Goldberg concurring in *Pointer v. Texas* (1965). Emphasis added.

[79]Henry J. Abraham, *Freedom and the Court: Civil Rights and Liberties in the United States* (Oxford University Press, 1967), p. 75.

champion of the poor and oppressed and quotes approvingly the views of the late Edmond Cahn: "Be not reasonable with inquisitions, anonymous informers, and secret files that mock American justice. . . . Exercise the full judicial power of the United States; nullify them, forbid them, and make us proud again." Justice Black, long a champion of total incorporation and vigorous enforcement of the Bill of Rights, would not allow members of the Court to impose on the country their own notions of fundamental rights except those specified in the Constitution. He quotes approvingly from Judge Learned Hand: "For myself it would be most irksome to be ruled by a bevy of Platonic Guardians, even if I knew how to choose them, which I assuredly do not."[80]

How just is our system of justice?

What are the major criticisms of the American system of justice? How have they been answered?

TOO MANY LOOPHOLES

It is argued that in our zeal to protect the innocent and place the burden of proof on the government, we have established so many elaborate procedures that justice is delayed, disrespect for the law is encouraged, and guilty men are allowed to go unpunished. Justice should be swift and sure without being arbitrary. But under our procedures a criminal may go unpunished because (1) the police decide not to arrest him, (2) the judge decides not to hold him, (3) the prosecutor decides not to prosecute him, (4) the grand jury decides not to indict him, (5) the jury decides not to convict him, (6) the judge decides not to sentence him, (7) an appeals court decides to reverse the conviction, (8) a federal judge decides to release him on a habeas corpus writ, (9) if he is retried and convicted, the executive decides to pardon, reprieve, or parole him. As a result, some complain, the public never knows whom to hold responsible when laws are not enforced. The police can blame the prosecutor,

[80]*Griswold v. Connecticut* (1965).

"How do I feel about being mugged? Well, naturally I didn't enjoy it and I certainly don't condone violence or threats of violence as a means toward social change. However, I can empathize with my assailant and realize that in his terms this is a valid response to the deteriorating socioeconomic situation in which we find ourselves."

Drawing by Lorenz; © 1972 The New Yorker Magazine, Inc.

the prosecutor can blame the police, and they can all blame the judges.

What one has termed "the hottest theme in criminal justice literature today," is what he describes as "the vertical fragmentation in policy-making (caused by the existence of parallel court systems) and the horizontal fragmentation in policy-making (caused by police-court-corrections relationships and what might be called the 'accused's shuttle system'."[81] Some argue that in our impossible pursuit of perfect justice, we are not achieving effective justice.[82] Many critics blame the Supreme Court for imposing its own inflexible notions of justice on the country and imposing so many disabilities on police and prosecutors that they are finding it increasingly difficult ever to bring any cases to closure.

Others take a different view. They doubt that the decisions of the Supreme Court have had that much impact on actual police and prosecutors that the Court can be blamed for the law's delays. And they point out that there is more to justice than simply securing convictions. All the steps in the administration of criminal laws have been developed out of centuries of trial and error and each of them has been constructed to provide protection against particular abuses. History warns against entrusting the instruments of criminal law enforcement to a single functionary. For this reason responsibility is vested in many officials.

TOO UNRELIABLE

Critics who complain that our system of justice is unreliable often point to trial by jury as the chief source of trouble. Trial by jury, they argue, leads to a theatrical combat between lawyers who base their appeals on the prejudice and sentiments of the jurors. "Mr. Prejudice and Miss Sympathy are the names of witnesses whose testimony is never recorded, but must nevertheless be reckoned with in trials by jury."[83] Too often, it is charged, verdicts are influenced by the jurors' dislike of an attorney's personality or a defendant's appearance. Too, untrained jurors are easily swayed by the prejudices and sentiments of the community. Juries lack the training to distinguish between fact and fiction. No other country relies so much on trial by jury as does the United States. And jury trials are time consuming and costly and unduly delay the administration of justice.

Defenders of the system reply that trial by jury provides an invaluable check by nonprofessionals over the actions of judges and prosecutors. As to the charge that juries are unreliable, there is no evidence to support it. On the contrary, decisions of juries do not systematically

[81]William C. Louthan, review of Macklin Fleming, *The Price of Perfect Justice*, in *Perspective* (May 1974), p. 84.

[82]Macklin Fleming, *The Price of Perfect Justice* (Basic Books, 1974).

[83]Jerome Frank, *Courts on Trial* (Princeton University Press, 1949), p. 122. See Harry Kalven, Jr., and Hans Zeisel's *The American Jury* (University of Chicago Press, 1971) for findings of the University of Chicago's massive study of the jury system.

differ with those of judges.[84] The jury system, moreover, helps to educate citizens and enables them to participate in the application of their own law. The jury trial, said Justice Murphy, has the beneficial effect of "leavening justice with the spirit of the times."

Another instrument that many critics believe contributes to the unreliability of our criminal justice system is the grand jury, provided for by one of the few provisions of the Bill of Rights that has not been incorporated into the Fourteenth Amendment. In theory the grand jury has two functions: to protect the innocent from having to stand trial by requiring the prosecutor to demonstrate behind closed doors that he has sufficient evidence to justify forcing a suspect to stand trial; and to provide an independent agency to investigate wrongdoing that is uncontrolled by those in power. Critics charge, however, that the grand jury has become a tool of the prosecutor. Said Justice Douglas, "It is, indeed, common knowledge that the grand jury, having been conceived as a bulwark between the citizen and the Government, is now a tool of the Executive."[85] During the early 1970s, critics from the left side of the political spectrum charged that grand juries had become instruments to intimidate radicals, blacks, and antiwar militants. By 1973 grand juries were being used to investigate the executive branch. And it was through the use of the grand jury that the special prosecutor was able to get before the courts his contention that the president had no constitutional right to withold information about wrongdoing. As the editors of the *Congressional Quarterly* have pointed out, "liberals can applaud grand juries for investigating Watergate and denounce them for intimidating militants. Conservatives might just as easily reprove them for the former and commend them for the latter. The important question about grand juries is whether they are an effective instrument for protecting the innocent and bringing the guilty to trial. . . . On these questions, the jury is still out.[86]

DISCRIMINATION AGAINST MINORITIES AND THE POOR

Perhaps on no problem has the Supreme Court worked harder during the last several decades than to give reality to the ideal of equal justice under the law. At the trial level, persons accused of crime who cannot afford an attorney must be furnished one at state expense. If a state requires transcripts for appeals, it must see that such transcripts are made available to those who cannot afford to purchase them.[87] If the state provides for appeals as a matter of right, it must provide indigents with legal assistance. That is as far, however, as a state's constitutional obligation to provide legal counsel goes. It has no constitutional duty to

[84]Kalven and Zeisel, *ibid.*, pp. 57 ff.

[85]*United States v. Mara*, dissenting, (1974).

[86]"The Supreme Court: Justice and the Law," *Congressional Quarterly* (1973), p. 93.

[87]*Griffin v. Illinois* (1956); *Douglas v. California* (1963).

continue to furnish legal counsel at state expense for indigents who wish to continue their legal appeals at the state or federal levels—for example, by asking for a review of the state decision by the Supreme Court of the United States.[88] Once an indigent person is sentenced, a state may not keep that person in jail beyond the term of the sentence because the person cannot afford to pay a fine, or imprison him or her for inability to do so.[89]

The Supreme Court has also started to move against fee systems that keep the poor from pursuing civil justice—for example, divorce proceedings. The Court, however, did not find it unconstitutional for a state to impose a small fee as a condition to petition a court for discharge from one's debts as a bankrupt.[90]

Congress, too, has acted. Each United States district court must now have a plan to provide counsel and investigative, expert, and other services necessary for an adequate defense for those unable to afford such help. Each district must provide for private attorneys (paid from the federal treasury) to serve indigents, but it may in addition establish a federal public defender system with a full-time, publicly paid staff or, if it prefers, create a community defender organization through the help of a federal grant to provide defense counsel.

Discrimination against minorities, especially blacks, in the administration of justice remains a major defect of our system. In some parts of the nation blacks may be subject to more severe punishment than whites for the same crimes, and whites who commit crimes against blacks are not as likely to be indicted by grand juries or convicted by jurors who share the defendants' attitudes. Still, Supreme Court decisions have gone a long way toward ensuring that juries are selected without respect to race.

The major area of difficulty arises outside the courtroom, for one of the most acute problems of our society is the tension between the police officer and the black community congregated in the ghettos of our large cities. The President's Commission on Law Enforcement and Administration of Justice and the President's National Advisory Commission on Civil Disorders have amply documented the observation, "Most Negro citizens do not believe that we have equal law enforcement in any city in this country. Whether the stated belief is well founded or not is at least partly beside the point. The existence of the belief is damaging enough."[91] Black Americans see the policeman as the enforcer of the white man's law; the documented studies of prejudice on the part of some white police officers and the examples of undignified, if not brutal, police treatment of blacks are numerous.

[88]*Ross and North Carolina v. Moffit* (1974).

[89]*Williams v. Illinois* (1970); *Tate v. Short* (1971).

[90]*Boddie v. Connecticut* (1971); *United States v. Kras* (1973).

[91]George Edwards, *The Police on the Urban Frontier* (Institute of Human Relations Press, The American Jewish Committee, 1968), p. 28. See also Arthur Niederhoffer, *Behind the Shield: The Police in Urban Society* (Doubleday, 1967).

As a result of mutual hostility between police and the communities they are to protect, there has developed a wall of isolation that blocks understanding. Police officers tend to work together and to play together, not only in isolation from the black community but from the entire community. Too often police have been recruited from sections of the city that exhibit the strongest antiblack attitudes, are trained by law officers who reinforce such attitudes, and are first assigned to areas of high crime rate, where blacks are the prime suspects.

Yet it would be as faulty of us to overgeneralize about the behavior of the police officer as it is of some police to overgeneralize about those who live within slum areas. The issue is the conditions that produce both kinds of behavior; there is too much at stake to content oneself with charges of police brutality. For "the policeman," wrote former Attorney General Ramsey Clark, "is the most important American. . . . He works in a highly flammable environment. A spark can cause an explosion. He must maintain order without provocation which will cause combustion."[92] The police officer has a vital role in preserving (or restricting) civil liberties. He determines who shall be arrested, he gives daily reality to the protections of our Constitution, and, as recent events in our large cities make clear, he has much to do with preventing or causing riots. Yet this person on whom we depend for so much, the only one in our civil society whom we arm with deadly weapons, is grossly underpaid. In performing his tasks, he often discovers that the public is indifferent, even hostile. Little wonder that he is sometimes impatient with reformers and academics who talk about the complexities of the cycle of poverty or the refinements of the law governing search and seizure, for it is the police officer and not the scholar who at 2 A.M. must go into an area of high crime rate in the middle of a hostile population to search a dark alley in response to a call about a prowler.

Until recently the role of the police officer was generally ignored. But finally, in the late 1960s, for a variety of reasons—fear of riots, concern about organized crime, desire to provide better and more understanding protection for the rights of persons black and white—there was initiated a sustained drive to improve the quality of police services and to understand better the problems the police face. In the larger cities steps have been taken to professionalize the police, improve their training, provide them with a better opportunity to understand the complexities of social problems, and to establish community relations programs in order to open communications between the police and the communities they serve. This is a beginning, but much remains to be done.

Courts and police are inevitably composed of people who reflect the prejudices and values of the society of which they are a part. When poverty and prejudice exist in the community, they will affect all institutions of the community. And yet there are few agencies that do as much as the courts to isolate prejudice and to compensate for poverty. As the

[92]Foreword to Edwards, *ibid.*, p. viii.

Commission on Civil Rights states, "There is much to be proud of in the American system of criminal justice. For it is administered largely without regard to the race, creed, or color of the persons involved. . . ."[93]

The Supreme Court and civil liberties

In our discussion of civil liberties and civil rights, it has become clear that the judges, especially those on the Supreme Court, play a significant role in enforcing constitutional guarantees. In fact, this combination of judicial enforcement and written guarantees of enumerated liberties is one of the basic features of the American system of government. As Justice Jackson wrote: "The very purpose of a Bill of Rights was to withdraw certain subjects from the vicissitudes of political controversy, to place them beyond the reach of majorities and officials and to establish them as legal principles to be applied by the courts. One's right to life, liberty, and property, to free speech, a free press, freedom of worship and assembly, and other fundamental rights may not be submitted to vote: they depend on the outcome of no elections." Or as Samuel Krislov has pointed out: "One is reminded of Godfrey Cambridge's nightmare: A telephone rings and a voice announces: 'We've had a referendum on slavery in California and you lost. Report to the auction block in four hours.' "[94]

The Minutemen, a militant anti-Communist organization, shown here in "training maneuvers" in Illinois.

This emphasis on constitutional limitations and judicial enforcement is an example of the "auxiliary precautions" that James Madison felt were necessary to prevent arbitrary governmental action. Other free nations rely more on elections and political checks to protect their rights, but in the United States we look to judges to hear appeals from people who feel that their freedoms are being jeopardized. All judges, not only those on the Supreme Court, have taken an oath to measure the actions of public officials against the appropriate constitutional, as well as legislative, provisions.

British judges have authority to restrain executive officials from depriving people of their legal rights, but they do not have the power to declare legislative acts unconstitutional. Moreover, Englishmen place primary reliance on an alert and aroused public opinion, operating through elected officials, to safeguard their liberty. Justice Jackson once commented: "I have been repeatedly impressed with the speed and certainty with which the slightest invasion of British individual freedom or minority rights by officials of the government is picked up in Parliament, not merely by the opposition but by the party in power, and made the subject of persistent questioning, criticism, and sometimes

[93]United States Commission on Civil Rights, *Report on Justice* (U.S. Government Printing Office, 1961), pp. 26 ff.

[94]*The Supreme Court and Political Freedom* (Free Press, 1968), p. 35.

rebuke. There is no waiting on the theory that the judges will take care of it. . . . In Great Britain, to observe civil liberties is good politics and to transgress the rights of the individual or minority is bad politics. In the United States, I cannot say this is so."[95]

In the United States, our emphasis on judicial protection of civil liberties focuses attention on the Supreme Court. But only a small number of controversies are carried to the Court, and a Supreme Court decision is not the end of the policy-making process; compliance with its rulings "does not necessarily, universally, or automatically follow their enunciation."[96] Only now are political scientists beginning to analyze the complex process by which the policies announced by the Supreme Court justices are or are not translated into changes in the political system.[97] It is the judges of lower courts, the policemen, the superintendents of schools, and the local prosecutors who translate the doctrines enunciated by the Court and who do or do not apply them.

And the Supreme Court is of little consequence unless its decisions reflect a national consensus. The judges by themselves cannot guarantee anything. Neither can the First Amendment. As Justice Jackson once asked: "Must we first maintain a system of free political government to assure a free judiciary, or can we rely on an aggressive, activist judiciary to guarantee free government? . . . [It] is my belief that the attitude of a society and of its organized political forces, rather than its legal machinery, is the controlling force in the character of free institutions. . . . [Any] court which undertakes by its legal processes to enforce civil liberties needs the support of an enlightened and vigorous public opinion. . . ."[98] In short, only so long as we desire liberty for ourselves and are willing to restrict our own actions in order to preserve the liberty of others can freedom be maintained.

[95]Robert H. Jackson, *The Supreme Court in the American System of Government* (Harvard University Press, 1955), pp. 81–82; Jonathan D. Casper, *The Politics of Civil Liberties* (Harper & Row, 1973).

[96]See Richard M. Johnson, *The Dynamics of Compliance: Supreme Court Decision-Making from a New Perspective* (Northwestern University Press, 1967), p. 3; "Interrogations in New Haven: The Impact of *Miranda*," *Yale Law Journal* (July 1967), pp. 1519–1648; Stephen L. Wasby, *The Impact of the United States Supreme Court: Some Perspectives* (Dorsey Press, 1970), Part II.

[97]Krislov, *The Supreme Court and Political Freedom*, pp. 166–220.

[98]Jackson, *The Supreme Court*, p. 82.

Part Four The people in politics

A PROBLEM GUIDE

A central problem in realizing government by the people in a mass society is popular representation. Part Four raises the crucial questions: Who really governs in democratic society? Do all people take part? Do small elite groups have more political influence than others? Through what instruments do people express themselves politically—interest groups, mass media, political parties, demonstrations, violence? How are the people organized to take part in government by the people? And how do these different types of political organizations and forms of representation square with the ideals of democratic government?

The basic inquiry in Chapter 9 concerns the formation and expression of political attitudes. What is the nature and role of public opinion in a free society? Who are the shapers of opinion—TV news commentators, newspaper editors and columnists, politicians? How much influence do such persons have over our political behavior? Do they really represent popular political opinion? Do elites control public opinion?

Chapter 10 develops the problem of popular representation in its principal forms—voting and interest-group activity. One key issue is the extent of representation. Some Americans do not vote because they are barred from the polls; millions do not vote because going to the polls does not seem worth the effort. How well do candidates understand the needs and attitudes of the persons they seek to represent? How much equality of political influence do we have in our society? Do elites have undue influence?

Chapter 11, concerning political parties, deals with this same problem of fair representation but in connection with another part of our political system. Under a two-party system, in theory at least, the party that wins most of the votes then proceeds to represent the interests of that popular majority in government. How effectively does the winning party speak for the voters that elected it? That raises another question: can the parties be strengthened so that they may represent their supporters more effectively? And what about the minority party—can it do the job of opposing the majority as well as it should?

A final problem of Part Four is the fairness and efficiency of the electoral system. We might think that electoral machinery could be neutral, but in point of fact it is not. Some election arrangements make it difficult for people to vote. Others—for example, the electoral college—give some voters more weight than others in the election of office seekers. How fair is our system of nominating political candidates—especially the president? Chapter 12 raises such problems, which all relate to the basic question in Part Four—the question of equality of political influence for the sake of fair representation in government.

Chapter 9 Public opinion and popular government

Government by the people is supposed to be government in accordance with the will of the people. But *is* there a popular will? Or are there many wills—of many people, of many *groups* of people, of especially powerful interests or elites? What does government do when people disagree, as they usually do? Should government itself try to influence public opinion? To what degree?

These questions sound theoretical, but consider them from the standpoint of a senator in Washington. He wants to do what his constituents want him to do, if only so he can stay in office. But he is not sure what they want him to do. He cannot really tell from his mail, because he suspects that the letter-writers generally reflect extreme opinion rather than the majority viewpoint. He knows that public opinion polls have their limitations. He is not sure just what issues he was elected on, if any. He listens for the voice of the people—but the people speak with many voices. No wonder he straddles the fence; from his standpoint his *constituents* are straddling the fence.

To examine public opinion in relation to government by the people, we need to understand not only the substance, but also the making of public opinion. How are people's attitudes shaped? What is the influence of the mass media? How is political opinion measured? We must ultimately be concerned with the fact that public opinion is a dynamic force that can change rapidly and powerfully. Thus American opinion in the 1950s was marked by agreement and consensus; President Eisenhower seemed to be a fitting spokesman for this feeling. Popular attitudes changed during the Kennedy and Johnson Administrations, with their emphasis on innovation and reform. There followed a period of deepening division and conflict over Vietnam and then of corroding cynicism during the Watergate scandals. In the mid-seventies we may be entering a new period in which the relations of government and public opinion may take on new forms and new urgencies. We will return to this question in this and subsequent chapters, and especially in Chapter 19.

The warp and woof of opinion

There is no one "public opinion." This might seem rather obvious, but how often have you heard a politician claim that "the public" wants such and such, or a columnist contend that "the people" reacted in a certain way?

A group of students invites a notorious criminal to speak on "crime and punishment." Think of this incident in terms of the "public opinion" it creates. The public is actually made up of a number of publics—the rest of the student body (itself divided into subpublics), the administration, the faculty, the local townspeople, parents, the taxpayers. And all react in different ways. Some don't react at all; others shake their heads and promptly forget about it; others write to the governor or their state legislator. Many approve the invitation but for conflicting reasons.

Translate the student episode into a national issue. When the president makes a speech about labor legislation, his words fall differently on the ears of union members, businessmen, union leaders, farmers, Democrats, Republicans, and so on. When a secretary of state proposes two billion dollars of United States aid to Vietnam, his words may be viewed with alarm by the same person who is calling for two billion dollars of aid to Israel—and vice versa. When a senator calls for the end of government subsidies, many businessmen applaud because they want lower taxes, but businessmen receiving subsidies—ship operators, for example—are critical. Most likely they cry out that "the American public" wants a strong merchant marine.

Instead of one public opinion, we must think in terms of the diversity of opinion within a particular population. We must ask: What portion of the people is on one side of an issue, what portion on the other? What portion feels strongly, what does not? How, in short, is opinion *struc-*

tured?[1] Then we can move on to the *qualities* of structured opinion, as follows:

1. *Saliency.* Different types of issues and problems are more or less salient for different types of people. By "salient" we mean that people feel involved in these issues, connected with them, relevant to them. For many people politics itself is not salient—it is not "at the focus of attention, crowding out other items, a pivot for organizing one's thoughts and acts."[2] Most people are more concerned about personal matters: their health, children, income, job. For other persons, political salience is extremely high; political issues dominate their lives.

Salience may change over time. Issues relating to their economic security and social welfare were highly salient to most people during the 1930s. Over the past decade, questions of race relations and public order, along with the involvement of the United States in far-off wars, have become salient to large portions of the public. Such changes have a vast impact on American political life.

2. *Stability.* Some kinds of political opinions are fairly stable. People's attitudes toward certain matters may change slowly, if at all, even though the world may be changing around them. This is especially true of loyalty toward one's own group and hostility toward competing groups. Thus, for many people political party preferences vary little over the years, as Table 9–1 suggests. In general, people remain more loyal to their groups, including their political parties, than to issues or policies that they cannot relate to those groups.

To what extent does one set of strong political opinions—support for the Democratic Party, for example, or a particular concern for social wel-

[1]For a significant exploration of the distribution and structure of recent political attitudes in relation to parties and elections, see Richard E. Dawson, *Public Opinion and Contemporary Disarray* (Harper & Row, 1973).

[2]Robert E. Lane and David O. Sears, *Public Opinion* (Prentice-Hall, 1964), p. 15.

9–1
Party self-identification, 1952–1974

Party preference	1952	1956	1960	1964	1966	1968	1970	1972	1974
Strong Democrat	22%	21%	21%	26%	18%	20%	20%	15%	18%
Weak Democrat	25	23	25	25	28	25	24	25	21
Independent Democrat	10	6	8	9	9	10	10	11	13
Independent	5	9	8	8	12	11	13	13	16
Independent Republican	7	8	7	6	7	9	8	11	8
Weak Republican	14	14	13	13	15	14	15	13	14
Strong Republican	13	15	14	11	10	10	9	10	8
Apolitical	4	4	4	2	1	1	1	2	2
	100%	100%	100%	100%	100%	100%	100%	100%	100%

SOURCE: Center for Political Studies, University of Michigan.

fare—help stabilize other political attitudes? Evidence on this question seems mixed. Certainly strong partisanship colors our response to what political leaders do; strong partisans are even likely to feel that their political leaders view issues the same way they do, when the leaders in fact do not. But consistency among various sets of related issues often seems low, especially on the part of the mass of people but just as often on the part of their leaders as well.[3]

3. *Fluidity.* Certain kinds of political attitudes can change dramatically, almost overnight. Isolationist feeling in 1941, for example, practically disappeared following the attack on Pearl Harbor; recently it has intensified again. Changes occur less in response to the exhortations or even the acts of political leaders than to *nonpolitical* events—a depression, frustrations in Vietnam, the movement of people from country to city. The intensity and durability of an opinion turn largely on its *saliency.*

Riots, a frequent occurrence in the 1960s, have all but disappeared in the 1970s.

4. *Intensity.* People vary greatly in the fervency of their beliefs. Some are mildly in favor, for example, of gun-control legislation; others are mildly opposed; still others are fanatically for or against. Some people may have no interest in the matter at all. Such variations in intensity have important political results. The attitudes of the passive can probably be easily changed. And those with strong feelings may try to organize in groups, to campaign, to win votes.

5. *Latency.* Public opinion may merely exist as a potential. Even though public attitudes on a particular issue have not crystallized, they are important, for they can be evoked and converted into action. Latent public opinion may have little direct impact on political decisions, but it has long-run political consequences; it sets rough boundaries within which the attentive publics and political leaders must operate. When leaders conclude that a public policy would give their opponents an opportunity to activate latent opinion, the issue is seldom debated. Thus for many years leaders assumed, rightly or wrongly, that the issue of United States recognition of the People's Republic of China would provoke such hostile reactions from the public that it was too hot to handle.

But latent opinion is an opportunity for political leaders as well as a danger. Especially in time of crisis, presidents or other leaders "may capture the attention of the ordinarily inattentive public, provide cues of direction and clarification, and amass . . . support" for their policies.[4] Or, as Lasswell has summed it up, "Crisis concentrates attention; noncrisis disperses it."

6. *Distribution.* The extent to which opinions on certain issues are widely and evenly distributed through many different sectors of the public has major political implications for party rivalry, electoral com-

[3]Norman R. Luttbeg, "The Structure of Beliefs Among Leaders and the Public," *Public Opinion Quarterly* (Fall, 1968), pp. 308–400.

[4]V. O. Key, Jr., *Public Opinion and American Democracy* (Knopf, 1961), p. 285, which is also the source of the Lasswell quotation.

petition and outcomes, and political polarization between parties and candidates. Opinions may be structured within the public by such social factors as geography, race, class, occupation, age. Do people in different social groupings tend to have the same or different opinions on different issues? How important are factors such as race, class, age, and the like in ordering political conflict and consensus? How does the distribution of opinions change over time or from issue area to issue area?[5]

The shaping of early political attitudes

By the age of about ten, American children typically are showing political interest and indicating political preferences. "By the early teens political interest is quite high, and by the late teens it is the equivalent of adult interest . . . . Thus the learning of opinions and beliefs begins when people are very young—religious affiliation quite early, political beliefs a little later—and what is learned hardens into the opinions and beliefs of adults."[6] What most influences the early forming of attitudes? In the United States, the family and the school.

THE INFLUENCE OF THE FAMILY

Obviously the family has a pervasive impact on the shaping of early political opinions. "Foremost among agencies of socialization into politics is the family," wrote Herbert Hyman,[7] and this has been confirmed by later investigations. We begin to form our picture of the world listening to our parents talk at breakfast or to the tales our older brothers and sisters bring home from school. What we learn in the family at the start are not so much specific political opinions, but the basic attitudes that will shape our future opinions—attitudes toward our neighbors, toward other classes or types of people, toward society in general. Some of us may rebel against the ways of the close little group in which we live, but most of us conform. The family is a sort of link between the past and the present. It translates the world to us, but it does so on its own terms.

A study of twelfth-graders, for example, indicated a high correlation between parents and children in the political party they support.

[5]For recent changes in opinion distribution and implications see Dawson, *Public Opinion and Contemporary Disarray;* also Robert S. Erikson and Norman R. Luttbeg, *American Public Opinion: Its Origins, Content, and Impact* (John Wiley, 1973), esp. pp. 40–57.

[6]Bernard Berelson and Gary A. Steiner, *Human Behavior,* Shorter Edition (Harcourt Brace Jovanovich, 1967), p. 105. See generally Fred Greenstein, *Children and Politics* (Yale University Press, 1965) and David Easton and Jack Dennis, *Children in the Political System* (McGraw-Hill, 1969).

[7]*Political Socialization* (Free Press, 1959), p. 69. For a different view see R. W. Connell, "Political Socialization in the American Family: The Evidence ReExamined," *Public Opinion Quarterly* (Fall 1972), pp. 323–33.

Lyndon Johnson takes the oath of office as vice-president shortly before John Kennedy is sworn in. (1) Jacqueline Kennedy; (2) Adlai Stevenson; (3) Dwight D. Eisenhower; (4) Earl Warren; (5) Dean Rusk; (6) John F. Kennedy; (7) Sam Rayburn; (8) Frank Dryden; (9) Lyndon B. Johnson; (10) Richard M. Nixon.

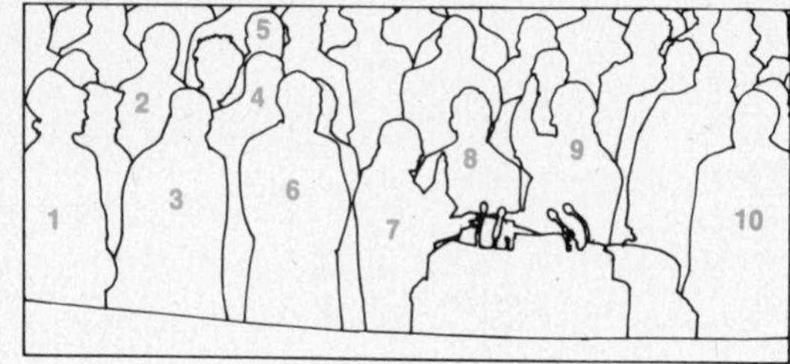

Throughout life this relatively high degree of correspondence continues. Investigators expected that the inheritance of party feeling would be much less frequent than, say, inheritance of church preference, because religion is typically a more highly organized and intense family activity than party participation. But they discovered that one was about as frequent as the other.[8] This kind of finding raises an interesting question: Is it the *direct* influence of parents on their children's political attitudes that creates the congruence? Or is it the fact that most children grow up in the same social situation that their parents do, and that parents and children are equally influenced by their environment?

Another question is the relative influence of the mother and of the father over their childrens' political opinions. It used to be assumed that the father had the dominant role. But a recent investigation suggests that the role of the mother may have been underestimated—perhaps because male dominance in political matters has simply been assumed. The influence of mothers on party identification, for example, at least rivals that of fathers. What happens when father and mother disagree

[8]M. Kent Jennings and Richard G. Niemi, "The Transmission of Political Values from Parent to Child," *American Political Science Review* (March 1968), p. 179, See also J. Leiper Freeman, "Parents, It's Not *All* Your Fault, But . . . ," *Journal of Politics* (August 1969), pp. 812–17.

politically? The child is likely to favor the party of the parent with whom he has had closer ties.[9]

POLITICAL IMPACT OF THE SCHOOLS

Schools are also potent opinion-shapers—one study concluded that they were the most important of all.[10] At an early age schoolchildren begin to pick up specific political values and to acquire basic attitudes toward our system of government. Even very small schoolchildren know the name of the president and his party affiliation and have strong attitudes toward him, and children as young as nine or ten begin to have a fairly precise knowledge of what a president stands for, though this will vary with the personality of the president. For example, one researcher found that "the Kennedy image was rich, specific, and considerably more politicized than we had anticipated. He was particularly well remembered for his efforts on behalf of peace and civil rights."[11]

Do school influences tend to give young people a greater faith in existing political institutions? Probably yes. "The thrust of school experience is undoubtedly on the side of developing trust in the political system in general," according to one study. "Civic training in schools abounds in rituals of system support in the formal curriculum."[12] In one school that stressed the pluralist democratic creed—equality, tolerance, civic participation—there was a decided increase of support for that creed among students.[13]

In short, scholars are confirming what every high school student knows—that schools have a certain, usually rather establishmentarian, point of view. But here again the political scientist must look more closely at what shapes attitudes. Is it the teachers, the other students, the formal classes, or the fact that *both teachers and students* are subject to *common* stimuli? These are difficult factors to untangle. One study found no evidence that the civics curriculum has a significant effect on the political orientations of the great majority of American high school students. Of course students differed in their interest in politics, but

[9]M. Kent Jennings and Kenneth P. Langton, "Mothers versus Fathers: The Formation of Political Orientations Among Young Americans," *Journal of Politics* (May 1969), p. 357.

[10]Robert D. Hess and Judith V. Torney, *The Development of Basic Attitudes and Values Toward Government and Citizenship During the Elementary School Years*, Part I (U.S. Office of Education, 1965), p. 193.

[11]Roberta S. Sigel, "Image of a President: Some Insights into the Political Views of School Children," *American Political Science Review*, (March 1968), pp. 216–26. See also F. Christopher Arterton, "The Impact of Watergate on Children's Attitudes Toward Political Authority," *Political Science Quarterly* (June 1974), pp. 269–88.

[12]Jennings and Niemi, "The Transmission of Political Values," p. 178.

[13]Edgar Litt, "Civic Education, Community Norms, and Political Indoctrination," *American Sociological Review*. (February 1962), pp. 69–75. See also Elizabeth Léonie Simpson, *Democracy's Stepchildren* (Jossey-Bass, 1971).

this resulted not from taking (or not taking) civics or government courses, but from the students' backgrounds and life plans. Students planning to attend college were more likely to be knowledgeable about politics, to be more interested in politics, to be more in favor of free speech, to talk about politics, and to read about politics.[14]

Once again we see how complex are the forces operating on the developing political attitudes of young people.[15] Moreover, as youths get older they of course become more and more subject to forces that affect adults. Perhaps the most important of these is the mass media.

The mass media and politics

In November 1969, a year after being elected to office, President Nixon launched a campaign against the television networks which, he felt, had long treated him unfairly. Vice-President Agnew spearheaded the attack. Agnew termed the television news industry a "tiny and closed fraternity of privileged men" and declared that no medium had a more

[14]Kenneth P. Langton and M. Kent Jennings, "Political Socialization and the High School Civics Curriculum in the United States," *American Political Science Review.* (September 1968), pp. 852–67. These generalizations do not apply to black students, some of whom, according to this study, were significantly influenced by their courses.

[15]Sophisticated analysis is being conducted in the general area of political socialization of adolescents; see, for example, Richard M. Merelman, "The Development of Policy Thinking in Adolescence," *American Political Science Review* (December 1971), pp. 1033–47; and a follow-up research note by the same author, same journal (March 1973), pp. 161–66; Donald D. Searing, Joel J. Schwartz, and Alden E. Lind, "The Structuring Principle: Political Socialization and Belief Systems," *American Political Science Review* (June 1973), pp. 415–32.

"You're wasting your time! . . . My mind is totally controlled by what the mass media feeds into it."

By Lichty; © Field Enterprises, Inc., 1973.

powerful influence over public opinion. "Nowhere in our system are there fewer checks on vast power." Agnew's resignation four years later did not deter the campaign. During the Watergate trials the Nixon White House repeatedly charged that television was distorting the news, unduly emphasizing the scandal, exploiting leaked information, and condemning administration officials in the newscasts before all the evidence was in.

This was by no means the first time that embattled politicians had attacked the news media, or at least tried to turn it to their own uses. Jefferson was so perturbed by the pervasive influence of the Federalist press that he founded a Republican newspaper. During the nineteenth century most newspapers were proudly and blatantly partisan. In recent decades the main attack against the news media has not been the Nixon accusation but the contention of liberals that the newspapers were overwhelmingly biased toward supporting conservative policies and candidates. Finding the press in mainly Republican hands, Franklin Roosevelt turned to radio and made adroit use of it, as John Kennedy did televised news conferences.

AN IRRESISTIBLE FORCE?

On the face of it, the influence of the media on political opinion would indeed seem to be immense. It is estimated that 40 million Americans watch the weekday evening newscasts on the three networks. Americans buy about 65 million newspapers a day, and there are countless foreign-language newspapers, thousands of weeklies, and a freewheeling "underground" press. Walter Lippmann has called the newspaper the "bible of democracy, the book out of which a people determines its conduct." And radio continues to reach tens of millions of persons, though its political impact is somewhat muted compared with the other media.

Yet political scientists and other opinion analysts are not certain that the mass media have the powerful effect on public opinion that many have assumed. Attitudes "built into" the slowly developing person through a long process of socialization are too strong to be easily overcome. The influence of family and school and church hangs on for many years and resists easy conquest by the mass media. Three forces are especially important:

1. *Selective perception.* People are not empty vessels to be filled up by torrents of television talk or acres of newsprint. Attention is always selective. Out of all the speeches, articles, news stories, and political pamphlets, many voters pay attention to very little. We all tend to concentrate on those speeches and those news stories and subscribe to those magazines that support our own predispositions or biases. We have an enormous capacity, as social psychologists have demonstrated over and over, to perceive phenomena in ways that stem from our own

9-2.
How the public views the media (regular readers' and viewers' ratings of the performance of the media in keeping people informed about important problems)

	Newspapers	TV news	Newsmagazines	Radio news
Excellent	15%	18%	26%	14%
Good	47	49	49	54
Fair	28	24	18	21
Poor	9	8	2	4

SOURCE: "The People and the Press," *Newsweek* (November 9, 1970) p. 22. Copyright Newsweek, 1970.

social and attitudinal development; that is, the "facts" we see are filtered through spectacles that distort in an infinite variety of ways. An accurate estimate of the impact of mass media requires paying attention to what the communicators said, what the audience saw or heard, and how the audience was affected.[16] The difference between *exposure* and *effect* can be enormous.

2. *Popular suspicion of the media.* Most Americans, according to a recent survey, seemed satisfied with the amount of news they were getting from the media, but more than half the people polled felt that some events were not being adequately reported. This credibility gap broadened when it came to comparing news stories with events that people had directly witnessed or participated in. People who knew something directly of the subject were especially critical of the newspapers; television and newsmagazines got a somewhat better rating (see Table 9–2).[17] Popular skepticism of the accuracy of reporters and of the objectivity of editors is of course an old phenomenon in the United States. To a degree that skepticism is doubtless a good thing in a republic; but intense suspicion of the press could have serious implications for the maintenance of faith in the free, fair, and open exchange of information and ideas in a democracy.

3. *Primary groups as filters.* The family and other primary groups that, as we noted, heavily influence the growing child also screen adults against the full and direct impact of the media. It is direct, face-to-face contacts that reach people, whether in families, neighborhoods, or small groups. The more *personal* the means of communication, according to many studies, the more effective it is in influencing opinions. Thus the average face-to-face conversation probably has more effect than a tele-

[16]Kurt Lang and Gladys Engel Lang, *Television and Politics* (Quadrangle Books, 1968).

[17]"The People and the Press," *Newsweek* (November 9, 1970), pp. 22–25.

vision speech, and a television speech more influence than a newspaper account.

Does this mean that personal methods of communication have more effect on opinions than organized methods such as newspapers? Possibly, but the situation is not that simple. For the local "opinion leaders"—the lawyer next door, the bartender, the campus politician, the ward leader, the head of the local League of Women Voters—may have received some of their ideas from a newspaper or magazine. If a friend drops in and sells me on the need for a sales tax, and if he in turn got the idea from a popular magazine, what is the source of the influence on me? Opinions are the product of the interplay of many forces.

PROPAGANDA

We have been discussing the routine dissemination of news and opinion; what about planned, intensive, and systematic efforts to change people's political ideas in a certain direction? We live in what has been called a propaganda age. "A new skill group has come into existence in modern civilization," Harold Lasswell has said. "Skill in propaganda has become one of the most effective roads to power in modern states."

Propaganda has been treated as an unmitigated evil, but that is a simplistic approach. Indeed, it is hard to say just where propaganda ends and education starts. Effective education may include some propaganda (in favor, say, of democratic values, the virtues of which must be taken in part on faith). And if propaganda is defined as a "method used for influencing the conduct of others on behalf of predetermined ends," then almost every person who writes or talks with a purpose becomes a propagandist. Lasswell has described propaganda as a technique for social control—"the manipulation of collective attitudes by the use of significant symbols (words, pictures, and tunes) rather than violence, bribery, or boycott." Obviously propaganda in these terms may be used for good causes as well as bad.

Americans are almost constantly exposed to propaganda techniques, especially those used by advertisers. Popular advertisements are designed to appeal to our basic attitudes, especially to our desire for recognition and approval by others, for prestige, and for security. The hallmarks of effective propaganda have been described as repetition, insistent exaggeration, identification with the person being persuaded, appeal to authority, false association (linking certain political beliefs, for example, with patriotism or God), and appeal to the herd instinct.[18]

Propaganda is often denounced as dishonest and dangerous, but it is also part of the currency of pluralistic politics. As Murray Edelman has written, "If politics is concerned with who gets what, or with the authoritative allocation of values, one may be pardoned for wondering

[18]Charles A. Siepmann, "Propaganda Techniques," in Reo M. Christenson and Robert O. McWilliams, eds., *Voice of the People*, 2nd ed. (McGraw-Hill, 1967), pp. 331–39.

why it need involve so much talk. An individual or group can most directly get what it wants by taking it or by force and can get nothing directly by talk." But force leads to counterforce, and the employment of language "is exactly what makes politics different from other methods of allocating values. . . . Force signals weakness in politics, as rape does in sex. Talk, on the other hand, involves a competitive exchange of symbols . . . through which values are shared and assigned and coexistence attained. It is fair enough to complain that the politician is not deft in his talk, but to complain that he talks is to miss the point."[19]

A free marketplace for ideas?

Many observers are not so sanguine about the influence of the media. They believe that political power over voters' opinions is so concentrated in newspaper publishing and in the television industry that democracy itself may be threatened. They echo Justice Holmes's classic dictum that "the best test of truth is the power of the thought to get itself accepted in the competition of the market." What kind of competition is possible, critics demand, when three networks dominate the television news media and a few newspapers or newspaper chains dominate the press?

THE POLITICS OF THE PRESS

Ideally in a free society, newspapers should be independent, fearless, politically unbiased, not overly dependent on stockholders, advertisers, government, or even subscribers. Three basic tendencies dominate the press, according to critics:

1. *Concentration.* This century has been one of "dying dailies." "In 1910," one authority reports, "there were 2,200 dailies published in 1,200 cities; 53 percent of all urban places had their own paper. Today less than a quarter of urban places have their own paper, mostly because there are many more cities, partly because the number of papers is down to 1,750. . . . In 1910 the majority of cities with papers had competing ones; today less than 3 percent have." Most dailies today are controlled by chains and hence by "absentee owners."[20]

2. *Commercialism.* A newspaper is a business and must depend on selling advertisements and copies. Many publishers feel that they must give the public what it wants. If readers like screaming headlines, sex, comics, scandal, and crime at the expense of full and balanced news stories and editorial comment, a newspaper can hardly hold out against

[19] *The Symbolic Uses of Politics* (University of Illinois Press, 1967), p. 114, p. 522.

[20] Ben H. Bagdikian, *The Effete Conspiracy* (Harper & Row, 1972), p. 10.

the customers. If the publisher caters to the social and political prejudices of his readers, however, he may deny them a chance to break out of their parochialism and apathy. Or he may block off the expression of controversial views for fear of alienating his customers.

3. *Conservatism.* Newspaper publishers are businessmen. They are worried by the things that worry every businessman—labor demands, costs, sales, taxes, dividends, profits. As businessmen they tend to take a conservative point of view. Nor is it surprising that most newspapers tend to support the more conservative candidate—Nixon had 83 percent of daily circulation with him in 1960 and 78 percent in 1968. Most congressional districts defined as "liberal" have no or very few liberal or pro-Democratic newspapers.[21]

Are these criticisms accurate? Some argue that concentration, or the absence of competition, is not necessarily bad. If a single newspaper has a monopoly, they contend, it does not need to pander to the lowest taste of the public in order to compete for readers. The editor need not fear that if he antagonizes local advertisers or political groups within the community he will lose business to a rival newspaper.

As for press conservatism, some contend that this tends to be offset by the liberalism of the reporters. Daniel P. Moynihan sees a growing tendency for journalists to be recruited from among college graduates, and especially those graduates who hold hostile attitudes toward middle-class Americans. Building on a long muckraking tradition, many journalists take a highly critical attitude toward public officials.[22] Perhaps we secure some protection in this counterbalancing of reporters' values with those of their publishers.

Certain newspapers such as *The New York Times* and the *Washington Post* "serve a special function in communication among the major political actors and the lesser activists."[23] These papers are prime instruments for supplying political leaders with forums for political debate and for reflecting the attitudes of their readers. Readers of these newspapers tend to be "more affluent and more liberal than the rest of the nation," and both as a result and a cause our most influential newspapers tend "to set a tone of pervasive dissatisfaction with the performance of the national government, whoever the presidential incumbent may be and whatever the substance of the policies."[24]

It has long been said that the editorial columns of newspapers do not affect opinion very much because editors think one way and people vote the opposite. Franklin D. Roosevelt's four presidential victories in a row, against heavy editorial opposition, are cases in point; so, to a

[21]*Ibid.*, pp. 147–48.

[22]"The Presidency and the Press," *Commentary* (March 1971), p. 43. See also John W. C. Johnstone, Edward J. Slawski, and William C. Bowman, "The Professional Values of American Newsmen," *Public Opinion Quarterly* (Winter 1972–73), pp. 522–40.

[23]Key, *Public Opinion and American Democracy*, p. 405.

[24]Moynihan, "The Presidency and the Press," p. 44.

lesser degree, is Kennedy's victory in 1960. Although it is significant that Roosevelt or Kennedy won despite heavy press opposition, the central question is the extent to which they had to modify their political views in order to minimize the effect of that opposition.

The real question is not only whether editorials directly influence our political attitudes and voting decisions; it is whether the press (and the media as a whole) shapes our political opinions through its overall news and editorial posture. The newspaper—in its front-page makeup, its headlines, its use of pictures, its playing up of some items, its distortion of important information, its lack of attention to problems that may be evolving into crises—influences the "picture in our heads," the very basic attitudes that predispose us to interpret news one way or another. The press has a long-run, continuous influence on opinions that may not be obvious in a particular election. "The steady flow of the propaganda of the media between elections probably strikes people at a time when their defenses are less effectively mobilized than they are during presidential campaigns."[25]

Criticism of newspapers has been abundant; practical remedies have been few. Some have suggested that newspaper chains be broken up through antimonopoly legislation. Others have proposed that the government subsidize competing newspapers—a kind of "T.V.A. yardstick" for the opinion industry. Such proposals have received little support because many Americans oppose any action that might, in their view, threaten the freedom of the press under the First Amendment. Better a biased, uncompetitive, commercially oriented press, they feel, than a government-controlled one. So the problem of dealing with press bias has been left to self-policing. A National Press Council, financed by a private foundation, was set up in 1973 to serve as an independent watchdog of press fairness. Some newspapers boycotted the council, and its effectiveness is in doubt.

TELEVISION NEWS: BIG BROTHER?

Some observers believe that television in general, and TV news in particular, is a much greater threat to popular government than has been recognized. Television, they contend, is not just another medium. Its influence is far more pervasive than that of the other media. Numerous newspapers that cross state lines provide considerable choice for the reader, they note, but only three networks dominate the American television scene, each with about 200 local affiliates. And people seem exceptionally vulnerable to the tube. They *trust* television far more than they do their newspapers; hence they are more vulnerable to it. They get far more of their political campaign information from television than from newspapers. Television news exposure cuts across age groups, educational levels, social classes, and races to an astonishing

[25]Key, *Public Opinion and American Democracy*, p. 403.

degree. The TV audience is often a captive one, compared to newspaper subscribers who can read selectively. And video, with all its concreteness, vividness, and drama, has an emotional impact that print cannot hope to match.[26]

The great fear of television as "big brother" is that it may become allied with "big government"—indeed, that this is already happening in the relationship between the president and television. The chief executive can command the television networks at prime time, as he wishes. He can speak directly to the nation. He does not need to answer questions, except in a televised press conference, and he can minimize his press conferences, as Nixon did. As a result of its linkage with executive power, according to one study, television has been converted into an "electronic throne."

"No mighty king, no ambitious emperor, no pope, or prophet ever dreamt of such an awesome pulpit. . . . At best the wizardry of radio had been an artery of audio communication which sent a voice into the living room. Television was a comprehensive transportation which carried the viewer to the convention floor, to the Vietnam battlefield, to the face of the moon, and to the White House, wherever the camera was directed. The president, in his ability to command the national attention, diminished the power of all other politicians and, in the case of Richard Nixon, fostered a distortion of our systems of safeguards."[27] By the mid-seventies the nation had not even begun to cope with such awesome electronic power.

POLICING THE ELECTRONIC MEDIA

Since their infancy, radio and television have been under some kind of government regulation. When radio broadcasting first began in the early 1920s, a free-for-all occurred because broadcasters sometimes used the same wavelengths at the same time, deafening the listener with a chaos of sound. By 1927, sharp protests had brought government action. Today, by law, a broadcaster or a telecaster cannot operate without a license from the Federal Communications Commission. Those granted such licenses are obliged to use the public-owned airwaves and to conduct their operations in the public interest. The FCC has the power to refuse to grant or renew a license if it decides the station is not providing programs that serve the public interest.

The FCC has the ticklish task of *policing* the broadcasters without *cen-*

[26]Gary L. Wamsley and Richard A. Pride, "Television Network News: Re-Thinking the Iceberg Problem," *Western Political Quarterly* (September 1972), pp. 434–50; see also Edward C. Dreyer, "Media Use and Electoral Choices: Some Political Consequences of Information Exposure," *Public Opinion Quarterly* (Winter 1971–72), pp. 544–53.

[27]Newton M. Minow, John Bartlow Martin, Lee M. Mitchell, *Presidential Television* (Basic Books, 1973), pp. vii–viii; see also Harold Mendelsohn and Irving Crespi, *Polls, Television, and the New Politics* (Chandler, 1970); James Aronson, *Deadline for the Media: Today's Challenges to the Press, TV, and Radio* (Bobbs-Merrill, 1974).

The nationally televised Nixon-Kennedy debate in 1960 was helpful to Kennedy but hurt Nixon.

soring them. On the one hand, the Communications Act of 1934 specifies that nothing therein shall be understood to give the Commission the power to interfere with the right of free speech by radio and television. And the Commission has no power to regulate the content of particular programs. On the other hand, in considering applications for the renewal of licenses, the Commission may and does take into account the content and character of the broadcaster's past programs in order to determine if he has used his license in the public interest. For instance, in 1968 the practices of a Mississippi television station, WLBT, in reporting race relations and civil rights became a factor in the renewal of its license. Network control over local programs is regulated indirectly by the limit on the number of local stations each network is permitted to own; and the FCC discourages excessive concentrated control over newspaper, television, and radio facilities in a community. In general, however, the FCC has not vigorously regulated television and radio broadcasting, and the industry operates largely under its own rules.

The FCC is also responsible for enforcing the statutory requirement that if air time is made available to one candidate for a public office it must be made available to all candidates for that office on the same terms. This section of the broadcasting act has caused difficulties, particularly in the years when national elections have been held, and Congress has occasionally suspended the rule to the extent of permitting television stations to give equal time to the presidential candidates of the two major parties without their having to give equal time to candidates of the splinter parties.

Broadcasters also have developed ways of avoiding the equal time requirement—for instance, by use of the news-interview format. The networks do broadcast editorials—on the grounds that their right to present a point of view labeled as such is comparable to the right a newspaper has to print editorials. Under present regulations, station owners may speak their own minds, but within reasonable limits they must also make time available to persons or parties of contrasting views. This is known as the Fairness Doctrine (see p. 153).

Taking the pulse of the people

"What I want," Abraham Lincoln once said, "is to get done what the people desire to have done, and the question for me is how to find that out exactly." This perplexing question faces every politician, in office or out. Another president, Woodrow Wilson, once complained to newspapermen that they had no business to say, as they often did, that all the people out their way thought so and so: "You do not know, and the worst of it is, since the responsibility is mine, I do not know, what they are thinking about. I have the most imperfect means of finding out, and yet I have got to act as if I knew. . . ."

How can the politician find out what the people are thinking? The usual way, of course, is to look at the election results. If John Brown wins over James Smith, presumably the people want what John Brown stands for. If Brown is an unequivocal advocate of gun regulation and Smith is 100 percent against any form of control, evidently the majority of the people support some kind of firearms regulation. But we know that in practice things do not work this way. Elections are rarely fought on single issues, and candidates rarely take clear-cut stands. It is impossible, moreover, to separate issues from candidates. Did Nixon win in 1972 because of Vietnam, crime, taxes, his personality, or shifts in party support? The answer is that he won for some of these reasons and for many others. Which brings us back to the question – what do the people want?

This is where straw votes and public opinion polls come in. In this country public opinion polls are over a century old, but their main development has taken place in the last three decades. Some of the techniques were originally worked out by market research analysts hired by businessmen to estimate potential sales for their products and then were adapted to measuring opinions on general issues. Today there are over a thousand polling organizations.

METHODS OF SAMPLING

Everybody conducts polls, or more precisely, most of our judgments are based on samples of evidence. The choice is not between polling (sampling) and not polling, but between biased and representative sampling. Most of us, in a majority of cases, draw conclusions from biased samples. For example: The congressman who reports that he is opposed to H.R. 506 and who is sure that the voters are too because his mail has been running six to one against the bill; the reporter who writes that students are becoming less radical, based on interviews with a dozen students on the Yale campus; the coed who predicted that McGovern would win, based on her discussions with several of her classmates. We can have little confidence in such assessments.

If a politician or a social scientist wants to measure opinion more precisely, the first thing he must determine is the *universe,* that is, the whole group whose opinion he is interested in – every adult, all students on this campus, all students in the United States, voters in City X. If the universe consists of only thirty units – all students in a particular class – the most precise way to find out what they think on a particular issue would be to poll every one of them. But for most politically significant problems this is impossible, so pollsters *sample* the universe they are interested in. The accuracy of the results of the poll turns largely on securing a sample *representative* of the total universe. If drawn properly so that each unit in a universe has an equal chance to be included, a relatively small sample can provide accurate results. Beyond a certain point, an increase in the size of the sample reduces only slightly the *sampling error*—that is, the range between the divisions found in the sample and those of the universe.

One way to develop a representative sample would be to draw the sample completely at random. But this type of *random sampling* is impossible for most political surveys. Instead we use *census tracts* (where these are available) which give the number of residences and their locations. By shuffling census tracts, drawing out at random the required number, and then sending interviewers to every fifth or tenth or twentieth house, we get a random sample. A less complicated, but less reliable, sample is *quota sampling*. Here an attempt is made to secure a sample that reflects those variables among the population that might affect opinion. One polling organization, in testing opinion that is thought to be affected by income status (for example, views on the income tax), makes up a sample based on two wealthy persons, fourteen members of the upper-income class, fifty-two from the middle-income groups, and thirty-two from the poor. Interviewers are instructed to interview people in each group until they have reached the quota for that group.

People are often suspicious of results based on what appears to be a small sample. Is it really possible, they wonder, to generalize about the opinions of 215 million persons on the basis of a few thousand interviews? Can such a small sample be truly representative? The answer is yes. In a comparison of demographic characteristics based on census results and those based on a carefully drawn sample, the differences were very small. The census reported that 18.8 percent of the population was between the ages of 21 and 29, 23.5 percent was between 30 and 39, and 20.9 percent was between 40 and 49. The sample results were 18.4, 23.8, and 21.5, respectively.[28] Social scientists assume that if a sample chosen by modern techniques reproduces such characteristics of the population so precisely, it will replicate the attitudes and opinions of the total population equally well.

ASKING THE RIGHT QUESTIONS

A major difficulty in securing accurate results from a survey is in phrasing the questions. If you ask a question in a certain way, you can get the answer you want. Ask a man if he favors labor unions and he may say No. Ask him if he favors organized efforts by workers to improve their well-being, and chances are he will answer Yes. Also, trouble may arise in the alternatives that a question presents. Clearly, asking a person "Do you favor the United States entering a world government, or do you prefer our traditional independence in determining our own affairs?" is loading the dice. Polling organizations go to great efforts to make their questions fair; some of them conduct trial runs with differently worded questions.

One way to avoid this difficulty is to ask a multiple-choice question. For example, a Gallup poll asked, "How far do you, yourself, think

[28]Samuel A. Stouffer, *Communism, Conformity, and Civil Liberties* (Doubleday, 1955), p. 238.

"Good morning, sir. I'm making a survey. Could you tell me which Presidential candidate you're—uh—against?"

Drawing by Ştevenson; © 1960 The New Yorker Magazine, Inc.

the federal government should go in requiring employers to hire people without regard to race, religion, color, or nationality?" The respondent could answer: All the way; None of the way; Depends on type of work; Should be left to state governments; or Don't know. A variation of this type—the open-ended question—allows the respondent to supply his own answer. He may be asked simply, "How do you think we should deal with the problem of air pollution by automobiles?" (The answers to this type of question are, of course, hard to tabulate accurately.)

Interviewing itself is a delicate task. The interviewer's appearance, clothes, language, and way of asking questions may influence the replies. Inaccurate findings may result from the bias of the interviewer or from his failure to do his job fully and carefully. And the persons interviewed may be the source of error. Respondents suspicious of the interviewer's motives may give false or confused answers. Their memories may be poor. To cover up ignorance they may give neutral answers or appear undecided. Or they may give the answers that they think the interviewer would like them to give.

Polls may give a false impression of the firmness and intensity of opinion; as we have seen, opinions may be volatile and fleeting. Moreover, polls do not differentiate among people—they give equal weight to a follower and to an opinion leader who may in the end influence other voters. Studies at the Survey Research Center at Michigan suggest that public opinion is not like an iceberg, where the movement of the top indicates the movement of the great mass under the water. The visible opinion at the top may be moving in a different direction—indeed it may even be differently located—from that of the great mass of opinion that is far less visible. In short, it is far easier to measure the surface of public opinion than its depth and intensity.

INTERPRETING THE RESULTS

To the average American, preelection forecasting is the most intriguing use of surveys, for everyone likes to know in advance how an election will turn out. During the campaign, pollsters submit regular "returns" on the position of the candidates. On the whole, the record of the leading forecasters has been good, as Table 9–3 shows. The most sensational slip came in 1948, when, during the presidential battle between President Truman and Governor Dewey, the polls repeatedly indicated that Mr. Truman was running far behind. The president denounced these "sleeping polls," but the pollsters stood pat on their statistics. Early in September one of them actually announced that the race was over. Gallup gave the president 44.5 percent of the popular vote in his final forecast and Roper's prediction was 37.1 percent. Actually Mr. Truman won 49.4 percent of the popular vote, and the pollsters were subjected to general ridicule. Since then they have been more cautious in making predictions from their polling data, and more careful in their methods.[29]

[29]See Mendelsohn and Crespi, *Polls, Television, and the New Politics*, Chap. 2.

9–3
Some recent presidential polls (by percentage)

Year	Actual Dem. vote	Roper Poll	Gallup Poll	Harris Poll
1936	60.2	61.7	53.8	–
1940	54.7	55.2	55.0	–
1944	53.8	53.6	53.3	–
1948	49.4	37.1	44.5	–
1952	45.+	43.0	46.0	–
1956	42.0	40.0	40.5	–
1960	49.4	47.0	49.0	–
1964	61.4	–	61.0	–
1968	42.7	–	40.0	43.0
1972	37.7	–	35.0	34.8

Political polls have taken on increasingly significant functions in our political system. Candidates use polls to determine where to campaign, how to campaign, and even whether to campaign. In the years and months preceding a national convention, politicians watch the polls to determine which among the hopefuls has political appeal. John F. Kennedy used polls systematically in both his preconvention and election campaigns, as have most of the presidential candidates since then. Questions have been raised about this use of polls. Should candidates run for office only when it seems safe to do so? If a candidate believes in a cause, should he not defend it publicly in order to present a meaningful choice to the voters?[30]

Surely the polls at best are no substitute for elections. Faced with his ballot, the voter must translate his opinions into concrete decisions between personalities and parties. He must decide what is important and what is unimportant. Then, out of the welter of views of all the voters, a decision emerges for some candidate who will act in terms of some program (however vague), and who will have the people's trust (again vague) to act on future problems. For democracy is more than the expression of views, more than a simple mirror of public opinion. It is also the *choosing* among issues—and the governmental action that must follow. Democracy is the thoughtful participation of people in the political process; as Lasswell says, it means using heads as well as counting them. Elections, with all their failings, at least establish the link between the many voices of the people and the decisions of their leaders.

[30]Critical analyses of public opinion polling are C. W. Roll, Jr. and A. H. Cantril, *Polls: Their Use and Misuse in Politics* (Basic Books, 1972); and Leo Bogart, *Silent Politics: Polls and the Awareness of Public Opinion* (John Wiley, 1972).

Public opinion in summary

Summarizing this chapter, we find:

1. Public opinion is not one opinion but a complex mixture of opinions characterized by stability and fluidity, interest and apathy, intensity and latency, and different degrees of distribution – so much so that no elected official can be at all sure what his constituents really believe.

2. Despite its diversity, public opinion acquires a certain orderliness or structure from the fact that most Americans are subjected to common influences – family, schools, the mass media, and so on.

3. Despite many assertions that some specific force – the mother or father, the family as a whole, early schooling, television, and so on – has the dominant role in moulding opinion, people actually seem to be shaped by many forces; research on the relative influence of these forces is continuing.

4. Some public opinion is formed by deliberate manipulation of attitudes by influential persons with all sorts of purposes. The development of highly efficient means of communication and persuasion has enlarged the role of the propagandist, but this influence is limited.

5. In the diffusion of ideas and opinions we do not have a wholly free market. In the press and other mass media, we find tendencies toward concentration, commercialization, and conservatism partly offset by the liberalism of many journalists and some of the most prominent newspapers.

6. We have fairly reliable methods for roughly measuring people's attitudes at a given time, but there is a vast difference between expressing a great variety of views on a great variety of subjects and making a choice between two candidates at election time.

Chapter 10 Political behavior: the american voter

"Elections are a mystery," writes Gerald M. Pomper. "Although we consider elections crucial to the functioning of democracy, we have little knowledge of their true significance. Americans choose half a million public officials through the ballot, but the extent of popular control of government policy decisions is undetermined. Throughout the world as well, governments proclaim themselves democracies and hold mass elections, but the meaning of the ballot remains cloudy to the Soviet worker and the Mississippi Negro."[1]

The mystery deepens when we try to look inside the mind of the voter. What causes some people to go to the polls and vote when others do not? Why are so many Americans merely spectators? How do we decide to vote the way we do? Does voting have any kind of rational pattern, or is it a crazy-quilt of vagrant and emotional actions?

[1]*Elections in America* (Dodd, Mead, 1968), p. 1.

The right to vote as one wishes, without interference from the government or from other persons, is supposed to be the great glory of democracy and the ultimate safeguard of it. The fact that Americans choose half a million public officials, according to some critics of American political arrangements, does not necessarily mean popular control of government. They contend that voters do not generally see the relation between elections and their own interests; that they do not usually get a meaningful choice between candidates; that what candidates promise and what they do in office is often quite different; in short, that voting is not the great foundation of democracy that many Americans assume it to be.

One reason for the controversy over the importance of voting is that scholars are making only slow progress in unraveling the nature of it. But we are steadily gaining new insights into the way relations among members of groups, between leaders and followers, and among members of families affect political activity.

Who votes?

The history of suffrage in the United States has been a long struggle to extend the right to vote from a small group of property-owning males—perhaps one person out of every twenty or thirty—to the great mass of the people. In this chapter we will consider who actually votes and how and why, rather than who has the right to vote. But note that we could not even be discussing voting behavior if many men and women had not fought to extend the right to vote over the last century and a half.

Three great struggles have been fought over this issue. The first was against *property tests* for voting. Conservatives like Chancellor Kent of

The great struggle for equal voting rights for women (left) was finally rewarded with passage of the Nineteenth Amendment. The women at right are voting for the first time.

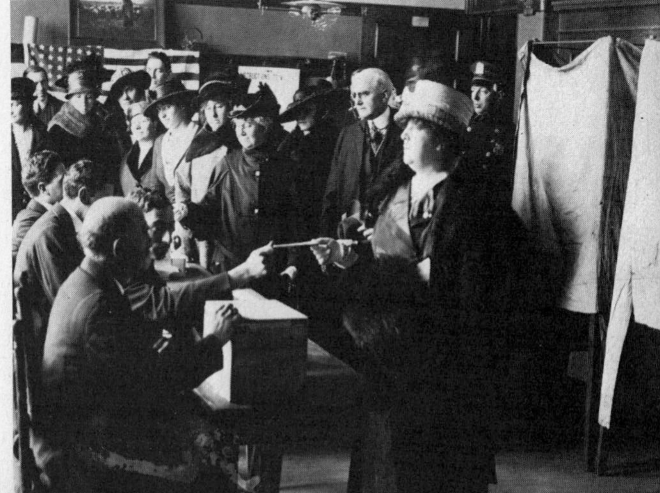

New York argued that universal male suffrage would jeopardize the rights of property, that if poor people gained the right to vote they would sell their votes to the rich. The democratic, egalitarian mood of America, eastern immigration and the western frontier, and the eagerness of politicians to lower voting barriers so they could pick up votes—all these led to the end of property (and taxpaying) restrictions by the middle of the nineteenth century.

The second great struggle was for *women's suffrage*. Husbands and fathers once argued that women had no place at the polling booth, that husbands could vote for the interests of the whole family—but these arguments had a hollow ring. The aroused women conducted noisy parades, drew up petitions, organized a Washington lobby, picketed the White House, got arrested, went on hunger strikes in jail. They won the vote in some states and finally achieved a breakthrough with the passage of the Nineteenth Amendment in 1920.

The third great struggle—for the right of black Americans to vote—has been mainly won (see Chapter 7). The most recent major extension of the suffrage has been to youths eighteen to twenty years old. Unlike the earlier expansions of the suffrage, this was hardly the result of a struggle by young people. It was in part a recognition by those twenty-one and older that younger persons were being educated to a point where they could vote intelligently. It was also a response to the widespread protest during the 1960s among the young, especially college students, against governmental and other "establishments"; adults realized that they could hardly urge young persons to forsake violence and confrontation and use peaceful political processes if the young lacked even the right to vote. It also seemed unfair that those "old enough to die for their country" could not "vote for their country." This most recent extension of suffrage was embodied in the twenty-sixth Amendment, ratified in 1971.

By the mid-seventies the overwhelming number of Americans, including women, blacks, and the young, possessed the right to vote. What do they do with it?

MILLIONS OF NONVOTERS

On the average, the proportion of Americans who vote is smaller than that of the British, French, Italians, West Germans, Scandinavians, or Canadians. Talk as we will about democratic suffrage, the fact remains that millions of Americans do not choose to vote or somehow fail to get to the polls on election day. Our record has not always been so poor. Voting was generally high (among those legally *able* to vote) during the latter nineteenth century; in 1876, 86 percent of the adult enfranchised males voted. In this century our voting ratio has been erratic. Turnout dropped between the early 1900s and the mid-twenties, rose in the late 1920s and 1930s, declined in the mid- and late 1940s, climbed in 1952 and 1956, and has decreased in the last three presidential elections—

three elections, incidentally, that were thought to be unusually significant and compelling.

Americans have an absolute right *not* to vote. But in a democracy where voting is considered a civic virtue and a prudent means of self-defense, the extent of nonvoting is startling. In the last two presidential elections about 40 percent of the eligible voters did not go to the polls. *Over 60 percent* of them stayed home in the congressional elections of 1974. Participation in state and local elections is usually even *lower.*

Why do people fail to vote? Aside from outright denials of the right to vote—happily no longer a significant factor—important reasons are registration requirements and being absent from the voting district on election day. As we noted in Part Three, registering to vote (not required in many other democracies) is bothersome and time-consuming and often compels a potential voter to initiate action long before he or she faces election issues.[2] Although the Supreme Court has ruled that states may not impose residency requirements of longer than fifty days, almost a third of the potential voters are not even registered to

[2]See Stanley Kelley, Jr., Richard E. Ayres, and William G. Bowen, "Registration and Voting: Putting First Things First," *American Political Science Review* (June 1967), pp. 359–77.

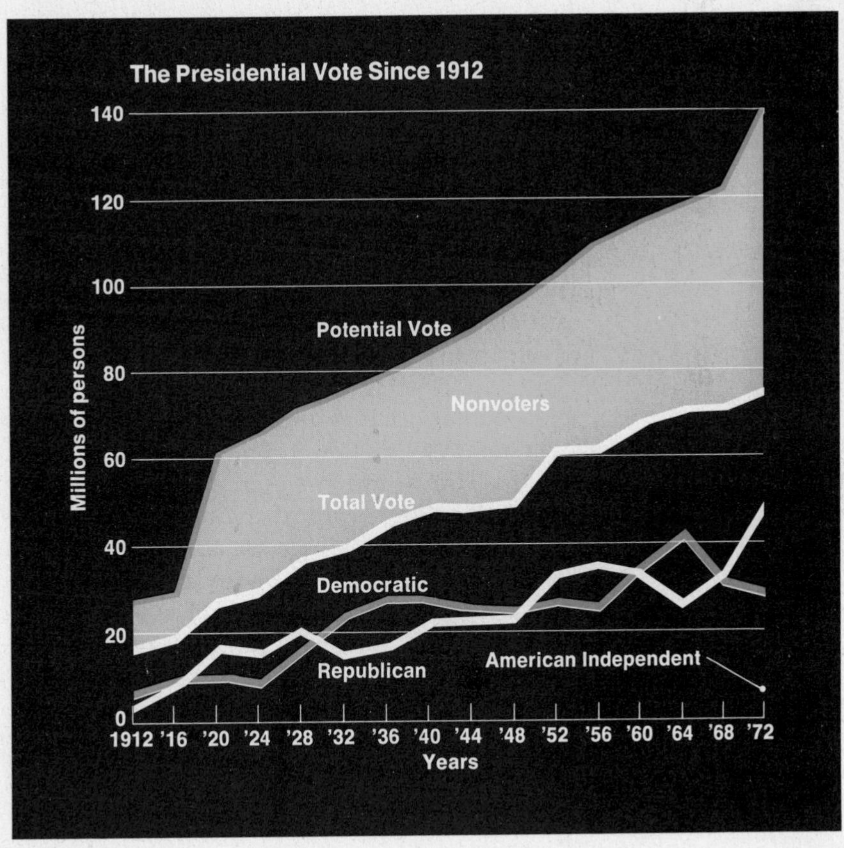

vote. Disturbed by the low turn-out, Congress in 1970 established for *presidential elections* a uniform thirty-day residency requirement and set simpler procedures for absentee voting.

The *prime* reasons for not voting, however, are not institutional. They are *personal.* Millions of Americans are just not interested enough to go to the polls to vote for president, and even fewer vote for state and local candidates. They feel—if they think about the matter at all—that politics is not important, or that there is no real choice between candidates, or that they do not know enough to vote, or that they are "disgusted with politics." Some fear losing business or wages if they go to the polls. Much nonvoting probably results from a combination of low interest and inconvenience: An elderly person might vote if the polls were around the corner—but actually they are two miles away and he or she lacks transportation. Of course, sometimes the inconvenience is simply a rationalization for basic lack of interest.

Should such apathy surprise us? When students mobilized for action after President Nixon's Cambodia "incursion" of 1970, it was estimated that half a million of them would take part in the ensuing national elections. In fact only a tiny minority was active. That minority was effective in a number of congressional elections, but the vast majority of interested students did more talking than electioneering. Some were alienated from the whole election process; most were simply not interested in the issues of the day.[3] Indeed, of all major categories of voters, the lowest percentage of voter turnout in the 1964 and 1968 presidential elections was among the eighteen to twenty-year-olds in the states that permitted them to vote.

WHO FAILS TO VOTE?

The extent of voting varies among different types of persons, areas, and elections. Voting studies generally agree on the following patterns, which are listed here roughly in order of declining importance:

1. People with high incomes are more likely to vote than people with low ones. Why do low-income people vote in fewer numbers than the wealthy? They have less economic security; they feel less of a sense of control over their political environment; they feel at a disadvantage in social contacts; and their social norms tend to deemphasize politics. Their nonvoting thus is part of a larger political and psychological environment that discourages political activity, including voting.[4]

2. The college-educated are more likely to vote than the noncollege-

[3]Walter T. Murphy, Jr., "Student Power in the 1970 Elections: A Preliminary Assessment," *Political Science* (Winter 1971), pp. 27–32. See also Sidney Hyman, *Youth in Politics* (Basic Books, 1972).

[4]See Angus Campbell, Philip E. Converse, Warren E. Miller, and Donald E. Stokes, *The American Voter* (John Wiley, 1960).

educated. High school alumni are more likely to vote than those with only a grade school education. "Practically speaking," writes Warren Miller, "almost everybody who has been to college votes."[5] Even college-educated persons who profess little interest in or knowledge about political issues turn out to vote. People with college backgrounds exist in a climate of opinion in which voting is considered a civic duty; they tend to be more exposed to ideas, active people, newspapers, political leaders. The college education itself may have an independent effect in exposing the graduates to political ideas and personalities.

3. Middle-aged people are more likely to vote than the younger and older. Many young people are busy getting established, moving about, having babies, raising young children. The new husband is occupied with getting ahead; the young wife is immersed in home affairs, or has a job of her own. They find little time for politics. The more established, between thirty-five and fifty-five, are more active; then voting falls off sharply in the sixties and seventies, owing partly to the infirmities of old age.

4. Men are more likely to vote than women. This variation—not very great in most elections—exists in many foreign countries as well. In recent presidential elections about 61 in every 100 women have voted, about 75 in every 100 men. Women feel less social pressure to vote than men. Morality issues such as birth control, however, generally bring out a high women's vote, and college-educated women tend to be more active in political party work than college-educated men. There are indications that the traditional difference in the rate of voting between men and women is decreasing.

5. Partisans are more likely to vote than independents. "By far the most important psychological factor affecting an individual's decision to vote is his identification with a political party."[6] When the election outcome is doubtful, strong partisanship is even more likely to induce a person to vote. A partisan is likely to have a personal interest and to be concerned about the outcome. If partisanship has this influence, however, the recent decline in party feeling and loyalty could bring a decline in voting turnout.

6. Persons who are active in organized groups are more likely to vote. This is especially true when the organized groups are themselves involved in community activity.[7] People in groups are more likely to be exposed to stimuli that engage them with civic and political problems.

Summing up, if you are a young woman with a low income and little

[5]Warren Miller, "The Political Behavior of the Electorate," *American Government Annual, 1960–1961* (Holt, Rinehart & Winston, 1960), p. 50.

[6]*Report of the President's Commission on Registration and Voting Participation* (U. S. Government Printing Office, 1963), pp. 9–10.

[7]Sidney Verba and Norman H. Nie, *Participation in America* (Harper & Row, 1972), pp. 197–200.

Choosing a presidential candidate at the Democratic convention in 1972. Robert Abrams reads the New York delegation's vote for the presidential nomination.

sense of partisanship, the chances that you will turn out even for an exciting presidential election are far less than if you are a wealthy man in your fifties, a strong partisan, and a member of a civic group. Thus nonvoting influences are cumulative. But there also appear to be psychological or attitudinal differences between nonvoters and voters. Even when sex, age, education, and income are controlled, the chronic nonvoter, more characteristically than the voter, is a person with a sense of inadequacy, more inclined to accept authority, more concerned with personal and short-range issues, less sympathetic toward democratic norms, and less tolerant of those who differ from himself.

EFFECT OF DIFFERENT TYPES OF ELECTIONS

Political institutions have their impact on nonvoting. So does the total political context. Note these tendencies:

1. National elections bring out more voters than state or local campaigns. Presidential elections attract the greatest number of voters. Off-year congressional elections almost invariably draw fewer persons to the polls. City and other local elections tend to attract an even smaller number.[8] And participation is lowest in party primaries. Even when voters are marking a ballot that offers a variety of national and local contests, some voters will check their presidential choice but not bother with others.

[8]On the variation of turnout in cities, and some reasons for it, see Robert R. Alford and Eugene C. Lee, "Voting Turnout in American Cities," *American Political Science Review* (September 1968), pp. 796–813.

2. Elections for chief executives attract more voters than elections for legislators. Turnout for representatives is considerably higher in years when a president is elected than in off-presidential years, as the chart below indicates. A somewhat similar difference exists at the state level between gubernatorial and legislative elections. The difference in executive and legislative turnout has major implications for governmental policy.

3. Voting is lowest in areas where there is little two-party competition. Thus, the lowest voting figures are likely to be found in states such as Mississippi, Alabama, and South Carolina. Recently there has been a marked upswing of voting in the South. The growth of two-party politics (under the impetus of Goldwater Republicanism) and greater participation by blacks are having their effect.[9]

How serious is the low rate of voting? Does it indicate that our democratic system is in danger? Should we encourage—perhaps even force—everyone to vote? No, answer some authorities. It is not a low rate of

[9]Philip E. Converse, Angus Campbell, Warren E. Miller, and Donald E. Stokes, "Stability and Change in 1960: A Reinstating Election," *American Political Science Review* (June 1961), pp. 269–80.

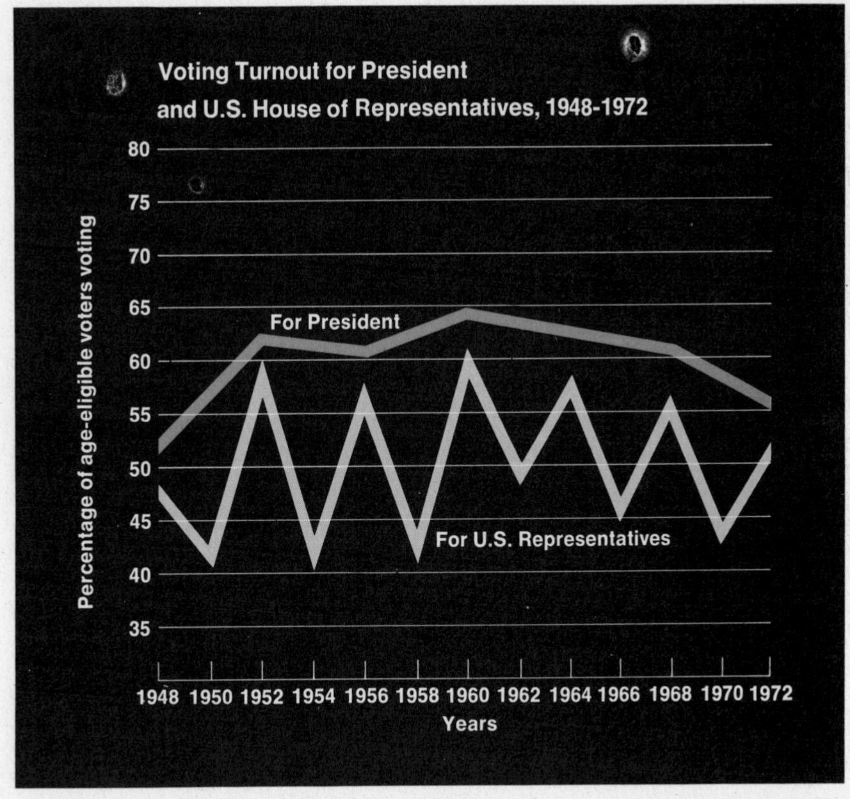

voting that signals danger to a democracy, they contend, but a high rate. They see a measure of nonvoting as a sign of some satisfaction with the state of affairs. Others strongly disagree. The decreased voting turnout in the presidential elections from 1964 through 1972, they say, hardly could indicate increased satisfaction with the American political situation. Rather it would suggest that people were disgusted, cynical, increasingly "turned off" and "tuned out" of the political system.

An acute dilemma for democrats emerges from the problem of voting turnout. On the one hand, nothing would be gained from forcing to the polls people who had little knowledge about, or interest in, an election. And sudden upsurges in voting triggered by a social crisis or the appeal of an authoritarian leader may be a danger sign, since large numbers of nonvoters hostile to democratic values would be mobilized. For there is much evidence that persons with low levels of political sophistication tend to take a simplified view of politics, fail to show tolerance toward people who disagree with them, and find it hard to grasp democratic norms. On the other hand, persons low in income and social status are precisely the ones who should be involved in voting and other political activity—both because they need to have more influence over government for their own welfare, and because a central idea of democracy is to include all citizens in its processes. How to integrate persons with low information and interest and limited democratic values into a system of self-government in a manner that will both advance their interests *and* strengthen the whole democratic system remains one of the major challenges to a government by the people.

One answer may be to increase voting gradually but systematically, especially in the low socioeconomic levels. How to do this? Moralistic preaching about the duties of citizenship fails to reach its chief target. Increased educational opportunity across the board may help, though the expansion of education during this century hardly seems to have brought increased voting. Much could be accomplished through *political* changes. Shorten the ballot by cutting down the number of unimportant elective positions: Simplify residence and registration requirements (permanent registration, or registration by postcard, are possibilities here). Make absentee voting easier. Declare election day a big holiday and dramatize the importance of voting. Above all, make the parties more competitive in state and local as well as national elections.

So much for the nonvoter. What about the people who *do* vote?

How we vote

Sometimes Americans are called fickle voters who blithely switch from party to party. Actually, the great majority of Americans stay with one party year after year, and their sons and grandsons vote for the same party long after that. Politically, these voters are "set in their ways."

Thus, both parties count on the support of an almost irreducible minimum of voters who will go Republican or Democratic almost by habit.

Of course, there are still millions of so-called independent voters. They help make our elections the unpredictable and breathless affairs that they so often are. Still, even in the variations from year to year one finds certain persistent elements. Looking closely at the complex mosaic of American politics, we can see patterns of voting habits that help us understand how we vote and a little about why we vote as we do.

1. A pattern of *sectional* voting. The South is the most famous example. The Democratic solidarity of the states that formed the Confederacy lasted over eighty years in presidential elections, and continues today in congressional elections. Republican sectionalism was not so clear-cut, but northern New England and parts of the Midwest have been dependable areas for the GOP. Thus Vermont has given its electoral votes to the Democrats only once since the Civil War (to Johnson in 1964); and Maine, only twice since 1912. More recently the South has become more Republican and the Northeast more Democratic.

2. A pattern of *national* voting. Even so, these traditional sectional alignments give way to national trends. One of the striking aspects of a great national swing is the way in which virtually all areas are part of that movement. The Franklin Roosevelt Administration, for example, ushered in a new age of Democratic party popularity that affected even the most traditionally Republican enclaves (Maine voted against Roosevelt all four times but the Democratic vote did increase in that state). States and sections are subject to a variety of local influences but they cannot resist the great political tides that sweep the nation. There has not been such a tide, however, in the four decades since FDR's reelection triumph of 1936. (In 1972 Nixon carried every state except Massachusetts and the District of Columbia, but other Republicans did not fare so well.)

3. A pattern of *similar* voting for *different* offices. Sectional and national forces affect voting for different candidates and offices in the same election. Well over half the voters usually vote a straight ticket—that is, they throw their support to every one of their party's candidates. If one candidate is an especially able vote-getter, the party's whole slate may gain. This is the famous "coattail" effect, whose precise nature is one of the challenging problems in the study of political behavior. Evidently popular presidential candidates like Roosevelt or an Eisenhower have long coattails that help elect many other candidates on their respective party tickets. But congressional and state candidates may have helpful coattails too, and it is not easy to tell which candidate rides on whose coattails or just how important the relation is.[10] This pattern

[10]For an example of some of the complex factors at work, see Barbara Hinckley, "Incumbency and the Presidential Vote in Senate Elections: Defining Parameters of Subpresidential Voting," *American Political Science Review* (September 1970), pp. 836–42. See also William B. Moreland, "Angels, Pinpoints, and Voters: The Pattern for a Coattail," *American Journal of Political Science* (February 1973), pp. 170–76.

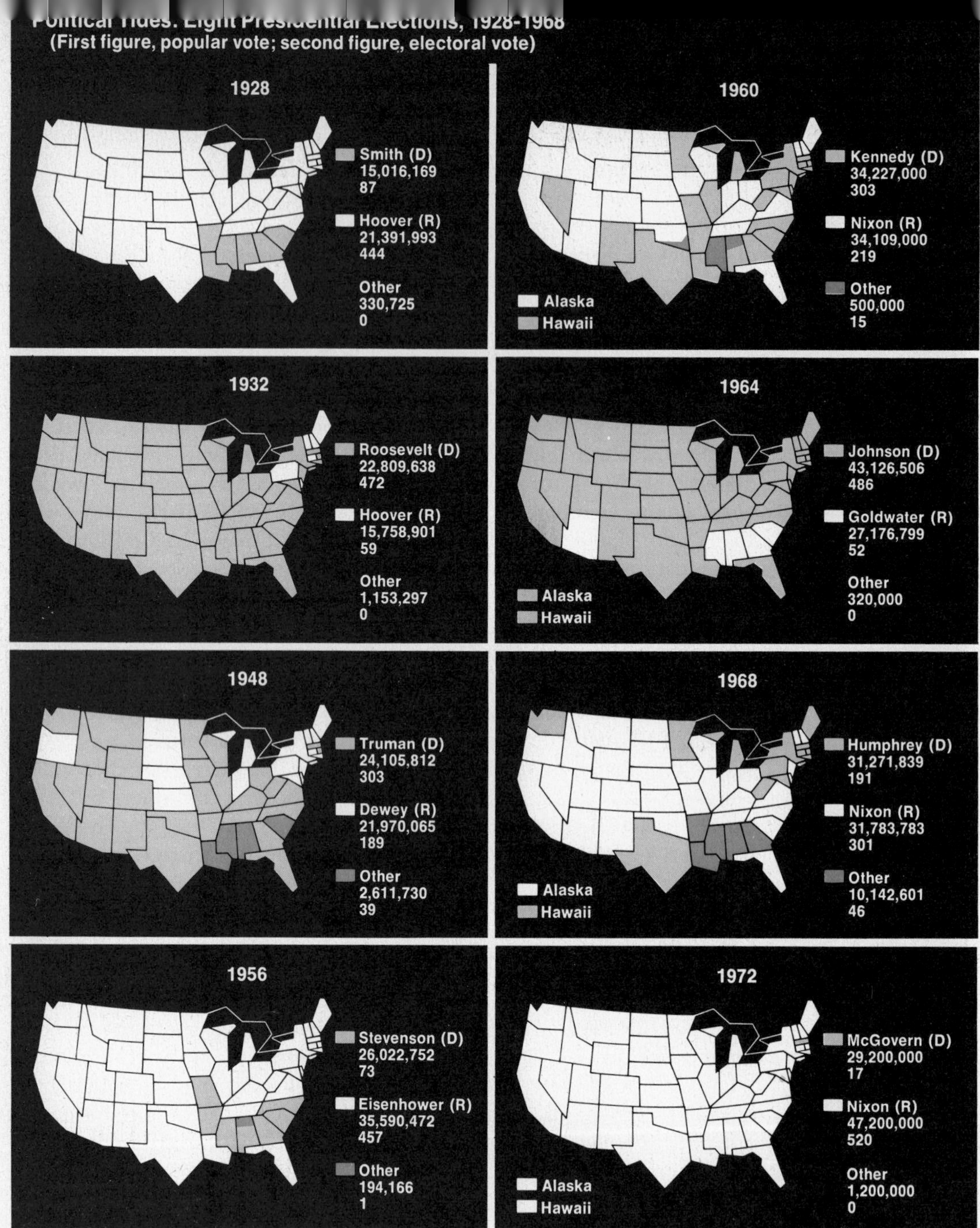

recently seems to have eroded, with a sharp increase in split-ticket voting. Thus Nixon won overwhelmingly for reelection in 1972, but Congress remained decisively in Democratic hands, and Republican candidates fared poorly in many states.

4. A pattern of voting over *time*. Great political tides seem to flow back and forth across the generations. Most presidential elections are *maintaining* elections—the pattern of partisan support of the preceding period persists. Long periods of maintaining elections are occasionally interrupted by *deviating* elections, which the "out" party wins because it has an especially attractive presidential candidate or because the existing administration has lost the nation's confidence. In these elections the underlying division of party support is not long disturbed. Wilson's victories in 1912 and 1916 are cases in point. Very occasionally, however, there occurs a *realigning* election that brings a basic and long-lasting transformation of party loyalties. A whole new balance of parties comes into being, as it did in the 1930s.[11] Some have predicted that we are on the eve of another series of realigning elections and a historic realignment of the parties. Others see mainly a pattern of confusion and dislocation today—a pattern that defies easy categorization such as deviation or realignment. We will return to this question in Chapter 11.

Why we vote as we do

What causes the political tides to rise and fall? Why do some voters stick with one party while others shift back and forth from election to election, while still others vote a split-party ticket in every election? A vast amount of effort has been devoted by political scientists in recent decades to answering such questions as these.

A traditional explanation for the great political tides has been economic. A drop in business activity has often preceded a loss of congressional seats and then a presidential defeat for the party in power. But we cannot be sure that business cycles *cause* political cycles. Sometimes the two cycles diverge in erratic fashion. Psychological, political, traditional, sectional, international, and other forces may muddle the effect of economic factors. It was not primarily economic issues but the sharply rising concern over slavery that precipitated the break-up of the Democratic-Whig party system in the 1850s. On the other hand, the Great Depression in the early 1930s doubtless was the main reason the GOP was toppled after its long period of supremacy.

So if there are patterns in American politics, these patterns are rough and are often blurred by capricious and unexplained variations. Indeed, the patterns may exist for years and then disappear. Thus before the 1948 election a change in party control of Congress in an off-year election had regularly preceded a change in party fortunes in the following presidential election. But the Democrats, who lost control of Congress in 1946, won both houses of Congress and—to the suprise of everyone and especially Thomas Dewey and perhaps even Harry Truman—won the presidency in 1948. And despite a 1954 congressional victory for the

[11]These three types of elections are defined and discussed in Angus Campbell, Philip E. Converse, Warren E. Miller, and Donald E. Stokes, *Elections and the Political Order* (John Wiley, 1966); see also Walter Dean Burnham, *Critical Elections and the Mainsprings of American Politics* (Norton, 1970).

Democrats, the GOP won the presidential election of 1956. So we have heard less of this "pattern" since then.

VOTING PATTERNS

Still, despite the murkiness of voting tendencies and the occasional "capriciousness" of American voters, analysis of massive amounts of voting data has uncovered some basic patterns.

1. Voting as members of *groups.* Most Americans vote the same way that their families or friends or workmates vote. On election day they mark their ballots or check off their voting machine levers in private but voting is essentially a group experience. The most homogeneous of all groups in moulding political opinions and ultimately the voting behavior of its members is doubtless the family. The reasons are twofold: members of the family shape one another's attitudes (often unintentionally); and members of the same family are naturally exposed to similar economic, religious, class, and geographical influences.[12]

As young adults move away from their families they may become members of many different groups. Some of their group memberships may mutually *reinforce* their voting decisions. Thus a young engineer who has grown up in a Democratically inclined family may marry a more conservatively inclined woman, associate on his job with Republican executives, socialize a good deal with fellow members of a country club, and join a taxpayer's organization. The engineer will probably become a Republican, though he will long feel a Democratic tug from his family years. Or group memberships may have conflicting impacts on a person's vote. Thus a woman factory worker may associate with Democrats in her local union but with Republicans in her social group or ethnic organization. Such persons are said to be "cross-pressured" and sometimes take the easiest way out by not voting at all!

Group influences on voting may change over time. The blue-collar worker, the black, and the urban ethnic tended to rally round FDR and the New Deal in the 1930s in part because they felt that the Republican party had failed them, in part because the New Deal Democrats recognized them and gave them concrete social and economic benefits. Business and professional men and women tended to be members of group interests opposed to New Deal "experimentation" and "waste." In the 1960s and 1970s newer issues—Vietnam, race, law and order, Watergate—cut across group alignments, created new group allegiances to Republican candidates, and caused severe splits within the Democratic party coalition.

2. Voting as members of *parties.* In this century most voters have

[12]See generally Richard E. Dawson and Kenneth Prewitt, *Political Socialization;* and for a specific example of an intrafamily relationship, M. Kent Jennings and Richard G. Niemi, "The Division of Political Labor Between Mothers and Fathers," *American Political Science Review* (March 1971), pp. 69–82.

identified with one or the other major parties. Many support their party almost automatically, simply looking for the "D" or the "R" next to a candidate's name, no matter who the candidate or what the issues. Party identification was relatively stable over the years; between 1952 and 1968 Democratic identification varied between a high of 51 percent and a low of 43 per cent, Republican between a high of 32 percent and a low of 23 percent.[13] This traditional allegiance is not necessarily blind or irrational. A person may vote for the same party over the years because he has thoughtfully concluded that that party serves his interests best.

Is party loyalty declining? A large number of voters, especially Democrats, ignored their long-time party identification in 1972. Democratic and Republican party self-identifiers (that is, persons who state that they are to some degree "Democrats" or "Republicans" when queried by pollsters) have dropped sharply in recent years – the Democrats to 36 percent by late 1973, the Republicans to 21 percent. Many voters identify with one of the major parties but vote for the opposition candidate, as millions of Democrats did in supporting Nixon in 1972. People usually do not openly and suddenly repudiate their party membership; rather they talk more about voting "for the person and not the party." Whether the drop in party identification is a short-run or long-run development remains to be seen.

3. Voting in terms of class, occupation, income, socioeconomic status. Most studies of voting behavior confirm what everyday observation has already indicated. The highest proportion of persons who prefer the Republican party are in the upper income brackets, especially with incomes over $15,000 a year. But we cannot make too much of this factor, indeed of any single factor. Eisenhower's great personal popularity seemed to blur differences in income, and the correlation between income and voting preference that developed out of the 1932 Depression tended to diminish. While the tendency of the lower socioeconomic groups to vote Democratic and of the higher to vote Republican reappeared somewhat in the 1960s, the relation of social class to party choice has declined over the whole span of post-World War II years. Older voters, with their memories of the Depression, tend to vote still on the basis of socioeconomic status, but younger voters are much less influenced by social and economic factors.[14]

4. Voting by *religion* and *race*. Analysis of the 1960s shows that "religion remained a potent source of political cleavage in the United States. . . . The detailed coding of the religious variable revealed that it

[13]Center for Political Studies, University of Michigan, 1974. See also Judson L. James, *American Political Parties in Transition* (Harper & Row, 1974), pp. 126–30; and William R. Shaffer, "Partisan Loyalty and the Perceptions of Party, Candidates, and Issues," *Western Political Quarterly* (September 1972), pp. 424–33.

[14]On economic and social factors in voting in general, in the United States and elsewhere, see Robert R. Alford, *Party and Society* (Rand McNally, 1963); on generational aspects see Paul R. Abramson, "Generational Change in American Electoral Behavior," *American Political Science Review* (March 1974), pp. 93–105.

10–1
The demography of the vote in recent presidential elections

Demographic characteristic	1948 Dem.	1948 Rep.	1956 Dem.	1956 Rep.	1960 Dem.	1960 Rep.
Religion						
Protestant	47†	53†	37	63	38	62
Catholic	66†	34†	51	49	78	22
Jewish			75	25	81	19
Race						
White	53†	47†	41	59	49	51
Black	81†	19†	61	39	68	32
Union labor families	74‡	26	57	43	65	35
Young voters (age 21-29 yrs.)	62‡	38	43	57	54	46
Sex						
Women	53†	47†	39	61	49	51
Men	56†	44†	45	55	52	48

†Figures accompanied by a dagger are taken from Angus Campbell et al., *The Voter Decides* (New York: Harper & Row Publishers, 1954), pp. 70–71. Data given there were converted from a percentage of the total sample to a percentage of those voting, ignoring the "Other" column. All other data are taken from releases of the American Institute of Public Opinion (the Gallup Poll), and from NBC and CBS samples as reported in *Congressional Quarterly Weekly Reports*, November 11, 1972, p. 2949.

‡Includes Democratic, Progressive, and States' Rights votes.

was the single most important of four predictors of political party identification, and was comparable to, if not more important than the *combined* effects of education, occupation, and income."[15] John Kennedy's campaign for the presidency tended to align Catholics even more with the Democrats, and Protestants with the GOP. The influence of religion declined in the next two elections, and there is some evidence that "religious cleavages in American politics continue on a downward trend from past polarization."[16] The most conspicuous effect of race in American politics is black support for Democratic candidates but this tendency too could change in the 1970s.

To identify the political preferences of sociological groups may give a misleading picture of voting behavior, for over time these distinctions alter; and they fail to take into account the impact of national and international developments and the personality factors of the individual voter and the way he responds to candidates. "Events, communications, and attitudes—may all be more or less independent of group memberships and social classifications," points out Warren Miller. They all make important contributions to the individual's political behavior. But their importance is inevitably minimized in group-oriented

[15]David Knoke, "Religion, Stratification and Politics: America in the 1960s," *American Journal of Political Science* (May 1974), p. 344.

[16]*Ibid.*, p. 344.

1964		1968			1972	
Dem.	Rep.	Dem.	Rep.	AIP*	Dem.	Rep.
55	45	35	49	16	30	70
75	25	59	33	8	48	52
90	10	83	17	—	61	39
59	41	38	47	15	32	68
94	6	85	12	3	87	13
—	—	—	—	—	46	54
64	36	47	38	15	48	52
62	38	45	43	12	38	62
60	40	41	43	16	37	63

*The American Independent party, headed by George Wallace.

descriptions of electoral behavior. To know someone's party affiliation does not tell us for sure how he will behave politically.

Is it a healthy sign that our political parties do not reflect too accurately basic social, economic, geographical, and religious differences? Or does this lead to a blurring of party lines, leading in turn to fuzzy programs and a failure of American government to deal with crises and problems? The fact that many Jews are Republicans, that some wealthy people are Democrats, that neither party can claim a monopoly of any group, keeps the parties from reinforcing and exaggerating differences. Lipset observes, "Where parties are cut off from gaining support among a major stratum, they lose a major reason for compromise."[17]

WHO ARE THE INDEPENDENTS?

Roughly a quarter to a third of the voters can be classified as independents—but "independent" is a tricky term. Some persons are called independent because they are "party-switchers"—they cross and recross party lines from election to election. Some are "ticket-splitters"—at the same election they vote for candidates of different parties.[18] Some

[17]S. M. Lipset, *Political Man* (Doubleday, 1960), p. 31.

[18]Walter De Vries and V. Lance Tarrance, *The Ticket-Splitter: A New Force in American Politics* (Erdmans, 1972).

"Me, I vote the man, not the party. Hoover, Landon, Dewey, Eisenhower, Nixon, Goldwater, Nixon . . ."

© 1956 Crowell Collier Publishing Company; reproduced by courtesy of Bill Mauldin.

are independents because they *feel* independent. Some call themselves independents because they think it is socially more respectable, but actually they vote with the same degree of regularity for one party as do others who are not so hesitant to admit party loyalty. A study indicates that younger voters with above-average incomes and college educations tend to be more independent than other groups but that the independent vote is rather evenly distributed throughout the population. And the number of independents, whether "switchers" or "splitters," has sharply increased in recent years, and this is a fact for any politician to reckon with.

Is the independent voter the more informed voter? There has been heated debate over this question, but much of it is fruitless because everything depends on what kind of independent we are talking about. If independents are defined as those who fail to express a preference between parties, the independent voter tends to be less well informed than the partisan voter, for such independents include chronic nonvoters, apathetic people, and the like. But if we mean those who switch parties between elections, we find some who are highly informed and who carefully pick and choose at the polls.

A much-discussed question is whether campaigning influences the votes of independents or even party regulars. From our discussion of voting behavior, we might conclude that all the speeches of vote-seekers and all the hullabaloo of their campaigns have little effect compared with the other forces at work. In part, this conclusion would be true. A campaign usually *converts* only a small fraction of the electorate. But it has other important effects. It *reinforces* the convictions of those already tending one way or another. And it *activates* people—that is, it arouses their interest, exposes them to particular candidates and ideas, shapes their attitudes, and stimulates them to vote on election day.

Still, events between elections and underlying attitudes, traditions, and pressures are far more important than the campaign. Does this situation discourage the vote-seeking politician? Not at all. He knows that he is dealing in margins, often in close margins. He knows that dozens of unknown intangibles will shape the final outcome. Massive political forces may be delicately balanced—perhaps a good push by his party and himself will tip them in the right direction.

Apathetics, participants, leaders

Students interviewing a cross-section of a population are often surprised to find people who seem to know nothing about the questions they are asked. The newspapers may be full of headlines and discussion about a Jackson or a Percy, but some citizens can place the names only vaguely in politics. "The first noteworthy fact about citizen participation in a democracy is that it is thin. Most citizens are little interested in

© 1961 United Feature Syndicate.

playing even a small policy-making role; fully a third of American citizens neither vote, join interest groups, do party work, communicate with their representatives, nor talk politics with their friends except occasionally in a vague and uninformed way.[19] The completely uninvolved are called isolates, apathetics, or even "chronic know-nothings."

On the other hand some citizens are influential enough to manipulate other people's political behavior. City bosses, student leaders, local newspaper editors, national columnists sometimes have this kind of power imputed to them. The classic statement of political influence is one attributed to Boss Plunkitt, a Tammany district leader, years ago:

> There's only one way to hold a district; you must study human nature and act accordin'. You can't study human nature in books. Books is a hindrance more than anything else. If you have been to college, so much the worse for you. You'll have to unlearn all you learned before you can get right down to human nature, and unlearnin' takes a lot of time. Some men can never forget what they learned at college. Such men may get to be district leaders by a fluke, but they never last.
>
> To learn real human nature you have to go among the people, see them and be seen. I know every man, woman, and child in the Fifteenth District, except them that's been born this summer—and I know some of them, too. I know what they like and what they don't like, what they are strong at and what they are weak in, and I reach them by approachin' at the right side.
>
> For instance, here's how I gather in the young men. I hear of a young feller that's proud of his voice, thinks that he can sing fine. I ask him to come around to Washington Hall and join our Glee Club. He comes and sings, and he's a follower of Plunkitt for life. Another young feller gains a reputation as a baseball player in a vacant lot. I bring him into our baseball club. That fixes him. . . . I don't trouble them with political arguments. I just study human nature and act accordin'. . . .
>
> As to the older voters, I reach them, too. No, I don't send campaign literature. That's rot. People can get all the political stuff they want to read—and a good deal more, too—in the papers. Who reads speeches, nowadays, anyhow? It's bad enough to listen to them.[20]

THE RANGE OF ACTIVITY

In between the highly influentials—the leaders—and the apathetics are the participants who follow politics, talk about issues, and vote. But even these three groupings are oversimplified. Actually we find a *range* or *spectrum* of political participation, as Table 10–2 suggests.

A range of activity (or inactivity) is also to be found among apathetics. Some literally never vote or talk politics. Others might vote occasionally and, if not talk politics, influence the talkers by their responsiveness or indifference. Apathy and participation also vary over time. A person may ignore one national election and become intensely in-

[19]Charles E. Lindblom, *The Policy-Making Process* (Prentice-Hall, 1968), p. 44.

[20]W. L. Riordon, *Plunkitt of Tammany Hall* (McClure, Phillips, 1905), pp. 33–34.

10–2
Approximate percentage of American citizens participating in various forms of political activity

Activity	Percentage
Holding public and party office	Less than 1
Being a candidate for office	
Soliciting political funds	
Attending a caucus or a strategy meeting	4–5
Becoming an active member of a political party	
Contributing time in a political campaign	
Attending a political meeting or rally	
Making a monetary contribution to a party or candidate	10
Contacting a public official or a political leader	13
Wearing a button or putting a sticker on the car	15
Attempting to talk another into voting a certain way	25–30
Initiating a political discussion	40–70
Voting	
Exposing oneself to political stimuli	

SOURCE: Charles E. Lindblom, *The Policy-Making Process* (Prentice-Hall, 1968), p. 45.

volved in the next; he may vote in fall elections but ignore the primaries that occur earlier in the year. And a person might be highly active in town or city elections and uninterested in state or national.

In general, to be sure, people active at one level of politics tend to be active at other levels. But we must be careful about generalizations concerning political apathy, such as "the poor don't take part in politics." This may be good polemics, but as analysts we must think in terms of specific elections, types of individuals, and political situations, as well as broad patterns.

WHY PEOPLE PARTICIPATE IN POLITICS

A vast amount of study has gone into the questions of how and why people get involved in politics. After an exhaustive study of the literature, Lester Milbrath identified a number of widely agreed-on generalizations about the nature and causes of political participation.[21] He sees participation as a function of the following factors:

1. *Political stimuli.* Citizens contacted personally are more likely to vote and show interest in the campaign. Persons lacking education and understanding about politics tend to shut out political stimuli. Middle-

[21]The generalizations about political participation in this section are mainly from Lester W. Milbrath, *Political Participation* (Rand McNally, 1965); see this book also for its extensive bibliography. Milbrath's findings have been generally confirmed, and the implications extensively examined, in Sidney Verba and Norman H. Nie, *Participation in America* (Harper & Row, 1972), pp. 31–32 ff.

class persons, men, and urban dwellers are exposed to more stimuli about politics than, respectively, working-class persons, women, and country dwellers. Children growing up in a politically involved home are more likely to maintain a high level of exposure to stimuli about politics when they become adults.

2. *Personal factors.* Those psychologically involved in politics are more likely to feel effective in political action. Persons of higher income and social status are more likely to become highly involved psychologically in politics than persons of lower status. "Perhaps the surest single predictor of political involvement," according to one study, "is number of years of formal education."[22]

3. *Political setting.* Persons contacted by party workers are more likely to participate in political activity. The relation works the other way too—persons who are more interested in politics are more likely to know party workers. Again, there is an *effectiveness* or *efficacy* factor—persons who see themselves or their group as having an impact on public policy are more likely to inform public officials of their views than are those who feel ineffective.

4. *Class status.* Persons at the higher socioeconomic levels tend to take advantage of the many different modes of political participation to a greater degree than those in the lower brackets. A major conclusion of a recent intensive study of participation is that "class" relates strongly to participation rates. "Indeed—and we think these data are quite surprising—social status has a closer relationship to political participation in the United States" than in eight other leading democracies. This is true of political participation in its many different forms; voting alone, according to this study, tends to be less class oriented.[23]

In general persons who feel nearer the center of society are more likely to participate in politics than those who feel near the periphery. Farmers are less likely to be involved in politics than businessmen. Union members are more likely to participate in some form than nonunion workers. Those who feel most insecure, vulnerable, and fearful of some kind of retaliation are the least likely to be politically involved or even to vote.[24]

Many of these generalizations are obvious or a matter of common sense. And they do not necessarily explain the deeper causes of interest or lack of interest in political activity. But these correlations and interrelationships do help us understand how to get to the deeper causes. Paralleling as they do our earlier generalizations about voting and nonvoting, they indicate the complex factors affecting participation and so help us to avoid glib stereotypes.

[22]Angus Campbell, "The Passive Citizen," *Acta Sociologica*, VI (1962), 20.

[23]Verba and Nie, *Participation in America*, pp. 339–40.

[24]Lester M. Salamon and Stephen Van Evera, "Fear, Apathy, and Discrimination: A Test of Three Explanations of Political Participation," *American Political Science Reveiw* (December 1973), pp. 1288–1306.

Noting the *range* of activity—from completely uninvolved persons to heavily "politicized" persons—helps also to deal with the central issue between elite-theorists and pluralists. Some elitists believe that American society is divided between an elite or a few elites, who dominate political activity, and the "masses," who are virtually detached from the political process. In fact, Americans are active in a multitude of ways and in many different degrees, as Table 10–2 suggests. A minority are completely apathetic or inactive, just as a minority are completely involved; in between is the great number of Americans who are involved in various ways, becoming more or less active as elections come and go, and depending on the particular election. It may be that not enough Americans are sufficiently interested, but this is quite a different argument from the claim that the great mass of Americans are simply impotent.

Conclusion: rational political man?

In summary, our review of the political behavior of the American voter suggests that:

1. Voting and nonvoting are complex processes influenced by historical, institutional, and psychological factors.
2. Higher-income, better educated, more middle-aged, and more partisan persons are more likely to vote than are their opposites.
3. Voting turnout tends to be higher for national elections than for state or local ones, for "executive" elections than for "legislative" ones, and for competitive elections than for less competitive ones.
4. Voting as a whole tends to follow roughly sectional, national, and interoffice patterns over time.
5. *How* Americans vote is heavily influenced by their party feeling, group memberships, and income.
6. A sizable minority of Americans are almost completely withdrawn from the political process, and another minority are intensely active politically and very influential. In between is the great mass of Americans who usually vote, often attend meetings or wear a party button or give money to a candidate or at least listen to political stimuli in the media and talk to their friends about politics.
7. People take part in politics—or fail to take part—for a variety of personal, political, and social factors; there is no single decisive factor that leads them to be active or inactive.

ARE VOTERS FOOLS?

A vitally important question emerges from these conclusions—a question that goes to the heart of the nature of political participation and also to the elitist-pluralist debate. Are voters fools? Or to put it more elegantly: Are the great mass of American voters like sheep, led hither and thither by propagandists and other manipulators? Are they so affected by a candidate's winning face or television style that they forget their "real" interests and vote for the most engaging personality? Are they so bored by politics or otherwise withdrawn from it that they leave the crucial decision-making to the few who *are* interested in politics—even just to the elites? Are they so "locked into" their family, school, party, group, and other "cells" of their social background that they cannot view parties, candidates, and issues realistically and self-protectively?

In posing this question of voting rationality, note the questions that are *not* at issue. All admit that a number of Americans—too large a number—*are* passive, withdrawn, ignorant, emotional, locked in, manipulated. The question is whether *most* Americans are, and to what degree, and whether this degree decisively affects the distribution of power in a government by the people. Second, we cannot settle the question of *ultimate* rationality—whether a whole nation, masses and elites alike, makes decisions that are right in the "long campaign of history." Nor should we evaluate the voting behavior of Americans in terms of some utopian model of angelic citizenry—or even a citizenry that agrees with us. For the great advantage of the democratic process is that it does not require for its successful operation a nation of selfless citizens. All we can ask, probably, is whether most Americans bring to politics a fair degree of knowledge of issues and candidates, an ability to make choices between alternatives at the polls, a "follow-up" capacity to learn whether the leadership they supported actually performed as they wished—in short, an ability overall, and in the long run, to figure out their own interests in relation to politics.

Many are skeptical about the capacity of men and women to cut through misty symbols and foggy rhetoric and perceive the reality of politics. The way in which voters react to symbols—dramatic acts, speeches, leadership styles, and the like—was stated by Edelman: "Mass publics respond to currently conspicuous political symbols; not to 'facts,' and not to moral codes embedded in the character or soul, but to the gestures and speeches that make up the drama of the state. . . . It is therefore political actions that chiefly shape men's political wants and 'knowledge,' not the other way around. . . ."[25]

Doubt about the capacity of Americans to govern themselves rationally was intensified as a result of voting studies conducted in the 1950s, a period of increasing sophistication and broadening activity in the field of voting and public opinion research. People seemed to know little about candidates, especially candidates for Congress. Less than half knew which party controlled Congress. Above all, voters were ill-informed on the issues. They did not know where the candidates stood, and often they did not know where they themselves stood because they were foggy about the nature of the issue, where the parties stood on the

[25]Murray Edelman, *The Symbolic Uses of Politics* (University of Illinois Press, 1967), p. 172.

issue, and the relation of the issue to themselves. When people bothered to vote at all, they were more influenced by candidate images or by their traditional party affiliation, as noted above, than by the positions that candidates or parties took on the issue. Truly the voters seemed "locked in" to their parties, groups, occupations, religion.[26]

THE INTELLIGENT STANDPATTER

More recent studies have modified this portrait of the American voter. About a decade ago V. O. Key, Jr., perhaps the leading political scientist of his day, began to go through a wealth of public opinion and voting data with these prime questions in mind. He did not pretend to come to definitive findings; indeed, he died before finishing the book. But Key did conclude that the picture of an ignorant, apathetic, manipulated, and locked in electorate had been greatly exaggerated. He looked especially at "standpatters"—those who clung to the same party year after year—and to "switchers"—those who changed parties. Both types of voters had been often viewed as irrational—the former because they stuck to the same old party or candidate no matter how much the interests of the standpatter or the nature of the party or candidate had changed, and the latter because they seemed to oscillate fecklessly and unthinkingly back and forth between parties and candidates.

Key found that standpatters often stood pat for a very good reason—they understood the policies of a particular party, felt that those policies favored their own interest, and stuck with their proven friends in office. Nor were most switchers irrational. They were people of more than average education, information, and interest. Election outcomes were also influenced by a third factor—the entrance or reentrance of millions of new voters into the political arena—but new voters too showed a capacity to deal with candidates in relation to issues that had meaning for them.[27]

The most recent research tends to support Key's view. Analysis of voting studies, mainly in the 1960s, indicated a significant shift in the voters' ability to comprehend issues and the stand of the major parties on these issues. Thus, voters seemed to be becoming increasingly aware that the Democratic party was more favorable, and the Republican less favorable, to federal government activism. Why the change? The answer did not seem to lie in educational or other social or economic developments, according to one study. The change was more likely to be caused by the coming of several presidential campaigns—especially 1964 and presumably 1972 as well—in which the candidates and parties seemed to offer a real and compelling choice to the voters.[28]

[26]See generally Angus Campbell et al., *The American Voter* (John Wiley, 1960).

[27]V. O. Key, Jr., *The Responsible Electorate* (Harvard University Press, 1966); see also Michael J. Shapiro, "Rational Political Man: A Synthesis of Economic and Social-Psychological Perspectives," *American Political Science Review* (December 1969), pp. 1106–19.

[28]Gerald M. Pomper, "From Confusion to Clarity: Issues and American Voters, 1956–1968," *American Political Science Review* (June 1972), pp. 415–28.

How lasting will this change be? Another study indicated that the importance of issues varies from election to election. Issues were highly related to voting decisions in 1968 because people were aroused about Vietnam, law and order, urban problems, Johnson's personality and his performance as president. The importance of issues also varied with the nature of the issues themselves. Some issues like inflation are close to the voters—they can "feel, see, and taste them"—and voters perceive the relation between the issues, the positions of candidates and parties, and what government finally does. On other issues that interrelation seems very hazy.[29] Finally, different types of political participation may stimulate different degrees of rationality. A person might be somewhat irrational in his voting but fairly intelligent and effective in—say—contacting his congressman about a personal need or helping some candidate in the campaign.[30]

Clearly, whether or not "voters are fools" is a question that cannot be answered by a simple Yes or No. Certainly the capacity of the great number of less-educated, less-informed persons to think analytically or conceptually is sharply limited. Their views are often not very consistent internally; for example, they may demand that taxes be lowered and at the same time that government spend more on housing, education, and health. Average people are not ideologues, not conceptualizers, not philosophers. But they have shown some capacity—and probably an increasing capacity in recent years—to calculate (1) how a specific government policy can hurt or help them; (2) where the two parties broadly stand on such government policies; (3) whether the main group or groups they belong to will benefit more from one party or the other; and to some degree (4) whether the nature of the times is good enough or bad enough so that the party or administration in power should be retained or voted out.[31]

Obviously our knowledge of these complex matters is still limited. Political scientists and other scholars stand on a research frontier. We must know much more than we do about the workings of the average voter's "political mind" and we must test our findings on a large scale. Even more important—for political scientists, at least—we must see how the voters' thinking is influenced by political phenomena and institutions, as presently constituted—by political parties, registration laws, the media, the nature of the opposition to the existing government, the issues facing the people.

[29]Richard W. Boyd, "Popular Control of Public Policy: A Normal Vote Analysis of the 1968 Election," *American Political Science Review* (June 1972), pp. 429–49. See also comments on the Pomper and Boyd articles by Richard A. Brody and Benjamin I. Page, and by John H. Kessel, and rejoinders by the two authors., *ibid.*, pp. 450–70.

[30]Verba and Nie, *Participation in America*, Chap. 7.

[31]See Campbell et al., *The American Voter, passim;* and Philip E. Converse, "The Nature of Belief Systems in Mass Publics," in David E. Apter, ed., *Ideology and Discontent* (Free Press, 1964), pp. 210–45.

Chapter 11 Parties in crisis

Our two big political parties are in trouble. They have suffered a drastic loss of popular support. Increasingly voters ignore party lines and "split their tickets." Parties evade the issues, critics charge; they renege on their promises; they are bankrupt of ideas; they follow public opinion rather than lead it. They fail to help the governors to govern; they fail to help the opposition oppose. Their organization is feeble in most states and localities; where it is strong, it consists of antiquated oligarchs. The two parties are dissolving, perhaps dying.

© 1972 by The New York Times Company. Reprinted by permission of Abner Dean.

These are not the charges of scaremongers. Most of them are advanced by sober political analysts. Consider the popular support of parties. The membership of the Republican party has dropped off sharply in the past decade; by 1974 the number of persons calling themselves Republicans had reached an all-time low of 25 percent.[1] But those deserting the GOP had not flocked into the Democratic party, for Democrats had lost ground too. The number of independents has almost doubled during the past decade. Or consider the state of party organization, machinery, and purpose. Several recent studies picture the parties as weak and disorganized. Some observers contend that the parties must

[1]Harris Survey, *Current Opinion*, 2, 1 (January 1974), 5; see also Walter Dean Burnham, *American Politics in the 1970s: Beyond Party?* (Cambridge, Mass., 1974).

"I can't believe I ate the whole thing."

Copyright © 1973 The Chicago Sun-Times; reproduced by courtesy of Wil-Jo Associates, Inc., and Bill Mauldin.

either be drastically reformed or they will disappear as major forces in American politics.[2]

Watergate dramatized the problem. The president is expected to be the leader of his party—both to guide it and be sustained by it. In 1972, however, President Nixon largely bypassed the Republican party and depended on his personal organization, the Committee for the Reelection of the President—the famous C.R.E.E.P. Many of the Watergate "horrors" grew out of the excesses of C.R.E.E.P.—its illegal actions, its secrecy, its financing, and its overweening personal loyalty to Mr. Nixon. Some Republicans pointed out, quite rightly, that recent Democratic presidents had often favored their personal organization over the needs of the Democratic party.

So our political parties are in crisis. Does it matter? What are the functions of parties? How well do they perform them? Are parties relevant to a "government by the people"? Why not let them die?

Parties: their rise and their role

Our two major parties are so big and ponderous that they remind us of the blind men and the elephant—each man felt a different part of the elephant and pictured the whole animal in a different way. By "parties" we do *not* mean two solid organizations confronting each other in a kind of continuous town meeting. We define party as (1) a structure of national, state, and local organizations; (2) inner circles of leaders holding or seeking public office; (3) networks of leaders—sometimes called "bosses"—who tend the organizational machinery around the clock, around the year; (4) party activists—usually called "party regulars"—who give money, time, and enthusiasm to the party's candidates; and (5) voters who identify with the party, almost always support its candidates, and break away from the party only as a result of major events, such as depression, an unpopular war, or a scandal like Watergate.

THE RISE OF THE "GRAND COALITIONS"

One way to see parties is to look at them historically, as a series of "grand coalitions" of groups and sectional leaders and interests that slowly shifted their allegiances over time. First was the Federalist grouping under Washington and Hamilton, a group dominated by the bankers, traders, big landowners, and small manufacturers of the day. This rather narrow coalition was challenged by the first Republican party, under the leadership of Jefferson and Madison, and later Jackson. Embracing small farmers, frontiersmen, laborers, debtors, slaveowners,

[2]John S. Saloma III and Frederick H. Sontag, *Parties: The Real Opportunity for Effective Citizen Politics* (Knopf, 1972), and David S. Broder, *The Party's Over* (Harper & Row, 1972) present the case for reformed and reorganized parties.

and with its base in the southern and central states, this coalition was ascendant in American politics for two generations.

Another party—the Whigs—rose to challenge the Republicans. But the Democratic party, exploiting its Jeffersonian symbols and holding on to its component groups, was able to overcome the Whig opposition in most elections. Neither party, however, was able to deal effectively with the explosive issue of slavery. Out of the Civil War came a new major party, the second Republican party. As the "party of the Union," the Republicans won the support not only of financiers, industrialists, and merchants, but also of large numbers of workers, farmers, and newly freed Negroes. For five decades after 1860, this Republican coalition was to win every presidential race for the Republicans, except for Cleveland's victories in 1884 and 1892. The Democratic party survived with its durable base in the South. For all their noisy battles during the century, both parties remained true to the rule that under a two-party system neither side can afford to be extremist. Both parties contained liberal and conservative elements and both appealed for support from all major interests, including business and labor.

These delegates to the National Black Political Convention form a present-day left-wing coalition.

Would the Republicans rule forever? The Democrats were unable to build a durable winning countercoalition against the "Grand Old Party" until the early 1930s, when the Hoover Administration had been overwhelmed by the Great Depression. Franklin Roosevelt not only strengthened the farm-labor-Southern alliance that Woodrow Wilson had begun to build; he put together a "grand coalition" of these groups plus Negroes, unemployed middle-class persons, national and racial minorities. This coalition reelected Roosevelt three times and brought presidential victories to the Democrats (except when Eisenhower ran) for two decades after Roosevelt died.

Then it was the Republicans' turn. Richard Nixon brought together a coalition of middle-class voters, "hardhat" workers, Southern conservatives, suburbanites, and business elements. Neither Hubert Humphrey in 1968 nor George McGovern in 1972 was able to organize a Democratic countercoalition big enough to overcome the Nixon organization, though the Democrats retained large majorities in Congress. In the wake of Watergate the Democrats hoped to capitalize on the GOP's troubles, but with their ranks eroded neither party had created a new grand coalition that showed promise of dominating American party politics for years to come.

NEW WINE IN OLD BOTTLES?

Both major parties are middle-aged—the Republicans have celebrated their centennial and the Democrats will soon mark their bicentennial (they contend that the Democratic party grew directly out of the first Republican party, which was born—they also claim—when Thomas Jefferson departed from the Washington Administration). The longevity of the two parties is remarkable, considering the depressions, wars, social changes, and political crises they have survived. But if the name and the symbols of the parties have stayed the same, what they represent has changed markedly. There have been extensive shifts in the policy positions of the major parties and in their social bases and electoral support.

Not only have the two big parties lasted for at least a century, they have dominated American party politics. The American pattern has been the absence of major third, fourth, or fifth parties. To be sure, third parties have had a role in our politics. They have drawn attention to controversial issues that the major parties either ignored or straddled. They have provided an electoral base to important leaders such as Eugene Debs, Robert La Follette, Norman Thomas, Henry Wallace, and George Wallace. They have organized special-interest groups, such as antislavery people, prohibitionists, vegetarians, left-wing trade unionists, New York State conservatives, Southerners opposing the national thrust toward integration. But they have never beaten both major parties at the polls, and hence they have never shaped national government policy from inside.

Why do we have a two-party system? Largely because of the nature of the *electoral* system. Most of our election districts have a single incumbent, and the candidate with the most votes wins. Because only one candidate can win, the largest and second-largest parties have a near-monopoly of office. In particular the system of electing the president operates in this fashion, on a national scale.[3] The presidency is the supreme prize in American politics; a party that cannot attain it, or show promise of attaining it, simply does not operate in the political big leagues. The ability of some third parties, such as the Farm Laborites, to last for two or three decades has been largely due to their hold on congressional and state offices in certain sections of the country.

Another pattern has been the *moderation* of party programs and policies. Successful party leaders must be group diplomats; they must find a middle ground among more or less hostile groups so that agreement can be reached on general principles. Moreover, each party, assuming that voters are distributed across an ideological spectrum from left to right, can take its extremist supporters more or less for granted and woo the voters in the middle of the spectrum.[4] This is one reason college students on the far left or far right are impatient with the major political parties. Both parties seem to such students to operate in the center—and in fact they do.

Parties have been part of the very fabric of our history. But have the parties helped *make* history? Some scholars have argued that our parties did not play the part in national development that many parties have in other countries, especially in the developing nations. The early parties did help mobilize support for Jeffersonian and Jacksonian measures, but they did not originate ideas and programs. They tended to *reflect*

[3]V. O. Key, Jr., *Politics, Parties, and Pressure Groups*, 5th ed. (Crowell, 1964), p. 274.

[4]See generally, Anthony Downs, *An Economic Theory of Democracy* (Harper & Row, 1957).

rather than *influence* political developments in the new nation; they expressed a politics of pragmatic adaptation to more basic currents of economic and social change. Innovation came mainly from outside the parties—from congressional and presidential leaders, rising business elites, intellectuals, western expansionists.

If that is true, then the grand coalitions that seemed to usher in new periods of party power appeared to be more influential historically than they really were. They gave the voters a sense of taking part in a great period of upheaval and reform, but they had little impact on people's lives. Some scholars disagree and contend that the parties served at least as gateways for new cadres of leaders to come into power.[5] We can judge this question better if we consider what parties actually do.

Party functions: the heavy burden

American political parties are expected to carry heavy burdens—so many that they might be excused for not carrying all of them very well. Historically, one of the key functions of our two-party system has been to unify the electorate and conciliate groups, sections, and ideologies by serving as "aggregators of national interest."[6] However, the parties failed to conciliate the sections in 1860 and broke up under the pressure of the North-South rupture. And such events as the Chicago Democratic convention in 1968 raised doubts as to the parties' ability to conciliate protest groups such as some blacks and some students.

The functions of the parties have also changed over time. Party activity used to be an important source of *public welfare*. Local party organizations, in their desire to win votes, gave the needy jobs, loans, free coal, picnics, and recreation, and they helped those in trouble over pensions, taxes, and licenses. The boss of the Republican machine in Philadelphia bragged that his organization was "one of the greatest welfare organizations in the United States . . . without red tape, without class, religion, or color distinction." The take-over of welfare by the government during the New Deal and later administrations drained this function away from most city organizations, but not entirely. In Kansas City, for example, Boss Pendergast got control of New Deal agency patronage and greatly increased his power.[7]

[5]See generally, W. N. Chambers, "Party Development and the American Mainstream," in W. N. Chambers and W. D. Burnham, eds., *The American Party System* (Oxford University Press, 1967); and Walter Dean Burnham, "The End of American Party Politics," in Bernard E. Brown and John C. Wahlke, eds., *The American Political System* (Dorsey Press, 1971), pp. 168–69.

[6]Charles G. Mayo and Beryl L. Crowe, eds., *American Political Parties: A Systemic Perspective* (Harper & Row, 1967), p. 487. See in this volume Leo D. Cagen's "Manifest Functions, Latent Functions, and the Democratic Policy" for an examination of some of the theoretical aspects of party function.

[7]Lyle W. Dorsett, *The Pendergast Machine* (Oxford University Press, 1968).

PARTY FUNCTIONS TODAY

1. To gain votes, parties simplify the people's choices. Usually they present the voters with two relatively different alternatives. Hence they allow voters to choose between a few options instead of a bewildering variety of them. But in many respects, some argue, parties confuse rather than simplify alternatives—again for vote-getting purposes.[8] On a popular issue the parties may try to appeal to such a wide electorate that no difference between them is very evident.

2. Parties help to stimulate interest in public affairs. An election contest is exciting. It makes politics look like a big prizefight, or world series, and draws millions of people into controversy. And after a polite interval following the election, the opposition party begins a drumfire of faultfinding against the party in power. But the opposition often fails to perform this role very effectively. It tends to break up into opposing factions that take potshots at the government from all directions, or to mute its criticism on the grounds that some issues—foreign policy, religion, education, and so on—should be "above" politics. It also mutes its criticism because too open partisanship is bad politics in that it offends voters.

3. Parties recruit political leadership and personnel. In the past they were important channels of upward mobility for integrating those "on the outside" into American public life. Irish-Americans and Italian-Americans are good examples. Whether or not the parties today can perform this role so well in recruiting blacks and Latinos into their cadres remains to be seen.

4. Parties, under most conditions, are key instruments for uniting persons of differing races, religions, and classes. Parties have a vested interest in playing down religious, racial, class, and other controversial issues. Despite the fact that most Americans are white Protestants, party leaders and candidates for public office seek to please Catholics, blacks, Jews, if only because they represent a large number of votes.

Of course parties at times are *divisive*, as when Democrats play up issues that divide the country, such as civil rights or social welfare, in order to win support. Just when parties should *unite* people and when they should *divide* people is a major tactical, strategic, and moral question facing party leaders.

5. Parties potentially serve as the link between the wishes of the mass public and what government finally does. They help organize the machinery of government and influence the men and women they have helped put into office. The president serves as party leader; Congress is organized on party lines; even bureaucrats are supposed to respond to new party leadership. Thus parties serve in some degree to bridge the separation of powers and prevent the constitutional checks and balances from unduly fragmenting government. But the parties have only limited success in this role.

[8]See Donald E. Stokes, "Spatial Models of Party Competition," in Angus Campbell, et al., *Elections and the Political Order* (John Wiley, 1966), especially on valence and position issues, pp. 170–71.

Of all these party functions, the average citizen probably feels that among the most important is confronting, posing, and clarifying issues. Many citizens have been skeptical of the ability of parties to state issues clearly and offer concrete alternatives. Scholarly studies of voting during the "bland" Eisenhower era have fortified this skepticism. Scholarship covering more recent times, however, has found a marked increase in the relation between party identification and opinion on a number of major issues such as social welfare and foreign aid.[9] "Contrary to what has been found in the past," one study concludes, "there is indeed considerable party-relatedness of vote based on specific issues."[10]

CHOOSING CANDIDATES

Certainly the function that takes most of a party's energy and interests is the recruiting and selecting of candidates for office. From the very beginning, parties have been the mechanism by which candidates for public office are selected. The earliest method was the *caucus.* A closed meeting of party leaders, it was the method used in Massachusetts only a few years after the *Mayflower* landed, and it played an important part in pre-Revolutionary politics. After the Union was established, party groups in the national and state legislatures served as the caucus for several decades. The legislators in each party simply met separately to nominate candidates. Our first presidential candidates were chosen by senators and representatives meeting as party delegates.

The legislative caucus soon fell into disrepute. Its meetings smacked of secret deals and logrolling; moreover, it could not be fairly representative of the people in areas where a party was in a minority, because only officeholders were members. Although there were efforts to make the caucus more representative, gradually during the 1830s and 1840s a system of *party conventions* took its place. The conventions were made up of delegates, usually chosen directly by party members in towns and cities, and served several purposes. They chose the party standardbearers. They debated and adopted a platform. And they provided a chance to whip up party spirit and perhaps to paint the town red. But the convention method in turn came in for grave criticism. It was charged—often quite rightly—that the convention was subject to control by the party bosses and their machines. At times, delegates were freely bought and sold, instructions from rank-and-file party members were ignored, and meetings got completely out of control.

To make party selections fairer and more democratic, the *direct primary*, first used by Wisconsin on a statewide basis in 1903, was adopted by state after state during the next fifteen years. This system gives every

[9]Gerald M. Pomper, "From Confusion to Clarity: Issues and American Voters, 1956–1968," *American Political Science Review* (June 1972), pp. 415–28.

[10]David E. RePass, "Issue Salience and Party Choice," *American Political Science Review* (June 1971), p. 400.

member of the party the right to vote on candidates in a primary election. The state usually supplies the ballots and supervises the primary election, which takes place some time before the general election in November. The direct primary was hailed by many Americans as a major cure for party corruption, but it did not cure all the existing evils, and it led to new ones.

Today the primary is the main method of picking party candidates, but the nominating convention is available in one form or another in a few of the states. The convention has also been retained nationally, of course, for picking presidential candidates. In either case, the party carries the main burden of activity, although many of its electoral activities are closely regulated by law. In the general election, too, the party has a role. It campaigns for its candidates, mobilizes its machinery in their behalf, helps finance them, and, on election day, produces cars, advice to the voters, and workers at the polls to watch the counting of the ballots.

The clanking party machinery

If you look at an organization chart of the Democratic or Republican parties, everything seems neat and tidy and organized. At the top is the presidential convention, which meets every four years and sets policy for the party. Below it is the national committee, and then the pyramid widens out to state committees on top of hundreds of county and city committees on top of thousands of ward, town, and precinct committees. But the organization chart is deceptive. In fact the national organizations have little power over the state and local ones; power flows up rather than down. Our parties are essentially loose coalitions of state and local committees, with little national machinery, cohesion, or discipline.

Why are our parties so decentralized? The main reason is the *federal* basis of our government. The Constitution has shaped our political system, just as the political system shaped governmental structure. Parties are a prime example of this circular relation. They tend to be structured around elections and officeholders, and because our federal system sets up elections and offices on a national-state-local basis, our parties are organized on a similar basis. Thus, the Constitution has given us federalism in our *parties* as well as in our government.

WEAKNESS AT THE TOP

In both major parties the supreme authority is the *national presidential convention.* The convention meets every four years to nominate the party's candidates for president and vice-president, to ratify the party's national platform, and to elect officers and adopt rules. But the convention in fact has limited power: the delegates have only three or four days

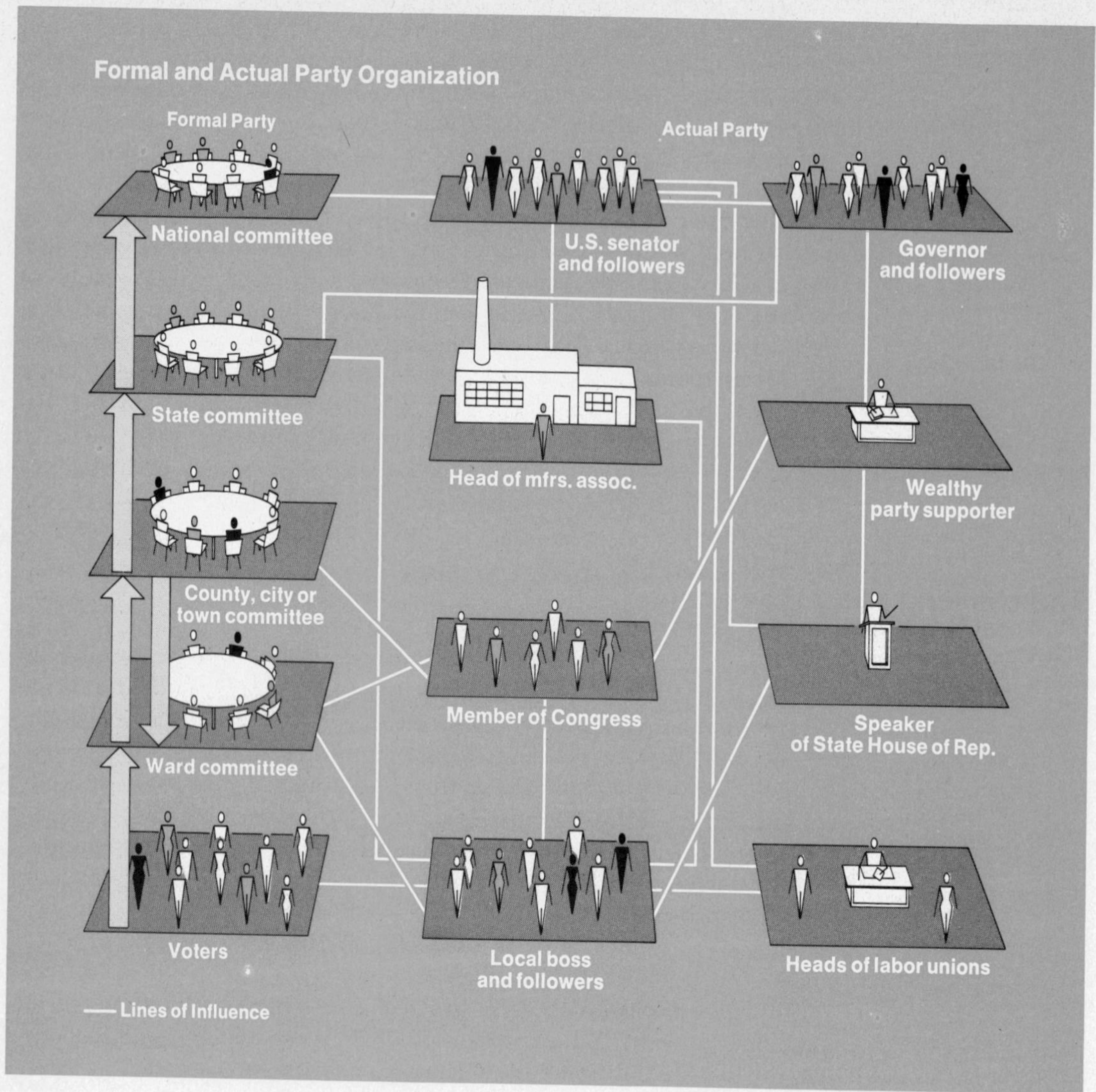

to accomplish their business; many key decisions have been made ahead of time; and the convention is usually dominated by office holders and office-seekers rather than by the mass of rank-and-file delegates.

More directly in charge of the national party—at least on paper—is the *national committee*. In the past, the national committee was "impotent and invisible." The committees gave large states only a little more representation than small ones; committee members were usually influential in their states but had little national standing, and the committees rarely met. However, the Republicans recently made their national committee more representative; and the Democrats, largely as a result of the reform impetus of 1968, enlarged their national committee to render it more responsive to areas in the country that tended to be more populous and more Democratic. More representative committees, however, will not necessarily bring stronger leadership.

The main job of the *national party chairperson* is to manage the presidential campaign. Although in form he or she is elected by the national committee, actually he or she is chosen by the party's presidential candidate at the close of the quadrennial convention. It is through the chairperson that the presidential candidate—and perhaps later the president—dominates the party nationally. By the same token, a defeated presidential candidate may have little control over the national chairperson, or the national committeepersons may elect a new head who responds to the balance of forces within the committee. Usually the national chairperson serves at the pleasure of the president. The basic tasks have been well summarized as image-maker, fund-raiser, campaign manager, administrator, and hell-raiser.[11]

It is the national chairperson, backed by the president, who gives the party a measure of unity and direction when the party is in power. When the party loses a presidential race, it often has no real central leadership. The defeated nominee is the titular leader, but he usually has little power over the organization, in good part, of course, because he has no jobs or other rewards to hand out. As a result, the party out of power nationally may come under the control of congressional leaders.

The *congressional* and *senatorial campaign committees* aid congressmen in their campaigns for reelection. Today, both the Republican and Democratic Senatorial Campaign Committees are composed of senators chosen for two-year terms by their respective party members in the Senate. After candidates have been nominated, the committees send them money, provide speakers, supply campaign material. During *presidential* election years, the activities of the national committee tend to overshadow the work of the congressional and senatorial campaign committees. But during *off-year* elections, these committees often provide the only campaign that is nationally directed.

Both a cause and a result of party disorganization is the manner in which candidates are nominated. Ordinarily, politicians seeking the party nomination run on their own, while the party remains, outwardly at least, neutral toward the aspirants. Lacking organized party support, each candidate builds a *personal* organization; thus, because scores of candidates are usually running for a dozen or more offices, from governor to local jobs, the party becomes a confused arena. Candidates campaign on their own, raising their own money and putting out their own publicity. In the hurly-burly of the primary campaigns there often develop sharp rivalries between Democrats or between Republicans—rivalries that may carry over into the general election, even though the

[11]Cornelius P. Cotter and Bernard C. Hennessy, *Politics Without Power: The National Party Committees* (Atherton Press, 1964), p. 67.

party should be unified in order to put up a strong fight. Such individualistic politics is not always the case; indeed, contests within the primaries are not always the rule.[12] When a heated primary contest does take place, it may seem democratic. But it can also be damaging to party unity.

PARTIES AT THE GRASS ROOTS

Governor George Wallace and former Governor Ronald Reagan are examples of strong local leaders with influence on mainstream American politics.

At the next lower level in the party hierarchy are the state committees, which in general resemble the national committees but are manned by committeemen chosen locally in counties or other areas. Most state committees are not powerful; they are often dominated by the governor, a United States senator, or a coalition of strong local leaders, just as the president dominates his party's national committee. The state chairman is sometimes chosen by the governor or senator; occasionally, however, he is really the party's boss on the state level and is able to heavily influence the nomination of governors, senators, and other key officials. Many state parties are as undisciplined and decentralized as the national party.

Below the state committees, each party hierarchy broadens out into countless district and county committees. These, too, vary tremendously in their functions and power. Some county chairmen (they are almost all men) are often powerful bosses such as Mayor Daley has been in Cook County; and many county chairmen make up the party slates for a host of offices such as county commissioner, sheriff, treasurer. Some county chairmen, however, are mere figureheads.

It is at the base of the party pyramid—at the city, town, ward, and precinct level—that we find the grass roots of the party in all its richness and profusion and variety. In a few localities, party politics is a round-the-clock, round-the-year occupation. The party's sergeants and corporals—the local ward and precinct leaders—do countless favors for their constituents, from fixing parking tickets to organizing clambakes. But such strong local party organization is exceptional. Most local party committees are small, poorly financed, and inactive except during the few hectic weeks before election day. Party activities are not professional but amateurish.[13]

Our party systems are highly complex. For example, a state party or-

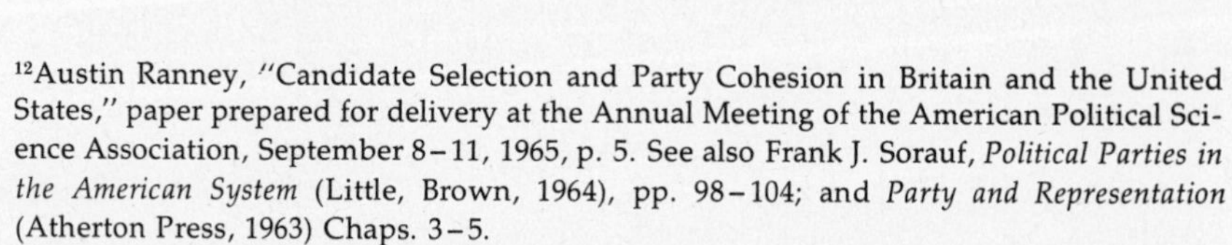

[12]Austin Ranney, "Candidate Selection and Party Cohesion in Britain and the United States," paper prepared for delivery at the Annual Meeting of the American Political Science Association, September 8–11, 1965, p. 5. See also Frank J. Sorauf, *Political Parties in the American System* (Little, Brown, 1964), pp. 98–104; and *Party and Representation* (Atherton Press, 1963) Chaps. 3–5.

[13]Local party effort is hard to measure, but it probably has significant influence; see Phillips Cutright, "Measuring the Impact of Local Party Activity on the General Election Vote," *Public Opinion Quarterly* (Fall 1963), pp. 372–86; Raymond E. Wolfinger, "The Influence of Precinct Work on Voting Behavior," *ibid.*, pp. 387–98; William J. Crotty, "Party Effort and Its Impact on the Vote," *American Political Science Review* (June 1971), pp. 439–50.

ganization may embrace a state committee, congressional district committees, county committees, state senatorial district committees, state judicial district committees, and precinct committees. Why such complexity? Partly because party politics tends to be highly individualistic and personalized (it would be more nearly correct to say that we have *candidate* or *officeholder* politics rather than party politics); partly because our constitutional arrangements provide for a multiplicity of officeholders at a number of levels of government; and partly because the diversity of our country and the absence of strong direction and control by the national party headquarters mean that party systems vary a good deal from state to state.

This situation inevitably opens a gulf between national party headquarters and state and local parties. Deepening this gulf is the fact that elections—which constitute the main activity of parties—are actually regulated and run by the states, not by the national government. Moreover, some states hold their state and local elections in different years from national elections (mostly in an effort to insulate state politics from national). New York State, for example, elects its governors for four-year terms in even-numbered years between presidential elections, and New York City elects its mayors every four years in *odd*-numbered years.

LEADERS AND FOLLOWERS

The party is made up of a variety of people ranging from committed activists to nominal party members. The leadership of a party, like that of any group, almost always comprises the full-time officials, a core of activists, and a larger number of fairly active members. The most important party leaders are usually the president, senators, governors, the elected state and local party chairmen, and other party officials.

Just as the Republican rank-and-file differs from Democratic members in socioeconomic background, so do the leaders of the two parties differ from one another. A study of the occupational backgrounds of candidates for nomination for county office in three Indiana counties, for example, showed that a quarter of the Republican candidates had professional backgrounds and half had managerial, while over 12 percent had been manual workers; of the Democrats, on the other hand, over 40 percent had been manual workers, and only one-fourth managerial.[14] Such contrasts, although suggestive, are not striking; it may be much more significant that most leaders in both parties come from middle-class, white-collar backgrounds.

What about leadership in the minority or opposition party? This party has very special duties: to probe, to criticize, to present alternative

[14]Frank Munger, "Two-Party Politics in the State of Indiana" (unpublished master's thesis, Harvard University, 1955), p. 275, cited in S. M. Lipset, *Political Man* (Doubleday, 1959), p. 289. See also M. Margaret Conway and Frank B. Feigert, "Motivation, Incentive Systems, and the Political Party Organization," *American Political Science Review* (December 1968), p. 1161.

approaches, and to act on those alternatives if elected. But the opposition party is not well organized to perform these functions. At the national level it has no authorized leader—except after it has named a presidential nominee. Its leadership is usually dispersed among congressional leaders, governors, former presidents, future hopefuls. During Eisenhower's administration, the Democrats established an advisory council composed of eminent Democrats such as Truman and Stevenson, and this council did a good job of proposing alternative policies to those of the Republican administration. But Democratic congressional leaders ignored the council, and it was dropped when President Kennedy took office (though he adopted many of its ideas). An all-Republican conference was established in 1962 and 1964, but Republican congressional leaders viewed it with suspicion.

Are the parties worth saving?

Clearly there is a big gap between what American parties *might* do and what they *actually* do. Ideally, parties build a bridge between the great mass of people and their government. They shore up national unity by bringing conflicting groups into harmony. They soften the impact of extremists at both ends of the political spectrum. They stimulate and channel public discussion. They find candidates for the voters and voters for the candidates. They help run elections. In short, parties shoulder much of the hard, day-to-day work of democracy. But parties do not perform these tasks very effectively, and hence they are under attack from persons who believe that parties should be the great mainspring of popular government.

The main charges against the American party system are twofold: they do not take meaningful and contrasting positions on issues, especially the rising issues of the 1970s; organizationally they are in such disarray that they could not achieve their goals even if they wanted to; hence parties are not vehicles for popular expression and social progress. How valid are these charges?

TWEEDLEDUM AND TWEEDLEDEE?

The typical party platform, it is alleged, seems designed to pick up every stray vote rather than speak out in a convincing manner on the vital questions of the day. Pity the poor voter! Platforms are so vague, and candidates' statements so ambiguous, that he has no basis on which to choose. According to an old saying, party platforms are like train platforms—something to get in on, not to stand on.

This charge may once have been valid, but recent scholarship indicates that it overstates the problem. By the 1960s, at least, many voters *saw* their own party or the opposition party as standing for something. "People tend to have a broad image of parties," Key reported. "They see a party as generally dedicated to the interests of a particular set of groups within society, or as committed to a broad range of policy objectives."[15] Their ideas of party position may be rather crude but they seem to make sense. Thus most businessmen and professional people see the Republican party as the party that best serves their interests, whereas workers tend to look on the Democrats as the party most helpful to them. When polled, workers often offer such comments as: "The Democratic party is for the working people"; "Poor people have a better chance with the Democrats"; or as one respondent put it, "Yes, they don't be no depressions, when them Democrats is in. They just lets that money roll on and that's what I likes!"

Many people, moreover, see important differences between the two parties. The Survey Research Center found that about 40 percent of their national sample responded affirmatively to the question: "Do you think there are any important differences between what the Democratic and Republican parties stand for." Another 10 percent indicated that there are differences but none of great moment. It is very likely that this proportion seeing important differences increased sharply from 1964 to 1972, when parties seemed to become more polarized. Of course there may be some *mis*perception involved. People who are strong Democrats or Republicans tend to look at events through the eyes of their party. This tendency is called *perceptual* distortion: the more partisan a person is, the more he may selectively perceive and distort his party's position.[16]

One scholar took the trouble to study recent party platforms to determine how similar they were. "Democrats and Republicans are not 'Tweedledee' and 'Tweedledum,' " Pomper concluded.[17] The difference between the two parties is not sharp but it is significant. Parties do share a consensus on many matters but their platforms are hardly identical. Although senators and representatives often vote with the opposition, party lines do generally hold in Congress on votes relating to platform pledges.

PARTIES IN DISARRAY?

The general indictment here is that our national parties are badly led at the top, weakly structured in the middle, and disorganized at the foundations. Some critics of our major parties believe that the root of all this trouble lies at the base of the parties—in the absence of big, solid, rank-and-file memberships. They note that anyone eighteen or over can "join" a party simply by registering as a party member or (in some states) by simply attending a party primary and asking for the ballot

[15] V. O. Key, Jr., *Public Opinion and American Democracy* (Knopf, 1961), p. 433.

[16] Angus Campbell *et al.*, *The American Voter* (John Wiley, 1960), p. 133.

[17] Gerald M. Pomper, *Elections in America* (Dodd, Mead, 1968), p. 200.

of a particular party (which automatically registers him in that party). Critics point out that these party "members" assume no obligations, pay no dues, do no work for the party, rarely take part in party discussions or activities. They become party members "on the cheap." Such persons are usually more active in their favorite social club than in the organization—the Democratic or Republican party—that assumes responsibility for governing the nation, the states, and most of the big cities.

Some local party organizations do have active memberships. The motive for joining and participating in parties varies widely. Some active workers are in the party mainly for personal and material incentives—jobs, favors, access to government officials. Others belong mainly for social reasons—the local party committee or club gives them a chance to meet other people. Quite differently motivated are those who in effect use the party to advance public policies or candidates that they support. The former types are the "professionals" or "regulars"; they stick with their party through thick and thin, support all its candidates, and keep the organization going between elections. The latter are the "volunteers," or "amateurs," who see party activity not as just an end in itself, nor as a means of personal advancement, but as a *means* to a greater good, such as governmental policies or social programs.

Tension and hostility sometimes develop between the two types of party members. The party "pros" often come from low-income backgrounds; the amateurs may be better educated and more ideological. Over a period of time, however, amateurs may gradually assume the political style and motive patterns of the professionals, with the result that the party becomes less concerned with ideology and programs.[18] Some fear that the "defection" of the amateurs to the professional style may make the party less vigorous as an agency of the "masses," but this view assumes that the well-educated, issue-oriented amateur is more representative of the general population than the "bread-and-butter-oriented" professional.

Others fear that if both parties are taken over by amateurs the resulting intense social conflict would greatly imperil the democratic system. Certainly the involvement of amateurs has had in the past consequences unintended by the amateurs. In 1964, for example, Goldwater Republicans were so convinced of the rightness of their cause, so anx-

[18]James Q. Wilson, *The Amateur Democrat* (University of Chicago Press, 1962), p. 5.

"I understand the new politics now—they're in an' we're out."

Dennis Sullivan et al., *The Politics of Representation*, St. Martin's Press, Inc.

ious to provide the country with "a choice, not an echo," that they antagonized more moderate Republicans.[19] In 1972 McGovern Democrats, embracing thousands of persons embittered by the Vietnam War and furious in general with the "Establishment," alienated large numbers of professionals, including leaders of labor and ethnic groups. In both cases the opposition candidate—Johnson in 1964 and Nixon in 1972—won in a landslide.

All this reminds us that there are different kinds of party membership. The professional and the amateur each offers certain strengths and handicaps to the party. The party base will have fissures in it as long as the party appeals—as a major party must—to a great range of persons with widely different motivations. But different kinds of membership may also provide the parties with greater resilience and durability.

PARTIES VERSUS PROGRESS?

American parties, some charge, are not vehicles for social reform. The fact that both major parties must be such big, widely inclusive, and moderate organizations means that neither one can act boldly and singlemindedly on behalf of the great mass of lower-class, low-income, and politically vulnerable persons. Hence the parties siphon off social and political energies that might be better used for other strategies of change. Much, of course, depends on the nature of the times. "Over the course of American history," Ladd says, "this party passiveness before social change has probably had a salutary effect, contributing to the capacity of the parties to perform a 'peacemaking' or 'reconciling' function. But in a period of exceptionally rapid and extensive change—and none has been more pronounced in this regard than our own—it also has the adverse effect of heightening the sense of unresponsiveness in the political system."[20] Since rapid social change seems continuous these days, it can be argued that parties were useful only in past times and are now outdated and should be scrapped.

The central argument of those who espouse this view is that weak parties that cannot vigorously advance the welfare of the mass of people simply end up strengthening the status quo. The rich and well-placed have plenty of political weapons of their own such as lobbyists, money, and influence over the media to advance their interests; the

[19]David Nexon, "Asymmetry in the Political System: Occasional Activists in the Republican and Democratic Parties, 1956–1964," *American Political Science Review* (September 1971), pp. 716–30, found that Republican activists were substantially more conservative than rank-and-file Republicans. Doubtless a similar study of Democratic activists from 1968 to 1972 would show that they were to the left of the rank-and-file Democrats. See Arthur H. Miller, Warren E. Miller, Alden S. Raine, Thad A. Brown, "A Majority Party in Disarray: Policy Polarization in the 1972 Election" (Center for Political Studies, University of Michigan, 1974).

[20]Everett Carll Ladd, Jr., *American Political Parties: Social Change and Political Response* (Norton, 1970), pp. 307–8.

political party is peculiarly the vehicle of collective popular action. It is the "people's lobby." If the party is insipid in its doctrine, ineffective both when in power and when in opposition, and disorganized from top to bottom, it blights the people's hopes instead of realizing them. Others contend that parties are more effective than the critics admit; that voters can always turn to popular candidates—men like Franklin or Theodore Roosevelt, John Kennedy, Dwight Eisenhower—if parties fail them; and that pluralistic, decentralized parties are appropriate for a pluralistic, individualistic people. Why, they ask, try to "Europeanize" or "Anglicize" parties that have their roots in the American tradition and cannot and need not change?

The argument has not been left there. Parties, no matter how flabby or sluggish, are nevertheless growing and living institutions. Party reform is in the air, if only because the Democrats suffered stunning defeats in 1968 and 1972 and the Republicans are reassessing their party in the wake of Watergate and their 1974 defeat.

Can the parties be saved?

To some, the Democratic party in 1968 seemed to be falling apart. President Johnson, stalemated militarily and politically by Vietnam, had announced he would quit at the end of his first full term. Robert F. Kennedy had been shot down in a Los Angeles hotel. Eugene McCarthy and his followers had polarized the party, while the Republicans, in contrast, seemed united behind the candidacy of Richard Nixon.

Passions exploded when the Democrats met for their party convention in Chicago. Out of this same convention, however, came a strong impetus to reform. A group of delegates led by Senator McCarthy and others won passage by a bare majority of a resolution to make the election of delegates to the 1972 convention a more open process. In the following years a series of Democratic party commissions proposed basic changes for the party. These proposals were of four basic types:[21]

First, *procedural reforms*. It was found that state and local parties occasionally ignored the requirements of fair play. Hence state parties were instructed to forbid proxy voting; to ban the use of the unit rule (under which the vote of a whole delegation was cast as the majority voted, no matter how strongly the minority differed); to insure that party meetings were held with proper advance notice, in public places, and at set times; to require proper quorums, amid other reforms.

[21]These proposals are drawn mainly from the report of the McGovern Commission: *Mandate for Reform: A Report of the Commission on Party Structure and Delegate Selection to the Democratic National Committee* (Commission on Party Structure and Delegate Selection, Democratic National Committee, 1970).

Second, *broadening participation.* Here the commissions proposed two basic changes. One was uncontroversial—ensuring that party rules specified no discrimination on the basis of race, color, creed, sex, or national origin. Another was a bit controversial (since some adults had become fearful of "youth power")—allowing and encouraging all persons eighteen years or older to take part in all party affairs. Another was *very* controversial—taking specific steps to encourage representation in party affairs (and especially nomination decisions) of young people, women, and minority groups "in reasonable relationship to their presence in the state's population." The quoted words were seen by critics as requiring *quotas* imposed from above, and the critics flatly opposed such a requirement.

Third, *alter delegate selection process.* These proposals will be discussed in the next chapter.

Fourth, *party modernization.* The emphasis here was on turning the Democratic party into a more activist, policy-oriented organization. This feeling came to a head in a movement to call a "charter conference"—virtually a constitutional convention—of the Democratic party to reorganize the party structure and to consider a proposal to set up *national policy conferences* midway between presidential conventions. Such conferences would bring the party platform up to date, select new party officers if necessary, modernize the party rules, and in general do everything presidential conventions do except nominate candidates. It was hoped that such conferences could be a "shot in the arm" for Democrats, many of whom felt frustrated and helpless during the long period between presidential conventions.

These proposals were hotly opposed by more centrist Democrats, especially after McGovern, who had led and symbolized the reform drive, was badly beaten at the polls in 1972. The centrists argued that party democracy could not be created by administrative fiat nor by imposing restrictions on the power of the rank and file to choose whom they wished. While they favored broadening the party, they feared that too much effort would be made to bring young people and women into the party councils but not working-class people, labor unionists, elderly people, and others. They opposed the curb on the role of officeholders in the party because they believed that the officeholders, having been selected in fair and open elections, were more representative of the rank-and-file than many of those who urged a more "participatory" party. Indeed, the emphasis on a "participatory" rank-and-file party, they declared, was really "elitist" and undemocratic, because those who would attend open, grass-roots caucuses were the more educated and affluent persons who had time to attend such meetings and the stamina and interest to debate all night, while the working man and the poor person lacked the leisure, energy, and self-confidence to express their interests at meetings or even to attend them. Above all, the critics opposed the quota system—"democracy by demography"—as

Evidence of the efforts of an extreme right-wing faction, the John Birch Society, to impeach former Supreme Court Justice Earl Warren.

arbitrary, elitist, and basically unrepresentative.[22] So vigorous was the opposition to the quota system that its revival seemed unlikely.

These opposing ideas came into direct confrontation in December 1974 in Kansas City at an unprecedented meeting—a Democratic party "charter conference" to draw up a constitution for the party. The two thousand delegates approved an "affirmative action" program that excluded quotas but was designed to encourage participation by women, blacks, young people, and others in party processes. The Democrats also adopted provisions to make party organs more representative of the rank-and-file. But the delegates, by a fairly close vote, refused to mandate future biennial policy conferences; these could be called by the Democratic National Committee if it was so minded. Proponents of such conferences feared that it might not be so minded. The charter convention, in short, reformed the party at the top; the job of strengthening the party as a structure and at the grass roots remained to be done.

All these reforms relate to the Democratic party; what about changes in the Republican party? A reform movement developed in the GOP following Goldwater's rout in 1964—defeat is a great stimulus to fresh thought—but the impetus slackened when Richard Nixon took office. Some Republicans contended that the GOP did not require as much change as the Democratic party because, as one Republican professional put it, "Many of the things the Democrats are now trying to reform the Republicans took care of one hundred years ago."[23] He noted that the Republicans had abolished the unit rule many years ago and today adopt new rules well in advance so that everyone is familiar with them. Watergate, which underlined the failure of the Republican party to prevent campaign excesses by C.R.E.E.P., seemed likely to trigger a movement for Republican party reform. Some Republicans contended, indeed, that the GOP might be an exciting place for young persons during the 1970s because of the party reconstruction and the dropping of "old guard" elements that will be inevitable after Watergate.

In summary then, how can we answer our questions about American parties? Certainly they are old and rather flabby organizations. They have reflected history more than they have made history. They serve their varying functions with widely differing success. They are weak at the top, poorly organized in the middle, and lack rank-and-file strength at the base. They are not instruments of steady social change. But they *have* survived. They *do* offer voters rough sets of alternatives. They *do* live up to their promises more than we think. They *do* draw strength from both professionals and amateurs. They march with the people, if not ahead of them. Above all, they are under close reassessment and significant changes may be in the offing.

[22]"Toward Fairness and Unity for '76" (Coalition for a Democratic Majority, Task Force on Democratic Party Rules and Structure, 1974).

[23]Quoted in Saloma and Sontag, *Parties*, p. 35.

Chapter 12 Appeal to the voters

We have noticed how opinions are born and shaped, the various publics that hold these opinions, the way opinions can be measured. We have looked at voting behavior—which people vote, how they vote, and why. We have considered parties as grand coalitions of interest groups, doing a variety of important jobs though not always doing them well, sometimes powerful in local activities but poorly coordinated as national agencies. All these forces interact in the crucible of the election process.

Free and fair elections are the ultimate bulwark of democratic government, and the ultimate test of it. Indeed, many democrats have considered such elections as a solution to the ills of a democracy. When reformers have proclaimed that "the cure for democracy is more democracy," they have usually meant more frequent elections, for more offices. On the other hand, as noted in Chapter 10, elections in America have been pictured as meaningless, corrupt, or elite-dominated—at best as symbolic exercises that delude the masses into thinking they share power with elites when actually they do not.

Election mechanics

Americans seem to love elections; we hold over one hundred thousand of them a year. In contrast to other democratic countries we like to elect a great variety of local officials—district attorney, county commissioner, village fence viewer, even judges—rather than giving such functions to appointed officials. Under the Constitution, moreover, the *state legislatures* regulate the time, place, and manner of federal as well as state and local elections, though Congress has considerable power to intervene. The result is an endless profusion and variety of electoral arrangements.

WHAT YOU DON'T KNOW *CAN* HURT YOU

This complexity makes voting a chore as well as a privilege. The voter ideally should know not only the names and positions of a score of candidates in the polling booth but the way candidates are nominated, what citizens have to do in order to vote, and the intricacies of paper ballots and voting machines. The political "pros" know these things. Since election arrangements differ from state to state, the conscientious voter must study the laws and practices in his own community.

Registration: "You must register if you want to vote." Despite this oft-repeated warning, many citizens find themselves unable to vote on election day because they are not on the registration list. And failure to register is perhaps the main cause of low voting turnout in American elections. "In round numbers, some 40 million Americans failed to get their names on registration lists in 1972. Another 23 million who were registered failed to vote. . . . Thus, with all the talk of voter disenchantment with candidates . . . there were twice as many unregistered citizens as registered nonvoters."[1]

Registration requirements vary from state to state, but the Supreme Court has said states may not impose "unreasonable" durational residency requirements and has hinted rather strongly that fifty days is about the most a state may constitutionally require. Furthermore, Congress has set aside residency requirements for voting for president; a person who moves within thirty days before a presidential election may vote in the place from which he or she came; otherwise, he is eligible to vote for President in the state to which he has moved.[2]

Every state except North Dakota now provides for some kind of permanent registration system, although in two states registration is not required statewide.[3] The problem is that the voter in most places must take the initiative, for drives by private groups and political parties to get people to go down to city hall or the court house to register have not been very effective. For this reason many are urging that Congress take over from the states and provide for registration by post card or estab-

[1]Penn Kimball, "The Case for Universal Voter Enrollment," in Richard J. Carlson, ed., *Issues of Electoral Reform* (National Municipal League, 1974), p. 25.

[2]Richard Claude, *The Supreme Court and the Electoral Process* (Johns Hopkins Press, 1970), p. 108; also Claude in Carlson, *Electoral Reform*, "The Federal Voting Rights Acts," pp. 49–70.

[3]National Municipal League, *A Model Election System* (National Municipal League, 1973), p. 4.

lish a system in which public officials have the responsibility to go out and place qualified persons on the voting rolls. This would not be the first initiative by Congress to regulate registration; in the Voting Rights Act of 1965 Congress actually set up procedures to supersede state registration in areas that have had a past record of using such procedures for discrimination. As Claude has pointed out, "The structure of our electoral system has been affected not only by a trend toward its democratization but also by an associated turn toward nationalization."[4]

Voting: Nowhere are fairness and accuracy more important than in the handling of elections. It took years to work out procedures to circumvent old-fashioned skullduggery at the polls. Thus in the old days tissue-paper ballots were issued, so that sharp-eyed party workers could see where a voter put his mark after the ballot was folded. Election reforms were passed, known as the Australian ballot system, under which ballots are given to voters only on election day, only at the official polling place, and only by public officials. Today voting machines have replaced ballots in most precincts, but the use of voting machines must also be carefully regulated to prevent abuses.

Stickers and write-ins: These are devices for making last-minute changes in the ballot or voting machine—for example, when a candidate withdraws or dies after the ballots have been printed or voting machines readied. The voter may either paste in a gummed sticker or write in the name of a candidate.

Party and candidate placement: Just where a party or candidate may be listed on a ballot or voting machine might seem of interest only to the professionals. Actually placement is very important. Under the *office-group* (or Massachusetts) type of balloting, the ballot or voting machine lists together the names and party designations of all candidates for the same *office*. Because this type of arrangement makes it difficult to vote a straight party ticket, it encourages split-party voting. The *party-column* (or Indiana) arrangement groups candidates by *party* in columns. A voter can vote for all the candidates of one party simply by making one mark or pulling the lever for the party's candidates as a block. The party-column alternative encourages straight party voting. Candidates are also interested in where their name is placed—whether their name will be close to a popular candidate, whether they can be listed under two or more parties and not just under one, and, most especially, whether their name will be listed at the top of the ballot.

PRIMARIES

Taking part in the selection of the parties' *nominees* is often as important as voting in the election itself. In almost all the states candidates are

[4]Claude, "Voting Rights Acts," p. 50.

chosen in direct primary elections rather than in conventions. These primaries are financed by the public treasury, run by regular election officials, and held in the same polling places as the regular election; moreover, the voters are protected by the same legal safeguards. To get on the primary ballot a candidate usually must file a petition signed by a required number of voters. In practice this means that almost anyone can get on the ballot if he or she does enough legwork, and the voter may find a large number of names listed on the primary ballot.

Who can vote in a party primary? In most states voters must publicly acknowledge membership in a party in order to help pick that party's nominees, but party membership in the United States is a rather ambiguous matter, and the requirements are not very strict. In some states a voter may declare his party allegiance when he or she registers to vote; in others the voter enrolls as a party member simply by showing up at the party primary to vote. In some states, mainly in the South, voters appearing at the primary must pledge, before receiving the ballot, that they supported the party's nominee at the last election, or will at the next, or both. In any case, a voter may change party affiliation between elections.

This discussion refers to the *closed primary*, in which the party seeks to allow only those who are, in one way or another, party adherents to vote. But a few states have an *open primary* system under which any qualified voter may participate in the primary of any party without having to reveal publicly his party affiliation. In some open systems the voter receives the ballots of all the parties and then fills out the one he prefers; in the state of Washington the voter receives one ballot that lists the candidates of all parties for all offices.

Several states use a combination convention-primary system. Party conventions—usually called *preprimary conventions*—or committees propose a candidate for each office. The candidate gaining the convention's endorsement then runs in the primary along with any other aspirants who may wish to compete without that endorsement. This procedure informs the voter of the official party choice but leaves him free to support any other candidate.

Most primary systems allow supporters of one party to enter—or "raid"—the primary of another. The aim may be to nominate the weakest candidate in the rival party. Probably more often the aim is merely to vote against a particularly disliked candidate, even though one does not expect to vote in the general election for the person supported in the primary. The open primary, exposed to the depredations of "one-day" Republicans and Democrats, makes raiding particularly easy. It is preferred by those who like to have a free choice on primary day as to the party contests in which they vote or who for some reason prefer not to reveal their party affiliation.

The open primary is deplored by party officials. It is also disfavored by advocates of party responsibility who believe that if parties are to be held accountable for the people they select to represent them, the party should be able to limit those who participate in the selection of its candidates to the party faithful. Research has not uncovered any relation between the openness of primaries and subsequent support for the party in the general election, at least with respect to election of state legislators.[5] Yet after the courts struck down Illinois's closed primary provision (which in effect kept persons from voting for twenty-three months in the primary of one party if they had voted in another party's primary), most observers felt that the Democratic organization's candidate for governor was defeated because of the movement into the primary of many Republicans. (If the aim was to select the weaker Democratic candidate, the raiders may have guessed wrong, for the Democratic nominee, Daniel Walker, defeated the Republican candidate in the subsequent fall election).[6]

In Southern states in the past, winning the Democratic nomination was usually tantamount to being elected because of the weakness of the Republican opposition. The surge of Republican strength in the South in recent years has made the primary less decisive. In either party, when several candidates run for nomination and so split the vote that no candidate wins a majority, a *runoff* primary is held between the two contestants with the most votes.

THE LONG BALLOT AND THE SHORT

A ballot has been known to be as long as twelve feet and to contain almost five hundred names. In filling out a long ballot—the form used by most states—the baffled voter must decide among a fantastic array of candidates for many offices. The more insignificant the office, the fewer the voters who know the qualifications of the candidates and the greater the likelihood that party organizations or interested groups can elect their favorites. And along with the candidates to be voted for, there are usually lengthy questions or propositions to be accepted or rejected.

There has long been a movement to shorten the ballot by restricting officials popularly elected to those concerned with broad policy determination, but progress has been slow. Most states have, however, adopted the *presidential short ballot*, which, instead of listing the names of all the electors of each party, carries only the names of the presidential and vice-presidential candidates to whom the electors are pledged. By casting one vote for president and vice-president, the voter in effect chooses the entire party slate of electors. But the long ballot seems certain to remain in state and local elections for a long time to come, if only because of the old-fashioned—many political scientists would say misguided—view that in a democracy voters have the ability and the desire to make the most minute decisions in filling offices.

To conclude: As political scientists, we should understand that most

[5]Ira Ralph Telford, "Types of Primary and Primary Responsibility," *American Political Science Review* (March 1965), pp. 117–18.

[6]See in general, Thomas W. Madron and Carl P. Chelf, *Political Parties in the United States* (Holbrook Press, 1974), esp. Chs. 5, 12.

of the voting arrangements discussed have some effect, planned or not, on voting behavior and hence on the allocation of political power. Unfortunately, research on these effects has been so limited and scattered that we still lack solid evidence and conclusions. There is indication that registration requirements and procedures are a major factor in the extent of nonvoting in the United States[7]; that party *primaries* tend to divide parties and their leaderships to a greater extent than do party *conventions;* that different types of ballots encourage or discourage *straight-party* voting. Further analysis of these problems, exploiting the vast amount of data available through polls and election returns, represents a major research frontier in political science.

Political money

The shadowy world of campaign finance has been briefly illuminated in recent years by the Watergate revelations, the resignations of President Nixon and Vice-President Agnew, "launderings" of money, secret campaign donations, and many, many earlier episodes. But the world of political money still remains shadowy. How much does election campaigning cost and should it cost that much? Who gives? Why? Where does the money go? Is political money a serious problem? If so, what has been done about it? What *can* be done about it?

Big round figures would suggest that political campaigns do indeed cost too much. The total cost of all campaigns in 1972 was perhaps $350 million—up (with the help of inflation) from $300 million in 1968. Some individual campaigns seem extremely costly. The Republicans spent about $17 million in the 1972 election campaign on television and radio alone; the Democrats spent more than this. A New York Democratic congressman spent for campaign expenses about $4,500,000 in an unsuccessful effort to win a seat in the United States Senate. One of Nelson Rockefeller's campaigns for governor was *officially* reported at $7,500,000; Democrats charged that he spent two or three times as much.

Staggering figures, to be sure. Yet if we put the question of campaign finance in broader perspective, the problem dwindles a bit. The $350 million spent on all campaigns in 1972 was but a fraction of a percent of the total cost of government. One Trident submarine costs hundreds of millions. Any large corporation spends a good deal of money recruiting its executives and decision-makers—why shouldn't government? Or

[7]For example, Donald R. Matthews and James W. Prothro in two articles in *The American Political Science Review*, "Social and Economic Factors and Negro Registration in the South," (March 1963), pp. 24–44, and "Political Factors and Negro Voter Registration in the South," (June 1963), pp. 355–67, find that political and legal factors have a probable effect on black registration but socioeconomic factors have an even greater probable effect. See also, in the same journal, Stanley Kelley, Jr., Richard E. Ayres, and William G. Bowen, "Registration and Voting: Putting First Things First" (June 1967), pp. 359–77; and Kimball, "Universal Voter Enrollment."

compare the cost of political campaigns with the money spent on commercial advertising. One big soap company will budget in 1976 almost as much as the cost of all campaigning for that presidential year. Or compare political expenditure per voter in the United States with the same in other countries. Americans spent $1.12 per capita in a recent year—much less than most countries and far less than the cost for Israelis of $21.20 per voter.[8]

The peculiar nature of American elections also raises the cost of campaigns. There are really two campaigns—one for nomination and one for election—and each of them lasts months. A presidential aspirant may campaign for at least a year before the elections, as Goldwater did in 1964, Nixon in 1968, McGovern in 1972, Udall and Jackson in 1976. Another reason for the high cost of getting elected (or defeated) is the growing use of professional campaign managers. In earlier decades a candidate might rely on an old-fashioned party organization staffed by hundreds of persons eager to get jobs or favors. Today, partly as a result of the key role of television in many campaigns, candidates are using merchandising techniques. It is not unusual for a candidate to hire a professional campaign firm, a computer expert, a polling organization, an advertising agency, a specialist in film-making, an expert in direct-mail campaigns, and other specialists in big-time promotion.

[8]These examples are from Herbert E. Alexander, *Political Financing* (Burgess, 1972), pp. 1–4, 38–39; see also David W. Adamany, *Campaign Finance in America* (Wadsworth, 1972), Chs. 2, 3.

Major Campaign Expenses:

Entertainment	$ 5,381.57	Stamps	$ 4,228.00
Travel	8,656.00	Telephone Charges	9,783.71
Advances for Expenses	4,732.00	Telephone Deposits	17,100.00
Hotels	538.50	Tickets for Dinners, etc.	5,376.00
Hq. Equipment, Furniture	7,626.00	Staff Payroll	54,955.00
Rents	9,025.00	Direct Mail Campaign	49,521.00
Media Consultant	19,326.00	Advertising	17,102.00
Printing	33,013.00	Polls	11,600.00
Research	1,122.00	Voter Surveys	15,000.00
New York State Income Tax	8,630.00	Mail & Vote List Computerizing	8,200.00
Soc. Security & Federal Taxes	17,592.38	Video-Tape Machines	1,267.95

These services cost a lot of money. (Whether merchandisers will replace party "professionals" is another and important subject).

The problem is not so much the amount of money; politics inevitably will be expensive. The problem in a democracy is *inequality* — whether the doctrine of one person-one vote becomes meaningless when one person can give tens of thousands of dollars and another can give nothing. How does this inequality square with the doctrine of government by the *people?* The question itself assumes that political money generates great political power — a proposition that has not been wholly proved.

WHO GIVES AND WHY?

Broadly speaking, those who give most are those who have the most. Ideally in a democracy, millions of average citizens might give a pittance or more to their candidates and parties, but this has not been the tradition in the United States. A number of experiments in mass fund-raising have been tried, but they were not very successful. However, presidential candidates with highly involved and loyal supporters have succeeded in gathering most of their money from small contributions. Barry Goldwater raised about $20 million in 1964 through television appeals combined with large-scale, direct-mail drives. During a nine-month period in 1968, George Wallace collected over $6 million, of which more than 75 percent was made up of contributions of less than $100. A record was set by George McGovern, who raised a total of $33 million, almost two-thirds of which came in donations of $100 or less.[9]

But the great bulk of the money comes from businessmen and professional people and from labor unions. Most of the money comes in large donations. The size and number of the gifts have been escalating: between 1952 and 1968 the number of contributors giving over $10,000 quadrupled. Federal law prohibits both unions and corporations from making contributions or expenditures in connection with candidacy for federal elective office, so donations are made by "individuals" even though they may come from corporations. In 1972 some corporations did give money directly (however camouflaged) to the Nixon campaign and more than a dozen executives were prosecuted and fined. Some individuals and families made huge donations, in the hundreds of thousands, and these were legal.

The money, whether legal or not, is not always given openly, of course. Watergate has made us familiar with the obscure channels through which political money flows: the use of "fronts" and "drops," the "laundering" of money to hide its real origin, and other devices. A far more common — and legal — device is the $100- or $1,000-a-plate dinner, for which large contributors buy whole tables or blocks of tables — and perhaps buy an expensive ad in a dinner "program" to boot. Party dinners tend to be a bit more plebian. The Democrats run a series of

[9]Stephen Schlesinger, "Running for Office: All You Need Is an Issue," *Washington Monthly* (October 1973), pp. 45 – 48.

Jackson Day dinners throughout the country, charging as low as $5 or $10 a plate; the Republicans have Lincoln Day dinners, also for a wider clientele. The Democrats in recent years have had considerable success with day-long "telethons" featuring party bigwigs and Hollywood actresses, punctuated by fervent appeals for direct-mail contributions.

The reasons for giving political money are multifold. Most givers want something specific. Business, labor, and other groups want certain laws passed or repealed, certain funds appropriated, certain administrative decisions rendered. Persons holding government jobs want to stay in office (and in certain cities pay the party an assessment to do so). Some big donors want ambassadorships or other prestigious posts. Some want recognition—an invitation to a White House dinner, a low license plate number, an honorific appointment. Others simply want *access* to officeholders. They neither expect nor get specific government rewards for their "cash on the barrelhead"; what they *do* expect and usually get is the opportunity to see the officeholder after the election and present their proposal and their case.

Many givers are moved by somewhat loftier motives. They believe that their candidate or party will govern best for them and their country. Their motives range from the vaguest idealism to hardheaded calculation that certain candidates, parties, or government actions would be best for the nation. Goldwater, McGovern, Wallace, and others have demonstrated how powerful this appeal can be when sounded by candidates who, whatever their political frustrations, are seen as genuinely committed to the doctrines they preach.

Is giving worthwhile? Is there a payoff? This question is unanswerable because the causal relation between giving money and the passage of an act, for example, is extremely obscure and tenuous; too many other factors are involved (including the giving of money by people on the other side of an issue). Perhaps it is enough to say that most politicians and most donors *think* that giving money brings results. Many successes and failures could be cited. The payoff may be intangible but very satisfying. Alexander cites the case of a Democratic contributor who claimed that his $1,000 donation was the best *social* investment he ever made. "He and his wife went free to a dinner dance and another event in California, his home state. While attending the national convention in Atlantic City, he was invited to a special event for big contributors each day: on Sunday night, a cocktail party with music and hors d'oeuvres; on Monday, a brunch at a choice of two hotels and an exhibition golf match in the afternoon; on Tuesday, an old-fashioned clambake; on Wednesday, a day at the races, followed by cocktails and dancing . . . ; on Thursday, a birthday party for the president followed by a buffet supper-breakfast. At all these affairs, there was bountiful food and drink." Other benefits for the contributor included an invitation to the Inauguration, the Inaugural gala and dinner, and a dinner at the White House.[10] Not a bad deal, the donor concluded.

[10] Alexander, *Political Financing*, p. 35.

REFORM OF POLITICAL MONEY

For many years the national and state governments have been trying to "sanitize" campaign finance, with very mixed results. The reformers have assumed that big donors were able to buy political influence and that, in any event, the image of "fat cats" gaining undue political power was an affront to American notions of equality and probity. Concern has risen in recent years along with the inflation of political money. One scholar contends that money has become so important candidates must conduct *three* campaigns—for a party nomination, for the election, and for campaign finance. This third campaign begins before the candidate starts running, continues all through the primary and the election contests, and is revived at the end of the campaign when the winners and losers contemplate their campaign debts.[11]

Reformers have tried three basic strategies in trying to prevent abuse: *limitations* on the giving, receiving, and spending of political money; *disclosure* of the sources and uses of political money; and governmental *subsidies* of campaigns, including incentive arrangements. Recent campaign finance laws have tended to use all three strategies, as reformers have tried desperately to deal with a problem that sometimes seems insoluble.

Limiting campaign spending is one of the older methods. Under the 1925 Corrupt Practices Act, a candidate for United States representative could not spend more than $2,500, a candidate for senator not more than $10,000. While higher amounts were allowed for larger states or districts, the act was utterly unrealistic and easily evaded. Later amendments limited spending by any political committee to $3 million a year and contributions by individuals to each candidate or nationally affiliated party committee to $5,000 annually. But the limitations on giving were no more effective than the restrictions on spending. Reporting was inadequate; often reports were filed after the election was over. Policing was almost nonexistent. Much of the corrupt-practice legislation did not cover primary elections. President Johnson called the 1925 act "more loophole than law."

In 1971, Congress decided on a different emphasis: *disclosure* of all receipts, expenditures, and debts. All political committees that anticipated receiving or spending more than $1,000 on behalf of federal candidates in any year were required to register with the government; periodic reports had to be filed including full data on every contributor of more than $100 and every expenditure of more than $100; one person was not allowed to contribute in the name of another person. In contrast to earlier laws, *ceilings* on political contributions were abolished (except for candidates, or their immediate families, contributing to their own campaigns). Candidates for federal office were also limited in the amounts they could spend on campaign advertising (television, radio, billboards, etc.) to ten cents per voting-age person. The main thrust of

[11]Delmer D. Dunn, "Contributors in the American Electoral Process," *American Politics Quarterly* (April 1974), pp. 221–29.

the act was to throw the "pitiless light" of full publicity onto the sources and uses of political money. While it is too early to evaluate the full influence of the legislation, its impact to date seems to be limited.

In another act of 1971, Congress turned to a different strategy: subsidy tax incentives. The purpose was to draw into politics more money with no strings attached. The law provided that political donors might claim a tax credit against federal income tax for 50 percent of their contributions, up to a maximum of $12.50 on a single return or $25 on a joint return; or they might claim a deduction on the full amount of the contributions, but not more than $50 on a single return or $100 on a joint return. The 1971 law also provided a tax *check-off* that allowed taxpayers to designate that $1 of his tax obligation would go into a fund to subsidize presidential election campaigns.

Watergate gave a sharp push to further regulation of political money. Late in 1974, after prolonged debate, Congress passed and President Ford signed the most sweeping campaign reform measure in American history. The new act established more realistic limits on campaign contributions and spending—for example, a spending limit of $20 million for each presidential candidate in the general election, and $70,000 for each congressional candidate. It tightened disclosure, reporting, and accountability and created a new full-time bipartisan elections commission to administer the act. But what made the new measure a "breakthrough" was a wholly new set of provisions for *public financing* of presidential campaigns. Major party candidates automatically qualify for full funding before the campaign. Public funding is also available to national parties for their presidential nominating conventions. Matching public funds of up to $4.5 million will be available to each candidate in presidential primaries.[12]

Critics noted that public funding for campaigns would be granted to *candidates*, not to parties. They argued that if subsidies went only to candidates, the result might be an even more fragmented, personalistic, and individualistic politics than already exists. If candidates' campaigns were publicly funded through political parties, some contended, the national parties, at least, would become more organized and responsible, especially if the parties had to match public funding with their own fund-raising. Critics also noted that public funding under the act would not be available to *congressional* candidates. Congress, it was said, feared a subsidy program that might encourage persons to run against incumbent congressmen. Almost all agreed, however, that the new measure was a landmark act—though much would depend on the probity and wisdom with which it would be administered by the new elections commission.

The argument over political money continues. "Who really owns America?" Senator Edward Kennedy demanded. "Is it the people, or is it a little group of big campaign contributors?" He cited links between

[12]Provisions of the new act are reported fully in *Congressional Quarterly Weekly Report*, Oct. 12, 1974, pp. 2865–70.

the energy crisis and oil industry contributions, between the American Medical Association and the inadequate health insurance programs, between the National Rifle Association and the lack of gun control, between the "demoralization" of the foreign service and the "sale" of ambassadorships to big donors. Others contend that federal subsidies will simply mean more governmental interference and bureaucracy, will be costly to the taxpayers, weaken the party system, and above all would have little effect in purifying politics. Still others believe that none of these reforms will work; they argue in favor of more fundamental reform strategies such as reducing the number of elected officials, shortening the length of campaigns, giving United States representatives and state officials four-year rather than two-year terms. We will return to the issue of Who Owns America and the allied question of election reform in Chapter 19.

Running for congress

The immense diversity of local factors makes it hard to generalize about congressional and senatorial campaigns, but there is some pattern to election outcomes. For example—and of crucial importance to policy-making in Congress—most congressional districts are noncompetitive (that is, the division of the vote falls outside the 45 to 55 percent "competitive" range); the competitiveness has been decreasing, dropping from about one-fifth of all House seats in 1952 to one-eighth in 1972. There is some evidence that Republican candidates for representatives are more successful when running as moderates than as strong conservatives.[13] Congressional campaigns seem much less connected with policy and program, and certainly ideology, than presidential campaigns.[14]

But when it comes to actual campaigning, conditions vary widely. Much depends on the candidate—whether he or she is an incumbent, a novice running for the first time, an old veteran attempting a comeback. Much depends on the time and the region, the urban, suburban or rural make-up of the district, and local conditions.

CAMPAIGNING FOR THE HOUSE

Still, there are certain patterns and rules of thumb, especially in campaigns for a seat in the House of Representatives.[15] For a person with

[13]Robert S. Erikson, "The Electoral Impact of Congressional Roll Call Voting," *American Political Science Review* (December 1971), pp. 1018–32.

[14]Walter Dean Burnham, "American Politics in the 1970s: Beyond Party?" unpublished paper, 1974.

[15]These generalizations are drawn in part from David A. Leuthold, *Electioneering in a Democracy: Campaigns for Congress* (John Wiley, 1968); the illuminating studies of primary and election campaigns, *Eagleton Institute Cases in Practical Politics*, sponsored by the

some political experience and a moderate number of contacts throughout the district, the first question is one of timing. Does the year look good for the candidate and his party? Is there any kind of groundswell against incumbents? If it is a presidential election year, will the party's ticket be headed by attractive national or state candidates, and if so, can he or she get a firm hold on their coattails? Would it be better to wait two or four years until the candidate has broadened his own range of acquaintances? Or will it be too late by then?

If he decides to "go," the candidate must first plan a primary race, unless there happens to be no opponents for the party's nomination—a piece of luck that is more likely when a party has little chance of carrying the district. The first step in running for the nomination is to build a personal organization, because the party organization is supposed to stay neutral until the nomination is decided. A candidate can build an organization as a holder of a lesser office such as state representative, or by deliberately getting to know people, serving in civic causes, helping other candidates, and being conspicuous without being overly controversial. The next step is to enlist the support of as many interest groups and party leaders as possible. (The latter may give their personal support even though their party committees are supposed to keep out of the contest.) A major problem for the candidate is how to divide resources—mainly money—between a primary effort and the final race.

Once nominated, the candidate comes into a rich inheritance—the large bloc of votes of the party faithful who will almost automatically support their party's nominee. He will also get considerable recognition from the press and from state and national leaders of the party. But the candidate for Congress usually has some woes. The party will provide him or her with far less financial support than needed. Except in a few localities, such as Chicago, the party organization is either feeble or strained to the limit in trying to help all its candidates on the long ballot, and the candidate finds that he must depend on a personal organization. But the main problem usually is one of *visibility*. If the campaign is in a large metropolitan area it is hard to get attention in the crowded press and on television, both of which are paying attention chiefly to the major candidates. And in rural areas the press may play down political news. The candidate cannot afford much television, which in any event usually covers a far larger area than a district, thus wasting much of his money.

As a result congressional candidates often conclude that their best tactic is stressing personal contact—shaking hands, canvassing house to house, emphasizing local problems. This is one reason national representatives seem rather parochial—their elections are often locally instead of nationally oriented.

Eagleton Foundation Advisory Board at Rutgers University (McGraw-Hill); Lewis A. Froman, Jr., "A Realistic Approach to Campaign Strategies and Tactics," in David W. Abbott and Edward T. Rogowsky, eds., *Political Parties: Leadership, Organization, Linkage* (Rand McNally, 1971), pp. 280–98; and Donald G. Herzberg and J. W. Peltason, *A Student Guide to Campaign Politics* (McGraw-Hill, 1970).

RUNNING FOR THE SENATE

Because states vary in population so widely, generalizing about Senate campaigns is most difficult. But running for the Senate is big-time politics. The six-year term and the national exposure make a Senate seat a particularly glittering prize, so competition is likely to be intense. The race may easily cost several hundred thousands of dollars, at the least, whereas congressional campaigns typically cost considerably less.[16] The candidate for Senate is far more visible—he finds it more important to take positions on national problems; he cannot duck tough issues very easily; and he is likelier to have better access to the news media.

Otherwise Senate races tend to be much like those for the House. The essential tactics, Froman has summed it up, are to get others involved, use as much personal contact as possible, be brief in statements to the public, don't publicize the opposition if you can help it, have a simple campaign theme. Persuade people through the basic methods of *reinforcement* of present feelings, *activation* of latent attitudes, *conversion* of opposing views to the extent possible. Remember that facts do *not* "speak for themselves"—an intellectual and psychological framework must be provided.[17]

All other things being equal, it seems evident that *incumbency* weighs heavily in the balance in Senate elections. The reason is not wholly clear. "It may simply be," says Barbara Hinckley, "that an incumbent is more widely known than his opponent—due to the publicity available as a member of the Senate, the franking privilege, etc.—and that with generally low levels of voter interest and information about Congress, voters will tend to vote for the more familiar (less unfamiliar) name." Or it may be "that senators accumulate electoral support with increasing years of service, in contrast to governors who accumulate grievances, an interesting hypothesis of difference between legislators and executives."[18]

But incumbents are not unbeatable. In 1974 Senator William Fulbright, a national figure, a thirty-year veteran member of the Senate, and probably its most distinguished spokesman on foreign policy, was trounced in the Democratic primary in Arkansas by a young, vigorous, and popular governor, Dale Bumpers. Some attributed the defeat to general disillusionment with incumbents whether or not they had anything to do with Watergate. But, many remembered too that in 1966 a young Republican business executive named Charles Percy ran a highly streamlined campaign that effectively used television, and he defeated a

[16]Leuthold, *Electioneering*, Ch. 6.

[17]"A Realistic Approach to Campaign Strategies." See also John W. Kingdon, *Candidates for Office: Beliefs and Strategies* (Random House, 1968).

[18]Barbara Hinckley, "Incumbency and the Presidential Vote in Senate Elections: Defining Parameters of Subpresidential Voting," *American Political Science Review* (September 1970), pp. 841–42.

three-term seemingly unbeatable incumbent, Paul Douglas. This of course is the old political cycle of young persons coming along to oust the old, but campaigns against incumbent senators are rarely easy ones.[19]

Is there any place for rational calculation in all this? Or is it simply a matter of following a few obvious rules of thumb like those listed above? Most politicians would argue that victory is nine-tenths perspiration and one-tenth inspiration. But careful calculation may pay off, especially in the very tricky business of picking a good year to run, and a good presidential candidate to run with or against. In 1964 Republican candidates faced the difficult decision of whether to cling tightly to the coattails of Barry Goldwater or conduct independent campaigns. Those who thought Goldwater a sure winner and climbed aboard his bandwagon fared worse at the polls than those who pursued a somewhat separate campaign from Goldwater. A decade later, Republican candidates in most districts did their best to disassociate themselves from President Nixon, Watergate, and inflation and tried to establish their own independent images. But the results in most elections are also affected by factors over which candidates have little control – party column ballots that emphasize the link between presidential and congressional candidates, national trends, as well as factors such as party registration and the influence of local candidates.[20]

We may be entering a period in which campaigns will become more significant in determining election outcomes, not merely because of the greater effectiveness of new political techniques, but also because of what appears to be a growing number of young voters who are not predisposed to vote for one party over another. They enter the campaign periods ready to be persuaded. Although party loyalties will probably not disappear altogether, there are likely to be fewer voters to whom one can appeal in terms of party loyalty alone.

Nominating a president

To attain the presidency a person has to run two races and win them both. First he must be nominated at his party's national convention (and this is sometimes the harder of the two jobs), and then he must get a majority of the nation's electoral votes.

[19]For a full description of another high-powered campaign – that of Edward M. Kennedy for the Democratic nomination for senator from Massachusetts in 1962 – see Murray B. Levin, *Kennedy Campaigning* (Beacon Press, 1966).

[20]Robert A. Schoenberger, "Campaign Strategy and Party Loyalty: The Electoral Relevance of Candidate Decision-Making in the 1964 Congressional Elections," *American Political Science Review* (June 1969), pp. 515 – 20. See also Robert J. Huckshorn and Robert C. Spencer, *The Politics of Defeat* (University of Massachusetts Press, 1971), which emphasizes the difficulty of challenging incumbents in noncompetitive districts.

Probably the first convention was held in 1808, when a few Federalist leaders met secretly in New York to nominate candidates for president and vice-president. In 1831, under Jackson's leadership, the first real national convention was held by a major party. Today the national convention is a famous and unique political institution. Every four years each party enjoys – usually for about a week – world attention; covered by batteries of cameras and by battalions of newsmen, every incident in the great convention hall is carried to millions in this country and abroad.

The preconvention campaign usually starts at least a year before the convention itself; early in 1975 candidates for nomination by the 1976 party conventions were already hard at work. Candidates must choose among several preconvention strategies: announcing early and going "all out"; keeping silent in order not to show one's strength (or weakness) too early; concentrating on gaining a following among the party's rank-and-file; quietly trying to win over party leaders throughout the states – leaders who may be able to deliver solid delegate support at the crucial moment in the convention battle.

All these tactics, however, are dominated by the rules of the presidential nomination game. In each national convention the object is simple – to win a straight majority of the votes cast on the first or any other ballot. All the candidates know that the delegates will arrive at the convention in all stages of commitment, noncommitment, or semicommitment to one candidate or another. Some delegates will be pledged to a candidate only on the first ballot; others pledge themselves (or are pledged by virtue of their election) to one person for all ballots; others have highly mixed and divided commitments to candidates. Further complicating the situation will be the variety of contending candidates; these will be "favorite sons," who have at least the initial support of their delegations; "stalking horses," who are used as fronts by strong candidates wishing to hold some strength in reserve; and "dark horses," who hope that the leading contenders may kill one another off.

CHOOSING DELEGATES

The key factor in the national convention is the make-up of the state delegations. Each party convention represents the states roughly in proportion to the *number of voters* in the state and at the same time gives a bonus to states with heavier concentrations of the *party's strength*. The two parties have often changed their rules for apportioning the votes among the states in an attempt to satisfy both these requirements. Democrats grant some delegates only half a vote, whereas Republicans favor arrangements that give delegates a single vote, with the result that Democratic conventions have more delegates.

The method of selecting delegates is set by state law and varies considerably from state to state. In about half the states, delegates are chosen by party *conventions* or committees. In the other states, including

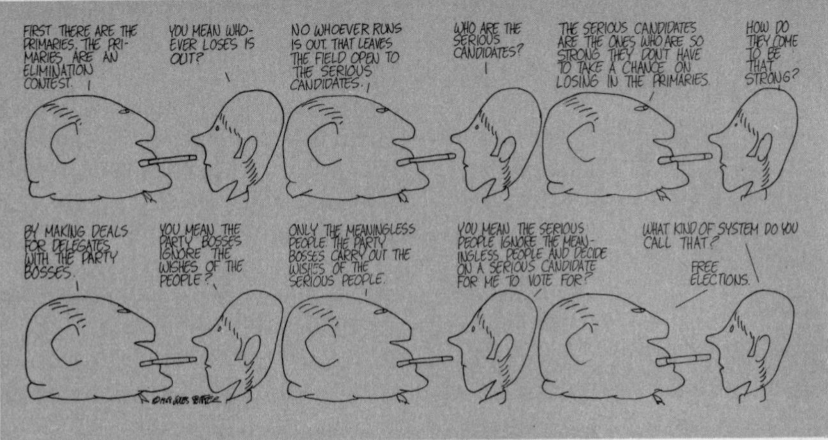

Courtesy Jules Feiffer and Publishers-Hall Syndicate.

most of the populous states, delegates are picked in state *presidential primaries.* A few states use a combination of the two methods. More states are substituting presidential primaries for conventions; fewer than one third of the delegates to the 1976 national conventions will be chosen in state conventions.

The state *convention* system tends to let the party's inner circles select the delegates. This may be no problem where the party leadership is representative, but that is sometimes not the case. Most Republican party organizations in the South, for example, were in the past controlled by a few Republican officeholders in Washington with the help of patronage. In such situations the question of who speaks for the rank-and-file of the party becomes very obscure. This was a main cause of the fierce fight between the Taft and Eisenhower supporters in the 1952 Republican convention, culminating in the unseating of the Taft delegations from Georgia, Louisiana, and Texas and the seating of the Eisenhower forces. Since that time the Republican party has greatly broadened its base in the South.

The presidential *primaries* provide most of the excitement and conflict of preconvention politics; these are the election contests that are so dramatically covered by television. The battles of Robert Kennedy and Eugene McCarthy in the 1968 presidential primaries and of Hubert Humphrey and George McGovern in the 1972 primaries will long be remembered in the Democratic party, as will Barry Goldwater's victories in 1964 in the Republican. With increased use of presidential primaries, moreover, they seem more and more important in forecasting—and perhaps influencing—the outcome of the convention balloting.

PRESIDENTIAL PRIMARIES: VARIETIES

Presidential primaries come in so many different forms in different states that it is almost impossible to generalize about them. The voters must master the specific arrangements in their own states—*and the significance of those arrangements for political outcomes.* Here are the key variations to look for:

1. Direct election of *delegates*. Under this alternative, persons voting in the party presidential primary choose from a list (or slates) of candidates for delegate to the national convention. Voters do not necessarily know what *presidential* candidates those *delegate* candidates favor. In effect the voter says: "I will vote for you to go as a delegate to the national convention and I will depend on you to choose a good presidential candidate for me."

2. Voting one's *presidential preference*. In this kind of presidential primary the voters can indicate their choice among the party's presidential candidates. The ballot will list those candidates and the voter simply puts his X or pulls the lever for the person he favors. Much depends on whether the outcome of these presidential votes is *binding* on the delegates to the national convention. It may or not be binding in a particular state. If it is, the delegates must vote for the preferred candidate on at least the first ballot at the convention. If it is not, the preference vote becomes merely a popularity contest—but one that may influence the candidate's national standing with press and public even though it does not bind delegates.

These two basic elements are found in primary states in different combinations and *how* they are combined can be crucial. Some states—notably California and Ohio—closely link delegate election and presidential preference. By a single X at the top of the column headed, say, "Delegates preferring Gerald Ford," the voter can both indicate the person he or she wants *and* vote for a delegate (or delegate slate) pledged to that candidate at the convention. But other states *separate* the two processes. Voters indicate their presidential preference in one part of the ballot and their delegate selection in another—and there may be no relation between the two. Whether these processes are linked or separate has profound implications both for practical presidential politics and for theories of representation.

These are not the only differences among presidential primary states. Here are other variations:[21]

Delegates may be elected from *congressional districts* or from the *whole state*, or some from each. Delegates from the whole state tend to be tied in with statewide party leaders; congressional-district delegates tend to be more locally oriented.

Some states require a presidential candidate to give his approval before he can be voted for in the primary. This may be hard on some presidential hopefuls who are holding back their final decision and do not wish to be "smoked out" by the exigencies of a single primary.

The extent of a delegate's *commitment* to a presidential candidate, even when that candidate has won a binding preference poll, may vary widely. Some delegates may be pledged to a candidate only on the first ballot or first two ballots; others to none; while still others may feel

[21]For a fuller summary of selection systems, see Frank J. Sorauf, *Party Politics in America, 2nd ed.*, (Little Brown, 1972), pp. 269–74.

morally or politically (but not legally) committed to stick by their candidate "until hell freezes over."

The variety of methods of choosing delegates, along with the variety of power patterns in state parties, makes it impossible to generalize about the nature of the final delegations. Some may be under the thumb of a powerful state party leader; others may be split wide open; still others may operate as a unit to support a favorite son or to maximize their bargaining power. Most state delegations mirror the factions in the state party, but sometimes a strong and well-organized faction will gain control of the whole delegation.

Electing the president

The convention adjourns immediately after the presidential and vice-presidential candidates deliver their acceptance speeches to the aroused and enthusiastic delegates. The presidential nominee may choose a new party chairman, who usually serves as his campaign manager. After a rest, the candidate spends the final days of the summer binding up party wounds, gearing the party for action, and planning campaign strategy. By early fall the presidential race is on.

Strategy differs from one election to another, but politicians, pollsters, and political scientists have collected enough information through experience in recent decades to agree broadly that a number of basic factors affect it. The great bulk of the electorate votes on the basis of party, candidate appeal, and issues. Much depends on voter *turnout* as well as on habitual party disposition. Nationally the Democrats have a great advantage in party registration and support; but the Republicans have an advantage in that their partisans are more likely to turn out on election day, and they have better access to money and usually a somewhat more favorable press. Pledges on policy and program may not arouse the mass electorate, but they do help activate interest groups and party organizations, which in turn help get out a favorable vote.

The course of the presidential campaign has become familiar over time. First there is a postconvention breathing spell while the candidates and their entourages plan strategy. One crucial question is *where to stump*, with the electoral college influencing the decision. *Building group support* calls for a major effort, with each candidate setting up hosts of veterans, farmers, and other campaign groups—labor, black, ethnic, religious—to operate within the big interest-group organizations such as the American Legion, the AFL-CIO, and the organized doctors. The question of *offensive* or *defensive* tactics plagues the tacticians: Do Americans vote *for* or *against* candidates? Should the opposition be attacked or ignored? Should the candidate campaign aggressively or seem to stay above the battle? And always there is the need to furbish—or refurbish—the image of the candidate; this was a major, and evidently highly effective, effort of the 1968 Nixon campaigners, who knew that the Republican nominee must shed his old image of divisive campaigning and, indeed, of failure as a campaigner.[22]

No one has captured the spirit of presidential campaigning better than Adlai E. Stèvenson, the unsuccessful Democratic candidate in 1952 and 1956:

> You must emerge, bright and bubbling with wisdom and well-being, every morning at 8 o'clock, just in time for a charming and profound breakfast talk, shake hands with hundreds, often literally thousands, of people, make several inspiring, "newsworthy" speeches during the day, confer with political leaders along the way and with your staff all the time, write at every chance, think if possible, read mail and newspapers, talk on the telephone, talk to everybody, dictate, receive delegations, eat, with decorum—and discretion!—and ride through city after city on the back of an open car, smiling until your mouth is dehydrated by the wind, waving until the blood runs out of your arm, and then bounce gaily, confidently, masterfully into great howling halls, shaved and all made up for television with the right color shirt and tie—I always forgot—and a manuscript so defaced with chicken tracks and last-minute jottings that you couldn't follow it, even if the spotlights weren't blinding and even if the still photographers didn't shoot you in the eye every time you looked at them. (I've often wondered what happened to all those pictures!) Then all you have to do is make a great, imperishable speech, get out through the pressing crowds with a few score autographs, your clothes intact, your hands bruised, and back to the hotel—in time to see a few important people.
>
> But the real work has just commenced—two or three, sometimes four hours of frenzied writing and editing of the next day's immortal mouthings so you can get something to the stenographers, so they can get something to the mimeograph machines, so they can get something to the reporters, so they can get something to their papers by deadline time. (And I quickly concluded that all deadlines were yesterday!) Finally sleep, sweet sleep, steals you away, unless you worry—which I do. . . .[23]

"The big guy in front is Joseph T. Cochrane. Call him Joe. You met him in Marysville three weeks ago. Talk about hunting. He goes after deer every fall. Man on left is Leo Brown. Sixteenth District in his pocket. Don't ask about his wife. She's ditched him. Fellow with mustache is Jim Cronin. Watch your step with him. He's Cochrane's brother-in-law, and . . ."

Drawing by Peter Arno; copyright © 1946 The New Yorker Magazine, Inc.

THE ELECTORAL COLLEGE SYSTEM: MECHANICS

To win the presidency, a candidate must put together a combination of electoral votes that will give him a majority in the electoral college. This unique institution never meets and serves only a limited electoral function. Yet is has an importance of its own. The framers of the Constitution devised the electoral college system because they wanted the president chosen by electors exercising independent judgment, but subsequent political changes have transformed the electors into straight party representatives who simply register the electorate's decision.

[22]On the key factor of personality in presidential campaigning, see Richard W. Boyd, "Presidential Elections: An Explanation of Voting Defection," *American Political Science Review* (June 1969), pp. 498–514.

[23]Adlai E. Stevenson, *Major Campaign Speeches*, 1952 (Random House, 1953), pp. xi–xii. Copyright 1953 by Random House, Inc.

The system today works as follows: In making his presidential choice on election day, the voter technically does not vote directly for a candidate but chooses between slates of *presidential electors*. Each slate is made up of persons selected by the state party (in most states in party conventions) to serve this essentially honorary role. The slate that wins the most popular votes throughout the state gets to cast all the electoral votes for the state (a state has one electoral vote for every senator and representative).

The electors on the winning slate travel to their state capital the first Monday after the second Wednesday in December, go through the ceremony of casting their ballots for their party's candidates, perhaps hear some speeches, and go home. The ballots are sent from the state capitals to Washington, where early in January they are formally counted by the House and Senate and the name of the next president is announced.

Counting the electoral votes has not always been just a formality. In 1876 there was a serious and potentially explosive dispute over which slate of electoral votes from several Southern states should be counted. The election was so close that the outcome was at stake. The Senate was Republican; the House, Democratic. Finally a Commission of Fifteen was elected, composed of eight Republicans and seven Democrats. By a vote of eight to seven, the Commission ruled that the Republican electors in the disputed states had been properly elected; so Hayes became president over Tilden.

The House and Senate also must act when no candidate secures a majority of the electoral votes. This is not likely so long as there are only two serious contending parties, but it has happened twice in the case of president and once in the case of vice-president and almost happened in the very close 1960 election. When the situation occurs, the House chooses the president from among the top three candidates; each state delegation has one vote, and a majority is necessary for election. If no man receives a majority of the electoral vote in the vice-presidential contest, the Senate picks from among the top two candidates; each senator has one vote, and again a majority is required.

THE ELECTORAL COLLEGE SYSTEM: POLITICS

The operation of the electoral college, with its statewide electoral slates, sharply influences the presidency and presidential politics. A Republican candidate usually enters the fray sure of the backing of rural states such as Vermont, Kansas, Oregon, and the Dakotas. Until the 1960s the Democratic candidate knew that he could depend on the support of the Solid South and some of the border states. But in order to win a presidential election, a candidate must appeal successfully to urban and suburban groups in populous states such as New York, California, Pennsylvania, Illinois, and perhaps a dozen others. Under the electoral college system, as we have seen, a candidate wins either *all* a state's electoral votes or *none*. Hence the presidential candidate ordinarily will not waste his time campaigning in states unless he has at least a fighting chance of carrying them; nor will he waste time in states that are assuredly on his side. Consequently, the fight usually narrows down to the medium-sized and big states where the balance between the parties tends to be fairly even.

Obviously the presidential candidate must win over—or at least not antagonize—masses of voters in industrial centers. He must show sensitivity to their problems—inflation, housing, wages, social security, and relations with foreign nations, especially nations whose sons and daughters have come by the million to our shores. Moreover, the candidate's appeals must at the same time transcend local and petty matters and dramatize the great national issues. The candidate, in short, strikes out for a national majority rooted in the largest states and sacrifices many narrow issues in order to exploit the broader ones. Candidates for Congress, on the other hand, often win votes by pressing local and sectional claims against those of the rest of the nation.

Both the mechanics and politics of the electoral college can be unpredictable. In 1972 an elector in Virginia chosen on the Republican ticket refused to cast his electoral vote for Nixon and gave it to the Libertarian party candidate. Although such departures from constitutional custom are rare and have never affected the outcome of an election, most people agree that it is dangerous to have a system that allows individual electors to vote for whomever they wish despite the results of the popular vote in their state. In a close election a small group of persons could frustrate the wishes of the majority of the electorate. Although under the present system some states attempt by law to bind electors to vote for the presidential and vice-presidential candidates of their party, these laws may not be enforceable.[24]

All the states except Maine now provide for the selection of electors on a general, statewise, straight-ticket basis. This makes it possible for a person to receive a majority of the popular vote without receiving a majority of the electoral vote. This very thing happened in 1876 when Tilden received more popular votes but lost the electoral vote to Hayes, and again in 1888 when Cleveland, despite his larger popular vote, got fewer electoral votes than Harrison.

The existence of the electoral college could also lead to an election being thrown into the House of Representatives. This has happened only twice in our history—both times before the establishment of our present two-party system—but if it did occur again, a minority of Representatives could elect a president, since every state delegation in the House, no matter how large, could cast only one vote.

[24]Wallace S. Sayre and Judith H. Parris, *Voting for President: The Electoral College and the American Political System* (Brookings, 1970), p. 41.

Elections: rule by the people?

Elections seem to lie at the very heart of democratic government, but do elections actually put power in the hands of the great majority of the people? Some critics say No. They contend: The great mass of voters do not know the issues or even the candidates. They do not choose between clearly stated alternatives. They do not even vote to the degree that the more affluent do. And winning candidates and parties do not follow through on their promises to the people. Critics are especially scornful of party platforms. According to a history professor, platforms "are like college catalogue descriptions: never the same as the course, but designed for appeal."[25]

Is there a case *for* elections as Americans operate them? A political scientist, Gerald M. Pomper, took a closer look at the old charges that politicians make all sorts of reckless promises and then abandon them, that the great mass of voters exercise no direct control of policy through elections, that elections do not serve as a link between the people and their government. By carefully comparing what parties and candidates had promised with what governments did later, he discovered that these charges have been considerably overstated. To be sure, he did not find that the mass of voters spontaneously and independently used elections to control the government. Initiatives lay with the politicians, not with the voters. But the great mass of voters were crucially important because of their power retrospectively to throw out of office politicians who had not followed through on their promises or who had simply not governed very well. And politicians could not govern effectively without having constantly in mind what the voters might do at the next election. "Politicians," concluded Pomper, "are free from popular dictation, but not from popular responsibility. . . . The voters authoritatively command: Attention must be paid."[26]

Obviously this analysis implies that there will be a heavy burden on *leadership* in a democracy. Government by the people is not directly by the people but by leaders acting with the eventual consent of the people. Hence leaders must know how to *govern*—that is, to initiate, to innovate, to act before the people may know what the real issues are—but they must not lose contact with the great mass of voters.

Although Pomper's careful analysis seems to undermine the critics' central contention that elections are meaningless, yet there is still a need to be concerned about how to improve election arrangements—particularly the convention system for choosing presidential nominees and the electoral college system for electing presidents.

[25]Quoted in Denis G. Sullivan, Jeffrey L. Pressman, Benjamin I. Page, and John J. Lyons, *The Politics of Representation: The Democratic Convention 1972* (St. Martin's, 1974), p. 74.

[26]*Elections in America: Control and Influence in Democratic Politics* (Dodd, Mead, 1968), pp. 255, 266.

The candidates shown here, George McGovern, Adlai Stevenson, and Charles Percy used different strategies to campaign for political office, but meeting with the rank-and-file voter was essential for each of them.

REFORMING THE NATIONAL CONVENTION

The national presidential convention has long been one of the most criticized of our election arrangements. Through unprincipled deals in smoke-filled rooms, it has been charged, the candidate is picked by party bosses, who often come up with a compromise candidate representing the dead level of party mediocrity. The manner of choosing the delegates is also under attack. Both conventions and primaries are rigged and run by state bosses, it is said, and presidential primaries are so complicated that they baffle the voter and discourage him from taking part.

The main defense of the convention system is simple: It works. During the past hundred years, the convention system has brought before the country men of the caliber of Lincoln, Cleveland, McKinley, Wilson, Smith, Willkie, both Roosevelts, Stevenson, Eisenhower, and Kennedy. The genius of the convention system is that it usually produces a candidate who represents party consensus instead of merely some wing of the party. This is important, for only such a man can enjoy the united support of the party in the campaign and in the White House. Moreover, it is said, the convention increasingly manages to select the man who is the overwhelming choice of the party rank-and-file and who is, indeed, a national favorite rather than a dark horse. When a party convention nominates a candidate lacking consensus and moderate support at the grass roots, as the Republicans did in choosing Goldwater in 1964, and the Democrats in picking McGovern in 1972, the party pays a heavy price in the November election.

Some favor the convention but would like to see it improved in operation. President Eisenhower, for example, called for cutting down the number of delegates to about a thousand; restricting demonstrations to five minutes; maintaining absolute order in the hall; and keeping all reporters and cameramen off the floor. Experienced politicians opposed such changes on the grounds that Americans liked the conventions the way they were, tumult and all, and that both the delegates and the public wanted reporters and cameramen on the floor—the delegates because they liked the publicity and the public because it wanted an intimate close-up of what was supposed to be happening in state delegations and smoke-filled rooms.

These questions came to a head in the crisis of the Democratic convention in Chicago in August 1968. The open combat between protesters and police outside of the convention stemmed from many factors, but it focused attention on the issue of whether conventions fairly represent the rank-and-file and whether they are open enough to rank-

and-file participation and influence. Inside, the Democrats managed to conduct a relatively orderly convention: A full-dress debate was held on Vietnam in which several sides were heard and the issues were intensely argued; there is no evidence to suggest that the candidates chosen were not the choice of a majority of the rank-and-file Democrats. But the general turmoil was so intense and well publicized as to bring the whole convention system under a cloud.

Before adjourning, the Democrats took two steps toward reform: They abolished the unit rule (under which all delegates must vote as a block if so instructed by a state party convention or by a majority of the delegation), and they also required that all delegates be selected during the year in which the convention is held (so that party leaders could not "lock up" the delegation long before even the candidates might be known). The Democrats also promised to consider other reforms.

During the early 1970s, the momentum for reform peaked in the Democratic party, under the leadership of Senator McGovern. Reformers were especially eager to open the party up to groups they felt had been prevented from playing their full role in the party—especially women, young persons, and minority groups. In a bold move, it was decided in effect that state delegations to presidential conventions must include women, young people, and minority-group members "in reasonable relation to the groups' presence in the population of the state." In some states this provision was interpreted in such a way that mandatory *quotas* were imposed. There the established leaders such as union officials were sometimes kept off slates in favor of housewives, college students, and others who had had little experience in the Democratic party.

The smoldering battle between regulars and reformers in the Democratic party reached a climax in the 1972 convention in Miami. Established labor, black, and other group leaders looked on in helpless rage while the "new politics" dominated the convention. Following McGovern's defeat, the pendulum swung back against reform. Mandatory quotas were repudiated. The effort to minimize the influence of officeholders—that is, the so-called hierarchy, or establishment—in the party was blunted. But the reform impetus was still considerable. Instead of quotas, Democrats backed "affirmative action programs" under which state party officials were required actively to welcome and recruit women, young persons, and minority-group members into the party. Slate-making was to be allowed but not to be given preferential treatment. And in a move that might have major and unanticipated consequences, "winner-take-all" presidential primaries were barred under proposal rules. Instead, states with presidential primaries must apportion delegate votes according to the popular preference for rival candidates.[27] Critics immediately charged that this type of "proportional representation" would mean that only wealthy candidates could run for president in 1976 because only such candidates would mount major

[27]On Democratic party reforms, see Sullivan et al., *Politics of Representation*, and John G. Stewart, *One Last Chance: The Democratic Party, 1974–76* (Praeger, 1974), esp. Chs. 2, 6.

campaign efforts in all states—and such efforts would be required if candidates were to have a chance to win sizeable blocks of votes before the convention, and if the convention itself was not to degenerate into guerrilla warfare.

The Republicans too were reform-minded. A party committee recommended a radical increase in the number of women delegates, more representation for blacks and other minority groups, regional platform hearings prior to the convention, and a curb on floor demonstrations except for the more serious candidates. While the Republican National Committee generally supported such reforms, they were not binding on state parties. Reform efforts languished during the Nixon presidency, but Watergate brought a new surge of reform in the GOP—especially since many Republicans felt that a major reason for Watergate itself was the supremacy of Nixon's personal organization, headed by C.R.E.E.P., over the national party organization.

A NATIONAL PRESIDENTIAL PRIMARY?

Many critics hold that such piecemeal reforms will never be enough to "democratize" the nomination method: indeed, that the convention system, no matter how operated, will always be "exclusive," "elitist," and "controlled." In order to avoid chaos, a convention consisting of thousands of delegates coming together briefly from all parts of the nation obviously has to be "managed," delegations have to have leaders, and prominent party officials such as governors and senators are likely to have more influence than rank-and-file delegates. Some of these critics would abolish the convention completely and substitute a *direct presidential primary system.*[28] Under this plan there would take place simultaneously throughout the states—probably in the spring of every presidential election year—primary elections in which the voters in each party would directly vote for their favorite without the intervention of nominating conventions.

This proposal, which might require a constitutional amendment, has been criticized on the grounds that it would: (1) favor rich candidates by enlarging the role of the mass media and minimizing party organization, so that candidates would have to spend an enormous amount of money for television and radio, especially if they were running against celebrities; (2) disrupt party solidarity and effectiveness by divesting the national parties of their key role in the nominating process; (3) probably attract so many candidates that no one candidate would win a majority in the presidential primary, thus requiring a second, expensive primary in the form of a run-off. Although the proposal for national presidential primaries has been advanced time and again over the last several decades, it has not attracted a great deal of support and its adoption continues to be unlikely.

[28]For a commentary on the Mansfield-Aiken proposed constitutional amendment embodying this plan, see *Congressional Record,* 119, No. 39 (March 13, 1973).

It is possible that more states will adopt the *state* presidential primary as a means of selecting delegates to the national presidential conventions. These primaries fall short of serving as "plebiscitarian democracy," but depending on how they are conducted—for example, how binding the results are on the delegates' presidential preferences at the convention—the state primaries introduce a strong popular voice into the nomination of presidential candidates.[29]

REFORMING THE ELECTORAL COLLEGE

"You go first, sonny, then point me toward him."

From *The Herblock Gallery* (Simon & Schuster, 1968).

The electoral college system has long been criticized on the grounds that: (1) small states and large "swing" states are overrepresented; (2) the winner-take-all aspect distorts equal representation of all voters and could elect the candidate who received fewer popular votes than his opponent; (3) electors could vote for some other person than the candidate they were pledged to vote for; (4) if no candidate won an electoral college majority the issue would be thrown into the House of Representatives, where each state delegation, no matter how large or small, would have one vote, thus perverting the representative process even further.

Of the many proposals for reform, the least drastic and simplest is to abolish the individual electors but to retain the winner-take-all method of counting the electoral vote. This proposal has never got very far, in part because it meets only part of the objection to the present system. Another reform proposal is the *proportional* plan, under which each candidate would receive the same proportion of the electoral vote of a state as he won of its popular vote; actual electors would be abolished. Thus if a candidate gained one-third of the popular vote in a state having twelve electoral votes, he would win four of the electoral votes. This proposal has been opposed by liberal Democrats because they fear it would augment the influence of rural, small-town conservatives. Since the present system compels presidential candidates to fight especially hard for the big, urban, balance-of-power states, many liberals feel the man who would be president must be especially responsive to the needs and hopes of the working class, black, ethnic, and other groups who make up the urban electorate. Liberals are even less enthusiastic over another proposal, the *district plan*, which would choose electors on the basis of congressional districts (plus two electors elected statewide from each state to correspond to the state's two senators). It is contended that this plan would overrepresent rural and suburban areas in the electoral college just as they are overrepresented in Congress.

The most forthright alternative to the present electoral college system is the *direct election* of the president. Presidents would be elected by direct popular vote just as governors are; there would be neither an

[29]James W. Davis, Jr., *Presidential Primaries: Road to the White House* (Crowell, 1967), pp. 4, 274; Harvey Zeidenstein, "Presidential Primaries—Reflections of 'The People's Choice'?," *Journal of Politics,* (November 1970), pp. 856–74.

electoral college nor individual electors. Typically this kind of plan provides that if no candidate receives at least 40 percent of the total popular vote, a run-off election would be held between the two contenders with the most votes. The arguments for this plan are that it would give every voter the same weight in the presidential balloting, in accordance with the one person-one vote doctrine; the winner would take on more credibility because of his predominance in one big national balloting; and the dangers and complications of the present electoral college would be ended in favor of a simple, visible, clear-cut decision. Opponents of direct election argue that the plan would require a national election system, thus further undermining federalism; that it would encourage "naked, unrestrained majority rule," and hence political extremism; and that the smaller states would be submerged in a vast electorate and hence would lose much of their present influence.[30]

How likely is electoral college reform? Despite much sentiment for change—especially for adoption of direct election—no reform proposal has been adopted. Both the defenders and opponents of the electoral college system have been so divided over their many proposals, and variants of proposals, that it has been impossible to muster two-thirds of the senators and of the representatives behind any proposed constitutional amendment. Conservatives in both parties, moreover, are strongly against direct election of the president. A major effort to pass a constitutional amendment for direct election failed in 1970 in the face of a determined filibuster by Southern and other conservatives.

Part of the trouble, no doubt, is that the very complexity of the electoral college system defeats efforts to persuade people to understand it and its dangers. When "people in the street" were polled about their views toward the electoral college, two (not typical) replies were:

> "Every boy and girl should go to college and if they can't afford Yale or Harvard, why, Electoral is just as good, if you work."
>
> "The guys at the bar poor-mouth Electoral somthin' awful. Wasn't they mixed up in a basketball scandal or somethin'?"[31]

[30]Neil R. Peirce, in *The People's President* (Simon and Schuster, 1968), describes and advocates the direct-vote alternative; Sayre and Parris, in *Voting for President*, argue for retaining the present electoral college system.

[31]Quoted in Lawrence D. Longley and Alan G. Braun, *The Politics of Electoral College Reform* (Yale University Press, 1972), p. 1. This study is a comprehensive treatment of the subject.

Part Five
Policy-makers and policy-making

The main problem posed by Part Five is responsible leadership. By *leadership* we mean the readiness and ability of policy-makers to act effectively in meeting public problems. By *responsible* we mean the ability of voters sooner or later to hold policy-makers accountable for their actions, and the obligation of officials to safeguard both the processes and the substance of democracy when threatened by emotional mass opinion.

Our assessment of responsible leadership begins properly with the treatment of Congress in Chapter 13. How quickly and effectively can Congress take the lead in meeting complex contemporary problems? What are the obstacles to a revitalized, reformed Congress? To whom is Congress responsible? Mainly to the voters, of course. But to which voters? Should Congress respond more strongly to a broader interest, such as a majority of the *national* electorate?

Chapter 14 treats federal judges and the judicial process. Judges, although not directly chosen by the voters, are frequently in the business of making policy. Yet to whom are they responsible? To the president? To Congress? To the electorate? To the Constitution? To their own professional standards or consciences? To all these, of course. But what if they must choose between different kinds of responsibilities?

The presidency, discussed in chapters 15 and 16, poses the problems of accountable leadership sharply. The powers of the office, combined with the fixed four year term, generally give enormous leadership resources to a president. Most strong presidents have used these tools purposefully. Yet, as we now know, the enlarged political leadership resources of the modern presidency can be abused and misused, just as they can be underused. What is the proper balance that would ensure in this great office both imaginative, progressive leadership *and* responsible use of power?

What about the civil servants and the sprawling federal bureaucracy? To whom are they responsible? To the president? To Congress? To the law? To their own perspectives and judgments? Bureaucrats are not expected to lead in the usual sense of that term. In fact, however, government administrators are constantly helping to fashion policy as they execute and implement it. Chapter 17 examines the growing importance of the bureaucrats and what factors or forces help to keep them accountable and within the Constitution.

Chapter 18 considers the major institutions of government as they interact and clash with one another. If, in the earlier chapters of this Part, we have looked at major national institutions in a somewhat compartmentalized fashion, we now view these same institutions *in motion*. That is, how do they contribute to the larger policy-making system? What institutions or groups are most important in shaping national policy? What skills and resources are needed to influence *policy outcomes?* What is the importance of lobbying and the lobbyists? What about the much discussed public interest lobbying groups? To whom are they responsible? What do they achieve?

In short, how can we make the various participants in national policy-making responsible to the majority of voters? Because most of our central policy-makers win power through political parties seeking majority support, this problem raises again the question of how strongly, if at all, the winning party should control the people in office. Should we make legislative and executive branch officials more responsible to the majority of the people? If so, how best to achieve such ends? Or do we want a looser, more decentralized policy-making system that gives more power to shifting coalitions of minority groups, working through and around parties?

In studying the question of responsibility in the context of national policy-making, we are trying to discover which voters and which interests the leaders are responsible to and just how they exercise that responsibility.

Chapter 13 Congresspersons and the congress

When a new set of "representatives of the people" convened in Washington in January 1975, there were hopes that the 94th Congress would continue in the new direction set by the 93rd. In the summer of 1974, as Congress began its historic televised proceedings against President Nixon, Americans were told that "the system works." Congress, originally conceived as the *first branch* of government, was at last reasserting itself. Almost all agreed that it met its awesome responsibility in the impeachment proceedings. But when President Nixon chose to resign rather than face trial in the Senate, and when the new president pardoned his predecessor, Congress once again sat on the sidelines. Then, as economic problems intensified in the fall of 1974, Congress made some effort, in cooperation with President Ford, to shoulder its share of the job of calming inflation and averting recession.

When the new Congress convened Americans still wondered. With one or two crises overcome, would Congress continue to reassert itself as a source of leadership? Or would the eclipse of Congress by the executive branch continue as part of a worldwide trend toward strong executives—as in Britain, France, Latin America, the Middle East, Russia, and China—and also within many of our states and cities?

Many still wanted to dream the dream of Congress as the *people's branch*, the seat of *republican* government, the agency of *popular action*.

Congress, of course, has both supporters and detractors. And—as in everything else—one's attitudes are often shaped by what kind of policies and programs one supports. Where activist liberals once viewed Congress as a roadblock to progress in the early 1960s, they often praised its deliberative virtues in the early 1970s. Note, for example, the view of a decidedly liberal senator in 1973: "I think there's a certain value to delay, and to the aging of an issue, that one perhaps appreciates only after one has been around here for a while. I think that in a democracy there's some value in allowing time for issues to be ventilated, for digging out facts, for having the debates, for having the efforts to compromise, which take time and for which Congress is given little credit, because what people say is 'What are you producing?'"[1]

Yet Congress is continually criticized. Many charge that congressmen augment government of elites, by elites, and for elites, adding that Congress actually comprises two "Houses of Misrepresentatives." As elected elites beholden to "fat cats" and "special interests," legislators are portrayed as obsessed chiefly with staying elected and as near-impotent in exercising independent control over the sprawling executive branch and the spiralling budgets. Delegation of more authority to the executive is their standard solution to major problems. And Congress seems irresponsible in foreign policy matters, if only because it is not involved. Diplomacy is now handled in this country as in every other country: by the executive in secret.

"It's called separation of powers—we separate you from your powers."

Herblock Special Report (W. W. Norton & Co., Inc., 1974).

Perhaps the most controversial and contested complaint revolves around the question of representation, since Congress was designed especially to reflect the people's needs and interests. Here again, disillusioned critics charge that the accommodations congressmen make to get elected and the folkways they observe once elected all combine to undermine what was supposed to have been its cardinal virtue.

Whatever its defects, few people dispute that Congress is the most powerful legislature in any large complex society. This chapter describes the job of congressmen and the structure of Congress, its subsystems and its relations with the larger political system. Whether one wishes to change Congress or keep it pretty much as is, it is first important to understand how it operates and why it functions as it does.

Who are the legislators?

All members of Congress are successful politicians—men and women who have risen through the political processes of their localities and states. The entire membership of the House of Representatives is elected every even year. Elections for the six-year Senate terms are staggered, so that one-third of the Senate is chosen at each congressional election.

[1]Sen. Walter F. Mondale (D. Minn.) quoted, *The New Yorker* (May 19, 1973), p. 129.

The Capitol

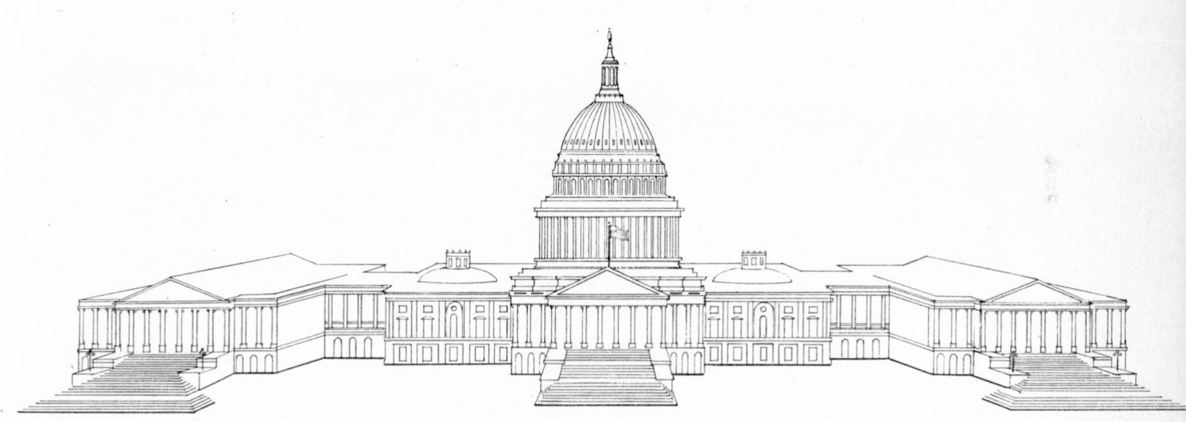

Congress is the seat of legislative authority, the center of public debate, a carry-over of folksy political traditions from earlier days—and a collection of several hundred relatively independent politicians with separate but overlapping constituencies. The architecture of the Capitol bespeaks its ways—two chambers, endless corridors, ornate rotundas and galleries, and a rabbit warren of grand rooms, tiny offices, winding passageways. There is no culminating point of authority but a multiplicity of decision centers.

PUBLIC AREAS

18 Statuary Hall
19 Rotunda
20 Senate Rotunda
21 Old Senate Chamber
*(being restored as old Senate Chamber)

SENATE

Washington, D.C. 20510

22 Senators' Offices
23 Executive Clerk
24 Senate Conference Room
25 Senate Disbursing Office
26 Minority Leader
27 Majority Leader
28 Office of the Vice President
29 Senators' Reception Room
30 Cloakrooms
31 Senate Chamber
32 Marble Room
33 President's Room
34 Office of the Secretary
35 Chief Clerk
36 Bill Clerk and Journal Clerk
37 Official Reporters of Debates

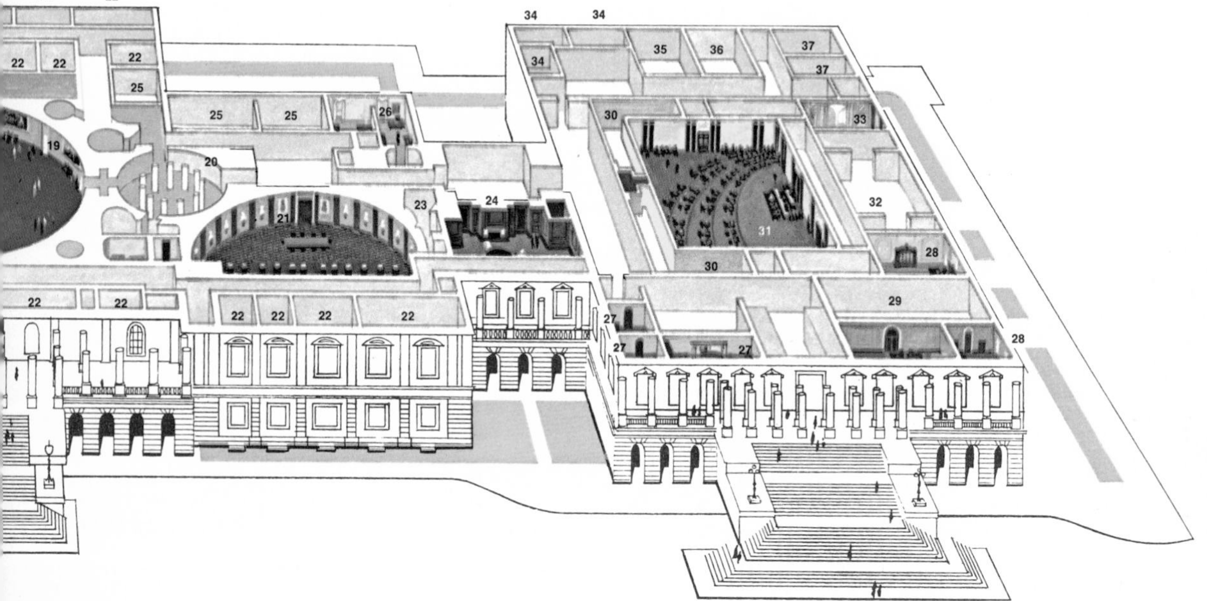

HOUSE OF REPRESENTATIVES
Washington, D.C. 20515

1 Speaker's Office
2 Committee on Ways and Means
3 Parliamentarian
4 House Floor Library
5 Cloakrooms
6 Members' Retiring Room and Lobby
7 House Chamber
8 Committee on Appropriations
9 Minority Whip
10 House Reception Room
11 House Minority Conference Room
12 House Majority Conference Room
13 House Document Room
14 Subcommittee on Foreign Affairs
15 Representatives' Offices
16 Prayer Room
17 Minority Leader

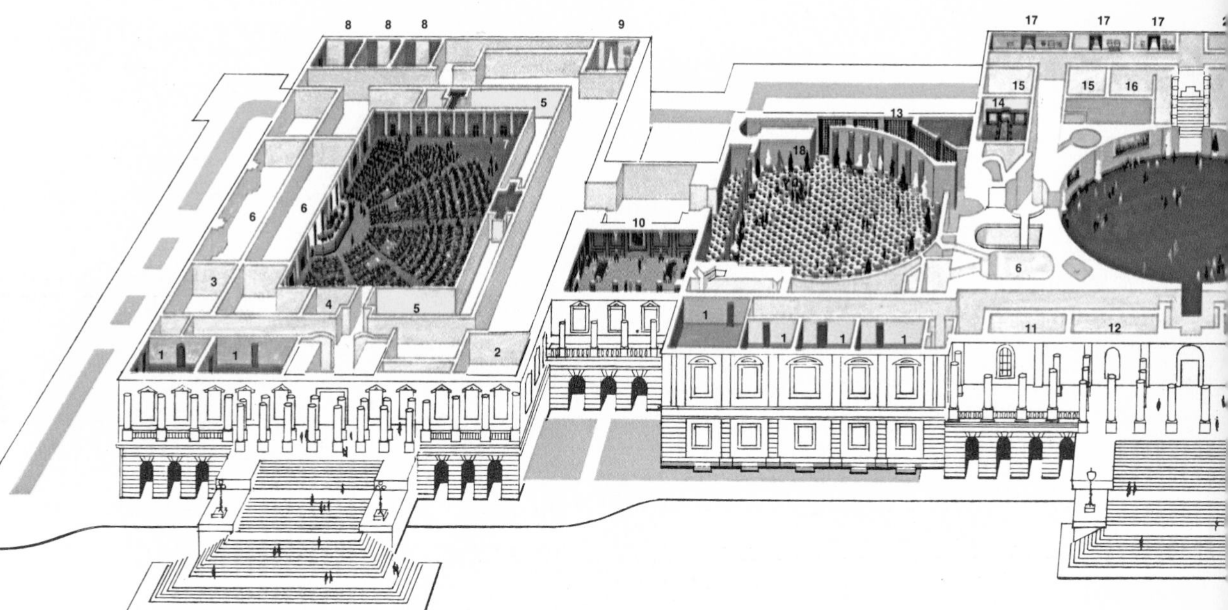

THE SOCIOECONOMIC MAKE-UP OF CONGRESS

"From log cabin to the White House"—that any youth can rise to high national office—is one of the most pervasive ideals in American politics. The Constitution, at least, sets up no major barriers except age. Members of the House must be at least twenty-five years old and have been citizens for seven years. Senators must be at least thirty and have been citizens for nine years. But in fact neither senators nor representatives mirror the socioeconomic make-up of the people as a whole.

The overwhelming number of national legislators are WASPs—white Anglo-Saxon Protestants. There has been a significant increase in the number of Catholics and Jews over recent decades, and a modest increase of women and blacks over recent years. Still the number of the latter two groups is disproportionately small. Of the 535 members of the 94th Congress (1975–77), for example, 18 were women, 18 were blacks, and about two dozen Jews, while Protestants numbered nearly 400 and Catholics about 125. Although most members were born and raised in their districts, a survey of the 93rd Congress indicated that an increasing number moved into their states or districts: 25 percent of those in the Senate and 42 percent of those in the House moved from elsewhere. Other distinguishing characteristics:

1. Senators and representatives come overwhelmingly from *upper- and middle-class* families. Their fathers tend to be professional men, businessmen, officials, and farmers rather than industrial wage-earners or farm laborers.

2. Members of Congress are far *better educated* than Americans as a whole. More than four-fifths of the members of recent Congresses were college educated; only about one-fifth of the voting age population had college educations.

3. Members come disproportionately from *rural areas*. Congress still abounds with "small-town boys," though this is beginning to change. The rural, or small-town, backgrounds can affect later attitudes toward urban problems.

4. Members *occupationally* do not accurately reflect the occupations

Conferring before the House Judiciary Committee are (from left) Representatives Edward Mezvinsky, R. H. Thornton, Jr., and Barbara Jordon with Walter Flowers and Jerome Waldie in the background.

of the electorate. Over half of them are lawyers. Business and banking are the next most represented occupations in the Congress. Rarely does a member of Congress emerge out of our trade unions or the so-called "blue collar" occupations. Hence, there is a notable overrepresentation of high-prestige professional and business occupations.

How important is this "misrepresentation?" Critics say that it offers damning proof of the elitist make-up of Congress. Pluralists point out that we would hardly expect to find the national percentage of high-school or college dropouts reflected in Congress. Elitists reply that whereas formal education may be related to political capacity, it is not clear that race, father's income, or place of birth has any such relationship. Other critics are bothered less by the socioeconomic mix of Congress than the socioeconomic interests that are represented there. Whatever the make-up, however, the question is whether legislators drawn from a restricted segment of the population will be *systematically* and *inexorably* biased in favor of certain points of view.

THE POLITICS OF DISTRICTING

There is also a *political* bias in Congress. The framers intended the Senate to represent areas rather than numbers, while the House was roughly to reflect population. By act of Congress the membership of the House is set at 435; these seats are distributed by Congress among the states according to population, with each state receiving at least one. After each ten-year census the Bureau of the Census submits a suggested allocation of the seats, which becomes final unless Congress acts to the contrary. But Congress has left almost complete control over the drawing of congressional districts to the state legislatures.

People hold conflicting notions about the proper basis for representation in the House of Representatives. Some argue that distinct geographic areas such as rural or inner-city districts should be the basis for representation, whether or not each district consists of the same number of people or voters. Others hold that representation should be based on compact districts that are as nearly equal in population as possible and do not cut across homogeneous areas such as cities.

For decades Congress left it to the state legislatures to determine how congressional districts should be drawn. In most states the party in control openly engaged in gerrymandering—that is, it tried to draw the boundaries of districts in such a way as to secure for itself as many representatives as possible. Congressional districts took on a variety of weird shapes and wildly varying populations.

The major consequence of leaving "districting" to the state legislatures was to reduce the number of competitive seats in the House and to overrepresent the *rural* areas, chiefly at the expense of the suburbs. Because the population had shifted from rural to inner-city and suburban areas, failure to redistrict used to automatically strengthen rural representation. Too, in most states the legislatures, themselves products of gerrymanders that overrepresented rural areas, favored their own rural supporters when drawing congressional district boundaries.

City and suburban people were of course unhappy about this arrangement, but their protests were ineffective. State legislatures were unresponsive to reforming themselves and Congress had no interest in doing so. And for decades the Supreme Court ruled that the drawing of congressional districts was a political judgment and not subject to judicial supervision (*Colegrove v. Green*, 1946).

Then in 1964 the Supreme Court came to the rescue. In *Wesberry v. Sanders*, the Court ruled that the Constitution requires that, as nearly as is practicable, one person's vote in a congressional election should be worth as much as another's.[2] (The Court used to talk about one man, one vote, but in more recent decisions it shows that it too can keep up with the times and now sometimes talks about one *person*, one vote.) Many critics accused the Supreme Court of being simplistic, of imposing on the nation its own view of how best to secure a "representative" Congress. The Supreme Court refused to retreat so far as congressional districts are concerned. (It has a less rigid standard for state legislatures and city councils, although it still holds to the principle of equal population among districts.)[3] In the case of congressional districts, the Court has laid down very stringent standards: A state legislature must justify any variance from precise mathematical equality by showing that it made a good-faith effort to achieve equality among districts. The desire to maintain the specific interests of particular districts—for example, urban or rural or suburban or minority-group—is no justification. As a result state legislatures have grudgingly redrawn congressional districts to meet the Supreme Court's standards.

How much difference have these actions made? Population inequalities have been ended. The voice of suburban populations has been enhanced in the House of Representatives, chiefly at the expense of rural areas but in some instances at a loss to the inner city. Gerrymandering, however, has continued unabated since the *Wesberry* decision. Indeed, without the flexibility accorded by population inequalities, politicians often find that the only way to protect incumbents is to draw lines even more cunningly than before. The Supreme Court simply insists that congressional districts be equal in population. One critic of the Supreme Court's insistence on mathematical equality believes that the results in New York were that "a bipartisan set of congressional districts with minimal population deviation was voided, and a partisan set of districts authorized—districts I might add which are characterized by zero deviation and very unhappy Democrats."[4]

[2]*Wesberry v. Sanders* (1964); *Wells v. Rockefeller* (1969); and *Kirkpatrick v. Preisler* (1969).

[3]*Mahan v. Howell* (1973).

[4]Robert G. Dixon, Jr., "Who Is Listening? Political Science Research in Public Law," *Political Science* (Winter 1971), p. 23. See also A. Spencer Hill, "The Reapportionment Decisions: A Return to Dogma?" *Journal of Politics* (February 1969), pp. 186–213.

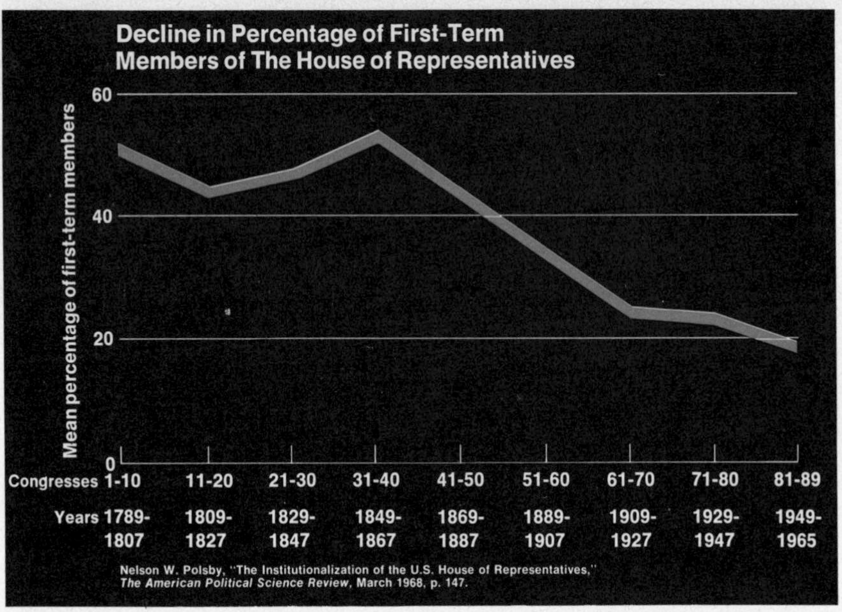

Senator Barry Goldwater campaigning.

SAFE SEATS AND CAREERISM

Senators and representatives are largely the product of the political forces in their states and districts. They are national officials locally chosen. Since they have power bases independent both of the president and of their party's leadership in Congress, they know that as long as they can keep "the folks (and the interests) back home" happy they can stay in office almost indefinitely. Redistricting of House seats, by responding to local pressures, augments congressional independence.

Localism and gerrymandering have other effects. In every election the vast majority of senators and representatives are returned to office. In the 1972 elections, for example, 85 percent of all Senate incumbents who ran were reelected, and 96 percent of all House incumbents who ran were reelected. These figures are typical. (The 1974 elections are outside the pattern, reflecting the repercussions of Watergate and stagflation.) Between 1956 and 1966, less than 2 percent of the House members seeking reelection lost their seats in this fashion.[5] Most House seats are "safe" in that incumbents typically win by such sweeping majorities that the chances of challengers defeating them are minimal.

There is a striking contrast in this aspect between House elections and presidential elections. Although presidential elections have been highly competitive in recent decades, the number of competitive con-

[5]Charles O. Jones, *Every Second Year: Congressional Behavior and the Two Year Term*, (Brookings, 1967), p. 68.

gressional seats has declined sharply in the past fifty years.[6] Senate elections have tended to be more competitive than House elections, partly because senators represent far more varied areas than many representatives, whose districts are often homogeneous enclaves. The *relative* homogeneity of House districts, as compared to entire states, and to the nation as a whole, makes it easier for representatives to stress local interests—one of the reasons that reelection to the House is somewhat more frequent than reelection to the Senate, and, of course, to governorships.

Critics of Congress point to this lack of competition as one of the causes of congressional conservatism. The whole election system, they contend, guarantees that Congress will be more tied to the status quo than will the president, and that the House will be more resistant to political change than the Senate. Pluralists hold that this failing can be remedied by the people, who can always vote an incumbent out of office if he loses touch with his constituents or with national needs. Unhappily, popular ignorance about candidates for Congress and congressmen in office is overwhelming. Few people even know the name of their congressman. Voters all too rarely evaluate legislators on their stands or votes on issues. More frequently, they are judged on their constituency service, their communications with the district, their attendance records, and other such nonlegislative matters.

A "safe" seat, on the other hand, also permits a congressman or a senator to become a national leader without having to worry too much about cultivating his district or state. Senator Frank Church, for example—as long as he does not take issue with sensitive domestic concerns of the people of Idaho—can count on a base from which he has become a national spokesman for certain foreign policy attitudes. Representatives of highly competitive states or districts, on the other hand, find it more difficult to ignore local concerns, and tend to concentrate their time and energies on more parochial matters.[7]

The job of the legislator

National legislators lead a hectic life. Congress now meets year round, whereas a hundred years ago it often met for just a few months each year. There is never enough time to digest the flood of information, letters, complaints, reports, and advice that pours into their offices. *Staying elected* is the chief priority for most members, and some members seem to have few if any other interests. But for most, there are the constantly demanding secondary tasks of *keeping on top of their committee*

[6]Nelson W. Polsby, "The Institutionalization of the U.S. House of Representatives," *American Political Science Review* (March 1968), pp. 145–47.

[7]See Roger H. Davidson, *The Role of the Congressman* (Pegasus, 1969), esp. Ch. 4.

responsibilities, staying in touch with key leaders and activists back home in their districts, and *striving to comprehend national problems* and their possible remedies. Most congressmen, most of the time, are extremely hard-working. They drive themselves at a pace far above that of the typical professional or business man. Of necessity their travel commitments are like those of airline pilots and cross-country truck drivers. The average member stays elected about eleven or twelve years, but the job description defies easy summary. Depending on the kind of district, the personality of the member, and issues of the day, the legislator may emphasize *representation, law-making and committee work,* or *reelection tasks.*

LEGISLATORS AS REPRESENTATIVES

Whom does the congressman represent—his geographical district and its immediate interests? his party? the nation? some special clientele? his conscience? How the legislators define their representative roles has been one of the major questions in political science—and for good reason. Congress was intended to serve as a forum for registering the diverse interests and values that make up the nation. It was never intended that the congressional branch would represent the identical viewpoints as the executive. But to whom does the congressman listen?

Certain patterns are evident, but they are murky and sometimes baffling. For one thing, congressmen perceive their roles differently. Some believe that they should serve essentially as *delegates* from their districts; they should find out what the "folks back home" need or want and serve those needs as effectively as possible. In a sense they would simply represent—*re-present*—the voters who sent them to Washington. The I'm-here-to-represent-my-district orientation, studies show, is often assumed by Republicans, nonleaders, non-Southerners, and members with low seniority.[8]

Others see their proper role as a *trustee;* their constituents, they argue, did not send them to Congress to serve as slavish agents, but as free-

[8]Roger H. Davidson, *The Role of the Congressman* (Pegasus, 1969), p. 140.

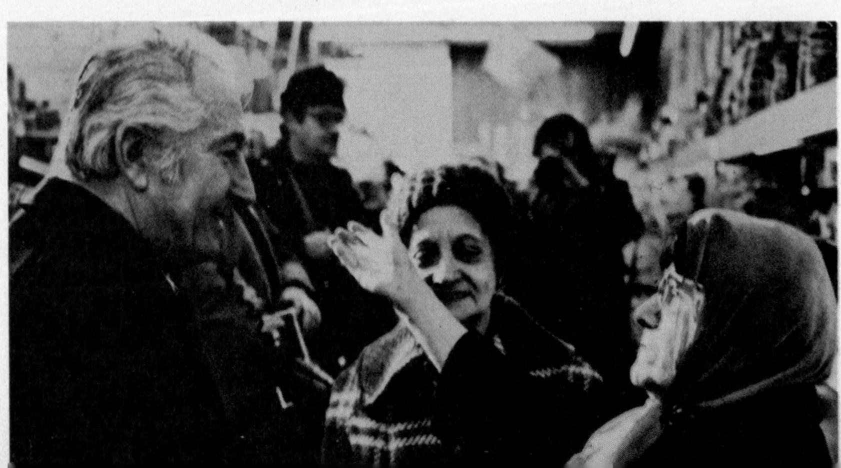

Representative Peter Rodino (D–N.J.), a man whose personalized attention to his constituents has helped keep him in Congress for twenty-five years, talks with a woman during a grocery store visit in Newark.

thinking legislators who would vote independently, on the basis of their own superior information and experience, for the welfare of the whole nation. This view echoes the classic stand once championed by Edmund Burke, who contended his judgment and conscience ought not to be sacrificed to the unenlightened and usually biased views of anyone else.[9] A legislature was a place, in his view, for deliberation and learning so mature opinion would result. A legislature should not, he believed, be a mere congress of ambassadors from localities. Interviews with members of the House of Representatives suggest that the *trustee*, or *national*, focus is more common among Democrats, House leaders, Southerners and high-seniority members.

While the question of instructed delegate versus statesman-trustee is an old one, it is somewhat misleading. Representatives cannot follow detailed instructions from their constituents because seldom are there such instructions. On many important policy questions, a member hears nothing from his constituents. And congressmen hear most often from those who agree with them. On the other hand, it is rather unrealistic to expect any legislator to define the national interest explicitly if this means comprehending all the needs and aspirations of millions of people. Most legislators, then, shift back and forth in their representative role depending on the opportunities, electoral facts of life, and pressures of the moment.

LEGISLATORS AS LAWMAKERS

Ultimately the major role of both senators and representatives is that of *law-maker*. How they perceive the nation's key problems and what can be done about them; how they respond to the interests of their constituents; the extent to which they follow cues from the president, from colleagues within the Congress, from lobbies—all these factors influence the law-writing and voting decisions in both Houses.

Most of the time the main single influence on the average legislator is his perception of how his constituents feel about the matter. This in itself does not exclude influence of other factors such as party and executive branch pressures, because the legislator may see his constituents as influenced by those pressures. But when all is said and done, the political future of the congressman depends on how a majority of his district's voters feel about his performance (to the extent that they know much about it). It will be a rare congressman who consistently and deliberately votes against the wishes of the people back home, and if too many did so it would break the major democratic link between the electorate and the decision makers.

This commonsense observation is supported by several studies. On domestic issues such as social welfare and civil rights, there is a mea-

[9]See Heinz Eulau, *et al.* "The Role of the Representative: Some Empirical Observations on the Theory of Edmund Burke." *American Political Science Review* (September 1959), pp. 742–56.

surable degree of congruence between the legislator and his district. Congressmen, especially junior members from competitive seats, vote their constituencies' attitudes, as they perceive them, with an eye on the next election. But even a member who wins by a substantial margin is not necessarily free to ignore the concerns of his constituents: "Indeed, the fact that he abides by their wishes, at least in matters about which they have an attitude of some intensity, may be one reason why he wins by substantial margins and has little primary opposition. Even if constituents are rarely interested in the congressman's actions, furthermore, he may anticipate their possible reactions to his votes and take those potential reactions into account. Indeed, his reasonably accurate anticipations could be one reason why constituents normally remain inattentive."[10] Of course, the extent to which members try to respond to their constituents' views also depends to some degree on the type of measures under consideration; for example, legislators might defer to constituent attitudes more on social and economic matters, where the voters have direct experience with government, than on less tangible policies on which mass opinion is not so well informed.[11]

Something of a paradox is evident here. Congressmen feel that their individual law-making actions may have considerable impact on the voters, yet the voters' ignorance of their congressmen's actions implies that the impact can be small. A member may think the folks back home like (or dislike) what he is doing when actually they have little if any idea of what he is doing. In part this contradiction is explained by the tendency of legislators to overestimate their visibility. Partly, too, a congressman must constantly be concerned about how he will explain his votes, especially if he fears they may be unpopular with influential citizens back home. Also, on election day, the member is dealing in increments and margins. Even if only a few of the voters are aware of his stand on a given issue, he fears that alienating this group might make the difference between victory and defeat.

Congressmen's voting decisions are also affected by the advice they obtain from their *colleagues—fellow congressmen*. Severe time limitations and the frequent necessity to make decisions with only a few hours or even minutes notice force legislators to depend on trusted peers. Most members develop friendships with people who think like themselves. Members often ask one another what they think of a piece of pending legislation, and in particular, they ask respected members of the committee working on the bill.

[10]John W. Kingdon, *Congressmen's Voting Decisions* (Harper & Row, 1973), p. 31. His interviews with a sample of members of the 91st Congress (1969) indicated that fellow congressmen and constituency factors were the most important influences on voting decisions, followed in importance by interest group, staff, and more weakly, by executive branch and party leadership factors.

[11]See in general, W. Wayne Shannon, *Party Constituency and Congressional Voting: A Study of Legislative Behavior in the United States House of Representatives* (Louisiana State University Press, 1968).

Members are also influenced by their home state colleagues, especially if the legislation appears to benefit certain states and disadvantage others. A handful of informal groups of congressmen have formed over time, some for substantive reasons, others for fraternal reasons; but nearly always bonds develop, information is traded and the norm of reciprocity often takes hold: "It's a matter of 'if you respect my work, I'll respect yours.' "

Unlike most of his or her constituents back home, a member's peers usually have detailed knowledge about many of the issues coming before Congress. Their views are often public, they may have voted on the matter in previous sessions, or in committee, and sometimes their public statements have been placed in the *Congressional Record.* Sometimes a member is influenced to vote one way merely because he or she knows another colleague is on the other side of the issue. More often, a legislator finds out how his or her friends stand on an issue, listens to one's party leadership's advice, takes into account the various committee reports and if still in doubt, consults yet additional friends.

The congressmen consulted are generally selected because they represent similar districts or the same region or state; or they are like-minded members of the same party or ideological faction. Of special importance, however, is whether they are known to be well informed and respected on the substance of the legislation; this factor alone sometimes sways a member to change his mind, to vote against his party, and sometimes even to vote contrary to what he thinks is the mood of his constituency.

Another continuing source of influence on legislative behavior is the political party. Friendship groups tend to be *intra*party more than interparty; and partisan leaders in both the executive and legislative branches apply rewards and penalties mainly to members of their own party. On some issues the pressure for conformity to a party position is immediate and direct, whereas constituency pressures may be distant, vague, and contradictory. Congressmen are always under some pressure to go along with their party, whenever possible. In the Senate "party 'discipline' may be weak, but party 'identification' is strong."[12]

The result of party pressures is a tendency, on major bills, for *most* Democrats to be arrayed against *most* Republicans. In party-line votes in the 1973 session, for example, the average Democratic senator voted with the majority of his party 69 percent of the time, and the average Republican senator voted with his party 64 percent of the time. In the House, the average Democrat voted with his party 68 percent of the time; the average Republican also voted 68 percent of the time. But here again the pattern is very uneven. Senators seem to be more independent of partisan constraints than representatives.[13] Party influence

[12]Malcolm E. Jewell and Samuel C. Patterson, *The Legislative Process in the United States* (Random House, 1966), p. 417.

[13]Aage R. Clausen and Richard B. Cheney, "A Comparative Analysis of Senate-House Voting on Economic and Welfare Policy, 1953–1964," *American Political Science Review,* (March 1970), p. 151.

Members of Congress reporting on meeting with the president.

seems to vary over time; it was probably much stronger during the nineteenth century than it has been in this century. Party influence varies by issue; recent studies indicate that party differences have been stronger over domestic, regulatory, and welfare measures than over foreign policy and civil liberty issues.[14] Much depends, of course, on what one means by party—the presidentially led party outside Congress, state, or local parties, or the congressional party leadership within Congress.

Many forces—regional, local, ideological—can override party influence. One important voting pattern in Congress reflects a *conservative coalition* of Republicans and Southern Democrats. A majority of Southern Democrats and a majority of Republicans have voted against the majority of Northern Democrats on about a quarter of the important roll call votes in recent years. This conservative coalition is most likely to appear on domestic issues, especially social welfare legislation, but its overall strength in Congress cannot be measured by voting decisions alone, because the many committee chairmen who are members of this group are often able to prevent legislation they oppose from ever being voted on. But this pattern may be changing too, as the Republican party strengthens its congressional membership from the South and the Democrats weaken their ties with it.[15]

Presidents and the executive branch can also influence how legislators vote. Some critics, for example, Ralph Nader, say Congress has yielded to virtually exclusive policy initiation and budgetary planning by the administrative branch: "No matter how hard the Congress may struggle on one issue, it is overwhelmed by the vastly greater forces of the presidency. Whether Congress wins or loses, the president ends up on top."[16] Even a fair number of congressmen complain that as now organized and staffed, Congress is incapable of really coming to grips with the enormously complex major questions central to the making of national policy.

Even if Congress were revitalized, or better organized, or even if it recaptured lost powers, the growing significance in our national lives of foreign policy issues means that the role of the president has been enhanced at the expense of the Congress. The president has the tools of foreign policy-making in his hands; and even those he shares with the Congress, such as the treaty-making power, have become less significant.

Note the following table which shows that presidents have resorted increasingly to executive agreements in arranging affairs with other nations rather than treaties which require Senate approval.

"First of all, Mr. President, we want our dome back!"

Editorial cartoon by Paul Conrad. Copyright Los Angeles Times. Reprinted with permission.

[14]Shannon, *Party, Constituency and Congressional Voting*. See also Aage R. Clausen, *How Congressmen Decide* (St. Martin's, 1973).

[15]See John F. Manley, "The Conservative Coalition in Congress," *American Behavioral Scientist* (December 1973), pp. 223–47.

[16]Mark J. Green, James M. Fallows, David R. Zwick, *Who Runs Congress?* (Bantam, 1972), p. 94.

13–1
Treaties and Executive Agreements (1789–1970)

Period	Treaties	Executive Agreements	Totals
1789–1839	60	27	87
1839–1889	215	238	453
1889–1939	524	917	1,441
1940–1970	310	5,653	5,963
	1,109	6,835	7,944

Louis Fisher, *President and Congress* (New York: The Free Press, 1972), p. 45.

Crises and emergencies have strengthened the hand of the White House vis à vis Congress. In 1973 the Senate created a special committee to look into the reasons why Congress has approved so many national emergency power statutes, especially since 1933. These statutes authorize the president to declare national emergencies and in effect to legislate by executive order.[17]

Although the president and the presidency, through executive orders, by executive agreements, through the full use of emergency, constitutional, and political powers, have become major agencies of legislation, congressmen are reluctant to admit that in deciding how to vote they are influenced by pressures from the White House. Studies suggest, however, that presidential influence on the voting decisions of congressmen may not be as significant as most political science literature previously made it appear. For example, in 1969, the positions of the executive branch did not appear to be particularly important in influencing legislators. Congressmen of the president's party did pay greater attention to the White House, but the differences between Republican and Democratic legislators were muted.[18]

"Don't put up any resistance! Just keep in step."

Ed Valtman '73, The Hartford Times.

There is evidence that a president has a more significant impact on congressional votes in the area of international politics than on domestic policies. As far as key domestic issues are concerned, congressmen are more likely to be influenced by what the voters back home want (or what he or she thinks they want), by considerations of party, than by what the White House wants.

The legislative obstacle course

From the very beginning, Congress has been a system of multiple vetoes. This was in part the intent of the framers, who wanted to disperse

[17]*Emergency Powers Statutes*, Report of the Special Committee on the Termination of the National Emergency, United States Senate, November 19, 1973, pp. 6, 7.

[18]Kingdon, *Congressmen's Voting Decisions*, p. 190.

powers so they could not be assembled by any would-be tyrant. But to cope with its legislative and other duties, Congress has developed an even more elaborate system that distributes political influence in different ways to different people.

TO ENACT A LAW

To follow a bill through the congressional labyrinth is to see the *dispersion* of power in Congress. Procedures and norms in the two chambers are somewhat different, but the basic distribution of power, in its effect on the shaping of legislation, or inactivity, is roughly the same. Every bill, including those drawn up in the executive branch, must be introduced in either chamber by a member of that body. The vast majority of the 20,000 or so bills introduced every two years die in committee for lack of support. On major legislation which has significant backing, the committee will hold hearings to receive opinions, meeting then to "mark up" (discuss and revise) and vote on the bill. If the committee votes in favor of the bill, it reports—or sends—it to the full chamber, where it is debated and voted on. If passed, it then goes to the other chamber, where the whole process is repeated. If there are differences between the bills as passed by House and Senate—and there often are—the two versions must go to *conference* committee for reconciliation.

In 1789–90 a mere 142 bills were introduced in the House of Representatives and only 85 reports were filed from committees. By the 92nd Congress (1971–72), over 17,000 bills were introduced and some 1,637 committee reports prepared. An indication of the contemporary workload of the House is shown in Table 13–2.

13–2
The Average House Legislative Workload 80th through 92nd Congress (1946–1972)

Category	Average Per Congress
Bills introduced	13,711
Committee reports	2,456
Public laws passed	790
Private laws passed	618
Total laws and resolutions	1,408
Presidential messages to Congress	185[1]
Presidential messages referred to committee	167[1]
Executive branch communications	2,372

[1]Figures for 89th through 92nd Congress only (1965–1972)

SOURCE: Final House Calendars. Reprinted from *Report* of the Select Committee on Committees, U.S. House of Representatives, to Accompany H. Res. 988, 93rd Congress (March 21, 1974).

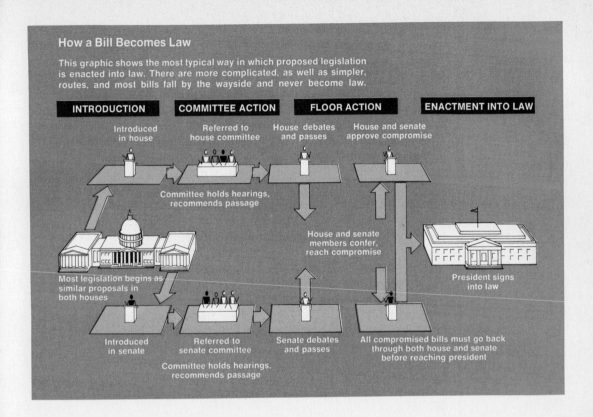

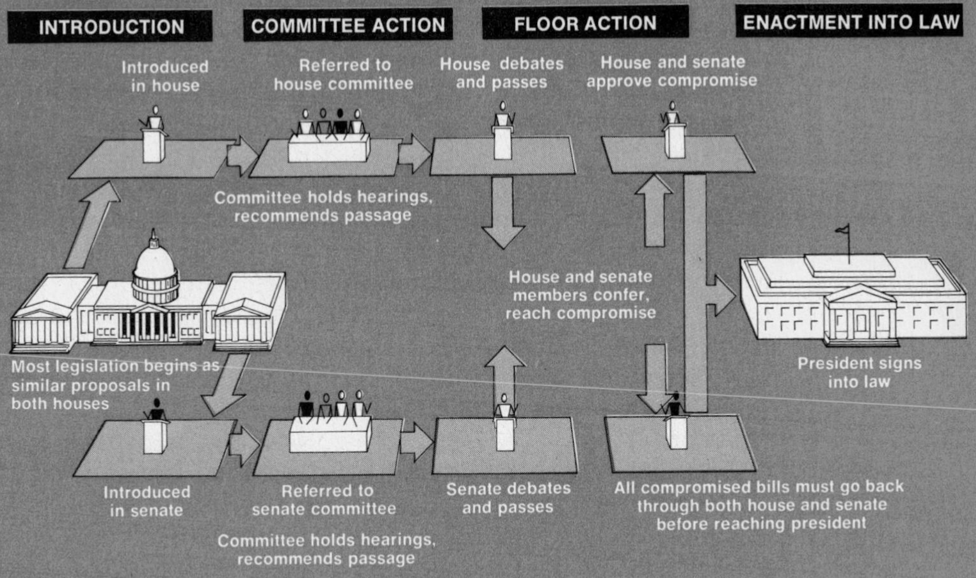

How a Bill Becomes Law

This graphic shows the most typical way in which proposed legislation is enacted into law. There are more complicated, as well as simpler, routes, and most bills fall by the wayside and never become law.

INTRODUCTION | **COMMITTEE ACTION** | **FLOOR ACTION** | **ENACTMENT INTO LAW**

Introduced in house

Referred to house committee

Committee holds hearings, recommends passage

House debates and passes

House and senate approve compromise

Most legislation begins as similar proposals in both houses

House and senate members confer, reach compromise

President signs into law

Introduced in senate

Referred to senate committee

Committee holds hearings, recommends passage

Senate debates and passes

All compromised bills must go back through both house and senate before reaching president

MULTIPLE OPPORTUNITIES FOR DELAY

The complexity of the congressional system provides a tremendous built-in advantage for the *opponents* of any measure. Proponents of new legislation must win at every step; the opponents need win only once. Multiple opportunities for vetoing legislation exist because of the dispersion of influence and because at a dozen points in committee or in the chamber a bill may be killed, or allowed to die through inaction.

One veteran student of national policy-making suggests our legislative obstacle course is so designed that only every twenty or thirty years has the American system really worked effectively in terms of bringing forth innovative legislation—and then only for brief periods. "A legislative idea whether good or bad, can be vetoed by any one of the following: (1) the chairman of the House substantive committee, (2) the House substantive committee, (3) the chairman of the House rules committee, (4) the House rules committee, (5) the House, (6) the chairman of the Senate committee, (7) the Senate committee, (8) the majority of the Senate, (9) one-third plus one of the Senate in event of a filibuster, (10)

The influence of powerful members of Congress, such as that of Republican Senators Hugh Scott and Barry Goldwater, is important in pushing, pulling, or slowing legislation through Congress. The minority party, especially, must have strong leaders to mold party unity.

the House-Senate conference committee if the Houses disagree, and (11) the president. If the concurrence of still other committees is required—appropriations, for example, the points of possible veto are multiplied."[19]

Getting a bill through Congress requires more than a majority at any one time or place. Majorities must be mobilized over and over again, in committee and in chamber. And these are ever shifting and changing majorities, involving different legislators in different situations at different points in time. Hence new coalitions must be built again and again.[20]

Clearly a controversial bill cannot go through without some astute legislative generalship. One tactical question at the start is whether to push for initial action in the upper or lower house. Complex calculations are involved. If a bill is expected to face rough sledding in the Senate, for example, its sponsors may seek House passage, hoping that a sizable victory might spur the Senate into action. Another question is what committee the bill should be assigned to for favorable action. Normally referral to a committee is automatic but sometimes a bill cuts across more than one jurisdiction leaving some room for writing the bill in such a way that it is bound to be referred to one committee rather than another. A recent civil rights bill, for example, was referred to the Senate Commerce Committee rather than the Judiciary Committee because the chairman of the former was more pro-civil rights than the chairman of the latter, but in the House it was sent to the Judiciary Committee and not the Interstate and Foreign Commerce Committee for precisely the same reason!

The houses of congress

The single most important fact about Congress is the *dispersion* of power between its two chambers. The Senate and the House each has an absolute veto over the law-making of the other. Each house runs its own affairs, sets its own rules, conducts its own investigations, but the *law-making* role is shared by the two chambers. Thus each chamber must be seen as a separate institution even though it reflects somewhat similar political forces and shares organizational patterns with the other.

THE HOUSE OF REPRESENTATIVES

Organization and procedure in the "lower" chamber is somewhat dif-

[19]James Sundquist, "Four More Years: Is Deadlock the Only Prospect?" *Public Administration Review* (May/June 1973), p. 280. For useful legislative case studies, see Robert Peabody, *et al. To Enact A Law* (Praeger, 1972) and Eric Redman, *The Dance of Legislation* (Simon and Schuster, 1973).

[20]Lewis A. Froman, Jr., *The Congressional Process: Strategies, Rules and Procedures* (Little, Brown, 1967), p. 19.

ferent from that in the "upper," if only because the House is over four times as large as the Senate. *How* things are done usually affects *what* is done. The House assigns different types of bills to different calendars; for example, finance measures—tax or appropriations bills mainly—are put on a special calendar that can expedite action. The House has worked out other ways of speeding up law-making, including an electronic voting device. Ordinary rules may be suspended by a two-thirds vote, or immediate action on a measure may be won by unanimous consent of the members on the floor. By sitting as the Committee of the Whole, the House is able to operate more informally and expeditiously than under its regular rules. For example, a quorum in this committee is only 100 rather than a majority of the whole chamber, and voting is quicker and simpler. Members are sharply limited in how long they can speak. In contrast to the Senate, debate may be cut off simply by majority vote.

THE SPEAKER AND THE ROLE OF PARTY

Former House Speaker John W. McCormack (left) with Carl Albert, present Speaker of the House.

The speaker's formal authority is not what it was sixty or seventy-five years ago when he could control committee assignments and wield almost complete control over House deliberations. Revolts by the rank-and-file "Progressives" in 1910 stripped the speaker of most of his old-time authority. Still, he remains the single most important member of the House.

The speaker's formal authority grows out of the fact that he can grant recognition to or withhold it from those who wish to speak, he settles parliamentary disputes (with the help of a specialist in procedure), he appoints members of select and conference (but not standing) committees, and in general he directs the business on the floor. Much more significant is the speaker's political and behind-the-scenes influence. Although formally chosen by the House of Representatives, he is in fact picked by the majority party. Once in office, the speaker is openly a party leader and is expected, subject to the rules of the game, to use his office to support the program of his party.[21]

traffic director of Congress

The powers of the speaker have been somewhat enlarged in recent years, through efforts of reformers to strengthen the congressional party as a policy-making instrument. For example, the speaker (and two other party leaders) now enjoy more leeway in influencing committee appointments; he has a steering and policy committee; and he has come to dominate the Rules Committee, once a roadblock in House transactions. If so disposed, a speaker can make use of these tools.

Next to the speaker, the most important party officer in the House is the *majority floor leader*, who, like the speaker, is chosen by the majority party caucus but, unlike the speaker, is an officer only of his *party* and not of the House proper. The majority floor leader helps plan party

[21]For a study, rich in implications, of the speakership as part of the evolving House structure of power, see Nelson W. Polsby, "The Institutionalization of the U.S. House of Representatives," *American Political Science Review* (March 1968), pp. 144–68.

strategy, confers with other party leaders, and tries to keep members of his party in line. The minority party elects a *minority floor leader*, who usually steps into the speakership when his party gains a majority in the House. Assisting each floor leader are the party *whips* (the term derives from the whipper-in, who in fox hunts keeps the hounds bunched in the pack). The whips serve as liaison between the House leadership of each party and the rank-and-file; they inform members when important bills will come up for a vote, exert mild pressure on them to support the leadership, and try to ensure maximum attendance on the floor when critical votes are imminent.

At the beginning of the session and occasionally thereafter, each party holds a *caucus* (or conference, as the Republicans call it). The caucus, composed of all the party's members in the House, meets privately to elect party officers, approve committee assignments, discuss important legislation, and perhaps try to agree on party policy. Decisions are usually made by simple majority. In theory, the caucus is the directing party agency; in fact, this party group plays a small part in law-making. A decision of the Democratic caucus is binding only when approved by two-thirds of the members. When it involves a matter of constitutional interpretation (as do most measures) or when conflicting promises have been made back home (and all sorts of promises have been made), the decision is not binding at all. Republicans are not bound by any conference decision. Hardly more important than the caucus are the *steering committees*, made up of the party leadership, which do little steering but have some influence on party policy and tactics.

THE HOUSE RULES COMMITTEE: TRAFFIC COP OR ROADBLOCK?

One important way in which the House differs from the Senate is the procedure for deciding the flow of business. In the House this power is largely vested in the House Rules Committee. This committee is one of the regular standing committees of the lower chamber, but in the normal course of events, a bill cannot come up for action on the floor of the House without a rule from the Rules Committee. By failing to act or refusing to grant a rule, the committee can kill a bill. Furthermore, the rule granted stipulates the conditions under which the bill will be discussed, and these conditions may seriously affect the chance of passage. The Rules Committee may grant a rule that makes it easy for a bill to be "amended to death" on the floor. A special rule may prohibit amendments altogether or provide that only members of the committee reporting the bill may offer amendments. And the rule also sets the length of debate.

Up to about the mid-1960s, the Rules Committee was dominated by a coalition of conservative Republicans, and Democrats and liberals denounced it as being unrepresentative, unfair, and dictatorial. Today it is seldom able to block legislation as it once did because of several procedural reforms. Even more important, its membership has come to reflect the view of the total membership of the House. Still the Committee remains part of the structure for the dispersion of power in the House and part of the structural bias in favor of the status quo.

THE SENATE

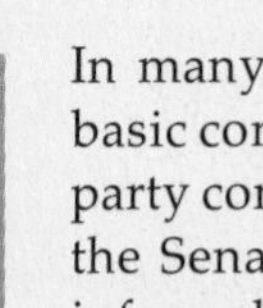

"So far, my mail is running three to one in favor of my position."

Drawing by Robt. Day; © 1970 The New Yorker Magazine, Inc.

In many respects the Senate resembles the House. There is the same basic committee structure, the elected party leadership, the rather weak party committees—in short, the same dispersion of power. But because the Senate is a smaller body, its procedures can be considerably more informal and it has more time for debate.

The president of the Senate (the vice-president of the United States) has little influence. He can vote only in case of a tie and is seldom consulted by the leadership when important decisions are made. The Senate also elects from among the majority party a *president pro tempore*, who is the official chairman in the absence of the vice-president. But presiding over the Senate is a thankless task and is generally carried out by a junior member of the chamber.

Party machinery in the Senate is somewhat similar to that of the House. There are party conferences (in the Senate, both parties have given up the term *caucus*), majority and minority floor leaders, and party whips. In the Senate each party has a *policy committee*, composed of the leaders of the party, which is theoretically responsible for the party's overall legislative program. (In the Senate the party steering committees handle only committee assignments.) Unlike the House steering committees, the Senate's policy committees are formally provided for by law, and each of them has a regular staff and a significant budget. Although the Senate policy committees exercise some influence on legislation, they have not asserted strong legislative leadership or managed to coordinate party policy.

The majority leader, however, is usually a person of influence within the Senate and sometimes in the nation. He has the right to be the first senator to be heard on the floor and, in consultation with the minority floor leader, determines the Senate's agenda. He has much to say about committee assignments for members of his own party. But the position confers less authority than the speakership in the House, and the leader's influence depends on his political skill and the national political situation. Some majority leaders had little influence in the Senate and were relatively unknown in the nation. Others made it an important post. It was as majority floor leader that Senator Taft became "Mr. Republican" and Lyndon Johnson won a national reputation.

THE POLITICAL ENVIRONMENT OF THE SENATE

Senators are a somewhat different breed of political animal from the average representative, and the upper chamber has a character all its own. If only because of their six-year term, senators have more political elbow room than representatives, who, elected by smaller constituencies, may feel cramped by the necessity of devoting themselves to the needs of relatively few interest groups. In addition, senators are more likely to wield political power in their state parties. The average senator becomes visible and politically significant earlier in his career than the average congressman. A senator's visibility often results in his or her incubating and exploring issues for public reaction and national approval or in running for the presidency, all of which contrasts sharply with the greater subject-matter specialization in the House. Part of this is due to the relative smallness of the Senate and easier access to the media; part also is due, no doubt, to their larger staffs.

To a degree, the Senate is a mutual protection society. Each member tends to guard the rights and perquisites of his fellow senators—so that his own rights and perquisites will be protected in turn. Members learn to live together. Two senators may attack each other rather sharply on the floor, only to be seen a short time later strolling together in the corridors outside. Like any close-knit social or occupational group, the Senate has developed a set of informal folkways—standards of behavior to which new members are expected to conform. Courtesy in debate is a cardinal rule, for example, and debate takes place in the third person.

Two publicly active senators with "high visibility" are Edmund Muskie of Maine and Edward Kennedy of Massachusetts.

By far the most important and pervasive of the folkways is *reciprocity*. A senator requests and receives many favors and courtesies from his fellows—always with the understanding that he will repay the kindness in some form. A senator may be out of town and request that the vote on a particular bill be delayed. A senator requests unanimous consent to suspend the rules so that he may insert material into the *Congressional Record*. A senator asks a committee chairman how a given bill will affect his constituents—and relies on his colleague's judgment. Reciprocity may involve seemingly trivial pleasantries—or it may involve millions of dollars in traded votes for public works appropriations. Logrolling is an institutionalized way of life.

Liberal senators and freshmen used to complain of a conservative "Establishment" or "club" that dominated the upper chamber through the power of these folkways and through its control of key committees and processes. But the Senate has changed. The urban influence continues to be strong in the upper chamber. A young, vigorous, attractive senator, especially one representing a large state, is almost bound to become a national political figure and to be treated as a possible candidate for the presidency. The key aspect of the Senate today is not so much the concentration of power in some Old Guard or Establishment as the dispersion of power among party leaders, a dozen committee chairmen, senators from the larger states, and young activists. The contemporary Senate is individualistic: committee chairmen have more power than nonchairmen, "but they are not strong enough to threaten the basic independence or substantive power of individual members."[22] And

[22]Randall B. Ripley, *Power in the Senate* (St. Martin's 1969), p. 229.

where once new members were expected to serve quiet apprenticeships they now often follow the model of Hubert Humphrey, Paul Douglas, Charles Percy, or William Proxmire who early on sensed the possibilities in the Senate for longer range public education—"incubating ideas that in a better climate, could hatch into programs."[23]

Huey P. Long, governor of Louisiana and later senator from that state, is shown here in a typical arm-waving pose while leading a filibuster in the early 1930s.

RULE 22: THE FILIBUSTER

One major difference between the Senate and the House is that debate is sharply limited in the House and is almost unlimited in the Senate. Once a senator gains the floor, he has the right to go on talking until he relinquishes it voluntarily or through exhaustion. This right to unlimited debate may be used by a small group of senators to *filibuster*—to delay the proceedings of the Senate in order to prevent a vote.

How may a filibuster be defeated? The majority can keep the Senate in continuous session in the hope that the filibustering senator will have to give up the floor. But if three or four senators cooperate, they can keep going almost indefinitely. They merely ask one another long questions that permit their partners to take lengthy rests. So long as they keep on their feet, debate can be terminated under Senate Rule 22 only by *cloture*. Under the rule of cloture, if sixteen members sign a petition, two days later the question of curtailing debate is put to a vote. If two-thirds of the senators on the floor vote for cloture, no senator may speak for more than one hour; then the motion before the Senate must be brought to a vote.

At one time the filibuster was the favorite weapon of Southern senators to block civil rights legislation. But now that the filibuster has diminished usefulness as an instrument of obstruction against civil rights legislation, attitudes toward it have become moderated. In 1971, for example, when Senate *liberals* threatened to filibuster against extension of the draft law, Rule 22 was successfully invoked even before the filibuster could begin. This vote marked the first occasion that Southerners such as Senator Strom Thurmond of South Carolina and John Stennis of Mississippi voted to limit debate in the Senate. Today, those who were critics of the filibuster when it was the final retreat of Southern conservatism, are more tolerant of it when used by liberals against a conservative majority.

The threat of a filibuster by an organized minority obviously affects Senate business, for the knowledge that a bill might lead to a filibuster is often enough to force a compromise satisfactory to its opponents. Sometimes the Senate leadership, knowing that a filibuster would tie up the Senate and keep it from enacting needed legislation, does not bother to bring a bill to the Senate floor.

Since Rule 22 was adopted in 1917, it has been invoked by the Senate

[23]Nelson Polsby, "Goodbye to the Inner Club" *Washington Monthly* (August 1969), p. 34. See also Paul Douglas, *In the Fullness of Time* (Harcourt Brace Jovanovich, 1971); and William Proxmire, *Uncle Sam: The Last of the Bigtime Spenders* (Simon and Schuster, 1972).

about eighty-five times. Only seventeen of these have been successful, most of them in the last decade. Various proposals have been offered to make it easier to terminate debate, and the Senate is presently considering making the vote a three-fifths rather than two-thirds majority. If such had been in effect in the past, another 20 cloture votes would have been successful.

The filibuster, and the threat of it, remains an important device available to Senate minorities. Still, a really determined majority can overcome a filibuster, either by wearing the speakers down or by mobilizing the necessary votes for cloture.

SPECIAL RESPONSIBILITIES OF THE SENATE

The Senate also differs from the House in two important ways. First, the Senate has the power to confirm presidential nominations—more than 65,000 of them each year. We shall discuss how the Senate meets this important responsibility in Chapter 18.

Second, the Senate has the responsibility of giving consent, by a two-thirds vote of the senators present, before the president may ratify a treaty. This gives the Senate a special role in foreign policy making.

Committees: the little legislatures

The main struggle over legislation takes place in committees and subcommittees, for this is where the basic work of Congress is done. Deluged by several thousand bills in a year, Congress could not do its job unless it delegated work to these "little legislatures."

The House of Representatives has twenty-two standing committees with an average membership of about thirty, and these are divided into more than 130 subcommittees. The committees are, as Speaker Reed once said, "the eye, the ear, the hand, and very often the brain of the House." Among the most important of them are the spending and taxing committees—namely, Appropriations and Ways and Means.

Standing committees have great power, for to them are referred all bills introduced in the House. They can defeat bills, pigeonhole them

Members of the Senate Rules Committee.

for weeks, amend them beyond recognition, or speed them on their way. Typically a committee reports out favorably only a small fraction of all the bills referred to it. Although a bill can be forcibly brought to the floor of the House through a *discharge petition* signed by a majority of the House membership, congressmen are reluctant to bypass committee action. For one thing, they regard the committee members as experts in their field. And there is a strong sense of reciprocity—you respect my committee's jurisdiction and I will respect yours. It is not surprising that few discharge petitions gain the necessary number of signatures.

The Senate has seventeen standing committees, each composed of seven to twenty-seven members. Whereas congressmen hold only one or two committee assignments, each senator normally serves on three committees and often on as many as nine or ten subcommittees. Among the most important Senate committees are Foreign Relations, Finance, and Appropriations. Senate committees have the same powers over the framing of legislation as do those of the House, but they do not have the same degree of power to keep bills from reaching the floor.

Partisanship factors shape the control and staffing of standing committees. The chairman and a majority of the members are elected from the majority party, and the minority party is represented roughly in relation to the proportion of its members in the entire chamber. Getting on a politically advantageous committee is important to members of Congress. A representative from Nebraska, for example, would usually much rather serve on the Agriculture or Public Works Committee than on the Merchant Marine and Fisheries Committee. Members usually stay on the same committee from one Congress to the next, but freshmen, who have been on undesirable assignments often bid for a better committee when places become available.

How are committee members chosen? In the House of Representatives a Committee on Committees of the Republican membership allots memberships to Republican freshmen. This committee is composed of one member from each state having Republican representation in the House, and this member, chosen by his state's delegation, is almost always the senior member of the delegation. Because he has as many votes on the committee as there are Republicans in his delegation, this committee is dominated by the senior members from the large-state delegations. On the Democratic side, assignment to committees is, as of 1975, handled by the Steering Committee of the Democratic Caucus, together with the speaker and majority leader, in negotiation with senior Democrats from the respective state delegations. In the Senate, veterans also dominate the committee-assignment process, with each party having a small steering committee for the purpose.

In making assignments, the leaders of Congress are guided by various considerations. The major considerations are the leaders' estimates of a member's talents and cooperativeness, whether his state or region is already well represented on a committee, and whether the assign-

A Day's Activities in Congress

Senate

Meets at 11:15 a.m. on campaign financing.

Committees:

Aeronautical & Space Sciences—10 a.m. Open:NASA auth. Dr. John Naugle. 235 Russell Office Bldg.

Appropriations Subcomte. on Interior—10 a.m. Open: Indian education & health services. 1114 Dirksen Office Bldg.

Appropriations Subcomte on Agriculture—10 a.m. Open: Consumer Product Safety Commission. S 128 Cap.

Appropriations Subcomte on HUD-Space Sciences—10 a.m. Open:NASA budget. 1224 DOB.

Appropriations Subcomte on Public Works—10 a.m. Closed:Naval nuclear reacotrs. Adm. Rickover. S 126 Cap.

Banking Subcomte on INTL Finance—10 a.m. Open: Ex-Im Bank & export controls. Elmer Staats, GAO; Wm. Casey, Ex-Im Bank. 5302 DOB.

Armed Services Subcomte on R&D—10 a.m. Closed: Mil. procurement auth. 224 ROB.

Commerce—10 a.m. Closed: Comte bus. 5112 DOB.

Commerce Subcomte on Consumer; Interior; Public Works—2:30 p.m. Closed: Deepwater ports construction & operation. 5110 DOB.

District of Columbia—9:30 a.m. Open: HR 12109, advisory neighborhood council. 6226 DOB.

Finance—10 a.m. Open: HR 10710, trade reform. Rep. Harrington. 2221 DOB.

Finance—2 p.m. Open: Compensation for energy-related unemployment. 2221 DOB.

Interior Subcomte on Minerals, Materials & Fuels—10 a.m. Open: Mineral leasing law revisions. 3110 DOB.

Interior—2:30 p.m. Open: S 3267, standby energy emergency authority & contingency plan. S 146 Cap.

Foreign Relations—10 a.m. Open: S 3117, State Dept. auth. S 116 Cap.

Foreign Relations Subcomte on Surveillance—3 p.m. Closed: Forthcoming hearings on warrantless wiretapping. S 116 Cap.

Judiciary Subcomte on Separation of Powers—10 a.m. Open: S 2903, independent Justice Dept.; S 2978, indep. special prosecutor. Archibald Cox. 2228 DOB.

Judiciary Subcomte—9 a.m. Open: Nomins. of Joseph Morris & Murray Schwartz to be district judges. 2228 DOB.

Joint Comte on Atomic Energy—2 p.m. Closed: AEC auth. H 403 Cap.

Republican Policy—12:30 p.m. Closed: Luncheon mtng. S 207 Cap.

Conferees—2:30 p.m. Closed. HR 7824, legal services. S 407 Cap.

House

Meets at noon.

Agriculture Subcomte on Dom. Marketing & Consumer Relations—10 a.m. Open:

Committees:

Meat costs. MC, USDA & publ witns. 1301 Longworth Office Bldg.

Appropriations Subcomte on Treasury-Postal-Genl Govt.—2 p.m. pen: Executive residence. Outside witns. 3 p.m. Advisory Comm. on Intergovt. Relations H 164 Cap.

Appropirations Subcomte on Defense—10 a.m. Open: AF McLucas, Chie f of Staff Gen. Brown H 140 Cap.

Appropriations Subcomte on Labor-HEW—10 a.m. Open: HEW budget. 2358 Rayburn House Office Bldg.

Appropriations Subcomte on HUD-Space-Science-Veterans—10 a.m. Open: NSF H 143 Cap.

Appropriations Subcomte on Transport—10 a.m. Open: FAA-Aerosat. 2358 RHOB.

Appropriations Subcomte on Public Works-AEC—1/80 a.m. Closed: Weapons. Open session will follow on program support. 2362 RHOB.

Appropriations Subcomte on Interior—10 a.m. Open: Office of Territories. H 305 Cap.

Appropriations Subcomte on Agri., Environ. & Consumer Protection—1 p.m. Open: EPA. 2362 RHOB.

Armed Services Subcomte No. 1—10 a.m. Closed: Title II (RDT&E) of DOD auth. AF Asst. Sec. LaBerge, Dep. Chief of Staff Gen. Evans. 2212 RHOB.

Armed Services Subcomte No. 2 and Post Office — Civil Service Subcomte on Manpower—10 a.m. Open. Title V (civilian personnel) of DOD auth. Carl Crewlow, DOD, 2118 RHOB.

Armed Services Subcomte NO. 3—10 a.m. Closed: Brfng on anti-sub warfare by J. Brackett Hersey, ONR, & Capt. Dempster Jacskon, Naval Material Ofc. 2337 RHOB.

Banking Subcomte on Housing—10 a.m. Open: Mark Up housing & community dev. legisl. 2222 RHOB.

District of Columbia—9:30 a.m. Open: HR 13608, WMATA. D.C. govt. & pub. witns. 1310 LHOB.

Education & Labor Subcomte on Equal Opportunity—9 a.m. Open: Mark up HR 12464, econ. oppor. extension. 2257 RHOB.

Govt Operations Subcomte on Equal Monetary Affairs—10 a.m. Open: CLC-FEO-petroleum increase. Chas. Owens, FEO, 2203 RHOB.

House Administration—10 a.m. Open: Mark up campaign reform legis. 2172 RHOB.

Interior Subcomte on Water & Power Resources—9:45 a.m. Open: Mark up HR 12165, Colorado River basin salinity. 1324 LHOB.

Interior Subcomte on Territorial & Insular Affairs — 10 a.m. Open: Problems of American Samoa. Gov. Haydon; reps of legis.; Interior Dept. witns. 2261 RHOB.

Interior Subcomte on Public Lands—2 p.m. Open: Wilderness legis. MC & pub. witns. 1324 LHOB.

Internal Security—10 a.m. Open: Exec. Branch domestic intelligence. Kevin Maroney & Richard Roberts, Justice; Peter Velde, LEAA. 311 Cannon House Office Bldg.

Commerce — 10 a.m. Open: HR 13834, energy emergency. 2123 RHOB.

Commerce Subcomte on Public Health & Environ.—2 p.m. Open: Mark up HR 13176, solid waste disposal amends. 2322 RHOB.

Public Works Subcomte on Transport.—10 a.m. Open: Trans. legis. MC: Gov. Wilson, N.Y.; pub witns. 2167 RHOB.

Public Works Subcomte on Oversight & Review—10 a.m. Open: Oversight hrngs on natl water pollution control. Pub. witns. 2253 RHOB

Rules—10:30 am Open: HR 13163, consumer protection; HR 12565, DoD supple; HR 11321, public safety officers' benefits. H 313 Cap.

Science—10 a.m. Open: Mark up HR 12689, NASA auth., & HR 12816, NSF auth. 2318 RHOB.

Veterans Subcomte on Edu. & Training—10 a.m. Open: Vietnam veterans' tuition. MC & pub. witns. 334 CHOB.

Ways & Means—10 a.m. Open: Mark up windfall profits legis Comite Rm. LHOB.

ment will aid in reelection. In general, leaders like to comply with members' preferences, and evidence indicates about three-fourths of the freshmen are granted some committee they requested.[24]

One reason Congress can cope effectively with its huge workload is that its committees and subcommittees are organized around subject-matter specialties. This allows members to develop considerable technical expertise in specific areas and to recruit skilled staffs. One consequence is that Congress is better able to criticize, challenge, and resist the experts in the executive bureaucracy. Members of interest groups and lobbyists realize the great power a specific committee has in areas of special interest to them and focus their attention on its members. Similarly, members of executive departments are careful to cultivate the chairmen and members of "their" committees. One powerful Senate committee chairman reminded his constituents of the amount of federal tax money being spent in their state: "This does not happen by acci-

[24]David W. Rohde and Kenneth A. Shepsle, "Democratic Committee Assignments in the House of Representatives," *American Political Science Review* (September, 1973), pp. 889–905.

dent," the Senator's campaign folder says. "It takes power and influence in Congress."

COMMITTEE DIVERSITY AND PERSISTENCE

Most committees are separate little centers of power, with norms, patterns of action, and internal processes of their own. Analyzing the House Appropriations Committee, Fenno discovered that it is characterized by a remarkable agreement among its members on key issues and the role the committee should play. Leadership in the committee is stable and its members tend to remain a long time; they have worked out a way of life emphasizing conformity, give-and-take, and hard work. The subcommittee chairmen of the House Appropriations Committee become specialists on the budgets and programs of the agencies within the scope of their subcommittee's jurisdiction and often exercise more influence over administrative policy than does any other single congressman. For example, the chairman of the Appropriations Subcommittee on Foreign Aid has more influence over that program than the chairman of the House Committee on Foreign Affairs. The several appropriations subcommittees defer to one another's recommendations and back up the decisions of the parent committee.[25]

Committees, however, differ. Some are powerful, others are notably less important. Because of the Senate's special role in foreign policy-making, for example, the Senate Foreign Relations Committee is often more influential than is the House Committee on Foreign Affairs. Within the two Appropriations Committees, however, the reverse is true, with the House Committee usually having a more significant role than the Senate Committee. Committees differ, not only for institutional reasons, but also to an important degree according to the desires and abilities of their members. As an astute student of the congressional committee process observed, "We have gotten oversight activity only when random individuals have found an incentive for doing so. . . . Similarly, I suspect that our current interest in exhorting all committees to acquire more information with which to combat the executive may be misplaced. Information is relatively easy to come by—and some committees have a lot of it. What is hard to come by is the incentive to use it, not to mention the time and the trust necessary to make it useful."[26]

ing by Richter; © 1972 New Yorker Magazine, Inc.

How the Congress uses its committees is critical in sustaining it as an equal partner in national policy-making. Notable progress has been made in recent years to open hearings to the public and to improve the quality of committee staffs. But efforts to modernize committee jurisdictions to give coherent consideration to broad, pressing national prob-

[25] See generally, Richard F. Fenno, Jr., *The Power of the Purse: Appropriations Politics in Congress* (Little, Brown, 1966).

[26] Richard F. Fenno, Jr., "If, as Ralph Nader Says, Congress is 'The Broken Branch,' How Come We Love Our Congressmen So Much?" Paper delivered in Boston, Massachusetts (December 12, 1972). See also his comprehensive comparative study of congressional committees, *Congressmen in Committees* (Little, Brown, 1972).

lems were dealt a setback in May of 1974. Missouri's Richard Bolling and nine other congressmen had been working in a bipartisan effort to overhaul the House committee system, which had not been altered significantly since 1946. Jurisdictional overlap is common. For example, eighteen different committees deal with educational programs. And no committee has primary responsibility for energy policy. Bolling's House Select Committee on Committees called for reassigning jurisdiction of several key committees, abolishing two long-time standing committees, and splitting another in two. By a vote of 111 to 95, House Democrats meeting in caucus sent the plan to another reform study committee for "further study." This effectively killed its chances. What started out as an effort to make the House more effective soon became viewed as a threat to the highly delicate balance of power within the House. Bolling, however, vowed to continue his fight: "I started working on reorganization nearly 20 years ago . . . and I have no intention of this being the killing of it. . . . "[27] But to date very little has been achieved.

BUDGET REFORM AND CONGRESS

The Congressional Budget Reform Act, adopted in 1974, was designed to encourage Congress to evaluate the nation's fiscal situation and program spending priorities in a comprehensive way. Congress felt that it had become too dependent on the president's budget proposals. Said one member: "Congress has seen its control over the federal purse strings ebb away over the past fifty years because of its inability to get a grip on the overall budget, while the Office of Management and Budget has increased its power and influence."[28] The fact is that there has been no congressional budgetary system—only a lot of separate actions and decisions coming at various intervals throughout the year with little or no relationship between them.

The Act creates a standing Budget Committee for each chamber. In the House, it is a twenty-three-member committee: five members from the Ways and Means Committee (the committee that handles tax bills); five members from the Appropriations Committee; one member from each of eleven legislative committees; one member from the majority leadership; and one member from the minority leadership. No member is allowed to serve on the House Budget Committee for more than four years out of a ten-year period. The Senate Committee is a fifteen-member Committee picked in the regular fashion.

Under the Reform Act, Congress has also established a Congressional Budget Office. It provides experts and computers and gives Congress

[27]Bolling, quoted in the *Christian Science Monitor*, May 24, 1974. For a sample of staff papers and suggestions considered by the Bolling Committee, see the special issue of *The Annals*, January, 1974, "Changing Congress: The Committee System." See also *Hearings on Committee Organization in the House*, Select Committee on Committees, House of Representatives, Vol. 3, 1973.

[28]Quoted in Joel Havemann, "Budget Reform Legislation Calls for Major Procedural Change," *National Journal Reports* (May 18, 1974), p. 734. This discussion also draws on this article, pp. 734–42.

the technical assistance and analytical help it needs to go over the information in the president's budgetary proposals. Also as a result of this Act, the General Accounting Office will be more actively involved in evaluating new spending proposals.

When the Act becomes fully effective in 1976 it will shift the federal fiscal year to begin on October 1. This will give Congress three additional months to consider a president's recommendations. As under existing practice, a president will submit his recommendations on January 20. By May 15, Congress, after receiving reports from its Budget Committee and its Budget Office, will adopt an initial tentative budget that will set target totals for spending and taxes. And if Congress so choses, this resolution can direct that appropriation bills when cleared by Congress will not be presented to the president for his action until Congress has completed its budget consideration in September. This initial target budget will be broken down by categories and will serve as a guide for the various committees and subcommittees considering detailed appropriation measures. Then by September 15, after detailed study, Congress will again look at the overall picture and either affirm or revise the budget set in its initial resolution.

How will it work? In 1946, Congress tried to get a coordinated "handle" over appropriations but the procedures were ineffective. The complex and political nature of the appropriations process, which is close to the heart of the democratic process, makes it difficult for a legislative body to organize itself and operate through any kind of comprehensive plan. What is to one congressional district a valuable project, is often a "boondoggle" to another. People are likely to favor limiting federal spending in the abstract, but unlikely to be in favor of closing down a military base in their own home town or limiting expenditures in the area of their own special concern. One of the key points in our political system to watch in the years immediately ahead will be how Congress implements the Budget Reform Act of 1974.

THE IMPORTANCE OF CHAIRMANSHIPS

Crucial in protecting the power of congressional committees and in widening the dispersion of power in the whole Congress are the committee chairmen. They still can exercise considerable power over both the operations of their committees and the final output of Congress. "It is generally the chairman who sets the pace that determines the total workload of the committee, the chairman who hires and fires staff, the chairman who forms subcommittees and assigns them jurisdictions, members, and aides. It is generally the chairman who manages the most important bills that are assigned to his committee, and at his own option oversees the endless tinkering with the substance of major bills that goes on in committee, on the floor, and in conference."[29]

[29]Nelson W. Polsby, Miriam Gallaher, and Barry Spencer Rundquist, "The Growth of the Seniority System in the U.S. House of Representatives," *American Political Science Review* (September 1969), p. 789.

Senator Robert A. Taft demonstrated his powerful position in the Eightieth Congress when he maneuvered the Taft-Hartley labor act through the Senate and House. Congress later overrode Truman's veto of the act.

"Events have not served to outdate the description by Woodrow Wilson of those who command the committees: petty barons who 'may at will exercise an almost despotic sway within their own shires, and may sometimes threaten to convulse even the realm itself.' . . . The most awesome power of a chairman is his ability to prevent his committee from acting and thus prevent Congress from acting."[30]

Chairmanships are usually awarded on the basis of seniority. The member of the *majority party* who has had the *longest continuous* service on the committee ordinarily becomes committee head. The chairman may be at odds with his fellow partisans in Congress, he may oppose his party's national program, he may even be incompetent—still, he usually wins the chairmanship under the working of seniority.

MODERATING THE CUSTOM OF SENIORITY

Committee chairmanships as well as committee assignments are the responsibility of the party caucuses in both chambers. The custom of seniority still prevails, but it is nowhere written down as a "rule," and factors other than seniority are beginning to be taken into account. In 1971, for example, the House Republican conference adopted the practice that ranking Republicans on committees would be elected by the Conference in a secret ballot. In the same year, House Democrats agreed that any ten members of a committee could force a record vote in the Democratic caucus on committee chairman. In 1973 they adopted a resolution which authorized a secret ballot vote on chairmanships if 20 percent of the caucus demanded it. In 1975, rank and file House Democrats, their ranks swollen and resolve stiffened by 75 mostly liberal newcomers, tried to remove several aging and "autocratic" chairmen. Even before they met, the once powerful Wilbur Mills stepped aside.

Senate Republicans in 1973 adopted a plan to have the Republican members of standing committees elect the "ranking Republican" rather than to follow the practice of seniority. Presumably if Republicans were to secure a majority in the Senate, they would use the same procedures to pick chairmen. Meanwhile, however, Senate Democrats still make their chairmanship and top-ranking committee selections pretty much in accordance with the seniority custom. Modifications in seniority reform are subtle, but already the impact seems clear. Said one junior Democrat, "Those guys (the chairmen) are going to have to go out and work, and I mean work, to lobby for their jobs." Proponents of congressional reform hail these new practices as a major step in the direction of enhancing chairmen's accountability to their party caucuses. However, Representative Robert F. Drinan saw it this way: "The first meeting of the Democratic caucus of the 93rd Congress consumed seven hours in an elaborate ritual calculated to tell the world that the House is reforming itself. Actually, the processes were designed to extend and enhance the power of the powerful and to confirm the powerlessness of those who are expected only to sit and wait."

[30]Daniel M. Berman, *In Congress Assembled* (Macmillan, 1964), pp. 121, 122.

The seniority practice tends to bestows the most influence in Congress on those constituencies that are politically stable or even stagnant—where party competition is low or where a particular interest group or city or rural machine predominates. It stacks the cards against areas where the two parties are more evenly matched, interest in politics high, the number of votes large, and competition between groups keen. These are the very areas most likely to reflect quickly and typically the political tides that sweep the nation.[31]

Seniority has its friends. It is defended on the grounds that elevating the most experienced members to leadership positions is automatic and impersonal and prevents disputes among congressmen. Basically the argument about seniority is one of self-interest. Rural interests tend to favor the system, while it is opposed by such groups as organized labor, advocates of civil rights legislation, and other urban-based interests who feel that it gives rural interests and their conservative representatives too much power in Congress. Yet liberal groups have not always been reluctant to profit from the system when it was within their power to do so. For example, the public outcry in response to the Supreme Court's school-prayer decision (p. 127) was loud; a constitutional amendment to permit prayer in the public schools almost certainly would have been supported by the required two-thirds of each house, yet the liberal Democratic chairman—much to the relief of liberals and civil libertarians—was able to kill the bill at least temporarily in his House Judiciary Committee.[32] If reapportionment and the passage of time cause the rule of seniority to enhance the influence of suburban- and urban-based Northern interests, it will be interesting to see if those defending and those opposing the rule of seniority switch sides.

Seniority remains because it supports the interests of congressional leaders. Many legislators have concluded that "the longer I'm here, the better I like the system." Thus, those who are most anxious to change the system have the least power to produce such changes. Most liberals have fewer quarrels with seniority as a principle than with the fact that they have not been able to control seniority posts. As liberals have come to dominate Democratic caucuses on both sides of Capitol Hill, therefore, they have sought to limit committee chairmen's power and enhance the power of *sub*committee chairmanships. These latter positions are controlled by members with somewhat less seniority who, moreover, are more apt to represent liberals than the committee chairmen. In the Senate, all but a handful of Democrats chair their own subcommittee; in the House, more than 100 Democrats are subcommittee chairmen. This provides staff perquisites and gives the members added

[31]For the view that the "bias" in chairmanships largely reflects a more basic bias in congressional membership itself toward certain regions, see Barbara Hinckley, "Seniority in the Committee Leadership Selection of Congress," *Midwest Journal of Political Science* (November 1969), pp. 613–30.

[32]William M. Beaney and Edward N. Beiser, "Prayer and Politics: The Impact of Engel and Schempp on the Political Process," *Journal of Public Law*, 13 (1964), 475–503.

leverage against committee chairmen. At the same time, there have been moves, soon after the 1974 election in particular, to strengthen the powers of the party leaders and caucuses—again at the expense of the committee chairmen's independence.

COMMITTEE INVESTIGATIONS

One of the most controversial activities of Congress in recent years has been the committee investigation, especially such well-publicized open hearings as those of the Senate Foreign Relations Committee. Why does Congress investigate? Hearings by standing committees, their subcommittees, or special select committees are an important source of information and opinion. They provide an arena in which experts can submit their views, statements and statistics can be entered into the record, and congressmen can quiz a variety of witnesses.

But committee investigations serve other functions as well. Public hearings are an important channel of communication and influence. A committee or committee chairman may use a hearing to address his colleagues in Congress—thus Senator Estes Kefauver's exposé of the drug industry in the 1950s was one way of impressing upon Congress the need for regulatory legislation. Committee hearings may also be used to communicate with the public at large. Senator Sam Ervin's Watergate Committee's televised investigations into election practices and campaign finance abuses in 1973 were not intended merely to obtain new information; the Senators were attempting to arouse citizens and to promote public support for election reforms.

Some investigations by regular committees are related to the overseeing of administration. A committee can summon administration officials to testify in public or private hearings. Some officials greatly fear these inquiries; they dread the loaded questions of hostile congressmen and the likelihood that some administrative error in their agency may be uncovered and publicized.

Are there any constitutional limits to Congress's power to compel private citizens to answer questions? The Supreme Court in 1957 *(Watkins v. United States)* cautioned Congress that the First Amendment limits its power to investigate, that no committee has the power "to expose for the sake of exposure," that Congress and its committees are not courts to try and punish individuals, and that "no inquiry is an end in itself; it must be related to, and in furtherance of, a legitimate task of Congress." Nonetheless, only a minority of the Supreme Court has shown any disposition to provide a judicial check on legislative investigations in behalf of First Amendment rights.[33] The judicial checks used so far are only two: The Fifth Amendment protection against self-incrimination has been construed broadly to protect witnesses who are

[33]*Barenblatt v. United States* (1969); *Wilkinson v United States* (1961); *Braden v. United States* (1961). For an excellent discussion of this issue, see Martin Shapiro, *Law and Politics in the Supreme Court* (Free Press, 1964), Ch. 2.

willing to risk public censure by invoking the amendment to refuse to answer questions; and the Supreme Court has narrowly construed the crime of contempt of Congress in order to avoid punishment of witnesses for refusing to answer questions unless these questions were clearly pertinent to the functions of an authorized committee.

The house versus the senate

When the framers created a bicameral national legislature, they anticipated that the two chambers would represent sharply different interests. The Senate was to be a small chamber of men elected indirectly by the people and holding long, overlapping terms. It would have the sole power to confirm nominations. Proposed treaties required the approval of a two-thirds vote in the Senate. Presumably, then, the Senate was to be a chamber of scrutiny, a gathering of "wise men" who would counsel and sanction presidents—whether the president liked it or not.

The House of Representatives, elected *in toto* every two years, was to be the direct instrument of the people. The Senate provided a conservative check on the House, especially in the late nineteenth and early twentieth centuries when it was a bastion of conservatism and something of a rich man's club. But many factors, chiefly political, have altered the characters of the House and Senate. In recent years, especially since World War II, the House has become a conservative check on the Senate, except for civil rights legislation. With only rare exceptions, executive departments and agencies view the Senate as a court of appeals for their appropriations that have been "shot down" by the House.[34]

How has this come about? One reason is that at least until recently, the number of safe, noncompetitive House districts has been increasing, while the number of safe, noncompetitive Senate seats has been decreasing. The urbanization of the nation, moreover, has left most states with large and growing metropolitan areas. Hence a senator's constituency nearly always consists of a wider variety of interests. But the Senate's behavior is also partly a result of the appropriation sequence and institutionalized norms. As Fenno has noted: "The House Committee follows a decision pattern that regularly anticipates Senate Committee action; Senate Committee decisions regularly take the form of reactions to prior House decisions. Their self-prescribed goals, as budget cutter or appeals court, take into account the order in which they act relative to one another."[35]

[34]Lewis A. Froman, Jr., *Congressmen and Their Constituencies* (Rand McNally, 1963), p. 142. But see also Richard F. Fenno, Jr., *The Power of the Purse* (Little, Brown, 1966). For a study of a possible exception, an instance when the Senate Finance Committee blocked the Family Assistance Program, see Daniel P. Moynihan, *The Politics of a Guaranteed Income* (Random House, 1973).

[35]Fenno, *ibid.*, pp. 690–91.

Given the differences between House and Senate, it is not surprising that the version of a bill passed by one chamber may differ substantially from the version of the same bill passed by the other. Only if both houses pass an absolutely identical measure can it become law. As a general rule, one house accepts the language of the other, but about 10 percent of all bills (usually major ones) passed must be referred to a conference committee.

If neither house will accept the other's bill, a *conference committee*—a special committee of members from each chamber—settles the differences. Both parties are represented, with the majority party having a larger number. The proceedings of this committee—not open to the public—are usually an elaborate bargaining process. Brought back to the respective chambers, the conference report can be accepted or rejected (often with further negotiations ordered), but it cannot be amended. Each set of conferees must convince its colleagues that any concessions made to the other house were on trivialities and that nothing basic in their own version of the bill was surrendered.

"Man, if you want to stay in this game, you'd better get in shape."

© 1973 by Herblock in *The Washington Post.*

How much leeway does a conference committee have? Ordinarily the conferees are expected to stay somewhere between the alternatives set by the different versions, but on matters where there is no clear middle ground, conferees are sometimes accused of exceeding their instructions and producing a new measure. Indeed, the conference committee has even been called a "third house" of Congress—one that arbitrarily revises Senate and House policy in secret session. Conference committees are also criticized on the grounds they are unrepresentative, even of the committees approving the bill, and because they disproportionately represent the senior committee leaders. Critics also complain that there is little remedy for biases that may creep into the bill via the conference committee, since the houses are usually confronted with a "take-it-or-leave-it" situation.[36]

Despite such criticism, however, some kind of conference committee is indispensable to the workings of a bicameral legislature. Conference committees integrate the two houses, help resolve disputes, and assist in formulating compromise bills for final consideration.

Congressional reform

Criticism of Congress is so extensive that we can only briefly review the main charges against the national legislature:

1. Congress is *inefficient.* The House and Senate are simply not suited to modern demands, according to this view. Bills require an endless amount of time to get through the labyrinthine legislative process and

[36]David J. Vogler, *The Third House: Conference Committees in the United States Congress* (Northwestern University Press, 1971).

are often blocked en route. Congressmen are not as well informed as they should be. The basic dispersion of power in Congress guarantees slowness, if not inertia.

Much of this criticism is exaggerated. And evaluation of *procedure* and *structure* is difficult to separate from views about how they affect *specific policies.* It is often a matter of whose ox is being gored. For example, from the White House vantage point, Congress is inefficient when it does not process the president's bills with speed. Measured simply in terms of work load, Congress deals with and rejects or passes an enormous number of highly complex measures. Many procedures in the two houses expedite handling of bills. The committee and subcommittee system is about the most reasonable device for hearing arguments and compiling information. Still, the question of efficiency remains. Many congressmen themselves feel defeated by the system. "I am appalled," one congressman said, "at how much congressmen are expected to do for the nation. . . . We just don't have the time to keep informed properly."[37] Time and again study groups inside and outside Congress have urged the chambers to reduce the number of committee assignments, establish better information systems, acquire better staffs, and strengthen majority rule.[38]

2. Congress is *unrepresentative* and *elitist.* The committee system responds unduly to organized regional and minority interests. The seniority system, at least in the past, has biased both houses toward conservatism. Particular arrangements, notably the Rules Committee in the House and the filibuster in the Senate, skew Congress even more toward the status quo. Defenders of Congress contend that there should be a strong institution to guarantee minority rights, to act as a brake on headlong government, to check straight majority rule. Critics of Congress answer this by arguing that minorities should have a right to publicize and delay what the majority proposes to do, but not to defeat it.

Both houses, critics hold, overrepresent locally organized elites at the expense of the mass of people. Congressmen, they contend, are products of upper-class or upper middle-class backgrounds, and cannot see the real needs of low-income groups. Within Congress an Establishment—actually an elite system—puts real control of Congress in the hands of a small number of members, and usually conservative members at that.[39]

3. Congress is *irresponsible.* The main problem in Congress is the dispersion of power among committee leaders, elected party officials,

[37]Donald R. Matthews, *U.S. Senators and Their World* (University of North Carolina Press, 1960), p. 89. See also Donald Riegle, *O Congress* (Doubleday, 1972).

[38]See, for example, Saloma, *Congress and the New Politics*, Ch. 8; and Research and Policy Committee, Committee for Economic Development, *Making Congress More Effective* (1970), "Summary of Conclusions and Recommendations," pp. 17–20.

[39]See, for example, Green, Fallows, and Zwick, *Who Runs Congress?* Ch. 3. For a different view, see Barbara Hinckley, *The Seniority System in Congress* (Indiana University Press, 1971).

factional chieftains, and other legislators. This dispersion of power means that to get things done congressional leaders must bargain and negotiate. The result of this "brokerage" system is that measures may be watered down or defeated or delayed, too much discretion is conferred on unknown bureaucrats, accountability for action or inaction is confused and responsibility thus eroded, and organized, narrow, special interests who know how "to work the system" are given an unfair advantage.

Those charging irresponsibility fear that Congress is the tool of no single interest but responds to so many minorities that it cannot speak for the great majority or for the nation as a whole. It cannot anticipate problems, plan ahead, mobilize legislative power to deal with entrenched social problems. Those concerned about congressional irresponsibility do not blame a few conservative interests or elitist elements. They recognize that the brokerage system is mainly the result of our constitutional and political system that divides up authority, checks power with power, and disperses and thwarts political leadership.

SUMMARY

Most students of Congress agree that Congress performs, more or less, six functions: law-making, representation, consensus-building, overseeing, policy clarification, and legitimizing. Law-making refers to conflict over substantive policies; representation is expressing the divergent and conflicting views of the economic, social, racial, religious, and other interests making up the United States; consensus-building is the bargaining process by which these interests are reconciled; overseeing is the surveillance of policy implementors; policy clarification is the identification and publicizing of issues; and legitimizing is the formal ratification of policies by what are widely accepted as proper and acceptable channels.[40]

Which of these functions are important? Which should be strengthened? Observers tend to divide into three schools of thought. First, those who support presidential government would make the "reforms" necessary to permit Congress to cooperate with the White House, make it less "obstructionist" and more a reflection of presidential policies. They favor such changes as having all congressmen elected at the same time as the president.

A second school approaches congressional reform from the perspective of party government. It would make Congress a copartner with the president but would make both of them agents of the *national political majority* as embodied in the national party in power. A third approach is called the "literary," or "Whig," school and holds that Congress should be an *independent, representative* law-making body that responds to different political forces from the president. Besides dispersion of

[40]Drawn from William L. Morrow, *Congressional Committees* (Scribner's, 1969), pp. 4–5.

authority, it favors, for example, giving Congress more professionalized staffs, resisting party controls over individual members, and encouraging the widest possible representation of divergent positions within Congress.

The presidential government school emphasizes legitimization, overseeing, and representation as the primary functions of Congress; the party government theorists give higher priority to policy clarification and representation; the literary school, or Whigs, stresses law-making, representation, consensus-building, and overseeing.[41] Some of the adherents of these various schools have changed sides in recent years. More skepticism exists, for example, among presidential government theorists because their traditional liberal assumptions about Congress and the presidency have not always been validated. As a result of the Vietnam War (as well as various Nixon Administration initiatives), many once enthusiastic "presidentialists" grew less so; and Congress won new allies from unexpected quarters.[42]

Our discussions of the president and the Congress indicate that we have a system of *dual representation* in which both Congress and president can and do legitimately claim to be the voice of the people. But since "the people" seldom if ever speak with a single voice, the structure and character of the two representative systems tend to give us a Congress that speaks for one majority and a president who speaks for another. Between the two we sometimes get a kind of balance—sometimes a deadlock. If, as some say, "the anxieties of American life speak through the Congress, then perhaps the urgencies speak through the presidency."[43] Sometimes, of course, the reverse is the case.[44]

It is fashionable, and has long been so, to damn Congress. There obviously is much that could be done to make our national legislature serve its several roles more effectively. Some things *are* being done: redistricting and reapportionment are shaping a legislature that more accurately reflects all segments of the population; the filibuster in the Senate seems to be losing some of its bite; with the spread of the two-party system into more and more of the states, the Senate has become more responsive; Congress is getting better staff; both the Congressional Research Service and the General Accounting Office provide increas-

[41]See, Saloma, *Congress and the New Politics*, pp. 37–47; Roger H. Davidson, David M. Kovenock, and Michael K. O'Leary, *Congress in Crisis: Politics and Congressional Reform* (Wadsworth, 1966).

[42]See for examples, Richard Goodwin, *The American Condition* (Basic Books, 1974); Arthur M. Schlesinger, Jr., *The Imperial Presidency* (Houghton Mifflin, 1973).

[43]Arthur M. Schlesinger, Jr., and Alfred de Grazia, *Congress and the Presidency: Their Role in Modern Times* (American Enterprise Institute, 1967), p. 2.

[44]Willmore Kendall, "The Two Majorities," *Midwest Journal of Political Science* (November 1960), pp. 317–45; and Paul J. Halpern, "The Two Majorities Revisited: Representativeness and Rationality in the Presidency and the Congress," a paper delivered at the 1974 annual meeting of the American Political Science Association (Chicago, Illinois).

ingly improved information services; and the seniority system for picking committee chairmen is slowly being modified.

Changes are taking place. But the critical image of Congress as a static or decaying institution is far from being put to rest. Its greatest strengths—its diversity and deliberative character—also serve to weaken its capacity to be a match for the executive branch. Congress will probably never be well enough organized to bargain effectively with presidents determined to press their powers to the full. The 535 members divided into two chambers, two parties, and hundreds of committees and subcommittees have little way of arriving at a common strategy to combat any present or future president with a penchant for secrecy and the temperament of a monarch.

If the checks are not checking and the balances are not balancing, basic improvements in our constitutional system are likely only if the Congress is willing to exercise powers it already has. Its members must be willing to reorganize their procedures and be willing to delegate to their leaders in the Congress the authority to bargain and persuade on their behalf. Congress, of course, will always be improved by the recruitment and election of gifted politicians who value Congress as a policy-maker and are willing to work rigorously to prevent presidential abuses of public power. In the end, however, if our Congress is to legislate wisely and oversee the government effectively, the public will have to monitor its performance more closely, with a keen eye on who should be reelected and who should be turned out of office.

Chapter 14 Judges and the judicial process

Foreigners are often amazed at the great power Americans give their judges, especially federal judges. In 1848, after his visit to America, the French aristocrat Alexis de Tocqueville wrote, "If I were asked where I place the American aristocracy, I should reply without hesitation . . . that it occupies the judicial bench and bar. . . . Scarcely any political question arises in the United States that is not resolved, sooner or later, into a judicial question."[1] A century later the English laborite Harold Laski observed, "The respect in which federal courts and, above all, the Supreme Court are held is hardly surpassed by the influence they exert on the life of the United States."[2]

Contemporary research suggests that perhaps Tocqueville and Laski exaggerated the extent of public veneration for our judges. Over time the Supreme Court does not appear to command significantly more respect among either the mass public or the elite than do the other two branches.[3] Nonetheless, the Supreme Court remains one of the most

[1]*Democracy in America*, ed. Phillips Bradley (Knopf, 1944), I, 278–80.

[2]*The American Democracy* (Viking Press, 1948), p. 110.

[3]See the research of such scholars as Murphy and Tanenhaus, Dolbeare and Hammond, Richard Johnson, findings of Gallup Polls and Harris Surveys as reported and cited in David Adamany, "Legitimacy, Realigning Elections, and the Supreme Court," *Wisconsin Law Review* (1973), pp. 808–20.

The Supreme Court justices

Making up the High Bench are, from left, front row: Associate Justices Potter Stewart, William O. Douglas, Chief Justice Warren E. Burger, Associate Justices William J. Brennan, Jr., and Byron R. White. Back row: Associate Justices Lewis F. Powell, Jr., Thurgood Marshall, Harry A. Blackmun, and William H. Rehnquist. Justices Powell and Rehnquist are the newest members of the Court, having taken their seats in January 1972.

important arenas for the making of public policy. Judges in no other governmental system have such a vital part in the political life of the nation as do our federal judges.

Should our judges play such a central role in our political life is a question to which we shall return. A prior question is: *Why* do they have such great influence? One reason is their power of judicial review—that is, their power to make the authoritative interpretation of the Constitution. Only a constitutional amendment (and the judges would interpret the amendment) or a later High Court itself can modify the Court's doctrine. Justice Frankfurter once put it tersely: "The Supreme Court is the Constitution."

Even without the power of judicial review, however, judges would be influential members of the policy-making elite. Indeed, constitutional questions are not involved in most of the cases that come before them. But when judges construe statutes and resolve conflicts, they often formulate rules that affect the conduct of millions of persons beyond those who happen to be parties to the litigation.

The law

The Constitution does not require judges to be lawyers. Yet all Supreme Court justices, as well as other federal judges, have been members of the bar. The reason for this is obvious: The business of courts is law, and law is a professional discipline, a technical subject whose mastery requires specialized training. What kind of law do federal judges apply? Where do they find it?

TYPES OF LAW

In many instances, a judicial decision is based on *statutory law*. This is law formulated by the legislature, although it also includes treaties and executive orders; it is law that comes from authoritative and specific law-making sources. The legislature has no choice but to state rules in general terms, for it cannot anticipate all the questions that will arise over their meaning. Therefore, although the initial interpretation is often made by an administrator, the final interpretation is made by judges.

If there is no statutory law governing a case that comes before a court the judges must apply the *common law*. Common law is judge-made law. It has an ancient lineage reaching back through centuries of judical decisions and originated in England in the twelfth century when royal judges began traveling around the country settling disputes in each locality according to prevailing custom. Gradually these customs became the same for the entire nation. The common law continues to develop according to the rule of *stare decisis*, which means "let the decision stand." This is the rule of precedent, which requires that once a rule has been established by a court, it shall be followed in all similar cases. The common law governs many disputes, and even where it has been superseded by statute, the statutory law is usually a modification and codification of the old common-law rules and is normally interpreted according to the common-law tradition.

The American common law began to branch off from the English system in the seventeenth century. Today we have forty-nine separate common-law systems, or fifty, counting the federal interpretation of state law. (In Louisiana the legal system is based on the other great Western legal tradition, the *civil law*. The civil law gives more emphasis to codes of law-givers and less to past judicial decisions. In Louisiana the civil law has been greatly influenced by and intermingled with the common law.) Whenever federal judges have to decide disputes between citizens of two states and there is no applicable state statute, they apply the common law as interpreted by the state courts. Only if there is no state interpretation do federal judges strike out for themselves.

Federal judges also apply *equity*. Like common law, equity is a system of judge-made law that had its origins in England. Early in the development of the common law, it was discovered that in certain circumstances it did not ensure justice. For example, under the common law, a person whose property rights are about to be injured has no choice but to wait until the injury has taken place and then to seek money damages. But the injury may do irreparable harm for which money damages cannot provide adequate compensation. Accordingly another set of rules was worked out to be used where the law was inadequate. Under equity, a person may go to a judge, show why the common-law remedy is inadequate, and ask for equitable relief—an injunction, for example, to prevent an act that threatens irreparable harm. If the wrongdoer persists, he may be punished for contempt of court.

Sometimes judges apply *constitutional law*. Because the Constitution contains only 7,500 words or so and can be read in a half-hour, it might be assumed that any person could learn constitutional law after a little study. But the document itself sheds little light on constitutional law. Constitutional law is full of phrases like "the clear and present danger rule" and "selective absorption" that are not to be found in the written words of the Constitution. They come from the decisions of the Supreme Court. Constitutional law, in other words, consists of statements about the interpretation of the Constitution that have been given Supreme Court sanction.

Admiralty and maritime law is also applied by federal judges. This is a highly complex and technical body of rules applicable to cases arising in connection with shipping and water-borne commerce on the high seas and, by decision of the Supreme Court,[4] on the navigable waters of the United States.

A relatively new kind of law that has become increasingly prominent in the decisions of federal judges is *administrative law*. Within the past several decades, Congress has delegated to administrators and administrative agencies so much rule-making authority that today there is, in volume, more administrative than statutory law. The rules and decisions of administrators may be reviewed by federal judges, and judges are often called on to determine whether the administrators have acted properly and within their authority.[5]

Law may also be classified as criminal or civil. *Criminal law*, which is almost entirely statutory, defines crimes against the public order and provides for punishment. Government has the primary responsibility for enforcing this type of law. The great body of criminal law is enacted by states and is enforced by state officials in the state courts, but the criminal business of federal judges is by no means negligible, and it is growing.

Civil law governs the relations between individuals and defines their legal rights. For example, Jones, who has a trademark for Atomic Pills, discovers that Smith is advertising Atomic Tablets in national magazines. If Jones wishes to protect his trademark, he may proceed against

[4]*The Genesee Chief* (1852).

[5]Martin Shapiro, *The Supreme Court and Administrative Agencies* (Free Press, 1968).

Smith before a federal judge. But the government can also be a party to a civil action. Under the Sherman Antitrust Act, for example, the federal government may initiate civil as well as criminal action to prevent violations of the law.

THE SCOPE OF JUDICIAL POWER: THE FIGHT THEORY

The American judicial process is based on the *adversary system.* A court of law is viewed as a neutral arena, in which two parties fight out their differences before an impartial arbiter. The underlying logic of the adversary system is that the best way for the court to discover the truth is for each side to strive as hard as it can to present its point of view. Macaulay said that we obtain the fairest decision "when two men argue, as unfairly as possible, on opposite sides," for then "it is certain that no important considerations will altogether escape notice."[6] Whether or not the fight theory is an adequate way of arriving at the truth—and there are those who believe it is not—the fact that it lies at the basis of our judicial system is crucial, because, first, the logic of the adversary system imposes formal restraints on the scope of judicial power and, second, the rhetoric of the adversary system leads us to conceive the role of the judge in a very special way.

If courts are to judge existing conflicts, then judicial power is essentially *passive*—that is, courts cannot act until combatants come to them. The judiciary is said to lack a self-starter.[7]

Furthermore, not all disputes are within the scope of judicial power. Judges decide only *justiciable disputes*—those that grow out of actual cases and that are capable of settlement by legal methods. Not all governmental questions or constitutional problems are justiciable. For example, judges will not determine which government of a foreign state should be recognized by the United States. The Constitution gives this authority to the president, and judges will not question his decision. Similarly, the Supreme Court has ruled that some claims of unconstitutionality raise political and not justiciable questions. What does the Court mean by "political"? It means an issue that requires knowledge of a nonlegal character, that requires the use of techniques not suitable for a court, or that the Constitution addresses to the political branch of government. Examples of political questions are: Which of two competing state governments is the proper one? What is a republican form of state government?[8]

Judges are not supposed to use their power unless the controversy is a real one. Two people cannot trump up a suit merely to contest legislation. For example, in 1889 a man named Wellman tried to purchase a railway ticket the day after the Michigan legislature had fixed the rates.

[6]Quoted in Jerome Frank, *Courts on Trial* (Princeton University Press, 1949), p. 80.

[7]Walter F. Murphy, Jr., *Elements of Judicial Strategy* (University of Chicago Press, 1964), p. 21.

[8]*Luther v. Borden* (1849); *Coleman v. Miller* (1939).

The ticket agent refused to sell a ticket at the new rate and Wellman brought suit. During the trial Wellman did not challenge the railway company's testimony. It became clear that Wellman wanted the railway company to win; he made no attempt to present fully the facts in the case. The Supreme Court refused to allow federal courts to decide the case, saying, "It was never thought that, by means of a friendly suit, a party beaten in the legislature could transfer to the courts an inquiry as to the constitutionality of a legislative act."[9] (This, of course, is exactly what is done in a nonfriendly suit. In such cases, however, the two parties have an interest in getting the full facts before the court.)

May anybody challenge a law? No, he or she must have "standing to sue" – that is, must have "sustained or is immediately in danger of sustaining a direct injury. It is not sufficient that he has merely a general interest common to all members of the public."[10] Furthermore, the injury must be substantial.

In recent years the Supreme Court and Congress have somewhat liberalized the doctrine of "standing" in order to permit a wider range of persons to resort to the courts to challenge the actions of the government or to attack corporate practices. Yet the Supreme Court has not gone as far as would Justice Douglas. He would give standing to sue to trees and other inanimate objects "about to be despoiled, defaced, or invaded by roads and bulldozers."[11] Nor will the judges give advisory opinions to Congress or to the president.

The logic of the adversary system requires that the judges decide only what is necessary to dispose of the specific case before them. The Supreme Court has expressed its reluctance to go beyond the case at hand, especially when constitutional questions are involved. As Justice Brandeis wrote,

> It is not the habit of the court to decide questions of a constitutional nature unless absolutely necessary to a decision of the case. . . . The Court will not "formulate a rule of constitutional law broader than is required by the precise facts to which it is applied. . . ." The Court will not pass upon a constitutional question although properly presented by the record, if there is also present some other ground upon which the case may be disposed of. . . . [It] is a cardinal principle that this Court will first ascertain whether a construction of the statute is fairly possible by which the question [of constitutionality] may be avoided.[12]

Judges do not always remain strictly within the limits set by these restrictions. The real significance of restrictions is not that they limit judicial power, but that they give the Supreme Court considerable lati-

[9]*Chicago & Grand Trunk Railway Co. v. Wellman* (1892).

[10]*Ex parte Levitt* (1937); *Schlesinger v. Reservists Committee* (1974).

[11]*Sierra Club v. Morton* (1972).

[12]Concurring opinion in *Ashwander v. T.V.A.* (1936).

tude to avoid deciding cases it does not want to confront. The first Justice Harlan made this quite clear: "The courts have rarely, if ever, felt themselves so restrained by technical rules, that they could not find some remedy, consistent with the law, for acts . . . that violated natural justice. . . ."[13]

DO JUDGES MAKE LAW?

Dred Scott, the elderly slave whose suit for freedom over a century ago pushed America toward civil war, is shown with his wife in this painting owned by Scott's great-grandson. The Supreme Court denied Scott his freedom, ruling that slaves were property and protected as such, even on free soil, by the Constitution.

"Do judges make law? 'Course they do. Made some myself," remarked Jeremiah Smith, former judge of the New Hampshire Supreme Court.[14] Although such statements are now quite common, they are somehow disquieting; they do not conform to our notion of the proper judge. Why should this be? Why is it that so many still cling to the notion that judges do not make law?

The conception many people have of the role of a judge—a conception that follows quite naturally from the adversary system of adjudication—is that it is similar to that of a referee in a prizefight. What do we expect of the referee? He must be impartial; he must be disinterested; he must treat both parties as equals. Referees do not make rules; they apply the rules the boxing commission has established. Insofar as the function of a judge is analagous to that of a referee, these same expectations may be legitimately applied to him. But the analogy must not be pushed too far. The referee need do nothing more than apply the boxing commission's rules, because the boxing commission has anticipated practically every conceivable situation in the ring. But the situations with which the legislature must deal are infinitely more complex.

Herein lies the answer to the question: Do judges make law? Not only do they, but they must. Legislatures make law by enacting statutes, but judges apply the statutes to concrete situations; inevitably discretion is involved. Indeed there will be some cases to which general expressions are clearly applicable: "If anything is a vehicle, a motor-car is one."[15] But does the word *vehicle* in a statute include bicycles, airplanes, and roller skates? A judge is constantly faced with situations that possess some of the features of the similar cases—but lack others. "Uncertainty at the borderline is the price to be paid for the use of general classifying terms." Statutes are drawn in broad terms: Drivers shall act with "reasonable care"; no one may make "excessive noise" in the vicinity of a hospital; employers must maintain "safe working conditions." The reason broad terms must be used is that legislators cannot have knowledge of all the possible combinations of circumstances the future may bring. Thus a statute does not settle many questions, because it could

[13]Quoted by Murphy, *Elements of Judicial Strategy*, p. 30.

[14]Quoted in Paul A. Freund, *On Understanding the Supreme Court* (Little, Brown, 1949), p. 3.

[15]This discussion is based on H.L.A. Hart, *The Concept of Law* (Oxford University Press, 1961), Chap. 7.

not have been anticipated that they would be raised. "In every legal system a large and important field is left open for the exercise of discretion by courts and other officials in rendering initially vague standards determinate, in resolving the uncertainties of statutes, or in developing and qualifying rules only broadly communicated by . . . precedents."[16]

These problems are further magnified when judges are asked—as American judges are—to apply the Constitution, written nearly 200 years ago. If Congress passed a law extending the terms of senators beyond six years, its unconstitutionality would be apparent to everyone. But if constitutional interpretation amounted only to this, judges would have no special function as interpreters of the Constitution, nor would they have much discretion. The Constitution abounds with generalizations: "due process of law," "equal protection of the laws," "unreasonable searches and seizures," "commerce among the several states." It is not likely that recourse to the intent of the framers will help judges faced with cases involving electronic wiretaps, General Motors, or birth-control pills. Because the rules by which society is governed cannot interpret themselves, judges cannot avoid making law.

STARE DECISIS

One element of the English common law that pervades our judicial system is *stare decisis*, the rule of precedent. A judge is expected to abide by all previous decisions of his own court and all rulings of superior courts. Although the rule of precedent imposes considerable regularity on the legal system, it is not nearly so restrictive as some people think.[17]

Consider, for example, the father who, removing his hat as he enters a church, says to his son,"This is the way to behave on such occasions. Do as I do."[18] The son, like the judge trying to follow a precedent, has a wide range of possibilities open to him: How much of the performance must be imitated? Does it matter if the left hand is used, instead of the right, to remove the hat? That it is done slowly or smartly? That the hat is put under the seat? That it is not replaced on the head inside the church? The judge can *distinguish* precedents by stating that a previous case does not control the immediate one because of differences in context. In addition, in many areas of law, there are conflicting precedents, one of which can be chosen to support a decision for either party.

The doctrine of *stare decisis* is even less controlling in the field of constitutional law. Because the Constitution, rather than any one interpretation of it, is binding, the Court can reverse a previous decision it no longer wishes to follow. Therefore Supreme Court justices are not seriously restricted by the doctrine of *stare decisis*. As the first Justice Harlan

[16] *Ibid.*, p. 125, 132.

[17] Benjamin Cardozo, *The Nature of the Judicial Process* (Yale University Press, 1921).

[18] This discussion is based on Hart, *Concept of Law*, pp. 121, 122.

told a group of law students: "I want to say to you young gentlemen that if we don't like an act of Congress, we don't have much trouble to find grounds for declaring it unconstitutional."[19]

The shape of federal justice

The Constitution provides for only one Supreme Court, leaving it up to Congress to establish inferior federal courts. (The Constitution also allows Congress to determine the size of the Supreme Court as well as of lower courts.) A Supreme Court is a necessity if the national government is to have the power to frame laws superior to those of the states. The lack of such a tribunal to maintain national supremacy, to ensure uniform interpretation of national legislation, and to resolve conflicts among the states was one of the glaring deficiencies of the central government under the Articles of Confederation.

The First Congress divided the nation into districts and created lower national courts for each district. That decision, though often supplemented, has never been seriously questioned. Today the hierarchy of the national courts of general jurisdiction consists of *district courts, courts of appeals*, and one *Supreme Court.*

THE ORGANIZATION OF FEDERAL COURTS

Judge Learned Hand.

The workhorses of the federal judiciary are the eighty-nine district courts within the states, one in the District of Columbia, and one the territorial district court in Puerto Rico. Each state has at least one district court; the larger states have as many as the demands of judicial business and the pressure of politics require (though no state has more than four). Each district court is composed of at least one judge, but there may be as many as twenty-seven. District judges normally sit separately and hold court by themselves. There are 403 district judgeships, all filled by the president with the consent of the Senate; all district judges hold office for life.

District courts are trial courts of *original jurisdiction*. They are the only federal courts that regularly employ *grand* (indicting) and *petit* (trial) juries. Many of the cases tried before district judges involve citizens of different states, and the judges apply the appropriate state laws. Otherwise, district judges are concerned with federal laws. For example, they hear and decide cases involving crimes aginst the United States—suits under the national revenue, postal, patent, copyright, trademark, bankruptcy, and civil rights laws.[20]

[19]Quoted by E. S. Corwin, *Constitutional Revolution* (Claremont and Associated Colleges, 1941), p. 38.

[20]Glendon A. Schubert, *Judicial Policy-Making*, rev. ed. (Scott, Foresman, 1974).

District judges are assisted by clerks, bailiffs, stenographers, law clerks, court reporters, probation officers, and United States magistrates. All these persons are appointed by the judges. The magistrates, who serve eight-year terms, handle some of the preliminaries. They issue warrants for arrests and often hear the evidence to determine whether an arrested person should be held for action by the grand jury. If so, the magistrate may set the bail. Magistrates may even conduct trials for petty offenses. A United States marshal, appointed by the president, is assigned to each district court. Although marshals no longer exercise general police jurisdiction, they maintain order in the courtroom, guard prisoners, make arrests, and carry out court orders, such as serving summonses for witnesses;[21] at times, as in the fall of 1962 in

[21]Rita W. Cooley, "The Office of United States Marshal," *Western Political Quarterly* (March 1959), pp. 123–40.

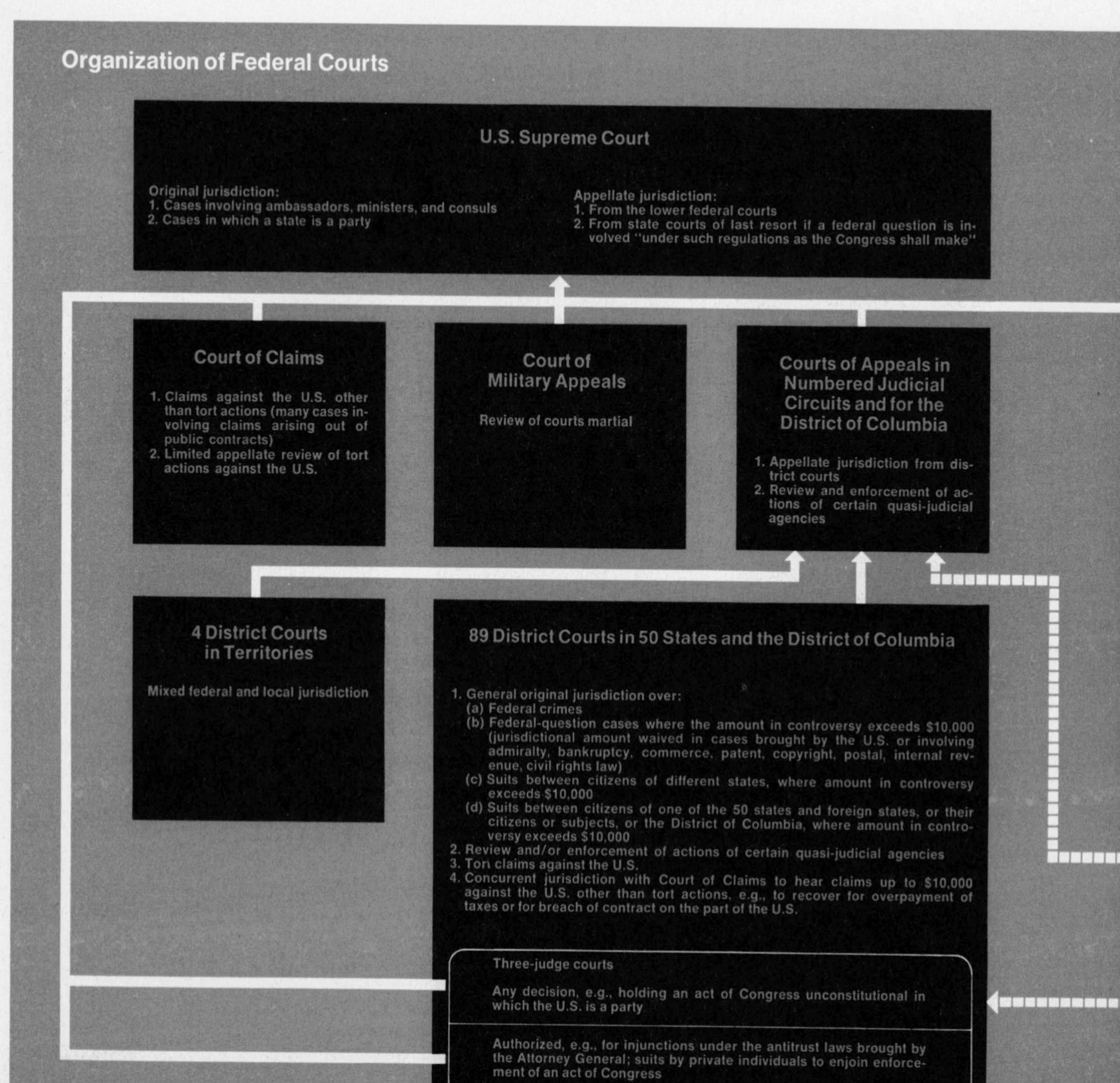

Organization of Federal Courts
U.S. Supreme Court
Original jurisdiction:
1. Cases involving ambassadors, ministers, and consuls
2. Cases in which a state is a party
Appellate jurisdiction:
1. From the lower federal courts
2. From state courts of last resort if a federal question is involved "under such regulations as the Congress shall make"
Court of Claims
1. Claims against the U.S. other than tort actions (many cases involving claims arising out of public contracts)
2. Limited appellate review of tort actions against the U.S.
Court of Military Appeals
Review of courts martial
Courts of Appeals in Numbered Judicial Circuits and for the District of Columbia
1. Appellate jurisdiction from district courts
2. Review and enforcement of actions of certain quasi-judicial agencies
4 District Courts in Territories
Mixed federal and local jurisdiction
89 District Courts in 50 States and the District of Columbia
1. General original jurisdiction over:
(a) Federal crimes
(b) Federal-question cases where the amount in controversy exceeds $10,000 (jurisdictional amount waived in cases brought by the U.S. or involving admiralty, bankruptcy, commerce, patent, copyright, postal, internal revenue, civil rights law)
(c) Suits between citizens of different states, where amount in controversy exceeds $10,000
(d) Suits between citizens of one of the 50 states and foreign states, or their citizens or subjects, or the District of Columbia, where amount in controversy exceeds $10,000
2. Review and/or enforcement of actions of certain quasi-judicial agencies
3. Tort claims against the U.S.
4. Concurrent jurisdiction with Court of Claims to hear claims up to $10,000 against the U.S. other than tort actions, e.g., to recover for overpayment of taxes or for breach of contract on the part of the U.S.
Three-judge courts
Any decision, e.g., holding an act of Congress unconstitutional in which the U.S. is a party
Authorized, e.g., for injunctions under the antitrust laws brought by the Attorney General; suits by private individuals to enjoin enforcement of an act of Congress

Oxford, Mississippi, they carry out orders of a federal court even in the face of violence.

Although a few kinds of decisions of a district court may be appealed directly to the Supreme Court, especially those that are required to be heard by three judges, most decisions must first be appealed to a United States court of appeals. (In fact, the majority of district court decisions are not appealed at all.) The United States is divided into eleven judicial circuits, including the District of Columbia as a circuit, each of which has a court of appeals consisting of three to fifteen circuit judges, ninety-seven in all. Congress is presently considering a revision of the boundaries of the circuits, most especially the possibility of dividing into two circuits the Fifth Circuit—the Deep South—which Chief Justice Burger has labeled "an unmanageable administrative monstrosity," and the Far West Ninth Circuit which includes Alaska and Hawaii as well as the mainland western states.

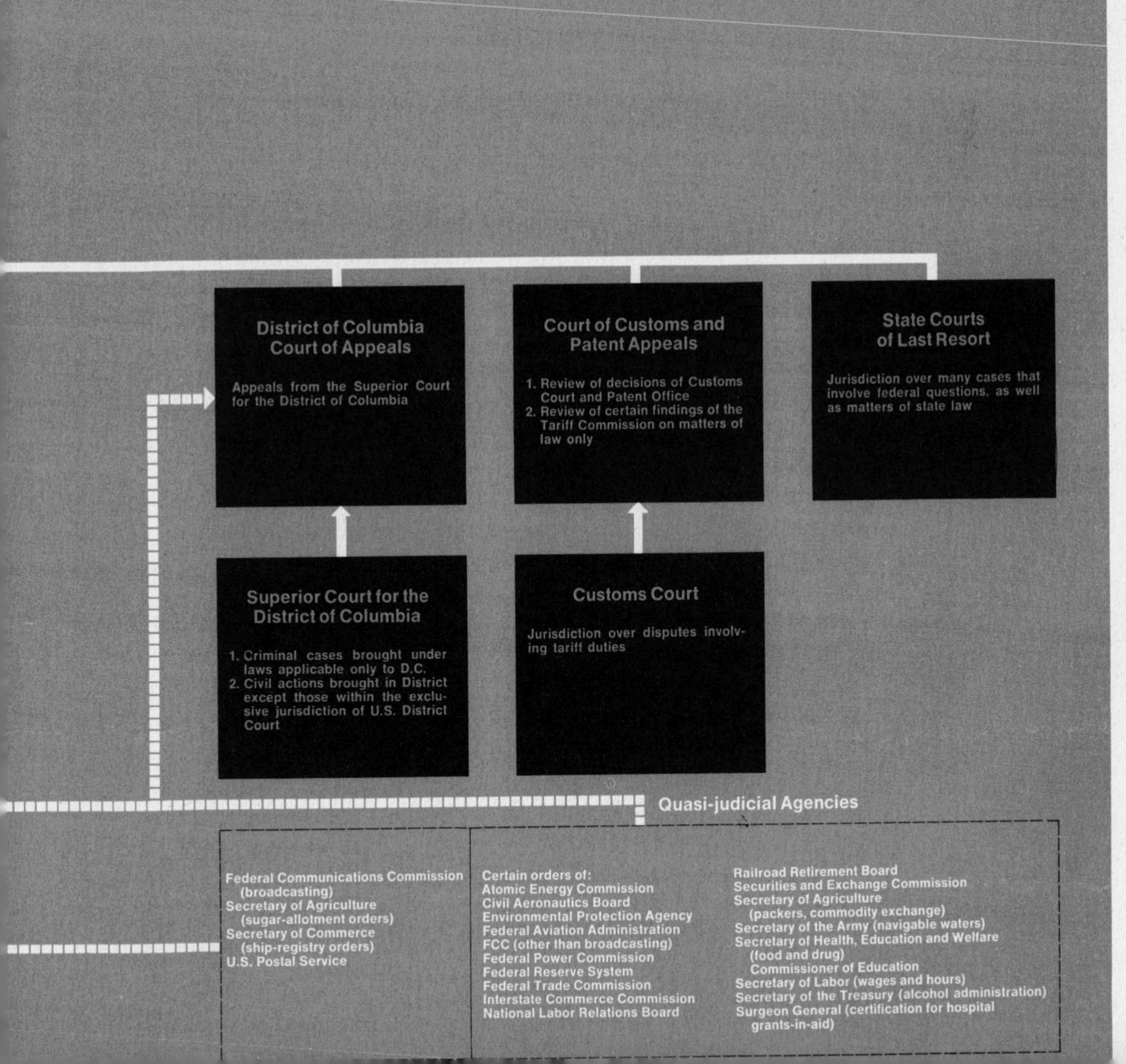

Like all judges of courts exercising Article III power—that is, the judicial power of the United States—circuit judges are appointed for life by the president with the consent of the Senate. The United States courts of appeals have only *appellate* jurisdiction—they review decisions of the district courts within their circuit and also some of the actions of the independent regulatory agencies such as the Federal Trade Commission. Each court of appeals normally utilizes panels of three judges to hear cases, although in the event of especially important and controversial cases the court may sit en banc. One Supreme Court justice is assigned to each circuit, but his duties as circuit justice are only nominal.

Administering—reforming—the federal judicial system

Chief Justice Burger has challenged bench, bar, nation, and Congress to modernize the federal court system so that the judges may more expeditiously and thoughtfully handle the constantly expanding volume of litigation. During the last quarter century, we have almost doubled the number of federal judges, but cases may still take months to be disposed of. More than 80,000 cases are pending in the federal system, and one-fourth of them are more than two years old.[22] Although the adoption of Rule 50 (b), the so-called speedy trial rule, requiring district courts to specify a time limit within which defendants must be tried, has advanced the processing of criminal trials, thousands of persons still wait endlessly for their day in court.[23] (Even more thousands maneuver to delay their day in court, for this is a tactic that often works to the advantage of the accused.)

We do not have a ministry of justice with overall responsibility for the operation of our courts; such a centralized system is contrary to our traditions. Rather each federal judge, appointed to hold office during "good behavior," is an independent person over whom no one has administrative authority. What happens if a judge fails to decide cases promptly or if in one district the judges are overworked while in another they have too little to do? Who proposes changes in regulations to make judicial business flow more smoothly?

In recent decades Congress has cautiously introduced an administrative structure to the federal judicial system while still leaving considerable district and circuit court autonomy. With the help of a recently created position of administrative assistant, the chief justice now spends

[22]James O. Monroe, Jr., "The Urgent Case for American Law Reform: A Judge's Response to a Lawyer's Pleas," *DePauw Law Review* (Spring 1970), pp. 466–89; see also Commission on Revision of the Federal Court Appellate System, *The Geographical Boundaries of the Several Judicial Circuits: Recommendations for Change* (Washington, D.C., 1973).

[23]Mark W. Cannon, "Administrative Change and the Supreme Court, "*Judicature* (March 1974), p. 341. Mr. Cannon is the administrative assistant to the chief justice of the United States, the first person to hold this new post.

a third of his time on administrative duties. He presides over the Judicial Conference of the United States, which consists of the chief judge of each of the courts of appeals and one district judge from each circuit.[24] The Conference, through its many committees, makes recommendations for the general procedural rules to be followed by the federal courts. The Supreme Court transmits these recommendations to Congress, and the rules become effective unless vetoed by either house of Congress within a stipulated time.

The Conference is assisted by the Administrative Office of the United States Courts whose director prepares budgets, develops reports, and handles financial transactions. The chief justice also supervises the Federal Judicial Center, the research arm of the federal courts, designed in the words of President Johnson "to enable the courts to begin the kind of self-analysis, research, and planning necessary for a more effective judicial system."

For each circuit there is a judicial council consisting of all the judges of the court of appeals. The council may assign work among the several district courts; it may determine whether a judge is sufficiently disabled so that he cannot perform his duties (in which case the president may appoint an additional judge.) One council has even gone so far as to order that no additional cases be assigned to a particular district judge because of doubts as to the continued propriety of his hearing cases. (The Supreme Court sidestepped the question of whether such action conflicts with the constitutional requirement that judges be allowed to serve "during good behavior.")[25] Each court of appeals is also assigned a professionally qualified circuit executive to help the council and to assist the court of appeals itself with the administration of its business.[26]

What of the Supreme Court? Although Justice Douglas insists that there is no problem, all the other justices and most observers are concerned that the Court lacks the time to be properly reflective and meticulous in its work. In the 1974 term the Supreme Court reviewed three times as many cases as it did twenty years before. Its written output amounted to 5,000 pages, more than twice as many pages as a decade ago, and more than 50 percent additional opinions. The work has become more complicated; the number of constitutional cases has doubled in a decade. If the growth rate should increase in the next decade at the same rate as the last one, each justice will have to consider more than 7,500 cases.[27]

What might be done? An additional law clerk has already been as-

[24]Peter Graham Fish, *The Politics of Federal Judicial Administration* (Princeton University Press, 1973), pp. 379–426.

[25]*Chandler v. Judicial Council* (1970).

[26]Robert J. Martineau, "The Federal Circuit Executives; An Initial Report," *Judicature* (May 1974), pp. 438–45.

[27]Mark W. Cannon, "Administrative Change," pp. 338–39.

signed to each justice, and a legal officer has been appointed to the staff of the court. Among other suggestions being considered – not just for the benefit of the Supreme Court but to lighten the load of all federal courts – are:

1. eliminate three-judge courts with direct appeals to the Supreme Court;
2. abolish diversity jurisdiction (cases between citizens of different states), thereby eliminating about 25 percent of the civil work caseload of the federal courts;
3. reform the system of workmen's compensation for railroad workers, longshoremen, and seamen and thus eliminate another 7 percent of the civil case load;
4. create an additional court of special jurisdiction to handle technical issues like antitrust, tax, and patent questions;
5. make greater use of computers for the processing of data;
6. assign more administrators to take from the judges the burdens of courtroom administration so that they can spend more of their time judging.
7. reduce the size of juries.[28]

Chief Justice Burger has even suggested that the bar might concentrate upon improving the caliber and capacities of those who advocate before the bench, perhaps something along the lines of the English system where a select group of specialists, known as barristers, argues cases while the rest of the lawyers, known as solicitors, take care of the legal work outside of the courtroom.

The most controversial of all the proposals presently being discussed by the bench, bar, and Congress is the recommendation of the so-called Freund Study Group (appointed by the chief justice and named after its chairman, a distinguished Harvard law professor, but then all Harvard professors are distinguished) that a national court of appeals be established. The new national court of appeals would consist of rotating membership drawn from the judges of the courts of appeals. It would screen cases and allow only the most important ones to be sent on to the Supreme Court. There are variants of this proposal, depending on how far the proposers would go in allowing such a court to dispose finally of matters presently being handled by the Supreme Court.

Once again, as we have so often noted, although everybody may agree in the abstract that it would be desirable to modernize the federal court system and to provide for faster processing of cases, actual changes will involve policy choices about which there are considerable differences of opinion. Judicial reform is likely to be a slow and cautious effort.

[28]See Henry J. Friendly, *Federal Jurisdiction: A General View* (Columbia University Press, 1973), for a federal judge's recommendations.

SPECIAL COURTS, LEGISLATIVE COURTS, AND ADMINISTRATIVE TRIBUNALS

In addition to the federal constitutional courts of general jurisdiction, Congress has created constitutional courts of special jurisdiction—the Court of Claims, the Customs Court, and the Court of Customs and Patent Appeals. The Court of Claims consists of a chief and six associate judges, with jurisdiction over all property and contract damage suits against the United States. The court sits in Washington, but commissioners of the court travel throughout the United States taking evidence. The United States Customs Court, consisting of nine judges, has jurisdiction to review rulings of collectors of the customs. Its decisions in turn may be appealed to the Court of Customs and Patent Appeals, a five-member court, which also reviews decisions of the Patent Office and, on a more restricted scale, certain rulings of the United States Tariff Commission.

In addition to constitutional, or *Article III*, courts that carry out the judicial power vested by the Constitution in the Supreme Court and such inferior courts as Congress may create, Congress may also establish *legislative*, or *Article I*, courts to carry out legislative powers granted to *Congress*. The main difference between legislative and constitutional courts is that the judges of the former need not be appointed "during good behavior" and may be assigned other than purely judicial duties.

The United States Court of Military Appeals, the GI Supreme Court, is a legislative, or Article I, court. It is composed of three civilian judges appointed for fifteen years by the president with the consent of the Senate. This Court applies military law, which is separate from the body of law that governs the rest of the federal court system.

The Constitution specifically exempts "cases arising from the land or naval forces, or in the Militia, when in actual service in time of War or public danger" from grand jury indictment. And the weight of opinion, though there is considerable dissent, is that all of the other Fifth and Sixth Amendment rights of persons accused of crime are not constitutionally applicable to military trials. But the Supreme Court has narrowly construed the words "arising in the military forces" even to the extent of exempting from military trials members of the armed services serving in the United States charged with off-the-post nonservice-connected crimes.[29] And Congress by law has imposed on military courts many of the procedural safeguards required by the Constitution in the regular courts.

In 1970 Congress disentangled the Article III courts operating within the District of Columbia from the court system designed to serve the people of the District on matters of local jurisdiction. It did this by creating a separate Article I, or legislative, court system for the District. This system consists of a trial court—the Superior Court of the District of Columbia—from which appeals may be carried to the District of Columbia Court of Appeals (not to be confused with the United States Court of

[29] *O'Callahan v. Parker* (1969); *Relford v. Commandant* (1971).

Appeals for the District of Columbia), which serves for the people of the District in the same fashion as does a state supreme court for the people of a state.

With the coming in 1974 of limited home rule to the District, the president was left with authority to appoint judges for the local district court system, with the consent of the Senate, for fifteen-year terms. But the president must nominate from a list of three candidates suggested to him by a seven-person commission, two of whom must be active practitioners of the bar of Washington. At the end of fifteen years, if the sitting judge desires to serve again and is rated by a special tenure commission as either "exceptionally well-qualified" or "well-qualified," he or she will be automatically reappointed. If given a lesser rating, the president may renominate or else select a new candidate from among a list presented to him by the nominating commission.

Many administrators and administrative agencies also hear and decide cases and exercise what is called *quasi-judicial* power, even though these agencies rank as neither constitutional nor legislative courts. For example, a person or company injured by the alleged unfair competitive practices of a business engaged in interstate commerce may bring a charge before the Federal Trade Commission. Attorneys appear, present briefs, introduce evidence, and carry out regular courtroom routines; eventually the commissioners hand down a decision—just as do judges. Appeals on questions of law and procedure in these hearings may be taken to a court of appeals and eventually to the Supreme Court.

STATE AND FEDERAL COURTS

In addition to this complex structure of federal courts, each of the fifty states maintains a complete judicial system of its own. And many of the large municipalities have independent judicial systems as complex as those of the states. This dual system of courts is not common—even among nations with federal systems. "The usual pattern in such countries is to entrust the enforcement of the federal law to the state courts. At the time of the adoption of our Constitution, however, the states and the federal government were too jealous of each other to accept a unitary judicial system."[30] The framers gave the national courts the power to hear and decide cases in law and equity if:

1. The cases arise under the Constitution, a federal law, or a treaty.
2. The cases arise under admiralty and maritime laws.
3. The cases arise because of a dispute involving land claimed under titles granted by two or more states.
4. The United States is a party to the case.
5. A state is a party to the case (but not including suits commenced or prosecuted against a state by an individual or a foreign nation).

[30]Milton D. Green, "The Business of the Trial Courts," in Harry W. Jones, ed., *The Courts, the Public, and the Law Explosion* (Prentice-Hall, 1965), pp. 8–9.

6. The cases are between citizens of different states.
7. The cases affect the accredited representatives of a foreign nation.

What is the relation between the federal and state courts? The common impression that all federal courts are superior to any state court is wrong. The two court systems are related, but they do not exist in a superior-inferior relationship. Over some kinds of cases only the state courts have jurisdiction; over other kinds both court systems have jurisdiction; and over others only the federal courts have jurisdiction. Moreover, except for the limited habeas corpus jurisdiction of the district courts, the Supreme Court is the only federal court that may review state-court decisions, and it may do so only under special conditions.

State courts have sole jurisdiction to try all cases not within the judicial power granted by the Constitution to the national government. As to the judicial power that is granted to the national government, Congress determines whether it shall be exclusively exercised by national courts, concurrently exercised by both national and state courts, or denied to either or both national and state courts. For example, Congress has stipulated that prosecutions for violations of federal criminal laws, suits for penalties authorized by federal laws, and cases involving foreign ambassadors are within the exclusive jurisdiction of national courts. On the other hand, legal disputes between citizens of different states involving more than $10,000 may be tried in either national or state courts. If the amount is less, the case can be tried only in state courts. (Of course, federal courts may have jurisdiction over suits between citizens of different states for some other reason, for instance if the dispute arises under national law.)

FEDERAL PROSECUTIONS

Judges decide cases; they do not prosecute persons. That job, on the federal level, falls to the Department of Justice and, more specifically, to the attorney general, the solicitor general, and the hundreds of United States attorneys and assistant attorneys throughout the country. A United States attorney is appointed to each district court by the president with consent of the Senate; he is appointed for a four-year term, but he may be dismissed by the president at any time. These appointments are of great interest to senators, who, through senatorial courtesy, exercise significant influence over them. Assistant attorneys are appointed by the attorney general. Assisted by the Federal Bureau of Investigation, the district attorneys start criminal proceedings against persons who break federal laws; they also initiate civil actions for the government. In a criminal case, the district attorney presents to a grand jury evidence that a national law has been violated. If the jury brings an indictment, the district attorney conducts the government's case against the accused.

The "prosecutor rather than the judge . . . plays the key role in the administration of criminal justice. The prosecutor must make or contribute to each of the key decisions: whether to charge an offense, which offense to charge, . . . whether to prosecute concurrently or separately if several charges are pending, and what sentence to recommend to the judge. Most of these decisions are made in the privacy of the prosecutor's office; neither newspapers nor television intrude to report the results."[31]

Although judges are the most thoroughly studied group of the federal judicial system, the role of the Department of Justice should not be underestimated. Attorneys from the Department and from other federal agencies participate in well over half the cases on the Supreme Court's docket.[32] Within the Department of Justice special divisions—such as the criminal division, civil division, antitrust division and civil rights division—coordinate the work of the attorneys in the field, develop cases, and send out specialists to assist the attorneys. Of special importance is the solicitor general, who appears for and represents the government before the Supreme Court. Moreover, no appeal may be taken by the United States to any appellate court without his approval.

In the aftermath of Watergate there has been some discussion within Congress and the country about taking the Department of Justice and the attorney general from the president's cabinet and making it an agency along the model of the General Accounting Office under the comptroller general—that is, under the control of a long-time career officer and responsible to Congress, or at least not directly responsible to the president.[33]

The arguments for such an organizational structure are clear: to minimize the danger that justice will be administered for partisan or political reasons, and to protect the independence of prosecutors and others investigating allegations of misconduct on the part of executive officials. On the other hand, the arguments for continuing to hold the president, the nation's elected chief executive, accountable for federal police and prosecutors are also compelling. There are grave dangers to a democracy from an independent, politically powerful prosecuting and police agency not directly accountable to the nation's elected chief executive.

In some of our states where the attorney general is elected independently of the governor, justice has not been administered with fewer political considerations than in those states where the attorney general is responsible to the governor.

[31]Herbert Jacob, *Justice in America: Courts, Lawyers, and the Judicial Process* (Little, Brown, 1965), p. 161.

[32]Nathan Hakman, "Lobbying the Supreme Court—An Appraisal of 'Political Science Folklore,'" *Fordham Law Review* (1966).

[33]Report of the National Academy of Public Administration, *Watergate: Its Implications for Responsible Government* (Basic Books, 1974), Chs. 4 and 5.

All things considered, major changes in the structure of the Department of Justice or its relation to the president are not likely; it *is* likely that as the result of Watergate, future presidents will be more careful not to fuse the responsibilities of running political campaigns with the duties of the attorney general.

Who are the judges?

The Constitution places the selection of federal judges in the hands of the president, acting with the advice and consent of the Senate. But political reality imposes constraints on the president's appointment power. The selection of a federal judge is actually a complex bargaining process, in which the principal figures involved are the candidates for the judgeship, the president, United States senators, the Department of Justice, the Standing Committee on Federal Judiciary of the American Bar Association, and political party leaders.[34]

THE POLITICS OF JUDICIAL SELECTION

The practice of senatorial courtesy gives a senator veto power over the appointment of a judge who is to sit in his state, if that senator is a member of the president's party. Even if he is from the opposition party he must be consulted. And, when the Senate is controlled by political opponents of the president, both senators from the state must be negotiated with regardless of their party affiliation. If negotiations between the senators and then between the senators and the Department of Justice deadlock, a seat may stay vacant for years.[35]

Since the end of World War II, the American Bar Association's Committee on the Federal Judiciary has come to play an important role in the appointment process. All federal judicial appointments are automatically sent to the committee for its evaluation. Presidents Eisenhower and Nixon agreed never to nominate a candidate rated unqualified by this twelve-man committee. Presidents Johnson and Kennedy were unwilling completely to substitute bar association politics for senatorial politics, but even they hesitated to nominate a person so classified.

The rule of senatorial courtesy does not apply to appointments to the Supreme Court and is somewhat less rigorously applied to the selection of judges for the courts of appeals—the judges do not serve in any one

[34]Harold W. Chase, *Federal Judges: The Appointing Process* (University of Minnesota Press, 1972), pp. 3–47; Henry J. Abraham, *Justices and Presidents: A Political History of Appointments to the Supreme Court* (Oxford University Press, 1974). See also Victor S. Navasky, *Kennedy Justice* (Atheneum, 1971), Ch. 5.

[35]Joel B. Grossman, *Lawyers and Judges: The ABA and the Politics of Judicial Selection* (John Wiley, 1965), p. 27. See also Chase, *Federal Judges*, and Jerry Landauer, "Shaping the Bench," *Wall Street Journal* (December 10, 1970), p. 1.

Justice Oliver Wendell Holmes.

senator's domain—so the president has considerably more discretion in making these appointments than he does in appointments to the district courts. It is not surprising that judges in the district courts often reflect a different consensus of values from those of the men appointed to the Supreme Court or to the courts of appeals.

Candidates for judicial office may "campaign" vigorously, attempting to drum up support from men in positions to influence the decision. Alphonso Taft wrote to Chief Justice Morrison R. Waite:

> My dear Judge, I have sometimes hoped, that if Judge Swayne should retire, there might be a possibility of my being thought of for that place. I should like it. . . . If . . . you should think favorably of it, and should find opportunity [*sic*] to encourage it, I should certainly be under great obligation whatever the result might be.[36]

The chief justice promised to "lose no opportunity" to let the president know what a fine judge Taft would make.

State and federal judges too are often active in promoting candidates. Sometimes their advice is solicited by the president, but it may well come uninvited. "When a recent proposed nomination to the . . . court of appeals was delayed for two years because of an intraparty dispute between the senators and the attorney general, a number of prominent jurists, including at least two Supreme Court justices, sought to break the deadlock."[37]

All this is the operation of the *political* process in the selection of judges. To some it may be a shocking picture. They would like to think that judges are picked without regard to party or ideology. But as a former Justice Department official, Donald Santarelli, has said, "When

[36]Quoted in Alpheus T. Mason, *William Howard Taft: Chief Justice* (Simon and Schuster, 1965) p. 18.

[37]Grossman, *Lawyers and Judges*, p. 39.

14–1
Federal judgeships as political patronage

	Number of judges appointed	
President	**Democrats**	**Republicans**
Roosevelt	203	8
Truman	129	13
Eisenhower	11	176
Kennedy	113	11
Johnson	170*	11
Nixon	16	213†

*One New York Liberal was appointed.
†As of May 3, 1974.

SOURCE: Department of Justice.

courts cease being an instrument for political change, then maybe the judges will stop being politically selected."[38]

THE ROLE OF PARTY

As Table 14–1 indicates, party considerations have always been important in the selection of judges. Presidents seldom choose a judge from the opposing party, and the use of judgeships as a form of political reward is openly acknowledged by those involved.[39] A state party leader wrote to the attorney general:

> If —— is not named [to the court of appeals] this would damage seriously the Kennedy forces in [this state.] —— was openly for Kennedy before L.A. and stood strong and voted there. He is known as one of my closest friends. He is an excellent lawyer—and on the merits alone, better qualified than Judge ——.
>
> The Senators will give you no trouble, but we have put this on the line in public, and if —— is not appointed it will be a mortal blow.

The desired candidate was appointed.[40]

THE ROLE OF IDEOLOGY

But finding a fellow partisan is not enough. Presidents want to pick the "right" kind of Republican or "our" kind of Democrat. Especially when the appointment is to the Supreme Court, the policy orientation of the nominee is important. As President Lincoln told Congressman Boutewell when he appointed Salmon P. Chase to the Court, "We wish for a Chief Justice who will sustain what has been done in regard to emancipation and legal tender." (Lincoln guessed wrong on Chase and legal tender; historical analysis suggests that presidents guess wrong about a fourth of the time—that is, the men they appoint do not conform to their expectations.)[41] Theodore Roosevelt voiced this attitude in a letter to Senator Lodge about Judge Oliver Wendell Holmes of the Massachusetts Supreme Judicial Court, whom he was considering for the Supreme Court: "Now I should like to know that Judge Holmes was in entire sympathy with our views, that is with your views amd mine. . . . I should hold myself guilty of an irreparable wrong to the nation if I should [appoint] any man who was not absolutely sane and sound on the great national policies for which we stand in public life."[42]

[38]Landauer, "Shaping the Bench."

[39]Jack W. Peltason, *Federal Courts in the Political Process* (Doubleday, 1955), p. 32.

[40]Sheldon Goldman, "Judicial Appointments to the United States Courts of Appeals," in Thomas P. Jahnige and Sheldon Goldman, eds., *The Federal Judicial System: Readings in Process and Behavior* (Holt, Rinehart & Winston, 1968), p. 19.

[41]Robert Scigliano, *The Supreme Court and the Presidency* (Free Press, 1971), pp. 146–47. Quoted in Peltason, *Federal Courts in the Political Process*, p. 41.

[42]Henry Cabot Lodge, *Selections from the Correspondence of Theodore Roosevelt and Henry Cabot Lodge* (Scribner's, 1925), 1, 518–19.

Roosevelt was even more specific in a letter to Lodge concerning the possible appointment of Horace Lurton: "[He] is right on the negro [*sic*] question; he is right on the power of the Federal Government; he is right on the insular business; he is right about corporations; and he is right about labor. On every question that would come before the bench he has so far shown himself to be in . . . touch with the policies in which you and I believe. . . . " Senator Lodge's reply is of equal interest: "I am glad that Lurton holds all the opinions that you say he does. . . . Those are the very questions on which I am just as anxious as you that judges should hold what we consider sound opinions, but I do not see why Republicans cannot be found who hold those opinions as well as Democrats."[43] The appointment went to Republican Attorney General William Moody.

President Nixon from the first was straightforward in his attempt to turn the courts in a more conservative direction. During his campaign he made it clear that he would appoint to the bench "strict constructionists." His difficulty after election in redirecting judicial policy-making stemmed from his lack of both a political and an ideological majority in the Senate.

Even before the 1968 election it was clear that the winner would have an unusual opportunity to influence the course of constitutional interpretation. Several members of the Supreme Court were reaching advanced ages. Moreover, in June of 1968 Chief Justice Earl Warren announced that he would retire as soon as his successor could be appointed. Although a Republican, Warren had a constitutional philosophy more consistent with that of President Johnson than with the views of Richard Nixon. By timing his retirement before the election, Warren gave President Johnson an opportunity to pick the next Chief Justice. Johnson promptly nominated Justice Abe Fortas, but the Senate refused to confirm his promotion. Hostile to President Johnson, displeased with the Warren Court's constitutional interpretations, and believing that the newly elected president should make the nomination, the senators were also responding to allegations that Justice Fortas had engaged in financial transactions thought to be improper for a member of the Supreme Court. In 1969 Justice Fortas resigned from the Supreme Court after further charges.

As a result, in his first year President Nixon had an opportunity to appoint Chief Justice Warren's successor and to fill the Fortas vacancy. The president appointed and the Senate quickly confirmed Warren Earl Burger to become Chief Justice of the United States. At the time of his appointment, Justice Burger was a judge of the Court of Appeals for the District of Columbia. His comments on and off the bench suggest that his constitutional views are less "liberal" than those of his predecessor, especially in the area of the administration of criminal justice.

[43]Quoted in Glendon A. Schubert, *Constitutional Politics* (Holt, Rinehart & Winston, 1960), pp. 40–41.

To replace Justice Fortas, President Nixon nominated Judge Clement Haynsworth, Jr., Chief Judge of the Court of Appeals for the Fourth Circuit. The Senate refused to confirm because of objections by labor and civil rights leaders and allegations about certain financial transactions. President Nixon tried again. This time he nominated Judge Harold Carswell of the District Court in Florida. Again the Senate refused to confirm because of revelations that earlier in his career Judge Carswell had supported racial segregation and because of charges that he lacked the ability to serve as a Supreme Court justice. Finally, President Nixon secured the confirmation of Harry A. Blackmun of the Court of Appeals for the Eighth Circuit. Justice Blackmun, unlike Haynsworth and Carswell, is a non-Southerner.

Then in the fall of 1971 Justice Black died and Justice Harlan resigned. To replace them President Nixon nominated Lewis Franklin Powell, Jr., a forty-year veteran of private practice and bar leadership from Virginia, thought to be a constitutional moderate, and William H. Rehnquist, a youngish (then forty-seven) Arizonian who had served the Nixon Administration in the Department of Justice and was thought to be a "Goldwater" Republican. In December 1971, the Senate finally confirmed both appointees, although Justice Rehnquist faced considerable opposition because of his previously expressed views on some civil liberties and civil rights issues.

The impact of the Nixon appointments is being felt. In many cases Burger, Blackmun, Powell, and Rehnquist are on one side with the three remaining judicial liberals left from the Warren Court—Marshall, Douglas, and Brennan—on the other side. Justices White and Stewart are the "swing men." Although the differences between the Warren and the Burger Courts should not be exaggerated, the Court has significantly altered its course in certain areas, such as the administration of justice, where the Burger Court is more likely than its predecessor to give state governments leeway to determine how justice should be administered. It has also granted states and cities more discretion to decide what movies and what periodicals are to be considered obscene.

Judicial ideology is also significant in the creation of vacancies. Because federal judges serve for life, a judge may be able to schedule his retirement so as to allow a president whose views he approves to appoint his successor. Chief Justice Taney stayed on the bench long after he was frail to prevent Lincoln from nominating a Republican. Justice Holmes wrote to a friend that Chief Justice White had delayed having an operation, in part because of a "determination not to give the appointment to Wilson," and Holmes himself was pleased by Calvin Coolidge's election in 1924, which "relieves my conscience from the doubt whether I ought to resign so as to give the appointment to him."[44] In 1929 Chief Justice Taft wrote, "I am older and slower and less acute and more confused. However, as long as things continue as

[44]Mark De Wolfe Howe, ed., *Holmes-Laski Letters* (Atheneum, 1963), I, 264, 453.

they are, and I am able to answer in my place, I must stay on the court in order the prevent the Bolsheviki from getting control. . . ."[45] And if, as many assume, the older, liberal Democratic sitting justices such as Douglas are holding off retirement until after a Republican has been replaced in the White House by a president more likely to nominate someone who reflects their own constitutional ideology, they are following well-established precedents.

CREATION AND ABOLITION OF JUDGESHIPS

Party politics is intimately involved in the creation of new judicial posts.[46] One of the first acts of a political party that has been out of power once it regains control of Congress and the White House is to increase the number of federal judgeships. When one party controls Congress and the other the White House, there is likely to be a stalemate, so that relatively few new judicial positions are created. Even after President Eisenhower promised that half the additional appointments would go to Democrats, he was unable to convince the Democratic leadership of Congress that there was a need for more judgeships. When President Kennedy took office, Congress promptly created new positions. During his first year in office, President Kennedy appointed eighty-five federal judges, eighty-four Democrats and one a member of New York's Liberal party. Although President Nixon was able to pry more than sixty additional judgeships out of Congress, conflicts between the White House and the Senate kept a large number of them vacant.

Justice Felix Frankfurter.

Congressional control over the structure and jurisdiction of the federal courts has been used successfully to influence the course of judicial decisions. Although thwarted in their attempts to impeach the judges, the Jeffersonians abolished the circuit courts that the Federalist Congress had created just prior to leaving office. In 1869 the radical Republicans in Congress used their constitutional power to alter the Supreme Court's appellate jurisdiction in order to snatch from the Court a case it was about to review involving legislation of dubious constitutionality *(Ex parte McCardle)*. They also reduced the size of the Court to prevent President Andrew Johnson from filling two vacancies. After Johnson left the White House, Congress returned the Court to its prior size to permit Grant to fill the vacancies, and the men Grant selected made it possible to reverse the Supreme Court invalidation of the Legal Tender Act. Historians are still debating whether Grant packed the Court. Certainly he was not unaware that his two appointees shared his sentiments about the desirability of reversing the earlier decision.

[45]Letter to Horace Taft, November 14, 1929, quoted in H. Pringle, *The Life and Times of William Howard Taft* (Farrar, 1939), II, 967.

[46]Richard J. Richardson and Kenneth N. Vines, *The Politics of Federal Courts* (Little, Brown, 1970), p. 17.

President Franklin D. Roosevelt's battle with the Supreme Court in 1937 is a most dramatic attempt by a political leader to influence judicial decisions by changing the size of the Court. Although Roosevelt did not succeed in packing the Court, it began to uphold New Deal legislation in the midst of the debate over his attempt to do so.

WHAT MANNER OF MEN?

Who are the judges? Because all federal judges are lawyers, it is not surprising that the judges are something of an educational elite.[47] Federal judges and Supreme Court justices have tended to come from middle- or upper-class backgrounds, and except for the appointment of Thurgood Marshall by Lyndon Johnson, Supreme Court justices have been white. They have all been male. Over 85 percent of Supreme Court members have been of British ethnic origin, and over 85 percent have been Protestant. But in recent years, a tradition of a Catholic seat and a Jewish seat on the Court has developed. Basically, though, critics' charge that the Supreme Court is a WASP institution is correct.

Federal judges at all levels are usually actively engaged in politics prior to their selection; a substantial majority of the justices have been drawn from politically active families and "every member of the Supreme Court except George Shiras held a political post of some kind prior to his appointment to the High Bench."[48] However, prior judicial experience has not been a major criterion in the selection of Supreme Court justices; only one-quarter have had really extensive judicial careers. Service on a federal district court often leads to promotion to the court of appeals, but there is no such stepping-stone to the High Court. Moreover, there is little in the history of the Supreme Court to suggest that prior judicial experience produces better qualified or more objective justices. Some of the Court's most distinguished members—for example, John Marshall, Taney, Miller, Hughes, Brandeis, Stone, and Frankfurter—had no judicial experience at the time of their appointments. The clamor in recent years for a requirement that only persons with judicial experience be considered for appointment to the Supreme Court is, according to one student of the Court's history, "only the most recent of the manifestations of the fact that advocacy of particular methods of judicial selection is inexorably related to desires for ideological control of the Court."[49]

[47]This section is based on John R. Schmidhauser, *The Supreme Court: Its Politics, Personalities, and Procedures* (Holt, Rinehart & Winston, 1960), and Sheldon Goldman, "Characteristics of Eisenhower and Kennedy Appointees to the Lower Federal Courts," *Western Political Quarterly* (December 1965), pp. 726–55.

[48]Schmidhauser, *ibid.*, p. 51.

[49]*Ibid.*, p. 52, See also Henry J. Abraham, *Justices and Presidents*, pp. 44–48.

How the Supreme Court operates

The justices are in session from the first Monday in October through June. In their gleaming Corinthian building, they listen to oral arguments for two weeks and then adjourn for two weeks to consider the cases and write their opinions. Six justices must participate in each decision, and cases are decided by a majority. In the event of a tie vote, the decision of the lower court is sustained, although the case may be reargued.

At 10 A.M. on the days when the Supreme Court sits, the eight associate justices and the chief justice, dressed in their judicial robes, file into the Court. As they take their seats – arranged according to seniority, with the chief justice in the center – the clerk of the Court introduces them as the "Honorable Chief Justice and Associate Justices of the Supreme Court of the United States." Those present in the courtroom are seated, with counsel taking their places along tables in front of the bench; the attorneys for the Department of Justice, dressed in morning clothes, are at the right. The other attorneys are dressed conservatively; sport coats are not considered proper. This is all part of what Richard M. Johnson has called the "'dramaturgy' of the Court – the majesty of its courtroom; the black robes of the justices; the ritual of its proceedings at oral argument and on decision day; the secrecy and isolation of its decision-making conferences; the formal opinions invoking the symbols of Constitution, precedent, and framers' intent; and all the other elements of setting and conduct that distinguish the Supreme Court, a body of constitutional guardians, from all other officials whose actions they may find wanting when tested against the national covenant."[50]

WHAT CASES REACH THE SUPREME COURT?

When an irate citizen vows he will take his case to the highest court of the land even if it costs him his last penny, he perhaps underestimates the difficulty of securing Supreme Court review, overestimates the cost (although it costs plenty), and reveals a basic misunderstanding of the role of the High Court. The rules for appealing a case to the Supreme Court are established by act of Congress and are exceedingly complex. Certain types of cases are said to go to the Supreme Court *on appeal;* in theory, the Court is obligated to hear these cases. Other appellate cases come before the Court by means of a discretionary *writ of certiorari.* In addition, the Constitution stipulates that the Supreme Court has original jurisdiction in specified situations. But one basic fact lies behind all the technicalities – the Supreme Court has control of its docket and decides which cases it wants to consider. The justices closely re-

[50]Richard Johnson, *The Dynamics of Compliance* (John Wiley, 1967), pp. 33–41. This summary of Johnson's comment is taken from David Adamany, "Legitimacy, Realigning Elections," p. 792.

view fewer than two hundred of the approximately four thousand cases annually presented to them.[51]

It is not enough that Jones thinks he should have won his case against Smith. There has already been at least one appellate review of the trial, either in a federal court of appeals or in a state supreme court. If the High Court had to review all cases from the courts of appeals, it would still be deciding cases today that originated in the 1920s. The Supreme Court will review Mr. Jones's case only if his claim has broad public significance. It may be that there is a conflict between the rulings of two courts of appeals on a legal point; by deciding Jones's case, the Supreme Court can guarantee that one rule is followed throughout the judicial system. It may be that Jones's case raises a constitutional issue on which a state supreme court has presented an interpretation with which the High Court justices disagree. The crucial factor in determining whether the Supreme Court will hear the case is its importance—not to Jones—but to the operation of the governmental system as a whole.

The Court accepts a case if four justices are sufficiently interested in it to request its consideration. Although the justices officially insist that their refusal to take a case does not signify that they agree with what the lower court has decided, it is probably correct to say that they tend to reject cases in which they are satisfied that a correct decision has been rendered. However, the refusal to hear a case may also indicate that the justices do not wish to become involved in a political "hot potato" or that the Court is so divided on an issue that it is not yet prepared to take a stand.

THE BRIEFS AND ORAL ARGUMENT

Prior to the presentation of the case in open court, the justices receive printed *briefs*, perhaps running into hundreds of pages, in which each side presents legal arguments, historical materials, and relevant precedents. In addition the Supreme Court may receive briefs from *amici curiae*—friends of the court; these may be individuals, organizations, or government agencies who claim to have an interest in the case and information of value to the Court. This procedure guarantees that the Department of Justice is represented if a suit between two private parties calls the constitutionality of an act of Congress into question. Although a brief brought by a private party or interest group may help the justices by presenting an argument or point of law that the parties to the case have not raised, often the briefs are filed as a means of "pressuring" the Court to reach a particular decision. In the school desegregation cases, twenty-four amicus briefs were filed; in the Defunis case re-

[51]Detailed figures as well as a review of the Court for the preceding term can be found in an article by Paul C. Bartholomew in each March issue of the *Western Political Quarterly*, in each November issue of the *Harvard Law Review*, and in an annual analysis of important decisions edited by Philip Kurland under the title *The Supreme Court Annual Review*, published by the University of Chicago Press.

lating to a university program designed to increase the numbers of blacks entering a law school, twenty-six such briefs were presented, including one in behalf of sixty law school deans.[52]

Formal oratory before the Supreme Court, perhaps lasting for several days, is a thing of the past. As a rule, counsel for each side is now limited to a one-hour argument—in some cases even less—and the Court scrupulously enforces the time limits. (Extremely important cases will occasionally be given additional time.) Lawyers use a lectern to which two lights are attached; a white light flashes five minutes before time is up and when the red light goes on, the lawyer must stop instantly, even in the middle of an "it."[53]

The entire procedure is formally informal. Sometimes, to the annoyance of the attorneys, the justices talk among themselves or consult briefs or legal volumes during the oral presentation. Justice Holmes occasionally napped during oral argument. When he found a presentation particularly bad he would frequently and ostentatiously consult his watch.[54]

The justices freely interrupt the lawyers to ask questions, and to request additional information. If a lawyer seems to be having a difficult time, they may try to help him present a better case. Occasionally the justices bounce arguments off a hapless attorney, at one another. During oral argument in the school desegregation cases, Justice Frankfurter was grilling an NAACP lawyer: "Are you saying that we can say that 'separate but equal' is not a doctrine that is relevant at the primary school level? Is that what you are saying" he demanded. Justice Douglas tried to help the lawyer out. "I think you are saying," he ventured, "that segregation may be all right in streetcars and railroad cars and restaurants, but . . . education is different from that." The lawyer found the Douglas paraphrase to his liking. "Yes, sir," he replied. Douglas continued, "That is your argument, is it not? Isn't that your argument in this case?" Again a grateful "yes" from counsel. Frankfurter, however, was not even moderately impressed. "But how can that be your argument . . .?" he cried, and the lawyer was once again on his own.[55]

The participants in oral argument are by no means equal. The solicitor general, who represents the federal government, probably enjoys a situational bias as the result of his more frequent, more intensive interaction with the justices. Similarly, though to a lesser extent, lawyers of great reputation can communicate with the Court more effectively than

[52]Samuel Krislov, "The *Amicus Curiae* Brief: From Friendship to Advocacy," *Yale Law Journal* (March 1963), pp. 694–721.

[53]Henry J. Abraham, *The Judicial Process*, 2nd ed. (Oxford University Press, 1968).

[54]Walter F. Murphy, *Wiretapping on Trial: A Case Study in the Judicial Process* (Random House, 1965), p. 93.

[55]Berman, *It Is So Ordered: The Supreme Court Rules on School Segregation* (Norton, 1966). p. 69.

can a young lawyer who has been specially admitted to the Supreme Court bar to make his first appearance.[56]

THE CONFERENCE

Each Friday the justices meet in conference. During the week they have heard the oral arguments, read and studied the briefs, and examined the petitions. Before the conference, each justice receives a list of the cases that will be discussed. Each brings to the meeting a red leather book in which the cases and the votes of the justices are recorded. The Friday conferences are highly secret affairs; what goes on in these meetings has to be gleaned from the infrequent comments of members of the Court.

Although the procedure varies, the conferences are marked by informality and vigorous give-and-take. The chief justice presides, and usually opens the dicussion by briefly stating the facts, summarizing the questions of law, and making suggestions for disposing of the case. He then asks each member of the Court, in order of seniority, to give his views and conclusions. After full discussion a vote is taken. The case is decided by majority vote, and one justice is designated to write the *opinion of the Court.* If the chief justice votes with the majority, he decides who writes the opinion. If he does not, the senior justice among the majority makes the decision. More often than not the opinion-assigner will assign the opinion either to himself or to the justice whose position is closest to his own.[57] Justices who are among the minority normally select one of their number to write a *dissenting opinion,* although each dissenter is free to write his own. If a justice agrees with the majority on the decision but differs on the reasoning, he may write his own opinion; this is known as a *concurring opinion.*

OPINION WRITING: MARSHALING THE COURT

The justice selected to write the Court's opinion is faced with an exacting task. He must produce a document that will win the support of at least four—and hopefully eight—intelligent, strong-willed men, all of whom may have voted the same way he did but perhaps for very different reasons. Assisted by his law clerks, recent honor graduates from law school, the justice tries his hand at a draft and sends it to his colleagues for their comments. If he is lucky, the majority will accept his formulation, perhaps suggesting minor changes. But it may be that his original draft is not satisfactory to the Court. If this is the case, he is forced to redraft and recirculate his opinion until a majority can reach agreement.

[56]Glendon A. Schubert, *Quantitative Analysis of Judicial Behavior* (Free Press, 1959), p. 109.

[57]David W. Rohde, "Policy Goals, Strategic Choice and Majority Opinion Assignments in the U.S. Supreme Court," *Midwest Journal of Political Science* (November 1972), pp. 652 ff.

There is considerable fluidity in the judicial process at this point.[58] In fact, there are "numerous instances on record in which the justice assigned the opinion of the Court has reported back that additional study had convinced him that he and the rest of the majority had been in error.[59] Sometimes he is able to convince the Court to change its mind. Moreover, a dissenting justice can sometimes persuade the opinion writer of the merits of his protest. For example, shortly after Harlan Fiske Stone came on the Court, the justices divided seven to one in a particular case, with Stone the lone dissenter. He did not give up, however, and took to Chief Justice Taft (who had assigned the opinion to himself) relevant articles from a dozen volumes of the Columbia and Harvard law reviews and a memorandum requesting reconsideration. Taft's draft opinion was circulated some time later, with the following note appended: "Dear Brethren: I think we made a mistake in this case and have written the opinion the other way. Hope you will agree. W.H.T." The new revised Taft opinion became the decision of a unanimous court.[60]

If the opinion writer's initial formulation is not acceptable to a majority of the Court, an elaborate bargaining process occurs. The opinion ultimately published is not necessarily the opinion the author would have liked to write—like a committee report, it represents the most common denominator. Holmes bitterly complained to Laski that he had written an opinion "in terms to suit the majority of the brethren, although they didn't suit me. Years ago I did the same thing in the interest of getting a job done. I let the brethren put in a reason that I thought bad and cut out all that I thought good and I have squirmed ever since, and swore that never again—but again I yield and now comes a petition for rehearing pointing out all the horrors that will ensue from just what I didn't want to say."[61]

The two major sanctions a justice can use against his colleagues are his vote and his willingness to write a separate opinion that will attack a doctrine the majority wishes to see adopted. A dissenting opinion is often written and circulated for the specific purpose of convincing the majority. If the opinion writer is persuaded by the logic of the dissenter, the dissenting opinion may never be published. Sometimes, however, an unpersuaded justice will be forced to give in to the demands of one of his colleagues. Especially if the Court is closely divided, one justice may be in a position to demand that a given argument be included in—or removed from—the opinion as the price of his swing vote. Sometimes this can happen even if the Court is not closely divided. An opin-

[58]J. Woodford Howard, "On the Fluidity of Judicial Choice," *American Political Science Review*, (March 1968), pp. 43–56. See also Murphy's *Elements of Judicial Strategy*.

[59]Howard, *ibid.*, p. 44

[60]Alpheus T. Mason, *Harlan Fiske Stone: Pillar of the Law* (Viking, 1956), p. 222. Murphy, *Elements of Judicial Strategy*, and Howard, *ibid.*, contain dozens of similar examples.

[61]Howe, *Holmes–Laski Letters*, II, 124, 125.

The Supreme Court

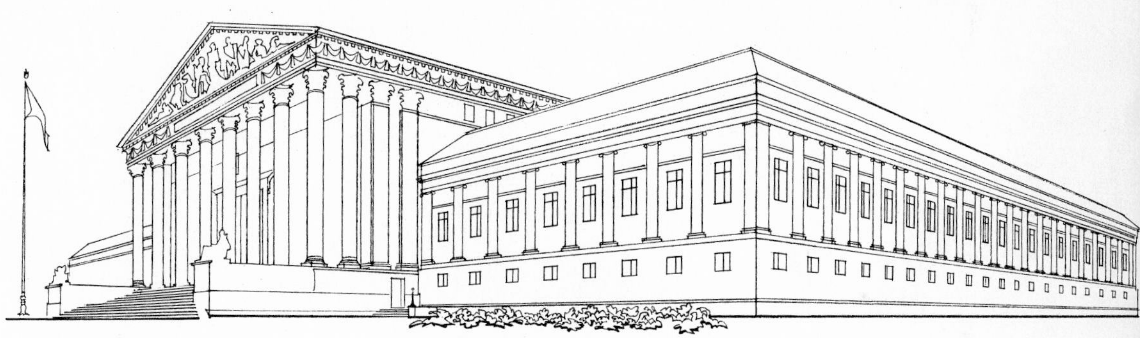

"We are very quiet there but it is the quiet of a storm center. . . ."
—Oliver Wendell Holmes, Jr.

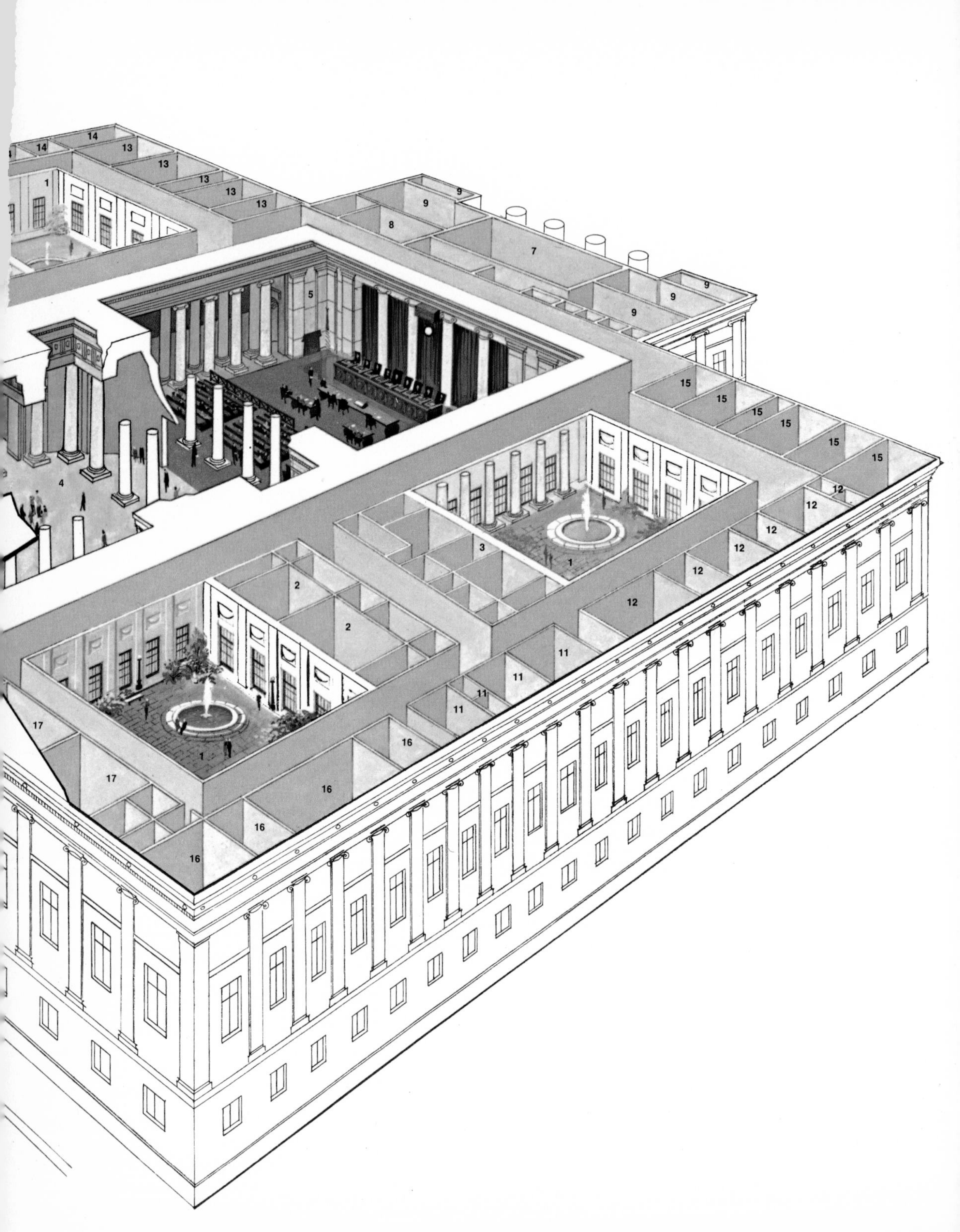

14
14
13
13
13
13
13
1
9
9
8
7
9
9
9
5
15
15
15
15
15
15
4
12
12
12
12
12
12
3
1
2
2
12
11
11
11
11
17
16
1
17
16
16
16

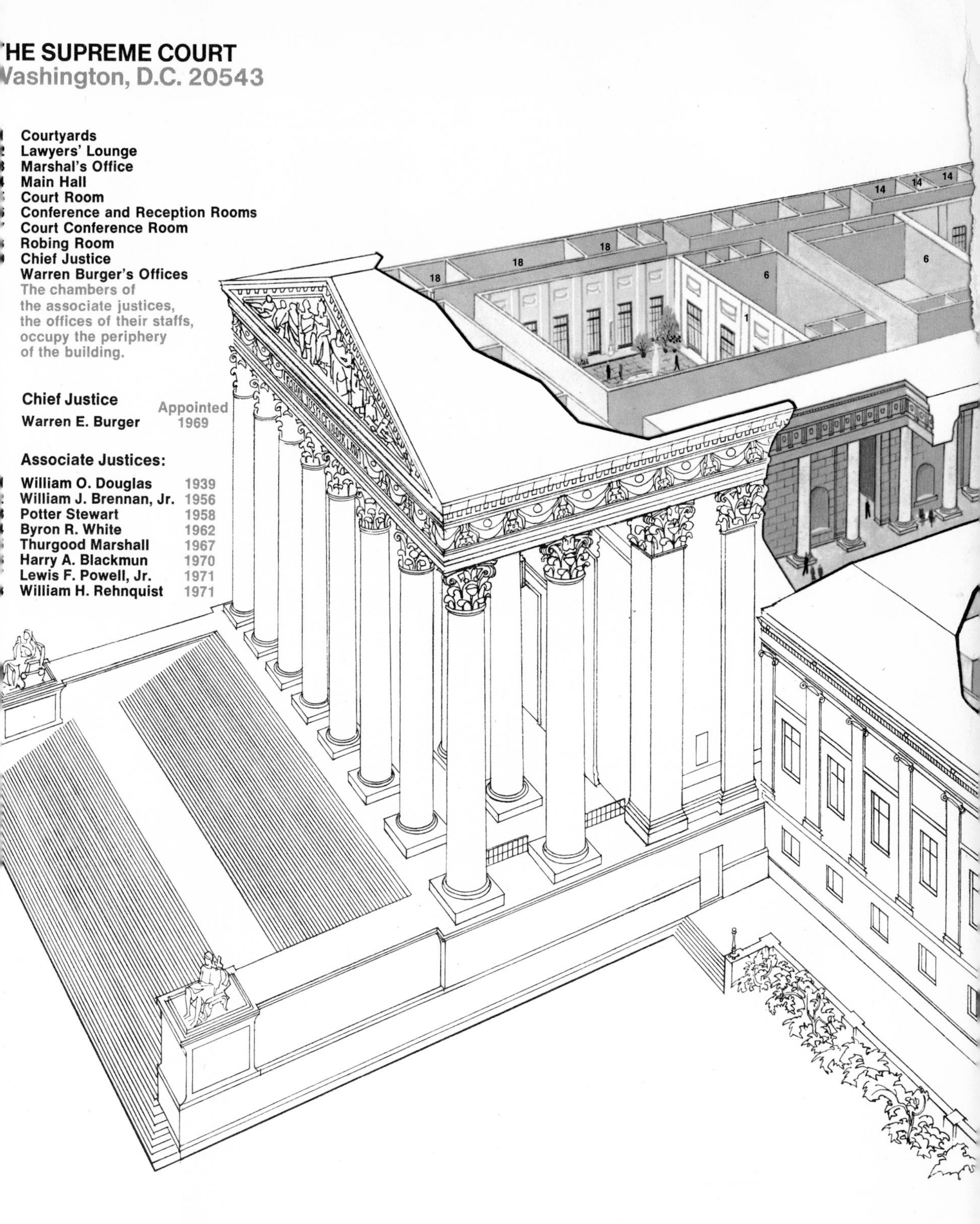
'HE SUPREME COURT
Vashington, D.C. 20543
Courtyards
Lawyers' Lounge
Marshal's Office
Main Hall
Court Room
Conference and Reception Rooms
Court Conference Room
Robing Room
Chief Justice
Warren Burger's Offices
The chambers of
the associate justices,
the offices of their staffs,
occupy the periphery
of the building.
Chief Justice
Warren E. Burger
Appointed
1969
Associate Justices:
William O. Douglas 1939
William J. Brennan, Jr. 1956
Potter Stewart 1958
Byron R. White 1962
Thurgood Marshall 1967
Harry A. Blackmun 1970
Lewis F. Powell, Jr. 1971
William H. Rehnquist 1971
14
14
14
18
18
18
6
6
1

ion writer who anticipates that his decision will elicit a critical public reaction may very much wish to have it presented as the view of a unanimous court and may be prepared to compromise to achieve unanimity.

OPINIONS AS MEDIA OF COMMUNICATION

As a general rule, Supreme Court decisions are accompanied by opinions that state the facts, present the issues, announce the decision, and, most important, attempt to justify the reasoning employed by the Court. Judicial opinions are the Court's principal method of expressing itself to the outside world, and it addresses them to various audiences. Perhaps the most important function of opinions is to instruct the lower courts and the bar how to act in future cases.

Sometimes judicial opinions are used to "drum up trade." A statement in the form "Nothing in this opinion should be taken to preclude a case in which . . ." is an invitation to attorneys and lower-court judges to act in a certain way. A dissenting or concurring opinion may be used to throw cues to the bench and bar. Judicial opinions may be directed at Congress or the president. If the Court regrets that "in the absence of action by the Congress, we have no choice but to . . ." or insists that "relief of the sort that petitioner demands can only come from the political branches of government," it is clearly asking Congress to act. Sometimes the Court will interpret existing statutes so narrowly as to render them ineffective, in the hope of forcing fresh legislative action. Such a hope once prompted the following dissent from Justice Clark: "Unless the Congress changes the rule announced by the Court today, those intelligence agencies of our government engaged in law enforcement may as well close up shop. . . ." Within three months, new legislation was on the statute books.[62]

Finally, the justices use published opinions to communicate with the public. Hopefully, a well-handled opinion may increase support among specialized publics—especially lawyers and judges—and among the general population for a policy the Court is stressing. For this reason the Court delayed declaring school segregation unconstitutional until unanimity could be secured. The justices understood that any sign of dissension on the bench on this major social issue would be an invitation to evade the Court's ruling.

The various functions of a judicial opinion are nicely illustrated by the following memorandum that Justice Frankfurter sent to Justice Murphy, discussing a dissenting opinion:

> This is a protest opinion—a protest at the Bar of the future—but also an effort to make the brethren realize what is at stake. Moreover, a powerful dissent . . . is bound to have an effect on the lower courts as well as on the officers of the law. . . . And so in order to impress our own brethren, the lower courts, and

[62]Berman, *It Is So Ordered*, p. 114; Murphy, *Elements of Judicial Strategy*, p. 66.

enforcement officers, it seems to me vital to make the dissent an impressive document.[63]

THE POWERS OF THE CHIEF JUSTICE

President Johnson's unsuccessful nomination in 1968 of Associate Justice Abe Fortas to the position of chief justice and the furor that followed led many people to ask what special powers the chief justice has. The chief justice has only one vote, and in terms of formal power, he is merely the first among equals.[64] However, his position gives him a unique opportunity to exercise leadership. The chief justice presides in open court and over the conferences, where it is he who usually presents each case to his associates—thus setting the tone of the discussion. Also, as we have seen, he assigns the writing of the opinion of the Court in all cases when he votes with the majority. This role—choosing the opinion writer—is significant because the writer determines whether an opinion is based on one ground rather than another and whether it deals narrowly or broadly with the issues. These choices may make a decision more or less acceptable to the public, may affect the decision of other justices to dissent, and may affect the value of a decision as a precedent. The chief justice is also the key figure in the Court's certiorari procedure; in practice, he is generally able to eliminate from the Court's docket those cases he considers trivial.

The ability of the chief justice to influence his Court has varied considerably. Chief Justice Hughes ran the conferences like a stern schoolmaster, keeping the justices talking to the point, moving the discussion along, and doing his best to work out compromises. Frowning on dissents, he tried to achieve a unanimous vote in order to give greater weight to Court decisions. Chief Justice Stone, on the other hand, encouraged each justice to state his own point of view and let the discussion wander as it would. Chief Justice Burger has devoted much of his time to judicial reform, speaking to bar and lay groups, and trying to build political support for modernizing the judicial structure. As Danelski reminds us, "the Chief Justiceship does not guarantee leadership. It only offers its incumbent an opportunity to lead. Optimum leadership inheres in the combination of the office and an able, persuasive, personable judge."[65]

AFTER THE LAWSUIT IS OVER

Victory in the Supreme Court does not necessarily mean that a litigant

[63]Quoted in Berman, *ibid.*, pp. 60, 61.

[64]This discussion is based on David Danelski, "The Influence of the Chief Justice in the Decisional Process of the Supreme Court," in Jahnige and Goldman, *Federal Judicial System*, pp. 147–60.

[65]"The Influence of the Chief Justice," p. 148.

will get what he wants. As a rule the High Court does not implement its own decision, but "remands" the case to the lower court with instructions to act in accordance with the Supreme Court's opinion. The lower courts have considerable leeway in their interpretation of the High Court's mandates.

The impact of a particular ruling announced by the Supreme Court on the behavior of those who are not immediate parties to a lawsuit is even more uncertain. Many of the more important decisions require further action by administrative and elected officials before they become the effective law of the land. Sometimes Supreme Court decisions are simply ignored: Despite the Supreme Court's holding that it is unconstitutional for school boards to require prayers within the schools, many school boards continued their previous practices.[66] For years after the Supreme Court held public school segregation unconstitutional, a great number of school districts remained segregated. The Constitution may be what the Supreme Court says it is, but a Supreme Court opinion, for the moment, at least, is what a trial judge or a police officer or a prosecutor says it means.

The most difficult Supreme Court decisions to implement are those that require the cooperation of large numbers of officials. For example, a Supreme Court decision announcing a new standard for police arrest procedures is not likely to have an impact on the way police make arrests for some time. Not many police officers subscribe to the *United States Supreme Court Reports.* Rather the process is more complex: Local prosecutors, state attorneys general, chiefs of police, and state and federal trial court judges must all participate in giving "meaning" to Supreme Court decisions.

Although Congress or a president has occasionally "ignored" or "construed" a Supreme Court ruling to avoid its impact, by and large decisions whose implementation requires only the action of a central governmental agency become immediately effective. For example, when the Supreme Court held that President Truman lacked constitutional authority to seize steel companies temporarily to avoid a shutdown during the Korean War, the president promptly complied. Of course other presidents retain wide discretion in determining how that particular precedent should be applied to guide their own behavior.

As we will also see in the case of the presidency, what appears to be a neat hierarchical system often turns out to be a confused mass of mutual controls and reciprocal influence, not at all like the disciplined chain of command of a military organization. So, too, are the relations of the Supreme Court with the judicial bureaucracy and other decisionmakers.[67]

[66]Theodore L. Becker, ed., *The Impact of Supreme Court Decisions* (Oxford University Press, 1969); and Stephen L. Wasby, *The Impact of the United States Supreme Court* (Dorsey Press, 1970), and the literature cited therein.

[67]Richardson and Vines, *The Politics of Federal Courts,* p. 161; Bradley C. Canon, "Reactions of State Supreme Courts to a U.S. Supreme Court Civil Liberties Decision," *Law and Society Review* (Fall 1973), pp. 108ff.

The judges: guardians of the Constitution

Judicial review—the power of a court of law to set aside an act of the legislature that in its opinion violates the Constitution—is an American contribution to the art of government. Although only a small portion of the business of the courts involves constitutional issues, this is surely one of the most exciting and politically significant aspects of the judicial process. If an Englishman or an American is thrown into prison without cause, either can appeal to the courts of his respective country for protection. When Parliament passes a law, however, no English judge has the authority to declare it null and void because he believes it to violate the English constitution. Not the courts but Parliament is the guardian of the English constitution. But in the United States the courts, ultimately the Supreme Court, are the keepers of the constitutional conscience—not Congress and not the president. How did the judges get this tremendous responsibility?

ORIGINS OF JUDICIAL REVIEW

The Constitution itself says nothing about who should be the final arbiter of disputes that might arise over its meaning. It does not specifically grant such power to the Supreme Court. Whether the members of the Convention of 1787 intended to bestow on the courts the power of judicial review is a question that has long been debated. There is little doubt that the framers intended the Supreme Court to have the power to declare state legislation unconstitutional, but whether they intended to give it the same power over national legislation is not clear. Edward S. Corwin, an outstanding authority on the American Constitution, concluded that unquestionably "the framers anticipated some sort of judicial review. . . . But it is equally without question that the ideas generally current in 1787 were far from presaging the present vast role of the Court."[68] Why, then, did the framers not specifically provide for judicial review? Probably because they believed the power rested on certain general provisions that made specific statements unnecessary.

The Federalists—the men who wrote the Constitution and controlled the national government until 1801—generally supported the courts and favored judicial review, but their opponents, the Jeffersonian Republicans, were less enthusiastic. In 1798 and 1799 Jefferson and Madison (the latter by this time had left the Federalist party) came very close in the Virginia and Kentucky Resolutions to arguing that the state legislatures and not the Supreme Court had the ultimate power to interpret the Constitution. This would seem to imply that the Supreme Court did not even have the final authority to review state legislation, something about which there had been little doubt.

[68]"The Constitution as Instrument and as Symbol," *American Political Science Review*, (December 1936), p. 1078.

When the Jeffersonians defeated the Federalists in the elections of 1800, it was still undecided whether the Supreme Court would actually exercise the power of judicial review. "The idea was in the air, the ingredients to support a doctrine of judicial review were at hand, an a few precedents could even be cited"; nevertheless, judicial review was not an established power. Then in 1803 came the case of *Marbury v. Madison*, a case intimately related to the political struggles between the Federalists and the Jeffersonians.

MARBURY V. MADISON

The elections of 1800 marked the rise to power of the Jeffersonian Republicans. President John Adams and his fellow Federalists did not take their defeat easily; indeed, they were greatly alarmed at what they considered to be the "enthronement of the rabble." But there was nothing much they could do about it before leaving office—or was there? The Constitution gives the president, with the consent of the Senate, the power to appoint federal judges to hold office during "good behavior"—virtually for life. If the judiciary should be manned by good Federalists, reasoned Adams and his party followers, they could stave off the worst consequences of Jefferson's victory.

The Federalist lame-duck Congress created dozens of new federal judicial posts. By March 3, 1801, Adams had appointed, and the Senate had confirmed, deserving Federalists to all these new positions. Adams signed the commissions and turned them over to John Marshall, the secretary of state, to be sealed and delivered. Marshall had just received his own commission as chief justice of the United States, but he was continuing to serve as secretary of state until Adams' term expired. Working right up to nine o'clock on the evening of March 3, Marshall sealed but was unable to deliver all the commissions. The important ones were taken care of, however, and only those for the justices of the peace for the District of Columbia were left undelivered. The chief justice retired to his lodgings and left the commissions to be delivered by his successor.

Jefferson was highly aroused by this Federalist packing of the judiciary. When he discovered that some of the commissions had not been delivered, he told the new secretary of state, James Madison, to hold up seventeen of those still in his possession. Jefferson could see no reason why the District needed so many justices of the peace, especially Federalist justices.

Among the commissions that were not delivered was one for William Marbury. After waiting in vain, Marbury decided to seek action from the courts. Searching through the statute books, he came across Section 13 of the Judiciary Act of 1789, which authorized the Supreme Court "to issue writs of mandamus, in cases warranted by the principles and usages of law, to . . . persons holding office, under the authority of the United States." A *writ of mandamus* is a court order directing an official

"He was preparing a writ of mandamus or habeas corpus or something, and we left him pretty much alone."

Drawing by Richard Decker; © 1956 The New Yorker Magazine, Inc.

Chief Justice John Marshall.

to perform a nondiscretionary or ministerial act. Delivering a commission is a ministerial act; the secretary of state is a person holding office under the authority of the United States; so why not, thought Marbury, ask the Supreme Court to issue a writ of mandamus to force Madison to deliver the commission? He and his companions went directly to the Supreme Court and, citing Section 13, they so asked.

What could Marshall do? If the Court issued the mandamus, Madison and Jefferson would probably ignore it. The Court would be powerless, and its prestige, already low, might suffer a fatal blow. On the other hand, by refusing to issue the mandamus, the judges would appear to vindicate the Republican party's claim that the Court had no authority to interfere with the executive. Would Marshall issue the mandamus? Most people thought so; angry Republicans talked of impeachment.

On February 24, 1803, the Supreme Court published its opinion. The first part was as expected. Marbury was entitled to his commission, said Marshall, and Madison should have delivered it to him; a writ of mandamus could be issued by the proper court against even such an august officer as the secretary of state.

Then came the surprise. Although Section 13 of the Judiciary Act purports to give the Supreme Court original jurisdiction in just such cases, this section, said Marshall, is contrary to Article III of the Constitution, which gives the Supreme Court original jurisdiction in *only* those cases in which an ambassador or other foreign minister is affected or in which a state is a party. This is a case of original jurisdiction, but Marbury is neither a state nor a foreign minister. If we follow Section 13, wrote Marshall, we have jurisdiction; if we follow the Constitution, we have no jurisdiction.

Then, in characteristic fashion, Marshall stated the question in such a way that the answer was obvious—namely, should the Supreme Court enforce an unconstitutional law? Of course not, he concluded; the Constitution is the supreme and binding law, and the courts cannot enforce any action of Congress that conflicts with it.

The real question remained unanswered. Congress and the president had also read the Constitution, and according to their interpretation (which was also reasonable), Section 13 was compatible with Article III. Where did the Supreme Court get the right to say they were wrong? Why should the Supreme Court's interpretation of the constitution be preferred to that of Congress and the president?

Marshall, paralleling Hamilton's argument in *Federalist No. 78*, reasoned that the Constitution is law, that judges—not legislators or executives—interpret law; therefore, the judges should interpret the Constitution. "If two laws conflict with each other, the courts must decide on the operation of each," he said. Obviously the Constitution is to be preferred to any ordinary act of Congress.

Case dismissed.

Jefferson fumed. For one thing, Marshall had said that a court with the proper jurisdiction could issue a writ of mandamus even against the secretary of state, the president's right-hand man. But there was little Jefferson could do about it, for there was not even a specific court order that he could refuse to obey. Thus, in a single stroke Marshall had given the Republicans a lecture for failing to perform their duties and had gone a long way toward acquiring for the Supreme Court the power of judicial review of acts of Congress—all in a manner that made it difficult for the Republicans to retaliate.

Marbury v. Madison is a masterpiece of judicial strategy. Marshall, contrary to modern canons of judicial interpretation, went out of his way to declare Section 13 unconstitutional. He could have interpreted the section to mean that the Supreme Court could issue writs of mandamus in those cases in which it did have jurisdiction. He could have interpreted Article III to mean that Congress could add to, though not subtract from, the original jurisdiction that the Constitution gives to the Supreme Court. He could have dismissed the case for want of jurisdiction without discussing Marbury's right to his commission. But none of these would have suited his purpose. Jefferson and his fellow Republicans had been threatening to use the impeachment power to remove Federalist partisans from the federal bench. Marshall was fearful for the Supreme Court's future, and he felt unless the Court spoke out it would become subordinate to the president and Congress.

Marshall's decision, important as it was, did not by itself necessarily establish for the Supreme Court the power to review and declare unconstitutional acts of Congress. *Marbury v. Madison* could have meant that the Supreme Court had the right to interpret the scope of *its own* powers under Article III but that Congress and the president had the authority to interpret their own powers under Articles I and II, respectively. However, Marshall's decision has not been interpreted by court or country in this way (though it was not until the *Dred Scott* case in 1857 that another act of Congress was declared unconstitutional). Had Marshall not spoken when he did, the Court might not have been able to assume the power of judicial review. The precedent had been created. Here we have a classic example of constitutional development through judicial interpretation. There is no specific authorization in the Constitution for the Court's power to declare congressional enactments null and void; yet today it is a vital part of our constitutional system.

JOHN MARSHALL'S LEGACY

Several very important consequences followed from the fact that America has accepted John Marshall's argument that courts are the final arbiters of the meaning of the Constitution. Because the courts refuse to give advisory opinions, the nation is often in doubt about the constitutionality of laws of Congress, acts of the president, regulations of administrative agencies until properly challenged in the courts. And in most instances an individual citizen who wishes to challenge the constitutionality of a statute must violate it. Publisher Ralph Ginzburg's gamble that the Supreme Court would rule that the federal obscenity statute violated his constitutional rights won him a five-year jail sentence (*Ginzburg v. United States,* 1966). A more generous construction of the 1934 Declaratory Judgment Act may make it easier to challenge statutes without first having to violate them (*Steffel v. Thompson,* 1974).

Yet the most important consequence of judicial review is that even a law solemnly enacted by the Congress and approved by the president may be challenged by a single individual. Those who lack the support of the Congress or those who wish to challenge the authority of the president through the device of a lawsuit may secure a hearing before the courts. In the United States, litigation supplements (at times, supersedes) legislation as an instrument for the making of public policy.

Judicial review in a democracy

An independent judiciary is rightly considered to be one of the hallmarks of a free society. As impartial dispensers of equal justice under the law, judges should not be dependent on the pleasure of the executive, the legislature, the parties to a case, the electorate, or a mob outside the courtroom. But the very independence that is essential to protect the judge in his role as a legal technician raises basic problems when a society decides – as ours has – to allow judges to make politically significant constitutional decisions.

Ours is a government of laws, not of men, we are often told, and therefore the policy views of our independent judges are (or at least should be) irrelevant. The absurdity of the assumption that law is so certain and clearly known that the human factor need not enter – that jurisprudence is a mechanical operation – is indicated by the fact that the Supreme Court of the United States divides so frequently, with each side declaring it has the appropriate interpretation of the law. In many cases, a judge has no clear mandate to decide one way or the other.

To recognize the facts of judicial life – that judges must choose between competing values – is not to criticize the judges. Nor is it to say that judges have unlimited discretion in deciding cases or that they give free rein to their own views. They are restricted, as we have seen, by procedural limitations. The doctrine of *stare decisis* imposes some constraints. But the total political system of which they are a part is probably the most significant restriction. If the Court is too far out of step, it is likely to get slapped down by the president or Congress. It is limited by the necessity to maintain the allegiance of the judicial bureaucracy.[69]

The never-ending task of determining what the Constitution means today, and tomorrow, is one in which the voters participate – if only

[69]Walter F. Murphy, *Congress and the Court* (University of Chicago Press, 1962); John R. Schmidhauser and Larry L. Berg, *The Supreme Court and Congress: Conflict and Interaction 1945–1968.*

indirectly. Although the public lacks precise knowledge about or even much awareness of the work of the Supreme Court, and although it is doubtful if many voters cast ballots for presidential candidates because of their stands toward the Court, elections do have consequences for constitutional interpretation. And it is not primarily because of Mr. Dooley's charge, "the Supreme coort follows th' iliction returns."[70] Rather, after each major realigning election when new party coalitions come into being and a new one takes over the White House and the Congress, they have clashed with the representatives of the old regime still in control of the federal courts. Or as one unknown wag put it, "The good presidents do dies with them, the bad lives after them on the Supreme Court." But after some delay, the new electoral coalitions by one device or another "win" and secure interpretations of the Constitution that reflect the new dominant political ideology.[71]

Even when no major realigning election appears to be in process, the voters still have an impact on the course of constitutional development. For example, both in 1968 and in 1972 President Nixon made it perfectly clear that if elected he would "turn the Court around." Although his views toward the Court probably had little to do with his winning the elections, the voters did put him into office and he did proceed to do as promised—appoint conservative "strict constructionists" to the court. Again in the next presidential election electors will have an opportunity to influence the course of constitutional development. The federal bench is presently balanced between judges who are sympathetic to the constitutional views as expressed by the Warren Supreme Court and those who tend to support the constitutional doctrines of the Nixon appointees. So in 1976, the voters will help to decide by their choice for president whether to continue to "turn the Court around" or to restore the direction the Court had taken under Chief Justice Warren.

JUDICIAL ACTIVISM VERSUS JUDICIAL SELF-RESTRAINT

In recent years, there has been considerable public debate over the proper role of the Supreme Court in our political system. Some critics, roughly characterized as judicial activists, insist that political choice is inevitable and inherent in judging and that judges should not make a false pretense of objectivity. Rather, they should recognize that they are making policy, and they should consciously exercise their judicial power to achieve social justice.[72]

[70]Finley Peter Dunne, Mr. Dooley, "The Supreme Court's Decisions" taken from John Bartlett, *Bartlett's Familiar Quotations,* 14th edition (Little, Brown 1968), p. 890.

[71]Adamany, "Legitimacy, Realigning Elections," p. 841–43; Stuart S. Nagel, "Court-Curbing Periods in American History," *Vanderbilt Law Review* (June 1965), p. 925; Sheldon Goldman and Thomas P. Jahnige, *The Federal Courts as a Political System* (Harper & Row, 1971), p. 263.

[72]Arthur S. Miller and Ronald F. Howell, "The Myth of Neutrality in Constitutional Adjudication," *University of Chicago Law Review* (Summer 1960), pp. 661–95.

Judicial self-restrainers take another view. They recognize a judge's difficulties in rising above his own biases, but they insist that objectivity is the goal he should aim for. They argue that legislators and executives, as the people's political representatives, have the chief responsibility for working out the accommodation of interests that is the essence of legislation. The self-restrainers insist that judges must be very careful to avoid injecting their own wishes into the judicial process, because it is not their responsibility to determine public policy.[73]

Some take a position midway between the activists and the self-restrainers. They believe that judges should exercise restraint in using their authority to review economic and social laws affecting property rights but not hesitate to void laws that the judges believe restrict civil liberties such as free speech. Their argument for this compromise position goes like this: The political majority should not be stopped from experimenting with social and economic arrangements. If mistakes are made, new majorities will arise to correct them. But majorities should not be permitted to tamper with basic liberties. For if they go too far, the very instruments for publicizing and correcting the mistakes—such as free speech and free press—will not be able to operate effectively. The Constitution does not embody any particular economic theory, and legislative majorities are free to adopt any economic policies they wish. But the Constitution is committed to the political theory of an open society, and it is the judges' special responsibility to prevent legislative tampering with the democratic process. These activists also argue that the judges have a special responsibility to protect discrete racial or religious minorities since such groups lack the political weapons to protect themselves from discriminatory treatment.

THE PEOPLE AND THE COURT[74]

The Supreme Court is able to make its decisions effective only to the extent that these decisions are supported by a considerable portion of the electorate. The main thrust of judicial policies cannot remain too far outside the main channels of American public life. Our system has reached a pragmatic compromise between the desire for the independence of judges from the political forces of the moment so that they may do justice, and the desire to provide political checks on the judges so that their policy-making activities will reflect the wishes of the society. Judges have no armies or police to execute their rulings. They have no authority to levy taxes. Ultimately, the power they enjoy rests on their retention of public support. No better criterion for determining the legitimacy of a governmental official has ever been invented.

[73]Learned Hand, *The Bill of Rights* (Harvard University Press, 1958).

[74]This is the title of a book by Charles L. Black: *The People and the Court: Judicial Review in a Democracy* (Prentice-Hall, 1960); See also, David F. Forte, ed., *The Supreme Court in American Politics* (D.C. Heath, 1972), for anthology of historical review.

Chapter 15 Presidents and the presidency

Even in a democracy—perhaps especially in a democracy—the people yearn for a leader. People seek a leader with the foresight to anticipate the future, the personal strength to unite us, to steel our moral will, to move the country forward, to make the country governable. In short, people want someone who will personalize government and authority, who will simplify politics, who will symbolize the protective role of the state, who will seem to be concerned with *them.* But has this tendency to turn to the president reached an undesirable state of dependency on the executive? Does the human heart ceaselessly reinvent royalty? How else can one explain the passionate support and retribution accorded presidents?

Americans applaud and practically worship presidents when things go well. But we castigate and break them when peace and prosperity elude us. Disasters as well as triumphs are credited to presidents—Hoover's Depression, Johnson's Vietnam War, Nixon's Watergate, Wilson's League of Nations, Roosevelt's New Deal. An exaggerated sense of presidential wisdom and omnipotence has caused us to forget that there are limits to what presidents can accomplish. The tragedies of U.S. involvement in Vietnam and of presidential involvement in the

Watergate scandals have deglamorized the presidency. Nevertheless, the vitality of our democracy still depends in large measure on the sensitive interaction of presidential leadership and popular participation. Carefully planned innovation usually is impossible without leadership.

Critics see the presidency as a seemingly essential institution that is fast becoming inconsistent with cherished democratic ideals. They view it as a remote, autocratic institution, the citadel of the staus quo, the center of the industrial-military-political complex, the very heart of the Establishment. They complain further:

Presidents have become near absolute monarchs on issues of war and peace.

Presidents neither dominate nor counterbalance elites; rather, they voluntarily serve elite interests or else they soon become pawns of strategic business and professional elites.

Presidents are less accountable today than ever before. They are able to transgress formal checks and balances designed by the framers, and even to bend or avoid laws to advantage their friends and punish their opponents.

Presidents now manipulate the public's sense of reality by relying on secrecy, emergency powers, and the "electronic throne" of television.

Presidents undermine constructive partisan debate and dissent by personalizing their office and proclaiming consensus or bipartisan politics.

The strong presidency reappraised

Some critics care less about the extent of presidential authority than the *purposes* for which it is used. In whose behalf, they ask, is presidential power exercised? If the president acts in behalf of what they consider to be improper interests or for what they describe as personal power, then they argue his power should be curbed. If, on the other hand, the president appears to represent interests of which they approve, then they argue his power should be left unchecked.

Other critics are more concerned about *process*. If the president appears to act in a fashion that reflects the wishes of the majority of the people most of the time, then they contend he is acting within the proper framework of democracy and the process is working properly. On the other hand, if he acts in a fashion contrary to the wishes of most of the people most of the time, then the process is not working and his power should be checked.

Most liberals in both parties look to the president as the potential spokesman of popular majorities, as a "tribune of the people." Throughout our history active presidents have tended to act in behalf of

Franklin D. Roosevelt (center), shown here with Joseph Stalin and Winston Churchill, was president for 12 years, years in which both the presidency and the national government experienced notable expansion.

changes pleasing to the liberal-progressive forces. This was not so much because activist presidents are liberals as that the constitutional and political circumstances of the presidency make it more probable that active presidents will be liberal ones.

There is no guarantee, of course, that a strong president will be liberal in orientation or pleasing to the liberal critics. Vietnam provides us with a classic example to the contrary. (Whether Nixon should be considered as an activist president, is a question of judgment. He certainly played an active role in foreign policy and not all of his ventures pleased liberals, although it is probably more accurate to say that the liberal wing of the Republican party was more pleased with Nixon's foreign policy initiatives than were his conservative supporters.)

On balance, however, as pluralists see it, the great presidents have been the strong presidents who have moved outside the elite system to reach the masses and mobilize wide popular support. That was how Jefferson and Jackson overcame the Adamses of their day; that is how the two Roosevelts overcame the "economic royalists" of their day. To be sure, pluralists grant, presidents often have to compromise with existing elites. But presidents know—and elites know—that the president often has substantial power to defy minority interests however strong they may be and appeal to the great majority. They like to quote Franklin Roosevelt who, after the economic elites had castigated him for his "radical" New Deal policies, cried out at the height of his 1936 reelection campaign: "I should like to have it said of my first Administration that in it the forces of selfishness and of lust for power met their match. I should like to have it said of my second Administration that in it these forces met their master!"

Both elitists and pluralists are concerned about the question of *representation* – for whom directly does the president speak and act? Perhaps there is an even more important criterion, *responsibility*. By this test the question is not what part of the population, large or small, elites or masses, the president most represents. The question is how effectively he advances the interests of the nation in the long run. Sometimes he acts before public opinion is fully prepared. And he often may initiate changes that neither complacent majorities nor conservative minorities wish to accept.

But if it is obvious that presidents must be permitted substantial power to govern, so it is obvious that no president can be blindly trusted with power. The potential for abuse is there as it is for any office entrusted with significant power. Watergate taught us that new checks and balances may be needed as the presidency evolves as an even more centralized and dominant political influence.

The president's constitutional position

With the specter of George III still looming over the land, the framers of the Constitution created a presidency of limited powers. They wanted a presidential office that would stay clear of parties and factions, enforce the laws passed by Congress, deal with foreign governments, and help the states put down disorders. They seemed to have in mind – and that is the way President Washington acted – that the president should be an elected king with substantial personal power, acting above parties.

The delegates rejected a plural or collegial executive. They also rejected an unlimited term. The term would be for four years with presidents eligible for reelection. Independent from the legislature, presidents would nevertheless share considerable powers with Congress. The essence of the arrangement would be an *intermingling* of powers. To achieve change the separate branches would have to work in cooperation and consultation with one another. A president's major appointments had to be approved by the Senate; Congress could override his veto by a two-thirds vote; he could make treaties only with the advice and consent of two-thirds of the senators; and, of course, all appropriations would be determined by Congress, not the president. Even a presidency with such limited powers, hemmed in by the system of checks and balances, worried some Americans in 1787. But the concerned were reassured by the fact that the wise and magisterial George Washington was to be the first chief executive.

Such was the origin of the presidency. It was designed neither to be an autocratic office nor the "people's" office. The questions, dilemmas, and compromises that preoccupied the framers are still with us. How strong should the executive be? How may its responsiveness and accountability be assured?

THE SWELLING OF THE PRESIDENCY

For decades American presidents have been extending the limits of executive powers, and Congress and the courts have been willing partners. Whenever emergencies occur, Congress rushes to delegate rule-making discretion to the executive branch. Congress seems incapable of dealing with matters that are highly technical, or that require constant management or consistent judgment. Lack of competent experts and the slowness with which Congress works contribute to the abdication of responsibility. Many people feel that what it lacks most is the will to use the power it has. Congress does try occasionally to stem the flow of delegated powers to the executive, but time and again it acquiesces in presidential declarations of a national emergency.

During the last two centuries in all democracies, and at all levels, power has drifted away from legislators to executives. The English prime minister, the French president, the governors of our states, the mayors of our cities are all playing a more dominating role in their respective governments than was true, generally speaking, one hundred years ago. There are strong forces at work that help to explain this beyond the mere lack of will in Congress. In fact, if you talk to most congressmen they wish to see their role enhanced.

When crises are proclaimed, Congress often enacts bills drafted by the White House with only the most perfunctory review and usually with little or no consideration of their effect on civil liberties, economic equity, and the separation of powers. Economic measures in the early New Deal and during the Nixon Administration are illustrative. And this pattern of hasty and inadequate consideration was repeated also during World War II, the Korean War, and with the Tonkin Gulf Resolution.

The danger of war also increases a president's impact on the nation's affairs. The Cold War badly shattered any remaining nostalgia for the once-cherished traditions against standing armies and entangling alliances. The combination of an enormous standing army, nuclear weapons, and the nation's Cold War commitments (to quote President Kennedy) "to pay any price, bear any burden, meet any hardship, support any friend, oppose any foe . . ." invited presidential dominance in national security matters.

Television, that singularly personalized communications medium, contributes immeasurably to presidential powers. With access to coverage nearly any time he wants it, a president can take his case directly to the people. The invitation to bypass and thus ignore Congress, the

Washington press, and even his own party leaders, weakens the checks once posed by the necessity of securing cooperation from other political leaders.

The great growth of the federal role in domestic and economic matters has enlarged presidential responsibility. It has also contributed to the swollen presidential establishment. Problems that are not easily relegated to any one department often get delegated to the White House. When new federal programs concern several federal agencies, someone near the president seems to be required to fashion a consistent policy and reconcile conflicts. White House aides, with some justification, claim the presidency is the only place in government where it is possible to set and coordinate national priorities. And presidents repeatedly set up central review and coordination units—some to help formulate new policies, some to help settle jurisdictional disputes among the departments, and some merely to placate well-organized interest groups who want their spokesmen to be present in the internal councils of decision-making.

The swelling of the presidency has been encouraged as well by the public's expectations of the office. Although we may dislike or condemn individual presidents, especially late in their terms, popular attitudes toward the institution of the presidency border on religious veneration. Perhaps it is because we have no royal family, no established church, or no common ceremonial leadership divorced from executive responsibilities. In an effort to live up to unrealistic expectations, some presidents overextend themselves; maintaining the presidential image requires them to expand their power, and so a circle of rising expectations is at work. The old schoolboy adage that the presidency evokes the incumbent's sense of history may today just as easily be offset by the temptation for a president to undertake ill-considered and unworthy ventures in search of historic renown.

"WHAT IS GOOD FOR THE PRESIDENCY . . ."

Circumstances—mainly scarcity of resources—usually dictate that a president can break new ground in only a few policy areas during his term in office. If the delegated powers and institutionalized trappings of authority have increased dramatically, it does not automatically follow that a president's powers are a match for his responsibilities. Especially is this the case in domestic and economic matters. Nor is there any guarantee that the increased powers are used for ends desired by the majority of the people. Hence, although strengthening the presidency is an old practice, many Americans now question the blind assumption that what is good for the presidency is good for the nation.

Is it possible to create a strong presidency that is leaner, more open, and more responsive to the electorate than it is at present? And how much of the needed leadership in the nation should we expect solely from a president?

People often do not know at the time that they stand at turning points in history. Perhaps we stand at a time when the political and constitutional currents are flowing away from the White House. We seem to be in a period of diminished presidential leadership, at least within domestic affairs. For certainly, one of the aftermaths of Watergate is a long and lingering suspicion of the presidency. And while presidents have grown in power and influence over the last several decades, the critical attitude toward them has also grown.

Hoover left the White House in disgrace; Roosevelt was subjected to severe criticism, especially by the media; Truman was vilified while in office; Kennedy was assassinated; Johnson was driven from office; Nixon was forced to resign. Only Eisenhower, the one inactive president of the last half century who did not use his office to initiate changes in domestic policy, left his post with honor.

Again, historical trends do not move all in the same direction. Who knows? A few years from now publicists and political scientists may be writing books about the lack of initiative in Washington because of the diminished presidency. We can return to these questions only after we have looked at the diverse functional responsibilities we expect a president to perform today.

Symbolic leadership

A president is the nation's number-one celebrity, and almost anything he does is news. Merely by going to church or to a sports event a president commands attention. A cult of personality often develops as even a bland or a personally unattractive president may become a hero to millions of supporters.

The Founding Fathers did not fully anticipate the ceremonial, even civil-religious, functions a president must perform. Certain magisterial functions such as the granting of pardons were conferred. But the presidency over time has acquired enormous symbolic powers against which there seem to be inadequate countervailing voices. The Constitution pays these powers little heed.

THE POPULAR NEED FOR LEADERSHIP

A president's personal conduct affects how millions of Americans view their political loyalties and civic responsibilities. Of course the symbolic influence of presidents is not always evoked in favor of worthy causes, and sometimes presidents do not live up to our expectations of moral leadership. But even in this highly secular nation, the people yearn for a sense of purpose, a vision of where the nation is going, to be provided, presumably, by our highest elected officeholders. This is a real, although often overstated, need: "The Presidency is the focus for

1901

the most intense and persistent emotions. . . . The President is . . . , the one figure who draws together the people's hopes and fears for the political future. On top of all his routine duties, he has to carry that off —or fail."[1]

It would be much easier for everyone, says Michael Novak, if our president were a prime minister, called on merely to manage the affairs of government in as efficient and practical a way as possible. But this is not the case. We have not found a way to separate the function of symbolizing the hopes and aspirations of the nation from the office of exercising executive power.[2] Yet this implies that prime ministers are not equally sanguine about how much better things will be next year. In fact, however, nearly everybody in positions of authority makes promises for a brighter, better tomorrow. Indeed it can be argued that an important part of leadership is to offer hope.

1923

Presidential chief-of-state duties often seem trivial and unimportant. For example, taken alone, pitching out the first baseball of the season, buying Christmas seals, pressing buttons that start big power projects, and visiting the scene of national disasters, do not require executive talents. Yet a president is asked continuously to accentuate our common heritage, to help unify the nation, and to create an improved climate within which the diverse interests of the nation can reason together. He is expected also to see that the nation fulfills the idealistic values it presents to other countries.

If the nation holds great expectations of its president, disappointed expectations lead people to turn against him. No president can fully satisfy the public's yearning for inspirational leadership.

1945

A PRESIDENTIAL DILEMMA

Under ordinary conditions, the president as leader of all the people, or symbolic leader of the nation, keeps running headlong into the president who tries to act for *part* of the people. Some presidential functions are fundamentally inconsistent with one another. On the one hand he is *party* leader, the spokesman and representative of a popular majority

[1]James David Barber, *The Presidential Character* (Prentice-Hall, 1972), p. 4.

[2]For a more extensive treatment of the symbolic implications of the presidency, see Michael Novak, *Choosing Our King* (Macmillan, 1974).

1963

Vice-presidents who moved into the White House

1969

1974

In this century, the U.S. has had fourteen presidents, starting with McKinley, and seventeen vice-presidents. Six of those vice-presidents subsequently became Chief Executive. From top: Theodore Roosevelt, Calvin Coolidge, Harry Truman, Lyndon Johnson, Richard Nixon, and Gerald Ford.

that is more or less organized in the party that he heads. As party chief he not only directs the national party organization; he also uses his powers as chief legislator to affect the party's program. On the other hand, as *symbolic* leader and *chief of state* he must act for all the people, regardless of group or faction. As chief executive he must faithfully administer the laws, whether these laws were passed by Democratic or Republican majorities in Congress; yet in choosing his subordinates and in applying the law, he tends to think first of the interests of his popular majority.

The relationship between these diverse presidential roles is uneasy. For example, the president may wish to address the nation on a problem. As president he is entitled to free time on the radio and TV networks. But if an election is in the offing, the opposition often charges that the president is really acting in his capacity as party chief and that his party should pay for the radio or TV time. The same question comes up in connection with the president's inspection trips, especially when he uses them as occasions for political talks and general politicking.

Most of the time, a president manages to combine his roles of chief of state and party leader without too much difficulty. The people expect him to hold both roles, and he moves from one to the other as conditions demand. There is nothing intrinsically wrong with ceremonial power; it becomes a problem only when it leaves the public believing ceremony equals accomplishment. Or it can be harmful if ceremonial and symbolic responsibilities inhibit a president from performing his real and often less dignified political leadership duties.

Priority-setting and policy formulation

Presidents, by custom, are responsible for proposing new initiatives in the areas of foreign policy, economic growth and stability, and the quality of life in America. This was not always the case. But beginning with Woodrow Wilson and especially since the New Deal, the president is expected to promote peace, prevent depressions, and propose reforms to enhance domestic progress. The trend in national policy-making is toward greater centralization. "Increasingly, federal programs are conceived by the President in his search for campaign issues or legislative program material, and they are planned by his Executive Office or special task forces and commissions that he has appointed."[3]

NATIONAL SECURITY POLICY

Presidents have more leeway in foreign and military affairs than they have in domestic matters. This is partly due to grants of authority stipu-

[3]Martha Derthick, *New Towns In-Town* (The Urban Institute, 1972), p. 96.

lated in the Constitution, and partly due to the character of diplomatic and military activity. The framers foresaw a special need for speed and single-mindedness in our dealings with other nations. And the Constitution vests in a president command of the two major instruments of foreign policy—the diplomatic corps and the armed services. It also gives him responsibility for negotiating treaties and commitments with other nations.

Congress has granted presidents wide discretion in initiating foreign policies, for diplomacy frequently requires quick action. A president can act swiftly; Congress usually does not. Even aside from his vast constitutional powers as commander in chief, Congress thus has given up tremendous amounts of its powers over foreign policy to the president.

The Supreme Court has repeatedly upheld strong presidential authority in this area. In the *Curtiss-Wright* case in 1936 the Court referred to the "exclusive power of the President as the sole organ of the Federal Government in the field of international relations—a power which does not require as a basis for its exercise an act of Congress, but which, of course, like every other governmental power, must be exercised in subordination to the applicable provisions of the Constitution." These are sweeping words. Yet a determined Congress *that knows what it wants to do* and can agree on it does not lack significant power in foreign relations. It must authorize and appropriate the funds that back up our policies abroad. It is a forum of debate and criticism. And, as it at least tried to do after the Vietnam War, it can specify the conditions of war-making.

ECONOMIC POLICY

Ever since the New Deal, presidents have been expected to initiate action to prevent unemployment, to fight inflation, to keep taxes down, to insure economic growth and prosperity, and to do whatever they think necessary and proper to prevent depressions. The Constitution does not place these duties on the White House, but a president knows that if he fails to act he will suffer the fate of Herbert Hoover who was denounced for years by the Democrats for his alleged inaction during the Great Depression. And there is considerable evidence that former President Nixon's drop in popularity stemmed as much from inflation as from Watergate.

The chief advisers to the president on economic policy—at least the organization charts so indicate—are the three members of the Council of Economic Advisers. Presidents often get their economic advice elsewhere; but the Council, established under the Employment Act of 1946, advises the president as to what actions he should take, or propose to the Congress, to maintain full employment and stabilize the economy.

The growth and complexity of economic problems have placed even more initiative in the hands of the president. Clearly, the delicate balancing required to keep a modern economy operating means that the presidency plays a central role.

MAKING DOMESTIC POLICY

A leader is one who knows where the followers are. Lincoln did not invent the antislavery movement; Roosevelt hardly instigated the Depression. Similarly, Kennedy and Johnson did not begin or lead the civil rights movement. But they all, in their respective times, became embroiled in these controversies, for a president cannot ignore what divides the nation. Presidents, like all political leaders in a democracy, try to stay out of controversies as long as they can.

But the essence of the modern presidency lies in its institutional capability to resolve societal conflicts. To be sure, a president most of the time will avoid conflict where possible, seeking instead to defer, delegate, or otherwise delay controversial decisions. The effective president, however, will clarify the major issues of the day, define what is feasible, and enlarge and vivify the governmental structure so that important goals can be realized as fully as possible.

A president—with the cooperation of Congress—can set a few national goals and propose legislation. Close inspection indicates, however, that in most instances a president's "new initiatives" in domestic policy are measures that have been under consideration in previous sessions of Congress. Just as the celebrated New Deal legislation had a fairly well-defined prenatal history extending back several years before its espousal by Franklin Roosevelt, so also most New Frontier and Great Society legislative programs were the fruits of long compaigns by congressional activists and special-interest campaigns.[4]

The Constitution ordains that the president "shall from time to time give to the Congress information of the State of the Union, and recommend to their Consideration such Measures as he shall judge necessary and expedient." From the start, strong presidents have exploited this power. Washington and Adams came in person to Congress to deliver information and recommendations. Jefferson and many presidents after him sent written messages, but Wilson restored the practice of delivering a personal, and often dramatic, message. Franklin Roosevelt used personal appearances (as have most presidents since then) to draw the attention of the whole nation to his programs—with the invaluable help of radio and the television camera.

Less obvious but perhaps equally important are the frequent written messages dispatched from the White House to Capitol Hill on a vast range of public problems. Often mumbled indistinctly by a clerk, these messages may not create much stir at the moment, but they are important in defining the administration's position and giving a lead to friendly legislators. Moreover, these messages are often accompanied

[4]Lawrence H. Chamberlain, *The President, Congress and Legislation* (Columbia University Press, 1946); and James L. Sundquist, *Politics and Policy* (Brookings Institution, 1968).

by detailed drafts of legislation that may be put into the hopper with hardly a change. These administration bills, the products of bill-drafting experts on the president's own staff or in the departments and agencies, as well as from extensive "conversations" with leading congressmen, may be strengthened or diluted by Congress—but many of the original provisions may survive unscathed.

THE POWER TO SAY NO

A president can veto a bill by returning it with his objections to the house in which it originated. Congress, by a two-thirds vote in each chamber, may then pass it over his veto. If the president does not sign or veto the bill within ten weekdays after he receives it, the bill becomes law without his signature. If Congress adjourns within the ten weekdays, however, the president, by taking no action, can kill the bill. This is known as the pocket veto.

The veto is sometimes a strong, sometimes a feeble, weapon. Its strength lies in the ordinary failure of Congress to muster a two-thirds majority of both houses in favor of a policy that the president has told the people he dislikes. Historically Congress has overridden only about 3 percent of the president's vetoes.[5] Yet a Congress that can repeatedly mobilize such a majority against a president can virtually take command of the government. Such was the fate of President Andrew Johnson.

In ordinary times, Congress can manipulate legislation to reduce the likelihood of a presidential veto. For example, it can attach irrelevant but controversial provisions, called *riders,* to vitally needed legislation; the president must either accept or reject the whole bill, for he does not have the power to strike out individual items in the bill—that is, he does not have the *item veto.* Appropriations are a special case in point. In one appropriations bill the lawmakers may combine badly needed funds for the armed forces with a host of costly pork-barrel items, but the president must take the whole bill or not at all.

For his part, the president can use the veto power in a postitive as well as a negative way. He can announce openly or let it be known quietly that a bill under consideration by Congress will be turned back at the White House door unless certain changes have been made. He can use the threat of a veto against some bill Congress badly wants in exchange for another bill that he wants. But the veto is essentially a negative weapon, of limited use to a president who has a positive program. For it is the president who usually is pressing for action.

Crisis management and commander in chief

Nearly two centuries of national growth and recurrent crises have in-

[5] Carlton Jackson, *Presidential Vetoes: 1792–1945* (University of Georgia Press, 1967).

creased the powers of the president over those explicitly allowed by the Constitution.[6] The institutional characteristics of Congress usually do not lend themselves as well as do those of the presidency to the requirements of disciplined teamwork, speed, and secrecy needed in times of emergency. The complexity of its decision-making procedures, its unwieldy numbers, and its constitutional tasks of debate, discussion, and authorization make Congress a more public, deliberative, and diffuse organization. When major crises occur, Congress traditionally holds debates but just as predictably delegates vast authority to a president, charging him to take whatever actions are necessary to restore order or regain control over the situation.

"The President shall be Commander in Chief of the Army and the Navy of the United States," reads Section 2 of Article II of the Constitution. Even though this is the first of the president's powers listed in the Constitution, the framers intended that his military role be a limited one. His *powers* were to be far less than a king's. It was as if he would be a sort of first general and first admiral. As it turns out, his military role has become much more important. He has his finger on the nuclear button and appears to have sole authority over limited wars as well.

The primary factor underlying this transformation in the president's function as commander in chief has been the changed role of the United States in the world, especially since World War II. In the postwar years we rapidly became the assertive spokesman for preserving the "free world" from Communism. Every president argued and won widespread support for the position that military strength, especially military superiority over the Soviet Union, was the primary route to national security. Nations willingly grew dependent on our assistance, which rapidly became translated into a multitude of treaties, pacts, and executive agreements. From then on, nearly every threat to the political stability of our far-flung network of allies became a test of whether we would honor our commitments in good faith.[7] These commitments plus the fear of nuclear war and the importance of deterrence all prompted Congress to give a lot of leeway to presidents in this area.

Drawing by Lurie, *Life* Magazine; © Time, Inc.

THE PRESIDENT'S WAR POWERS

The Constitution delegates to Congress the authority to *declare* war (with the consent of the president), but in practice the commander in chief *precipitates* war. This power of making war has been used by the chief executive time and time again. Polk in 1846 ordered American forces to advance into disputed territory; when Mexico resisted, Polk informed Congress that war existed by act of Mexico, and a formal declaration of war was soon forthcoming. McKinley's dispatch of a battleship to Havana, where it was blown up, helped precipitate war with

[6]See Arthur M. Schlesinger, Jr., *The Imperial Presidency* (Houghton Mifflin, 1973), esp. Chs. 1–7.

[7]William P. Rogers, "Congress, the President, and War Powers," *California Law Review* (September 1971), pp. 1207–8.

Spain in 1898. In 1918, when no state of war existed between the United States and Russia, Wilson sent American forces to Siberia to join Allied troops fighting the Bolsheviks. The United States was not formally at war with Germany until late 1941, but prior to Pearl Harbor Roosevelt ordered the Navy to guard convoys to Great Britain and to open fire on submarines threatening the convoys. Truman had no specific authorization from Congress in 1950 when he ordered American forces to resist aggression in Korea. Nor did President Kennedy when he ordered a troop build-up during the Berlin crisis of 1961, when he sent forces into Southeast Asia in the spring of 1962, and when he ordered a naval quarantine of Cuba in the fall of 1962. Nor did President Johnson when he bolstered American forces in Vietnam from 1965 to 1968. Nor did Nixon in his "incursion" into Cambodia in 1970, or in his support for Saigon's invasion of Laos in 1971.

Under modern conditions, some believe, Congress's formal authority to declare war has become obsolete. In Korean and Vietnamese type wars, it seems, formal declarations of war are no longer made. If a total war should come, an aggressor is unlikely to make a formal declaration of war before he launches the missiles. Yet people are justifiably fearful of unhampered presidential war-making powers. Normal checks and balances do not operate because a crisis usually produces a sharp if fleeting solidarity in the otherwise divided political system. And the "loyal party opposition" has failed to oppose the president largely because of bipartisan understandings about "adjourning politics in time of national crises" and "politics must stop at the water's edge."

"I've never known a people so hard to deal with, except maybe Congress."

Courtesy Publisher's Hall Syndicate.

Until 1969 Congress had usually failed to check presidential war-making powers. Beginning in 1969, however, Congress passed a number of resolutions and statutes aimed at reasserting itself. Congress began to build an independent expertise to monitor and question foreign commitments. But as Louis Fisher suggests, "To complement this new congressional expertise, there must be a new temperament and set of attitudes: a courage to resist being stampeded into granting power simply because the President waves the flag; an ability to distinguish between a need for speed and mere recklessness; a strength and resolve to defer to no one in the exercise of independent judgment." Fisher, however, questions whether Congress "has the will and the staying power to contribute from one year to the next, in times of crisis as well as relative calm, without reverting to its former acquiescence in the President."[8]

But this emphasis on the need for will and courage strikes some observers as naive or hazy. They feel that, under most circumstances, whenever a president takes a foreign policy initiative, he is likely to have most of the country behind him, including the elites, the media, and the masses. Only after the initiative is shown "not to work"—that

[8]Louis Fisher, "War Powers: A Need for Legislative Reassertion," Rexford G. Tugwell and Thomas E. Cronin, eds., *The Presidency Reappraised* (Praeger, 1974), pp. 71–72. See also Schlesinger, *The Imperial Presidency*.

is, after the deaths and the inflation—do segments of the country get "turned off" and the Congress begins to reflect the popular feeling. Thus, many political scientists warn that we ought to avoid remythologizing Congress merely because the presidency is becoming dymythologized. And they question whether future members of Congress are going to be more courageous, able, or resolved than those in the past.

CONGRESSIONAL RELUCTANCE AND PRESIDENTIAL SECRECY

Congress had been reluctant to use its appropriation power as a restraint on a president's power as military chief, but in 1970 it stipulated that no funds should be used to send ground troops into Cambodia or Laos, an unprecedented restraint on the president's discretion. In the War Powers Act of 1973, Congress attempted to impose curbs on the president's power to use the armed forces for hostile purposes without congressional approval. By such devices Congress could, if it wished, terminate hostilities. It probably could not prevent them from being started, however.

In wartime the White House becomes a general headquarters for governmental as well as for military and industrial mobilization. Political power, ordinarily dispersed throughout the national government, is then largely centered in the president. He becomes a sort of constitutional dictator. He makes secret diplomatic agreements with foreign powers, far surpassing in importance many treaties that in peacetime would require senatorial consent. He authorizes the allotment of billions of dollars of funds appropriated by Congress. He takes final responsibility for crucial military decisions—as in the case of Roosevelt's decision in World War II to concentrate our armed might against Hitler before turning to Japan. Opposition congressmen may continue to snipe at the commander in chief's nonmilitary plans or policies such as domestic economic policy or postwar peace goals; but they will not ordinarily obstruct his war program, even though they may lack confidence in it, as many senators did in the case of Vietnam.

These vast powers of the president in wartime are not a recent development. It was Lincoln, struggling to overcome the crisis of civil war, who set the vital precedents for presidential quasi-dictatorship. Congress was not in session when Lincoln was inaugurated in March 1861; despite the emergency (or perhaps because of it), the new president did not even call Congress into session for four months. Congress itself has handed the presidency great chunks of authority during wartime. In World War II, Congress delegated vast power to the president, who redelegated it to price, production, manpower, and transportation czars, who in turn were coordinated by superczars. Roosevelt used Lincolnian as well as Wilsonian precedents.

The maintenance of democratic controls over foreign and military policy has been increasingly difficult in the Cold War and the nuclear age. Secrecy is at the heart of the problem; President Nixon argued: "You cannot in today's world have successful diplomacy without secrecy. It is impossible. . . . And it is particularly impossible when you are dealing not with your friends, but with your adversaries."

But executive secrecy is subject to abuses as Watergate has dramatically illustrated. People could understand, even if they might oppose, the use of secrecy and suspension of dialogue in the president's negotiations with China or in his diplomatic initiatives with Middle Eastern nations. But most people found it difficult to understand the use of secrecy in dealing with congressional leaders. The tapping of telephones to prevent security leaks, the breaking into offices—these are the tactics not of politics, but of *war*. These practices may be appropriate ways to deal with enemies but they are not appropriate ways to deal with domestic political opponents.

How to prevent what may be a necessary evil—secrecy for diplomatic purposes—from secrecy to cover up obstructions of justice? Many Americans feel that even at the risk of a less effective foreign policy—and they have doubts whether exclusively presidential initiatives in this area are more likely than congressional sharing to produce good policy—what is needed is a greater power-sharing with the Congress over foreign policy.

Politician as coalition-builder

An effective president is an effective politician—the most visible and potentially the strongest mobilizer of influence in the American system of power. *Politician* is a nasty word to many Americans; it denotes a scheming, evasive person who is out for his own self-interest. Little wonder many politicians claim they are "above politics."

There is, however, a more constructive definition of *politician:* one who helps manage conflict, one who knows how to negotiate, bargain, and fashion compromises required in making the difficult and desirable become a reality. A president cannot escape these tasks. As a candidate he has made promises to the people. To get things done he must work with many people who have differing loyalties and responsibilities. Inevitably, the president is embroiled in legislative politics, judicial politics, bureaucratic politics.

Despite his tremendous powers a president can rarely command: he spends most of his time persuading people. Potentially he has great persuasive power—it is not easy for the average politician or official to resist a president—but in the long run people think mainly of their own interests and obligations. In a government of separated institutions that share powers,[9] some congressional and bureaucratic leaders are beyond the political reach of the president because they have their own constituencies—a House committee, for example, or a powerful interest

[9]Richard E. Neustadt, *Presidential Power* (John Wiley, 1968), p. 33.

group. Presidents cannot simply bark out orders like a first sergeant. Before Eisenhower became president, Harry Truman said of him: "He'll sit here, and he'll say, 'Do this! Do that!' And nothing will happen. Poor Ike—it won't be a bit like the Army. He'll find it very frustrating."[10] *All* Presidents have found it frustrating.

But a president is not without resources. Besides the authority and trappings of his office, the president has two other special sources of political influence—his influence over public opinion and his role as party chief.

No other politician (and few television or film stars) can achieve a closer contact with the people than does the president. Typically, he has been a prominent senator or a vice-president and has built up a host of followers. He has won a nomination and an election and hence has been under the public gaze for years. But the White House is the finest platform of all—a "bully pulpit," as Theodore Roosevelt called it; and now an "electronic throne" as well. The president has his television studio, which he can use to appeal directly to the people. He can summon the press when he wishes, accept an invitation to speak, choose a sympathetic audience, arrange a "nonpolitical" speaking tour—and he can time all these moves for maximum advantage.[11]

The press conference is an example of how systematically the president can employ the machinery of communication. Years ago the con-

[10]Quoted *ibid.*, p. 9.

[11]See Newton W. Minow, John B. Martin, and Lee M. Mitchell, *Presidential Television* (Basic Books, 1973).

Gerald Ford in close contact with the public. "Nonpolitical" speaking tours have often been used by presidents to bolster their public approval ratings and to garner support for their reelection. Since September of 1975, however, the secret service and many members of Congress have urged President Ford to avoid announced tours where potential assassins might take a shot at him.

ferences were rather casual affairs. Franklin Roosevelt ran his conferences informally and was a master at withholding information as well as giving it. Under Truman, the conference became "an increasingly routinized, institutionalized part of the presidential communications apparatus. Preparation became elaborately formalized, as did the conduct of the meetings themselves."[12] Kennedy authorized the first live telecast of a press conference and used it frequently for direct communication with the people. That Nixon held big televised conferences less frequently led to much grumbling by the Washington correspondents. In contrast, Ford's easy manner and openness with the press did much to explain his early popular support.

Several presidents have commissioned private polls to gauge public opinion on public controversies. Every president, says a former White House aide, must be a "keen judge of public opinion. He must be able to distinguish its petty whims, to estimate its endurance, to respond to its impatience, and to respect its potential power."

Despite these advantages, the president finds difficulties in both gauging and shaping public opinion. A president must know not only what to do but *when* to do it. Public opinion can be unstable and hence somewhat unpredictable. President Johnson recognized that his wide popular support of the mid-1960s had melted away by 1968 when he decided not to run again. President Nixon's drop in public opinion polls, a result of the Watergate scandals, contributed to his resignation. And nearly every president loses support the longer he is in office. Dissatisfaction sets in; interest groups grow impatient; promises seem to be unkept; the presidency gets blamed for whatever goes wrong.

PARTY LEADERSHIP

A second main source of influence for the president is his political party. Most presidents since Washington have been party leaders, and generally the more effective the president, the more use he has made of party support. Men such as Wilson and the two Roosevelts fortified their executive and legislative influence by mobilizing support within their party. Yet no president has fully led his party, and the history of all presidents includes party failures as well as triumphs.

The president has no formal position in the party structure, but his vast influence over vital national policies and over thousands of appointments commands respect from national party leaders. Both president and party need each other. He needs the party's backing throughout the government in order to enact his program. The party needs his direction, his prestige, and the political "gravy" that flows from the White House.

The strings of the national organization all lie in a president's hands. Formally, the national party committee picks the national party chairman; actually, the president lets the committee know whom he wants—

[12]Elmer E. Cornwell, Jr., *Presidential Leadership of Public Opinion* (Indiana University Press, 1965), p. 175.

and they choose that person. Today the president can hire or fire national party chairmen much as he shifts department heads or even his own staff. Usually his pronouncements on national party policy are more authoritative than any party committee's, even more significant than the party platform itself.[13] He can give a candidate a good deal of recognition and publicity in Washington. He can grant—or deny—campaign assistance and even financial assistance.

THE LIMITS ON PRESIDENTIAL PARTY LEADERSHIP

Yet the president's practical power over his party is sharply limited, and it often comes to an end precisely when he needs it most. He has little influence over the selection of the party candidates for Congress and for state and local office. In part the reason is his limited control of state and local organizations; but even more, it is that party organizations themselves do not control their candidates in office. They do not control them because most candidates win office less through the efforts of the organized party than through their own individual campaigning in both the primary and general elections. Of course, the situation varies from place to place, but in most instances *a personalized politics* emphasizing the candidate triumphs over *a programmatic politics* emphasizing party and issues.

Franklin Roosevelt's "purge" of 1938 is a dramatic example of the limits of the president's power. Despite his own sweeping victory in the 1936 election and the lopsided Democratic majorities in Congress, Roosevelt ran into heavy opposition from many Democratic senators and representatives in 1937 and 1938. Angered by this opposition within the party, Roosevelt decided to use his influence to bar the nomination of anti-New Deal candidates in the 1938 congressional primaries. He announced that not as president but as "head of the Democratic party, charged with the responsibility of carrying out the definitely liberal" 1936 Democratic party platform, he would intervene where party principles were clearly at stake. Roosevelt won a significant victory in New York City when he repudiated the anti-New Deal chairman of the House Rules Committee and he helped a pro-administration Democrat win nomination. But elsewhere—mainly in the South—he was defeated.

A president must *bargain* and *negotiate* with party leaders as he does with other independent power centers. Lacking full support from the whole party, the president usually falls back on his own personal organization that originally enabled him to gain the presidential nomination.

President Nixon's 1972 campaign was separated almost entirely from regular Republican party campaigns of that year. Few Republican party professionals were involved in his campaign; most of the Committee to Reelect the President (C.R.E.E.P.) were people who owed their loyalities and their jobs to two or three top presidential lieutenants. Few seemed

[13]David Broder, *The Party's Over* (Harper & Row, 1971).

to have long-standing allegiances to the programs and goals of the Republican party. From a management point of view C.R.E.E.P. had the same advantages as secret diplomacy: everything was under control, the employees followed orders. Yet C.R.E.E.P. ended up sponsoring exploits the likes of which the Republican National Committee doubtless would have repudiated. This was not so much because of different moral standards in the two groups, as because of the political professionals' principles of fair party combat and organizational protectiveness.

Summary

We have seen, then, a variety of diverse presidential responsibilities. Presidents must act alternately, and often simultaneously, as *symbolic*, *priority-setting*, *crisis-managing*, and *coalition-building* leaders. No president can divide his job into tidy compartments. Ultimately all of his responsibilities interrelate with one another. To complicate matters, "the President," writes one student of the office, "is more like a juggler, already juggling too many eggs, who often, at the most anxious moments, is forever having more eggs tossed at him."[14]

One other major presidential responsibility—*administrative* and *organizational* leadership—will be treated in the following chapter. How does a president attempt to organize and control the executive branch? What constitutes the presidential Establishment? And how can we make presidents and the presidency safe for democracy?

[14]Richard J. Walton, *Cold War and Counter-Revolution: The Foreign Policy of John F. Kennedy* (Penguin Books, 1972), p. 201.

Chapter 16 The presidential establishment

When Jefferson was president, the federal government employed 2,120 persons—Indian commissoners, postmasters, collectors of customs, tax collectors, marshals, lighthouse keepers, and clerks. Today, by latest count, the president heads an executive branch of nearly three million civilians and well over two million military employees, who work in at least 2,000 units of federal administration—departments, services, bureaus, commissions, boards, governmental corporations, and others. The president also sits on top of a formal bureaucracy of his own, known since 1939 as the Executive Office of the President.

To gain control over the highly dispersed federal executive bureaucracy and make it work with the White House is simultaneously one of the most crucial and most frustrating of presidential responsibilities. Presidents and their staffs are almost always more keenly interested in generating new policy ideas than in the tedious and less glamorous task of enforcing legislatively approved policies.

There is seldom enough time available to plan effectively or think profoundly about program implementation. As one Kennedy aide put it, the White House "is always too much in a rush, moving from one thing to the next. It is just about all you can do to get things started. The burden of the presidency is to get things started. The presidency is not an executive agency with clout to carry out the goals of the President. It perhaps ought to have been done, but we didn't have time for it . . ."[1]

[1]Quoted in T. E. Cronin, "Presidents as Chief Executives," R. G. Tugwell and T. E. Cronin, eds., *The Presidency Reappraised* (Praeger, 1974), p. 237.

Administrative and organizational leadership

The Constitution charges the president to "take care that the laws be faithfully executed." A president, however, can be only a part-time administrator, for other responsibilities demand most of his attention. He is, then, dependent on his dependents. Theoretically, at least, orders flow down a hierarchical administrative *line*, from president to department heads, to bureau chiefs, and down to smaller offices. The president, like all top executives, is assisted by a *staff*, who advise him from *his* point of view. This line and staff organization is inherent in any large administrative entity, whether the Army, General Motors, or the United Nations.

Presidents have come to rely heavily on their personal staffs. Nowhere else—not in Congress, not in his cabinet, not in his party—can he find the loyalty, the single-mindedness, and the team spirit that he can build among his closest aides. Moreover, presidents come to view most cabinet heads as advocates, peddling ideas that would benefit the particular clientele or programs of their department. Presidents apparently feel their own aides will provide them with more neutral and objective advice. But there are substantial costs to listening only to one's closest aides.[2] Presidential staff often develop a shared frame of reference or a consensus that inhibits rather than encourages critical thinking. George Reedy, a former press secretary to President Johnson, depicts the White House as a palace court with strong presidents creating an environment in which any assistant who persists in presenting irritating thoughts is weeded out. "Palace-guard survivors learn early to camouflage themselves with a coating of battleship grey. . . . Inevitably in a battle between courtiers and advisers, the courtiers will win out. This represents the greatest of all barriers to presidential access to reality. . . ."[3] And an astute British writer notes: ". . . if a president needs to be protected by his White House staff against the departments, he also needs to be kept on guard by the departments against his White House staff, who may all too easily begin to think only they know the purposes and the needs and the mind of their president, until *he* becomes *their* creature and believes that his interests are safe with them."[4]

THE EXECUTIVE OFFICE OF THE PRESIDENT

The Executive Office of the President consists of the White House office and a variety of other agencies (see page 457). One lesson Richard Nixon felt he had learned from his predecessors; The president was not really in control of the Executive Office, and the Executive Office was not really in control of the executive branch as a whole. The Executive Office had become both a big staff agency for the president

[2]Max Ways, "A Management Critique of the Watergate Disaster," *Fortune* (November 1973), p. 200.

[3]George Reedy, *The Twilight of the Presidency* (World, 1970), p. 98.

[4]Henry Fairlie, *The Kennedy Promise* (Doubleday, 1973), pp. 167–68.

The White House

1600 Pennsylvania Ave., N.W.
Washington, D.C. 20500

EAST WING

WEST WING

MANSION

The White House is an executive office, a ceremonial mansion, and a home. Several presidents have viewed it almost as a jail, preferring to spend as much time as possible at other presidential retreats outside of Washington. But most Americans view the rather elegant White House as the center of political and social activity in the nation's capital. It is also something of a national shrine as millions of people from America as well as around the world visit and inspect it each year.

EAST WING

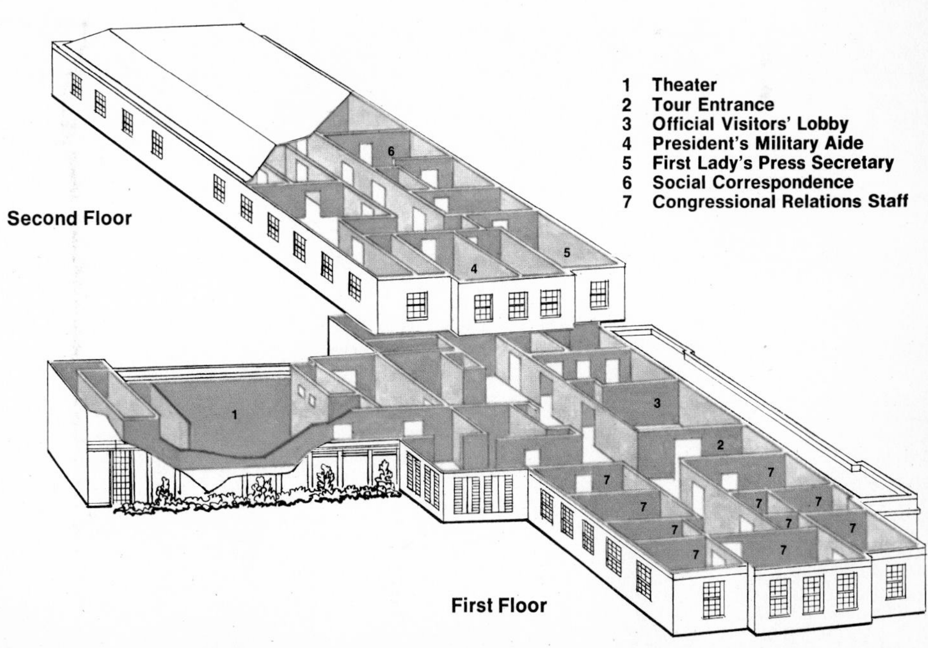

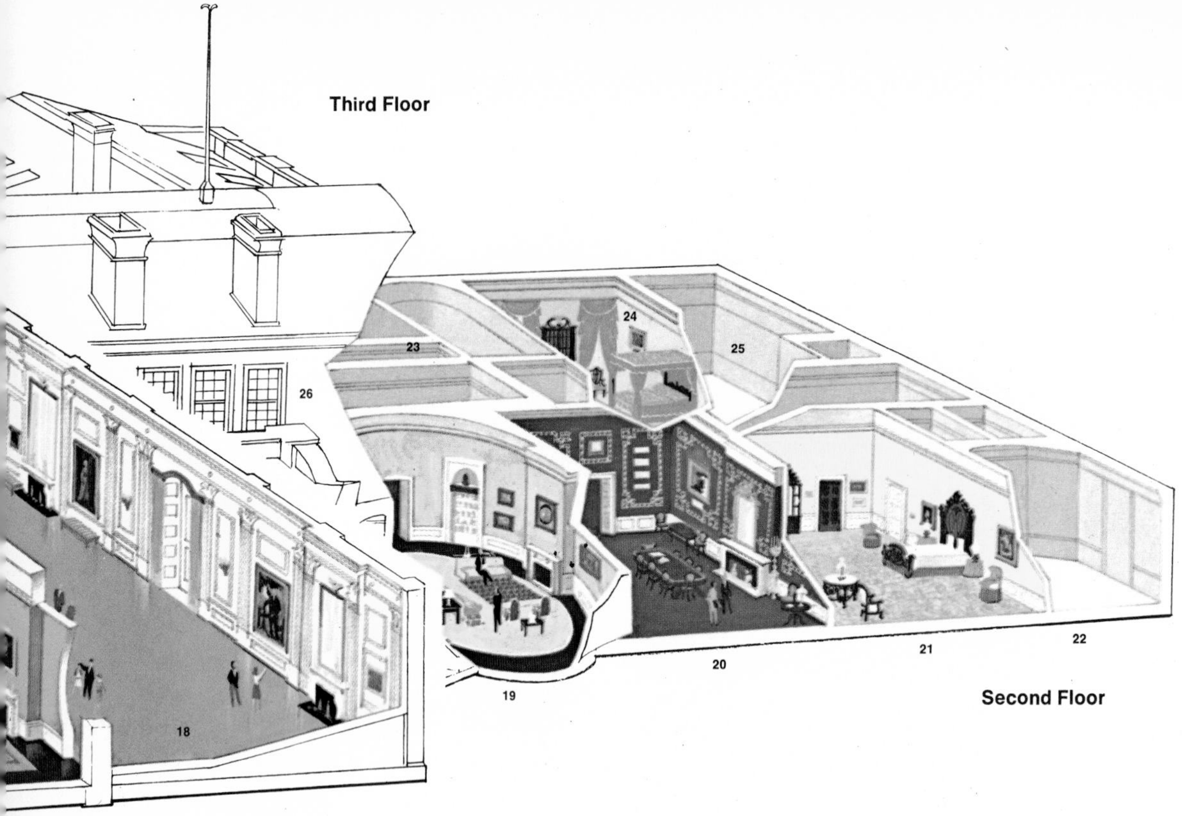

Third Floor

26

23

24

25

18

19

20

21

22

Second Floor

First Floor

MANSION

Ground Floor
1 Housekeeper
2 Secret Service
3 Doctor's Office
4 Diplomatic Reception Room
5 China Room
6 Gold Room
7 Kitchen
8 White House Curator
9 Library
10 Vaulted Arch Hallway

First Floor
11 State Dining Room
12 Red Room
13 Blue Room
14 Green Room
15 Private Dining Room
16 Main Lobby
17 Cross Hall
18 East Room

Second Floor
19 Yellow Oval Room
20 Treaty Room (Monroe Room)
21 Lincoln Bedroom
22 Lincoln Sitting Room
23 Presidential Family Living Quarters
24 Queen's Room (Rose Room)
25 Queen's Sitting Room

Third Floor
26 Staff Living Quarters

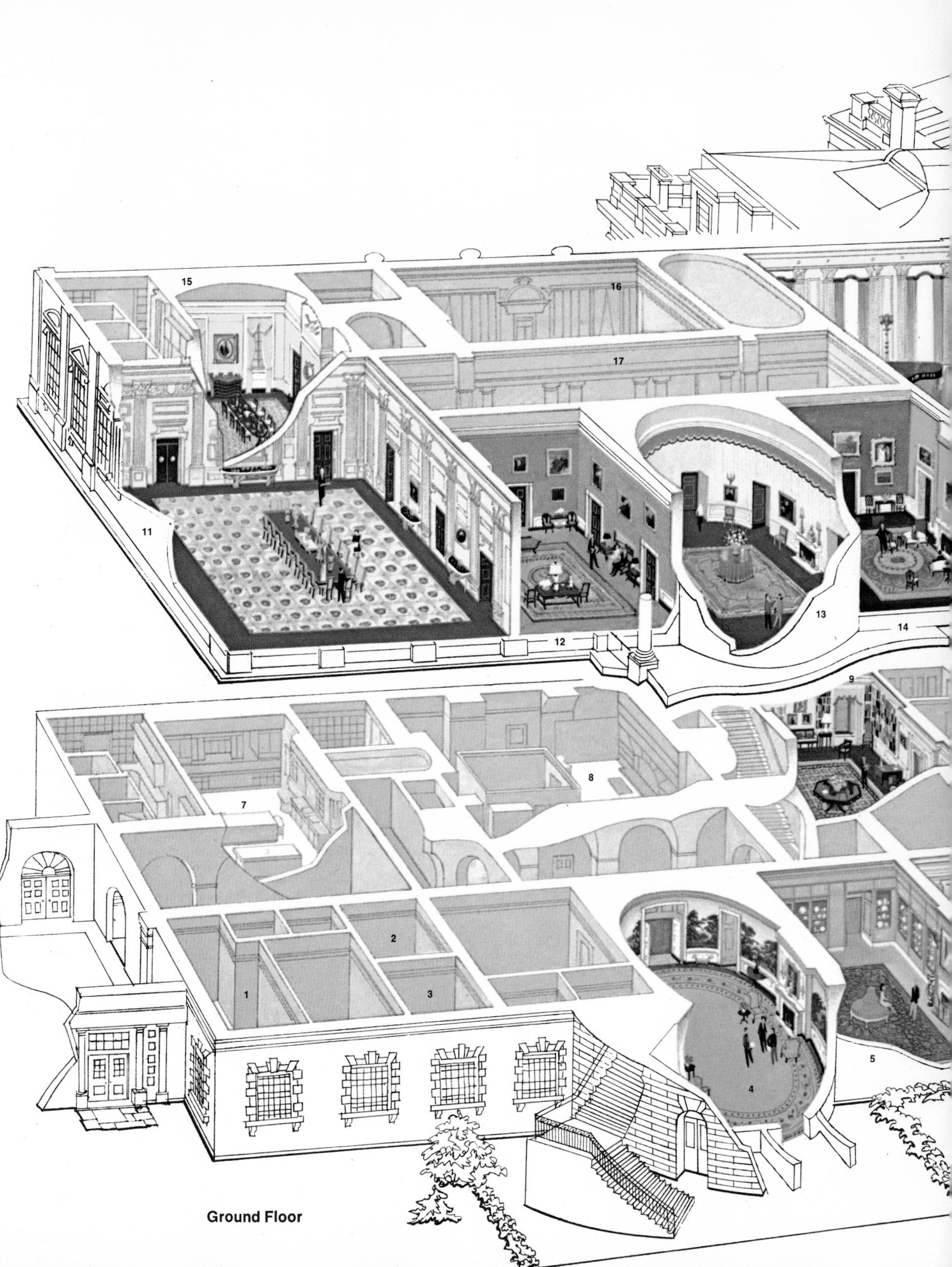
15
16
17
11
12
13
14
9
8
7
2
1
3
4
5
Ground Floor

WEST WING

1 Situation Room
2 National Security Council Staff
3 Oval Office
4 Cabinet Room
5 West Lobby
6 Roosevelt Room (conference room)
7 Assistants to the President
8 Presidential Press Secretary
9 Press Room

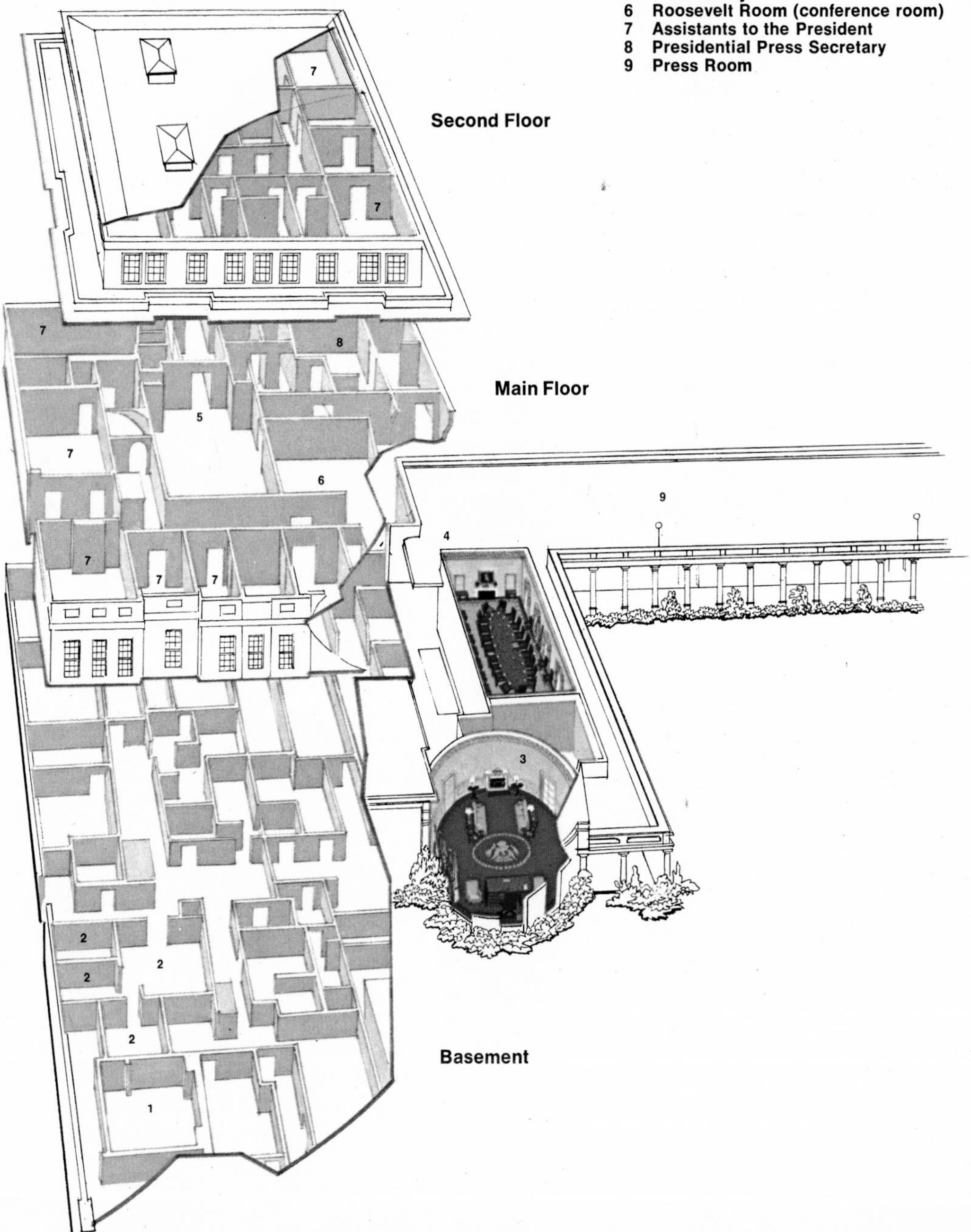

Second Floor

Main Floor

Basement

and a management office for the whole bureaucracy. So many low-level decisions were crowding upward into the Executive Office that the president, paradoxically, was losing control. Decision-making, he felt, had been unduly hoarded in the Executive Office rather than delegated to the agencies. "A president whose programs are carefully coordinated," he told Congress, "whose information system keeps him adequately informed, and whose organizational assignments are plainly set out, can delegate authority with security and confidence."

One unit in the Executive Office, Nixon came to believe, was a model for the rest. This was the National Security Council. He had special confidence in its staff chief, Henry Kissinger, and in the way the group of experts under Kissinger marshaled information and presented options that enabled Nixon to preserve a wide choice and make effective decisions. In setting up the new Domestic Council in 1970, the president hoped these experts would continually assess national needs, identify alternative ways of meeting those needs, and maintain a continuous review of policies and programs. Nominally headed by the president and chiefs of big domestic agencies, the Council actually does its work through subcommittees that bring together White House staff officials and agency officials working on concrete policy proposals. The Domestic Council under Nixon did build up a larger staff than had existed under Kennedy and Johnson, but improvements in planning and advising were not apparent. Rather than earning distinction as a policy-planning staff, it gained notoriety as the home base for many of those convicted of Watergate-related crimes.

The Office of Management and Budget continues to be the central presidential staff agency. Its director advises the president in detail about the hundreds of government agencies—how much money they should be allotted in the budget and what kind of job they are doing. The director and his assistants try to pare down the appropriations requested by the agencies to fit the president's fiscal program. They also try to improve the planning, management, and statistical work of the agencies. The Office makes a special effort to see that each agency conforms to presidential policies in its dealings with Congress by requiring clearance for policy recommendations to the legislature.

A budget is many things, for it deals with the purposes of people in a highly political environment. "Serving diverse purposes, a budget can be . . . a political act, a plan of work, a prediction, a source of enlightenment, a means of obfuscation, a mechanism of control, an escape from restrictions, a means to action, a brake on progress, even a prayer that the powers-that-be will deal gently with the best aspirations of fallible men."[5] But to a president the budget is usually a means of control over administrators who can join ranks with congressional or state politicians or interest groups to thwart presidential priorities. Through the long budget-preparing process the president uses the Office of Management and Budget as a way to conserve and centralize his own influence.

[5]Aaron Wildavsky, *The Politics of the Budgetary Process* (Little, Brown, 1964), p. v.

NIXON'S CABINET CONSOLIDATION PROPOSAL

To control the White House staff was one thing, to control the whole executive branch quite another. During his first term, President Nixon urged Congress to join him in a comprehensive reorganization of the executive branch. "Let's face it," he told Congress. "Most Americans today are simply fed up with government at all levels. They will not—and should not—continue to tolerate the gap between promise and performance. . . . The fact is that we have made the Federal Government so strong it grows muscle-bound and the states and localities so weak they approach impotence."

He proposed that the existing eleven cabinet departments be reduced to eight. The Departments of State, Treasury, Defense, and Justice would remain, but the others would be consolidated into four:

1. Human Resources—a department dealing with the concerns of *people*, as individuals and as members of families, a department focused

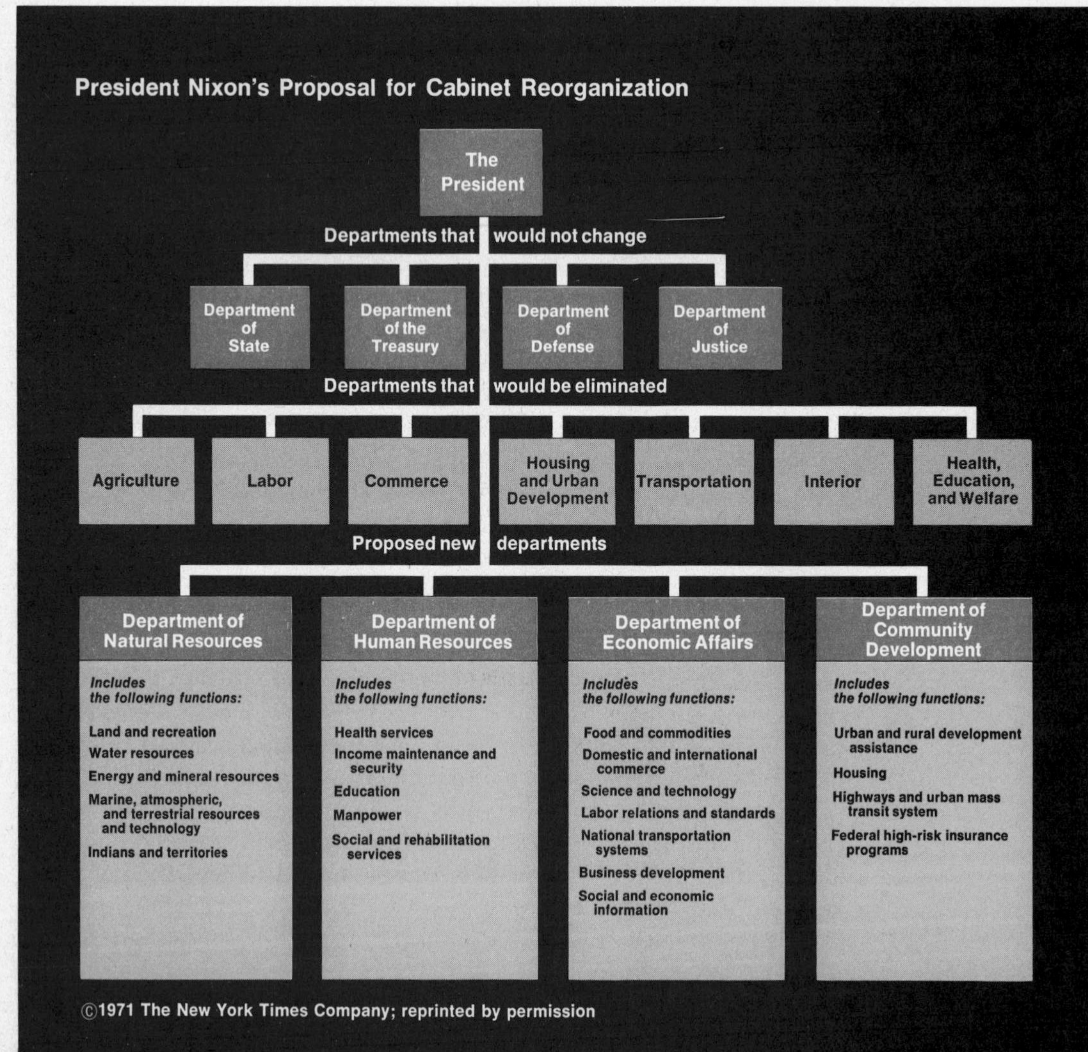

©1971 The New York Times Company; reprinted by permission

on human needs. The new department would have about 120,000 employees.

2. Community Development—a department concerned with the *community*, rural and urban, and with all that it takes to make a community function effectively. About 30,000 employees.

3. Natural Resources—a department concerned with the *physical environment*, with the preservation and balanced use of the nation's natural resources. About 110,000 employees.

4. Economic Affairs—a department concerned with maintaining high and stable *employment*. About 120,000 employees.[6]

The "revolutionary" new plan, as President Nixon termed it, ran into strong opposition in Congress, which had close ties to the old-line departments. At the start of his second term, Nixon by executive order established a "supercabinet." He elevated the secretaries of Agriculture, of Health, Education and Welfare, and of Housing and Urban Development to the level of White House counsellor, while retaining them in their cabinet posts, and gave them responsibility for the three areas of natural resources, human resources, and community development. But in the wake of Watergate this organizational innovation was disbanded.

Nearly every method employed by presidents to regain control over the bureaucracy, it seems, has promoted new difficulties. Setting up new organizations takes a long time. Reorganizations, if and when they are approved by Congress, seldom achieve everything intended—and some unanticipated consequences often are more unsettling than the organizational chaos that encouraged the reorganization in the beginning. And setting up yet further operational activities in the Executive Office of the President makes the already bureaucratic presidential establishment even more top-heavy.

Presidents cannot bypass or ignore the federal bureaucracy for very long without great costs to their reputations and programs. If the White House is to have any impact on existing policies run by the vast federal departments, a president and his lieutenants have no choice but to become wholly familiar with the routines of government—the budget, the personnel system, the advisory processes, evaluation and assessment operations, the legislative clearance and liaison activities. For these routines are both the "guts" and the tools of government. And only with a mastery of them come the skills of effective organizational leadership.

The presidential establishment

Tourists passing by 1600 Pennsylvania Avenue often remark about the beauty and simplicity of the White House. The executive mansion is

[6]Message to Congress on the State of the Union, January 22, 1971; White House Announcement, March 25, 1971.

small compared to those of many foreign potentates. But the pomp and trappings of elegance, the very expensive upkeep costs of the White House as well as other presidential retreats, and the idea of the red-costumed Marine Band constantly playing "Hail to the Chief" annoy some ardent democrats who are uneasy about the leader in a democracy living like a king. More important is the real fear that these monarchic trappings may erode the integrity of men who are not independently wealthy. President Ford, more than most recent presidents, has tried to deroyalize the presidency.

The famous West Wing of the White House contains the president's main office and the offices of about a dozen key presidential aides. Most of the presidential bureaucracy, however, is located in a complex of buildings surrounding the White House—one of the two main ones, called the Old Executive Office Building, is west of the West Wing across a small closed-off driveway; and a second, the New Executive Office Building, is located a block away from the White House and adjacent to Lafayette Park.

The expansion of the presidential establishment is by no means a phenomenon only of recent administrations. The number of employees in the presidential entourage has been growing steadily since the early 1900s when only a few dozen people served a president at a cost of less than a few hundred thousand dollars annually. The Executive Office of the President, approved by Congress in 1939, was the recommendation of President Roosevelt's Committee on Administrative Management. The Executive Office was to provide the president help he obviously needed in carrying out the growing responsibilities imposed by the Depression, and the enlarged role of the government. Little did people know that thirty-five years later the Executive Office would house nearly five thousand employees and more than a dozen advisory and review councils.

The most prominent and controversial component in the Executive Office is the White House office. A president's immediate staff, working out of the White House itself, does not have fixed form; indeed, part of its value lies in its flexibility and adaptability. Most presidents, however, have an appointments secretary, who lets the "right" people see the president and keeps the others away; a press secretary, who handles announcements and deals with the scores of newsmen and photographers assigned to the White House; a correspondence secretary, who watches the president's mail and often drafts important letters; a legal counsel, who advises the president on a variety of matters of broad policy; a foreign policy aide who acts as the president's eyes and ears on the many-sided diplomatic front in Washington; military aides; and several other key legislative, administrative, and political assistants.

The staff of the White House office can be categorized by functions: those whose primary concern is with (1) domestic policy, (2) economic policy, (3) national security or foreign policy, (4) administration and personnel matters (as well as personal paper work and scheduling for the president), (5) congressional relations, and (6) public relations.

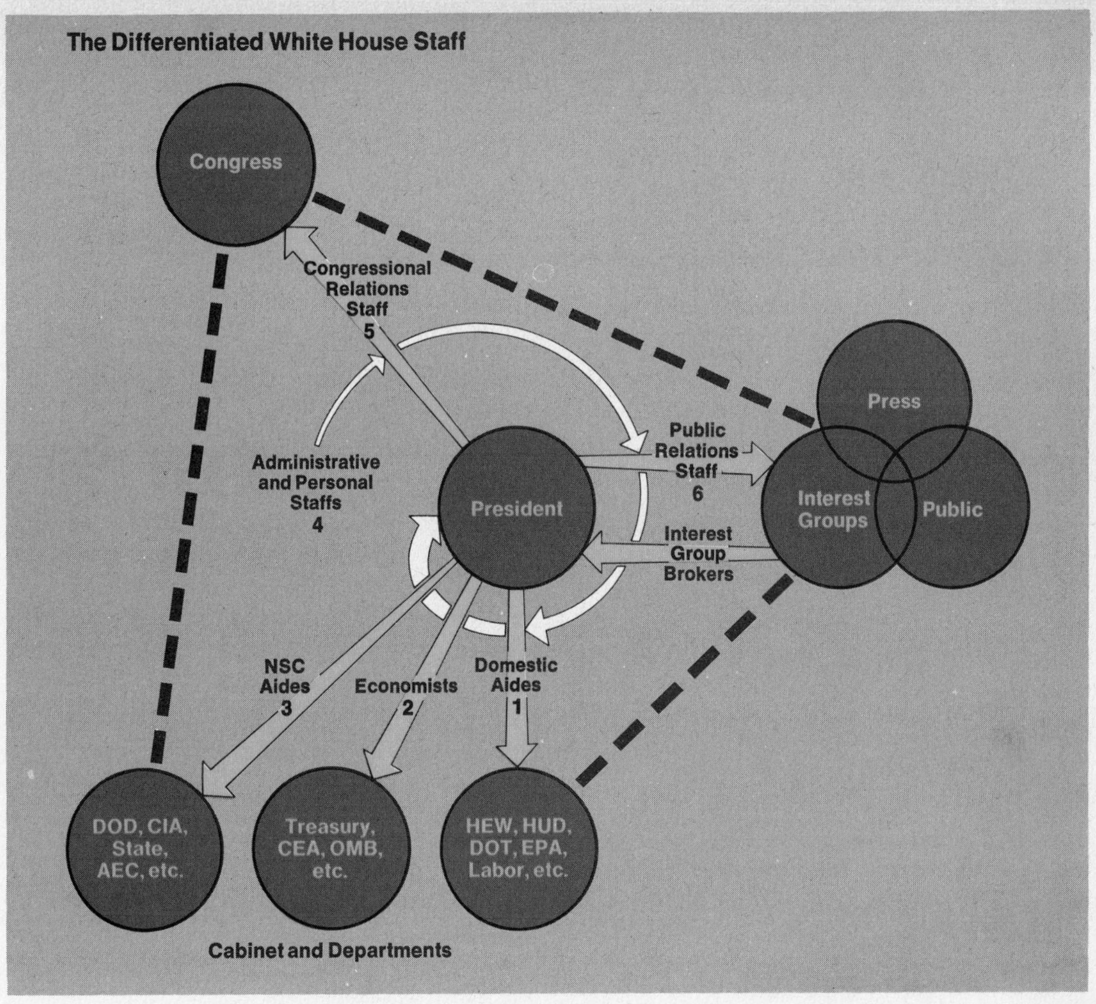

Presidential aides sometimes insist that they are simply the eyes and ears of the president, that they make few important decisions, and that they never insert themselves between the chief executive and the heads of departments. But the burgeoning White House staff has made this traditional picture nearly obsolete. Some White House aides, impatient with what they viewed as bureaucratic and congressional slowdowns and even sabotage, came to view the presidency as if it alone was *the* government. Separation of powers has meant little to them. They may have lost sight of their location within the larger constitutional system. Listen to Nixon's John Ehrlichman:

> There shouldn't be a lot of leeway in following the President's policies. It should be like a corporation, where the executive vice-presidents [the cabinet officers] are tied closely to the Chief Executive, or to put it in extreme terms, when he says jump, they only ask how high.[7]

[7]John Ehrlichman, interview published in *The Washington Post* (August 24, 1972). See also Jeb Stuart Magruder's account of White House life in the Nixon administration, *An American Life: One Man's Road to Watergate* (Atheneum, 1974).

THE PRESIDENTIAL CABINET

It is hard to find a more unusual, even nondescript institution than this one. It is nowhere mentioned by name in the Constitution. Yet, since early in Washinton's administration, every president has had a cabinet. Washington's consisted of his secretaries of state, treasury, and war plus his attorney general. Today the cabinet consists of the president, the vice-president, the officers who head the eleven executive departments, and usually a few others. The cabinet has always been a loosely designated body, and it is not always clear who belongs to it. In recent years, for example, certain executive branch administrators and White House counsellors have been accorded cabinet rank as well.

Cabinet government as practised in parliamentary systems simply does not exist in America. In fact a president is not required by law to form a cabinet or hold regular meetings. Kennedy, Johnson, Nixon, and Ford all preferred smaller conferences with those specifically involved in a problem to formal cabinet meetings. Kennedy saw no reason to discuss defense department matters with his secretaries of agriculture and labor present. He simply thought cabinet meetings were wasting valuable time for too many already busy people. Crucial decisions were more often reached in informal conferences between the president, the heads of two or three major departments, and staff members.

Presidents seldom turn to the cabinet as a collective board of directors for advice; votes are rarely taken and a president sometimes ignores cabinet sentiment. Lincoln, finding the whole cabinet opposed to him on one occasion, could say with impunity, "Seven nays, one aye—the ayes have it." Nixon went ahead and proposed his Family Assistance Plan in 1969 despite opposition or indifference to it from at least half his cabinet.

Under recent presidents, the cabinet as a collectivity often seems nonexistent. Personal presidential advisers and the heads of various

President Lyndon Johnson (right) meets with Vice-President Hubert Humphrey and other government officials aboard the president's plane.

central review units such as OMB, the Domestic Council, the National Security Council, and others have gained superior status over most of the department heads. This has happened in part because presidents feel their domestic department heads adopt narrow, parochial advocate views. Rapport between presidents and these cabinet members weakens, as presidents, in frustration, turn more and more to their close, trusted staffs to settle jurisdictional and interdepartmental conflicts. Tension inevitably builds up between domestic staff aides and the domestic cabinet members.

The head of a large domestic department under both Kennedy and Johnson said:

> There is a tendency on the inside to guard the president too much—they [White House aides] develop considerable power by tightening up the ring around the president. They all play on the fact that he hasn't any time for this or that, etc. But a good cabinet member—one who isn't filling some political niche—can be a very excellent corrective to the White House "hot house" staff who are confined there and are virtually locked up fourteen hours a day. . . . The president needs to hear from his cabinet. . . . A president should occasionally sit down in a leisurely way with his cabinet members and listen and ask that important question: "What do you think?" But this occurred very rarely with either President Kennedy or Johnson.

The cabinet may someday become a team that both sustains the president and renders him more responsible to the people. But at present the American cabinet bears little resemblance to the cabinet described by Harold J. Laski as "a place where the large outlines of policy can be hammered out in common, where the essential strategy is decided upon, where the president knows that he will hear, both in affirmation and in doubt, even in negation, most of what can be said about the direction he proposes to follow."

THE VICE-PRESIDENCY

Though the vice-presidency is now part of the presidential establishment, it has not always been so. Most vice-presidents served mainly as president of the Senate. And in the absence of additional assignments, this kept them more in the legislative orbit than the executive. In most administrations the vice-president was at best a kind of fifth wheel and at worst a political rival who sometimes connived with party factions against the president. The office was often dismissed as a joke. The main reason for the vice-president's posture as outsider was that presidential nominees usually chose as running mates men who were geographically, ideologically, and in other ways likely to "balance the ticket."

In recent decades, however, presidential candidates have selected more like-minded men for their running mates and have made somewhat more use of them. Eisenhower gave to Nixon a fairly prominent role in his administration, as did Kennedy to Johnson, and Johnson to Humphrey. Before offering Humphrey the vice-presidency, according to one report, Johnson made him understand that he could disagree with the president privately before a decision was made but afterwards must support him publicly. And Humphrey did remain loyal.[8] On becoming a presidential candidate himself, Humphrey was widely criticized for having been a "White House puppet," especially on the issue of Vietnam; he replied that a vice-president must be a firm supporter of presidential policy. Spiro Agnew, Gerald Ford, and Nelson Rockefeller in their different ways, were used chiefly to rally the party faithful.

Ideally a vice-president serves several roles in addition to the largely ceremonial functions of acting as president of the Senate. Because he succeeds to the president's job should the president die or resign, a vice-president works as understudy, preparing to assume presidential responsibilities. He can assume some of the president's party and ceremonial duties thereby easing some of the president's burden. A vice-president can also perform several specialized assignments, for example, chairing advisory councils, cabinet-level committees, or a White House conference, or undertaking goodwill missions abroad.

In practice few vice-presidents ever earn the full confidence of a president. Perhaps presidents have been jealous of their vice-presidents' getting favorable attention without having to take blame for anything. Presidents are jealous too when a vice-president tries to maintain his independence and identity as a public figure.

Tensions usually develop between top presidential aides and the vice-president and his staff. Part of the problem arises because presidents prefer not to give up any ceremonial duties for which they themselves can win credit or favor. Neither do cabinet members like to share their responsibilities with vice-presidents, a factor that makes it very hard for vice-presidents to gain administrative experience. Then too, presidents often delegate highly divisive political chores to a vice-president. Such assignments are characteristically "unpresidential."

The search for a better way to select and use vice-presidents is made more urgent by the fact that eight presidents have died in office, four by assassination, four by natural death, and one president has resigned. Lending urgency also is the fact that the vice-presidency is an especially good position from which to gain publicity for future campaigns for the presidency: one-third of our presidents were once vice-presidents, including four of our last six presidents.

Some feel that a vice-presidency is no longer needed. Most who advocate its abolition recommend that some officer, like the secretary of state or the Speaker of the House of Representatives, serve as acting president in the event the office becomes vacant until 60 or 90 days later when a special election for a president would be held. The hope or intent in such proposals is to affirm the view that the president must, except for the briefest periods, be a person elected to that office by the people.

[8]Theodore H. White, *The Making of the President 1964* (Atheneum, 1965), pp. 285–86.

If most people feel the office should be continued, this does not mean they are wholly satisfied with it. There is substantial support for devising better ways to pick vice-presidential nominees as well as for making the vice-presidency a less insignificant office.[9] Both major parties are considering practical means of making the selection procedures for the vice-presidency more democratic. Under the existing system, presidential nominees have virtually a free hand in choosing their running mates. While there are some notable advantages of the present system—especially the possibility that the ticket will be ideologically compatible—drawbacks are also clearly present, notably: ". . . the pressure of time (which contributed to the abortive choice of Senator Thomas F. Eagleton by George McGovern in 1972), the lack of formalized consultation within the party, the rubberstamp role for convention delegates, and the absence of public scrutiny and judgment of prospective vice-presidential candidates before the nomination."[10]

What is likely to come of the vice-presidency? The office will remain attractive to aspiring politicians if only because it is one of the major paths to the presidency. The Twenty-second Amendment, by imposing an absolute two-term limit on the incumbent, means that the vice-president now has even a better chance to move up; the Twenty-fifth Amendment and political party practice seem to ensure he will be the president's personal choice. It is almost certain, however, that vice-presidents will continue to have an anomalous and always underdefined role.

THE EXPANDING EXECUTIVE OFFICE

More than three dozen councils, offices, or planning boards have existed at varying times since 1939 in the president's Executive Office. Roosevelt created eight. Truman added seven, Eisenhower four, Kennedy three, Johnson two, Nixon eleven, and Ford several more. Each president, except Johnson, has dropped at least two of these review, or coordination, units. Official members of the Executive Office of the President by the mid-1970s were (with their date of creation):

The White House Office (1939)
Council of Economic Advisers (1946)
National Security Council (1947)
Office of the Special Representatives for Trade Negotiations (1963)
Council on Environmental Quality (1969)
Office of Management and Budget (1970)
Domestic Council (1970)

[9]A notable study of the Agnew vice-presidency and its ending is found in Richard M. Cohen and Jules Witcover, *A Heartbeat Away: The Investigation and Resignation of Vice-President Spiro T. Agnew* (Viking, 1974).

[10]John Etridge, "Nation's No. 2: Is He Always the Second Best?" *Los Angeles Times* (October 28, 1973), Part VII. See also Arthur Schlesinger, Jr., "Is the Vice-Presidency Necessary?" *Atlantic Monthly* (May 1974), 37–44.

Office of Telecommunications Policy (1970)
Council on International Economic Policy (1971)
Special Action Office for Drug Abuse Prevention (1971)
Council on Economic Policy (1973)
Federal Property Council (1973)
White House Council on Wage and Price Stability (1974)
Economic Policy Board (1974)
White House Labor-Management Committee (1974)

The presidential establishment is enlarged further by a network of consultants, experts on loan from executive departments, and countless ad hoc task forces, presidentially appointed commissions, an occasional White House conference, and other temporary study groups. Recent presidents have sought outside advice and relied on these newer mechanisms partly because they need people with new knowledge and partly because they distrust the old-line departments with their image of being special pleaders. The description of these hundreds, and sometimes thousands, of presidential experts can sound very impressive. Theodore White, for example, has called them the "action-intellectuals" and America's "new priesthood." But these "best and the brightest" are sometimes no match for the problems they are advising on.

Moreover, there are some basic problems in the relationship between experts and politicians. Knowledge is power and the political aides around a president are jealous when it comes to preserving the president's power. They want to *use* the experts, but are seldom skilled in rewarding and cultivating the intellectual. Intellectuals have a different problem. To practice their critical and creative function, they must in part be outsiders, immune to the seductions of power. Presidents, as career politicians, are accustomed to being surrounded by supporters and often find it difficult to hear criticism of their programs. The temptation is always great to listen only to the like-minded or the cheerleaders.

As the presidential establishment has become a large, complex bureaucracy in itself, it has rapidly acquired many dubious characteristics of large bureaucracies: layering, overspecialization, communication gaps, inadequate coordination, and a tendency to become consumed with short-term operational concerns at the expense of thinking systematically about important long-range problems and estimating the consequences of various policies.

How should the Executive Office of the President be organized? Nobody is sure. Many agree that it is too large, that there are too many *operational* as opposed to staff, or advisory, units. Critics are also concerned about the quality of advice and how the office could be better organized to ensure better policy-making and more effective presidential leadership. On this there is little consensus.[11] Nearly everyone recog-

[11]Aaron Wildavsky, "The Presidency in the Political System," *The Presidency* (Little, Brown, 1975), introductory essay. But, see also Alexander L. George, "The Case for Multiple Advocacy in Making Foreign Policy," *American Political Science Review* (September 1972), pp. 780–81; and Irving L. Janis, *Victims of Groupthink* (Houghton Mifflin, 1973).

nizes two realities: Different presidents will be served best by different personal staff arrangements; and even the best possible organizational and advisory structures never ensure that a president will recognize and use good advice when he receives it. As Aaron Wildavsky put it, "You can lead a President to advice, so it seems, but you can hardly make him take it." He adds, "Could it be that a creative and flexible structure for advice calls for a President with the same qualities?"

Making the presidency safe for democracy

The startling series of events in the Watergate scandals sharpened the old questions: How much executive power can a democracy afford? Is a strong presidency a tool of elites, or an advocate of majoritarian interests *against* elites? New questions also were raised: Was the swelling of the presidency due to presidential strength or an attempt to compensate for institutional weaknesses? Was a bigger presidency necessarily better? Did presidential powers grow because they were usurped by presidents or abdicated by Congress?

Specific complaints against the presidency were many: impoundment of billions of congressionally approved funds, alleged obstruction of justice, abuse of the doctrine of executive privilege, White House lying about the conduct of the Vietnam War, and excessive secrecy and duplicity. Trust in the president plunged downward. People lost confidence, first in Johnson's, then in Nixon's brand of leadership. The very legitimacy of the presidency was being tested.

How much formal authority does and should a president have? The Constitution, which is silent on so many issues and political struggles of today, is vague on the matter. It seems to grant broad executive authority without defining boundaries. Some scholars hold that in emergencies the president has wide powers to protect the public interest without specific legal authority and even at the cost of overriding existing laws. There seems to be a kind of *inherent* power in the presidency, vast but undefined, that an aggressive president can exploit in times of crisis. The problem is that crisis is now the rule rather than the exception.

Franklin Roosevelt's conception of his powers—sometimes called the *prerogative theory*—was that, in the face of emergencies, a president had the same power John Locke once argued kings had—the power, in Locke's words, "to act according to discretion for the public good, without the prescription of the law and sometimes even against it."[12] The World War II destroyer-bases agreement, for example—in which the president on his own initiative traded naval destroyers to England in return for some military bases—conflicted with several laws.

[12]E. S. Corwin, *The Constitution and What It Means Today*, 10th ed. (Princeton University Press, 1948), p. 85. See also Clinton Rossiter, *Constitutional Dictatorship* (Harcourt Brace Jovanovich, 1948).

PRESIDENTIAL CHARACTER

What about presidential personality? If the presidency has too much power for the safety of the country (and the world) and yet not enough to solve some of the nation's toughest problems, what kind of person do we need in this highest office? Political scientist James David Barber writes that because the issues are always changing, we should be concerned somewhat less with the stands a candidate takes than with the candidate's character. The character, Barber claims, will stay pretty much the same. The people best suited for the presidency, according to his view, are the politicians who creatively shape their environment and savor the give-and-take exchanges in political life. He calls them "active-positive" types.[13]

Our understanding of personality and character, however, is not yet developed to the stage where accurate predictions can be made about suitable presidential candidates. Using strict character criteria to screen candidates, for example, probably would have prevented the moody and often depressed Abraham Lincoln from winning office. Nor can we be sure that a president's character will stay the same through his term or even over the lifespan of an issue. And just as we need to learn more about a presidential candidate's character, we need more clearly defined issues. And it would help also to know the kind of people a candidate would seek out as advisers.

NEW CHECKS AND BALANCES NEEDED?

Presidential power is doubtless greater today than ever before. It is misleading, however, to infer from a president's capacity to drop an H-bomb that he is similarly powerful in most other policy-making areas.

The more political analysts study policy developments over time and engage in revisionist treatments of past presidents, the more it is clear that presidents, in fact, are seldom free agents in effecting basic social change. We have seen that as priority-setter, politician, and executive a president must share power with congressmen, bureaucrats, and

[13]James David Barber, *The Presidential Character* (Prentice-Hall, 1972). But see a critique of this study by Alexander L. George, "Assessing Presidential Character," *World Politics* (January 1974), pp. 234–82.

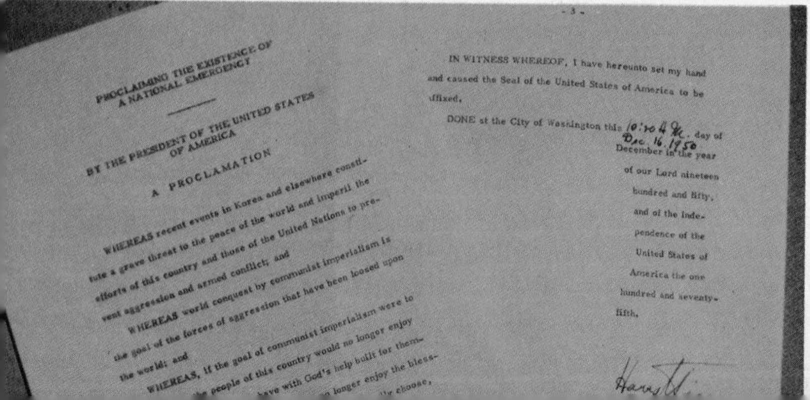

PROCLAIMING THE EXISTENCE OF A NATIONAL EMERGENCY

BY THE PRESIDENT OF THE UNITED STATES OF AMERICA

A PROCLAMATION

WHEREAS recent events in Korea and elsewhere constitute a grave threat to the peace of the world and imperil the efforts of this country and those of the United Nations to prevent aggression and armed conflict; and

WHEREAS world conquest by communist imperialism is the goal of the forces of aggression that have been loosed upon the world; and

WHEREAS, if the goal of communist imperialism were to ... the people of this country would no longer enjoy ...

- 3 -

IN WITNESS WHEREOF, I have hereunto set my hand and caused the Seal of the United States of America to be affixed.

DONE at the City of Washington this ... day of December in the year of our Lord nineteen hundred and fifty, and of the Independence of the United States of America the one hundred and seventy-fifth.

President Truman's proclamation of national emergency in 1950.

interest-group elites, among others. The ability to set priorities and even to pass laws is not the same as being able to enforce and administer them properly. A president who wants to be effective in implementing policy changes must know explicitly what he wants to achieve, and must know how to motivate and strengthen the bureaucracy to that end.

This is an exceedingly tough assignment in a political system held together in such large measure by compromise, ambiguity, and contradictory goals. Not only must a president deal with key congressmen, cabinet members, important bureaucrats, a vice-president, party chiefs, and even leaders of the opposition party, but he must also cope with the great political forces operating around the White House—public opinion in all its complexity, pressures from organized interests, demands from his own party. He must negotiate endlessly among individuals and among interests. He will constantly be in battle with investigative reporters and the muckrakers. And he must respond to public sentiment at the same time he educates it. The fierce light of public opinion, magnified by the press and the electronic media, always beats down upon the White House.

The Twenty-second Amendment, which bars a president from being elected for more than two terms, also curbs his power. The amendment weakens a president during his second term because powerful political leaders in Congress and in the bureaucracy feel less obliged to support a leader they know will be out of power by a certain date. As Clark Clifford, a former counselor to three presidents, put it, "A President who can never again be a candidate is a President whose coattails are permanently in mothballs."

Reaction to Watergate took at least two forms. Cynics with an elitist perspective said here was irrefutable evidence of an isolated, autocratic presidency. And they charged that Watergate could occur in part because of the inadequacy of our checks and balances. Pluralists, or supporters of the American system of dispersed powers, saw in the system's response to Watergate at least some evidence that the system could work—that is, they felt the courts, the press, and even Congress *did* reassert themselves when put to a critical test. The Watergate disclosures and investigations led to public outrage and reprimand. And future presidents were, in effect, served notice by the public at large of what is acceptable and just what is not acceptable.

There is a danger, too, in abstracting the presidency from history, and in overreacting to Vietnam and Watergate. Probably no foolproof safeguard against the abuse of presidential power exists. And the imposition of a vast new array of checks and balances might cripple the important potential of the institution for creative leadership.

If, as is frequently said, President Johnson led the nation into an undeclared and unwanted war, it should be remembered that Congress and the prevailing public mood encouraged him. Our Indochina policies were in large measure a reflection of the widespread belief that America should act as a world policeman, keep its commitments to its allies, and halt Communism wherever possible. Johnson felt he was

"Remember how we all grew up wanting to be President?"

Copyright © 1974. Reprinted by permission of Saturday Review/World and Herbert Goldberg.

providing the kind of restrained but firm leadership Americans wanted. Like most presidents he was not about to change fundamental American sentiments; rather, he felt he was to respond to and mirror its mood.[14]

NEEDED: A NEW ATTITUDE TOWARD THE PRESIDENCY

In one sense, the best safeguard and restraint on the most dangerous of presidential powers rests with the attitudes of the American people. Citizens have far more power than they generally realize. Presidents usually hear them when they are "sending a message," to borrow George Wallace's apt phrase. Citizens can also "vote" between elections in innumerable ways—by changing parties, by organizing protests, by their votes in off-year special elections.

Unrealistic expectations of the presidency have helped to weaken the institution. Part of the reason presidents turn to secrecy, to subordinating substance to style, has been the overburdening of the office with exaggerated expectations. We elect a politician and then insist on a superhuman, statesman-kinglike performance. As currently designed, the presidency is an institution that manipulates its occupants, and accentuates their *shortcomings* as well as their virtues.[15] It seems cruel to put someone in a position where it is nearly certain he will fail and then condemn him for not succeeding, but this is what we usually do to our presidents.

We need a healthy skepticism toward presidential decisions. An ability to get elected, for example, is not the same as an ability to govern and lead the nation. The glamor that surrounds the great drama of "the making of the president" too often distracts from the far less exciting but still more important struggle of "the running of the presidency." The promise of the presidency lies in the capacity to symbolize the best aspirations of the nation and to act wisely and rapidly to make the executive branch work effectively.

[14]See John Mueller, *War, Presidents and Public Opinion* (John Wiley, 1973).

[15]See Magruder, *An American Life;* and Carl Bernstein and Bob Woodward, *All the President's Men* (Simon and Schuster, 1974).

We are less likely to fashion a more democratic presidency by constitutional changes than by *political* reforms. Proposals for a six-year term with reelection forbidden hold little promise of making presidents more accountable. Parliamentary structural features such as a "vote of no confidence," although beguiling, do not seem necessary or practical. Existing counterbalances are available: impeachment, power of the purse, congressional investigations, and freedom-of-information statutes. The remedy to an imperial and overextended presidency lies in citizen insistence that Congress and the parties revitalize their processes and effectively use their powers. Persistence and intensity will have their impact, especially if we can recast our political institutions to serve as vehicles for two-way communications. It might be well to remind ourselves that the presidency has not grown in function and power only because presidents, elites, or the masses wanted it to. It has grown mainly in response to historic, economic, and social forces.

Another problem in making presidents accountable remains the possibility, if it is carried too far, that a presidency could be devised whose occupants would merely register the boisterous, emotional whims in the nation. And, we must ask ourselves, would making the presidency *immediately* accountable to the majority of the people make it any more effective in dealing with such issues as racial injustice and poverty, problems that are often sustained, consciously or not, by the preferences or fears of the majority?

In sum, the presidency is an amalgam of the huge presidential establishment, presidential personality, and heavy demands and expectations on the chief executive. It is still being reshaped as new presidents, with ideas of their own, move into the White House. To elitists, it is part of the system of elites that runs the nation. To pluralists it is an agency that can work in behalf of a great variety of groups and at times for popular majorities; to conservatives it is often too much the instrument of liberal-radical egalitarian majorities. All three groups fear its potential for too much concentrated power, even for becoming a dictatorship.

The overriding task of American democrats is to bind a president to the majority will of the nation without shackling him as a source of intelligent leadership. To require immediate accountability may well be to paralyze the presidency and to leave it a hollow shell. Presidential power, properly defined, must be more than the power to persuade, and less than the power to coerce—it must be the power to achieve results acceptable to the people and by democratic means.

Chapter 17 Bureaucrats and bureaucracy

A Washington story tells of a government clerk who received dozens of papers daily, which he read, initialed, and deposited in his out basket. One day a report meant for another office found its way to his desk, and he followed the usual reading, initialing, and dispatching routine. Two days later the report was returned with the following memorandum attached: "This document was not designed for you to handle. Please erase your initials and initial the erasure."[1]

What Americans call red tape is a universal complaint. All large organizations—governmental or not—are bureaucracies and are run by bureaucrats. It's more or less part of the human condition. Specialization of function and hierarchical relationships are necessary in an organization of any size. Why then is the criticism of bureaucrats in government so loud and persistent? Partly because public officials work in a goldfish bowl under the sharp eyes of congressmen, columnists, radio and television commentators, and lobbyists; and partly because some interest groups wage massive public-relations campaigns to convince us that bureaucracy is inherently evil.

In this chapter, we are mainly interested in the 5 million civilians and

[1]Quoted in Charles E. Jacob, *Policy and Bureaucracy* (Van Nostrand, 1966), p. 47.

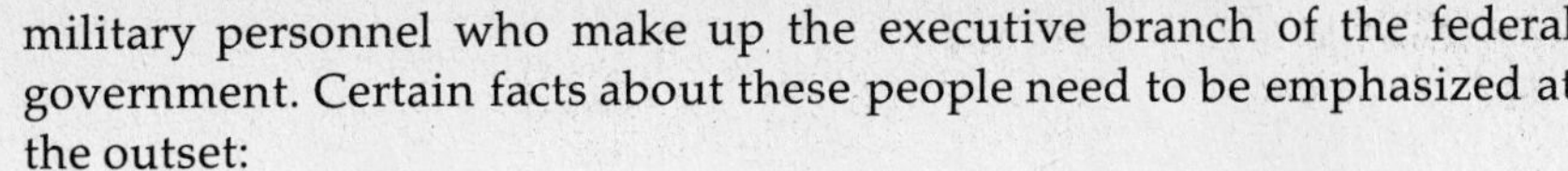

military personnel who make up the executive branch of the federal government. Certain facts about these people need to be emphasized at the outset:

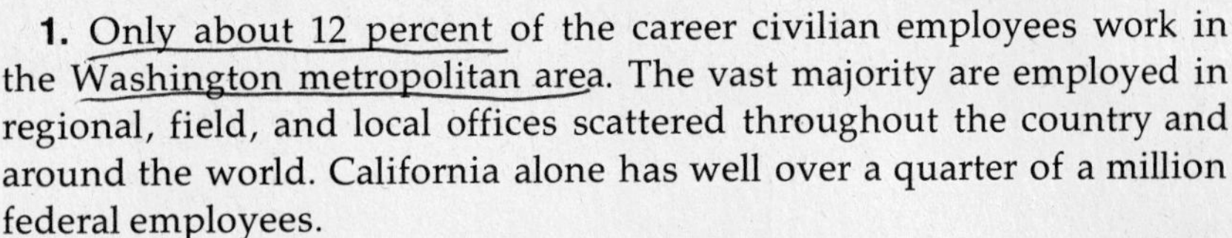

1. Only about 12 percent of the career civilian employees work in the Washington metropolitan area. The vast majority are employed in regional, field, and local offices scattered throughout the country and around the world. California alone has well over a quarter of a million federal employees.

2. Almost half of the civilian employees work for the Army, Navy, Air Force, or other defense agencies. The continuing world crisis has put its stamp on our bureaucracy.

The Pentagon.

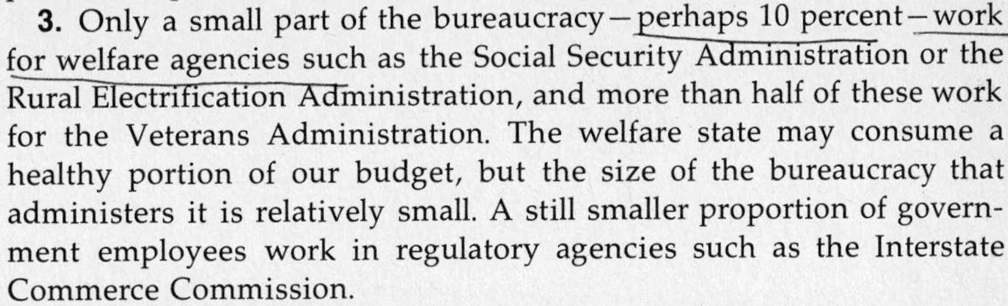

3. Only a small part of the bureaucracy—perhaps 10 percent—work for welfare agencies such as the Social Security Administration or the Rural Electrification Administration, and more than half of these work for the Veterans Administration. The welfare state may consume a healthy portion of our budget, but the size of the bureaucracy that administers it is relatively small. A still smaller proportion of government employees work in regulatory agencies such as the Interstate Commerce Commission.

4. Federal employees are not any one type. Indeed, in terms of social origin, education, religion, and other background factors, bureaucrats are more broadly representative of the nation than are legislators or politically appointed executives.

5. Federal civilian employment has decreased slightly in recent years and, relative to state and local growth rates, has leveled off. State and local civilian forces on the other hand continue to grow.

6. Their work in government is equally varied. Over 15,000 different personnel skills—about two-thirds as many as are found in all private business—are represented in the federal government. Unlike Americans as a whole, however, most federal employees are white-collar workers—stenographers, clerks, lawyers, office heads, inspectors, and the like.

How important are the bureaucrats? In a sense, of course, they are all-important. They are the core of government. Without officials and employees, government would be a collection of politicians and lawmakers—generals without armies. So influential are the officials that sometimes the political heads seem insignificant. As Alexander Pope wrote over 200 years ago,

For forms of government let fools contest,
Whate'er is best administer'd is best.

But this sentiment goes too far. "Forms of goverment" help shape the political world in which the administrator lives; they influence the kind of decisions made and the way they are carried out.

Actually we cannot separate the administration of policy from politi-

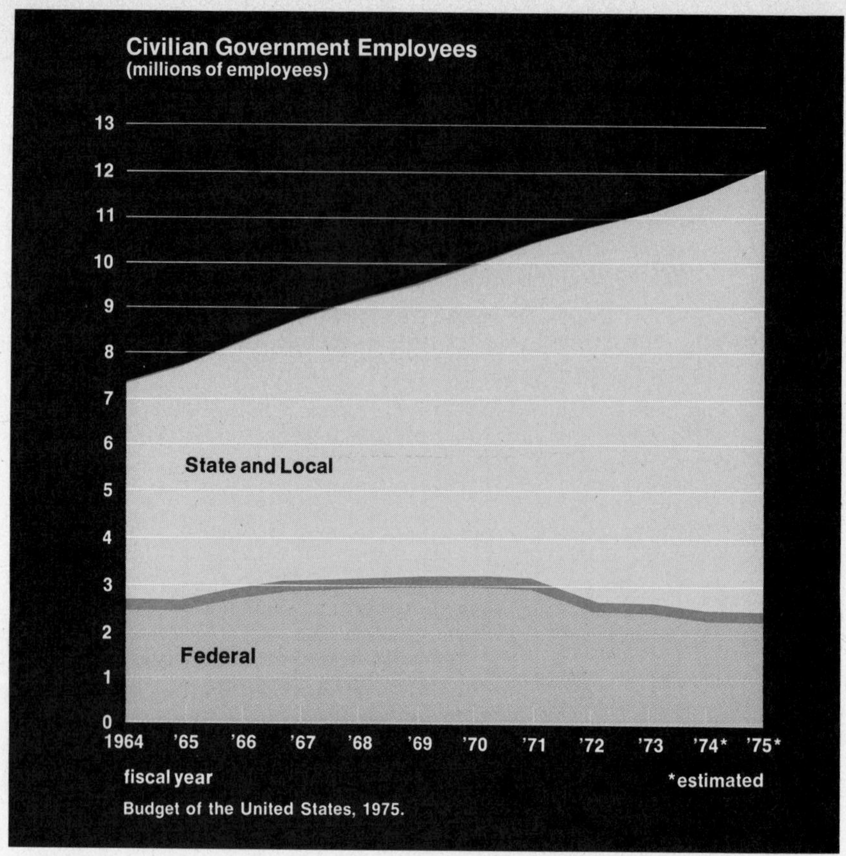

cal conflicts over what the policy should be. Congress passes a law setting federal standards for safety of automobiles and designates the Department of Transportation to implement the program. But conflicts over standards – or politics – do not stop with the enactment of the law. Or a president announces dramatically that we are about to "make war on poverty" or "become energy self-sufficient," and Congress creates new agencies to carry out certain programs and appropriates funds, but politics – conflicts over who is to get what and who is to do what – do not stop. They are merely transferred temporarily from legislative to administrative areas.

Our purpose is not to put administration and politics in separate spheres, but to see why the administrative process is an integral part of the policy process. What kinds of problems do administrators face? What are their options? To whom are they accountable? How does the structure of administrative organization serve to promote some interests to the disadvantage of others? How much and under what conditions are bureaucrats subject to effective control by Congress, the president, special-interest groups? Are they "agents of elites" or "servants of the masses" – or something else?

The shape of administration

Big government is complex government. The executive branch is a cluster of eleven departments and at least thirty-five independent agencies, together embracing over 2,000 bureaus, divisions, branches, offices, services, and other subunits. In size, five big agencies – the Departments of Army, Navy, and Air Force, the Postal Service, and the Veterans Administration – tower over all the others. Most of the agencies are responsible to the president, but some are partly independent of him. Virtually all the agencies exist by act of Congress, and the legislators could abolish them either by passing a new law or by withholding funds. The power of Congress to set up departments and agencies is implicit in the Constitution. The framers presumably assumed – without actually specifying – that Congress might establish such functions and reorganizations as it saw fit.

FORMAL ORGANIZATION

A soldier writes to his family that he is a member of the first squad of the second platoon of Company B of the 1st Battalion of the 426th Regiment of the 95th Division of the III Corps of the Ninth Army. A friend of his works in the personnel office of the parts section of the Flint Division of the Buick Department of General Motors. A woman in Washington, D.C., tells her brother that she is a behavioral scientist currently helping to run the Population and Reproduction Grants Branch, Center for Population Research, in the National Institute of Child Health and Human Development of the Public Health Service in the Department of Health, Education, and Welfare.

The larger the number of people and the more complex the job, the more highly organized an agency will be. In establishing a new agency, Congress may lay down a general structural plan in legislation, the president may give further shape to it in executive orders and in private instructions, and the head of the agency and his assistants will extend the organizational skeleton of the new agency down to small units. But the executive branch as a whole, it has been said, grew up "without plan or design like the barns, shacks, silos, tool sheds, and garages of an old farm." Although different functions produce various kinds of organization, in general the main agencies of government are composed of departments, corporations, independent agencies, and their subunits – bureaus, divisions, offices, and so on down the line – together with a network of regional and field offices.

The departments are headed by secretaries (except Justice, which is headed by the attorney general). These secretaries are also cabinet members (except for the secretaries of the Army, Navy, and Air Force, who report to the president through their chief, the secretary of defense) and thus are directly responsible to the president. Although the departments vary greatly in size, they have certain features in common:

Often a deputy or an undersecretary takes part of the administrative load off the secretary's shoulders, and one or more assistant secretaries direct major programs. Like the president, the secretaries have various subcabinet-level assistants who help them in planning, budget, personnel, legal services, public relations, and other staff functions. The departments are, of course, subdivided into bureaus and smaller units, but the basis of division may differ. The most common basis is *function*; for example, the Commerce Department is divided into the Bureau of the Census, the Patent Office, the Office of Minority Business Enterprise, and so on. Or the basis may be *clientele* (for example, the Bureau of Indian Affairs of the Interior Department), or *work processes* (for example, the Economic Research Service of the Agriculture Department), or *geography* (for example, the Alaskan Air Command of the Department of the Air Force). The basis of organization of most departmental units—and indeed of the departments themselves—is mixed.

The score or more of *government corporations*, such as the Tennessee

Formal and Informal Lines of a Bureaucratic Organization

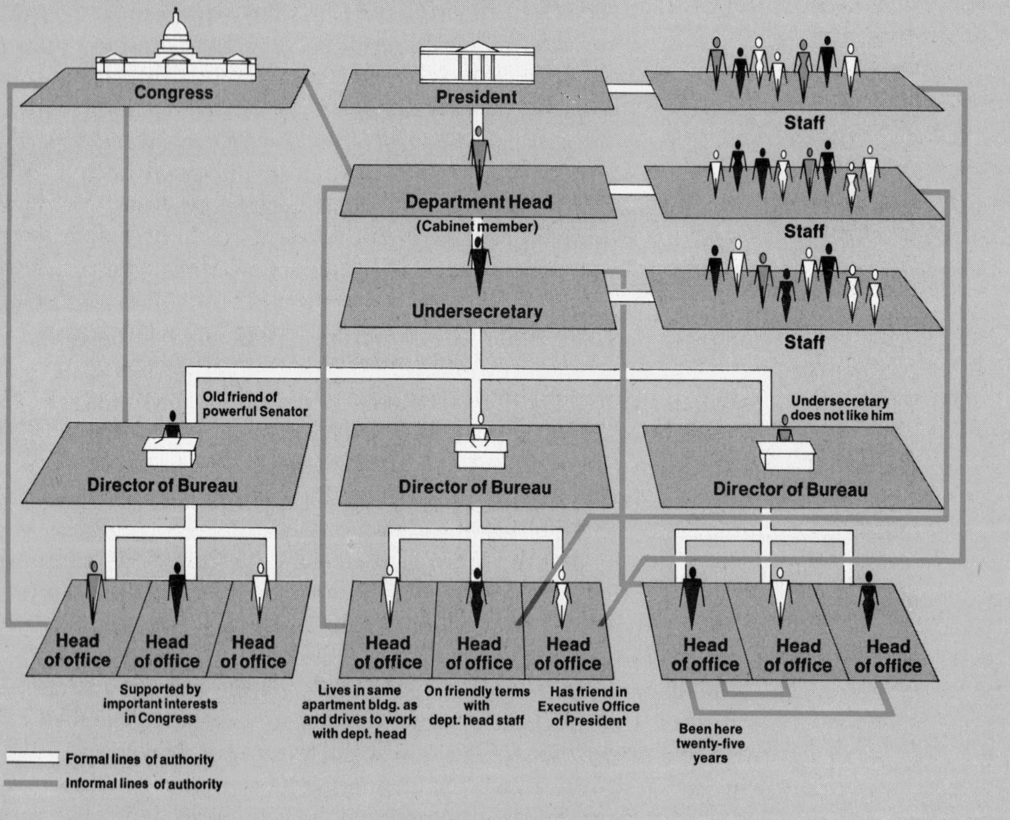

Hierarchy- Change of command -highest to lowest

Valley Authority and the Federal Deposit Insurance Corporation, are a sort of cross between a business corporation and a regular government agency. Government corporations were designed to make possible a freedom of action and flexibility not always found in the regular federal agencies. These corporations have been freed from certain regulations of the Office of Management and Budget and the Comptroller General. They also have had more leeway in using their own earnings as they pleased. And yet the fact that the government owns the corporations means that it retains basic control over their activities. Recently, Congress has deprived the corporations of much of their freedom, and they have taken on some of the character of regular departments—they are no longer free from the need to get annual congressional appropriations, for example. However, they remain useful means of keeping certain government activities (especially financial) apart from the routine, congested, and centralized federal agencies and from excessive congressional and presidential control, particularly in time of emergency.

The *independent agencies* comprise many types of organization and many degrees of independence. Broadly speaking, all agencies that are not corporations and that do not fall under the executive departments (such as Treasury or Interior) are called independent agencies. Many of these agencies, however, are no more independent of the president and Congress than are the executive departments themselves. The huge Veterans Administration is not represented in the cabinet, for example, but its chief is directly responsible to the president.

Russell Means presents the views of some Indians in the Wounded Knee dispute to the Bureau of Indian Affairs.

Another type of independent agency is the *independent regulatory board* or *commission*—agencies like the Securities and Exchange Commission, the National Labor Relations Board, the Interstate Commerce Commission. Congress deliberately set up these boards to keep them somewhat free from White House influence in exercising their quasi-legislative and quasi-judicial functions. Congress has protected their independence in several ways. The boards are headed by three or more commissioners with overlapping terms, they often have to be bipartisan in membership, and the president's power of removal is curbed.

Within the departments, corporations, and independent agencies are a host of subordinate units. The standard name for the largest subunit is the *bureau*, although sometimes it is called an office, administration, service, and so on. Bureaus are the working agencies of the federal government. In contrast to the big departments, which are often mere holding companies for a variety of agencies, the bureaus usually have fairly definite and clear-cut duties as the names of some of them attest: the Bureau of Customs and Bureau of the Mint of the Treasury Department, the Bureau of Indian Affairs of the Interior Department. Most bureaus are overshadowed by their mother agencies, but some of them, like the Federal Bureau of Investigation and the Bureau of Reclamation, enjoy a popular prestige and political position of their own. Below the bureaus are hundreds of branches, services, sections, and other units that perform even more specialized operations.

The *field service* of the federal government embraces a vast number of regional, state, county, and local units. The local post office is part of the field service, as is the local recruiting center for the armed forces or the local office of the Social Security Administration.

At the action end of government cluster many of the same kinds of problems of politics and administration as are found in Washington. Despite the efforts, with some considerable success, of concentrating federal offices in a relatively few regional centers, most large cities continue to contain many federal offices, each of which reports to its own regional and national headquarters.

Recently greater efforts have been made to involve the local citizenry in the administration of federal programs. The rhetoric of this "grassroots federalism" is often "to humanize" the government, to bring it "closer to the people" but the political consequence may be to permit the local interest groups to undermine federal standards. Under other conditions citizen participation may provide a new power base for groups who previously had little impact on community politics. In any event the form of organization and the nature and extent and kind of local involvement are not politically neutral decisions.

CONTRACTING OUT

In recent decades important areas of federal policy have been delegated to quasi-federal employees—individuals who spend federal funds and implement federal policy but are not directly employed by the United States: hospital or welfare administrators, defense contractors, university officials, directors of local community action organizations. The organizations may be not-for-profit corporations such as RAND: mixed public and private corporations such as COMSAT; government-sponsored corporations such as the Federal National Mortgage Association; and government organizations such as the National Science Foundation and the National Institutes of Health that make grants to or contracts with other organizations such as universities and individuals.

These structures are the result of struggles for power and position. Under such euphemisms as "decentralization," "grassroots administration," and "freedom from politics," as Seidman has pointed out, various groups strive to manipulate the structure of the organization so as to maximize their ability to obtain federal funds and minimize federal control over the use of those funds.[2] University scientists, for example, have successfully argued for forms of federal funding that give to scientists maximum discretion how the funds will be used. The scientists sincerely believe that such arrangements promote the public interest. The same can be said of railroads, airline companies, defense contractors, and others who favor organizational forms that will give them maximum support with minimum restraints.

[2]Harold Seidman, *Politics, Position, and Power: The Dynamics of Federal Organization* (Oxford University Press, 1970), pp. 34 ff.

INFORMAL ORGANIZATION

All this elaborate organization of the executive branch gives order and system to administration. It assigns certain functions to certain units, places one official (or sometimes more) at the head of each unit and makes him responsible for its performance, allows both specialization and coordination, permits ready communication, and in general makes our farflung administration somewhat controllable and manageable. But this formal organization can be highly misleading if taken too seriously. The detailed organization chart on the office wall of some administrator may represent hope and intention rather than reality.

Why? Because people differ—in attitude, motive, ability, experience, and political influence. And their very diversity leads to all sorts of complications. Relationships among officials in an agency may be based on influence rather than on formal authority. Leadership may be lodged not at the top but in a variety of places. A certain group of officials may have considerable influence, whereas another group, with the same formal status, may have much less. The loyalties of some officials may cut across the formal aims of the agency.

Consider an imaginary but typical bureau. The bureau chief is an oldline administrator who has served through four presidential administrations. He is cautious and unimaginative. He has a rival in the person of an assistant to the secretary who heads the whole department. Some officials in the bureau look to this assistant for leadership; they share his enthusiasm and support his plans, and they hope that he may take over the department some day and give them the power and position they feel they deserve. But the bureau chief has his own set of motives and attitudes; moreover, he enjoys the backing of a powerful bloc in Congress that will defend him if he is attacked. He has built a personal organization made up of two or three division chiefs, an attorney, the personnel officer, and his own staff, and this personal following is intensely loyal to him.

This, perhaps, is an extreme case, but it shows how informal organization can have a major effect on administration. A subordinate official in an agency might be especially close to his chief simply because they went to the same college or play poker together, or because the subordinate knows how to ingratiate himself with his chief. A staff official may have tremendous influence, not because of his formal authority, but because his experience, fairness, common sense, and general personality lead men to turn to him for advice. In an agency headed by a chief who is weak or unimaginative, a vacuum may develop that encourages others to try to take over. Such informal organization and communication cutting across regular channels is inevitable in any organization, public or private. Even the Army, with all its hierarchy and regimentation, abounds with these elements.

BUILDING AND MANAGING THE TEAM

The government administrator is not nearly so free in building his team as is the private businessman. Government has long followed prescribed methods of recruiting, examining, classifying, promoting, and dismissing personnel. For many years America had a notorious appointment system that was summed up in the slogan "To the victor belong the spoils." When a new party came to power, its leaders and followers felt they had a right to take over desirable government jobs. Parties should have patronage, it was said, to encourage members to work for the party and to answer the people's demand for a new broom to sweep Washington clean. Moreover, some argued that a frequent turnover of officials would keep government democratic. Besides, they said, the duties of public officials were so plain and simple that any intelligent person could perform them.

Later in the nineteenth century a sharp reaction set in against the spoils system. The job of government was becoming increasingly complex, and interested citizens, some of them organized in the National Civil Service Reform League, were agitating for reform. Presidents, too, were chafing under the pressures of hordes of job-seekers. Public opinion crystallized when President James A. Garfield was assassinated in 1881 by a disappointed office-seeker. Two years later Congress passed the Pendleton Act, which set up the beginnings of a merit system under a three-man bipartisan board, the Civil Service Commission. The act placed certain types of employees under a new classified service, which could be entered only by passing a competitive examination. Congress put relatively few employees under the new merit system, but it gave the president power to expand the classified service. As a result of a series of executive orders over the years, about three-quarters of the federal employees today hold jobs that are covered by a merit system and protected from patronage.

© 1958 United Feature Syndicate.

Today the administrator must work closely with the Civil Service Commission in staffing his agency. With about 7,000 employees of its own, the Commission acts as a central agency for recruiting, examining, and appointing government workers. It advertises for new employees, prepares and administers oral and written examinations throughout the country, and makes up a register of names of those who pass the tests. When an agency wishes to employ a person, the Commission certifies to it three names taken from the top of the appropriate register. The administrator has some voice in the type of examination given, and he has some freedom of choice among the three job applicants, but obviously his discretion is greatly limited.

The centralization of personnel direction in the Civil Service Commission disturbs administrators eager for freedom and flexibility in their agency operations. They charge that the Commission is entangled in red tape, uses old-fashioned personnel methods, and lacks initiative and imagination. Certainly the Commission has no monopoly over basic personnel policy. The White House has taken increasing leadership, as noted above, and the departments have some autonomy. But despite its defects, over the years the Civil Service Commission has helped to keep most federal jobs out of the spoils system.[3] Still designed to be nonpartisan, the Commission is composed of three members (no more than two of the same party) with six-year terms.

Hiring is only the first step in building the administrative team. The administrator must place, train, and supervise appointees. Effective administration requires much more than knowledge of the formal legalities and power relationships. In any organization an official endowed with manipulative skills may well be able to dispense almost entirely with coercive sanctions and secure compliance by creating personal relationships and social obligations.

REFORMING THE FEDERAL ADMINISTRATIVE STRUCTURE

The framers of our national Constitution, unlike those of most state constitutions, did not fix into the Constitution the precise structure of the administrative branch. They knew that as conditions in society changed, the federal structure should be altered, and so Congress was given (or at least has taken) the authority to create and abolish federal agencies and to determine their functions.

The process of adapting the federal administrative structure never stops even though it moves at a slow pace. Since the days of President Franklin Roosevelt, every president, operating under limited authority delegated by Congress, has reorganized parts of the executive branch. And every president has appointed a task force or two to recommend how the administrative structure could be made more effective. But most of the recommendations that would upset existing political arrangements and power balances have gone unimplemented.

From the days of FDR, conservatives and business groups have tended to attack big government and Washington bureaucracy as tyrannical and inefficient, whereas liberals and union leaders customarily have argued that the attacks merely screened the desire of business and other conservative groups to escape government regulation.[4] In recent years, however, the attacks on big government have come from all segments of the political spectrum. Liberal reactions to the federal bureaucracy are at best in a state of confusion and reflect a widening gulf in attitudes toward the functions performed by the government. On the one hand, some liberals are now sensitized to the potential threats of big "impersonal" government to personal liberties; on the other hand, they continue to support the basic functions of the "service state," especially when some of these functions fall under attack from a president who advo-

[3]Wallace S. Sayre, ed., *The Federal Government Service*, 2nd ed. (Prentice-Hall, 1965), considers these and related problems. See also John W. Macy, Jr, *Public Service* (Harper & Row, 1971).

[4]For an example of the businessman-managerial consultant critique of big government, see Peter Drucker, *The Age of Discontinuity: Guidelines to Our Changing Society* (Harper & Row, 1969). For a more neutral analysis, see Herbert Kaufman, *The Limits of Organizational Change* (University of Alabama Press, 1971).

cates major cutbacks. Yet, by the early 1970s some liberals as well as most conservatives began to question the effectiveness of large social service bureaucracies in alleviating the conditions of poverty and welfare dependency.[5]

President Nixon once proposed to Congress that it abolish seven departments, primarily those organized to serve particular "clients," and replace them by four new departments organized in terms of general missions (see chart on p. 450). He argued that this restructured federal bureaucracy could provide coherent planning, resolve agency conflicts more sensibly, and deliver governmental services more effectively and efficiently.

Congress did not approve President Nixon's recommendations. For as we have noted, the "shape" of government is not neutral as between conflicting interests. Changing the shape of administration is more than a matter of efficiency and economy; it also involves considerations of policy outcomes. Spokesmen for agriculture, for labor, for business, for education, for housing, and all those who identify with and believe they have access to, if not control over, particular agencies are likely to oppose any reorganization that threatens to break the connections between their group and the agency with which they have been working many years. Furthermore, congressional leaders are not unmindful of the fact that if they restructure federal administration they may have to restructure the congressional system. Powerful congressional committees are now organized to appropriate funds for and supervise existing departments; their power too is threatened by reorganization.

Only if a president is able to capitalize on widespread and intensively felt public dissatisfaction with governmental performance and can put together coalitions of political interests will he be able drastically and quickly to alter the bureaucracy. For the shape of administration is both a cause and a consequence of political realities and public needs.

ADMINISTRATION: THE CLASSICAL MODEL

Early in this century under the banner of the science of public administration many pioneering scholars developed a formal model of administration from which they deduced certain principles: *unity of command*—every officer should have a superior to whom he reports and from whom he takes orders; *chain of command*—there should be a firm line of authority running from the top down and of formal responsibility running from the bottom up; *line and staff*—the staff advises the executive but gives no commands, whereas the line has operating duties; *span of control*—a hierarchical structure should be established so that no one person supervises more agencies directly than he can effectively handle; *decentralization*—administrators should delegate decisions and responsibilities to lower levels.

[5]Alice M. Rivlin, *Systematic Thinking for Social Action* (Brookings Institution, 1971), and Daniel P. Moynihan, *The Politics of a Guaranteed Income* (Random House, 1973).

These classical principles of public administration were thought to promote efficiency and economy, to secure firm control by superiors over subordinates, and, by establishing links between politically accountable policy-makers and administrative agencies, to make administration responsive to the demands of the elected officials.

HOW GOOD IS THE CLASSICAL MODEL?

The classical model remains the most influential ideal for those involved in administration. However, scholars have become increasingly skeptical of the validity of these principles either as guides for practitioners or as models for investigators. As Herbert A. Simon wrote in his highly influential *Administrative Behavior:*

> Administrative description suffers . . . from superficiality, oversimplification, lack of realism. . . . It has refused to undertake the tiresome task of studying the actual allocations of decision-making functions. It has been satisfied to speak of "authority," "centralization," "span of control," "function," without seeking operational definitions of these terms. . . . A fatal defect of the current principles of administration is that, like proverbs, they occur in pairs. For almost every principle one can find an equally plausible and acceptable contradictory principle.[6]

Another and related challenge to this rational approach to decision-making is *incrementalism.* The incrementalists question the idea that people rationally approach problems with definite objectives in mind and with a clear sense of alternative ways of reaching those objectives. Individuals—even public administrators—simply do not know enough about the alternatives, their own goals and values are not clear enough, and the situations they face are too complex for such a broad and "rational" approach, according to this argument. Rather, they are likely to go one step at a time, to feel their way, to cling to one familiar method rather than to consider carefully all the other methods, to attack problems piecemeal, to adjust and compromise with institutions rather than overturn them and reconstruct them. Not only is this the way people *do* act, according to the incrementalists, this so-called "muddling through" approach is the way they *should* act if they wish to go about their affairs in a sensible and effective manner.[7]

PPBS—A NEW TECHNIQUE OR THE OLD POLITICS?

Not all critics of government or students of public administration are happy with the incrementalist view of bureaucratic operations. Some

[6](Macmillan, 1947), p. xiv.

[7]David Braybrooke and Charles E. Lindblom, *A Strategy of Decision* (Free Press, 1963). See also C. E. Lindblom, *The Policy-Making Process* (Prentice-Hall, 1968). Vincent Ostrom, *The Intellectual Crisis in American Public Administration* (University of Alabama Press, 1973).

believe that it attempts to make a virtue out of logrolling, trial-and-error approaches and that it is a mindless way to plan and manage government. Public institutions, they charge, are often wasteful, inefficient, and ineffective, and what is needed is the adoption of modern, businesslike, management techniques. One of the most prominent of these new approaches is known as the Planning, Programming, and Budgeting System, PPBS, which was first introduced in the Department of Defense in 1961 and, as a result of a White House directive, to other civilian agencies in 1965.

Program budgeting is an attempt to require agencies to specify more precisely their several objectives—that is, program goals, or outputs—and then to relate to these objectives the resources that are needed—that is, the inputs. Adherents of PPBS contend that it encourages openness, explicitness, objectivity, the use of empirical data, quantification, and makes it more difficult for bureaucrats to conceal from Congress and the public when the programs they administer are not worth the funds invested in them. Instead of just going to Congress—and the public—and asking for so many millions for personnel and so many to purchase commodities, under PPBS, agencies have to stipulate what they are trying to accomplish and then put a price tag on their requests so that Congress and the public can better decide what they are paying for and what they are getting for their money.

Adherents of PPBS contend that it provides a more systematic way to discuss complex issues by concentrating debate on *what* is right rather than *who* is right.[8] The more sophisticated advocates of PPBS recognize that it is not a substitute for old-fashioned politics, but an addition to them. It "can help focus debate upon matters about which there are real differences of value, where political judgments are necessary. It can suggest superior alternatives, eliminating, or at least minimizing, the number of inferior solutions. Thus, by sharpening the debate, systematic analysis can enormously improve it."[9]

Many remain skeptical of PPBS. They argue that it provides a misleading impression of being "scientific" and that it gives an aura of quantification to what are basically *qualitative* issues. After more than a decade of experience with PPBS, and its milder variant of "management-by-objectives" (MBO) introduced by the Nixon Administration, it has neither introduced a significantly higher level of rational choice-making nor given analytic or systems experts an advantage over the politicians either in Congress or the administration.

[8]For a defense of PPBS, see A. C. Enthoven and K. W. Smith, *How Much is Enough? Shaping the Defense Program, 1961–1969* (Harper & Row, 1971). For a discussion of difficulties in making it work, see F. C. Mosher and J. E. Harr, *Programming Systems and Foreign Affairs Leadership: An Attempted Innovation* (Oxford University Press, 1970).

[9]Charles L. Schultze, *The Politics and Economics of Public Spending* (Brookings Institution, 1968).

Administrators as decision-makers

A police officer stops a student who fails to bring his car to a full halt before crossing a highway. The student admits that he did not come to a full halt, but he argues that he did look both ways before entering the highway. The officer lets him off with a lecture and a warning. Why? The law requires that the student be arrested and pay a fine. But the officer knows that a full halt is not necessary at this particular corner as long as the driver is reasonably careful.

Here is a simple example of administrative discretion and decision-making. The officer is an experienced person of good sense. In this case she exercised two functions basic in the administrative process—she established her own rule and she made a judicial decision. In her own way she was participating in *administrative legislation* and *administrative adjudication.*

To say that bureaucrats make important decisions, however, is not to say that they have unlimited alternatives from which to choose. An administrator may have been given broad discretion by both Congress and the president and yet feel constricted by other forces. He or she must take into account all kinds of complex organizational and psychological relationships. Furthermore, the administrator often must act in a hurry and on the basis of incomplete knowledge. Congress has long realized that as governmental problems become more numerous and complex, important decisions increasingly must be made by administrators. One reason for this is the greater technical sophistication required. The granting of a license to operate a television channel by the FCC or the establishment of fair rates to be charged for electric power by the FPC demand technical training that congressmen could not readily provide. Congress is primarily composed of generalists; the delegation of rule-making authority to commissions permits legislation by specialists.

Furthermore, if Congress passed laws with very precise wording, it would get so bogged down in details that it could never complete its work. For example, assume that Congress is concerned that there be enough truck lines in operation to ensure prompt transportation services for shippers, but not so many as to lead to ruinous competition. If it attempted to specify the exact circumstances under which a new truck line should be licensed, a statute would have to read as follows:

> Keokuk, Iowa, needs four truck lines unless that new superhighway that they have been talking about for ten years gets built. Then they will need five unless, of course, Uncle Charlie's Speedy Express gets rid of its Model T and gets two tractors and vans. Then they will only need three as long as two freight trains a day also stop there.
>
> On the other hand, Smithville, Tennessee, needs eight truck lines unless. . . .[10]

[10]Martin Shapiro, *The Supreme Court and Administrative Agencies* (Free Press, 1968), p. 4.

Of course, Congress does not and cannot write statutes like these. Instead, it declares its policy in general terms, and empowers the Interstate Commerce Commission to license new truck lines when such action would be warranted by "public convenience and necessity." The ICC then judges the situation in Keokuk and Smithville, and makes specific rules.

Another example: Congress by law has recognized the right of employees engaged in organizations impacting on interstate commerce to "organize and bargain collectively through representatives of their own choosing." Such a general provision leads to hundreds of new questions and definitions, such as the nature of unions, the rights of employers, the definition of unfair labor practices, the rights of nonunion employees, the scope of collective bargaining, and so on. And these all-important policies are made by the National Labor Relations Board.

Well over 100 agencies have the power to issue rules and regulations affecting the public. Most of these are the independent regulatory agencies like the Interstate Commerce Commission, which has power to regulate the nation's railroads, or the Federal Communications Commission, which polices the nation's radio and television waves. But Congress has assigned regulatory responsibilities to several executive departments such as Agriculture, which, among other things, issues regulations for the nation's stockyards, and Transportation, which licenses pilots and regulates the air traffic control system.

ADMINISTRATORS AS JUDGES

Administration of all kinds and at all levels must settle disputes or mediate among conflicting claims. The secretary of defense, for example, has to reconcile the demands among the rival services such as the Navy and Air Force. But the independent regulatory agencies bear the main burden of making judicial decisions when disputes arise between two or more private interests or between private interests and the government. Congress has delegated power to regulatory agencies to make such decisions, a power that transforms them into courts, the administrators into judges. They receive complaints, hold hearings, listen to witnesses and lawyers, study briefs, and make decisions, much like any other court.[11]

Much of this judicial business is handled informally, through the voluntary settlement of cases at lower levels in an agency. Informal settlements make life a lot easier in the bureaucratic jumble of Washington. They dispose of disputes relatively quickly and inexpensively, and they take an immense burden off the courts. Moreover, they are handled supposedly by "experts" in technical areas. And yet many persons have expressed concern over the extent of the judicial power vested in

[11]See Victor G. Rosenblum, "How to Get into TV: The Federal Communications Commission and Miami's Channel 10," in Alan F. Westin, ed., *The Uses of Power* (Harcourt Brace Jovanovich, 1962), pp. 173–228.

the agencies as well as the obvious lack of visibility and accountability. They complain that elite-oriented administrators violate due process of law by holding private and informal sessions, by failing to give interested parties an adequate hearing, by basing their decisions on insufficient evidence.[12]

Partly in response to similar complaints there was passed the Administrative Procedures Act of 1946 providing for broader judicial review of administrative decisions. The courts have always had the power to overturn the agency's judgments on points of *law*, as in cases where an agency had exceeded its authority, or misinterpreted the law, or simply been unfair. Under the 1946 act, however, the courts acquired more authority to examine questions of *fact*—that is, to go over the mass of technical evidence examined by the agency. Though this tendency has not gone very far, it points up the problem of maintaining the balance between judicial control and administrative efficiency and expertness. The 1946 law also provided for procedural safeguards, such as more formalized hearings and proper notice of action.

Those who worry about the concentration of judicial power in the agencies usually express the fear that administrators will do too much prosecuting and not enough impartial judging. Yet the opposite tendency may prevail. In some cases regulatory agencies become so occupied with umpiring disputes that they pay insufficient attention to prosecuting offenders. The result of this tendency may be inadequate protection of the very groups these agencies were set up to safeguard.

THE POLITICS OF ADMINISTRATIVE DECISION-MAKING

One of the arguments in favor of delegating policy-making to independent agencies was that railroad rates, the quality of television signals, and the elimination of stock frauds are technical questions to be settled by experts—not politicians. In fact, of course, these issues cannot be isolated from politics. Which one of six competitors should operate a TV station in Miami? Should utility profits be based on the initial investment or on replacement costs? Decisions such as these, which can greatly benefit a corporation or impair the economy of a congressman's district, will inevitably lead to tremendous pressures being exerted on the decision-maker.

One of the most interesting phenomena in the field of independent regulatory agencies is the relationship that has tended to develop between the agency and the industry it is supposed to regulate. The ICC, for example, was set up to check railroad abuses and was initially opposed by the railroads. Today the ICC views itself as the protector of the railroads' interests, and they are its chief supporters.[13] Indeed, it often is

[12]See Joseph C. Goulden, *The Superlawyers* (Weybright & Talley, 1972), Ch. 5. See also Louis K. Kohlmeier, Jr., *The Regulators* (Harper & Row, 1969), and Theodore J. Lowi, *The End of Liberalism* (Norton, 1969).

[13]Peter Woll, *American Bureaucracy* (Norton, 1963), pp. 36–40.

said that commissions in time are captured by the interests they regulate. This is not a question of corruption—though occasionally that does occur—but of excessive interaction between the regulated and the regulator. Federal Communications Commissioners are in constant contact with members of the broadcasting industry—at conventions and conferences and in their day-to-day activities. It would be strange indeed if they were not sympathetically inclined toward the problems of the industry. Also, there is considerable personnel interchange between regulatory bodies and industry. This is not surprising. The agencies require people with technical skills; they find them in industry. Young men in government may look forward to jobs in industry. A House Armed Services Subcommittee investigation revealed that the 100 largest corporations receiving defense contracts employed more than 1,400 former officers, of which 261 were of general or flag rank. General Dynamics, which had the most government contracts when the study was made, employed 187 former officers and was headed by a former secretary of the Army. Presumably these men still maintained close social contacts, at least, with their old comrades-in-arms.[14]

The relationship between a regulatory agency, its clientele industry, and "its" congressional committee is a symbiotic one. The agency does favors for the industry and for the committee and in turn makes demands on them both. The problem with this relationship is that the decision-maker—the regulatory agency—is responsible to very limited and specialized constituencies. The broadcasters have influence with the FCC, but who speaks for the viewing public? Defense industries have highly placed friends in the Pentagon, but who represents the taxpayer? The decentralization of decision-making throughout the bureaucracy is related to the general dispersion of leadership in our political system. Plainly, this serves to benefit some groups at the expense of others.

LIMITATIONS ON ADMINISTRATIVE LAW-MAKING

Despite wide discretion, administrators are not free to make any rules they wish or to decide disputes any way they please. Limitations are of several kinds:

1. The agencies interpret and enforce laws of Congress; if they misinterpret a statute, Congress can always amend it to make its intent clearer. The basic legislative power of Congress compels the agencies to identify the will of Congress and to interpret and apply laws as the congressmen would wish. Congress can also exercise this control through investigations, and especially through appropriations.

2. Congress had closely regulated the procedures to be followed by

[14]Quoted in Jacob, *Policy and Bureaucracy*, p. 178. See Grant McConnell, *Private Power and American Democracy* (Knopf, 1966), for a general discussion of this problem.

regulatory agencies. Under the Administrative Procedures Act of 1946, agencies must publicize their machinery and organization, must give advance information of proposed rules to interested persons, must allow such persons to present information and arguments, must allow parties appearing before the agency to be accompanied by counsel and to cross-examine witnesses.

3. Under certain conditions, final actions of agencies may be appealed to the courts.

4. Other federal agencies place constraints on the administrator's activities, for example, the Office of Management and Budget and the General Accounting Office. In addition to reviewing an agency's budget requests annually in the name of the president, OMB has a management section to review management, organization, and practices on a more or less continuous basis. The GAO conducts postaudits of agency spending, and in recent years has moved into investigations of the effectiveness of alternative programs designed for similar ends. Also, the General Services Administration (GSA), an organization of nearly 40,000 people, sets up procedures for the procurement of supplies, maintains buildings, and supervises construction of federal facilities.

5. Administrators in regulatory agencies, as in all agencies, are surrounded by informal political checks as well as formal ones. They must keep in mind the demands of professional ethics, the advice and criticism of experts, and the attitudes of congressmen, the president, interest groups, political parties, private persons, and so on. In the long run, these safeguards are the most important of all.

PRESSURES AND PROBLEMS

The obligations of a federal executive are many, not the least of these is to understand what is expected by administrative superiors, by fellow professionals, and by the dictates of conscience. Career administrators, even more than their political superiors who generally have short tenures, are in a good position to know when a program is not operating properly and what corrective action is needed. But that career administrators often do not go out of their way to "make things better" is one of the major complaints about bureaucrats.

The problem is that bureaucrats often operate in an environment in which they learn by hard experience that they are more likely to get into trouble by attempting to improve programs than if they just do nothing. In fact, despite the charge of administrative aggressiveness, scholarly investigation indicates that the hardening of administrative arteries is a more likely occurrence.

When administrators are aggressive they probably seek to increase the size and scope of their agency. Often the fiercest battles in Washington are not over principles or programs but over territorial boundaries, personnel cuts, and fringe benefits. "Career officials come naturally to believe that the health of their organization is vital to the nation's security."[15] Administrators become more skillful at building political alliances to protect the integrity of the organization than at building alliances to protect the integrity of the programs the organization is supposed to administer. This is a phenomenon not peculiar to governmental institutions, as faculty and students can often testify to, especially as it concerns other departments and colleges on their campus.

Bureaucrats, like all who work in complex organizations, tend to use the resources at their command on "flashy programs," and to give priority to issues that help focus favorable attention on their activities. We hear much of the Defense Department's efforts "to sell the Pentagon," but except for the sheer size of its efforts it is not exceptional; for organizations, public and private, all work to promote a favorable image.

Organizations, again public and private, also tend to resist change and to resent "outside" direction by the president or other "external" central controls. A bureau chief, whether he works for the government, a large corporation, or a university, is likely to consider the president, whether of the United States, a corporation, or a university, to be an outsider whose authority in matters affecting his or her bureau is always suspect.

ADMINISTRATORS AS ALLIANCE-BUILDERS

Administrators often have more bargaining and political alliance-building skills than the elected and appointed officials to whom they report. In one sense, agency leaders are at the center of action in Washington. Administrative agencies over time come to resemble entrenched pressure groups in that they continually operate to advance *their* interests.

An administrator, like a congressman or a president, works amid a complex set of political pressures. In making a major decision, he must try to anticipate the attitudes of his own subordinates, of his clientele, of experts inside and outside the agency, of other agencies involved in the decision, of the communications media, of the attentive public as a whole, of the party in power and the opposition party, of Congress and the president, perhaps even of foreign governments.

Careerists develop a keen sensitivity to the political pressures playing on their bureaus. The degree to which an administrator becomes an attorney for his or her clientele varies with the policy area, with personality and other circumstances. But many bureau chiefs no longer meekly submit to superiors, if they ever did. If they are not defending some specialized constituency, they are arguing that government should be helping the weak and the underprivileged. Whatever their values, the picture of the bureaucrat as subservient and timid is misleading. Their leverage and importance can be substantial. "Bureaucratic politics rath-

[15]Morton Halperin, "Why Bureaucrats Play Games," *Foreign Policy* (May 1971). See also I. M. Destler, *Presidents, Bureaucrats, and Foreign Policy* (Princeton University Press, 1972).

er than party politics has become the dominant theatre of decision in the modern state."[16]

The bureau chief, then, is at the center of the phenomenon which has been variously described as a "subgovernment," "policy whirlpool" or "cozy little triangle"—the triads linking relevant bureaucrats with key congressional committees and their staff and then their clientele groups.[17] These subgovernments may cut across various federal layers, if intergovernmental transfers of funds are involved.

It is such alliances, made for self-protection and for promotion of mutually advantageous federal programs, that cause much of bureau-

[16]Francis E. Rourke, *Bureaucracy, Politics and Public Policy* (Little, Brown, 1969), p. 153.

[17]See Ernest Griffith, *Congress: Its Contemporary Role*, 3rd ed. (New York University Press, 1961); J. Leiper Freeman, *The Political Process*, rev. ed. (Doubleday, 1965); Douglass Cater, *Power in Washington* (Random House, 1964); and Dorothy James, *The Contemporary Presidency* (Pegasus Books, 1969).

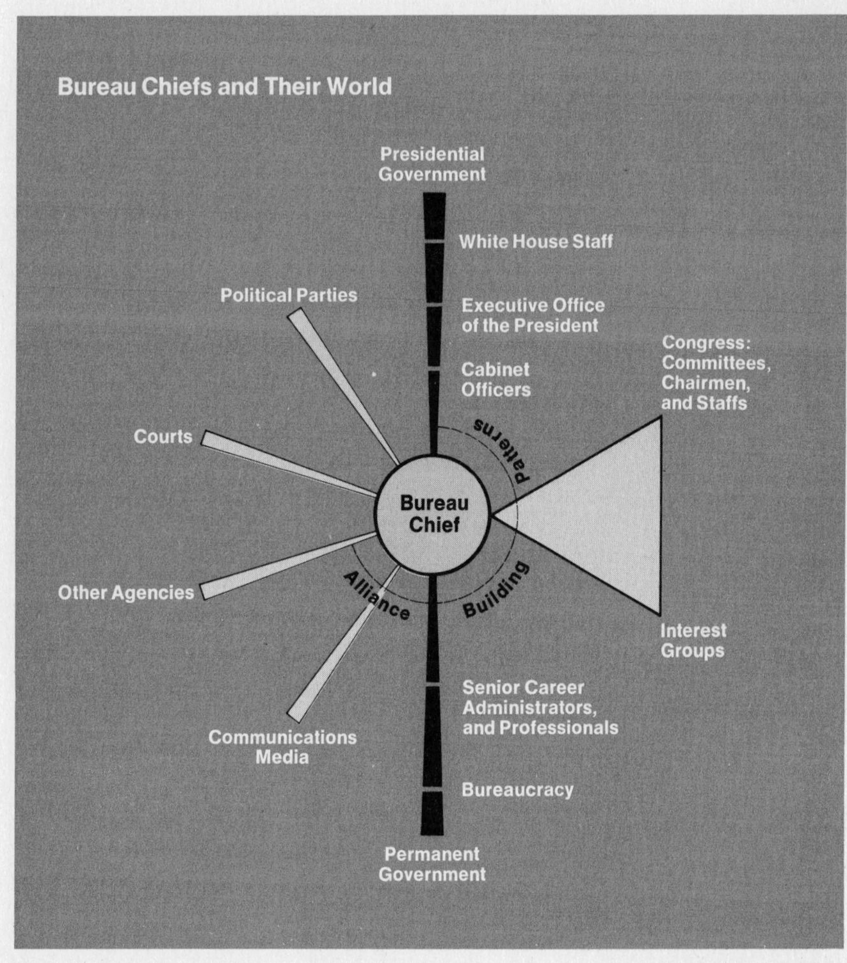

cracy's resistance to change and direction from appointed or elected political "superiors." A bureau chief's loyalty to his agency and programs often competes with loyalty to his administrative superiors. Some people view such external relations as a sort of administrative guerrilla warfare—and as a serious roadblock in the way of fulfilling electoral or party responsibility or of holding elected leaders to account. Others view this as merely an inevitable clash over values in a system that should provide ample opportunities for such clashes. After all, the bureaus themselves are merely one more forum for registering the diverse will that makes up the people's will.

Congressmen are also heavily involved. They pressure and cultivate bureau officials just as special interests nurture close ties with both the Congress and bureau heads. Congressmen have considerable leverage because of their control over agency budgets and the power to approve or deny agency requests for needed legislation. A bureau is especially careful to develop good relationships with the members of the committees handling its legislation and appropriations, as is seen from the following exchanges:

OFFICIAL OF THE FISH AND WILDLIFE SERVICE: Last year at the hearings . . . you were quite interested in the aquarium there [the Senator's state], particularly in view of the centennial coming up. . . .

SENATOR MUNDT: That is right.

OFFICIAL: Rest assured we will try our best to have everything in order for the opening of that centennial.

SUBCOMMITTEE CHAIRMAN: I wrote you gentlemen . . . a polite letter about it . . . and no action was taken. . . . Now, Savannah may be unimportant to the Weather Bureau but it is important to me. . . .

WEATHER BUREAU OFFICIAL: I can almost commit ourselves to seeing to it that the Savannah weather report gets distribution in the northeastern United States [source of tourists for the subcommittee chairman's district].[18]

ADMINISTRATORS AS PROGRAM IMPLEMENTORS

A policy is never completely fixed; almost always it is being defined and redefined as it is being carried out. Everyday in hundreds of ways federal bureaucrats make decisions that affect our jobs, our investments, our lives. Safety officials in the Department of Transportation issue a more stringent set of air-safety regulations in response to airline personnel union demands. FBI officials at the scene decide strategy for handling a hijacker or kidnapper. An admiral resists White House and Defense Department cabinet wishes and remarks: "Now Mr. Secretary,

[18]Quoted in Aaron Wildavsky, *The Politics of the Budgetary Process* (Little, Brown, 1964), pp. 80, 81.

if you and your Deputy will go back to your offices, the Navy will run the blockade."[19] Despite a federal policy against racial discrimination or a presidential order to enforce federal antipollution laws, the biases and prejudices and political values of the federal agents who must administer "the law" will affect what happens to whom, what interests will be promoted, which will be disadvantaged.

Often in American politics those who work to bring about adoption by Congress of a certain policy fail to be concerned with how that policy will be implemented. In fact, "The typical American politician . . . squarely faces conflict only when he must,"[20] and Congress displaces, defers, or delegates conflict wherever possible. Some believe that such a system of decentralizing implementation to bureaucrats and the interest groups to which they respond makes for a system in which policy is most wisely made and enforced. Others decry such a system, as for example, T. J. Lowi who contends that interest-group liberalism, as he calls it, "transforms logrolling from necessary evil to greater good." He would have Congress be more precise in its delegation of authority to bureaucrats.

Whatever might be, the fact is that as our system operates, policy is not firmly made and cleanly implemented at the national level. Local politics intrude. "In the process of adjustment to local interests, purely 'federal' purposes are compromised: ideals expressed at the federal level are revised to suit local realities. Yet the adaptation is not on the federal part alone. Federal action does influence what happens on the local level, with the net result that domestic programs are neither 'federal' nor 'local,' but a blend of the two."[21]

What often happens is that political coalitions work very hard to get a program adopted by Congress, but fail to set clear performance standards or methods by which to evaluate the success of the programs enacted into law. Today there is much talk in Washington about *performance evaluation*. But again as we have seen so often, performance evaluation is not only, or even primarily, a technical problem. It too depends upon political judgments. Whether or not one concludes that programs of compensatory education, urban renewal, welfare programs, or aid to the farmers are great successes or obvious failures, often depends upon differences of values. With regard to most issues that matter, it is a lot easier to determine how much something costs than how much it is worth.

[19]Elie Abel, *The Missile Crisis* (Bantam Books, 1966) p. 156. Also see a useful discussion of this episode and crisis management problems in Graham T. Allison, *Essence of Decision* (Little, Brown, 1971).

[20]Theodore J. Lowi, *The End of Liberalism* (Norton, 1969), p. 76.

[21]Martha Derthick, *New Towns In-Town* (Urban Institute, 1972), pp. 97–98. See also Jeffrey L. Pressman and Aaron Wildavsky, *Implementation: How Great Expectations in Washington Are Dashed in Oakland . . .* (University of California Press, 1973).

Administrators in action: a case study

We have seen the complex of pressures and loyalties amid which a bureaucrat must work. We have seen that an administrator must have some of the qualities of the politician, the law-maker, the judge, the expert, the team quarterback. Day after day he must make decisions involving issues of policy, problems of organization, matters of law—and, above all, people. The following case, based on actual administrative experience, illustrates some of the painful choices a bureaucrat may have to make, whether he is in Washington or in the field.

George Brown is chief of the Bureau of Erosion in the Department of Conservation.[22] He is still in his early forties; his appointment to the post was a result of both his ability and luck. When the old bureau chief retired, the president wanted to bring in a new chief from outside the agency, but influential members of Congress pressed for the selection of a former senator who had represented a farm state. As a compromise, Brown, then a division head, was promoted to bureau chief. A graduate of a Midwestern agricultural college, Brown is a career official in the federal service.

Early in March of Brown's second year in the new post, his boss, the secretary of conservation, summoned him and the other bureau heads to an important conference. The secretary informed the group that he had just attended a cabinet meeting in which the president, in order to fight inflation, had called on each department to effect at least a 10 percent cut in spending in the coming fiscal year. The president, the secretary reported, was convinced that there was a great popular demand for federal fiscal restraint.

Brown quickly calculated what this cutback would mean for his agency. For several years, the Bureau of Erosion had been spending about $90 million a year to help farmers protect their farmland. Could it get along on about $80 million, and where could savings be made? Returning to his office, Brown called a meeting of his personnel, budget, and management officials, and his four division chiefs. After several hours of discussion it was agreed that savings could be effected only by decreasing the scope of the program—which would involve ending the jobs of about 1,200 of the bureau's employees. He asked his subordinates to prepare a list of 20 percent of the employees who were the least useful of the Bureau. He would decide which to drop after checking with the affected congressmen, judging whom he could and could not afford to hurt.

A few weeks later Mr. Brown presented an $80 million budget to Secretary Jones, who approved it and passed it along to the White House. The president then went over the figures in a conference with the director of the Office of Management and Budget, and a few weeks later the White House transmitted the budget for the whole executive de-

[22]The persons and agencies (except for the OMB) in this case are fictitious, but the general facts of the case are drawn from actual happenings in Washington.

partment, incorporating the Erosion Bureau's $80 million, to Congress.

Meanwhile Brown was running into trouble. News of the proposed budget cut had leaked immediately to the personnel in the field. Nobody knew who would be dropped if the cut went through, and some of the abler officials were already looking around for other positions. Morale fell. Hearing of the cut, farmers' representatives in Washington notified local farm organizations throughout the country. Soon Brown began to receive letters asking that certain services be maintained. Members of the farm bloc in Congress were also becoming restless.

Shortly after the president's budget went to Congress, Representative Smith of Colorado asked Brown to see him. Smith was chairman of the Agriculture Subcommittee of the House Appropriations Committee and thus was a potent factor in congressional treatment of the budget. Brown immediately went up to the Hill. Smith began talking in an urgent tone. He said that he had consulted his fellow subcommittee members, both Democratic and Republican, and they all agreed that the Erosion Bureau's cut must not go through. The farmers needed the usual $90 million and even more. They would practically rise up in arms if the program were reduced. Members of Congress from agricultural areas, Smith went on, were under tremendous pressure. Leaders of farm groups in Washington were mobilizing the farmers everywhere. Besides, Smith said, the president was unfair in cracking down on the farm program; he did not understand agricultural problems, and he failed to understand that programs designed to increase agricultural output were the best way to fight inflation. Besides, the cuts in federal programs should be made elsewhere.

Then Smith came to the point. Brown, he said, must vigorously oppose the budget cut. Hearings on appropriations would commence in a few days and Brown as bureau chief would of course testify. At that time he must state that the cut would hurt the bureau and undermine its whole program. Brown would not have to volunteer this statement, Smith said, but just respond to leading questions put by the congressmen. Brown's testimony, he felt sure, would help clinch the argument against the cut because congressmen would respect the judgment of the administrator closest to the problem.

Smith informed Brown that other bureaucrats were fighting to save their appropriations. Obviously, said Smith, they are counting on public reaction to get them an exemption from the 10 percent cutback. Brown would be foolish not to do the same.

Brown returned to his office in a state of indecision. He was in an embarrassing position. He had submitted his estimates to the secretary of conservation and to the president, and it was his duty to back them up. An unwritten rule demanded, moreover, that agency heads defend budget estimates submitted to Congress, whatever their personal feelings might be. The president had appointed him to his position, he reflected, and had a right to expect loyalty. On the other hand, he was on the spot with his own agency. The employees all expected their chief to look out for them. Brown had developed happy relations with "the field," and he squirmed at the thought of having to let more than a thousand employees go. What would they think when they heard him defend the cut? More important, he wanted to maintain friendly relations with the farmers, the farm organizations, and the farm bloc in Congress. Finally, Brown was committed to his program. He grasped its true importance, whereas the president's budget advisers were less likely to understand it. And he knew that his pet project—to aid rural poverty areas in Appalachia, a program he had nurtured for several years—would be most likely to be sacrificed because it was not supported by a powerful constituency.

Brown turned for advice to an old friend in the Office of Management and Budget. This friend urged him to defend the president's budget. He appealed to Brown's professional pride as an administrator and career servant, reminding him that every student of administration agreed that the chief executive must have central control of the budget and that agency heads must subordinate their own interests to the executive program. He argued that the only way to stop inflation would be for all agencies to make program cuts. As for the employees to be dropped—well, that was part of the game. A lot of them could get jobs in defense agencies; civil service would protect their status. Anyway, they would understand Brown's position. In a parting shot he mentioned that the president had Brown in mind for bigger things.

The next day Brown had lunch with the senator, wise and experienced in Washington ways, who had helped him get his start in the government. The senator was sympathetic. He understood Brown's perplexity, for many similar cases had arisen in the past. But there was no doubt about what Brown should do, the senator said. He should follow Representative Smith's plan, of course being as diplomatic as possible about it. This way he would protect his position with those who would be most important in the long run.

"After all," the senator said, "Presidents come and go, parties rise and fall, but Smith and those other congressmen will be here a long time, and so will these farm organizations. They can do a lot for you in future years. And remember one other thing—these people are elected representatives of the people. Constitutionally, Congress has the power to spend money as it sees fit. Why should you object if they want to spend an extra few million?"

Leaving the Senate Office Building, Brown realized that his dilemma was deeper than ever. The arguments on both sides were persuasive. He felt hopelessly divided in his loyalties and responsibilities. The president expected one thing of him. Congress (he was sure Smith reflected widespread feeling on Capitol Hill) expected another. As a career man and professional administrator, he sided with the president; as head of an agency, however, he wanted to protect his team. His future? Whatever decision he made, he was bound to alienate important people and interests. There was no way to compromise, because he would have to face a group of astute congressmen.

It was Brown's realization that the arguments in a sense canceled one another out that in the end helped him to make his decision. For he decided finally that the issue involved more than loyalties, ambitions, and programs. Ultimately it boiled down to two questions. First, to whom was he, Brown, legally and administratively responsible? Formally, of course, to the chief executive who appointed him and who was accountable to the people for the actions of the administration. And second, which course of action did he, Brown, feel was better for the welfare of all the people? Looking at the question this way, he felt the president was right in asking for fiscal restraint. As a taxpayer and consumer himself, Brown knew of the strong sentiment for doing something about inflation. To be sure, Congress must make the final decision. But to make the decision, Brown reflected, Congress had to know the attitude of the administration, and the administration should speak with one voice for the majority of the people or it should not be speaking out at all. With mixed feelings, Brown decided to support the president. Being a seasoned alliance-builder, however, he hedged his bets somewhat. He came out strongly for the president's budgets, but at the very same time he sent to friendly congressmen some questions to be asked of himself in future hearings, so that he might be able to give some hint of the impact of the cutbacks.

Who controls the bureaucrats?

The case study we have just considered leads to three important generalizations:

1. Bureaucrats are people, not robots, and as people they are subject to many influences.

2. Bureaucrats do not respond merely to orders from the top but to a variety of motives stemming from their own personalities, formal and informal organization and communication, their political attitudes, their educational and professional background, and the political context in which they operate.

3. Bureaucrats are important in government. Some of them have tremendous discretion and make decisions of great significance—and the cumulative effect of all their policies and actions on our daily lives is enormous.

Put these factors together and a crucial question arises. To which people should the bureaucrats be held accountable—the majority who elected the president, the majority as reflected by the Congress, the organized interests?

CHAINS OF COMMAND

An important, but by no means the only, school of thought is that the

Former Attorney General William Saxbe (right) is shown here with FBI Director Clarence Kelley (center) and former Special Prosecutor Leon Jaworski (left). All three served as Justice Department officials under Nixon and Ford.

president should be placed unequivocally in charge, for he is responsive to the broadest constituency. The presidential office, it is argued, must see that popular needs and expectations are converted into administrative action. If the nation votes for a conservative president who favors restricted intervention in the economy by federal agencies, that policy can be effected only if the bureaucracy responds to presidential direction. Or if the electorate chooses a president who favors a more vigorous regulation of business, the majority's wishes can be translated into action only if the bureaucrats support the presidential policies.

Yet as we have seen over and over again, under the American system of constitutional checks and political balances a single political majority winning a presidential election does not acquire control of the national government, not even the executive branch itself. For under our Constitution the president is not the undisputed master of the executive structure. Congress too has its say and wishes to keep it. Congress sets up the agencies, broadly determines their organization, provides money, and establishes the ground rules. Congress constantly reviews the activities of the bureaucrats by appropriations hearings, special investigations, or informal inquiry. And as we have seen, the Senate helps choose the people who run the agencies. Then, too, a presidential "mandate" is hard to apply directly to specialized issues—such as the fate of the Bureau of Erosion programs cited in the preceding case study.

Moreover, it is not Congress as a whole that shares the direction of the executive structure with the president. More accurately, it is the individual congressmen to whom Congress has delegated its authority. These men, primarily chairmen of committees, usually specialize in the appropriations and policies of a particular group of agencies—often the agencies serving constituents in the congressmen's own districts. But some legislators stake out a claim over more general policies; the late Congressmen Carl Vinson, for example, made the Navy Department his specialty. Congressmen, who see presidents come and go, come to feel that they know more about agencies than does the president (and often they do). Although Congress as an institution may prefer to have the president in charge of the executive branch so they can hold him responsible for its operation, the senior congressional leaders often prefer to seal off the agencies from presidential direction in order to maintain their own influence over public policy. Sometimes this is institutionalized—the Army Chief of Engineers, for example, is given authority by law to plan public works and report to Congress without referring to the president.

As we have seen, Congress has deliberately decided that the independent regulatory agencies should not be responsive to the president's control. Because these agencies make rules and decide disputes, Congress wants them to be arms of the Congress. So in addition to making these commissions multiple in membership, Congress has given their commissioners long and staggered terms. Although the president fills vacancies with the consent of the Senate, Congress has restricted his right to remove the members of these quasi-legislative, quasi-judicial agencies. The Supreme Court, in *Humphrey's Executor v. United States* (1935), upheld the right of Congress to do so and subsequently went further (*Wiener v. United States,* 1958) to rule that the president lacks any power to remove the officers of such agencies unless Congress has specifically authorized him to do so.

Important as these institutional breaks in the president's chain of command are, they are only part of the picture. In addition, *political* checks block the president. Some of the agencies have so much support among interest groups and Congress that a president would hesitate to move against them. The Federal Bureau of Investigation, for example, and the so-called clientele agencies such as the Rural Electrification Administration or the Veterans Administration have powerful backing.

Another and very important factor limits the extent of presidential control. Every day thousands of bureaucrats are involved in making thousands of decisions. The president has limited time, limited resources, and limited political influence to expend. He and his staff can become involved only in matters of significant political interest. Congressmen can operate in areas far from the presidential spotlight.

What of the bureaucrat? He is not merely an innocent bystander, but there are those who think he should be. They believe that federal administrative employees—at least those in the lower ranks—should be neutral in partisan politics. They are fearful that the party in power will use the federal civil service to perpetuate itself at election times. Not only has the federal civil service largely overcome the patronage system, but the Hatch Acts of 1939 and 1940, whose constitutionality was reaffirmed by the Supreme Court in 1973 *(United States Civil Service Commission v. National Association of Letter Carriers)*, extend the idea of neutrality by forbidding federal civil servants "to take any active part in political management or political campaigns." Moreover, the Lloyd-LaFollette Act, which was upheld by the Supreme Court in 1974 *(Arnett v. Wayne Kennedy, et al.)*, permits a federal civil servant to be dismissed if he makes statements in his official capacity of such a critical nature about his agency that it endangers its operations. Even stricter rules prohibit military personnel from involvement in political party matters.

The aim of all this legislation and regulation is to prevent the building of gigantic political machines controlled by federal office-holders. It is also to protect career public servants against having to donate money to parties or candidates in order to retain their jobs. They may discuss politics in private and may vote, but they cannot engage in open, active, obviously partisan action. Despite some criticism that it is unwise to isolate millions of people from politics, and despite the conviction of some that it is unfair, perhaps even unconstitutional, to deny public employees the same political freedoms as anyone else, the neutralization of the civil service in political party battles seems to be a fixed feature of the operations of the national government. (The Hatch Act also applies to most state government employees whose salaries are paid even in part with federal funds. Now that residents of the District of Columbia have a measure of home rule, Congress has had to exempt federal employees who are candidates for local office within the District from compliance with the Hatch Act.)

The neutralization of the civil service from partisan politics does not mean, however, that federal bureaucrats are neutralized from issue politics, nor does it mean that they are passive recipients of orders from above which they carry out independent of their own views.

SOME ALTERNATIVES

To many people the federal administrative structure seems to be a self-defeating morass of contradictions; a many-splintered thing with field officers unable or afraid to make decisions; of agencies not only unable to work together but fighting with one other. Sometimes it seems virtually no one, anywhere, can establish priorities and exert leadership over the diverse executive departments.

The president is often looked to to serve as a counterweight to the otherwise powerful centrifugal forces within the executive bureaucracy. But as we have seen, this is more of a wish than an actual accomplishment. And presidential direction also presupposes that a president knows what he wants. Again, often as not, we are faced with a political rather than a technical problem. The same confusion and conflict within the country over values, ends, and priorities are likely to be reflected within the bureaucracy.

Blaming bureaucracy and damning bureaucrats for our troubles, an increasingly fashionable pastime, is not likely to make for more effective or responsive administration. Reforming the bureaucracy and the bureaucrats, another fashionable pastime, has led to a variety of proposals. Two deserve mention.

Some propose that we develop, along the English pattern, an *independent senior civil service* of career officials who would be moved from agency to agency in order to ensure that they develop no strong attachments to any particular agency but rather develop a more comprehen-

Career military. From left: Chairman of the Joint Chiefs of Staff, General George S. Brown; Air Force Chief of Staff, General David C. Jones; and chief of Naval Operations, Admiral James L. Holloway.

sive view of the world. We have made some progress in this direction. But more than half of the senior civil servants serve most of their careers within one agency or bureau. Specialization is, of course, vital to modern organization. But, it is contended, rotation would be a freshening device. It might loosen up stiffened joints, bring new blood to agencies, encourage a sense of breadth rather than fixed routines. It might even break alliances among senior civil servants and outside client groups. "A profession of public administration, as distinct from a career within a specific agency, is vital to the proper centralization of a democratic administrative process."[23] But before congressmen or presidents are likely to give much support to establishing an independent corps of civil servants, they will want a clear perception of what the consequences of the creation of such a group might do to the power structures of our political system.

A second proposal goes to the very heart of the democratic process. It is concerned not with making bureaucrats more effective, but ensuring that they are responsive to the electorate. The emphasis is upon *strengthening* the *political parties* as devices to link what the electorate wants done with what the federal administrative agencies do. As V. O. Key noted,

> The problem of bureaucracy is in part not a problem of bureaucracy at all. It is rather a question of attracting into party service an adequate supply of men competent to manage and control the bureaucracy from their posts as the transient but responsible heads of departments and agencies. . . . It is through such persons who owe their posts to the victorious party that popular control over government is maintained.[24]

In summary, the role of the bureaucrats in the American system of government is not to be determined merely by structural alterations. For the system of command will always end not just in the White House, but in many places on Capitol Hill, and in the offices of various interest groups in Washington. The executive and legislative branches have conflicting claims, including those of the bureaucrats themselves, each insisting that the administrator act "in the public interest" but each with a different definition of that interest. *Defining the public interest* is the crucial problem.

[23]Lowi, *End of Liberalism*, p. 304.

[24]V. O. Key, Jr. *Politics, Parties and Pressure Groups*, 5th ed. (Crowell, 1964), pp. 711–12.

Chapter 18 Making policy: conflict and cooperation

George Bernard Shaw once suggested that progress comes about because unreasonable people dream dreams of a different kind of world. Reasonable people, he observed, would adjust themselves to reality. But unreasonable people try to adjust the world or adapt the world to themselves. Thus when progress does come about it is often due to the efforts of these unreasonable or often disagreeable people. Shaw may be right. Yet there is more to making policy than just the presence of stubborn people, however important they may be. Policy is made in a variety of contexts. And the world of Washington policy-making is comprised of all kinds of people—reasonable and unreasonable, complacent and outraged. The patterns of conflict and cooperation among them are the subject of this chapter.

Policy-making in America is neither simple nor tidy. There is no recipe book for resolving political disputes, no standard way to settle conflicting claims. As previous chapters suggest, our government is not a "top down" structure of authority. Rather ours is a system of dispersed powers, shared *across* branches and *among* various levels of government. All the branches and all the levels participate in making policy. To achieve significant changes in policy often requires sustained cooperation among a rather large number of public officials. Hence when a new issue arises and policy changes are needed, politicians, bureaucrats, and concerned activists in a variety of settings must negotiate with one another. *Policy* politics is the activity, usually involving negotiation, argument, persuasion, bargaining, and sometimes even the use of force, by which an issue is defined, agitated, or settled.

Who are the nation's policy-makers? How do they acquire the positions and skills needed to influence the making of public policy? How do new issues get placed on the public agenda? And what are some of the major characteristics of our policy formulation, enactment, and execution processes?

We have just examined in the last several chapters the major institutions for national policy-making. To understand how policy is made, however, we need to understand how these institutions interact with one another: sometimes embroiled in heated battles over what should be done, sometimes engaged in cooperative bargaining to reach a mutually agreeable compromise. To discuss the strengths or weaknesses of any one institution as a policy-maker in a compartmentalized way, without constant reference to the other participants in the larger political system, is to ignore the dynamics and realities of our highly interdependent processes of national leadership.

Policy-makers: elected, appointed, and self-designated

Other things being equal, elected officials usually are more influential in making policy than the nonelected. Other things, however, are not always equal. Exceptions to this rule are many. Supreme Court justices and hundreds of presidential appointees, for example, can be very influential in making certain policies. So also there are hundreds of staff aides, expert advisors, Washington reporters, lobbyists, and self-appointed agents for all kinds of causes who often exercise considerable influence over particular public policies. They are important either because they hold key positions or they possess critically needed skills and resources. How do such people gain entry to what some have termed "the governing class"?

The Senate and the president often struggle over control of the top personnel in the executive and judicial branches. The Constitution leaves the question somewhat ambiguous, stating that "The President . . . shall nominate, and by and with the Advice and Consent of the Senate, shall appoint Ambassadors, other public Ministers and Consuls, Judges of the Supreme Court, all other officers of the United States. . . ." However, presidents have never enjoyed full control over hiring and firing in the executive branch. The Senate jealously guards its right to confirm or reject major appointments; and during the period of congressional government after the Civil War, presidents had to struggle to keep their power to appoint and dismiss. In recent years presidents have gained more control of personnel, in part because organizational experts have warned that the chief executive cannot really be held accountable unless he can hire the top policy-making executives he wants.

SENATORIAL COURTESY

There is one area, however, where the Senate remains on top: if the president wants to appoint a person to serve in a state, unless he has the approval of the senator or senators from that state who are members of the president's political party, his nominations are likely to come to naught, especially if his party controls the Senate. This is known as the practice of *senatorial courtesy*—the unwillingness of the Senate to confirm any person "personally obnoxious," that is, politically objectionable—to the senator or senators from the state if they are of the same party as the president. A president whose appointees are looked upon with disfavor by the senators of the state in which they are to serve, regardless of party, is likely to have trouble, but senatorial courtesy is seldom so rigidly applied that it requires a president to consult with members of the other party in making his nominations.

A curious consequence of the rule of senatorial courtesy is that President Eisenhower was able to appoint federal district judges in the South more liberal in their views on civil rights than was President Kennedy. Kennedy had to clear his appointments with Democratic senators from the Southern states: Republican Ike seldom had Republican senators to deal with.

THE POLITICS OF CONFIRMATION

Related to senatorial courtesy but not to be confused with it, is the ordinary practice of a president to consult widely before making key appointments. After all, presidents and senators have to do business with each other. No president likes to offend a powerful senator, and he will not want to push through someone if it costs too much political goodwill. In some circumstances where the president needs all the support that he can get, for example as did Nixon in 1974 when impeachment was threatened, he will often make no appointments that will offend key senators. Thus, in 1974, President Nixon withdrew a nomination of a person as assistant secretary of Defense in order to avoid offending Senator Goldwater.

Each year the Senate receives more than 65,000 appointments and confirms 99 percent of them; most of them are routine military promotions in the officer ranks, or appointments to civilian positions such as the foreign service corps and United States attorneys. The Senate concentrates its attention on the approximately 500 major nominations to key policy positions.

The Senate is not bashful. Historically, it has refused to approve one out of five presidential nominations to the Supreme Court. Most were in the last century, but in recent times Senate confirmation hearings toppled the appointment of Justice Fortas to Chief Justice and turned back two Nixon appointees. The Senate tends to defer to the president on cabinet nominations, although even here it has rejected a few.

When a president faces a Senate controlled by members of the opposition party, he is likely to have even more trouble in securing confirmation of his choices. President Nixon's batting average was especially bad: the Senate rejected two of his choices for the Supreme Court, one FBI Director nominee, an assistant secretary of state nominee, and several to regulatory commissions.

Perhaps the severest blow to presidential authority to appoint came with the adoption by Congress, over Nixon's objection, of the requirement that henceforth future directors and deputy directors of the Office of Management and Budget be confirmed by the Senate, positions previously thought to be of such a special relationship to the president that no Senate confirmation was required.

The struggle over who shall be appointed is just the beginning of the contest to win the allegiance of the top appointees. Even when a president gets his first choice approved, he can never underestimate the immediate pushing and shoving that will tempt his appointee to adopt contrary policy views. Every president has believed that at least a few members even of his own cabinet have "sold out" to clientele or special congressional views.

Placing new issues on the public agenda

Who sets the agenda for national policy-making? Policy is certainly not formulated in a vacuum. Organized interests representing varied points of view press their claims and counterclaims. Some groups and people clearly enjoy more access, more opportunities to get their cases heard, and more possibilities for vetoing measures that would hurt their interests. Still, why some issues become prominent national controversies and others do not is unpredictable.

Some issues are given considerable attention, others are slow to win it, and still others seem victims of involuntary neglect. Some critics hold that, "The most significant fact about the distribution of power in America is not who makes such decisions as are made, but rather how many matters of the greatest social importance are not the objects of anyone's decision at all."[1] That is, matters of great importance to many people do not get on the public agenda.

[1]Robert Paul Wolff, *The Poverty of Liberalism* (Beacon Press, 1968), p. 118. See also M. A. Crenson, *The Un-Politics of Air Pollution* (Johns Hopkins Press, 1971); and Peter Bachrach and Morton S. Baratz, "Decisions and Nondecisions: An Analytical Framework," *American Political Science Review* (September 1963), pp. 632–42. See too Jack L. Walker, "The Diffusion of Knowledge and Policy Change: Toward a Theory of Agenda Setting," Paper delivered at the 1974 annual meeting of the American Political Science Association.

Whether government is inactive in some area, however, does not mean it is without a policy in that area. Unconscious or implicit though it may seem, *this is still a policy.* Inattention to issues and the avoidance of conflict can be as important as decisive governmental action. Indifference to racial or sexual discrimination clearly was policy—very important policy for those affected by it.

A former Nixon domestic counsellor, Daniel P. Moynihan, once called for a policy of "benign neglect" toward minority problems, not, apparently, because he was indifferent to racial discrimination but rather because he felt that less governmental assertiveness was a better way to handle problems of racial discrimination. Hence, we must distinguish between the instances when there is a plain lack of national attention to certain problems and those when the indifference is the result of a policy decision, but the issue in question commands national attention. Thus in the South for many decades the government did nothing about racial segregation, but the policy most surely received plenty of attention. Still, everything has political consequences, including doing nothing.

still a policy

no policy is a policy

SHARED POLICY-MAKING LEADERSHIP

Inaction by other policy-makers often forces an issue to another part of the political system. All three branches of the national government as well as the bureaucracy, media, and interest groups seem to take turns initiating public policy changes.

The Supreme Court's *Brown v. Board of Education* (1954) is a classic example of a landmark civil rights and education policy decision with reverberating implications for the other components of the political system. This same court decision was itself the result, not so incidentally, of a variety of economic, social, and political changes in the country, and it in turn triggered actions and reactions that ricocheted back on the Court.

Groups pressing for policy changes will seek to exert their influence where they are most likely to succeed. If you have large sums of money to contribute to a political campaign, you are more likely to have influence with Congress and the presidency than with the courts. If you lack funds and a large political base, you may find it more effective to resort to litigation. The NAACP, for example, has instituted and won numerous cases in its long-term efforts to improve the legal protection of blacks.

One of the virtues of our system's influence dispersion and separation of powers is that when things get clogged in one part of the system, a safety valve can often be found elsewhere in the system. The safety valve is sometimes found in the courts, sometimes in a president, sometimes in the administrative agencies. In practice then, interests, groups, and individuals will seek to exploit the system and exert pressures on the branch most favorable to them. Ordinarily farmers repair to the Senate, trade union leaders to the White House. In recent years blacks have gone to the courts, and "public interest" groups have discovered the administrative and regulatory agencies. Ralph Nader, for example, was able to exert considerable pressure on the FTC.

Just as Congress delegates extensive legislative power to the president, so he delegates policy-making power to hosts of administrators down the line. Obviously, a secretary of state can have a distinct influence on policy, as do other department heads and bureau, division, and section chiefs. In a sense, there is no level in the administrative hierarchy at which discretion ends. At any time the most routine matter may be called to the public's attention, perhaps by a newspaper columnist or a congressman. Then the matter will be pulled out of the lower echelon and given consideration by a bureau or department chief—perhaps even by the White House.

In short, there are thousands of people throughout the government (and millions more such as editors, lobbyists, and ordinary citizens, outside) who exert direct pressure on legislators, legislation, and policy. Control of legislation cannot be diagramed neatly—with Congress on top, the president in the middle, and a pyramid of department, bureau, and division heads below. Rather, it is a *circular* system, with president and congressmen cooperating on some matters, fighting over others, and both influencing—and being influenced by—the administrators throughout the government and political forces outside.

Thus, the president shares his policy-making power not only with Congress but also with administrators in the executive branch that he himself heads. The extent to which he wields legislative power turns not only on his formal constitutional position and powers but also on his political position and powers. His political powers turn on many factors. How effective is he in appealing to the public? How good is his timing? How active and articulate are his lieutenants—his cabinet members and key agency heads? How close are his relations with congressional leaders? Can he mobilize public opinion? Does his influence reach into states and districts throughout the country? Does his party control Congress? Is the country in a depression? A time of prosperity?

Obviously a president's power turns to a great extent on his public prestige and standing. But in the daily task of getting things done in Washington, his effectiveness turns also on his professional reputation in a city peopled by thousands of expert politicians. Because the president's power, and his employment of it, is customarily the most impor-

President Eisenhower (left) talking with Secretary of State Dulles (center) and Assistant Secretary of State Holland (right). Key decisions are often made in small groups such as these, drawn from different levels in the bureaucracy.

tant single influence in Washington, these professionals must watch him closely. Does he carry through on his promises? Does he reward those who help him and punish—or at least withhold favors from—those who do not? How well does he bargain with other power centers? To what extent, in short, is he on top of the struggle for power, or submerged in it, or remote from it? The president's political skill and his political power are interrelated; Washington politicians must anticipate as best they can his ability and will to make the most of the bargaining advantages he has. Out of what others think of him and his power emerge his opportunities for influence with them.[2]

The role of the Washington lobbyists

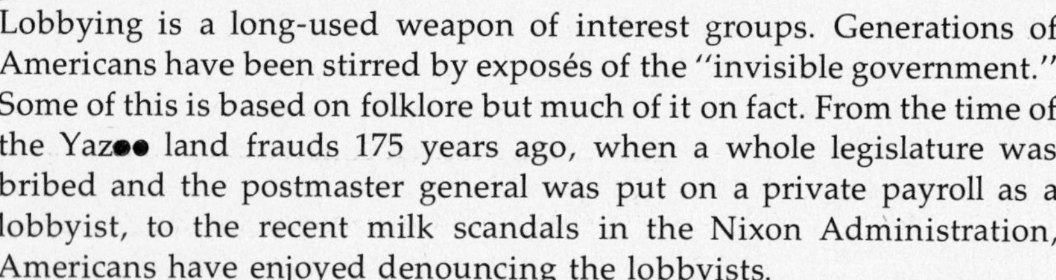

Lobbying is a long-used weapon of interest groups. Generations of Americans have been stirred by exposés of the "invisible government." Some of this is based on folklore but much of it on fact. From the time of the Yazoo land frauds 175 years ago, when a whole legislature was bribed and the postmaster general was put on a private payroll as a lobbyist, to the recent milk scandals in the Nixon Administration, Americans have enjoyed denouncing the lobbyists.

Thousands of lobbyists are active in Washington today, but few of them are glamorous, unscrupulous, or very powerful. Most of the organizations maintaining lobbyists are highly specialized such as the National Fertilizer Association, Retired Officers Association, American Federation of Scientists, and Institute of Shortening and Edible Oils. Lobbyists for these associations are often hard-working attorneys, with long experience in Washington ways; their job is to watch a handful of bills and to keep in touch with a few administrative officials. Because law-making today is a highly technical matter, these lobbyists—or legislative counsels, as they like to be called—play a useful part in modern government. The harried congressman or administrator, threading his way through mountains of paper and seeking to appease conflicting interests, gladly turns to them for their views and information.[3]

Lobbyists for well-financed economic interests operate on a loftier scale. Their specialty is knowing just how to throw their political weight around. These lobbyists are better known throughout the country than some congressmen, better paid, better staffed, and more secure in their position. The groups they represent have such broad interests that lobbyists must watch a wide variety of bills touching every phase of government. They are expert in raising such a clamor that they seem to be speaking for vast numbers of people. They exert pressure in Con-

[2]Richard E. Neustadt, *Presidential Power* (Signet Books, 1964), Ch. 3.

[3]On lobbying as a communication process, see Lester W. Milbrath, *The Washington Lobbyists* (Rand McNally, 1963). Also see L. Harmon Zeigler and G. Wayne Peak, *Interest Groups in American Society*, 2nd ed. (Prentice-Hall, Inc., 1972); and Lewis A. Dexter, *How Organizations are Represented in Washington* (Bobbs-Merrill Company, Inc., 1969).

gress wherever they can find vulnerable points—regular committees, appropriations committees, individual legislators, even on the floor of the House and Senate. They know how to mobilize their organizations back home to send a storm of letters, telegrams, and petitions down on Washington. They know how to draw up laws, to testify before committees, to help speed a bill through its long legislative journey, or to slow it down. They are experts in the art of influence. They also have the money to contract out some of their work to those Washington law firms that specialize in highly refined technical matters.

The Tobacco Institute, Inc., a lobbying-public relations organization formed in 1958, is an example of how an important economic industry organizes to combat government regulation.[4] The Institute is comprised of fourteen of the leading tobacco producers. Presidents of the major tobacco companies sit on its board; and it is financed by these companies, who contribute according to their share of the market (a practice that is widespread).

The Tobacco Institute's major efforts have been to overturn, modify, and delay government warnings to the public about the hazards of smoking. Led by retired congressmen, it has battled, often successfully, to weaken stricter regulations that would ban cigarette sales. And it continues to battle against more stringent regulation of cigarette usage. It hires top Washington lawyers and contracts work to noted public relations firms. It also hires its own experts to conduct studies that often run counter to reports put out by the government.

An advanced form of persuasion today is cooperative lobbying. A number of "specialized" organizations form a "peak" association to press for legislation—or to block it—in a general policy area. The Food Group, for example, a twenty-five-year-old informal conference group in Washington, represents more than sixty business associations such as the National Canning Association and the International Association of Ice Cream Manufacturers and works closely with the National Association of Manufacturers and the National Farm Bureau Federation. This group spawned an Information Committee on Federal Food Regulations to fight truth-in-packaging legislation. Sixty food groups would seem to be a pretty formidable coalition, but a study of cooperative lobbying indicates the frustrations as well as the opportunities involved in cooperation. The various specialized organizations differed over priorities, with the result that strong and unified pressure on Congress and the government agencies was often hard to achieve.[5]

THE WASHINGTON "SUPERLAWYERS"

Lobbying, loosely defined, is any intentional effort to influence legislation. But the Washington law firms that specialize in selling influence

[4]See the useful case history, A. Lee Fritschler, *Smoking and Politics: Policymaking and the Federal Bureaucracy* (Appleton-Century-Crofts, 1969).

[5]Donald R. Hall, *Cooperative Lobbying—The Power of Pressure* (University of Arizona Press, 1969).

and insight concern themselves with all kinds of government activity besides legislation. Their clients want early warnings about government action that might weaken their economic position. They also want any information that can improve their tax circumstances, win federal licenses or contracts, lessen troublesome federal regulation.

There are thousands of Washington lawyers who specialize in helping clients to advance their interest before various agencies of the federal government. They are generally well educated, well connected, and well heeled. The successful ones work very hard and are very sought after. Much of what they do is not easily recognized as practicing law. Sometimes they serve as political science instructors, educating their clients about how a bill becomes a law, about the politics of regulatory commissions, or about the significance of White House executive orders and budgetary priorities. Often, too, they merely stay in touch with their friends who work in key government positions. Said one prominent lobbyist who serves Wall Street interests:

> You can't practice securities law from your desk in New York. You must get down to Washington at least once a week. . . . I'll go see a Commissioner even when I don't have anything specific to talk about. Hell, you can't let them forget who you are, because the time may come when you want to get a message across in a hurry. And I'm not talking about "fixing" any proceedings, either, so don't get any wrong ideas. But there are times in a securities practice when you want to get something through the Commission in a hurry, and, my boy, that's when you'd better have close acquaintances. And I don't mean any GS-13 staff attorney, either; I mean a mover.[6]

"Public interest" groups

The American people are organized in all kinds of ways, by occupation, by nationality, by race, by ethnic origin, by hobby. There is an organization speaking for almost everything and everybody. All organizations, of course, insist that what they want is in the public interest and that they are representing "the people," or at least what is in the people's interest.

Washington has also long seen so-called "public interest" groups, groups speaking for no particular economic class, no particular occupation. The League of Women Voters, the Americans for Democratic Action, the Poor People's Lobby, are examples of such groups. In recent years Ralph Nader, Common Cause, the Environmental Defense Fund, and Friends of the Earth have popularized the public interest lobby and have often resorted to litigation. They turn to the lawsuit in part because they lack a mass base and because they feel underrepresented in state and national legislatures.

[6]Quoted in Joseph C. Goulden, *The Superlawyers: The Small and Powerful World of the Giant Washington Law Firms* (Weybright and Talley, 1972), p. 8.

"*That* ought to satisfy Ralph Nader!"

Drawing by Ed Fisher; © 1970 The New Yorker Magazine, Inc.

Groups also gain a forum for presenting their points of view by seeking permission to file *amicus curiae* (friend of the court) briefs even in cases in which they are not direct parties. Thus, the American Civil Liberties Union files many such briefs with the Supreme Court in cases that raise questions of constitutional liberty. Another technique is to publish in legal periodicals. Judges read these journals to keep abreast of legal scholarship and sometimes even cite them as authority for their rulings. Publication in these journals gets one's view before the courts.

Motivated by a mixture of principle, ideology, and perhaps a need for recognition, they see themselves as redressing the balance and representing the unrepresented or at least the underrepresented. They also view themselves as dedicated to winning *collective benefits*—available to everyone—as opposed to special, or parochial, benefits.

These groups are crucially dependent on a favorable press. Their reports and court battles are often prepared with a close eye on generating publicity. Some temptation doubtless exists for them to oversimplify and resort to moralistic rhetoric. In one such encounter Nader pointed out that, "The best way to build government is to attack government." These strategies quite naturally grate on those in government and sometimes provide stubborn opposition, especially among those who are trying to make programs work under difficult conditions. Criticism of Nader's Raiders comes from both right and left. Nader has learned how to use effectively the techniques of investigation, publicity, and litigation, and he has captured the imagination and support of lots of people. He has had unquestionable impact; some think it is a constructive impact but obviously those who have been affected adversely think Nader is a troublemaker. Defenders of Nader argue that most of the criticism he gets is unfair and misleading. Nader pursues his objectives on many levels and through many stages of action, including hard pressure for fundamental legislative and administrative reforms. He has helped mobilize thousands of people at all levels of government. And thousands of people in government agencies and corporations have been affected by his studies. Thus, Nader is given credit by many on Capitol Hill for doing much to strengthen or initiate such legislation as the Natural Gas Pipe Line Safety Act, the Federal Coal Mine Health and Safety Act, the Wholesome Meat Act, the Radiation Control Act, and the Occupational Safety and Health Act.

COMMON CAUSE AS A POLICY-ACTIVIST

Common Cause, created and led by John W. Gardner, a former cabinet secretary for the Department of Health, Education, and Welfare, is among the most prominent of the citizen lobbies with about 350,000 members across the nation. Common Cause spends about $7 million a year. With intense fervor it calls for limits on campaign contributions and expenditures and for substantial public financing of campaigns. It asks for full-disclosure laws at all levels of government. It also de-

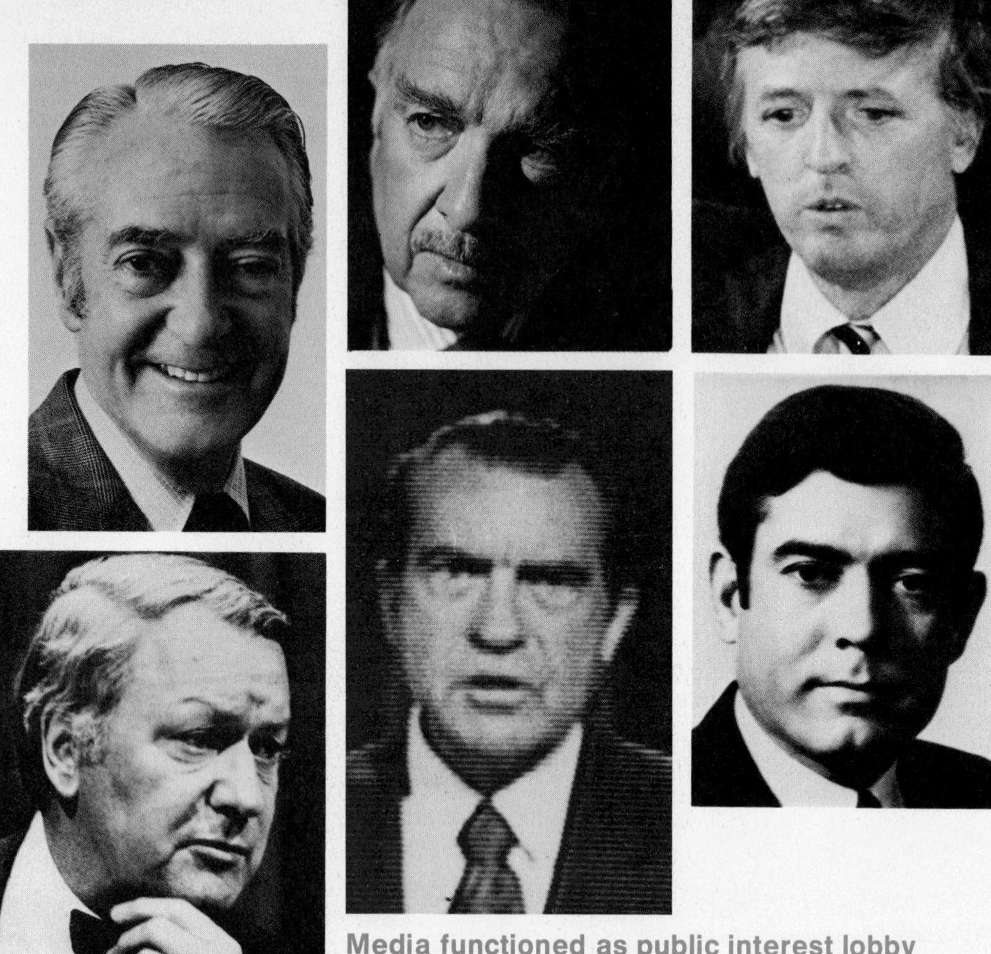

Media functioned as public interest lobby during Watergate

Among those who wrote or talked about the Watergate coverup and President Nixon's leadership failures therein and kept these issues constantly before the public were (clockwise from lower left) James Reston, Howard K. Smith, Walter Cronkite, William F. Buckley, Jr., and Dan Rather.

mands open hearings and an end to secrecy in legislatures at every level. With timely assistance from Watergate—some claim that Common Cause was saved by Watergate—it has made headway in some areas long immune to serious change.

It was a Common Cause lawsuit that finally forced the Committee to Reelect the President to disclose the sources of $20 million in contributions it has been determined to keep secret. Common Cause was also among the most vigorous proponents of measures that have sharply curbed private contributions and introduced a mixed system of public and private financing for some federal primary and general election campaigns. By the mid-1970s Common Cause state units claimed credit for helping pass laws in twenty-five states that curb legislative secrecy or reform campaign financing.

Common Cause has moved away from its early rhetoric about serving as "the people's lobby" and now merely proclaims that "we only represent our own members . . . we don't claim to represent everybody." Its central thrusts of inveighing against secrecy and the influence of money in government are aimed at making government more responsive. And Common Cause's strategy of emphasizing the substance of policy through procedural reform demonstrates once again the interrelationship of politics, process, and policy.

Many people feel that the citizen lobbies have begun to balance the scales of justice in Washington. But these organizations are still no match, either in numbers or influence for the far better financed and well-established corporate, union, farm, and professional lobbies. Most citizen lobbies exist on a precarious financial base. Turnover among their staff is high due in part to low salaries and the fact that moral gratifications are not enough to motivate most people for extended service. Moreover, the issue attention span of even the attentive public is relatively short, hence concern with government integrity and consumer protection can lapse after a while, quite apart from whether the fundamental problem has been addressed. Then too, so many of these reform movements depend on supplies of recent college and law school graduates, yet young people form an unstable base for long-term support of a policy change. Most are lured, by mood or necessity, to move on after a while, and this dissipates the accumulated staff skills.

Among the major organizational problems facing the public interest lobbies are the maintenance of high morale and avoiding the deadening effects of bureaucratization. There is a tendency among high-minded organizations, after awhile, either to talk or organize themselves to death. For a time, however, many of these groups do act as guardians of that valued human trait—the sense of righteous outrage. Still, those who are merely committed, but not particularly competent soon find that outrage is not sufficient, especially if, as often is the case, they are middle- or upper middle-class individuals who really do not have that much personally to be outraged about. Blacks, American Indians, and groups with serious grievances—that is, self-interested groups, and the well-established special interests such as oil companies, Dow Chemical, and the AMA—are likely to be there long after the more generally outraged have turned to something else. In short, the more intense the interest, the easier to organize and sustain, the interest group.

We have a long and rich history of reform movements that build up after some scandal, but after awhile all returns to "normal." Even so, reformers eventually did "knock over" the corrupt city machines, Nader and his allies have turned around a few of the regulatory agencies. And campaign reforms did come about in 1974 as contemporary reformers took advantage of the public outrage toward the Watergate scandals.

These self-appointive guardians of the public interest sustain themselves because substantial numbers of people are willing to support them. And this support comes precisely because enough people believe in the need for what the Swedish have called an *ombudsman*—a person who will handle citizen complaints. Extra-institutional groups undoubtedly will carry on, bringing suits, issuing reports, and more generally, exposing what they feel are illegitimate practices. Such groups and movements splendidly manifest the First Amendment Constitutional privilege "of the people peaceably to assemble, and to petition the Government for a redress of grievances."

These groups have become important in mobilizing and directing political efforts and attention. They are different from both political parties and the more conventional interest groups. They generally operate outside the political parties, and for some segments of the population they may have supplanted political parties in terms of political group identification and allegiance. Their single-minded attention to particular issues make them, in some senses, antiparty. Some of this indifference or antagonism to parties comes from their more populist nature—less concerned with politicians than with bills, less concerned with winning elections and staying in office than with ideals of peace, environment, and equal rights. In any event, they may drain contributions of time, energy, and money away from the major parties and may weaken them over the long run.

Control of lobbying

Copyright © 1974. Reprinted by permission of Saturday Review/World and Randy Glasbergen.

In general, Americans have been far more concerned about concentrated private power than divided government power. And the obvious problem of overrepresentation of some groups at the expense of others is a source of deep concern. For years reformers have been trying to curb the excesses of "pressure groups." The attempt to control lobbying—the primary weapon of interest groups—is a revealing example of the difficulties involved in trying to regulate dynamic groups in a democracy.

Attempts to control lobbying began at least a century ago. In 1877 Georgia wrote into its constitution the simple provision that lobbying is a crime. Early in this century a number of states passed acts to regulate lobbyists, requiring that legislative counsels, or agents, officially register as such and that they file statements of expenses paid or promised in connection with promoting legislation. Under the Federal Regulation of Lobbying Act of 1946, every person hired to influence or defeat bills in Congress must register and disclose the name and address of his employer, how much he is paid, and who pays him. Every three months he must file a further statement listing the names of publications that have carried his publicity and the bills he supports or opposes. Organizations whose main purpose is to influence legislation also must furnish information that is printed regularly in the *Congressional Record.*

The prime aim of such legislation is to turn the spotlight of publicity on the expenditures and activities of lobbyists. The national lobby law has furnished a vast amount of detailed information about lobbyists—who they are, who sponsors and finances them, what bills they seek to pass or block. This information has given the public some idea of the amounts and sources of money involved, although the acknowledged loopholes in this legislation are great.

Some hold that publicity is not enough, that what we need is actual regulation of lobbying. Most lobbyists, these critics argue, not only have no fear of publicity but, on the contrary, actually welcome it. There is much doubt, however, that Congress will try to restrict lobbyists. For one thing, such an attempt might drive the lobbyists underground, where their influence might be more insidious and just as effective, and regulation might run into serious constitutional objections based on the rights guaranteed by the First Amendment. But more important, most students of the problem feel that lobbyists serve an important and desirable function and that nothing more than publicity is needed.

These observers point out that lobbyists are a sort of "third house" of Congress. While the Senate and House are set up on a geographical basis, lobbyists represent people directly in terms of their economic or other interests. Small but important groups, such as Indians, can get representation in this third house that they might not be able to get in the other two. In a nation of large and important interests, this kind of functional representation, if not abused, is highly useful as a supplement to geographical representation.

Group conflict and direct action

Policy issues often arise because people feel they are being cheated or threatened. So they band together with like-minded people. Invariably they discover other groups either within or outside of the government who oppose their point of view. Trying to win friends and influence politicians becomes a prime goal.

Government is both a struggle among those already holding considerable political power and a struggle between those who hold it and those who *want* it. Politicians and policy-making administrative officials become conflict brokers and conflict managers not so much because they want to, but because this is the very heart of policy politics. The skillful policy-maker usually understands interest-group dynamics and knows when and how to arbitrate among conflicting interests. To effect change he usually needs to (1) identify the combination of interest groups that will produce enough support to win agreement with his proposal, (2) marshall the symbolic and real support of the identified groups, (3) fight off opposition groups, and (4) sustain his own capacity to play an effective entrepreneurial role.[7] Governmental civil servants themselves serve increasingly as major sources of policy initiative as they guide the development of knowledge and mobilize public support for policy change.

PROTEST POLITICS

Policy change rarely happens without agitation, pressure, and visions of how conditions can be improved. Rational arguments, coalition-building, compromise, and bill writing are the conventional ways to secure policy change. But the tactic of protest also has a rich legitimate history in America. Political scientist James Q. Wilson points out that protest occurs for one or more of several reasons:

> First, it may be a strategy designed to acquire resources with which to bargain. . . . Second, protest may be a strategy designed to make credible the willingness of a group to use the bargaining resources it already has. . . . Third, a protest may be designed to activate third parties. . . . Finally a protest activity may be carried on in order to enhance the protesting organization.[8]

Opposition to the Vietnam War was so widespread in the 1960s that the government could not fail to recognize it.

Dramatic direct action is sometimes required to win recognition of a grievance or to gain attention from policy-making elites. Direct action embraces a variety of activities ranging from passive resistance and mass demonstrations to sit-ins, strikes, and heckling of speakers. Traditionally, strikes have been used in the United States mainly by unions to win concessions from employers, but strikes and other kinds of economic pressure can also be used for political purposes. The different forms of direct action have been used by many types of groups. In some places blacks active in the civil rights movement have been denied credit or dismissed from their jobs and blacklisted, and in recent years white and black civil rights activists have counterattacked their foes by organizing boycotts of buses and stores. College students also organized freedom rides to bring about compliance with ICC regulations on intercity buses.

Protest against the war in Vietnam in the late 1960s stimulated direct action throughout the nation, especially on college campuses. In dozens of communities mass demonstrations and marches dramatized suppression of the right to vote, police brutality, and denial of job opportunity. Using Gandhian nonviolent methods as their guide, some leaders sought to restrain their followers from violence; but, like the great Gandhi, they sometimes created situations in which violence easily erupted.

President Nixon's "incursion" into Cambodia in the spring of 1970,

[7]Drawn from Eugene Bardack, *The Skill Factor in Politics: Repealing Mental Commitment Laws in California* (Berkeley: University of California Press, 1972). See also R. W. Cobb and C. D. Elder, *Participation in American Politics: The Dynamics of Agenda-Building* (Allyn and Bacon, 1972).

[8]James Q. Wilson, *Political Organizations* (Basic Books, 1973), pp. 282–83.

along with the Kent State and Jackson State killings, brought direct action to a new pitch on and off campuses. Students struck their classes, closed many colleges and universities (often in cooperation with the faculties), organized demonstrations, massed in Washington. Like much direct action, however, the early momentum soon dissipated.

VIOLENCE

The Whiskey Rebellion of 1794 and the Civil War are sober reminders that force is an old weapon in American politics. And these are not the only times that force has been used. For decades labor disputes were marked by bloodshed. The history of the relations between the black and white races is marked by episodes of the use of force. Violence has been used to repress blacks; lynching and persecution were once a way of life. And no doubt the fear and threat of violence remain part of race relations. Many whites are afraid of blacks and vice versa.

Some have advocated that force and violence be elevated as major instruments of politics. Terrorists in Northern Ireland and the Middle East are examples. Some have even argued that these tactics are appropriate in the United States. Although the overwhelming majority of blacks have flatly repudiated such doctrines, in the late 1960s a few black militants, responding to murders, arson, and other terrors inflicted on them, preached the use of force as a weapon of last resort. They contended that without violent action, the poor and the disposed would not be able to seize enough power to influence the course of events.

The use of force has not been very productive in American politics; in fact more often than not it has been counterproductive. It was the violence, for example, of some southern police officers and apologists for them that led to reaction in Washington and to the mobilization of national political power in behalf of civil rights. And those who have espoused revolutionary doctrines of force and violence have never had much of a following.

Caution—direct peaceful action should not be confused with the use of force and violence. The former is protected by our Constitution; the latter is not. A peaceful march on city hall or a school or even the Pentagon—the tactics of mass protest—can lead to violence but should not be confused with it. Similarly, a strike or a boycott is the application of economic coercion, but is of a different order than violence or acts of terrorism.

On the one hand, the importance of individual revolutionary leaders and activities in history is obvious. On the other, efforts since the Revolution to overturn the system in our country have failed, and it is hard to recall issues that have been resolved in recent times by recourse to violence.[9]

[9]J. M. Burns, *Uncommon Sense* (Harper & Row, 1972), p. 73.

The issue-attention cycle and incrementalism

The public's interest in even the most pressing problems may wax and wane. The span of the public's attention is notoriously short. Shifting public moods and the personal incentives of elected officials encourage the adoption of new policies rather than basic restructuring of existing policies. To rally support for a new program, given our existing arrangements, is easier than to cut back on-going programs. Too many beneficiaries, both the target of the programs and those who administer them, will usually fight to oppose any changes in programs already "on the books." Thus, reworking or even rethinking old programs over the long term becomes subordinate to what might be called an "add-on" approach to public policy-making.

In Anthony Down's words, "Each of these new problems suddenly leaps into prominence, remains there for a short time, and then—though still largely unresolved—generally fades from the center of public attention."[10] Public boredom, he suggests, often sets in when large numbers of people realize the cost of solving the underlying root problem would be very high indeed. (Perhaps boredom is the most underrated force in history.) For example, vast amounts of smog are produced by increased automobile usage, but few voters are ready to campaign actively for drastic remedies like public transportation and prohibiting the use of cars.

Policy-makers, especially those in a democracy, do not like to make anybody mad if they can help it. There is not much point to losing votes. Therefore, they would rather enlarge the size of the national economic pie and give new groups funds without having to take them from old groups—that is, to increase the pie rather than to redistribute it. Like fathers and mothers and university administrators, anybody who has the responsibility for allocating scarce resources would rather make everybody happy than take allowance back from one child and give it to another, or take funds from one university department and redistribute them to another. The more likely the electorate is to have some way of controlling those who govern, the more likely those who govern are going to be sensitive to these matters. If the group that is presently getting "the short end of the stick" lacks political clout, it is likely not to get its fair share of the economic goods of the society.

Congressmen of both parties and nearly all persuasions have incentives for not closely examining certain parts of the budget. Liberals, for example, are especially upset with budget cuts in social programs, often seeing them as an abandonment of social responsibility. Conservatives view cuts in military spending as especially unwise—even dramatic cost overruns in military procurement seldom arouse the customary conservative wrath against waste. In their favorite but different spheres, then, the goal of most liberals and conservatives is to increase

[10]Anthony Downs, "Up and Down With Ecology—The Issue-Attention Cycle," *Public Interest* (Summer 1972), p. 38.

federal spending, regardless, sometimes, of whether or not funds are spent efficiently. To question existing efforts just yields headaches and ammunition for the opposition. "It is much easier to pick some major problem that [is new and not now funded], hold hearings that dramatize the unmet need, and then propose new programs without replacing any old ones."[11]

The character of policy systems in Washington also promotes incrementalism. People involved in one phase of policy-making are usually not involved in other phases. A person who writes a provocative article suggesting the idea of a National Teacher Corps, for example, contributes to the dialogue and incubation of a policy, but that same person seldom is involved in the subsequent stages of bill-writing, legislative hearings, presidential message-writing, congressional authorization, funding decisions, or setting up the administrative apparatus to enforce the bill—each of which is likely to modify or greatly recast the original proposal. Hence, our system of separation of powers, widespread dispersal of functional authority, and the complex labyrinth of policy subsystems promotes a seeming addiction to piecemeal policy change. Planning comprehensively is difficult in a system such as ours, which is glued together with alliance politics, majorities of the moment, and constant compromising. Immediate clientele pressures tend to displace the original objective of the legislation and comprehensive planning for it.

Thinking comprehensively, however, is not impossible in our system; the problem is that in order to get something done and enforced, it takes the approval of lots of different and often differing people; and as we develop consensus, there is much compromising and bargaining. The democratic process which requires a calculus of consent makes comprehensive and integrated action more difficult than in nondemocratic systems such as in the Soviet Union. Our democratic society is especially difficult, as compared with small countries such as Sweden where there is a more homogeneous population and hence usually a broader consensus. We have to get by so many different veto groups that the policy proposals that come out are almost always different from what sponsors desired.

Policies are customarily based on the extension of past practices, worked out step-by-step, and nearly always with the intent of placating vested interests. Policy-makers bend over backwards to design programs in such a way as to cultivate interest-group support, and to neutralize possible antagonists. This results, not surprisingly, in watered-down objectives and laws that are extremely general and vague. To be sure, laws often are complex and detailed, yet they are deliberately written to permit discretionary interpretation. And in any event, objectives are seldom spelled out clearly.

Too, there is the fact that in a democracy political leaders are not like-

[11]Alice Rivlin, "A Counter-Budget for Social Progress," *New York Times Magazine* (April 8, 1973), p. 86.

ly to be risk-takers and not likely to call upon the people to sacrifice today in order to avoid some problem decades from now. We are not likely to do much about a fuel crisis until we run out of gasoline, or to do much about pollution until people start choking. But then again, as we look around the world, other nations are not doing much better at solving long-range problems either—the Soviet Union and Japan and all industrial nations have nearly the same problems; and even the old standard we measured ourselves against, England, with its disciplined parties, no separation of powers, and concentration of responsibility, is not making much progress with inflation or pollution or race (and religious) relations.

The move to decentralize authority to states and localities, a major thrust of the Nixon Administration, also fostered incrementalism. With such strategies, Washington officials were in effect saying, "Let local elites decide what is proper policy in their locality. Let us not interfere." Some people argue, and they are partly correct, that efficiency and promoting a smaller federal bureaucracy were the prime motivations. But decentralization and "disaggregation" (dividing up policy-making into fragmented, functional units) are also a means of getting Congress and federal bureaucrats to relinquish their power of using federal funds to bring about what they deem to be desired, purposeful change. Thus, policy-making by localization is still another way for Washington officials to make people happy. Yet it is often at the expense of national objectives, comprehensive planning, swift action.

Policy-making processes in democratic countries are, except in matters of foreign relations, rarely insulated from localism. Our party system and popular values concentrate power at the state and local levels. Numerous case studies document how our structural arrangements of government in general are "better suited to protect the local status quo . . . than to force any unpopular local action. . . . Even when a congressional majority favoring national action against a local vested interest has finally been obtained, localities have commonly been able to modify policy through intervention in the administrative process."[12]

The relationship between citizens' issue-attention spans and incrementalism is not entirely clear. From past experience it seems that politicians count on a little real or symbolic change to satisfy the urgent, emotional demands of most people. The very exercise of working on some new plan or legislating some additional initiative takes the edge off public alarm. "Don't just stand there: Do Something!" But the *something* does not have to be very much. And, in any event, authority is so fragmented both vertically and horizontally, that even radical actions by one set of policy-makers can be restrained or pared back elsewhere in the policy-making system. This is the essence of incrementalism. Critics yearn for a better way to get things done. Defenders of incrementalism suggest that it is not a policy choice, but a fact of life. Second, they note, 5 percent compounded annually "is lots of change."

[12]Gary Orfield, *The Reconstruction of Southern Education* (John Wiley, 1969), p. 356.

Contests between the branches and often *within* the branches (House vs. Senate, cabinet officer vs. White House staff) capture our interest much as do sports events. We can identify with the side we want to win and then follow the contest to wait for a final outcome.

If we follow the way national policy is made as reported in the newspapers or on television, we rarely see behind bill-signing ceremonies, press conferences, or formal statements. And, very often, we mainly hear about the struggles and contests between the branches. Congress refuses to go along with the president. The courts overrule presidential impoundment of highway trust funds. Or the president vetoes a bill passed by Congress. These contests are of great new interest, and the clash among the branches gets firmly lodged in the public mind.

Washington journalism feeds on such contests because it makes for more interesting copy than the numerous cooperative and collaborative efforts to make policy. Box scores indicating how many of the president's legislative measures pass Congress are tabulated but the scores often conceal as much as they reveal. They are helpful up to a point, but they do not really tell us why a president has not been successful. Neither do they tell us much about the quality of measures proposed,

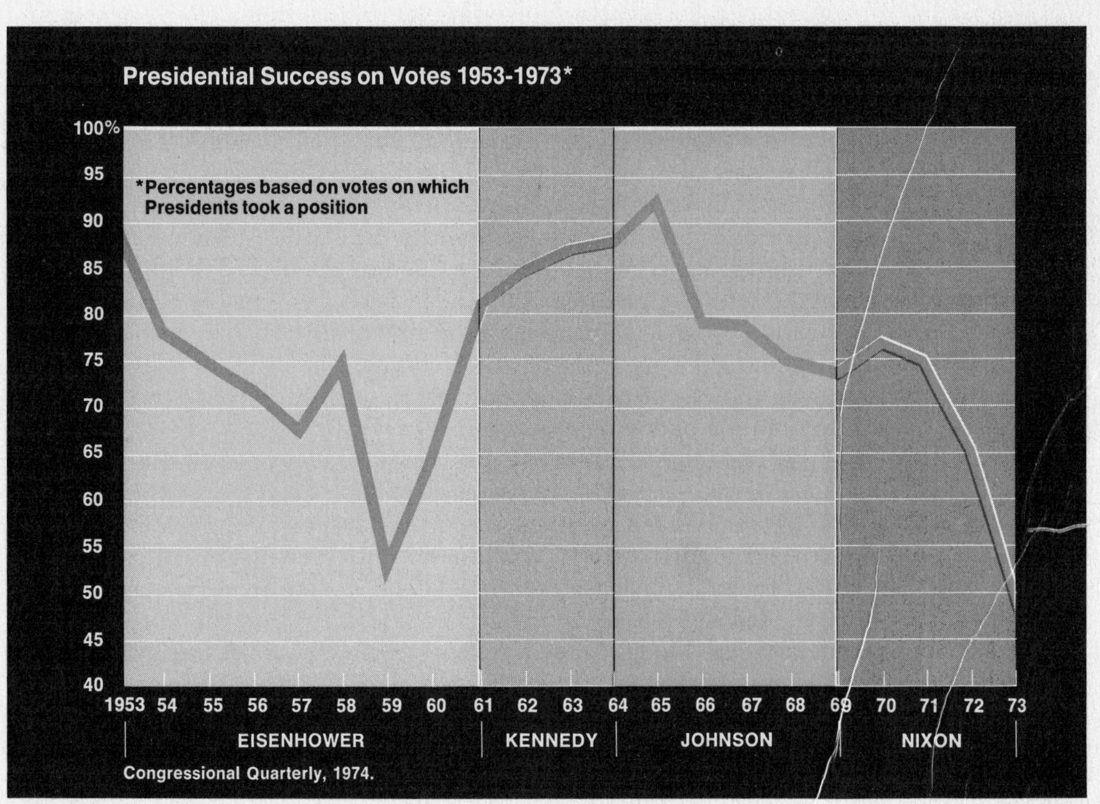

Congressional Quarterly, 1974.

passed, and rejected. A president with an eye solely on the box score, for example, can avoid endorsing measures that are unlikely to pass. Moreover, the higher box score successes may be due more to rapidly increasing federal revenues than to adroit presidential leadership with the Congress. But the box score approach to stories about the president and Congress is likely to remain because it helps simplify reporting.

Another example of this penchant for contest-watching is the concern over the character of voting blocs within the Supreme Court. How many five-to-four decisions? Who are the judicial activists? Who are the practitioners of judicial restraint? And who are the swing voters?

THE ROLE OF EXPERTISE AND STAFF

Beneath and behind "the ruling class," one finds thousands of individuals at work in the Washington policy-making process. They help resolve conflicts, harmonize diverse interests, and facilitate cooperation *across* institutions. Only by understanding these people can we fully appreciate the patterns and eccentricities of Washington policy-making.

Sometimes just being in the right place at the right time enables an individual to contribute significantly to policy decisions. More likely, however, people who *make a difference* occupy formal positions or command needed expertise, or both. Specialists drawn from various professional communities are often looked to for counsel in the early stages of deliberation when policy makers in Washington are assigning relative importance to various competing policy issues. Thus, they are often in a strategic position to define what the issues are. It is, of course, also essential to be familiar with *the rules of the game* as played in Washington's bureaucratic and congressional subsystem politics.

Senior committee staff positions, which before 1946 were filled on a patronage basis, are increasingly filled on the basis of competence. The ability of these professional staffs to select and analyze information for hearings and legislation gives them considerable impact on policy-making. They become a major center of communication that links Congress, the executive branch, interest groups, and diverse constituencies around the nation.[13]

Federal biomedical policy was substantially recast in the 1960s by a small group of medical researchers, philanthropists, and members of Congress assisted by staffers both in Congress and the White House. Writers, academics, and professional entrepreneurs are often the catalysts for policy change: "The development of the Economic Opportunity Act, the Family Assistance Plan, the Safe Streets Act, the Tax Reform Act of 1969, the Model Cities Program, revenue-sharing, the TVA, the unsuccessful Brannan Plan for agriculture in 1949, the National Traffic and Motor Vehicle Safety Act, and the Consumer Credit Protection Act

[13]See, for example, Samuel C. Patterson, "The Professional Staff of Congressional Committees," *Administrative Science Quarterly* (March 1970), pp. 25 ff.

("truth-in-lending") all illustrate an essentially nonorganizational policy-development process."[14]

Some policy-making entrepreneurs are highly educated economists, lawyers, or scientists who began their careers in government and have risen to positions of importance within departments, in the Executive Office of the President, or within congressional staffs. Sometimes within a few years they can become strategic information brokers, knowing a vast amount of detail about ongoing operations, case histories of actual practices, as well as plausible alternatives for future change. Moreover they are likely to keep informed of professional developments in their disciplines, to meet with their counterparts in other departments and branches, and to maintain acquaintances in the trade associations and at the state level.

Washington is abundantly peopled with staff specialists who have served long periods within a policy area and in a variety of strategic positions. The career ladders are neither tidy nor predictable. An economist at the OMB moves to the nongovernmental Brookings Institution and a few years later is back in government service within the Congressional Research Service. An aide to a senator goes to HEW and then back to elective state government positions and later returns to cabinet posts at HEW, Defense, and Justice, and then becomes ambassador to Great Britain. A young lawyer works in the office of the secretary at the Department of Defense, then joins the White House National Security Council Staff, leaves to become counsel for the Senate Armed Services Committee, and three years later enters private practice in Washington, D.C.

Still another example of mobility is the instance of a graduate of law school becoming first a law clerk to a Supreme Court justice, then joining the Justice Department, and after a year or two there being invited to join the domestic staff at the White House. These four real case illustrations are by no means unusual. Mobility in Washington is extensive and career ladders diverse; as a result complex networks of *friendships, influence* and *loyalties* characterize the policy-making process.

One of the more fascinating aspects of Washington politics is the way in which policy activists in different branches of government, or associated with various nongovernmental organizations (such as research

[14]Wilson, *Political Organizations,* p. 331.

institutes, foundations, lobbyist units, or media), join forces and fashion working alliances. Policy subsystems grow up around a set of interrelated issues, as much a response to the process of getting things done as to the issues that define the subsystem. Age and formal position are less important than information, imagination, energy, and persistence. Policy activists learn how to capture support from members of Congress and senior White House aides. This, it turns out, is not difficult, for certain congressmen and White House aides are always looking for new ideas with which to promote their careers.

Then, too, there is usually some newspaper or journal willing to provide a forum for debate of a new issue. There are countless opportunities for testifying at hearings, bringing suits in court, or convincing staff people who serve cabinet or high Executive Office officials. The access points, or "cracks," in the larger political system are many.

THE ROLE OF THE INTELLECTUAL

Intellectuals have often been involved in governing countries—sometimes, like Aristotle, as tutors to the political class. But today the complexity of programs and technology enlarges the need for intellectual participation. In a free society politicians always try to win over the intellectuals and they need help from other intellectuals. However, intellectuals tend to be critical of politicians, although most of them are by no means averse to power or influence. Many intellectuals, such as Socrates was, are proud and determined critics of politicians. To retain his or her credentials as a professional, an intellectual must be able to prove considerable independence from all authority. An intellectual, then, is often found indicting public policy actions, complaining about the low quality of decision-making, and decrying wrong choices or the absence of national priorities.

Working relations between intellectuals and public officials are often precarious. Intellectuals are not accustomed to placing loyalty to an officeholder above the free exchange of ideas. They are inclined instead to want public credit for their ideas. (John Kenneth Galbraith once said, aptly, "modesty is a vastly overrated virtue"—a view not uncommon among intellectuals.) Intellectuals nonetheless, are nearly always involved in charting national goals, forecasting policy needs, and trying to devise models for better policy performance. But they are often hostile to the pressures that invariably arise to compromise and "sell a program."

OUTSIDE ADVISERS

The role of outside advisers splendidly illustrates both the conflict and cooperation inherent in making policy. In recent years somewhere between 30,000 and 40,000 people served the executive branch as part-time consultants or advisory council members. They are used to review grant applications, offer feedback about general policy operations, and lend professional legitimacy to ongoing programs. But they can be a source of dissent and constraint as well as a helpful counsel.

Scientists, economists, educators, or various other professionals, like anyone else, find it difficult to be completely objective participants in national policy councils. Most of these outside advisers favor special theories or levels of research; most are particularly mindful of the resource needs of their disciplines or institutions. And invariably they favor and vigorously promote an acceleration of federal funds for their fields. Some advisers who have become involved in certain areas of government policy do not want to threaten the bureau or programs on which they advise. An incestuous and symbiotic relationship often develops; advisers provide support, legitimacy, visibility, and even lobbying assistance. In return, advisers receive enhanced status, ego-gratification, and more funds, grants, and federal support for their university or professional discipline.

News columnists and commentators as well as all kinds of journalists also act as policy brokers in Washington. Their impact is difficult to measure, but at least is recognized by their critics who complain that public affairs coverage is being corrupted by advocacy journalism. Such writers as James Reston, I. F. Stone, David Broder, George Will, Seymour Hersh, and William F. Buckley, Jr., influence which issues are discussed and help define and clarify policy problems for the attentive public. Such programs as *Today, Meet the Press,* and *Firing Line* often can be important forums for both proposing and criticizing public policies. The best of journalists are skilled in handling complex policy

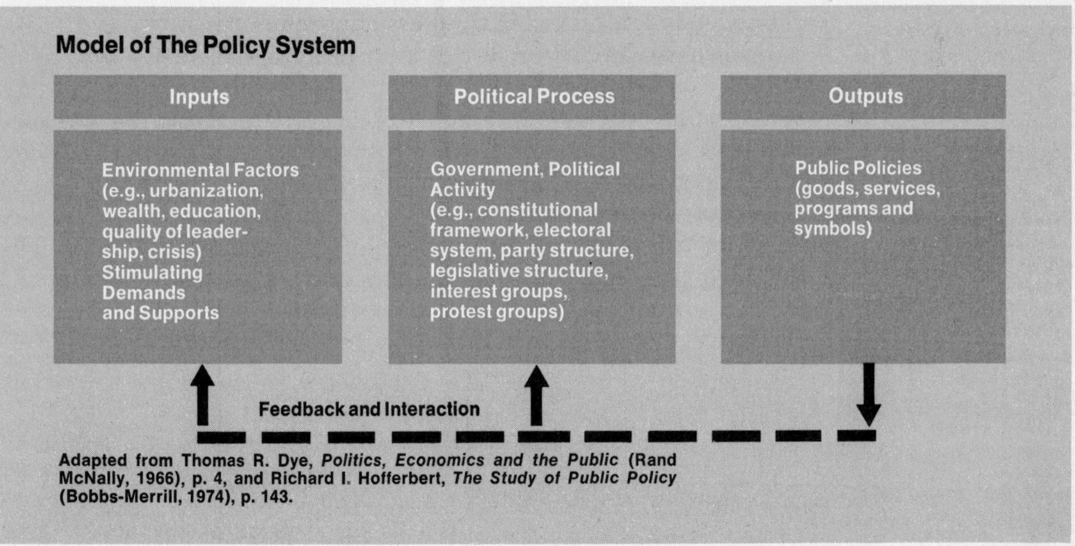

Adapted from Thomas R. Dye, *Politics, Economics and the Public* (Rand McNally, 1966), p. 4, and Richard I. Hofferbert, *The Study of Public Policy* (Bobbs-Merrill, 1974), p. 143.

information and can translate it into valid terms of public debate. Properly performed, this is an invaluable contribution to policy making.[15]

Program oversight—the policy process continues

As we have noted, the adoption of a policy is only the beginning of the policy process. After Congress passes a law and the president signs it, what happens next? Who watches, who evaluates, who decides the details of how the policy will be put into effect?

The answer is everybody and nobody. Just as planning in a comprehensive fashion is difficult to achieve in any free nation, and especially in the United States, so we have a diffuse system for following through after Congress passes a law.

An ideal public organization, some think, would be one that continuously monitors and evaluates its own activities to determine whether it is accomplishing its goals and whether the goals are worth achieving. But this is obviously utopian. Organizational leaders, like the rest of us, are not the best ones to evaulate their own accomplishments.

Those favoring programs and those responsible for administering them often prefer to concentrate their energies on getting the programs through the Congress (and also funded fully) rather than evaluating their own success. Funds are scarce. Evaluation is fraught with difficulties and dangers to the organization, and when it does occur, tends to be conducted more with an eye on enlarging one's budget or ensuring organizational survival than on determining whether an organization's objectives and goals are appropriate. *Bring us the success stories!* Crudely put, that seems to be the standing operating procedure. And then the success stories are paraded before the Office of Management and Budget and appropriate congressional committees.

Bureaus and agencies often cast their proposals in such a way as to persuade, not to report systematic evaluation. Program "evaluation" reports coming into the White House or the Congress from the bureaucracy have long been suspect, since the success of the programs they administer, to a considerable extent, puts their own performance on the line. In this sense, evaluation can never be, and probably should not be, entirely apolitical—it will be used by one party or branch of government against another. Evaluation will also be used by one department or agency against another. This in-fighting within the executive branch poses additional incentives on an agency to politicize their evaluation efforts.[16]

[15]See Leon V. Sigal, *Reporters and Officials: The Organization and the Politics of Newsmaking* (D. C. Heath, 1973). But see also Timothy Crouse, *The Boys on the Bus* (Random House, 1973).

[16]Aaron Wildavsky, "The Self-Evaluating Organization" *Public Administration Review* (September-October 1972), pp. 509–20. Our discussion draws from this article.

Some bureaus become so preoccupied with marginal activities that enhance their prestige that they neglect the less visible work which makes up their true purpose. Plainly, delays and deficiencies in evaluation sometimes occur because an agency purposely wants to camouflage the real costs of its operations. More often, however, the problem is due to the fact that it is difficult and expensive to develop outcome or impact measures. Sometimes, too, it is nearly impossible to relate governmental expenditures with policy outcomes, or to be precise about what has caused social change if change can even be noticed.

Political and social scientists have turned their attention to the *product* side of public policy. Instead of being concerned only with what affects government, or with what goes on inside governmental institutions, more attention is being given to what comes out of the policy-making processes. Defining success becomes a major concern. And the test of a program is not input but *output.* "It is interesting, and at times important, to know how much money is spent on schools in a particular neighborhood or city. But the crucial question is how much do the children learn. Programs are for people, not for bureaucracies."[17]

Why have Congress and the White House not insisted on more systematic policy-planning and evaluation? The short-term political incentives seem to propel their energies in an opposite direction. *Pass now, plan later!* The election is just around the corner. Presidents, especially, are ever eager for fast results. They seldom appreciate the need for more analysis, testing, small-scale pilot experiments, and systematic reappraisal of ongoing programs. They say they were elected *not to study* and research policies, *but to get things done,* and to put ideas into operation.

LEGISLATIVE OVERSIGHT

As Congress has been eclipsed by the executive in more and more policy formulation areas, there has been a move to strengthen it as a focus for program oversight. Congress has gradually accepted both its policy-initiating eclipse as well as its new after-the-fact assessment role, although even its staunchest defenders readily admit Congress performs this responsibility with only modest success.

The Legislative Reorganization Act of 1946 assigned to each standing committee the responsibility to "exercise continuous watchfulness of the execution by the administrative agencies concerned of any laws, the subject matter of which is within the jurisdiction of such committee." Oversight is neither constant nor systematic, however, for a variety of reasons, not the least of which is that comprehensive oversight of all federal program implementation would demand all the time of all the

[17]Daniel P. Moynihan, "Policy vs. Program in the '70's," *Public Interest* (Summer 1970), p. 100.

staff and members of Congress, but in fact, oversight is not the top priority most of the time.[18]

Congressmen exercise the oversight function when they are particularly upset with the way they are being treated by executive branch officials and when it serves their constituents in a tangible way. Certain standing committees have created specific oversight subcommittees, but there is little knowledge of whether such subcommittees make any appreciable difference on the quality of policy-making. What is frustrating, of course, is not that oversight is performed intermittently but that it necessarily comes after the fact, such as when the Air Forces's C-5A had its motors fall off and its landing gears collapse.

Evaluation of programs, like their adoption, however, is not primarily a technical problem, but a political one. Of course, all can agree that there is something wrong with Defense Department procurement when the cost of buying a weapons system is much more than Congress anticipated, but for most evaluations the issues are choices between costs and benefits for which there is no expert answer. Is the welfare program worth the expenditures? Should we abolish subsidies to farmers? Has the highway program produced good or bad results for the nation? Are the funds spent on grants for students to attend medical schools worth it to the taxpayer? If experts could tell us whether these programs were "good" or "bad," we would need a government of experts. But in fact, there are no precise answers, and this is why we rely on the democratic system and on politicians chosen by popular vote.

Politicians in legislative and executive branches may benefit from the growing number of policy experts in fields around operating agencies, consulting firms, and professional societies. Political scientist Jack Walker suggests that these producers of ideas and policy evaluators can serve the commonweal and not just the vested interests:

> The power of organized interests to shape the early stages of problem definition and policy formulation may be reduced substantially by the steady, abrasive influence of ideas and social theory. The great significance of the growing role of experts in democratic systems may not be, as is often feared, their ability to manipulate elected representatives and gain irresponsible control over the routine operations of public bureaucracies, but rather their ability to provide the intellectual underpinnings of public policy. The political significance of the rise of communities of policy professionals may lie not so much in how they affect the daily struggle for bureaucratic authority, but in the subtle and portentous manner in which they are changing the relationship between knowledge and power.[19]

Senator Jacob Javits (R–N.Y.) directs a question to an oil company executive during an investigation into the energy crisis. Congressmen may also exercise the oversight function to counter the force of the executive branch.

Many within and outside of Congress feel Congress should not yet retreat merely to oversight functions. They feel that program oversight

[18]For other obstacles to comprehensive oversight, see Morris S. Ogul, "Legislative Oversight of Bureaucracy," Working paper, *Hearings,* Select Committee on Committees, U.S. House of Representatives, 93rd Cong. 1973, Vol. 2, 701–9.

[19]Jack L. Walker, "The Diffusion of Knowledge and Policy Change," p. 29. See also Heinz Eulau, "Skill Revolution and Consultative Commonwealth," *American Political Science Review* (March 1973), pp. 169–91; and Thomas E. Cronin and Sanford Greenberg, eds., *The Presidential Advisory System* (Harper & Row, 1969).

has a low priority compared with the need to strengthen Congress in other ways. Yet, oversight, properly conducted, can be a major means for Congress to retain its role in policy-making. For the present, incentives for conducting more comprehensive program oversight are great in the abstract but modest in concrete situations. The Office of Technology Assessment was recently established by the Congress as a staff agency to assist it in policy formulation and oversight. This office will be closely watched to see if it can work as a creative and constructive countervailing force to executive branch domination of information and evaluation. From it and similar congressional innovations may come the much-needed debates over national priorities, program design alternatives, and diverse strategies for implementing national policy goals.

What about the people?

Many people today contend that in the present state of complexity the citizen is increasingly disengaged and unable to have significant impact on government policies. Concentration of economic power in the hands of ever-larger corporations is accompanied, so it is argued, by a corresponding concentration of power at the top levels of the executive branch. The rich get richer. The powerful get more power. In short, "them what has—gets." A policy-making elite governs the nation. Closer inspection of policy-making suggests, however, that in most cases no one institution or group is able to exert its will without the support or acquiescence of some others. The policy-making arena is highly differentiated, and power is dispersed widely. Policy is seldom the outcome of any particular battle, but rather the cumulative outcome of a number of battles fought over time. Policy is, moreover, rarely decreed from on high. More than just a small group of people are involved in making national policy in nearly all areas.

Moreover, there is among most policy activists still a great sense of doing what is best for the people. Numerous agents in and out of government act as guardians of the public interest, vigorously trying to redress citizen grievances.

Some critics argue that the conflict and cooperation inherent in policy-making occur mainly *among elites* within the institutions and groups. These elites may fight over minor points while ignoring (or cooperating on) broad crucial issues affecting the public interest, such as poverty, environment, or defense. Elites may not compete in any confrontation over central national priorities; hence, these critics argue, there is no real "clash of groups."

Other critics hold that through the arrangement of checks and balances, government is fragmented almost to the point of paralysis. Meanwhile, powerful private groups—corporations, unions, banks, and the oil companies, among others—exercise concentrated private power that can usually overcome the dispersed public power. So these critics

"Remember, son, if at first you don't succeed, re-evaluate the situation, draw up various hypotheses for your failure, choose reasonable corrective measures, and try, try again."

Copyright © 1974. Reprinted by permission of Saturday Review/World and Randy Glasbergen.

say that a majority of the people are essentially left out: government is not responsible to most of the people because it is so fragmented; private elites are not responsible because the public has no direct control over them.

While none of these criticisms can be dismissed, divergent policy views are represented in many ways in the policy-making process. Enough examples exist of policy-making in behalf of redistribution of wealth and opportunities to undermine the cynical verdict that policy is made mainly to help the rich get richer. How else explain medical care, the Voting Rights Act of 1965, food stamp programs, veterans' benefits, consumer protection measures, welfare expenditures, federal warnings against cigarette smoking, and affirmative action programs?

Summary

In short, our policy-making processes are often in fact very porous, permitting large numbers of groups and individuals to join battle and change the status quo. Our political system, like all such systems, almost by definition, is undoubtedly weighted in favor of the status quo and against radical changes in policy. But those who know better ways of doing things and are willing to partake of the pulling and hauling that characterize national policy-making *can* make a difference. Skill, knowledge, the ability to build coalitions of like-minded supporters and attract sympathetic press coverage are critical preconditions for change. All of these, together with unusual stamina, are needed to place new issues on the public's agenda and to get diverse policy actors *across* the political system to cooperate in effecting purposive change in public policy.

Part Six Democratic government in America reappraised

Chapter 19 The ordeal of change

As Americans prepared to celebrate their 200th birthday as a nation, some expected—or perhaps feared—that the bicentennial would mark a period of change almost as profound as the signing of the Declaration. A decade or more of assassinations, Vietnam, inflation, recession, confrontations, riots, and finally the prolonged anguish of Watergate culminating in the resignation of a president had left many Americans and their leaders confused, upset, but above all, determined to do better. It had all seemed, as the old engineer would say, "one hell of a way to run a railroad."

But how to do it better? Each of the political crises had been followed by an outpouring of reform proposals. Struggles in the streets and on the campuses brought new plans for forms of participatory democracy that would bring people into the political process at every level. Vietnam and other adventures abroad produced many proposals for modifying presidential power over war-making, as we have seen. The deep divisions within the Democratic party inspired recommendations for reform of party processes and organization. Failures in dealing with knotty problems of inflation, recession, environmental deterioration, and cultural blight gave rise to proposals ranging from minor tinkering with the machinery of government to drastic reconstruction of the whole system. Watergate prompted major recommendations from congressional groups and private commissions, and it aroused a deeply felt resolution among Republicans, both regulars and reformers that their party must never be stained in this fashion again.

To some it seemed time for a new and fruitful collaboration between "principle democrats" and "process democrats" (See Chapter 1)—a collaboration rivaling that of 1776 and 1787. Reform proposals fell into three broad categories: (1) changes in the *political* system, especially political parties; (2) changes, both constitutional and mechanical, in the *governmental system*, especially the relationship of president and Congress; (3) comprehensive and drastic reshaping of the *whole* system, especially in its relation to economic power, to make it more responsive to the masses of people and less to elites.

Toward a new majority?

Perhaps the most striking aspect of American politics in the mid-seventies was the shifting, volatile nature of public opinion in contrast with the stability—some would say inertia—of the party system. That popular attitudes were not only fluid but virtually in a state of disarray, in relation to political institutions, was attested to by virtually all public opinion analysts.[1] The last few years, wrote Dawson, "have witnessed the rise of a growing disquiet, and even a sense of frustration, among many people. This disquiet has been associated with alterations in basic opinion relationships and with the breakup of some of the social and political coalitions that have given meaning and structure to political life over the past few decades. There is a sense of change or pressure for change, but a lack of focus and structure to the various pressures. . . ."[2] This disarray had a number of causes; one of the most important was a vast loss of confidence in governmental leadership following Vietnam and Watergate.

In the cloudiness of disorganized, churning public opinion, however, one trend was as clearly visible as it was potentially significant. This was the heightened public concern with *issues*, with *policies*, with what government actually *does*. Not so long ago many if not most Americans took a position on issues depending on their (often inherited) *party identification*. Now millions of persons were choosing parties—or moving back and forth between parties—largely on the basis of *issues*. But many Americans found the major political parties irrelevant to the political problems that increasingly were exciting or provoking them.

CHANGING ISSUES AND PARTY REALIGNMENT

Most adult Americans today grew up in a period when two major par-

[1]See, for example, Richard E. Dawson, *Public Opinion and Contemporary Disarray* (Harper & Row, 1973); Louis Harris, *The Anguish of Change* (Norton, 1973); Walter Dean Burnham, "American Politics in the 1970s: Beyond Party?" unpublished paper, 1974; Arthur H. Miller, Warren E. Miller, Alden S. Raine, and Thad A. Brown, "A Majority Party in Disarray: Policy Polarization in the 1972 Election" (Center for Political Studies, University of Michigan, 1974).

[2]Dawson, *Contemporary Disarray*, p. 3.

ties competed over issues arising directly from the Great Depression and the New Deal. Parties and candidates tended to build election coalitions around the hotly debated issues of government regulation of business, rights of labor, taxation, social welfare. The less affluent generally lined up behind the Democrats favoring the New Deal and at least a modicum of redistribution of wealth and aid to the poor; wealthier people naturally opposed "soaking the rich" in behalf of the poor. This was a very rough tendency; there has rarely been anything neat and tidy about American politics. Some of the wealthy, perhaps a bit conscience stricken about their affluence, supported the New Deal, while some of the poor voted for conservative Republicans. Some Southern Democrats were more conservative than most Republicans. Foreign policy often cut across the party equilibrium and united Democratic and Republican interventionists against Democratic and Republican isolationists. But the basic economic and social tendencies were strong enough for the two parties to offer a meaningful choice to voters on issues and policy and to assume some responsibility for what government finally did. Parties and issues were relevant to each other.

The political ordeals of the last decade and a half have brought a sharp change in the relation of issues to the present party alignment and election coalitions. The old differences over economic questions are still important, but they have been augmented by so-called *social* issues —notably government corruption, race, urban blight, law and order, rights of defendants, rights of Indians and other ethnic minorities —that have mobilized and to some degree polarized people in coalitions different from the old ones. On such issues the party cleavage has cut *through* existing classes and status groups instead of cutting between them; or, conversely, divisions over issues have become more acute *within* each of the parties than *between* them. Class or occupational status was no longer such a dependable guide to how he or she would choose between parties. The increasing conservatism of the mass public on the new issues such as public order and civil rights (i.e., school desegregation and busing) and the rising polarization lay behind the collapse of the old FDR-New Deal-Democratic party coalition, the political rise of men like Robert Kennedy, Eugene McCarthy, George McGovern, and George Wallace, and the unexpected political resurrection and triumph of Richard Nixon.[3]

How effectively did the two major parties lead in—or at least adjust to—the change in dominant issues? The shift in issues from the New Deal orientation to the new emphasis on "social" issues benefited the Republicans, but the party was too weak to win a majority in the House or Senate. The Democrats, after exploiting for years the issue of the "Republican-made" depression and GOP "standpattism," became embroiled in a violent internal conflict, mainly over social issues. The furious contests in the Democratic conventions of 1968 and 1972 overshadowed even the struggle within the Republican convention of 1964,

[3]Burnham, "Politics in the 1970s," pp. 7–8. On party realignment see also the major work, James L. Sundquist, *Dynamics of the Party System* (Brookings Institution, 1973).

when Barry Goldwater triumphed as a dedicated conservative. And the fact that Americans today, partly as a result of their rising distrust of government and politicians, are demanding that candidates take clearer, more definite stands on issues, increased the pressures on the major parties.

Given these pressures, the situation might seem ripe for a *realigning* of the parties so that they offered voters a meaningful choice on key social issues such as law and order, civil rights, reform of campaign finance. By taking a more liberal stand on such issues, the Democrats could consolidate a new coalition that might keep them in power for years. Or the Republicans, by taking a tougher stand on public order and related issues, might hope to pick up the support of centrist elements—most notably the "hard hat" workers—and forge a new coalition that could keep the GOP in power for years. At critical times in the past, the two parties had realigned the foundations of their support in the face of voters' changing attitudes toward developing issues, as in the 1890s and 1930s. Why not again in the 1970s?

The prospects for realignment in the 1970s seemed less promising, however. Most office-holding Democrats preferred to stick with the safe old economic issues on which they had won elections for forty years. Many Republicans feared that their image as a party that "protects the taxpayer's dollar" and opposes "big government" would be compromised if they brought into the Republican tent hosts of workers taking the "right" position on law and order but also favoring more social welfare and governmental control.

There were other, more complex obstacles to party realignment. Instead of deserting the party that their parents bequeathed to them, that they "grew up in," many voters found it easier to support a third party, such as George Wallace's American Independent party or a new left-wing party; to split their tickets among several candidates at election time; or to shift back and forth from party to party from election to election; or to vote for personable *candidates* rather than parties; or not to vote at all, perhaps out of disgust or cynicism. Finally, in contrast to the New Deal coalition, there were no longer two basic groupings for voters to fall into; voters were divided in many different ways and not just into the natural camps of liberals and conservatives. Political conflict had become *multidimensional,* as reflected in the strength of the Wallace movement and the deep divisions especially among the Democrats.

Will party dissolution lead to candidate marketing firms and heavily financed interest groups?

PARTY DISSOLUTION VERSUS PARTY REORGANIZATION

Many political observers believe that the basic response of the parties to shifting issues will be not to change at all. Parties will continue as awkward, somewhat illogical combinations of interests concerned more with brokering, bargaining, and election-winning than taking positions on issues. The two big parties will survive in part *because* they are undoctrinaire, sprawling, many-sided, and essentially disorganized and unstructured. Others are far less hopeful. They see the main alternative to party realignment to be party *dissolution.*[4] Parties will continue to decline in membership, voter support, financial strength, organization, morale, and influence. These observers do not welcome the dissolution of parties, for it means that politics will be even more dominated by candidates, candidates' personal organizations, candidate marketing firms, professional fund-raisers, heavily financed interest groups, and a highly individualistic, personalistic leadership—and possibly by a new version of the old-fashioned "man on horseback." But they see no alternative.

Still others feel that this kind of rootless politics is the very antithesis of government by the people and that there is indeed a hopeful alternative—party reform and modernization. Their specific proposals—procedural reforms, broadened participation, democratized delegate selection, and general party modernization—were discussed in Chapter 11. But party modernizers hope that certain of these proposed reforms might be especially promising for a new emphasis on *issues* and *policy:*

1. *Citizen involvement.* Modernized parties, it is urged, would provide rank-and-file citizens with a mechanism for the discussion of issues. This is the *party caucus,* one of the oldest political institutions in America. The caucus, like the convention, was popular in nineteenth-century America but later was attacked for coming under the control of bosses. A rejuvenated and democratic caucus system would provide a place in every community where party members could debate issues, take positions on policy questions, and choose delegates to party caucuses or conventions at higher levels where party issues and planks could be further acted on. Caucuses, unlike the typical party committee today, would be open to all registered members of the party; and every member, whether a grizzled old party veteran or a college junior, would have one vote.

2. *Policy councils.* Party debate and discussion would be much improved if it had the benefit of advice from informed specialists. The national Democratic party established in the 1950s an advisory council, assisted by an unusually able staff of economists, lawyers, former government officials, and others, and this council helped develop many of the ideas that animated the Kennedy and Johnson Administrations. The Republican party has experimented with somewhat similar devices. Party modernizers today would extend this idea to every level of the party—especially to the state and congressional level.

3. *Congressional district organization.* Party reorganizers are especially concerned with the condition of parties at the congressional district level, in part because that condition varies generally between fair and poor, and in part because they see a huge potential there. It is because party organization in the congressional districts is either nonexistent or badly related to the structure of the presidential party, as they see it,

[4]On aspects of the question of party dissolution, see Walter Dean Burnham, "Politics in the 1970s"; Arthur H. Miller, Warren E. Miller, Alden S. Raine, and Thad A. Brown, "Party in Disarray."

that the political foundations of the presidency are so separated from those of Congress. A member of the House of Representatives rarely has to deal with a district party that (a) helps him get elected; (b) helps maintain support for him after he gets elected; (c) takes a position on issues so that he knows how his party stands back home; (d) lets him understand when the district party feels he is violating the party platform or his promises to his party supporters; (e) opposes him for renomination if he consistently deserts his party on issues before Congress; and (f) is nationally oriented.

Building strong congressional district parties would be particularly significant for the question of *policy output*—what government actually does. It is because parties are so weak in the districts, according to the reorganizers, that parties are so weak in Congress. Strengthen the district parties, encourage the congressmen to be more loyal to the parties that nominated them and helped elect them, make the senators more responsive to the state parties for the same reason—and then the party caucus in the House, the party conference in the Senate, the party whips, party leadership, and party discipline could mean something on Capitol Hill. And if in the meantime presidents had a greater sense of loyalty to parties because of the strengthened national machinery and morale and platform of the parties, the parties might finally serve the great role that the reformers hoped for: strong bridges between the executive and legislative branches, powerful links between the whole presidential establishment and the rank-and-file of Congress, unifying machinery that would produce more coordination on issues *within* parties and a clearer difference and more rational competition *between* parties.

The parties should go back to the people

6 #

PARTY RULE AS MAJORITY RULE OR AS BROKER RULE?

Those who call today for stronger national parties speak in the spirit of the Jeffersonians and Jacksonians who believed in political parties in large part because they believed in majority rule and its egalitarian implications. But not all Americans have favored majority rule in either theory or practice. They favor a different kind of representation, one that is more responsive to group pressures, to shifting coalitions of major organized groups. The latter alternative, which has borrowed intellectually from American thinkers such as John Calhoun, has been called *broker rule*, for it is based on varying degrees of combat and collaboration among endlessly changing and brokering group interests rather than on conflict between a well-organized majority party and a well-organized minority party.

Which is better: a government that represents coalitions of minorities? or a government that represents a relatively clearcut majority and has no obligation to the minority (except to guarantee its right to try to become a majority at the next election)? The answer depends on one's basic values—first of all, on what one expects from government. A system that represents coalitions of minorities usually reflects the trading, collaborating, and compromising that must take place in order to reach agreement among the various groups. Government acts essentially as a go-between, as a mediator among organized groups that have definite policy goals. Under broker rule, leaders cannot get too far ahead of the groups; they must tack back and forth, shifting in response to the changing equilibrium of group pressures. Instead of acting for a united popular majority with a fairly definite program (either liberal or conservative), the government tries to satisfy all major interests by giving them a voice in decisions and sometimes a veto over actions. In the pushing and hauling of political groups, the government is continually involved in delicate balancing acts.

Some political scientists believe that the most representative of all systems is straight majority rule. They believe that when a majority of the voters elects a set of leaders to power, the new government essentially represents the majority and is responsible for enacting its views into law. It leaves the minority only the right, as noted above, to try to become a majority. Many Americans fear strict majority rule. They believe that the majority holds in it the seeds of tyranny. Broker rule, on the other hand, minimizes conflict by absorbing forces on the far right and the far left. Majority rule would result in violent wrenches as first one set of leaders and then an opposing set came to power.

The majoritarians deny this. They maintain that majority rule must be safe because the majority, by definition, embraces a tremendous variety of attitudes and interests, even though it does not include every group across the political spectrum. Because the majority is a broad one, the leaders must act in the interests of a tremendous diversity of voters. Thus a popular majority carries built-in checks and balances.[5] Minorities—not majorities—tend to be extremist.

It is one thing for theorists to argue that the two major parties must stand for more definite programs or policies if they are to give the voters a real choice and empower the winning party to set a firm course for government. It is something else for hard-headed party leaders to take this step, for politicans often prefer to evade tough issues rather than carry them into political battle. Heightened public interest in issues is likely, however, to compel parties to take more definite stands. In that event, which major party will take what kind of stand? On this issue opinions differ widely.

A young Republican columnist, Kevin Phillips, has urged his party to steer firmly in a moderately conservative direction, thus winning long-term support in the South, in many of the border states, in "sunbelt" states such as California and Florida, and in the midwest and prairie-state heartland.[6] A long-time socialist, Michael Harrington, maintains that the Democratic party must move strongly to the left and build a new and powerful coalition of blacks, industrial workers, young people,

[5]The classic statement of this view is Henry Steele Commager, *Majority Rule and Minority Rights* (Oxford University Press, 1943), pp. 55ff.

[6]*The Emerging Republican Majority* (Doubleday, 1970).

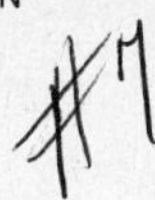

middle-class liberals, and the great mass of the poor. "Don't form a fourth party," he urges radicals, "form a new first party."[7] Two "mainstream" Democrats, Richard Scammon and Ben Wattenberg, contend that if either party goes in a strongly conservative or radical direction it will simply allow another party to dominate the center of the political spectrum—and the party that dominates the center, they say, wins national elections. The Democrats, they hold, must attract or retain the support of the "real majority," which is not simply composed of the poor, the black, and the young. The old Roosevelt coalition is not really dying; rather it needs to be rejuvenated and expanded.[8]

Many political analysts, on the other hand, renounce the idea of stronger and more doctrinal parties.[9] They believe that, given the conditions of American politics, the party-rule model is irrelevant to the United States. They fear that more discipline and doctrine in parties would cut down on party competition in certain areas, for the national leaders of a strong party might enforce sectionally unpopular doctrines (such as integration in the South). They note that office-holders in particular oppose stronger parties because the office-holders fear being unduly pressured by the party organization and prefer a less structured, more "manageable" political base they can hope to control through personal appeal and effective fund-raising.

Recast the Constitution?

For still more reasons party reform leaves critics cold. Stronger, more policy-minded parties would be impossible and undesirable, they feel, because the American political environment is inhospitable to "party government." Parties in particular could never "bring government together"—that is, create teamwork between president and Congress and among different levels of government—because our Constitution was carefully designed to fragment governmental authority and to blunt popular power. Parties could not unite government; rather government, with its separated, competitive, and counterbalancing institutions, tends to divide parties. The choosing of three different sets of officials at the national level alone, the staggering of elections, federalism, the "long ballot"—these and other structural features virtually pulverize parties.

[7]*Toward a Democratic Left* (Macmillan, 1968); and, by the same author, "Don't Form a Fourth Party: Form a New First Party," *New York Times Magazine* (September 13, 1970), p. 28. See also David S. Broder, *The Party's Over* (Harper & Row, 1972).

[8]*The Real Majority* (Coward-McCann, 1970). See also Ben J. Wattenberg, *The Real America* (Doubleday, 1974), esp. Ch. 21.

[9]For a trenchant critique of the ideas of a group of political scientists who called twenty-five years ago for "more responsible political parties," see Evron M. Kirkpatrick, "Toward a More Responsible Two-Party System: Political Science, Policy Science, or Pseudo-Science?" *American Political Science Review* (December 1971), pp. 965–90, and sources cited therein.

These critics agree with the party reorganizers that the main problem is the fragmentation of governmental power at a time when the people need a powerful agency to provide a concerted antiinflation and antirecession policy, a coordinated energy policy, a unified military and foreign policy, a coherent national growth policy, a globally relevant food policy, an integrated system of intergovernmental relations, and more. But the way to achieve this kind of integration, they insist, is not to pursue the will-o'-the-wisp of party government but by striking at the heart of the problem. And the heart of the problem, as they see it, lies in the original decision of 1787 to create a government of separated institutions sharing power. That system has succeeded in preventing activist presidents from planning, putting through, and carrying out concerted policy; but it did not succeed in preventing the Nixon White House from bursting temporarily through the "fences" around power that the framers had built into the Constitution. (Although in most ways the system did ultimately work: Nixon was forced to resign, and those who worked for him and who were allegedly responsible for the abuse of power were forced to stand trial.)

REBUILDING THE STRUCTURE

Some of these critics content themselves with proposals less to change the structure than to make it more efficient. Certain of these proposals have been noted in earlier chapters: improving the performance of Congress by modifying the seniority system; reorganizing the committee structure; abolishing the electoral college; strengthening administrative leadership; streamlining the Cabinet; granting the president the item veto. Other critics would go farther; they would fundamentally reorganize the leadership structure without changing the basic system of distribution of power and checks and balances.

Such plans come in different combinations, but one will illustrate the sweep of the proposals. Rexford Tugwell, former New Deal brain-truster and governor of Puerto Rico, has proposed a "model Constitution" under which a more limited president would have a nine-year term; one vice-president would be in charge of "internal" affairs and another, new vice-president in charge of "general" affairs and would succeed the president in event of a vacancy; the fifty states would be reorganized into about twenty "new states" of equal size, requiring the regrouping of small states into larger ones; the House of Representatives with a strengthened speakership would become the basic law-making branch, and the Senate, enlarged to take in the veteran leadership of the nation, would have essentially the role of the House of Lords in Britain; and the new constitution could be changed—and indeed whole new constitutions could be adopted—by straight majority vote of the people.[10]

Other critics would go farther still. If the framers basically failed to

[10]Rexford G. Tugwell, *The Emerging Constitution* (Harper's Magazine Press, 1974). A less sweeping but equally thought-provoking argument for a new constitution is Charles M. Hardin, *Presidential Power and Accountability* (University of Chicago Press, 1974).

contain power by fragmenting it, they contend, then the solution for twentieth-century America is to reverse that decision and create a more effective set of controls by the legislature and executive over each other. Such a reversal means establishing exactly what the framers did *not* establish—a parliamentary form of government.

Under this form the voters elect only a legislature at the national level, and the legislature in turn chooses the prime minister, who in turn selects a cabinet from his party leadership in the legislature and proceeds to run the country. During the Watergate crisis, when the impeachment process was proceeding with agonizing slowness and strain, some Americans watched with admiration as Canada, West Germany, Britain, Israel, and several other democracies changed their leadership with ease and dispatch. It was widely agreed that if any Western prime minister had run into political and legal difficulties as severe as President Nixon's, that prime minister would have had to resign, call an election, take his and his government's case to the people, and let the voters decide. It all seemed so simple and fair. Why not adopt it in America?

"That's the trouble with a monarchy—they can't vote you out of office."

Copyright © 1956. Reprinted by permission of Saturday Review/World and Joseph Mirachi.

The easy answer to this question is that the American people, whatever their current disillusionment with the presidential (or better, presidential-congressional-judicial) form of government, simply are not (and probably never will be) convinced enough of the superiority of parliamentary government to go through the long, laborious, and complex process of drastically amending the Constitution and repudiating a basic decision of the framers. That may be a correct answer, but it is not a sufficient one. The political scientist must analyze the merits of the proposal, whatever the practical possibility of its adoption.

But few in the profession—and not many outside it—support such a basic alteration. Most fear that the parliamentary alternative might produce in the United States the kind of "hair-trigger" government that caused unstable and weak regimes in prewar Europe. They believe that the unity and representativeness of parliamentary governments rests more on the quality of their *party* systems than on the nature of their parliamentary processes. They remind us that in Britain, for example, virtually all changes in government in this century have been caused not by votes of confidence in Parliament but by decisions by the electorate—and that aside from the more flexible timing of parliamentary elections, the basic system is not all that different from the American.

AGAIN—ENDS AND MEANS

The debate over basic constitutional reform raises in acute form the issue of the differences between *principle* democrats and *process* democrats first discussed in Chapter 1. If the framers combined brilliantly the perspectives of both process and principle democrats, can Americans today equally well appreciate the interlinkage of ends and means in considering changes in the processes of democracy? The process democrat is willing to abide by constitutional procedures even when he loathes the result—for example, the impeachment and removal of a president. The principle democrat believes that processes must always be tested against their actual consequences for the facing of issues and the output of policy.

These conflicting views provide a crucible for democratic leadership. Is a leader a person who can override established processes in pursuit of some higher goal, who can withstand current majority feeling when he is convinced that that feeling violates fundamental democratic principles? Or does a leader try mainly to protect democratic processes? Can a leader do both?

Process democrats reason as follows: A governmental system should be tested basically on *how* it governs rather than on *what* it does. Does it protect the right of everyone to take part in the choice of policies and of leaders? Does it broadly represent the views of the general citizenry in what it does? Does it ensure that due procedure is observed in the enactment of policy—for example, that measures are fully debated in Congress and that citizens can challenge enacted measures in the courts? Process democrats may wholly disapprove of the actions that result from all these due procedures. But they believe that in the long run these procedures on the "input" side of government will lead to good policies on the "output" side of government.

Principle democrats reason as follows: Leaders must be concerned about the general welfare of the whole nation in the long run, not just the immediate interests of their constituents at any one time. Leaders must meet the test not only of current majorities but also of history. In the first decade of this century, not many Americans were intensely concerned about conservation, but Theodore Roosevelt was, and we feel that he acted responsibly in setting aside areas for recreation for all the generations that followed. Most Americans in 1941 were either isolationist or unaware of the menace of Hitlerism; Franklin Roosevelt acted on the basis of principle, not representation, when he prepared the country as much as possible for war. Vice-President Nixon wanted the United States to intervene to help the French in Indochina back in 1954; by the hindsight of history most feel that President Eisenhower did the right thing by not sending in the bombers. Various senators have recently been urging a substantial redistribution of income, though they have not felt much pressure for this policy from the poor in their states.

Process democrats are skeptical of all this. How does one know at the time where virtue lies, on whose side history (which, after all, is written by historians with all their own defects of vision) will be written? Was Herbert Hoover acting responsibly when he stuck to his principle of limited government action in the Depression, when many people wanted him to act? Did President Nixon act responsibly in ordering the secret, unauthorized bombings in Cambodia? Beware, say the process democrats, of sticking to your principles because you think you know better than the people and their current leaders who work through the usual processes of government. History has seen many examples of reactionary and revolutionary groups—wholly sincere and principled—that have gained power under the banner of some grand doctrine but then come to believe that they know better than the people and end up imposing their will *on* the people—all in the name of principle and the public interest.

Principle democrats concede the force of this point. But they insist that they are not talking about just *any* set of principles. A Joseph McCarthy might be wholly sincere in his inquisitorial and bullying tactics, but his "principles" would violate both the premises and the processes of American democracy. There must be some test of principle—some higher standard, some "public philosophy" in Walter Lippmann's term—against which the actions of leaders must be measured. The measuring rod must be the long-term, fundamental, deep-seated principles of a people—in the American case, the ideas of freedom, individual liberty, due process, fair representation, equality, and opportunity that have been spelled out in countless speeches, manifestos, and doctrines since the beginnings of the republic. To be sure, these principles are hazy and often disregarded. But they are the only yardsticks we have for measuring what governments do.

The authors of this book differ on the question of how much emphasis should be given to the whole concept of responsibility. Burns, perhaps out of his long study of presidential leadership, believes that public officials must always keep before them a sense of responsibility for the on-going nation, for humanity, for history, and asks that they not be so overwhelmed by short-run popular pressures that they submerge the long-run good.[11] Peltason, perhaps out of his skepticism of leaders, believes that the concept of responsibility, like that of patriotism or virtue, can be the refuge of scoundrels as well as saints. He would distinguish between the use of the concept for his own personal values and its use as an analytical instrument for evaluating governments and leaders. Cronin, noting that bursts of creative innovation in our system have come from persons who respected constitutional means *as well as* democratic ends, believes that the truly great leader in a democracy must be both a process and a principle democrat.

A new "revolution"?

"Would you like to write out the ticket?"

Copyright © 1970. Reprinted by permission of Saturday Review/World and Robert Minter.

A few Americans would like to celebrate the bicentennial, which, they remind us, commemorates the start of a *revolution*, by revolting against the whole present system and changing it root and branch. They are convinced that fast and comprehensive change in American society can be achieved neither through party and other political reforms nor through constitutional recasting. Very few of these modern radicals want or expect any kind of violent revolution. But they would like to see a fundamental "democratization" of American politics.

Radical critics of American government disagree strongly among themselves as to both the right diagnosis and the right prescription.

[11]For a parallel theme, see John F. Kennedy, *Profiles in Courage* (Harper & Row, 1955).

Some see American government as autocratic, fascistic, oppressive, tyrannical—in essence a police state. Those who hold this view differ over who really controls the government: some say an economic oligarchy made up of corporation heads; others point to the military; some blacks see a tyrannical rule by whites; other critics see some combination of these and other "sinister" forces—for example, mass media executives, munitions makers, reactionary political leaders, heads of a few giant corporations. But whatever group or combination of groups holds power, it is said, the result is the same: control by oligarchs, impotence of the great popular majority, suppression of civil liberties, oppression of students, blacks, and other powerless minorities. And these critics point to calamities such as the killing of students at Kent State and Jackson State as proof of the inherent iniquity of the "system."

Elitism & Pluralism explain how power is divided

THE CHARGE OF ELITISM (Theories of power distribution)

Others contend that the American system is not "government by the people" but actually government by an *elite*. This critique is less sharp and sweeping than the first but perhaps even more unsettling to "conventional wisdom" about the existing system. The elite is seen as a comparatively small number of people who exert a tremendous amount of economic, social, and political power. They may be wise or stupid, benign or cruel, concerned about the problems of the masses or blind to them, representative of the people as a whole or concerned only about themselves, responsible before the "bar of history" or as frivolous and heedless as Marie Antoinette; whatever their character or virtue or lack of it, the members of the elite make the great decisions and the people as a whole remain essentially impotent. Elites dominate the mass media, organized interest groups, the courts, legislatures, and bureaucracies; elites wrote the Constitution originally and now dominate the interpretation of it; elites are powerful enough to keep the great "popular" instrumentalities such as elections, political parties, and the presidency from having much control over government.

It is important to note what this charge of elitism does *not* say. "Elitists" (who believe that elites in fact govern but who do not necessarily believe they *should* do so) do not all claim that the American government is despotic or totalitarian, that a few men at the top rigidly control the great mass at the bottom, that the masses are completely downtrodden and impotent, or that a socialist or communist or highly decentralized system would necessarily be any better. They *do* see a sharp constrast between the claims and the rhetoric of "government by the people" on the one hand and its actual substance and achievements on the other.[12] (4)

[12]An extensive elite-theorist literature has developed. See especially C. Wright Mills, *The Power Elite* (Oxford University Press, 1956); Peter Bachrach, *The Theory of Democratic Elitism* (Little, Brown, 1967); Lewis Coser, *The Functions of Social Conflict* (Free Press, 1964); Ralf Dahrendorf, *Class and Conflict in Industrial Societies* (Stanford University Press, 1959); and Thomas R. Dye and L. Harmon Zeigler, *The Irony of Democracy* (Wadsworth, 1970).

Not only do elites make the key decisions, according to this view; they tend to perpetuate themselves. While there may be a slow circulation of persons out of the mass and into the elite, and out of the elite and back into the mass, the elite largely comes from the upper socioeconomic levels of society and sees to it that new members of the elite do likewise. In the relatively few cases when others are admitted to the charmed circle, the price of admission is acceptance of the basic values of the elite. Hence elitism means conservatism and even stagnation in government.

THE PLURALISTS' REBUTTAL

Those who see power as widely distributed among individuals and groups, leaders and followers, and governmental and political officials in American society are sometimes called "pluralists," a much-abused term that usually means the *decentralization* of power. Most pluralists are not at opposite poles from most elite theorists. Pluralists generally do not contend that American government can be run or should be run by the great mass of people. No one favors government by public opinion, for example. Pluralists may favor full citizen participation, but they do not believe that the masses should take part in actual decision-making over foreign affairs or monetary policy or farm programs. Like elite theorists, they see great differences in political power between the people at the top and at the bottom of the class system; they grant that elites, considering their small numbers, have disproportionate control over public opinion and governmental decisions; they recognize that there is no free and easy access to the elites on the part of the masses.[13]

The pluralists contend, however, that the elite theorists have exaggerated the extent of elitism in American society and government, and also the significance of it. Instead of one central, powerful, unified set of elites, the pluralists see a variety of shifting elites in politics, government, business, labor, and education, along with a host of "out" elitist groups that operate through antiestablishment newspapers, through demonstrations and other forms of protest, or even through violence. Some elite groups are closed to the masses, pluralists grant, but other elites are open to newcomers and gain in vigor and influence through infusions of new blood. Some elites are conservative and unresponsive to the people as a whole, but others are highly "public regarding." Different elites, moreover, compete with one another for status and influence, and in doing so they draw more and more participation from the masses. In a system where elections determine who will take formal authority, elites are constantly tested by their capacity to appeal to popular favor and to support popular leaders. The balance between elitist and pluralist tendencies is not fixed and static; it varies from year to

[13]The pluralist literature is extensive. See, for example, Robert A. Dahl, *Pluralist Democracy in the United States* (Rand McNally, 1967); David B. Truman, *The Governmental Process* (Knopf, 1951); Arnold Rose, *The Power Structure* (Oxford University Press, 1967); and Robert A. Dahl, *Who Governs?* (Yale University Press, 1961).

year, from place to place, from issue to issue, from government to government. Contending groups, especially political parties, have a vested interest in exposing and attacking those in positions of authority.

The pluralists concede that the American system has not adequately taken into account the views and needs of certain groups who have been denied the right to participate in the political process. Until recently blacks have been so oppressed that their aspirations and needs could be and were ignored by those who governed. The poor have often been underrepresented, and consumer needs have not been adequately presented. But the pluralists contend that these are not faults *of* the system but *in* the system, faults that can and should be corrected. What is needed is *more* pluralism so that the interests of all and all the interests are recognized in the political process.

THE ARGUMENT JOINED

The crux of the elitist belief is that the most conspicuously democratic institutions, in Edelman's words, "are largely symbolic and expressive in function" rather than a means through which the mass public achieves goals that represent its real, concrete interest. Party battles, combat among interest groups, exciting elections, presidential conventions watched by tens of millions of people—all these may seem to be life-and-death matters to the voters but they are essentially matters of appearance. "A dramatic symbolic life among abstractions," says Edelman, "becomes a substitute gratification for the pleasure of remolding the concrete environment."[14] The people only *think* they are governing themselves.

This elitist conception turns essentially on a view of the great public as largely uninformed, apathetic, credulous, and unable to see below the surface of things. It also minimizes the public's ability to learn through experience, to evaluate the politics of the *deed,* even if it is fooled by the propaganda of the *word.* In short, it reminds us of the point made earlier that the expert may know all about the shoe but only the shoe-*wearer* can tell whether the shoe pinches. The elitists do not accept this argument. They contend that the shoe-wearer may be talked into thinking that a shoddy pair of shoes is really the latest thing in style, and that it is worth a little pinching of his feet, which he is only imagining anyway.

Is there any empirical evidence to throw light on this question of the political efficacy of the mass public? In their classic study of Elmira, New York, Berelson and his colleagues concluded that *individual* voters were indeed uninvolved in politics, not well informed, parochial, and unable to think clearly and "rationally." But they also found that the qualities of interest and understanding that might be missing in a particular individual could be found in a society or community *as a whole.* Thus in the community as a whole they found balances between in-

[14]Murray Edelman, *The Symbolic Uses of Politics* (University of Illinois Press, 1967), pp. 9, 19.

volvement and indifference, stability and flexibility, progress and conservatism, consensus and cleavage, individualism and collectivism.[15] This conclusion parallels a point made earlier in this volume that while some persons are intensely active and effective in politics, and others are withdrawn and impotent, the great number of people is characterized by a *range* of involvement, semi-involvement, and noninvolvement.

A comparable conclusion was reached by Almond and Verba after an intensive study of five Western nations, including the United States. These investigators, too, found a contrast between the classic ideals of civic interest and participation and rational thinking and the *existence* in these nations of political apathy, narrowness, and irrationality. But they concluded that tendencies toward political apathy and intensity, toward support of the status quo and support of change, toward consensus and cleavage, and toward other conflicting qualities are distributed widely through societies and even within individuals. Hence these "good" and "bad" qualities tend to cancel each other out. For a democracy cannot thrive when all the citizens are passionately aroused politically any more than it can when all the citizens are inert and ignorant.[16] Thus, according to such studies, it is in the balancing of opposite tendencies in large publics that we find the safeguards of democracy. These are the *social* and *psychological* checks and balances that parallel—and strengthen—the constitutional ones.

PARTICIPATORY DEMOCRACY

Those who view American government as fundamentally more elitist than pluralist are typically far more precise in their critiques than in their proposals for change. Many critics, especially on the left, agree, however, on the need for sharply increasing the role of *direct popular participation* in discussing issues and making decisions, if a society is really to support its claim of being a government by the people.

What many people would regard as the most perfect form of democracy, as Dahl says, exists when every person within a given set of persons "has a full and equal opportunity to participate in all decisions and in all the processes of influence, persuasion, and discussion that bear on that decision."[17] Direct participation in decision-making, its advocates contend, will serve two major purposes. It will enhance the dignity, self-respect, and understanding of the individual by giving him responsibility for the decisions that shape his life. And it will act as a "safeguard against anti-democratic and undemocratic forms of govern-

John Gardner, chairman of Common Cause—a notable "cause" group.

[15]Bernard R. Berelson, Paul F. Lazarsfeld, and William N. McPhee, *Voting* (University of Chicago Press, 1954), p. 312.

[16]Gabriel A. Almond and Sidney Verba, *The Civic Culture* (Princeton University Press, 1963), Chap. 15. On the political intelligence of the American public, see also V. O. Key, Jr., *The Responsible Electorate* (Harvard University Press, 1966).

[17]Robert A. Dahl, *After the Revolution?* (Yale University Press, 1970), p. 67.

ment and prevent the replacement of democracy by dictatorship or tyranny. This rests upon a theory of self-protection which maintains that interests can be represented, furthered, and protected pre-eminently by those whom they concern directly."[18]

Supporters of participatory democracy see three areas of high potential. One is in the *workplace:* employees should have a central role in decisions about health and safety regulations, pace and quality of work, rest time, pollution control, choice of supervisors. A second is the *community:* the aim here is to achieve local, grassroots control of public institutions and services. Town or neighborhood meetings would control spending and administration in medical clinics, publicly financed child care centers, planning of open space and land use, the running of parks, recreation areas and zoos. Third, *electoral politics:* here participatory democracy calls for more extensive use of the initiative and referendum, especially at the local level; greater participation in local party caucuses and committees; quick creation of local "cause groups" when some issue becomes acute. Local initiative campaigns are seen as potentially powerful means of stimulating community interest, mobilizing activity, and creating informal caucuses and councils.[19] Some believe that the electoral effort should be linked with local party committees; others contend that becoming involved in old-line party organizations would be the "kiss of death."

Experience with many forms of participatory democracy suggests it has limitations as a form of decision-making. In an age of burgeoning population, increasingly complex economic and social systems, and enormously wide-ranging decision-making units of government, direct participation has come to have only a marginal place in self-government. As a practical matter, people simply cannot put in endless hours taking part in every decision that affects their lives. The larger and more complex the political unit, the more citizens must delegate to representatives. Even New England towns find that they must give up the old town meeting and change to representative town meetings (wherein a limited number of members are chosen by their neighbors) when the town population goes beyond 15,000 or 20,000. Widespread participatory democracy could be achieved only if we reversed the economic, political, and social trends of the last two centuries and reverted to a nation of thousands of small, neighborhood-sized, largely self-governing units.[20]

Involvement of large numbers of citizens in civic affairs is, of course, a worthy goal, especially at the local level within party committees, city

[18]Peter Y. Medding, " 'Elitist' Democracy: An Unsuccessful Critique of a Misunderstood Theory," *Journal of Politics* (August 1969), p. 642. See generally Peter Bachrach, *The Theory of Democratic Elitism: A Critique* (Little, Brown, 1967).

[19]Stewart Burns, "The Struggle for 'Unlimited Democracy,' " unpublished paper, University of California, Santa Barbara, 1974, pp. 7–12.

[20]For reflections on such tendencies in a different political culture, see Benjamin R. Barber, *The Death of Communal Liberty: A History of Freedom in a Swiss Mountain Canton* (Princeton University Press, 1974).

councils, school boards, airport authorities, conservation districts. And we have long seen a tendency through unionization and other organizational efforts by workers to win for employees a stronger voice in working conditions and factory decisions. But we must distinguish between democracy *as* participation and a greater role for participation *in* a democracy. The immediate answer to the question "participation or representation?" is enlarging the role of participation *in* representation—that is, broadening the power of all people to take part in local decision-making and to take part in choosing their representatives in larger units of government.

Conclusion: the changelessness of change

No one could have predicted the course of the last fifteen years—the assassinations, political crises, burned cities, endless wars, the resignation of a president under fire, the pardoning of the old president by the new, and all the rest. The next decade or so is equally unpredictable. We do not know what pressures and crises await us. In half an hour our daily lives and hopes, our social and political institutions, the very fabric of our lives, could become a cinder. Even without a nuclear war, we may be headed for cataclysmic events. An environmentalist has suggested that the 1970s may be characterized by a Politics of Despair; the 1980s by a Politics of Desperation; the 1990s by a Politics of Catastrophe; the twenty-first century as an Era of Annihilation.[21] An economist has predicted that the population explosion in poor lands, the looming shortage of food and raw materials, the spread of nuclear weapons to small countries, and the stupendous pressures for redistributing wealth between poorer and richer nations will produce a literally unbearable burden on democracy as we know it.[22] The result might be far less "government *by* the people" than "government *of* the people" by authoritarian, even tyrannical leaders.

Some may dismiss such "prophets of gloom and doom." Has not the nation survived depression, world wars, Vietnam, inflation, the near-impeachment and the resignation of a president? The consequences, intended and unintended, of events are hard to anticipate. The crucial influences of our history may be a mixed bag of political and nonpolitical developments—the invention of the transistor, the jet age, the "pill" and its effect on population, the continuing emancipation of women, the assumption that an eighteen-year-old is legally an adult. One of the most interesting developments, reflected in recent public opinion research, is that Americans are increasingly interested in political issues and governmental policy, and that they now can approach policy less as prisoners of their group, party, or occupational status.

[21]Richard Falk, *This Endangered Planet* (Random House, 1971), pp. 420f.

[22]Robert L. Heilbroner, *An Inquiry into the Human Prospect* (Norton, 1974).

Thus the political party, for good and for ill, acts less as a guiding and stabilizing force; the voter thinks and decides more on his own.

Even more remarkable is the reversal by income groups of their traditional position on issues. We expect the rich to be generally more conservative (that is, in favor of the status quo), the poor to be more liberal. But on new types of issues that are becoming salient in the United States, the affluent are more liberal and the working class more conservative. Thus a higher percentage of those making over $15,000 a year than those making under $5,000 a year:

Are favorable to Ralph Nader.
Believe abortions should be legalized.
Feel that blacks are not demanding more than they are ready for.
Would not turn in a son or daughter possessing marijuana.
Would not ban newspapers that preach revolution.

On the eve of the bicentennial, the focus in American politics, according to this analysis, had moved away from both the old economic and social issues to a heightened appreciation of liberty, privacy, and pluralism. In 1970 the public condoned the Kent State killings; less than four years later most Americans viewed the episode as "repressive and unjustified." In 1970 most Americans considered student protesters, black civil rights protesters, homosexuals, and atheists as harmful and dangerous to the country; four years later only a minority did. The villains in the mid-1970s in the popular mind were vigilante groups, businessmen making illegal campaign contributions, generals conducting and then covering up secret bombing raids, government officials trying to use official intelligence agencies, like the CIA and FBI, for political advantage.[23] Yet no more than 5 percent of the people wanted to "overthrow the system."

Perhaps these were temporary shifts of attitudes in response to Watergate and its blatant threats to individual liberty, due process, and privacy. Yet there were strong indications that those holding the more libertarian position were gaining in numbers and political power, while those groups opposing—generally the less educated and lower income—were dropping in relative strength. On traditional "bread and butter" issues the lower-income groups were taking a strong stand for more welfare programs, tax reform, comprehensive federal health insurance—but those making over $15,000 were taking an almost equally strong stand in favor of these. The old political guidelines seemed truly to be in disarray.

One other trend particularly concerns students reading this book. By 1976 over one-fourth of the electorate will be in their teens and twenties, and this group will be more highly educated (at least in years) than ever.[24] So a college student of politics seeking to divine the winds of

[23]Source: Louis Harris, June 1974.

[24]Burnham, "Politics in the 1970s," pp. 40–41.

change could do a lot worse than listen to the talk around him — as well as to the talk of the large number of his or her contemporaries *not* in college.

One thing is certain amid all the murk. The celebrations and the traumas, the advances and failures, the processes and institutions of a "government by the people," as contrasted with something called the State in other lands, are inseparable from the daily lives and hopes and needs of 215,000,000 Americans. No one has made this argument more eloquently than Walt Whitman, in his "By Blue Ontario's Shore":

O I see flashing that this America is only you and me,
Its power, weapons, testimony, are you and me,

Its crimes, lies, thefts, defections, are you and me,
Its Congress is you and me, the officers, capitols, armies, ships are you and me,
Its endless gestation of new states are you and me,
The war (that war so bloody and grim, the war I will henceforth forget), was you and me,
Natural and artificial are you and me,
Freedom, language, poems, employments, are you and me,
Past, present, future, are you and me.

I dare not shirk any part of myself,
Nor any part of America good or bad. . . .

Part Seven Government in action: functions and performance

A PROBLEM GUIDE

In Part Seven we come to what the national government actually does. Here we will reappraise the more important federal functions, ranging from central decisions about defense weapons systems and SALT-talk negotiations to matters of taxation, consumer protection, and anti-inflation battles. As we analyze these functions and governmental performance in these areas, we shall see that they raise anew many of the theme concerns already explored in this book. Here we shall see how they relate to the functions of the national government.

In these times of crisis, can there really be a government by the people? Do national responsibilities—the tasks now carried out by national policy-makers—prove that democratic government is merely a cloak for rule by the few rather than the people as a whole? Do the complex operations of the federal government suggest that a democratic system cannot effectively perform the critical tasks of strengthening and stabilizing the economy? That it can protect and enhance national resources, cope with the energy crisis, provide for an adequate and financially fair system of national health insurance? Chapter 23, 24, and 25 provide factual background necessary for considering these charges.

Is our nearly two-hundred-year-old Constitution still viable in this age of international tensions and increasing world scarcities? The early 1970s witnessed heightened expectations for an era of détente, but more recently we hear mainly of the world population crisis, world food shortages, continuing energy and precious mineral scarcities, and, of course, extreme inflation. Because of the often anarchical balance of power relation among nations, our policy-makers must be able to move quickly to head off crisis or to meet it head on. They have the power to mobilize and manage our armed forces without getting the consent of the voters or event the consent of the Congress—and sometimes without announcing their plans ahead of time. Under these new conditions, what happens to traditional constitutional processes of open debate and deliberative action? Does the unity of purpose and action required in an age of nuclear diplomacy make democratic practices obsolete? Or can new processes of foreign and military policy-making be fashioned to fit the age? What about the traditional supremacy of civilian over military leaders? What about the unusual counterrevolutionary activities of the CIA? These are some of the problems addressed in Chapters 20, 21, and 22.

What about the people—how do they get taken into account in the way our government functions? The increasing role of the national government in almost every aspect of our lives raises the basic question of whether big government narrows or enhances individual liberty and initiative. Are we more free today, or less free? In our quest for greater equality and affirmative action do we risk a leveling down and an oppression that may deprive us of creativity and individuality? And for whom does the national government performs its immense variety of tasks? Does it serve major needs of the people as a whole, or does it actually operate on behalf of the fatcats and well organized elite interests? Does federal regulation and taxation, ostensibly undertaken for the general welfare, actually turn out to protect the industry or profession being regulated and taxed at the expense of the public interest? Chapters 23, 24, and 25 investigate these and related questions.

What ensures that national policy-makers will act responsibly? Those administering federal functions have great discretion and power. In matters of foreign and defense policy, should officials be accountable to the people merely through periodic elections, or is something else needed to prevent the abuse of power? Can the political system, as it is now designed, be made to work for underrepresented groups such as women, blacks, the elderly, and the poor? Do we need policy-makers who are more specifically instructed by their parties as to what is to be done and how it should be done, or should our governmental system allow our leaders more leeway to act quickly and comprehensively when such action is needed?

This section will also extend our earlier treatment in Chapter 18 of how various interests, institutions, ideas, and individuals interrelate in the policy-making process. Does policy result from extensive planning and rational analysis of all the alternatives? Or does it result from bargaining among individuals and groups who work out compromises that are acceptable to the major power brokers that make up our system? Or is policy the result of changing coalitions in which groups and individuals combine with one another to give one group what it wants in return for what another group wants?

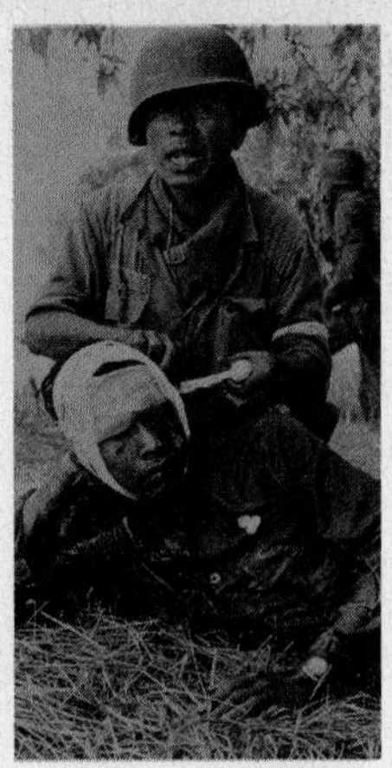

Chapter 20 Foreign policy: politics and problems

Every nation seeks peace, or at least claims to, but must be ready to wage war. On no set of problems are leaders of nations more involved than those of foreign policy. The United States is no exception. Most of our presidents of this century, whatever their personal preferences, have found that our relations with other nations take priority over all other issues. Most of our recent presidents have spent more than half of their time on foreign policy matters.

The United States is prepared for fighting even while working for détente because of the one momentous fact that dominates all foreign policy-making—the world is made up of sovereign and independent nations, each pursuing its own national self-interest.

Critics charge that our nation becomes embroiled in overseas military activity because we have come to see many of the world's problems exclusively in military terms. In the words of one critic: "Creating a controlled global environment for the number one nation is merely an extension of the principle of prudent corporate management. The uncertainties and the unknown quantities are great."[1] Yet the mid-

[1]Richard J. Barnet, *Roots of War: The Men And Institutions Behind U.S. Foreign Policy* (Penguin Books, 1972), p. 145.

1970s witnessed at least the appearance of U.S. withdrawal from overseas conflicts. With the gradual reduction of tensions in Indochina and perhaps also in the Middle East, an era of détente seemed possible. But a major paradox of U.S. foreign policy was summed up by former President Nixon when he said "Détente does not mean the end of danger. . . . These processes are not automatic or easy. They require vigilance and firmness and exertion. Nothing would be more dangerous than to assume prematurely that the dangers have disappeared."[2] President Ford has consistently expressed these same cautions.

American foreign policy does not function in a vacuum. It must take into account our national goals and supply the means of attaining them. It must consider our immediate needs as well as our long-range interests; our adversaries as well as our allies; our strategic requirements as well as our political ideals.

Dramatic changes in recent years have transformed America's position in the world. For a generation we were preoccupied with preventing the Cold War from escalating into a hot war. Our interventions in Cuba, Vietnam, the Dominican Republic, Cambodia, and elsewhere caused great discontent worldwide and deeply divided our nation. In the 1970s, in the wake of almost ten years of war in Indochina, most Americans in and out of public office welcomed an end to the war and the beginning of negotiations.

The substance and effect of American foreign policy is widely debated today. What officials and agencies actually make foreign policy? Have we relied too heavily on presidential leadership? Is American foreign policy overly dominated by military considerations? What role do and should intelligence agencies assume in our relations with other nations? Does foreign policy-making differ from domestic policy-making as far as the roles of experts, the news media, and mass public are concerned?

These are hard questions, but answers must be sought if the United States is to share constructively in the leadership of the world. Nearly everyone agrees that the United States must maintain its strength if it is to help achieve peace among nations. At the same time it must preserve *and improve* its own system of responsive, popular government or it loses what it is trying to safeguard.

The United States in a changing world

The chief objective of American foreign policy has been to preserve the security of the United States. To be sure, American politicians have often preferred to speak in high moral terms about safeguarding world

[2]Richard M. Nixon, "United States Foreign Policy for the 1970's: Shaping a Durable Peace," President's Report to the Congress, May 3, 1973. On related problems see Alec Nove, "Can We Buy Détente?" *New York Times Magazine*, October 13, 1974.

peace rather than to talk the blunt language of power politics. But beneath the high-flown rhetoric, the central purpose of protecting national interests has been fairly consistent.

But promoting the national interests of the United States provides no better guidelines to foreign policy-makers than the standard of the public interest furnishes to those who make domestic policies. Total security is never obtainable much less definable. Our policy-makers try to influence, direct, and shape events—but the rest of the world shapes and influences us. And in recent decades the world about us has been in a process of constant upheaval and regeneration.

SECURITY IN THE SEVENTIES

The world continues to grow smaller in the mid-1970s. Technical progress—satellite communications, for example—and growing food, fuel, and mineral shortages have profoundly changed the international scene. Common interests and mutual problems are forcing traditional conflicts and rivalries aside. Resource scarcities are creating new ones. The old order is changing.

Western Europe, gradually moving toward greater economic and political integration, is more than ever a vital force in world affairs. African and Middle Eastern nations have cast off their colonial ties. For decades in Latin America, more than 300 million people have been combating poverty, disease, and political chaos in an attempt to gain prosperity and dignity. Japan has risen from ashes to become the economic giant of Asia. China, for decades a pariah among nations, has established diplomatic ties with the West. Relations with Castro's Cuba have mellowed. And the various accords among Middle Eastern nations seem, at least temporarily, to have achieved a foundation for stability there. There are hopeful signs about some old problems but other unresolved problems and new crises abound.

NEW TIMES, NEW PROBLEMS AND OLD

By the mid-1970s hopes for a "full generation of peace" seemed overly optimistic. Tension continued to characterize Soviet-Western relations. In Africa racial hatred threatened to ignite half the continent. Energy needs and poverty still fanned the conflict in the Middle East. In Southeast Asia three decades of war diminished chances for a lasting peace.

There was a widespread conviction on the part of many Americans that their government had misinformed them about the events and reasons leading to our involvement in the war in Indochina. The publication of the classified Pentagon Papers opened a new phase in the debate that so often follows an unsuccessful war: who caused it, who is to blame, how can we avoid it in the future?

American involvement in Vietnam had clearly eroded the faith, especially of younger Americans, in the competence and fairness of their public leaders. They challenged the "foreign policy establishment," charged that this elite was fearful of dissent and that it had manipulated public opinion.

Previously, most Americans felt enormous wealth and power markedly increased their responsibilities to make the world safe for democracy and to spread the gospel of American Values. Now, growing numbers of people appeared to favor isolationist policies. However, many others feel that while our wealth and power should be used with restraint we still have a great responsibility for egalitarian action on a global level.

As new and different national priorities and foreign policy were debated, the "lessons of involvement" threatened to become for many Americans what the "lessons of Munich" has been a generation earlier. Chants of "No More Vietnams" resembled the former slogan, "No More Munichs." But just as the indoctrination with the lessons of Munich proved excessive, so too "it would be no less dangerous to make too much of the lessons of Vietnam and allow one failure to condemn a quarter century of diplomacy."[3] On the other hand, might not both slogans be helpful for the future? They may not contradict so much as complement each other; perhaps we have learned that we should now view our relations with foreign nations in less simplistic terms than those of *ally* and *enemy*.

"*My* idea of an American presence in the Mediterranean stops at Jackie's yacht."

Drawing by Alan Dunn; © 1970 The New Yorker Magazine, Inc.

The makers of foreign policy must face all the facts of domestic and internal politics. In deciding what to do, they must consider the political situation in the nations throughout the world and the uncertainties and complexities of politics at home. At this time, when American power makes us the leading actor on the world scene whether we wish the role or not, and when our mistakes may have catastrophic and irreversible consequences, foreign policy-making is one of the most critical tasks facing Americans.

The "lessons of Munich" and memories of Hitler's rise to power in the 1930s were part of American public mood in the 1950s and 1960s.

WHO MAKES FOREIGN POLICY?

It is the awesome responsibility of those who formulate our foreign policies to determine the basic objectives vital to our national interests and to devise programs to achieve these objectives. American foreign policy-makers are neither omnipotent nor omniscient, and they do not control the events that create problems and set limits to solutions. But to the best of their ability and resources these people must decide how to use (or not use) the instruments available to them—bargaining or negotiation, persuasion or progaganda, economic assistance or pressures, and the threat and actual use of armed force.

The responsibility for foreign policy-making was fixed in the Constitution at the national level. However, it did not divide the powers over

[3]Laurence W. Martin, "Military Issues: Strategic Parity and Its Implications" in R. Osgood et al., *Retreat From Empire?* (Johns Hopkins Press, 1973), pp. 170–71.

foreign relations cleanly and evenly. In England control over foreign relations had been vested in the king and his ministers. The framers tried to redress the balance a bit. Many of the powers given to Congress by the Constitution reflect the decision by the framers to take them from the executive branch; they wanted to make what had heretofore been a prerogative of the executive into a more shared relationship with the legislature. Congress was given the power to declare war, to appropriate funds, and make rules for the armed forces. But the president was left as commander in chief of the armed forces and the director of those who negotiate in behalf of this nation with other countries. The courts have the power to interpret treaties, but by and large they have ruled that our relations with other nations are "political" and not judicial issues.

Executive domination of foreign policy-making is a fact of the political life of all nations, including democratic ones. Presidential dominance over American foreign policy has been constant in our history. Since the dawn of the nuclear age it has become one of the central issues of our time. But first we must look at the people within the executive departments who make up the foreign policy establishment—the men and women and organizations through which the president acts.

THE PRESIDENT'S RIGHT-HAND MAN

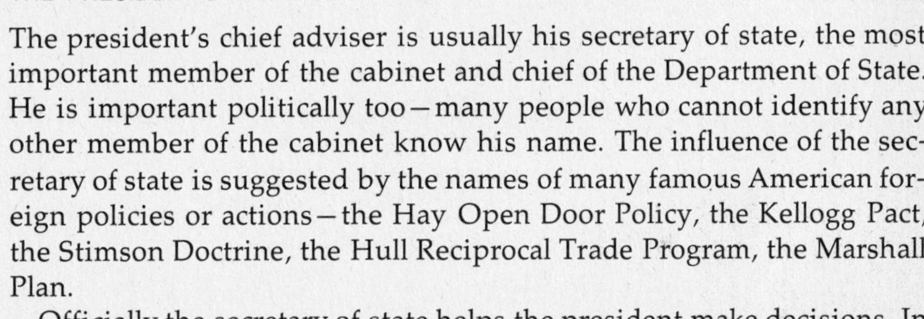

The president's chief adviser is usually his secretary of state, the most important member of the cabinet and chief of the Department of State. He is important politically too—many people who cannot identify any other member of the cabinet know his name. The influence of the secretary of state is suggested by the names of many famous American foreign policies or actions—the Hay Open Door Policy, the Kellogg Pact, the Stimson Doctrine, the Hull Reciprocal Trade Program, the Marshall Plan.

Officially the secretary of state helps the president make decisions. In actual practice the secretary formulates a great deal of foreign policy himself and then secures the president's backing. Just how much influence the secretary exercises depends largely on the president's personal desires. Presidents Harding, Coolidge, Hoover, Eisenhower, and Ford, at least in his first year, turned over to their secretaries of state almost full responsibility for making important policy decisions. Other presidents—for example, Wilson, both Roosevelts, Kennedy, and Nixon—have taken a more active part themselves; indeed, at times they were their own secretaries of state. Even so, important decisions on foreign policy are so numerous that both president and secretary of state play important roles.

The secretary has a large department to administer and multiple roles to fill. He receives many visits from foreign diplomats. He attends international conferences and usually heads our delegation in the General Assembly of the United Nations. He makes key statements on foreign policy, sometimes speaking directly to the people. He appears before congressional committees to explain and justify the administration's policies. He visits other nations to confer with chiefs of state and foreign ministers, sometimes for explicit diplomatic negotiations, as in the case of Henry Kissinger's Middle East "shuttle diplomacy." He also deals directly with our own diplomats in other countries.

The secretary of state, as a leading member of the president's cabinet, sometimes has a hand in shaping general administration policy. He attempts to serve as the president's chief agent in coordinating all the governmental actions that affect our relations with foreign nations. This role is one that, despite presidential directives, secretaries of state have nearly always found difficult to perform, especially when they must deal with the activities of the president's own inner staff or those of some powerful agency head who has close rapport with the president.

The secretary of state is dependent on the support of the president, but he must also command considerable backing in the Congress. Unless he enjoys congressional confidence, the foreign policies proposed by the president may have rough going on Capitol Hill.[4] For this reason, one of the secretary's top assistants is assigned to keep congressmen in touch with the secretary's policies and to serve as a channel of communication between the legislators and the secretary. Broadly speaking, however, the secretary is at the mercy of power relationships in Washington—the relations between president and Congress—all reflecting the temper of the country. And in recent years his impact abroad has depended largely upon his influence at home. The secretary of state must defend and promote his nation to the world while securing and advancing his position in the Congress and with the American people.

THE PRESIDENT'S LEFT-HAND MEN

Decades ago, the president need call only on the secretary of state for advice in formulating foreign policies. Today, foreign policy is intimately related to and affected by every phase of governmental activity—finance, education, agriculture, commerce, and, of course, military affairs. Suppose, for example, the president has to make a decision on a matter of international trade. The specialized knowledge and help he would need are scattered throughout the executive structure, in the Departments of Treasury, Commerce, Labor, and Agriculture, in the Federal Trade Commission, and in the United States Tariff Commission. Fifty agencies are concerned with foreign policy, and all of them are called upon from time to time to furnish advice and make decisions. The secretary of the treasury, for example, not the secretary of state, ordinarily is responsible for discussions with other nations on the flow of international payments and trade.

[4]For an illustration of how important congressional confidence in the secretary of state is for the president's program, see Richard F. Fenno, Jr., *The President's Cabinet* (Harvard University Press, 1959), pp. 203 ff.

In addition to the secretary of state, the secretary of defense is also a major source of advice to a president. Because the main goal of American foreign policy is maximum security for the United States, it is not surprising that the military and defense agencies have a strong voice in the shaping of that policy. Moreover, the line between military and foreign policy is almost impossible to draw, and indeed the National Security Council was even created to help integrate and coordinate the two. A secretary of defense can often have more to say than the secretary of state about our policies toward Cuba, Vietnam, and the Dominican Republic, for example. Also frequently called upon for advice is the chairman of the Joint Chiefs of Staff, the principal military adviser to the president and the secretary of defense. And generals who have been assigned to command international military forces are invited to testify before Congress and to speak in behalf of controversial foreign policies. The influence of a MacArthur, a Marshall, or a Westmoreland on foreign policy is hard to measure but obvious to see.

THE PRESIDENT'S OWN MEN

The secretaries, agency chiefs, and their subordinates are chosen by the president and are expected to support and carry out his decisions. Yet at the same time they retain a measure of independence, and they naturally tend to reflect the views of and to defend the departments and agencies they head.[5] As a result, our presidents have found a need to appoint personal advisers whose loyalties in the making of foreign policy lie solely with the chief executive. Wilson had his Colonel House; Roosevelt, his Harry Hopkins; Eisenhower, his Sherman Adams; Kennedy, his brother Robert and McGeorge Bundy; Johnson, his Walt Rostow; Nixon and Ford, their Henry Kissinger. Since each president views responsibility in a personal way, the special adviser has played a loosely defined role.

Under Nixon, this position was formalized into the office of assistant to the president for national security affairs. Heading a staff of forty to fifty professionals, this assistant was assigned advisory, coordination, and negotiation duties. Originally, this assistant merely kept the president apprised of important developments within the government and around the world. Nixon gave considerably more authority to Henry Kissinger. If Johnson's staff assistants in this post were criticized for shielding him from reality, Kissinger was criticized for shielding the rest of the government from secret negotiations of one kind or another. Perhaps in an attempt to overcome these liabilities Nixon appointed Kissinger as secretary of state. But Kissinger continued to hold the position of assistant to the president for national security affairs, spending mornings at the White House and afternoons at State. This brought to a close, at least for a while, a much-debated controversy over the

[5]See Morton Halperin, *Bureaucratic Politics and Foreign Policy* (Brookings Institution, 1974).

usurpation of State Department authority by White House staff.[6]

INTELLIGENCE AND FOREIGN POLICY

Clearly, policy-makers must have some idea of the direction in which other nations are going to move in order to be able to counter those moves. They need, in other words, high-level foreign policy intelligence. Therefore, those who gather and analyze material are among the most important assistants to the policy-makers—they often become policy-makers themselves.

What is the significance of yesterday's coup in Portugal or Chile? How many trained infantrymen are there in Czechoslovakia? What are the weapons and air strength of the North Korean military? What should we do about Soviet pressure on Poland? Before policy-makers can answer such questions, they want to know a great deal about other countries—their probable reactions to a particular policy, their strengths and weaknesses, and, if possible, their strategic plans and intentions. Moreover, the makers of foreign policy must be familiar with the geographical and physical structure of the nations of the world; with the people—their number, skills, age distribution; the status of their arts, technology, engineering, and sciences; and their political and social systems.

Although most of the information comes from open sources, the term *intelligence work* conjures up visions of spies and undercover agents, and secret intelligence often does supply the crucial and coordinating data. Intelligence work involves three operations—surveillance, research, and transmission. *Surveillance* is the close and systematic observation of developments the world over; *research* is the attempt "to establish meaningful patterns out of what was observed in the past and attempts to get meaning out of what appears to be going on now,[7] and *transmission* is getting the right information to the right people at the right time.

Many agencies engage in intelligence work, among them the State Department's Bureau of Intelligence and Research, the Defense Intelligence Agency, the supersecret National Security Agency (which works on code-breaking and electronic communications systems), the Atomic Energy Commission, the FBI, and, most important, the Central Intelligence Agency. These six agencies form the United States Intelligence Board, which prepares encyclopedic intelligence surveys on most countries of the world.

The CIA was created in 1947 to coordinate the gathering and analysis of information that flows into the various parts of our government from all over the world. Yet organization alone cannot ensure that our policy-

[6]Dean Acheson, "The Eclipse of the State Department," *Foreign Affairs* (July 1971), pp. 593–606. This controversy is also discussed in I. M. Destler, *Presidents, Bureaucrats, and Foreign Policy* (Princeton University Press, 1972).

[7]Sherman Kent, *Strategic Intelligence for American World Policy* (Princeton University Press, 1949), esp. p. 4. On the limits and abuses of intelligence activities, see R. H. Blum, ed., *Surveillance and Espionage in a Free Society* (Praeger, 1972).

makers will know all they need to know. As a close student of intelligence operations has pointed out:

> In both the Pearl Harbor and Cuban crises there was plenty of information. But in both cases, regardless of what the Monday morning quarterbacks have to say, the data were ambiguous and incomplete. There was never a single, definitive signal that said, "Get ready, get set, go!" but rather a number of signals that, when put together, tended to crystallize suspicion. The true signals were always embedded in the noise or irrelevance of the false ones.[8]

When the CIA was established, Congress recognized the dangers to a free society inherent in a secret organization not accountable in the ordinary way for what it does (its funds, for example, are hidden through out the federal budget). Hence it was stipulated that the CIA *is not to engage in any police work or to perform operations within the United States.* But owing to the nature and scope of CIA activities, there is the danger that the CIA may overstep itself—as Nixon tempted it to do during Watergate and related affairs and in Chile.

Employing more than 16,000 persons, the CIA spends over $750 million annually. The CIA director, as head of the U.S. foreign intelligence community, oversees research, military intelligence operations, spy satellites, and U-2 and SR-71 exercises that may cost $6 billion annually.[9] Critics charge, with reason, that CIA operations amount to a clandestine foreign policy that is insulated from public control and even public scrutiny. In some nations the local CIA chief has more staff, more agents, a larger budget, and more influence than the U.S. ambassador.

Since its creation in 1947, the CIA has left a trail of covert activities and deposed governments such as those in Iran and Guatemala. The ill-fated 1961 Bay of Pigs invasion of Cuba was CIA directed, and later the CIA organized and trained anticommunist forces in Laos, and contributed considerable support to the anti-Allende political forces in Chile. Because of its past record and because it must act when our government cannot officially intervene in another nation's affairs, there has been a growing tendency to credit (or blame) the CIA for any coup, purge, and revolt whether or not it was actually involved. The CIA has become "the whipping boy" of American foreign policy.[10]

In 1967 several CIA "front groups" were discovered supporting a variety of research and political action programs, both domestic and foreign.[11] Some observers feel such activities represent an "integral part

[8]Roberta Wohlstetter, *Cuba and Pearl Harbor: Hindsight and Foresight* (Rand, 1965), p. 36.

[9]This is the estimate of a former National Security Council staff member, Andrew Hamilton, in his "The CIA's Dirty Tricks Under Fire—At Last" *The Progressive* (September 1973). See also J. McGarvey, *C.I.A.: The Myth and the Madness* (Saturday Review Press, 1972); and V. Marchetti and J. D. Marks, *The CIA and the Cult of Intelligence* (Knopf, 1974).

[10]Harry Howe Ransom, *The Intelligence Establishment* (Harvard University Press, 1970), p. xiii.

[11]Richard M. Hunt, "The CIA Disclosures: End of an Affair," *Virginia Quarterly Review* (Spring 1969), pp. 211–29.

of our diplomacy," while others have denounced them as "jeopardizing the very values we are resolved to defend."[12] Understandably secrecy and interference in the internal political affairs of Third World nations offends the American sense of fair play, yet Congress has resisted efforts to curb the CIA's activities or its autonomy.[13]

As long as the United States must deal with other nations, our policymakers need up-to-date, concise intelligence. Because the intelligence must be collected and evaluated before it is usable, those who supply such information will remain powerful. The CIA's political leverage, its information, its secrecy, its speed in communication, its ability to act, and its enormous size make it a potent force. And we must therefore be certain that this power is used by our publicly accountable decision-makers, and does not itself become a source of politically unaccountable decision-making. The CIA must be on tap, not on top.

COORDINATING THE FOREIGN POLICY ESTABLISHMENT

With so many officials and agencies involved in foreign policy, the problem of coordination is immense. One of the key coordinating agencies is the National Security Council, created by Congress in 1947 to help the president integrate foreign, military, economic, fiscal, internal security, and psychological policies that affect our national security. It consists of the vice-president, secretary of state, secretary of defense, and such other officers as the president shall appoint to it. The chairman of the Joint Chiefs of Staff regularly attends meetings of the council, as does the director of the CIA (on organization charts, the CIA is an agency of the National Security Council). The assistant to the president for national security affairs serves as the executive secretary for the council staff. Members of the council are expected to act nor merely as representatives of their departments "but as a collegiate body seeking over-all policies rather than compromises of agencies' positions."

President Eisenhower relied heavily on the National Security Council and elaborated under it a whole series of suborganizational units. President Kennedy, partly in response to charges that the system had become too rigid, and partly because of his desire to maintain firm personal control over national security policy, came to use the NSC much less than did his predecessor. Kennedy abolished most of the subcommittees of the NSC and relied heavily on his special assistant for national security affairs and a small personal staff.[14] Yet before his admin-

[12]Christopher Felix, "Secret Operations Are an Integral Part of Our Diplomacy," and J. William Fulbright, "We Must Not Fight Fire with Fire," in Young Hum Kim, ed., *The Central Intelligence Agency: Problems of Secrecy in a Democracy* (D. C. Heath, 1968), pp. 36–46, 96–108.

[13]Ransom, *The Intelligence Establishment,* Chap. 7. See also T. M. Franck and E. Weisband, eds., *Secrecy and Foreign Policy* (Oxford University Press, 1974).

[14]For an example of President Kennedy's use of the staff system, see Robert F. Kennedy, *Thirteen Days: A Memoir of the Cuban Missile Crisis* (Norton, 1969).

istration was over he found it necessary to create a variety of special task forces working under the NSC. President Johnson continued the Kennedy pattern. President Nixon revived the NSC as the principal forum for the consideration of policy issues, but Nixon seemed to rely more on the NSC staff than on formal NSC meetings; under his administration subunits for coordination and planning were recreated much as they had existed under Eisenhower, all under the chairmanship of the president's assistant.[15]

The NSC evolved from its original role of reviewing national security issues such as defense spending and foreign aid into a policy-making body. Opponents of foreign policy as made by Johnson and Nixon claimed the NSC had grown in authority far beyond Congress' original intent. Late in Nixon's first term, the NSC had enlarged so much in size and dimension that observers cited Kissinger's own pre-Nixon era cautions about the decrease in staff effectiveness as size increases: "The staffs on which modern executives come to depend develop a momentum of their own. What starts out as an aid to decision-makers often turns into . . . [an] organization whose internal problems structure and sometimes compound the issues which it was originally designed to solve."[16] Perhaps this was among the reasons Kissinger was sent to the State Department.

Other critics of the NSC structure note that this "little State Department" is highly disposed toward military solutions and lacks sufficient diplomatic influence.[17] Some say the NSC is both a symbol and cause of the ascendence since World War II of military policy over "diplomatic" initiatives. But the Kissinger-Ford, or Ford-Kissinger, strategies in the mid-1970s tend to undermine this sterotype.

On January 19, 1971, President Nixon established the Council on International Economic Policy and made it responsible for developing foreign economic policy consistent with domestic economic policy. Organized to be similar to the NSC, it was a recognition both of the growing importance of trade, foreign investment, and sensitive international monetary questions, and the need for a central review staff to help the president oversee the more than sixty government departments, agencies, and committees dealing with trade and economic policy.[18]

The history of the National Security Council suggests that it has been built more around people than abstract organizational principles. Each

[15]Keith C. Clark and Laurence J. Legere, eds., *The President and the Management of National Security* (Praeger, 1969); and Destler, *Presidents, Bureaucrats and Foreign Policy*.

[16]H. A. Kissinger, "Domestic Structure and Foreign Policy," *Daedulus* (Spring 1966), p. 509.

[17]John Franklin Campbell, *The Foreign Affairs Fudge Factory* (Basic Books, 1971), p. 268. See also, R. J. Barnet, *Roots of War* (Penguin Books, 1972).

[18]On the origins and role of this council, see Harald Malmgren, "Managing Foreign Economic Policy," *Foreign Policy* (Spring 1972), pp. 42–63.

president has shaped its structure and adapted its staff procedures to suit personal preferences. The NSC has been less important for the subjects it has treated than as an arena where options are lined up, opinions articulated, and predictions made. Under different administrations since 1947, and often within the same administration, the NSC has been variously the center stage for foreign policy deliberations, relegated to the wings, or tolerated intermittently as an "educational" forum to which issues were brought after decisions had already been made. The need for a National Security Council seems logically inescapable. "Yet," as a former NSC staff member aptly said, "what logic makes necessary, it does not necessarily make effective."[19]

The politics of foreign policy-making

President Nixon and King Faisal. Economic policy and the Arab-Israeli war were subjects of much negotiation between the U.S. and Saudi Arabia.

Foreign policy flows through much the same institutional and constitutional structures as does domestic policy. Like domestic policy, basic foreign policy is made within the context of our constitutional and political system. Public opinion, pressure groups, political parties, elections, separation of powers, federalism—all these are also part of the politics of foreign policy-making. But they operate somewhat differently from the way they do in internal affairs.

PUBLIC OPINION AND FOREIGN POLICY

Different foreign policy issues evoke different degrees of public involvement. In crisis situations—the Cuban missile crisis or the 1973 Arab-Israeli war—decisions are made by a small group of men. "Only command post positions were involved; the public and its institutions were far removed; the decisions made by the elite were highly legitimate; public and semipublic responses were largely ceremonial and affirmative. In sum, there was hardly any politics at all."[20] The conduct of the war in Vietnam is the prime example of many of these tendencies. Yet even in these situations the president and his advisers make their decisions with the knowledge that what they decide will ultimately have to command support from the public and its institutions, especially Congress. And although there may be no large-scale public involvement, those who participate in making these crisis decisions report that "When decisions are made on the big questions . . . there is struggle and conflict . . . a push for accommodation, for compromise."[21]

[19]Robert H. Johnson, "The National Security Council: The Relevance of the Past to Its Future," *Orbis*, (Fall 1969), p. 709.

[20]Theodore J. Lowi, "Making Democracy Safe for the World," in James N. Rosenau, ed., *Domestic Sources of Foreign Policy* (Free Press, 1967), p. 300.

[21]Roger Hilsman, *To Move a Nation: The Politics of Foreign Policy in the Administration of John F. Kennedy* (Doubleday, 1967), p. 541.

In noncrisis situations the public appears to consist of three "publics." The largest, comprising perhaps as much as 75 percent of the adult population, is the *mass public;* this group knows little about foreign affairs, despite the grave importance of the subject.[22] During the Berlin Crisis in 1959, a *New York Times* survey showed that many people did not even know where Berlin was.[23] In 1964 the Survey Research Center found that 28 percent of the people interviewed did not know there was a Communist regime in China. And studies in 1970 revealed that even during the widely publicized Vietnam War, most Americans remained ignorant of major events abroad.[24]

The second public is the *attentive public.* Comprising perhaps 10 percent of the population, it maintains an active interest in foreign policy. The *opinion-makers* are the third and smallest public, transmitting information and judgments on foreign affairs and mobilizing support in the other two publics.

To illustrate the relationship between these three publics, one analyst has developed this instructive analogy of a huge theater with a tense drama being played out on the stage:

> The mass public, occupying the many seats in the balcony, is so far removed from the scene of action that its members can hardly grasp the plot, much less hear all the lines or distinguish between the actors. Thus they may sit in stony silence or applaud impetuously, if not so vigorously as to shake the foundations of the theater. Usually, however, they get thoroughly bored and leave. . . . The attentive public, on the other hand, is located in the few choice orchestra seats. Its members can not only hear every line clearly, but can also see the facial expressions of the actors. Thus they become absorbed in the drama, applauding its high spots and disparaging its flaws. Indeed, their involvement is such that during the intermission they make their views known to any occupants of the balcony who may have wandered into the lobby. As for the members of the opinion-making public, they are the actors on the stage, performing their parts with gusto and intensity, not infrequently in an effort to upstage each other. Many are directing their performance at some specific portion of the orchestra audience. Others, those with especially strong vocal cords, try to make themselves heard as far as the balcony. All are keenly aware that the quality of their performance will greatly affect their bargaining power when they seek higher salaries or better parts in future productions.[25]

Over the years the plot may change, but the drama continues as the majority in the balcony remain uninvolved.

Why are so many people indifferent or uninformed? First, foreign affairs are usually more remote than domestic issues. People have more

[22]Alfred O. Hero, *Americans in World Affairs* (World Peace Foundation, 1959), p. 10.

[23]*New York Times* (March 22, 1959), Part IV, p. 8.

[24]Don D. Smith, " 'Dark Areas of Ignorance' Revisited: Current Knowledge about Asian Affairs," *Social Science Quarterly,* (December 1970), pp. 668–73.

[25]James N. Rosenau, ed., *Public Opinion and Foreign Policy* (Random House, 1961), pp. 34–35.

first-hand information about inflation than about Chilean land reform or Turkish political problems. The worker in the factory and the boss in the front office know what labor-management relations are about, and they have strong opinions on the subject. They are likely to be less concerned about the internal struggles for power within Ethiopia or our policy on Cambodia—or to feel that they could not do much about it anyway. Only when American soldiers, especially drafted soldiers, are being killed does the mass public become concerned with foreign affairs. And the relatively fewer citizens trying to influence foreign than domestic policies is a phenomenon not unique to the United States—it is found in other democratic nations also.[26]

Lack of widespread citizen concern, knowledge, and involvement in the politics of foreign policy should not be confused with lack of intense feelings about aspects of the international scene. Since World War II, with the obviously growing importance of our foreign commitments, questions about our relations with other nations have been high on the list of public concerns. And when issues such as the Vietnam conflict become domesticated—that is, when they visibly, directly, and immediately affect the people of the United States—the debate over such policies produces demonstrations campaigns, hearings—all the trappings of the ordinary political process.[27] Until a foreign policy issue becomes critical most Americans are unconcerned with it, but when they can see that it directly affects them they can and often do become highly and intensely concerned about it.

PUBLIC MOODS: THE UNSTABLE BASE

The movement from no interest to intense feeling means that the public reaction to foreign policy issues is often based on moods that have little intellectual structure or factual content.[28] The common denominator of the mass public oversimplifies the problems of foreign politics. It tends to reduce all issues to the one issue that is most urgent at the moment. It thinks of the participants in terms of heroes and villains. It favors quick and easy remedies—fire the secretary of state, lower trade barriers, get rid of Castro and all will be well. Although this "mood theory," claiming that the public's interest in foreign affairs is low and volatile, has been challenged, it is conceded that the American people are extremely "permissive" with the U.S. foreign policy-makers

[26]Gabriel A. Almond and Sidney Verba, *The Civic Culture: Political Attitudes and Democracy in Five Nations* (Princeton University Press, 1963).

[27]Rosenau, *Domestic Sources of Foreign Policy*, p. 49.

[28]This material is drawn from Gabriel A. Almond, *The American People and Foreign Policy* (Harcourt, 1950); Rosenau, *Public Opinion and Foreign Policy;* and Hero, *Americans in World Affairs.* In a more recent edition of his book (Praeger, 1960), Almond has noted a "greater stabilization in foreign policy awareness and attention" in recent years.

on international issues.[29] And although members of the attentive public and the decision-makers are also subject to mood responses and oversimplification, as the level of interest and information rises so does the degree of sophistication.[30]

Popular indifference toward international politics means that the official policy-makers often have to dramatize issues in order to arouse public support for their programs. On the other hand, in periods of public excitement, fear of rash public opinion causes policy-makers to be overcautious. To secure American participation in the United Nations, for example, the State Department carried on an intensive publicity campaign but, in so doing, gave many people the impression that the United Nations would ensure peace and order in the world. To arouse public support for the Truman Doctrine, people were told of the looming "crisis." But then officials had to cool down public opinion to ease demands for hasty action.

The instability of public moods makes it difficult for official policy-makers to plan ahead, to take the long view after fully considering the military, political, diplomatic, psychological, and other subtle factors involved in every major decision. The unorganized mass public does not, of course, make foreign policy. Yet public opinion determines the broad limits within which others make the decisions. Public attitudes—the political climate in general—determine the political possibilities open to the policy-makers. The president and his advisers know they must eventually secure active public support for programs that call for large expenditures of money or for commitments that involve risk of grave danger to the national security.

Congressmen are sensitive to what they perceive to be popular feeling. The relations between the public and congressmen are direct, well known, and influential. What of the Department of State? "The Department . . . and the American public are neither old nor intimate friends," writes John Dickey.[31] Until recently, those responsible for foreign policy regarded themselves as answerable only to the president. Now the Department of State makes a systematic effort to keep the public informed, and, just as important, to keep itself informed about the state of public opinion.

On major issues of foreign policy, the president, through television addresses, messages to Congress, and public speeches, tries to persuade the public. A president doubtless enjoys more leeway in shaping public opinion in support of his foreign policy in the early years of his admin-

[29]William R. Caspary, "The 'Mood Theory': A Study of Public Opinion and Foreign Policy," *American Political Science Review* (June 1970), pp. 536–46.

[30]Rogers et al detect no significant increase in awareness among the college educated in their study of the general public's knowledge of foreign affairs. William C. Rogers et al., "A Comparison of Informed and General Public Opinion on U.S. Foreign Policy," *Public Opinion Quarterly* (Summer 1967), pp. 242–52.

[31]John S. Dickey, "The Secretary and the American Public," in Don K. Price, ed., *The Secretary of State* (Prentice-Hall, 1960), p. 139.

The plight of starving children such as these victims of the Biafraian-Nigerian civil war in 1967–70, brought to our attention by the press and citizen groups, heightened worldwide concern in the world food shortage crisis.

istration. Most presidents suffer a decline in popularity over time as dissatisfaction and disillusionment with one or more policies sets in.[32] Television, for example, was of little help to Lyndon Johnson as he tried to prolong support for his Vietnam policy. Support steadily declined and opposition steadily rose. And, as he found out, time in office forecloses options. Thus it was more creditable and far easier for a new president to reverse the war and to initiate diplomatic exchanges with China—policies seemingly impossible for Johnson to sponsor.

The State Department is as interested in finding out what the public thinks as it is in explaining its policies to the public. The policy planning and guidance staff analyzes polls, reads resolutions and publications of organized groups, and digests daily more than ninety newspapers and sixty magazines. At one time the staff contracted for surveys so that it would be able to learn public views. But in 1957, after one poll showed general public support for foreign aid at a time when congressional mail was critical, congressmen cut off funds for these surveys. Although this incident merely demonstrated the well-known fact that congressional mail may be unrepresentative of general opinion, congressmen felt that the survey information was being used by the Department of State to discredit congressional attitudes and as propaganda in behalf of the foreign aid programs.[33]

THE ATTENTIVE PUBLIC AND FOREIGN POLICY

Group and opinion leaders sprinkled through the political society—priests and preachers, newspaper editors, radio and TV commentators, professors, and public speakers—form an attentive public whose support is actively sought by the official policy-makers and who have an influential voice in the shaping of our foreign policy. These men and women serve as a national pulse for our decision-makers. One source calls these opinion-making elites "the decent, kindly cross that democratic governments carry around their necks in the contest with the dictatorships."[34]

The press is extremely powerful in shaping public opinion, a fact reflected in frequent disputes between the "fourth estate" and the government. The case of *New York Times Company v. United States,* in June 1971, over that newspaper's publication of the Pentagon Papers, ex-

[32]See John E. Mueller, *War, Presidents and Public Opinion* (John Wiley, 1973).

[33]See the full account in MacAlister Brown, "The Demise of State Department Public Opinion Polls: A Study in Legislative Oversight," *Midwest Journal of Political Science* (February 1961), pp. 1–17.

[34]"The Way We Go to War," *The Economist* (June 26–July 2, 1971), p. 16.

posed the basic conflict between the freedom of the press and government's need for secrecy, between the public's right to know and its "right to have its business transacted in a responsible fashion."[35] Hostility between the press and the Department of State is an issue of long standing. According to many observers there are not one but three foreign offices in Washington—one at the *New York Times*, another at the *Washington Post*, and one at the State Department.

Another segment of the attentive public consists of citizens' organizations dedicated to increase public awareness of U.S. foreign policy. Thus the Foreign Policy Association designs community and media programs to encourage citizens to study and discuss major foreign policy controversies. The Council of Foreign Relations, sometimes called the cornerstone of the Eastern Establishment, publishes *Foreign Affairs* magazine and several books a year; it also provides a forum for bringing business leaders and government elites together for talks on new directions in foreign policy. More doctrinal groups like the World Federalists argue for world government. The Navy League, comprised of friends of the Navy, devotes its energy to increase the strength of the Navy believing this to be essential for the nation's security. Similarly, defense contractors sometimes try to promote certain kinds of foreign policies, though their educational campaigns are necessarily more veiled.

Religious and national-origin publics are particularly interested in certain phases of foreign policy. These groups sometimes have intense feelings about issues, and they are often strategically located to affect the outcome of elections. Although some scholars are skeptical about the influence of these groups, politicians appear to be sensitive to their wishes.[36] Many Americans of German origin voted against Roosevelt in 1940 because of his strong stand against Germany.[37] The attitude of Roman Catholic officials helped shape American policy during the Spanish Civil War and in the early support of the Diem regime in South Vietnam. Studies tend to confirm, however, that one's religious affiliation has only a marginal impact on one's views on specific foreign policy issues. And pronouncements by denominations or ecumenical organizations on public issues have little impact on the views of their members.[38]

It is difficult to generalize about the impact of special interest groups on American foreign policies. Their influence appears to vary by type of

[35]Dean Rusk, former secretary of state, interviewed in "Pentagon Study: The Other Side," *U.S. News and World Report* (July 19, 1971), p. 69.

[36]Louis L. Gerson, *The Hyphenate in Recent American Politics and Diplomacy* (University of Kansas Press, 1964), p. 243.

[37]See Lawrence H. Fuchs, "Minority Groups and Foreign Policy," *Political Science Quarterly* (June 1959), pp 161–75.

[38]See Alfred O. Hero, Jr., *American Religious Groups View Foreign Policy: Trends in Rank-and-File Opinion 1937–1969* (Duke University Press, 1973). See also W. O. Chittick, *State Department, Press and Pressure Groups* (John Wiley, 1970).

issue and from time to time. At moments of international crisis the president is able to mobilize so much public support for his policies that specialized groups find it difficult to exert much influence. And outside the crisis areas, careful investigations into some areas of policy, such as reciprocal trade, find that special groups have had no decisive role in the formulation of foreign policy.[39] One investigation came to the conclusion that "interest group influence on foreign policy is slight,"[40] even weaker than in internal politics. Of course, what is more difficult to determine is the impact on policy caused by the policy-makers' *anticipations* of group reactions.

PARTIES AND FOREIGN POLICY

Parties, as such, do not play a major role in shaping foreign policy, for two reasons: First, many Americans would prefer to keep foreign policy out of politics. Second, parties take less clear and candid stands on foreign policy than they do on domestic policy. All the party weaknesses discussed earlier operate in full measure in foreign policy-making. Party platforms often obscure the issues instead of highlighting them; many congresspersons fail to follow even a very general party line; and the parties fail to discipline even the most outspoken rebels.

Should parties be concerned with foreign policy? At the end of World War II sentiment grew stronger for a bipartisan approach to foreign policy. An ambiguous term, *bipartisanship* seems to mean (1) collaboration between the executive and the congressional foreign policy leaders of both parties; (2) support of presidential foreign policies by both parties in Congress; (3) withdrawal of foreign policy issues from debate in political campaigns. In general, bipartisanship is an attempt to remove the issues of foreign policy from partisan politics. In its defense, it is argued that despite the internal differences that divide Americans, we share a common interest with respect to other nations. During times of national danger we should unite behind policies necessary to preserve the national well-being, and such unity is needed to support our foreign policies. American foreign policy, it is asserted, was ineffective following World War I because it became entangled in the partisan struggle between Democrats and Republicans.

Bipartisanship has appeal. In this era of chronic crisis, it seems to symbolize people standing shoulder to shoulder as they face an uncertain and potentially hostile world. It provides more continuity of policy, and it ensures that a wider variety of leaders and interests are consulted

[39]Raymond A. Bauer, Ithiel de Sola Pool, and Lewis Anthony Dexter, *American Business and Public Policy: The Politics of Foreign Trade* (Atherton, 1963), p. 396. See also Bernard C. Cohen, *The Press and Foreign Policy* (Princeton University Press, 1963), p. 2.

[40]Lester W. Milbrath, "Interest Groups and Foreign Policy," in Rosenau, *Public Opinion and Foreign Policy*, p. 251. See also the analysis of group influence on foreign policy in Bernard C. Cohen, *The Influence of Non-Governmental Groups on Foreign Policy-Making* (World Peace Foundation, 1959).

in foreign policy-making. Psychologically, it helps to satisfy the instinct of people to turn to one another for reassurance. Its motto—partisan politics stops at the water's edge—is comforting to the many Americans worried about disunity.

But the idea of bipartisanship has come under sharp attack. Some feel that bipartisanship is merely a smokescreen for presidential usurpation of foreign policy-making powers. They suggest too that it obscures the fact that foreign policy is made by a relatively small, self-perpetuating elite of national security managers who are essentially nonpartisan *and* unelected, thus unaccountable to the political process. Other critics charge that it denies a basic tenet of democracy—the right of a people to choose between alternative lines of action. According to this argument, in a free society people should be allowed and even encouraged to differ. The need in a democracy is not to stifle differences, or to ignore them or to elude them. The need is to express the differences in a meaningful way, to find the will of the majority, to permit the government to act and the opposition to oppose.

Major divisions have also developed *within* the political parties. Thus debates over our role in Indochina, when they finally did take place, occurred primarily within the Democratic party, not between Democrats and Republicans. And recent presidents seeking renomination have been challenged from within their own parties by candidates who advocate alternative directions in foreign policy. And there are usually "third party" movements that propose other policies. If our major parties do not always present us with a clear *choice*, they at least offer us *a chance* for changing officials and policies. To win as many votes as possible, the major parties search for common denominators among the voting public. They strive to distill the essence of agreement from the medley of conflicting opinions. And when the winning party takes office, the losing party has the equally important task of furnishing "loyal" opposition.

Thus parties—and partisanship—are vital to democracy. "Why should we abandon them at the water's edge?" ask the opponents of bipartisanship. Certainly not because Americans are agreed on foreign policy—the nation abounds with different opinions, as recent crises have made clear. Surely not because we hope to show a united front to the rest of the world—we cannot deceive them with a pretense of agreement; they know our differences as well as we do. Besides, our party divisions should be something to flaunt with pride—not something to be hidden in the closet whenever foreigners seem to be looking at us.

Even more serious, critics conclude, bipartisanship erodes responsibility. A great virtue of partisan government is that those in office can be held to account simply because they hold authority. But when the leaders of both parties work together, responsibility fades. After things go badly, the leaders of each party maintain that it was the other party's fault. Instead of a sober consideration of alternative courses of action, there is a frantic hunt for scapegoats.

CONGRESS AND FOREIGN POLICY

It may seem strange to discuss our national legislative body as part of the attentive public rather than as part of the formal foreign policy establishment. But despite the importance of foreign policy, despite the fact that Congress can block the president's policy and undermine his decisions, Congress as an institution does not directly *make* much foreign policy. In the making of foreign policy, the power of Congress is mainly *consultative* and *punitive*—although it sometimes does take the initiative in foreign economic and military assistance questions. It is also a link between the policy-makers and the public. Like many of us, however, Congress wants a meaningful relationship, especially "meaningful consultation" with the president in matters of foreign relations.[41]

Because of congressmen's sensitivity to public opinion, because of their expertise, and because of their prominence, individual congressmen (in contrast to Congress) are sometimes included within the circle of those who make the decisions. For example, the chairman of the Senate Committee on Foreign Relations has been involved at times, though usually his main role is either helping to educate the public or educating the president on what will or will not run into congressional opposition. When the chairman is out of sympathy with the policies of the president, as former Senator Fulbright was on Vietnam, he may use the committee to focus attention on the differences.

During the 1930s and after World War II, the almost unanimous opinion of academics and the attentive public favored strengthening the hand of the president and limiting the role of Congress in the foreign policy area. It was generally thought that *only the president* had the knowledge, the political base, and the broad, global perspective from which to develop coherent and sensible foreign policies. Congress was thought to be too responsive to the parochial and uninformed attitudes of the public. When conservative leaders tried to alter constitutional arrangements in order to limit the president's power to make executive agreements and to implement treaties, they ran into solid opposition from the intellectual and academic elites.

But in recent years, with popular sentiment and intellectual opinion so opposed to the Vietnam policies of Presidents Johnson and Nixon, many have urged Congress to strengthen its role in the foreign policy process. Some feared that the imbalance between executive and legislative authority was causing "a crisis in constitutional relationships." Congress, especially the Senate, became more assertive: The restriction by Congress on the use of funds for ground warfare in Laos, the 1973 vote to cut off funds for bombing in Cambodia, and the War Powers Act of 1973—all these were clear signs of a growing restiveness of congressmen and their constituents over presidential supremacy in foreign policy-making.

[41]Jacob K. Javits, "The Congressional Presence in Foreign Relations," *Foreign Affairs* (January 1970), p. 233. See also Walter F. Mondale, "Beyond Détente: Toward International Economic Security," *Foreign Affairs* (October 1974), pp. 1–23.

THE WAR POWERS ACT OF 1973

Congress has the constitutional power to declare war; but a president as commander in chief can send the troops where he wishes. In fact if not in theory the decision whether or not Americans will fight has been left to the president. Congress may or may not, after the fact, bring into existence the legal state of war, now perhaps a somewhat obsolete practice since seldom do nations today bother to declare war formally; they just start shooting at each other.

In an attempt to redress the balance, in 1973 Congress took an unprecedented step, even to the extent of overriding a presidential veto, and enacted the War Powers Act of 1973. Nixon called the act an unconstitutional intrusion into the president's constitutional authority and an "action that seriously undermines this nation's ability to act decisively and convincingly in times of international crisis." Nevertheless, the Congress has declared that henceforth the president can commit the armed forces of the United States (1) only pursuant to a declaration of war by Congress, (2) by specific statutory authorization, or (3) in a national emergency created by an attack on the United States or its armed forces. After committing the armed forces under this third condition the president, by the act, is supposed to report immediately to Congress; and within sixty days, unless Congress has declared war, the troop commitment is to be terminated, with the president being allowed another thirty days if he certifies to Congress that unavoidable military necessity for the safety of U.S. forces requires their continued use. Ninety days having elapsed, the act then permits Congress, by concurrent resolution not subject to a presidential veto, to direct the president to disengage such troops.

Not everyone was pleased by the passage of the War Powers Act. Some members of Congress supported President Nixon's stand. Still another group in Congress felt that this act granted a president *more power* than he already had, even to the extent of perhaps encouraging short-term interventions.[42] Whether or not this act of Congress will make any difference, it reflects the determination by the Congress in 1973 to try to control the president's formerly unlimited discretion to decide when and where and under what conditions American troops shall be engaged. Any future president who remembers the reaction of Congress and the nation to Korea and to Vietnam and the 1973 War Powers Act will know that commitment of American troops to foreign combat is subject to the approval of Congress and he will have to persuade the nation that his actions are justified by the gravest of national emergencies.

Whether the intensity of this reaction will last much longer than the disenchantment over Indochina remains an open question. But Con-

[42]See, for example, Thomas F. Eagleton, *War and Presidential Power: A Chronicle of Congressional Surrender* (Liveright, 1974).

gress has the constitutional authority to intervene whenever it has the political will to do so.[43]

In summary, the politics of foreign policy-making involves the public, interest groups, political parties, elections, and the same agencies of government that are involved in the American system of government generally. There are differences of course: A president and his advisers are subject to fewer immediate political constraints, and the publics are likely to have less concern and less voice in foreign policy than in domestic policy. The political parties and the Congress—the agencies most likely to be responsive to the impact of interest groups and the mass public—have less to do with the making of foreign than domestic policies.

[43]See the various views in *Congress, the President and the War Powers,* Hearings before the Subcommittee on National Security Policy and Scientific Developments, House of Representatives, 1970; Louis Henkin, *Foreign Affairs and the Constitution* (Foundation Press, 1972); and Arthur M. Schlesinger, Jr., *The Imperial Presidency* (Houghton Mifflin, 1973).

Chapter 21 To provide for the common defense

In late October 1962, some wondered if the end of the world was near. Soviet ships carrying offensive missiles steamed toward Cuba after the president of the United States had announced that this nation would not permit a nuclear threat to exist ninety miles from our shores. The world held its breath as the missile-laden ships drew closer to the American quarantine zone. A series of portentous messages flew back and forth between the White House and the Kremlin.

Even as we sought a peaceful solution to the crisis, American bombers lumbered down runways, loaded with their awesome weapons. On the western plains, missile silos swung open their massive doors. At sea, sleek fighter-bombers shot from carrier decks, circling, watching. And throughout the United States, Americans listened and waited, some in basements and fallout shelters, thinking that perhaps the unthinkable had arrived. The world seemed on the very brink of nuclear war.

Not since August 9, 1945, when an atomic bomb destroyed the Japanese city of Nagasaki, had this source of energy been unleashed in combat. Almost twenty years later, with ever more powerful nuclear weapons involved, the world was spared the knowledge of their true destructive power. Estimates of possible casualties varied, but no fewer than 130 million Americans would have perished in the first minutes of nuclear combat. President Kennedy estimated that as many as 500 million total deaths would have occurred during the first hours of such an exchange. The number would continue to mount over a longer period as fallout and lack of food, shelter, and medicine took their toll.[1]

Is it any longer possible for "nations to fight each other and survive as nations, or even for armies to fight a battle and have at the end enough men on either side to fight another"?[2] In this age of absolute weaponry, this "fail-safe" era of "overkill" and "second strike capability," some are optimistic. They believe that our recognition of the horror and destruction of nuclear war will enable us to avoid such madness. For others, the proliferation of nuclear warheads portends the end of civilization unless these weapons can be brought under some form of international control.

The politics of defense

In a nationwide television and radio address in October 1962, President Kennedy advised the American people that the U.S. was setting up a naval blockade against Cuba.

Both the president and Congress are responsible for the common defense, and both have constitutional authority to discharge that responsibility. Congress appropriates the money and determines the size, structure, and organization of the fighting forces; the president is the commander in chief of these forces and determines when military power will be used.[3] In defense policy as in foreign policy, the president is the decision-maker of last resort, the ultimate decision-maker.

Since World War II, Americans have fought long, costly, and bitter wars in Korea and Indochina; but Congress, although in both instances confirming and supporting the president's decisions to use military force, did not declare a *formal state of war* in either. In these days when an all-out use of military force by a superpower could *destroy* the world in minutes and where limited wars engaging millions of men can be conducted without either protagonist declaring war, it may be that formal declarations by nations of a state of war are obsolete. Since 1945 there have been no declarations of war, though there have been at least sixty incidents of major fighting between nations.[4]

[1]Richard J. Barnet, "The Illusion of Security," *Foreign Policy* (Summer 1971), p. 72. See also Graham T. Allison, *Essence of Decision: Explaining the Cuban Missile Crisis* (Little, Brown, 1971).

[2]Paraphrase of Winston Churchill by Roger Hilsman, in *Military Policy and National Security*, ed. William Kaufmann (Princeton University Press, 1956), p. 44.

[3]Arnold Kanter, "Congress and the Defense Budget: 1960–1970," *American Political Science Review* (March 1972), pp. 129–43; and James Clotfelter, *The Military in American Politics* (Harper & Row, 1973), Chap. 7.

[4]See George Thayer, *The War Business: The International Trade in Armaments* (Simon and Schuster, 1969), p. 17; Merlo Pusey, *The Way We Go to War* (Houghton Mifflin, 1969), pp. 149–65; and Adam Yarmolinsky, *The Military Establishment: Its Impacts on American Society* (Harper & Row, 1971).

The president, the Congress, the National Security Council, and the State Department make overall policy and integrate our national security programs. But the day-by-day work of developing and implementing our programs is the job of the Department of Defense, the DOD.

PENTAGONIA

The sheer magnitude of our defense establishment is difficult to comprehend. DOD spends about $90 billion a year. The Pentagon, its headquarters, is the world's largest office building, and houses within its miles of corridors nearly 30,000 military and civilian personnel. The offices of several hundred generals and admirals are there, as is the Office of the Secretary of Defense (OSD), symbolizing civilian control of the armed services.

Prior to 1947 there were two separate military departments, War and Navy. But the difficulty of coordinating them during World War II led to demands for unification. In 1947 the Air Force, already an autonomous unit within the War Department, was made an independent unit, and the three military departments—Army, Navy, Air Force—were placed under the general supervision of the secretary of defense.[5] The Unification Act of 1947, a hesitant first step, was a bundle of compromises between the Army, which favored a tightly integrated department, and the Navy, which wanted a loosely federated structure. It also reflected compromises between congressmen who felt that disunity and interservice rivalries were undermining our defense efforts, and congressmen who, on the other hand, feared that a unified defense establishment would defy civilian control and smother dissenting views.

The 1947 act had not been long in operation before it became apparent that the Department of Defense, which was supposed to be the nation's sword, looked more like a pitchfork. All that the act had really accomplished was to bring the military services under a common organization chart. Instead of moving from two military departments to one,we had ended up with three.

In 1958, Eisenhower urged Congress to appropriate all funds to the secretary of defense rather than to the separate military departments and to give the secretary full control over the armed services, including the authority to transfer or abolish combatant functions and to establish direct lines of command between his office and operational forces in the field. The president also asked that the Joint Chiefs of Staff be strengthened by giving its chairman a vote, that the staff be enlarged, and that each service chief be allowed to delegate his command duties so that he could devote most of his time to the work of the Joint Chiefs.

The president's plan to unify the Defense Department by increasing the authority of the secretary of defense and by centralizing the Joint Chiefs was subjected to heavy congressional fire. Many congressmen,

[5]For a comprehensive analysis, see Paul Y. Hammond, *Organizing for Defense: The American Military Establishment in the Twentieth Century* (Princeton University Press, 1961).

fearful of creating a Prussian military establishment, argued that instead of concentrating greater authority in the defense secretary, what was needed was a streamlining of the layer upon layer of civilian staffs, and all their attendant red tape.

President Eisenhower felt so strongly about his proposals for Defense Department reorganization that he used the prestige and influence of his office to promote their acceptance. In the end, the Defense Department Reorganization Act of 1958 gave the president most of what he wanted. Congress, however, refused to approve the appropriation of funds to the secretary of defense. Furthermore, at the prompting of the Naval Air Force, Marine Corps, and National Guard (which groups, it was pointed out, live in constant fear that somebody will abolish them)[6] Congress insisted that the secretary of defense notify the House and Senate armed services committees if he contemplates any major change in combatant functions.

Congress also refused to repeal a provision, which Presient Eisenhower called legalized insubordination, authorizing a secretary of a military department or a member of the Joint Chiefs to make any recommendations he wishes to Congress about Defense Department matters even if his recommendations are contrary to Defense Department policy. Eisenhower's view, like that of other presidents, was that he was the commander in chief, that the secretary of defense was his deputy, and that it was the duty of all military officials to support before Congress and the country the agreed-on policies of the Defense Department regardless of their own judgment.

McNAMARA AND CREEPING UNIFICATION

Under Presidents Kennedy and Johnson there were no legislative changes in the structure of the Department of Defense, but the fact that Robert McNamara was secretary of defense led to greater changes in the operation of the Department of Defense than had been effected by any act of Congress. Secretary McNamara brought to the department a small group of men, trained chiefly as economists and analysts. "Perhaps never before had so much civilian talent, sophisticated in military strategy, been assembled under a Defense Secretary himself known for exceptional intellect combined with the ability to make difficult decisions with dispatch."[7] Secretary McNamara and his "whiz kids," as they came to be called, with strong support from the White House, proceeded to coordinate the supply and intelligence activities of the services, create unified military commands, and bring more unification to the Department than Congress had been willing to sanction by legislation. Systems analysis and program budgeting were introduced as

[6]Ivan Hinderaker, "The Eisenhower Administration: The Last Years," in *American Government Annual, 1959–1960* (Holt, Rinehart & Winston, 1959), p. 82.

[7]Harry Howe Ransom, *Can American Democracy Survive Cold War?* (Doubleday, 1963). See also Charles J. Hitch, *Decision-Making for Defense* (University of California Press, 1966), pp. 22–58; Henry L. Trewhitt, *McNamara: His Ordeal in the Pentagon* (Harper & Row, 1971).

means of evaluating weapons and allocating funds among various commands and services. Secretary McNamara and his staff had their own ideas about strategic policies; unlike many past civilian leaders of the Defense Department, they raised questions about military strategy and overruled military men when they felt that the "top brass" lacked sound reasons. The secretary, supported by Presidents Kennedy and Johnson, even redistributed military funds in order to redress what he believed had been an unbalanced reliance by the Eisenhower Administration on nuclear power.[8]

NIXON, FORD, KISSINGER, AND THE MILITARY

McNamara's performance, while pleasing to his presidents, was deeply resented by a great many military chiefs and their friends in Congress. Once the former Ford Motor Company head had left, however, many people wondered how much he had achieved. Nixon and his lieutenants lost little time in reversing the pattern, granting the service heads more leeway in shaping their budgets and consulting with them more often. "The experience of the last twenty-five years," one participant-observer concluded "suggests that the effort to reorganize the Pentagon and then to demand 'unified' military advice from the Joint Chiefs of Staff had been a failure."[9] Nixon and Ford and their defense secretaries, Laird and Schlesinger, gave the military chiefs a stronger voice in budget and weapon system decisions. They downgraded the various "whiz-kid" civilian review staffs that were so central to McNamara's battles with the military.

Yet, in many respects, Nixon and Ford imposed Henry Kissinger between themselves and the Pentagon. Whether Kissinger was at the White House or at State, he acted as an alternative source of information and options on a broad range of military and national security matters. He served in fact as a channel for various kinds of military advice and often found himself in battle with the secretaries of defense.

Has the political influence of the military and the Pentagon been reduced in recent years? Some people think so. This was probably less due to the presidential intent than a general public reaction to Vietnam on the one hand and the reality of détente politics on the other. No longer does agreement among the Joint Chiefs guarantee congressional support. The central role of Kissinger in the Nixon-Ford decision-making for national security was doubtless another factor. Thus, during the Arab-Israeli 1973 war, Kissinger at times seemed to be acting as secretary of defense as well as secretary of state.[10]

[8]William K. Kaufmann, *The McNamara Strategy* (Harper & Row, 1964); Alain C. Enthoven and K. Wayne Smith, *How Much Is Enough? Shaping the Defense Program, 1961–1969* (Harper & Row, 1971). For a more critical view see Sidney Lens, *The Military Industrial Complex* (Pilgrim Press, 1970).

[9]Morton H. Halperin, "The President and the Military," *Foreign Affairs* (January 1972), p. 320. See also James Clotfelter, *Military in American Politics.*

[10]Marvin and Bernard Kalb, *Kissinger* (Little, Brown, 1974).

The nation's top military commanders and defense department officials meeting in the National Military Command Center at the Pentagon to discuss plans, policies, and procedures.

THE JOINT CHIEFS OF STAFF

The Joint Chiefs of Staff (JCS) serve as the principal military advisers to the president, the National Security Council, and the secretary of defense. They comprise the military heads of the four armed services and a chairman, all appointed by the president with the consent of the Senate for a two-year term and eligible in peacetime for only one reappointment. Behind double steel doors in the Pentagon, the Joint Chiefs shape strategic plans, work out joint supply programs, review major supply and personnel requirements, formulate programs for joint training, make recommendations to the secretary of defense on the establishment of unified commands in strategic areas, and provide American representation on the military commissions of the United Nations, NATO, and the OAS.

The chairman of the Joint Chiefs takes precedence over all other military officers. He presides over the meetings of the Joint Chiefs, prepares the agenda, directs the staff of some 400 officers in an overall JCS organization of about 2,000 people, and informs the secretary of defense and the president of issues on which the Joint Chiefs have been unable to reach agreement.

At times, the Joint Chiefs are unable to develop united strategies or to agree on the allocation of resources. There is more to disputes among military services, however, than mere professional jealousies. The technological revolution in warfare has rendered obsolete existing concepts about military missions. In the past, it made sense to divide command among land, sea, and air forces, but today "technology makes a mockery of such distinctions."[11] Defense research and development (R&D) is constantly altering formerly established roles and missions. Yet the individual services are most reluctant to relinquish their traditional functions. Each branch supports weapons acquisitions that bring it "prestige and sustenance." This often leads to interservice rivalries such as

[11]Henry A. Kissinger, *Nuclear Weapons and Foreign Policy* (Doubleday, 1958), p. 228.

The battleship "Arizona," part of the U.S. fleet that sank in the first wave of the Japanese attack on Pearl Harbor, December 7, 1941.

the Army and Air Force quarrel over which should provide air support for ground troops, and the Air Force and Navy dispute over land versus sea-based missiles.[12]

Sometimes interservice rivalries break out in the Congress and the press. Quasi-official organizations, such as the Association of the United States Army, the Navy League, and the Air Force Association, lobby openly in behalf of their particular service. Behind the scenes the military men themselves are active. The president tries to keep interservice disputes inside the administration, but the military commander who feels that administration policy threatens the national security is in something of a quandary. He is taught to respect civilian supremacy and to obey his civilian superiors. But which civilian superiors? The president as commander in chief? Or should he—as he has a legal right to do—report to Congress, which is also a civilian superior? A few officers resolve the dilemma of conflicting loyalties to president, Congress, and conscience by resigning so that they will be free to carry their views to the nation. More commonly, military personnel who wish to dissent from official policy get their views to Congress by resorting to the Washington practice of "leaking" information to the press. Furthermore, when testifying before congressional committees it is not difficult for officers to support the policies of the Defense Department only in a formal sense and to allow their real views to come across.

The continuation of interservice differences has led some to advocate the replacement of the Joint Chiefs by a single chief of staff, the complete integration of all military into a single branch, and the reassignment of forces in terms of strategic missions rather than means of locomotion. Although such a system has had the support of many high-ranking Army and some Air Force officers, it is opposed by most Navy officers and most congresspersons.

Strategic defense policy, much like policy in any other area, is the result not of a collective process of rational inquiry but of a mutual process of give and take.[13] Whether strategic policies are worked out within the Defense Department, the White House, or Congress, the decisions result from a political process in which some measure of consensus is essential; and some conflict among the participants is not necessarily evil. As one admiral put it: "How curious it is that the Congress *debates*, the Supreme Court *deliberates*, but for some reason or other the Joint Chiefs of Staff just *bicker!*"[14]

[12]Bruce M. Russett, *What Price Vigilance? The Burdens of National Defense* (Yale University Press, 1970), p. 15.

[13]Samuel P. Huntington, *The Common Defense: Strategic Programs in National Politics* (Columbia University Press, 1961), preface and *passim*.

[14]Quoted *ibid.*, p. 170. See also David W. Tarr, "Military Technology and the Policy Process," *Western Political Quarterly* (March 1965), pp. 135 ff.

The Joint Chiefs engage in the same type of logrolling tactics as used in Congress. On budget issues, they tend to endorse all of the programs desired by each service. On questions relating to Vietnam, the Joint Chiefs nearly always simply endorsed the recommendations of Generals Westmoreland and Abrams. "When forced to choose on an issue of policy, the Chiefs compromise among the different service positions rather than attempting to develop a position based on a unified military point of view."[15]

Arms control and national defense

People have dreamed for centuries of a world in which conflicts would be resolved without force. But in reality, as long as the United States exists in a world of sovereign, independent nations, it will look to its own defenses. The policy of deterrence suggests that a strategic equilibrium between the U.S. and the U.S.S.R., or "mutual deterrence," is the best realistic safeguard of U.S. security. (Effective deterrence is commonly measured by the usable strength of the *survivable second strike force*.) The policy of deterrence is based on the idea that a conflict in values is the root cause of the East-West confrontation, and that military force is but a reflection of that basic conflict. Moreover, proponents argue, we need to have a reserve military strength to back up our position in arms control negotiations.

Proponents of disarmament argue that armaments themselves are a fundamental cause of international tension. They warn of the immense risks of the deterrence system—human error, a failure in the warning network, a misguided missile, the inevitable expansion of the number of nations with nuclear weapons. But they paint an even grimmer picture of a future without arms control—one with heightened tension as the result of the development of more devastating nuclear warheads and longer-ranged, more accurate delivery vehicles; the threat of biological, chemical, and even radiological weapons; the constant surveillance of spy satellites; ever-increasing defense budgets and commitments of human resources to weapons technology.

Some advocates of disarmament feel this possibility can be forestalled only by general and complete renunciation of force with the elimination of all military power. The Soviets have favored disarmament in general terms, but until recently avoided specific proposals.[16] A vocal minority in the West proposes that in order to save the world from nuclear destruction, the West must unilaterally take a significant first step in disarmament. A skeptical majority suspects that the Soviet Union would not reciprocate but rather take advantage of our vulnerability.

[15]Morton H. Halperin, "President and Military" p. 321.

[16]Ralph E. Lapp, *Arms Beyond Doubt: The Tyranny of Weapons Technology* (Cowles, 1970), p. 185.

21–1
The U.S.–U.S.S.R. Strategic Balance

Weapon Category	Mid-1973 Estimates		Maximum Permitted by 1977 Under First SALT Accords		
Offensive:	U.S.	U.S.S.R.	U.S.	U.S.S.R.	
ICBMs	1,054	1,527	1,054	1,618 +	*or* 1,408 +
SLBMs	656	628	710	740	950
Total long-range missiles	1,710	2,155	1,764	2,358	
Submarines equipped with nuclear missiles	41	48	44	62	
Strategic bombers	442	140	(not covered by SALT)		
Deliverable warheads	6,560	2,280	(not covered by SALT)		
Defensive: ABMs	0	64	200*	200*	

*Amended to 100 by 1974 accords.

A more feasible alternative to the arms race is limited disarmament, generally known as arms control. Beginning with nuclear weapons, gradual arms reduction by both sides has two immediate objectives: first, to reduce the likelihood of war and, if unsuccessful in this, second, to diminish the violence of armed conflict. Within this policy, mutual arms reduction would be accomplished through negotiations.

On August 5, 1963, the United Kingdom, the Soviet Union, and the United States agreed on a treaty to ban nuclear explosions in the atmosphere or in any other place where there was danger of radioactive debris. The treaty permits nations to test underground and has an escape clause allowing any signer to withdraw from the treaty on three months' notice, but its ratification by the United States and the Soviet Union and the subsequent adherence to it by more than one hundred nations was the first concrete step toward nuclear disarmament.

The test-ban treaty was followed in 1967 by the International Treaty on the Peaceful Uses of Outer Space, banning the use of satellites as vehicles or platforms for the launching of nuclear weapons, and in 1968 by the signing of the Nonproliferation Treaty and its presentation to the U.S. Senate for ratification. The Nonproliferation Treaty pledges the nuclear powers not to disseminate nuclear devices to nonnuclear powers for at least twenty-five years and the nonnuclear nations not to seek to acquire such devices.

In February of 1971, an international treaty was signed that banned the location of nuclear weapons on the seabed or ocean floor. In September 1971, the United States and Soviet Union agreed on measures to reduce the likelihood of accidental war. And in April of 1972, another treaty was signed that banned the development, production, and stockpiling of biological weapons and toxins. The cumulative impact of these agreements, many of which had been discussed for several years, helped set the stage for détente and an era of negotiations.

SALT TALKS AND SUMMIT ACCORDS

Strategic Arms Limitation Talks, and SALT negotiations, began in Helsinki, Finland, in November 1969. Discussions lasted two and a half years. It produced two agreements that were signed by President Nixon and Soviet leader Leonid Brezhnev on May 26, 1972, in St. Catherine's Hall in the Kremlin. The United States and the Soviet Union agreed by *treaty* to limit their defensive nuclear arsenal of antiballistic missiles to 200 ABMs and no more—one system of 100 to defend the national capital and the other to defend an offensive-missile site. (See Table 21–1). In July of 1974, Nixon and Brezhnev agreed to limit the ABM defensive systems to one location in each nation.

Nixon and Brezhnev also signed an *interim agreement* to freeze each country's offensive missile forces for a five-year period. Pressures in both nations to restrict war expenditures led many people to hope the SALT talks would lead to a major breakthrough in curbing the arms race. Most observers feel that the record of "Round One" SALT talks is neither reassuring nor disappointing; it is inconclusive.[17] Modest steps have been taken, but military budgets continue to rise.

Meanwhile the Pentagon is adding some very costly items to its strategic force, including trident submarines and a fleet of B-1 supersonic bombers. Critics question the need to push ahead with construction of these "unnecessary, immensely expensive, and desperately dangerous" weapons. Two specific charges are made. First, that in the name of accumulating "bargaining chips" for further SALT talks, we are really making negotations on arms control more difficult by creating powerful vested constituencies for the preservation of weapons. Second, critics suggest that our most important problems today are domestic ones. And unnecessary defense spending will contribute importantly to a further loss of confidence in America's financial and economic integrity.

HOO-BOY! WHAT A MILITARY BUDGET!
DON'T THEY KNOW THERE'S A PEACE ON?
2-28
BRICKMAN

Washington Star Syndicate, Inc.

President Ford and defenders of our military budgets say that SALT I provides a foundation of confidence and a process for more extensive and permanent agreement on arms limitation. Still, they argue, the key factor in the present détente policy is a perceived balance of strategic nuclear power between ourselves and the Soviet Union. If either felt vulnerable, détente would simply be out of the question. Nixon's 1975 budget request summed up his view: "The Soviet Union continues to pursue an aggressive program to develop new military weapons. As U.S. forces and defense spending, measured in dollars of constant purchasing power, have been reduced, Soviet forces and spending have been increased. In order to prevent a serious imbalance from developing, the United States must continue to modernize and to improve the readiness of its combat forces."[18] (See Figure 21–1.)

Nixon and Brezhnev met again in the summer of 1974 in Russia to

[17] See John Newhouse, *Cold Dawn: The Story of SALT* (Holt, Rinehart & Winston, 1973).

[18] *The United States Budget in Brief, Fiscal Year 1975* (U.S. Government Printing Office).

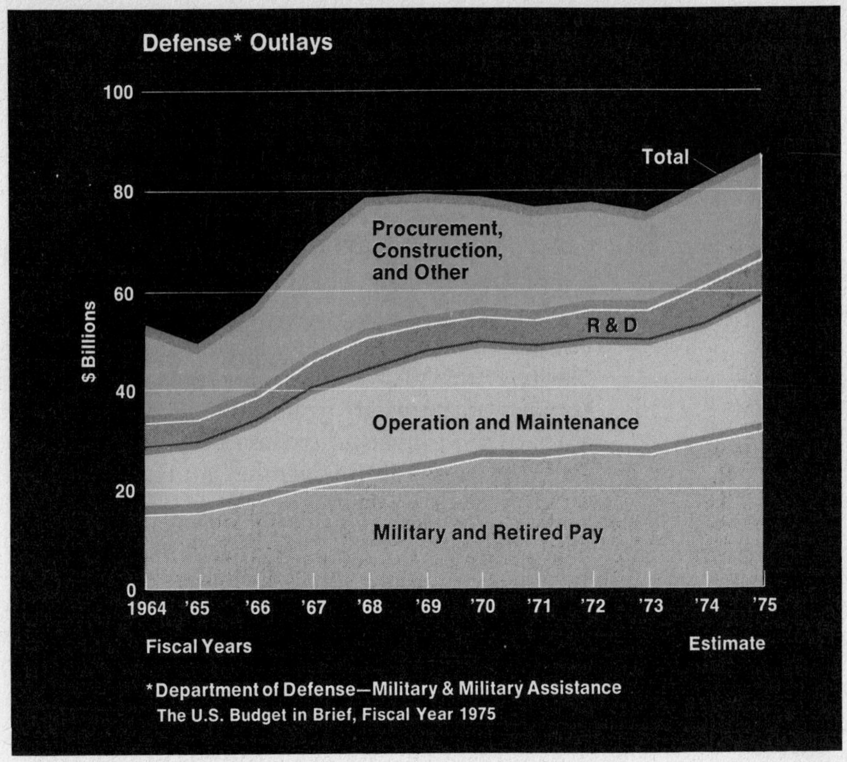

*Department of Defense—Military & Military Assistance
The U.S. Budget in Brief, Fiscal Year 1975

sign additional accords and agreements. They sought a relaxation of tension in general and arranged a partial underground nuclear test ban accord in particular. Nixon and Brezhnev also signed a ten-year agreement to facilitate economic, industrial, and technical cooperation. Senator Edward Kennedy summed up the generally supportive American mood toward these Soviet-American agreements on arms control: "Clearly, we in the United States cannot stop the arms race alone. Just as clearly, neither can they. . . . There is, I believe, a basic continuity in American interests concerning the Soviet Union that goes beyond today, beyond any one set of leaders, and beyond any one political party. It is to find some way of putting the cold war behind us for all time, and to improve relations step by step through a series of agreements that are truly in the mutual interests of both countries."[19]

President Ford met again, in late 1974, with Brezhnev, this time at Vladivostok. They negotiated agreements about arms limitations which would take effect after SALT I in 1977 and run through 1985. Reaction to the Vladivostok accords was at best mixed. Kissinger hailed them as a great breakthrough. Others contend that it merely allows both sides 10 more years of competitive buildup before agreeing to cut back.

[19]Edward M. Kennedy, *Los Angeles Times* (June 30, 1974), Part X, p. 1.

Security and liberty: not by power alone

As long as the United States exists in a world of sovereign, independent nations, it must look to its defenses. The nation has neither the sufficient resources nor the desire to control the destinies of the international community. Politics is conflict but it is also cooperation, and power should be used to help build the kind of world community in which armies and wars will be archaic. This view is heightened as we assume a more realistic view of China.

What should be the role of the military in a democratic society? A fear of the military is deeply rooted in American traditions. And the unpopularity of the Vietnam War, together with the belief that the vast military expenditures are giving undue influence to the military and their allies in the industrial community, has aroused concern about how to ensure civilian control over the "military-industrial complex."[20]

The framers of the Constitution, recognizing that military domination is incompatible with free government, wove into the Constitution several precautions. The president, an elected official, is the commander in chief of the armed forces; with the Senate's consent, he commissions all officers. Congress makes the rules for the governance of the military services; and appropriations for the Army are limited to a two-year period. Congress has supplemented these precautions by requiring that the secretary of defense and the heads of the military departments be civilians and by devising elaborate procedures to prevent the military from controlling the selection of men for West Point, Annapolis, and the Air Force Academy.

"I'll never forget his ringing words: 'Damn the Appropriations Committee —full speed ahead!'"

Copyright © 1963. Reprinted by permission of Saturday Review/World and Ed Fisher.

Maintaining civilian supremacy over the military today is harder than it has ever been before. There is no longer a clear separation between military and civilian spheres of activity. As national security problems are brought to the fore, the generals, often reluctantly, are called upon to pass judgment on issues that in the past have not been thought to be within the scope of their competence. At the same time, their civilian superiors find it more difficult to secure the information they need to exercise control. In many cases it is the military who decide what information must remain top secret. Congressmen and the general public are at a disadvantage in exercising supremacy over the military.

When a nation maintains a large military establishment, there tends to be an increase in centralization and in executive power, and a corresponding reduction in judicial and legislative control. A nation preoccupied with defense from an external threat is also more prone to suppress domestic dissent and to label critics as unpatriotic or subversive. Commenting on this ominous phenomenon in the early years of the Cold War, Harold D. Lasswell noted that the nation at large usually

[20]For opposing views on this issue, see John Kenneth Galbraith, *How to Control the Military* (Signet Broadside, 1969); and Albert L. Weeks, "The Pentagon's Alliance with Industry," *American Legion Magazine* (June 1971), pp. 24 ff.

"acquiesces in denials of freedom that go beyond the technical requirements of military security."[21]

Critics also argue that the military conspires with defense contractors and other strategic elites to maintain a vast network of bases and fleets around the world. (See Figure 21 – 2.) In the mid 1970s, it is charged, the defense budget is deliberately being used as a weapon to increase federal spending with which to keep the economy from a full-scale recession. Why the defense budget? ask the critics. Some have despaired, "It is sadly evident in Washington that the political leaders and other Americans who were outraged by the war in Vietnam, frightened by the implications of the ABM, and transfixed by the Pentagon Papers controversy have for some reason — weariness perhaps — lost their taste for battle with the always moving, always advancing military juggernaut."[22]

[21]"Does the Garrison State Threaten Civil Rights?," *Civil Rights in America, Annals of the American Academy of Political and Social Science* (May 1951) p. 111.

[22]Julius Duscha, "Military Spending: The Juggernaut Rolls On," *The Progressive* (April 1974), p. 33. For related interpretations see J. C. Donovan, *The Cold Warriors: A Policy-Making Elite* (D. C. Heath, 1974); and S. Melman, *Pentagon Capitalism* (McGraw-Hill, 1970).

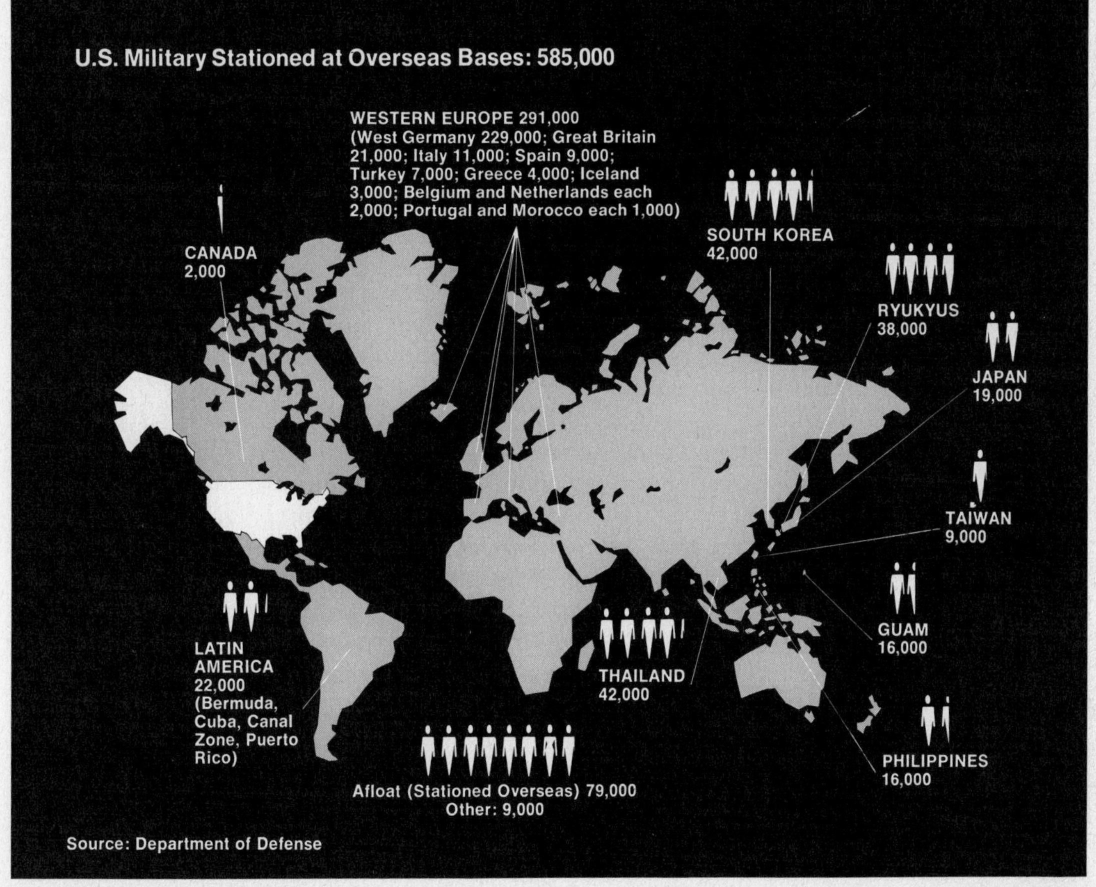

President Kennedy looks into East Berlin across the Brandenburg Gate. The East Germans, who are sensitive to any seeming "threat" to their security, draped red flags from the gate arches to curtail Kennedy's view into the East.

Yet it may be less the case that the military is to blame for pushing large budgets than that civilian leaders, elected and appointed, acquiese too readily. Congress has the undeniable power to control defense policy and defense spending, but it has apparently encouraged the tremendous growth in military responsibilities because leading congressmen have by and large followed the line of reasoning of the military leaders.[23]

Defenders of the defense budget feel that those who would reduce it are naive, or neo-isolationists. They point out that with the help of more analytical GAO audits, military procurement has been improved. They argue that defense programs in recent fiscal years have exacted the smallest percentage of the gross national product and the smallest percentage of the federal budget since 1950. They explain that the military budget must include increasing expenditures necessary to establish and maintain an all-volunteer army. This is the first time this has been tried since World War II and it is costing considerably more than was expected.

National debates about the military budget, weapons systems, force

[23]Clotfelter, *Military in American Politics*, p. 234.

levels, and troops in Europe are now common. The objectives of a leaner, less costly, and more efficient military force are being pressed upon the military, particularly as we appear to be moving into an era of detente and negotiations and away from the Cold War. Basic to most of these trends is the recognition that true national security resides in something more than troops and hardware.

In his last official address to the nation, President (and former General of the Army) Dwight D. Eisenhower warned against "the acquisition of unwarranted influence . . . by the military-industrial complex."[24] President Eisenhower's faith in the nation's future lay with "an alert and knowledgeable citizenry," who would guard against "the disastrous rise of misplaced power."

[24] *The New York Times* (January 18, 1961), p. 22.

Chapter 22 Foreign relations and national security

Quite apart from our foreign policy ideals, we now know that the actual conduct and implementation of policy is often of strategic importance. The nuclear age leaves only the smallest margin for error in matters of national security. Yet foreign relations and national security responsibilities are dispersed among hundreds of thousands of Americans who together make up the Departments of State, Defense, and related agencies. Upon them we place more responsibilities than we like to realize; perhaps more than many of them wish to acknowledge.

American foreign and defense policies are shaped in a great variety of ways—by the speeches, military actions, administrative operations, negotiations, as well as routine diplomatic intercourse. The State Department, its agencies, and personnel represent American interests to the world, and it plays a crucial though often unglamorous role in helping execute, and helping to change our policies in light of the political and bureaucratic realities of other nations.

A close look at the Foreign Service of the United States will reveal the problems in the diplomatic corps, and a look at our involvement in international organizations will reveal our frustrations in seeking peace through world organizations. Finally our review of foreign policy-making would be incomplete if we failed to consider that most important event in America's recent past—the Vietnam War.

The role of the state department

The United States Department of State has been variously maligned as a "a fudge factory," "a foggy bottom," "a machine that fails," or "a bowl of jelly." Yet it is also the key agency in the day-to-day routine of foreign affairs. This executive department, our nation's oldest, has five traditional duties:

1. To inform the president and his advisers of current international developments through information gathered and transmitted by our embassies and missions abroad.

2. To assist the president in forming and implementing foreign policy.

3. To conduct the official relations of the United States and to deliver official communications.

4. To negotiate with nations and international organizations. It must approve all negotiations and agreements with foreign governments. A business agreement between an American company and the Soviet Union, for example, cannot be legally concluded without State Department approval.

5. To coordinate the activities of all governmental groups, agencies, and committees that formulate and execute foreign policy.

ORGANIZATION

As the diplomatic arm of a superpower, the State Department has responded to our new global concerns with continuous growth and reorganization. Many critics insist, however, that the more it changes, the more it stays the same. One detractor diagnoses the State Department's ills as chronic "elephantiasis and fragmentation."[1] However, though frequently ridiculed for its large size, it is actually Washington's "bureaucratic pygmy." Among the cabinet departments, State's annual budget is the lowest—less than 1 percent of that of the Department of Defense. Considering the State Department's role and prestige, its staff of 24,000 is still among the executive branch's smallest departments—especially when compared with the *3.4 million* civilian and military in DOD.

The policy-making and advisory functions are performed by the sec-

[1]Paraphrase of George F. Kennan in Stanley Hoffmann, *Gulliver's Troubles, or, The Setting of American Foreign Policy* (McGraw-Hill, 1968), p. 254, cited in John Franklin Campbell, *The Foreign Affairs Fudge Factory* (Basic Books, 1971), p. 13. For a balanced view, see Francis E. Rourke, *Bureaucracy and Foreign Policy* (Johns Hopkins Press, 1972).

retary, a deputy secretary, undersecretaries for political affairs, for economic affairs, and security assistance, and a deputy undersecretary for economic affairs and management. These five officials are supported by about fifteen assistant secretaries and a staff of several hundred specialists, and a planning and coordination staff that formulates long-range programs. An executive secretariat coordinates work between the policy-making and advisory levels and maintains the Operations Center, the State Department's crisis room, which was established in 1961 when the Bay of Pigs invasion exposed critical communications problems within the department and between our posts overseas.[2] The twenty secretaries, all political appointees, often meet to discuss current developments.

The day-to-day operations of the department are organized along functional and geographic lines. Responsible for activities that cut across geographic boundaries are nine bureaus, each headed by an assistant secretary: International Organizations Affairs, Security and Consular Affairs, Economic Affairs, International Scientific and Technological Affairs, Intelligence and Research, Public Affairs, Educational and Cultural Affairs, Congressional Relations, and Legal Adviser.

Five geographic bureaus, also headed by assistant secretaries, embrace specific regions: Inter-American Affairs, European Affairs, East Asian and Pacific Affairs, Near Eastern and South Asian Affairs, and African Affairs. These bureaus are divided into offices headed by country directors, and these are subdivided into about five hundred desk officers who cover specific countries and functions. This "layering" has plagued efficiency, for the State Department has become top-heavy with administrators who now comprise almost 40 percent of the personnel in each bureau. When informed of this "management-labor" imbalance, Secretary Rusk retorted, "We're a policy business. We *need* more Chiefs than Indians."[3]

SPECIAL AGENCIES

Within the Department of State, but with only loose ties, is the Agency for International Development (AID), which operates under a director who reports directly to the secretary of state. With a staff of over 9,000 AID handles the nation's economic and technical assistance and coordinates most military aid programs. AID operates on the assumption that using our economic power to strengthen independent nations will improve our own security.

Since the end of World War II, we have organized, reorganized, and renamed the agency responsible for the administration of economic assistance more than a dozen times. Under Nixon and Ford still further

[2]Burton M. Sapin, *The Making of United States Foreign Policy* (Brookings Institution, 1966), pp. 110–25, esp. p. 111.

[3]Campbell, *Foreign Affairs Fudge Factory*, p. 123.

changes occurred, the most prominent of which established a new undersecretary of state post to coordinate security-related economic aid programs and the military assistance and sales programs run by the Defense Department.

Economic assistance, or "foreign aid," as it is commonly called, is a controversial and unpopular program. In the post-Vietnam years, neo-isolationists wonder why we have become so involved in other people's affairs. Others contend that the United States too often subordinates serious economic and social development goals to short-term political objectives, such as buying diplomatic support and strengthening friendly incumbent governments. Critics charge, too, that much of our aid is given under stringent conditions, one of which is that the recipient country buy only U.S. products. Many people also claim that economic and military aid is often used as a weapon of coercion, forcing less developed countries to accept U.S. policies they otherwise would not accept. Thus Johnson cut off economic aid until the Indian government agreed to reform its agricultural programs and, among other things, agreed to use vast supplies of fertilizers sold by U.S. firms. "I kept the 'short tether' on," said Johnson as he placed Indian aid on a month-to-month rather than year-to-year basis. "I decided to reshape our policy to meet the changed situation in the world. We would insist that our friends make a concerted effort to help themselves before we rushed in with food, money and sympathy."[4]

U.S. aid to Chile before and during the Marxist Allende regime also illustrates the manipulative use of foreign aid. We cut off nearly all economic and social aid to Allende but continued to give substantial financial support to the Chilean military, over whom Allende had only fragile control. Meanwhile, the CIA was apparently funding other anti-Allende groups. Allende's government soon fell and the military took over in bloody coup. Such usage of "foreign aid" obviously outrages some Americans, yet few actually want to cut foreign assistance programs that provide humanitarian assistance and disaster relief. And the U.S. currently spends nearly a billion dollars a year for multilateral development assistance, provided through the United Nations and international lending institutions such as the World Bank.

The Arms Control and Disarmament Agency (ACDA), officially independent but housed in the State Department, is another major special agency. ACDA's director reports to the secretary and the president on arms control and disarmament negotiations. Created in 1961 to cope with the wide range of disarmament problems, the ACDA conducts research, briefs our disarmament negotiators, and participates directly in disarmament talks and projects. The 1963 test-ban treaty was based on an ACDA draft. The agency promoted and secured the hot line communication system between Washington and Moscow, and it helped shape the Antarctic Treaty, the Nuclear Nonproliferation Treaty,

[4]Lyndon B. Johnson, *The Vantage Point* (Holt, Rinehart & Winston, 1971), p. 223.

and the Outer Space Treaty. The ACDA is a major participant in the SALT talks and related détente negotiations. The agency, often viewed as both an arms limitation advocate and a "State Department orphan," is not a policing agency, and its patient efforts are often thwarted by larger and more powerful interests within the government.[5]

VOICES OF AMERICA

The United States Information Agency (USIA) functions under the secretary of state and the NSC, but its director, appointed by the president, maintains a separate Washington headquarters. USIA staff (known overseas as the U.S. Information Service, or USIS) serve in each of our 129 embassies and are subordinate to the respective ambassadors. Included in the USIA's activities are the Voice of America, which broadcasts in forty languages; publication of sixty-six magazines in twenty-seven languages; and financing the production and distribution of books. Its 200 overseas libraries are visited by twenty million people each year.

World War II awakened the United States to the uses of propaganda as an instrument of policy. Under the Office of War Information all shades of propaganda ("white," factual; "black," fictional; "gray," mixed) were used to soften enemy morale and gain the support of neutral countries. During the Cold War, "Campaigns of Truth" have been waged by both sides, but some people now feel these activities should be greatly deemphasized if not eliminated. They claim our successes and failures abroad are more related to *what we do* than to *what we say*. Advocating turning off "the Great Wind Machine," one former USIA officer speculated that "without the USIA the course of recent history would have been the same, except a bit less noisy."[6]

Radio Free Europe is an operation similar to Voice of America although RFE is a private organization and VOA is an operation of the USIA. Popular RFE programs consist of political satire, songs, and dialogue satirizing Communist regimes.

The creation of semiautonomous units under the secretary of state, such as ACDA and USIA, reflects a compromise in the never-ending debate between those who believe the State Department should make policy but, except for the traditional instrument of diplomacy, leave its execution to others, and those who insist that all facets of foreign policy should be coordinated into a single agency (as we did for defense policy in creating the Department of Defense).[7]

Conducting and managing foreign affairs is a big business. Foreign affairs create great problems and require precise workable solutions. Red tape and disorder in the State Department have caused modern presidents to create "bypass mechanisms"—personal state departments of their own. When this occurs, other agencies such as the CIA and

[5]George Thayer, *The War Business: The International Trade in Armaments* (Simon and Schuster, 1969), p. 191.

[6]Bruce Oudes, "The Great Wind Machine," *Washington Monthly* (June 1970), pp. 31–33.

[7]Perhaps the best discussion of the organizational problems of the State Department and foreign policy-making can be found in I. M. Destler, *Presidents, Bureaucrats and Foreign Policy* (Princeton University Press, 1972).

DOD become more independent of traditional sources of foreign policy-making.[8] In times of urgency, officials cannot wait for decisions to travel up and down the bureaucratic ladder. Organization, speed, and efficiency are needed. If they are frustrated by the Department of State, decision-makers act through alternative means, with the result, as an anonymous Washington official complained, that "State is being run all over town."[9]

Americans overseas

American diplomacy is older than the United States. Even before the Revolution, Benjamin Franklin was sent as our representative to France by the Continental Congress. Today the United States maintains nearly three hundred posts abroad, with missions in the capital cities of almost all nations with whom we carry on diplomatic relations. In addition, we maintain permanent missions at the North Atlantic Treaty Organization, the Organization of American States, European regional organizations, the United Nations, and other units such as the International Civil Aviation Organization. The heads of these missions, designated by the president with the consent of the Senate, hold the rank of ambassador, minister, or chargé d'affaires. Historically, ambassadors were sent to the larger and more important countries, but now we maintain embassies (each headed by an ambassador) in almost all countries. Until recently, diplomatic posts were filled primarily by political appointees, some of whom had little knowledge of foreign affairs. Today more than two-thirds of the chiefs of missions are Foreign Service officers.

During our early years as a nation, the caliber of our overseas representation was high. Men like John Adams, Thomas Jefferson, and James Monroe served American interests in foreign capitals. But, following the War of 1812, diplomatic posts were used mainly to reward persons for political activities. High diplomatic assignments were given to wealthy men who had contributed to the campaigns of victorious presidents. Because the salaries of diplomats were small and their expenses large, only men of independent means could afford to take posts in the more important nations. Various minor reforms were made, but it was not until 1924 that a modern career service was established. In that year, the Rogers Act consolidated the diplomatic and consular service and provided for a Foreign Service of the United States established on a career basis. The service was further modernized and reorganized by the Foreign Service Act of 1946.

[8]Richard Holbrooke, "The Machine that Fails," *Foreign Policy* (Winter 1970–1971), p. 70.

[9]Quoted in Campbell, *Foreign Affairs Fudge Factory*, p. 228.

THE AMERICAN FOREIGN SERVICE

The American Foreign Service is the eyes and ears of the United States in other countries. Although a part of the State Department, the service represents the entire government and performs jobs for many other agencies. Its main duties are to carry out foreign policy as expressed in the directives of the secretary of state, gather data for American policy-makers, protect Americans and American interests in foreign countries, and cultivate friendly relations with foreign peoples.

The Foreign Service is composed of ambassadors, ministers, officers, reserve officers, and staff.[10] At the core of the service are the Foreign Service officers, comparable to the officers of the regular army in the military services. They are a select, specially trained body of men and women who are expected to take an assignment any place in the world on short notice. There are approximately 3,500 such officers; in recent years less than one hundred junior officers won appointment. Competition to gain appointment is now tougher than ever and it is generally agreed that "this is as bright and talented a group as any to be found in government."[11] They have their own training school, the Foreign Service Institute, where new officers are briefed and where experienced officers get advanced instruction.

The Foreign Service is one of the most prestigious *and* most criticized branches of the national government. During the 1950s the criticism seemed to outweigh the respect, and the service's morale suffered accordingly. In loyalty-security hearings, officers were asked to justify remarks sometimes taken out of context from confidential reports made years ago to their superiors. Critics accused the service of being infiltrated by Communist sympathizers; others charged that it was dominated by a high-society elite who were still under the impression that diplomacy was the near monopoly of gentlemen. The charges about Communist infiltration were obviously overdrawn, as were claims that the service was preoccupied with refined manners. Still, most of the personnel of the service did come from the same general social background—a fact that cut down on the effectiveness of their reporting, for every reporter, no matter how objective, selects and evaluates what he sees on the basis of his or her own attitudes and life experiences.

Since 1954 the State Department has attempted to fill its major positions with Foreign Service officers wherever possible and has expanded its categories of specialists, but the Department has had to rely on civil service employees to a substantial extent to fill positions calling for special skills and backgrounds not available with the Foreign Service. A comprehensive study of the Foreign Service by the Carnegie Endow-

[10]See the Epilogue for a discussion of the method of appointment and preparation for entering the Foreign Service, and for a detailed background, William Barnes and John Heath Morgan, *The Foreign Service of the United States* (Department of State, 1961).

[11]See the perceptive assessment by James Fallows, "The Foreign Service as Mirror of America" *Washington Monthly* (April 1973), pp. 5–14.

ment's Committee on Foreign Affairs Personnel (the Herter committee) looked at the overseas service of all the other agencies of the federal government and called for the creation of a single family of foreign affairs services. The Herter committee discovered that earlier reforms were working fairly well, but urged additional expansion of training, a broader basis of selection, and further integration of civil service and Foreign Service personnel.[12] In 1964, following the Herter committee's report, the secretary of state and the director of the United States Information Agency announced the integration into the Foreign Service of most of the key officials of the USIA.

In more recent years, criticism of the Foreign Service has come as much from within as from outside.[13] Most of the criticism claims the Foreign Service: (1) stifles creativity with its clannish "don't-rock-the-boat" and "minimize risk-taking" mentality (2) attracts officers who are, or at least become, concerned more about *being* or *becoming* somebody than *doing* something, and (3) requires its new recruits to wait fifteen to twenty years before being considered for positions of responsibility. These problems are well recognized in Washington and the task of improving the Service continues. More women and minorities have been recruited in recent years, and other managerial innovations have been tried. But the career service features of the Foreign Service Corps—entry at the bottom, rank in the person rather than in the position, resistance to lateral entry, advancement through grades as determined by senior officers' evaluations, and the tendency towards self-government—make it resistant to easy change. "We can expect," writes one critic, "the Foreign Service exposés to keep rolling out." Its problems of overstaffing, empty jobs, and tedious apprenticeships are in fact common in most bureaucracies. It is just that "The Foreign Service's situation is exaggerated—because its prestige is so high, and the value of its work inherently so hard to quantify. . . ."[14]

In spite of efforts to professionalize the Foreign Service, it continues to suffer the high winds and tides of Washington's turbulent political climate. A veteran of these storms has pointed out that "President Kennedy was angry because he thought the Foreign Service was too conservative. Nixon thinks they're too liberal. They're both wrong. The Foreign Service is just the Foreign Service."[15]

[12]*Personnel for the New Diplomacy* (Carnegie Endowment for International Peace, 1962). In addition, the Carnegie Endowment has published six monographs, collectively known as the Foreign Affairs Personnel Studies, prepared for use by the Herter committee.

[13]See, for example, Chris Argyris, *Some Causes of Organizational Ineffectiveness Within the Department of State* (Department of State Occasional Paper, U.S. Government Printing Office, 1967); John E. Harr, *The Professional Diplomat* (Princeton University Press, 1969), and *Toward a Modern Diplomacy* (1968), a report of the American Foreign Service Association.

[14]Fallows, "Foreign Service as Mirror," p. 14.

[15]Anonymous source quoted in Holbrooke, "The Machine that Fails," p. 75.

In order to get a better idea of the many duties of the Foreign Service, let us consider the activities of a typical American mission.

AMERICANS IN NEW DELHI

On Shantipath – Path of Peace – in New Delhi stands a handsome modern building designed by an American architect in an Eastern style. This is the American embassy, in its diplomatic enclave in India's capital city. The entire United States mission operates from eight office buildings in this enclave and outside, spends over $3 million a year directly on its own activities, helps administer several hundred millions in loans and grants to India, and employs about sixteen hundred Americans and three thousand Indians. A dozen local units of major Washington departments and agencies – Commerce, Agriculture, and the Peace Corps, for example – are attached to the embassy. The ambassador – and New Delhi has received such notable American envoys as J. Kenneth Galbraith, Chester Bowles, and Daniel Patrick Moynihan, – is the ranking American representative in India and is responsible for coordinating all activities of the mission.[16]

The embassy's Division of Political-Economic Affairs, created in 1965, is divided into an External Section, which informs the State Department of developments in India's political, military, and economic relations with other nations, and an Internal Section, which analyzes and reports on India's internal economic policies and political affairs – for example, parliamentary debates, election results, Bangladesh, language and communal problems, Kashmir.

One key agency is organized separately from the embassy but operates under the ambassador's general direction. The United States Information Service sponsors exchanges of persons and cultural programs in India; visits by American specialists; science, art, and book exhibits; and film shows. The Information Section is a huge publishing operation in itself. It puts out several large-circulation magazines and numbers of pamplets, press releases, texts of important speeches, feature stories, and photographs for use by Indian newspapers and magazines.

Former U.S. Ambassador to India John Kenneth Galbraith, his wife, and two Indian officials during a visit to the giant Bhakra Dam in Northwest India.

The USAID (United States Agency for International Development) used to operate in India, again under the ambassador's general direction, and was one of the largest missions. It gave development grants and loans for industry, agriculture, health, and education. It made grants for malaria and smallpox eradication, craftsman training, dairy development, crop production. Since the India-Pakistan War and the cooling off of friendly relations between India and the United States, U.S. aid programs to India have been reduced markedly – chiefly at India's request. As relations between the two nations slowly return to normal, the USAID will probably once again build up a staff in India.

And then there is the Peace Corps. India has sometimes had more

[16]For an enlightening as well as entertaining memoir, see John Kenneth Galbraith, *Ambassador's Journal* (Houghton Mifflin, 1969). See, for contrast, Charles Bohlen, *Witness to History, 1929–1969* (Norton, 1973).

PCVs (Peace Corps Volunteers) than any other country—around 500. As in other countries, the PCVs work at the grass roots level on such matters as auto mechanics, health, rural community action, and farming.

OTHER AMERICANS OVERSEAS

During World War II, several departments and agencies set up their own overseas offices. The diplomatic missions in many cases were overshadowed, and friction and lack of coordination resulted. The American ambassador in London was not even kept informed of various matters affecting Anglo-American relations and was all but superseded by the American lend-lease expediter. After the war many of these agencies were abolished, and some of their duties and personnel were assigned to diplomatic and consular missions. But as postwar programs developed, the principle that the United States should have but one overseas arm was again violated, and separate overseas missions were frequently established. The Agency for International Development, the CIA, the Peace Corps, and the Foreign Agriculture Service have their own overseas career services. In many countries a Military Assistance Advisory Group reports directly to the Pentagon, and in some countries there are operating military commands.

As a matter of official protocol, an ambassador is the president's representative and outranks all other Americans, including even the vice-president and secretary of state when they visit the country of his mission. Recent presidents have issued directives to clarify the ambassador's primacy and his responsibility for coordinating all American activities in the country of his mission. But in fact the primacy of the ambassador remains a polite fiction. Overseas personnel continue to deal directly with their organizational superiors in Washington, especially on important matters of budget and programs. It is unlikely that coordination of our agencies overseas can proceed any faster than the coordination of programs in Washington.

The United States and international organizations

The United States belongs to all the important world organizations, and its representatives attend all major international conferences. These organizations and conferences are major instruments of American diplomacy. In addition to the United Nations and its related agencies, the United States is a member of more than two hundred international organizations of various types. Slowly but steadily, certain functions are being transferred from the national to the international level.

THE ORGANIZATION OF AMERICAN STATES

In its own hemisphere, the United States is a member of the Organization of American States (OAS), a regional agency of twenty-four American republics. The OAS Charter was amended in February 1970, changing the original structure established in 1948 in the Charter of Punte del Este. The General Assembly, replacing the Inter-American Conference, is the supreme OAS organ. It meets annually at the ministerial level and deals with the OAS budget, members' contributions, coordination, and applications for new membership.

Three councils are responsible to the General Assembly: the Inter-American Economic and Social Council, the Inter-American Council for Education, Science, and Culture, and the Permanent Council, which directs the affairs of specialized agencies such as the Inter-American Judicial Committee, the Inter-American Indian Institute, and the Pan-American Health Organization. In addition to fostering economic and social progress, the OAS seeks to preserve unity and harmony among the sister republics. The Inter-American Committee on Peaceful Settlement has been created to this end.

THE UNITED NATIONS

The United Nations is an organization designed to bring nations together to maintain international peace and security, to achieve international cooperation in solving world problems, to promote and encourage respect for human rights. Although basically an association of nations, the United Nations is an international legal personality with the power to make treaties and the competence to claim reparations for injury to its agents. It maintains its own legal staff, operates its own headquarters, and has its own flag. The major United Nations organs are the Security Council, the General Assembly, the Economic and Social Council, the Trusteeship Council, the Secretariat, and the International Court of Justice.

The United States maintains a permanent diplomatic mission at the headquarters of the United Nations. This mission is headed by a chief who has the rank of ambassador and sometimes cabinet status. In addition, the president, with the consent of the Senate, appoints five representatives to the General Assembly; these representatives serve for the duration of a particular session. The chief of the mission is re-

A general view at the opening of a conference of foreign ministers of the Organization of American States.

sponsible for coordinating the actions of our many delegates to the other divisions of the United Nations. Within the Department of State, the Bureau of International Organization Affairs coordinates the policies and activities of our United Nations delegation with those of other federal agencies, helps to prepare instructions to our representatives in the delegation, serves as technical adviser to them, disseminates information to the public about the United Nations, and assumes general responsibility for American participation.

The United Nation's failure to solve each and every dispute among nations and its inability to eradicate global problems such as famines or the arms race have caused some Americans to become disillusioned with it. The United Nations suffers also from "creeping irrelevance" and a highly calcified international civil service that makes our Foreign Service look very healthy. We witness the "defeat of an ideal" says one critic—the members pay lipservice while at the same time pursue their short-term interests at its expense.[17] Timidity, bureaucracy, and "geographical" appeasement reign supreme. Gunnar Myrdal concludes that "On the whole the United Nations system of intergovernmental organizations have become less and less effective as matrixes for international co-operation, particularly in regard to problems where substantial interests of the great powers . . . are directly or indirectly involved."[18]

The United Nations, like every other agency of international politics, is dominated by the fact the world is divided into separate nations acting, most of the time, in their own self-interest. The United States, like most nations, cites the U.N. Charter when it suits its short-term interest and ignores it when it does not. The U.S. has usually found that on important matters it is easier to deal with involved nations directly. The United Nations, with 142 member nations, can only do *what the member nations want it to do*. Rarely can it move fast. And rarely can it achieve solutions if there is no broad consensus.

Critics are divided over whether we have expected too much of it or too little. Certain conservatives have long opposed our involvement in it, fearing the U.S. would lose its sovereignty and risk being trapped by the Communists or the Third World nations, or both. Surely some of the U.S.'s disillusionment has come about because the U.N. is so large and unwieldy and it seemingly accomplishes so little. Yet there are many who feel the U.N. fails because we have had so little faith in it. They counsel us to expect more: *try to make it work*. And, they note, as the U.S. shifts away from strategies of interventionism and toward détente, the U.N. could provide the foundation for *constructive internationalism*. Whether the U.S. moves in this direction or not, the U.N. is a useful and perhaps a necessary organization for diplomatic consultation. It is easy

[17]Shirley Hazzard, *Defeat of an Ideal: A Study of the Self-Destruction of the United Nations* (Little, Brown, 1973).

[18]Foreword, p. 13, in Mahdi Elmandjra, *The United Nations System: An Analysis* (Faber and Faber, 1973). For a different view see the diary by William F. Buckley, Jr., *United Nations Journal* (Putnam, 1974).

to scorn the United Nations, but can anyone suggest an alternative? Meanwhile, the U.N. remains a vital forum for working out joint programs on the law of the sea, economic development, world population problems, global energy supplies, and the protection of international environment.

Vietnam: a case study[19]

Foreign policy is not made according to any set formula, but represents various traditions, organized interests, and constitutional—and sometimes extraconstitutional—processes. Our democracy has vested the primary responsibility for making foreign policy in the chief executive. But he in turn, is dependent on accidents of history, on his advisers, and in the long run, on the American people. When there are no obvious solutions to international problems, our decision-makers must predict, act, and wait—sometimes successfully, but sometimes with unforeseeable and catastrophic consequences. Since the end of World War II, no single event so dominated American life as the Vietnam War. How did it happen?

Who made our Vietnam policy? Did the Congress participate in that decision? Or did our civilian and military elites "advise" us into war?

To what degree should the people be involved in decision-making in such a war? Can they be informed without aiding our enemies? Does concern for security threaten our democratic system?

Why were American soldiers in Vietnam? How did our commitment change over three decades of involvement? What led to the ultimate collapse of 1975 of the U.S.-supported South Vietnamese government? Why did we not succeed in achieving our goals in Southeast Asia? Historians will be arguing about some of these questions for decades. We can begin to outline here some of the factors that must be considered in answering them.

A DECISION NOT TO GO TO WAR

In March, 1954, some months before the Geneva Conference was to be held, the French chief of staff arrived in Washington, D.C., to tell President Eisenhower, Secretary of State Dulles, and Chairman of the Joint Chiefs of Staff Admiral Radford, that unless the U.S. intervened, Indochina would be lost to the Communists.[20] Some time later, the National Security Council (NSC), with Radford, Dulles, and Vice-President Nixon, agreed that Indochina must not be allowed to fall into Communist

[19]Jay Fahn drafted background material on which this case study draws.

[20]The materials on Indochina are drawn from Chalmers M. Roberts, "The Day We Didn't Go to War," *The Reporter* (September 14, 1954), pp. 31–35; and "The Pentagon Papers," disclosed by the *New York Times*, the *Boston Globe*, and *Newsweek* in June–July 1971. See Neil Sheehan, et al. *The Pentagon Papers* (as published by the *New York Times* [Quadrangle Books, 1971]).

hands lest it set off a "falling row of dominoes" across all Southeast Asia. The Council decided that if necessary the United States should intervene, provided it could obtain the support of its allies and the French would grant Indochina its independence. A policy paper was prepared, initialed by the president to make it official.

Although the president had the constitutional power to put this policy into effect, Eisenhower usually wanted prior congressional approval. So in April 1954, Dulles told a small group of congressmen and foreign policy leaders from both parties that Eisenhower wanted a joint resolution from Congress permitting the use of air and naval power for a single strike to attempt to break the siege of Dienbienphu.

The congressmen – both Republicans and Democrats – asked, "Would this mean war?" Would Communist China intervene on the other side? Radford, who long believed that a showdown with the Chinese Communists was inevitable and who felt that the sooner it came the better, minced no words: "Yes." Would land forces have to be used? No one could say for sure. As the talk continued, it became clear that the other chiefs of staff did not agree with Radford, and that Dulles, moreover, had not consulted our allies. Finally, the congressmen told Dulles that before they would try to get a joint resolution from Congress that would in effect commit the nation to war, the secretary should first line up the allies.

Within a week Dulles had talked with the diplomatic representatives in Washington of Britain, France, Australia, New Zealand, the Philippines, Thailand, and the three associated states of Indochina. Except for France, the allies were opposed. Dulles flew to London to talk personally with Prime Minister Churchill and Foreign Secretary Eden, but they were unenthusiastic even after Dulles proposed the creation of a Southeast Asia Treaty Organization to serve as a vehicle for united action. Eden said that coming on the eve of the Geneva Conference – which had been called in part to discuss means to end the seven-year Indochina war – American military action would be disastrous. He was convinced it would lead to the use of ground troops and the spread of fighting to Communist China. The British cabinet voted no support. There was no American strike, and Dienbienphu fell after a bloody siege.

Early in May, 1954, President Eisenhower repeated that under certain conditions – Indochinese independence and continued French military support – the United States would seek congressional approval for armed intervention.[21] The Joint Chiefs of Staff completed military blueprints for preventing a Communist takeover in Indochina, and this time British cooperation was not required. Now, however, the French were war-weary and willing to negotiate with the Vietminh, the local Communist-led anticolonial forces. Eisenhower was infuriated. Threatening to exclude the French from the Big Three (the United States,

[21]Memorandum by Robert Cutler, Special Assistant to President Eisenhower, May 7, 1954, reprinted in the *New York Times* (July 5, 1971), p. 10.

United Kingdom, and France), the NSC warned that in the event of a Communist victory all U.S. aid to France would end.[22] Distressed by what he viewed as French weakness, the president sent a team of saboteurs to Hanoi to conduct clandestine operations in the North.[23]

The Geneva Agreements were eventually concluded on July 21, 1954, and provided for French withdrawal from Indochina and authorized a temporary military demarcation line to divide North Vietnam from South Vietnam. It was agreed too that Vietnam was to be unified through national elections to be held in July of 1956.[24] Almost everyone seemed pleased except the United States. Dulles, alarmed by the terms of the accords, called the settlement a disaster, a sellout to communism. The NSC and JCS quickly established a program of American military and economic aid to the temporary Saigon government in South Vietnam. If France would not plug the dike against a Communist flood in Asia, then the United States would. Thus was born our commitment, out of a decision not to go to war.

President Kennedy shared his predecessors' beliefs that the United States must resist Communist expansion in Southeast Asia, and that the U.S. should assist the South Vietnam government in defending its freedom and independence. Especially because of his liberal image and perhaps in part due to his Bay of Pigs fiasco, Kennedy did not want to appear "soft" on Communism.

In the late fifties, South Vietnam had been weakened by constant pressure from the Viet Cong (a derogatory contraction of "Vietnamese Communist," used, except by the Communists, to describe the Communist subversive movement in the South after 1954), the successors to the Vietminh. In the North, Ho Chi Minh was a charismatic populist who was turning more and more to Communist support. Ho Chi Minh still sought the elections promised at Geneva and ultimately the reunification of Vietnam.

Meanwhile, ravaged by terror and instability since the French defeat in 1954, South Vietnam authorities looked to the United States for help. Was North Vietnam the main cause of the gradually weakened South Vietnamese government? Or was the opposition to the Saigon temporary government in the late fifties merely a loosely organized group, including Buddhists, Saigon intellectuals, trade-unionists, neutralists as well as Communist party activists? People differed in their judgment, though U.S. advisers invariably emphasized the guiding hand of the North Vietnamese Communists. Blaming North Vietnam was, many people feel now, a smokescreen to hide Saigon's inability to win the loyalty of the people in its half of Vietnam.

[22]Fox Butterfield, "Pentagon Papers: Eisenhower Decisions Undercut the Geneva Accords, Study Says," *The Pentagon Papers*, p. 13.

[23]Excerpts from the report of the Saigon Military Mission, an American team headed by Edward G. Lansdale, 1954–1955, reprinted *ibid.*, p. 11.

[24]See George Kahin and John W. Lewis, *The United States in Vietnam* (Dial Press, 1967), Chaps. 2 and 3.

"FLOOD RELIEF"

In October 1961, Kennedy sent General Maxwell Taylor to South Vietnam to survey the military and political situation. Taylor was to report directly to Kennedy with specific proposals for American support. Taylor met with President Ngo Dinh Diem. He recommended Kennedy send a Mekong Delta flood-relief "task force," largely military in composition, including "combat troops" for protection. Taylor added, "The risks of backing into a major Asian war by way of SVN are present but are not impressive. NVN is extremely vulnerable to conventional bombing, a weakness which should be exploited diplomatically in convincing Hanoi to lay off SVN."[25] He urged that up to 8,000 troops be sent and forcefully argued that our program "to save the SVN" could not survive without them.

Even before the Taylor mission, President Kennedy had initiated several important changes in American policy. In May 1961, Kennedy authorized covert operations against North Vietnam and the use of American advisers in guerrilla action against enemy bases in neighboring Laos. At the same time, the president sent Vice-President Lyndon Johnson to Saigon with instructions to "encourage" the South Vietnamese to request U.S. ground forces. South Vietnam's President Diem was reluctant to make such a request because the presence of American forces would serve his critics' charges that Diem was only an American puppet. Furthermore, the 1954 Geneva Agreements prohibited the introduction of foreign troops into Indochina. By the time General Taylor visited Saigon in October, Diem finally saw fit to make the request for American troops.

The Taylor fact-finding mission was a crucial turning point. Taylor spent several weeks in Vietnam, and his reports to Kennedy reportedly so "shocked" Kennedy that the president kept them suppressed. And contrary to Taylor's real proposals, almost all news accounts of his trip held that Taylor had recommended against combat troops.[26]

The situation was rapidly deteriorating *within* the Saigon government and *in the countryside* of South Vietnam. Kennedy finally decided against Taylor's suggestion for a large ground force, but eagerly complied with Diem's "request" for additional logistical and advisory support. During the next two years—1962 and 1963—Kennedy proceeded to raise the number of American advisers from 685 to almost 16,000, a figure that meant American participation in combat operations. It also meant American casualties.

Early in 1961, the new president had informed the world that the United States was prepared "to pay any price" to preserve freedom at

[25]Cable from General Maxwell Taylor to Kennedy on Introduction of U.S. troops November 1, 1961, in Neil Sheehan, et al., *Pentagon Papers*, pp. 146–48.

[26]See David Halberstam, *The Best and the Brightest* (Random House, 1972), p. 169. For Taylor's own version, see his memoir: *Swords and Plowshares* (Norton, 1972), Chaps. 17 and 18.

home and around the world. Now the down payment had been made, and the installments were just beginning to come due.

HOPING FOR THE BEST

When Lyndon Johnson became president, conditions in South Vietnam had further deteriorated. Diem had been ousted and murdered, and "a sad series of revolving-door juntas" had led the nation to the point of dissolution.[27] While it was not certain that United States aid alone could save South Vietnam, it was believed that to pull out would mean leaving South Vietnam to the Viet Cong and North Vietnamese and would bring cruel retribution for our supporters in the South.

Secretary of Defense McNamara, reporting to Johnson in December 1963, termed the situation in South Vietnam disturbing. The Viet Cong had made vast progress, yet the secretary did not feel that more U.S. aid alone could help. Instead, McNamara advised covert operations against the North (Plan 34-A). He felt the United States should watch and wait, "running scared, hoping for the best."

But hoping for the best does not win wars. In January 1964, the JCS proposed a major "Americanization" of the war, including American control of all combat operations, use of American forces, and air strikes against the North. The Joint Chiefs did not expect that hitting the North would hurt the Viet Cong in the South, but felt strongly that bolder action was necessary to demonstrate American resolve to oppose Communist wars of national liberation. The senior officers emphasized that "the United States must make plain to the enemy our determination to see the Vietnam campaign through to a favorable conclusion."[28]

A few high officials and Kennedy advisers suggested that the United States withdraw. John Kenneth Galbraith had warned Kennedy along this line as early as 1961. Ex-New Dealer Benjamin V. Cohen had urged withdrawal. Even Robert Kennedy, then the attorney general asked, "if we can't win with Diem and we can't win without him, . . . why . . . not disengage?" Robert Kennedy's suggestion came at an NSC meeting at which Secretary of State Dean Rusk presided in President Kennedy's absence. Rusk stood on existing policy; Rusk's view was that "we will not pull out of Vietnam until the war is won."[29] We would stick to our commitments *and our guns* regarding the future of South Vietnam.

Most influential was McNamara's report of March 1964, which echoed the earlier JCS proposals that "higher levels of effort" were necessary to win the war. The secretary spelled out a plan for "Graduated Overt Military Pressure"—use of American ground and air forces to retaliate

[27]The quote comes from *Newsweek* (June 28, 1971), p. 17. But for an insightful discussion of this period, including the U.S. role in the coup against Diem, see Chester L. Cooper, *The Lost Crusade* (Dodd, Mead, 1970), Chaps. 8 through 12.

[28]Memorandum from General Taylor, January 22, 1964, reprinted in Neil Sheehan, et al., *Pentagon Papers*, pp. 282–85.

[29]Neil Sheehan, et al., *Pentagon Papers*, pp. 180–81.

against North Vietnam for its increasing support of the Viet Cong. McNamara proposed that plans be completed to allow for such responses within a seventy-two hour period and for a full-scale strike capability within thirty days. (This required beefing up all U.S. ground, air, and naval forces in the western Pacific to meet any possible reaction by Hanoi or Peking.)

The buck stopped in the White House. President Johnson trusted his highest military advisers, who assured him that more pressure would end, not widen, the conflict. Would the United States allow South Vietnam's freedom to disappear beneath the "tide of Communist domination" in Asia? Did the American people want victory in Vietnam, or peace and safety for only themselves in "Fortress America"? "Anti-Communism has been and still is a potent force in American politics, and most people who were dealing with the Vietnam problem believed that the Congress and the public would 'punish' those who were 'soft on Communism.' "[30] Johnson delayed any increase in our commitment but ordered the plans drawn up. Johnson took McNamara's advice to hope for the best, but as commander in chief he prepared for the worst.

THE DAYS WE WENT TO WAR

For both Vietnam and Washington, 1964 and 1965 were decisive years. On August 2, 1964, North Vietnamese allegedly "attacked" American warships in the Gulf of Tonkin. This controversial Tonkin Gulf Affair has been widely debated ever since, and the so-called "attack" has never been proven.[31] Within hours American planes were hitting preselected targets in North Vietnam, thanks to the retaliation planning of March and April.

In Washington, D. C., Secretaries Rush and McNamara, informed congressional leaders that the Gulf of Tonkin attack was "unprovoked." Although fully aware of McNamara's plan for covert operations in the North, they denied any United States involvement there. Before the week's end, both houses authorized the president to take "all necessary measures" to protect American forces and to prevent further aggression. More important, however, Congress called upon the chief executive to use armed force to assist any SEATO member or protocol state (such as South Vietnam) "in defense of its freedom." The legislative branch advised and *consented* with little debate. The Gulf of Tonkin Resolution passed through the Senate 88–2, and through the House 416–0. The American people, believing that our ships had been attacked without cause on the high seas, were prepared to respond in kind. The stakes and the risks rose rapidly.[32]

[30]Leslie Gelb, "Vietnam: The System Worked," *Foreign Policy* (August 1971), pp. 166–67.

[31]See Joseph C. Goulden, *Truth Is the First Casualty* (Rand McNally, 1969); and E. G. Windchy, *Tonkin Gulf* (Doubleday, 1971).

[32]For different interpretations of the role of public opinion and the Vietnam war, see Richard Barnet, *Roots of War* (Penguin Books, 1972), Chaps. 9 and 10; and John E. Mueller, *War, Presidents and Public Opinion* (John Wiley, 1973), Chaps. 2–5.

With a congressional blank check in hand and an optimistic military at his ear, President Johnson amplified the content and scope of the American commitment. Following attacks on American bases in February 1965, Johnson ordered Operation Rolling Thunder—the sustained bombing of North Vietnam—and, in March, U.S. Marines waded ashore at Danang to protect our airstrip. But no sooner had the Marines landed than the president ordered a change in mission from perimeter defense to a more active combat role. In taking that important step in early April 1965, President Johnson insisted that the switch be made without publicity.[33] On the same day the president even told a reporter that "no far-reaching strategy . . . is being suggested or promulgated."[34]

With the infusion of American forces, the war grew hotter, and calls for more troops louder. While General Westmoreland, U.S. Commander in Vietnam, assured Johnson that more men would turn the tide, Undersecretary of State George Ball sounded the discordant note of reducing, not increasing, the American effort. This experienced diplomat expressed grave doubts about the wisdom of U.S. policy, and stated bluntly that for all our intensive efforts, South Vietnam was still losing the war. In withdrawing, Ball could not envision any lasting blow to our credibility as an ally, except for parochial fears in Southeast Asia. (The CIA had previously discredited the domino theory.) Certain friends would raise eyebrows, and we could expect "some catcalls from the sidelines," but in the long run, continuing the war would cause greater damage to our honor and prestige than would "pursuing a carefully plotted course toward a compromise solution. . . ."[35]

Ball's message was delivered and read, but the NSC considered it a "throwaway alternative." Johnson listened to his hawks, and by the end of July 1965, 200,000 American troops were violating the long-standing dictum against fighting a land war in Asia.

SECOND THOUGHTS

With every increase in men, Americans were assured that the job could be done. But the job kept demanding more men. Top civilian and military minds wanted the president to "widen" the bombing in the North to include vital port and oil facilities. Walt Rostow, the president's national security adviser, informed Johnson that heavier damage was needed "for more decisive results." So more bombs fell. General Westmoreland, facing a determined foe in the South, boosted his troop requests from 175,000 in June to 443,000 in December 1965. The U.S. commander claimed that with more American men the enemy could be

[33]Neil Sheehan, et al., *Pentagon Papers*, p. 453.

[34]*Newsweek* (June 28, 1971), p. 21.

[35]Memorandum, "A Compromise Solution in South Vietnam," from Undersecretary of State George W. Ball for President Johnson, July 1, 1965, reprinted in Neil Sheehan, et al., *Pentagon Papers*, pp. 459–64.

defeated within two years. At every crucial stage, more force was prescribed as the remedy, yet every increase brought only more requests.

Second thoughts began to appear about our course of action. In January 1966, Assistant Secretary of Defense John McNaughton told McNamara that the American dilemma was caused by an "enormous miscalculation." Most important, McNaughton observed, U.S. policy had shifted from preserving freedom and fulfilling commitments to preventing defeat and avoiding humiliation. He warned against pushing American obligations *beyond* our reputation.[36]

McNaughton's doubts were confirmed that summer when studies by the Defense Intelligence Agency disclosed that our intensified bombing of the North had had no measurable direct effect on Hanoi, and appeared only to have increased the opposition's will to resist. The CIA had warned earlier that such would be the case, but its estimates were bypassed by the military. Disenchantment spread further when casualty reports of the bombings in North Vietnam showed the majority to be civilians. Still other reports indicated that "pacification" efforts in South Vietnam had failed. In October, the secretary of defense himself finally urged the president to restrict the bombing and to seek a political settlement to the war. Secretary McNamara noted that such a settlement was the only alternative to a longer, costlier war. Further escalation would raise casualties but not achieve any acceptable solution.[37] Neither power nor pacification had worked. At best, military defeat had been avoided.

The JCS were alarmed by this view, and they quickly (the same day) presented their position to the president. They did not share the secretary's pessimism, and they countered McNamara's call for restricting Operation Rolling Thunder with a plea for broadening the bombing.[38] Again the president, the "ultimate decision-maker," was the middleman. This internal debate intensified early in 1967 when General Westmoreland requested a total force of more than half a million men. Now the president hesitated. The military argued that more troops and better targets could hurt the enemy and give the United States the upper hand in negotiations, but the president was still puzzled over our inability to make progress in the South. Then Westmoreland asked for another 200,000 men—a total of 671,616—which would have required mobilization of the reserves. The Vietnam commander even suggested extending the war into Cambodia, Laos, and perhaps North Vietnam.[39]

[36]Assistant Secretary of Defense John McNaughton to Secretary of Defense McNamara, January 19, 1966, reprinted in Neil Sheehan, et al., *Pentagon Papers*, pp. 502–04.

[37]Draft memorandum for President Lyndon B. Johnson, "Action Recommended for Vietnam," from Secretary of Defense Robert S. McNamara, October 14, 1966, reprinted *ibid.*, pp. 554–63.

[38]Joint Chiefs of Staff memorandum, General Earle G. Wheeler, Chairman, to Secretary of Defense McNamara, October 14, 1966, reprinted *ibid.*, pp. 564–65.

[39]Notes on Johnson's discussion with Wheeler and Westmoreland, April 27, 1967, *ibid.*, pp. 579–81.

An ever-growing number of dissenters within the government were incensed at the mention of an invasion of the North. We had fought China in Korea. Had we not learned that lesson? We could not rely upon conventional means to repel a Chinese attack. And we were not prepared to do otherwise. Even Rostow suddenly suggested a bombing cutback. McNamara and McNaughton repeated their earlier "compromise" positions. But the generals prevailed, and the troops and targets increased to some degree.

By now Vietnam was convulsing the home front. Ever-increasing draft calls and military funerals brought the war closer to the American people, while Congress grew restless over the endless spending of "blood and treasure" in an undeclared war halfway around the world. Senators Morse and Fulbright launched repeated attacks on the administration for conducting a "presidential war," a war by proxy, and peace demonstrators laid seige to the Pentagon in protest of our conduct in Asia. As many citizens demanded why we fought in Vietnam when the battle was at home, America's cities exploded in racial violence, requiring federal troops to restore order. "Guns and butter" threatened to dominate the coming election campaign, while events in Korea, Europe, and the Middle East reminded us that American interests were worldwide. The war continued.

THE MAN AND THE WAR: A CHANGE

When Tet, the Vietnamese New Year, began in late January 1968, there was renewed hope that a ceasefire might lead to negotiations, but the Viet Cong and the North Vietnamese celebrated by attacking every large city in the South. Only weeks before, allied officials had boasted that the VC controlled only limited rural areas. These small areas suddenly included the American Embassy in Saigon, where the staff had to fight with pistols as terrorists lobbed grenades into the compound. Opposition forces captured Hue, the ancient capital, and set about massacring the South Vietnamese.[40] American forces had finally to destroy the city in order to "save" it.

The Tet offensive was a stunning political victory for Hanoi in the U.S. as well as a crippling blow to South Vietnam. It signaled a major shift in American public opinion against the war, for it proved that after years of fighting the enemy could still hit and hit hard. General Wheeler, chairman of the JCS, secretly labeled the attacks a complete surprise, "a very near thing."[41] Publicly, however, officials maintained that it

[40]Civilians suffered wanton deaths throughout the war, from both U.S. and enemy attacks. See Seymour M. Hersh, *My Lai 4: A Report on the Massacre and Its Aftermath* (Random House, 1970); and by the same author, *Cover-up: The Army's Secret Investigation of the Massacre at My Lai 4* (Random House, 1972).

[41]General Earle G. Wheeler to President Johnson, February 27, 1968, "Report of Chairman, JCS, on Situation in Vietnam and MACV Requirements," reprinted in Neil Sheehan, et al., *Pentagon Papers*, pp. 628–34.

represented the VC's "last gasp," and General Westmoreland proclaimed an allied victory. With another 200,000 men, said the generals, the United States could complete that victory.

Thousands of lives had been spent, yet progress had been terribly slow. Intelligence sources reported that the enemy could maintain combat regardless of American troop strength. In the center stood the president. His generals and admirals had promised victory, yet every escalation had brought only more promises, only more devastation to the people and land of South Vietnam. And now the military wanted more men, more lives.

In late February 1968, after granting only a fractional increase in American forces, the president flew to Fort Bragg, North Carolina, to say good-bye to the 82nd Airborn Division who were leaving for Vietnam. The commander in chief met with no excitement, no flair, no bravado. These paratroopers were veterans, and they shared no illusions of glory. Johnson had ordered them back to Vietnam, and they were going. But they knew, and he knew, that many of them would not return. That day and the following ones were to be a turning point for Johnson and for the war. For only a month later the president announced "the promotion" of General Westmoreland to Army Chief of Staff and his *removal* from Saigon. There would be no military victory, no dictated peace.

On March 31, Johnson informed the nation of his decision. He would not send any more troops to Vietnam. He disclosed a partial bombing halt as proof of his desire to end the war. He called upon Hanoi for some gesture of its willingness to negotiate. And finally, he announced he would not seek or accept the Democratic presidential nomination. He would devote what time and energy remained to the search for peace in Vietnam.

Preisdent Johnson's "abdication" did not reflect a basic change in his Vietnam policy. Three years later, in his memoir, he said he had inherited presidential commitments in Indochina and that holding South Vietnam was the key to holding Southeast Asia because the "domino theory" was sound; that Vietnam was not a civil war but a case of naked aggression on the part of the Communists; that he was following a "middle way" in Vietnam between doves and hawks, a middle way that represented a consensus of American public opinion; and that he was always willing to negotiate and that Hanoi was absolutely unyielding.[42] The doves disputed every one of these arguments, save perhaps the first.[43]

Polls showed that a majority of people were against the way the war

[42]Lyndon B. Johnson, *The Vantage Point: Perspectives of the Presidency, 1963–69* (Holt, Rinehart & Winston, 1971), pp. 43, 120, 156, 250, 420.

[43]See, R. J. Barnet, *Roots of War* (Penguin Books, 1972); J. C. Donovan, *The Cold Warriors* (D. C. Heath, 1974); J. W. Fulbright, *The Crippled Giant* (Vintage, 1972); the Senator Gravel Edition of *The Pentagon Papers*, Vol. 5, N. Chomsky and H. Zinn, eds., (Beacon Press, 1972); and D. Halberstam, *The Best and the Brightest.*

was being handled. To be sure, that majority was made up of some who wanted escalation as well as many who wanted disengagement. This in part demonstrates the loneliness of the president and shows that Johnson was indeed somewhere in the middle. But the "dump-Johnson" movement within the president's own party was attracting considerable support as people looked to the 1968 election. The emotion of antiwar demonstrations, the beginning of the day-long folk music protest festivals, the appeal of the urbane and witty Eugene McCarthy, and the dramatic entry of Senator Robert Kennedy into the election race—all these and more encouraged a war-weary Johnson to step aside, himself now a casualty of the war he had inherited. Johnson had once had a consensus, all right, but a very frail one indeed.

DENOUEMENT

Prior to his unexpected announcement to retire from public office, President Johnson had expressed his belief that the South Vietnamese should shoulder more of the fighting, a doctrine that later emerged as the core of President Nixon's "Vietnamization" program, in which the war was gradually turned over to the Vietnamese while American forces were brought home. Peace talks finally began in Paris after lengthy disagreement over the shape of the negotiating table, but diplomacy could not yet take over from war.

Following the Cambodian incursion in May 1970, Congress sought to limit the president's war-making power, a power granted the legislative branch by the Constitution. The unpopularity of the wartime draft also led the House and Senate to end the draft system and adopt the "volunteer army" plan. Still, domestic opposition to the war continued to mount as did dissatisfaction with the pace of Vietnamization.

Thousands of Vietnam veterans returned home in the early 1970s embittered by the war and disillusioned with their government. Some were addicted to heroin; many could not find jobs. The debate over Vietnam was stirred again in the summer of 1971 when the top-secret Pentagon papers were reprinted in part by the national press. The government, alarmed by the publication of highly classified information, sought to prohibit further disclosures. But the Supreme Court ruled in a landmark decision that the freedom of the press, guaranteed by the First Amendment, transcended the needs of government secrecy. And despite fears that the national security was irretrievably endangered, the republic survived. The nation was exhausted, divided, and tired. "No more Vietnams" was now the watchword.

The war, however, was still far from over. The incursion of Cambodia in May 1970, extensive secret bombing raids in Cambodia from 1969 on, the invasion of Southern Laos in February 1971, the permanent use of South Vietnamese armies for full-scale fighting in Cambodia and Thais for the war in Laos, and finally, the bombing of Hanoi and mining of Haiphong all illustrated that the Kennedy-Johnson War had also become the Nixon War. Reports indicated, moreover, that more than 3 million tons of bombs had been dropped by the U.S. on Indochina in Nixon's first term.

Gradually, however, Nixon did withdraw the troops until by election 1972 he could claim that he had "brought the boys home." The United States still provides enormous air and weapon supplies to the Saigon government, and even as late as 1974 the U.S. was giving more than $3 billion in economic aid to the Thieu regime. Thieu was reelected in a one-man election in October 1971, adding one more blow to the premise that American involvement had been designed to bring about a more democratic and free South Vietnam.

Fifty thousand Americans dead, 300,000 Americans wounded, and estimates of 200 billion American dollars spent. Generations would debate the lessons of Vietnam. At the very least, Vietnam rekindled concern over the president's power as chief foreign and national security policy-maker for a democracy. What happened in Vietnam? "The overriding evidence in the Pentagon papers quite apart from the timing of decisions or the candor with which they were disclosed, is that the United States Government involved itself deeply and consciously in a war that its leaders felt they probably could not win but that they also felt they could not afford to lose."[44]

Halberstam argues that Johnson and his advisers wanted to be defined as strong and tough. They had been swept forward, he contends, by their anti-Communist beliefs and by an unusual sense of power and glory, and the omnipotence and omniscience of an American century: "They knew the right path and they knew how much could be revealed, step by step along the way. They had manipulated the public, the Congress and the press from the start, told half truths about why we were going in, how deeply we were going in, how much we were spending, and how long we were in for. When their predictions turned out to be hopelessly inaccurate, and when the public and the Congress, annoyed at being manipulated, soured on the war, then the architects had been aggrieved . . . [and they turned upon the media]. . . . The faults, it seemed, were not theirs. . . ."[45] This was, of course, only one view, but it is a popular view and leads to the conclusion that what is needed is a more open presidency that is less isolated, less surrounded by like-minded advisers, less "imperial."

Meanwhile, as the debates continued over how we became involved, the nation gladly accepted Henry Kissinger's phased pull-out. Kissinger was rewarded with a Nobel Prize. Nixon was able to defuse the issue, even if an attentive citizenry noted that the war was still going on and was using up American money and equipment at rates much higher than most Americans wished to be reminded. But people *wanted* to be-

[44]Max Frankel, "The Lessons of Vietnam," in Neil Sheehan, et al., *Pentagon Papers*, p. 651. See also J. C. Thomson, Jr., "How Could Vietnam Happen?" in R. Manning and M. Janeway, eds., *Who Are We?* (Little, Brown, 1969), pp. 196–211.

[45]David Halberstam, *Best and Brightest*, pp. 655–56.

lieve the war was over. World opinion also seemed to breathe a sigh of relief that we were out, and we did not apparently suffer in other foreign developments. Indeed the deescalation of the war in Vietnam clearly opened up the possibility for improved relations with China and Russia.

The legacy of Vietnam for the United States was disappointment, cynicism, and a new though still hard-to-define type of isolationism. The legacy for the presidency was an increase in secrecy and a credibility gap that knew no partisan lines. As noted in earlier chapters, the Congress moved to regain some measure of control over war-making and foreign policy, but to date these efforts seem eclipsed by presidential actions in the Middle East, in international monetary and trade affairs, and in summitry negotiations in arms control. Thus the lessons of Vietnam are many, yet they are in part inconclusive and in part still unfolding. The fall of the Thieu government in the Spring of 1975 signalled the end of our involvement in Vietnam.

Can we have a democratic foreign policy?

A great paradox exists in conducting the foreign relations of a modern democracy. In the last century Tocqueville wrote that foreign relations "demand scarcely any of the qualities which are peculiar to a democracy; they require, on the contrary, the perfect use of all those in which it is deficient."[46] Morgenthau has observed more directly that policy-makers in our democracy "either . . . must sacrifice what they consider good policy upon the altar of public opinion, or they must by devious means gain support for policies whose true nature is concealed from the public."[47] Not a few voices have charged our leaders with misleading the people, the experts with misleading our leaders, and ideologies with blinding all of us, especially in Indochina.

Where shall we draw the line? How *do* our policy-makers reconcile public rights with political realities?

In Vietnam our apparent policy was to stop Communist expansion. Our policy-makers guessed wrong in thinking gradual military pressure would deter the North. They miscalculated the character of the war as well as the commitment of those who opposed the Saigon governments. Finally they tried to get out with some face-saving gestures. And because they recognized mistakes or believed that the American people and Congress might not support them in what they thought necessary, they sought to conceal difficulties.

Perhaps our biggest disappointment—as a system of government—was that our institutions did not make up for these failings or at least

[46]Alexis de Tocqueville, *Democracy in America* (Knopf, 1945), I, 224–35.

[47]Hans Morgenthau, "The Conduct of American Foreign Policy," *Parliamentary Affairs* (Winter 1949), p. 147.

did not warn us of them sooner. Students of government must of necessity ask themselves and search for the answer to the central, lingering question: How can we fashion our institutions and processes so as to prevent these human failings from exacting such a large toll again?

If one believes that the American people were kept in the dark, then one ignores the fact that no group of citizens has ever had access to more information about a war than we had about Vietnam. We did not have all the information, but, because of a free press and independent judiciary, more was shown, written, and said about Vietnam than in any other war from the Revolution to Korea. "We knew what we were doing when we went into Vietnam."[48]

American democracy has vested primary responsibility for the making of foreign policy in its chief executive. A president can usually act swiftly and decisively. He is in a good position to see the nation's long-run interests above the tugging of bureaucratic and special interests. He must face the people in elections—but not so often that he must follow public opinion instead of leading it. Yet the desired presidential accountability between elections can only be achieved if the people are willing to inform themselves and insistently demand answers, explanations, and honest reporting from their leaders.

War, said Clausewitz, is merely the extension of diplomacy by other means, still "a part of political commerce."[49] Perhaps future generations will be able to eliminate this alternative entirely, but in our own time our leaders must deal with realities, not dreams, with the world as they see it, not as they wish it. Greater restraints upon decision-makers might undermine our security, and fewer restraints might endanger our freedom. In the end, if the Vietnam War has had any value, it is to make us aware of the limits of our power as a world policeman, to demythologize the notion of an omniscient presidency, and to question the balance of power both among our institutions and between nonelected advisers and our elected representatives.

[48]See an essay so titled by Henry Fairlie in the *Washington Monthly* (May 1973), pp. 7–26.

[49]Karl von Clausewitz, *On War* (Penguin Books, 1968), p. 119.

Chapter 23 Government as regulator

It is impossible to draw a sharp line between the activities of the national government in waging war and peace on the one hand and its economic and domestic functions on the other. They are inextricably intertwined. The foreign policies administered by the State Department have a direct impact on American businessmen and farmers. Fighting a war makes major demands on the nation's economy. Our foreign economic policies directly affect employment, wages, prices, and taxes at home. We discuss domestic and economic activities separately from foreign affairs only for purposes of convenience.

Americans have always been quick to criticize their country's foreign policy, but no one seriously questions that foreign policy must be made by the national government. Even the most reactionary critic of bureaucratic inefficiency has never urged that foreign affairs be turned over to business leaders, for example, or that the job of defending the country against attack be turned over to state governments. But on domestic questions, people differ not only over *what* policies should be adopted, but also over *whether* government should act at all and, if so, *which* government. And if they agree that government should act, the dispute shifts to: How far should government go? What kinds of control or procedure should it use?

This chapter and the next two will describe some of the functions of our national government and will provide illustrations of the major techniques of governmental action. Our concern is not so much what particular governmental bureaus do or the precise description of a particular agency's organization; it is to describe and assess the general forms of the national government's activities and to indicate persistent problems.

In this chapter we shall explore the national government's regulatory role—regulatory in the narrow sense of trying to limit the activities of some of its citizens, to prevent unfair practices, to restrict one interest from interfering with the rights of others (as defined, of course, by the people in power). This is government in a somewhat negative or restrictive sense. In the next chapter we shall turn to some of the promotional functions of government. But it is really impossible to make a sharp distinction between regulation and promotion. *Regulation* means setting restraints on individuals and groups, directly compelling them to take, or not to take, certain actions. *Promotion* means encouraging, strengthening, safeguarding, or advancing the interests of particular persons, groups, industries, or sectors of the economy. But to regulate one interest may be to promote another. Similarly, promotion can be used to regulate interests. Often either one, or a combination, can be used to carry out a public policy.

The main regulatory task of the national government is the policing of powerful interests such as business and labor. But, of course, government is not the only regulating agency. Regulatory control is also exercised by families, friends, churches, and the overall social environment. Governmental regulatory agencies, especially those presumed to be "watchdogs" for consumers, have in recent years come under harsh criticism. Critics call them "lap dogs" for the industries they are supposed to regulate. Even Federal Trade Commission Chairman Lewis A. Engman warns that our protected industries are a major cause of inflation. In an October 1974 appeal for reform Engman said, "Our airlines, our truckers, our railroads, our electronic media, and countless others are on the dole. . . . We get irate about welfare fraud. But our complex system of hidden regulatory subsidies makes welfare fraud look like petty larceny." Both Ralph Nader and President Ford have suggested that some regulatory agencies' outmoded rules and regulations cost the consumer millions of dollars in increased prices. In short, the role of government as regulator is nearly always controversial.

Regulating business

Business leaders today operate in a complex web of national, state, and local laws. This was not always so. Business has never been altogether free of restrictive legislation, of course, but during much of the latter part of the nineteenth century our national policy was to leave business pretty much alone. Most of the nation's leaders believed broadly in laissez faire—"hands off." With considerable freedom, businessmen set about developing (as well as exploiting) a nation that was enormously rich in natural resources. The heroes of the 1870s and 1880s were not politicians but the business magnates—the Rockefellers, Morgans, Carnegies, and Fricks. "From rags to riches" became the nation's motto.

Yet many businessmen in the late nineteenth century were not just given their freedom, they often were given prime sections of land to subsidize expansion of rail systems, tariffs to protect infant industries, and implicit if not explicit police assistance to prevent rapid unionization. In effect, government was helping to *promote* many of these businesses. These subsidies encouraged arbitrary behavior and opened the door to government regulation. If government was involved as a promoter, it also had the responsibility of stepping in to curb abuses.

Toward the end of the last century, a reaction set in. Sharp depressions rocked the nation's economy and threw people out of work. Millions labored long hours in factory and field for meager wages. Muckrakers revealed that some of the most famous business leaders had indulged in shoddy practices and corrupt deals, taking a "public-be-damned" attitude. A demand for government regulation of business sprang up, and a series of national and state laws were passed attempting to correct flagrant abuses. Such laws, however, followed no methodical plan or philosophy; rather they were adopted on the pragmatic assumption that each problem could be handled as it arose.

ANTITRUST POLICY

Americans have had mixed feelings about big business. On one hand, we have sometimes been impressed by bigness—the tallest skyscraper, the largest football stadiums, the biggest corporation—and the efficiency and power that seemed to go with it. On the other hand, today we are somewhat more skeptical about the benefits and side effects of giant enterprises. Moreover, we often believe that our economic system functions best under conditions of fair competition among small—or reasonably small—businesses. This dichotomy has long been reflected in our attempts to prevent monopoly and restraint of trade.

The popular clamor for government control late in the nineteenth century culminated in attacks on monopoly. Trustbusters argued that small business was being squeezed out by huge trusts in oil, sugar, whiskey, steel, and other commodities. In 1890 Congress responded to this sentiment by passing the Sherman Antitrust Act. Designed to foster competition and stop the growth of private monopolies, the act made clear its intention "to protect trade and commerce against unlawful restraints and monopolies." Henceforth, persons making contracts, combinations, or conspiracies in restraint of trade in interstate and foreign commerce could be sued for damages, required to stop their illegal practices, and subjected to criminal penalties.

The Sherman Antitrust Act had little immediate impact. Presidents made little attempt to enforce it, and the Supreme Court's early construction of it limited its scope.[1]

During the Wilson Administration Congress added the Clayton Act to the antitrust arsenal. This act outlawed specific abuses such as the charging of different prices to different buyers in order to destroy a weaker competitor, granting rebates, making false statements about competitors and their products, buying up supplies to stifle competition, bribing competitor's employees, and so on. In addition, interlocking directorates in large corporations were banned and corporations were prohibited from acquiring stock (amended in 1950 to include assets) in competing concerns if such acquisitions substantially lessened interstate competition. At the same time Congress established a five-person Federal Trade Commission (FTC) to enforce the Clayton Act and to prevent unfair competitive practices. The FTC was to be a traffic cop for competition.

"It so happens, Gregory, that your Grandfather Sloan was detained by an agency of our government over an honest misunderstanding concerning certain anti-trust matters! He was not 'busted by the Feds'!"

Drawing by W. Miller;
© 1971 The New Yorker Magazine, Inc.

But antitrust activity continued to languish during the 1920s. Times were prosperous: Republican administrations were actively pro-business. The FTC consisted of men who opposed government regulation of business. The Department of Justice, charged with enforcing the Sherman Act, paid little attention to it.

Then came the Depression. Popular resentment mounted against big business as abuses were revealed. At first the Roosevelt Administration tried to fight the Depression by setting aside the antitrust laws, but by the late 1930s the modern period of trustbusting began in earnest. Since then the Supreme Court has shown a more sympathetic attitude toward the purposes of the Sherman Act and the FTC has acted with more vigor. The "beefed-up" Antitrust Division of the Department of Justice has won some notable victories.

But how effective has all this activity been? Have antitrust suits and FTC proceedings and the fear of them kept our system more competitive than otherwise might have been the case? It is difficult to give a precise answer, even to find out what is happening to the economic marketplace. But there is no argument that one third of the nation's manufacturing capacity is controlled by fifty companies and well over two-thirds of all manufacturing assets are owned by only five hundred corporations.

Monopolies—where one firm dominates an industry—have virtually disappeared from the economic arena (except for governmentally regulated *natural* monopolies like the telephone company). In place of the monopolies of old, two new threats have emerged: the *oligopoly*—where a *few* firms jointly dominate a market, like the automobile industry; and the *conglomerate*— a firm that owns businesses in many unrelated industries, like ITT. Present antitrust tools have been seriously put to the test by these relatively recent developments. Federal prosecutors have generally believed that the Sherman Act and the Clayton Act could be

[1] *United States v. E. C. Knight Co.* (1895).

applied only to the traditional single-firm monopoly. But, in recent years, the FTC and the Department of Justice have begun to expand the interpretation of existing legislation to attack oligopolies; they have moved against the major breakfast cereal producers and large oil companies, for example. Some critics view these actions as merely political "potshots" attacking once again the "economic royalists" because it is good politics. Other critics view these actions as cosmetic. They believe that if the goal is to break up large concentrations of economic power it can be accomplished only if Congress enacts new legislation.

What should the government do about big business? Few policymakers agree on the answer to this question. Some say that we are doing too much. And even those who think we are doing too little do not agree on the correct solutions. Economist Neil Jacoby, for example, sees no need for new initiatives. He feels that the damage done by big business is vastly overestimated, that even the extent of concentration is exaggerated. He rejects the view that the United States has become a corporate state as pure myth. He sees the increasing size of business as an indication of increased economies of scale. The market is still as competitive as before, only the companies are bigger. According to Jacoby, we, as consumers, benefit from the technology provided by the large modern corporation.[2]

Another view, held by John Kenneth Galbraith, among others, agrees with Jacoby that bigness contributes to efficiency, provides the capital necessary for innovation, and spurs economic growth. But those of this view also recognize the potential abuses that can occur when economic power is concentrated in the hands of a few corporate managers. They think the benefits of size need to be channeled more toward the needs of society. Galbraith suggests three new tasks for government:

1. Provide assistance to the segment of our economy that is still considered to be competitive—for example, the corner grocery store or the independent TV repairperson.

2. Control the direction of big business by restricting the use of resources in areas that are already overdeveloped; by setting limits on the use of technology; and by establishing stringent standards on the byproducts of industry—for example, pollution—*and* enforcing the standards once they set them.

3. Manage the economy directly by implementing wage-price controls in all the industries that are dominated by big business and big unions.[3]

"But this would be socialism!" exclaim many economists and policy-

[2]Neil H. Jacoby, *Corporate Power and Social Responsibility* (Macmillan, 1973), pp. 138, 145, 249.

[3]John Kenneth Galbraith, *Economics and the Public Purpose* (Houghton Mifflin, 1973), pp. 221–22.

makers. "No," says Galbraith. He argues that government already plays a major role in the development of individual firms, and in the distribution of economic rewards between different industries. He writes, "Where the industry is powerful government responds strongly to its needs. And also to its products. It gives the automobile industry roads for its cars, the weapons industry orders for its weapons, other industries support for research and development."[4] In the early 1970s the government even guaranteed a loan for the Lockheed Corporation when it was near bankruptcy. All Galbraith calls for, or so he claims, is the *redirection* of government subsidies. "If these proposals are socialism," he would reply to his critics, "socialism already exists."

Still another group of reformers want to break up large corporations, not just regulate them. These individuals believe that the market can work, all it needs is a chance. They are against bigness, charging that bigness leads to irresponsibility and misconduct. In its study of antitrust policy, Ralph Nader's Center for the Study of Responsive Law concludes that economic power is inevitably translated into political power.[5] They argue, therefore, that all attempts to control large corporations will be almost impossible. (As Watergate has shown, many politicians are very dependent on big business or big labor for campaign contributions.) Only by cutting the giants down to size, says Nader, will government be able to exercise control over their actions.

Senator Philip Hart, Chairman of the Senate Antitrust and Monopoly Committee, agrees with Nader. He has introduced legislation—the Industrial Reorganization Act—that would make the possession of monopoly or *oligopoly* power illegal; it would also establish an Industrial Reorganization Commission to study certain concentrated industries and to prosecute violations of the act; and it would set up an Industrial Reorganization Court to try cases and devise remedies under the act. Probably the most important item in the bill is the establishment of a rebuttable presumption that oligopoly power exists in a market in which any four or fewer corporations account for 50 percent or more of the sales.[6] Corporations, if this were enacted, would have to prove that they were not violating the provisions of the act, instead of the government having to prove they were in violation. Whether or not such a provision could survive a challenge to its constitutionality probably depends on the details of how the law is written and the penalities it imposes.

Are the nation's antitrust laws, drawn up sixty years ago and earlier,

[4] *Ibid.*, p. 294.

[5] Mark Green et al., *The Closed Enterprise System* (Bantam Books, 1972). For similar criticism, see Morton Mintz and Jerry S. Cohen, *America, Inc.* (Dial, 1971); and John M. Blair, *Economic Concentration* (Harcourt Brace Jovanovich, 1972).

[6] Philip A. Hart, "Restructuring the Oligopoly Sector: The Case for a New Industrial Reorganization Act," *Antitrust Law and Economics Review* (Fall 1972), pp. 47–66. See also "The Industrial Reorganization Act," *Columbia Law Review* (March 1973), pp. 635–76.

still applicable to a 1970s economy? This question evokes markedly different responses. At the center of activity in this area is the Justice Department's Antitrust Division. About 320 lawyers spend all their time preparing select government cases in an overall effort to protect the free enterprise system. In one recent four-and-a-half-year period, this division brought nearly 350 civil and criminal cases. Corporate conduct that may be illegal comes to their attention through complaints by a competitor, customer, or supplier.[7]

Veteran observers feel the Antitrust Division does a reasonably fair and adequate job. Yet it is understaffed, and considering its responsibility it must work with an exceedingly small budget. In recent years a rejuvenated Federal Trade Commission also has been active in investigating the structure of concentrated industries. Many of the FTC's important cases, as with the Goodyear Tire and Rubber Company case in 1973, are settled during consent negotiations. *Consent decrees* are orders to cease anticompetitive conduct. With a consent decree there is no punitive government action, and in addition the company is able to avoid the unfavorable publicity that usually attends antitrust litigation. This and related complexities lead many to conclude that well-established corporations can nearly always get around antitrust prohibitions.

Antitrust politics, like most high-energy economic controversies, resembles a tug of war. Major new battles in this arena are inevitable. Leading participants will include private antitrust lawyers, the FTC, the Justice Department, Senate and House Antitrust and Monopoly Subcommittees, the courts, lawyers representing corporate interests, and various public-interest and consumer advocate lawyers who call for procedural reform, more aggressive enforcement, and even federal "chartering" (federal licensing) as an alternative to conventional antitrust policies. Traditionally, producer interests rather than consumer interests dominated and shaped the actions of the government. Thus, strong corporate opposition to the proposed Industrial Reorganization Act, the Nader-backed federal chartering idea, and similar deconcentration measures can be expected. Sustained and imaginative consumer advocacy activity is likely to provide a countervailing force.

PROTECTING THE CONSUMER

Most Americans believe in vigorous but fair and open competition. In a simple economy, competition virtually polices itself; buyers and sellers know one another, and the old principle of *caveat emptor*—"let the buyer beware"—is sufficient. But with large business enterprises, a national marketplace, a strongly organized work force, who will protect the consumer?

[7]See articles by Jonathin Cotlin, "Antitrust Report/Justice Division: Congress Monitors New Developments in Big Business," *National Journal* (February 10, 1973), pp. 177–88; and "Increased Corporation Antitrust Suits Prompt Industry Fears of New Federal Policy," *National Journal* (September 15, 1973), pp. 1367–73.

Among the forty or so federal agencies sharing the responsibility for enforcing more than a dozen consumer protection statutes, the most important are the Consumer Product Safety Commission, the Office of Consumer Affairs in the Department of Health, Education, and Welfare, the Consumer Protection Section of the Antitrust Division of the Department of Justice, the Food and Drug Administration in HEW, the Federal Communications Commission and especially the Federal Trade Commission. These agencies are likely to be joined soon by a Consumer Protection Agency.

Originally the FTC had as its major focus the protection of businessmen against the unfair practices of their competitors. The consumer was expected to benefit from this enforced competition, but that was more or less an incidental consequence. During the past several years, however, the FTC has been given additional authority, and even more significantly has started to construe its existing authority in order to protect consumers from fraud, shoddy and dangerous goods, misleading warranties, and deceptive advertising practices.[8] Here are some examples of FTC actions:

1. *Dangerous practices.*The FTC regulates the interstate marketing of apparel in order to prevent the use of highly flammable materials. The commission has also tried, with some success, to protect consumers from the hazards of cigarette smoking. This has been a hard battle. The tobacco industry is important in the economy of many states and has considerable clout in Congress. In 1963, when the FTC ordered tobacco companies to place a rather severe health warning on cigarette packages and in advertisements, Congress intervened and substituted an innocuous and inconspicuous warning.[9] Three years later, the FTC reported to Congress that this warning had had no impact on consumption. Finally, in 1970 Congress made it unlawful to advertise cigarettes on radio and television, strengthened the language of the required warning on cigarette packages, and specifically authorized the FTC to issue health-related regulations for the cigarette industry and its advertising.

2. *Unfair or deceptive practices.* It is against the law for a business person who sells in interstate commerce to misrepresent products. But the marketplace is vast, there are thousands of products, and the FTC has a relatively small staff. Until recently it tried to police the marketplace by proceeding complaint by complaint. For example, after a rather elaborate hearing it enjoined a television commercial that allegedly showed sandpaper being shaved to demonstrate the "supermoisturizing power" of a shaving cream. The demonstration had utilized not sandpaper but sand applied to plexiglass, which of course made the job easier.

In 1971, prompted by Ralph Nader and other consumer advocates, the FTC changed its procedures. It now requires all major industries to file

[8]See Mark Nadel, *The Politics of Consumer Protection* (Bobbs-Merrill, 1971).

[9]See A. Lee Fritschler, *Smoking and Politics* (Appleton-Century-Crofts, 1969).

data with the commission to substantiate their advertising claims for safety, performance, efficacy, quality, and comparative prices. The information is available to the public. If it does not substantiate the claims made in advertisements, the firm is subject to commission charges of false advertising.

This "ad substantiation" program was also supplemented by a "corrective advertising" program. The average American child watches over 5,000 commercials a year, many of which are false, misleading or both—such as Wonder Bread's promise to "build strong bodies 12 ways." Although it is still too early to evaluate the FTC's campaign to clean up false advertising, most observers agree that the problem is both considerable and legally very tricky.[10]

3. *Truth in packaging.* The FTC shares with the Department of Health, Education, and Welfare responsibility for the enforcement of the 1966 act that requires those who sell in the interstate market to adopt standards that will not mislead the consumer as to the amount or price of a product he or she is purchasing.

4. *Truth in lending.* The FTC shares with the Board of Governors of the Federal Reserve System the responsibility for enforcing the 1968 act designed to protect consumers from misleading advertisements about the rate of interest they will pay when they purchase homes or other products on credit or when they borrow from banks or other lending institutions. Thus, the Supreme Court, in upholding the 1968 Truth in Lending Act, has ruled against deceptive magazine subscription sales practices (*Mourning v. Family Publications Services, Inc.*, 1973).

5. *Discriminatory advertisement of housing.* The 1968 Open Housing Act empowers the FTC to prevent advertisers from offering rentals or houses for sale on a racially discriminatory basis. Prior to receiving this authority, the FTC had taken an even more vigorous step; it used its general powers to prevent false and deceptive advertising by interstate advertisers who purport to have rentals available to all persons but who refuse to rent to blacks.

How effective has the FTC been in protecting the consumer? The American Bar Association, President Johnson's National Commission on Product Safety, President Nixon's Advisory Council on Executive Organization, the Urban Coalition, and Ralph Nader appeared to agree that at least until recently it has not been as effective as it should be. They also agreed that the fault is not exclusively that of the commission. In 1969 the FTC opened only 192 new investigations of deceptive consumer practices, although it received 12,000 complaints; more de-

[10]"Corrective Advertising and the FTC: No, Virginia, Wonder Bread Doesn't Help Build Strong Bodies Twelve Ways," *Michigan Law Review*, Vol. 70 (1971); "Corrective Advertising: The New Response to Consumer Deception," *Columbia Law Review*, Vol. 72 (1972); and James Rowen, "How to Keep Them Buying Even Though They Know You're Lying," *Washington Monthly* (April 1973), pp. 55–60.

tailed and stringent laws are needed, as well as more vigorous consumer advocacy. Almost all those who have looked into the matter seem to agree that the FTC should be given authority to seek preliminary injunctions in federal courts against what it deems to be an unfair or deceptive business practice, that its jurisdiction should be expanded to include those activities "affecting" interstate commerce as well as activities "in" interstate commerce, and that it should be specifically authorized to protect consumers against deceptive guarantees and warranties.

The FTC serves both as an impartial hearing agency to determine if a business is engaging in an unfair practice and as a prosecutor in behalf of the consumer. It tends to give more emphasis to the former responsibility. Thus many urge the creation of some federal agency that would provide adequate representation and legal talent for consumer interests on all pending federal legislation and to initiate proposals of its own. A department of consumer affairs is one suggestion. More probable is a consumer protection agency designed to offset the weighty lobbying resources of special interests, to redress the imbalance of representation and to make sure that the views of consumers are considered before a federal agency or court decides to act or not act on important health, safety, or economic matters. This new agency would have no explicit regulatory authority, but would help ensure that consumer interests are spelled out in federal proceedings where the buying public has a stake. Conservatives and certain business interests vigorously opposed this legislation, but such an agency is likely to be created eventually.

The Consumer Product Safety Commission, potentially a very powerful and independent body, was set up in late 1972. This commission is authorized to issue and enforce product-safety rules governing performance, composition, design, finish, and packaging of a consumer product. It also can fix requirements for marketing and warning labels. An injury-information clearinghouse is maintained by the commission to provide nationwide accident statistics about hazardous products. Recently this activist, five-person commission widely publicized its findings and issued warnings about certain defects in some bicycles, a prominent cause of several hundred thousand injuries annually.

Consumerism is a growing political force. Historically, consumers had to depend for the protection of their interests upon competition among contending producer groups. But even conservative economists now emphasize how consumers have suffered: "competition among producers in the political arena proved to be an unreliable protection of consumer interests. Producer groups found that collaboration brought them more benefits from government than did competition. If one group supported other groups in exchange for their support of its interests, a compliant Congress would bow to the combined pressure of the coalition. Congressional solicitude for producers' demands has cost the American consumer dearly in high prices and high taxes."[11] Thus countermeasures have been adopted and more seem likely.

[11]Jacoby, *Corporate Power and Social Responsibility*, p. 159.

PROTECTING THE ENVIRONMENT

We know now that our natural resources are limited, that industrial and agricultural production cannot be allowed to proceed unhindered by a federal ecology policy, that smog, noise, oil-clogged beaches, chemical wastes, and random timber and strip-mining activity not only offend our senses but also threaten our health and lives. Political battles, however, are less about *whether* the national government should do something, than *what* it should do, to *whom*, and at *what* price.

Cleaning up the environment often comes into direct conflict with other important social goals. In recent years, many policy-makers have been forced to choose between clean air and jobs for their constituents. Put yourself in their place. What would you do if you were a legislator faced with the following situation? Your district has an unemployment rate above 10 percent; industry is desperately needed to provide jobs. A company applies for a permit to build a new factory in your district. If it is allowed to build, many jobs will be created. But, there is one problem: the plant the company intends to build will worsen an already serious pollution problem. To make things even tougher, there are no pollution control devices for this particular type of industry, and there are no other "clean" industries that can be attracted to the district in place of this polluting one. Which problem do you give priority to: employment or pollution?

In early periods it was thought that environmental concern should be a state or local function. But it is now widely recognized that the politics of enviromental protection involves a struggle to control the exercise of public power in the United States. "Ecologists know that their movement's energy will dissipate into a futile spasm of arrested reform unless the firm, continuing weight of federal authority is brought to bear."[12] Thus we now have a rather elaborate set of federal regulations and agencies concerned with the ecosystem. The national government's approach is both promotional and regulatory. Funds are available to stimulate research as well as to assist states and localities in building

[12]Walter A. Rosenbaum, *The Politics of Environmental Concern* (Praeger, 1973) p. 4.

Results of an unclean environment: birds coated with oil off the coast of Santa Barbara, California, and New York City covered with a heavy blanket of smog.

waste treatment plants and in taking other preventive actions; federal regulations also establish minimum standards.

However, once an environmental problem is identified, correcting it is more complicated than merely calling upon the experts to design a solution and then persuading the federal government to implement it. In many cases, today's problems are the result of yesterday's experts' recommendations. Thus, the interstate highway system—one of the largest public works projects in the world's history—is the grand culmination of federal promotion of the automobile. It brought many benefits in the form of jobs and the easy movement of people and goods. It has also brought or contributed to many problems—air and noise pollution and population concentration. In the judgment of some of today's experts, it has also caused land misuse, community disruption, and by diverting the movement of many goods from railroads to the highways, perhaps the energy crisis. Today, in response, we promote auto safety, subsidize urban mass transit, mandate pollution control devices, sometimes ration fuel, and fund research on electric automobiles—all with the same tax dollars. We hope our actions will not produce greater problems tomorrow than those we are trying to solve today.

The primary federal agencies concerned with the environment are the Council on Environmental Quality, in the Executive Office of the President, that develops and recommends policies to Congress and the president; and the Environmental Protection Agency, which is responsible for enforcement of federal laws and regulations. EPA enforces much of the National Environmental Policy Act of 1969 and its controversial requirement of environmental impact statements for federal projects.

Federal regulations to protect the environment are becoming progressively more stringent; they now cover more kinds of activity and secure wider public support. Hardly anyone or any group openly and directly opposes the idea of federal action to protect the environment. No one comes out in favor of pollution. But questions of costs, priorities, and choices are very much part of the political scene.

One of the more important federal environmental protection laws of recent years is the Air Pollution Act of 1970. The act sets air quality standards to promote health and authorizes federal funds for research and grants to states and localities. Its most controversial provision sets a 1975 deadline for automobiles sold in the United States to emit 90 percent less carbon monoxide, hydrocarbons, and nitrogen oxides than did 1970 model cars. The law permits manufacturers to petition for delay; and in view of the substantial technical difficulties in meeting the standards set by the law, and the political power of both the automobile manufacturers and the United Auto Workers, the postponement of the effective date of 1975 did not surprise many people.

Another example of federal regulation is the Water Quality Improvement Act of 1970, which imposes liability for cleanup costs for oil spills on those responsible for them, and supplements other federal acts by stimulating investment by states and localities in water control and sewage treatment programs.

The politics of environmental protection furnishes an excellent example of the difference between securing the passage of a law and changing human behavior. It takes some political muscle to get Congress to pass a law; but without a sustained political force to monitor the implementation of that law, there could well be merely a "symbolic payoff," while the air continues to be polluted and the environment irreversibly damaged.

ENERGY REGULATION

Until the 1960s, business and government generally assumed that America's natural resources were virtually unlimited. Then, a few scientists began to examine these resources in light of our exponential rate of growth. Their conclusion: Unless we moderate the speed at which we consume resources like oil, minerals, and even water, we will soon be facing a crisis of tremendous proportions. Most business leaders and some scientists scoffed at these doomsday predictors. But by 1972, respected government officials, scientists, and even businessmen, began to fear a major energy shortage.

Their fears were realized. Beginning in the winter of 1972–73, several parts of the country experienced shortages in oil and gas. In the early part of January 1973, fuel oil and propane shortages forced Denver to close down 121 schools. Factories and plants in many cities also closed. In the summer things got worse. Nearly 20,000, or about 10 percent, of the nation's service stations went out of business between June 30, 1973 and June 30, 1974 because they could not get enough gas. Stations that remained open raised their prices markedly. Many states and counties adopted different kinds of rationing so that the available gas could be distributed equitably. Speed limits were reduced to conserve energy. In one way or another, all Americans were affected.

"Who was navigating, anyhow?"

Copyright 1973 Herblock in *The Washington Post.*

What caused the crisis? A number of answers have been suggested. First, many attribute the shortage to the mass-consumption lifestyle of the Western world. Big cars, home appliances, neon signs—all these require large amounts of energy as do air conditioning and central heating. And, as the population has increased and the standard of living improved, people are demanding more things that use up energy. The people in the United States make a special claim on these scarce resources: we represent less than 6 percent of the world's population, but we consume over 32 percent of the energy it produces.

A second reason why the crisis became acute in the winter of 1973 was that the Middle Eastern oil countries used their control over oil as a foreign policy weapon. The United States had been importing approximately 20 percent of its oil from the Arab nations. Western Europe and Japan are even more dependent on these sources. The Arab nations' decision to stop temporarily supplying oil to those countries and permanently to increase its price causes extreme hardship, especially in Europe. The United States has been forced to find alternate supplies, or—as more often the case—make do with less oil. Finally, people like

Ralph Nader and Senator Henry Jackson, accused the major oil producers of deliberately creating the crisis. They felt that the companies intended to use the crisis as a justification for asking the government to relax pollution control standards, pass the Alaskan Pipeline bill, and retain the oil-depletion allowance.

Beyond the energy crisis remains the fact that industrial nations and developing nations everywhere are demanding more energy than is available. The creation of the Federal Energy Administration and a multibillion-dollar research program were our initial responses. But what are the alternatives for the longer run? We can *cut down on demand.* Many people have advocated this, but is it realistic for us to expect the rest of the world to give up its desires for a better standard of living? Most of those who demand that the United States and the developing nations reduce their dependence on energy-consuming conveniences are middle class, warm, and comfortable. It is possible to *find alternative sources* of energy, but there has been very little research into this problem. No easy solutions exist because either we do not know what to do or we cannot agree on what to do. Who is going to pay what costs for whose benefit? How much are people really willing to sacrifice? How much are we willing to compromise environmental improvement for increased energy production?

The Energy Supply and Environmental Coordination Act of 1974 typifies a compromise response to the energy crisis. Its chief purpose is to reduce demand for oil and gas and stimulate coal production by requiring certain utilities to convert to coal for their primary fuel. In effect this legislation allows the Federal Energy Administration, with EPA approval, to order coal conversions in certain regions where such conversion would not cause major violation of the Clean Air Act Standards. "Another major provision of the act is the long-anticipated postponement of strict auto emission standards. The 1975 interim standards for carbon monoxide and hydrocarbons will be extended to 1976, with exceptions allowed to 1977. Deadlines for limits on nitrogen oxides are being pushed back from 1976 to 1978."[13]

Labor-management relations

Governmental regulation of business has been essentially restrictive. Most of the laws and rules have curbed certain business practices and steered the dynamic force of private enterprise into socially useful channels. But regulation cuts two ways. In the case of American workers, most laws in recent decades have tended not to restrict but to confer rights and opportunities. Actually, many labor laws do not touch labor directly; instead, they regulate its relations with employers.

[13]Constance Holden, "Clean Air: Congress Settles for a Restrained Coal Conversion Plan," *Science* (June 21, 1974), p. 1270.

LABOR AND THE GOVERNMENT

Labor leaders generally favor federal regulation. They fear that business might impose far stricter regulations on labor if governmental regulations did not exist. Moreover, the federal government in recent years has become a major ally in the campaign to improve job safety and working conditions.

During the first half of this century, governmental protection and promotion were gradually extended over the whole range of labor activity and organization. This was the result of two basic developments: labor's growing political power and the awareness of millions of Americans that a healthy and secure nation depends in large measure on a healthy and secure labor force.

Labor's basic struggle was for the right to organize. For many decades trade unions had been held lawful by acts of state legislatures, but the courts had chipped away at this right by legalizing certain antiunion devices. The most notorious was the *yellow-dog contract*, by which antiunion employers, before they would hire a new worker, made him promise not to join a labor organization. If labor organizers later tried to unionize the worker, the employer, on the basis of yellow-dog contracts, could apply for injunctions from the courts to stop the organizers. Chafing under this restriction, labor in 1932 secured the passage of the Norris–La Guardia Act, which made yellow-dog contracts unenforceable in federal courts. Granting labor the right to organize, the act also drastically limited the issuance of labor injunctions in other respects.

By 1932 unions had won other kinds of protection from the federal government, especially over conditions of labor. Almost a century before, in 1840, the government had established the ten-hour day in its navy yards, and later Congress shortened the working day of government employees to eight hours and required the eight-hour day for railroad employees and for seamen. Nevertheless, progress was slow. Then came the New Deal. Congress began to enact a series of laws to protect workers and their right to form trade unions.

PROTECTING WORKERS

Among the more important areas of federal regulations designed to protect workers are the following:

1. *Public contracts.* The Walsh–Healey Act of 1936, as amended, requires that all contracts with the national government in excess of $10,000 provide that no worker employed under such contracts be paid less than the prevailing wage; that he or she be paid overtime for all work in excess of eight hours per day or forty hours per week; that convict labor and child labor (boys under sixteen and girls under eighteen) not be employed.

Beginning in the 1940s by executive order, and since supplemented by legislation, all contractors and subcontractors of the federal government have been required to take affirmative action to ensure equal job opportunities for minorities and for women. Since unions are not direct parties to contracts with the federal government, contract compliance efforts have been less successful in forcing affirmative action on unions and eliminating union practices that restrict minority employment. However, unions that discriminate are in violation of other federal laws.

2. *Wages and hours.* The Fair Labor Standards Act of 1968 set a maximum work week of forty hours for all employers engaged in interstate commerce or in the production of goods for interstate commerce (with certain exemptions). Work beyond that amount must be paid for at one and one-half times the regular rate. Mimimum wages, first set at 25 cents an hour have been progressively increased, the most recent amendment was in 1974, so that for most nonfarm employees and federal employees it is $2.10 for 1975 and $2.30 for 1976. For most farm workers the rate is $1.80 for 1975 and to increase gradually to $2.30 by 1978. Congress has also extended the coverage of the act so that it now includes more than forty million workers. The most notable extension came in 1966 when, for the first time, Congress overcame the opposition from rural districts and brought under the act certain farm workers, although at a rate less than for nonfarm employees. The 1974 Amendment extended coverage to government employees and to most domestic household workers. The Equal Pay Act of 1963 amended the Fair Labor Standards Act to compel employers to pay equal wages to women and men for doing equal work. It in turn has been extended to cover most jobs.

Federal acts prohibiting child labor and regulating industrial safety and occupational health came too late to protect this boy who was put to work in a West Virginia coal mine in 1908.

3. *Child labor.* The Federal Labor Standards Act prohibits child labor (under sixteen years of age or under eighteen in hazardous occupations) in industries that engage in, or that produce goods for, interstate commerce.

4. *Industrial safety and occupational health.* The Occupational Safety and Health Act of 1970 created the first comprehensive federal industrial safety program. It gives the secretary of labor broad authority to set safety and health standards for workers of companies in interstate commerce, and creates a Safety and Health Review Commission consisting of three members appointed by the president with the consent of the Senate to hear appeals from the secretary's orders. The Nixon Administration and most employer groups had wanted two presidentially appointed boards, one to set standards, the other to enforce them. They argued that it would be unfair to employers to give the secretary of labor authority to make and enforce standards. Labor spokesmen opposed such a move because of the fear that an independent regulatory agency would become captured by the industry it was supposed to regulate. Congress supported labor in giving rule-making authority to the secretary, but labor failed to secure for the secretary authority to close down a plant when he believes an "imminent danger" threatens the lives of workers. He must seek a court order to do so.

The enforcement of occupational safety is currently one of the most important and controversial areas of business-labor-government relations. Worker representatives contend that the federal effort is underfunded and too slow. Business leaders argue that some of the federal requirements border on the impossible, others on the inscrutable. A Ralph Nader study group report concluded that: "The goal of the job health and safety movement should be to put scientific knowledge and modern technology to the human task of eliminating from the workplace all unreasonable and unnecessary hazards to life and limb. This is not going to happen overnight. It will take sustained effort over a considerable period of time and a total mobilization of available resources to counter the encrustations of decades of neglect and the ever-burgeoning perils spawned by modern industry."[14] Meanwhile, it is estimated that 75,000 inspections will be made to enforce the act in 1974 by federal officials and 150,000 more by agencies in thirty states with approved ongoing programs. By 1975, federal inspections are expected to increase to 105,000, and state inspections will increase to 250,000. To be sure, it will take more than research, standard-setting, and inspections to fulfill this landmark legislation. But a beginning has been made.

PROTECTING UNIONS

Do unions need federal laws to protect their right to organize? Much of the record of union efforts before 1933 suggests that organizing the unorganized without federal protection was extremely difficult. Indeed, union membership and strength was waning fast until New Deal measures granted workers the right to organize and bargain collectively, free from the interference and coercion of employers. The National Labor Relations Act of 1935 made these guarantees permanent. In the preamble, this act, usually called the Wagner Act after its sponsor, declared that workers in industries affecting interstate commerce (with certain exemptions) should have the right to organize and bargain collectively and that inequality in bargaining power between employers and workers led to industrial strife and economic instability. The act made five types of action unfair for employers to practice: (1) interfering with workers in their attempt to organize unions or bargain collectively, (2) supporting company unions (unions set up and dominated by the employer); (3) discriminating against membership in unions; (4) firing or otherwise victimizing an employee for having taken action under the act; (5) refusing to bargain with union representatives. The act was intended to prevent open-shop employers from using violence, espionage, propaganda, and community pressure to resist unionization of their plants.

To administer the act, a board of three (now five) members, holding overlapping terms of five years each, was set up. Under the act, the National Labor Relations Board (NLRB), an independent regulatory

[14]Joseph A. Page and Mary-Win O'Brien, *Bitter Wages* (Grossman, 1973), p. 256.

commission, has the ticklish job of determining the appropriate bargaining unit—that is, whether the employees may organize by plant, by craft, or on some other basis. The board operates largely through regional officers, who investigate charges of unfair labor practices and may issue formal complaints, and through trial examiners, who hold hearings and submit reports to the board in Washington.

STRIKING A BALANCE

From the start the Wagner Act was a center of controversy. It strengthened the unions and helped them seize greater economic and political power. In 1936 a committee of eminent attorneys declared it unconstitutional. Taking heart from this opinion, many corporations simply ignored NLRB decisions. Unions, unwilling to wait for the slow-moving procedures of the law, organized violent strikes, including the much-criticized sit-down strikes. In April 1937, during President Roosevelt's campaign to pack the Supreme Court, the Court by a five-to-four vote upheld the constitutionality of the act.[15] The fight then shifted to Congress, where senators and representatives attacked the NLRB through denunciations, investigations, and slashes in its appropriations.

What had caused all this uproar? First, from the outset the board vigorously applied the prolabor provisions of the act. Second, the board got caught in the struggle between AFL and CIO. Whichever way it decided certain representation cases, it was bound to antagonize one labor faction or the other. Third, the purpose of the act was widely misunderstood. Employers and editorial writers solemnly charged the measure and the board with being biased in favor of labor, when the very aim of the act had been to improve the workers' bargaining power.

The controversy was sharpened by criticism of several union practices. These practices were not new, but now that labor was achieving greater power they came in for more public attention. One was *featherbedding.* Faced with labor-saving devices that cut down on the number of workers needed to do a given job, some unions demanded that the original number of workers be paid, even if they had nothing to do and merely stood around. Then there was the charge that unions were in the hands of dictators. Some union leaders stayed in office for years, even decades, and then passed control to other members of their family. To be sure, many union leaders had no more control over their unions than did many business executives over their enterprises, but unions are supposed to be run in a democratic manner. Moreover, protected by the *closed shop*—a contract under which only union members can be hired—some union heads seemed to have as much power to discipline members as had the more ruthless employers of old. And a few unions were rackets, and had connections with the underworld.

Most unions continued to be run honestly and responsively. Never-

[15]*National Labor Relations Board v. Jones & Laughlin Steel Corp.* (1937).

theless, public opinion seemed to swing against labor after World War II. Not only labor excesses but a wave of great industrywide strikes intensified demands in Congress for a law that would equalize the obligations of labor and management. In 1946 the Republicans won majorities in both the House and Senate, paving the way for modification of the Wagner Act.

THE TAFT-HARTLEY ACT

The upshot was the Labor–Management Relations Act of 1947, commonly called the Taft–Hartley Act after its sponsors. This act, which applies with certain exceptions to industries affecting interstate commerce:

1. Outlaws the closed shop and permits the *union shop* (under which newly employed workers must join the union within a stated time period) only under certain conditions.
2. Outlaws jurisdictional strikes (strikes arising from disputes between unions over which has the right to do a job), secondary boycotts, political expenditures by unions in connection with federal elections, excessive union dues or fees, and strikes by federal employees.
3. Makes it an unfair labor practice for unions to refuse to bargain with employers.
4. Permits employers and unions to sue each other in federal courts for violation of contracts.
5. Allows the use of the labor injunction on a limited scale.

Organized labor greeted the new measure as a "slave-labor" act and vowed that it would use its political power to wipe the act from the statute books. Senator Taft saw the bill as "an extraordinary reversal along the right lines toward equalizing the power of labor unions and employers." Since 1947, organized labor has kept up its drive to repeal the Taft–Hartley Act, especially the section that permits states to outlaw union shops. Union leaders contend that these laws undermine their organizing efforts, especially in the South, where most of the states have taken advantage of it to pass so-called right-to-work laws.

THE LABOR REFORM ACT OF 1959

During the late 1950s a Senate rackets committee investigating labor activities found in some unions glaring cases of corruption, dictatorial control by a few bosses, loose financial practices, and other deplorable conditions. Heavily publicized, the committee's disclosures aroused popular demand for reform. At the same time, business and other interests, with the backing of the Eisenhower Administration, wanted new restrictions on labor's use of the boycott and picketing. Union leaders opposed reform on the grounds that it would harass good unions and have no effect on the bad ones. After two years of deadlock over the issue, Congress passed the Labor Reform Act of 1959 (often called the Landrum–Griffin Act), which, among other things:

1. Requires labor organizations to file comprehensive reports with the secretary of labor on all financial transactions and on the workings of their constitutions and bylaws.

2. Under a bill-of-rights section, grants union members the unqualified right to vote in union elections by secret ballot, to speak up freely in union meetings, to get open hearings in discipline cases, and to sue in federal courts if they feel that they are not getting fair play under union rules.

3. Requires secret elections at least every three years for local union officers and at least every five years for national union officers.

4. Outlaws organizational picketing if the employer has validly recognized another union or if there has been an NLRB election within the preceding year.

KEEPING LABOR-MANAGEMENT PEACE

The Federal Mediation and Conciliation Service, with mediators located in seven regional offices, stands ready to help settle labor-management disputes in any industry affecting interstate commerce (except railroads and airlines, which are covered by the Railway Labor Act), either on request of one of the parties to the dispute or whenever the dispute threatens to cause a substantial interruption of interstate commerce. Through tact and persuasion, the troubleshooters of the Federal Mediation and Conciliation Service induce unions to call off strikes and persuade employers to make concessions. The service noted that in July of 1974 there were more strikes, 588, involving more workers, 230,000, than at any time since the organization started keeping records in 1959.

The Taft–Hartley Act also set up machinery for handling disputes affecting an entire industry or a major part of it, where a stoppage would threaten national health or safety. When such a strike breaks out, the following steps are authorized:

1. The president appoints a special board to investigate and report the facts.

2. The president may then instruct the attorney general to seek in a federal court an eighty-day injunction against the strike.

3. The court grants this injunction if it agrees that the national health or safety is endangered.

4. If the parties have not settled the strike within the eighty days, the board informs the president of the employer's last offer of settlement.

5. The NLRB takes a secret vote among the employees to see if they will accept the employer's last offer.

6. If no settlement is reached, the injunction expires, and the president reports to Congress with such recommendations as he may wish to make.

How successful has the Taft–Hartley Act been in helping maintain labor peace? It has been invoked several times – sometimes successfully, sometimes not – against strikes in vital sectors of the economy such as atomic energy, coal, shipping, steel, and telephone service. Often the president and the secretary of labor attempt to mediate strikes without resorting to the act. Its effectiveness is difficult to assess because legislation is only one of the many factors that affect industrial peace.

Still, the basic issue remains unresolved – strikes are part of the price we pay for the system of collective bargaining. But under what conditions does the price become so high that the federal government should intervene, stop the strike, and force a settlement either by setting the terms or insisting on compulsory arbitration? The country will be dealing with this issue for a long time and increasingly so with the rapid spread of unionism in government. Since 1960, the number of government workers in unions has doubled. Today more than 4,500,000 public employees belong to unions or collective bargaining associations, and a growing militancy has already been felt.

The policies of collective bargaining are but part of a broader set of issues. Labor is deeply concerned not only with the traditional conditions of work such as hours, wages, and pensions, but also with job security itself, now threatened by technical change and automation. Business is faced not only with rising costs but with intense foreign competition. The public is directly affected by altered patterns of competition, quality of goods, prices, and unemployment. The impact of monopoly power of either a business or a union is felt throughout society. A healthy labor-management climate seems to require a willingness on the part of the immediate participants, the people, and their government to take a broad view of specific problems.

The politics of regulation

Karl Marx, the theorist of capitalist decay, maintained that the long-run interests of all capitalists were the same. He argued that the proletariat had a similar unity of interest and that eventually the exploiting class would give way to a government of the workers. Relations among the new proletarian rulers would be so harmonious that eventually the state would just wither away.

A look at the American economy today is enough to dispel the idea of a united group of businessmen facing a united group of workers. Admittedly, there is conflict between businessmen and workers. But such conflict is obscured by a vast complex of antagonistic interests operating *within* economic groups. The American political scene reflects not only the struggle of employer against worker, but also the struggles of consumer against producer, of business against business, of labor against labor, of section against section. And all these interests are intertwined and interlocked in such a way as to make the whole picture complex indeed.

President Truman's seizure of the steel industry in April 1952 in order to prevent a strike rocked the business world. The Supreme Court ruled the seizure unconstitutional and a prolonged strike followed, ending only when the government allowed substantial price increases to compensate the steel companies for higher wages in the union agreement.

THE CLASH OF INTERESTS

Some of the sharpest contests among interest groups take place within the world of business. Early attempts to regulate the railroads, for example, reflected chiefly a struggle between the railroads and consumers. But other interests were drawn into the struggle—for example, financial control groups, railroad investors, and railroad equipment and supply industries. Later, the railroads began to meet intense competition from other forms of transportation, and railroad politics became even more intricate. Today a political battle between railroad carriers and the trucking business simmers constantly. The railroads argue that the trucking business offers unfair competition. The fact that government builds and maintains the nation's highways, they protest, means that motor transportation is subsidized, whereas the railroads must provide their own facilities; the truckers reply that they contribute heavily to highway maintenance through gasoline and other taxes—and so the battle rages. The railroads also complain of the subsidies granted airlines and water shippers.[16]

The internal rivalries of labor also affect the politics of regulation. Labor, as noted, is by no means a unified, monolithic body; it is a cluster of unions of all kinds, sizes, and interests, along with many unorganized workers. For example, the Railroad Brotherhoods and the Teamsters' Union often clash on national transportation policy simply because industrially these two groups compete with each other. And the "liberal" industrial unions such as UAW and the Electrical Workers, often clash with such "conservative" unions as the Teamsters or the building trades over social welfare legislation and the support of liberal Democrats.

WHO REGULATES THE REGULATORS?

In creating each of the more than twenty regulatory commissions, Congress issued a broad policy directive but left it up to each commission, within the scope of its authority, to make the rules and issue the orders necessary to carry out the congressional mandate. Commissioners were given long, staggered terms; the president's power to remove them was limited; and he often must, in selecting commissioners, appoint individuals from both parties. In general, Congress clearly prefers to make

[16]Andrew Hacker, "Pressure Politics in Pennsylvania: The Truckers vs. the Railroads," in Alan F. Westin, ed., *The Uses of Power: 7 Cases in American Politics* (Harcourt, 1962), pp. 323–75.

regulatory agencies insulated from the president *and* relatively responsive to Congress.

Just how independent, then, are these *independent* commissions? Who regulates the regulators? Are regulatory agencies frequently *captured* by the industries they are supposed to regulate? An answer requires consideration of separate but frequently confused questions. *Have the commissions operated without regard to partisan politics? Have they carried on their duties uninfluenced by improper pressures?* For example, the Federal Communications Commission is supposed to decide which applicant should be licensed to use a television channel uninfluenced by personal favor, partisan preference, or the wishes even of the president of the United States. The Federal Trade Commission, in deciding if a particular company has violated the regulations concerning misleading advertising, is not supposed to be influenced by the intervention of a senator or the views of presidential assistants. By and large, the independent regulatory commissions have been insulated from partisan politics and have operated in accord with standards of propriety.

A far more difficult question is: *Have the commissions discharged their duties in terms of a broad concept of the public interest?* Obviously the independent regulatory commissions have not and cannot be made independent of politics in the broader and more important sense of the word. No agency operating within a democracy and vested with important decision-making duties can be removed from the political system. Because independent regulatory commissions must decide big political questions calling for the adjustment of a variety of interests, their independence from the White House often makes them more dependent on the interests they regulate. For the groups most immediately affected by the decisions of a commission naturally have a more sustained interest in the regulations than does the general public. As Edelman has observed, "The organizational and psychological embrace of the industry around the regulatory commissioners go hand in hand. To be part of the organization in the sense of incessant exposure to its problems and decisional premises is to come to share its perspectives and values. This is not 'pressure'; it is absorption."[17] Consumer spokesperson Ralph Nader and his associates have made similar charges.

A regulatory commission that offends a highly organized interest may discover that it is not quite as independent as its formal charter indicates. For the interests frequently work through the Congress and often can exert pressures on a commission more easily by moving through a congressional committee than by direct pressures on the commission.

Could it be, however, that many industries have been "captured" by their regulatory agency just as agencies are thought to be captured by the industry? This is in part the view of one student of regulation: "An agency is established, sometimes with industry support and sometimes

[17]Murray Edelman, *The Symbolic Uses of Politics* (University of Illinois Press, 1964), p. 66.

over industry objections, and then gradually creates a regulatory climate that acquires a life of its own. Certain firms will be helped by some of the specific regulatory decisions making up this climate, others will be hurt. But the industry as a whole will adjust to the climate and decide that the costs of shifting from the known hazards of regulation to the unknown ones of competition are too great; it thus will come to defend the system."[18]

To be sure, the capture of a regulatory agency by the regulated interests is not unknown in Washington.[19] Overall, however, the record of recent commission experience suggests that even though regulators often consider too narrow a range of issues, information, and interests, they usually are reasonably free of industry domination and control. And some of the commissions, such as FTC, SEC, and the Consumer Product Safety Commission, receive relatively high marks from all kinds of observers.

Almost all presidents, at least since the day of Franklin Roosevelt, have called on Congress to restructure the regulatory commissions. They have also appointed study groups that recommend reductions in the commissions' independence from policy direction of the president.[20] President Ford, as part of his program to combat inflation, has called for the creation of a National Commission on Regulatory Reform. The commission is to undertake "a long overdue total reexamination of independent regulatory agencies" in order to "identify and eliminate existing federal rules and regulations that increase costs to the consumer, without good reason. . . ."[21]

The independence of regulatory commissions from the president is often exaggerated. A president may not be able and should not be allowed to influence a particular decision of a commission any more than of a court, but the general thrust of policies of an independent regulatory commission is very much a part of the president's responsibilities. A president dedicated, let us say, to more vigorous government involvement in the enforcement of consumer protection objectives must make his influence felt. Despite their formal independence, a president's influence can often be exercised through the shrewd use of his appointment power, budgetary control, support or opposition on substantive legislation affecting a commission's work, and more generally through his influence in Congress and the nation.[22]

Independent regulatory commissions—even though their members

[18]James Q. Wilson, "The Dead Hand of Regulation," *Public Interest* (Fall 1971), p. 47.

[19]See for example, Louis M. Kohlmeier, Jr., *The Regulators: Watchdog Agencies and the Public Interest* (Harper & Row, 1969); and Erwin G. Krasnow and Lawrence D. Longley, *The Politics of Broadcasting Regulation* (St. Martin's Press, 1973).

[20]The Nixon proposals and criticism of them are summarized in Roger G. Noll, *Reforming Regulation: An Evaluation of the Ash Council Proposals* (Brookings Institution, 1971).

[21]Gerald R. Ford, Message to Congress on The Economy, October 8, 1974.

[22]See William L. Cary, *Politics and the Regulatory Agencies* (Prentice-Hall, 1967), esp. Ch. 1.

are influenced by the executive, their powers derive from legislative delegation, and their decisions are subject to review in the courts—have a scope of responsibility to the American economy that often exceeds that of the three regular branches of government. In short, the influence of the regulatory commissions is pervasive and their actions have vital consequences on personal rights. Aside from the many operational problems of the commissions, such as delay in processing cases, increasing judicialization of procedures, overlapping jurisdiction, and lack of interagency coordination, the key issues today involve *efficiency*, *equity*, and *integrity*. Are commissions achieving their goals at a reasonable cost? Are they treating those subject to them fairly? Are they responsive to the larger political system yet responsible to broad "public interest" concerns? To strengthen popular government, we must continually raise these questions and reappraise the performance of regulatory agencies.

Chapter 24 Government as promoter

Government promotion—subsidies or special assistance for segments of the population—is by no means a recent development. In his very first annual address to Congress, President Washington called for a tariff to protect business. Alexander Hamilton, his secretary of treasury, proposed that government help develop business by giving bounties to new enterprises. The new government promoted commerce in countless ways—by establishing a money system and a postal service, granting charters, enforcing contracts in court, subsidizing roads and waterways. Subsidizing businesses, farmers, veterans, and a myriad of other activities has long been standard operating procedure.

Yet great controversies rage over the role of the government in the economy. Conservatives sharply criticize the welfare state on the ground that "we need more economy in government and less government in the economy." Critics from the right contend that spendthrifts in Washington are undermining our "way of life" through a variety of give-away programs. Critics from the left charge that Washington bureaucrats are ineffective and that the welfare state is merely a symbolic gesture in which the powerful distribute a few crumbs to keep the powerless quiet, or—worse—that it is really a "warfare state" run by elites.

In fact, however, almost all groups at one time or another have benefited from government help. Many professed economic conservatives plainly seek government aid to fund an SST, to bail out Lockheed Aircraft, to support government-backed loans to railroads, to subsidize the merchant marine industry, and so on.[1] Just as plainly, spokespersons for the have-less sectors of society seek a larger government role in insuring personal health, in establishing an economic floor below which people are not allowed to fall, and in promoting improved housing and employment opportunities. Clearly, governmental promotion can be used to help any group. The main questions are: Who shall be aided? In what way? And with what consequences?

Helping business

A government that protects property and enforces contracts enables owners of business to operate in a stable situation where agreements can be enforced. A government that promotes a prosperous economy enables businesses to enjoy a large volume of sales and good profits. The kind of monetary system established by government—for example, tight or easy money—is of direct interest to business. Aside from these obvious aids, the national government supplies a number of specific services and assists individual sectors of the business community.

THE DEPARTMENT OF COMMERCE

The Department of Commerce is the nation's "service center" for businesses, and its secretary is nearly always a person with an extensive business background who serves as an advocate of the business community's interests. The department assists business in many ways: its Social and Economic Statistics Administration reports on business activity and prospects at home and around the world; the National Bureau of Standards makes scientific investigations and standardizes units of weight and measure.

The Bureau of the Census has been called the greatest fact-finding and figure-counting agency in the world. The Constitution requires that a national census be taken every ten years; the results of this census, and of others in between, supply business executives with valuable information on business and agricultural activity, incomes, occupations, employment, housing and homeownership, and governmental finances.

The Patent Office is also in the Commerce Department. The first article of the Constitution authorized Congress to secure to authors and inventors, for a limited period, "the exclusive right to their respective writings and discoveries." A patent, conferring the right of exclusive

[1]See Louis Fisher, "Big Government, Conservative Style," *The Progressive* (March 1973), pp. 22–26.

use of an invention for seventeen years, is a valuable property right. On receiving an application for a patent, the Patent Office must study its records to see if any prior patent might be infringed and if the invention is sufficiently original and useful to be patentable; meanwhile the applicant marks his product "patent pending." Although most patent problems are technical, patent policy also invokes such broad problems as the stimulation of invention and the threat of monopoly and economic concentration.

Through the Maritime Administration, the government directly and indirectly subsidizes the American merchant marine by several hundred million dollars a year. National security considerations are the primary justification for this subsidy program. "The operating subsidies and cargo preference laws sustain a fleet of U.S. flag ships to be available in time of war to carry essential cargoes. The shipbuilding subsidies presumably maintain shipyard capacity that might be needed in wartime."[2] Critics point out, however, that this subsidy program is so designed as to discourage competition, limit the freedom of subsidized operators, and jack-up the cost of ships (because they must be built in the U.S.) to more than double the price of those built in foreign shipyards.[3] Thus, here again is a government promotion program that probably causes as many problems as it resolves. Then, too, this is the kind of program that prompts some people to remark that "Industry would very much like to nationalize its losses and privatize its gains."[4]

OTHER HELP FOR BUSINESS

In addition to the activities of the Department of Commerce, the government assists business through such other agencies as the Small Business Administration, an independent agency headed by an administrator appointed by the president. The SBA is designed to aid small companies through such services as financial counseling, research, loans to victims of natural disasters such as floods and hurricanes.

The government also aids business through research and experimentation carried on by a variety of agencies. Examples include new commercial wood products resulting from work done in the laboratories of the U.S. Forest Service and diversified uses of bituminous coal arising from research in the Department of the Interior.

Through a wide range of tax benefits for certain segments of the population—especially businessmen, but others as well—government encourages certain types of activity and investment such as exploring for oil. The money foregone by the government through such provisions in the tax code is now called "tax expenditure." In this sense, many economists say, it should be considered as much a part of the federal budget

[2]Charles L. Schultze, *Setting National Priorities: The 1971 Budget* (Brookings Institution, 1970), p. 175.

[3]*Ibid.*, pp. 174–77

[4]A remark attributed to Admiral Rickover, among others.

as money directly appropriated for, say, the Forest Service. Estimated tax expenditures of this kind in the calendar year 1972 were almost $60 billion. Major categories include: energy depletion allowances, $1.7 billion; business investment credits, $3.8 billion; individual capital gains deductions, $7 billion; deductibility of mortgage interest, $3.5 billion; deductibility of property taxes, $3.25 billion; and so on.[5]

DELIVERING THE MAIL

The government assumed the responsibility for the delivery of the mails even before the Revolution. For many years, the postmaster general was more important for his political than for his administrative responsibilities. Presidents appointed to the post the national chairman of his own party or one of his key campaign managers. The reason was obvious: the Post Office Department had thousands of patronage jobs to parcel out to the local party workers. Over the years postal employees were gradually brought under the Civil Service, and continuing efforts have been mounted to restructure the Post Office as a self-supporting business enterprise. In spite of such efforts, however, the Post Office is still heavily subsidized and many people believe it always will be. Some people believe it should be subsidized by the government so that communications may flourish, advertisers may better advertise, and literary and public affairs magazines may enjoy lower postal rates and higher circulations (and survival).

In response to the recommendations of a presidential commission, and after two years of heated debate in Congress in which postal workers and their unions bargained hard to protect their positions, Congress in 1970 abolished the Post Office Department and created a new independent agency, the United States Postal Service.

The Postal Service is governed by an eleven-member board of governors, nine of whom are appointed by the president with the consent of the Senate, no more than five of whom may be from the same political party. These nine members in turn appoint a postmaster general, and he in turn joins them in selecting a deputy postmaster general. These two administrative officers also serve on the board of governors. The appointed members serve for staggered nine-year terms, but the postmaster general and the deputy postmaster general serve at the board's direction.

Postal employees retain their Civil Service status, but the board has authority to set compensation and determine fringe benefits. Employees are permitted to engage in collective bargaining, but may not legally strike. In the event of a deadlock between the board and its employees, there is to be compulsory arbitration.

In time, the Postal Service is *expected* to become self-supporting. But

[5]See U.S. House of Representatives, Committee on Ways and Means, *Estimates of Federal Tax Expenditures* (June 1, 1973).

during the transitional period which, at the earliest, will run to 1984, Congress is to make appropriations from tax funds. Like a business, the Postal Service is permitted to sell bonds to purchase capital equipment. Unlike a business, however, it may set the rates that it charges only after a recommendation from the presidentially appointed five-member Postal Rate Commission. Moreover, the Civil Aeronautics Board and the Interstate Commerce Commission retain power to approve payments to air and rail carriers of the mails.

The United States Postal Service is *the largest single business* in the world, the biggest nonmilitary department of the national government. It handles over 90 billion pieces of mail every year, operates more than 32,000 post offices, and has more than 700,000 employees.

The new business organization reflects the businesslike nature of the Postal Service's functions. But it also reflects the fact that the decisions made by the Postal Service have a major impact on our economy and our political system. Its structure—especially the presidential appointment of most members of the board of governors—is designed to promote proper consideration of these political factors, and to avoid the service's making its decisions solely from a perspective of how to maximize profits.

Will the government continue to involve itself in this kind of direction promotion and management, or does there seem to be a trend away from such arrangements? It seems likely that we will see more governmental management of enterprises. Technology and economics seem to be working in that direction. When the private sector finds it unprofitable to provide essential services or when policy considerations make it seem inappropriate to permit them, government steps in.

Among other examples of government management or involvement are the National Aeronautics and Space Administration (NASA), Communications Satellite Corporation (COMSAT), Corporation for Public Broadcasting (CPB), and the National Railroad Passenger Corporation (Railpax or Amtrak). NASA took over the responsibility for our space program simply because no private enterprise could undertake it, although 80 percent of its work is done by private industrial and university contractors. COMSAT is a business enterprise whose stock is sold to the public, but the federal government and American Telephone and Telegraph Company are the major stockholders and appoint the controlling directors of the firm. COMSAT was created to develop, launch, and operate communications satellites and to keep the business from becoming a monopoly of AT&T. CPB's responsibility for providing funds for public service broadcasting has been previously mentioned. Amtrak provides intercity railroad passenger service because privately owned and operated railroads were unwilling and unable to do so. The stock of Amtrak is owned by railroad companies and the public, and its board of directors, like that of COMSAT, is selected by a combination of presidential appointment and stockholders. All these enterprises show an interlacing of public and private finance, public and private control.

Promoting trade vs. protectionism

Rapid changes in the world have brought several new external challenges to American trade policies. First, if we are to maintain our economic growth and high standard of living, we must increase our exports. But, unprecedented economic development in certain segments of the world has introduced a new kind of foreign competition. In Europe, American business no longer faces a weak and fragmented competitor, but an established and growing European Common Market. This entity has a potential industrial capacity equivalent to our own, and a population—and hence a market—significantly larger than ours. Japan, which has experienced tremendous industrial expansion, already effectively competes with many American manufacturers.

Communist bloc nations have also registered some significant industrial advances and have begun to make inroads in world trade. The less-developed, or developing, nations pose yet different challenges. They want economic, social, and technical assistance and also markets for their products. Smaller, less-developed countries have been concerned about U.S. companies operating within their borders. Some countries want to impose greater taxes or even to nationalize such firms. Then, too, many of the world's less industrial nations have discovered that they can charge higher prices for raw materials needed by the U.S. (About 20 percent of the raw materials we use are now imported, and this percentage is rising.) The Middle Eastern nations rather dramatically demonstrated this with oil price escalation and export restrictions.

Other developments affecting U.S. trade policy have been *balance of payments* deficits and major *trade deficits* which in recent years have run into the billions. The rise of the *multinational corporation* has also jolted the way we view our trade agreements. A so-called "multinational corporation" is a company that through foreign direct investments organizes subsidiary production or marketing offices in other nations. I.T.T., Singer, Colgate-Palmolive, National Cash Register, and Goodyear, for example, have half of their fixed assets outside the United States. Critics, especially from affected labor unions, call such overseas investing the exporting of American jobs. Others charge that the interdependence of the world economy as well as its health is increasingly dependent—dangerously so—upon the investments and decisions of the multinational corporate managers. Leaders of big business counter that our multinational corporations are essential to the health of our economy, actually help our balance of payments problem, and generate jobs at home. Debate over proper controls and taxation on the multinationals is likely to continue for some time to come.[6]

Has the United States turned basically isolationist? Its new economic

[6]For different views, see Anthony Sampson, *The Sovereign State of I.T.T.* (Stein and Day, 1973); Hugh Stephenson, *The Coming Clash* (Saturday Review Press, 1972); Raymond Vernon, *Sovereignty at Bay* (Basic Books, 1971); and the Emergency Committee for American Trade, *The Multinational Corporation: American Mainstay in the World Economy* (1973). Also, R. J. Barnet and R. E. Muller, *Global Reach: The Power of the Multinational Corporations* (1975).

policies of the early and mid-1970s raised fundamental questions, but they must be understood in the perspective of longer-term strategies.[7] The principal device used by all governments to aid their nation's business has been the *tariff*, and Congress has often favored interests that desire high protective tariffs. To be sure, in the years of rich surplus, we usually denounced the restrictive and protectionist policies of other nations as an evil infringement upon the freedom of trade. Yet over the years, our own businesses were jeopardized by foreign competition, and they and their employees successfully petitioned Congress to curb competitive imports.

By the beginning of this century many industries protected by high tariffs had expanded to a point where sales of their own products in foreign markets were imperative. And Americans discovered that foreign trade is a two-way proposition: if you want people in a foreign market to buy your goods, you must be willing to buy theirs.

In 1934 Congress empowered the president to negotiate mutual tariff reductions with other nations, subject to certain restrictions. By 1970 tariffs on industrial products had been substantially reduced. But restrictions on agricultural commodities remain, along with nontariff limitations such as quotas, minimum import prices, and even outright prohibitions on sales of certain kinds of products. American business firms are finding it more difficult to compete in certain markets, especially in Japan and inside the Common Market. They also face competition from industrial giants in countries where there are no antitrust regulations. Because of restrictions on American sales abroad and tougher competition from foreign products inside the United States, protectionist sentiment clearly has revived.

The legislative struggle over tariffs and international trade policies reflects some unusual interest-group alignments. Despite some reservations, the Chamber of Commerce, the AFL-CIO, and the Farm Bureau have in general opposed measures that would limit foreign trade. Pressures to restrict imports arise from both organized labor and management in industries such as textiles where foreign competition is especially severe.[8] Thus the issue cuts across and within interest groups.

One of the more difficult, and complicated, problems of recent years is our unfavorable balance of international payments. Our unfavorable balance of payments has resulted in an outflow of gold reserves and a surplus of dollars in the hands of European bankers. The reasons for the unfavorable situation are not primarily an imbalance between our exports and imports, although this exists especially since the Arabs have raised the price of oil which we must import, but our large expenditures for foreign aid and overseas military activity. Other nations are con-

[7]C. Fred Bergsten, "The New Economics and U.S. Foreign Policy," *Foreign Affairs* (January 1972), p. 199.

[8]See Raymond A. Bauer, Ithiel de Sola Pool, and Lewis Anthony Dexter, *American Business and Public Policy: The Politics of Foreign Trade* (Atherton, 1963), pp. 73–81, for the broad context in which trade policy is made.

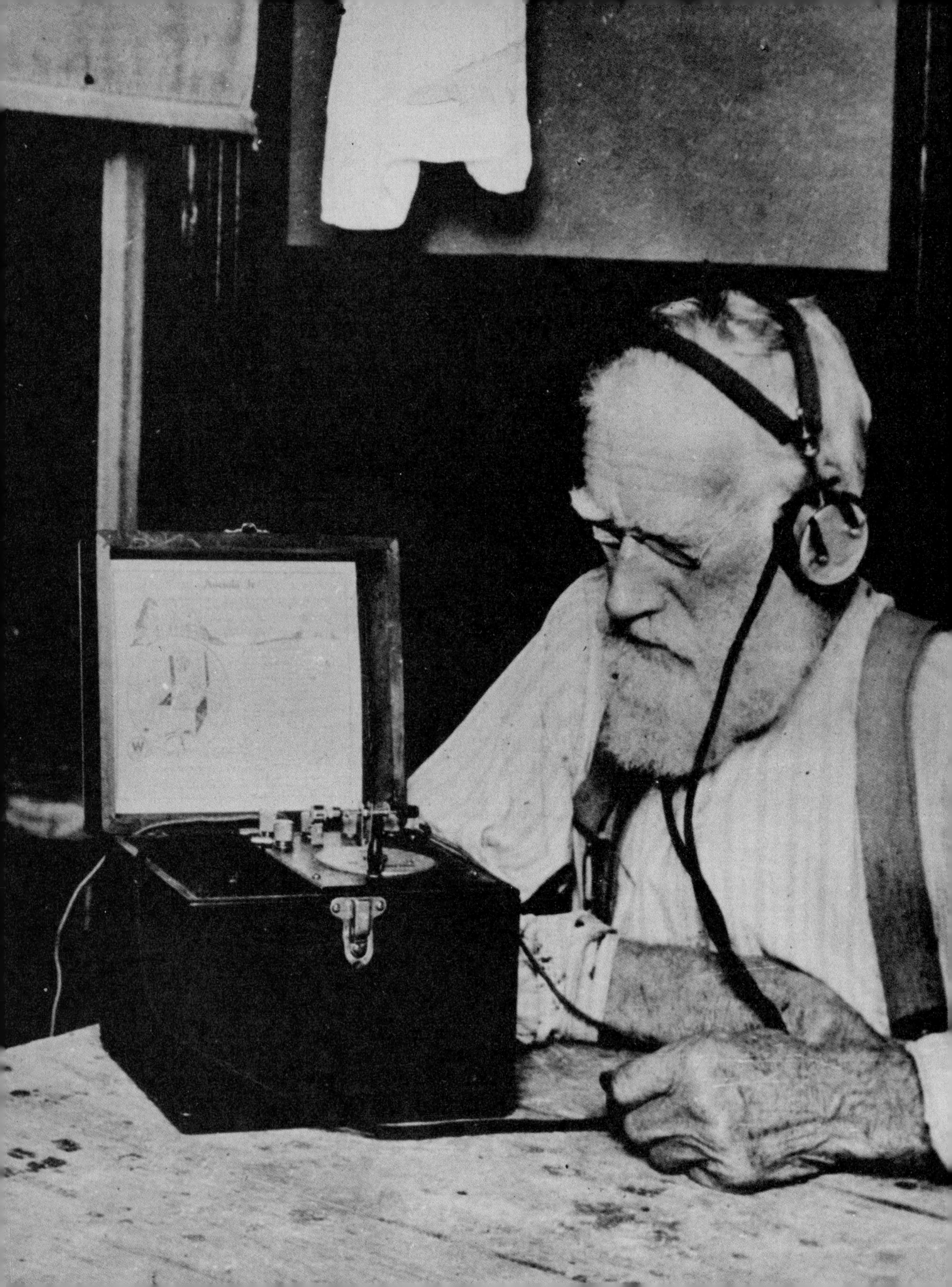

A farmer listens on his crystal set to a 1923 market news broadcast by the U.S. Department of Agriculture. Information farmers heard through their earphones helped them decide what to raise and when to sell their products. The USDA began its market news reports in 1915 and has supplied the service ever since. Today's reports, conducted through about 220 field offices, furnish information on prices, supply, and market conditions for all major agricultural products.

cerned about the American balance of payments because of the inflationary pressure it places on their economies. They are fearful that we will try to solve our economic problems without regard to the impact of our actions on their economic situation. These developments led to the devaluation of the dollar as well as renewed efforts by some elements of the labor movement to raise tariffs and curb the power of the multinational corporations.

Aiding farmers

Nowhere is the diversity of American life more apparent than in agriculture. American farmers grow an amazing variety of crops. There are big farmers employing scores of workers on many hundreds of acres of land; there are farmers operating family-sized farms of 100 to 200 acres, with the help of one or two hired hands; there are tenant farmers working other people's farms for a share of the produce and profits; there are, finally, millions of farm laborers, many of whom move from farm to farm as the seasons change.

This wide diversity is reflected in the highly complex set of problems commonly identified simply as the "farm problem." There are actually many interrelated problems, but the basic difficulty is that American agriculture is *out of balance* with the rest of society. The general features of this imbalance are:

1. *Internal imbalance.* All farms are not equally successful. In most cases, successful farms use more capital, more land, and less labor than the marginally prosperous ones. The big farms, which have kept pace with technological developments and have made the best use of resources, constitute a minority of farms in America. A third of all farms produce almost 90 percent of all food and fibers; the least productive 50 percent are responsible for only 6 percent of the product. A half million farm owners who work full time get so small a return that they are classified as living below the poverty line.

2. *Social imbalance.* Many rural communities are being bypassed by social and economic development. Some are hard pressed to provide adequate schools, fire protection, and sanitation. A quarter of all rural homes are classified as substandard, compared with 15 percent of urban homes. In the cities, one person in eight is poor, in the suburbs, one in fifteen; but in rural America, one in every four is poor. The million migrant farm workers constitute probably the most economically and socially deprived group in the United States. They are largely excluded from the protection of minimum-wage legislation; in most states they are not eligible for unemployment compensation; and they are not covered by laws that protect their right to form trade unions.

3. *Economic imbalance.* From a world perspective, inadequate agricultural production remains acute and because of the population explosion is becoming even more serious despite American productivity. One farm worker supplied sixteen persons with farm products in 1950. Just twenty years later his counterpart supplied food and fiber for forty-three persons. But the adoption of improved production methods—mechanization, fertilizers, pesticides, and the like—has brought increased costs. Farm prices have tended not to increase at the same rate as costs for what the farmer buys. As a result, the American farmer has not in general shared in the nation's economic growth. All these facts closely affect the relation of government to agriculture.

The principal agricultural role of the federal government during the nineteenth century was to promote production. In 1862 the Homestead Act gave settlers 160 acres of public land in exchange for a promise to occupy the land for five years; Congress granted huge tracts of land to the states for the establishment of colleges; and it created the Department of Agriculture. In later years agricultural research stations were set up, conservation and reclamation programs undertaken, and farm cooperatives encouraged.

World War I increased governmental intervention in agriculture; the prices of food, cotton, and farmland skyrocketed, and the farmers enjoyed a boom. In 1920 the bubble burst. Prices plummeted and millions of farmers were left with surplus land, unpaid-for machinery, high taxes, and burdensome debts. Farmers turned to Washington, and Congress responded by passing measures to police the trading in contracts for future delivery of agricultural commodities, to encourage agricultural cooperatives, and to ease credit. These proved ineffectual in stemming the agricultural depression.

The Great Depression sharply intensified agricultural stagnation. Unlike industrial firms, the farmers could not retrench, lay off workers, cut down orders for materials, and decrease output. Most of the farmers' expenses continued at the same level no matter what the state of the market was. So when the price of agricultural commodities dropped, the farmers tried to grow even more—with the result that prices fell even further. And farmers were so numerous that there was no way that by themselves they could control markets.

The Roosevelt Administration tried to do for farmers what businessmen were doing for themselves—restrict production in order to increase or maintain prices. It tried to create new demands and shift farm production toward commodities for which there was a better market. And since the 1930s, the federal government has developed—haltingly—a whole arsenal of devices to bring some order into agricultural markets, sustain farmers' incomes, and achieve a balance between supply and demand.

Some of these more important devices or subsidies (not all of which are used each year) are:

1. *Acreage allotments.* Government experts estimate the probable demand for staple commodities such as cotton, wheat, and rice. Then, using an elaborate system, they may break down the national acreage allotments into individual allotments for each farm. Such allotments have not been used in recent years.

2. *Marketing quotas.* If production becomes high and a price collapse threatens, farmers by a two-thirds vote may approve the establishment of marketing quotas. Each producer is allotted his share and pays a penalty if he markets more. During recent years of inflation and shortages, quotas have not been used.

3. *Price supports.* The government, through loans, in effect may take commodities off the farmers' hands if it appears that excess production may cause prices to fall below a certain minimum. The farmers store their commodities in government warehouses and allow their loans to expire if the market falls below the loan price; the government then takes over the commodities. By discouraging farm commodities from flooding into the market after each harvest, these loans encourage orderly marketing and eliminate sharp price changes.

4. *Conservation payments.* These are grants to farmers to induce them to take certain lands from production and plant them in grass or trees or to adopt other soil-conservation practices.

5. *Food for the poor.* Through the food stamp program, the National School Lunch Act, and the school milk program, food is distributed to the needy.

By the early 1960s the results were a continuing decline of the small farm, restiveness in the cities over the high cost of food, and soaring farm surpluses that cost billions of dollars each year just to handle and store. As of 1970, the farm controls and subsidy program—and world conditions—seemed to work. A relative balance began to appear between supply and demand. More recently, however, increased international demands, along with inefficient and complex distribution methods, resulted in rising prices and sporadic shortages of foodstuffs in our own supermarkets. The government apparently has been somewhat sluggish in changing over from policies designed to limit production to those adaptive to the new market conditions.

Who benefits from government farm subsidies? Whatever the merits of our farm policies, subsidies seldom amount to a welfare program in the sense that they transfer income to poor farm families. The bulk of the subsidies go to the twenty percent whose net incomes already average $20,000 or more. ". . . They tend, at least roughly, to be distributed in proportion to the volume of production on each farm. The more a farm produces, the greater the value of price supports. Moreover, most of the cash payments a farmer receives from the government depend on the size of his acreage allotment or his production, both of which vary directly with the size of his farm."[9]

Critics charged too that a 1972 grain sale to the Soviet Union, negotiated by the Department of Agriculture, was also notable for its subsidy to a few wealthy corporations at the expense of U.S. consumers. A Senate investigation of this historic sale—the largest in history—of 700 million bushels of grain, concluded the sales created a shortage in domestic supplies that drove up the price of bread and flour-based products. Senator Henry Jackson termed it the "Great American Grain Robbery." The shortage created increases in the price of feed grains which led to higher prices for beef, pork, poultry, eggs, and dairy products. "At virtually every step, from the initial planning of the sales to the subsidy that helped support them, the grain sales were ineptly managed. The result was public confusion, waste of taxpayers' dollars, and higher food prices."[10] In the Midwest, however, most farmers disagree with Senator Jackson and in general approve the grain sales, arguing that it is good for business and helps relieve our balance of payments problem. They see no reason why farmers cannot sell their products overseas just as businessmen do.

Debates over both the equity and effectiveness of the present farm policy will almost surely intensify in the next few years. The political power of the farm bloc may be somewhat diminished, but it is far from puny. Farmers quickly won reversal of Nixon's plan to consolidate and restructure the Department of Agriculture. The power of the agricultural lobby is well established in the political arena. Still, adjustments and revision of our overall farm strategies seem to be in order.

Government as the patron of science

The Founding Fathers were aware of the importance of science. Congress was given specific authority to provide for the census, to establish weights and measures, and to encourage scientific endeavors by regulating patents. But of more importance has been the broader power to appropriate money for the general welfare and for the common defense. Our government has long been involved in scientific exploration and development. The Lewis and Clark Expedition during the Jefferson period, the Army Corps of Engineers, the National Academy of Sciences, and the Morrill Act of 1862 mark important commitments. But, of course, the biggest expansion came after World War II.

[9]Charles L. Schultze, *The Distribution of Farm Subsidies: Who Gets the Benefits?* (Brookings Institution, 1971), p. 2.

[10]Quote from a report of the Senate permanent investigations subcommittee, *Rocky Mountain News* (July 29, 1974), p. 40

SCIENCE AGENCIES

The national government filters support for science through many agencies; the most important are the National Science Foundation, the Department of Defense, the Energy Research and Development Administration, the National Aeronautics and Space Administration, and the Department of Health, Education, and Welfare.

The National Science Foundation (NSF), under the leadership of a director appointed by the president with the consent of the Senate and the guidance of a twenty-four person board of scientists, each year provides matching funds for research facilities, makes available graduate fellowships, and grants funds to thousands of scientists to support their investigations.

HEW's National Institutes of Health (NIH) now spends more than $2 billion each year to support the health sciences. The government's "war on cancer" is run under NIH auspices. Like the NSF, the NIH is primarily an agency to support scientific work of nongovernment scientists, although it does operate its own hospitals and extensive research laboratories, most of which are located in Bethesda, Maryland.

The National Oceanic and Atmospheric Administration (NOAA), located in the Department of Commerce, offers another example of extensive government involvement in science. This 12,000-member agency is charged, among other things, with: (1) hurricane modification research, (2) weather and sea prediction and warning system research, (3) charting the nation's coastal and Great Lake regions with the aim of producing aeronautical maps for safe and efficient commercial and general aviation, and (4) the operation of a national environmental satellite services system. Its Weather Service makes forecasts on the basis of data funneled to it by its hundreds of field stations. Its services are utilized especially by farmers, airlines, and the resort industry. The use of computers, weather satellites, and a variety of weather modification technologies suggest that NOAA unquestionably will have even a greater role for both civilian and military activities in years to come.[11]

What are some of the consequences of aid to science? It has not *as yet* led to intensive federal control. The government is using grants and contracts as a lever for promoting affirmative action policies in hiring practices. And, of course, changing research priorities established at the national level have had a strong effect in attracting researchers into certain fields.

University administrators, much as they welcome federal support, are alarmed by the fact that federal grants to the natural sciences could lead to an imbalance in university programs. Federal grants cover the direct cost of research but only partly the indirect or overhead costs. The universities must divert other funds to cover this research and thus have less to spend on the other departments. To offset imbalances in availability of federal research funds, the National Science Foundation has

[11]Howard J. Taubenfeld, ed., *Controlling the Weather* (Dunellen, 1970).

expanded its support to include the social sciences, and Congress in 1965 established the National Foundation for the Arts and the Humanities.

PROMOTING ATOMIC AND NUCLEAR ENERGY

Originally, the main job of the Atomic Energy Commission (AEC) was to build and stockpile atomic bombs. In its three decades of existence, the AEC did this task so well that today the nation's military arsenal is loaded with nuclear weapons, and a huge surplus of fissionable material is on hand for building even more bombs. The AEC also guided and promoted the development of the peaceful use of the atom. Today, in part because of our concern with energy needs, we have a strong commitment to the use of nuclear power and thus to the construction of an extensive network of nuclear power plants. One thousand nuclear power plants should be operating by the year 2000.

How did a conservative Congress in 1946 happen to create this vast public enterprise? In 1945 Congress found itself in the remarkable position of being able to provide in advance for the control of a gigantic new resource—atomic energy. Some voices were raised in favor of private control, but most members of Congress decided that the goal of public responsibility was too precious to surrender. Scientists testified that the use of fissionable, fusionable, and radioactive materials would lead to further significant discoveries, which in time would create numberless and unpredictable problems. Without some kind of control and planning, chaos would set in. So certain was Congress of the need for government development that, in the end, it socialized atomic energy with virtually no dissension at all.

Legislative battles did break out, however, over several provisions of the bill. Civilian versus military control was the most controversial issue. As first introduced, the atomic energy bill explicitly provided that members of the proposed Atomic Energy Commission might be officers of the Army or Navy. Shortly, a new kind of pressure group sprang into action—atomic scientists. Many of them had chafed under military control during the war, and they feared that such control might be authoritarian, or at least harmful to the spirit of free scientific inquiry. The scientists organized citizens' committees, testified before Congress, made speeches, put out propaganda, and lobbied on Capitol Hill. Partly as a result of this skillful political action, the bill was changed. The commission would be entirely civilian, but it would be advised on military matters by a military liaison committee.

The development of policy by the commission has been overseen by the Joint Congressional Committee on Atomic Energy, that has taken its statutory "watchdog" responsibilities seriously.[12] The hearings of this committee are a valuable source of information on many aspects of

[12]For an instructive interpretation of AEC's passage and the development of this joint committee, see Harold Green and Alan Rosenthal, *Governing the Atom* (Atherton, 1964).

nuclear energy. But many people, especially environmentalists, think that for careful checks and balances the public must look elsewhere; for the joint committee and the AEC have evolved a cooperative (some say cozy) relationship over the years. AEC and its clients, like most governmental enterprises, have been unreservedly enthusiastic proponents of its activities—in this case, nuclear energy. This is perhaps as it should be, but there are those who feel AEC's boosterism and promotion have come at the expense of safety and the environment.

In part the basic problem was that AEC had been charged to regulate and *promote* the use of nuclear power. While striving to achieve a balance between the two, the AEC was never able to satisfy everyone (including some of its own scientists) that, for example, it paid as much attention to safety as to promotion. The release of radioactivity into the environment is a problem that promises to grow exponentially as more reactors are put in operation. The design for nuclear power plants is such that they will undoubtedly produce large quantities of radiation and radioactive waste known as "fission products." Some experts contend that these products are a million to a billion times more toxic than any industrial pollutant yet known.

Congress, in late 1974, abolished the Atomic Energy Commission and established the Energy Research and Development Administration and the Nuclear Regulatory Commission. This, in effect, separated the AEC's promotional and regulatory functions. The research administration will explore all possible energy sources, with simultaneous projects in nuclear fission and fusion, coal gasification and liquification, and solar, geothermal, wind, tidal, and ocean current power. The new regulatory unit will absorb AEC's regulatory division with separate units supervising licensing of nuclear fuel facilities, reactor safety, materials safeguards, and regulatory research.

Nuclear energy will remain the object of intense public interest because of the conflict arising from overlapping federal and state safety codes, the extent of permissible competition from private nuclear enterprises, the impact of this source upon other power sources, the effects on the economy of the location of nuclear facilities, as well as the considerable opposition by environmental groups over safety hazards. Nonetheless, it is safe to assume that this multi-billion-dollar program for developing nuclear energy will continue to be managed directly by the government.

SCIENCE, SCIENTISTS, AND PUBLIC POLICY

Scientific considerations infuse every aspect of public policy. No federal agency today considers itself properly equipped without an assistant secretary for science and technology or some such science adviser. Until 1973 an Office of Science and Technology existed in the Executive Office of the President. The functions of this office, which included advice on overall science policy and responsibilities to coordinate science problems that are broader than the jurisdiction of a single agency, are now lodged with the director of the National Science Foundation. Meanwhile, Congress has created the Office of Technology Assessment to strengthen its capacity to formulate new technology legislation and to review ongoing federal research and development activities.[13]

With scientists occupying key policy-advising positions in government, it is sometimes difficult for the nonscientists who are responsible for making public policy to sort out scientific advice from what may merely reflect the personal values of the scientists. Just as military domination of civilians would undermine the democratic system, so would scientific domination of politicians. And on the other hand, just as it would be dangerous for civilians to ignore their military advisers, it would be even more disastrous for them to ignore science advisers. Some scientists complain that the latter is happening today. Decisions, they say, such as our current commitment to build a large number of nuclear power plants or our past investments in the man-on-the-moon program, are often based on political rather than scientific considerations. But scientists, like other mortals, often disagree with one another, even on the scientific questions involved in the larger questions of public policy.[14] This is at least a partial safeguard against the dangers to democracy that might flow from a scientific elite.

The state of welfare[15]

Until the Great Depression the prevailing public sentiment was that except for veterans and a few special groups the national government had no responsibility for taking care of persons in need. America was thought to be a land of unlimited opportunity. Millions of acres of free land, enormous resources, and technical advances all helped take care of people who otherwise might not have made a go of it. If a man failed to get ahead, people said, it was his own fault. The "worthy poor," widows, and orphans were taken care of through private or county relief. Rather grudgingly, the state governments—mainly during the early twentieth century—extended relief to needy old people, blind persons, and orphans, but the programs were limited. No work, no food was the ruling ethic.

[13]On the role of scientific advice in the White House and in Congress, see David Z. Beckler, "The Precarious Life of Science in the White House," and Emilio O. Daddario, "Science Policy: Relationships Are the Key," both in *Daedalus* (Summer 1974), pp. 115–34, and pp. 135–42 respectively.

[14]Don K. Price, *The Scientific Estate* (Harvard University Press, 1965). See also Marvin Blissett, *Politics in Science* (Little, Brown, 1972).

[15]The heading of this section is the title of a book by Gilbert Y. Steiner, *The State of Welfare* (Brookings Institution, 1971), a comprehensive analysis of our welfare programs on which we have drawn in the discussion that follows.

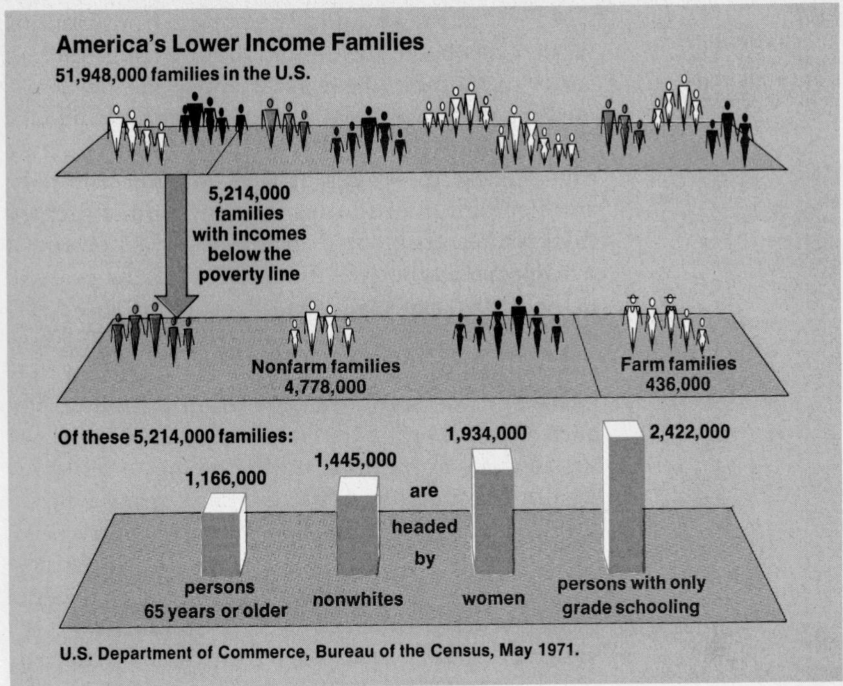

Then the nation was struck by the Great Depression. Unemployment mounted to sickening heights; in the early 1930s between ten and fifteen million people were without jobs. Breadlines, soup kitchens, private charity, meager state and local programs—these were pitifully inadequate gestures. The Roosevelt Administration created an elaborate series of emergency relief programs.

What started as an emergency response to a "temporary" condition has become a permanent feature of our governmental system. During the past forty years the national government has become progressively and deeply involved in welfare activities. Even after three decades of national economic expansion, there are more than fifteen million Americans receiving welfare and an additional twelve million needing but not getting it. At least seven million families live on incomes below the poverty line. And the numbers being added to welfare rolls, and the cost of the programs, are increasing at accelerating rates.

That the national government should do something about the persistence of poverty is not a much-debated issue, but *what* it should do is. There is not even agreement about the dimensions of the problem—how many poor exist, who they are, and why they are poor. But it is clear that prosperity has passed by a substantial number of Americans, perhaps thirty million of them. These are often the hidden poor, those who remain invisible to the majority of Americans because they exist in the dark slums of the city and in the mountains and valleys of rural America.

A third of the chronically poor are from families in which the breadwinner has been without a job for a long time. Some are headed by a father or mother whose skills are so meager that he or she cannot support the family. A large portion of the poor live in families headed by a person over sixty-five years of age or one with little or no education. Because black Americans have been subject to pervasive discrimination and denied opportunities for education, a greater percentage of blacks than whites are poor. Nevertheless, 70 percent of the poor are white.

Almost everybody is unhappy about the present state of national welfare policies, especially the largest of the so-called categorical relief programs, Aid to Families with Dependent Children. (There is less criticism of programs providing help for the aged, the blind, the disabled.) Conservatives argue that the drain on the taxpayer is beyond endurance. Liberals argue that it is immoral for a rich nation to spend billions for defense, to put men on the moon, to build highways, to subsidize wealthy farmers, to assist business firms when millions are in want. Radicals argue that the poor are in poverty because of the deliberate design of the powerful. The National Advisory Commission on Civil Disorders (the Kerner Commission) summarized much of this dissatisfaction when it concluded: "The Commission believes that our present system of public assistance contributes materially to the tensions and social disorganization that have led to civil disorders. The failures of the system alienate the taxpayers who support it, the social workers who administer it, and the poor who depend on it. As one critic told the Commission: 'The welfare system is designed to save money instead of people and tragically ends up doing neither.' "[16]

In short, as Theodore Marmor points out:

> Both hostile critics and sympathetic analysts of public assistance seem to agree that there is a "crisis." What this crisis consists of differs from analyst to analyst, but the following issues emerge: (a) inadequacy of payment levels; (b) disparity of payments between one geographical area and another . . . , and among various categories of public assistance recipients; (c) administrative injustices and arbitrariness, including the alleged stigma of being on welfare, which also serves to deter eligible and deserving persons from applying; (d) the financial costs of increasing the benefits . . . ; (e) the unfortunate effects of public assistance upon family cohesiveness and work behavior; (f) the social divisiveness and inequity of welfare programs aiding only certain groups of the poor and excluding others, most notably the working poor.[17]

The celebrated exchange between F. Scott Fitzgerald and Ernest Hemingway continues to set the framework within which we debate welfare policies. Fitzgerald is reported to have said, "The rich are different from the poor," to which Hemingway responded, "Yes, they have more

[16] *Report of the National Advisory Commission on Civil Disorders* (U.S. Government Printing Office, 1968), p. 252.

[17] Theodore Marmor, "On Comparing Income Maintenance Alternatives," *American Political Science Review* (March 1971), pp. 84–85.

money." On the Fitzgerald side of the argument are social scientists like Herman Miller, Oscar Lewis, and Michael Harrington, who believe that we must make a distinction between those without money and the poor. A student at college from a middle-class background or a space scientist out of work may be without much money, but he or she is not "poor." To be "poor" is to be part of the "culture of poverty," a subculture with its own system of values and behaviors that make it possible for those living in poverty to exist but make it difficult for them to "succeed" by the standards of the larger society. As Harrington has written, "There is . . . a language of the poor, a psychology of the poor, a world view of the poor. To be impoverished is to be an internal alien, to grow up in a culture that is radically different from one that dominates the

In the 1930s, programs were funded to reduce the poverty of the Depression by substituting work for welfare. Billions went to the Works Progress Administration (WPA) which financed a variety of conservation and public works programs. Right, men work on one of the 116,000 buildings erected or improved by the WPA. Above, the first National Recovery Administration (NRA) flag is raised in Chicago in 1933.

society."[18] Although modern Fitzgeraldites vary in their political ideologies—some think the culture of poverty deserves to be maintained—they tend to emphasize that welfare dependency is unlikely to be reduced unless persons are given the education, the training, and the skills they will need to break out of the culture of poverty. They also tend to favor measures to enhance the political power of the poor so that they will be better equipped to secure their share of governmental resources.

Those who take the Hemingway position—and in this category there are political conservatives and political liberals and political radicals—argue that what the poor need most is money. With more money they will be able to provide decent housing, secure education for their children, and in time become capable of taking care of themselves.

During the last several decades we have had several waves of welfare reform which can be loosely categorized as having the following thrusts:

1. Trying to substitute workfare for welfare. In November 1934, President Roosevelt wrote, "What I am seeking is the abolition of relief altogether. I cannot say so out loud yet but I hope to be able to substitute work for relief."[19] He hoped that, with economic recovery and full employment, people would move from relief to employment. And many did so. But five presidents later, Richard Nixon announced, "What America needs now is not more welfare but more workfare."[20]

Jobs do remove from relief those who are temporarily unemployed because of economic dislocations and who have the skills required for employment. But the problem is that many of those on welfare are unemployable, unskilled, or have skills that even if put to work are not likely to provide wages sufficient to avoid some kind of additional help.

2. Trying to substitute social services. In the early 1960s the major thrust of welfare reform was to provide professional help for those on welfare. It was believed that with this kind of assistance those in need could become able to take care of themselves. For example, if the problem appeared to stem from illness, a caseworker was to see to it that adequate health care was provided, or if a family was about to lose its breadwinner because of a marital dispute, a caseworker would be assigned to see what could be done to resolve the conflict and keep the family together.

The difficulty, however, is that there are not enough trained caseworkers to provide help for all those on relief. Even more discouraging is that experiments in which one group received intensified caseworker

[18]Michael Harrington, *The Other America* (Penguin, 1963), pp. 23–24.

[19]Quoted in Steiner, *The State of Welfare*, p. 1.

[20]Quoted in Daniel P. Moynihan, *The Politics of a Guaranteed Income: The Nixon Administration and the Family Assistance Plan* (Random House, 1973), p. 225.

services and another group merely received welfare payments demonstrated that at the end of the period the former group was not any less dependent on welfare than the latter.

3. Trying to increase the political influence of the poor. Strayer has written, "As the political power and the political resources of the affected public in the area of poverty and ghetto problems are minimal, likewise their success in generating remedial action is minimal. . . . Those who need to use government the most so as to regulate the environment, are the least able to do so."[21]

To correct this condition, a primary thrust of President Johnson's War on Poverty was to involve the poor in working out community action programs, to create structures outside of the regular channels that the poor could use to make their claims for a more adequate share of governmental services, to provide funds for legal assistance to protect rights against landlords and welfare agencies, and to mobilize the poor for political action.

There is little doubt that the War on Poverty did enhance the political voice of the poor, especially in the urban centers, and the formation of groups such as the National Welfare Rights Organization has added new forces to the political scene. As one congressional aide commented about community action agencies created by the Economic Opportunity Act of 1964, "We've funded a monster in community action. The programs are a bunch of Boston Tea Parties all around the country. They're creating a third force."[22] On the other side, as Daniel P. Moynihan has pointed out, "The apparent function of many of these programs as they actually came into being was to raise the level of perceived and validated discontent among poor persons within the social system . . . without improving the conditions of life of the poor in anything like a comparable degree."[23]

4. Trying to increase the cash income available to the very poor. These reforms, the most recent, involve some kind of income maintenance program such as a family allowance, a negative income tax, or a guaranteed minimum annual income.[24] Here the emphasis is on providing those in need with more dollars. More about these programs later.

Forty years of experimentation, tinkering, and development have brought us a system that reflects all these several approaches and more. What is the national government doing now?

[21]John Adrian Strayer, "The American Policy Process and the Problems of the Ghetto," *Western Political Quarterly* (March 1971), pp. 50–51.

[22]Quoted in *Time* (May 13, 1966), p. 29.

[23]"The Professors and the Poor," in *A Commentary Report* (Commentary, 1970), p. 12.

[24]Income Maintenance Programs, *Hearings* Before the Subcommittee on Fiscal Policy of the Joint Economic Committee, 90th Cong., 2nd sess., Vol. 1, June 1968.

SOCIAL INSURANCE

The least controversial aspects of the social welfare system in the United States are the several social insurance programs, programs which Steiner refers to as "subtle relief" in contrast to "crude relief."[25] These programs are available to those who are covered not on the basis of need, but on the basis of legal right as insurance against the risks of unemployment, old age, sickness, or disability.

Unemployment insurance This system is operated jointly by the national and state governments. Congress levies on all employers of four or

[25]Steiner, *The State of Welfare*, Ch. 1.

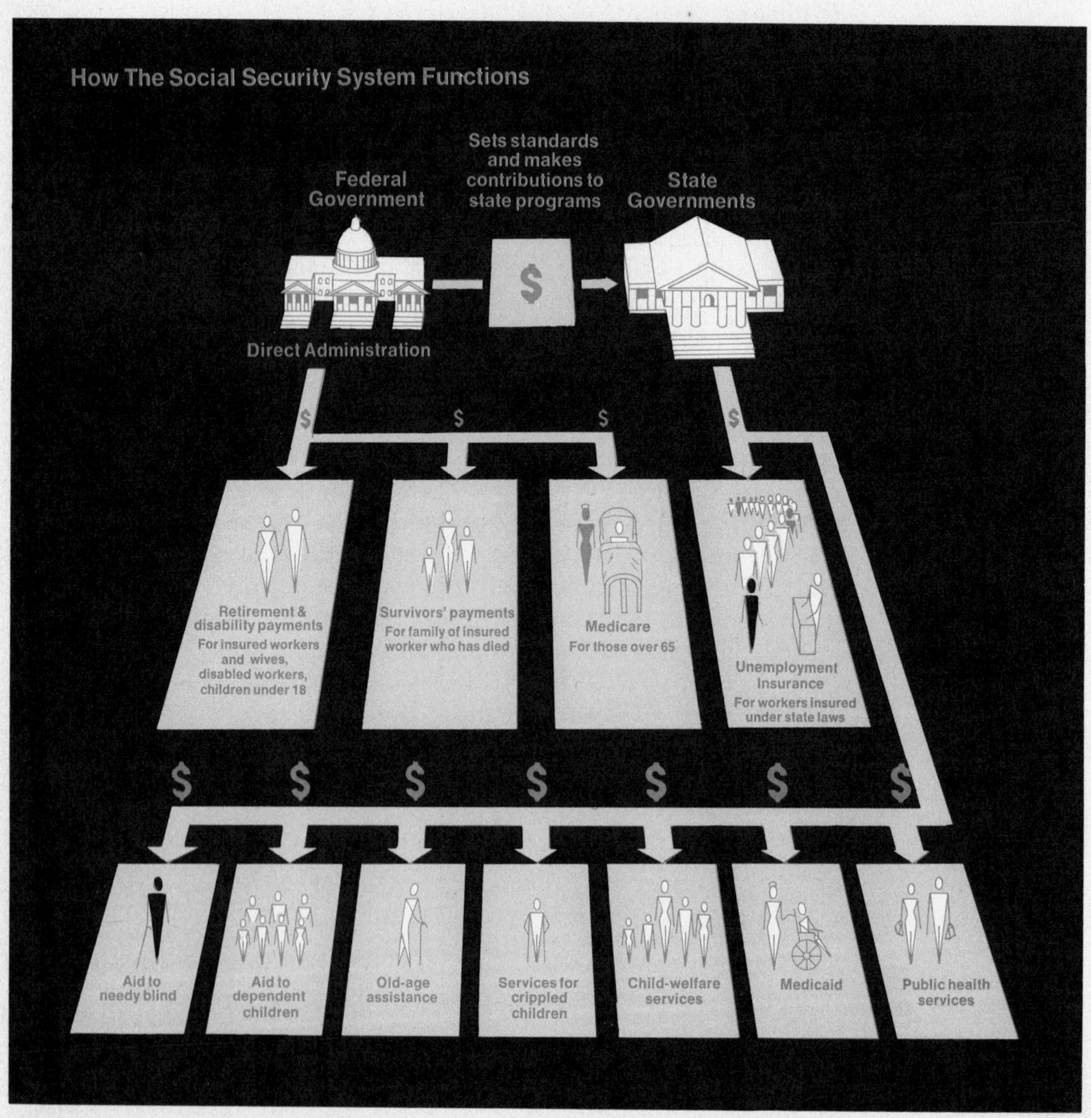

more a payroll tax. However, if an employer contributes to a state unemployment program that meets federal standards, he may deduct from his federal payroll tax all that he pays to the state fund, provided it is no more than 90 percent of his federal tax. A state could refuse to participate, but none has done so because its employers would have to pay the tax anyway and its unemployed workers could secure no benefits.

About half the states cover firms with fewer than four workers, and Congress has extended unemployment benefits to federal civilian employees and servicemen and made them available to employees of nonprofit organizations, including state institutions of higher education. Congress in 1970 made a further extension of coverage to include farm workers on large farms. By the mid-1970s, 74 percent of the working population was covered by some kind of unemployment insurance. (About thirteen million remained unprotected, including most farm workers, domestic workers, state and local government employees, the self-employed, and, in half the states, employees of firms that have fewer than four workers.) Railway workers are covered under a separate system administered by the Federal Railroad Retirement Board.

The national government helps defray administrative costs, but each state administers its own program subject to federal standards. The money collected by each state is deposited to that state's account in the United States Treasury. From this fund each state pays benefits to workers who report to state public employment agencies and are willing and able to work, but for whom there are no jobs. Each state sets its own scale of benefits and determines who is eligible to receive them.

Amendments adopted in the 1970s to the unemployment compensation program provide federal funds to extend the period of unemployment benefits during periods when national unemployment rates remain high for an extended period of time.

Federal-state operation of unemployment insurance keeps it flexible, but is also results in benefits varying considerably among the states. Administrative services in some states are less efficient than in others, and there is variation in the extent to which a state effectively gets benefits to those who are entitled to them. The Manpower Administration in the Department of Labor attempts to coordinate efforts among the states to place jobless workers.

Old-age, Survivors', and Medicare Insurance Unlike unemployment insurance, these risks are covered by a nationwide contributory system into which employers and employees each pay a certain amount.

The system pays men and women sixty-two years of age or older monthly retirement benefits that vary in accordance with the worker's contributions and the number of persons in his family entitled to secondary benefits. (If the insured has a wife sixty years old or older or a disabled husband fifty or older or dependent children or disabled children, the family receives secondary benefits.) Full benefits are paid between the ages of sixty-two and seventy-two only if the recipients are not earning more than a certain amount, presently $2400, a year from jobs covered by social security. (Income from dividends, interest, rents, and annuities is not counted.) After age seventy-two a person is entitled to retirement benefits regardless of his wages. Survivors' benefits for spouses, dependent parents, and children include a lump sum of money and monthly payments.

In 1965, after intensive debate, Congress added medical benefits for those sixty-five years of age or older. *Medicare,* as it is called, consists of two separate but related provisions. Hospital payments, nursing-home care, certain kinds of home nursing care, and outpatient services are financed by an addition to the social security tax which is noted separately on worker's withholding slips so that everyone may see where his money is going. The funds then go into a trust fund separate from other social security funds—a concession to quell the fears of those who felt that Medicare might threaten the soundness of the entire Social Security System. Participation of the two million people sixty-five or older who are not covered by social security is financed by a general revenue.

Doctors' fees, mental hospital care, and a number of other health services are also available under Medicare through a voluntary payment of a monthly premium. The government matches the amount of the premium from general revenues. A person does not have to be covered by social security to participate in the voluntary medical insurance plan.

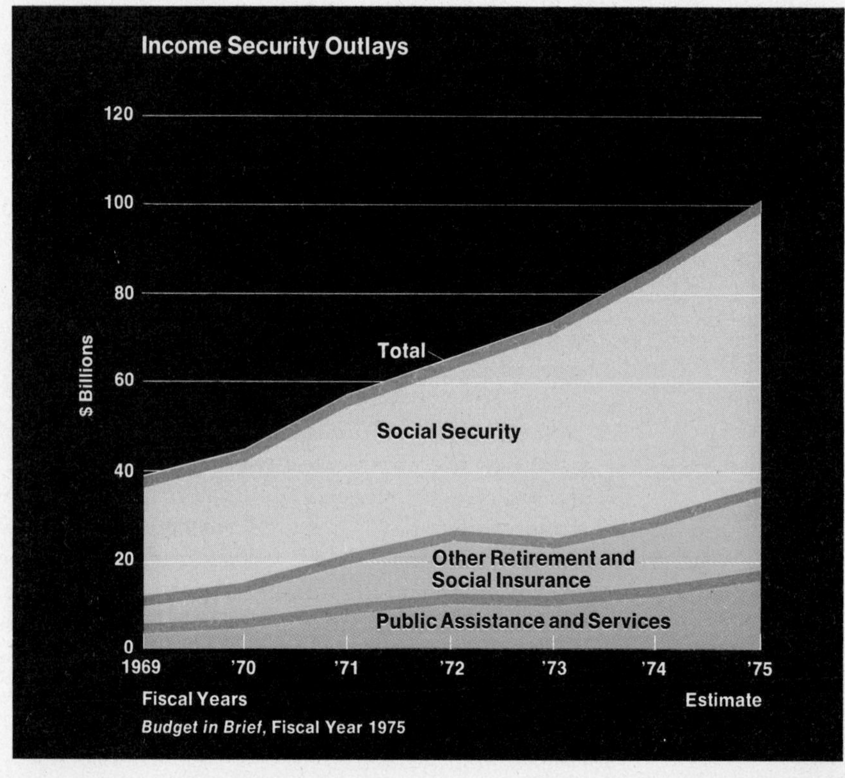

Budget in Brief, Fiscal Year 1975

Retirement, survivors', and medicare insurance now covers almost all workers, either on a mandatory or on a permissive basis. The only major category not covered on a mandatory basis is public employees, many of whom have their own retirement systems. The fact that the program has been broadened extensively under both Republican and Democratic administrations suggests that the basic system is now outside the area of party battle. There is much agreement that the system should be extended to cover other risks—for example, medical care for those under sixty-five—a proposal we will discuss later in this chapter.

Toward a guaranteed income?

At the time the Social Security System was inaugurated in 1935, there were millions of people for whom the insurance benefits were of little help. So the national government also made available substantial grants to the states to help make welfare payments to certain needy persons. That there would always be some who would need welfare—those too handicapped to work, for example—was anticipated, but it was expected that, with the return of prosperity and the build-up of social security insurance benefits, the federal government in time could retire from the welfare field and leave to the states the burden of providing assistance to the blind, the handicapped, and orphans.[26] This has not been so!

In good times as well as bad, one out of every nineteen Americans receives some kind of public assistance. Unemployment insurance is of little help to a person who is too unskilled to get a job or to earn enough for his family to live on; old-age insurance is not sufficient for those who have no other resources. And a mother with small children finds it difficult when her husband dies or deserts her, especially if she lacks a basic education, to support her family.

AID FOR FAMILIES WITH DEPENDENT CHILDREN

The fastest growing, most costly, and most controversial of these programs is Aid for Families with Dependent Children. A dependent child, defined by federal law, is one under eighteen who has been deprived of parental support but who is living with the other parent or with a close relative. AFDC helps about six and one-half million children and two and one-half million adults. The program's aim is to keep together families with children under eighteen despite the death, disability, or desertion of the breadwinner. Many critics have charged that because families with fathers are not eligible for assistance, AFDC encourages fathers to desert so that their wives and children may receive help; the

[26]Gilbert Y. Steiner, *Social Insecurity: The Politics of Welfare* (Rand McNally, 1966), p. 21; Edgar May, *The Wasted Americans* (Harper, 1964).

program has also been charged with encouraging immorality and breeding persons for whom welfare becomes a way of life. Some states have attempted to deny assistance to families where the mother is unwed, where there is a man living in the house, where a family has just moved to the state, or where it is headed by an alien. But Congress and, more important, the Supreme Court have ruled against such restrictions on AFDC. The Court has even ruled that a recipient may not have welfare taken away without first being provided with a hearing in which the state indicates why the recipient should be rendered ineligible and gives him or her an opportunity to confront any adverse witnesses.[27]

Congress has been hospitable to amendments requiring mothers of children over six years old to participate in a job-training or work program to qualify for federally assisted welfare. To this end Congress has increased federal grants to provide child care centers and has exempted from taxation a certain percentage of a mother's income so that she is not penalized by loss of assistance because of earning a salary. The trouble is that nearly half of AFDC mothers have gone no further than the eighth grade in school; and, as Steiner has pointed out, even if AFDC children under six years of age were given a place in every licensed day care facility in the country, there would still be one million of such AFDC children left over. "After a few years," he concludes, "it will inevitably be discovered that work-training and day-care have had little effect on the number of welfare dependents and no depressing effect on public relief costs. Some new solution will then be proposed, but the more realistic approach would be to accept the need for more welfare and to reject continued fantasizing about day-care and 'workfare' as miracle cures."[28]

In contrast to AFDC, which requires applicants to demonstrate a need before they are qualified to receive help, are other "welfare-type" programs such as aid to student housing. As a result of this federal program, thousands of college students secure subsidized rent whether they are in need or not.

A MINIMUM INCOME FOR MANY

Effective in 1974, the federal government guaranteed a minimum income to Americans at least sixty-five years old, and to the blind and disabled *of any age.* This guarantee is an *absolute right.* An eligible individual may receive $146 a month, and a couple both of whom are eligible will receive $219 per month. This program replaces state-administered programs of assistance to the aged, blind, and disabled. About 4.6 million aged and 1.6 million blind or disabled people will be covered. This program, called the Supplemental Security Income Pro-

[27]*Goldberg v. Kelly*

[28]*The State of Welfare*, p. 74.

"If God hadn't wanted there to be poor people, He would have made us rich people more generous."

Drawing by Dana Fradon; © 1973. The New Yorker Magazine, Inc.

gram, is administered by the Social Security Administration. Its money, however, will come not from the Social Security Trust Fund, but from general funds of the U.S. Treasury. Is this income guarantee a major step toward a universal cash income guarantee? Some people think so. "Supplemental Security Income, for the first time, makes the cash income of millions of Americans—the aged, the blind, the disabled—a *legal obligation* of the Federal Government. For a bewildering and unfair variety of state rules to decide who is 'needy' enough to be helped, SSI substitutes objective and national standards of income and resources. In philosphy, procedures, and financing, the new law represents a quiet revolution in American welfare."[29]

Promoting equality

Welfare politics and welfare policies have remained high on the public agenda for more than a decade. Improvements have been realized. The number of families living below the poverty line has been reduced substantially since 1964. The number of substandard housing units has also been lowered markedly. More and more minority persons have entered and graduated from colleges. Moreover, equity and dignity are stated at high levels to be the primary goals of welfare policy. So there have been many successes. But the welfare and antipoverty offensives have always been very controversial. And many measures once proposed have been

[29]Vincent J. and Vee Burke, "The Minimum Income Revolution," *The Progressive* (December 1973), p. 36.

allowed to die, were later scuttled, or are still on the Congressional agenda for action. The beleaguered War on Poverty, the unsuccessful battle to pass a family assistance program, and the campaign for national health insurance are illustrative.

THE WAR ON POVERTY

The Economic Opportunity Act of 1964 created the Office of Economic Opportunity, within the Executive Office of the president, as a coordinating command post to distribute federal funds to other agencies and to operate a variety of programs through its own staff. Each program was aimed at a specific poverty-creating condition or a special clientele. Among the more important of these programs were:

1. *Operation Headstart.* Designed to get preschool children into school before the impact of a disadvantaged environment so disabled them that they would be unable to profit from formal instruction when they reach the age of five or six.

2. *Neighborhood Youth Corps.* For teenagers who dropped out, or were in danger of dropping out, of high school. Operated by the Department of Labor, the corps provided work experiences after school hours and during the summer.

3. *Community Action Programs.* The most controversial of the programs, this was an attempt to overcome what the drafters of the act thought to be the basic weaknesses of welfare programs—fragmentation and middle-class bias. To overcome these deficiencies, the federal government made grants to local community action groups covering most of the costs for coordinated programs "that are developed and administered with maximum feasible participation of the residents of the areas and members of the group for whose benefit the Act was passed."

In its first ten years, the Economic Opportunity Act was subjected to intense criticism from many quarters. Some charged that the programs did not call for enough participation by the poor and provided inadequate funds for a serious attack on the overwhelming problems of chronic poverty. Others said the act was used to support unsavory "rip-offs." Still others contended that much of the federal money never really benefited the poor for whom it was intended.

The Nixon Administration sought in vain to close down the Office of Economic Opportunity. The War on Poverty had become unpopular with many (including even some at the White House) before the end of the Johnson Administration. Critics noted that too many programs were organized too fast, promised too much, and in the end achieved too little. The gap between promise and performance soured many of the agency's early sponsors. Too, there was often preciously little hard evidence to prove that its programs were helping to eliminate the causes of poverty.[30]

In 1975 the OEO was still in existence. Some of its programs, however, were assumed by other departments. Thus, the migrant worker program was delegated to the Department of Labor and health projects to HEW. The Legal Services Corporation was created as an independent agency to carry on the controversial but highly praised legal-aid programs previously financed through the OEO. But if the once-proclaimed and widely heralded promise of "an end to poverty" in America plainly had not been realized, the battle was still being waged.

FAMILY ASSISTANCE PROGRAM

President Nixon for a time made a minimum or guaranteed income plan his top domestic priority. "The present system [of welfare]," he charged, "has become a monstrous, consuming outrage—an outrage against the community, against the taxpayer, and particularly against the children it is supposed to help."[31] He proposed that the bulk of the existing welfare system, with its differing benefit levels, eligibility rules, and procedures, be abolished and replaced with a federally administered plan. The federal government would provide benefits on a uniform basis ensuring that every family, including those with working fathers, received at least a minimum income (for a family of four, the proposed figure was $2,400.) As earned income increased, federal assistance would be gradually reduced. States could supplement federal grants if they wished, but would not be required to do so. Families headed by an incapacitated adult or by women with children under six would be paid full benefits, but refusal by an eligible breadwinner to take work or work training would result in an $800-a-year reduction in benefits.

By late 1972 the Nixon Family Assistance Plan was dead. Nixon had termed it "the most important single piece of social legislation in the decades." What had gone wrong? Some objected because of the low federal payments, the stringent work and training requirements, and the fact that the states need not supplement federal payments. Others objected because they believed that the cost of including the working poor eventually would require extraordinarily large budgetary outlays.

The measure passed easily in the House of Representatives, but it failed to make any serious headway in the Senate. Divisive ideological conflict took hold. "Within the Senate Finance Committee liberals flayed the bill as inadequate and inhumane, using as their standard a

[30]See Daniel P. Moynihan, *Maximum Feasible Misunderstanding: Community Action in the War on Poverty* (Free Press, 1969); and Robert A. Levine, *The Poor Ye Need Not Have With You: Lessons from the War on Poverty* (M.I.T. Press, 1970).

[31]State of the Union Message, January 22, 1971. *Congressional Quarterly Weekly Report* (January 29, 1971), p. 263.

Copyright © 1967 The Chicago Sun-Times.
Reproduced by courtesy of Wil-Jo Associates, Inc. and Bill Mauldin.

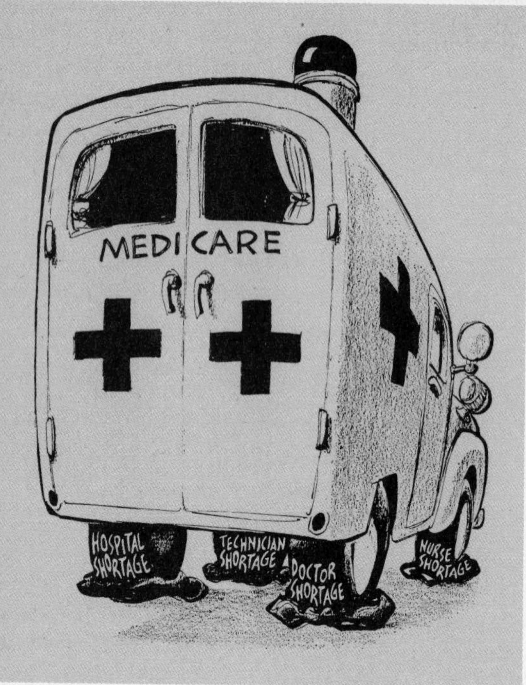

generous income guarantee which the majority of American voters would surely have rejected. The conservative senators on the commitee . . . divested FAP's pretensions to consistent welfare reform. They dissected the process of compromise by which conflicting program features were fused and structural reform frustrated. 'Work incentives?' exclaimed Senator Williams [of Delaware] 'what work incentives?' "[32]

Nixon gradually abandoned his commitment to income maintenance. He was unable to sell the whole program to a majority within his own party. The idea of federalizing welfare and beginning a nationally financed income floor for all apparently was too bold a measure for most Republicans. It is possible, too, that some liberal Democrats resented a Republican stealing credit by proposing their kind of policy. Whatever the reasons it appeared that for the moment the existing system would be essentially kept in operation. Our complex welfare system may be "patchworky," but it does serve millions of people, and (or so many specialists now feel) improvements can be made within the present categories. Even so, there doubtless will be renewed efforts in the next few years to reformulate, recast, and enact some kind of negative income tax or guaranteed income.

[32]Theodore R. Marmor and Martin Rein, "Reforming the Welfare Mess: The Fate of the Family Assistance Plan, 1969–72," in Allan P. Sindler, ed., *Policy and Politics in America* (Little, Brown, 1973), p. 19. For another view, see Daniel P. Moynihan, *Politics of a Guaranteed Income.*

PAYING THE HOSPITAL BILLS

Health care has become one of the nation's most controversial issues. Costs for health care are rising steeply. The average family spends well in excess of $600 a year on health care—the largest percentage going for hospitalization costs. Most rich people receive better care than do most poor people. Few Americans are protected adequately against catastrophic illnesses.

What about the multitude of insurance programs? Don't they cover most people? Ninety percent of families with incomes over $10,000 are covered. But about 50 percent of families earning less than $7,000 do not have hospital insurance coverage. Most of the population 65 and over is covered by Medicare, and a substantial portion of poor families benefits from state-run Medicaid programs. However, state-set benefits vary widely. Ironically, part of the steep rise in medical care costs is related to the growth of insurance coverage. Economists point out that when a third party is paying most of the bill, neither the patient nor the doctor is encouraged to economize.

Hence, the battle to enact a national health insurance system has become very intense and serious. National health insurance programs are by no means new. At least as early as 1914 labor leaders pressed state legislatures to enact them. Labor leaders tried again in 1935 and 1943—this time at the national level. President Truman pushed for a limited

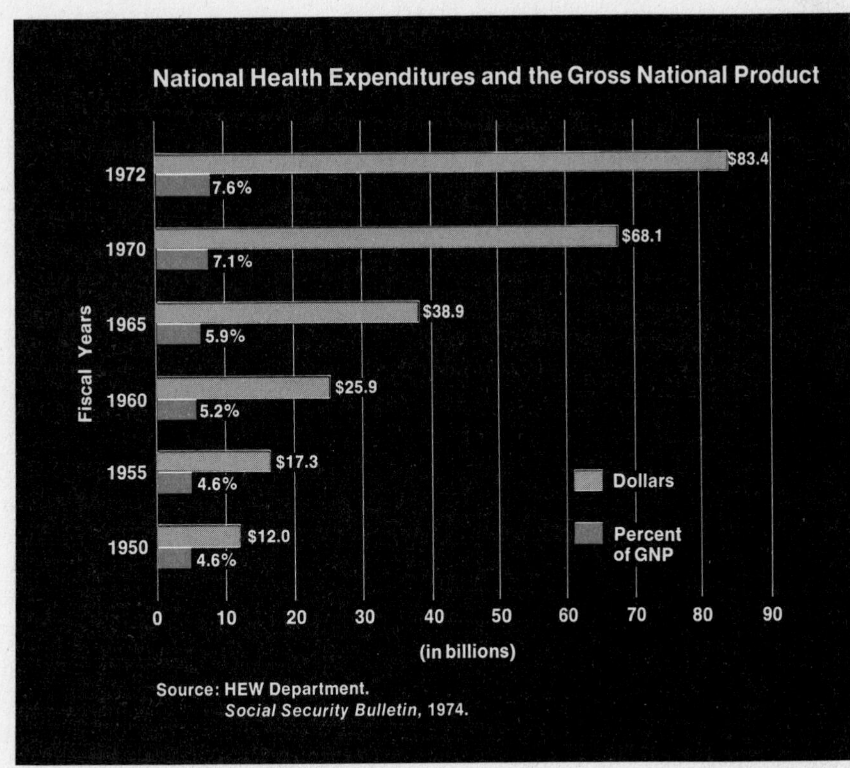

national health insurance scheme in 1948, but the measure died in congressional committee.

Is the time coming when a family's medical bills will be paid by national health insurance? Very likely. Numerous plans are under consideration. But fundamental differences among proponents and the lack of any groundswell of public support for any of the various proposals have combined to forestall passage.

According to one close observer, most proponents of national health insurance now agree on the following three objectives:[33]

1. To cover low-income people so that they can have access to needed care without financial hardship.

2. To protect all persons, including the middle and upper-income, against catastrophic expense that could take a large share of their income.

3. To increase incentives for using preventive medicine and managing health institutions efficiently.

The American Medical Association's proposal is commonly known as *medicredit.* AMA's plan would have the government pay 100 percent of the part of the insurance company premium allocated to "catastrophic" benefits. The government would also pay part of the premium for basic benefits—ranging from 100 percent for the poor to 10 percent for the well-off. Government contributions toward insurance premiums would come from general tax revenues. And this plan would ensure that medical expenses would not exceed 10 percent of the family's taxable income in any year.

A White House plan as proposed by the Nixon-Ford Administrations provides for unlimited hospital and physician services; 100 days of post-hospital extended care; 100 home health care visits; outpatient prescription drugs, children's dental, eye, and ear care, and limited mental health care services. The administration's bill would mandate the creation of a privately financed program for the bulk of the population. The administration plan favors a limited federal role and primary roles for state governments and the insurance industry. Private insurance firms would supply the policies that would enable most citizens to be covered under one of the following possible options: (1) most wage-earners could enroll, as many already do, in group policies provided by their employers; (2) Medicare would continue to provide for the elderly; and (3) for those ineligible for either of those approaches, insurance firms would make coverage available at rates related to enrollees' income, by arrangement with state authorities. The White House plan would ensure that no family would have to pay in excess of $1,500 for medical expenses in any year. Some people feel that this proposal's

[33]Alice M. Rivlin, "Agreed: Here Comes National Health Insurance—Question: What Kind?" *New York Times Magazine* (July 21, 1974), p. 35.

chief defect lies in its financing, especially that provision of a private head tax that would fall more heavily on low-wage earners than high-wage earners.

Congressman Wilbur Mills and Senator Edward Kennedy are the authors of a third major plan. Their plan calls for virtually compulsory coverage and for covering a worker continuously whether he moves from job to job or becomes unemployed. The Mills-Kennedy bill differs from the Nixon-Ford proposal in that it sets up a single federal health insurance program that would be administered by HEW's Social Security Administration. It would be financed by increased social security taxes. The government would collect from employers a 4 percent tax on every employee's pay check, and the rest would be paid by the employer. The self-employed and those with unearned income would pay a new tax. Welfare recipients would be handled under a separate formula. The Mills-Kennedy plan incorporates several features from both the White House plan and from a much more expensive labor-backed "liberal" plan.

Many state governors back the Mills-Kennedy plan, mindful of the tremendous costs states absorbed as a result of the Medicaid program. Medicaid, passed in 1965, grew rapidly from a $200 million program in 1966 to a massive endeavor that today finances the basic health care needs of about 30 million poor people at a cost to states of well over $4 billion. The states say that the responsibility to finance health insurance for all should be left to Washington. They do not mind a monitoring and planning function, so long as it is free of financial obligation.

By 1975 there were at least a dozen proposals for various health care programs before Congress. President Ford at one time had hoped to make some kind of health program one of his first achievements. Even the major insurance companies now find it is in their best interest to push for a limited national health insurance system. The battle lines are well drawn. Heated debates are taking place. Some plan seems likely to pass. And its adoption will mark another major development since the inauguration of federal welfare and insurance programs in 1935.

Other health care issues will be with us for a good many years. A new debate has arisen recently contending that the effectiveness of medical care is a lot less than presumed. Some feel that federal money spent on nutrition research, education, or environmental improvements would actually improve our medical condition more than money for hospitalization, drugs and doctors. These people believe strongly that a disproportionate amount of resources is given to *treating* rather than *preventing* diseases.

Housing and urban development

Since the Depression, the federal government has helped Americans rent or build decent housing. The FHA (Federal Housing Administration), by insuring mortgages, made it possible for persons of middle-income levels to buy homes. And the government, by guaranteeing (through the Federal Deposit Insurance Corporation) the savings accounts of depositors in savings and loan institutions, helped these institutions to provide mortgage funds to millions of Americans. But what of the other millions who are unable to purchase a home or pay rentals for a house or an apartment? What of urban decay? What of blacks who are trapped in ghettos?

Since 1937 the federal government has had a public housing program, which, working with local housing authorities, has made available more than 800,000 units for more than 2,500,000 people. But what Catherine Bauer wrote twenty years ago is still true today: "Public housing, after more than two decades, still drags along in a kind of limbo, continuously controversial, not dead but never more than half alive."[34] Public housing has been termed "high-rise slums for the poor" and "an improper environment for the raising of children." Tenants in public housing projects often do not like them, neighbors of the projects are often opposed to them. The destruction by city authorities of the huge Pruitt-Igoe complex in St. Louis in 1973 was an example of the ultimate disillusionment with traditional high-rise public housing projects. Many who live in suburbs do not want public housing in their neighborhoods; they fear reduction in property values and increased school taxes, and they want to remain segregated from black people.

Rent subsidies for the poor and scattered site location for public housing, instead of high-density projects, are the public housing reforms of the 1970s. It will be difficult to secure any considerable expansion of public housing, however, as long as governmental authority in the metropolitan areas is scattered among so many different agencies and suburbanites use their governments to keep public housing confined to the central cities. As more and more communities require a public referendum before accepting a public housing project, the obstacles to public housing become even greater. For these reasons many, including several HUD officials, now advocate that, instead of trying to provide subsidized housing, governments should make cash payments to the poor so they can compete for housing in the regular market.[35]

Congress also makes funds available to cities for urban renewal and rehabilitation. Cities are to acquire and clear slum properties, then resell the land to private builders who agree to develop it according to an approved plan. Federal grants and loans are also available to improve municipal services such as mass transit systems.

Urban renewal, despite some success, is criticized for replacing the slum homes of the poor with units that the poor cannot afford to rent or

[34]"The Dreary Deadlock of Public Housing," *Architectural Forum* (May 1957), p. 140, quoted in Steiner, *Social Insecurity*, pp. 134–35.

[35]See, for example, Henry J. Aaron, *Shelters and Subsidies* (Brookings Institution, 1972), Ch. 10.

buy. And whatever is being done is not enough, for slums are being created faster than they are being replaced. Until recently more housing units were being destroyed for highways and other civic projects than were being built. Federal laws now stipulate that no federal funds will be granted for any project that will displace persons from homes until the federal administrator is assured that assistance will be given to those displaced and that replacement homes will be found.

In 1966, through the Demonstration Cities and Metropolitan Development Act, Congress tried a new technique: a select number of cities (Model Cities) were invited to submit plans for federal support for a coordinated attack on certain target areas within the cities. The plans were to be developed with the aid of the people living in the areas concerned. This approach, similar to that of the War on Poverty, recognized past failures in which housing, education, transportation, and recreation were each approached in a segmented and uncoordinated fashion. It was hoped that a coordinated attack on all phases of the urban environment, especially one that involved the people, would result in more progress.

In 1968, Congress adopted the Housing and Urban Development Act, whose goal was to provide six million units of new or rehabilitated housing each year for ten years and to make these units available to those with low incomes. The act was an attempt to do for the poor what the FHA had done for those with middle incomes. By a variety of devices, the federal government subsidizes mortgage or rental payments so that persons with low incomes can afford to live in these units. The act is designed to provide not massive high-rise public housing buildings, but those that, from the outside, are indistinguishable from other houses and apartments.

By the mid-1970s, political debates in the housing area generally focused on two proposals. First, the idea of some kind of *housing allowance* for low-income families. Many problems remain to be ironed out before this is put into effect, but on grounds of both equity and efficiency this proposal was picking up support.[36] A second, and far more controversial plan, called for *opening up the suburbs.* One objective of this is to help save the inner cities from further decay. The premise is the need for economic integration in both the central cities and the suburbs. Thus the trick is to attract some middle and upper-middle households back to the cities while encouraging—through various government incentives to builders, communities, and poor people—modest dispersal of low-income families throughout the suburban area.

The current "trickle-down" process of providing housing for the poor, contends Anthony Downs, compels families with the lowest incomes and often the least competence to live concentrated together in our worst urban housing. This invites high rates of crime, vandalism, broken families, mental illness, delinquency, and drug addiction. To be

[36]See the discussion of it in Edward R. Fried, et al., *Setting National Priorities: The 1974 Budget* (Brookings Institution, 1973), pp. 138–45.

sure, many well-to-do suburbanites will question and oppose what Downs calls a strategy of dispersed economic integration. They will see it as a proposal to tax the middle income brackets to disperse "slums" to the suburbs. Yet his forecast of the probable benefits is likely to gain consideration. Opening up the suburbs, he says, would produce:

> **1.** Better access to expanding job opportunities for workers in low and moderate-income households—especially the unemployed.
>
> **2.** Greater opportunities for such households to upgrade themselves by moving into middle-income neighborhoods, thereby escaping from crisis ghetto conditions.
>
> **3.** Higher quality public schooling for children from low-income households who could attend schools dominated by children from middle-income households.
>
> **4.** Greater opportunity for the nation to reach its officially adopted goals for producing improved housing for low and moderate-income households.
>
> **5.** Fairer geographic distribution of the fiscal and social costs of dealing with metropolitan-area poverty.
>
> **6.** Less possibility of major conflicts in the future caused by confrontations between two spatially separate and unequal societies in metropolitan areas.[37]

People may well agree on the desirability of these benefits, but for the foreseeable future, there will be considerable disagreement on how to attain such goals.

Responsibility for administering housing programs is vested in the Department of Housing and Urban Development (HUD), which was established in 1965. HUD is still searching to develop its role. Its responsibilities are broader than housing, but it has yet to emerge as the principal focus for the federal government's attack on the urban crisis.

The welfare state?

A cataloging of the federal government's promotional activities could be continued almost indefinitely, if space and patience allowed. The government as promoter is not a new role; it is as old as the federal union itself. The intention was embodied in the preamble to the Constitution when it stated that one of the aims of "We the people" is to "promote the general welfare." We are now witnessing the latest of several surges of intense governmental concern with health, education, and welfare. But even these programs, extensive as they are, do not begin to tell the story of government promotional activities in recent

[37]Anthony Downs, *Opening Up the Suburbs: An Urban Strategy for America* (Yale, 1973), p. 26.

years. We have said nothing about the major debate over transportation programs, the now long-standing battles to secure more federal aid to education, development of new parks, river, and recreation areas, and a variety of projects to develop national growth and population distribution policies and to promote the arts and protect the natural beauty of the United States.

Many disagree with these efforts by the national government to improve the quality of life, to focus resources and attention on the problems of the poor, to improve the environment. They view with distaste the bureaucracy required for these programs, and they allege that the programs are ineffective interferences with individual initiative. But although most of these programs have been initiated under Democratic presidents, they have secured bipartisan support. Regardless of the party in power in Washington, these activities of the national government are destined to become more significant. The pressures are for more, not less, involvement by the national government, and the problems are becoming more overwhelming and not less so. (However, there is a countermovement for more state and local involvement, highlighted by the various revenue-sharing proposals.) The national welfare state seems to be a lasting part of the American society.

Chapter 25 The politics of taxing and spending

We have looked at two of the main methods by which government influences society—regulation and promotion. Through *regulation*, government lays down the rules that control what people may and may not do. Through *promotion*, government directly or indirectly advances the interests of certain groups. We have also looked at a third method, though more briefly, namely the *direct management* of certain enterprises such as handling the mail and developing nuclear energy. The government could allow a private company to process and deliver the mail, and it could regulate the company in the public interest, or susidize it, or both. Instead, the government itself took over the job long ago.

But perhaps the most important influence the government has upon the economy is the way in which it *taxes* and *spends* money. Enormous sums are involved; with a current national budget well over $300 billion, our government spends more than 20 percent of the GNP, more than one-fifth of the value of everything the country produces. Government has come to intervene in the economy in so many ways with such broad powers and diverse instruments of control that governmental leaders are to a very real extent economic leaders as well.

Tax and budgetary decisions are especially important because they determine in large measure the division of resources between public and private goods and the distribution of private resources among different families and individuals. Tax and budget choices determine the government's priorities. Will domestic spending be cut? Will national security and defense spending be increased? Ought we have tax reform or a tax rate increase? In short, the politics of taxing and spending centers about the questions of what we want to accomplish as a nation and who will actually bear the burden of paying for it.

By the middle of the 1970s the ability of the national government to control inflation without at the same time creating massive unemployment had become perhaps the most important question before the nation. A worldwide inflation, a change in balance of international economic power as the oil-producing nations began to accumulate billions, growing problems of international exchange, questions about the nature of international credit and banking mechanisms—these were the issues on the agendas of all the major nations. Obviously, the government of the United States, and most importantly, the president of the United States, could not escape the basic responsibility of trying to maintain the economic health of the nation.

Many have hailed the trend that gives the government of the United States such an important role in managing this country's (and the world's) economic well-being. Others deplore it because they consider it a dangerous drift toward totalitarianism. Whether desirable or undesirable, the government cannot escape the responsibility of managing the economy.

Raising money

Big government is expensive. Federal, state, and local governments spend almost $450 billion yearly. This is almost a third of the income of all Americans; in short, our governments pay out about 30 cents of every dollar we earn. The national government is the biggest spender of all. In recent years Washington has disbursed more than all state and local governments combined.

Where does all this money come from? The federal government gets most of its funds from taxes and the rest from loans, commercial revenues from governmental enterprises, income from special fees and fines, and grants and gifts.

LEVYING TAXES

"In this world," Benjamin Franklin once said, "nothing is certain but death and taxes." Tax collecting is one of the oldest activities of government. Indeed, one of the few contacts that many people in earlier societies had with government was through the tax collector. He was the dread figure who symbolized the demands and authority of some far-off ruler. Putting power over taxation into the hands of the people was a landmark in the rise of self-government. "No taxation without representation" has been the war cry not only of early Americans but, in effect, of the people in countries the world over.

The new Constitution in 1787 clearly provided that Congress "shall have power to lay and collect taxes, duties, imposts, and excises." But duties and excise taxes had to be levied uniformly throughout the United States; direct taxes had to be apportioned among the states according to population; and no tax could be levied on articles exported from any state. Except during the Civil War, the federal government for a century relied on the tariff for most of its revenue. This hidden tax—which many people mistakenly thought to be a tax on foreigners—fluctuated with the rise and fall of trade and tariff levels. Congress supplemented these taxes with excise taxes on the manufacture or sale of certain goods, and in 1894 an income tax law was enacted (such a tax had been used during the Civil War but given up shortly afterwards). The 1894 tax was not drastic—only 2 percent on all incomes over $4,000—but it seemed a portent of worse things to come. One fiery opponent of the bill scorned it on the floor of the Senate as "an attempt to array the rich against the poor, the poor against the rich . . . Socialism, communism, *devilism.*" The next year, in *Pollock v. Farmers' Loan and Trust Co.*, the Supreme Court declared the tax measure unconstitutional on the ground that it was a direct tax and therefore had to be apportioned among the states according to population. Twenty years later, in 1915, the Sixteenth Amendment was adopted authorizing Congress "to lay and collect taxes on incomes, from whatever source derived, without apportionment among the several States, and without regard to any census or enumeration."

Raising money is only one important objective of taxation; regulation and, more recently, promotion of economic growth and controlling inflation are others. Taxation as a device to promote economic growth will be discussed later. In a broad sense, all taxation regulates human behavior; for example, a graduated income tax has a leveling influence on incomes, and a tariff act affects foreign trade. More specifically, Congress has used its taxing power to prevent or regulate certain practices. Years ago, Congress laid a 10 percent tax on the circulation of notes by state banks, immediately putting an end to such issues.

Today federal taxes are as follows:

1. *Income taxes on individuals.* Levies on the income of individuals account for more than 40 percent of the federal government's tax revenue. Originally set at a low rate, the income tax was greatly increased during World War I and went to new heights during World War II and the Korean conflict. Over the years the income tax has grown increasingly complex as Congress has responded to claims for differing kinds

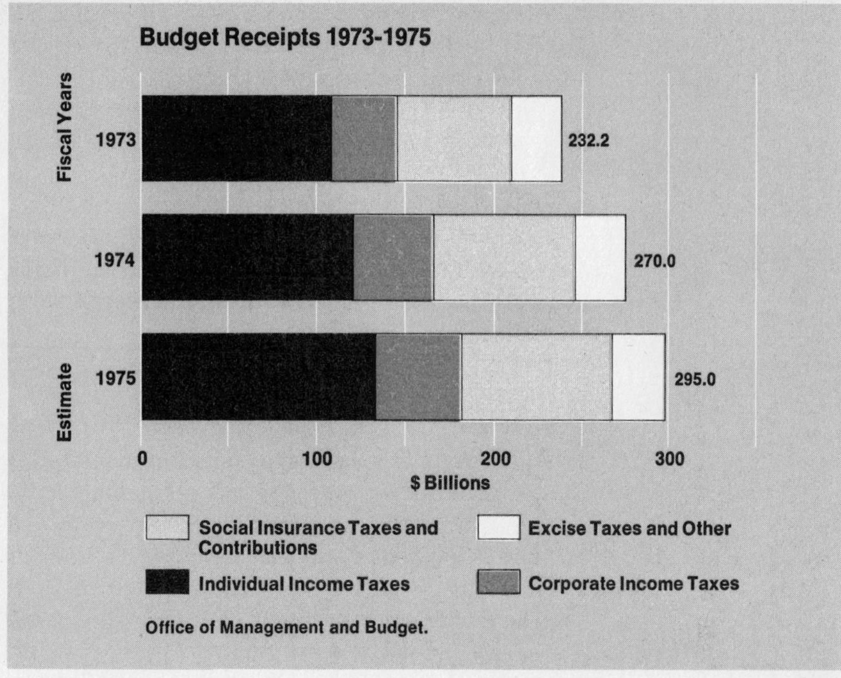

of exemptions and rates, but the tax has one great advantage in its flexibility. The schedule of rates can be raised or lowered in order to stimulate or restrain economic activity. The income tax is moderately progressive. People with high incomes generally pay larger fractions of their income than lower-income people, though many of the wealthy do benefit from tax loopholes.[1]

2. *Income taxes on corporations.* These account for about 16 percent of the national government's tax dollar. As late as 1942, corporate income taxes amounted to more than individual income taxes, but returns from the latter increased more rapidly during World War II.

3. *Social insurance or payroll taxes.* This is the second largest and most rapidly rising source of federal revenue. From a mere $4 billion in 1950 this tax has grown to raise nearly $90 billion in fiscal year 1975. These are the moneys collected mainly from our payroll deductions to finance the Social Security System and related insurance programs that were discussed in the previous chapter. They are, economists point out, highly regressive; low-income people generally pay larger fractions of their income than do high-income people. "The rapidly increasing importance of payroll taxes as a source of federal revenue means that

[1]See Philip M. Stern, *The Rape of the Taxpayer* (Random House, 1973); and Joseph Pechman, *Federal Tax Policy*, rev. ed. (Brookings Institution, 1971).

low-income earners bear a growing share of the federal tax burden. The growth in the share of payroll taxes has been offset by a decline in excise and corporation profits taxes. . . ."[2]

4. *Excise taxes.* Federal taxes on liquor, tobacco, gasoline, telephones, air travel, and other so-called luxury items are scheduled to be reduced in stages until they are eliminated. However, the date for the elimination of these taxes is continually postponed by Congress, so that they still account for about 6 percent of total tax revenue each year.

5. *Customs duties.* Though no longer the main source of federal income, these taxes provided in recent years an annual yield of more than $3 billion.

THE POLITICS AND MACHINERY OF TAXATION

When a young law assistant once commiserated with Justice Holmes on the taxes he had to pay, the old gentleman replied, "With taxes I buy civilization." Most of us are less philosophical. We complain that our tax load is too heavy and that someone else is not carrying his fair share. People with large incomes naturally grumble about income taxes as high as 70 percent or more of their net income. Low-income people

[2]Edward R. Fried, et al., *Setting National Priorities: The 1974 Budget* (Brookings Institution, 1973), p. 7.

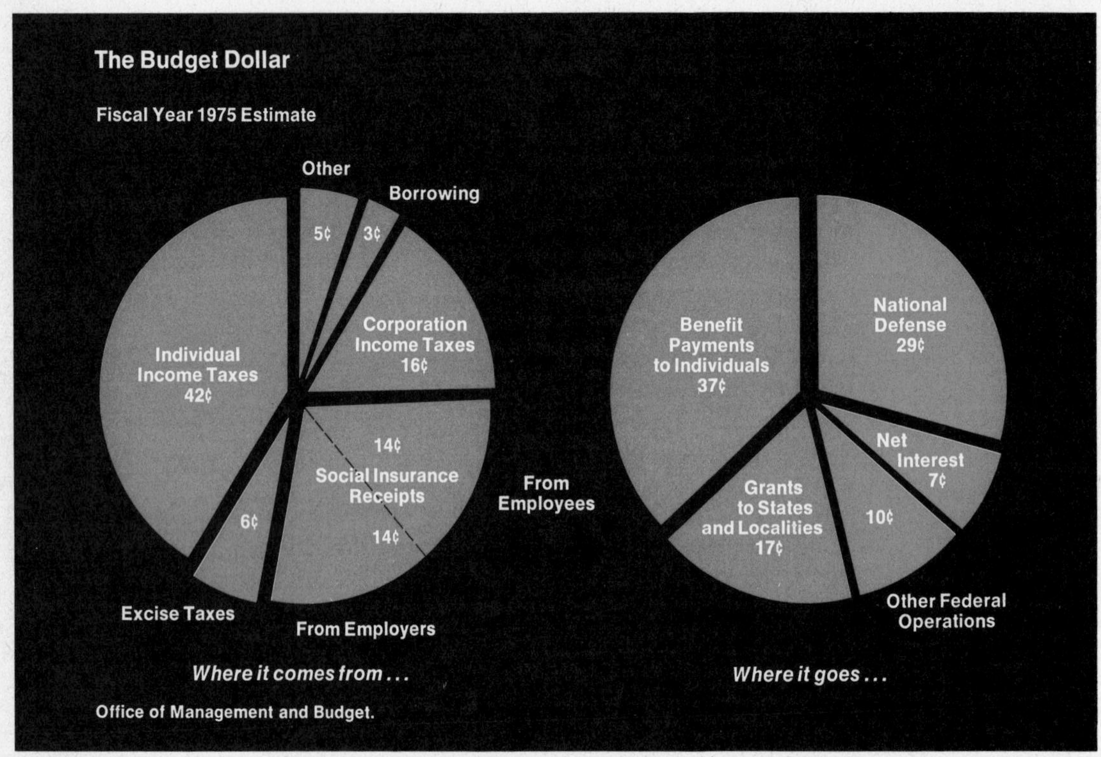

Office of Management and Budget.

point out that even a low tax may deprive them of the necessities of life. People in the middle-income brackets feel that their plight is worst of all—their incomes are not high but their taxes are.

What is the best type of tax? Some say the *graduated income tax*, because it is relatively easy to collect, hits hardest those who are most able to pay, and hardly touches those at the bottom of the income ladder. Others argue that *excise taxes* are the fairest, because they are paid by people who are spending money for goods—especially luxury goods—and thus obviously have money to spare. Furthermore, by discouraging people from buying expensive goods, excise taxes have a desirable deflationary effect in time of rising prices. On the other hand, excise taxes are more expensive to collect than income taxes, and in some cases, such as the tax on tobacco, they may hit the poor the hardest. Most controversial of all taxes is the *general sales tax*, which resembles the excise tax except that it is levied against the sales of all goods. Labor and liberal organizations denounce this form of tax as regressive—that is, it hurts the poor person more than the rich person, because the former uses all his earnings to buy goods, whereas the latter may devote more of his income to buying personal services or to savings. Proponents of the sales tax stress its anti-inflationary effect and point to its successful use in a number of states.

A recent tax bill illustrated the wide impact of taxes on a variety of individuals and groups. Testifying on proposed tax changes before a congressional committee, 138 witnesses expressed their views; and scores of briefs were submitted. The printed testimony covered more than sixteen hundred pages. Business representatives opposed new taxes on corporations. Small businessmen complained that existing taxes favored big business. Spokesmen for tobacco growers, transportation interests, the wine and spirits industry, movies, the legitimate theater, candymakers, telephone companies, and bowling alley proprietors argued that the proposed tax would discriminate against them. Labor demanded a lighter burden for low-income groups and higher taxes on business. Unorganized workers and consumers however, were not represented.

Although the Constitution provides that all revenue bills must be initiated in the House of Representatives, it is usually the president who originates tax legislation. With the help of tax experts on his staff and in the Treasury Department, he draws up a tax program not only designed to meet the government's revenue needs for the coming fiscal year but also taking into consideration the current and projected state of the economy. Often the representatives of interest groups are consulted while the bill is being formulated. Then the president submits his tax program to Congress, often along with his budget message. The powerful House Ways and Means Committee next holds hearings on the bill; administration representatives, headed by the secretary of the treasury, usually lead off the parade of witnesses, followed by representatives of interested groups, taxation experts, and others. Following committee consideration, tax measures go through Congress in much the same manner as other bills. Although the Senate cannot initiate tax legislation, it refuses to take a backseat in tax matters. It often differs with the House and forces extensive changes of bills coming from the lower chamber. Sometimes Congress refuses to follow the president's recommendations and works out a tax measure largely on its own.[3]

The Treasury Department has the job of collecting the taxes levied by Congress. One of the original departments set up in 1789 and headed by the second-highest-ranking secretary, this department today is a large agency employing about 116,000 people. The actual tax-collecting job falls mainly to the Internal Revenue Service. Fifty-eight district directors are located throughout the country, and taxes are paid into district offices rather than directly to Washington. The service takes in over $150 billion a year at the cost of less than 50 cents for each $100 in returns. Customs duties are collected by the Treasury Department's Bureau of Customs, which maintains ports of entry, inspects the discharge of cargo, assesses the value of merchandise, and through the services of the United States Coast Guard, prevents smuggling.

UNCLE SAM, BORROWER

When a person is suddenly faced with expenses too heavy to meet out of his regular income, he may have to borrow money. The same is true of government. During military and economic crises, the federal government has gone heavily in debt. It borrowed $23 billion during World War I, about $13 billion more during the 1930s, and over $200 billion more during World War II. Between crises, the government has tried to pay off its debts, but progress has been slow. By 1975 the gross federal debt was more than $500 billion.

Borrowing costs money. The federal government can borrow at a relatively low rate—because no security is safer than a government bond. Nevertheless, the federal debt is so huge today that the interest alone is approaching $30 billion a year. The size of the debt and of the interest payments alarms many Americans. How long can we allow the debt to grow at this staggering rate? Two considerations must be kept in mind. In the first place, the government owes most of the money to its own people rather than to foreign governments or persons; and second, the economic strength and resources of the country are more significant than the size of the public debt.

How does the government borrow money? The Constitution says that Congress may "borrow money on the credit of the United States"; it puts no limit on either the extent or method of borrowing. Under congressional authorization, the Treasury Department sells securities to banks, corporations, and individuals. Usually these securities take the form of long-term bonds or short-term treasury notes. Some bonds may

[3]See John F. Manley, *The Politics of Finance* (Little, Brown, 1970); and Lawrence C. Pierce, *The Politics of Fiscal Policy Formation* (Goodyear, 1971).

be cashed in at any time, others not until their maturity. Because the United States government guarantees these bonds, they are in great demand, especially by banks and investment companies. However, the government, particularly in time of inflation, likes to induce as many individuals as possible to buy bonds, because individuals who buy bonds have less money with which to buy goods and so will not contribute to inflationary pressures.

A third source of federal funds consists of administrative and commercial revenues. The fee paid to the State Department for a passport and the fine paid by a criminal are administrative revenues that account for a portion—though a very small portion—of federal income. More important are the funds paid to the federal government in exchange for direct services—payments to the Post Office for stamps, to the Park Service for recreation, to the Government Printing Office for pamphlets.

Finally, some public-spirited people actually give money or property to the government. Mr. Justice Holmes, who did not mind taxes, left the government almost his entire estate when he died. But gifts, needless to say, are an infinitesimal source of federal revenue.

Spending the money

Federal power projects are a major form of outlay to develop or create (though some say destroy) regional resources.

All the billions of dollars the government takes in are funneled into the treasury and then rapidly move out through hundreds of channels to points throughout the nation and, indeed, throughout the world. Nothing reflects the rise of big government more clearly than the change in the amounts and methods of its spendings. As recently as 1933 the federal government spent only $4 billion, about $30 per capita. By 1975 the respective figures were more than $300 billion and over $1,500. The machinery for spending has changed, too. At one time spending was loosely administered. Records show, for example, that in an early year of the republic one Nicholas Johnson, a Navy agent of Newburyport, Massachusetts, was handed several thousand dollars to supply "Cpt. Brown for recruiting his Crew."[4] Today Mr. Johnson would have to make out detailed forms and wait for a check.

Where does the money go? Much of it, of course, is for national defense. The $305 billion unified budget estimated for the fiscal year 1975 allots about 29 percent to national security; 7 percent to interest on the national debt; 37 percent to social insurance, education, and other major social programs; 17 percent to States and localities, and 10 percent to other programs such as space and agriculture. Much of the federal debt is for payments for past wars, and defense-related expenditures such as veteran's pensions and benefits are buried in non-"national security" categories. Even in the past three decades interesting changes have tak-

[4]L. D. White, *The Federalists* (Macmillan, 1948), p. 341.

en place. In 1939 total expenditures of the federal government amounted to $9 billion. Of this, national defense took about $1 billion, interest less than $1 billion, and veterans about $600 million. It is hard to realize today that as recently as 1939 most federal expenses were for domestic relief and welfare functions. Significantly, in 1939 we spent only about 0.5 percent of the budget on international activities. The proportion has risen manyfold as we became deeply involved in world developments.

The sheer fact of spending $305 billion a year is most significant of all. Years ago, federal revenues and outlays were so small that national taxing and spending had little impact on the overall economy. But today the federal government cannot drain billions of dollars from certain areas of the economy and pump them back into other areas without its having a profound effect on the economy of the nation and of the world at large. This problem will be considered later in the chapter. First we must see how the federal budget is drawn up and made into law.

FORMULATING THE BUDGET

As we have seen, Congress must authorize the spending of funds, but the initiation of appropriations is a responsibility of the president. The first step in preparing a federal budget is for the various departments and agencies to estimate their needs.[5] This process starts early; while Congress is debating the budget for the fiscal year immediately ahead, the agencies are making budget estimates for the year following. The estimating job is handled largely by budget officers working under the direction of the agency chiefs. The agency officials must take into account not only their needs as they see them, but also the overall presidential program and the probable reactions of Congress, especially those of the House Appropriations Committee.[6] Departmental budgets are highly detailed; they include estimates on expected needs for personnel, supplies, office space, and the like.

The Office of Management and Budget handles the next phase of budget-making. A staff agency of the president, the OMB scrutinizes each agency budget to see if it is in accord with the president's budget plans. This job is done by experienced budget examiners who usually have been long acquainted with a particular agency and can look over its requests with a sharp eye for accuracy, economy, and good program planning. Hearings are then held to give agency spokesmen a chance to clarify and defend their estimated needs. The director and his aides, who make the final decision, very frequently prune the agencies' requests rather severely.

For months the director has been conferring with the president or top presidential lieutenants and has been trying to keep the agencies below

[5]For a discussion and graphic presentation of the budgetary cycle, see Aaron Wildavsky, *The Politics of the Budgetary Process,* rev. ed. (Little, Brown, 1974).

[6]*Ibid.* Ch. 2; and Richard F. Fenno, Jr., "The House Appropriations Committee as a Political System," *American Political Science Review* (June 1962), pp. 310–24.

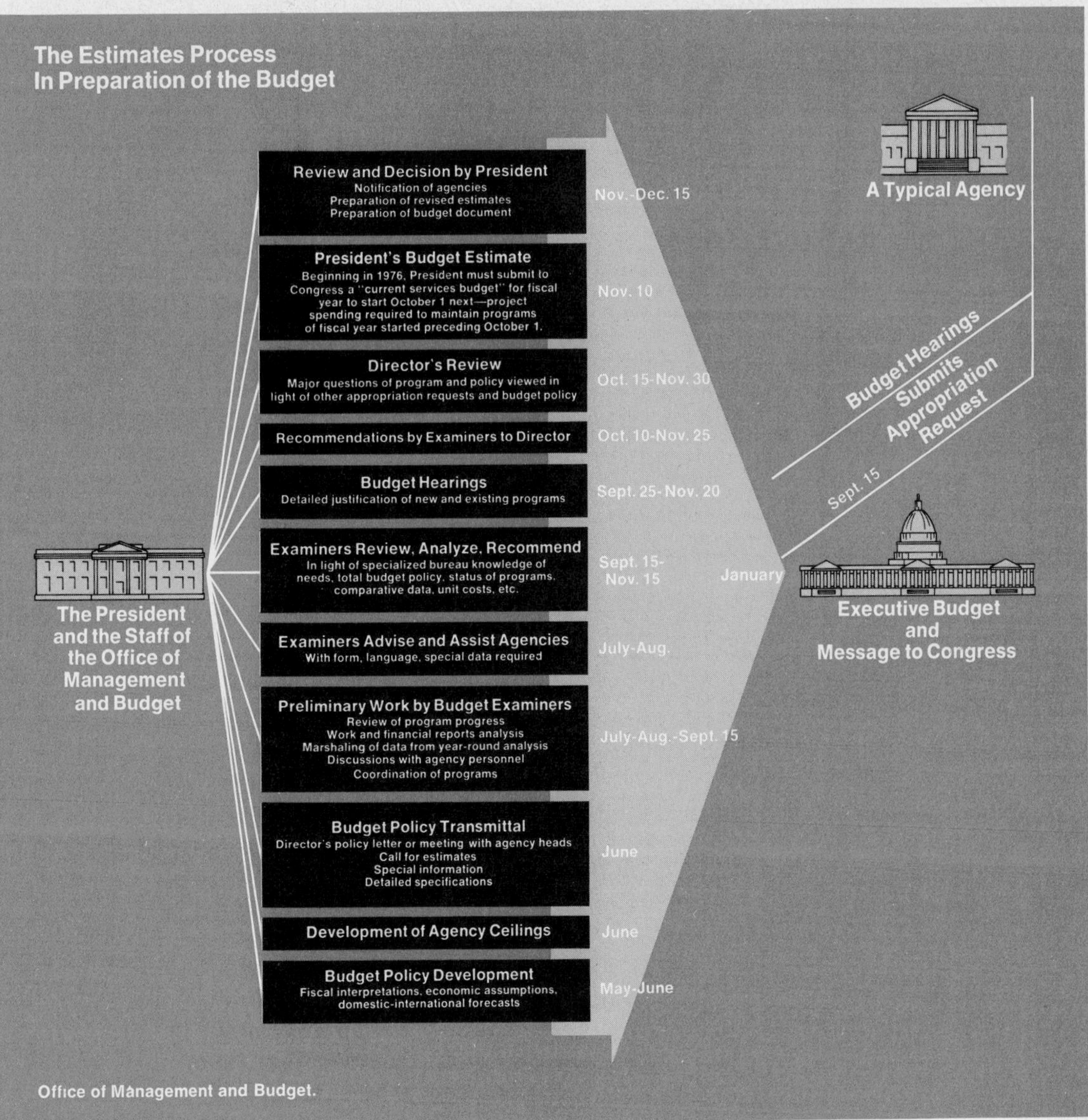

Office of Management and Budget.

the budget ceilings set by them. Finally—it is probably December by now—the director arrives at the White House with a single consolidated set of estimates of both revenue and expenditures, the product of perhaps a year's work. The president has reserved a day or two for a final review of the budget, and the two check the consolidated figures. The budget director also helps the president prepare a budget message that will stress key aspects of the budget and tie it in with broad national plans. By January, soon after Congress convenes, the budget and the message are ready for the legislators and the public.

PRESENTING THE BUDGET

A budget as big and complex as that of the national government is not easy to understand; it is not even easy to present in a manner that makes possible comprehension of the financial picture of the national government. Until 1968 three separate budgets—the administrative budget, the consolidated cash budget, and the national income accounts budget—were presented, but the administrative budget was the one that received public attention.

In 1968 President Johnson added a new method of presenting the budget—the unified budget—in accordance with the proposals of the bipartisan Commission on Budget Concepts. The *unified budget* includes trust-fund revenues and expenditures in addition to ordinary revenues and expenditures; it also includes as an expenditure *net lending*—that is, the amount the government lends for the fiscal year in excess of what it is paid. In other words, a net lending is considered for the fiscal year as if it were an expenditure for that year.

PROCESSING THE BUDGET

The president merely proposes. Under the Constitution only the Congress can appropriate funds. In 1974 Congress adopted the Budget Reform Act designed to give it a more effective role in the budgetary process. The act calls on the president when submitting his proposals to include proposed changes in tax laws, estimates of amounts of revenue lost through existing preferential tax treatments, and more important, five-year estimates of the costs of new and continuing federal programs. The act also calls on the president to seek authorizing legislation—authority to do something—a year before he asks Congress for the funds to do it.

The Impoundment Control Act passed at the same time (1974) contains a variety of highly complex provisions designed to curtail the president's ability to impound funds once appropriated by Congress, to curtail the use of backdoor appropriations, and to bring under some kind of congressional surveillance measures that call for automatic and continuing appropriations.

CHECKING UP ON EXPENDITURES

After Congress has appropriated money, it reserves the right to check up on the way the money is spent. Under the Budget and Accounting Act of 1921, the General Accounting Office (GAO) does the national government's accounting job. The GAO is headed by a comptroller general, who is appointed by the president with the approval of the Senate. The comptroller general enjoys some measure of independence, however, for his term of office is fifteen years, he is ineligible for reappointment, and he can be removed only for specific cause by a joint resolution of Congress.

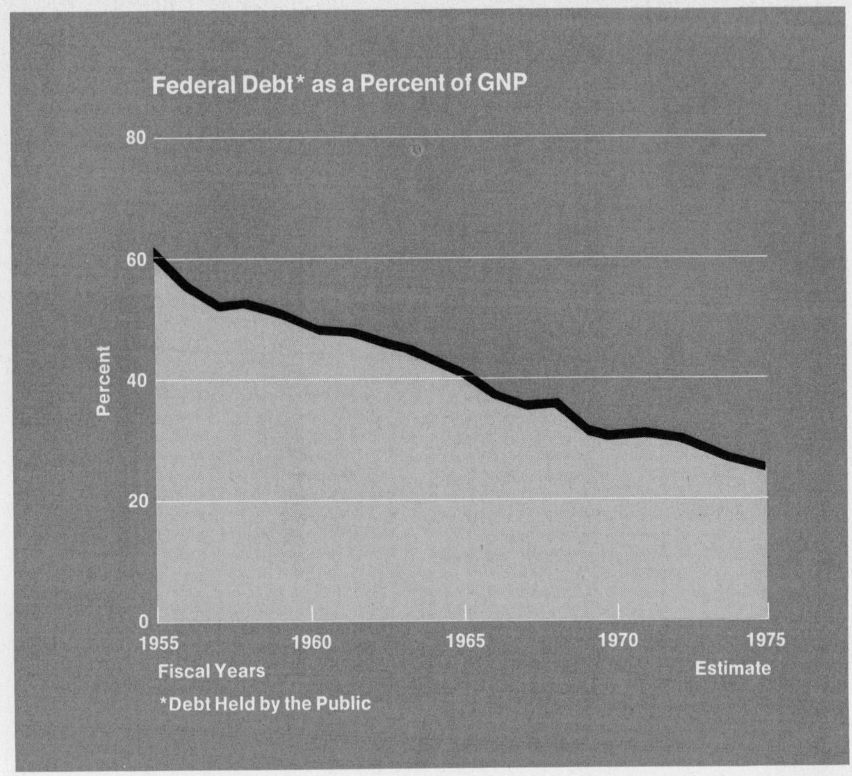

The comptroller general was originally intended to operate as an independent auditory serving as an arm of Congress to guard against improper and unauthorized expenditures. But as time went on, he was swamped by a gigantic accounting job that forced him to handle administrative matters in the executive branch even though he was not responsible to the chief executive. At the same time, overall management in the executive branch suffered, because daily accounting, an important instrument of administrative control, had been placed in a separate agency.

Improvements have been made in recent years. The GAO, with almost 5,300 employees, now uses spot sampling methods to check vouchers and makes its audits in the field rather than in Washington. Although the comptroller general still has the authority to disallow expenditures, his approval is no longer needed prior to the disbursement of funds. Being relieved of personal responsibility for payments that may subsequently be disallowed, disbursing officers (provided they have acted in good faith and with reasonable diligence) have been encouraged to make their own decisions about the legality of expenditures.

The General Accounting Office has—as a result of the Legislative Reorganization Act of 1970—taken on broader responsibilities in inves-

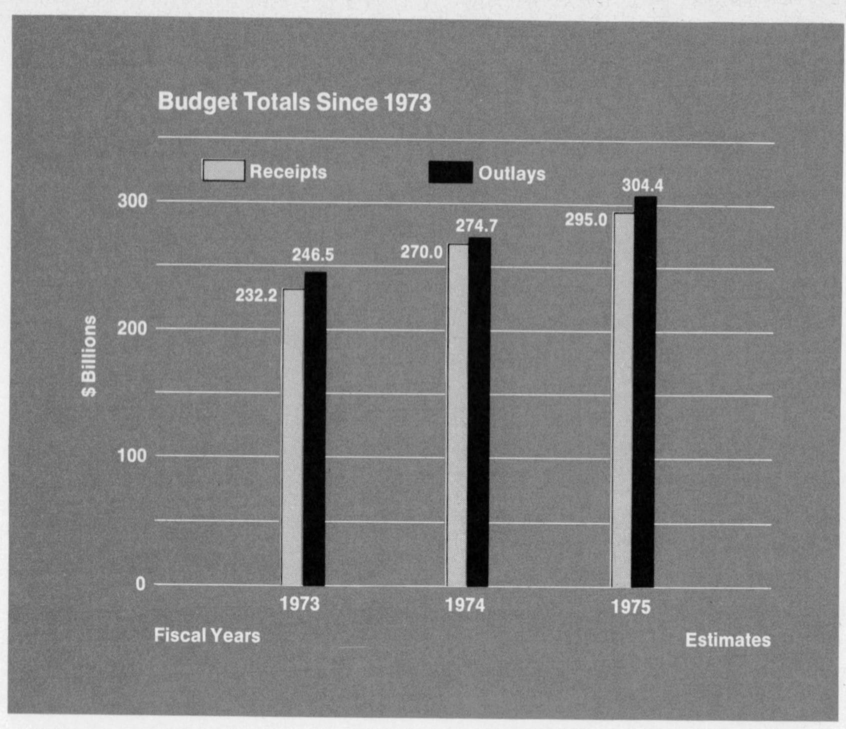

tigating and even evaluating programs. With the passage of the Federal Election Campaign Act of 1972, the GAO also supervised (1) the monetary limitations placed on spending by candidates for federal elective office for use of the communications media, and (2) the disclosure of campaign receipts and expenditures by candidates for the offices of president and vice-president. However, GAO's Office of Federal Elections, which handles these responsibilities, was replaced by the independent Federal Elections Commission established by the Federal Election Campaign Act of 1974.

It might seem that accounting is a technical matter that could be settled without much argument. On the contrary, accounting is a political problem too, for it reflects two struggles in Washington—the attempt of Congress as a whole to maintain as much control as possible over the still mushrooming bureaucratic machine and the struggle of individual legislators to maintain a system that checks individual administrative payments.

Managing money

Today's economy is essentially a money economy. Instead of using a system of barter, "civilized" peoples exchange commodities through a vast system of money and credit. We have seen the tremendous role the federal government plays in this system, simply because it gets and spends well over $300 billion a year. But aside from its role as the biggest buyer and seller of goods and services, the federal government has a more direct impact on our money economy. It manufactures money; it regulates the value of money; it controls the nation's credit system; and it can devalue the dollar,—as was done in 1971 and again in 1973.

Manufacturing money is the easiest of these jobs. The Bureau of Engraving and Printing in the Treasury Department, using carefully designed plates and special types of paper, turns out millions of dollars in the form of bills, bonds, and postage stamps every week; this "folding-money" is fed into general circulation through the Treasury and the Federal Reserve banks. The Bureau of the Mint in Philadelphia, Denver, and San Francisco (also under the Treasury) manufactures various coins that together make up about one-twentieth of the country's cash.

In itself, this money is only so much paper and metal. How does the government maintain its value?

THE CURRENCY SYSTEM

The Constitution gives the federal government the right to manage the nation's monetary system. Under the Articles of Confederation, the na-

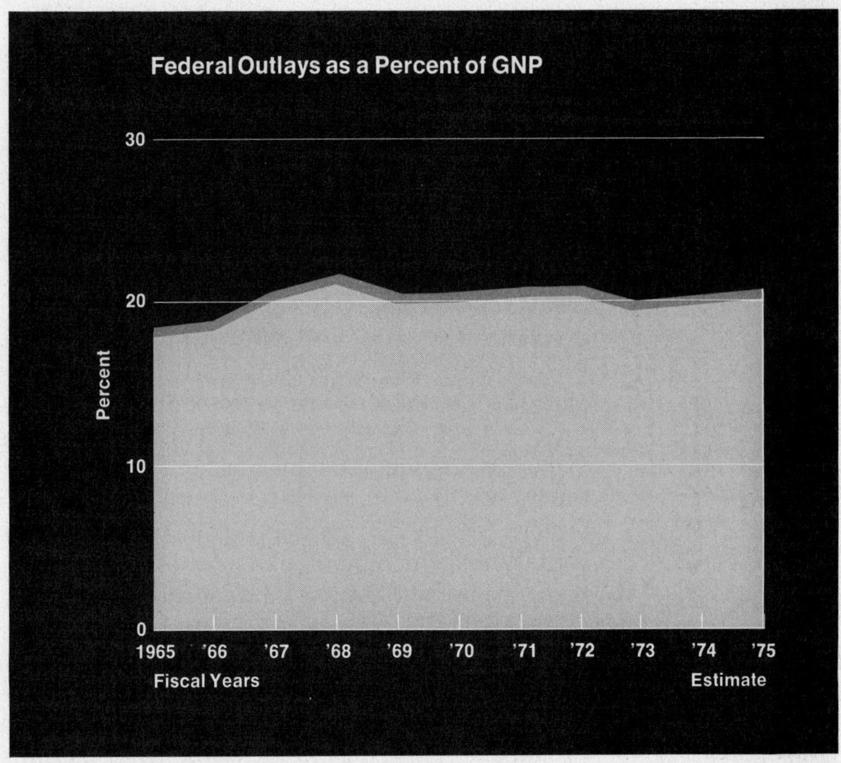

tional currency had consisted mainly of almost worthless paper money, and the individual states had maintained separate currencies. To correct this, the Constitution of 1787 vested in Congress authority to coin money and to regulate its value, carefully withholding this power from the states. Thanks partly to Secretary of the Treasury Hamilton, the early Americans scrapped the former confusing British system of guineas, pounds, shillings, and pence and adopted a decimal system.

Today the United States is on a highly modified gold standard – the money and credit supply is backed up in small part with gold, and the unit of monetary value is defined in terms of gold. But all the currency of the United States – Federal Reserve Notes and coins – is legal tender and cannot be freely exchanged for gold or silver. In short, the money of the United States is freely redeemable only for other money of the United States. (Although, since 1975, Americans are once more free to purchase and own gold as well as silver if they so wish.)

Money makes up only a part of the circulating medium and is less important to our economy than credit. In the expansion and contraction of credit, the most important institutions are the banks and the Federal Reserve System.

BANKS AND LENDING INSTITUTIONS

Banking, though a private business, is subject to close government supervision. There are over 14,000 banks in the United States; 4,600 are chartered by the national government, the rest by the states. The national banks have custody of 50 percent of all bank deposits. The comptroller of the currency in the department of the Treasury supervises their operations. Each national bank must file reports on its financial condition four times a year and must permit bank examiners to inspect its books at least three times every two years – at unannounced times.

Although state authorities have the primary responsibility to supervise state-chartered banks most of these banks are also subject to federal regulation, because their deposits are insured by the Federal Deposit Insurance Corporation (FDIC). All national banks must participate in this program, and state banks that meet approved standards are also permitted to do so. All but a few hundred of the commercial bank and trust companies in the United States have their deposits insured by the FDIC, as do some of the over 500 mutual savings banks. The FDIC routinely examines banks that are not members of the Federal Reserve System (see below) and establishes rules designed to keep them solvent. When a member bank becomes insolvent, the FDIC takes over its management and pays each depository up to $40,000.

The Federal Savings and Loan Insurance Corporation, operating under the supervision of the Federal Home Loan Bank Board, protects investors in federal savings and loan associations and those state-chartered institutions approved for participation. Like the FDIC, it guarantees savings up to $40,000 for each account.

THE FEDERAL RESERVE SYSTEM

In many nations, a central bank owned and operated by the national government determines general monetary policies. The Constitution does not specifically authorize the national government to create such a bank—indeed, it says nothing at all about banking. But Alexander Hamilton believed that some such institution was necessary, and in 1791, on his initiative, the United States Bank was incorporated by the national government and given a twenty-year charter. This bank was partly private and partly public; the national government owned only a minority of the shares and had only a minority voice in its management. Jefferson and his supporters opposed the bank on monetary, political, and constitutional grounds; nevertheless, President Madison found it necessary to have the bank rechartered for another twenty years in 1816, after the Jeffersonians had refused to do so in 1811. In 1819 the Supreme Court in *McCulloch v. Maryland* (see Chapter 4) upheld the constitutionality of the bank as a necessary and proper way for the national government to establish a uniform currency and to care for the property of the United States.

After the bank closed its doors in 1836, state banks, which had previously been restrained by the second United States Bank embarked on an orgy of issuing notes that often could not be redeemed. A military crisis forced a house cleaning. To stabilize an economy beset with war demands and to support the desires of the "dear money" groups, Congress authorized in 1863 the chartering of national banks. These are privately owned corporations not to be confused with a central bank or an institution like the United States Bank. State banks were permitted to continue in business, but a 10 percent federal tax on their notes quickly drove state bank notes out of existence.

The national bank system created during the Civil War was stable—indeed, so stable that it was inflexible. Financial crises during the late nineteenth century and in 1907 revealed an unhappy tendency of banks to restrict their loans and of national banks to contract their issuance of notes, just at the times when an *expansion* of money was needed. In order to furnish an elastic currency, and for other reasons, Congress in 1913 established the Federal Reserve System.

The act of 1913 was a compromise. Some wanted a strong central bank, but many feared that this would centralize control over currency in too few hands. So a system was established that gives us a modified central banking program with considerable decentralization. The country is divided into twelve Federal Reserve districts, in each of which there is a Federal Reserve bank (most Federal Reserve banks have branches). Each Federal Reserve bank is owned by member banks. All national banks must join the system, and state banks that meet standards are permitted to do so. Today approximately 5,700 of the 14,000 banks are members of the system; these are the largest banks and have over 85 percent of total deposits.

Each Federal Reserve bank is headed by a board of directors, of which six members are elected by the member banks and three appointed by the board of governors in Washington. Three of the directors elected by the member banks must be bankers, and three must be active in business and industry. The three directors appointed by the board of governors may not have any financial interest in and may not work for any bank. The board of governors designates one of its appointees chairman of the board of directors, and this board in turn selects a president to serve as its chief executive officer.

A seven-person board of governors sitting in Washington supervises the entire system. They are selected by the president with the consent of the Senate for fourteen-year terms, and the president designates the chairman, who has a four-year term. The board of governors—advised by the Federal Advisory Council, which is composed of a member from each Federal Reserve district—meets in Washington at least four times a year and determines general monetary and credit policies. It has four major devices to tighten or loosen the financial activities of the nation's banks and, in turn, of the whole economy:

1. To increase or decrease within legal limits the reserves that member banks must maintain against their deposits in the Federal Reserve bank.
2. To raise or lower the rediscount rate charged by Federal Reserve banks to member banks. The rediscount rate is the price member banks must pay to get cash from the Federal Reserve banks for acceptable commercial notes that the banks hold.
3. Through the Open Market Committee (composed of all members of the board of governors and five representatives of the Reserve banks), to sell or buy government securities and certain other bills of exchange, bank acceptances, and so on.
4. To exercise direct control over the credit that may be extended in order to purchase securities (called margin requirements). From time to time Congress has given the board of governors temporary authority to fix terms of consumer credit.

Through these and other devices, the board of governors may affect the flow of money by tightening or loosening credit. For example, if inflation is threatening, the board can depress the economy by raising member-bank reserve requirements (thus cutting down on the cash they have available for lending), by raising rediscount rates (thus forcing member banks to raise the rates for which they will lend money), by selling government securities in the open market (thus absorbing funds from the economy), and by raising margin requirements (thus reducing credit available to bid up the prices of securities). In addition, the Federal Reserve banks serve as depositories for government funds, clear checks and transfer funds among member banks, and may, in case of economic emergency, lend money directly to businesses.

The Federal Reserve System is intentionally isolated from influence by the president, and, because it does not depend on annual appropriations, even Congress exercises little control over it. "Devised as a service agency for banking and commerce—to achieve a semi-automatic adjustment of the money supply—the Federal Reserve has become as well a policy-making institution with major responsibility for national economic stabilization."[7] And many observers feel that it is improper to vest this important new responsibility in an agency so divorced from public accountability. The board of governors, for example, often has to make a choice between fighting inflation, which may cause unemployment, and promoting employment at the expense of creating inflation. As Gardiner C. Means has said, "There is a good deal of question whether such a momentous decision should rest with the Federal Reserve Board."[8] Yet many, including most bankers, want to preserve the system's independence. They believe that only an agency insulated from political pressures can take the often unpopular steps needed to prevent inflation.

Today all agree that monetary policy must be considered as but one weapon to combat depression, control inflation, foster full employment, and encourage economic growth. Whether or not we can retain a system in which the central banking authorities "can legally . . . tell the head of [their] own Government to go fly a kite"[9] remains a moot issue.

Managing the economy

Does the government have the same direct control over the national economy that it has, say, over atomic energy and national forests? No. Only if we had a socialized economy administered from Washington would we have a managed economy in that sense. We still have an economy in which a great deal of power is left to private individuals and enterprises. And yet the government keeps a firm hand on all the gears and levers that control the general direction in which the economy will head and the rate at which it will move. These gears and levers are taxes, spending, credit, and the like. If these levers were operated in a haphazard, whimsical way, they might have a catastrophic effect. Operated in a carefully synchronized manner, however, they can help keep the economy on an even keel.

It is only rather recently that Americans have recognized the part that government could play in stabilizing and invigorating the economy. (There are still differences of opinion over the part that it *should* play.)

[7]See Michael D. Reagan "The Political Structure of the Federal Reserve System," *American Political Science Review* (March 1961), pp. 64–76, for a detailed analysis of the present structure and policy implications of the Federal Reserve System.

[8]Quoted *Ibid.*, p. 75.

[9]Elliot V. Bell, quoted *ibid.*, p. 76.

The slow development of our understanding, the political struggle over the question of whether the federal government should take responsibility for full employment, the enactment of the Employment Act of 1946, the Ford administration's "economic summit" in late 1974—these are fascinating episodes in the trend toward overall control of the economy by the federal government.

ECONOMIC GROPING

Austerity is a hard teacher. The Depression of the 1930s had a tremendous impact on American thinking about the role of government in economic matters. We have had long, severe depressions before—for example, in the 1870s and 1890s. But by 1929 the United States had become a rich and powerful nation, and prosperity seemed here to stay. Then the Great Depression struck. Millions of unemployed, falling prices and income, plummeting production—all added up to mass misery. "One vivid, gruesome moment of those dark days we shall never forget," wrote one observer. "We saw a crowd of some fifty men fighting over a barrel of garbage which had been set outside the back door of a restaurant. American citizens fighting for scraps of food like animals!"[10]

Despite a wide range of initiatives on the part of the New Deal to cope with the Depression, it hung on. Faint signs of recovery could be seen in the mid-1930s, but the recession of 1937–1938 indicated that we were by no means out of the woods. Eight or nine million people were jobless in 1939. Then came the war, and unemployment was cured—for a while. Millions of people had more income, more security, a higher standard of living. Lord Beveridge in England posed a question that bothered many thoughtful Americans: "Unemployment has been practically abolished twice in the lives of most of us—in the last war and in this war. Why does war solve the problem of unemployment which is so insoluble in peace?"[11] Worried that the economy might collapse after the war, thousands of people came up with plans to ensure jobs for all.

One school of thought was that the Depression persisted because the New Deal was hostile to business and intruded government too long and too extensively into the economic life of the nation. Proponents of this theory urged the government to reduce spending, lower taxes, curb

[10]Quoted in F. L. Allen, *Since Yesterday* (Harper, 1940), p. 64.

[11]W. H. Beveridge, *The Pillars of Security* (Macmillan, 1943), p. 51.

Research projects, such as that being conducted here by a biologist at Oak Ridge National Laboratory in Tennessee, may not produce an immediate effect on the national economy, but in the long run, they may provide major industrial breakthroughs and hence contribute to economic stabilization.

the power of labor, and generally leave business and the economy alone except for traditional regulation and aids to certain businesses. Another large group, made up of economists, labor representatives, government officials, and others, took a different tack. They said that the trouble with the New Deal was not that it had done too much but that it had done too little. The thinking of this group was deeply influenced by the work of John Maynard Keynes, the English economist. In visits to the United States during the 1930s, Keynes warned that if people did not consume enough or invest enough, national income would fall. The way to increase national income is either to spend money on consumption goods (such as clothes or food or automobiles) or on investment goods (steel mills and dock facilities) or on both. Finally, *government must do the spending and investing if private enterprise by itself would not or could not.* The Keynesian approach was related to concepts involving governmental influence on public works, wages, prices, credit, taxation, and the like. Congress, through the passage of the Employment Act of 1946, gave formal acceptance to it.

THE EMPLOYMENT ACT OF 1946

Congressional enactment of a measure that specifically recognized the primacy of the national government in the maintenance of full employment was bound to be difficult.[12] The bill as presented by the Truman Administration embodied the viewpoint of Keynesian economists and had the support of organized labor, many senators, and members of several Senate committee staffs. Arrayed against the bill were such organizations as the NAM, chambers of commerce, the American Farm Bureau Federation, and a number of key conservatives in Congress. Although the bill fairly easily passed the Senate in close to its original form, the conservative House Rules Committee ensured that only a much weaker version would pass the lower House. Enacted in February 1946, the act declared:

> It is the continuing policy and responsibility of the Federal Government to use all practicable means consistent with its needs and obligations and other essential considerations of national policy, with the assistance and cooperation of industry, agriculture, labor, and state and local governments, to coordinate and utilize all its plans, functions, and resources for the purpose of creating and maintaining, in a manner calculated to foster and promote free competitive enterprise and the general welfare, conditions under which there will be afforded useful employment, for those able, willing, and seeking to work, and to promote maximum employment, production, and purchasing power.

If this declaration sounds like double talk, the reason may be that the bill had to be built on a series of compromises; in effect, the bill made

[12]For the full history of the bill, see Stephen K. Bailey, *Congress Makes a Law* (Columbia University Press, 1950).

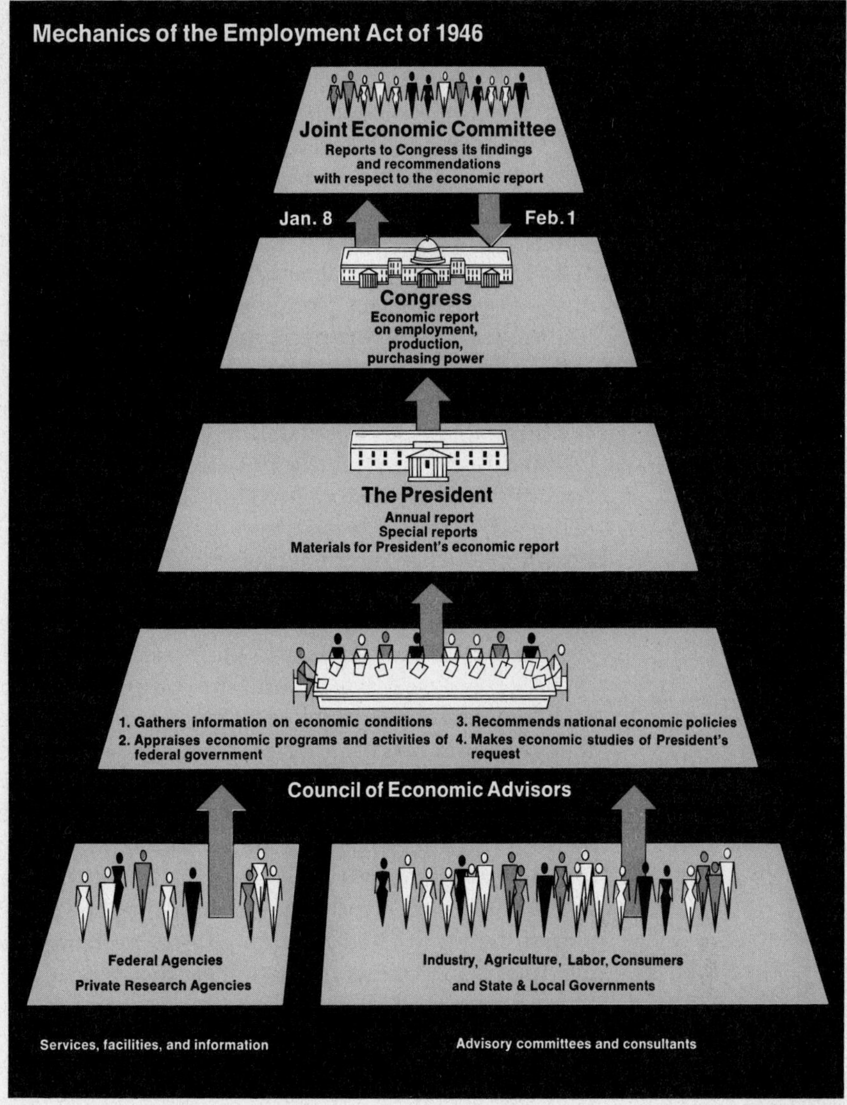

the federal government responsible for acting in the face of rising unemployment instead of relying wholly on nongovernmental forces. Equally important, the act established machinery to carry out that responsibility:

1. *The Council of Economic Advisers* (CEA). Composed of three members appointed by the president with the consent of the Senate and located in the Executive Office of the President, this council with a small staff studies and forecasts economic trends, assesses the contribution of federal programs to maximum employment, and recommends to the president "national economic policies to foster and promote free competition, to avoid economic fluctuations or to diminish the effects thereof, and to maintain employment, production, and purchasing power."

2. *The Economic Report of the President.* Every January the president must submit to Congress an economic report based on the data and forecasts of the council. The report must include a program for carrying out the policy of the act; it can also include recommendations for legislation if the president sees fit.

3. *Joint Economic Committee* (JEC). This is a committee of Congress authorized by the act. Composed of seven senators and seven representatives, it must report early in each year its findings and proposals in respect to presidential recommendations. Aside from publishing various reports, the JEC is able to give Congress an overview of the economy. In this sense it is an anomaly in Congress: "a planning and theory group in a culture fiercely devoted to the short run and practical. It is committed to the panoramic view in a system that stresses jurisdictional lines. It signifies recognition that economic problems are related, in a body that deals with them piecemeal."[13]

How has the Employment Act worked in practice? The CEA has emerged as a high-level presidential advisory body, with its chairman serving both as an adviser to the president and as a spokesman for the president before Congress and the country. The annual economic report and the budget message are major presidential statements on the role that governmental fiscal policies will play in the economy in the coming year. The JEC has played a significant role in developing information on important economic problems. The machinery established under the act is providing both the president and Congress with the type of information and advice needed to shape the government's fiscal policy.[14]

The various mechanisms established by the act work, but is the information being utilized and the advice implemented? Certainly the Employment Act is more significant for the basic ideas it embodies than for the procedures it created. The Keynesian economic underpinnings of the act have gained wide acceptance in Washington and elsewhere; governmental fiscal policy is being used in a straightforward fashion to stimulate the economy and cope with its fluctuations. No longer, for example is a balanced budget viewed by Washington decision-makers as a national goal always to be pursued. It is seen that in certain instances it is better for the government to spend more than it takes in and to run a budget deficit. This is the widely recognized course of action when the economy is not operating at full capacity. When the economy is operating at full capacity, other measures may be called for—a budget surplus, for instance, may be required to check inflationary pressures

[13]Commission on Money and Credit, *Money and Credit: Their Influence on Jobs, Prices, and Growth* (Prentice-Hall, 1961), pp. 268–69.

[14]For an account of performance and politics under the Employment Act, see Harvey C. Mansfield, "The Congress and Economic Policy," in David B. Truman, ed., *The Congress and America's Future*, 2nd ed., (Prentice-Hall, 1973), Ch. 6.

under conditions of full employment. This sort of Keynesian rationale provided the basis for the $12 billion personal income tax cut in 1964 and the nearly $2 billion cut in excise taxes in 1965. Although unemployment in 1964 was moving steadily downward as the gross national product moved upward, the economy was still not at full capacity, and more stimulus from the federal government was required. The increased governmental spending and the lower taxes resulting from the 1964 cut put more money in the hands of the American public, which spent more money, thus creating more jobs. The economy boomed. Indeed, so successful was this action that though taxes were cut by $12 billion, $12.7 billion more was collected from personal taxes in 1964.

When the 1964 tax cut bill was passed, it was viewed by most people as a definite success. The "new" economics of the 1960s won praise from nearly all sides. But within just two years, the victory was beginning to lose its glow, and new economic problems emerged.

A growing economy usually means rising prices; and when the expansionary effects of war are added, it means inflation. The increased purchasing power created by the tax cut, and the increased government purchases that occurred with greater Vietnam involvement, created a demand for goods that exceeded the supply. The CEA chairman, Gardner Ackley, warned President Johnson of the impending problem and suggested that a tax increase might be necessary.

Now Johnson was faced with the unpleasant side of Keynesian economics—taking dollars away from consumers. As the 1966 elections approached, however, few members of Congress wanted to campaign on a record of having just increased taxes. Johnson was reluctant to call for a tax increase. He, like most people, kept hoping the war might soon end, thus forestalling the need for a tax increase.

Everyone nearly always dislikes tax increases. And the tax increase controversy in the late 1960s was compounded by political considerations. On what would the new tax revenues be spent? Liberal Democrats did not want to pass an increase if it was going to the Vietnam War. Conservatives did not want to support an increase if it meant more Great Society programs. Many liberals wanted *tax reform* to accompany the tax increase; many conservatives wanted cuts in the federal budget to accompany the increase. Everyone wanted something, and with almost every group objectives differed. In the end Congress in 1968 passed a 10 percent surcharge tax and set out to cut budget expenditures by $6 billion.

The tax increase helped slow inflation—but only slightly. Most economists think the tax cut came too late. Originally recommended in December 1965, it became law only in June of 1968. This kind of delay represents a major problem in governmental management of the economy. While economists can sometimes determine fairly rapidly what the appropriate fiscal actions should be, the political process often responds more slowly. First, the economic advisers have to make the president aware of the problem and suggest policy responses. Second, the president must decide how and when to act. Next begins the formal presentation and unveiling of policy initiatives. Finally, Congress must be persuaded, and the measure guided through the legislative labyrinth of committees. Few shortcuts exist.

Known remedies are seldom as available as the Kennedy-sponsored tax cut was in the early 1960s. Moreover, we are limited in that if we are to execute new policies we must do so by democratic procedures. And everything we do has consequences we never intend. The lessons of history show that we are seldom as smart as we think. All too often our "solutions" become our children's problems.

WHAT SHOULD BE DONE?

Some observers have suggested that the president be given standby authority to raise and lower taxes, within certain limits, without the approval of Congress. Cumbersome congressional procedures clearly preclude the quick injection of money into the economy by means of a tax cut even when such a policy may be economically warranted. With such authority, for example, the tax increase of 1968 probably would have occurred a year earlier. But many in the Congress see this proposal as an encroachment upon their constitutional responsibilities.

After the tax increase of 1968, inflationary pressures continued to build. The Federal Reserve tightened the money supply; but this did not halt the surging inflation. Nixon took office amidst continued inflation. He sought for his first two years in office to curb inflation with traditional monetary and fiscal policies. Yet the rate of advance in prices and the cost of living climbed still higher, as did unemployment. Soon he faced the problem of simultaneous inflation *and* rising unemployment.

What brought about these conditions? Many economists attribute it to the shift from *excess-demand* inflation to *cost-push* inflation. In the

Copyright, 1974, G. B. Trudeau/distributed by Universal Press Syndicate.

mid-1960s the demand for goods and services *pulled* up the price level—more people were willing to pay more for products. In the late 1960s, labor unions began to seek wage increases to compensate for the increased production costs, and as a result the increased costs *pushed* up the price level. Monetary and fiscal policies are not as adept at slowing cost-push inflation as they are at halting demand-pull. Too, the oligopolistic power of many corporations allowed them to maintain high prices even when demand was declining. Thus, the car industry was able to keep prices high because the "big three" (GM, Ford, and Chrysler) together refused to lower prices. Consumers in turn had little choice—they either bought at the higher prices, or did without. Each of these choices posed an added problem for the managers of the nation's economy.

RESTRAINING WAGES AND PRICES

President Johnson attempted to deal with the cost-push problem by instituting wage-price guidelines. These guidelines were recommendations to business and labor on what price and wage increases seemed reasonable—reasonable, that is, to the president's economic advisers. Compliance with these guidelines was sought through *jawboning*—the application of public pressure or threat to recalcitrant industries. When Nixon took office, he had declared vehemently his intention to avoid wage-price guidelines, especially enforced governmental controls.

In 1971, as economic conditions worsened, the clamor for wage-price controls was unrelenting. Even Arthur Burns, chairman of the Federal Reserve Board, advocated some kind of wage-price policy. Nixon stood firm. The situation grew severe in mid-1971. Inflation was undermining the value of the dollar abroad; our balance of payments crisis was threatening to weaken our overall international position. The president was forced to reconsider. On August 15, 1971, he announced his revised economic policies, consisting of:

1. a ninety-day wage and price freeze,
2. a 10 percent surcharge tax on imports,
3. suspension of dollar convertibility, and
4. tax cuts designed to increase investment.

Few Americans directly realized the effect of the import surcharge, the suspension of dollar convertibility, or the investment tax cuts, but most of us were affected by the dramatic ninety-day freeze. The freeze had two main purposes. First, to convince the public, business, and labor that the administration was serious about stopping inflation. Second, to buy time to work out the specifics of the wage-price controls that were to follow.

Because of the complexity of the American economy it is both impossible and impractical to freeze prices for very long. Some prices are un-

"You BET I'm hopping mad! When inflation begins to affect the well-to-do, it's time something was DONE about it!"

Reprinted by permission of Newspaper Enterprise Association.

controllable—for instance, the freeze excluded raw agricultural products because the large number of supplies, and the many ways of setting up black markets would have prohibited effective enforcement. But the freeze was effective in buying time.[15]

The freeze went into effect on very short notice. Time was not available to set up a new enforcement organization. Instead, enforcement was delegated mainly to the Internal Revenue Service. The Cost of Living Council was created; it was composed of the chairman of the CEA, the secretaries of treasury, agriculture, labor, commerce, and housing and urban development, the director of the OMB, the director of the now defunct Office of Emergency Preparedness, and the special assistant to the president for consumer affairs. This group had final say on all questions of policy relating to the price-wage freeze.

By the time Gerald Ford assumed the presidency, the outlook for controlling inflation had again worsened. The Republican administrations had long since dumped serious wage and price controls, and a toothless variant of jawboning, substituted in its place, had proved unsuccessful. "Double-digit" inflation and unprecedented interest rates plagued the country—and most other nations as well. Our economic problems were being duplicated, especially in Europe.

As President Ford, the Congress, and the nation faced the double problems of inflation and recession, Ford and his advisers had the

[15]Arnold R. Weber, *In Pursuit of Price Stability: The Wage-Price Freeze of 1971* (Brookings Institution, 1973)

delicate task of trying to propose the right combination of tax reductions on some items, perhaps tax increases on others; increased spending in some areas, cutbacks in others; restraining money and credit at one moment but being ready to increase money supplies at the next moment, as everyone concerned tried to fine tune the economy and steer the nation between double-digit inflation and double-digit unemployment. At first, President Ford and his advisers gave their prime attention to the dangers of inflation and proposed a series of measures to brake the economy, even at the risk of increasing unemployment. But as the recession deepened and unemployment increased faster than anticipated, the president, the 94th Congress, and the Federal Reserve System came forward with another series of proposals to get the

Business at the White House: The power of the presidency and of the federal government can be brought to bear on the business community so as to affect major decisions, as in President Kennedy's 1962 dispute with the steel industry Here, Kennedy poses with Roger M. Blough, chairman of the board of U.S. Steel. Also pictured are Henry C. Alexander, chairman of Morgan Guaranty Trust Company of New York City; Secretary of the Treasury Douglas Dillon; and H. Greenewalt, president of DuPont.

economy moving forward but at the same time to restrain inflation.

Plainly, the problem in a democracy is how to mobilize the government so that it can respond flexibly to changing economic conditions, but to do so in a fashion that keeps government accountable to the people. What we witness is not unwillingness to accept governmental responsibility for maintaining employment; the act of 1946 specifically recognized that responsibility. The problem in part is whether a governmental system such as ours can act effectively when action is needed. But the problem is also one of knowing what to do, and when to do it.

The political economy: a case study

In these last three chapters we have observed that economic and political life in our society are inextricably interwoven. There are no easily discerned boundaries between private and public sectors of the economy. A few still insist that government and the economy must be kept strictly separated, that government should not interfere in private economic affairs. Whatever its theoretical merits, this view is unrealistic. In modern American society we confront a political economy in which a decision in one area inevitably affects decisions in others. This political economy is a mixed economy—mixed in that it blends private and public enterprise, individual initiative and government promotion, personal responsibility and public regulation, federal and state governments.

We have also discovered that government regulation, promotion, and economic management are not really distinct. Promotion may be used for regulatory purposes and regulation for promotional; government taxing and spending in the broadest sense always entails both. A single case serves to demonstrate these relationships—President Kennedy's dispute with the steel industry in 1962.[16]

For a year the Kennedy Administration had been trying, mainly through exhortation, to induce both labor and employers to hold the price line. Early in April 1962 the big steel companies and the labor unions had signed a contract that the president greeted with enthusiasm as noninflationary. A few days later Roger Blough, chairman of the board of the United States Steel Corporation, went to the White House and informed the president that his corporation was raising the price of steel. The president knew that other steel companies would follow suit, the whole dike against inflation might be breached, and his policies of conciliation and persuasion would be repudiated. He knew that he must act, that he must act quickly, and that he must act across a wide front.

The events that occurred during the next three days at the White

[16]A succinct account of this event is found in Grant McConnell, *Steel and the Presidency, 1962* (Norton, 1963).

House have been the subject of much scholarly and journalistic attention. They can be summarized as follows:

First, the president summoned cabinet members, economic advisers, staff assistants, statisticians, and congressional advisers to his office to plan an all-out counterattack.

Statisticians brought up to date a fact book on steel that had been put out by the Eisenhower Administration two years earlier—both to be armed with the facts and to demonstrate the continuity with Eisenhower's anti-inflation policies.

The president asked congressional leaders publicly to register dismay about the steel price increase. They promptly did so.

The Justice Department announced an investigation of the steel price rise for possible violations of the antitrust laws.

The chairman of the Federal Trade Commission told reporters that his agency had begun an informal investigation to determine whether the steel companies had violated a consent decree of 1951.

The Democratic National Committee telephoned Democratic governors to ask them to issue statements supporting the president and to ask steel producers in their own states to hold the price line. But the national committee made no statement of its own so that this would not seem to be a party issue.

Before newsmen and television cameras at a press conference, the president denounced the price increase with controlled fury as a "wholly unjustifiable and irresponsible defiance of the public interest."

Several liberal Republicans attacked Big Steel's action. Administration leaders with connections in high places in the business world tried to induce business leaders to pressure steel against its decision.

All this was part of the administration's tactic of mobilizing public pressure on the steel companies. But its main tactic was to divide and conquer. Much depended on how many other steel companies would follow the lead of United States Steel in raising prices. Some already had. Administration officials had networks of contacts with officials in the other companies. The government also held some economic leverage because of its huge contracts with steel companies, especially defense contracts; indeed, the Defense Department announced that it was ordering defense contractors to shift steel purchases to companies that had not raised prices. The precise nature of the negotiations between administration officials and steel company officials is not clear, but this tactic evidently turned the tide. Inland Steel and several other companies announced that they would not raise prices. Bethlehem Steel rescinded its announced increase. Soon United States Steel was left isolated, and it quickly capitulated to these market pressures. Just seventy-two hours after Blough visited the White House, he announced that his company would withdraw its price increase.

Plainly, it was a resounding immediate victory for a president pledged to hold the price line on behalf of the people as a whole. It demonstrated the power of the president—at least when a president felt that economically and politically his back was against the wall. Yet there were misgivings. Republican leaders in Congress, in a joint statement, said that a fundamental issue had been raised: "Should a president of the United States use the enormous powers of the federal government to blackjack any segment of our free society into line with his personal judgment without regard to law?" Much was made of an unfortunate action on the part of FBI agents, who routed reporters from bed to check the accuracy of certain statements of business officials; although there was no threat to the reporters themselves, for many observers the action smacked too much of the "early-morning knock on the door" in police states. A few weeks later, the blame for a series of sharp dips in the stock market was laid by some to the president's action—thus linking the steel price fight to the broader question of the government's relation to economic prosperity.

Six years later, President Johnson also ordered federal agencies to refuse to buy steel from companies that had announced what the president considered to be an inflationary price increase. The steel companies again reduced their previously announced prices, although not back to the original level. But this time little was made of the president's intervention.

Twelve years later, liberal members of Congress called on President Ford to use the powers of his office, as Kennedy had, to roll back steel prices. In a two-and-a-half-year period, steel prices had climbed nearly 25 percent. Senator Proxmire termed the increase "totally unjustified and unconscionable." The steel companies in question contended that they need higher prices to be assured sufficient profits for future modernization and expansion. Ford's Council on Wage and Price Stabilization jawboned with the steel interests, but with limited apparent success this time.

As the case illustrates, the complex relationship between government and the economy, plus the mutual connections between governmental techniques, makes policy evaluation complicated. But we can at least begin with the knowledge that the goals of personal and national welfare are pursued in a highly political setting—a setting inevitable in a government by the people.

Epilogue: Citizenship as an office

Drawing by Richter; © 1970. The New Yorker Magazine, Inc.

Government of, by, and for the people is the most exacting venture mankind has ever undertaken. Exhilarating, demanding, and frustrating, the burden falls on each of us if we would make it work. Those who want a better America will not realize it by sitting around and waiting for it. If government of, by, and for the people is to be more than an abstract ideal, citizen activists must be willing to stretch their imaginations, clarify the issues for debate, demand accountability, form political alliances, and be willing to serve as activist citizen-politicians. This Epilogue suggests a variety of opportunities and strategies for citizen-politicans to put their knowledge and skills to work to help fashion a more democratic government.

Help needed: citizen-activists

There is always the danger that political scientists will overvalue the contributions of the politically active and undervalue the contributions of those who choose to leave politics to others. In some societies the government actually compels people to engage in political action, attend political classes, and even makes the right kind of political response and precondition for getting a good job or attending college. In our society, however, the choice of whether to be politically active belongs to each citizen. And those who choose to take care of the sick, grow the food, teach foreign languages, take care of the young, sell cars, establish insurance agencies, but limit their politics to paying their taxes and voting also make important contributions to our society. In fact, a nation in which every citizen gave highest priority to political action might not be very pleasant to live in.

But a democracy needs many people who are more involved in government than merely voting and who give political matters a high claim on their talents and energies. We need especially to insure that active citizenship is not concentrated in those who come only from a part of the community. Fortunately, the talents, time, and energies required for democratic government are not the monopoly of any organized interest, any particular group, class, sex, race, or section of the nation.

There is no recipe for preparing effective citizen-activists. Playing an effective part in politics depends on more than mere participation, commitment, and a desire to make things better. It demands political shrewdness and a comprehension of access points and political system slack.

Those dedicated to what has come to be called "movement politics" recognize the possibilities for creative participation. As Michael Walzar observes:

> In almost every area of social life [new activists] are certain to encounter entrenched and efficient bureaucracies which evade, resist and wear down, or simply absorb the force of their protest. The decline of political parties and of legislative authority has clearly reduced the accessibility of the political system and made the work of the newly activated citizens much harder than it once was. Nevertheless, there is abundant evidence to suggest that access is still possible and that bureaucracies can be pushed this way or that (even when they can't be seized and transformed).[1]

Many of the procedures of American politics may seem dull and complex—and they often are. The routines of both electoral and pressure politics can indeed be tedious, frustrating, and unrewarding. But there is much that is important, fascinating, inspiring—and even entertaining—in the patterns of American politics. Registration drives, for example, may seem of little import until someone publicly challenges your right to vote, or your candidate loses an election by an especially slim margin. Limitations on campaign spending may seem unimportant—until the opposition accuses your candidate of trying to buy the election. And organizing protests and petitioning public officials may seem a waste of time—until finally the day comes when the officials in question come to see the merits of your complaints and reverse their policies.

To be sure, radical or revolutionary changes in our political system seldom occur, but the range of challenges and opportunities for the would-be citizen-activist is plentiful: party politics, electoral politics, advisory politics, pressure, or movement, politics, and, of course, careers in the civil and military services.

Party politics

Though many young people may have little interest in seeking political or career administrative jobs in government, even so they can and should consider taking an active role in one of the two major or several fringe parties. As we have seen earlier, the American parties badly need strengthening at every level. The country needs more party politicians to hunt out quality candidates and help elect them, and then to remind the elected of their responsibilities to the people.

Jeffersonians and Jacksonians dreamed a great dream—that a party system could be effective, could raise issues for rational deliberation, and build coalitions to achieve a more just and decent society. Seldom have parties lived up to the Jeffersonian dream. Seldom have they served to discipline the whims and arbitrariness of those in public office who have lost touch with the people. But if we have not lived up to the Jeffersonian hopes, it does not mean that parties are unimportant, nor that we cannot still realize a healthy, competitive party system that would recruit the ablest of public servants, spur the most provocative of debates over national priorities, and inspire honesty and accountability in government.

The first step for the citizen-activist is to find the name of the local chairperson of his party; someone will know at city hall or at the local county courthouse. He should call the local party officials, find out their views, objectives, and organizational routines. If he disagrees with their views, his initial work is already cut out for him. If he agrees with their views and intentions, they will doubtless welcome him and sign him up for some subcommittee or future campaign assignment.

Voting lists must be checked, letters stamped, leaflets distributed, meetings arranged, publicity sent out, posters put up. Keeping track of new registration and campaign finance laws alone is now a time-consuming task. Special skills are always needed. Artists and painters can design visual aides and advertisements. Communication specialists and writers are needed to draw up documents and to organize media campaigns. Fund-raisers, speech-writers, typists, and door bell ringers—all are needed. One should be prepared for odd assignments. College graduates often are most interested in helping out on "research activities," and though there are numerous research assignments involved in party and election activities, academic research about the great issues of the day often gets subordinated to the more urgent tasks of organizing coffee hours, testimonial dinners, and driving around town on countless errands.

One of the important jobs in party politics is of course enlarging the number of the party faithful. The task of getting party loyalists out to vote is equally important. Identification systems have to be devised. Names and addresses of those not regis-

[1]Michael Walzer, *Political Action: A Practical Guide to Movement Politics* (Quadrangle Books, 1971), p. 122.

"That's the way our system works—each branch of government watches the other two, and the people watch dumbfounded."
Editorial cartoon by Frank Interlandi. Copyright, Los Angeles Times. Reprinted with permission.

tered must be obtained. Continual records of those who have moved away and those who have moved into the community must be continually updated. City directories, police lists, and even the telephone book will all be helpful. Another common practice is to check the membership lists of local organizations such as the American Legion or a labor union for names not on the voting list. The citizen-activist ought to approach the unregistered person by mail, over the phone, or, best of all, at home.

Registration laws vary from state to state. The unregistered voter is often apathetic, but our complex system of registration also inhibits many people who are interested in voting; they may not know when or where they can register, what the registration deadlines are, and when and how they must affiliate with a particular party in order to participate directly in party caucuses and primaries. The shrewd party activist will know the answers to these questions and will be able to provide both the cues and incentives needed to get ever larger numbers of people to participate more fully in party and election activities.

The heart of registration and voting drives lies in approaching the individual voter in person, but the approach is much more effective if it comes as part of a general effort. Often the most fruitful procedure is a nonpartisan community-wide program. The drive is carried on through the press, radio, television, posters, civic groups, trade unions, veterans' organizations, window displays, churches, door-to-door canvassing, rallies. In some communities police cars have carried "get-out-the-vote" signs and "votemobiles" have toured with sample voting machines or ballots.

Much of this work would be simple drudgery under any other circumstances. In the heat of a campaign, however, this work often takes on an aura of the dramatic. Volunteers are part of a team engaged in the keen struggle. Party headquarters are always crowded; the phone seems always to be ringing. Crisis follows crisis. Candidates dash in to make arrangements for coming meetings and rush out to speak at the Kiwanis Club's annual barbecue. Rumors flow thick and fast.

Taking part in party politics can be a rewarding business, especially if, ideally, the names on the ballot are those of flesh-and-blood persons you have helped to nominate and—hopefully—elect. In practice, however, no new activists should go into party politics with any illusions of how parties operate. On the local level, organizations are often stagnant, if not moribund. Committees rarely meet, attendance is often low, the parties are run, by and large, by small groups of people who by virtue of their part-time activities find it easier to operate in an undemocratic manner, passing on many of their responsibilities to leaders higher up in the organization. Often the powers over crucial matters such as candidate selection and important allocations of convention delegates and campaign finances become centralized in the hands of remote city and state party veterans.

Party veterans, moreover, often try to run campaigns offering something for everyone, while at the same time saying nothing that will offend anyone. Precisely because Americans are not strongly ideological, the two major parties usually have played down the divisive issues and instead have tried to capture as many differing viewpoints and fence-sitting independents

Ed Valtman '73. The Hartford Times.

as they can. It becomes all the more of a challenge for the citizen-activist to ensure that all issues receive a fair hearing, that none be considered beneath the dignity of their party's candidates. If parties today are often not very democratic in their internal activities, this does not necessarily have to be the case. It has often been the case that parties have not been major sources of new programs and fresh thinking about the critical issues of the day, but this should provide a challenge and a point of departure to prove otherwise.

Vitally important decisions are made between elections and newly recruited party activists will have little trouble getting a foothold in the local or county party organization at such times. Occasionally, the oldline leaders may try to close out newcomers to keep their organization as a kind of private preserve. Such incumbents should not be allowed to succeed without a struggle. Turnover in local and state party posts is higher than most people think. And in many states there are a variety of factions within the two major parties. So, if necessary, one can often work with another part of the organization, or join or form auxiliary groups like the Young Democrats or Young Republicans or the Ripon Society.

Abundant opportunities await the party-activist. The tasks of rebuilding and reshaping the parties to become more participatory themselves, and more effective in achieving their goals are tasks that cry out for concerned citizens. And it is by these activities that citizens can win back for themselves the right not to be bossed, but to direct their government and its officials. This can happen, however, only if large numbers of people are willing to dirty their hands and become involved on a sustained basis at the grass roots of party politics.

Electoral politics

We will never have effective government at all levels until we can persuade many skilled members of our communities that they must take a personal responsibility for what happens. Just as a nation is never finished, so also nations and institutions can decay. Even the best structural processes and the most effective checks and balances cannot ensure the free and just society envisaged by the framers of the Constitution. The citizen-activist, critical and concerned, can provide the vitality and the vision required for democratic self-government.

For those interested in making a career of electoral politics, there are few set rules; it is more like an obstacle course full of temptations and dangers. One of the persistent and usually fashionable traditions in America has been to deride and make light of the career politician. Intellectuals and foreign visitors decry the lack of brilliant and inspiring people in public life. Clergymen and young idealists despair of the lack of morality and vision in politics. And even major participants in politics laugh at the hyperbole and evasiveness toward critical issues. Said one: "a politician is a statesman who approaches every question with an open mouth."

It is well to remember, however, what Plato once noted: "What is honored in a country will be cultivated there." We need now, just as we did two hundred years ago, a class of politicians who have objectives in view beyond the enlargement of their own careers. They will need to love politics, respect people, and delight in the tough give-and-take that should be the hallmark of democracy—the national conversations between leaders and the public. *Politics is not only the art of the possible, but also the art of making the difficult possible.*

A surprisingly large number of Americans do not want to seek office. There will always be many more who are willing to serve than to run. The personal sacrifices political life demands—loss of privacy, loss of family life, loss of leisure, dangers to one's health, and so on—are far more than most people are willing to pay. Thus, one of the major difficulties in our democracy is finding talented people to run for office.

Certainly chance plays an enormous role in determining whether one succeeds in a political career. This, along with the obvious lack of job security, often dissuades able people from even considering electoral politics. "One who enters politics must realize that he is to live dangerously," a former candidate has said. "In business, the line between the red and the black divides anxiety and comfort, but a businessman can survive a bad year; in politics 0.1 percent on one's biennial gross vote can mean the difference between prosperity and ruin."[2] It might be added that before entering politics, the prospective candidate would be wise to reflect on his personal strengths and weaknesses. If he or she is sensitive to criticism, shy, short of temper, and prefers to lead a quiet, peaceful life, the chances are strong that he or she would neither be happy in politics nor be able to develop the kind of democractic temperament so essential for elective public service today.

What can the citizen-activist do who chooses to seek political office? He or she can work actively in the campaigns of others and see first hand the ordeal of winning nomination and subsequent election. The would-be politician should also read widely in history, politics, and philosophy, know the use of parables, develop an excellent memory, study the major issues of the day, cultivate the leadership of major organizations in the region, and develop as fully as possible the capacity to listen and to learn.

[2]Stimson Bullitt, *To Be A Politican* (Doubleday, 1959), p. 53

Senator Hugh D. Scott, Jr., long-time minority leader in the Senate and a former chairman of the Republican National Committee, once listed the following personality traits as especially helpful for men and women who would like to be active in politics:

1. Be politically informed.

2. Integrity. Despite cynicism about politics, a dishonest politician is almost always exposed sooner or later.

3. Patience. Scott spent "twenty years or so of being stopped several times a day by people with something on their mind, of having my lapels seized so firmly or my sleeve tugged by someone who wants something done that he feels I may be able to do, of long interviews with people with a grievance, a petition, a plan, an invention, or just a two-way ball-bearing tongue."

4. Courtesy. "On Ballot Boulevard there's no market at all for the sour stuff."

5. Gregariousness.

6. Hard work. "To know your neighborhood and to help your neighbors is a 365-day-a-year job."

7. A sense of humor. Freshman members of Congress are warned by their elders, "Don't violate Rule Six." And what is Rule Six? "Don't take yourself too seriously." And Rules One to Five? "Don't take yourself too seriously." A sense of proportion, a sense of humor.

8. Courage.[3]

An important lesson learned time and again during the 1960s and early 1970s was that by finding out the rules and simply getting enough people to the right caucuses, preconvention meetings, party gatherings, and to the polls, new people can get themselves elected to important posts.[4] But the rules are very complex and often difficult to figure out. Rarely is a candidacy successfully launched and brought to fruition in a few weeks, except in occasional special elections held to fill vacancies created by death or unexpected retirement. And very long is the list of celebrated successful politicians who won office only after losing election bids one or several times.

A candidate for office should also learn how to use multiple advisers and know well the dangers of listening to only one set of counsellors. Many younger politicians can find themselves surrounded by people who act more like cheerleaders than candid and perceptive analysts. On the other hand, many an effective politician is driven by compulsions and intuitive guesswork that he himself may very well not comprehend, since few people can be their own analysts. Too much introspection and too much advice-soliciting can paralyze.

Advisory politics

For many, party and electoral politics will not be the best way to contribute to government by the people. Those who have specialized knowledge that might improve governmental performance may prefer other alternatives. As the late Justice Robert H. Jackson suggested, "It is not the function of our government to keep the citizen from falling into error; it is the function of the citizen to keep the government from falling into error."

Public officials and career public servants at all levels of government customarily welcome advice on public policy. If they don't welcome it, they should not be allowed to ignore new ideas or inhibit open scrutiny of their operations. In practice, most officials conduct hearings, appoint study groups, establish advisory committees, and frequently have small sums of money available for consultant studies. For the citizen-activists who wants to change existing policies or help pass and establish new policies, there are almost limitless opportunities to obtain a hearing and press one's arguments.

It is important to appreciate, however, that especially in a democracy the academically well-researched argument will carry less weight than the political argument—that is, whether an adviser believes that a policy is "right" may be less important to many officials than how the policy will affect their career or reelection chances. Hence advisory work does not take place in a political vacuum. Usually, some people will be advantaged and some disadvantaged by whatever new initiative the candidate is recommending.

An ideal place for the citizen-adviser to start out is right in his or her home area.

Every community needs a loose coalition of people, willing to work together, often on a nonpartisan basis, to examine and offer policy advice on urgent city problems. City councilmen and their staffs cannot do it alone, nor can local business elites or minority leaders. What is needed are citizen-advisers who will apply their professional skills as well as common sense to such issues as crime, integration, housing, and ecology and assist those in office in evolving equitable and effective programs.

Citizen-advisers, to be sure, will often be disillusioned by the clumsiness with which politicians and bureaucrats use advice; but the adviser will learn, too, that knowledge is power. Most people holding public office are receptive to constructive ideas. Anyone willing to under-

[3]Hugh D. Scott, *How To Go Into Politics* (John Day, 1949) pp. 26 ff.

[4]William T. Murphy, Jr. and Edward Schneier, *Vote Power: How to Work for the Person You Want Elected* (Doubleday, 1974). For another view, see Stephen C. Shadegg, *The New How To Win An Election* (Taplinger, 1972).

take systematic policy and program evaluations and who can present a convincing rationale for dealing with the seemingly intractable realities finds a ready audience. The person who can design cars that will cause less smog, invent better ways to produce energy and conserve natural resources, or formulate better foreign policies will find politicians knocking at his or her door.

As one becomes better known as a creative adviser, the outlets for policy advice will grow rapidly. Party platform committees will ask you to testify; departmental officials at state and national levels may appoint you to advisory panels; television and newspaper journalists will seek interviews. Citizen-advisers learn too that once they have gained recognition and visibility in their field, their ability to influence officials and make governments more responsible is measurably enhanced. They can help organize opposition coalitions of experts. Then, too, they can use their positions of acknowledged expertise to educate fellow citizens to support or oppose government programs. Citizen-advisers who closely watch government programs doubtless will become concerned with the often inadequate means of program implementation. In the best of situations they will not only come up with new ideas but also develop new ways of turning these ideas into successful programs.

Pressure or movement politics

The best insurance system for honest government is an alert citizenry, ever watchful of its leaders, and increasingly imaginative in developing new means to keep public officials and party leaders accountable and within the Constitution. Government by the people need not be a utopia unrelated to present-day processes and politics.

The difficulty with pressure politics is that not all the pressures are represented. As we saw from our study of the American political system, it is biased in favor of producer interests against those of the consumers, in favor of the wealthy and educated as against the poor and ignorant. This has become well recognized, but it does not have to be accepted as the way things have to be. Those who claim to speak for the consumer and for the poor, the depressed, and the discriminated against have organized. "Public interest" lobbies, citizen-activist movements, and countless consumer groups have sprung into action in recent years. Their prime goal is not to elect people to office but to influence those who hold public office, to change policies, to increase accountability, and to lessen the secrecy that so often grows up as a barrier to the people's right to know.

"To choose pressure politics," writes Michael Walzer, "means to try to influence those people who already hold power, who sit in official seats, who may even be responsible for the outrages against which the movement is aimed."[5] Here again there are few established rules. Tactics differ markedly—from the SDS and Saul Alinsky kind of militance on the one hand to the more approved techniques of a Ralph Nader study report and of the League of Women Voters on the other. Certain general strategies are similar: Do not presuppose the hostility of all officials, media people, and outsiders. Neither look up to anyone nor down on anyone. Attack the people's leaders, not the people. (In politics, of course, everybody claims to speak for the public interest and to represent the people.) Alliances and coalitions with other related groups should be explored. Every effort should be made to increase the membership's understanding of how government works and what the issues are. What they do not know about, they can't object to. As H. L. Mencken said, "Conscience is the inner voice which warns us that someone may be watching." As Ralph Nader and Common Cause have found: accountability is at the very heart of free self-government.

On occasion, pressure groups and "public interest" lobbies support certain candidates with profit. "The independent, single-issue candidate is another easy choice. He is unlikely to win, but his campaign can serve to spread the word, and a good vote can have significant demonstration effect. A single-issue campaign may also put considerable pressure on one of the major parties to make the cause its own and so win the support of whatever constituency is being mobilized.[6] Educational campaigns, boycotts, petitions, strikes, marches, and nonviolent civil disobedience activities all must be considered.

Those who choose pressure politics do so in large part because they despair of realizing their main aims merely by electing new people to public office. As Common Cause's John W. Gardner often put it, his group was not above politics, it was merely nonpartisan. It was his view that elected officials are limited by the accommodations they made to get elected, limited again by their desire to be reelected, and limited by biased structural constraints in the institutions they must work with. Gardner added: "Clearly we cannot organize our society in

[5]Walzer, *Political Action*, p. 26

[6]*Ibid.*, p. 104.

such a way that we are dependent on inspired presidential leadership, because most of the time it won't be there. We must build creative strength in other parts of the system. And in fact that's the kind of system it was intended to be. It was never intended that we should seek a Big Daddy and lean on him. We shall save ourselves—or we won't be saved."[7]

Just as in election work, most citizen-action work will be tedious, routine, and repetitive. Stamina is essential. Membership maintenance and internal communications will sometimes seem urgent, exhilarating, and highly rewarding, but most of the time they will not. Strategies will vary from one region to another and from one set of policy issues to the next. But one has only to look at the considerable impact of Ralph Nader and the many public interest research groups he helped start to see that a few individuals—*when they know what they are doing*—can bring about significant change. These Nader-encouraged local student pressure groups have brought about such changes as the following:

1. The appointment of an ombudsman for prisoners in the St. Louis jails.

2. New regulations that forbid lumber companies to cut swaths of forest without federal approval.

3. A new plan in Detroit that forces landlords to repair dilapidated housing.

4. Successfully challenged utility rate increases in Massachusetts and Vermont.

5. The conception of a new Minnesota law that regulates the selling of hearing aids.

6. The passage of a truth-in-lending law in New York State.

Futures in public service

Public employment has been the most rapidly growing segment of the American work force. More than one out of every seven people in the American work force serve as employees of more than 78,000 entities of government formed to provide public services at the federal, state, county, or municipal levels.[8] Most of the positions in government service are open to qualified people, regardless of their political persuasions. The career services at every level constantly need to recruit able newcomers. To meet these needs, governments are increasingly competitive with private employers for highly educated professionals.

Over 90 percent of the positions in the federal executive branch are open to qualified citizens by appointment. Most of these positions are filled through civil service examinations. Veterans receive preferences on these examinations, which are held at the various regional headquarters of the Civil Service Commission.

Contrary to popular belief only about 12 percent of federal civilian positions are in Washington, D.C. The rest are scattered throughout the fifty states and in over 100 countries around the world. Positions calling for professional training are filled through interviews and questionnaires that enable the Civil Service Commission and the appointing agencies to examine the competence and experience of the individual.

Several federal agencies have their own personnel systems and are not covered by regular civil service rules. The TVA, FBI, National Security Agency, United States Information Agency, CIA, and Foreign Service Officer Corps, for example, recruit and hire their own employees.

The Foreign Service Office Corps deserves special mention because of its more specialized testing and its important diplomatic responsibilities. Written, oral, and language tests are required, and intensive interviews are used to eliminate candidates who seem "shy, aggressive, boorish, unable to defend their views, who give evidence of low standards of conduct, and who show a lack of knowledge of the United States." Only about 5 percent of all applicants pass the diplomatic exams. Persons who wish to take the examinations may receive application forms from the Board of Examiners for the Foreign Service, Department of State, Washington, D.C. 20520.

Civil service jobs are now graded in a general schedule of eighteen grades with competitive salaries and attractive fringe benefits, retirement programs, and vacation time. The Hatch Act "officially" protects civil servants from being obliged to contribute to political funds, but it also bars them from directly participating in any partisan political activities. As might be expected, the Hatch Act is still viewed as a mixed blessing, in part because it prevents such a large number of people from vigorous participation in party politics.

Those who seek work in the federal career services should do so without illusions. Three federal agencies—Defense, Post Office, and the Veterans Administration—account for nearly 75 percent of all federal positions. Despite valiant efforts to make the merit system work, a tacit seniority system often takes root. Despite assertions that government service is removed from politics, recent administrations have manipulated promotions and abolished jobs. Departments and bureaus do develop a political life of their own—a passion

[7]John W. Gardner, *In Common Cause* (Norton, 1971), p. 84.

[8]John W. Macy, Jr., *Public Service: The Human Side of Government* (Harper & Row, 1971).

for size, growth, and jurisdictional integrity invariably develops.[9]

There has been considerable discussion in the 1970s about decentralization, or regionalization, of the federal government. Some devolution of authority to federal regional offices or to state and local authorities has occurred. Still, most civil servants would agree that the key positions of power in the civil service are those at their respective headquarters offices in Washington, D.C. To move up the hierarchical ladders, according to many now in the civil service, "you have got to be willing to move to Washington and work at the center. A whole raft of people get stuck in the provinces and become very frustrated." On the other hand many of those in the public service prefer to work in other parts of the country, and it is undeniable that people in a very real sense can make of their jobs what they want—the highly motivated public servant, no matter where he or she is located, nearly always can seize opportunities to improve the quality of government performance.

One of the fastest growing segments of public employment is in state and local governments. The passage of the Intergovernmental Personnel Act of 1971 opened opportunities for inservice training, including assignments in a variety of governmental levels. Salaries generally are not as high in state and local positions as those in federal government, but they are improving as these governments expand their services and raise the standards. The positions of city manager and of city-planning director are especially challenging and demand talented executives with well-developed political and managerial capabilities.

Young people interested in sampling public service may participate in a wide variety of government internship programs at the federal, state, and local levels. Intern programs provide people with short term government experience and a first-hand look at the process. Many members of Congress take on college students as summer interns. Most states and many cities operate intern programs within the state or territorial legislature. Legislative intern programs are usually open to students majoring in political science or in public administration and, of course, law. Information about intern opportunities can usually be obtained from any department of political science or local student government officers.

Citizen-volunteer service

The Peace Corps recruits from a wide range of skilled Americans for overseas work. After screening and training, volunteers are assigned to countries that request Peace Corps services. Applicants must be citizens of the United States and eighteen years of age or older. Volunteers receive no regular salaries but get allowances to cover the cost of clothing, housing, food, and incidental expenses so that they live at an economic level equivalent to their clients in the host country. Upon completion of service, Peace Corps volunteers receive a separation allotment based on time spent overseas. The payment accumulates at the rate of $75 a month. Peace Corps questionnaires are available at most colleges, universities, and post offices.

Volunteers in Service to America (VISTA) is the domestic counterpart of the Peace Corps. Volunteers lend their talents for a year to the service of communities that are striving to solve pressing economic and social problems. After a training period that stresses field experience and discussions of the nature and causes of poverty in the United States, volunteers are sent to work in migrant worker communities, Indian reservations, rural and urban community action programs, hospitals, schools, and mental health facilities. In short, workers may be sent wherever poverty exists. VISTA volunteers are paid only subsistence expenses and a modest monthly stipend and personal allowance.

The several volunteer federal programs have been consolidated under a new national agency, ACTION. ACTION administers the Peace Corps, VISTA, the National Student Volunteer Program, Foster Grandparents, the Retired Senior Volunteer Program, the Service Corps of Retired Executives, and HUD's Office of Voluntary Action. Inquiries about these programs should be addressed to ACTION Recruiting Office, Washington, D.C. 20525. Or, you may call ACTION toll free at 800-424-8580. A nationally sponsored Teacher Corps also exists for teachers or potential teachers who want to devote several years of service to poverty area schools. Inquiries about this program, which in addition offers teacher-training fellowships, should be directed to the Teacher Corps, U.S. Office of Education, Washington, D.C. 20202.

Last word

Citizen-activists can have an impact on governmental and political processes. Progress in civil rights, consumerism, ecology, women's liberation, and countless other areas came about only when concerned groups had aquired numbers and force that could no longer be ignored. To

[9]For some interesting discussions about bureaucracy and career service, see John Franklin Campbell, *The Foreign Affairs Fudge Factory* (Basic Books, 1971); Anthony Downs, *Inside Bureaucracy* (Little, Brown, 1967)

have impact, however, people must be willing to concentrate their energies, enlarge the number of people sharing their views, and work hard to channel their activities into effective political action. The essence of democracy is participatory and advocacy politics. And politics without party and pressure politics is really not democratic and open politics at all. Beware of those people who try to remove critical public issues and problems from politics. Some political leaders boast they are above politics. This is like a bishop saying he is above religion.

Winning power must always be subordinate to knowing the proper purposes to which it should be put. But a better America will never result if tens of millions of us become spectators rather than active, vital participants. Ogden Nash once summed it up this way:

They have such refined and delicate palates
That they can discover no one worthy of their ballots
And then when someone terrible gets elected
They say, There, That's just what I expected!

As we have tried to suggest, there is more than one way to become politically active and to serve one's country. What is important is that citizen-activists understand both the assets and responsibilities of our system. Our era is more antipolitical than perhaps any in the past hundred years. Our ideals and aspirations are still valid. The trouble comes when we fail to live up to our own abiding values. The distinguished jurist Elihu Root spoke aptly about the role of political life in America when he said:

> Politics is the practical exercise of the art of self-government, and somebody must attend to it if we are to have self-government; somebody must study it, and learn the art, and exercise patience and sympathy and skill to bring the multitude of opinions and wishes of self-governing people into such order that some prevailing opinion may be expressed and peaceably accepted. Otherwise, confusion will result either in dictatorship or anarchy. The principal ground of reproach against any American citizen should be that he is not a politician. Everyone ought to be.

Every individual in a democracy contributes to its success or failure. Those who, because of ignorance, indifference, or self-complacency, stay on the sidelines, nevertheless influence the course of events, negative though their influence may be. In a very real sense, the quality of commitment and concern of the people broadly determine the type of leadership they get. Citizen-activist programs need to command the allegiance of not only the young but of all the hopeful who dream of a better America and a just world. Citizenship itself should be viewed as nothing less than *an office*—an office for which people must prepare and to which people must devote their time and talent.

Keeping informed: Bibliography

Newspapers, radio, and television are important sources of information, but the person who depends solely on these sources will have an imperfect picture of the world around him. They give only a disconnected story of the sensational—the newsworthy—events. They tell little of the whys and wherefores.

Magazines of general circulation contain useful material, but they do not go deeply into particular questions. Where do you find a law? How do you look up a court decision? Where can you find information on the United Nations? How do you find out how your congressman has voted? What are some good books on the U.S.S.R.? Many aids and services have been designed to make such information readily available.

Important information-dispensing centers are the more than seventy-five hundred public libraries and the many hundreds of private libraries that are open to the public. In these libraries can be found, in addition to magazines of general interest, many specialized journals such as *The American Political Science Review*. There are also a number of periodical indexes, of which the *Public Affairs Information Service* is useful because it indexes books, pamphlets, and reports, as well as articles from hundreds of periodicals on topics in a broad range of current public interest. Major political science journals are included in the *Social Sci-*

ence and Humanities Index. The *International Political Science Abstracts,* edited by the International Political Science Association, provides précis of articles from all major political science journals throughout the world. The *Reader's Guide to Periodical Literature* includes mainly popular magazines with mass or family circulation. The *Index to Legal Periodicals* and *Business Periodicals Index* are also useful.

The *Universal Reference System* is the most comprehensive reference to books, papers, journals, and reviews. Most of these indexes are published monthly and indexed cumulatively at the end of the year; they can help you locate materials on most subjects. In addition to these periodical guides, Robert B. Harmon's *Political Science: A Bibliographical Guide to the Literature* (1965) which is kept up to date by supplements, No. 1 (1968), No. 2 (1971), No. 3 (1973). Lubomyr Wynar's *Guide to Reference Materials in Political Science,* Vol. 1 (1967), Vol. 2 (1968), and the *ABS Guide to Recent Publications in the Social and Behavioral Sciences* (1965), also kept up to date with annual supplements, are useful. Other bibliographies you might consult are Robert Harmon's *Political Science Bibliographies* (1973), and *ABC Pol Sci; Advance Bibliography of Contents: Political Science and Government,* a monthly service which reproduces the tables of contents of periodicals in the field of political science. The card catalog in the library will reveal the books that are available there. You may be able to learn something about an author's reputation or a particular book in the *Book Review Digest;* but reviews in this digest are taken from a limited group of publications and may therefore not be complete. You will also find the *Book Review Index* helpful; it complements the *Book Review Digest* but is more current and complete. It lists sources of all reviews in periodicals indexed, and it comes in monthly and quarterly issues with annual cumulations.

One of the most useful volumes is the *United States Government Manual,* an annual publication. This manual, which can be obtained from the Superintendent of Documents, U.S. Government Printing Office, Washington, D.C. 20402, covers the authority, organization, and functions of all branches of the government. It has up-to-date organization charts, tells who holds the higher executive positions, and gives a brief description of the work of each unit of government. The *Congressional Directory,* also published annually, has some of the materials found in the *Manual,* and it includes autobiographical sketches of members of Congress, lists of congressional committees and committee assignments, election statistics for the last several congressional elections, and maps of congressional districts. The *Directory* is the place to find out the name of your congressman, a short sketch of his life, what committees he is on, and the boundaries of the district he represents. The *Almanac of American Politics,* published by Gambit, contains current biographies, voting records, lobbying interests, as well as political, demographic, and economic profiles on a member's district.

Of special interest to persons interested in social sciences is the *Encyclopedia of the Social Sciences,* published in 1930 under the editorship of

Edwin R. A. Seligman and Alvin Johnson; it contains articles on various topics—political parties, sovereignty, representation, John Locke, for example—that are among the best short treatments to be found. The *International Encyclopedia of the Social Sciences*, which was edited by David L. Sills and published in 1968, complements its predecessor and brings the information up to date.

Although both encyclopedias contain a great deal of biography, the *Dictionary of National Biography* and the *Dictionary of American Biography* are the prime sources for this type of data. Included are some outstanding articles; one by Carl Becker on Benjamin Franklin, for example, is found in the *Dictionary of American Biography*. In *Current Biography* you can find materials and background information on men in the news, and there is a companion set, *Biography Index*, in case specific information has not been written up fully in *Current Biography* for ten years or so. Also of help will be *Who's Who in American Politics* and *Who's Who in Government*.

Certain important tools for quick reference to current events are available, such as *Facts on File*, the *New York Times Index*, the *Wall Street Journal Index*, and *Keesing's Contemporary Archives*.

If you want raw figures, consult the *Statistical Abstract of the United States*, another yearly publication of the Government Printing Office. The reference librarian will be able to point out other useful tools of this nature, such as the *Historical Statistics of the United States*, the *Congressional District Data Book*, and the many publications from the Bureau of the Census. The *American Statistical Index* is a comprehensive guide to the statistical publications of the U.S. government. It is useful in locating which of the numerous statistical publications issued by the government contain the statistics a student may be looking for.

Where can you find a law? We often hear people talk about some statute without having seen it. Where can the actual text be found? The laws of the United States as passed by Congress are first printed individually and are known as slip laws. Each law has a number; in recent years public laws have been numbered according to the term of Congress in which they were enacted. At the end of each year the laws are collected and published by the Government Printing Office under the title of *United States Statutes at Large*. Each year's collection is separately numbered, though there are two separate parts of each number. Part One contains *public laws*—that is, laws affecting the people generally or having to do with governmental organization. Part Two contains *private laws*, those having to do with particular groups or individuals. The laws in the *Statutes at Large* are listed chronologically, each law constituting a separate chapter. The Taft-Hartley Act, for example, is Chapter 120 of Volume 61, on page 136; it is cited as 61 Stat. 136.

The volumes of *Statutes at Large* are useful for research, but they include many laws of only specialized interest. Furthermore, many of the measures modify earlier legislation and are themselves modified by later legislation. To find *current* laws on a topic, it is best to go the *United*

States Code, which contains the public laws of the United States that are in force at the present time. The official edition of the *United States Code* is published every six years. Supplements are issued annually between editions. The laws are arranged according to fifty titles; each title is divided into sections, and each section into paragraphs that are consecutively numbered for each title. The fifty titles cover such subjects as Congress, Title 2; Armed Forces, Title 10; Bankruptcy, Title 11; Labor, Title 29; and so on. The *Code* is cited by title and paragraph. The citation of the Taft-Hartley Act, for example, is 29 U.S.C. 141 ff.

The *Code*, like the *Statutes at Large*, is printed by the Government Printing Office, but there are also commercially published editions known as *United States Code Annotated* (U.S.C.A.) and the *Federal Code Annotated* (F.C.A.). These annotated editions include notes on judicial interpretations of the law as well as the law itself. If available, they are more useful than the *Code* itself.

The series *Treaties in Force* is the best source of information about treaties and executive agreements. These volumes are published annually and are organized chronologically.

Where does one find the rules and regulations issued by the president and the executive agencies? Every day except Sunday and Monday the government publishes the *Federal Register*, which contains executive orders, regulations, and proclamations issued by the president, as well as the orders and regulations promulgated by the executive agencies (including the independent regulatory commissions). These administrative rules and regulations are collected, codified, and kept up to date in the *Code of Federal Regulations*, organized on the same plan as the *United States Code*. The *Code of Federal Regulations*, the *Federal Register*, along with the *United States Government Manual* previously mentioned and the annual publication, *Public Papers of the President*, are part of what is known as the Federal Register System. The *Weekly Compilation of Presidential Documents*, which contains public messages, speeches, and statements of the president, is published every Monday.

The laws as they finally appear on the statute books give, however, only part of the story. Where do you find out what went on before the laws were passed or why certain laws were not passed? This information can, in part, be found in one of the most edifying and interesting items of American letters—the *Congressional Record*. The *Record* is issued every day Congress is in session and is bound and indexed at the end of each session. It contains everything that is said on the floors of the two chambers, plus a lot that is not said. Congress freely gives its consent to requests of its members "to revise and extend their remarks," which is a polite way of saying that congressmen are permitted to include in the *Record* statements they did not make before Congress. These speeches are then reprinted and distributed to the folks back home. Congressmen, with the unanimous consent of their colleagues, also place in the *Record* poems, articles, letters, editorials, and other materials they find interesting. Each day's *Record* is now accompanied by a *Daily Digest* that highlights the events both on the floor of Congress and in committees. Action on specific items can be traced by searching through the index. An easier method is to use the *Digest of Public General Bills* which gives a brief summary of all the public bills and traces their progress in the legislative assembly line.

There are several commercial services that provide convenient references to congressional activities. The *Congressional Quarterly Weekly Report* contains voting records, legislative action, reports on lobbying, and other materials about Congress in action. This is the best source for materials on lobbying activity. The materials are indexed and collected in the *Congressional Quarterly Almanac*, an annual publication. The *United States Code: Congressional and Administrative News* and the *Congressional Index* also provide ready reference to congressional activity. Another helpful way to monitor congressional activity is through the *CIS/Index*, an index to publications of Congress issued monthly with annual cumulations by the Congressional Information Service. It indexes and abstracts committee hearings, prints chamber reports and other congressional documents, and contains a brief summary of the statement of each witness in a hearing and includes page numbers on which particular testimonies appear.

Because most of the real work of Congress is done in committees, the reports of these committees and the printed records of hearings are important sources of information. The hearings and reports may be found in any of the 1,122 depository libraries in the United States. (A depository library is one that receives regularly publications issued by the Government Printing Office.) All depositories are now on a selective basis with the exception of those designated as regional depositories, of which there are thirty-nine. However, there are very few libraries which do not elect to receive congressional hearings.

Congress is not the only branch of the federal government that keeps a record of its work. All the other agencies have their own publications, describing their work and supplying the citizen with general and specialized information. These can be obtained from the Superintendent of Documents, Government Printing Office, Washington D.C. 20402, at a nominal price. They are indexed in the *Monthly Catalog of United States Government Publications.* One of the several general guides to government publications is Laurence F. Schmeckebier's and Roy B. Eastin's *Government Publications and Their Use*, 2nd. rev. ed., (Brookings, 1969).

Activities of the executive branch of the federal government as well as the Congress and the courts are analyzed in the *National Journal Reports*, a weekly publication. This is the best single source on developments within the federal executive. *The Washington Monthly* provides critical essays on policy politics and bureaucracy in Washington.

Where can you find the reports of the federal judiciary? Legal bibliography is a complex subject, but the law is too important to leave to lawyers. The decisions of the Supreme Court are published by the government in numbered volumes known as the *United States Reports.* Cases are cited by volume and page number. *Communist Party of Indiana v. Whitcomb,* 414 U.S. 441 (1974), means that this case can be found in the 414th volume of the *United States Reports* on page 441 and that the opinion was handed down in 1974. Decisions of the Court prior to 1875 are cited by the name of the Supreme Court reporter. Thus, *Marbury v. Madison,* 1 Cranch 137 (1803), can be found in the first volume of Cranch's Supreme Court reports on page 137; the opinion was announced in 1803. Two other editions of Supreme Court opinions are commercially published, and each has its own form of citation. Some of the federal district court rulings are now commercially published in volumes known as the *Federal Supplement.* Those of the federal courts of appeals are now also published by the same commercial publisher in volumes known as the *Federal Reporter.* These reports are not available in many general libraries, but in many communities a special law library, usually located in the courthouse, contains the reports of the cases plus other materials needed by lawyers in their professional work.

Selected bibliography

This bibliography makes no pretense of including all the good books pertinent to American government. Its purpose is to provide an initial guide to the literature. With few exceptions, the rich periodical literature is not mentioned, nor are all the works cited in footnotes to the text included.

Part one Democratic government in America

Government by the people?

Agger, R. E., D. Goldrich, and B. E. Swanson, *The Rulers and the Ruled* (1964). A critique of community power literature.

Bachrach, P., *The Theory of Democratic Elitism* (1967). An appeal for the revitalization of democratic participation.

Banfield, E. C., *Political Influence* (1961). A pluralist view of metropolitan decision-making.

Beam, G. D., *Usual Politics* (1970). A critique of pluralistic analysis and "process democracy."

Bottomore, T. B., *Elites and Society* (1964). A broad approach to elitist theory.

Dahl, R. A., *Who Governs? Democracy and Power in an American City* (1961). Pluralist democracy in New Haven, Connecticut.

———, *After the Revolution? Authority in a Good Society* (1970). An examination of the principles on which the authority of democratic government rests.

Domhoff, G. W., *Who Rules America?* (1967). Concludes that a power elite rules at the national level even if there may be more pluralistic elities at the community level.

Friedenberg, E. Z., *The Anti-American Generation* (1971). Some of the causes of generational conflict.

Gravel, M., *Citizen Power* (1972). Proposal for a "people's platform," by a U.S. senator.

Green, P., and S. Levinson, eds., *Power and Community: Dissenting Essays in Political Science* (1970). Critiques of conventional political science by the "counterestablishment."

Held, V., *The Public Interest and Individual Interests* (1970). Reconciliation of conflict between these two forces.

Hunter, F., *Community Power Structure* (1953). The business community as the center of power in Atlanta, Georgia.

Kariel, H. S., *The Decline of American Pluralism* (1961). A challenge to the assumption that individual freedom is best maintained in a pluralist system.

King, R., *The Party of Eros: Radical Social Thought and Realm of Freedom* (1972). Probing, scholarly critique of sexual radicals.

Lindblom, C. E., *The Intelligence of Democracy* (1965). The role of many interacting groups and individuals in the formation of public policy.

Lowi, T. J., *The End of Liberalism* (1969). An analysis of "interest group liberalism" and a call for authority and standards in government.

Lynd, R. S., and H. M. Lynd, *Middletown* (1929) and *Middletown in Transition* (1937). Classic studies in the stratification of power in Muncie, Indiana.

Mailer, N., *St. George and the Godfather* (1972). Pungent comment on 1972 politics and personalities.

Miliband, R., *The State in Capitalist Society* (1969). The impossibility of political equality under the conditions of advanced capitalism.

Mills, C. W., *The Power Elite* (1956). The domination of American society by the "power elite."

Newfield, J., and J. Greenfield, *A Populist Manifesto* (1972). Populist call for a new majoritarianism.

Nisbet, R. A., *Community and Power* (1953). The drift toward centralization and the eclipse of community.

Polsby, N. W., *Community Power and Political Theory* (1963). A critique of stratification studies of community power from a pluralist perspective.

Presthus, R., *Men at the Top: A Study in Community Power* (1964). Decision-making in two small communities.

Riesman, D., *et al., The Lonely Crowd* (1950). An influential assessment of American social character.

Rose, A. M., *The Power Structure: Political Process in American Society* (1967). A pluralist view of American politics by a sociologist.

Roszak, T., *The Making of a Counter Culture* (1969). A discussion of the new culture being created by the youth of America.

Skolnick, J. H., and E. Currie, eds., *Crisis in American Institutions* (1970). A critical look at American life.

Truman, D. B., *The Governmental Process: Political Interests and Public Opinion* (1951). Politics as group conflict: a widely used analysis.

Political analysis

Bentley, A. F., *The Process of Government* (1967). A seminal study in methodology and a systematic treatment of the role of interest groups in the political process.

Buchanan, W., *Understanding Political Variables* (1969). An introduction to empirical political analysis.

Buehrig, E. H., ed., *Essays in Political Science* (1966). Readings on the state of the discipline.

Charlesworth, J. C., ed., *Contemporary Political Analysis* (1967). Eight approaches to political study.

Claunch, J. M., ed., *Mathematical Applications in Political Science* (1965). Four essays concerning the use of mathematics in political science.

Cnudde, C. F., and D. E. Neubauer, eds., *Empirical Democratic Theory* (1969). A good collection of recent efforts in empirical democratic theory.

Connolly, W. E., *Political Science and Ideology* (1967). Toward a neutral definition and application of ideology.

Crick, B., *The American Science of Politics: Its Origins and Conditions* (1959). A critical study of American political science.

Dahl, R. A., *Modern Political Analysis* (1970). Second edition of an excellent short introduction to the systematic study of politics.

Davies, J. C., *Human Nature in Politics: The Dynamics of Political Behavior* (1963). Argues that political behavior is rooted in man's organic needs.

Deutsch, K. W., *The Nerves of Government: Models of Political Communication and Control* (1963). Toward a general theory of politics through the use of communication systems metaphor.

Downs, A., *An Economic Theory of Democracy* (1957). A deductive model for analysis and investigation.

Easton, D., *A Framework for Political Analysis* (1965). Seeking a general theory of politics.

———, *A Systems Analysis of Political Life* (1965). Seeking a general theory of politics.

Edelman, M., *The Symbolic Uses of Politics* (1964). A provocative analysis of the meanings of political acts.

Ellul, J., *The Political Illusion* (1967). Opinions on modern politics.

Flanigan, W., and D. E. Repass, *Electoral Behavior* (1968). Exercises in data analysis for beginning students.

Flathman, R. E., *The Public Interest: An Essay Concerning the Normative Discourse of Politics* (1966). The relation between reason and morals in decision-making.

Friedrich, C. J., *Man and His Government: An Empirical Theory of Politics* (1963).

———, ed., *Nomos XII: Rational Decision* (1964). Papers on a wide range of problems dealing with the concept of rational decision-making.

Garceau, O., ed., *Political Research and Political Theory* (1968). Essays on theory and methodology.

Gibson, Q., *The Logic of Social Enquiry* (1960). An exposition of scientific method.

Gotshalk, D. W., *Human Aims in Modern Perspective* (1966). Human aims and their implications for public policy.

Gouldner, A. W., *The Coming Crisis of Western Sociology* (1970). Critique of functionalist sociology.

Hyneman, C. S., *The Study of Politics: The Present State of American Political Science* (1959). A survey of research problems, methods, and data.

Jouvenel, B. de, *The Art of Conjecture* (1967). The methodological problems of anticipating future developments.

———, *The Pure Theory of Politics* (1963).

Knutson, J. E., *The Human Basis*

of the Polity: A Psychological Study of Political Men (1972). Need requirements and political behavior.

Landau, M., *Political Theory and Political Science: Studies in the Methodology of Political Inquiry* (1972). Attempt to clarify the relation of science to political science.

Lasswell, H. D., *The Future of Political Science* (1963). A blueprint for the discipline by an eminent social scientist.

Leege, D. C. and W. L. Francis, *Political Research: Design, Measurement and Analysis* (1974). Important methodologv text.

Lenski, G. E., *Power and Privilege: A Theory of Social Stratification* (1966). Causes and effects of the distribution of political and economic power.

Lipset, S. M., ed., *Politics and the Social Sciences* (1969) On the current relationship between political science and related disciplines.

Maclver, R. M., *The Web of Government* (1947). An analysis of government.

Meehan, E. J., *Contemporary Political Thought* (1967).

———, *The Theory and Method of Political Analysis* (1965). A scientific approach to political phenomena.

Mills, C. W., *The Sociological Imagination* (1959). The promise of social research by a leading critic of American civilization.

Ranney, A., ed., *Political Science and Public Policy* (1968). The role of political science in policy analysis.

Servan-Schreiber, J. J., *The Radical Alternative* (1971). Problems of industrial society.

Simon, Y., *The Tradition of Natural Law: A Philosopher's Reflections* (1965). Basic philosophical questions of government.

Van Dyke, V., *Political Science: A Philosophical Analysis* (1960). Analysis of various approaches to the study of politics.

Woelfl, P. A., *Politics and Jurisprudence* (1966). Classical criticism of modern political science.

General treatments of American government and society

Bryce, J. B., *The American Commonwealth*, 3 vols. (1888). Ranks with Toqueville; more descriptive and less analytical.

Burns, J. M., *Uncommon Sense* (1972). Call for more principled and less "pragmatic" politics.

Clark, K. B., *Pathos of Power* (1974). Political power and human potential.

Clough, S. B., and T. F. Marburg, *The Economic Basis of American Civilization* (1968). The history of United States economy and its role in the shaping of American civilization as a whole.

Dietze, G., *America's Political Dilemma* (1968). Contends that America's democratic development has taken the system from bad to worse.

Ellul, J., *The Technological Society* (1967). A study in the motives for societal development and a commentary on the present state of society

Harrington, M., *The Accidental Century* (1965). A treatise on the state of man and society in the twentieth century.

Harris, L., *The Anguish of Change* (1973). Key changes in public opinion.

Havens, M. C., *The Challenges to Democracy: Consensus and Extremism in American Politics* (1965). A reappraisal of the moral bases of the American political system.

Kendall, W., and C. W. Carey, *The Basic Symbols of the American Political Tradition* (1970). Critique of American egalitarian tradition and scholars' emphasis on it.

Kennedy, R. F., *To Seek a Newer World* (1968). Propositions for social and political improvement.

Lerner, M., *America as a Civilization: Life and Thought in the United States Today* (1957). Wide-ranging study of American pluralism.

McCarthy, E., *First Things First: New Priorities for America* (1968). A suggested political course for the United States.

Myrdal, G., *An American Dilemma* (1944). Monumental study of American society with special attention to the problems of relationships between blacks and whites.

Niebuhr, R., *Man's Nature and His Communities* (1965). A study of man in society by a leading theologian.

Polsby, N. W., *Political Promises* (1974). Wide-ranging essays on contemporary American politics.

Toqueville, A. de, *Democracy in America*, 2 vols. (Phillips Bradley edition, 1964; first published in 1835.) Classic study of American government.

Wattenberg, B. J., *The Real America* (1974). Argument, based on census data, that America "never had it so good" domestically.

American political thought

Bailyn, B., *The Origins of American Politics* (1968). Colonial political thought.

Becker, C. L., *Modern Democracy* (1941). Study accenting the economic basis of democracy and the discrepancy between the ideal and the actual.

Benson, L., *The Concept of Jacksonian Democracy* (1961). The emergence of mass participation in politics.

Berg, E., *Democracy and the Majority Principle: A Study in Twelve Contemporary Political Theories* (1965). Study of the majority principle and its role in achieving popular government.

Boorstin, D., *The Genius of American Politics* (1953). On the lack of ideology in American politics.

Bunzel, J. H., *Anti-Politics in America* (1967). The growing negative strains in American politics.

Commager, H. S., *Majority Rule and Minority Rights* (1943). Defense of the majority-rule principle and attack on the limitations of judicial review.

———, *The American Mind* (1950). An attempt to discover a distinctively American way of thought and conduct.

Craven, W. F., *The Legend of the Founding Fathers* (1956). Emphasizes contributions of the Puritans.

Croly, H., *The Promise of American Life* (1909). Intellectual foundations of the Progressive movement.

Dahl, R. A., *A Preface to Democratic Theory* (1956) Constructs a model of democracy and finds Madisonian and populistic models inadequate.

Frankel, C., *The Democratic Prospect* (1962). An examination of democracy in an age of science and technology.

Gabriel, R. H., *The Course of American Democratic Thought*, 2nd ed. (1956). Interpretation of democratic thought from 1815 to the time of publication.

Hartz, L., *The Liberal Tradition in America: An Interpretation of American Political Thought since the Revolution* (1955). Emphasizes the uniqueness of the American liberal tradition.

Hofstadter, R., *The American Political Tradition and the Men Who Made It* (1954). Study of the ideology of American statesmen, emphasizing the basic agreement underlying their political conflicts.

———, *The Age of Reform: From Bryan to FDR* (1955). The American reform impulse, 1890–1940.

———, *Anti-Intellectualism in American Life* (1963). A historical essay on the unpopularity of intellect.

Kendall, W., *John Locke and the Doctrine of Majority Rule* (1941). Written by an exponent of the majority-rule principle.

Lane, R., *Political Ideology: Why the American Common Man Believes What He Does* (1962). Study of political belief systems.

Lindsay, A. D., *The Modern Democratic State* (1943). Statement of the nature of democracy, its development, its essence, and defense of it, by an English scholar.

Lippmann, W., *Essays in the Public Philosophy* (1956). Antiparliamentarian, Burkean defense of democracy.

Meiklejohn, D., *Freedom and the Public: Public and Private Morality in America* (1965). Governmental obligation concerning moral awareness.

Merriam, C. E., *A History of American Political Theories* (1903; reissued 1936). Standard classic.

Mill, J. S., *Representative Government* (1882). One of the most important books on the foundations and problems of democracy.

Niebuhr, R., *The Children of Light and the Children of Darkness* (1944). Short defense of democracy by the late theologian.

Parrington, V. L., *Main Currents in American Thought* (1927–1930). Interpretation of American literature, including the writings of the major political theorists and practitioners.

Pennock, J. R., *Liberal Democracy* (1950). Defense of democracy, major threats to it, and the limitation on the majority in democratic government.

Perry, R. B., *Puritanism and Democracy* (1944). A study of two American ideals, this book has been called a "thesaurus of democratic thought and an arsenal of democratic defense."

Riemer, N., *The Revival of Democratic Theory* (1962). Call for renewed theoretical efforts based on the democratic premise.

Rossiter, C. L., *Seedtime of the Republic* (1953). Political ideas of the men who founded the Republic.

Sandifer, D. V., and L. R. Scheman, *The Foundations of Freedom: The Inter-Relationship between Democracy and Human Rights* (1966). Theory and reality in the relation between human rights and democracy.

Sartori, G., *Democratic Theory* (1962). The concept of democracy as practiced by many different nations.

Spitz, D., *Patterns of Anti-democratic Thought* (1949). Refutation of the major critics of democracy from the right.

Thorson, T. L., *The Logic of Democracy* (1962). Stimulating attempt to justify democracy logically.

Tuccille, J., *Radical Libertarianism: A New Political Alternative* (1970). Right-wing libertarianism versus traditional conservatism.

Tussman, J., *Obligation and the Body Politic* (1960). Commitments of a democrat.

Watkins, F. M., *The Political Tradition of the West* (1948). Traces development of modern liberalism.

Part two **The rules and how they grew**

Revolution and confederation

Bailyn, B., *Ideological Origins of the American Revolution* (1967).

———, and J. N. Garrett, eds., *Pamphlets of the American Revolution, 1750–1776.* Vol. 1, 1750–1765 (1965). Colonial publications on conflicts immediately preceding the Revolution.

Becker, C. L., *The Declaration of Independence* (1942).

Boorstin, D. J., *The Americans: The Colonial Experience* (1958). Emphasis on the uniqueness of the colonial experience and its influence on the development of the American character.

Chambers, W. N., *Political Parties in a New Nation: The American Experience. 1776–1809* (1963). Development and role of the party system in a new polity.

Dumbauld, E., *The Declaration of Independence and What It Means Today* (1950). Phrase-by-phrase explanation of the Declaration, placing it in the context of the days in which it was written.

Greene, J. P., *The Reinterpretation of the American Revolution,*

1763–1789 (1968). Important anthology with interpretative essay by the editor.
Jameson, J. F., *The American Revolution Considered as a Social Movement* (1926).
Jensen, M., *The New Nation* (1950). Study of the Confederation; contains sharp criticism of the "chaos and patriots-to-the-rescue" interpretation.
Kurtz, S. G., and J. H. Hutson, eds., *Essays on the American Revolution* (1973). By eight distinguished historians.
Main, J. T., *The Social Structure of Revolutionary America* (1965). Life in America at the time of the Revolution.
Merritt, R. L., *Symbols of American Community, 1735–1775* (1966). Content analysis of colonial newspapers and the growth of American community in the prerevolutionary period.
Miller, H. H., *The Case for Liberty* (1965). Colonial origins of the basic constitutional freedoms.
Miller, J. C., *Origins of the American Revolution* (1943).
Pole, J. R., *Political Representation in England and the Origins of the American Republic* (1966). Analysis of English political activity and its effect on the political development of colonial America.
Wood, G. S., *The Creation of the American Republic: 1776–1787* (1969). Major study of the political values leading to the establishment of the Constitution.

The Constitutional Convention and the ratification campaign

Beard, C. A., *An Economic Interpretation of the Constitution of the United States* (1913). Caused a popular furor and has had a strong influence on historians and political scientists.
Brown, R. E., *Charles Beard and the Constitution: A Critical Analysis of "An Economic Interpretation of the Constitution"* (1956).
Eidelberg, P., *The Philosophy of the American Constitution: A Reinterpretation of the Intentions of the Founding Fathers* (1968). Philosophical interpretation of the Constitution.
Elliot, J., *The Debates in the Several Conventions on the Adoption of the Federal Constitution*, 2nd ed., 5 vols. (1835–1846). Contains the debates in the state ratifying conventions.
Farrand, M., *The Records of the Federal Convention of 1787*, 4 vols., rev. ed., (1966).
Jay, J., J. Madison, and A. Hamilton, *The Federalist* (1788). Basic source material, classic exposition of the Constitution.
Mason, A. T., *The States Rights Debate: Antifederalism and the Constitution* (1964). Antifederalist thought as seen through debates in state ratifying conventions.
Notes of Debates in the Federal Convention of 1787, reported by J. Madison (intro. by Adrienne Koch; 1966). James Madison's record of the Constitutional Convention.
Rossiter, C., *1787: The Grand Convention* (1966). Studies of the delegates and their accomplishments.
Rutland, R. A., *The Ordeal of the Constitution: The Antifederalists and the Ratification Struggle of 1787–1788* (1966). State-by-state, blow-by-blow account.
Smith, D. G., *The Convention and the Constitution: The Political Ideas of the Founding Fathers* (1965). Theories of government underlying the Constitution as it was originally formed.
Smith, J. A., *The Spirit of American Government* (1911). Spirited statement of the thesis that the Constitution is the platform of an antidemocratic movement.
Solberg, W. U., *The Federal Convention and the Formation of the Union of the American States* (1958). Interesting documentary account.
Warren, C., *The Making of the Constitution* (1937). Disputes the Beard thesis (see above), contains day-by-day account of the activities of the delegates.

The living Constitution

Baldwin, L. D., *Reframing the Constitution: An Imperative for Modern America* (1972).
Benedict, M. L, *The Impeachment and Trial of Andrew Johnson* (1973). Revisionist's argument that the action was justified because of Johnson's obstruction of congressional programs.
Berger, R., *Impeachment: The Constitutional Problems* (1972). From fourteenth-century England to America today.
Beth, L. P., *The Development of the American Constitution, 1877–1917* (1971).
Black, C. L., *Impeachment: A Handbook* (1974). Layman's guide: everything you wanted to know but didn't dare ask about impeachment.
Brant, I., *Impeachment: Trials and Errors* (1972). Prompted by opposition of the author to the movement to impeach Justice Douglas.
Chase, H. W., and C. R. Ducat, *Corwin's "The Constitution" and What it Means Today* (1973). Phrase-by-phrase explanation.
Dietze, G., ed., *Essays on the American Constitution* (1965).
Hardin, C. M., *Presidential Power and Accountability* (1974). Call for constitutional reform.
Jacobs, C. E., *The Eleventh Amendment and Sovereign Immunity* (1972).
Magrath, C. P., ed., *Constitutionalism and Politics: Conflict and Consensus* (1968). The nature of a living constitution.
Orfield L. B., *Amending of the Federal Constitution* (1942).
Peltason, J. W., *Corwin and Peltason's "Understanding the Constitution"* (1973). Phrase-by-phrase explanation written for college students and laypersons.
Pritchett, C. H., *The American Constitution* (1968). General treatment of our constitutional system.
Seaton Hall Law Review, *The Constitutional Doctrine of Separation of Powers* (Spring 1974).

Historical background and recent conflicts between President Nixon and the Congress.
Small, N. J., ed., *The Constitution of the United States of America: Analysis and Interpretation* (revised and annotated, 1964), Senate Document 39, 89 Cong., 1st sess., 1964.
Sutherland, A. E., *Constitutionalism in America: Origin and Evolution of its Fundamental Ideas* (1965). Papers marking constitutional development from the Petition of Right in 1628 to the present.
Tugwell, R. G., *The Emerging Constitution* (1974). Call for fundamental change in constitutional structures.
Wiecek, W. M., *The Guarantee Clause of the U.S. Constitution* (1972).

Federalism

An especially rich source of materials on American federalism is the reports of the Advisory Commission on Intergovernmental Relations. The commission, a permanent federal agency, has responsibility for continuing research and periodic recommendations in the area of intergovernmental relations.

Barton, W. V., *Interstate Compacts in the Political Process* (1967). Studies the formation of agencies or districts to help resolve interstate or state–national conflicts.
Bennett, W. H., *American Theories of Federalism* (1968).
Dahl, R. A., and E. R. Tufte, *Size and Democracy* (1973)
Earle, V., ed., *Federalism: Infinite Variety in Theory and Practice* (1968). Essays.
Elazar, D. J., *American Federalism: A View from the States* (1966). General text, essay, and report on a research project.
———, *et al.*, eds., *Cooperation and Conflict: Readings in American Federalism* (1969).
Farkas, S., *Urban Lobbying: Mayors in the Federal Arena* (1971). Federalism and the work of the U.S. Conference of Mayors.
Feld, R. D., and C. Grafton, eds., *The Uneasy Partnership: The Dynamics of Federal, State, and Urban Relations* (1973). Readings.
Fesler, J. W., *Area and Administration* (1949). Lectures on problems arising from functional and regional administration.
Friedrich, C. J., *Trends of Federalism in Theory and Practice* (1968). Comparative survey of modern federal systems.
Goldwin, R. A., ed., *A Nation of States: Essays on the American Federal System* (1963).
Graves, W. B., *American Intergovernmental Relations: Their Origins, Historical Development, and Current Status* (1964). Problems of twentieth century federalism.
Grodzins. M., *The American System,* ed. D. J. Elazar (1966). American federalism examined by a noted scholar. Edited after his death by a longtime friend.
Handler, J. F., *Reforming the Poor: Welfare Policy, Federalism, and Morality* (1972). Importance of "state power."
Key, V. O., Jr., *The Administration of Federal Grants to the States* (1939). Pioneering study.
Leach, R. H., *American Federalism* (1970). Comprehensive analysis.
Macmahon, A. W. *Administering Federalism in a Democracy* (1972). By a senior scholar.
May, R. J., *Federalism and Fiscal Adjustment* (1969). Empirical analysis emphasizing balance among constituent units.
Patterson, J. T., *The New Deal and the States: Federalism in Transition* (1969).
Reagan, M. D., *The New Federalism* (1972). Argues that states are dependents of the national government.
Reuss, H. S., *Revenue-Sharing: Crutch or Catalyst for State and Local Government?* (1970). Congressman's argument that revenue-sharing funds be conditioned on structural reform at the state and local levels.
Riker, W. H., *Federalism: Origin, Operation, Significance* (1964). Sophisticated study.
Schmidhauser, J. R., *The Supreme Court as Final Arbiter in Federal-State Relations, 1789–1957* (1958).
Sharkansky, I., *The Maligned States: Policy Accomplishments, Problems, and Opportunities* (1972).
Sundquist, J. L., with D. W. Davis, *Making Federalism Work: A Study of Program Coordination at the Community Level* (1969). Problem of coordinating programs in the federal system.
Wagner, R. E., *The Fiscal Organization of American Federalism* (1971). Favors flexibility in allowing citizens to create new states.
Wright, D. S., *Federal Grants-in-Aid: Perspectives and Alternatives* (1968). Broad assessment of the program of federal grants.

Part three Civil liberties and citizenship

Abernathy, G. M., *Civil Liberties under the Constitution,* 2nd ed. (1972). Casebook and commentary.
Abraham, J. J., *Freedom and the Court: Civil Rights and Liberties in the United States,* 2nd ed. (1972).
American Civil Liberties Union, *Annual Reports.* State of civil liberties.
Anastopolo, G., *The Constitutionalists: Notes on the First Amendment* (1971). Reflections of an informed and involved person.
Arendt, H., *Crisis of the Republic: Lying in Politics; Civil Disobedience: On Violence; Thoughts on Politics and Revolution* (1972).
Barker, L. J., and T. W. Barker, Jr., *Freedom, Courts, Politics: Studies in Civil Liberties* (1965). Problems of civil liberties placed in their political contexts.
———, *Civil Liberties and the Constitution,* 2nd ed. (1975). Cases and commentaries.
Emerson, T. I. et al., *Political*

and Civil Rights in the United States, 2 vols, 3rd ed. (1967) with 1971 supplement. Comprehensive collection of liberties materials.

Hand, L., *The Bill of Rights* (1958). Famous judge's statement of the need for judicial self-restraint in the area of civil liberties.

Krislov, S., *The Supreme Court and Political Freedom* (1968). Role of the Court.

Longaker, R. P., *The President and Individual Liberties* (1961). The role of the executive branch in the maintenance of civil liberties.

Rutland, R. A., *The Birth of the Bill of Rights, 1776–1791* (1962). Best single-volume history of origins and early years.

First amendment freedoms

Barker, C., and M. H. Fox, *Classified Files: The Yellowing Pages* (1972). Report on scholars' access to government documents.

Barron, J. A., *Freedom of the Press for whom? The Right of Access to Mass Media* (1973).

Bush, C. R., ed., *Free Press and Fair Trial* (1971). Studies of impact, if any, of publicity on trial outcomes.

Carmen, I. H., *Movies, Censorship, and the Law* (1966).

Casper, J. D., *The Politics of Civil Liberties* (1972). Litigation as part of, and reflection of, the views and values of the nation.

Chafee, Z., *Free Speech in the United States,* rev. ed. (1941). Most comprehensive study of restrictions on speech during and after World War I; discussion of dangers inherent in sedition laws.

Clor, H. M., ed., *Censorship and Freedom of Expression: Essays on Obscenity and the Law* (1971). Essays reflecting diversity of approach.

Commission on Obscenity and Pornography, *Report* (1970). Controversial report containing findings, conclusions, and recommendations.

Dolbeare, K. M., and P. E. Hammond, *The School Prayer Decision: From Court Policy to Local Practice* (1971). Linkages between Supreme Court decisions and local action.

Epstein, J., *The Great Conspiracy Trial: An Essay on Law, Liberty, and the Constitution* (1970). The trial of the "Chicago Eight."

Ernst, M. L., and A. V. Schwartz, *Censorship: The Search for the Obscene* (1964). Argument that the dangers inherent in censorship are greater than those in pornography.

Georgetown Law Journal, *Media and the First Amendment in a Free Society* (1973). Symposium.

Gilmor, D. M., *Free Press and Fair Trial* (1966). Survey of cases and problems.

Hohenberg, J., *Free Press/Free People: The Best Cause* (1971). History, principally of Europe and the U.S.

House Subcommittee on Foreign Operations and Government Information, *Administration of the Freedom of Information Act* (1973).

Lasswell, H. D., *National Security and Individual Freedom* (1950). Pressures created by the Cold War, with recommendations.

Latham, E., *The Communist Controversy in Washington—From the New Deal to McCarthy* (1966). Study of communist activity in the federal government.

Levin, M. B., *Political Hysteria in America: The Democratic Capacity for Repression* (1972). From the 1920s red scare to the 1970s.

Lofton, J., *Justice and the Press* (1966). Suggests voluntary restraints for the press in trial coverage.

Manwaring, D. R., *Render unto Caesar* (1962). A study of the flag-salute controversy.

Meiklejohn, A., *Free Speech and Its Relation to Self-Government* (1948). Attack on the clear-and-present-danger doctrine and defense of the absolute right of political speech.

Mill, J. S., *Essay on Liberty* (1859; many editions). Famous defense of free speech.

Morgan, R. E., *The Supreme Court and Religion* (1972). Review of the issues.

Muir, W. K., Jr., *Prayer in the Public Schools* (1968). Activities and attitudes of school officials in the aftermath of rulings on school prayer.

Murphy, P. L., *The Meaning of Freedom of Speech: First Amendment Freedoms from Wilson to FDR* (1972).

———, *The Constitution in Crisis Times, 1918–1969* (1972).

Pember, D. R., *Privacy and the Press: The Law, the Mass Media, and the First Amendment* (1972).

Perry, J. M., *Us & Them: How the Press Covered the 1972 Election* (1974).

Rosenbloom, D. H, *Federal Service and the Constitution* (1971). Constitutional and legal rights of federal employees.

Shapiro, M., *Freedom of Speech: The Supreme Court and Judicial Review* (1966). Argument for judicial activism in defense of free speech.

Small, W. J., *Political Power and the Press* (1972). By a CBS official.

Whalen, C. W., Jr., *Your Right to Know* (1973). Congressman's argument in favor of "shield" legislation for journalists.

Equality under the law

Barrett, R. H., *Integration at Ole Miss* (1965). Liberal Southerner's account of the desegregation crisis at the University of Mississippi.

Berman, W. C., *The Politics of Civil Rights in the Truman Administration* (1970).

Brophy, W. A., and S. Aberle, *The Indian: America's Unfinished Business* (1966). The injustices done to the American Indian.

Brotz, H., ed., *Negro Social and Political Thought: 1850–1920* (1966). An anthology of Negro thought on the dilemma of the black American.

Bullock, C. S., II, and H. R. Rodgers, Jr., *Black Political Attitudes: Implications for Political Support* (1972).

Burkey, R. M., *Racial Discrimina-*

tion and Public Policy in the United States (1971). Review of practices and policy responses.

Carmichael, S., and C. V. Hamilton, *Black Power: The Politics of Liberation in America* (1967). Influential formulation of the concept of black power.

Clark, K. B., *Dark Ghetto* (1965). Life in the black ghetto.

Claude, R., *The Supreme Court and the Electoral Process* (1970).

Curtis, J. C., and L. L. Gould, eds., *The Black Experience in America: Selected Essays* (1970). The black experience in America from colonial times to the present.

Daniel, P., *The Shadow of Slavery: Peonage in the South, 1901–1969* (1972).

Davidson, C., *Biracial Politics: Conflict and Coalition in the Metropolitan South* (1972). Case study of Houston, Texas.

Draper, T., *The Rediscovery of Black Nationalism* (1970). The historical roots.

Gillette W., *The Right to Vote: Politics and the Passage of the Fifteenth Amendment* (1965). A concise history of the passage of the Fifteenth Amendment.

Grimes, A. P., *Equality in America: Religion, Race, and the Urban Majority* (1964). Essays illustrating the impact of Supreme Court decisions in modern America.

———, *The Puritan Ethic and Woman Suffrage* (1967). On the origins of woman suffrage.

Hamilton, C. V., *The Bench and the Ballot: Southern Federal Judges and Black Voters* (1973). Role of trial courts in the enforcement of voting rights laws.

———, ed., *The Black Experience in America* (1973). Essays by black scholars and activists focusing on tactics and goals.

Handlin, O., *Race and Nationality in American Life* (1957).

———, *The Uprooted* (1952). Moving history of immigration from the perspective of the immigrants.

Hanes, W., Jr., *Black Politics: A Theoretical and Structural Analysis* (1972). From colonial times to the present.

Harris, R., *The Quest for Equality* (1960). Historical and constitutional study of events leading to the Brown decision.

Harvey, J. C., *Civil Rights During the Kennedy Administration* (1971).

———, *Black Civil Rights During the Johnson Administration* (1973).

Henderson, L. J., Jr., ed., *Black Political Life in the United States* (1972). Articles by black scholars, excellent bibliographical essay by editor.

Hertzberg, H. W., *The Search for an American Indian Identity* (1971).

Holden, M., Jr., *The Politics of the Black Nation* (1973), and *The White Man''s Burden* (1973). Companion volumes, unsentimental, pragmatic analysis addressed to leaders of both races.

Howard, J. R., ed., *The Awakening Minorities: American Indians, Mexican-Americans, and Puerto Ricans* (1970). The paradoxical position of "partial" minority groups.

James, J. B., *The Framing of the Fourteenth Amendment* (1965). The Fourteenth Amendment as viewed by its contemporaries.

Kalven, H., Jr., *The Negro and the First Amendment* (1965). The civil rights movement and interpretation of the First Amendment.

King, D. B., and C. W. Quick, eds., *Legal Aspects of the Civil Rights Movement* (1965). Essays on the civil rights movement.

Krislov, S., *The Negro in Federal Employment: The Quest for Equal Opportunity* (1967). On one of the important aspects of the civil rights movement.

Ladd, E. C., Jr., *Negro Political Leadership in the South* (1966). A report on Negro political activity, primarily on the urban level, in the South.

Leggett, J. C., *Class, Race, and Labor* (1967). Class consciousness and race relations, from a case study in Detroit.

Lester, J., *Look Out Whitey! Black Power's Gon' Get Your Mama!* (1968).

Malcolm X, *Autobiography* (1964). The evolution of black political consciousness.

Marx, G., *Protest and Prejudice: A Study of Belief in the Black Community* (1968). Black attitudes toward Jews.

Matthews, D. R., and J. W. Prothro, *Negroes and the New Southern Politics* (1966). Negro political participation in a changing South.

Mayer, R. R., *et al.*, *The Impact of School Desegregation on a Southern City* (1974).

McCoy, D. R., and R. T. Rultten, *Question and Response: Minority Rights and the Truman Administration* (1973). Presidential leadership.

Meier, A., and Rudwick, *Core: A Study in the Civil Rights Movement, 1942–1968* (1973).

Mendelson, W., *Discrimination* (1962). Based on reports of the United States Commission on Civil Rights.

Meyer, H. N., *The Amendment that Refused to Die* (1973). Defense of Justice Black's and the first Justice Harlan's interpretation of the Fourteenth Amendment.

Miller, E. W., and M. L. Fisher, *The Negro in America: A Bibliography* (1970). Over 6,500 entries.

Miller, L., *The Petitioners: The Story of the Supreme Court of the United States and the Negro* (1966). Struggle for racial justice in the courts.

Moreland, L. B., *White Racism and the Law* (1970). Study of the constitutional authority of the national government to protect civil rights and the Supreme Court's interpretation of that authority.

National Advisory Commission on Civil Disorders, Report (1968). The Kerner Commission's probing analysis, with recommendations, of the racial disorders of 1967.

Newby, I. A., *The Segregationists: Readings in the Defense of Segregation and White Supremacy* (1968). White supremacist thought since 1890.

Parsons, T., and K. B. Clark, eds., *The Negro American* (1966). Comprehensive survey.

Peeks, E. C., *The Long Struggle for Black Power* (1971).

Peltason, J. W., *Fifty-eight Lonely Men: Southern Federal Judges and School Desegregation* (1962; reissued 1971).

Rainwater, L., *Behind Ghetto Walls: Black Family Life in a Federal Slum* (1970).

Reitman, A., and R. B. Davidson, *The Electoral Process: Voting Laws and Procedures* (1972).

Rubin, L. B., *Busing and Backlash: White Against White in an Urban School District* (1972). Case study of Richmond, California, Unified School District.

Scott, R. L., and W. Brockriede, eds., *The Rhetoric of Black Power* (1969).

Sorkin, A. L., *American Indians and Federal Aid* (1971). A Brookings Institute evaluation of federal programs.

Sovern, M. I., *Legal Restraints on Racial Discrimination in Employment* (1966). The implementation of fair employment legislation from a lawyer's viewpoint.

Steiner, S., *La Raza: The Mexican Americans* (1970). Broad picture of Chicano life.

Strong, D. S., *Negroes, Ballots, and Judges* (1968). Federal pronouncements on Negro voting and Southern legislative and judicial resistance.

Taylor, W. L., *Hanging Together: Equality in an Urban Nation* (1971). By former staff director of the U.S. Commission on Civil Rights.

Ten Broek, J., *et al.*, *Prejudice, War, and the Constitution* (1954). Origins, politics, and legality of Japanese-American evacuations in World War II.

Wilhoit, F. M., *The Politics of Massive Resistance* (1973). History of Southern resistance to *Brown v. Board of Education.*

Woodward, C. V., *The Strange Career of Jim Crow* (1955). Account of the growth of segregation laws.

Wright, N., *Black Power and Urban Unrest* (1967).

Rights to life, liberty, and property

Bent, A. E., *The Politics of Law Enforcement* (1974).

Breckenridge, A. C., *Congress Against the Court* (1970). Congressional response to Supreme Court decisions in the area of criminal justice.

Cole, G. F., *Politics and the Administration of Justice* (1973). Based on research findings.

Corwin, E. S., *Liberty Against Government* (1946). Essays on the growth and decline of substantive due process.

DeCrow, K., *Sexist Justice: How Legal Sexism Affects You* (1974).

Ellift, J. T., *Crime, Dissent, and the Attorney General: The Justice Department in the 1960's* (1971). Criminal justice, black militancy, and anitwar dissent.

Fellman, D., *The Constitutional Right of Association* (1963). A legal scholar looks at case law pertaining to the constitutional guarantee.

Fleming, M., *The Price of Perfect Justice* (1974). Critical analysis by judge of California court of appeals of the work of the Warren Court in criminal justice.

Freed, D., *Agony in New Haven: The Trial of Bobby Seale, Eric Huggins, and the Black Panther Party* (1973).

Harris, R., *Justice: The Crisis of Law, Order, and Freedom in America* (1970). Pro-Ramsey Clark, anti-John Mitchell discussion of the role of the attorney general.

Jacob, H., *Urban Justice: Law and Order in American Cities* (1973). Judicial system in our cities.

Kalven, H., Jr., and H. Zeisel, *The American Jury* (1966). Differences between judge and jury in determining the guilt of criminal defendants.

LaFave, W. R., *Arrest: The Decision to Take a Suspect into Custody* (1965).

Landynski, J. W., *Search and Seizure and the Supreme Court* (1966). Historical and analytical account of the Court's interpretation of the Fourth Amendment.

Lewis, A., *Gideon's Trumpet* (1964). Exciting account of the landmark right-to-counsel decision from the perspective of the appellant.

Milner, W. A., *The Court and Local Law Enforcement: The Impact of Miranda* (1971).

Murphy, W. F., *Wiretapping on Trial* (1965). A case study of the *Osborn* case and the judicial development of the right of privacy.

Navasky, V. S., *Kennedy Justice* (1971). Critical account of the Department of Justice under Robert Kennedy.

Newman, D. J., *Conviction: The Determination of Guilt or Innocence without Trial* (1966).

President's Commission of Law Enforcement and Administration of Justice, *The Challenge of Crime in a Free Society* (1967). A report on crime in America and what can be done about it.

Silver, I., ed., *The Crime Control Establishment* (1974).

Stephens, O. H., *The Supreme Court and Confessions of Guilt* (1973). Impact of the *Miranda* rules.

Part four **The people in politics**

Public opinion

Of special interest is the *Public Opinion Quarterly*.

Berelson, B., and M. Janowitz, eds., *Reader in Public Opinion and Communication* (1966). Readings on all the major phases of the subject.

Choukas, M., *Propaganda Comes of Age* (1965). The massive role of propaganda in our age.

Christenson, R., and R. O. McWilliams, *Voice of the People*, rev. ed. (1968). Survey of current issues and research in public opinion.

Dawson, R. E., *Public Opinion and Contemporary Disarray* (1973). Sluggishness of party and electoral response to shifting public opinion.

Dewey, J., *The Public and Its Problems* (1927). Classic work.

Dicey, A. C., *Law and Public Opinion in England* (1905).

Erikson, R. S., and N. R. Luttbeg, *American Public Opinion: Its Origins, Content, and Impact* (1973).

Free, L. A., and H. Cantril, *Political Beliefs of Americans: A Study of Public Opinion* (1967). Broad survey of popular attitudes based primarily on 1964 survey data.

Katz, E., and P. F. Lazarsfeld, *Personal Influence: The Part Played by People in the Flow of Mass Communications* (1955). On the "two-step" theory of mass communications.

Key, V. O., Jr., *Public Opinion and American Democracy* (1961). Full-scale treatment of concepts and issues.

Lane, R. E., and D. O. Sears, *Public Opinion* (1964). Short but excellent examination of the dynamics of opinion formation.

Lippmann, W., *Public Opinion* (1922).

Lowell, A. L., *Public Opinion and Popular Government* (1913).

Luttbeg, N. R., ed., *Public Opinion and Public Policy: Models of Political Linkage* (1968). Mechanism by which public opinion is articulated to the policymakers.

Wilcox, A. R., *Public Opinion and Political Attitudes* (1974), wide-ranging essays.

Public opinion polls

Bogart, L., *Silent Politics: Polls and Awareness of Public Opinion* (1972). Uses and dangers of polls.

Glock, C. Y., ed., *Survey Research in the Social Sciences* (1967).

Mendelsohn, H., and I. Crespi, *Polls, Television and the New Politics* (1970). Critical study of polls of all sorts.

Rosenberg, M., *The Logic of Survey Analysis* (1968). The logic and reasoning underlying the analysis of survey research data.

Media of communication

Aronson, James, *Deadline for the Media: Today's Challenges to the Press, TV and Radio* (1974).

Cater, D., *The Fourth Branch of Government* (1959). Critical evaluation of the relations of the press with the national government.

Cohen, B. C., *The Press and Foreign Policy* (1963). A systematic examination of the interaction between the press and government officials.

Commission on the Freedom of the Press, *A Free and Responsible Press: A General Report on Mass Communication* (1958). Recommends that the mass media assume greater responsibility for the interpretation of contemporary events.

Dunn, D. D., *Public Officials and the Press* (1969). Interrelationships between news reporters and government officials at the state level.

Fagen, R. R., *Politics and Communication* (1966). Communications as a factor in the political process.

Janowitz, M., *The Community Press in an Urban Setting* (1952). The community press as a vehicle for social integration.

Lippmann, W., *Liberty and the News* (1920). Critical essay by one of America's famous journalists.

Minow, N., J. B. Martin, and L. M. Mitchell, *Presidential Television* (1973). Presidential influence via TV, as seen by experts.

Mott, F. L., *American Journalism* (1941). Standard history.

Nimmo, D. D., *Newsgathering in Washington: A Study in Political Communication* (1964). Interaction of government and the press.

Rivers, W. L., *The Opinion-makers* (1965). Relationship between reporters and government officials and a critical evaluation of the effect of the press on public opinion.

Rubin, B., *Political Television* (1967). Influence of television on elections and the presidency.

Small, W. J., *Political Power and the Press* (1973). Case study of news media, presidential management of news, and the Pentagon Papers.

Political behavior: voting

Berelson, B. R., P. F. Lazarsfeld, and W. N. McPhee, *Voting* (1954). Voting in 1948 in a New York community, with useful summary of findings of other voting studies.

Burkhart, J., J. Eisenstein, T. Fleming, and F. Kendrick *Strategies for Political Participation* (1972). Brief, practical, realistic guide.

Campbell, A., P. Converse, W. Miller, and D. Stokes, *The American Voter* (1960). Analysis of 1956 election on national sample data. Seminal work.

Campbell, A., G. Gurin, and W. E. Miller, *The Voter Decides* (1954). Study of 1952 election based on data gathered by sampling.

Commission on Civil Rights, *Political Participation: A Study of the Participation by Negroes in the Electoral and Political Processes in Ten Southern States since Passage of the Voting Rights Act of 1965.* (1968)

David, P. T., *Party Strength in the United States, 1872–1970* (1972). Comprehensive voting data, organized by state, year, and office.

De Vries, W., and V. L. Tarrance, *The Ticket-Splitter: A New Force in American Politics* (1972). Study of a rising phenomenon.

Eldersveld, S., *Political Parties: A Behavioral Analysis* (1963).

Flanigan, W. H., *Political Behavior of the American Electorate* (1968). Drawn from four major national surveys from 1952 to 1964.

Gosnell, H. F., *Democracy: The Threshold of Freedom* (1948). Discussion of theories of citizenship and of the premises of the right to vote.

Hyman, S., *Youth in Politics* (1972) Extravagent expectations of youthful participation compared with reality.

Isaacs, S. D., *Jews and American Politics* (1974).

Jennings, M. K., and H. Zeigler, eds., *The Electoral Process* (1966). Readings on the phenomenon of elections in a democratic society.

Key, V. O., Jr., *The Responsible Electorate* (1966). A defense of the much-maligned voting public.

——, *Southern Politics in State and Nation* (1949). The impact of the "Negro problem" on Southern politics; already a classic.

Ladd, E. C., Jr., *Negro Political Leadership in the South* (1969). Stability and change in Southern politics.

Lane, R. E., *Political Life: How People Get Involved in Politics* (1958).

Lazarsfeld, P. F., B. R. Berelson, and H. Gaudet, *The People's Choice* (1948). Demonstrates the technique of panel interviewing on "how the voter makes up his mind in a presidential campaign."

Lipset, S. M., *Political Man* (1960). Important series of articles on political sociology.

Merriam C. E., and H. F. Gosnell, *Nonvoting* (1924). Pioneering study.

Milbrath, L. W., *Political Participation: How and Why Do People Get Involved in Politics?* (1965). Catalogue of knowledge on the subject and a few propositions.

Novak, M., *The Rise of the Unmeltable Ethnics: The New Political Force of the Seventies* (1972). Quest for a new ethnic politics as against the Anglo-Saxon tradition.

Verba, S., and N. H. Nie, *Participation in America* (1972). Empirical and theoretical study of "political democracy and social equality."

Wallace, D., *First Tuesday: A Study of Rationality in Voting* (1964). Analysis of voting behavior and public opinion in suburban Westport, Connecticut.

Political parties

Agar, H., *The Price of Union* (1950). History stressing the thesis that loosely organized and undisciplined parties are essential to the preservation of the Union.

Binkley, W. E., *American Political Parties: Their Natural History*, 3rd ed. (1958). Stresses the role of parties as coalitions of interest groups.

Broder, D. S., *The Party's Over* (1971). Readable critique of U.S. parties and a call for reform.

Burner, D., *The Politics of Provincialism: The Democratic Party in Transition, 1918–1932* (1967).

Burns, J. M., *The Deadlock of Democracy: Four-Party Politics in America* (1963). Old and new political alignments.

Chambers, W. N., and W. D. Burnham, eds., *The American Party Systems: Stages of Political Development* (1968). History of United States competitive party politics.

Committee on Political Parties of the American Political Science Association, *Toward a More Responsible Two-Party System* (1950). Recommendations for strengthening the American party system.

Cosman, B., and R. J. Huckshorn, eds., *Republican Politics* (1968). The Republican party during and after the 1964 election.

Costikyan, E. N., *Behind Closed Doors: Politics in the Public Interest* (1966). Political and personal memoirs of a member of New York's Reform Democratic movement.

Cotter, C. P., and B. C. Hennessey, *Politics Without Power: The National Party Committees* (1964). Emphasis on the national chairman and the committee staffs.

Crotty, W. J., *Approaches to the Study of Party Organization* (1968). Problems of internal party organization.

Cunningham, N. E., *The Jeffersonian Republicans: The Foundation of Party Organization, 1789–1801* (1957).

Eagleton Foundation, *Case Studies in Practical Politics.* Continuing series of studies of concrete political situations.

Greeley, A. M., *Building Coalitions* (1974). Need for compromise and leadership within parties, especially the Democratic.

Greenstein, F., *The American Party System and the American People*, 2nd ed. (1970). Handy synthesis of recent research.

Herring, E. P., *The Politics of Democracy* (1940; reissued 1966). Interpretation and defense of the present system; interpretations contrary to those of the committee on political parties mentioned below.

Herzberg, D. G., and G. M. Pomper, eds., *American Party Politics: Essays and Readings* (1966). Political parties as factors in voting behavior, elections, and the governmental process.

Hofstadter, R., *The Idea of a Party System* (1969). The United States as the first nation to accept the idea of a system of opposed parties.

Holcombe, A. N., *The Political Parties of Today* (1924); *The New Party Politics* (1933); *The Middle Classes in American Politics* (1940). Interpretations of American politics as moving from sectional to urban, or "class," politics with the middle class holding the balance and preserving free government.

Jones, C. O., *The Republican Party in American Politics* (1965). The implications of being the minority party.

Ladd, E. C., Jr., *American Political Parties: Social Change and Political Response* (1970). Historical response of the party system to social and economic change.

Lasswell, H. D., *Politics: Who Gets What, When, How* (1946; reissued 1958). One of Lasswell's more popular treatments.

Leiserson, A., *Parties and Politics: An Institutional and Behavioral Approach* (1958).

Martin, R. G., *The Bosses* (1964). Political machinery in United States history.

Mayo, C. G., and B. L. Crowe, eds., *American Political Parties: A Systematic Perspective* (1967). Articles on the structure and function of political parties.

McCormick, R. *The Second American Party System* (1966). Party development and Jacksonian democracy.

Mazmanian, D. A., *Third Parties in Presidential Elections* (1974). Their role and history with special treatment of George Wallace.

Michels, R. *Political Parties* (1915; reprinted 1949). Important sociological study of the oligarchical tendencies of European democratic political parties.

Nash, H. P., Jr., *Third Parties in American Politics* (1958). Their role and history.

Nichols, R. F., *The Invention of the American Political Parties* (1967). Traces the old world origins of the American party system, which took shape in the 1850s.

Ostrogorski, M., *Democracy and the Organization of Political Parties*, 2 vols. (1908). Early, classic interpretation of development of parties in the United States and England.

Porter, K. A., and D. B. Johnson, *National Party Platforms, 1840–1964* (1966).

Ranney, A., *Curing the Mischiefs of Faction: Party Reform in America* (1974). An important review of reform efforts and their consequences by one of the leading scholars in this field.

Ripon Society, and C. W. Brown, Jr., *Jaws of Victory* (1974). Past and future GOP tactics viewed by young Republican liberals.

Saloma, J. S, III, and F. H. Sontag, *Parties* (1972). Sweeping indictment of U.S. parties, with explicit program for reform, to realize "opportunity for effective citizen politics."

Schattschneider, E. E., *Party Government* (1942); *The struggle for Party Government* (1948). Case for more centralized and disciplined parties by an outstanding scholar who virtually developed a school of thought about American politics.

Sorauf, F. J., *Party Politics in America* (1968). The parties as political structures in the political process.

Stewart, J. G., *One Last Chance* (1974). What the Democrats must do to win in 1976.

Turner, F. J., *The Significance of Sections in American History* (1937). The importance of sectionalism in American politics was first projected by Turner at the beginning of the twentieth century.

Nominations and elections

Adamany, D. W., *Campaign Finance in America* (1972). Brief but informative treatment, emphasizing costs, sources, reform.

Alexander, H. E., *Financing the 1964 Election* (1966). Study of party and campaign finance.

Burnham, W. D., *Critical Elections and the Mainsprings of American Politics* (1970). Perceptive analysis of aggregate voting data.

Campbell, A., P. E. Converse, W. E. Miller, and D. E. Stokes, *Elections and the Political Order* (1966). The functions of elections in the total political system.

Citizen's Research Foundation, Various studies in national and state campaign financing.

Cummings, M. C., Jr., *Congressmen and the Electorate: Elections for the U.S. House and the President, 1920–1964* (1964). The relationship between congressional and presidential elections.

David, P. T., R. M. Goldman, and R. C. Bain, *The Politics of National Party Conventions* (1960). Analysis of the nominating process.

———, et al., *Presidential Nominating Politics in 1952* (1954). Five-volume report undertaken by over 150 political scientists.

Davis, J. W., *Presidential Primaries: Road to the White House* (1967). The evolution of the primary system and a study of some past primary strategies.

Heard, A., *The Costs of Democracy* (1960). Authoritative study of campaign finance.

Huckshorn, R. J., and R. C. Spencer, *The Politics of Defeat* (1971). Systematic study of campaigning for Congress, including recruitment, campaign organization, problems.

Johnson, J. B., *Registration for Voting in the United States*, rev. ed. (1946). Survey of methods used.

Kelley, S., *Political Campaigning* (1960). A study in strategy and technique.

Kraus, S., ed., *The Great Debates* (1962). Analysis of the Kennedy-Nixon debates.

Lamb, K., and P. Smith, *Campaign Decision-Making* (1968)

Levin, M. B., *Kennedy Campaigning: The System and the Style as Practised by Senator Edward Kennedy* (1966). Documents the 1962 campaign for the Democratic senatorial nomination in Massachusetts.

Longley, L. D., and A. G. Braun, *The Politics of Electoral College Reform* (1972). Alternatives for electoral college reform, including direct vote for president.

Mileur, J. M., and G. T. Sulzner, *Campaigning for the Massachusetts Senate* (1974). "Electioneering outside the political limelight."

Napolitan, J., *The Election Game and How to Win It* (1972). Modern election techniques by a master, with emphasis on electronic media.

National Municipal League, *Presidential Nominating Procedures in 1964: A State-by-State Report* (1965). An analysis and questionnaire study.

Ogden, F. D., *The Poll Tax in the South* (1968). A complete study of the poll tax and its effect on the democratic process.

Parris, J. H., *The Convention Problem* (1972). Reform of presidential nominating procedures.

Peterson, S., *A Statistical History of the American Presidential Elections* (1963). Election returns by state for every presidential election up to 1960.

Pierce, N. R., *The People's President* (1968). The direct-vote alternative.

Polsby, N. W., and A. B. Wildavsky, *Presidential Elections*, 3rd ed. (1971). The context within which presidential elections are fought and the strategies employed.

Pomper, G. M., *Elections in America: Control and Influence in Democratic Politics* (1968). Elections, their effect on public policy, and the true efficacy of the American ballot.

Pool, I. de S., R. P. Abelson, and S. Popkin, *Candidates, Issues, and Strategies* (1965). Campaign technique and public response.

President's Commission on Campaign Costs, *Financing Presidential Campaigns* (1962). Recommendations on improved financing of national election campaigns.

Rae, D. W., *The Political Consequences of Electoral Laws* (1967). Relationship of electoral laws to legislative representation of political parties.

Rosenbloom, D. L., *The Election Men* (1973). Critique of the "political consultant" as threat to American party system.

Sayre, W. S., and J. H. Parris, *Voting for President: The Electoral College and the American Party System* (1970). An analysis of the existing electoral system and four leading alternatives.

Scammon, R. M., *America Votes.* Collection of recent election statistics, additional volumes every two years.

Schlesinger, A. M., Jr., ed., *The Coming to Power: Critical Elections in American History* (1972). Sixteen elections.

Sullivan, D. G., J. L. Pressman, B. I. Page, J. J. Lyons, *The Politics of Representation* (1974). Crisis and decision-making in Democratic national convention of 1972.

White, T. H., *The Making of the President, 1960* (1961). Pulitzer Prize account of the 1960 national campaign. See White's treatments of the 1964, 1968, and 1972 campaigns.

Part five **Policy makers and policy making**

Congressmen and the Congress

Bailey, S. K., *Congress Makes a Law* (1950). Detailed account of the enactment of the Employment Act of 1946.

Bibby, J. and R. Davidson, *On Capitol Hill: Studies in the Legislative Process,* 2nd ed., (1972). Case studies illustrating the legislative process in Congress.

Bolling, R., *House Out of Order* (1965). Personal account of the workings of the House by a liberal congressional reformer.

Brady, D., *Congressional Voting in a Partisan Era* (1973). Study of McKinley era in comparison to modern House of Representatives.

Burdette, F. L., *Filibustering in the Senate* (1940). Standard source.

Burnham, J., *Congress and the American Tradition* (1959). Congress viewed as losing its rightful authority.

Clapp, C. L., *The Congressman: His Work as He Sees It* (1963). The House as observed by a number of its members.

Clausen, A., *How Congressmen Decide: A Policy Focus* (1973). What are the determinants of congressional voting decisions?

Davidson, R. H., *The Role of the Congressman* (1969). Examination of legislative and representational roles and why they are adopted.

———, D. M. Kovenock, and M. K. O'Leary, *Congress in Crisis: Politics and Congressional Reform* (1966). The organization of the Congress and proposals for reform.

Douglas, P. H., *In the Fullness of Time* (1971). Instructive memoir by a former senator from Illinois.

Eagleton, T. F., *War and Presidential Power: A Chronicle of Congressional Surrender* (1974). An analysis of the War Powers Act of 1973 by one liberal who fought against it.

Eidenberg, E., and R. D. Morey, *An Act of Congress: The Legislative Process and the Making of Education Policy* (1969). Passage and implementation of the Elementary and Secondary Education Act of 1965.

Fenno, R. F., Jr., *Congressmen in Committees* (1973). Excellent comparative study.

———, *The Power of the Purse: Appropriations Politics in Congress* (1966). A complete study of the appropriations procedure and its political characteristics and implications.

Ferejohn, J. A., *Pork Barrel Politics: Rivers and Harbors Legislation, 1947–1968.* (1974).

Fishel, J. *Party and Opposition: Congressional Challengers in American Politics* (1973).

Fisher, L., *President and Congress: Power and Policy* (1972). Historical perspective on contemporary presidential-congressional relations.

Freeman, J. L., *The Political Process: Executive Bureau-Legislative Committee Relations* (1965). The interaction of bureaucrats, congressmen, and lobbyists in policy-making.

Froman, L. A., Jr., *The Congressional Process: Strategies, Rules, and Procedures* (1967). Studies the relation between formal and informal rule structures and policy outputs of the Congress.

Galloway, G. B., *History of the House of Representatives* (1962).

Goodwin, G., *The Little Legislatures* (1970). Analysis of the role of congressional committees.

Grazia, A. de, *Republic in Crisis: Congress Against the Executive Force* (1965). A study of the distribution of power at the federal level.

———, *et al., Congress: The First Branch of Government* (1966). Twelve studies of the organization and workings of Congress.

Green, M., *et al., Who Runs Congress?* (1972). The Ralph Nader study group's critical assessment of Congress's weaknesses.

Gross, B. M., *The Legislative Struggle* (1953). Probing analysis of Congress as the battleground of interest struggles.

Hacker, A., *Congressional Districting: The Issue of Equal Representation* (1963).

Harris, J. P., *The Advice and Consent of the Senate* (1953). A study of the confirmation of appointments by the United States Senate.

Hinckley, B., *The Seniority System in Congress* (1971). Puts sen-

iority in the context of the whole congressional system.
Horn, S., *The Cabinet and Congress* (1960). History and discussion of proposals to improve Cabinet-congressional relations.
Huitt, R. K., and R. L. Peabody, *Congress: Two Decades of Analysis* (1969). Collection of essays.
Jackson, J., *Constituencies and Leaders in Congress: Their Effects on Senate Voting Behavior* (1974).
Jones, C. O., *Party and Policy Making: The House Republican Policy Committee* (1964). The power of a party policy committee in Congress.
Kingdon, J., *Congressmen's Voting Decisions* (1973). Important assessment of major factors congressmen consider before they vote.
Kirby, J. C., Jr., and A. Rosencranz, *Congress and the Public Trust* (1970). A report of the Association of the Bar of the City of New York, Special Committee on Congressional Ethics.
Manley, J. F., *The Politics of Finance: The House Committee on Ways and Means* (1970). A study of one of the House's most important committees with special attention on the role of Chairman Wilbur Mills.
Matthews, D. R., *U. S. Senators and Their World* (1960). Study of the Senate as an institution and the behavior of its members.
Mayhew, D. R., *Congress: The Electoral Connection* (1974). A major original study of the link between elections and legislative power.
Miller, C., *Member of the House* (1962). Newsletters from a gifted congressman to his constituents.
Morrow, W. L., *Congressional Committees* (1969). Comprehensive view of the committee structure.
Patterson, J. T., *Congressional Conservatism and the New Deal* (1967). Origins of the Republican-conservative Democratic coalition in Congress.
Peabody, R. L., and N. W. Polsby, eds., *New Perspectives on the House of Representatives*, 2nd ed. (1969). Essays on the House as a political institution.
Polsby, N. W., *Congress and the Presidency*, 2nd ed. (1971). A study of the Congress and the division of powers.
Price, D., *Who Makes the Laws?* (1972). Case studies of policy initiation and influence in the Johnson Administration years.
Riegle, D., *O Congress* (1972). Reflections of a young House member.
Rieselbach, L. N., ed., *Congressional Politics* (1973). A useful collection of readings.
Ripley, R. B., *Party Leaders in the House of Representatives* (1967). Discussion of congressional majority-party leadership in this century.
———, *Majority Party Leadership in Congress* (1969).
———, *Power in the Senate* (1969).
Robinson, J. A., *Congress and Foreign Policy-Making*, rev. ed. (1967). Probing analysis of Congress in the foreign policy process.
Saloma, J. S., III, *Congress and the New Politics* (1969). Balanced and careful analysis.
Scoble, H. M., *Ideology and Electoral Action* (1967). Study of the National Committee for an Effective Congress.
Shannon, W. W., *Party, Constituency, and Congressional Voting: A Study of Legislative Behavior in the United States House of Representatives* (1968). Contains a good summary of congressional rollcall studies.
Sundquist, J. L., *Politics and Policy: The Eisenhower, Kennedy, and Johnson Years* (1968). Why the national government alternates between spurts of creative energy and long periods of inaction in policy-making.
Truman, D. B., ed., *The Congress and America's Future*, 2nd ed. (1973). Papers for an American Assembly on Congress.
———, *The Congressional Party: A Case Study* (1959). The party system in Congress, analyzed through studies of roll calls.
Turner, J., and E.V. Schneier, Jr., *Party and Constituency*, rev. ed. (1970). Measurement of the relative impact of parties and constituencies on congressional voting behavior.
U.S. House of Representatives, Select Committee on Committees, *Committee Organization in the House*, 3 vols. (1973).
Vogler, D. J., *The Third House* (1971). An analysis of conference committees and their significance.
Wilson, W., *Congressional Government* (1885). Classic interpretation.

The judges and the judicial process

See also the titles listed under "The Living Constitution" in the bibliography for Part Two.

Becker, T. L., *Political Behavioralism and Modern Jurisprudence* (1964).
Bishop, J. W., Jr., *Justice Under Fire: A Study of Military Law* (1974).
Cappelletti, M., *Judicial Review in the Contemporary World* (1971). Concentrates on Europe and the United States.
Cardozo, B. N., *The Nature of the Judicial Process* (1921). A classic.
Casper, J. D., *Lawyers Before the Warren Court: Civil Liberties and Civil Rights, 1957–1966* (1972).
Chase, H. W., *Federal Judges: The Appointing Process* (1972). Study of the process during the Eisenhower, Kennedy, and Johnson Administrations.
Davis, K. C., *Discretionary Justice: A Preliminary Inquiry* (1971). Problems of regulatory commissions.
Eisenstein, J., *Politics and the Legal Process* (1973). The legal system as an integral part of the political system.
Fish, P. G., *The Politics of Federal Judicial Administration* (1973). History of the administrative structure of the federal system.
Frank, J., *Law and the Modern Mind* (1930). Discussion of the various factors, especially psy-

chological, that affect men, including judges.

Frankfurter, F., *Law and Politics* (1939). Articles, book reviews, occasional papers written before the author became a justice.

Friendly, H. J., *Federal Jurisdiction: A General View* (1973). A federal judge's prescriptions for improvement.

Garvey, G., *Constitutional Bricolage* (1971). Urges judges to adopt a new decision-making framework.

Jacob, H., *Justice in America* (1965).

Jahnige, T., and S. Goldman, eds. *The Federal Judicial System* (1968).

James, H., *Crisis in the Courts* (1968).

Jones, H. W., ed., *The Courts, the Public, and the Law Explosion* (1965). Discrepancy between theory and practice in the judicial process.

Murphy, W. F., *Elements of Judicial Strategy* (1964). Judicial behavior analyzed from the perspective of strategems to maximize policy preferences.

Nagel, S., *The Legal Process from a Behavioral Perspective* (1969). Behavioral studies of the judiciary.

Peltason, J. W., *Federal Courts in the Political Process* (1955).

Rawls, John, *A Theory of Justice* (1971). Major philosophical work.

Richardson, R. J., and K. N. Vines, *The Politics of Federal Courts* (1970). Analysis of the policy role of the federal courts.

Schubert, G. A., *Judicial Policy-Making: The Political Role of the Courts*, rev. ed. (1974). Includes an excellent bibliographical essay on the literature in the field.

———, ed., *Judicial Behavior: A Reader in Theory and Research* (1964)

———, ed., *Judicial Decision-Making* (1963).

———, and D. J. Danelskki, *Comparative Judicial Behavior: Cross-Cultural Studies in Political Decision-Making in the East and West* (1969).

Sheldon, C. H., *The American Judicial Process* (1974). Models used in judicial policy research.

Stumpff, S. E. *Morality and the Law* (1966).

Tullock, G., *The Logic of the Law* (1971).

The Supreme Court and judicial review

Abraham, H. J., *Justices & Presidents: A Political History of Appointments to the Supreme Court* (1974).

Baker, L., *Back to Back: The Duel between FDR and the Supreme Court* (1967). An account of the Roosevelt court-packing fight.

Bickel, A. M., *The Least Dangerous Branch: The Supreme Court at the Bar of Politics* (1962). Discussion of the "proper" role of the Court.

———, *Politics and the Warren Court* (1965). Essays on the activities of the Warren Court, covering civil rights, reapportionment, and religion.

———, *The Supreme Court and the Idea of Progress* (1969). Essays critical of the Warren Court.

Black, C. L., Jr., *Structure and Relationship in Constitutional Law* (1969). The political setting of the court.

Corwin, E. S., *Court over Constitution: A Study of Judicial Review as an Instrument of Government*, 2nd ed. (1942).

———, *The Doctrine of Judicial Review* (1914). Essays, including a famous article on *Marbury v. Madison.*

Cox, A., *The Warren Court: Constitutional Decision as an Instrument of Reform* (1968).

Danelski, D., *The Appointment of a Supreme Court Justice* (1965). The story behind the appointment of Pierce Butler.

Davis, A. L., *The United States Supreme Court and the Uses of Social Science Data* (1973).

Dean, H. E., *Judicial Review and Democracy* (1966). The case for judicial review as an integral part of the democratic process.

Elliott, W. E. Y., *The Supreme Court's Role in Voting Rights Disputes, 1845–1964* (1974).

Ellis, R. B., *The Jeffersonian Crisis: Court and Politics in the Young Republic* (1971).

Fairman, Charles, *History of the Supreme Court: Reconstruction and Reunion, 1864–88, Part One, Vol. VI* (1971). Monumental volume in the monumental Holmes Devise History of the Supreme Court.

Forte, D. F., ed., *The Supreme Court in American Politics: Judicial Activism vs. Judicial Restraint* (1972). Collection of essays.

Frank, J. P. *Marble Palace: The Supreme Court in American Life* (1958).

Goebel, Julius, Jr., *History of the Supreme Court of the United States: Antecedents and Beginnings to 1801, Vol. I (1971).* First volume in the Holmes Devise History.

Goldberg, A. J., *Equal Justice: The Warren Era of the Supreme Court* (1972). Lectures by the former Supreme Court Justice.

Grossman, J. B., *Lawyers and Judges: The ABA and the Politics of Judicial Selection* (1965).

Haines, G. G., *The Role of the Supreme Court in American Government and Politics, 1789–1835* (1944). Detailed history of the formative years.

———, *The American Doctrine of Judicial Supremacy*, 2nd ed. (1932). Balanced investigation of the role of the Supreme Court and its use of judicial review.

Jackson, R. H., *The Struggle for Judicial Supremacy* (1941). Critical discussion of the Supreme Court, especially its activities during the New Deal period.

Johnson, R. M., *The Dynamics of Compliance* (1967). Analysis of the process by which decisions change behavior.

Krislov, S., *The Supreme Court and Political Freedom* (1968).

Kurland, P. B., ed., *The Supreme Court Review*, Annual collection, since 1959, of commentary articles on Supreme Court activity.

———, *Politics, the Constitution, and the Warren Court* (1970).

Lemert, E., *Social Action and Legal Change* (1970).

McCloskey, R., *The American*

Supreme Court, 1789–1960 (1960). Analytical history.

———, *The Modern Supreme Court* (1972). Essays by one of our most erudite scholars.

Miller, A. S., *The Supreme Court and American Capitalism* (1968).

Murphy, W. F., *Congress and the Court* (1962). Along with the Pritchett volume listed below useful for comprehensive coverage of a recent Supreme Court controversy.

———, and C. H. Pritchett, eds., *Courts, Judges, and Politics,* 2nd ed. (1974). An introduction to the organization and function of the American judiciary.

Pritchett, C. H., *Congress versus the Supreme Court* (1961).

Rosen, P. L., *The Supreme Court and Social Science* (1972).

Schmidhauser, J. R., *The Supreme Court* (1960). Internal politics.

———, and L. L. Berg, *The Supreme Court and Congress: Conflict and Interpetation, 1945–1968* (1972).

Schubert, G. R., *The Judicial Mind: Attitudes and Ideologies of Supreme Court Justices, 1946–1963* (1965). A study of eighteen Supreme Court justices and the causes and results of their actions.

Scigliano, R., *The Supreme Court and the Presidency* (1971). Natural allies against the Congress—at least before Watergate.

Shapiro, M., *Law and Politics in the Supreme Court* (1964).

———, *The Supreme Court and Administrative Agencies* (1968).

———, ed., *The Supreme Court and Public Policy* (1968). The Supreme Court's internal organization and external effect on the political process.

Shogan, R., *A Question of Judgment: The Fortas Case and the Struggle for the Supreme Court* (1972).

Simon, J. F., *In His Own Image: The Supreme Court in Richard Nixon's America* (1973).

Strum, P., *The Supreme Court and "Political Questions": A Study in Judicial Evasion* (1974).

Swindler, W. F., *Court and Constitution in the Twentieth Century: Vol. I., The Old Legality 1889–1932* (1969); *Vol. II, The New Legality 1932–1968* (1970); *Vol. III, The Modern Interpretation* (1974).

Swisher, C. B., *History of the Supreme Court of the United States: The Taney Period 1836–64, Vol. V* (1974). Another volume in the Holmes Devise series.

Warren, C., *The Supreme Court in United States History,* rev. ed., 2 vols. (1932). Standard history, sympathetic to the Court's use of judicial review.

Wasby, S. L., *The Impact of the United States Supreme Court: Some Perspectives* (1970). Comprehensive analysis of impact literature.

Wechsler, H., *Principles, Politics, and Fundamental Law* (1961). A controversial interpretation of judicial review.

Judicial biography

Asch, S. J., *The Supreme Court and Its Great Justices* (1971). Popular short biographical sketches.

Beveridge, A. J., *The Life of John Marshall,* 4 vols. (1916–1919). Has become the prototype of judicial biography.

Bland, R. W., *Private Pressure on Public Law: The Legal Career of Justice Thurgood Marshall* (1973).

Fairman, C., *Mr. Justice Miller and the Supreme Court* (1939). Contains account of the Court's work and Reconstruction politics during the critical years 1860–1890.

Frank, J. P., *Mr. Justice Black* (1949). By a leading legal thinker.

Friedman, L., and F. L. Israel, eds., *The Justices of the United States Supreme Court 1789–1969: Their Lives and Major Opinions,* 4 vols. (1970). 3,373 pages of essays written by thirty-eight scholars.

Griffith, K., *Judge Learned Hand and the Role of the Federal Judicary* (1973).

Hendel, S., *Charles Evans Hughes and the Supreme Court* (1951).

Howe, M. D., *Justice Oliver Wendell Holmes: Vol. I, The Shaping Years, 1841–1870* (1957); *Vol. II, The Proving Years 1870–1882* (1963).

Konefsky, S. J., *The Constitutional World of Mr. Justice Frankfurter* (1949). Collection of opinions with introductory notes by the editor.

———, *The Legacy of Holmes and Brandeis* (1957). Study of the constitutional philosophy of two outstanding justices.

Kurland, P. B., ed., *Felix Frankfurter on the Supreme Court: Extrajudicial Essays on the Court and Constitution* (1970).

Mason, A. T., *Brandeis: A Free Man's Life* (1946).

———, *Harlan Fiske Stone* (1956).

———, *William Howard Taft, Chief Justice* (1965).

Mendelson, W., *Justices Black and Frankfurter,* 2nd ed. (1966). Conception of the Court's role in terms of the careers of these two jurists.

Schick, M., *Learned Hand's Court* (1970). Work of one of the more important federal appellate courts.

Schubert, G., *Dispassionate Justice: A Synthesis of the Judicial Opinions of Robert H. Jackson* (1969).

Swisher, C. B., *Roger B. Taney* (1935).

———, *Stephen J. Field, Craftsman of the Law* (1930). Biography of a justice who had much to do with the development of substantive due process.

Williams, C., *Hugo L. Black* (1950).

Presidents, presidency, presidential establishment

Anderson, P., *The Presidents' Men* (1968). A useful journalistic appraisal of presidential counselors.

Bach, S. and G. Sulzner, eds., *Perspectives on the Presidency* (1974). Useful collection of trenchant essays.

Bailey, T. A., *Presidential Greatness: The Image and the Man from George Washington to the Present* (1966). Proposed and applied criteria for evaluating presidential greatness.

Barber, J. D., *The Presidential Character* (1972). Influential study of personality and performance.

———, ed., *Choosing a President* (1974). Wide-ranging essays on selection process.

Berger, R., *Impeachment: The Constitutional Problems* (1973). Major source on this topic.

———, *Executive Privilege* (1974). A history of its origin, use, and abuse.

Burns, J. M., *Presidential Government: The Crucible of Leadership* (1966). History and analysis of the presidential system.

Cornwell, E. E., Jr., *Presidential Leadership of Public Opinion* (1962). Presidential mobilization of public and congressional support.

Corwin, E. S., *The President: Office and Powers*, rev. ed. (1957). Historical and constitutional development of the office.

Cotter, C. P., and H. M. Smith, *Powers of the President During National Crises* (1961).

Cronin, T. E., *The State of the Presidency* (1975). Comprehensive analysis of contemporary presidency.

Cronin, T. E., and S. Greenberg, eds., *The Presidential Advisory System* (1969). The men and staff councils around the president.

Destler, I. M., *Presidents, Bureaucrats, and Foreign Policy* (1972). Assessment of varying ways to organize for effective foreign policy-making.

Donovan, R. J., *The Inside Story* (1956). Taken from notes on the Eisenhower Cabinet meetings; gives picture of this and other aspects of the Eisenhower Administration.

Eisenhower, D. D., *The White House Years: Waging Peace, 1956–1961* (1965). White House affairs from the viewpoint of the president and his staff.

Eisenhower, M. S., *The President Is Calling* (1974). Memoirs of service under eight presidents.

Fenno, R. F., *The President's Cabinet* (1959). Standard source; analysis of Cabinets from Wilson to Eisenhower.

Hargrove, E., *The Power of the Modern Presidency* (1974). Balanced, sensible reappraisal.

Herring, P., *Presidential Leadership* (1940). A classic essay on congressional-presidential relations.

Hughes, E. J., *The Living Presidency* (1973). Contemporary analysis by a former Eisenhower aide.

———, *The Ordeal of Power: A Political Memoir of the Eisenhower Years* (1963) A view from the inside.

Jackson, C., *Presidential Vetoes, 1792–1945* (1967). The historical utility of presidential veto power.

Johnson, L. B., *The Vantage Point* (1971). Presidential memoir.

Kallenbach, J. E., *The American Chief Executive: The Presidency and the Governorship* (1966). Treats both background and present-day status of the presidency and the governorship.

Koenig, L. W., *The Chief Executive* (1968). General analysis of the president performing many roles.

Laski, H. J., *The American Presidency* (1940). Dynamics of the presidency by a famous British political scientist.

May, E. R., ed., *The Ultimate Decision: The President as Commander in Chief* (1961). Analysis of presidential behavior during national emergencies.

McConnell, G., *The Modern Presidency* (1967). Brief study of the changing office.

———, *Steel and the Presidency* (1963). Story of the dramatic confrontation between President Kennedy and Big Steel.

Morgan, R. P., *The President and Civil Rights* (1970).

Mueller, J. E., *War, Presidents and Public Opinion* (1973). Analyzes linkages between major events and support for the president.

Neustadt, R., *Presidential Power* (1960). Influential work on presidential politics.

O'Brien, L. J., *No Final Victories* (1974). Memoirs of a Kennedy–Johnson political strategist.

Phillips, C., *The Truman Presidency: The History of a Triumphant Succession* (1966). A journalistic account of the Truman era.

Polsby, N., ed., *The Modern Presidency* (1973). Useful collection on presidents and their staffs from FDR to Nixon.

Reedy, G. E., *The Twilight of the Presidency* (1970). Provocative analysis of presidential isolation by one-time LBJ aide.

Rossiter, C., *Constitutional Dictatorship* (1948). Analysis of departures from constitutional provisions and a discussion of separation of powers.

———, *The American Presidency*, rev. ed. (1960). Analysis of the growth and uses of the presidency.

Schlesinger, A. M., Jr., *The Imperial Presidency* (1973). History of the growth of the president's role in foreign policy and recommendations for the future.

———, *A Thousand Days* (1965). The Kennedy Administration treated in historical depth by the "resident intellectual" in the White House.

Schubert, G. A., Jr., *The Presidency in the Courts* (1957). Study of the Supreme Court's interpretation of the office and powers.

Sorensen, T. C., *Decision-Making in the White House: The Olive Branch or the Arrows* (1963). With a foreword by John F. Kennedy.

Taft, W. H., *Our Chief Magistrate and His Powers* (1916). Presents a much more limited concept of the presidency.

Thomas, N. C., and H. Baade, eds., *The Institutionalized Presidency* (1972). Essays on the swelling of the modern presidency.

Tugwell, R. G., *The Enlargement of the Presidency* (1960).

———, and T. E. Cronin, eds., *The Presidency Reappraised* (1974). Analysis of the problems of the presidency in the 1970s.

Wann, A. J., *The President as Chief Administrator* (1968).

White, L. D., *The Federalists* (1948); *The Jeffersonians* (1951); *The Jacksonians* (1955); and *The Republican Era, 1869–1901* (1958). Cover the early years and emphasize the administrative organization of the executive.

Wildavsky, A., ed., *The Presidency*, 2nd ed., (1975). Comprehensive collection of presidency studies.

Wilson, W., *Constitutional Government in the United States* (reprinted 1921). Written before he became president; indicates his concept of the role and responsibility of the office.

Wough, E. W., *Second Consul: The Vice-Presidency—Our Greatest Political Problem* (1956). History and analysis of the office.

Young, D., *American Roulette: The History and Dilemma of the Vice-Presidency*, rev. ed., (1972). Useful histories of vice-presidents and their office.

Bureaucrats and bureaucracy

Altshuler, A. A., ed., *The Politics of the Federal Bureaucracy* (1968). The role of the bureaucracy in the political process.

Barnard, C. I., *The Functions of the Executive* (1938). Classic analysis of bureaucratic organization.

Bennis, W. G., ed., *American Bureaucracy* (1970). A useful collection on bureaucracy and democracy, and change and innovation in complex organizations.

Berkman, R. L., and W. K. Viscusi, *Damming the West* (1973). This Ralph Nader study group report illustrates how a federal bureau serves special interest groups.

Blau, P., *On the Nature of Organizations* (1974). Essays from a leading student of organized behavior.

Cleveland, H., *The Future Executive* (1972). A veteran public administrator offers useful advice and forecasts for those who will lead public organizations.

Downs, A., *Inside Bureaucracy* (1967) An important analysis of bureaucratic norms and incentive systems.

Gawthrop, L. C., *Bureaucratic Behavior in the Executive Branch: An Analysis of Organizational Change* (1969). Summary of the literature on administration in the federal executive.

Gellhorn, W., *When Americans Complain* (1966). Existing governmental procedures in handling grievances.

Goodnow, F. J., *Politics and Administration* (1900). A pioneering volume, an attempt to isolate administration from politics as a separate branch of study.

Gross, B. M., *The Managing of Organizations* (1964). A complete work on administration and its many forms.

Hyneman, C. S., *Bureaucracy in a Democracy* (1950). Study of the control and role of the bureaucracy with special attention to the question of legislative and executive responsibilities.

Jacob, C. E., *Policy and Bureaucracy* (1966). Study of administration and policy formulation.

Jacoby, H., *The Bureaucratization of the World* (1973). A survey of the spread and growth of bureaucracy throughout the world.

Kaufman, H., *Administrative Feedback: Monitoring Subordinates' Behavior* (1973). Assesses the ways in which bureau chiefs learn whether or not their directives are being carried out.

———, *The Limits of Organizational Change* (1971).

Kilpatrick, F. P., M. C. Cummings, Jr., and M. K. Jennings, *The Image of the Federal Service* (1964).

March, J. G., ed., *Handbook of Organizations* (1965). Twenty-eight papers covering many aspects of organizations and organization theory.

Merewitz, L., and S. H. Sosnick, *The Budget's New Clothes* (1971). A critique of planning-programming-budgeting and benefit-cost analysis.

Miles, R. E., Jr., *The Department of Helath, Education and Welfare* (1974). An examination of a major domestic executive department by a former sub-cabininet administrator.

Mosher, F. C., *Democracy and the Public Service* (1968). The appointive public service and the democratic process.

Ostrom, V., *The Intellectual Crisis in American Public Administration*, rev. ed. (1974). A revisionist examination of the orthodox doctrines of public administration with proposals for a system of democratic administration.

Parkinson, C. N., *Parkinson's Law* (1957). The "laws" of bureaucratic expansion.

Perrow, C., *Complex Organizations* (1972). A sociologist critically reviews major perspectives toward organizations and raises questions about the future of large, centralized organizations.

Pressman, J. L., and A. Wildavsky, *Implementation: How Great Expectations in Washington Are Dashed in Oakland* (1973). Case examination of the problems of enforcing federal Economic Development Administration programs.

Redford, E. S., *Democracy in the Administrative State* (1969). Fresh insights to fundamental questions.

Rourke, F. E., *Bureaucracy, Politics and Public Policy* (1969).

Sayre, W. S., ed., *The Federal Government Service: Its Character, Prestige, and Problems*, 2nd ed. (1965). An American Assembly symposium.

Schon, D. A., *Beyond the Stable State* (1971). Examines the possibilities for improved organizational response to an era of rapid change and increasing complexity.

Schultz, C. L., *The Politics and Economics of Public Spending* (1968). Policy analysis in the executive branch.

Seidman, H., *Politics, Position, and Power* (1970). A senior public official discusses the dynamics and politics of federal organizational structures.

Selznick, P., *Leadership in Administration: A Sociological Interpretation* (1957). Study of leadership in administrative organizations.

Simon, H. A., *Administrative Behavior* (1950). A study of decision-making processes in administrative organization.

Stanley, D. T., *The Higher Civil*

Service: An Evaluation of Federal Personnel Practices (1964). A study of a group of civil servants whose decisions have a great effect on American life.

———, D. E. Mann, and J. W. Doig, *Men Who Govern: A Biographical Profile of Federal Political Executives* (1967). A study of executive appointments covering five administrations.

Thompson, V., *Modern Organizations* (1961). Perceptive analysis which suggests political applications.

Tullock, G., *The Politics of Bureaucracy* (1965). The political relationships in an administrative structure.

United States Government Manual (published annually). Described in the introduction to this bibliography.

Van Riper, P., *History of the United States Civil Service* (1959). History of public employment in the United States; emphasis on the period since the beginning of civil service reform.

Vaughn, R. G., *The Spoiled System: A Call for Civil Service Reform* (1974). A critical Nader study of the U.S. Civil Service Commission and its deficiencies.

Waldo, D., *The Administrative State* (1948). The theory of American public administration; survey of the various schools of thought.

———, *Perspectives on Administration* (1968). Central issues in administrative theory and research.

Wildavsky, A., *The Politics of the Budgetary Process,* rev. ed., (1974). Study of the way in which federal budgetary decisions are made.

Wilensky, H. L., *Organizational Intelligence* (1967). The use and abuse of intelligence information in modern agencies.

Making policy: conflict and cooperation

Bailey, S., and E. Mosher, *ESEA: The Office of Education Administers a Law* (1968). Examines the enactment and process of implementation of major educational policy.

Bauer, R. A., I. de Sola Pool, and L. A. Dexter, *American Business and Public Policy* (1963). The politics of passing a major foreign trade bill.

Cater, D., *Power in Washington* (1964). Useful interpretative essays about how things get done in Washington.

Cobb, R. W., and C. D. Elder, *Participation in American Politics: The Dynamics of Agenda-Building* (1972). A new approach to understanding how issues gain attention and become prominent.

Crenson, M. A., *The Un-Politics of Air Pollution* (1971). A study of decision-avoidance or "nondecision-making" in a controversial policy area.

Deakin, J., *The Lobbyists* (1966). A history of lobbying, with brief character sketches of certain lobbyists.

Dexter, L., *How Organizations Are Represented in Washington* (1969). A useful survey of the practical strategies employed to represent interest groups in the Washington policy-making community.

Domhoff, G. W., *The Higher Circles: The Governing Class in America* (1970). Polemic claiming elite domination and control of national policymaking in America.

Dye, T. R., *Understanding Public Policy* (1972). A useful introductory text about policy analysis and particular public policies.

Engler, R., *The Politics of Oil* (1961). Review and analysis of the petroleum industry's political influence.

Fritschler, A. L., *Smoking and Politics* (1969). An account of the battles between the tobacco industry and various governmental policy-making units trying to regulate the sales and advertising of cigarettes.

Garceau, O., *The Political Life of the American Medical Association* (1941). Pioneering study of the political activities of doctors in America.

Goulden, J. C., *The Superlawyers* (1972). Portraits of the giant Washington law firms.

Greenberg, D. S., *The Politics of Pure Science* (1967). An examination of how scientists are involved both as policy-makers and lobbyists.

Hall, D., *Cooperative Lobbying—The Power of Pressure* (1969). The activities of the U.S. Chamber of Commerce and business lobbying in general.

Halberstam, D., *The Best and the Brightest* (1972). A vivid critical appraisal of the Kennedy-Johnson brain trust in national security policy-making.

Herring, E. P., *Group Representation Before Congress* (1929). Relations between interest groups and formal institutions of government.

———, *Public Administration and the Public Interest* (1936). Interaction between interest groups and administrative machinery.

Hofferbert, R. I., *The Study of Public Policy* (1974). Summarizes policy research by political scientists.

James, M., *The People's Lawyers* (1973). Examines wide range of "public-interest" lawyers and lets many of them speak about what they are doing.

Levine, R. A., *Public Planning: Failure and Redirection* (1974). A fresh examination of a continuing problem.

Lindblom, C. E., *The Policy-Making Process* (1968). Introductory text on administrative policy-making.

Maass, A., *Muddy Waters* (1951). Indictment of the Army Corps of Engineers as "the lobby that can't be licked."

Mahood, H. R., ed., *Pressure Groups in American Politics* (1967). Useful collection of contemporary readings.

Mann, D., and J. W. Doig, *The Assistant Secretaries* (1965). Useful analysis of backgrounds and recruitment of subcabinet policy-makers.

McConnell, G., *Private Power and American Democracy* (1966). Influence of private power groups on public policy.

Milbrath, L. W., *The Washington Lobbyists* (1963). The role of the lobbyist in the formation of national public policy.

Mitchell, W. C., *Public Choice in*

America (1971). Phases of public policy-making.

Monsen, R. J., Jr., and M. W. Cannon, *The Makers of Public Policy: American Power Groups and Their Ideology* (1965). Formal and informal power groups and their influence on public policy.

Nadel, M. V., *The Politics of Consumer Protection* (1971). The policy politics of consumer legislation and consumer advocacy.

Olson, M., Jr., *The Logic of Collective Action: Public Goods and the Theory of Groups* (1965). An explanation and investigation of the motivating forces in group action.

Parry, G., *Political Elites* (1969). Reviews various theories and perspectives toward the role and impact of political and professional elites.

Pechman, J. A. and B. A. Okun, *Who Bears the Tax Burden?* (1974).

Peters, C., and J. Rothchild, eds., *Inside the System* (1973). An excellent collection of articles drawn from *The Washington Monthly* analyzing policy-makers and policy-making.

Presthus, R., *Elites in the Policy Process* (1974).

Prewitt, K., and A. Stone, *The Ruling Elites* (1973). Another review of the policy-making significance of elites and an appraisal of the elite-pluralist debates in social science.

Ripley, R. B., ed., *Public Policies and Their Politics* (1966).

Roos, L. L., Jr., ed., *The Politics of Ecosuicide* (1971). Useful collection examining the politics of environmental policy-making.

Salisbury, R. H., ed., *Interest Group Politics in America* (1970). A collection of current readings.

Schneier, E. V., ed., *Policy-Making in American Government* (1969).

Sindler, A. P., ed., *Policy and Politics in America* (1973). Six original case studies focusing on different branches and different phases of policy-making.

Wilson, J. Q., *Political Organizations* (1973). Examines a wide variety of organizations, their incentives and efforts to contribute to public policy-making.

Wolman, H., *Politics of Federal Housing* (1971). A useful study of how national housing policies were made during the 1960s.

Ziegler, H., and G. W. Peak, *Interest Groups in American Society*, 2nd ed. (1972). An interpretation of the role of organized interest groups in policy-making.

Leadership and responsibility

Bennett, L., Jr., *What Manner of Man* (1964). The life of Martin Luther King.

Burns, J. M., *Roosevelt: The Lion and the Fox* (1956). Problems and practices of FDR as a Democratic leader.

———, *Roosevelt: The Soldier of Freedom, 1940–1945* (1970). FDR's wartime presidency and oscillation between roles of moral leadership and power politics.

Evans, R., and R. Novak, *Lyndon B. Johnson: The Exercise of Power* (1968). Perceptive analysis of LBJ's career.

Goldman, E. F., *The Tragedy of Lyndon Johnson: A Historian's Personal Interpretation* (1968).

Gottfried, A., *Boss Cermak of Chicago: A Study of Political Leadership* (1962).

Hardin, C. M., *Presidential Power and Accountability* (1974). Provocative proposals for a new constitution.

Heilbroner, R. L., *An Inquiry into the Human Prospect* (1974). Population and other massive crises ahead and implications for democratic government.

Jacobs, J., and the editors of American Heritage, *RFK: His Life and Death* (1968).

Johnson, H., and B. M. Gwertzman, *Fulbright: The Dissenter* (1968). One of the Senate's most outspoken members.

Lasswell, H., *Psychopathology and Politics* (1930); and *Power and Personality* (1948). Through use of interviews, observations, and psychological techniques, Lasswell has developed a typology of political leaders and related their public careers to their psychological characteristics.

McFarland, A. S., *Power and Leadership in Pluralist Systems* (1969). Deep-probing analytical and theoretical study.

Marvick, D., ed., *Political Decision-Makers* (1961). Diverse approaches to the study of political leadership.

Schlesinger, J. A., *Ambition and Politics: Political Careers in the United States* (1966). Behavior as a factor of goals and ambitions in a political career.

Verba, S., *Small Groups and Political Behavior: A Study of Political Leadership* (1961). Experimental findings related to notions of the political process.

Part seven
Government in action

Foreign policy: politics and problems

Acheson, D., *Present at the Creation: My Years in the State Department* (1969). Memoirs by a former Secretary of State.

Allison, G. T., *Essence of Decision: Explaining the Cuban Missile Crisis* (1971). Superb case study offering diverse theoretical interpretations.

Almond, G. A., *The American People and Foreign Policy* (1950). Analysis of the effect of the public, interest groups, and opinion leaders.

Barnet, R. J., *Roots of War* (1972). A critical revisionist review of the bureaucratic, economic and imperial aspects of U.S. foreign policy.

Campbell, J.F., *The Foreign Affairs Fudge Factory* (1971). Critical analysis of State Department and Foreign Service.

Clark, K. C., and L. J. Legere, *The President and the Management of National Security* (1969). A thorough defense-oriented view of critical decision making.

Cleveland, H., *The Obligations of Power: American Diplomacy in the Search for Peace* (1966). The unique task of American foreign policy, past attempts to meet this task, and future proposals.

Cohen, B. J., *The Question of Imperialism: The Political Economy of Dominance and Dependence* (1974). A critique of Marxist and radical theories of imperialism.

Destler, I. M., *Presidents, Bureaucrats, and Foreign Policy* (1972). Review of methods used by the White House to co-ordinate and control foreign policy making.

Donovan, J. C., *The Cold Warriors: A Policy-Making Elite* (1974). A cluster of case studies covering the period 1945 to 1969.

Feis, H., *Foreign Aid and Foreign Policy* (1964). Discussion of the relationship between assistance and diplomacy.

———, *From Trust to Terror: The Onset of the Cold War, 1945–50* (1970). Narrative account of the break-up of the wartime alliance.

Frankel, C., *The Neglected Aspect of Foreign Affairs: American Educational and Cultural Policy Abroad* (1965). United States cultural and educational foreign policy.

Fulbright, J. W., *The Crippled Giant: American Foreign Policy and Its Domestic Consequences* (1972). Essays and reappraisals by the then chairman of the Senate Foreign Relations Committee.

Gaddis, J. L., *The United States and the Origins of the Cold War, 1941–1947* (1972).

Gilbert, J. H., ed., *The New Era in American Foreign Policy* (1973). Useful collection of essays.

Graubard, S., *Kissinger: Portrait of a Mind* (1973).

Haas, E. B., *Tangle of Hopes: American Commitments and World Order* (1969). Recommendations for American adjustment to a changing international environment.

Halperin, M. H., *Bureaucratic Politics and Foreign Policy* (1974). Struggles, strategies and diverse interests among those who shape foreign policy.

———, and A. Kanter, eds., *Readings in American Foreign Policy: A Bureaucratic Perspective* (1973).

Henkin, L. *Foreign Affairs and the Constitution (1972).* Comprehensive coverage, including Congress versus President as well as federalism problems.

Hoffmann, S., *Contemporary Theories in International Relations* (1960).

Hoopes, T., *The Devil and John Foster Dulles* (1973). Critical assessment of Dulles and "brinkmanship" foreign policy.

Kennan, G. F., *Realities of American Foreign Policy* (1966). New edition of a 1954 work.

Kissinger, H. A., *American Foreign Policy*, rev. ed. (1974). Essays and speeches.

Kissinger, H. S., *Nuclear Weapons and Foreign Policy* (1957). Influential discussion of the strategic impact of nuclear technology & defense of policy of limited nuclear war.

Kirkpatrick, L. B., Jr., *The U.S. Intelligence Community: Foreign Policy and Domestic Activities* (1973). New look at the CIA by a former top CIA official.

Kolko, G., *The Roots of American Foreign Policy: An Analysis of Power and Purpose* (1969). Radical view of American foreign policy.

Liska, G., *Imperial America: The International Politics of Primacy* (1967). America as the dominant power in international relations.

Lowenthal, A. F., *The Dominican Intervention* (1972).

Mackinder, H. J., *Democratic Ideals and Reality* (1919; republished, 1942). Seminal study of what is too narrowly called geopolitics.

Marchetti, V., and J. D. Marks, *The CIA and the Cult of Intelligence* (1974). Argues that the CIA has grown fat, bureaucratic and ineffective.

McGarvey, P. J., *CIA: The Myth and the Madness* (1972). A critical account of the CIA by a former CIA employee.

Mueller, J. E., *War, Presidents and Public Opinion* (1973). Interpretation of the relationship between public opinion and presidential behavior.

Neustadt, R. E., *Alliance Politics* (1970). U.S.–British relationships.

Osgood, R. E., *et. al., Retreat From Empire?: The First Nixon Administration* (1973). Essays primarily on foreign policy and diplomatic relations.

Morgenthau, H. J., *A New Foreign Policy for the United States* (1968). An evaluation of past policy and future recommendations.

Price, D. K., ed., *The Secretary of State* (1961). Examination of the office.

Ransom, H. H., *The Espionage Establishment* (1970). Definitive and sympathetic look at the "invisible government."

Rieselbach, L. N., *The Roots of Isolationism: Congressional Voting and Presidential Leadership in Foreign Policy* (1966). An analysis of congressional action on foreign policy over the last twenty years.

Robinson, J. A., *Congress and Foreign Policy-Making: A Study in Legislative Influence and Initiative* (1967). Congress in the foreign-policy process.

Rosenau, J. N., ed., *Domestic Sources of Foreign Policy* (1967). A study of domestic policy as an ingredient in foreign-policy formulation.

———, *Public Opinion and Foreign Policy* (1961). Treatment of public's role in decision making.

Rostow, W. W., *The Diffusion of Power 1957–1972* (1972). Wide ranging examination, often with personal accounts, of foreign policy events and major decision-making case studies.

Tucker, R., *A New Internationalism: Threat or Promise?* (1972).

Waltz, K. N., *Foreign Policy and Democratic Politics: The American and British Experience* (1967). A comparison of American and British foreign policy formulation.

Ward, B., *The Lopsided World* (1968). Contends that international economic inequities are endangering the world's political and economic stability.

Westerfield, H. B., *Foreign Policy*

and Party Politics (1955). Role of the parties and bipartisanship in Congress.

Wise, D., *The Politics of Lying* (1973). Numerous examples of public opinion and press manipulation with special attention given to government secrecy in foreign policy-making.

To provide for the common defense

Barnet, R. J., *The Economy of Death* (1969). Recommendations for reducing military influence on government policy making.

Borklund, C. W., *The Department of Defense* (1968).

Brodie, B., *Escalation and the Nuclear Option* (1966). Political and military considerations of the thermonuclear age.

Caraley, D., *The Politics of Military Unification: A Study of Conflict and the Policy Process* (1966). Conflict over military unification from 1943 to 1947 and the resolution of the conflict as part of the policy process.

Clotfelter, J., *The Military in American Politics* (1973). Useful review of the military within the larger political system.

Davis, V., *Postwar Defense Policy and U.S. Navy, 1943–1946* (1966). The Navy's fight for survival in the immediate postwar period.

Derthick, M., *The National Guard in Politics* (1965). Study of a very successful pressure group.

Enthoven, A. C., and K. W. Smith, *How Much Is Enough?: Shaping The Defense Program, 1961–1969* (1971). Two McNamara advisers explain the workings of systems analysis and the defense budget process.

Feis, H., *The Atomic Bomb and the End of World War II* (1966). Causes and effects of the decision to drop the atomic bomb.

Fitzgerald, A. E., *The High Priests of Waste* (1972). A controversial Defense Department official offers strong criticism of cost overruns and related problems.

Fulbright, J. W., *The Pentagon Propaganda Machine* (1970). An analysis of the public relations effort of the Department of Defense by one-time chairman of the Senate Committee on Foreign Relations.

Galloway, K. B., and R. B. Johnson, Jr., *West Point: America's Power Fraternity* (1973). An attempt to trace military shortcomings to how West Point trains military elites.

George, A. L., *et al.*, *The Limits of Coercive Diplomacy: Laos, Cuba, Vietnam* (1971). Case studies with a useful overview of lessons learned and the likely conditions under which coercive diplomacy can work.

Gilpin, R., *American Scientists and Nuclear Weapons Policy* (1962). An analysis of participation in policy making by an important new elite.

———, and Christopher Wright, eds., *Scientists and National Policy Making* (1964). Essays by nine authors on the changing role of science in government.

Goulding, P., *Confirm or Deny* (1970). How the Pentagon informs and misinforms the American public and the world.

Green, P., *Deadly Logic: The Theory of Nuclear Deterrence* (1966). A scientific approach.

Hauser, W. L., *America's Army in Crisis: A Study in Civil-Military Relations* (1973). A soldier-scholar treats some problems confronting the Army in the post-Vietnam and volunteer army context.

Huntington, S.P., *The Common Defense: Strategic Programs in National Politics* (1961). Essays analyzing the dynamics of postwar defense policy making.

———, *The Soldier and the State* (1957). Study of civil-military relations in the United States.

Kaplan, M. A., *The Rationale for NATO: European Collective Security—Past and Future* (1973).

Knorr, K., *Military Power and Potential* (1970). The components of military power.

Kolodziej, E.A., *The Uncommon Defense and Congress, 1945–1963* (1966). Role of Congress in formulation of military policy.

Lapp, R. E., *Arms Beyond Doubt* (1970). The tyranny of weapons technology.

McBride, J. H., *The Test Ban Treaty: Military, Technological, and Political Implication* (1967). The hawk case for nuclear power.

Melman, S., *Pentagon Capitalism* (1970). A critical view of the Pentagon's activities.

Millis, W., *Arms and Men* (1956). History of American military institutions.

Newhouse, J., *Cold Dawn: The Story of SALT* (1973). Analysis of SALT talks and arms race agreements made in the early '70s.

Payne, J. L., *The American Threat: The Fear of War as an Instrument of Foreign Policy* (1970).

Russett, B. M., *What Price Vigilance? The Burdens of National Defense* (1970). Facts and figures on cause and effects of the military establishment.

Sapin, B. M., ed., *Contemporary American Foreign and Military Policy* (1970).

Sapolsky, H. M., *The Polaris System Development: Bureaucratic and Programmatic Success in Government* (1972). Examination of a major weapon project and its politics.

Schelling, T. C., *Arms and Influence* (1966). An analysis of international strategies.

Singer, J. D., *Deterrence, Arms Control, and Disarmament: Toward a Synthesis in National Security Policy* (1962).

Smith, B.L.R., *The RAND Corporation: Case Study of a Nonprofit Advisory Corporation* (1966). History, structure, operations, and future of famous "think tank."

Spanier, J. W., *The Truman-MacArthur Controversy and the Korean War*, 2nd ed. (1965). Study of wartime civil-military relationships.

Stern, P. M., *The Oppenheimer Case: Security on Trial* (1969). The famous scientist as security risk.

Stone, J. J., *Containing the Arms Race: Some Specific Proposals* (1966). Analysis and proposals on questions of national strategy.

———, *Strategic Persuasion: Arms Limitation Through Dialogue* (1968).

Taylor, M.D., *Swords and Plowshares* (1972). A former Chairman of the Joint Chiefs and military adviser to Kennedy and Johnson tells his side.

Thayer, G., *The War Business* (1969). Shows that war means low competition and high profits.

Trewhitt, H. L., *McNamara: His Ordeal in the Pentagon* (1971).

Wiesner, J. B., *Where Science and Politics Meet* (1965). By John Kennedy's science adviser.

Yarmolinsky, A., *The Military Establishment* (1971). A former DOD Deputy Assistant Secretary examines the impact of the armed forces upon our public policies and our lives.

York, H. F., ed., *Arms Control: Readings from Scientific American* (1973).

———, *Race to Oblivion: A Participant's View of the Arms Race* (1970). A former science adviser to several administrations criticizes recent U.S. arms race policies.

Foreign relations and national security

Alan, J., *The Politics of Peace-Keeping* (1969). The peace-keeping role of the UN.

Baldwin, D. A., *Economic Development and American Foreign Policy, 1943–1962* (1966). Domestic goals of foreign-aid recipients; conflicts between recipient and donor.

Beichman, A., *The "Other" State Department* (1968). A study of United States representation and activity in the UN.

Claude, I. L., Jr., *Swords into Ploughshares*, 4th ed. (1971). Analysis of the problems of international organizations.

Elder, R. E., *The Information Machine: The United States Information Agency and American Foreign Policy* (1968).

———, *Overseas Representation and Services for Federal Domestic Agencies* (1965). A discussion of problems involved when domestic agencies must reorient some segments of their institutions for foreign service.

Elmandjra, M., *The United Nations System: An Analysis* (1973). The UN as an intergovernmental political system within the international system.

Frankel, C., *High on Foggy Bottom* (1970). "An outsider's inside view of the government" by a former Assistant Secretary of State.

Galbraith, J. K., *Ambassador's Journal* (1969). Personal account of noted economist's service in India.

Haar, J. E., *The Professional Diplomats* (1969). A study of American professional diplomats.

Hazzard, S., *Defeat of An Ideal: A Study of the Self-Destruction of the United Nations* (1973). A study of some of the self-inflicted bureaucratic and organizational problems of the UN.

Hunter, R. E., and J. E. Reilly, eds., *Development Today: A New Look at U.S. Relations with the Poor Countries* (1972).

Johnson, R. A., *The Administration of United States Foreign Policy* (1971). A study of contemporary administrative processes.

Jones, A. G., *The Evolution of Personnel Systems for U.S. Foreign Affairs* (1965). A history of the Foreign Service from its inception to the present.

Kennedy, R. F., *Thirteen Days* (1969). The late Robert Kennedy's vivid account of the Cuban missile crisis of 1962.

Leacacos, J. P., *Fires in the In-Basket: The ABC's of the State Department* (1968). An excellent study of how the State Department was run under Dean Rusk in the 1960s.

Martin, J. B., *Overtaken by Events: The Dominican Crisis from the Fall of Trujillo to the Civil War* (1966). The United States embassy in the Dominican crisis.

Nelson, J. M., *Aid, Influence, and Foreign Policy* (1968). Foreign aid as an instrument of foreign policy.

O'Leary, M. K., *The Politics of American Foreign Aid* (1967). Domestic sources of foreign-aid policy.

Packenham, R., *Liberal America and The Third World* (1973). Analysis of attentive-public moods toward U.S. assistance programs.

Perloff, H. S., *Alliance for Progress: A Social Invention in the Making* (1969). Origins and an evaluation of the first seven years of the Alliance.

Rosi, E. J., ed., *American Defense and Detente: Readings in National Security Policy* (1973). A useful anthology.

Rourke, F. E., *Bureaucracy and Foreign Policy* (1972). Short, penetrating view of the role of bureaucracy in foreign policy making and execution.

Sterling, R. W., *Macropolitics: International Relations in a Global Society* (1974).

Stuart, G. H., *The Department of State* (1949). Comprehensive history.

Toma, P. A., *The Politics of Food for Peace* (1967). Origins and activities of a United States foreign aid program.

American foreign policy: Vietnam

Cooper, C. L., *The Lost Crusade* (1970). Revealing inside study of American Vietnam policy.

Corson, W. R., *The Betrayal* (1968). Critique of the United States in Vietnam by a Marine colonel.

Duncanson, D. J., *Government and Revolution in Vietnam* (1967).

Ellsberg, D., *Papers On The War* (1972). Analysis of why we went into Vietnam by one of the "Pentagon Papers" authors who worked for several years as Defense Department and RAND specialist on Vietnam strategies.

Falk, R. A., ed., *The Vietnam War and International Law* (1969).

Fall, B. B., *Hell in a Very Small Place* (1967). The story of the seige of Dien Bien Phu.

Fishel, W. R., ed., *Vietnam: Anatomy of a Conflict* (1968). History and analysis of United States activity in Vietnam.

Fitzgerald, F., *Fire in the Lake: The Vietnamese and the Americans in Vietnam* (1972). Excellent account of the difference between U.S. and Vietnamese cultures.

Goulden, J. C., *Truth is the First Casualty* (1969). Illusion and reality of the Gulf of Tonkin affair.

Halberstam, D., *The Best and the Brightest* (1972). Vivid account of the Kennedy advisers and their role in the Vietnam war.

Hersh, S. M., *My Lai 4* (1970). An account of the massacre in a South Vietnamese hamlet.

Lansdale, E. G., *In the Midst of Wars* (1972). Memoir by a key civilian adviser on land reform and guerrilla warfare in Southeast Asia.

Lemay, C. E., with D. O. Smith, *America is in Danger* (1968).

Randle, R. F., *Geneva 1954: The Settlement of the Indochinese War* (1969). Comprehensive description that includes the domestic determinants of the foreign policy positions of the participants.

Sheehan, N., *et al.*, *The Pentagon Papers* (as published by *The New York Times*) (1971).

Taylor, T., *Nuremberg and Vietnam: An American Tragedy* (1970). Some parallels between Nuremberg and Vietnam by the former chief American prosecutor at Nuremberg.

Walt, L. W., *Strange War, Strange Strategy: A General's Report on Vietnam* (1970).

Walton, R. J., *Cold War and Counterrevolution: The Foreign Policy of John F. Kennedy* (1972). A revisionist treatment of Kennedy as a foreign policy leader.

Government and the economy

Anderson, J. E., *Politics and the Economy* (1967). Trends and policy patterns in national economic policy.

Barber, J., *The American Corporation: Its Power, Its Money, Its Politics* (1970).

Berle, A. A., *Economic Power and the Free Society* (1957). Essay on the prevailing currents in economic life and their impact on individual freedom.

Burns, A. F., *The Management of Prosperity* (1966). A report on the Employment Act of 1946.

Canterbury, E. R., *Economics on the New Frontier* (1968). Important history of political and economic decision-making in the early 1960s.

Dahl, R. A., and C. E. Lindblom, *Politics, Economics and Welfare* (1953). Patterns of economic and political power; suggests new theoretical approaches.

Flash, E. S., *Economic Advice and Presidential Leadership: The Council of Economic Advisers* (1965). History of the Council of Economic Advisers.

Galbraith, J. K., *The New Industrial State* (1967). Controversial view of modern economic life.

Haveman, R. H., and R. D. Hamrin, eds., *The Political Economy of Federal Policy* (1973). Valuable introductory collection.

Kolko, G., *Wealth and Power in America* (1962). Examines social class and income distribution.

Okun, A. M., *The Political Economy of Prosperity* (1970). By a former chairman of the Council of Economic Advisers.

Shonfield, A., *Modern Capitalism: The Changing Balance of Public and Private Power* (1965). The change in capitalism since World War II.

Silk, L., et. al., *Capitalism: The Moving Target* (1974). Collection of diverse views.

Soule, G., *Planning U.S.A.* (1967). History and analysis of United States economic planning.

Tobin, J., *National Economic Policy* (1966).

Wilensky, H. L., *The Welfare State and Equality* (1975).

Government as regulator

Arnold, T. W., *The Folklore of Capitalism* (1937). Mythology of business and trust-busting, with emphasis on its futility, by a man who subsequently became an active trustbuster.

Bauer, R. A., I. de S. Pool, and L. A. Dexter, *American Business and Public Policy* (1963). A major study of public opinion and congressional activity on business politics.

Berle, A. A., and G. C. Means, *The Modern Corporation and Private Property* (1933). Analysis of the growth of large industry, the separation between ownership and control, and problems of social control.

Blair, J. M., *Economic Concentration* (1972). A former chief economist for the Senate Antitrust and Monopoly Subcommittee describes and assesses recent conglomerate activity.

Brayman, H., *Corporate Management in a World of Politics: The Public, Political, and Governmental Problems of Business* (1967). Corporate management and communication.

Cary, W. L., *Politics and the Regulatory Agencies* (1967). Analysis of the political relationships of six prominent independent regulatory agencies.

Cochran, T. C., *Business in American Life: A History* (1972).

Commoner, B., *The Closing Circle* (1972). The case for ecology and more rigorous environmental controls.

Commons, J. R., et al., *History of Labor in the United States*, 4 vols. (1935). One of the best labor histories covering the period before the New Deal.

Davies, J. C. III, *The Politics of Pollution* (1970). The role of Congress, public opinion, and interest groups in the formation of federal antipollution legislation.

Dubos, R., *Reason Awake: Science for Man* (1970). Essays on the threat to man's environment by technology and the population explosion.

Ehrlich, P. R., and A. H. Ehrlich, *Population, Resources, Environment*, rev. edition (1972). An analysis of the dangers posed by environmental deterioration, overpopulation, hunger, and war.

Friedlander, A. F., *The Dilemma of Freight Transport Regulation* (1969).

Friendly, H. J., *The Federal Administrative Agencies: The Need for Better Definition of Standards* (1962). Advocates improvement in commission personnel

and standards.
Galbraith, J. K., *Economics and the Public Purpose* (1973). Analysis and prescription by an outspoken and unconventional liberal economist.
Green, M. J., et al., *The Closed Enterprise System* (1972).
Greenstone, J. D., *Labor in American Politics* (1969). Broad evaluation of labor's role in American politics.
Jacoby, N. H., *Corporate Power and Social Responsibility* (1973). An economist's outline for government action and restraint.
Kohlmeier, L. M., Jr., *The Regulators: Watchdog Agencies and the Public Interest* (1969).
Krasnow, E. G., and L. D. Longley, *The Politics of Broadcast Regulation* (1973). Examines the subgovernment of the FCC and its allies and adversaries.
Linowes, D. F., *The Corporate Conscience* (1974). Argues for including socio-economic or social audit impact statement in every annual report.
Michael, J. R., ed., *Working on the System: A Comprehensive Manual for Citizen Access to Federal Agencies* (1974).
Nadel, M. V., *The Politics of Consumer Protection* (1971). A political history and assessment of consumer protection legislation and the role of the press, consumer advocates and executive agencies in the policy process.
Nader, R., and M. Green, eds., *Corporate Power in America* (1973).
Noll, R. G., *Reforming Regulation* (1971). An appraisal of recent proposals and suggestions of some others.
———, M. J. Peck, and J. J. McGowan, *Economic Aspects of Television Regulation* (Brookings, 1973).
Redford, E. S., *The Regulatory Process: With Illustrations from Civil Aviation* (1969). An important scholarly analysis of federal regulation.
Rosow, J. M., ed., *The Worker and the Job: Coping with Change* (1974). Essays on new attitudes toward and innovations in work.
Scott, R., *Muscle and Blood* (1974). An angry and fact-filled account of industrial hazards.
Silverman, M., and P. R. Lee, *Pills, Profits and Politics* (1974). The politics of drug dependence and the pharmaceutical business.
Taubenfeld, H. J., ed., *Controlling the Weather* (1970). On legal, technical and political implications of weather modification.
Wellford, H., *Sowing Thy Wind* (1972). A study of the Wholesome Meat Act of 1967 that argues that it has unintentionally helped the industry sometimes at the expense of the public.
Winslow, J. F., *Conglomerates Unlimited: The Failure of Regulation* (1974).
Zagoria, S., ed., *Public Workers and Public Unions* (1972). A useful collection sponsored by the American Assembly, with a special focus on New York City.

Government as promoter

Aaron, H. J., *Shelter and Subsidies* (1972). Examines who benefits from federal housing policies and advocates housing allowance.
Altmeyer, A. J., *The Formative Years of Social Security* (1966). A history of the program.
Benedict, M. R., *Farm Policies of the United States, 1790–1950* (1953). Origins and development of governmental policy.
Beyle, T. H., and G. T. Lathrop, eds., *Planning and Politics: Uneasy Partnership* (1970).
Brown, L. R., *In the Human Interest* (1974). A noted agricultural expert outlines a strategy to stabilize world population.
Davis, D. H., *Energy Politics* (1974). Examines major energy sources used in the U. S. and political implications.
Dienes, C. T., *Law, Politics and Birth Control* (1972). A study of how courts and legislatures handle a controversial issue in Connecticut, Massachusetts, and New York.
Donovan, J. C., *The Politics of Poverty* (1967). The formation of the Economic Opportunities Act of 1964.
Downs, A., *Opening Up the Suburbs* (1973). An analysis of housing policies.
———, *Who Are the Urban Poor?* (1970). A brief but comprehensive description of poverty in urban areas.
Ehrenreich, B. and J. Ehrenreich, *The American Health Empire: Power, Profits and Politics* (1971). Examines contemporary health care problems and politics.
Goodwin, L., *Do the Poor Want to Work?* (1972). A social-psychological study of the federal "work-incentive" program.
Harrington, M., *The Other America* (1963). An influential book that helped to make many people aware of the poverty problem in the early 1960s.
Kennedy, E. M., *In Critical Condition: The Crisis in America's Health Care* (1972). A prominent Senator's case for more federal action.
Kotz, N., *Let Them Eat Promises* (1969). Hunger in the affluent society.
Lakoff, S. A., ed., *Knowledge and Power: Essays on Science and Government* (1966). Essays covering varied aspects of science-government relations.
Levitan, S. A., *Programs in Aid of the Poor for the 1970's* (1970). Introduction to the federal welfare system.
Lewis, O., *La Vida: A Puerto Rican Family in the Culture of Poverty - San Juan and New York* (1966). The migrant life of a composite family.
Lilienthal, D. E., *TVA: Democracy on the March*, rev. ed. (1953). Defense of TVA as major instrument of grass-roots democracy. By a former director of TVA.
Macy, J. W., Jr., *To Irrigate a Wasteland: The Struggle to Shape a Public Television System in the United States* (1974). Analysis by a former chairman of the Corporation for Public Broadcasting.
Marris, P., and M. Rein, *Dilemmas of Social Reform: Poverty and Community Action in the United States* (1968). Contemporary problems and future

prospects of programs for social reform.

McKinley, C., and R. W. Frase, *Launching Social Security: A Capture and Record Account, 1935–1937* (1970). Exhaustive and informative survey.

McKinley, C., *The Management of Land and Related Water Resources in Oregon: A Case Study in Administrative Federalism* (1965).

Morgan, R. J., *Governing Soil Conservation: Thirty Years of the New Decentralization* (1966). The agricultural and administrative problems of soil conservation.

Moynihan, D. P., *Maximum Feasible Misunderstanding: Community Action in the War on Poverty* (1969). Origins of the War on Poverty.

______, *The Politics of Guaranteed Income* (1973).

National Association of Social Workers, *The Social Welfare Yearbook*. Annual collection of articles.

Penick, J. L., Jr., C. W. Pursell, Jr., M. B. Sherwood, and D. C. Swain, eds., *The Politics of American Science: 1939 to the Present* (1965). Policy and administration in the scientific community.

Perry, H., *"They'll Cut Off Your Project"* (1972). A vivid account of an Appalachian community's struggles to make an antipoverty program work.

Pinchot, G., *Breaking New Ground* (1947). Autobiography of a crusader for conservation.

Polsky, R. M., *Getting To Sesame Street* (1974). Examines how the enormously popular Sesame Street television series was launched and the role of the federal government in sustaining it.

Price, D. K., *The Scientific Estate* (1965). Analysis of the role of experts in a democracy.

Reagan, M. D., *Science and the Federal Patron* (1969). Study of the increasing dependence of science on the federal government.

Reilly, W. K. ed., *The Use of Land* (1973).

Richardson, E., *Dams, Parks and Politics: Resource Development and Preservation in the Truman-Eisenhower Era* (1973).

Rosen, G., *A History of Public Health* (1958). General review of programs through several centuries.

Rosenbaum, W. A., *The Politics of Environmental Concern* (1973). One of the best available studies of the politics of environmental reform.

Ruttenberg, S. R., *Manpower Challenge of the 1970's: Institutions and Social Change* (1970). History, administrative structure, and delivery of current manpower programs.

Selznick, P., *TVA and the Grass Roots* (1949). Sociological interpretation.

Shover, J. L., *Cornbelt Rebellion: The Farmers' Holiday Association* (1965). The protests of United States farmers during the Depression and the New Deal.

Somers, H. M., and A. R. Somers, *Doctors, Patients, and Health Insurance* (1961). Comprehensive, balanced examination.

Steiner, G. Y., *The State of Welfare* (1971). Reviewing a decade of welfare reform efforts.

Thomas, M., and R. M. Northrop, *Atomic Energy and Congress* (1956).

United States Social Security Administration, *Social Security Bulletin*.

Wengert, N. I., *Natural Resources and the Political Struggle* (1955). History and politics of conservation.

Wenk, E., Jr., *The Politics of the Ocean* (1972). Useful analysis of regulation and promotion.

Witte, E. E., *The Development of the Social Security Act* (1962).

Wolman, H., *The Politics of Federal Housing* (1970). A well researched study of how federal housing policy is shaped.

Taxing and spending: fiscal and monetary policy

The several reports resulting from the Employment Act of 1946 are primary sources for the problem of governmental fiscal and monetary policy. These include the President's Economic Report to the Congress, Report of the Council of Economic Advisers, and Reports and Hearings of the Joint Congressional Committee on Economics Report. These are issued regularly.

Bach, G. L., *Making Monetary and Fiscal Policy* (1971). An introduction to a complex process.

Blechman, B. M., et al., *Setting National Priorities: The 1975 Budget* (1974). An analysis of a U.S. Budget with a cogent analysis of alternatives.

Buchanan, J. M., *Public Finance in Democratic Process: Fiscal Institutions and Individual Choice* (1967). A discussion of individual decision making in public goods and expenditures and in future taxation policies.

Golembiewski, R. T., ed., *Public Budgeting and Finance: Readings in Theory and Practice* (1968). Budgeting technique and theory.

Grayson, C. J., Jr., and L. Neeb, *Confessions of a Price Controller* (1974). Memoirs by the former chairman of Nixon's Price Commission.

Heller, W. W., *New Dimensions of Political Economy* (1966). Memoir by Kennedy's chief economic adviser.

Keynes, J. M., *The General Theory of Employment, Interest, and Money* (1936). One of the most influential books of modern times; interpretation of economics that calls for governmental fiscal and monetary policy and public works to offset unemployment.

Kimmel, L. H., *Federal Budget and Fiscal Policy, 1789–1958* (1959). General survey of policies and procedures.

Morrison, R. J., *Expectations and Inflation: Nixon, Politics, and Economics* (1973).

Norton, H., *The Role of the Economist in Government Policymaking* (1969).

Office of Management and Budget, *The Federal Budget in Brief*. Summary of the budget, published annually; many illustrations.

Ott, D. J., and A. F. Ott, *Federal Budget Policy* (1965). A nontechnical study of the budget and its relationship to the economy.

Pechman, J. A., *Federal Tax Policy*, rev. edition (1971). The formation and implementation of tax policy.

Pierce, L. C., *The Politics of Fiscal Policy Formation* (1971).

Reagan, M. D., *The Managed Economy* (1963). The evolution of free-enterprise economy.

Sharkansky, I., *The Politics of Taxing and Spending* (1969). Text on taxing and spending at all levels.

Silk, L., *Nixonomics*, second edition (1973). Analysis of Nixon economic policy by an economics reporter.

Stern, P. M., *The Rape of the Taxpayer* (1973). Critique of tax loopholes.

Surrey, S. S., *Pathways to Tax Reform* (1973). A former Treasury official offers advice.

Thurow, L. C., *The Impact of Taxes on the American Economy* (1973).

Weber, A. R., *In Pursuit of Price Stability: The Wage-Price Freeze of 1971* (1973).

Wildavsky, A. B., *The Politics of the Budgetary Process*, rev. edition (1974). The strategies and calculations of participants in the budget-making process.

Epilogue: citizenship as an office

Alinsky, S., *Rules for Radicals* (1971). Suggestions from a veteran community organizer.

Bullitt, S., *To Be a Politician* (1959). A former candidate for office reflects on his experience with "practical politics."

Burns, J. M., *Uncommon Sense* (1972).

Cotter, C. P., ed., *Practical Politics in the United States* (1969). A useful collection of articles by professionals and academic activists.

Gardner, J. W., *In Common Cause* (1972). A description of one of the best-known citizen pressure groups by its chairman.

Herzberg, D. G., and J. W. Peltason, (1970). *A Student Guide to Campaign Politics* (1970). How to be effective in political campaigning.

Macy, J. W., *Public Service: The Human Side of Government* (1971). A former chairman of the Civil Service Commission probes the workings of the federal public service.

Mitchell, C., *Why Vote?* (1971). A political scientist argues the importance and impact of voting.

Murphy, W. T., and E. Schneier, *Vote Power: How to Work for the Person You Want Elected* (1974). A very helpful analysis of what must be done to help people get elected to major public offices.

Ross, D. K., *A Public Citizen's Action Manual* (1973). A product of Ralph Nader's Public Citizen, Inc., organization.

Scott, H., *How to Run for Public Office and Win* (1968).

Segal, R., *The Struggle Against History* (1973). A socialist's view of what type of system reforms and participatory politics is needed to transform democracy.

Shadegg, S. C., *The New How to Win an Election* (1972). A veteran Republican campaign manager and election consultant tells how a campaign should be run.

Walzer, M., *Political Action: A Practical Guide to Movement Politics* (1971). One of the best guides to citizen-activism.

Wilson, J. Q., *The Amateur Democrat* (1962). A discussion of the difficulties in organizing issue-oriented participatory partisan organizations.

Political novels

Books of fiction often provide useful insights into political life. Many novelists have developed specifically political themes whereas others have presented political implications for the broader human drama. Three general studies—Irving Howe, *Politics and the Novel* (1957); Joseph Blotner, *The Modern American Political Novel: 1900–1960* (1966); and Gordon Milne, *The American Political Novel* (1966)—discuss aspects of the interrelationship between politics and the novelists' art. Following is a brief listing of a few leading American political novels.

Adams, H., *Democracy* (1880). Classic in American political fiction.

Burdick, E., *The Ninth Wave* (1956). A powerful account of applied political psychology.

———, and H. Wheeler, *Failsafe* (1962). On policy-making and accidental war.

Dos Passos, J., *Number One* (1943). A study in the pathology of political corruption.

Drury, A., *Advise and Consent* (1960). A fictional version of the Senate's confirmation of a controversial presidential appointment.

Frank, P., *Affair of State* (1948). Dilemmas in the life of a foreign service officer.

Holland, H. M., Jr., ed., *Politics Through Literature* (1968). Selections on a worldwide basis.

Lederer, W. J., and E. Burdick, *The Ugly American* (1959). Vignettes of several types of Americans on overseas assignments.

O'Connor, E., *The Last Hurrah* (1955). A delightful portrait of a big-city boss and his machine.

Schneider, J. G., *The Golden Kazoo* (1956). Public relations men transform a presidential campaign.

Sheed, W., *People Will Always Be Kind* (1973). Examines the ambitions and values of a reflective, invalid senator seeking presidential nomination.

Sheehan, E., *The Governor* (1970). An impressive novel journey into the world of Massachusetts politics as seen through the ordeal of a young governor.

Warren, R. P., *All the King's Men* (1946). The rise and fall of a southern demagogue in the mold of Huey Long.

West, N., *A Cool Million* (1934). Satirizes several social and political values, especially shallow superpatriotism.

Wicker, T., *Facing The Lions* (1973). The rise and fall of a southern senator is recounted.

The Constitution of the United States

We the People of the United States, in Order to form a more perfect Union, establish Justice, insure domestic Tranquility, provide for the common defence, promote the general Welfare, and secure the Blessings of Liberty to ourselves and our Posterity, do ordain and establish this Constitution for the United States of America.

Article I

Section 1. All legislative Powers herein granted shall be vested in a Congress of the United States, which shall consist of a Senate and House of Representatives.

Section 2. The House of Representatives shall be composed of Members chosen every second Year by the People of the several States, and the Electors in each State shall have the Qualifications requisite for Electors of the most numerous Branch of the State Legislature.

No Person shall be a Representative who shall not have attained to the Age of twenty five Years, and been seven Years a Citizen of the United States, and who shall not, when elected, be an Inhabitant of that State in which he shall be chosen.

Representatives and direct Taxes shall be apportioned among the several States which may be included within this Union, according to their respective Numbers, which shall be determined by adding to the whole Number of free Persons, including those bound to Service for a Term of Years, and excluding Indians not taxed, three fifths of all other Persons. The actual Enumeration shall be made within three Years after the first Meeting of the Congress of the United States, and within every subsequent Term of ten Years, in such Manner as they shall by Law direct. The Number of Representatives shall not exceed one for every thirty Thousand, but each State shall have at Least one Representative; and until such enumeration shall be made, the State of New Hampshire shall be entitled to chuse three, Massachusetts eight, Rhode-Island and Providence Plantations one, Connecticut five, New-York six, New Jersey four, Pennsylvania eight, Deleaware one, Maryland six, Virginia ten, North Carolina five, South Carolina five, and Georgia three.

When vacancies happen in the Representation from any State, the Executive Authority thereof shall issue Writs of Election to fill such Vacancies.

The House of Representatives shall chuse their speaker and other Officers; and shall have the sole Power of Impeachment.

Section 3. The Senate of the United States shall be composed of two Senators from each State, chosen by the Legislature thereof, for six Years; and each Senator shall have one Vote.

Immediately after they shall be assembled in Consequence of the first Election, they shall be divided as equally as may be into three Classes. The Seats of the Senators of the first Class shall be vacated at the Expiration of the second Year, of the second Class at the Expiration of the fourth Year, and of the third Class at the Expiration of the sixth Year, so that one third may be chosen every second Year; and if Vacancies happen by Resignation, or otherwise, during the Recess of the Legislature of any State, the Executive thereof may make temporary Appointments until the next Meeting of the Legislature, which shall then fill such Vacancies.

No Person shall be a Senator who shall not have attained to the Age of thirty Years, and been nine Years a Citizen of the United States, and who shall not, when elected, be an Inhabitant of that State for which he shall be chosen.

The Vice President of the United States shall be President of the Senate, but shall have no Vote, unless they be equally divided.

The Senate shall chuse their other Officers, and also a President pro tempore, in the Absence of the Vice President, or when he shall exercise the Office of the President of the United States.

The Senate shall have the sole Power to try all Impeachments. When sitting for that Purpose, they shall be on Oath or Affirmation. When the President of the United States is tried, the Chief Justice shall preside: And no Person shall be convicted without the Concurrence of two thirds of the Members present.

Judgment in Cases of Impeachment shall not extend further than to removal from Office, and disqualification to hold and enjoy any Office of honor, Trust or Profit under the United States: but the Party convicted shall nevertheless be liable and subject to Indictment, Trial, Judgment and Punishment, according to law.

Section 4. The Times, Places and Manner of holding Elections for Senators and Representatives, shall be prescribed in each State by the Legislature thereof; but the Congress may at any time by Law make or alter such Regulations, except as to the Places of chusing Senators.

The Congress shall assemble at least once in every Year, and such Meeting shall be on the first Monday in December, unless they shall by Law appoint a different Day.

Section 5. Each House shall be the Judge of the Elections, Returns and Qualifications of its own Members, and a Majority of each shall constitute a Quorum to do Business; but a smaller Number may adjourn from day to day, and may be authorized to compel the Attendance of absent Members, in such Manner, and under such Penalties as each House may provide.

Each House may determine the Rules of its Proceedings, punish its Members for disorderly Behaviour, and, with the Concurrence of two thirds, expel a Member.

Each House shall keep a Journal of its Proceedings, and from time to time publish the same, excepting such Parts as may in their Judgment require Secrecy; and the Yeas and Nays of the Members of either House on any question shall, at the Desire of one fifth of those Present, be entered on the Journal.

Neither House, during the Session of Congress, shall, without the Consent of the other, adjourn for more than three days, nor to any other Place than that in which the two Houses shall be sitting.

Section 6. The Senators and Representatives shall receive a Compensation for their Services, to be ascertained by Law, and paid out of the Treasury of the United States. They shall in all Cases, except Treason, Felony and Breach of the Peace, be privileged from Arrest during their Attendance at the Session of their respective Houses, and in going to and returning from the same; and for any Speech or Debate in either House, they shall not be questioned in any other Place.

No Senator or Representative shall, during the Time for which he was elected, be appointed to any civil Office under the Authority of the United States, which shall have been created, or the Emoluments whereof shall have been encreased during such time; and no Person holding any Office under the United States, shall be a Member of either House during his Continuance in Office.

Section 7. All Bills for raising Revenue shall originate in the House of Representatives; but the Senate may propose or concur with Amendments as on other Bills.

Every Bill which shall have passed the House of Representatives and the Senate, shall, before it become a Law, be presented to the President of the United States; If he approve he shall sign it, but if not he shall return it, with his Objections to that House in which it shall have originated, who shall enter the Objections at large on their Journal, and proceed to reconsider it.

If after such Reconsideration two thirds of that House shall agree to pass the Bill, it shall be sent, together with the Objections, to the other House, by which it shall likewise be reconsidered, and if approved by two thirds of that House, it shall become a Law. But in all such Cases the Votes of both Houses shall be determined by Yeas and Nays, and the Names of the Persons voting for and against the Bill shall be entered on the Journal of each House respectively. If any Bill shall not be returned by the President within ten Days (Sundays excepted) after it shall have been presented to him, the Same shall be a Law, in like Manner as if he had signed it, unless the Congress by their Adjournment prevent its Return, in which Case it shall not be a Law.

Every Order, Resolution, or Vote to which the Concurrence of the Senate and House of Representatives may be necessary (except on a question of Adjournment) shall be presented to the President of the United States; and before the Same shall take Effect, shall be approved by him, or being disapproved by him, shall be repassed by two thirds of the Senate and House of Representatives, according to the Rules and Limitations prescribed in the Case of a Bill.

Section 8. The Congress shall have Power To lay and collect Taxes, Duties, Imposts and Excises, to pay the Debts and provide for the common Defence and general Welfare of the United States; but all Duties, Imposts and Excises shall be uniform throughout the United States;

To borrow Money on the credit of the United States;

To regulate Commerce with foreign Nations, and among the several States, and with the Indian Tribes;

To establish an uniform Rule of Naturalization, and uniform Laws on the subject of Bankruptcies throughout the United States;

To coin Money, regulate the Value thereof, and of foreign Coin, and fix the Standard of Weights and Measures;

To provide for the Punishment of counterfeiting the Securities and current Coin of the United States;

To establish Post Offices and post Roads;

To promote the Progress of Science and useful Arts, by securing for limited Times to Authors and Inventors the exclusive Right to their respective Writings and Discoveries;

To constitute Tribunals inferior to the supreme Court;

To define and punish Piracies and Felonies committed on the high Seas, and Offences against the Law of Nations;

To declare War, grant Letters of Marque and Reprisal, and make Rules concerning Captures on Land and Water;

To raise and support Armies, but no Appropriation of Money to that Use shall be for a longer Term than two Years;

To provide and maintain a Navy;

To make Rules for the Government and Regulation of the land and naval Forces;

To provide for calling forth the Militia to execute the Laws of the Union, suppress Insurrections and repel Invasions;

To provide for organizing, arming, and disciplining, the Militia, and for governing such Part of them as may be employed in the Service of the United States, reserving to the States respectively, the Appointment of the Officers, and the Authority of training the Militia according to the discipline prescribed by Congress;

To exercise exclusive Legislation in all Cases whatsoever, over such District (not exceeding ten Miles square) as may, by Cession of particular States, and the Acceptance of Congress, become the Seat of the Government of the United States, and to exercise like Authority over all Places purchased by the Consent of the Legislature of the State in which the Same shall be for the Erection of Forts, Magazines, Arsenals, dock-Yards, and other needful Buildings;-And

To make all Laws which shall be necessary and proper for carrying into Execution the foregoing Powers, and all other Powers vested by this Constitution in the Government of the United States, or in any Department or Officer thereof.

Section 9 The Migration or Importation of such Persons as any of the States now existing shall think proper to admit, shall not be prohibited by the Congress prior to the Year one thousand eight hundred and eight, but a Tax or duty may be imposed on such Importation, not exceeding ten dollars for each Person.

The Privilege of the Writ of Habeas Corpus shall not be suspended, unless when in Cases of Rebellion or Invasion the public Safety may require it.

No Bill of Attainder or ex post facto Law shall be passed.

No Capitation, or other direct, Tax shall be laid, unless in Proportion to the Census or Enumeration herein before directed to be taken.

No Tax or Duty shall be laid on Articles exported from any State.

No Preference shall be given by any Regulation of Commerce or Revenue to the Ports of one State over those of another: nor shall Vessels bound to, or from, one State be obliged to enter, clear, or pay Duties in another.

No Money shall be drawn from the Treasury, but in Consequence of Appropriations made by Law; and a regular Statement and Account of the Receipts and Expenditures of all public Money shall be published from time to time.

No Title of Nobility shall be granted by the United States: And no Person holding any Office of Profit or Trust under them, shall, without the Consent of the Congress, accept of any present, Emolument, Office, or Title, of any kind whatever, from any King, Prince, or foreign States.

Section 10. No State shall enter into any Treaty, Alliance, or Confederation; grant Letters of

Marque and Reprisal; coin Money; emit Bills of Credit; make any Thing but gold and silver Coin a Tender in Payment of Debts; pass any Bill of Attainder, ex post facto Law, or Law impairing the Obligation of Contracts, or grant any Title of Nobility.

No State shall, without the Consent of the Congress, lay any Imposts or Duties on Imports or Exports, except what may be absolutely necessary for executing its inspection Laws: and the net Produce of all Duties and Imposts, laid by any State on Imports or Exports, shall be for the Use of the Treasury of the United States; and all such Laws shall be subject to the Revision and Controul of the Congress.

No State shall, without the Consent of Congress, lay any Duty of Tonnage, keep Troops, or Ships of War in time of Peace, enter into any Agreement or Compact with another State, or with a foreign Power, or engage in War, unless actually invaded, or in such imminent Danger as will not admit of delay.

Article II

Section 1. The executive Power shall be vested in a President of the United States of America. He shall hold his Office during the Term of four Years, and, together with the Vice President, chosen for the same term, be elected, as follows

Each State shall appoint, in such Manner as the Legislature thereof may direct, a Number of Electors, equal to the whole Number of Senators and Representatives to which the State may be entitled in the Congress: but no Senator or Representative, or Person holding an Office of Trust or Profit under the United States, shall be appointed an Elector.

The Electors shall meet in their respective States, and vote by Ballot for two Persons, of whom one at least shall not be an Inhabitant of the same State with themselves. And they shall make a List of all the Persons voted for, and of the Number of Votes for each; which List they shall sign and certify, and transmit sealed to the Seat of the Government of the United States, directed to the President of the Senate. The President of the Senate shall, in the Presence of the Senate and House of Representatives, open all the Certificates, and the Votes shall then be counted. The Person having the greatest Number of Votes shall be the President, if such Number be a Majority of the whole Number of Electors appointed; and if there be more than one who have such Majority, and have an equal Number of Votes, then the House of Representatives shall immediately chuse by Ballot one of them for President: and if no Person have a Majority, then from the five highest on the List the said House shall in like Manner chuse the President. But in chusing the President, the Votes shall be taken by States, the Representation from each State having one Vote; A quorum for this Purpose shall consist of a Member or Members from two thirds of the States, and a Majority of all the States shall be necessary to a Choice. In every Case, after the Choice of the President, the Person having the greatest Number of Votes of the Electors shall be the Vice President. But if there should remain two or more who have equal Votes, the Senate shall chuse from them by Ballot the Vice President.

The Congress may determine the Time of chusing the Electors and the Day on which they shall give their Votes; which Day shall be the same throughout the United States.

No Person except a natural born Citizen, or a Citizen of the United States, at the time of the Adoption of this Constitution, shall be eligible to the Office of President; neither shall any Person be eligible to that Office who shall not have attained to the Age of thirty five Years, and been fourteen Years a Resident within the United States.

In Case of the Removal of the President from Office, or of his Death, Resignation, or Inability to discharge the Powers and Duties of the said Office, the Same shall devolve on the Vice President, and the Congress may by Law provide for the Case of Removal, Death, Resignation or Inability, both of the President and Vice President, declaring what Officer shall then act as President, and such Officer shall act accordingly, until the Disability be removed, or a President shall be elected.

The President shall, at stated Times, receive for his Services a Compensation, which shall neither be encreased nor diminished during the Period for which he shall have been elected, and he shall not receive within that Period any other Emolument from the United States, or any of them.

Before he enter on the Execution of his Office, he shall take the following Oath or Affirmation:-"I do solemnly swear (or affirm) that I will faithfully execute the Office of President of the United States, and will to the best of my Ability, preserve, protect and defend the Constitution of the United States."

Section 2. The President shall be Commander in Chief of the Army and Navy of the United States, and of the Militia of the several States, when called into the actual Service of the United States; he may require the Opinion, in writing, of the principal Officer in each of the executive Departments, upon any Subject relating to the Duties of their respective Offices, and he shall have power to grant Reprieves and Pardons for Offences against the United States, except in Cases of Impeachment.

He shall have Power, by and with the Advice and Consent of the Senate, to make Treaties, provided two thirds of the Senators present concur; and he shall nominate, and by and with the Advice and Consent of the Senate, shall appoint Ambassadors, other public Ministers and Consuls, Judges of the supreme Court, and all other Officers of the United States, whose Appointments are not herein otherwise provided for, and which shall be established by Law; but the Congress may by Law vest the Appointment of such inferior Officers, as they think proper, in the President alone, in the Courts of Law, or in the Heads of Departments.

The President shall have Power to fill up all Vacancies that may happen during the Recess of the Senate, by granting Commissions which shall expire at the End of their next Session.

Section 3. He shall from time to time give to the Congress Information of the State of the Union, and recommend to their Consideration such Measures as he shall judge necessary and expedient; he may, on extraordinary Occasions, convene both Houses, or either of them, and in Case of Disagreement between them, with Respect to the Time of Adjournment, he may adjourn them to such Time as he shall think proper; he shall receive Ambassadors and other public Ministers; he shall take Care that the Laws be faithfully executed, and shall Commission all the Officers of the United States.

Section 4. The President, Vice President and all civil Officers of the United States, shall be removed from Office on Impeachment for, and Conviction of, Treason, Bribery, or other High Crimes and Misdemeanors.

Article III

Section 1. The judicial Power of the United States, shall be vested in one supreme Court, and in such inferior Courts as the Congress may from time to time ordain and establish. The Judges, both of the supreme and inferior Courts, shall hold their Offices during good Behaviour, and shall, at stated Times, receive for their Services, a Compensation, which shall not be diminished during their Continuance in Office.

Section 2. The judicial Power shall extend to all Cases, in Law and Equity, arising under this Constitution, the Laws of the United States, and Treaties made, or which shall be made, under their Authority;-to all Cases affecting Ambassadors, other public Ministers and Consuls;-to all Cases of admiralty and maritime Jurisdiction;-to Controversies to which the United States shall be a Party;-to Controversies between two or more States; between a State and Citizens of another State;-between Citizens of different States;-between Citizens of the same State claiming Lands under Grants of different States, and between a State, or the Citizens thereof, and foreign States, Citizens or Subjects.

In all Cases affecting Ambassadors, other public Ministers and Consuls, and those in which a State shall be Party, the supreme Court shall have original Jurisdiction. In all the other Cases before mentioned, the supreme Court shall have appellate Jurisdiction, both as to Law and Fact, with such Exceptions, and under such Regulations as the Congress shall make.

The Trial of all Crimes, except in Cases of Impeachment, shall be by Jury; and such Trial shall be held in the State where the said Crimes shall have been committed; but when not committed within any State, the Trial shall be at such Place or Places as the Congress may by Law have directed.

Section 3. Treason against the United States, shall consist only in levying War against them, or in adhering to their Enemies, giving them Aid and Comfort. No Person shall be convicted of Treason unless on the Testimony of two Witnesses to the same overt Act, or on Confession in open Court.

The Congress shall have Power to declare the Punishment of Treason, but no Attainder of Treason shall work Corruption of Blood, or Forfeiture except during the Life of the Person attainted.

Article IV

Section 1. Full Faith and Credit shall be given in each State to the public Acts, Records, and judicial Proceedings of every other State. And the Congress may by general Laws prescribe the Manner in which such Acts, Records and Proceedings shall be proved, and the Effect thereof.

Section 2. The Citizens of each State shall be entitled to all Privileges and Immunities of Citizens in the several States.

A Person charged in any State with Treason, Felony, or other Crime, who shall flee from Justice, and be found in another State, shall on Demand of the executive Authority of the State from which he fled, be delivered up, to be removed to the State having Jurisdiction of the Crime.

No Person held to Service or Labour in one State, under the Laws thereof, escaping into another, shall, in Consequence of any Law or Regulation therein, be discharged from such Service or Labour, but shall be delivered up on Claim of the Party to whom such Service or Labour may be due.

Section 3. New States may be admitted by the Congress into this Union; but no new State shall be formed or erected within the Jurisdiction of any other State; nor any State be formed by the Junction of two or more States, or Parts of States, without the Consent of the Legislatures of the States concerned as well as of the Congress.

The Congress shall have Power to dispose of and make all needful Rules and Regulations respecting the Territory or other Property belonging to the United States; and nothing in this Constitution shall be so construed as to Prejudice any Claims of the United States, or of any particular State.

Section 4. The United States shall guarantee to every State in this Union a Republican Form of Government, and shall protect each of them against Invasion; and on Application of the Legislature, or of the Executive (when the Legislature cannot be convened) against domestic Violence.

Article V

The Congress, whenever two thirds of both Houses shall deem it necessary, shall propose Amendments to this Constitution, or, on the Application of the Legislatures of two thirds of the several States, shall call a Convention for proposing Amendments, which, in either Case, shall be valid to all Intents and Purposes, as Part of this Constitution, when ratified by the Legislatures of three fourths of the several States, or by Conventions in three fourths thereof, as the one or the other Mode of Ratification may be proposed by the Congress; Provided that no Amendment which may be made prior to the Year One thousand eight hundred and eight shall in any Manner affect the first and fourth Clauses in the Ninth Section of the first Article; and that no State, without its Consent, shall be deprived of its equal Suffrage in the Senate.

Article VI

All Debts contracted and Engagements entered into, before the Adoption of this Consitution, shall be as valid against the United States under this Constitution, as under the Confederation.

This Constitution, and the Laws of the United States which shall be made in Pursuance thereof; and all Treaties made, or which shall be made, under the Authority of the United States, shall be the supreme Law of the Land; and the Judges in every State shall be bound thereby, any Thing in the Constitution or Laws of any State to the Contrary notwithstanding.

The Senators and Representatives before mentioned, and the Members of the several State Legislatures, and all executive and judicial Officers, both of the United States and of the several States, shall be bound by Oath or Affirmation, to support this Constitution; but no religious Test shall ever be required as a Qualification to any Office or public Trust under the United States.

Article VII

The Ratification of the Conventions of nine States, shall be sufficient for the Establishment of this Constitution between the States so ratifying the Same.

Done in Convention by the Unanimous Consent of the States present the Seventeenth Day of September in the Year of our Lord one thousand seven hundred and Eighty seven and of the Independence of the United States of America the Twelfth. In witness whereof We have hereunto subscribed our Names.

[The first 10 Amendments were ratified December 15, 1791, and form what is known as the Bill of Rights]

Amendment 1

Congress shall make no law respecting an establishment of religion, or prohibiting the free exercise thereof; or abridging the freedom of speech, or of the press; or the right of the people peaceably to assemble, and to petition the Government for a redress of grievances.

Amendment 2

A well regulated Militia, being necessary to the security of a free State, the right of the people to keep and bear Arms, shall not be infringed.

Amendment 3

No Soldier shall, in time of peace be quartered in any house, without the consent of the Owner, nor in time of war, but in a manner to be prescribed by law.

Amendment 4

The right of the people to be secure in their persons, houses, papers, and effects, against unreasonable searches and seizures, shall not be violated, and no Warrants shall issue, but upon probable cause, supported by Oath or affirmation, and particularly describing the place to be searched and the persons or things to be seized.

Amendment 5

No person shall be held to answer for a capital, or otherwise infamous crime, unless on a presentment or indictment of a Grand Jury, except in cases arising in the land or naval forces, or in the Militia, when in actual service in time of War or public danger; nor shall any person be subject for the same offence to be twice put in jeopardy of life or limb; nor shall be compelled in any criminal case to be a witness against himself, nor be deprived of life, liberty, or property, without due process of law; nor shall private property be taken for public use, without just compensation.

Amendment 6

In all criminal prosecutions, the accused shall enjoy the right to a speedy and public trial, by an impartial jury of the State and district wherein the crime shall have been committed, which district shall have been previously ascertained by law, and to be informed of the nature and cause of the accusation; to be confronted with the witnesses against him; to have compulsory process for obtaining witnesses in his favor, and to have the Assistance of Counsel for his defence.

Amendment 7

In Suits at common law, where the value in controversy shall exceed twenty dollars, the right of trial by jury shall be preserved, and no fact tried by a jury, shall be otherwise reexamined in any Court of the United States, than according to the rules of the common law.

Amendment 8

Excessive bail shall not be required, nor excessive fines imposed, nor cruel and unusual punishments inflicted.

Amendment 9

The enumeration in the Constitution, of certain rights, shall not be construed to deny or disparage others retained by the people.

Amendment 10

The powers not delegated to the United States by the Constitution, nor prohibited by it to the States, are reserved to the States respectively, or to the people.

Amendment 11

[Ratified February 7, 1795]

The Judicial power of the United States shall not be construed to extend to any suit in law or equity, commenced or prosecuted against one of the United States by Citizens of another State, or by Citizens or Subjects of any Foreign State.

Amendment 12

[Ratified July 27, 1804]

The Electors shall meet in their respective states and vote by ballot for President and Vice-President, one of whom, at least, shall not be an inhabitant of the same state with themselves; they shall name in their ballots the person voted for as Presdient, and in distinct ballots the person voted for as Vice-President, and they shall make distinct lists of all persons voted for as President, and of all persons voted for as Vice-President, and of the number of votes for each, which lists they shall sign and certify, and transmit sealed to the seat of the government of the United States, directed to the President of the Senate;-The President of the Senate shall, in the presence of the Senate and House of Representatives, open all the certificates and the votes shall then be counted;-The person having the greatest number of votes for President, shall be the President, if such number be a majority of the whole number of Electors appointed; and if no person have such majority, then from the persons having the highest numbers not exceeding three on the list of those voted for as President, the House of Representatives shall choose immediately, by ballot, the President. But in choosing the President, the votes shall be taken by states, the representation from each state having one vote; a quorum for this purpose shall consist of a member or members from two-thirds of the states, and a majority of all the states shall be necessary to a choice. And if the House of Representatives shall not choose a President whenever the right of choice shall devolve upon them, before the fourth day of March next following, then the Vice-President shall act as President, as in the case of the death or other constitutional disability of the President.-The person having the greatest number of votes as Vice-President, shall be the Vice-President, if such number be a majority of the whole number of Electors appointed, and if no person have a majority, then from the two highest numbers on the list, the Senate shall choose the Vice-President; a quorum for the purpose shall consist of two-thirds of the whole number of Senators, and a majority of the whole number shall be necessary to a choice. But no person constitutionally ineligible to the office of President shall be eligible to that of Vice-President of the United States.

Amendment 13

[Ratified December 6, 1865]

Section 1. Neither slavery nor involuntary servitude, except as a punishment for crime whereof the party shall have been duly convicted, shall exist within the United States, or any place subject to their jurisdiction.

Section 2. Congress shall have power to enforce this article by appropriate legislation.

Amendment 14

[Ratified July 9, 1868]

Section 1. All persons born or naturalized in the United States, and subject to the jurisdiction thereof, are citizens of the United States and of the State wherein they reside. No State shall make or enforce any law which shall abridge the privileges or immunities of citizens of the United States; nor shall any State deprive any person of life, liberty, or property, without due process of law; nor deny to any person within its jurisdiction the equal protection of the laws.

Section 2. Representatives shall be apportioned among the several States according to their respective numbers, counting the whole number of persons in each State, excluding Indians not taxed. But when the right to vote at any election for the choice of electors for President and Vice President of the United States, Representatives in Congress, the Executive and Judicial Officers of a State, or the members of the Legislature thereof, is denied to any of the male inhabitants of such State, being twenty-one years of age, and citizens of the United States, or in any way abridged, except for participation in rebellion, or other crime, the basis of representation therein shall be reduced in the proportion which the number of such male citizens shall bear to the whole number of male citizens twenty-one years of age in such State.

*Section 3.*No person shall be a Senator or Representative in Congress, or elector of President and Vice President, or hold any office, civil or military, under the United States, or under any State, who, having previously taken an oath, as a member of Congress, or as an officer of the United States, or as a member of any State legislature, or as an executive or judicial officer of any State, to support the Constitution of the United States, shall have engaged in insurrection or rebellion against the same, or given aid or comfort to the enemies thereof. But Congress may by a vote of two-thirds of each House, remove such disability.

Section 4. The validity of the public debt of the United States, authorized by law, including debts incurred for payment of pensions and bounties for services in suppressing insurrection or rebellion, shall not be questioned. But neither the United States nor any State shall assume or pay any debt or obligation incurred in aid of insurrection or rebellion against the United States, or any claim for the loss or emancipation of any slave; but all such debts, obligations and claims shall be held illegal and void.

Section 5. The Congress shall have power to enforce, by appropriate legislation, the provisions of this article.

Amendment 15

[Ratified February 3, 1870]

Section 1. The right of citizens of the United States to vote shall not be denied or abridged by the United States or by any State on account of race, color, or previous condition of servitude.

Section 2. The Congress shall have power to enforce this article by appropriate legislation.

Amendment 16

[Ratified February 3, 1913]

The Congress shall have power to lay and collect taxes on incomes, from whatever source derived, without apportionment among the several States, and without regard to any census or enumeration.

Amendment 17

[Ratified April 8, 1913]

The Senate of the United States shall be composed of two Senators from each State, elected by the people thereof for six years; and each Senator shall have one vote. The electors in each State shall have the qualifications requisite for electors of the most numerous branch of the State legislatures.

When vacancies happen in the representation of any State in the Senate, the executive authority of such State shall issue writs of election to fill such vacancies: *Provided,* That the legislature of any State may empower the executive thereof to make temporary appointments until the people fill the vacancies by election as the legislature may direct.

This amendment shall not be so construed as to affect the election or term of any Senator chosen before it becomes valid as part of the Constitution.

Amendment 18

[Ratified January 16, 1919]

Section 1. After one year from the ratification of this article the manufacture, sale, or transportation of intoxicating liquors within, the importation thereof into, or the exportation thereof from the United States and all territory subject to the jurisdiction thereof for beverage purposes is hereby prohibited.

Section 2. The Congress and the several States shall have concurrent power to enforce this article by appropriate legislation.

Section 3. This article shall be inoperative unless it shall have been ratified as an amendment to the Constitution by the legislatures of the several States, as provided in the Constitution, within seven years from the date of the submission hereof to the States by the Congress.

Amendment 19

[Ratified August 18, 1920]

The right of citizens of the United States to vote shall not be denied or abridged by the United States or by any State on account of sex. Congress shall have power to enforce this article by appropriate legislation.

Amendment 20

[Ratified January 23, 1933]

Section 1. The terms of the President and Vice President shall end at noon on the 20th day of January, and the terms of Senators and Representatives at noon on the 3d day of January, of the years in which such terms would have ended if this article had not been ratified; and the terms of their successors shall then begin.

Section 2. The Congress shall assemble at least once in every year, and such meeting shall begin at noon on the 3d day of January, unless they shall by law appoint a different day.

Section 3. If, at the time fixed for the beginning of the term of the President, the President elect shall have died, the Vice President elect shall become President. If a President shall not have been chosen before the time fixed for the beginning of his term, or if the President elect shall have failed to qualify, then the Vice President elect shall act as President until a President shall have qualified; and the Congress may by law provide for the case wherein neither a President elect nor a Vice President elect shall have qualified, declaring who shall then act as President, or the manner in which one who is to act shall be selected, and such person shall act accordingly until a President or Vice President shall have qualified.

*Section 4.*The Congress may by law provide for the case of the death of any of the persons from whom the House of Representatives may choose a President whenever the right of choice shall have devolved upon them, and for the case of the death of any of the persons from whom the Senate may choose a Vice President whenever the right of choice shall have devolved upon them.

Section 5. Sections 1 and 2 shall take effect on the 15th day of October following the ratification of this article.

Section 6. This article shall be inoperative unless it shall have been ratified as an amendment to the Constitution by the legislatures of three-fourths of the several States within seven years from the date of its submission.

Amendment 21

[Ratified December 5, 1933]

Section 1. The eighteenth article of amendment to the Constitution of the United States is hereby repealed.

Section 2. The transportation or importation into any State, Territory, or possession of the United States for delivery or use therein of intoxicating liquors, in violation of the laws thereof, is hereby prohibited.

Section 3. This article shall be inoperative unless it shall have been ratified as an amendment to the Constitution by conventions in the several States, as provided in the Constitution, within seven years from the date of the submission hereof to the States by the Congress.

Amendment 22

[Ratified February 27, 1951]

Section 1. No person shall be elected to the office of the President more than twice, and no person who has held the office of President, or acted as President, for more than two years of a term to which some other person was elected President shall be elected to the office of the President more than once. But this Article shall not apply to any person holding the office of President when this Article was proposed by the Congress, and shall not prevent any person who may be holding the office of President, or acting as President, during the term within which this Article becomes operative from holding the office of President or acting as President during the remainder of such term.

*Section 2.*This article shall be inoperative unless it shall have been ratified as an amendment to the Constitution by the legislatures of three-fourths of the several States within seven years from the date of its submission to the States by the Congress.

Amendment 23

[Ratified March 29, 1961]

Section 1. The District constituting the seat of Government of the United States shall appoint in such manner as the Congress may direct:

A number of electors of President and Vice President equal to the whole number of Senators and Representatives in Congress to which the District would be entitled if it were a State, but in no event more than the least populous State; they shall be in addition to those appointed by the States, but they shall be considered, for the purposes of the election of President and Vice President, to be electors appointed by a State; and they shall meet in the District and perform such duties as provided by the twelfth article of amendment.

Section 2. The Congress shall have power to enforce this article by appropriate legislation.

Amendment 24

[Ratified January 23, 1964]

Section 1. The right of citizens of the United States to vote in any primary or other election for President or Vice President, for electors for President or Vice President, or for Senator or Representative in Congress, shall not be denied or abridged by the United States or any State by reason of failure to pay any poll tax or other tax.

Section 2. The Congress shall have power to enforce this article by appropriate legislation.

Amendment 25

[Ratified February 10, 1967]

Section 1. In case of the removal of the President from office or of his death or resignation, the Vice President shall become President.

Section 2. Whenever there is a vacancy in the office of the Vice President, the President shall nominate a Vice President who shall take office upon confirmation by a majority vote of both Houses of Congress.

Section 3. Whenever the President transmits to the President pro tempore of the Senate and the Speaker of the House of Representatives his written declaration that he is unable to discharge the powers and duties of his office, and until he transmits to them a written declaration to the contrary, such powers and duties shall be discharged by the Vice President as Acting President.

Section 4. Whenever the Vice President and a majority of either the principal officers of the executive departments or of such other body as Congress may by law provide, transmit to the President pro tempore of the Senate and the Speaker of the House of Representatives their written declaration that the President is unable to discharge the powers and duties of his office, the Vice President shall immediately assume the powers and duties of the office as Acting President.

Thereafter, when the President transmits to the President pro tempore of the Senate and the Speaker of the House of Representatives his written declaration that no inability exists, he shall resume the powers and duties of his office unless the Vice President and a majority of either the principal officers of the executive department or of such other body as Congress may by law provide, transmit within four days to the President pro-tempore of the Senate and the Speaker of the House of Representatives their written declaration that the President is unable to discharge the powers and duties of his office. Thereupon Congress shall decide the issue, assembling within forty-eight hours for that purpose if not in session. If the Congress, within twenty-one days after receipt of the latter written declaration, or, if Congress is not in session, within twenty-one days after Congress is required to assemble, determines by two-thirds vote of both Houses that the President is unable to discharge the powers and duties of his office, the Vice President shall continue to discharge the same as Acting President; otherwise, the President shall resume the powers and duties of his office.

Amendment 26

[Ratified June 30, 1971]

Section 1. The right of citizens of the United States, who are eighteen years of age or older, to vote shall not be denied or abridged by the United States or by any State on account of age.

Section 2. The Congress shall have the power to enforce this article by appropriate legislation.

Proposed Amendment 27

[Proposed March 22, 1972]

Section 1. Equality of rights under the law shall not be denied or abridged by the United States or by any State on account of sex.

Section 2. The Congress shall have power to enforce, by appropriate legislation, the provisions of this article.

Section 3. This amendment shall take effect two years after date of ratification.

Index